Fodor's 2007

Mexico

D1319560

Fodor's Travel Publications • New York, Toronto, London, Sydney, Auckland
www.fodors.com

CONTENTS

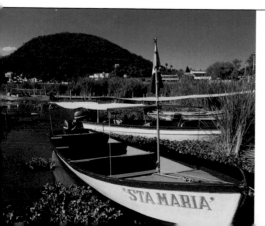

MAPS

Circled letters in text correspond to letters on the photographs. For more information on the sights pictured, turn
to the indicated page number Ⓐ➤ on each photograph.

DESTINATION
MEXICO

It could happen while you're climbing the Pyramid of the Magician at the magnificent Maya ruins of Uxmal in the Yucatán, descending into the formidable Barranca del Cobre (Copper Canyon), strolling through the shady plaza of a colonial Heartland town in the heat and torpor of siesta time, lolling on the beach in glittering Acapulco, snorkeling off Quintana Roo in the waters of the Caribbean, or gawking at the variety of chilies in Oaxaca's Central de Abastos market. And you won't be in Mexico too long before it does happen—you realize that what makes this country so alluring is its diversity. Mexico is a blend—of peoples, of cultures, of landscapes, of worlds new and old, of the legacies of the vanquished and the conqueror—and the mix is so enchanting that you'll hardly even notice that you're falling under its spell.

MEXICO CITY AND SIDE TRIPS

Ⓐ 44

Ⓑ 51

Ⓒ 45

Mexico City, population 24 million, is the largest metropolis on earth. And at 7,349 feet, it is North America's highest city. More to the point, however, Mexico is the oldest city in North America, and the past courses through it like the canals that cut through the hanging gardens the Aztecs built at outlying ⒻXochimilco. The past comes alive in the galleries of the ⒷMuseo Nacional de Antropología—where pride of place belongs to an arrestingly sophisticated Aztec calendar stone—and it surfaces in full force on the ⒸZócalo, the plaza that's the heart and soul of today's city, just as it was once the capi-

tal of the Aztec empire, Tenochtitlán. A stroll through this square takes you past the 16th-century Catedral Metropolitana, Latin America's oldest and largest cathedral, to the ruined Ⓐ**Templo Mayor,** the ceremonial Aztec center of human sacrifice. An adjacent museum displays the treasures unearthed during its excavation. Southeast of the city the gilded carvings in Ⓓ**Iglesia de Santo Domingo,** one of 224 churches the Spanish built in the valley of Puebla, hover over the faithful as if to promise a glittering life after death. Looming above the city and the Valley of Mexico, the rumbling 17,887-foot volcano

Ⓔ**Popocatépetl** is a constant reminder of forces mightier than any civilization, past or present, and an opportunity to hike off last night's rich chicken mole dinner beneath the crater, so long as you don't pass the 12,000-foot danger point.

BAJA

Ⓐ 143

Lively border traffic colors the culture of the upper reaches of Baja Norte, the half of the peninsula attached to the state of California, where Tijuana keeps right on living up to its raucous and rowdy reputation. Down the coast Rosarito and Puerto Nuevo open their doors for weekending Californians, likewise Ⓓ**Ensenada,** which also has a busy fishing port and fish market to show for it. But you can't say you've really experienced the 1,000-mile-long finger of land that is Baja California until you head south, off the beaten path. Here, in some of the most beautiful terrain on earth, quiet

Ⓑ 161

© 163

Ⓓ 126

fishing villages and pristine beaches punctuate two coastlines. On the Sea of Cortés you can dip your paddles into protected Bahía Concepción—or on the Pacific coast, off Ⓐ**San Ignacio,** pull up within petting distance of migrating gray whales. Inland, boulder-strewn wastes are dotted with cacti, mountain peaks soar to 10,000 feet, and the high sierra yields its wonders as you hike through Parque Nacional San Pedro Mártir. Galleries near Misión San Javier display ancient paintings left by Baja's earliest inhabitants. In their wake, explorers, missionaries, pirates, and movie stars have made their way here, trying to get away from it all. The silhouettes of golfers, anglers, and sunseekers stand out in today's crowds, which flock to the elegant hostelries of that still wonderfully natural area at Baja California's tip known as Los Cabos. And with secluded coves like Playa de Amor and a spectacular land's end at Ⓒ**El Arco,** it's no wonder that newlyweds are among the Los Cabos pilgrims—the hacienda-style Ⓑ**Palmilla** even has its own adobe wedding chapel.

SONORA

Imagine Arizona a hundred years ago, when cowboys drove cattle across wide-open ranges and lined up along the bars of saloons to sing *rancheras*, ballads right out of the storybooks of the Old West. Then add a coastline—a fringe of beach washed by a balmy turquoise sea—and you've conjured up Sonora, Mexico's northernmost state. South of Nogales, a sometimes-rowdy border town, relatively unspoiled coastal towns like Bahía Kino and Guaymas keep company with quiet, undiscovered seaside Ⓑ©**San Carlos,** for example. And arid coffee-colored hills tumble into the Sea of Cortés in a profusion of creosote bushes, saguaro, and organ-pipe cacti. Offshore, dolphins, pelicans, sea lions, and migrating whales thrive—as do swimmers, snorkelers, sea kayakers, and enthusiasts of just about every other aquatic stripe. Inland, Father Eusebio Francisco Kino's missions populate towns such as Magdalena, and deserts give way to stands of cottonwoods and evergreens rising into the foothills of the Sierra Madre. Their hidden treasures include Ⓐ**Alamos,** a former silver-mining center that is one of Mexico's loveliest and best-preserved colonial towns.

A 208

The high desert of the Sierra Madre gives way to high drama when it plunges into the four gorges known as the Barranca del Cobre—the Copper Canyon—a mile deep, a mile wide, and four times the size of the Grand Canyon. Most people see it from the Chihuahua al Pacífico railroad on its run between Los

COPPER CANYON

Mochis and Chihuahua City. From whistle-stops like the one at ©**Divisadero,** you'll see how this difficult terrain has pushed its resident Tarahumara Indians to master extraordinary skills—like superlong-distance running. Tarahumara ancestors left marks all around the Paquimé Ruins at Ⓐ**Casas Grandes.** Of the priests who worked among the tribes, creating missions like the one at Ⓑ**Cusárare,** Father Miguel Hidalgo began preaching Mexican independence in 1810. A hundred years later General Pancho Villa launched Mexico's civil war from his home in lively Chihuahua City.

B 204

C 203

Six million strong and growing, Mexico's second-largest metropolis fully lives up to its reputation for being *señorial y moderna* (lordly and modern). Spreading across a mile-high plateau of the Sierra Madre, the city retains a generous measure of colonial charm thanks to the landmarks of its 30-block historic center, such as the 17th-century Ⓐ**Catedral and Palacio de Gobierno,** a seat of local government. Down Plaza Tapatía at the Ⓑ**Instituto Cultural Cabañas,** galleries sur-

GUADALAJARA

round 23 patios and house such treasures as Jose Clemente Orozco's ceiling mural depicting the heavenward striving of the spirit of humanity. Strolling through the quarter's shady, plant-filled squares you're likely to encounter roving troubadours and sombrero-topped bands of mariachis. You'll begin to absorb the intriguing mix of the profound and profane pleasures of the city where the Spanish once endowed countless churches and monuments with vast sums—and invented such traditional Mexican mainstays as *el jarabe tapatío* (the hat dance) and *charreadas* (rodeos), in which cowboys still compete weekly. In the ⒟**Mercado Libertad,** one of Latin America's largest enclosed markets, with its thousand-odd stalls, you can haggle with local vendors for a piece of fruit or a gold watch. Locally made handicrafts are the reward for a

Ⓑ⟩**221**

Ⓒ⟩**237**

trip across the cactus-studded plains surrounding Guadalajara. In Tlaquepaque and nearby ⒞**Tonalá** thousands of artisans fashion artful ceramics and glassware, from the Baroque to the whimsical and contemporary. It's all sold in outdoor markets, studios in old adobe houses, and shops along pedestrian malls and plazas. The dusty cobblestone streets of these towns and their air of old-time Mexico make a refreshing antidote to Guadalajara's urban bustle. Nearby at Tequila you can drink at the source of Mexico's famous firewater.

Ⓓ⟩**234**

In this fertile swath of farm country, traditions cling as tenaciously as the prickly pear and other cacti that spring from the rolling landscape. On Ⓑ**Lake Pátzcuaro,** Purépecha Indians fish and ply their canoes as they have for hundreds of years. Even in

THE HEARTLAND

Ⓐ 282

mountainous San Miguel de Allende, known for its substantial English-speaking community, local women still gather at the public *lavandería* for laundry and gossip. These connections with the past keep the Heartland's turbulent history alive, as do a wealth of monuments, museums, and landmarks. In Ⓐ**Querétaro,** handsome mansions bespeak civic pride that stems in no small measure from the city's status as an eyewitness to history—it was here that Mexico's short-term Emperor Maximilian was executed and the Mexican constitution signed. In Ⓒ**Guanajuato,** musicians

Ⓑ 299

perform beside shady Jardín Unión's aerial hedges, and the massive stone Alhóndiga de Granaditas recalls victory against Spain in the War of Independence. Tiny ⒺGuadalupe is a model of *virreinal* (viceregal, or colonial) splendor—don't miss its Franciscan Ex-Convento de Guadalupe. Sleepy ⒹZacatecas, its cobblestone streets lined with pastel houses, was once the world's most prolific silver-producing city and is still known for the work of its silversmiths. Come nightfall, residents pour into the tidy streets for the *tambora*, a joyously clamorous musical procession.

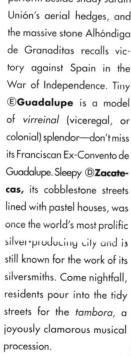

Ⓔ〉281

Ⓓ〉276

PACIFIC COAST RESORTS

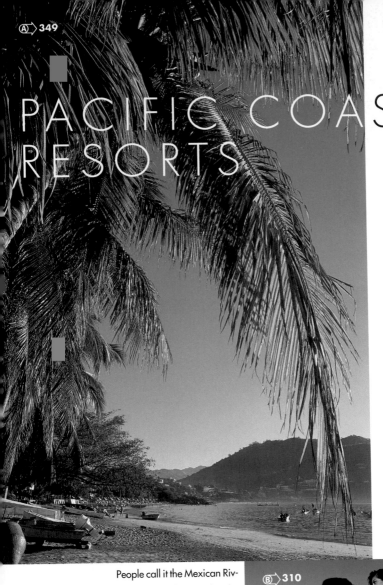

Ⓑ 310

People call it the Mexican Riviera and Gold Coast, but the most apt way to refer to this jungle-backed coastline might just be Tropical Paradise. Historical landmarks like the colonial church of Nuestra Señora de Guadalupe in the once-sleepy fishing village—now glittering resort—of Ⓒ**Puerto Vallarta** are few and far between. But the 900 miles of cove-scalloped white strands edging the Pacific provide more-than-ample diversion for sun worshippers and water-sports lovers, from angling in Ⓑ**Mazatlán,** to snorkeling off the white- or black-sand beaches of Manzanillo, to simply feeling sand between your toes in low-key Ⓐ**Zihuatanejo** or its glitzy neighbor, Ixtapa.

ACAPULCO

You may have heard the rumors, but word that this venerable resort on a spectacular bay is past its prime doesn't seem to have reached Ⓐ**Acapulco.** The sun shines as brightly as ever on beaches and golf courses nearly 365 days a year. And the city, as ever, rouses itself from its daytime torpor to a healthy nighttime glow—whether the setting is your own candlelit pool at the Ⓒ**Westin Las Brisas,** one of the hotels that set the gold standard for resort luxury, or some of the party-heartiest discos this side of the Pacific. Among Acapulco's myriad activities, one pastime best left to well-practiced locals is diving from the 130-foot-high cliffs at Ⓑ**La Quebrada,** a perennially thrilling sight in a city that's always been known for putting on a good show.

Ⓐ▷ 362

Ⓑ▷ 370

Ⓒ▷ 380

OAXACA

(A) 413

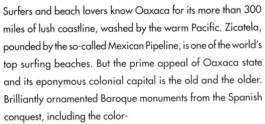

(B) 406

Surfers and beach lovers know Oaxaca for its more than 300 miles of lush coastline, washed by the warm Pacific. Zicatela, pounded by the so-called Mexican Pipeline, is one of the world's top surfing beaches. But the prime appeal of Oaxaca state and its eponymous colonial capital is the old and the older. Brilliantly ornamented Baroque monuments from the Spanish conquest, including the colorfully tile-domed ⑧**Catedral Metropolitana de Oaxaca**, pass almost for new, when magnificent remnants of civilizations long past are so near at hand. Mountaintop Ⓐ**Monte Albán,** with its still-intact ball court, temples, and observatory, was already a thriving city of 40,000 more than 2,500 years ago. A full millennium of civilization passed before the original Zapotec people were surpassed by the Mixtec, who turned the site into a rich necropolis that has yielded some of North America's greatest ar-

chaeological treasures. Today the descendants of both peoples enrich life in Oaxaca City. Festivals are lavish and intense, none more so than the macabre celebrations leading up to the Ⓒ**Día de Muertos** (Day of the Dead/All Souls' Day). Elegantly singsong native languages lend a distinctly musical note to the commotion in Saturday's Central de Abastos, Mexico's largest Indian market. Here and elsewhere, vendors sell everything from herbs and chilies to baskets, rugs, tin toys, and *huipiles* (embroidered tunics). After dark, strings of lights deck the 19th-century Ⓓ**Palacio de Gobierno** for no special reason. Every turn of a corner is likely to deliver a dose of local color that will etch itself into your memory.

Ⓒ➤404

Ⓓ➤407

19

These less-developed southern states are at the heart of Maya and Lacandon Indian country and are for most people a gateway to Guatemala. But if you linger here you'll discover what is arguably Mexico's most authentic culture, in

CHIAPAS AND TABASCO

Ⓑ 448

colonial San Cristóbal de las Casas and traditional villages around it such as ⒷSan Juan Chamula, whose daily life turns on centuries-old rituals. Make your way from the city through jungles and sinuous mountainscapes to verdant ⒶSumidero Canyon, a 4,000-foot-deep near-vertical gash carved by the Grijalva River. In all of Mexico there is nothing like the mesmerizing power of the 2,000-year-old Maya city of ⒸPalenque rising out of the lush forests, echoing in its stone-capped tower and temples the spirit of the surrounding hills.

Ⓐ 477

Ⓑ 483

If you were to work your way south from the Texas border, from souvenir-choked Nuevo Laredo through the mountain city of Saltillo and low-profile coastal Tampico, you'd get a taste of Mexico as heady as the brew from the coffee beans harvested in the tropical highlands outside the raffish city of Ⓐ**Veracruz.** In the antique city itself the diverse citizenry takes to the streets for entertainment and exuberant self-expression: trios slap away at tiny guitars and portable harps, singers belt out that famed local song, *La Bamba*, and, most alluring of all, evening strollers pause in the Ⓑ**Plaza de Armas** for a little *danzón*—the sensuous, once-scandalous dance brought to Mexico by 19th-century Cubans. Elegance of movement is an aerial affair in colonial Ⓒ**Papantla de Olarte,** where four *voladores* (fliers) enact the ancient Totonac Indian calendrical cycle, diving backwards while tethered to an 82-foot pole and circling it upside down 52 times. The sublime Pyramid of the Niches at El Tajín, nearby, is the architectural flower of the ancient Indian civilizations that once dominated the coast.

YUCATÁN

Ⓐ▷ 585

Beaches and ruins, beaches and ruins, beaches and ruins: Mexico's most-visited region will reward you with an embarrassment of both riches, sometimes simultaneously—on Ⓒ**Playa Chacmool** in Cancún, the Chichén Maya rain god Chac looks as much like a beachgoer as he does like the sacrificial altar he once was. Ⓓ**Tulum** may well be the most satisfying spot in the Yucatán (in spite of the crowds). Here, alongside the Caribbean, the local limestone of the temples has mellowed

©>516

in the salt air, and you can go for a swim from the perfect slip of sand where the ancients beached their canoes. But it was the sky, not the sea, upon which the Maya builders set their sights, and in their displays of might they erected monumental temple-pyramids to soar above their now-deserted cities. The enormous Ⓐ**Chichén Itzá,** which once dominated the Yucatán, is populated with hundreds of structures. Elegant, refined Uxmal is exceptional in another way—for the grace of its pyramids, courtyards, and relief carvings. And along the Puuc Route, satellite cities like Kabah, Sayil, and Labná help color the picture of one of the Americas' most intriguing civilizations. These cities once hummed with activity, but today many are quiet: at Ⓑ**Cobá,** the lonely silence is broken only by the shrieks of spider monkeys from the encroaching jungle. And Ⓔ**Cenote Dzitnup,** the swimmable, skylit sinkhole near colonial Valladolid, is as eerily mysterious as ever.

Ⓓ>571

Ⓔ>589

YUCATÁN

Ⓕ 537

Ruins of Maya civilizations may beckon, remnants of Spanish colonialism, like quirky Mérida and fortified Campeche and the formidable Ⓖ**Convento de San Antonio de Padua** at Izamal, may cry out to be explored, but let's face it—the reason you're thinking about the Yucatán is its irresistible mix of sun, sand, and sea. On much of the Quintana Roo coast between Cancún and Tulum, luxury hotel strips like those at Playa del Carmen preside over balmy, crystalline waters and unbroken beaches as white as alabaster. The world's second-largest barrier reef lies just off the island of Cozumel, luring divers and snorkelers, and nature reserves farther south at Sian Ka'an and Boca Paila and north at Parque Natural Río Lagartos attract migrating flamingos, herons, and other birds, as well as their binocular-toting admirers. To the west, along the shores of the Golfo de México, temperatures hover appealingly at 80 degrees, and the sun shines 240-plus days a year—even more than on the Caribbean—and you'll find relaxed coastal villages like ①**Celestún.** The epicenter of the peninsula, where your every whim can be satisfied both by day and by night, is Ⓗ**Cancún,** hacked out of the jungle three decades ago and purpose-built for pleasure. The let-the-good-

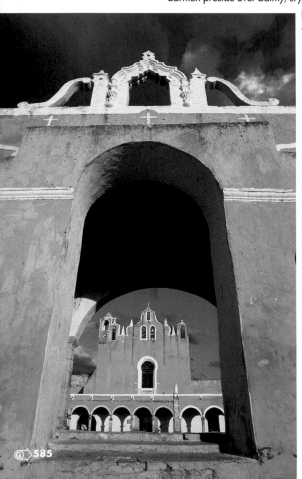

Ⓖ 585

Ⓗ 519

times-roll attitude of Mexico's top resort is so entrenched that even roadside art aims to amuse. For a bit more quiet— and more beach life than nightlife—tiny fish-shaped ⓕ**Isla Mujeres** is just the thing, a mere half hour by boat across the bay from Cancún. Or head down the coast to laid-back Paamul for great beachcombing, the midsummer hatching of sea turtles, and a lagoon that's ideal for snorkeling. Whatever your passion, you'll find a place to pursue it under the Yucatán sun—and you don't have to set your sights any farther than that point out there where the blue-green sea meets the cloudless sky.

GREAT ITINERARIES

Guaymas

San Ignacio

Mulege

BAJA
CALIFORNIA
SUR

La Poza

Loreto
Misión San Javier

San Carlos/
Bahía
Magdalena

120 km

234 km

La Paz

183 km

195 km

San José del Cabo/
Costa Azul
Cabo San Lucas
Playa Palmilla
Playa Solmar

Los Mochis

Basaseachi Falls
73 km
Cuauhtémoc
Chihuahu

128 km

104 km

Divisadero
Creel
Bacajipare

140 km

Cerocahui

240 km

Ⓐ 154

Canyons and Coasts
8 to 12 days

Natural wonders never cease in northern and western Mexico. From the heart-stopping views and hikes into the Barranca del Cobre—the Copper Canyon—to Baja Sur's inland deserts, its annual migrations of whales, and the beaches of Los Cabos, opportunities for adventure and relaxation are everywhere.

3 to 5 days. Riding the Chihuahua al Pacífico rail line from west to east affords the most stunning views of the Copper Canyon. So start off in Los Mochis and make the mountain village of Cerocahui your first stop. From here, views of Urique Canyon are superb, and the cave paintings at the Cueva de las Cruces are worth a

detour. Then head up the line to Divisadero, *the* place for sunset views, horseback trips to the Tarahumara Indian village of Bacajipare in the canyon, and the most luxurious lodgings on the way to Chihuahua City. Farther on, outside of Creel, the 806-foot Basaseachi Falls are one of North America's highest cascades. If a dose of urban life feels like the appropriate tonic after taking in the canyons, spend the night in Chihuahua before catching a plane for La Paz in Baja Sur. ☞ *Chapter 5*

5 to 7 days. Vast as it is, Baja is all about choices—whale-watching in Bahía Magdalena, sea-kayaking or fishing off Loreto, hiking among arid mountain ranges from Misión San Javier, windsurfing off the East Cape, diving and snorkeling or golf in Ⓐ Los Cabos—pick two or three and be sure to give yourself time to relax on the beaches of Costa Azul, Playa Palmilla, or Playa Solmar at the southern tip of the peninsula. Bahía Magdalena and Loreto are west and north of La Paz and the East Cape and Los Cabos are to the south, so figure travel time between them into the mix. ☞ *Baja California Sur in Chapter 3*

By Public Transportation
Distances here demand a fair amount of air travel: first from Mexico City to Los Mochis, then from Chihuahua to La Paz—which flies you over the canyons you just saw from cliff's edge—then from Los Cabos home. The rail trip from Los Mochis to Chihuahua is a 15-hour proposition straight through, but it's best to stop at towns along the way and reboard later in the day or the next day, or even the next. From La Paz, tour companies will take you to Bahía Magdalena to see whales. To get to Loreto (3 hrs north of La Paz), the East Cape (1 hr south), and Los Cabos (2 hrs south), renting a car will allow you to explore quieter coastal stretches on your own. Buses also run throughout Baja Sur.

Colonial Mexico
7 to 10 days

Remarkably well-preserved, these colonial cities are full of atmospheric haciendas and richly decorated cathedrals—along with intriguing juxtapositions of the colonial and the Indian that are classic Mexico.

B 284

QUERÉTARO

1 day. This Heartland city has been called the cradle of independence, and Querétaro's most beautiful area is the restored Plaza de la Independencia, filled with grand mansions once belonging to titled friends of the Crown. Amble around the square and a few of the nearby streets to see the Baroque BMuseo de Arte de Querétaro, the Casa de la Marquesa, the Palacio del Gobierno del Estado, the Jardín de la Corregidora, and 16th-century hermitages turned into museums. Then head for San Miguel de Allende for the night.
☞ *Querétaro in Chapter 7*

SAN MIGUEL DE ALLENDE

1 to 2 days. You can cover most of what you'll want to see around the pretty town plaza in half a day. Serving as a cultural hub of the region, this friendly city is full of bookstores, art galleries, and coffee shops where you'll run into some of the American expatriates. San Miguel's historic inns are perfect for soaking up more local ambiance. Take time to visit churches—the Gothic Revival Parroquia, the churrigueresque Iglesia de San Francisco, and the unique Oratorio de San Felipe Neri, built by Indians. The Casa de Ignacio Allende museum is the birthplace of the revered revolutionary hero. Consider a side trip to the historic village of Dolores Hidalgo and the Casa Hidalgo, home of the insurgent priest whose cry for independence from Spain started the

1810 war. If you're here for an extended stay, you might enroll in one of the town's art or language institutes.
☞ *San Miguel de Allende in Chapter 7*

GUANAJUATO

2 to 3 days. Splendid buildings rising above labyrinthine streets give Guanajuato its medieval appearance. Make your way to the main square and the impressive Teatro Juárez, headquarters of the annual Cervantes Festival (October), which draws noted international artists. El Museo Casa Diego Rivera, birthplace of the famed muralist, and the hulking Alhóndiga de Granaditas fortress are nearby. On day two, visit the Basílica Colegiata de Nuestra Señora de Guanajuato and La Valenciana churches—the former for its 8th-century statue of the Virgin, the latter for its elaborately carved pink facade and gilded altars. Don't miss the Mansión del Conde de Rul, owned by the richest colonial mine owners of the district, or a concert by an *estudiantina* (student) group dressed in old Spanish capes and caps.
☞ *Guanajuato in Chapter 7*

SAN CRISTÓBAL DE LAS CASAS

1 to 2 days. San Cristóbal in the southern state of Chiapas is a walking city, and on foot you can encounter the same mix of colonial and native cultures—from the iconic ochre-colored *catedral* to the *mercado municipal* bustling with Lacandon Maya merchants—that exists between the city itself

and the surrounding Indian villages. One of them, San Juan Chamula, is known for its colorfully trimmed white stucco church, named for John the Baptist. Here a devout syncretism of traditional Maya rituals and the Catholicism that the Spanish brought to the New World makes for a fascinating snapshot of Mexico.
☞ *San Cristóbal de las Casas in Chapter 11*

MÉRIDA

2 days. No city in Mexico comes close to Mérida's quirky self-confidence and its almost Continental flair. At the same time the jaunty metropolis is just as Maya as San Cristóbal. Urbane streets like Paseo de Montejo—styled late in the 19th century like Paris' Champs-Élysées—are offset by the chilies-to-crafts *mercado* (market). And the catedral, built with stone from a Maya temple, contains a dark-skinned Christ that aims to reconcile people of Maya and Spanish descent. In that spirit, Mérida is at once the largest city on the Yucatán Peninsula and, at heart, a typical Yucatecan town unafraid to welcome you into its midst.
☞ *Mérida in Chapter 13*

By Public Transportation
The easiest way to get to and between the Heartland cities of Querétaro, San Miguel, and Guanajuato is by luxury bus. From Mexico City the bus from the Observatorio or Northern bus terminals to Querétaro takes about two hours. From Querétaro it's another two hours to San Miguel; Dolores Hidalgo is 45 minutes from San Miguel. Return to San Miguel for the 2½-hour ride to Guanajuato. Nearby León's airport has flights to Mexico City (1 hr), from which you can fly to Tuxtla Gutiérrez (2 hrs), an hour west of San Cristóbal by bus. Then fly out of Tuxtla straight to Mérida (1 hr).

Léon

100 km Dolores Hidalgo

GUANAJUATO

Guanajuato   San Miguel de Allende

53 km   Querétaro

220 km   HIDALGO

Tula

Teotihuacán

Mexico City

Cuernavaca   Puebla

La Cocina Mexicana
8 to 11 days

Considering the poor representation that Mexican food gets in the United States, savoring the true flavors of Mexico can only deepen your appreciation of the country and its culture. By necessity—Mexico is a vast country—this gastronomic tour is limited to a few cities, but keep in mind that every region has its own excellent cuisine.

☞ *For descriptions of the foods mentioned below, see the La Cocina Mexicana box in the dining section of Chapter 1*

of the city's dining options—from quaint fondas to colonial mansions and elegant old haciendas.
☞ *Dining in Chapter 1*

PUEBLA
2 days. From Mexico City, make your way out to colonial convents like the Ex-Convento de Santa Rosa, where nuns invented the city's most famous dishes—mole and *chiles en nogadas*. Then tuck into the food itself in restaurants in Puebla's historic district, most of which are lavishly decorated with Talavera tile, for which Puebla is famous. Visit the Calle de los Dulces (Sweets Street), filled with shops selling the nuns' fruit, coconut, and sweet-potato candies. And don't miss the town's fruit wines.
☞ *Puebla in Chapter 2*

VERACRUZ
2 to 3 days. The transit from inland Puebla to coastal Veracruz will take you to the home of that notorious chili, Jalapa's jalapeño, and to the source of a dish that appears on menus throughout Mexico—*huachinango á la veracruzana* (red snapper covered in tomatoes, onions, olives, and herbs). In

Mexican *altura*, fuels a café society in Veracruz—look for Gran Café del Portal, a local stronghold of *café lechero* (coffee with hot milk).
☞ *The State of Veracruz in Chapter 12*

OAXACA CITY
2 days. Several native cultures merge in exotic Oaxaca City, where you can feast on the seven types of mole the city is known for, or taste its sweet and salty tamales. Try one of the traditional fondas under the *portales* (arcades) in the main square. You'll also find *quesillo*, Oaxaca's special cheese, as well as table chocolate and giant *totopos* (baked tortillas) in regional dishes and piled in heaps at the local mercado, an essential stop for its symphony of colors and smells. Mountaintop Monte Albán, where archaeologists found royal tombs full of splendid gold jewelry, makes an easy day trip from the city.
☞ *Oaxaca City in Chapter 10*

By Public Transportation
The best way to get from Mexico City to Puebla is by luxury bus (2 hrs), from the TAPO terminal or the international airport. The bus from Puebla over the mountains and into Veracruz City takes four hours. From Veracruz to Oaxaca it's best to fly: back to Mexico City (1½ hrs), then on to Oaxaca (2 hrs).

MEXICO CITY
2 to 4 days. Mexico City chefs turn out everything from colonial to *cocina Mexicana moderna* (modern Mexican cuisine) to pre-Hispanic dishes like chilied maguey worms for their *chilango* (Mexico City) clientele. Many restaurants focus on some regional cuisine, which means that you'll find the best of Veracruz seafood, Yucatecan *pibil*, Tampico *carne asada*, and Chihuahua *carnitas* within the confines of the capital. And luxury hotels often invite regional chefs to oversee gastronomic festivals in their restaurants. Take advantage

Veracruz City seafood is a way of life, and you can expect stunning sea bass, prawns, and lobster and dishes like crab *salpicón*—finely chopped with onion, cilantro, and lime. Coffee grown in the highlands around Jalapa, the famous

Map labels

Léon
Guanajuato
Dolores Hidalgo
100 km
San Miguel de Allende
53 km
Querétaro
220 km
Tula
53 km
Teotihuacán
Jalapa
Mexico City
133 km
Cuernavaca
Puebla
150 km
Córdoba
Orizaba
Veracruz
151 km
88 km
124 km
Tuxtepec
218 km
Monte Albán
Oaxaca City
Puerto Escondido
Tehuantepec
Puerto Angel

VERACRUZ
HIDALGO
TLAXCALA
MEXICO
PUEBLA
OAXACA
GULF OF MEXICO
PACIFIC OCEAN

The Lost Cities of Ancient Mexico
9 to 11 days

Once inhabited by numerous pre-Columbian cultures, Mexico has one of the world's most impressive collections of archaeological sites. The Maya are the standout. Their monumental cities are at their finest on the Yucatán Peninsula and in jungle-clad Tabasco and mountainous Chiapas.

TEOTIHUACÁN
1 day. For the 14th- to 16th-century Aztecs, this was the birthplace of the gods. At its 8th-century peak ©Teotihuacán hummed with as many as 250,000 people, its massive, spellbinding pyramids rising above their city as symbols of the ordered lives that they lived in the ancient Valley of Mexico. Just an hour outside of Mexico City by bus, these ruins of a people who to this day remain nameless are an essential first site.
☞ *Teotihuacán in Chapter 2*

VILLAHERMOSA
2 to 3 days. The banana and oil capital of Mexico, Villahermosa is a rough mid-point between ancient sites and ancient cultures. Head for the Parque Museo La Venta, with its enormous Olmec stone heads, for an in-depth look at a culture that preceded the Maya by several centuries. Later in the day, swing north out of town to Comalcalco, a Maya site with giant stucco masks and the only known brick temples in the Maya world. Save the best for last and make your way to Palenque in Chiapas the next day. With a classicism akin to Greek architecture, this site exudes an ethereal beauty that is nothing short of bewitching. It's also the first site in the Americas where the tomb of a pre-Hispanic ruler was discovered in a burial chamber within a pyramid.
☞ *Villahermosa, Comalcalco, and Palenque in Chapter 11*

MÉRIDA
6 or 7 days. A capital city of the Yucatán, Mérida is a perfect base for getting out to the ruins in the surrounding countryside. Here in the most Maya of all Yucatecan cities, take in the Museum of Anthropology for a preview of Maya art, and walk around the lively main square to see its colonial mansions, cathedral, and small churches set in shady plazas. On your second day, head to Chichén Itzá, an extensive site built by two different Maya empires. Climb to the top of the Temple of the Warriors for a glimpse of its famous Chacmool and a bird's-eye view of the site. Later in the afternoon you might visit the Cave of Balancanchén, with its ceremonial artifacts, and the Maya village of Izamal, on the way back to Mérida. Spend all of day three at beautiful Uxmal, the sterling example of the graceful Puuc architectural style. Optional overnights are possible at hotels near Chichén Itzá and Uxmal, which has an evening sound-and-light show. If time permits, you can spend a day at the smaller Puuc ruins of Kabah, Sayil, and Labná. Consider planning your trip around a local Maya festival to see the intriguing blend of pre-Hispanic beliefs and Catholic rituals.
☞ *The State of Yucatán in Chapter 13*

By Public Transportation
In Villahermosa you can take a cab to the Parque Museo La Venta but need to book an excursion to Comalcalco. Buses are unreliable. To get to Palenque you can catch a luxury bus from the ADO terminal; the trip takes about 2½ hours. There are also full-day excursions to Palenque from Villahermosa. From Tuxtla Gutiérrez there is a one-hour flight to Mérida. You can take day trips to the major Yucatán sites from Mérida. Second-class buses do run to Chichén Itzá and Uxmal from Mérida's main bus terminal, but they have no air-conditioning and are a bit uncomfortable.

FODOR'S
CHOICE

Even with so many special places in Mexico, Fodor's writers and editors have their favorites. Here are a few that stand out.

ARCHAEOLOGICAL SITES

El Tajín. The Pyramid of the Niches rises out of the jungle like the fantasy of a lost world. ☞ p. 491

Ⓔ **Palenque.** Nestled in a rain forest in Chiapas, these Maya ruins have a magical quality, perhaps because of their intimacy. The most magnificent royal tomb in the Maya empire was uncovered here. ☞ p. 454

Ⓗ **Teotihuacán.** Predating the Aztecs and believed by them to be the birthplace of the gods, this pyramid complex outside Mexico City was one of the largest cities in the ancient world. ☞ p. 94

BEACHES

Ⓒ **Playa de Amor, Cabo San Lucas.** From this secluded cove at the very tip of Baja California you can see the Sea of Cortés on one side, the Pacific Ocean on the other. ☞ p. 163

Playa Norte (Playa Cocoteros), Isla Mujeres. This beach on sleepy Isla Mujeres is ideal for water sports and lounging under grass-roofed *palapas.* ☞ p. 541

Zicatela, Oaxaca Coast. A long stretch of cream-color sand, Zicatela is one of the top 10 surfing beaches in the world. ☞ p. 418

SPECIAL MOMENTS

A *calesa* (horse-drawn carriage) ride through Mérida. Discover Old World graciousness by trotting slowly through the wide streets and French-style neighborhoods of Yucatán's capital. ☞ p. 577

Don Porfirio's Bar, Querétaro. After a day of exploring, stop in at the bar of the Casa de la Marquesa hotel for a drink, and to drink in the Old World elegance of this 18th-century house. ☞ p. 284

Ⓓ **Whale-watching, Baja.** Go out on a boat for the best views of the great gray mammals, who pass through Scammon's and San Ignacio lagoons en route from Alaska each winter. ☞ p. 142

MUSEUMS

Ⓘ **Museo de Arte Contemporaneo, Monterrey.** The best of postmodern Latin American art is gathered at this gallery. A chic coffeehouse attracts the city's intellectuals. ☞ p. 503

Museo de Frida Kahlo, Mexico City. The former home of the now-fashionable Kahlo is filled with her disturbing, surrealistic paintings and those of friends such as Klee and Duchamp. ☞ p. 57

Museo Na Bolom, San Cristóbal de las Casas. Franz and Gertrude Blom lived in a lovely, rambling home surrounded by gardens. Their former residence contains displays reflecting their extensive archaeological, ethnological, and ecological interests. ☞ p. 438

SHOPPING

Ⓐ **Casa de las Artesanías and Sna Jolobil, San Cristóbal de las Casas.** Stop here for some of Mexico's most striking Indian weavings, hand-embroidered blouses and tunics, multicolored *fajas* (sashes), and beribboned hats. ☞ p. 444

Old Town, Puerto Vallarta. Few Mexican cities have a collection of native crafts, among them clothing and household goods, as representative as that of Puerto Vallarta. ☞ p. 325

Zona Rosa, Mexico City. Antiques, crafts, and the latest fashions are abundant in this tony neighborhood. ☞ p. 81

FLAVORS

Cicero Centenario, Mexico City. The setting, in a restored 17th-century mansion, is superb, and the menu is enticing, featuring inventive versions of authentic colonial dishes. $$$ ☞ p. 64

La Cocay, Cozumel. The name is Maya for firefly and, like its namesake, this restaurant is a bit magical. Meals here are some of the most innovative and flavorful on Cozumel. $$$ ☞ p. 552

La Estancia de los Tecajetes, Jalapa. Local *cocina Mexicana* doesn't get much better than the enchiladas or *crepa consentida*—chicken crepes doused with a poblano-and-cheese sauce—served here. $$ ☞ p. 488

COMFORTS

Ⓕ **La Casa de Espiritus Alegres Bed and Breakfast, Guanajuato.** This renovated hacienda is a folk-art paradise filled with whimsical treasures from every state in Mexico. $$$$ ☞ p. 273

Ⓖ **Quinta Real, Guadalajara.** Colonial architecture and Spanish-style furnishings distinguish this luxury hotel in a quiet residential neighborhood. $$$$ ☞ p. 228

Ⓑ **Las Ventanas al Paraíso, Cabo San Lucas.** This waterside architectural wonder is the last word in earthy elegance—and reason enough to hop on the next plane to the southern tip of the Baja Peninsula. $$$$ ☞ p. 162

Ⓙ **Chan Kah, Palenque.** A resident monkey is among the charms of this jungle retreat near the Maya ruins; accommodations are in comfortable bungalows. $$$ ☞ p. 459

AFTER HOURS

Fantasy and Enigma discos, Acapulco. Two standouts in a city where Saturday-night fever still rages, Fantasy attracts an older crowd, and Enigma's great light-and-sound show comes with dropdead views of Acapulco Bay. ☞ p. 384

Gran Café del Portal, Veracruz. People-watch into the wee hours over a cup of *café con leche* at this renowned coffeehouse. ☞ p. 481

Joe's Lobster House, Cozumel. Beginning after 10 PM, live rollicking reggae and hot salsa spice up the music menu here. This quaint nightspot, popular with locals, hops into the wee hours. ☞ p. 556

1　MEXICO CITY

Two volcanoes and a pyramid complex flank Mexico's capital, once the center of Aztec civilization and now the country's cosmopolitan business, art, and culinary hub. From the Alameda, a leafy center of activity since Aztec times, to the Zona Rosa, a chic shopping neighborhood, Mexico City offers endless options to urban adventurers. Day trips might include the legendary pyramids of Teotihuacán, colonial Puebla, where mole sauce and Talavera tiles originated, or Xochimilco's floating gardens.

By Frank Shiell

Updated by
Paige Bierma
and Patricia
Alisau

Mexico City is a city of superlatives. It is both the oldest (675 years) and the highest (7,349 ft) metropolis on the North American continent. And with nearly 24 million inhabitants, it is the most populous city in the world. It is Mexico's cultural, political, and financial core—on the verge of the 21st century but clinging to its deeply entrenched Aztec heritage.

As the gargantuan pyramids of Teotihuacán attest—the name is Aztec, meaning "the place where one becomes a god"—the area around Mexico City was occupied from early times by a great civilization, probably Nahuatl in origin. The founding of the Aztec capital nearby did not occur until more than 600 years after Teotihuacán was abandoned, around 750. As the story goes, the nomadic Aztecs were searching for a promised land in which to settle. Their prophecies said they would recognize the spot when they encountered an eagle, perched on a prickly pear cactus, holding a snake in its beak. In 1325, the disputed date given for the founding of the city of Tenochtitlán, the Aztecs discovered this eagle in the valley of Mexico. They built Tenochtitlán on what was then an island in shallow Lake Texcoco and connected it to lakeshore satellite towns by a network of *calzadas* (canals and causeways, now freeways). Even then it was the largest city in the Western hemisphere and, according to historians, one of the three largest cities on earth. When he first laid eyes on Tenochtitlán in the 16th century, Spanish conquistador Hernán Cortés was dazzled by the glistening metropolis, which reminded him of Venice.

A combination of factors made the conquest possible. The superstitious Aztec emperor Moctezuma II believed the white, bearded Cortés on horseback to be the mighty plumed serpent-god Quetzalcóatl, who, according to a tragically ironic prophesy, was supposed to arrive from the east in the year 1519 to rule the land. Moctezuma therefore welcomed the foreigner with gifts of gold and palatial accommodations.

But in return, Cortés initiated the bloody massacre of Tenochtitlán, which lasted almost two years. Joining forces with him was a massive army of Indian "allies," gathered from other settlements such as Cholula and Tlaxcala, who were fed up with the Aztec empire's domination and with paying tribute, especially sending warriors and maidens to be sacrificed. With the strength of their numbers—along with the European tactical advantages of brigantines, horses, firearms, armor, and inadvertently, the introduction of smallpox and the common cold—Cortés succeeded in devastating Tenochtitlán. Only two centuries after it was founded, the young Aztec capital lay in ruins, about half its population dead from battle, starvation, and contagious European diseases against which they had no immunity.

Cortés began building the capital of what he patriotically dubbed New Spain, the Spanish empire's colony that would spread north to cover what is now the United States' southwest, and south to Panama. *Mexico* comes from the word *Mexica* (pronounced *meh*-shee-ka), which is the Aztecs' name for themselves. Aztec is the Spaniards' name for the Mexica. At the site of the demolished Aztec ceremonial center—now the 10-acre Zócalo—Cortés started building a church (the precursor of the gigantic Metropolitan Cathedral), mansions, and government buildings. He utilized the slave labor—and artistry—of the vanquished native Mexicans. On top of the ruins of their city, and using rubble from it, they were forced to build what became the most European-style city in North America. But instead of having the random layout of contemporary medieval European cities, it followed the sophisticated grid pattern of the Aztecs. The Spaniards also drained and filled in Lake Texcoco, preferring wheels and horses (which they introduced to Mexico) over canals and canoes for transport. The land-filled lake bed turned out to be a soggy support for the immense buildings that have been slowly sinking into it since they were built. For much of the construction material the Spaniards quarried the local porous, volcanic pink stone called *tezontle*.

The city grew during the colonial period, and the Franciscans and Dominicans converted the Aztecs to Christianity. In 1571 the Spaniards established the Inquisition in New Spain and burned heretics at its palace headquarters, which still stands in Plaza de Santo Domingo.

It took more than 200 years for Mexicans to successfully rise up against Spain. The historic downtown street 16 de Septiembre commemorates the "declaration" of the War of Independence. On that date in 1810, Father Miguel Hidalgo rang a church bell and cried out his history-making *grito* (shout): "Viva Ferdinand VII [king of Spain at the time]! Death to bad government!" Some historians conclude that Hidalgo's call to arms in the name of the Spanish monarch was just a facade to start an independence movement, which Hidalgo successfully accomplished. That "liberty bell," which now hangs above the main entrance to the National Palace, is rung on every eve of September 16 by the president of the republic, who then shouts a revised version of the patriot's cry: "Viva Mexico! Viva Mexico! Viva Mexico!"

Flying in or out of Mexico City, you get an aerial view of the remaining part of Lake Texcoco on the eastern outskirts of the city. At night the expanse of city lights abruptly ends at a black void that appears to be an ocean. In daylight you can also see the sprawling flatness of the 1,482-square-km (572-square-mi) Meseta de Anáhuac (Valley of Mexico), completely surrounded by mountains. On its south side, two usually snowcapped volcanoes, Popocatépetl and Iztaccíhuatl, are both well over 17,000 ft high. For decades, many thought the twin volcanoes were extinct, but Popocatépetl awakened. It began spewing smoke, ash, and even some lava in 1994 and has remained active on and off since then.

Unfortunately, the single most widely known fact about Mexico City is that its air is polluted. So you might picture the city, its streets packed with vehicles, wrapped daily in a cloak of black smog. In reality, in spite of the capital's serious pollution problem, it also has some of the clearest, bluest skies anywhere, especially in spring and summer. At 7,556 ft, it often has mild daytime weather perfect for sightseeing and cool evenings comfortable for sleeping. Mornings can be glorious—chilly and bright with the promise of the warming sun.

If Mexico City's smog brings Los Angeles to mind, so might the fault line that runs through the valley. In 1957 a major earthquake took a tragic toll, and scars are still visible from the devastating 1985 earthquake—8.1 on the Richter scale. The government reported 10,000 deaths, but the word around town put the toll at 50,000.

Growing nonstop, Mexico City covers a 1,480-square-km (570-square-mi) area of the valley. The city is surrounded on three sides by the state of Mexico and bordered on the south by the state of Morelos. Glossy magazine ads usually tout Mexico's paradisiacal beach resorts and ancient ruins, but cosmopolitan, historic Mexico City is a vital destination in itself—more foreign and fascinating than many major capitals on faraway continents.

Pleasures and Pastimes

Dining

Mexico City has been a culinary capital ever since the time of Moctezuma. Chronicles tell of the extravagant daily banquets prepared for the slender Aztec emperor by his palace chefs. More than 300 different dishes were served for every meal—vast assortments of meat and fowl seasoned in dozens of ways; limitless fruit, vegetables, and herbs; freshwater fish; and fresh seafood that was rushed to Tenochtitlán from both seacoasts by sprinting relay runners.

Until the 15th century, Europeans had never seen indigenous Mexican edibles such as corn, chilies of all varieties, tomatoes, potatoes, pumpkin, squash, avocado, turkey, cacao (chocolate), and vanilla. In turn, the colonization brought European gastronomic influence and ingredients—wheat, onions, garlic, olives, citrus fruit, cattle, sheep, goats, chickens, domesticated pigs (and lard for frying)—and ended up broadening the already complex pre-Hispanic cuisine into one of the most multifaceted and exquisite in the world: traditional Mexican.

Today's cosmopolitan Mexico City is a gastronomic melting pot with some 15,000 restaurants. You'll find everything from simple family-style eateries to five-star world-class restaurants. And international restaurants serve foods from around the world—although Spanish and French haute-cuisine are dominant.

In the past decade or so a renaissance of Mexican cooking has brought about a new wave known as *cocina mexicana moderna* (modern Mexican cuisine), which many Mexico City restaurants serve. Emphasis is on presentation, the delicate tastes of traditional regional dishes gleaned from colonial cookbooks, and ancient indigenous cooking techniques such as steaming and baking, which used a lot less fat, as there were no pigs for lard. Also, items such as crunchy fried grasshoppers and cooked *maguey* (cactus) worms now grace the menus of the best restaurants in town.

Lodging

As might be expected of a megalopolis, Mexico City has more than 25,000 hotel rooms—enough to accommodate every taste and budget. You can lodge in the quaint or the colonial, the smoked-glass-and-steel high-rise, or the elegant replica of an Italianate palace.

Museums

Mexico City is the cultural as well as political capital of the country, as evidenced by its 80-plus museums—some of the finest in Latin America. In buildings of architectural merit, you can see the sweeping murals of such native sons as Diego Rivera, José Clemente Orozco, and Juan O'Gorman; the gripping surrealism of Frida Kahlo; stunning pre-Hispanic ceremonial pieces; and outstanding collections of religious art.

Nightlife and the Arts

Mexico City is the cultural capital of Latin America and, with the exception of Río de Janiero, has the liveliest nightlife of the region. There's something for every taste, from opera and symphonies to a renowned folklore ballet and a lively square where mariachi play. You'll also find discos and offbeat places where salsa and *danzón* (Cuban dance music) are headliners.

Shopping

Native crafts and specialties from all over Mexico are available in the capital, as are designer clothes. You'll also find modern art by some of the best contemporary painters, many of whom are making a name for themselves in the United States. And of course Mexican goods are a far better deal here than they are in overseas outlets.

Sports and the Outdoors

Latin sports such as the *fiesta brava* (bullfighting)—brought to Mexico by the conquistadores—have enjoyed popularity for more than four centuries in the capital, which attracts the country's best athletes. And although the roots of soccer ("fútbol") are probably English, a weekend afternoon game at Mexico City's giant Estadio Azteca leaves no question that this is the sport Mexicans are craziest about. Adventure-travel agencies have also opened in Mexico City to offer great weekend getaways such as white-water rafting in nearby Veracruz. Tennis, golf, running—even rowing a boat in a park—are other outdoor pursuits to engage in while in town.

EXPLORING MEXICO CITY

Most of Mexico City is aligned on two major intersecting thoroughfares: Paseo de la Reforma and Avenida Insurgentes—at 34 km (21 mi), the longest avenue in the city. Administratively, Mexico City is divided into 16 *delegaciones* (districts) and about 400 *colonias* (neighborhoods), each with street names fitting a given theme, such as a river, philosopher, doctor, or revolutionary hero. The same street can change names as it goes through different colonias. Hence, most street addresses include their colonia (abbreviated as Col.). And, unless you're going to an obvious place, it is important to tell your taxi driver the name of the colonia.

The principal sights of Mexico City fall into three areas. Allow a full day to cover each thoroughly, although you could race through them in four or five hours apiece. You can cover the first two areas—the Zócalo and Alameda Central, and Zona Rosa and Bosque de Chapultepec (Chapultepec Park)—on foot. Getting around Coyoacán and San Angel in southern Mexico City will require a taxi ride or two.

Numbers in the text correspond to numbers in the margin and on the Zócalo and Alameda Central; Zona Rosa, Bosque de Chapultepec, and Condesa; and San Angel and Coyoacán maps.

Great Itineraries

You can spend a month in Mexico City and just begin to grasp the tip of its iceberg of sights, sounds, and tastes. For stays shorter than this, here are some highlights.

IF YOU HAVE 3 DAYS

Start with the **Zócalo** ①, with its exotic ruins, museums, and public buildings; then stroll to the **Palacio de Bellas Artes** ⑮ and surroundings—stopping at the **Casa de los Azulejos** ⑬ for a Mexican lunch—and end the day at **Alameda Central** ⑱. Day 2, head for the **Museo Nacional de Antropología** ㉖ in the morning and the **Zona Rosa** in the afternoon, when it starts to come alive. Visit the **Mercado Insurgentes** (☞ Markets *in* Shopping, *below*) for some fun shopping, or any of the stores on our list. Consider an evening in the pleasant **Colonia Condesa** for dinner; it is one of the city's up-and-coming neighborhoods. Day 3, go to **Bosque de Chapultepec** ㉑ to stroll the green pathways past the rowing lake and visit the **Castillo de Chapultepec** ㉒, the **Museo de Arte Moderno** ㉔, **Museo Rufino Tamayo** ㉕, and, of course, the **Zoológico** ㉗ to see the pandas. Visit downtown's **Plaza Garibaldi** (☞ Nightlife *in* Nightlife and the Arts, *below*) on your last night in town for a rousing mariachi send-off. If the Classic period site of **Teotihuacán** intrigues you, however, you could spend the third day there (☞ North of Mexico *in* Chapter 2).

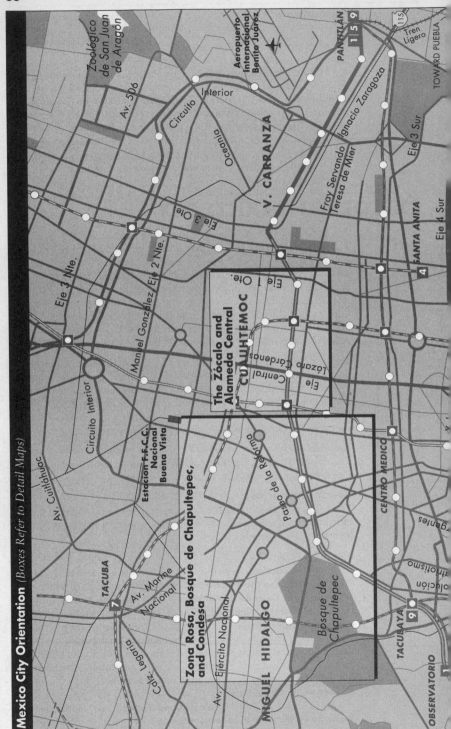

San Angel and Coyoacán

A. OBREGON

BARRANCA DEL MUERTO

COYOACÁN

UNIVERSIDAD

Ciudad Universitaria

Insurgentes

BENITO JUAREZ

IZTACALCO

TASQUEÑA

Country Club

Parque Nacional Cerro de la Estrella

TO XOCHIMILCO

Tren Ligero

2 miles

3 km

N

Rojo Gómez

Av. Lic. Javier

Av. Río Churubusco

Circuito Interior

Eje 5 Sur

Eje 6 Sur

Av. Cinco

Eje 3 Ote.

Eje 2 Ote.

Calz. de la Viga

Eje 1 Ote.

Av. Plutarco Elías Calles

Av. Eugenia

Av. del 4 Sur

Calz. de Tlalpan

Eje Central Lázaro Cárdenas

Av. División del Norte

Av. Río Churubusco

Av. Miguel Angel de Quevedo

Av. Santa Ana

Calz. Tasqueña

Eje 10 Sur

Av. A. Urraza

Eje 2 Pte.

Eje 7 Sur

Eje 8 Sur

Av. de los Ins.

Av. de la Re

Av.

Mexico City Subways

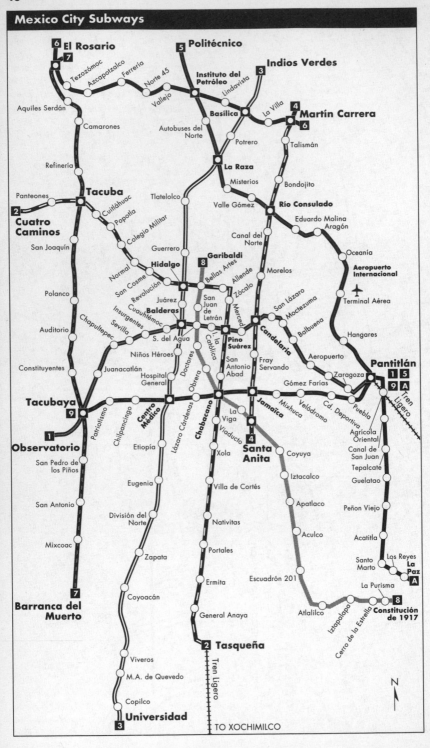

6 7 El Rosario

5 Politécnico

Indios Verdes 3

Instituto del Petróleo

Lindavista

Tezozómoc Azcapotzalco Ferrería

Norte 45

Aquiles Serdán

Vallejo

La Villa

Martín Carrera 4 6

Camarones

Basílica

Autobuses del Norte

Potrero

Talismán

Refinería

La Raza

Misterios

Bondojito

Panteones

Tacuba

Tlatelolco

Valle Gómez

Río Consulado

2 Cuatro Caminos

Cuitláhuac

Popotla

Eduardo Molina Aragón

San Joaquín

Colegio Militar

Canal del Norte

Oceanía

Guerrero

Garibaldi

Aeropuerto Internacional

Polanco

Normal

Hidalgo 8

Bellas Artes

Morelos

Terminal Aérea

San Cosme

Revolución

Allende

Zócalo

San Lázaro

Moctezuma

Auditorio

Juárez

Cuauhtémoc

San Juan de Letrán

Hangares

Insurgentes

Balderas

Merced

Candelaria

Balbuena

Chapultepec

Sevilla

S. del Agua

Pino Suárez

Aeropuerto

Constituyentes

Niños Héroes

San Antonio Abad

Fray Servando

Zaragoza

Pantitlán 1 5

Juanacatlán

Hospital General

Doctores

Obrera

Gómez Farías

9 A

Tacubaya 9

Patriotismo

Centro Médico

Chabacano

La Viga

Jamaica

Mixhuca

Velódromo

Cd. Deportiva

Puebla

Tren Ligero

Observatorio 1

Chilpancingo

Etiopía

Viaducto

Santa Anita 4

Coyuya

Agrícola Oriental

San Pedro de los Piños

Lázaro Cárdenas

Xola

Iztacalco

Canal de San Juan

San Antonio

Eugenia

Villa de Cortés

Apatlaco

Tepalcate

Guelatao

Mixcoac

División del Norte

Nativitas

Aculco

Peñon Viejo

Zapata

Portales

Acatitla

Coyoacán

Ermita

Escuadrón 201

Los Reyes La Paz A

Santo Marto

Barranca del Muerto 7

General Anaya

Atlalilco

La Purisma

Constitución de 1917 8

Tasqueña 2

Iztapalapa

Cerro de la Estrella

Viveros

Tren Ligero

M.A. de Quevedo

Copilco

Universidad 3

TO XOCHIMILCO

N

IF YOU HAVE 5 DAYS

Follow the three-day itinerary, going to **Bosque de Chapultepec** ㉑ on Day 3. On Day 4 spend time in **San Angel**—start with the Bazar Sábado if your plans bring you here on a Saturday—and in **Coyoacán,** with its lovely casa-museums, especially **Museo de Frida Kahlo** ㊲ and **Museo de Leon Trotsky** ㊳. On Day 5 take an excursion to the **Basílica of the Virgin of Guadalupe,** Latin America's holiest shrine, and the pyramids of **Teotihuacán** (☞ North of Mexico *in* Chapter 2), where a powerful regime held sway over the region more than a millennium before the arrival of the Spanish. Climb at least one pyramid, visit the museum, and head back to Mexico City.

IF YOU HAVE 10 DAYS

Follow the five-day option and add a visit to the resort town of **Cuernavaca** (☞ South of Mexico City *in* Chapter 2), about an hour's drive southeast of Mexico City. Spend the day in its museums and browsing its pretty main square, then overnight at one of the town's converted mansions. On Day 7 head back to Mexico City via Highway 95 and stop in **Xochimilco,** where you can ride through the floating gardens on a gondola-like boat and view an outstanding private collection of works by Diego Rivera and Frida Kahlo at the Dolores Olmedo Patino Museum. On Day 8 drive to the ancient Toltec ruins at **Tula** and continue to the village of **Tepotzotlán,** which has a beautiful Jesuit church. The next day, head to **Puebla** for a couple hours' tour, including the main square and the fine Amparo Museum, then pop over to the nearby town of **Cholula,** once a sacred ceremonial site. Climb to the top of the church built over a pyramid, and return to Puebla for the night. En route back to Mexico City on the last day, drive to **Cacaxtla** to see some of the best-preserved Mesoamerican murals in Mexico.

The Zócalo and Alameda Central

This area is all about history: the Zócalo, its surrounding Centro Histórico, and Alameda Park were the heart of both the Aztec and Spanish cities. Many of the streets in downtown Mexico City have been converted into pedestrian-only thoroughfares.

A Good Walk

An excellent point of departure for any tour of the city's center is the **Zócalo** ①, the heart and soul of old downtown. From here you can literally see the layers of history in the buildings around you. On the north side of this huge square you'll see the tilting **Catedral Metropolitana** ② and adjacent to it the comparatively small 18th-century Sagrario Chapel, even more angled than the cathedral. The **Templo Mayor** ③, ruins from the Aztec capital, is northeast of the cathedral, across the pedestrian plaza. If you're interested in modern art, walk south about half a block from the Templo Mayor to the end of Calle Seminario, then go two blocks east on Calle Moneda to Academia to find the **Museo José Luis Cuevas** ④. Take Moneda back (west) to the Zócalo. The first building you'll see on your left is the massive **Palacio Nacional** ⑤, covering two city blocks. Walk south past the palacio to the corner and turn right, crossing the street to get to the section of the Zócalo occupied by the 1722 **Ayuntamiento** ⑥. Recross the street and walk northwest through the open square to Calle Cinco de Mayo and the National Pawn Shop in the **Monte de Piedad** ⑦. Three-and-a-half blocks north is the historic **Plaza de Santo Domingo** ⑧. Walk one block east along Calle República de Cuba and one block south on Calle República de Argentina to get to Calle Justo Sierra and the **Conjunto de San Idelfonso** ⑨, now an art gallery. Turn west and follow Calle Justo Sierra three blocks—it will change into Calle Donceles—to Calle República de Chile, then turn left (south) a block

42

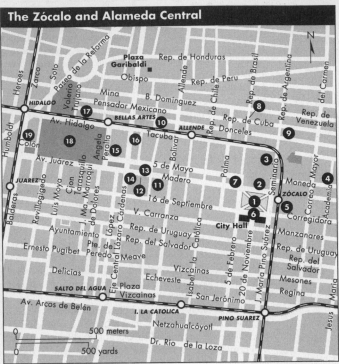

The Zócalo and Alameda Central

to Calle Tacuba. Turn right and walk one block to have a scrumptious lunch at the Café de Tacuba (☞ Dining, *below*) on the right side of the street. Or, you can continue west on Tacuba 1½ blocks to the **Museo Nacional de Arte** ⑩ in the colonial Plaza Manuel Tolsa.

From Calle Tacuba, head two short blocks south to Calle Madero, one of the city's most architecturally varied streets. On the south side of Madero, between Bolivar and Gante, is the 1780 Baroque **Palacio de Iturbide** ⑪. Go west along on the south side of Madero; less than a block past the palacio you'll come to the **Iglesia de San Francisco** ⑫, with its beautifully painted walls. The stunning tilework of the **Casa de los Azulejos** ⑬ will draw your eye across Calle Madero.

The ultimate goals of the remainder of this walk are an antiques museum and a Diego Rivera mural museum. From Calle Madero, walk less than a half block west to Eje Central Lázaro Cárdenas, a wide four-lane avenue. At the corner and on your left, you can't miss the 1950s-style skyscraper, the **Torre Latinoamericana** ⑭, which has one of the best aerial views of the city as well as a sky-high aquarium. Cross the avenue and turn right (north) to explore the beautiful **Palacio de Bellas Artes** ⑮ opera house, the long side of which skirts Lázaro Cárdenas (its entrance is on Juárez). The 1908 post-office building of **Dirección General de Correos** ⑯ is up Lázaro Cárdenas another 150 ft across from Bellas Artes.

Pass the post office to Calle Tacuba and cross Lázaro Cárdenas one last time, where Calle Tacuba turns into Avenida Hidalgo. One block west, you'll come to the antique-filled **Museo Franz Mayer** ⑰. Across Avenida Hidalgo is the north end of the leafy park **Alameda Central** ⑱. At its south end, on Avenida Juárez, **Fonart** is a government-owned handicrafts store (☞ Specialty Shops *in* Shopping, *below*). To get to the **Museo Mural Diego Rivera** ⑲, take Juárez west to Calle Balderas, about 3½ blocks from Fonart. Turn right and walk a short block to Calle Colón.

TIMING

The Zócalo area will be quietest on Sunday, when bureaucrats have their day of rest. But Alameda Park will be jumping with children and their parents enjoying a Sunday outing. The park will be particularly festive during Christmas, when dozens of "Santas" will appear with plastic reindeer to take wish lists from long lines of children. Although Mexicans do celebrate on Dec. 25, the traditional Mexican Christmas kicks in January 5, the eve of the Day of the Three Kings, and the Three Wise Men of biblical lore replace the Santas in the Alameda. Gorgeous Christmas paintings-in-lights deck the Zócalo from end to end and stream up Calle Madero past Alameda Park to Paseo de la Reforma beyond the museums in Bosque de Chapultepec.

During the daytime, the downtown area is filled with people and vibrant with activity. As in any big city, watch out for pickpockets, especially on crowded buses and subways, and avoid dark, deserted streets at night.

The streets in the walking tour are fairly close to one another and can be covered in half a day. The National Palace, Templo Mayor and its museum, and Franz Mayer Museum are worth an hour each of your time; you can cover the Palace of Fine Arts in a half hour.

Sights to See

THE ZÓCALO

6 **Ayuntamiento** (City Hall). The two buildings of Mexico's city hall stand on the south side of the Zócalo; colonial tiles of the arms of Cortés and other conquistadores decorate the one on the west. Originally built in 1532, it was destroyed by fire in 1692 and rebuilt in 1722. In 1935 the Distrito Federal needed more office space, and to maintain the architectural integrity of the Zócalo, the "matching" structure across the street (20 de Noviembre) was built. In 1997, for the first time in 70 years, Mexico City residents were allowed to elect their own mayor (the post had previously been appointed by the president). Thus did the city's first leftist mayor, Cuauhtémoc Cárdenas—son of Mexico's populist president Lázaro Cárdenas—take over the reins in these buildings until 2000.

2 **Catedral Metropolitana** (Metropolitan Cathedral). Construction on this oldest and largest cathedral in Latin America began in 1573 on the north side of the Zócalo and continued intermittently throughout the next three centuries. The result is a medley of Baroque and neoclassical touches. Inside are four identical domes, their airiness grounded by rows of supportive columns. There are five altars and 14 chapels, mostly in the fussy churrigueresque style, an ornate Baroque style named for Spanish architect José Churriguera (d. 1725). Like most Mexican churches, the cathedral itself is all but overwhelmed by the innumerable paintings, altarpieces, and statues—in graphic color—of Christ and the saints. Over the centuries, this cathedral has sunk noticeably into the spongy subsoil. Its list is evident when viewed from across the square, and engineering projects to stabilize the structure are constantly under way.

7 **Monte de Piedad** (Mountain of Pity). Now housing the National Pawn Shop—which sells jewelry, antiques, and other goods not reclaimed by their owners—this structure was built to help the poor in the late 18th century. It's on the northwest corner of the Zócalo, on what was once the site of an Aztec palace. ☎ 5/278–1800. ☉ *Mon.–Sat. about 10–7.*

4 **Museo José Luis Cuevas.** One of the newest museums downtown, installed in a refurbished former convent, it has a superb collection of contemporary art, as well as work by Mexico's enfant terrible, José Luis Cuevas, who is one of the country's best contemporary artists. Don't miss the sensational *La Giganta* (*The Giantess*), Cuevas's 8-ton bronze sculpture in the central patio. Up-and-coming Latin American artists appear in tem-

porary exhibits throughout the year. ⊠ *Academia 13,* ☎ *5/542–8959.*
▨ *80¢, free Sun.* ☉ *Tues.–Sun. 10–5:30.*

★ ❺ **Palacio Nacional** (National Palace). This grand government building
was initiated by Cortés on the site of Moctezuma's home and remodeled by the viceroys. Its current form dates from 1693, although a third
floor was added in 1926. Now the seat of government, it has always
served as a public-function site. In fact, during colonial times, the first
bullfight in New Spain took place in the inner courtyard.

Diego Rivera's sweeping, epic murals on the second floor of the main
courtyard have the power to mesmerize. For more than 16 years (1929–
45), he and his assistants mounted scaffolds day and night, perfecting
techniques adapted from Renaissance Italian frescoes. The result, nearly
1,200 square ft of vividly painted wall space, is grandiosely entitled *Epic
of the Mexican People in Their Struggle for Freedom and Independence.*
The larger-than-life paintings represent two millennia of Mexican history, filtered through Rivera's imagination. He painted pre-Hispanic
times in innocent, almost sugary scenes of Tenochtitlán. Only a few vi-
gnettes—a lascivious woman baring her leg in the marketplace, a man
offering a human arm for sale, and the carnage of warriors—acknowledge the darker aspects of ancient life. As you walk around the floor, you'll
pass images of the savagery of the conquest and the hypocrisy of the Spanish priests, the noble independence movement, and the bloody revolution. Marx appears amid scenes of class struggle, toiling workers,
industrialization (which Rivera idealized), bourgeois decadence, and nu-
clear holocaust. These are among Rivera's finest—as well as most accessible
and likely most visited—paintings. The palace also houses two minor museums—dealing with 19th-century president Benito Juárez and the Mexican Congress. And the liberty bell rung by Padre Hidalgo to proclaim
independence in 1810 hangs high on the central facade. It chimes every
eve of September 16, while from the balcony the president repeats the
historic shout of independence to throngs of *chilangos* (Mexico City residents) below. Usually the people demand that the chief executive continue shouting until he loses his voice. ⊠ *East side of the Zócalo.* ▨ *Free
(you will be asked to leave an I.D. at the front desk).* ☉ *Daily 9–5.*

❽ **Plaza de Santo Domingo** (Santo Domingo Plaza). The Aztec emperor
Cuauhtémoc built a palace here, where heretics were later burned at
the stake in the Spanish Inquisition. The plaza was the intellectual hub
of the city during the colonial era. Today, its most colorful feature is
the **Portal de los Evangelistas** (Portal of the Evangelists), filled with scribes
at old-fashioned typewriters who are most likely composing letters for
love-stricken swains. This age-old custom, which originated when quill
pens were in vogue, has successfully launched quite a few of Cupid's
arrows. The gloomy-looking **Palace of the Inquisition,** founded by the
Catholic Church in 1571 (50 years after the conquest) and closed by
government decree in 1820, is catercorner to the lively portal. It was a
medical school for many years and now serves as a museum portraying the history of both the Inquisition and medicine. The 18th-century
Baroque **Santo Domingo church,** slightly north of the portal, is all that
remains of the first Dominican convent in New Spain. The convent building was demolished in 1861 under the Reform laws that forced clerics
to turn over all religious buildings not used for worship to the government. Today, you can still see white-robed Dominican nuns visiting the
church. ⊠ *Between República de Cuba, República de Brasil, República
de Venezuela, and Palma.*

❸ **Templo Mayor** (Great Temple). The ruins of the ancient hub of the Aztec
empire were unearthed accidentally in 1978 by telephone repairmen
and have since been turned into a vast and historically significant ar-

chaeological site and museum. At this temple, dedicated to the Aztec cult of death, captives from rival tribes—as many as 10,000 at a time—were sacrificed to the bloodthirsty god of war, Huitzilopochtli. Seven rows of leering stone skulls adorn one side of the structure.

The adjacent **Museo del Templo Mayor** contains 3,000 pieces unearthed from the site and from other ruins in central Mexico; they include ceramic warriors, stone carvings and knives, skulls of sacrificial victims, a rare gold ingot, models and scale reproductions, and a room on the Spaniards' destruction of Tenochtitlán. The centerpiece is an 8-ton disk discovered at the Templo Mayor. It depicts the moon goddess Coyolxauhqui, who, according to myth, was decapitated and dismembered by her brother Huitzilopochtli for trying to persuade her 400 other brothers to murder their mother. ⊠ *Seminario 8, at República de Guatemala (entrance on the plaza, near Catedral Metropolitana),* ☎ *5/542–4784, 5/542–4785, 5/542–4786.* ☞ *$2.50, free Sun.* ☺ *Tues.–Sun. 9–5. Call 2 wks ahead to schedule free English-language tours by museum staff, or hire a freelance guide outside the museum.*

❶ **Zócalo** (formal name: Plaza de la Constitución). Mexico City's historic plaza and the buildings around it were built by the Spaniards, using Indian slave labor. This enormous paved square, the largest in the Western Hemisphere, occupies the site of the ceremonial center of Tenochtitlán, the capital of the Aztec empire, which once comprised 78 buildings. Throughout the 16th, 17th, and 18th centuries, the Spaniards and their descendants constructed elaborate churches and convents, elegant mansions, and stately public edifices, many of which have long since been converted to other uses. There is an air of Old Europe in this part of the city, which, in its entirety (the Centro Histórico), is a national monument that has been undergoing major refurbishing. Imposing buildings are constructed with the pink volcanic tezontle stone and the quarry stones that the Spaniards recycled from the rubble of the Aztec temples they razed. Throngs of small shops, eateries, cantinas, street vendors, and women in native Indian dress contribute to an inimitably Mexican flavor and exuberance.

Zócalo literally means "pedestal" or "base": in the mid-19th century, an independence monument was planned for the square, but it was never built. The term stuck, however, and now the word "zócalo" is applied to the main plazas of most Mexican cities. Mexico City's Zócalo (because it's the original, it is always capitalized) is used for government rallies, protest marches, sit-ins, and festive events. It is the focal point for Independence Day celebrations on the eve of September 16 and is spectacularly festooned during the Christmas season. Flag-raising and -lowering ceremonies take place here in the early morning and late afternoon. ⊠ *Bounded on the south by 16 de Septiembre, north by 5 de Mayo, east by Pino Suárez, and west by Monte de Piedad.*

ALAMEDA CENTRAL

⓲ **Alameda Central** (Alameda Park). This has been one of the capital's oases of greenery and centers of activity since Aztec times, when the Indians held their *tianguis* (market) on the site. In the early days of the Viceroyalty, the Inquisition burned its victims at the stake here. Later, national leaders, from 18th-century viceroys to Emperor Maximilian and President Porfirio Díaz, clearly envisioned the park as a symbol of civic pride and prosperity: over the centuries, it has been endowed with fountains; railings; a Moorish kiosk imported from Paris; and ash, willow, and poplar trees. Its most conspicuous man-made structure is the semicircular, white marble **Hemiciclo a Benito Juárez** (monument to Juárez) on the Avenida Juárez side of the park. It is a fine place for strolling, relaxing, and listening to live music on Sunday and holidays.

⑬ **Casa de los Azulejos** (House of Tiles). Built as the palace of the counts of the Valle de Orizaba, an aristocratic family from the early period of Spanish rule, this 17th-century masterpiece acquired its name from the tilework installed by a later descendant, a ne'er-do-well scion who married a rich woman. In addition to its well-preserved white, blue, and yellow tiles, the facade also has iron grillwork balconies and gray stonework. One of the prettiest Baroque structures in the country, it is currently occupied by Sanborns, a chain store–restaurant. The dazzling interior, which includes a Moorish patio, a monumental staircase, and a mural by Orozco, is worth seeing. If you have plenty of time—service is slow—this is a good place to stop for breakfast, lunch, or dinner. ✉ *Calle Madero 4, at Callejón de la Condesa,* ☎ *5/512–9820 ext. 103.* ⊙ *Daily 7 AM–1 AM.*

⑨ **Conjunto de San Idelfonso** (San Idelfonso Complex). This colonial building with lovely patios started out as a Jesuit school for the sons of wealthy Mexicans in the 18th century, then took life as a medical college, and finally became a public preparatory school. After a complete renovation, it reopened in 1992 with "Splendors of Mexico: 30 Centuries of Art" and has been showcasing outstanding traveling Mexican exhibits ever since. The interior contains extraordinary works by the big three of mural painting—Diego Rivera, David Alfaro Siqueiros, and Clemente Orozco. ✉ *Justo Sierra 16, almost at the corner of República de Argentina, 2 blocks north of the Zócalo,* ☎ *5/789–2505.* ▣ *$2.50, free Tues.* ⊙ *Tues.–Sun. 10–6, Wed. and Sat. 10–9.*

⑯ **Dirección General de Correos** (General Post Office). Mexico City's main post-office building is a fine example of Renaissance revival architecture. Constructed of cream-color sandstone in 1908, it epitomizes the grand imitations of European architecture common in Mexico during the Porfiriato—the rather long dictatorship of Porfirio Díaz (1876–1911). Upstairs, the **Museo del Palacio Postal** shows Mexico's postal history. ✉ *Calle Tacuba and Eje Central Lázaro Cárdenas,* ☎ *Museum 5/510–2999, post office 5/521–7394.* ▣ *Free.* ⊙ *Museum weekdays 9–4, weekends 10–2; post office weekdays 8–8, Sat. 9–1.*

⑫ **Iglesia de San Francisco.** Supposedly the site of Moctezuma's zoo, and certifiably built on the site of Mexico's first convent (1524), this iglesia's current 18th-century French Gothic incarnation is one of the newest buildings on the street. The paintings inside are beautiful. ✉ *Calles Madero and 16 de Septiembre,* ☎ *no phone.* ⊙ *Daily 7 AM–8:30 PM.*

⑰ **Museo Franz Mayer.** Opened in 1986 in the 16th-century Hospital de San Juan de Dios, this museum has exhibits that include 16th- and 17th-century antiques, such as wooden chests inlaid with ivory, tortoiseshell, and ebony; tapestries, paintings, and lacquerware; rococo clocks, glassware, and architectural ornamentation; and an unusually large assortment of Talavera ceramics and *azulejos,* or tiles. The museum also has an impressive collection of more than 700 editions of Cervantes's *Don Quixote.* The old hospital building is faithfully restored, with pieces of the original frescoes peeking through. ✉ *Av. Hidalgo 45, at Plaza Santa Veracruz,* ☎ *5/ 518–2267.* ▣ *$1.50, free Tues.* ⊙ *Tues.–Sun. 10–5. Call 1 day ahead for an English-speaking guide.*

⑲ **Museo Mural Diego Rivera.** Diego Rivera's controversial mural, *Sunday Afternoon Dream in the Alameda Park,* originally was painted on a lobby wall of the Hotel Del Prado in 1947–48. Its controversy grew out of Rivera's Marxist inscription, "God does not exist," which the artist later replaced with the bland "Conference of San Juan de Letrán" to placate Mexico's dominant Catholic population. The 1985 earthquake destroyed the hotel but not the poetic mural. This museum was built across the street from the hotel to house the work. ✉ *Calles Balderas and Colón,* ☎ *5/510–2329.* ▣ *$1, free Sun.* ⊙ *Tues.–Sun. 10–6.*

🔟 **Museo Nacional de Arte** (National Art Museum). This neoclassical building, built during the Porfiriato and turned into a museum in 1982, contains a superb collection from nearly every school of Mexican art, with a concentration on Mexico's artistic development from 1810 to 1950. The museum was undergoing restoration in 2000 and scheduled to reopen by October 2000. Works include Diego Rivera's portrait of Adolfo Best Maugard, José María Velasco's *Vista del Valle de México desde el Cerro de Santa Isabel (View of the Valley of Mexico from the Hill of Santa Isabel)*, and Ramón Cano Manilla's *El Globo (The Balloon)*. *El Caballito*, a statue of Spain's Carlos V on horseback, stands out front. ⊠ *Calle Tacuba 8,* ☎ *5/512–3224.* 🎫 *$2, free Sun.* ◐ *Tues.–Sun. 10–5:30.*

★ ⑮ **Palacio de Bellas Artes** (Fine Arts Palace). Construction on this colossal white-marble opera house was begun in 1904 by Porfirio Díaz, who wanted to add yet another ornamental building to his accomplishments. He was ousted seven years later after winning yet another rigged election. He died in 1915, and the building wasn't finished until 1934. Today the theater serves as a handsome venue for international and national artists, including such groups as the Ballet Folklórico de México (☞ The Arts *in* Nightlife and the Arts, *below*). The palace is indeed renowned for its architecture, the work of Italian Adamo Boari, who also designed the post office; it includes an art-nouveau facade trimmed in pre-Hispanic motifs. Inside are a Tiffany stained-glass curtain depicting the two volcanoes outside Mexico City and paintings by several celebrated Mexican artists, including Rufino Tamayo and Mexico's trio of muralists: Rivera, Orozco, and Siqueiros. Temporary art exhibits are also held here. ⊠ *Eje Central Lázaro Cárdenas and Av. Juárez,* ☎ *5/512–3633.* 🎫 *$2.50 for exhibits, free Sun. (no charge to look at the building and gift shops inside).* ◐ *Building Tues.–Sun. 10–9, exhibits Tues.–Sun. 10–5:30.*

OFF THE
BEATEN PATH

TLATELOLCO – At Avenida Reforma's northern end, about 2 km (1 mi) north of the Palacio de Bellas Artes, the area known as Tlatelolco (pronounced tla-tel-*ohl*-coh) was the domain of Cuauhtémoc (pronounced kwa-oo-*teh*-muck)—the last Aztec emperor before the conquest—and the sister city of Tenochtitlán. In modern times its name makes residents shudder, because it was here that the Mexican army massacred several hundred protesting students in 1968. In addition, the 1985 earthquake destroyed several high-rise apartments in Tlatelolco, killing hundreds. The center of Tlatelolco is the **Plaza de las Tres Culturas,** so named because Mexico's three cultural eras—pre-Hispanic, colonial, and modern—are represented on the plaza in the form of the small ruins of a pre-Hispanic ceremonial center (visible from the roadway); the Iglesia de Santiago Tlatelolco (1609) and Colegio de la Santa Cruz de Tlatelolco (1535–36); and the ultracontemporary Ministry of Foreign Affairs (1970). The *colegio* (college), founded by the Franciscans after the conquest, was once attended by the sons of the Aztec nobility. ⊠ *The plaza is bounded on the north by Manuel González, on the west by Av. San Juan de Letrán Nte., and on the east by Paseo de la Reforma, between Glorietas de Peralvillo and Cuitláhuac.*

⑪ **Palacio de Iturbide** (Emperor Iturbide's Palace). Built in 1780, this handsome Baroque structure—note the imposing door and its carved-stone trimmings—became the residence of Iturbide in 1822. One of the heroes of the independence movement, the misguided Iturbide proclaimed himself emperor of a country that had thrown off the imperial yoke of the Hapsburgs only a year before. His own empire, needless to say, was short-lived. Now his home is owned by Banamex (Banco Nacional de México) and sponsors cultural exhibits in the atrium. ⊠ *Calle Madero 17,* ☎ *5/225–0281.* 🎫 *Free.* ◐ *Inner atrium daily 9–3.*

⑭ **Torre Latinoamericana** (Latin American Tower). Touted as the tallest building in the capital before the Hotel de Mexico was built in the 1980s, this 47-story skyscraper was completed in 1956, and on clear days the observation deck and café on the top floors afford fine views of the city. The **Fantastic World of the Sea**, a sky-high aquarium, miraculously transported small sharks and crocodiles to the 38th floor. ⊠ *Calle Madero and Eje Central Lázaro Cárdenas,* ☎ *Observation deck 5/521–0844, aquarium 5/521–7455.* ☜ *Deck $3.20, aquarium $2.20.* ☉ *Deck daily 9:30 AM–11 PM; aquarium daily 9:30 AM–10 PM.*

Zona Rosa, Bosque de Chapultepec, and Colonia Condesa

Bosque de Chapultepec, originally called Cerro de Chapultepec, is the largest park in the city, a great green refuge from gray urban living. Housing five world-class museums, a castle, a lake, an amusement park, and the Mexican president's official residence, Chapultepec is a saving grace for visitors and locals. If you pick only one of these museums to visit, make it the Museo Nacional de Antropología—you won't find the likes of its exhibits anywhere else.

The Zona Rosa, once a cultural center of Mexico City, is now a first stop for shopping, where stores, hotels, travel agencies, and restaurants line the avenues. Nearby Colonia Condesa is the newcomer on foreigners' itineraries. This tranquil neighborhood is filled with casual cafés and the city's hottest new eateries.

A Good Walk

Emperor Maximilian built the Paseo de la Reforma in 1865, modeling it after the Champs-Élysées in Paris. Its purpose was to connect the Palacio Nacional (☞ Sights to See *in* Zócalo and Alameda Central, *above*) with his residence, the Castillo de Chapultepec. At the northern end of Reforma are Tlatelolco (☞ Sights to See *in* Zócalo and Alameda Central, *above*), the Lagunilla Market, and Plaza Garibaldi, where the mariachis gather. To the south, Reforma winds its leisurely way west into the wealthy neighborhoods of Lomas de Chapultepec, where most of the houses and estates sit behind stone walls.

Two areas of particular interest along Reforma are the Zona Rosa and Bosque de Chapultepec. Start your exploration of the Zona Rosa section at the junction of Reforma, Avenida Juárez, and Bucareli, just west of the Alameda Central. Along the stretch of Reforma west of this intersection are a number of statues erected at the request of former Mexican president Porfirio Díaz to honor illustrious men, including Simón Bolívar, Columbus, Pasteur, and the Aztec emperor Cuauhtémoc. The best known, the **Monumento a la Independencia** ⑳, also known as The Angel, marks the western edge of the Zona Rosa. To get the best of the area's sights, walk along Hamburgo, Londres, and Copenhague streets—like others in the Zona, named for Continental cities. There is a crafts market, Mercado Zona Rosa, on Londres.

Four blocks southwest of the Zona Rosa, at Avenida Chapultepec, you'll come to the main entrance of **Bosque de Chapultepec** ㉑, or Chapultepec Park. Uphill from the entrance is the **Castillo de Chapultepec** ㉒ and its National History Museum. Heading downhill again after leaving the Castillo, you'll go past the much smaller, also historical, **Museo del Caracol** ㉓. North of the Castillo on the near side of Paseo de la Reforma is the **Museo de Arte Moderno** ㉔. Almost directly across Paseo de la Reforma on its north side and west of Calle Gandhi, you'll see the **Museo Rufino Tamayo** ㉕, in which you'll find Tamayo's works as well as those of other modern artists. West of the Museo Tamayo on the same side of Reforma is the **Museo Nacional de Antropología** ㉖, with its world-

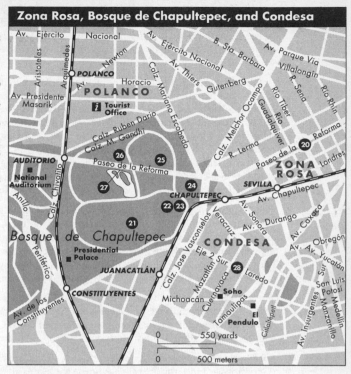

renowned collections of Mesoamerican art and artifacts. Cross Reforma again and you'll come to the entrance to the **Zoológico** ㉗.

Southeast of Bosque de Chapultepec, **Colonia Condesa** ㉘ is a tree-lined neighborhood where meandering streets make for pleasant strolling, especially in spring when jacaranda blossoms color the colonia. From the Bosque de Chapultepec, take a *pesero* (minibus) from beside the Chapultepec metro or a five-minute taxi ride to the trendy restaurant zone of Calle Michoacán. If you choose to walk, it'll take 15–20 minutes: walk up Calle Veracruz going away from the park, turn right on Avenida Mazatlán, then left onto Calle Michoacán.

TIMING

You can easily spend an hour at each Bosque de Chapultepec museum (☞ Sights to See, *below*), with the exception of the National Museum of Anthropology, which is huge compared with its sister cultural centers. You can have a quick go-through in two hours, but to really appreciate the fine exhibits, anywhere from a half-day to two full days is more appropriate. Tuesday to Saturday are good days to visit the museums and stroll around the park. On Sunday and Mexican holidays, when museum entry is free, the park and museums are packed with families. Adding Colonia Condesa to the end of a day of museum visits will make for a delightful evening.

Sights to See

BOSQUE DE CHAPULTEPEC

㉑ **Bosque de Chapultepec** ("The Woods of Chapultepec," or Chapultepec Park). This 1,600-acre green space, divided into three sections, draws families on weekend outings, cyclists, and joggers. And its museums—including the Museo Nacional de Antropología—are among the finest in Mexico. This is one of the oldest parts of Mexico City, having been inhabited by the Mexica (Aztec) tribe as early as the 13th century. The Mexica poet-king Nezahualcoyotl had his palace here and ordered construction of the aqueduct that brought water to Tenochtitlán. Ahuehuete trees (Moctezuma cypress) still stand from that era, when the woods were used as hunting preserves.

At the park's principal entrance, one block west of the Chapultepec metro station, the **Monumento a los Niños Héroes** (Monument to the Boy Heroes) consists of six marble columns adorned with eaglets. Supposedly buried in the monument are the six young cadets who wrapped themselves in the Mexican flag and jumped to their deaths rather than surrender to the Americans during the U.S. invasion of 1847. To Mexicans, that war is still a troubling symbol of their neighbor's aggressive dominance: the war cost Mexico almost half of its national territory—the present states of Texas, California, Arizona, New Mexico, and Nevada.

Other sights in the first section of Bosque de Chapultepec include three small boating lakes, a botanical garden, and the Casa del Lago cultural center, which hosts free plays, cultural events, and live music on weekends. **Los Pinos,** the residential palace of the president of Mexico, is on a small highway called Avenida Constituyentes, which cuts through the park. This is heavily guarded and cannot be visited.

The less-crowded second and third sections of Bosque de Chapultepec contain a fancy restaurant; ☞ **La Feria de Chapultepec;** ☞ **El Papalote, Museo de Niño;** the national cemetery; and the Lienzo Charro (Mexican rodeos) held on Sunday afternoon.

★ ㉒ **Castillo de Chapultepec** (Chapultepec Castle). On Cerro del Chapulín (Grasshopper Hill), the Castillo has borne witness to all the turbulence and grandeur of Mexican history. In its earliest permutations, it was a Mexica palace, where the Indians made one of their last stands against the Spaniards. Later it was a Spanish hermitage, gunpowder plant, and military college. Emperor Maximilian used the castle, parts of which date from 1783, as his residence, and his example was followed by various presidents from 1872 to 1940, when Lázaro Cárdenas decreed that it be turned into the **Museo Nacional de Historia** (National History Museum).

Displays on the museum's ground floor cover Mexican history from the conquest to the revolution. The bathroom, bedroom, tea salon, and gardens were used by Maximilian and his wife, Carlotta, during the 19th century. The ground floor also contains works by 20th-century muralists O'Gorman, Orozco, and Siqueiros, while the upper floor is devoted to temporary exhibits, Porfirio Díaz's malachite vases, and religious art. A 30¢ shuttle bus runs between this museum and the Museo del Caracol. ⊠ *Section 1 of Bosque de Chapultepec,* ☎ *5/553–6224, 5/286–9920.* ⊠ *$2, free Sun.* ☉ *Tues.–Sun. 9–5.*

☾ **La Feria de Chapultepec.** This children's amusement park has various games and more than 50 rides, including a truly hair-raising haunted house and a *montaña rusa*—"Russian mountain," or roller coaster. ⊠ *Section 2 of Bosque de Chapultepec,* ☎ *5/230–2112.* ⊠ *$7.50 day pass includes all rides.* ☉ *Tues.–Fri. 11–7, weekends 10–9.*

★ ㉔ **Museo de Arte Moderno** (Museum of Modern Art). Exhibits here focus on Mexican artists. One room is devoted to Mexican plastic arts from the 1930s to the 1960s; four other rooms feature revolving exhibits of contemporary painters, sculptors, lithographers, and photographers from around the world. ⊠ *Paseo de la Reforma and Calle Gandhi, Section 1 of Bosque de Chapultepec,* ☎ *5/553–6313.* ⊠ *$1.50, free Sun.* ☉ *Tues.–Sun. 10–6.*

☾ ㉓ **Museo del Caracol.** Officially it's the Galería de la Lucha del Pueblo Mexicano por su Libertad, but most people refer to it by the more fanciful
name Museum of the Snail because of its spiral shape. The gallery con-
centrates on the 400 years from the establishment of the Viceroyalty to
the Constitution of 1917, using dioramas and light-and-sound displays
that children can appreciate. ✉ *Section 1 of Bosque de Chapultepec, on
the ramp up to the Castillo*, ☎ 5/553–6285. 🎫 $2. ☉ *Tues.–Sun. 9–5:30.*

★ ㉖ **Museo Nacional de Antropología** (National Museum of Anthropology).
This is the greatest museum in the country—and arguably one of the finest
archaeological museums anywhere. Even its architectural design, by Pedro
Ramírez Vázquez, is distinguished. The museum is arranged on two floors,
surrounded by salons, each displaying artifacts from a particular geographic region and/or culture. The collection is so extensive—covering some
100,000 square ft—that you could easily spend a day here, and that might
be barely adequate. Labels and explanations are in Spanish, but you can
reserve and hire (for about $70 for up to 20 people) an English-speaking
tour guide by calling the museum one week in advance, or hire an unofficial bilingual guide outside the museum for about $10. The museum has
English audio guides for rent for $3.50, and English-language guidebooks
are available in the bookshop.

A good place to start is in the Orientation Room, where a film is shown
in Spanish nearly every hour on the hour during the week and every
two hours on the weekends. The film traces the course of Mexican pre-
history and the pre-Hispanic cultures of Mesoamerica. The 12 ground-
floor rooms treat pre-Hispanic cultures by region—such as Sala
Teotihuacána, Sala Tolteca, Sala Oaxaca (Zapotec and Mixtec peoples),
Sala Maya (Maya groups from many areas, including Guatemala), and
so on. The famous Aztec calendar stone, the original *Piedra del Sol*
(Stone of the Sun) is found in Room 7, the Sala Mexica, which describes
Aztec life. A copy of the Aztec ruler Moctezuma's feathered headdress
is displayed nearby in the same salon—strangely, the original headdress
is in Vienna. An original stela from Tula, near Mexico City, massive
Olmec heads from Veracruz, and vivid reproductions of Maya murals
in a reconstructed temple are some of the other highlights. The magnificent tomb of the 8th-century Maya ruler Pacal, which was discovered in the ruins of Palenque, is another must to explore (Sala Maya).
The perfectly preserved skeletal remains lie in state in an immense stone
chamber, and the stairwell walls leading to it are beautifully decorated
with bas-relief scenes of the underworld. Pacal's jade death mask is also
on display nearby. The ground floor is filled with everything from the
early remnants of nomadic societies to the statuary, jewelry, weapons,
figurines, and pottery that evoke the brilliant, quirky, and frequently
bloodthirsty civilizations that peopled Mesoamerica for the 3,000
years that preceded the Spanish invasion.

The nine rooms on the upper floor contain faithful ethnographic displays of current indigenous peoples, using maps, photographs, household objects, folk art, clothing, and religious articles. When leaving the
museum, take a rest and watch the famous Voladores de Papantla (fly-
ers of Papantla) as they swing by their feet down an incredibly high
maypolelike structure. ✉ *Paseo de la Reforma at Calle Gandhi, Section 1 of Bosque de Chapultepec*, ☎ 5/286–2923, 5/553–6381, 5/553–
6386 for a guide. 🎫 $2.50, free Sun. ☉ *Tues.–Sun. 9–7.*

★ ㉕ **Museo Rufino Tamayo** (Rufino Tamayo Museum). Within its modernist
shell, this sleek museum contains the paintings of the noted Mexican
muralist, works from his private collection, and temporary exhibits of
pieces by contemporary artists from around the world. The majority
of paintings are by Tamayo; those from his collection, which demon-

strate his unerring eye for great art, include a Picasso and a few works by Joan Miró, René Magritte, Francis Bacon, and Henry Moore. ⊠ *Paseo de la Reforma at Calle Gandhi, Section 1 of Bosque de Chapultepec,* ☏ *5/286–6519.* ▦ *$1.50, free Sun.* ☉ *Tues.–Sun. 10–6.*

☾ **El Papalote, Museo del Niño** (The Butterfly, Children's Museum). Five theme sections compose this excellent interactive museum: *Our World; The Human Body;* the pun-intended *Con-Sciencia,* with exhibits relating to both consciousness and science; *Communication,* on topics ranging from language to computers; and *Expression,* which includes art, music, theater, and literature. There are also workshops, an IMAX theater, a store, and a restaurant. ⊠ *Av. Constituyentes 268, Section 2 of Bosque de Chapultepec,* ☏ *5/237–1781.* ▦ *$4.* ☉ *Weekdays 9–1 and 2–6; weekends 10–2 and 3–7.*

☾ **Ripley's Museo de lo Increíble** (Ripley's Museum of the Incredible) and the **Museo de Cera de la Ciudad de Mexico** (Mexico City Wax Museum). Although these museums lack the polish of their equivalents in, say, New York, they are nonetheless fun for children of all ages. The Ripley's museum has 14 exhibit rooms chockablock with believe-it-or-not items, and in the wax museum, Placido Domingo and Mexican politicians come to life. ⊠ *Londres 4 (east of Zona Rosa),* ☏ *5/546–3784.* ▦ *$3 each museum or $4 for both.* ☉ *Weekdays 11–7, weekends 10–7.*

☾ ㉗ **Zoológico.** During the early 16th century, Mexico City's zoo housed a small private collection of animals belonging to Moctezuma II; it became quasi-public when he allowed favored subjects to visit it. The current zoo opened on this site in the 1920s and has the usual suspects as well as some superstar pandas. A gift from China, the original pair—Pepe and Ying Ying—produced the world's first panda baby born in captivity (much to competitive China's chagrin). The zoo also produced the first spectacled bears in captivity in 1998, the same year officials added the Moctezuma Aviary. The zoo is surrounded by a miniature train depot, botanical gardens, and lakes where you can go rowing. You'll see the entrance on Paseo de la Reforma, across from the Museo Nacional de Antropología. ⊠ *Section 1 of Bosque de Chapultepec,* ☏ *5/553–6263, 5/256–4104.* ▦ *Free; English audio guide $2.50.* ☉ *Tues.–Sun. 9:30–4:15.*

COLONIA CONDESA

㉘ **Colonia Condesa.** The neighborhood sprang up in the early 1900s around the city's elite, who quickly abandoned it in the '40s for other more-fashionable areas, leaving decaying mansions and parks behind. Today, the neighborhood is getting renovation from an influx of new residents, mostly young artists, entrepreneurs, and foreigners. Restaurants have sprung up everywhere in the colonia, quickly making Condesa a new center for cuisine.

Condesa doesn't have much in the way of museums or monuments, but it is the perfect place to break from a hectic day of sightseeing—just sit back in one of the neighborhood's relaxed sidewalk cafés and watch Mexico go by. And with a new restaurant opening nearly every week, it is the place to come for dinner. The main drag is Avenida Michoacán, from which restaurants radiate out in every direction. Avenida México loops the main park in the area, Parque México, and Avenida Amsterdam makes another loop around the area. The park area used to be a racetrack, which explains the looping roads.

There is also an abundance of hip and trendy clothing shops in the area. The most famous are on Michoacán: Soho (☏ *5/553–1730),* for example, is a clothing and music store whose name refers to the often-made comparison of Condesa to New York's Soho neighborhood in the 1950s; the trendy La Esquina clothing store (☎ 5/211–2951) down the street is similar. Another great shop to browse through is El Péndulo (✉ Nuevo León 115, ☎ 5/286–9493), a sort of cultural center. It has a large selection of Spanish books and an international collection of CDs, and the restaurant has a great breakfast menu, with classical guitarists playing on Sunday morning. El Péndulo often hosts other performers—jazz, classical, folk, or rock bands—on weekends.

Farther east on Michoacán, you can head to the Parque México or the smaller Parque España for a picnic or a stroll. There's a great movie theater right on the Parque España that shows Hollywood and Mexican films, the Plaza Condesa (☎ 5/286–4973); it has waiters who will serve you popcorn and drinks during the flick. From Michoacán, take Tamaulipas north about four blocks to arrive at the park and theater.

ZONA ROSA

For years the Zona Rosa has been a favorite part of the city because of its plethora of restaurants, cafés, art and antiques galleries, hotels, discos, and shops. With the mushrooming of fast-food places and some tacky bars and stores, the Zona—as it is affectionately called—has lost some of its former gloss, but nonetheless still draws the faithful. Most of the buildings in the Zona Rosa are on a very human scale, at two or three stories high: they were originally private homes built in the 1920s for the wealthy. All the streets are wistfully named after European cities; some, such as Génova, are garden-lined pedestrian malls accented with contemporary bronze statuary.

To enjoy the Zona Rosa, just walk the lengths of Hamburgo and Londres and some of the side streets, especially Copenhague—a veritable restaurant row. The large crafts market on Londres is officially Mercado Insurgentes, although most people call it either Mercado Zona Rosa or Mercado Londres. Just opposite the market's Londres entrance is Plaza del Angel, a small upscale shopping mall, the halls of which are crowded by antiques vendors on weekends.

㉒ Monumento a la Independencia (Independence Monument). A Corinthian column topped by a gold-covered angel is the city's most beautiful monument, built to celebrate the 100th anniversary of Mexico's War of Independence. Beneath the pedestal lie the remains of the principal heroes of the independence movement; an eternal flame burns in their honor. ✉ *Traffic circle between Calle Río Tiber, Paseo de la Reforma, and Calle Florencia.*

San Angel and Coyoacán

Originally separate colonial towns, San Angel and Coyoacán were both absorbed by the ever-growing capital. In the process they've managed to retain their original pueblo charm and tranquility.

San Angel is a little colonial enclave of cobblestone streets, stone walls, pastel houses, and gardens drenched in bougainvillea. It became a haven for wealthy Spaniards during the Viceroyalty period, around the time of the construction of the Ex-Convento del Carmen. The elite were drawn to the area because of its rivers, pleasant climate, and rural ambience, and proceeded to build haciendas and mansions that, for many, were country homes. Like neighboring Coyoacán, San Angel was just a suburb of Mexico City until the government decided to incorporate it into the capital.

Coyoacán means "Place of the Coyotes." According to local legend, a coyote used to bring chickens to a friar who had saved the coyote from being strangled by a snake. Coyoacán was founded by Toltecs in the 10th century and later settled by the Aztecs, or Mexica. Bernal Díaz Castillo, a Spanish chronicler, wrote that there were 6,000 houses at the time of the conquest. Cortés set up headquarters in Coyoacán during his siege of Tenochtitlán and at one point considered making it his capital. He changed his mind for political reasons, but many of the Spanish buildings left from the two-year period during which Mexico City was built still stand.

Coyoacán has had many illustrious residents from Mexico's rich and intellectual elite, including Miguel de la Madrid, president of Mexico from 1982 to 1988; artists Diego Rivera, Frida Kahlo, and José Clemente Orozco; Gabriel Figueroa, cinematographer for Luis Buñuel and John Huston; film star Dolores del Río; film director El Indio Fernández; and writers Carlos Monsiváis, Elena Poniatowska, and Jorge Ibargüengoitia. It is also the neighborhood where Leon Trotsky in exile met his violent death. Although superficially it resembles San Angel, Coyoacán has a more animated street life. Most of the houses and other buildings honor the traditions of colonial Mexican architecture, and the neighborhood is well kept by residents, many of whose families have lived here for generations.

A Good Tour

To explore the southern part of the city take a taxi or pesero down Avenida Insurgentes and get off at Avenida La Paz. On the east side of Insurgentes is the bizarre **Monumento al General Alvaro Obregón** ㉙. Cross Insurgentes on Avenida La Paz, and take the southern fork off Avenida La Paz (Calle Madero) until you come to San Angel's center, **Plaza San Jacinto** ㉚. Stroll to the **Casa del Risco** ㉛ on the north side of the plaza and, if it's a Saturday, head for the **Bazar Sábado** (☞ Markets *in* Shopping, *below*) on the north end. Retrace your steps on Avenida La Paz, to Avenida Revolución and Plaza del Carmen, which lies at the corner of Calle Monasterio. Inside is the colonial **Ex-Convento del Carmen** ㉜, interesting as an example of sacred architecture and for its religious artifacts. Now take Avenida Revolución one long block north to see the modern Mexican and European works at the **Museo Alvar y Carmen T. de Carrillo Gil** ㉝.

The next part of the tour goes to Coyoacán, which extends east of Avenida Insurgentes about 1 km (½ mi) from San Angel. Consider taking a taxi to the Plaza de Santa Catarina on Avenida Francisco Sosa, about halfway into the center of Coyoacan, because the tour involves a lot of walking.

If you decide to hoof it, make your way east to the corner of Avenidas Universidad and Francisco Sosa. Head east on Francisco Sosa until you come to the pretty 16th-century Iglesia de Santa Catarina, which dominates the tiny **Plaza de Santa Catarina.** The plaza also contains a bust of Mexican historian Francisco Sosa, who lived here and wrote passionately about Coyoacán. Across the street is the **Casa de Jesús Reyes Heroles** (Avenida Francisco Sosa 202); the former home of the ex-minister of education is a fine example of 20th-century architecture on the colonial model. It's now used as a cultural center. Continue east on Francisco Sosa and you'll pass Casa de Diego de Ordaz at the corner of Tres Cruces. This *mudéjar* (Spanish-Arabic) structure, adorned with inlaid tiles, was the home of a former captain in Cortés's army.

Now you're standing at the entrance of the **Jardín Centenario** ㉞. The Templo de San Juan Bautista and the picturesque **Casa de Cortés** ㉟ sit in the small Plaza Hidalgo adjacent to and north of the garden. Walk two blocks southeast of Plaza Hidalgo on Calle Higuera to the corner of Calle Vallarta, where you'll find the **Casa de la Malinche** ㊱. The house, darkened with age, faces an attractive park called Plaza de la Conchita.

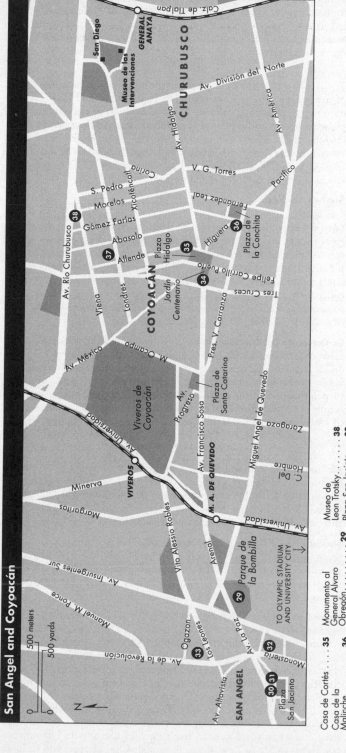

San Angel and Coyoacán

Return to Plaza Hidalgo and walk five blocks north on Calle Allende to the corner of Calle Londres and the **Museo de Frida Kahlo** ㊲. It is linked historically—or should we say romantically—with the fortresslike **Museo de Leon Trotsky** ㊳, east of it on Londres, then two long blocks north on Morelos.

TIMING

You're likely to want to linger in these elegant and beautiful sections of town, especially in Coyoacán. The Frida Kahlo and Leon Trotsky museums give intense, intimate looks at the lives of two famous people who were friends and lovers, and who breathed their personalities into the places where they lived. Allow at least an hour at each. The other museums are much smaller and merit less time. Weekends are liveliest at the Plaza Hidalgo and its neighboring Jardín Centenario, where street life explodes into a fiesta.

Sights to See

SAN ANGEL

㉛ **Casa del Risco** (Risco House). This 1681 mansion is one of the prettiest houses facing the Plaza San Jacinto. A huge free-form fountain sculpture—exploding with colorful porcelain, tiles, shells, and mosaics—covers the entire eastern wall of its patio. Although it's not ranked among the city's top museums, the **Museo de la Casa del Risco** houses a splendid collection of 17th- and 18th-century European and colonial Mexican paintings as well as period furnishings. ✉ *Plaza San Jacinto 15,* ☎ *5/616–2711.* *Free.* *Tues.–Sun. 10–5.*

㉜ **Ex-Convento del Carmen** (Carmelite Convent and Church). Erected by Carmelite friars with the help of an Indian chieftain between 1615 and 1628, this cloister, with its tile-covered domes, fountains, and gardens, is one of the most interesting examples of colonial religious architecture in this part of the city. The church still operates, but the convent is now the **Museo Regional del Carmen,** with a fine collection of 16th- to 18th-century religious paintings, icons, and 12 mummified corpses. ✉ *Av. Revolución 4, at Monasterio,* ☎ *5/616–2816, 5/616–1177.* *$2, free Sun.* *Tues.–Sun. 10–4:45.*

㉙ **Monumento al General Alvaro Obregón.** This somber gray granite monument marks the spot where reformer and national hero Obregón was gunned down by a religious zealot in a restaurant in 1928, soon before he was to begin his second term as president. ✉ *Parque de la Bombilla, east of Av. La Paz at Av. Insurgentes.*

㉝ **Museo Alvar y Carmen T. de Carrillo Gil.** This private collection contains early murals by Orozco, Rivera, and Siqueiros; works by modern European artists such as Klee and Picasso; and temporary expositions of young Mexican artists. ✉ *Av. Revolución 1608, at Desierto de los Leones,* ☎ *5/550–1254.* *$1.* *Tues.–Sun. 10–6.*

★ ㉚ **Plaza San Jacinto.** This cozy plaza with a grisly history is the center of San Angel. In 1847 about 50 Irish soldiers of St. Patrick's Battalion, who had sided with the Mexicans in the Mexican-American War, had their foreheads branded here with the letter *D*—for deserter—and were then hanged by the Americans. These men had been enticed to swim the Rio Grande, deserting the ranks of U.S. General Zachary Taylor, by pleas to the historic and religious ties between Spain and Ireland. As settlers in Mexican Texas, they felt their allegiance lay with Catholic Mexico, and they were among the bravest fighters in the war. They met their end when the American flag flew over Castillo de Chapultepec (☞ Sights to See *in* Zona Rosa, Bosque de Chapultepec, and Colonia Condesa, *above*) after the death of the *niños héroes.* A memorial plaque (on a building on the plaza's west side) lists their names and expresses

Mexico's gratitude for their help in the "unjust North American invasion." Off to one side of the plaza, the excellent handicrafts market, Bazar Sábado, is held on Saturday (☞ Markets *in* Shopping, *below*). ✉ *Between Miramon, Cda. Santisima, Dr. Galvez, and Madero.*

COYOACÁN

㉟ **Casa de Cortés** (Cortés's House). The place where the Aztec emperor Cuauhtémoc was held prisoner by Cortés is reputed to have been rebuilt in the 18th century from the stones of his original house by one of Cortés's descendants; the municipal government now has offices here. Dominating the little square on which it sits, this was almost the city's first city hall, but Cortés decided to rebuild Tenochtitlán instead. The two-story, deep-red house, with its wide arches and tile patio, is gorgeous. The house is not open to the public, but there is a tourist-information booth in the front room that's staffed by friendly employees eager to tell you about Coyoacán. ✉ *Plaza Hidalgo between Calles Carillo Puerto and Caballo Calco.*

㊱ **Casa de la Malinche.** One of the most powerful symbols of the conquest is located in Coyoacán but, significantly perhaps, is not even marked. It's the somber-looking, fortresslike residence of Malinche, Cortés's Indian mistress and interpreter, whom the Spaniards called Doña María and the Indians called Malintzín. Malinche aided the conquest by enabling Cortés to communicate with the Nahuatl-speaking tribes he met en route to Tenochtitlán. Today she is a much-reviled Mexican symbol of a traitorous xenophile—hence the term *malinchista*, used to describe a Mexican who prefers things foreign. Legend says that Cortés's wife died in this house, poisoned by the conquistador. ✉ *2 blocks east of Plaza Hidalgo on Calle Higuera at Vallarta.*

㉞ **Jardín Centenario** (Centenary Gardens). Small fairs, amateur musical performances, and poetry and palm readings are frequent occurrences in this large park surrounded by outdoor cafés. At the far end of the Jardín you'll see **Templo de San Juan Bautista,** one of the first churches to be built in New Spain. It was completed in 1582, and its door has a Baroque arch. ✉ *Between Calle Centenario, Av. Hidalgo, and Caballo Calco.*

★ ㊲ **Museo de Frida Kahlo.** The house where the painter Frida Kahlo was born (in 1907)—and lived with Diego Rivera almost continuously from 1929 until her death in 1954—is fascinating. Kahlo has become a cult figure, not only because of her paintings—55 of 143 are self-portraits—but also because of her bohemian lifestyle and flamboyant individualism. As a child Kahlo was crippled by polio, and several years later she was impaled on a tramway rail. She had countless operations, including the amputation of a leg; was addicted to painkillers; had affairs with Leon Trotsky and several women; and married Rivera twice. Kahlo's astounding vitality and originality are reflected in this house, from the giant papier-mâché skeletons outside and the painted tin *retablos* (ex-votos) on the staircase to the gloriously decorated kitchen and the bric-a-brac in her bedroom. Even if you know nothing about Kahlo, a visit to the museum will leave you with a strong, visceral impression of this pivotal feminist artist. ✉ *Londres 247, at Allende,* ☎ *5/554–5999.* 🎫 *$2.* ☉ *Tues.–Sun. 10–5:45.*

㊳ **Museo de Leon Trotsky.** Resembling an anonymous and forbidding fortress, with turrets for armed guards, this is where Leon Trotsky lived and was murdered. It is difficult to believe that it's the final resting place for the ashes of one of the most important figures of the Russian Revolution, but that only adds to the allure of the house, which is owned by Trotsky's grandson.

This is a modest, austere dwelling. Anyone taller than 5 ft must stoop to pass through doorways to Trotsky's bedroom—with bullet holes still in the walls from the first assassination attempt, in which the muralist Siqueiros was implicated—his wife's study, the dining room, and the study where the Mexican communist Ramón Mercader finally drove an ice pick into Trotsky's head. On his desk, cluttered with writing paraphernalia and an article he was revising in Russian, the calendar is open to that fateful day, August 20, 1940. The volunteers will tell you how Trotsky's teeth left a permanent scar on Mercader's hand, how he clung to life for 26 hours, what his last words were, and how his death was sponsored by the United States (others would say Stalin). Not all the volunteers, however, speak English. ⊠ *Río Churubusco 410,* ☎ *5/658–8732.* 🎟 *$1.* ☉ *Tues.–Sun. 10–5.*

🐾 **Nuevo Reino Aventura.** This 100-acre theme park on the southern edge of the city comprises seven "villages": Mexican, French, Swiss, Polynesian, Moroccan, the Wild West, and Children's World. Shows include performances by trained dolphins. The most famous of the playful swimmers was an orca whale named Keiko, star of the film *Free Willy,* who was sent to an aquarium in Oregon to recover his health before he was released into his native Icelandic waters in 1998. ⊠ *Southwest of Coyoacán on Carretera Picacho a Ajusco at Km 1.5,* ☎ *5/645–5434, 5/645–6232.* 🎟 *$14 includes entrance and all rides.* ☉ *Tues.–Thurs. 10–6, Fri.–Sun. 10–7.*

DINING

Mexico City restaurants open 7–11 AM for breakfast (*desayuno*), 1–5 for lunch (*comida*), and most locals start out at 9 PM for dinner (*cena*). Restaurants stay open till midnight during the week and a little later on weekends. At deluxe restaurants, dress is generally formal (jacket and tie), and reservations are almost always required; see reviews for details. (Even if a deluxe restaurant doesn't *require* a jacket and tie, men are likely to feel out-of-place if not well dressed.) If you're short on time, there are American-style coffee shops (VIPS, Denny's, Shirley's, and Sanborns) all over the city; some are open 24 hours.

Colonia Polanco is an attractive, upscale neighborhood on the edge of Chapultepec Park that has some of the best and most expensive dining (and lodging) in the city. Zona Rosa restaurants get filled pretty quickly on Saturday night, especially the Saturday coinciding with most people's payday, which falls on the 1st and 15th of each month.

CATEGORY	COST*
$$$$	over $40
$$$	$25–$40
$$	$15–$25
$	under $15

per person for a three-course meal, excluding drinks and service

Argentine

$$$ ✕ **Cambalache.** Before entering this ever-busy beef lover's dream, you can see the chefs preparing their thick cuts in the window. If you come with a few people, try the Super Lomo Cambalache, a steak big enough for three–four people. If you're not in the mood for beef, there are several chicken dishes on the menu, such as the Don Ignacio: a boneless chicken breast served in a mushroom sauce with pineapple and fresh sweet peppers. Vegetables *do* come with menu items, and potatoes, par-

LA COCINA MEXICANA

TO ENTERTAIN THE NOTION that Mexican food is little more than tacos, enchiladas, and burritos—or Tex-Mex or Taco Bell—would be culinary blasphemy to native gastronomes. Regional cooking is the heart and soul of Mexico, multiplied by the republic's 32 states and the provinces within them. Fresh ingredients abound, recipes are passed down through generations (think *Like Water for Chocolate*), and preparation requires much patience and loving care. With the staples—rice, beans, chilies, and tortillas—chefs are turning out ever more sophisticated variations on national dishes. But in terms of the Mexican chef's arsenal of ingredients, they're only the beginning.

Maize was sacred to the Indians, who have innumerable ways of preparing it—from faithful tortillas and tamales (cornmeal wrapped in banana leaves or corn husks) to tostadas (lightly fried, open tortillas topped with meat, lettuce, and the like) and tacos (tortillas briefly heated, filled, and wrapped into slim cylinders). *Pozole* (hominy) is most often served in pork-based soups. The sweet, corn-based drink *atole,* similar in consistency to hot chocolate, is a favorite breakfast or before-bed treat.

You'll find fish not just on the coasts but also in the lake regions around Guadalajara and in the state of Michoacán. *Huachinango* (red snapper), abalone, crab, and swordfish are all popular. And ceviche—raw *mariscos* (shellfish) marinated in lime juice then topped with chopped chilies, onions, and cilantro—is almost a national dish; just make sure it's fresh. Shrimp, lobster, and oysters can be huge and succulent; bear in mind the folk adage and eat oysters only in months with names that contain the letter *r.* Likewise avoid raw shellfish wherever cholera or water pollution might be a risk.

Mexicans love beef, pork, and *barbacoa* (barbecued lamb) with a variety of sauces. The complex, spicy mole—its ingredients can number more than 100, among them many kinds of chilies, and in one mole, chocolate—is one of Mexico's proudest culinary inventions. It is usually served over chicken or turkey. Chicken is often roasted, served in sauces like mole, or tucked in enchiladas, tacos, or burritos.

Fresh fruits and vegetables are another Mexican pleasure. Jicama, papaya, mamey, avocado, mango, guayaba, squash, and tomatoes are just some of the produce native to Mexico. (All fresh produce should be washed in water with a commercial disinfectant—bacteria exist in Mexico that your stomach might not be happy with.)

Other Mexican specialties are less common abroad: *antojitos* or *botanas* (appetizers), *chilaquiles* (breakfast dishes made with tortilla strips scrambled with chilies, tomatoes, onions, cream, and cheese), and *chiles en nogada* (a large poblano chili stuffed with beef or cheese, raisins, onion, olives, and almonds and topped with a creamy walnut sauce and pomegranate seeds). Soups are hearty—particularly pozole, *sopa azteca* (avocado, chicken chunks, and tortilla in a broth), and *sopa de flor de calabaza* (pumpkin-flower soup).

The astonishing assortment of breads, sweets, beers, wines (which are fast improving), and agave- (related to the cactus) based liquors goes on and on. Freshly squeezed fruit juices and fruit shakes (*licuados*) are safe to drink—if ordered in a restaurant with hygienic practices—and taste heavenly. And coffee ranges from Americano (black) to organic varieties to *café de olla,* which is laced with spices.

ticularly the soufflé, are a specialty. ✉ *Arquímedes 85, Col. Polanco,* ☎ *5/280–2080, 5/280–2957. AE, MC, V.*

$$$ ✕ **Rincon Argentino.** This most talked about Argentine restaurant in the city is known as much for its decor as for its exquisitely prepared cuts of beef. The interior is like the outdoors, with the ceiling painted into a sky, the bar covered by a thatch roof, and the dining areas turned into a stone-and-wood lodge. The focus here is beef—such as *lomo mignon,* filet mignon served with bacon and a rich mushroom sauce. Most Argentines prefer their beef *bien cocida* (well-done), but you can have it any way you like. ✉ *Presidente Masarik 177, Col. Polanco,* ☎ *5/531–8617, 5/254–8775. AE, MC, V.*

$ ✕ **Fonda Garufa.** Its tables spilling out onto a Condesa sidewalk, this is a perfect place for a relaxed meal after a day of sightseeing. Filet mignon, served with mushrooms and watercress, is especially delicious. There's also an extensive list of innovative pastas. A favorite with regulars is fettuccine Hindú: half a chicken breast bathed in a yogurt sauce laced with cilantro, ginger, onion, and chili, over fresh fettuccine. ✉ *Michoacán 93, Col. Condesa,* ☎ *5/286–8295. AE, MC, V.*

French

$$$$ ✕ **Fouquet's de Paris.** In the Camino Real hotel, this branch of the
★ renowned Parisian restaurant is an elegant haven of peace and tranquility. The best pâtés in Mexico and tender, juicy lamb chops are part of the diverse and stylish menu. Desserts are in a class of their own: sorbets, such as the delicately flavored passion fruit, are outstanding, and the cakes, mousses, and pastries are light and delicious. Monthlong gastronomic festivals are held here throughout the year, and each October or November chefs from the original Fouquet's in Paris take over the kitchen. ✉ *Hotel Camino Real, Mariano Escobedo 700, Col. Polanco,* ☎ *5/203–2121. Reservations essential. Jacket and tie. AE, DC, MC, V. Closed Sun. No lunch Sat.*

$$$ ✕ **Champs Élysées.** Commanding a superb view of the Independence
★ Monument is one of the bastions of haute cuisine in Mexico City. The variety of sauces served with both meat and fish dishes is impressive— hollandaise over sea bass or red snapper takes top honors. Regulars find either the roast duck (carved at your table) or the classic pepper steak hard to resist. The cheese board is particularly generous. ✉ *Paseo de la Reforma 316, at Estocolmo, Zona Rosa,* ☎ *5/525–7259. AE, DC, MC, V. Closed Sun.*

$ ✕ **El Buen Comer.** One of the more original Polanco eating spots, El Buen Comer (which means "eating well") consists of not more than 20 tables in the covered garage of a private house. The entrance is easily missed, and the atmosphere inside is that of a large, private lunch party. The emphasis is on French cuisine from Lyon. House specialties include an endive salad with a cream-and-nut vinaigrette served with scallops. The fondues and pâtés are excellent. The quiche royale with shrimp is a must for seafood lovers. Desserts include mango or chocolate mousse or raspberries smothered in cream. El Buen Comer makes a great stop after shopping in Polanco. ✉ *Edgar Allan Poe 50, Col. Polanco,* ☎ *5/282–0325. Reservations essential. AE, MC, V. Closed Sun. No dinner.*

Greek

$ ✕ **Agapi Mu** (My Love). This 16-table Greek bistro tucked in a converted Colonia Condesa home with a Greek flag out front and snug rooms inside attracts its share of actors, singers, and artists. Come for authentic Greek food in a casual, intimate setting and rambunctious Greek song and dance Thursday through Saturday nights. The menu includes *paputsáka* (stuffed eggplant), *kalamárea* (fried squid Greek style), and *dolmádes* (stuffed grape leaves). Wash it all down with a Hungarian Sangre de Toro wine, and finish it off with a smooth, sweet Greek coffee. ⊠ *Alfonso Reyes 96, Col. Condesa,* ☎ *5/286–1384. AE, MC, V.*

International

$$$$ ✕ **Maxim's de Paris.** Under the auspices of the original Parisian Maxim's, this spacious but intimate Art Deco restaurant sits under a stained-glass ceiling and serves classic Gallic cuisine spiced up with the best of Mexican ingredients. French chef Jacques Chretene uses his vast expertise to create such delicacies as tender veal in its juice accented with truffles and asparagus, and fresh Dover sole in white butter sauce studded with bits of lobster. The pastry chef's desserts include mouth-watering soufflés. The wine cellar is nonpareil, and the service impeccable. ⊠ *Hotel Presidente Inter-Continental México, Campos Elíseos 218, Col. Polanco,* ☎ *5/327–7700. Reservations essential. Jacket and tie. AE, DC, MC, V. Closed Sun. No lunch Sat.*

$$$–$$$$ ✕ **Les Célébrités.** In addition to its superb French fare, this elegant hotel
★ restaurant has refreshed the menu with Mediterranean selections. The sunny yellow decor and a profusion of flowers enhance the pleasing light-filled ambience. The restaurant is known for its one-of-a-kind combinations, such as an appetizer of king crab with asparagus cream, sauce of caviar, and passion-fruit vinaigrette; for dessert, there's sinfully rich chocolate mousse cake and light, flaky hazelnut pastry with profiteroles in a chocolate–coriander sauce. The restaurant is open for breakfast as well. ⊠ *Nikko México hotel, Campos Elíseos 204, Col. Polanco,* ☎ *5/280–1111. Reservations essential. Jacket and tie. AE, DC, MC, V. Closed weekends.*

$$$–$$$$ ✕ **Estoril.** In an exquisitely furnished 1930s town house in fashionable
★ Colonia Polanco, Rosa Martin serves French cuisine with a Mexican flair. *Perejil frito* (fried parsley) is a popular starter, and main dishes offer some unusual combinations: giant prawns in Chablis or curry sauce, and sea bass in fresh coriander sauce. If you have a sweet tooth, try either the delicious tart Tatin—an upside-down apple tart with caramel—or the homemade mint sorbet. ⊠ *Alejandro Dumas 24, Col. Polanco,* ☎ *5/280–9828. AE, DC, MC, V. Closed Sun.*

$$$–$$$$ ✕ **Hacienda de los Morales.** This Mexican institution, set in a former hacienda that dates back to the 16th century, is grandly colonial in style, with dark wood beams, huge terra-cotta expanses, and dramatic torches. The menu combines international and Mexican cuisines with imaginative variations on both. Walnut soup is delicate and unusual. Fish is seemingly unlimited, from sea bass *marinière* (in a white-wine sauce) to a mixed seafood gratin. The charcoal-broiled grain-fed chicken has a distinct flavor. Still, the chef can have his off days, in which case you can head for the tequila bar as consolation. Live mariachi music completes the atmosphere. ⊠ *Vázquez de Mella 525, Col. Chapultepec Morales,* ☎ *5/281–4554, 5/281–4703. AE, DC, MC, V. No dinner Sun.*

$$$ ✕ **Bellini.** While its great turntable slowly revolves on the 45th floor of the World Trade Center, executives from surrounding offices pack Bellini at lunch. At night it turns romantic, and the view of the city by lamplight is fantastic. The majority of the dishes here aren't Italian but Mexican and international. The house special is a lobster of your choosing from a tank brought tableside; it's prepared to your taste. Other favorites are filet mignon and homemade pastas served with classic Italian sauces. Finish with a flambéed dessert, such as strawberries jubilee or crêpes suzette. After dinner, work off the extra calories at the disco one floor above the restaurant. ⊠ *Av. de las Naciones 1, World Trade Center Tower, Col. Napoles, 20 mins by car south of Zona Rosa,* ☎ *5/628–8305. Jacket and tie. AE, DC, MC, V.*

Mexico City Dining

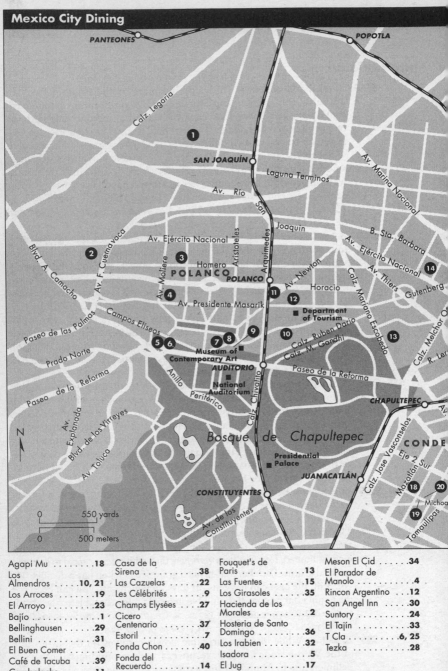

$$–$$$ ✕ **Bellinghausen.** This is one of the most beloved lunch spots in the Zona Rosa and practically a landmark of good eating for the locals; it's only open until 7 PM. The partially covered hacienda-style courtyard at the back, set off by an ivy-laden wall, is a midday magnet for executives and tourists. A veritable army of waiters scurries back and forth serving such tried-and-true favorites as *sopa de hongos* (mushroom soup) and *filete chemita* (broiled steak with mashed potatoes). The *higaditos de pollo* (chicken livers) with a side order of sautéed spinach is another winning dish. ⊠ *Londres 95, Zona Rosa,* ☎ *5/207–6149. AE, DC, MC, V. No dinner.*

$ ✕ **Los Arroces.** The name means "rices," and rice is exactly what you'll get at this trendy spot in Colonia Condesa—50 different rices from around the world in soups, salads, and main dishes—everywhere but desserts. There's *pastel de arroz,* for example, which is white Mexican rice prepared with *rajas* (green pepper strips), *flor de calabaza* (pumpkin flower), corn, and bacon; Maya rice, served with squid, chopped red onion, sour oranges, and beans; and Spanish paella with rice from Valencia. Noteworthy nonrice dishes include chicken with raspberry mole and blue-corn tortilla quesadillas stuffed with cheese, spinach, and chilies. ⊠ *Michoacán 126,* ☎ *5/286–4287. AE, MC, V.*

Italian

$–$$ ✕ **La Lanterna.** The Petterino family has run this two-story restaurant for more than three decades. The downstairs has the rustic feel of a northern Italian trattoria, with the cramped seating adding to the intimacy. Upstairs is more spacious. All pastas are made on the premises; the Bolognese sauce, in particular, is a favorite. Raw artichoke salad, *conejo al Salmi* (rabbit in a wine sauce) and *filete al burro nero* (steak in black butter) are all worthy dishes. Seasonal presentations include fungi in a variety of dishes plus homegrown arugula for salads and carpaccio. ⊠ *Paseo de la Reforma 458, Col. Juárez,* ☎ *5/207–9969. Reservations not accepted. MC, V. Closed Sun. and Dec. 25–Jan. 1.*

Japanese

$$$ ✕ **Suntory.** This main branch of the Suntory restaurants in Mexico transports you to Japan by way of a Zen garden at the entryway and a dense green garden that follows. In this enchanted world you are not absolved of the difficulty of choice. Will it be the teppanyaki room to watch your fresh meat or fish prepared with a variety of vegetables, or perhaps the sushi bar—or maybe you'll end up in the shabu-shabu room, with its wafer-thin sashimi and a copper pot of steaming vegetable broth in which elegant slices of beef are cooked? Prices are high, but the ingredients are of the best quality. ⊠ *Torres Adalid 14, Col. del Valle,* ☎ *5/536–9432. Second branch:* ⊠ *Montes Urales 535, Lomas Chapultepec,* ☎ *5/202–4711. Reservations essential. AE, DC, MC, V. No dinner Sun.*

Mexican

$$$ ✕ **Cicero Centenario.** This thoroughly Mexican restaurant occupies a
★   restored 17th-century mansion in the heart of the historic downtown. Elegant colonial antiques are strikingly posed against folk art and pastel walls, and the bar has an outstanding collection of tin ex-votos and other religious memorabilia. The enticing menu includes excellent versions of authentic colonial dishes such as *pollo en pipián verde* (chicken in green-pumpkin-seed sauce). Try the *chicharrón* (crispy pork rind) and guacamole appetizer, but be sure to leave room for dessert, such as rose-petal ice cream. An ebullient street-level cantina has afternoon

HOW TO USE THIS GUIDE

Think of this guide as your tool kit for a perfect trip. It's packed with everything you need—color photos, insider advice on hotels and restaurants, practical tips, essential maps, and more.

COOL TOOLS

As you're planning your trip, be on the lookout for our favorite features.

Fodor's Choice Look for entries marked with a star. Although all listings in this guide come highly recommended, these deserve special mention.

Great Itineraries Not sure what to see in the time you have? Mix and match our easy-to-follow itineraries to create a trip that suits you.

Good Walks Let us be your guide to the must-see sights. Follow the numbered bullets and you won't miss a thing.

Need a Break? Looking for a quick bite to eat or a spot to rest? These sure bets are along the way.

Off the Beaten Path Some lesser-known sights are definitely worth a special trip. We tell you which to detour for.

POST-IT® FLAGS

Note your favorite spots with these handy Post-it® flags.

"Post-it" is a registered trademark of 3M.

ICONS AND SYMBOLS

Look for these icons and symbols throughout the guide. Price charts for dining and lodging are strategically located—check the index to find the one you want.

★   Our special recommendations
✕   Restaurant
🏠   Lodging establishment

✕🏠   Lodging establishment whose restaurant warrants a special trip
☪   Good for kids
☞   Sends you to another section of the guide for more information
✉   Address
☎   Telephone number
🕐   Opening hours
💲   Admission prices
🖱   Sends you to www.fodors.com/urls for up-to-date links to the property's Web site

VACATION COUNTDOWN

Your *checklist for a* *perfect journey*

WAY AHEAD

- Devise a trip budget.

- Write down the five things you want most from this trip. Keep this list handy before and during your trip.

- Make plane or train reservations. Book lodging, rental cars, and other transportation.

- Arrange for pet care.

- Submit your passport application, or check that your existing passport is valid.

- Photocopy important documents and store in a safe place.

A MONTH BEFORE

- Make restaurant reservations and buy theater and concert tickets. Visit fodors.com for links to local events and news.

- Familiarize yourself with the local language or lingo.

TWO WEEKS BEFORE

- Replenish your supply of medications and contact lenses if necessary.

- Create your itinerary.

- Enjoy a book or movie set in your destination to get you in the mood.

- Develop a packing list. Shop for missing essentials. Repair and launder or dry-clean your clothes.

A WEEK BEFORE

- Stop newspaper and mail deliveries and pay bills.

- Acquire local currency and traveler's checks.

- Stock up on film and batteries.

- Label your luggage.

- Finalize your packing list— always take less than you think you need.

- Create a toiletries kit filled with travel-size essentials.

- Get lots of sleep. You don't want to get sick or run-down before your trip.

A DAY BEFORE

- Drink plenty of water.

- Check your necessary travel documents.

- Get packing!

DURING YOUR TRIP

- Keep a journal/scrapbook as a personal souvenir.

- Spend time with locals.

- Take time to explore. Don't plan too much. Let yourself get lost and use your Fodor's guide to get back on track.

serenades by a folk trio. ⊠ *República de Cuba 79,* ☎ *5/512–1510. Reservations essential. AE, DC, MC, V. No dinner Sun.*

$$$ ✕ **San Angel Inn.** In the south of the city, this magnificent old hacienda
★ and ex-convent, with elegant grounds and immaculately tended gardens, is both a joy to the eye and an inspiration to the palate. Dark mahogany furniture, crisp white table linens, and beautiful blue-and-white Talavera place settings strike a note of restrained opulence. Many dishes are to be recommended, especially the classic *huitlacoche* (corn fungus) served in crepes, as well as *sopa de tortilla* (tortilla soup). The *puntas de filete* (sirloin tips) are liberally laced with chilies, and the *huachinango* (red snapper) is offered in a variety of ways. Desserts— from light and crunchy meringues to pastries bulging with cream—can be rich to the point of surfeit. ⊠ *Calle Diego Rivera 50, at Altavista, Col. San Angel,* ☎ *5/616–0537, 5/616–2222, 5/616–1402. Jacket required. AE, DC, MC, V.*

$$–$$$ ✕ **El Arroyo.** This dining complex, complete with its own bullring, is an attraction in itself. At the south end of town near the beginning of the highway to Cuernavaca, it was founded more than 50 years ago by the Arroyo family and is now run by jovial Jesús ("Chucho") Arroyo. His loyal following includes celebrities, dignitaries, and bullfighters, along with local families, groups, and tourists; more than 2,600 people can dine simultaneously in a labyrinth of 11 picturesque dining areas. Typical Mexican specialties—chicken mole, a dozen types of tacos, and much more—are prepared in open kitchens. There's mariachi music and the full gamut of Mexican drinks, including *pulque,* a classic alcoholic Aztec beverage made from a plant related to the cactus. The small bullring is the forum for *novilleros,* or young bullfighters just beginning their careers, during the season (about April through October). Breakfast starts at 8 AM, and lunch is served until 8 PM. ⊠ *Av. Insurgentes Sur 4003, Col. Tlalpán, a 30–40-min drive south of Zona Rosa,* ☎ *5/573–4344. AE, DC, MC, V. No dinner.*

$$–$$$ ✕ **Fonda El Refugio.** Since it opened in 1954, this Zona Rosa restaurant in a converted two-story town house has served the best dishes from each major region of the country. Atmosphere is casual but elegant in the intimate colonial-decor dining rooms (the one downstairs is the prettiest). Along with a varied regular menu, there's a daily selection of appetizers and entrées; you might find a mole made with pumpkin seeds or *albóndigas en chile chipotle* (meatballs in chipotle sauce). Try the refreshing *aguas* (fresh-fruit and seed juices) with your meal and the *café de olla* (clove-flavored coffee sweetened with brown sugar) after dessert. ⊠ *Liverpool 166, Zona Rosa,* ☎ *5/207–2732, 5/ 525–8128. AE, DC, MC, V. No dinner Sun.*

$$–$$$ ✕ **Isadora.** Some of Mexico City's most inventive cooking takes place in this converted private house in Polanco. The three smallish dining rooms have a 1920s feel and are uncharacteristically ascetic—pale walls dabbed with minimal modern-artistic flourishes. The management sponsors cooking festivals, and every three months the kitchen produces dishes from a different country. The basic menu changes six times a year, and over that same period it will include three Mexican food fests. The set menu features duck pâté and excellent seafood pasta, with juicy prawns, shellfish, and squid. Ice creams, meringues, and chocolate cake benefit from the chef's delicate mint sauce. ⊠ *Moliere 50, Col. Polanco,* ☎ *5/ 280–1586. Jacket and tie. AE, DC, MC, V. Closed Sun.*

$$–$$$ ✕ **El Tajín.** Named after El Tajín Pyramid in Veracruz, this eatery serves the innovative Mexican cooking that has taken the metropolis by storm. El Tajín adds zest and style to many well-known dishes. Dazzling main dishes include soft-shell crab accented by sesame seeds and a tad of chipotle. This lovely restaurant is hidden behind the functional facade of the Veracruz Cultural Center in Colonia Coyoacán. Ancient

Huastecan faces grinning from a splashing fountain add a bit of levity to the dining experience. ⊠ *Miguel Angel de Queveda 687, Col. Coyoacán,* ☎ *5/659–4447, 5/659–5759. AE, MC, V. No dinner.*

$$ ✕ **Los Almendros.** If you can't make it to the Yucatán, try the peninsula's unusual and lively food at one of this restaurant's two locations. If the spacious, cool white interior and bubbling fountain don't transport you, then the habañero chilies, red onions, and other native Yucatecan ingredients will. Traditional dishes, such as a refreshing lime soup or *frijol con puerco* (tender pork pieces with black beans), share the menu with impossible-to-pronounce Maya cuisine. Especially worth trying is the *pescado tikinxic*—white fish in a mild red marinade of achiote seed and juice of bitter orange. This is a good place to sample a wide array of fine tequila, served with sliced jicama and a tangy tomato-juice chaser called sangrita. ⊠ *Campos Elíseos 164, Col. Polanco,* ☎ *5/531–6646;* ⊠

$$ ✕ **Fonda del Recuerdo.** A popular family restaurant, the *fonda* (mod-
★ est restaurant) also has a solid reputation among tourists and anyone celebrating anything. Every day 2–10, five lively marimba groups from Veracruz provide festive music. The place made its name with its fish and seafood platters from the gulf state of Veracruz, and the house special is huachinango *à la Veracruzano* (a whole red snapper in a succulent, mildly spiced sauce of tomato, chopped onion, and olives). Sharing its fame is the *torito,* a potent drink made from tequila and exotic tropical fruit juices. Meat from the kitchen's own *parillas* (grills) is always first-rate. Portions are huge, but if you have room for dessert, try *crepas de cajeta al tequila* (milk-caramel crepes lightly sauced with tequila). ⊠ *Bahía de las Palmas 39, Col. Anzures,* ☎ *5/260–7339, 5/260–1292. Reservations essential. AE, DC, MC, V.*

$$ ✕ **Los Girasoles.** Two prominent Mexico City society columnists own this downtown spot. Los Girasoles (which means sunflowers) is on a lovely old square in a restored three-story colonial home and serves nueva Mexicana cuisine—light, tasty, and innovative. Traditional Mexican bean soup is dressed up with noodles and a pinch of chilies. Meat, fish, and seafood dishes are blended with exotic herbs and spices. There are also pre-Hispanic delicacies such as *escamoles* (ant roe), *gusanos de maguey* (chilied worms), and *chapulines* (crispy fried grasshoppers). The desserts pay homage to local produce with such creations as *guanábana* (soursop) and *zapote* (a tropical fruit native to Mexico) mousses. One of the nicest places for dining is the covered street-level terrace. ⊠ *Plaza Manuel Tolsa on Xicoténcatl 1,* ☎ *5/510–0630, 5/510–3281. AE, MC, V. No dinner Sun.*

$$ ✕ **Los Irabien.** This beautiful dining area filled with plants and the owner's impressive art collection is a worthwhile stop for foodies and culture vultures. Chef Arturo Fuentes turns out nueva Mexicana and traditional Mexican dishes. His *ensalada Irabien* triumphs as a mixture of smoked salmon, abalone, prawn, quail eggs, and watercress. One outstanding entrée is nopal cactus stuffed with fish fillet. You'll also find less exotic dishes. Los Irabien is one of the city's breakfast spots par excellence—tempting you with *huevos de codorniz huitzilopochtli*—quail eggs with tortilla in a pumpkin-blossom sauce. ⊠ *Av. de la Paz 45, Col. San Angel,* ☎ *5/616–0014. Jacket and tie. AE, DC, MC, V. No dinner Sun.*

$$ ✕ **T Cla.** Since its 1998 opening, this see-and-be-seen newcomer has
★ been a welcome addition to Mexico City's growing nueva Mexicana scene. Named after an old-fashioned typesetting key, the restaurant's Polanco location and a newsprint collage set a hip tone. The artsy Roma locale has copped a bit of an attitude toward those who don't reserve, but the food is worth a little cheekiness. The appetizers are especially intriguing, including squash flowers stuffed with goat cheese in a

chipotle sauce and a spicy crab-stuffed chile relleno. The house special beef dish, *filete T Cla,* shows a flair for sauces, in this case combining Roquefort with huitlacoche. Best of all, the prices are still unpretentious. ✉ *Moliere 56, Col. Polanco,* ☎ *5/282–0010;* ✉ *Durango 186A, Col. Roma,* ☎ *5/525–4920. AE, MC, V. No dinner Sun.*

$ ✕ **Bajío.** This cheerful neighborhood bistro is a find when it comes to good eating. Decorated in bright colors, Bajío attracts Mexican families and is run by vivacious Carmen "Titita" Ramírez—a chef and culinary expert who has been featured in, among others, *Saveur* magazine. The restaurant specializes in classic down-home Veracruz cooking. The 30-ingredient mole, a Bajío signature dish, is to die for; also excellent are *empanadas de platano rellenos de frijol* (tortilla turnovers filled with bananas and beans) and *carnitas* (roast pork). You may have to go a little off the beaten track to get here, but it's worth it. ✉ *Cuitláhuac 2709, Col. Azcapotzalco, about a 20-min ride north of Zona Rosa,* ☎ *5/341–9889. AE, MC, V. No dinner.*

$ ✕ **Café de Tacuba.** An essential breakfast, lunch, dinner, or snack stop downtown, this Mexican classic has been charming all comers since it opened in 1912 in a section of an old convent. At the entrance to the atmospheric main dining room are huge 18th-century oil paintings depicting the invention of *mole poblano,* a complex sauce with a variety of chilies and chocolate that was created by the nuns in the Santa Rosa Convent of Puebla. Along with mole poblano, look for delicious tamales made fresh every morning. There are also pastries galore. A student group dressed in medieval capes and hats serenades Thursday–Sunday 3:30–11:30; mariachis play during lunch the other days. ✉ *Tacuba 28, Col. Centro,* ☎ *5/518–4950. Reservations not accepted. AE, MC, V.*

$ ✕ **Casa de la Sirena.** Dining is sublime here at the foot of the Templo Major ruins, which supplied some of the building blocks for this 16th-century mansion. A wandering Spanish monk named the home after a mermaid (*sirena*) carved into the facade of a nearby building. The atmospheric second-floor dining terrace is within sight and sound of numerous Indian dances honoring the spirits of the crumbling Aztec temples below. Lunch caters to the vast number of government workers in the area. At night, it's utterly romantic dining under the stars. The cuisine is nouvelle with such specialties as Cornish hen in mango mole sauce and a plethora of other innovative meat and fish dishes. If you've never tried it, order a smooth tequila liqueur as an after-dinner digestive. ✉ *Guatemala 32, Zócalo,* ☎ *5/704–3225,* FAX *5/704–3465. AE, MC, V. Closed Sun.*

$ ✕ **Las Cazuelas.** Traditional Mexican cooking at its best is the word at ★ one of the most famous of the capital's fondas. The large dining area is brightened by hand-painted chairs from Michoacán and green-and-white table linens. Ideal Mexican appetizers to share are *carnitas rancheras* (pork morsels in red sauce). The tortilla soup, with its dash of *pasilla* chili and bits of cheese, makes another excellent starter. Main courses center on various moles or the piquant sesame-flavored pipián sauce with pork or chicken. Finish with a café de olla and a domestic brandy. ✉ *San Antonio 143, at Illinois, Col. Napoles,* ☎ *5/563–4118. Reservations not accepted. AE, MC, V. Closed Sun. No dinner.*

$ ✕ **Fonda Chon.** This unpretentious family-style restaurant, deep in a downtown working-class neighborhood, is famed for its pre-Hispanic Mexican dishes. A knowledge of zoology, Spanish, and Nahuatl helps in making sense of a menu that takes in a gamut of ingredients—no processed foods among them—from throughout the republic. *Escamoles de hormiga* (red-ant roe), 97% protein, is known as the "caviar of Mexico" for its costliness, but you may have to acquire a taste for it. Among the exotic entrées are armadillo in mango sauce and crackling crisp fried grasshoppers with guacamole. More-traditional specialties include fried or chilied baby kid and barbecued ribs in a red chili sauce. The zapote flan is worth a try. ⊠ *Regina 160, near La Merced market, Col. Centro,* ☎ *5/542–0873. Reservations not accepted. MC, V. Closed Sun. No dinner.*

$ ✕ **Hosteria de Santo Domingo.** This genteel institution near downtown's Plaza Santo Domingo has been serving *authentico* colonial dishes for more than a century in an atmospheric late-19th-century town house. Feast on tried-and-true favorites such as stuffed cactus paddles, thousand-flower soup, pot roast, and a stunning array of quesadillas. Among what may be the best homemade Mexican desserts in town are the comforting flan and *arroz con leche* (rice pudding). The place is open for breakfast and is always full at lunch. Get there early to avoid standing in line. ⊠ *Belisario Dominguez 72, Col. Centro,* ☎ *5/510–1434, 5/526–5276. AE, MC, V. No dinner Sun.*

Spanish

$$–$$$ ✕ **El Parador de Manolo.** A two-story period house was remodeled into this Spanish restaurant in fashionable Polanco. The Bar Porrón on the ground floor serves Spanish tapas, including an excellent prawn mix in a spicy sauce; after 9, the bar has live music and flamenco. In the brasserie-style dining room upstairs, choose from a Spanish menu or from the list of the chef's recommendations. Specially cured Serrano ham is possibly the best in the city; *calamares fritos* (fried squid) and *crepas de flor de calabaza al gratin* (pumpkin-flower crepes) are other fine starters. Fish dishes make the most appealing main courses, although the chateaubriand Parador for two (in a black corn-fungus sauce) is truly original. Desserts are less notable. Wines are on display downstairs, as are the fresh fish of the day. ⊠ *Presidente Masarik 433, Col. Polanco,* ☎ *5/281–2357, 5/281–5762. AE, MC, V. No dinner Sun.*

$$ ✕ **Tezka.** This Zona Rosa restaurant is Mexico's first and only with nueva cocina Basque, created by famous Basque chef Arzac, who transposed many of his best dishes to Mexico from his restaurant in San Sebastían, Spain. It's always packed with a Spanish clientele. Feast on baked fish in parsley sauce and sweet garlic cream, or pheasant prepared with dates, pine nuts, and apple puree. Arzac disdains appetizers, which he believes ruin appreciation of entrées, so you won't find any starters here. There *are* tempting and original desserts, such as cheese tart with blueberries. There's a decent list of Spanish wines such as Cune, Vina Ardanza, and Reserva 904. ⊠ *Royal Hotel, Amberes 78, at Liverpool,* ☎ *5/228–9918. AE, DC, MC, V. Closed Sun. No dinner Sat.*

$–$$ ✕ **Meson El Cid.** This *meson* (tavern) exudes an atmosphere of Old Spain. During the week, classic dishes such as paella, spring lamb, suckling baby pig, and Cornish hens with truffles keep customers happy, but on Saturday night this place really comes into its own with a medieval banquet. The fun unfolds with a procession of costumed waiters carrying huge trays of steaming hot viands. A caged cat—the grandson of the first feline to play this role, the waiters will tell you—heads the parade as in olden days, when a king's food was tested for poisoning by letting a cat nose around in it first (cats being keen enough not to touch the stuff if it had been tampered with). Entertainment is provided by a student singing group dressed in medieval Spanish capes and hats. ⊠ *Humboldt 61, Col. Centro,* ☎ *5/521–1940, 5/521–8881, 5/512–7629. AE, MC, V. No dinner Sun.*

Vegetarian

$ ✕ **Las Fuentes.** About three blocks north of the U.S. Embassy on Calle Río Tiber, Las Fuentes is run by Philipe Culbert, a lifelong vegetarian who ascribes to the time-honored dietary dictates of ancient Persia in balancing his menu. A sample meal might be tacos stuffed with carrots and potatoes accompanied by apple salad and followed by whole-grain cookies made with honey. Don't be put off by the sterile Formica tables. The office and embassy workers who pack the place at lunchtime come for the food rather than the ambience. ⊠ *Río Panuco 27, at Calle Río Tiber, Col. Cuauhtémoc,* ☎ *5/525–0843. MC, V.*

$ ✕ **El Jug.** To duck the madding crowd, head for this small, tidy retreat near the Zona Rosa. You'll enjoy delicious vegetarian fare to the accompaniment of New Age music. Heaping salads, homemade soups, and entrées such as *chiles rellenos* (stuffed green peppers) come with whole-grain bread. You can choose the filling daily *comida corrida* (fixed-price menu) or order à la carte. After lunch, you might want to browse through the store on the premises and absorb the vibes of crystals, incense holders, aromatherapy pillows, and the like. ⊠ *Puebla 326-A (entrance on Calle Cozumel), Col. Roma,* ☎ *5/553–3872. Reservations not accepted. No credit cards. Closed Sun. No dinner.*

LODGING

Although the city is huge and spread out, most hotels are within a relatively manageable group of neighborhoods. Stylish Colonia Polanco and Bosque de Chapultepec are on the west side of the city. Paseo de la Reforma runs from Chapultepec, northeast through "midtown," and intersects with Avenida Juárez at the beginning of the downtown area. Juárez becomes Calle Madero, which continues east to the downtown historic district and its very core, the Zócalo. The Zona Rosa, replete with boutiques, cafés, restaurants, and nightspots, is literally across Reforma (south), in the western midtown area.

Business travelers tend to fill up deluxe hotels during the week; some major hotels discount their weekend rates. If you reserve through the toll-free reservations numbers, you probably will find rates as much as 50% off during special promotions. You can expect hotels in the $$$ and $$$$ categories to have purified water, air-conditioning, cable TV, radio, minibars, and extended (often 24-hour) room service.

CATEGORY	COST*
$$$$	over $160
$$$	$90–$160
$$	$40–$90
$	under $40

All prices are for a standard double room, excluding service charge and 15% sales tax. There is an additional 2% room tax.

Colonia Polanco and Bosque de Chapultepec

$$$$ ⊞ **Camino Real.** About the size of Teotihuacán's Pyramid of the Sun,
★ this sleek, minimalist, bright pink and yellow, 8-acre city-within-a-city attracts everyone from heads of state and celebrities to holiday travelers. Impressive works of art embellishing the endless corridors and lounges include Rufino Tamayo's mural *Man Facing Infinity* and a Calder sculpture. The fifth-floor executive level has 100 extra-large guest rooms with special amenities. Fouquet's de Paris restaurant (☞ Dining, *above*) holds culinary events, and the airy Azulejos serves Mexican fare and Sunday buffet brunches. A nightclub hosts top Latin American artists who perform Thursday through Saturday starting at 11 PM; there's dancing after the show. ⊠ *Mariano Escobedo 700, 11590,* ☎ *5/203–2121, 800/722–6466,* ⅎ⅍ *5/250–6897, 5/250–6723. 673 rooms, 36 suites. 3 restaurants, 4 bars, pool, 4 tennis courts, health club, nightclub, business services. AE, DC, MC, V.* ⊛

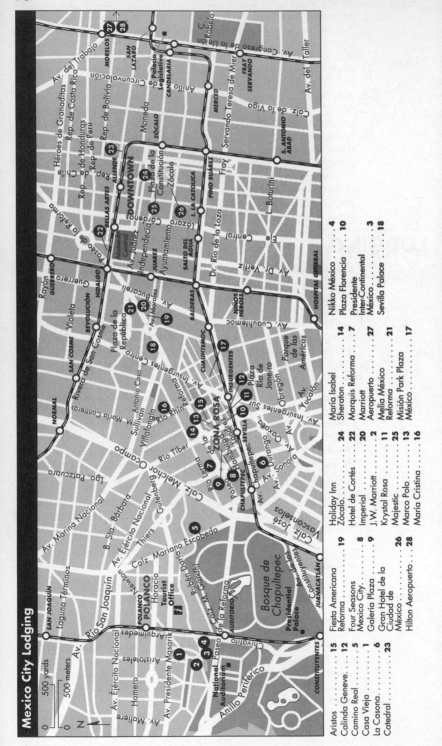

Mexico City Lodging

500 yards

500 meters

$$$$ 🖫 **Casa Vieja.** This classically elegant, sumptuously decorated Colonia Polanco mansion is the dream-come-true of a local businessman who took his love of things Mexican and expressed it in his all-suites (one and two bedrooms) hotel. Tastefully selected folk art, handsomely hand-carved furniture, and gilded wall trimmings complement patios and splashing fountains. Lively Mexican colors are a light-hearted touch in the 10 suites, all of them different. All have a full kitchen, fax machine, CD and video-cassette players, hot tub, and picture window overlooking an inside garden. The hotel's Mexican restaurant is named after its huge floor-to-ceiling *Arbor de la Vida (Tree of Life)* sculpture. Rates include breakfast. ⊠ *Eugenio Sue 45, Col. Polanco, 11560,* ☎ *5/282–0067,* 🖳 *5/281–3780. 10 suites. Restaurant, bar, concierge, free parking. AE, MC, V.*

$$$$ 🖫 **J. W. Marriott.** In posh Colonia Polanco, this hotel was designed as a boutique property with personalized service and small, clubby public areas; nothing overwhelms here. Rooms are done with plenty of wood and warm colors but are otherwise unremarkable in decor. Each has a work desk with an outlet for a personal computer and modem. The hotel has the best-equipped business center in the city, open 24 hours. Executive floors come with extra amenities. The pretty Thai House restaurant is also on site. ⊠ *Andrés Bello 29, at Campos Elíseos, Col. Polanco, 11560,* ☎ *5/282–8888, 800/228–9290,* 🖳 *5/282–8811. 312 rooms. 3 restaurants, bar, coffee shop, pool, exercise room, business services, meeting rooms, travel services, car rental. AE, DC, MC, V.* ⊛

$$$$ 🖫 **Nikko México.** Part of the Japanese Nikko chain, this glistening, 42-floor high-rise occupies a prime Polanco position: adjacent to Bosque de Chapultepec, just a five-minute walk from the Anthropology Museum. It has signage and menus in Japanese, English, and Spanish. Although it's the second-largest hotel in the city and has marvelous views from the top floor, its standard rooms are a little claustrophobic; executive floors have better rooms and extra facilities. Four top restaurants excel in their gastronomic specialties: Les Célébrités (International) (☞ Dining, *above*), Teppan Grill and Benkay (both Japanese), and El Jardín (international). The cozy Shelty's Pub is also a big hit with locals. ⊠ *Campos Elíseos 204, 11560,* ☎ *5/280–1111, 01–800/908–8800, 800/645–5687 in the U.S. and Canada,* 🖳 *5/280–9191. 724 rooms, 24 suites. 4 restaurants, 2 bars, indoor pool, 4 tennis courts, health club, jogging, dance club, business services, meeting rooms, travel services, car rental. AE, DC, MC, V.* ⊛

$$$$ 🖫 **Presidente Inter-Continental México.** This 42-story Inter-Continental, adjacent to Bosque de Chapultepec in Colonia Polanco, has a dramatic five-story atrium lobby—a hollow pyramid of balconies—with music performed daily at the lively lobby bar. Rooms are spacious, and all have work areas. On clear days, the top two floors have views of the nearby snowcapped volcanoes. The executive floors have a lounge, concierge, and extra amenities. A number of smart stores and six eateries are on the premises, including branches of Maxim's de Paris (☞ Dining, *above*) and the Palm and Alfredo Di Roma. ⊠ *Campos Elíseos 218, 11560,* ☎ *5/327–7700, 800/327–0200 in the U.S. and Canada,* 🖳 *5/327–7730. 627 rooms, 32 suites. 6 restaurants, coffee shop, lobby lounge, exercise room, baby-sitting, business services, meeting rooms, travel services, car rental, parking (fee). AE, DC, MC, V.* ⊛

Zona Rosa

$$$$ 🖫 **Galería Plaza.** Part of the Westin Hotel deluxe chain, this ultramodern
★ property is on a quiet street in elegant Zona Rosa—ideal for shopping, enjoying nightlife, and dining out. Standard rooms are relatively small, but service and facilities are faultless. Rooms on the executive floor,

where a special concierge desk provides personalized service and easy checkout, are larger. Other advantages include voice mail in all rooms, a heated rooftop pool with sundeck, a secure underground parking lot, and a 24-hour restaurant, which has a popular buffet breakfast. ⊠ *Hamburgo 195, at Varsovia, 06600,* ☎ *5/208–0370, 800/228–3000,* FAX *5/207–5867. 420 rooms, 19 suites. 3 restaurants, lobby lounge, room service, pool, exercise room, concierge, travel services, parking (fee). AE, DC, MC, V.* 🕭

$$$$ 🖬 **Krystal Rosa.** Part of the Mexican Krystal Hotel chain, this superbly run high-rise hotel is in the heart of the Zona Rosa and has an excellent view of the city from the rooftop pool terrace. There is a stylish lobby cocktail lounge, a bar with local entertainers, and a restaurant, Hacienda del Mortero, that serves excellent classic Mexican cuisine. Two club floors have VIP check-in and service, complimentary Continental buffet breakfast, and rooms with extra amenities. ⊠ *Liverpool 155, 06600,* ☎ *5/228–9928,* FAX *5/228–9929. 267 rooms, 35 suites. 2 restaurants, 2 bars, pool, concierge, business services, parking (fee). AE, DC, MC, V.*

$$$ 🖬 **Aristos.** On bustling Paseo de la Reforma a few blocks east of the U.S. Embassy and near the Mexican Stock Exchange, this 15-story Zona Rosa–fringe hotel wears its age well (it was one of the first luxury hotels in the area). Rooms are well supplied and attractively decorated in shades of peach and mauve, with brass and wood accents. The business center has a bilingual staff and a message service. ⊠ *Paseo de la Reforma 276, 06600,* ☎ *5/211–0112,* FAX *5/514–3543. 298 rooms, 29 suites. 4 restaurants, bar, beauty salon, sauna, exercise room, travel services, parking (fee). AE, DC, MC, V.*

$$$ 🖬 **Calinda Geneve.** A Quality Inn, referred to locally as El Génova, this five-story 1906 hotel is fitted with traditional colonial-style carved wood chairs and tables in the pleasant lobby; guest rooms are smallish but comfortable. The hotel's attraction as a gathering place has always been the Salón Jardín, a striking Belle Epoque gallery with a profusion of plants and a high stained-glass ceiling; it's been taken over by the popular Sanborns restaurant chain with little change to its decor. The hotel's informal street-front Café Jardín serves until 10 PM, and a branch of the Sanborns retail chain, which sells sundries, opens off the lobby. ⊠ *Londres 130, 06600,* ☎ *5/211–0071, 800/228–5151,* FAX *5/208–7422. 320 rooms. Restaurant, bar, café, room service, exercise room, coin laundry, business services. AE, DC, MC, V.* 🕭

$$$ 🖬 **La Casona.** This elegant, understated mansion, registered as an artistic monument by Mexico's Institute of Fine Arts, was turned into a charming 30-room hotel in 1996. Filled with sunny patios and sitting rooms, the hotel is finely decorated with antiques, expensive rugs, hardwood floors, and accessories in the spirit of the days of the Porfiriato, when the house was built. No two rooms are alike, but all have hair dryers, fluffy bathrobes and slippers, and good-size bathtubs. There's a small restaurant that serves old-style country cooking. The two-story hotel building, with its demure salmon facade, looks out on a tree-lined street in Colonia Roma, about a 10-minute walk south of the Zona Rosa and in easy reach of museums, restaurants, and Paseo de la Reforma. A Continental breakfast is included in the price of a room. ⊠ *Durango 280, at Cozumel,* ☎ *5/286–3001, 800/223–5652,* FAX *5/211–0871. 30 rooms. Restaurant, bar, room service, exercise room. AE, DC, MC, V.* 🕭

$$$ 🖬 **Marco Polo.** Ultramodern and intimate, the central Zona Rosa all-
★   suites Marco Polo has the amenities and outstanding personalized service often associated with a small European hotel. All rooms have climate control, cable TV, FM radio, minibar, and work desks; some suites have hot tubs. North-facing top-floor rooms have excellent views of Paseo de la Reforma and the Angel monument—the four penthouse suites

have terraces—and the U.S. Embassy is close by. In the street-level Bistro de Marco Polo, you can listen to sophisticated piano music evenings 7–9. ⊠ *Amberes 27, 06600,* ☎ *5/207–1893,* ℻ *5/533–3727. 60 suites. Restaurant, bar, business services. AE, DC, MC, V.* ⊛

$$$ 🖭 **Plaza Florencia.** This modern hotel is on a busy avenue that borders the Zona Rosa—and the low end of $$$. The lobby's heavy furniture and dark colors make it feel more like a lodge, in which guests relax after a day of exploring. Rooms are well furnished in hotel-modern style—cheerfully decorated, and soundproofed against the location's heavy traffic noise; higher floors have views of the Angel monument. Some large family suites are available. All rooms have air-conditioning, heat, color TV, and a phone. A business center offers fax, copy, computer, and Internet-access services. ⊠ *Florencia 61, 06600,* ☎ *5/ 211–0064,* ℻ *5/511–1542. 130 rooms, 12 suites. Restaurant, bar, coffee shop, business services. AE, DC, MC, V.* ⊛

$$ 🖭 **Misión Park Plaza México.** A part of the Misión chain, this very comfortable hotel a few blocks from the Zona Rosa's eastern end is well placed for shopping and sightseeing. Mirrors, good light, and like-new bathrooms make the rooms more pleasant; all have air-conditioning and color TV with U.S. channels. Sixteen rooms have been converted into executive units that have work areas, and Internet connection has been added to an office off the lobby for guests' use. Staff is friendly and accommodating, and breakfast is included in the room rates. ⊠ *Napoles 62, 06600,* ☎ *5/533–0535,* ℻ *5/533–1589. 50 rooms. Coffee shop, lobby lounge, exercise room, meeting rooms. AE, MC, V.* ⊛

Midtown and along the Reforma

$$$$ 🖭 **Four Seasons Mexico City.** This is—perhaps by definition—one of the
★   most luxurious hotels in the capital and accordingly has won the AAA Five Diamond Award three years running. Surrounding a traditional courtyard with a fountain, the eight-story building was modeled after the 18th-century Iturbide Palace downtown. Half the rooms overlook the lush inner courtyard garden. Huge bowls of flowers and lovely European furnishings fill the spacious marble lobby. Geared for business travelers, rooms have data ports and all the amenities you'd expect at a Four Seasons hotel. There's also a boardroom on the premises and a full-service business center with even a reference library. A well-stocked tequila bar off the lobby is a perfect pre-dinner option. Excellent cultural tours of the city are offered free to guests on weekends. ⊠ *Paseo de la Reforma 500, 06600,* ☎ *5/230–1818, 800/332–3442,* ℻ *5/230–1808. 200 rooms, 40 suites. 2 restaurants, 2 bars, pool, exercise room, health club, business services, meeting rooms. AE, DC, MC, V.* ⊛

$$$$ 🖭 **María Isabel Sheraton.** Don Antenor Patiño, the Bolivian "Tin King," inaugurated this Mexico City classic in 1969 and named it after his granddaughter, socialite Isabel Goldsmith. The hotel is constantly being remodeled, but the glistening brown marble and Art Deco details in the lobby and other public areas remain. All guest and public rooms are impeccably maintained; penthouse suites in the 22-story tower section are extra-spacious and exceptionally luxurious. The location—across from the Angel monument and the Zona Rosa, with Sanborns next door and the U.S. Embassy a half block away—is prime. It has the largest conference room (for 1,500) in town. ⊠ *Paseo de la Reforma 325, 06500,* ☎ *5/207–3933, 800/334–8484,* ℻ *5/207–0684. 681 rooms, 74 suites. 3 restaurants, bar, room service, pool, massage, sauna, health club, concierge floor, business services, meeting rooms, parking (fee). AE, DC, MC, V.* ⊛

$$$$ 🖭 **Marquis Reforma.** Opened in 1991, this plush, privately owned member
★   of the Leading Hotels of the World, and 1999 recipient of the Five

Stars and Five Diamonds Award given by the Mexican government, is within walking distance of the Zona Rosa. It has a striking pink-stone and curved-glass Art Nouveau facade, and its seventh-floor suites afford picture-perfect views of the Castillo de Chapultepec. The elegant lobby is fitted in a classic European style, with paintings, sculpture, and palatial furniture. Guest-room furniture and decor are Art Deco–inspired. The award-winning La Jolla restaurant serves Mexican cuisine. The fully staffed corporate center has state-of-the-art computer services, and guest-room phones feature a second plug for computers with fax modem. The health club has hard-to-find holistic, stress-busting massages. ⊠ *Paseo de la Reforma 465, 06500,* ☎ *5/211–3600, 800/235–2387, 877/818–5011 in Canada,* 𝔽𝔸𝕏 *5/211–5561. 133 rooms, 84 suites. 2 restaurants, bar, health club, business services, meeting room. AE, DC, MC, V.* 🐕

$$$$ 🏨 **Meliá México Reforma.** Perched at the junction of Paseo de la Reforma, Juárez, and Bucareli—convenient to downtown, the Zona Rosa, and the Stock Exchange—this flashy 22-story smoked-glass behemoth (formerly part of the Crowne Plaza chain) looks quite spectacular in its otherwise nondescript surroundings. It touts the ultimate in high-tech amenities for business travelers: a stock-market indicator, computers, cellular phones, and secretarial, translation, messenger, and shipping services. Executive rooms have PC- and fax-modem outlets and three telephone lines. Public areas include a coffee bar with 20 java concoctions, an oyster-and-jazz bar, and a French restaurant. The hotel also has limousine rental, a pharmacy, and boutiques. ⊠ *Paseo de la Reforma 1, Col. Tabacalera, 06030,* ☎ *5/128–5000, 800/336–3542,* 𝔽𝔸𝕏 *5/128–5050. 424 rooms, 30 suites. 2 restaurants, 2 bars, room service, beauty salon, shops, business services, travel services, car rental. AE, DC, MC, V.*

$$$ 🏨 **Fiesta Americana Reforma.** This immense hotel, built in the 1970s by a Mexican chain that billed it a "bar with a hotel," may be past its prime, but the business travelers and large groups that parade in and out of the lobby still keep it lively. There isn't much Mexican atmosphere except for the live Mexican music in the lobby bar, but there's something to say for being able to get a good tan on the sundeck, work out in the gym, and choose from two restaurants, one of which offers breakfast and lunch buffets. ⊠ *Paseo de la Reforma 80, 06600,* ☎ *5/705–1515, 800/343–7821,* 𝔽𝔸𝕏 *5/705–1313. 610 rooms. 2 restaurants, 2 bars, exercise room, business services, free parking. AE, DC, MC, V.* 🐕

$$ 🏨 **Imperial.** Opened in 1990, the Imperial occupies a stately late-19th-century European-style building right on the Reforma alongside the Columbus Monument. Quiet elegance and personal service are keynotes of this privately owned property. The hotel's Restaurant Gaudí has an understated, tony atmosphere and serves Continental cuisine with some classic Spanish selections. All rooms have safes. ⊠ *Paseo de la Reforma 64, 06600,* ☎ *5/705–4911,* 𝔽𝔸𝕏 *5/703–3122. 50 rooms, 10 junior suites, 5 master suites. Restaurant, bar, café, business services, meeting rooms, travel services. AE, DC, MC, V.* 🐕

$$ 🏨 **María Cristina.** Full of old-world charm, this Spanish colonial-style
★   gem is a Mexico City classic. Impeccably maintained since it was built in 1937 (it was last refurbished in January 1995), the building surrounds a delightful garden courtyard—the setting for its El Retiro bar. Three tastefully decorated apartment-style master suites, complete with hot tubs, were added in the early '90s. All rooms have safes. Located in a quiet residential setting near Parque Sullivan, the hotel is a block from the Paseo de la Reforma and close to the Zona Rosa. ⊠ *Río Lerma 31, 06500,* ☎ *5/566–9688,* 𝔽𝔸𝕏 *5/566–9194. 140 rooms, 8 suites. Bar, room service, beauty salon, travel services. MC, V.*

$$ ▦ **Sevilla Palace.** This glistening modern showplace has five panoramic elevators for its 23 floors, a covered rooftop pool with hot tub, a health club, a top-floor supper club with entertainment, a terraced rooftop lounge with a city view, and convention halls with capacities of up to 1,000. It's near the Columbus traffic circle and attracts lots of tourists from Spain. ✉ *Paseo de la Reforma 105, 06030,* ☎ *5/705–2800, 800/ 732–9488,* ℻ *5/703–1521. 413 rooms. 2 restaurants, 3 bars, pool, health club, nightclub, meeting rooms. AE, MC, V.* ✆

Downtown

$$$ ▦ **Majestic.** The atmospheric, colonial-style Majestic, built in 1937, is perfectly located if you're interested in exploring the historic downtown: on the Zócalo at the corner of Madero. This Best Western property is also perfect for viewing the Independence Day (September 16) celebrations, which draw hundreds of thousands of people to this square, and many people reserve a room a year in advance of the festivities. Rooms are decorated in the style of the 1940s and have no air-conditioning but are kept cool by high ceilings and the fact that you are in a high-mountain city; each has a remote-control color TV and a minibar. Although the front units have balconies and a charming view, they can be noisy with car traffic until about 11 at night. Service is efficient and courteous. The seventh-floor La Terraza dining room and terrace—which serve international and Mexican specialties—have marvelous panoramas of the Zócalo. The Sunday buffet (1–5) features live Mexican music. The fun El Campanario piano bar welcomes anyone who wants to make a singing debut, and has become a favorite with locals. ✉ *Madero 73, 06000,* ☎ *5/521–8600, 800/528–1234,* ℻ *5/512–6262. 85 rooms. Restaurant, bar, coffee shop, travel services. AE, DC, V.* ✆

$$ ▦ **Gran Hotel de la Ciudad de México.** Ensconced in what was formerly a 19th-century department store, this more traditional hotel has contemporary rooms. Its central location—adjacent to the Zócalo and near the Templo Mayor—makes it a good choice for local sightseeing. Its distinctive Belle Epoque lobby—with a striking stained-glass Tiffany dome, chandeliers, gilded birdcages, and 19th-century wrought-iron elevators—is worth a visit in its own right. The Mirador breakfast restaurant overlooks the Zócalo. The Del Centro restaurant-bar run by Delmónicos is one of Mexico City's best—a great place to stop for a drink while exploring nearby. The hotel has been undergoing a long-term, gradual refurbishing; be sure to request a renovated room that does not look out onto a brick wall. ✉ *16 de Septiembre 82, 06000,* ☎ *5/510–4040,* ℻ *5/512–6772. 125 rooms. 2 restaurants, bar, concierge, travel services, parking (fee). AE, DC, MC, V.*

$$ ▦ **Holiday Inn Select Zócalo.** Opened in 1998, this hotel couldn't have a better location—on the Zócalo and close to a gaggle of museums, restaurants, and historic buildings. It's actually in a historic building that dates back to colonial times. The interior is modern and has the feel of a Holiday Inn. Although the glass-front lobby lacks personality, there's more flavor to the terrace restaurant, which is set with old-fashioned wrought-iron tables and has an amazing view of the Metropolitan Cathedral and National Palace. Rooms are small but well-equipped with closet safe, coffeemaker, air-conditioning and heat, iron and ironing board, and bathroom amenities. All suites have data ports; five have Jacuzzi bathtubs. ✉ *5 de Mayo at Zócalo, Centro Histórico, 06000,* ☎ *5/521–2121, 800/465–4329,* ℻ *5/521–2122. 100 rooms, 15 suites. 2 restaurants, bar, room service, exercise room, meeting rooms, travel services, parking (fee). AE, MC, V.* ✆

$$ ⊞ **Hotel de Cortés.** This delightful small hotel, managed by Best Western, is housed in a 1780 colonial building that was designated a national monument. Colonial-decor rooms are small and simply furnished; they open onto an enclosed central courtyard. Two comfortable soundproof suites overlook Alameda Park across the busy street. A restaurant also looks onto the park, and a friendly bar opens to the tree-shaded central courtyard and fountain, a lovely setting for tea or cocktails. Friday evening at 7:30, there's a Mexican folkloric show with music and dance. The Franz Mayer Museum is just a block away, and it's an easy walk to Palacio de Bellas Artes. Loyal guests reserve many months in advance. ⊠ *Av. Hidalgo 85, 06000,* ☎ *5/518–2184, 800/334–7234,* 𝔽𝔸𝕏 *5/512– 1863. 19 rooms, 10 suites. Restaurant, bar. AE, DC, MC, V.*☜

$ ⊞ **Catedral.** In the heart of historic downtown, this refurbished older
★ hotel is a bargain, with many of the amenities of the more upscale hotels at less than half the price. Public areas sparkle with marble and glass. Guest rooms are done in a cheerful contemporary fashion, and all have color TVs (local channels only) and phones. You can get one with a view of the namesake Catedral, but keep in mind that its bells chime every 15 minutes late into the night. Service is friendly, the hotel restaurant is excellent, and El Retiro bar attracts a largely Mexican clientele to hear live Latin music. ⊠ *Donceles 95, 06000,* ☎ *5/512–8581,* 𝔽𝔸𝕏 *5/512–4344. 116 rooms. Bar, coffee shop, room service, nightclub, laundry service, dry cleaning, travel services. AE, MC, V.*

Airport

$$$$ ⊞ **Hilton Aeropuerto.** This luxury oasis opened in 1998, marking the arrival of the only hotel *inside* the airport. Cool and compact, with a distinctive gray marble lobby and a wide-angle view from the bar of landing planes, the hotel feels like a private club with its subdued elegance and attentive but unobtrusive staff. Rooms come with full working gear for a traveling executive: two phone lines, modem connection, ergonomic chairs, and coffeemaker. Rooms have four different views—airstrip, street, atrium, or garden (bamboo plants set along a concrete ledge). All units wrap around one floor. ⊠ *Benito Juárez International Airport, international terminal, 15520,* ☎ *5/133–0505, 800/445–8667,* 𝔽𝔸𝕏 *5/133– 0500. 129 rooms. Restaurant, bar, exercise room, business services, meeting room, parking (fee). AE, DC, MC, V.*☜

$$$ ⊞ **Marriott Aeropuerto.** Just over a short covered footbridge from the airport terminal is this deluxe hotel that's sleek and modern as well as comfortable. The hotel is convenient if you arrive late or have an early morning flight; you pay a price for this convenience, although discounted corporate rates are available. There's a pool on the eighth floor. Even if you're only between flights and don't overnight, you can sit in one of the overstuffed chairs in the soothing lobby to get away from the frantic energy of the airport, or catch a meal in the restaurant. ⊠ *Benito Juárez International Airport, 15520,* ☎ *5/230–0505, 800/228–9290,* 𝔽𝔸𝕏 *5/ 230–0555. 600 rooms, 8 suites. Restaurant, bar, coffee shop, pool, sauna, health club, meeting rooms, car rental, free parking. AE, DC, MC, V.*☜

NIGHTLIFE AND THE ARTS

Good places to check for current events include the Friday edition of *The News,* a daily English-language newspaper, and *Tiempo Libre,* a weekly magazine listing activities and events in Spanish. All are available at newsstands.

Citywide cultural festivals with free music, dance, and theater performances by local groups take place all year long but especially in July and August. A three-week spring cultural festival with international headliners takes place in the Historic Center between March and April. Check with the Mexico City Tourist Office (☞ Contacts and Resources *in* Mexico City A to Z, *below*) for dates and details.

The Arts

Dance

The world-renowned **Ballet Folklórico de México,** directed by Amalia Hernández, presents stylized Mexican regional folk dances and is one of the most popular shows in Mexico. Performances Wednesday at 8:30 PM and Sunday at 9:30 AM and 8:30 PM are at the beautiful Palacio de Bellas Artes (Palace of Fine Arts; ⊠ Av. Juárez at Eje Central Lázaro Cárdenas)—it's a treat to see its Tiffany-glass curtain lowered. Call the Palacio de Bellas Artes box office (☎ 5/512–3633) or Ticketmaster (☎ 5/325–9000) for information on prices and for reservations. Hotels and travel agencies can also secure tickets.

The **National Dance Theater** (☎ 5/280–8771), behind the National Auditorium on Paseo de la Reforma, and the **Miguel Covarrubias Hall** (⊠ National Autonomous University of Mexico [UNAM], Av. Insurgentes Sur 3000, Ciudad Universitaria, ☎ 5/622–7051 for university's dance department) frequently sponsor modern-dance performances.

Music

The primary venue for classical music is the **Palacio de Bellas Artes** (⊠ Eje Central Lázaro Cárdenas and Av. Juárez, ☎ 5/512–3633), which has a main auditorium and the smaller Manuel Ponce concert hall. The National Opera has two seasons at the palace: January–March and August–October. The National Symphony Orchestra stages classical and modern pieces at the palace in the spring and fall.

The top concert hall, often touted as the best in Latin America, is **Ollin Yolitzli** (⊠ Periférico Sur 5141, ☎ 5/606–7573); it hosts the Mexico City Philharmonic several times a year. The National Autonomous University of Mexico's Philharmonic orchestra performs at **Nezahualcoyotl Hall** (⊠ National Autonomous University of Mexico, Av. Insurgentes Sur 3000, Ciudad Universitaria, ☎ 5/622–7112).

For pop music stars such as Jamiroquai, Luis Miguel, Kiss, and Juan Gabriel, check newspapers for attractions at the following halls: **Auditorio Nacional** (⊠ Paseo de la Reforma 50, across from Nikko México hotel, ☎ 5/280–9234, 5/280–9979), **Teatro Metropolitano** (⊠ Independencia 90, downtown, ☎ 5/510–1035, 5/510–1045), **Palacio de los Deportes** (⊠ Av. Río Churubusco and Calle Añil, ☎ 5/237–9999 ext. 4264), and **Hard Rock Cafe** (⊠ Paseo de la Reforma and Campos Elíseos, Col. Condesa, ☎ 5/327–7171).

Theater

You might find some English-language plays by checking listings in *The News*. However, if you understand Spanish (or are content to watch), you'll be able to enjoy a wider range of theatrical entertainment in Mexico City, including recent Broadway hits. Prices are reasonable compared with those for stage productions of similar caliber in the United States. Although Mexico City has no central theater district, most theaters are within a 15- to 30-minute taxi ride from the major hotels. The top venues include **Hidalgo** (⊠ Av. Hidalgo 23, at Eje Central Lázaro Cárdenas, ☎ 5/521–5859), **Insurgentes** (⊠ Av. Insurgentes Sur 1587, ☎ 5/598–6894), **Silvia Pinal** (⊠ Yucatán 160, at Coahuila, Col. Roma, ☎ 5/264–1172), **Teatros Alameda** (⊠ Av. Cuauhtémoc at Av. Chapultepec, ☎ 5/514–2300, ext. 221 or 244), and **Virginia Fabregas** (⊠ Joaquín Velázquez de León 29, ☎ 5/566–4321). Theater tickets are available through **Ticketmaster** (☎ 5/325–9000).

Nightlife

Night is the key word to understanding the timing of going out in Mexico City. People generally have cocktails at 7 or 8, take in dinner and a show at 10 or 11, head to discos at midnight, then find a spot for a nightcap somewhere around 3 AM. The easiest way to do this if you don't speak Spanish is on a nightlife tour (☞ Contacts and Resources *in* Mexico City A to Z, *below*). If you set off on your own you should have no trouble getting around, but for personal safety absolutely avoid taking taxis off the street—take official hotel taxis or call a *sitio* (stationed) taxi (☞ Getting Around *in* Mexico City A to Z, *below*).

Niza and Florencia streets in the Zona Rosa are practically lined with nightclubs, bars, and discos that are especially lively Friday and Saturday nights. Big hotels have both bars and places to dance or be entertained, and they are frequented by locals. Outside the Zona Rosa, Paseo de la Reforma and Avenida Insurgentes Sur have the greatest concentration of nightspots. Mexico City has something for everyone in the way of night entertainment, but remember that the capital's high altitude makes liquor extremely potent, even jolting. Imported booze is very expensive, so you may want to stick with what the Mexicans order: tequila, rum, and *cerveza* (beer).

Dancing

Dance emporiums in the capital run the gamut from cheek-to-cheek romantic to throbbing strobe lights and ear-splitting music. Most places have a cover charge, but it is rarely more than $10. Some of the clubs require that reservations be made one to two days beforehand for Thursday through Saturday nights, if you want a table.

To really experience the nightlife Mexico has to offer, it's imperative to visit a dance club. **Bar León** (☒ República de Brasil 5, Col. Centro, behind the Catedral Metropolitana in the Zócalo, ☎ 5/510–2979) is a traditional salsa bar with great live music and a kitschy feel. **Salón Los Ángeles** (☒ Lerdo 206, Col. Guerrero, ☎ 5/597–5181) takes you back in time to the 1930s, with decor straight out of a movie. The grand, open dance floor swings to the rhythms of danzón and salsa. When renowned musicians such as Celia Cruz come to town, this is where they perform. The popular **Salón México** (☒ 2do Callejón San Juan de Dios 25, ☎ 5/518–0931) is a Colonia Guerrero danzón spot. **Meneo** (☒ Nueva York 315, Col. Napoles, just off Av. Insurgentes Sur, ☎ 5/523–9448) is a modern dance hall for live salsa and merengue with two dance floors. One of the capital's best-kept secrets is **Mama Rumba** (☒ Querétaro 230, at Medillín, Col. Roma, ☎ 5/564–6920), a 10-minute cab ride from the Zona Rosa. A nondescript Cuban restaurant during the day, it turns on the hot salsa, danzón, cha-cha-cha, and conga beat Thursday, Friday, and Saturday nights, when the top-rate Cuban house band takes the stand. Both Bar León and Mama Rumba are great if you aren't an expert dancer because the tiny dance floors are so packed that no one will notice mistakes.

If Latin music isn't your thing, two of the hippest discos in the city stand next to each other in the center. The **Pervert Lounge** (☒ Uruguay 70½, Col. Centro, ☎ 5/518–0976) and **Colmillo** (Fang; ☒ Versailles 52, Col. Juárez, ☎ 5/518–0976) are swank, upscale places where the young and beautiful come to see and be seen while shaking their exposed belly buttons on the dance floor. The Colmillo spins techno music downstairs and has an exclusive jazz bar upstairs.

Bars

Nice bars to sit and have a few drinks in are hard to come by in Mexico City. Often they are either too noisy or too seedy. Bars are usually open Tuesday–Saturday 8–3 and generally don't charge a cover. However, **La Nueva Ópera** (⊠ 5 de Mayo 10, at Filomeno Mata, downtown, ☎ 5/512–8959) is one of the city's finest cantinas, and it's brought in top personalities since it opened in 1870. The bar provides a relaxing atmosphere, Mexican appetizers and entrées, and an expansive drink list. Don't forget to have your waiter point out the bullet hole allegedly left in the ceiling by Mexican revolutionary hero Pancho Villa. **Bar Milán** (⊠ Milán 18, at General Prim, Col. Juárez, ☎ 5/592–0031) is a very casual, unpretentious local favorite. Upon entering you need to change pesos into *milagros* (miracles), which are notes necessary to buy drinks throughout the night. The catch is to remember to change them back for pesos before last call. The music tends to be the latest alternative grooves, Latin rock, and '80s singers such as Diana Ross. Make sure to check out the amazing cactus sculpture covering the wall behind the main bar. **Bar Mata** (⊠ Filomeno Mata 11, at 5 de Mayo, ☎ 5/518–0237) is on the fourth and fifth floors of a colonial building near Palacio de Bellas Artes in the centro. The atmosphere is conducive to dancing and mingling, especially in the rooftop (fifth floor) bar, which has great views of the night-lit city and is a place to escape from the cigarette smoke.

Dinner Shows

The liveliest shows are in clubs downtown and in the Zona Rosa. The **Feria de México** (⊠ Paseo de la Reforma 28, across from Melía México Reforma hotel, ☎ 5/535–1065) is the newest venue for enjoying traditional Mexican music and dance over dinner. Show times at this rustic dinner club are 4 and 10:30 daily, with an additional 6:30 show Thursday through Saturday. The show is free, but you pay for your meal (varied Mexican–American fare) à la carte. At **Focolare** (⊠ Hamburgo 87, at Río Niza, ☎ 5/207–8257), you can watch a cock fight, mariachi singers, and traditional folk dancers Thursday through Saturday nights. The show costs $7.50; Mexican dinner and drinks are separate. At the **Hotel de Cortés** (⊠ Hidalgo 85, downtown, ☎ 5/518–2184) you can take in the strains of marimba and mariachi players as well as watch traditional dancers on the beautiful patio. The show goes on Friday night only and for $20 includes a full meal.

Hotel Bars

The following hotel-lobby bars are all good bets for a sophisticated crowd and more-mellow music, about 7–1 daily: **María Isabel Sheraton** (⊠ Paseo de la Reforma 325, Col. Cuauhtémoc, ☎ 5/207–3933), **Presidente Inter-Continental México** (⊠ Campos Eliseos 218, Col. Polanco, ☎ 5/327–7700), **Camino Real** (⊠ Mariano Escobedo 700, Col. Nueva Anzures, ☎ 5/203–2121), and **Galería Plaza** (⊠ Hamburgo 195, Zona Rosa, ☎ 5/208–0370).

Mariachi Music

The traditional last stop for nocturnal Mexicans is **Plaza Garibaldi** (⊠ east of Eje Central Lázaro Cárdenas, between República de Honduras and República de Perú), where exuberant mariachis gather to unwind after evening performances—by performing even more. There are roving mariachis, as well as *norteño* (country-style) music and white-clad *jarocho* bands (Veracruz-style), peddling songs in the outdoor plaza, where you can also buy beer and shots of tequila. Well-to-do Mexicans park themselves inside one of the cantinas or clubs surrounding the plaza and belt out their favorite songs with the hired musicians.

The better cantinas are Guadalajara de Noche (☎ 5/526–5521) and Tenampa (☎ 5/526–6341). Choose a cantina and order a tequila; the musicians will be around shortly offering to serenade you (a song costs about $5). Mexicans typically buy songs by the dozen, so the bar is rarely without the wailing mariachis for more than 10 minutes. These places stay open Sunday through Thursday until at least 2 AM, and even later Friday and Saturday.

Note: The square was spruced up in the early '90s to rid it of its seedy image, but things can still get a bit raucous late at night. Furthermore, leaving Plaza Garibaldi can be dangerous—be sure to arrange for transportation ahead of time. You may call a travel agency (☞ Contacts and Resources *in* Mexico City A to Z, *below*), drive your car and park in the well-lighted ramp below the plaza, or call a safe sitio taxi (☞ Getting Around *in* Mexico City A to Z, *below*).

OUTDOOR ACTIVITIES AND SPORTS

Adventure Sports

A number of adventure-travel agencies have sprouted up to entice both tourists and natives out of the smog and chaos of Mexico City for a weekend of white-water rafting, rappelling, or biking. One of the best is **México Verde Expeditions** (⊠ Homero 526, Int. 801, Col. Polanco, ☎ 5/255–4400, 5/255–4465), whose guides speak English and lead tours to the pristine areas of such nearby states as Veracruz and Morelos. Call a week in advance to make reservations and bring a sleeping bag and sunblock. The small **Planeta Expeditions** (⊠ Amatlán 51-C, at Montes de Oca, ☎ 5/211–9020) is run out of a café in trendy Colonia Condesa. It has journeys to climb the Iztaccíhuatl volcano, as well as rafting and rock climbing. Three-day trips cost $100–$150.

Bullfighting

The main season is the dry season, around November through March, when celebrated *matadores* appear at **Plaza México** (⊠ Calle Agusto Rodín 241, at Holbein, Col. Ciudad de los Deportes, ☎ 5/563–3959), the world's largest bullring, which seats 40,000. Gray Line Tours offers bullfight tour packages (☞ Contacts and Resources *in* Mexico City A to Z, *below*). Otherwise, tickets, about $2–$25, can be purchased at hotel travel desks or at the bullring's ticket booths weekends 9:30–2 and 3:30–7. The ring is next to the Ciudad de los Deportes sports complex, and the show goes on at 4 Sunday.

Golf

All golf courses are private in Mexico City, but you can play if you are the guest of a member. If you stay at the Camino Real hotel, you can have the hotel arrange admittance to the **Bella Vista Golf Club** (☎ 5/360–3501), off the Querétaro Highway. Greens fees Tuesday through Friday are $85; weekends, $150.

Soccer

Fútbol is the sport that Mexicans are most passionate about, which is evident in the size of their soccer stadium, **Estadio Azteca** (⊠ Calzada de Tlalpan 3465), the second largest in Latin America. The World Cup Finals were held here in 1970 and 1986. You can buy tickets outside the stadium in the south of the city on the same day of any minor game. For more-important games, buy tickets a week in advance. The Pumas, a popular university-sponsored team, play at **Estadio Olímpica** (⊠ Av. Insurgentes Sur at Universidad Nacional Autónoma de México).

Tennis

Tennis clubs are private in Mexico, so if you want to play, consider staying at a hotel that has courts on site.

Water Sports
The best place for swimming is your hotel pool. If you're desperate to row a boat, however, you can rent one in the lakes of Bosque de Chapultepec, near the Zoológico.

SHOPPING

The finest, most concentrated shopping area is the **Zona Rosa,** a 29-square-block area bounded by Paseo de la Reforma on the north, Niza on the east, Avenida Chapultepec on the south, and Varsovia on the west. It's chock-full of boutiques, jewelry stores, leather-goods shops, antiques stores, and art galleries, as well as dozens of great restaurants and coffee shops. Day or night, the Zona Rosa is always lively.

Polanco, a choice residential neighborhood along the northeast perimeter of Bosque de Chapultepec, has blossomed into a more upscale shopping area with exclusive stores and boutiques. Many are in such malls as the huge ultramodern **Plaza Polanco** (✉ Jaime Balmes 11), the new upscale **Plaza Moliere** (✉ Moliere between Calles Horacio and Homero), and the **Plaza Masarik** (✉ Presidente Masarik and Anatole France).

There are hundreds of shops with more-modest trappings and better prices spread along the length of Avenida Insurgentes, as well as along Avenida Juárez and in the old downtown area.

Department Stores, Malls, and Shopping Arcades

The major department-store chains are **Liverpool** (✉ Av. Insurgentes Sur 1310; ✉ Mariano Escobedo 425; and in the Plaza Satélite and Perisur shopping centers), **Suburbia** (✉ Horacio 203; ✉ Sonora 180; ✉ Av. Insurgentes Sur 1235; and in the Plaza Satélite and Perisur shopping centers), and **El Palacio de Hierro** (✉ Calles Durango and Salamanca, Col. Condesa; and in the Plaza Moliere in Col. Polanco), which is noted for items by well-known designers at prices now on par with those found in the United States. **Santa Fe** mall is the largest in Latin America, with 285 stores, a movie theater, and several restaurants. It's in the elegant Santa Fe district, which in recent years has become the favored office real-estate property in the city. To get here, take the Periférico Expressway south to the exit marked CENTRO SANTA FE. The posh and pricey **Perisur** shopping mall is on the southern edge of the city, near where the Periférico Expressway meets Avenida Insurgentes. Department stores are generally open Monday, Tuesday, Thursday, and Friday 10–7, and Wednesday and Saturday 10–8.

Sanborns is a chain of mini-department stores with some 65 branches in Mexico City. The most convenient are at Madero 4 (its original store in the House of Tiles, downtown); several along Paseo de la Reforma (including one at the Angel monument and another four blocks west of the Diana Fountain); and in the Zona Rosa (one at the corner of Niza and Hamburgo and another at Londres 130 in the Hotel Calinda Geneve). They carry quality ceramics and crafts (and can ship anywhere), and most have restaurants or coffee shops, a pharmacy, ATMs, and periodical and book departments with English-language publications.

Plaza La Rosa, a modern shopping arcade (✉ between Amberes and Génova, Zona Rosa), has 72 prestigious shops and boutiques, including Aldo Conti and Diesel. It spans the depth of the block between Londres and Hamburgo, with entrances on both streets.

Bazar del Centro (✉ at Isabel la Católica 30, just below Calle Madero, downtown) is a restored, late-17th-century noble mansion built around a garden courtyard that houses several chic boutiques and prestigious jewelers such as Aplijsa (☎ 5/521–1923), known for its fine gold, silver, pearls, and gemstones, and Ginza (☎ 5/518–6453), which has Japanese pearls, including the prized cultured variety. Other shops sell Taxco silver, Tonalá stoneware, and Mexican tequilas and liqueurs. This complex is elegant and also has a congenial bar.

Portales de los Mercaderes (Merchants' Arcade; ⊠ extending the length of the west side of the Zócalo between Calles Madero and 16 de Septiembre) has attracted merchants since 1524. It is lined with jewelry shops selling gold (often by the gram) and authentic Taxco silver at prices lower than those in Taxco itself, where the overhead is higher. In the middle of the Portales de los Mercaderes is **Tardán** (⊠ Plaza de la Constitución 7, ☎ 5/512–2459), an unusual shop specializing in fashionable men's hats of every shape and style.

Markets

A "must"—even for browsers—is a visit to the **Bazar Sábado** (Saturday Bazaar) at Plaza San Jacinto in the southern San Angel district. It's been selling unique handicrafts at excellent prices for more than three decades. Outside, vendors sell embroidered clothing, leather goods, wooden masks, beads, *amates* (bark paintings), and trinkets. Inside the bazaar building, a renovated two-story colonial mansion, are the better-quality—and higher-priced—goods, including *alebrijes* (painted wooden animals from Oaxaca), glassware, pottery, jewelry, and papier-mâché flowers. There is an indoor restaurant as well. Market and restaurant are open 10–7.

Sunday 10–4, more than 100 artists exhibit and sell their painting and sculpture at the **Jardín del Arte** (Garden of Art) in Parque Sullivan, just northeast of the Reforma–Insurgentes intersection. Along the west side of the park, a colorful weekend mercado with scores of food stands is also worth a visit.

The **Mercado Insurgentes** (also called Mercado Zona Rosa) is an entire block deep, with entrances on both Londres and Liverpool (⊠ between Florencia and Amberes). This is a typical neighborhood public market with one big difference: most of the stalls (222 of them) sell crafts. You can find all kinds of handmade items—including serapes and ponchos, baskets, pottery, silver, pewter, fossils, and onyx, as well as regional Mexican dresses and costumes.

The Zona Rosa's pink neocolonial Plaza del Angel (⊠ Londres 161) has a **Centro de Antigüedades** (antiques center) with several fine shops. On Saturday, together with other vendors, the dealers set up a flea market in the arcades and patios. On Sunday, bibliophiles join the antiques vendors to sell, peruse, and buy collectors' books and periodicals.

The Zócalo and Alameda Park areas have interesting markets for browsing and buying handicrafts and curios; polite bargaining is customary. The biggest is the **Centro Artesanal Buenavista** (⊠ Aldama 187, by the Buenavista train station, about 1½ km [1 mi] northwest of downtown). **La Lagunilla** market (⊠ Libertad, between República de Chile and Calle Allende) attracts antiques hunters who know how to determine authenticity, as well as coin collectors. The best day is Sunday, when flea-market stands are set up outside. This market is known affectionately as the Thieves' Market: local lore says you can buy back on Sunday what was stolen from your home Saturday. Within the colonial walls of **La Ciudadela** market (⊠ Balderas and Ayuntamiento, about 4 blocks south of Av. Juárez), more than 300 artisans' stalls display a variety of good handicrafts from all over the country, at better prices than you can find at the rest of the markets.

Specialty Shops

Antiques

Antigüedades Coloniart (⊠ Estocolmo 37, Zona Rosa, ☎ 5/514–4799) has good-quality antique paintings, furniture, and sculpture. The store is open weekdays noon–3 and 4–7, Saturday 10–2. **Antigüedades Imperio** (⊠ Hamburgo 149, Zona Rosa, ☎ 5/525–5798) specializes in 19th-century European furniture, paintings, glass, and vases. It's open weekdays 11:30–2 and 3:30–7, Saturday 11:30–3.

Art

The **Juan Martín Gallery** (⊠ Dickens 33-B, Col. Polanco, ☎ 5/280–0277) is an avant-garde studio. The store and gallery of the renowned **Sergio Bustamante** (⊠ Nikko México hotel, Campos Elíseos 204, Col. Polanco, ☎ 5/282–2638; ⊠ Amberes 13, Zona Rosa, ☎ 5/525–9059; ⊠ Camino Real hotel, Mariano Escobedo 700, Col. Polanco, ☎ 5/254–7372) displays and sells the artist's wild sculpture, jewelry, and interior-design pieces. The **Oscar Roman Gallery** (⊠ Julio Verne 14, Col. Polanco, ☎ 5/280–0436) is packed with work by good Mexican painters with a contemporary edge. The **Nina Menocal de Rocha Gallery** (⊠ Zacatecas 93, Col. Roma, ☎ 5/564–7209) specializes in up-and-coming Cuban painters. **Misrachi** (⊠ Presidente Masarik 523, Col. Polanco, ☎ 5/250–4105), a veteran among galleries, promotes well-known Mexican and international artists.

Candy

Celaya (⊠ 5 de Mayo 39, ☎ 5/521–1787), in the downtown historic section, is a decades-old haven for those with a sweet tooth. It specializes in candied pineapple, papaya, guava, and other exotic fruit; almond-paste; candied walnut rolls; and *cajeta,* a typical Mexican dessert of thick caramelized milk.

Clothing

The Spanish designer store **Zara** (⊠ Londres 102, Zona Rosa, ☎ 5/525–1516; ⊠ Presidente Masarik 332, at Tennyson, Col. Polanco, ☎ 5/280–1529; ⊠ Plaza Moliere, Col. Polanco, ☎ 5/280–7572) has sleek women's fashions. **Guess** (⊠ Presidente Masarik 326, Col. Polanco, ☎ 5/282–0133) sells chic denim sportswear.

Designer Items

Cartier (⊠ Amberes 9, Zona Rosa, ☎ 5/207–6109; ⊠ Presidente Masarik 438, Col. Polanco, ☎ 5/281–5528) sells genuine designer jewelry and clothes, under the auspices of the French Cartier. **Gucci** (⊠ Hamburgo 136, Zona Rosa, ☎ 5/207–9997) has no connection with the European store of the same name; nevertheless, it has a fine selection of shoes, gloves, and handbags.

Jewelry

The owner of **Los Castillo** (⊠ Amberes 41, Zona Rosa, ☎ 5/511–8396) developed a unique method of melding silver, copper, and brass, and is considered by many to be Taxco's top silversmith. His daughter Emilia Castillo displays fine ceramic dishes with tiny inlaid silver figures, such as fish and birds. Taxco silver of exceptional style is sold at **Arte en Plata** (⊠ Londres 162-A, Zona Rosa, ☎ 5/511–1422), with many designs inspired by pre-Columbian art. **Pelletier** (⊠ Torcuato Caso 237, Col. Polanco, ☎ 5/250–8600) sells fine jewelry and watches. **Tane** (⊠ Amberes 70, Zona Rosa, ☎ 5/511–9429; ⊠ Presidente Masarik 430, Col. Polanco, ☎ 5/281–4775; ⊠ Santa Catarina 207, Col. San Angel, ☎ 5/616–0165; and other locations) is a treasure trove of perhaps the best silver work in Mexico—jewelry, flatware, candelabra, museum-quality reproductions of archaeological finds, and bold new designs by young Mexican silversmiths.

Leather

For leather goods you have a few choices in Mexico City. **Aries** (✉ Florencia 14, Zona Rosa, ☎ 5/533–2509) is Mexico's finest purveyor of leather goods, with a superb selection of bags and accessories for men and women; prices are high. **Gaitán** (✉ Calle Sarasete 95-B, at Tetracini, Col. Peralvillo downtown, ☎ 5/759–3393) carries an extensive array of leather coats, luggage, golf bags, and saddles. **Las Bolsas de Coyoacán** (✉ Carrillo Puerto 9, Col. Coyoacán, ☎ 5/554–2010) specializes in high-quality leather goods.

Mexican Crafts

Browse for folk art, sculpture, and furniture in the gallery **Artesanos de México** (✉ Londres 117, Zona Rosa, ☎ 5/514–7455). Handwoven wool rugs, tapestries, and fabrics with original and unusual designs can be found at **Tamacani** (✉ Av. Insurgentes Sur 1748B, Col. Florida, ☎ 5/662–7133). **Arte Popular en Miniatura** (✉ Hamburgo 85, Col. Juárez, ☎ 5/525–8145) is a tiny shop filled with tiny things, from dollhouse furniture and lead soldiers to miniature Nativity scenes. **Flamma** (✉ Hamburgo 167, Zona Rosa, ☎ 5/511–8499, 5/511–0266) is a town house that sells beautiful handmade candles. **Galerías del Arcángel** (✉ Estocolmo 40, Zona Rosa, ☎ 5/511–6303) is an exquisite crafts and furniture shop tucked away in the Zona Rosa. It specializes in carved wood furniture from Patzcuaro, Michoacán (brought to life with brightly painted sunflowers, calla lilies, and suns), as well as wooden angel decorations, pottery, and paintings.

Under the auspices of the National Council for Culture and Arts, **Fonart** (National Fund for Promoting Handicrafts) operates two stores in Mexico City, and others around the country. Prices are fixed (and high), but the diverse, top-quality folk art and hand-crafted furnishings from all over Mexico represent the best artisans. The best location is downtown (✉ Juárez 89, ☎ 5/521–0171), just west of Alameda Park. Major sales at near wholesale prices are held at the main store–warehouse (✉ Av. Patriotismo 691, Col. Mixcoac, ☎ 5/563–4060) year-round.

Feders (factory: ✉ Bufon 25, Col. Nueva Anzures, ☎ 5/260–2958; ✉ Bazar Sábado booth, Plaza San Jacinto 11, San Angel, ☎ no phone) has great handblown glass, Tiffany-style lamps, and wrought iron.

MEXICO CITY A TO Z

Arriving and Departing

By Bus

Greyhound (☎ 5/729–0707, 800/231–2222) buses make connections to major U.S. border cities, from which Mexican bus lines depart throughout the day. Reserved seating is available on first-class coaches, which are comfortable but not nearly as plush as the intercity buses. If you plan stopovers en route, make sure in advance that your ticket is written up accordingly. In Mexico, platform announcements are in Spanish only.

Within Mexico, buses are becoming the most popular way to travel: you can board ultramodern, superdeluxe motor coaches that show U.S. movies and serve soft drinks and coffee. **ETN** (Enlaces Terrestres Nacionales, ☎ 5/577–6529, 5/271–1262, 5/277–6529) serves cities to the west and northwest, such as Guadalajara, Morelia, Querétaro, Guanajuato, San Miguel de Allende, and Toluca. **ADO** (☎ 5/133–2424, 5/133–2444, 01–800/702–8000) buses depart southeast to such places as Puebla, Oaxaca, Veracruz, Mérida, and Cancún. Reserved-seat tickets can be purchased at Mexico City travel agencies.

Various other classes of intercity bus tickets can be purchased at virtually any travel agency in the city (there's an especially large number in the Zona Rosa). Buses depart from four outlying stations (*terminales de autobuses*), where tickets can also be purchased: **Central de Autobuses del Norte** (⊠ Av. Cién Metros 4907, ☎ 5/587–1552), going north; **Central de Autobuses del Sur** (⊠ Tasqueña 1320, ☎ 5/689–9745), going south; **Central de Autobuses del Oriente** (⊠ Ignacio Zaragoza 200, ☎ 5/762–5977), going east; and **Terminal de Autobuses del Poniente** (⊠ Río Tacubaya and Sur 122, ☎ 5/271–4519), going west.

By Car

Major arteries into Mexico City include Highway 57 to the north, which starts at Laredo, Texas, and goes through Monterrey and Querétaro. Highway 95 comes in from Cuernavaca to the south, and Highway 190D from Puebla to the east. Highway 15 via Toluca and Valle de Bravo is the main western route.

By Plane

THE AIRLINES

All flights lead to Mexico City. **Mexicana** (☎ 5/448–0990) has scheduled service from Chicago, Denver, Los Angeles, Miami, New York, San Antonio, San Francisco, and San Jose. It has direct or connecting service at 30 locations throughout the country. **Aeroméxico** (☎ 5/133–4000) serves Mexico City daily from Dallas, Houston, Los Angeles, Miami, Orlando, New Orleans, Atlanta, New York, Phoenix, San Antonio, San Diego, and Tucson (as well as Tijuana). Aeroméxico serves some 35 cities within Mexico. **Aerolitoral,** a subsidiary of Aeroméxico based in Monterrey, serves north-central cities as well as San Antonio, Texas, via Monterrey from Mexico City. **Taesa** (☎ 5/227–0700), a Mexican airline, has direct flights (but not nonstop) to Mexico City from Chicago and Oakland; directs and nonstops from Tijuana; and nonstops from Laredo, Texas.

North American carriers serving Mexico City include **Air Canada, Alaska Airlines, American, America West, Canadian, Continental, Delta, Northwest, Trans World Airlines, United,** and **US Airways. Air France** flies nonstop between Houston and Mexico City.

THE AIRPORT

The newest wing of Mexico City's **Aeropuerto Internacional Benito Juárez** is a high-tech, state-of-the-art elongation of the east end of the existing airport. It is occupied by American, Delta, and United airlines, as well as by all the major car-rental agencies; four banks and seven currency exchanges (*casas de cambio*); Cirrus and Plus ATMs that disburse pesos; places to rent cellular phones; and a food court, pharmacy, bookstore, and pricey shops. A multilevel parking garage for 2,500 cars has also been added (short-term parking is about $2 an hour).

Porters and free carts are available in the baggage-retrieval areas. Banks and currency exchanges rotate their schedules to provide around-the-clock service. Although dollar bills (not coins) are acceptable at the airport, you'll get the best exchange rate by changing dollars at the currency offices here. You can also use your ATM card to take pesos directly out of your U.S. account at ATMs (called *cajero automático* locally) here and throughout the city—and you'll get an even better exchange rate. Just remember that your home bank will probably charge $3 or more for the transaction. The Mexico City Tourist Office, Mexican Ministry of Tourism (Sectur), and the Hotel Association have stands in the arrival areas that can provide information and find visitors a room for the night.

BETWEEN THE AIRPORT AND CENTER CITY

If you're taking a taxi, purchase your ticket at one of the official airport taxi counters marked **Transportación Terrestre** (ground transportation), located in the baggage-carousel areas as well as in the concourse area and curbside; avoid *pirata* (taxi drivers offering their services). Government-controlled fares are based on which colonia you are going to and are usually about $7 (per car, not per person) to most hotels. A 10% tip is customary for airport drivers if they help with baggage. All major car-rental agencies have booths at both arrival areas.

By Train

The train system in Mexico is in the process of being privatized and is badly in need of refurbishing. At press time, only four lines were running between fairly obscure Mexican towns. We don't recommend train travel at this time, but if you're determined to go by rail, you can get information from English-speaking operators about schedules and prices from **Ferrocarriles Nacionales de Mexico** (National Mexican Railways; ☎ 5/547–1084) in Mexico City.

Getting Around

By Bus

The Mexico City bus system is used by millions of commuters because it's cheap and goes everywhere. Buses are packed during rush hours so, as in all big cities, you should be wary of pickpockets. One of the principal bus routes runs along Paseo de la Reforma, Avenida Juárez, and Calle Madero. This west–east route connects Bosque de Chapultepec with the Zócalo. A southbound bus may be taken along Avenida Insurgentes Sur to San Angel and University City, or northbound along Avenida Insurgentes Norte to the Guadalupe Basilica. Mexico City Tourism offices provide free bus-route maps. The price was raised at the end of 1996 from 1 to a maximum 3.50 pesos (about 35¢), depending on how far you're going—still a bargain, especially for foreigners.

By Car

Millions of intrepid drivers brave Mexico City's streets every day and survive, but for out-of-towners the experience can be frazzling. One-way streets are confusing, rush-hour traffic is nightmarish, and parking places can be hard to come by. Police tow trucks haul away illegally parked vehicles, and the owner is heavily fined. As in any large city, getting your car back here is a byzantine process. **Locatel** (☎ 5/658–1111) is an efficient 24-hour service for tracing vehicles that are towed, stolen, or lost (in case you forgot where you parked). There's a chance an operator on duty may speak English, but the service is primarily in Spanish. Visitors can hire a chauffeur for their cars through a hotel concierge or travel service such as American Express.

Also keep in mind that the strictly enforced law **Hoy No Circula** (Today My Car Can't Circulate) applies to all private vehicles, including your own. One of several efforts to reduce smog and traffic congestion, this law prohibits every privately owned vehicle (including out-of-state, foreign, and rental cars) from being used on one designated weekday. During emergency smog-alerts, which usually occur in December and January, cars are prohibited from circulating on two days of the week. Cars in violation are inevitably impounded by the police. Expect a hefty fine as well.

The weekday you can't drive is specified by the last number or letter of the license plate: on a non-emergency week, 5–6 are prohibited on Monday; 7–8 on Tuesday; 3–4 on Wednesday; 1–2 on Thursday; and 9–0 on Friday. For further information, contact the Mexican Government Tourism Office nearest you, and by all means plan your schedule accordingly.

By Pesero

Originally six-passenger sedans, then vans, and now minibuses, peseros operate on a number of fixed routes and charge a flat rate (a peso once upon a time, hence the name). They're a good alternative to buses and taxis; however, be prepared for a jolting ride because many drivers like to turn their buses into bucking broncos. Likely routes for tourists are along the city's major west–east axis (Bosque de Chapultepec–Paseo de la Reforma–Avenida Juárez–Zócalo) and north–south along Avenida Insurgentes, between the Guadalupe Basilica and San Angel–University City. Peseros pick up passengers at bus stops and outside almost all metro stations. Just stand on the curb, check the route sign on the oncoming pesero's windshield, and hold out your hand. Tell the driver where to stop, or press the button by the back door. If it's really crowded and you can't reach the back door in time, just bang on the ceiling and yell, "Baja," which means "getting off" in Spanish. Base fares are 2 pesos (about 20¢) with the price going up to 3.50 pesos (about 35¢) according to how far you travel. Exact change is appreciated by drivers.

By Subway

Transporting 5 million passengers daily, Mexico City's metro is one of the world's best, busiest, safest, and cheapest transportation systems—1.50 pesos (about 15¢). The impeccably clean marble-and-onyx stations are brightly lighted, and modern French-designed trains run quietly on rubber tires. Some stations, such as Insurgentes, are shopping centers. Even if you don't take a ride, visit the Zócalo station, which has large models of central Mexico City during three historic periods. Many stations have temporary cultural displays ranging from archaeological treasures to modern art; the Pino Suárez station has a small Aztec pyramid inside, a surprise discovery during construction.

There are 10 intersecting metro lines covering more than 160 km (100 mi). It's a bit confusing: the number 8 previously had been assigned to a line whose construction was canceled because it would have destroyed unearthed Aztec ruins. Line 9 was subsequently built. Now number 8 designates the newest (10th) line. The ninth line was A. Segments of Lines 1 and 2 cover most points of interest to foreigners, including the Zona Rosa, Bellas Artes, and the Centro Histórico. At the southern edge of the city, the Tasqueña station (Line 2) connects with the electric train (*tren eléctrico*) that continues south to Xochimilco. To the southeast, the Tren Ligero from the Pantitlán station (Lines 1, 5, and 9) heads east to Chalco in the state of Mexico. The various lines also serve all four bus stations, the Buenavista train station, and the airport; however, only light baggage is allowed on board during rush hours. User-friendly, color-coded maps are sometimes available free at metro-station information desks (if there's an attendant) and at Mexico City tourism offices; color-keyed signs and maps are posted all around.

Trains run frequently (about two minutes apart) and are least crowded 10–4 and at night. To reduce incidences of harassment during crowded rush hours, regulations (not strictly enforced) require men to ride separate cars from women and children. Hours vary somewhat according to the line, but service is essentially 5 AM–midnight weekdays; 6 AM–2 AM Saturday; 6 AM–1 AM Sunday and holidays.

By Taxi

The Mexico City variety comes in several colors, types, and sizes. Unmarked, or *turismo,* sedans with hooded meters are usually stationed outside major hotels and in tourist areas; however, they are uneconomical for short trips. Their drivers are almost always English-speaking guides and can be hired for sightseeing on a daily or hourly basis (always negotiate the price in advance). Sitio taxis operate out of stands, take radio calls, and are authorized to charge a small premium. Among these, **Servi-Taxis** (☎ 5/271–2560) and **Taxi-Mex** (☎ 5/538–0912, 5/538–0573), which accepts American Express, offer 24-hour service.

Serious dangers to your safety come from unscrupulous cab drivers who are preying on tourists, robbing and assaulting them or forcing them to withdraw money from ATMs. **Take only registered hotel taxis or have a hotel concierge call a sitio cab—do not hail taxis on the street under any circumstances.** Be sure to establish the fare in advance.

Taxi drivers are authorized to charge 10% more at night, usually after 10. Taking a taxi in Mexico City is extremely inexpensive and tips are not expected unless you have luggage—then 10% is sufficient.

Contacts and Resources

Consulates and Embassies

The **U.S. Embassy** (✉ Paseo de la Reforma 305, Col. Juárez, ☎ 5/209–9100) is open weekdays 9–2 and 3–5, but is closed for American and Mexican holidays; however, there's always a duty officer to take emergency calls on holidays and after closing hours. The embassy keeps a list of English-speaking local doctors on hand if you need to consult one. The **Canadian Embassy** (✉ Schiller 529, Col. Polanco, ☎ 5/724–7900) is open weekdays 9–1 and 2–5 and is closed for Canadian and Mexican holidays. The **British Embassy** (✉ Río Lerma 71, Col. Juárez, ☎ 5/207–2449) is open weekdays 8:30–3:30.

E-Mail

Many hotels have complimentary e-mail service for guests. There are also several Internet cafés in the Zona Rosa that charge as little as $3 an hour for access. At **Bits Café** (✉ Hamburgo 165-C, at Florencia, 1 block south of the Angel monument, ☎ 5/525–0144), you can have a cappuccino and cheesecake, or a beer and a sandwich, while you catch up on your electronic correspondence. It's open Monday–Saturday 10–10. Open 10–10 daily, **JavaChat** (✉ Génova 44-K, next to McDonald's, ☎ 5/514–6856, 5/525–6853) offers free bottomless coffee or soft drinks while you're on the computers.

Emergencies

Dial ☎ 060 or 080 for **police, Red Cross, ambulance, fire,** or other emergency situations. If you are not able to reach an English-speaking operator, call the Sectur hot line (☞ Visitor Information, *below*). For missing persons or cars call **Locatel** (☎ 5/658–1111).

HOSPITAL

American British Cowdray Hospital (✉ Calle Sur 136–116, corner of Observatorio, Col. las Américas, ☎ 5/230–8161 for emergencies, 5/230–8000 switchboard).

English-Language Bookstores and Publications

The best place for English- and foreign-language newspapers and magazines is **Casa de la Prensa,** which has two locations in the Zona Rosa (✉ Florencia 57; ✉ Hamburgo 141). **Sanborns** (☞ Department Stores, Malls, and Shopping Arcades *in* Shopping, *above*) carries a limited number of U.S. newspapers but an ample supply of magazines, paperbacks, and guidebooks. The **American Book Store** (✉ Calle Madero 25) has an extensive selection of publications. A daily English-language newspaper, *The News,* is available at hotels and at newsstands in the tourist areas; it provides a summary of what is happening in Mexico and the rest of the world with cultural and entertainment listings and daily stock-market reports. Remember that most U.S. or foreign-published publications are about double the price you'd pay for them at home.

The **Benjamin Franklin Library,** actually a part of the U.S. Embassy, was instituted to create greater understanding and cultural exchange between the United States and Mexico. The library has a substantial collection of English novels, a good reference section, and many U.S. periodicals. You must be at least 20 years old, fill out an application, and have a Mexican resident sign it in order to check out books, but anyone can browse through the stacks. ⊠ *Londres 16, Zona Rosa,* ☎ *5/209–9100, ext. 3482 or 3483.* ⊙ *Weekdays noon–7.*

Guided Tours

Except for the Tren Turístico, the tours described below can be booked through the agents listed in Travel Agencies (☞ *below*).

ORIENTATION TOURS

Various travel agencies run tourist-friendly, English-guided tours of Mexico City and surrounding areas. The basic city tour ($39) lasts eight hours and takes in the Zócalo, Palacio Nacional, Catedral Metropolitana, and Bosque de Chapultepec. A four-hour pyramid tour costs around $23 and covers the Basílica de Nuestra Señora de Guadalupe and the major ruins at Teotihuacán.

A good way to see the historic downtown—if you know some Spanish—is on **Tren Turístico's** (☎ 5/512–1012, 5/512–1013) charming replicas of 20-passenger trolleys from the 1920s. The 50-minute narrated tour ($2.50) includes the Zócalo, Colegio de San Idelfonso, Plaza de Santo Domingo, Plaza Manuel Tolsá (location of the Palacio de Minería and Museo Nacional de Arte), Plaza de la Santa Veracruz (Museo Franz Mayer), and the Palacio de Iturbide. Trolleys depart hourly 10–5 daily from the train's offices in front of Alameda Park (⊠ Av. Juárez 66, at Revillagigedo).

SPECIAL-INTEREST TOURS

Travel agencies offer various city tours. The most popular ones seem to fall in the following general categories:

Cultural: The seven-hour tour ($67) is run Sunday morning only and usually includes a performance of the folkloric dances at the Palacio de Bellas Artes, a gondola ride in the canals of Xochimilco's floating gardens, and a visit to the modern campus of the National University.

Bullfighting: On Sunday only are trips to the bullring with a guide who will explain the finer points of this spectacle. This three-hour afternoon tour ($30) can usually be combined with the Ballet Folklórico–Xochimilco trip ($85).

Nightlife: These tours are among the most popular tours of Mexico City. The best are scheduled to last five hours and include transfers by private car rather than bus; dinner at an elegant restaurant (frequently Bellini or at the Del Lago); a drink and a show at the Plaza Garibaldi, where mariachis play; and a nightcap at Guadalajara de Noche, which features Mexican folk dancers. Nightlife tours begin at $56.

Travel Agencies

Gray Line Tours (⊠ Londres 166, ☎ 5/208–1163), **American Express** (⊠ Paseo de la Reforma 234, ☎ 5/326–2831), and **Mexico Travel Advisors** (MTA; ⊠ Génova 30, ☎ 5/525–7520, 5/525–7534).

Visitor Information

The **Mexico City Tourist Office** (Departamento de Turismo del Distrito Federal, or DDF) maintains information booths at both the international and domestic arrival areas at the airport. In town, visit the city's tourism module at Amberes 54, at the corner of Londres in the Zona Rosa. This office also provides information by phone with its Infotur service (☎ 5/525–9380) 9–7 daily. Multilingual operators are available and have access to an extensive data bank.

The **Secretariat of Tourism** (Sectur) operates a 24-hour multilingual hot line (☎ 5/250–0123, 5/250–0493, 5/250–0027, 5/250–0589, 5/250–0151, 5/250–0292, 5/250–0741) that provides information on both Mexico City and the entire country. If lines are busy, keep trying. Outside Mexico City, call toll-free (☎ 01–800/903–9200, 800/482–9832) to reach the Sectur Tourist Information Center at Presidente Masarik 172 (in Colonia Polanco), open weekdays 8–8.

2 SIDE TRIPS FROM MEXICO CITY

If the pace—or smog—of the megalopolis begins to run you down, just an hour or two outside Mexico City lies a plethora of towns and archaeological sites guaranteed to make you feel that you've turned back the clock on the concrete jungle. Take a deep breath of fresh air while you hike up one of the twin volcanoes or water ski at Valle de Bravo, relax in the bougainvillea-scented town of Cuernavaca, or take in the spectacular pyramids at Teotihuacán.

By Frank Shiell

Updated by
Paige Bierma

Aican culture, you'll be pleasantly surprised to find that just a short drive or bus ride can place you in a traditional small-town church, in the middle of a gorgeous national park, or on top of breathtaking ancient ruins. Quaint towns such as Cholula or Tepoztlán give a taste of what life might have been like in Mexico City before its population began exploding with industrial growth in the 1960s and '70s. Cholula is famous for its friendly townsfolk and colonial churches. Tepoztlán has a curious cultural mix of its indigenous community and the New Age proselytes drawn by the town's pyramid. Just an hour north of the city, the famous Teotihuacán ruins have larger and more historically significant pyramids, as do the former Toltec capital of Tula and the splendid ruins at Cacaxtla and Xochitécatl to the southeast.

Two nearby state capitals, the medium-size cities of Cuernavaca and Puebla, are windows on the diversity of Mexican life. Cuernavaca's flower power and springlike climate have made this culturally hip city a favorite weekend getaway for *chilangos* (Mexico City residents), as well as a center for Spanish-language schools that draw people from around the world. Puebla, on the other hand, is a conservative city, surrounded by important agricultural valleys and populated with an abundance of churches, chapels, ex-convents, and monasteries.

NORTH OF MEXICO CITY

Hugging the roads to the north of Mexico City are several of the country's most celebrated pre-Columbian and colonial monuments. The Basílica de Guadalupe, a church dedicated to Mexico's patron saint, and the pyramids of Teotihuacán make an easy day tour, as does the combination of the ex-convent (now a magnificent museum of the viceregal period) at Tepotzotlán and the ruins at Tula, also to the north but in a slightly different direction.

There are no tourist offices in the area, but a good English-language guidebook to Teotihuacán is sold at the site.

La Villa de Guadalupe

"La Villa"—the local moniker of the site of the two basilicas of the Virgin of Guadalupe—is Mexico's holiest shrine. Its importance derives from the miracle that the devout believe transpired here on December 12, 1531, when an Indian named Juan Diego received from the Virgin a cloak permanently imprinted with her image so he could prove to the priests that he had indeed had a holy vision. On that date each year millions of pilgrims arrive, many crawling on their knees for the last few hundred yards, praying for cures and other divine favors. When Pope John Paul II visited Mexico in 1999, he blessed the new statue of Juan Diego located outside the **Antigua Basílica** (Old Basilica). The Antigua Basílica dates from 1536; various additions have been made since then. The altar was executed by sculptor Manuel Tolsá. The basilica now houses a museum of ex-votos (hand-painted tin retablos) and popular religious art, paintings, sculpture, and decorative and applied arts from the 15th to the 18th centuries.

Because the structure of the Antigua Basílica had weakened over the years and the building was no longer large enough or safe enough to accommodate all the worshipers, Pedro Ramírez Vázquez, the architect responsible for Mexico City's splendid National Museum of Anthropology, was commissioned to design a new shrine; it was consecrated

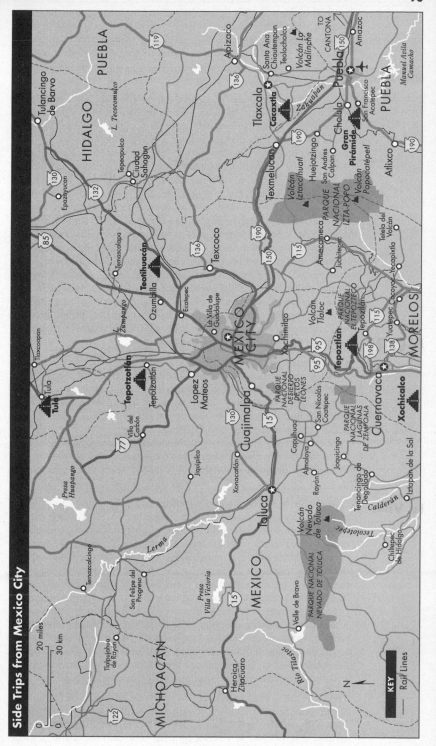

Side Trips from Mexico City

KEY
— Rail Lines

20 miles
30 km

PUEBLA

HIDALGO

Tulancingo
de Barvo

130

132

85

136

Texcoco

Teotihuacán

Ozumbilla

Ecatepec

La Villa de
Guadalupe

MEXICO
CITY

Xochimilco

Epazoyucan

L. Tecocomulco

Tepeapulco

Ciudad
Sahagún

Temascalapa

77

Tlaxcoapan

L. Zumpango

Tula

Tula

Tepotzotlán

Tepotzotlán

Tepotzotlán

Villa del
Carbón

Jiquipilco

Xonacatlán

Lopez
Mateos

Cuajimalpa

130

15

Capilhuac

Amoloya

Rayón

Joquicingo

MICHOACÁN

Tlalpujahua
de Rayón

Temazcalcingo

San Felipe del
Progreso

Presa
Huapango

Lerma

Presa
Villa Victoria

Valle de Bravo

Heroica
Zitácuaro

122

15

MEXICO

Toluca

Volcán
Nevado
de Toluca

PARQUE NACIONAL
NEVADO DE TOLUCA

Tecolotepec

Calderán

Chiltepec
de Hidalgo

Iztapán de la Sal

Tenancingo de
Degollado

119

Apizaco

Santa Ana
Chiautempan

Teolochoco

Tlaxcala

Cacaxtla

Zahuapan

Texmelucan

190

Volcán
Iztaccíhuatl

Huejotzingo

San Andres
Calpan

PARQUE
NACIONAL
IZTA-POPO

Volcán
Popocatépetl

Volcán La
Malinche

Puebla

Cholula

Gran
Pirámide

San Francisco
Acatepec

PUEBLA

Manuel Avila
Camacho

TO
CANTONA

150

Amazoc

Atlixco

190

190

136

115

Amecameca

Juchitepec

Tetela del
Volcán

Yecapixtla

Ozumba

Volcán
Tlaloc

PARQUE
NACIONAL
EL TEPOZTECO

Tepoztlán

Tepoztlán

95

95

198

138

Yautepec

Cocoyoc

MORELOS

Xochicalco

Cuernavaca

PARQUE
NACIONAL
DESIERTO
DE LOS
LEONES

San Nicolás
Coatepec

PARQUE
NACIONAL
LAGUNAS
DE ZEMPOALA

N

Río Tilostoc

in 1976. In this case, alas, the architect's inspiration failed him: the **Nueva Basílica** is a grotesque and most unspiritual mass of steel, wood, resinous fibers, and polyethylene. The famous cloak is enshrined in its own altar and can be viewed from a moving sidewalk that passes below it.

Teotihuacán

★   This Mesoamerican Giza is one of the most powerful sites in Mexico; from its size and scale, there's no doubting Teotihuacán's (*teh*-oh-tee-wa-*can*) monumental place in history. It was likely a small town already by 100 BC; four centuries later it had reached its zenith. At the time of its decline in the 8th century, it was one of the largest cities in the world, with possibly as many as 250,000 people. The sacred metropolis lay in the midst of rich obsidian mines, which provided the means for its rise as a major regional trading power and center for the arts—its influence on Maya pottery stretched as far away as Tikal in present-day Guatemala. The glasslike obsidian is still being fashioned into animal figures, which are sold in market stalls on the site. Just who lived here isn't exactly clear—even the original name of the city is lost. It is believed that water shortages and crises caused by local deforestation contributed to Teotihuacán's downfall. It was set on fire and destroyed by raiders around AD 650. Centuries later, the Aztecs arrived in the Valley of Mexico. Because the memory of the grandeur of this city survived the passage of time, these new settlers named the site Teotihuacán, which meant "place where the gods were born." It was here, the Aztecs believed, that the gods created the universe.

The awesome **Pirámide del Sol** (Pyramid of the Sun), with a base as broad as that of the pyramid of Cheops in Egypt, is off the center of Teotihuacán's main axis. Estimated to have been built between AD 100 and AD 250, it is the site's oldest structure. Its planes and angles were precisely built in relation to the movement of the sun—marking the equinoxes, for example—and the Pleiades constellation. The 242 steps of the 215-ft pyramid face west, the cardinal point where it was believed that the sun was transformed into a jaguar in order to pass nightly through the darkness of death.

The most impressive sight in Teotihuacán is the 4-km- (2½-mi-) long **Calzada de los Muertos** (Avenue of the Dead), the main axis of the ancient city along which six major structures lie. The Aztecs gave the avenue this name because of the stepped platforms lining it, which they mistook for tombs. The graceful 126-ft-high **Pirámide de la Luna** (Pyramid of the Moon) dominates the northern end of the avenue, and the compact, square **Ciudadela** (Citadel) flanks the opposite end. More than 4,000 one-story dwellings constructed of adobe and stone and occupied by artisans, warriors, and tradesmen once surrounded the avenue. On the west side of the spacious plaza facing the Pyramid of the Moon are the **Palacio del Quetzalpápalotl** (Palace of the Plumed Butterfly), **Templo de las Conchas Emplumados** (Temple of Plumed Conch Shells), and **Palacio de los Jaguares** (Palace of Jaguars), which is where the priests resided. The palaces are best known for the spectacular bird and jaguar murals in their winding underground chambers.

The Ciudadela, with its **Templo de Quetzalcóatl y Tlaloc** (Temple of the Plumed Serpent and Rain God), shows off the plastic arts of the time with its brawny toothed serpent heads jutting out of the temple facade. Quetzalcóatl and Tlaloc together represent the fusion of earth and sky.

Climbing one pyramid is probably enough for most people. The Pyramid of the Sun is the taller by 89 ft, and affords a spectacular view of

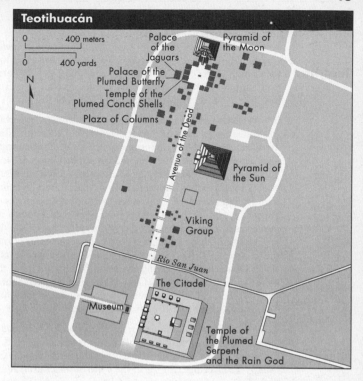

Teotihuacán

0 ——— 400 meters
0 ——— 400 yards

N

Palace of the Jaguars
Pyramid of the Moon
Palace of the Plumed Butterfly
Temple of the Plumed Conch Shells
Plaza of Columns
Avenue of the Dead
Pyramid of the Sun
Viking Group
Rio San Juan
The Citadel
Museum
Temple of the Plumed Serpent and the Rain God

the entire area. Wear comfortable clothes (especially shoes) and bring sunscreen or a visored hat when you visit.

Many of the artifacts uncovered at Teotihuacán are on display at the Museum of Anthropology in Mexico City. The **on-site museum,** opened in 1994 near the Pyramid of the Sun, contains fabulous pieces from the archaeological zone—such as the stone sculpture of Tlaloc, the goggle-eyed god of rain; black and green obsidian arrowheads; and simulated burial sites of exalted personages of the empire, their skeletons arranged as they were when discovered.

Seeing the ruins will take two–four hours, depending on how smitten you are by the place—or when your tour bus leaves. ☎ 595/60052 or 595/60276. ☞ $2.50, free Sun. ☉ Daily 7–6.

Many tour buses to the ruins stop briefly in **San Agustín Acolmán** to see the outstanding plateresque (an ornate 16th-century Spanish style) church and ex-convent, now a museum. The original Augustinian church (1539) is noteworthy for its vaulted roof and pointed towers. The ornate cloister and plateresque facade, set off with candelabralike columns, were added a century later by the monks.

Dining and Lodging

For price categories, see Dining and Lodging in Chapter 1.

$$ ✕▨ **Villa Arqueológica.** If you'd like to overnight at the pyramids, this Club Med stands across the road from the fenced-off site and has snug rooms and a huge garden and patio restaurant-bar surrounding a pool and tennis court. This is the only hotel that has permission to be in the area. ✉ Villa Arqueológica Teotihuacán, San Juan de Teotihuacán 55800, ☎ 595/60909, 5/203–3086 in Mexico City, 800/258–2633. 40 rooms. Restaurant, pool, tennis court. AE, MC, V.

Tepotzotlán

The Jesuit church and school of San Francisco Javier at Tepotzotlán (pronounced teh-po-tzot-*lan*) rank among the masterpieces of Mexican churrigueresque architecture. The unmitigated Baroque facade of the church (1682) is the first thing to catch the eye, but inside and out, every square inch has been worked over, like an overdressed Christmas tree. Note the gilded, mirrored Chapel of the Virgin of Loreto.

In pre-Hispanic times, the village was an important stop along the salt route—salt was used as money—between Toluca and Texcoco (near Teotihuacán) and had a prestigious school of dance and art. In 1580, four Jesuit priests arrived, learned the native language, and turned the village into a center of evangelization by setting up a school for the young nobles of the conquered nation. The church, of course, was built with Indian slave labor, but as a concession to the slaves, many of the angels decorating the chambers have been painted with dark-skinned indigenous faces. This is probably the only church in Mexico where you will find such paintings. There's also a museum of religious art in the complex. There are two notable restaurants for taking a light snack or lunch after viewing the Jesuit complex. One is the museum's coffee shop and the other is **Casa Mago,** directly across the square from the church. Casa Mago's owners will proudly recount how Elizabeth Taylor dropped by in 1963 to have a beer.

This village is also famous for its traditional Christmas *pastorela*, a charming and humorous morality play that has been taking place for more than 30 years, telling the story of the birth of Jesus Christ. Staged every year December 16–23 in the patio of the church at night, the cast includes a few professionals and loads of extras from the town who portray shepherds, angels, and, of course, the Devil. Tickets are available through Ticketmaster (☏ 5/325–9000 in Mexico City) or the church's offices in Tepotzotlán (☏ 5/876–0243).

Tula

 Tula, capital of the Toltecs—whose name for it was Tollán—was founded around AD 1000 and abandoned two centuries later. Quetzalcóatl was born in Tula and became its priest-king. Under his rule, the Toltecs reached the pinnacle of their civilization, with art, science, and philosophy flourishing. According to myth, Quetzalcóatl went into exile in Yucatán but vowed to return—on a date (1519) that unfortunately coincided with the arrival of Hernán Cortés, whom the Aztecs therefore fatefully welcomed. Visible from afar, Tula's 15-ft **warrior statues** (*atlantes*), rather than the ruins themselves, make the show. These basalt figures tower over Pyramid B, their strong geometrics looking vaguely totemic. Crocodiles, jaguars, coyotes, and eagles are also depicted in the carvings and represent the various warrior orders of the Toltecs. ▨ *$2, free Sun.* ☉ *Tues.–Sun. 9:30–4:30.*

North of Mexico City A to Z

Getting There

To get to **La Villa de Guadalupe** by car, take Paseo de la Reforma Norte until it forks into Calzada de Guadalupe, which leads directly to the shrine. Or take the No. 3 (red) metro line from downtown to the Basílica stop (the station symbol is the virgin's image). Buses run every 20 minutes between 7 AM and 3 PM from the Central de Autobuses del Norte to **Teotihuacán,** and the trip takes about one hour. Tour companies also offer combination visits to the two sights.

To get to **Tepotzotlán** from Mexico City, follow Periférico Norte. After 41 km (25 mi), you'll come to the exit for Tepotzotlán. **Tula** is about 8 km (5 mi) north of Tepotzotlán. Buses to Tula/Tepotzotlán leave Mexico City every 20 minutes, also from the Central de Autobuses del Norte.

SOUTH OF MEXICO CITY

Xochimilco (pronounced kso-chee-*meel*-co) is famous for its floating gardens, where you can ride in gondolalike boats and get a fleeting sense of a pre-Hispanic Mexico City. Beyond Xochimilco, in the neighboring state of Morelos, Cuernavaca is a weekend retreat for wealthy chilangos and foreigners. From Cuernavaca, consider a detour to the town of Tepoztlán, which has a 16th-century Dominican convent, a lively Sunday market, its own little pyramid, and plenty of New Age devotees.

Xochimilco

When the first nomadic settlers arrived in the Valley of Mexico, they found an enormous lake. As the years went by and their population grew, the land wasn't sufficient to satisfy their agricultural needs. They solved the problem by devising a system of *chinampas* (floating gardens), rectangular structures something like barges, which they filled with reeds, branches, and mud. They planted them with willows, whose roots anchored the floating gardens to the lake bed, making a labyrinth of small islands and canals on which they carried the flowers and produce grown on the chinampas to market.

Today Xochimilco is the only place in Mexico where the gardens still exist. Go on a Saturday, when the *tianguis* (market) is most active, or on a Sunday. (Note that Xochimilco is popular among families on Sunday.) On weekdays the place is practically deserted, so it loses much of its charm. Hire a *trajinera* (flower-painted launch); an arch over each spells out its name in flowers. As you sail through the canals, you'll pass mariachis and women selling tacos from other trajineras.

★ People also flock to Xochimilco for the **Museo Dolores Olmedo Patino,** which holds the largest private collection of works by flamboyant muralist Diego Rivera. It was put together by Olmedo, his lifelong model, patron, and onetime mistress (which she denies). The lavish display of nearly 140 pieces from his cubist, post-cubist, and mural periods hangs in a magnificent 17th-century hacienda with beautiful gardens. The museum also has works by Rivera's legal wife, Frida Kahlo, and his common-law wife, Angelina Beloff. ⊠ *Av. México 5843,* ☎ *5/555–1016.* 🖼 *$2,* 🕙 *Tues.–Sun. 10–6.*

Cuernavaca

The climate in Cuernavaca, a trifling 85 km (53 mi) from Mexico City, changes dramatically to lush and semitropical as the altitude descends almost 2,500 ft. In fact, it was this balmy springlike temperature that first attracted the rich and famous to what has become a resort: Cortés built the first summer place—read palace—here in the 16th century. There are spectacular restaurants and hotels, in addition to the beautiful Borda Gardens and Diego Rivera murals in the Palacio de Cortés. An overnight stay is recommended.

Cuernavaca is built on a series of small hills whose streets intertwine at a maddening pace. If you're not used to driving in San Francisco, say, it's better to get around by cab, especially on weekends, when the number of cars swells to disproportionate numbers.

Most sights are concentrated around the central **Plaza de Armas,** which is surrounded by crafts shops, sidewalk cafés, and government buildings. The square itself is filled with vendors from neighboring villages. Throughout the week they hawk local arts and crafts; on weekends, one side of the square is taken over by stalls in which you'll find silver and gold jewelry and leather goods from elsewhere in the country. **Jardín Juárez** (Juárez Gardens), a smaller square across the street from Plaza de Armas, puts on free band concerts Thursday evening at 6 under its colonial arcade. Either of these two squares is the perfect place for whiling away a pleasant afternoon after a visit to the tourist sights. After dark, the hip spot is the **Plazuela del Zacate** (⊠ Galeana and Fray Bartolomé de Las Casas, 2 blocks from the Plaza de Armas), where sidewalk cafés and bars open every night and young people gather.

The **Palacio de Cortés** (Cortés's palace-cum-fortress) houses the **Museo de Cuauhnáhuac**—Cuauhnáhuac being the native name for Cuernavaca—which focuses on Mexican history before and after the conquest. Diego Rivera painted some of his finest murals on the palace's top floor in 1930–32. Like those of Mexico City's National Palace, they dramatize the history and the horrors of the conquest, colonialism, and the revolution. Former U.S. Ambassador to Mexico Dwight Morrow commissioned Rivera to paint the murals for $30,000. ⊠ *Juárez and Hidalgo,* ☎ *73/12–81–71.* ☜ *$1.60, free Sun.* ☉ *Tues.–Sun. 10–5.*

The beautiful, spacious **Jardín Borda** (Borda Gardens) is the most visited sight in Cuernavaca. The jardín was designed in the late 18th century by a member of the Borda family—rich miners of French extraction—for one of his relatives; Maximilian and Carlotta visited the gardens frequently. Here Maximilian had a dalliance with the gardener's wife, La India Bonita, who was immortalized in a portrait by a noted painter of the time. In this century, novelist Malcolm Lowry turned the gardens into a sinister symbol in *Under the Volcano.* ⊠ *Av. Morelos 103, at Hidalgo, 3 blocks west of Palacio de Cortés,* ☎ *73/ 12–92–37.* ☜ *$1, free Sun.* ☉ *Tues.–Sun. 10–5:30.*

The **Catedral de la Asunción,** an eclectic structure begun in 1529 by Cortés, is noteworthy for the skull and crossbones over its main entrance and its 17th-century Japanese wall paintings. It's also famous for Sunday-morning mariachi masses. Paintings inside the **Palacio Municipal,** diagonally opposite the cathedral, depict pre-Hispanic city life. ⊠ *Hidalgo and Av. Morelos, opposite Borda Gardens.*

Near Plaza de Armas, the **Robert Brady Museum** is a delightful restored colonial mansion housing a diverse collection of art and artifacts assembled by the late Brady—an artist, antiquarian, and decorator from Fort Dodge, Iowa. You can see ceramics, antique furniture, sculptures, paintings, and tapestries, all beautifully arranged in rooms painted with bright Mexican colors. ⊠ *Calle Netzahuacóyotl 4, between Hidalgo and Abasolo,* ☎ *73/18–85–54.* ☜ *$2.* ☉ *Tues.–Sun. 10–6.*

The small ruins of **Xochicalco** ("place of flowers") include a pyramid and ball court. Showing Maya, Toltec, and Zapotec influences, the ancient fortified city reached its peak between AD 700 and 900. A solar-powered museum has six rooms of artifacts, including beautiful sculptures of Xochicalco deities found on site. The museum has a café, bookstore, and gift shop. ⊠ *23 mi southwest of Cuernavaca (take Hwy. 95D south; look for the sign for the turnoff).* ☎ *No phone.* ☜ *$2, free Sun.* ☉ *Tues.–Sun. 10–5.*

Dining and Lodging

If you've missed getting invited to one of the wealthy weekenders' mansions set in the hills on the edge of town, not to worry: there are a number of remarkable hotels and restaurants with equally remarkable gardens—several of them in restored colonial mansions and even haciendas—where you can get a taste of life behind the high stone walls. Many people come here to do just that, and many Cuernavaca hostelries that began as restaurants added on rooms to satisfy clients who felt too relaxed to drive back to Mexico City after their elaborate meals.

$$ ✕ **La Strada.** For a change from Mexican food, come to this old-timer to enjoy a good Italian meal on a colonial candlelit patio. You can't go wrong with the fish dishes, pizzas (ask for the pizza menu), or the house beef specialty—*filete de Estrada,* served with homemade pasta. A guitarist plays Wednesday and Friday night, and the chef whips up weekend specials each Friday. ✉ *Salazar 3, around the corner from Palacio de Cortés,* ☎ 73/18–60–85. AE, MC, V.

$ ✕ **Vienes.** Founded by an Austrian several generations ago, this Austro-Hungarian restaurant—which has grown up with the town—serves excellent Wiener schnitzel and goulash and irresistible pastries such as Sacher torte and apple strudel. ✉ *Lerdo de Tejada 302, at Comonfort, 1 block west of main square,* ☎ 73/14–34–04. AE, MC, V.

$$$$–$$$ ✕🏨 **Las Mañanitas.** Opened 41 years ago by an American expat, rooms and suites here are exquisitely decorated with traditional Mexican fireplaces, hand-carved bedsteads, hand-painted tiles in the bathrooms, and gilded handicrafts. Mexico City residents drive an hour on weekends just to dine at the restaurant, with its spectacular open-air terraces and garden inhabited by flamingos, peacocks, and African cranes. Portions are ample, as with the tried-and-true favorite Mexican Plate—enchilada, chile relleno, *carne asada* (thinly sliced oven-grilled beef), and tamale, served with side dishes of guacamole and refried beans. Don't miss the black-bottom (chocolate) pie. ✉ *Ricardo Linares 107, 62000,* ☎ 73/14–14–66, FAX 73/18–36–72. 1 room, 22 suites. Restaurant, bar, pool. AE.

$$$ 🏨 **Camino Real Sumiya.** The romantic hideaway, built by Woolworth heiress Barbara Hutton, was converted into a restaurant after she died. In 1993 new owners took over and turned it into a posh hotel. It's set amid formal Japanese gardens (including a contemplative rock garden) and contains an original Kabuki theater brought over from Kyoto. A concierge takes care of every need. The rooms, which are equipped with modern furniture, two queen-size beds, and color satellite TVs, are set in the far part of the garden for privacy. Nonguests can eat in the restaurant. ✉ *Morelos 62550, about 15 mins south of town at Interior del Fracc. Sumiya, Col. José Parres, Juitepec (take Civac exit on Acapulco Hwy.),* ☎ 73/20–91–99, 800/722–6466 in the U.S. and Canada, FAX 73/20–91–42. 163 rooms. 2 restaurants, bar, coffee shop, pool, 7 tennis courts, travel services. AE, DC, MC, V.

$$$ 🏨 **Clarion Cuernavaca Racquet Club.** This posh tennis club–turned-hotel is less expensive than most lodgings, and its appeal is in its beautiful gardens and spacious two-room suites equipped with romantic fireplaces. Families converge here on weekends. The restaurant admits nonguests. ✉ *Francisco Villa 100, Rancho Cortés, 62120,* ☎ 73/11–24–00, 800/228–5151 in the U.S. and Canada, FAX 73/17–54–83. 52 suites. Restaurant, bar, pool, 9 tennis courts. AE, DC, MC, V.

$$ 🏨 **Hacienda de Cortés.** This old hacienda dates from the 16th century and *did* belong to the conquistador. Rooms are decorated in traditional Mexican furnishings; they have lovely patios and gardens that will beckon you outdoors, as well as TVs and minibars inside. ✉ *Plaza Kennedy 90, Col. Atlacomulco, 62250,* ☎ 73/15–88–44, FAX 73/15–00–35. 22 rooms. Restaurant, bar, pool. AE, MC, V.

$$ ⊞ **Hotel Jacarandas.** Another former hacienda close to the downtown area, this hotel has the open, luxurious feel of an old-time Cuernavaca ranch. Huge laurel and fruit trees, jacarandas (of course), and poinsettias fill out the hotel's 98,000 square ft of terraced gardens, as do three pools, two tennis courts, and herb and vegetable gardens the hotel restaurant uses for its salads and herbal teas. This is a popular spot among Mexico City families. The rooms are simple, with TVs but no cable. ⊠ *Cuauhtémoc 33, Col. Chapultepec, 62450,* ☎ *73/15–77–77,* FAX *73/15–78–88. 80 rooms, 6 suites. Restaurant, bar, 3 pools, 2 tennis courts, squash. AE, DC, MC, V.*

Tepoztlán

🔺 Some say Tepoztlán, surrounded by beautiful sandstone monoliths that throw off a russet glow at sunset, is a magical place—Mexico's answer to Sedona, Arizona. It attracts practitioners of hatha yoga, meditation, crystal healing, herbal cures, astrology, and native sorcery. This town of 13,000, with a village atmosphere and cobblestone streets, is primarily known for its tiny **Tepozteco pyramid,** probably of Aztec origin, perched on top of a hill; hundreds of people come each weekend to climb it. Other things of interest include the lively **Sunday market,** with its fruits, vegetables, and handicrafts; and the **dances** held during the pre-Lenten Carnival, when celebrants don bright masks depicting birds, animals, and Christian figures. Anthropologists Robert Redfield and Oscar Lewis both did fieldwork here in the 1950s. Tepoztlán's landmark is the multibuttressed 1559 **Templo y Ex-Convento de la Natividad de la Virgen María** (Temple and Ex-Convent of the Birth of the Virgin Mary), its fine paneled doors adorned with Indian motifs. Yearly on September 8, the faithful assemble here to celebrate the birth of the Virgin Mary, the town's patron saint. The date also commemorates the baptism of the legendary ruler Tepoztecatl, for whom the pyramid is named.

Tepoztlán drew national attention in September 1995, when townspeople stormed city hall and took government officials hostage to protest the proposed building of a mega–golf resort on their revered Tepozteco terrain. They eventually ousted the mayor and town police and continued protesting until the developers abandoned the project. In 1997 they finally elected a member of the Party of the Democratic Revolution, but for more than a year they governed themselves.

Lodging

$$–$$$ ⊞ **Posada del Tepozteco.** Two pools, a tennis court, and terraced gardens brimming with bougainvillea are perched above the downtown area, providing great views of both the village and the pyramid. Most of this tranquil hotel's rooms have Jacuzzis. ⊠ *Calle del Paraíso 3, 62520,* ☎ *73/95–00–10. 18 rooms. Restaurant, bar, 2 pools, massage, tennis court. AE, MC, V.*

South of Mexico City A to Z

Arriving and Departing

To get to **Xochimilco** by car, take Periférico Sur to the extension of División del Norte. Xochimilco is 21 km (13 mi) from the Zócalo in Mexico City; the trip should take between 45 minutes and one hour, depending on traffic. If Xochimilco is your final stop, you are probably best off taking a taxi. By public transportation, take metro line No. 2 to Taxqueña and then any bus marked Xochimilco.

To continue south by car, return to Periférico Sur, turn left (south) on Viaducto Tlalpán, and watch for signs to **Cuernavaca** in about a half hour. The *cuota* (toll road, Route 95D) costs about $6 but is much faster than the *carretera libre* (free road, Route 95). On Route 95D, it will take you about 1½ hours to cover 85 km (53 mi).

Tepoztlán is 26 km (16 mi) east of Cuernavaca via Route 95D. Buses also run every 20 minutes from Mexico City's Metro Taxqueña.

Contacts and Resources

E-MAIL

The **Export Internet Café** (✉ Av. Morelos Sur 168, Local A–6, near the state tourist office, ☎ 73/12–16–56) is open daily 10–7 and charges $3 an hour.

VISITOR INFORMATION

The **Morelos State Tourist Office** (✉ Av. Morelos Sur 187, ☎ 73/14–38–72) in Cuernavaca is located in Colonia Las Palmas; it's open weekdays 8–3 and 6–9, weekends 9–2.

SOUTHEAST OF MEXICO CITY

Well-preserved colonial Puebla was once the center of the Spanish tile industry. Nearby Cholula is a sacred spot in ancient Mexico and home to an important pyramid and scores of churches. You can detour along the way to see the volcanoes, Popocatépetl (pronounced poh-poh-kah-*teh*-pettle) and Iztaccíhuatl (pronounced eesh-tah-*see*-wattle). On your way back to the capital, leave time—an entire day would be best—to visit the city of Tlaxcala, with its rare church and former convent, and an amazing archaeological site nearby.

The Volcanoes

Leaving Mexico City, you can view **Popocatépetl** and **Iztaccíhuatl** to the south—if the smog is not too thick. "Popo," 17,887 ft high, last erupted in 1802, but rumblings and bubblings in late 1994 were sufficiently strong to cause nearby villages to be evacuated temporarily. It continued to burp and belch and spew large clouds of smoke and ash during the following years—and even a bit of lava in 1998—although most seismologists found little cause for alarm. In any case, Popo is currently off-limits for climbing beyond the 12,000-ft point. Check with the U.S. State Department for the latest developments if you plan to climb Izta—a feat for serious mountaineers. The Parque Nacional, a verdant pine forest, makes a good spot for a picnic.

The legend states that Popocatépetl, an Aztec warrior, had been sent by the emperor—father of his beloved Iztaccíhuatl—to bring back the head of a feared enemy in order to win Iztaccíhuatl's hand. He returned triumphantly only to find that Iztaccíhuatl had killed herself, believing him dead. The grief-stricken Popo laid out her body on a small knoll and lit an eternal torch that he watches over, kneeling. Each of Iztaccíhuatl's four peaks is named for a different part of her body, and its silhouette conjures up its nickname, "Sleeping Woman."

Lodging

At the 12,000-ft marker on Popo, there's a park shelter with spartan dormitory accommodations (cement-slab beds), but it will only open when and if climbers are again allowed to scale Popo. You'll pay a few dollars a night here, and you must bring your own sleeping bag. You can drive here from the main highway, but this is the end of the road; if you want to go higher, you'll have to hoof it.

The venerable **Los Volcanes** (✉ Blvd. Los Volcanes, Popo Park 56970, at Km 66.5 on Carretera Mexico–Cuautla, ☎ 597/60294, $) is about an hour from Popocatépetl and Iztaccíhuatl, but it's the closest hotel and has nice views of both volcanoes. It has 38 rustic rooms, all with potbellied stoves.

Adventure Sports

If you're itching to climb Izta, the small **Planeta Expeditions** (✉ Amatlán 51-C at Montes de Oca, ☎ 5/211–9020) runs out of a café in trendy Colonia Condesa in Mexico City. Two-day trips cost $100.

Cholula

The town fathers claim that Cholula has 365 church cupolas, one for every day in the year. Alas, the 37 churches in Cholula are mostly in ★ poor condition. But 6½ km (4 mi) south of town, **San Francisco Acatepec** has one of the two most stunning, well-preserved churches in the country. Covered with Puebla tiles, it's been called the most ornate rococo Poblano facade in Mexico. Equally unusual is **Santa María Tonantzintla**'s church interior, on the way to Cholula. Its polychrome wood-and-stucco carvings—inset columns, altarpieces, and the main archway—are the essence of churrigueresque. Set off by ornate gold-leaf figures of plant forms, angels, and saints, the carvings were made by native craftsmen.

 The **Gran Pirámide** (Great Pyramid) was the centerpiece of Toltec and then Aztec religious centers. It consists of seven superimposed structures connected by tunnels and stairways. The Spaniards, as they often did, built a chapel to **Nuestra Señora de los Remedios** (Our Lady of the Remedies) on top of it. Behind the pyramid is a vast 43-acre temple complex, once dedicated to Quetzalcóatl. ✉ *Calzada San Andreas at Calle 8 Nte.*, ☎ *22/47–90–81,* ⌦ *$2 (includes museum), free Sun.* ☉ *Daily 10–5, museum 10–6.*

Puebla

Maize was first cultivated in the Tehuacán Valley around 5000 BC. Later, the region was a crossroads for many ancient Mesoamerican cultures, including the Olmecs and Totonacs. The young Spanish colony Puebla had the first glass factory, the first textile mill, and the second hospital. The battle of May 5, 1862—resulting in a short-lived victory against French invaders—took place just north of town. The national holiday, Cinco de Mayo, is celebrated yearly on that date in its honor, and the battle is reenacted.

Puebla today retains a strong conservative religious element and was one of the cities Pope John Paul II chose to visit during his 1978 Mexican tour. Overrun with religious structures, this city probably has more ex-convents and monasteries, chapels, and churches per square mile than anywhere else in the country. In fact, the valley of Puebla, which includes Cholula, was said to have 224 churches and 10 convents and monasteries in its heyday.

The city is full of idiosyncratic Baroque structures built with red bricks, gray stone, white stucco, and the beautiful Talavera tiles produced from local clay. Puebla is one of the few cities in Mexico declared a Patrimony of Humanities site by the United Nations because of the splendor of its colonial architecture.

Don't miss the **cathedral** (✉ Calle 2 Sur, south of the Zócalo), partially financed by Puebla's most famous son, Bishop Juan de Palafox y Mendoza—who donated his personal fortune to build its famous tower, the second-largest church tower in the country. Palafox was the illegitimate son of a Spanish nobleman who grew up poor but inherited his father's wealth. Onyx, marble, and gold adorn the cathedral's high altar, designed by Mexico's most illustrious colonial architect, Manuel Tolsá. The facade itself is gray and cheerless.

The **Iglesia de Santo Domingo** (Santo Domingo Church; ⊠ Av. Cinco de Mayo at Av. 4 Pte.) is especially famous for its Rosary Chapel, where almost every inch of the walls, ceilings, and altar is covered with gilded carvings and sculpture.

The **Museo Amparo,** filled with the private collection of pre-Columbian and colonial art of Mexican banker and philanthropist Manuel Espinoza Yglesias, is one of the most beautiful in Mexico. ⊠ *Calle 2 Sur at Av. 9 Ote.,* ☎ *2/246–46–46.* ☞ *$1.60, free Mon.* ☉ *Wed.–Mon. 10–6.*

The **Uriarte Talavera** pottery factory was founded in 1824 and is one of the few authentic Talavera workshops left today. To be authentic, the pieces must be hand-painted in intricate designs with natural dyes derived from minerals, which is why only five colors are used: blue, black, yellow, green, and a reddish pink. There is a shop on site, and free tours of the factory run Monday through Saturday 10–2. ⊠ *Av. 4 Pte. 911, between Avs. 9 and 11 Nte.,* ☎ *2/232–15–98.* ☉ *Weekdays 9–6:30, Sat. 10–6:30, Sun. 11–6.*

Visit the **Barrio del Artista** (⊠ Calle 8 Nte. and Av. 6 Ote.) to watch painters and sculptors working in the galleries 10–6 daily. You may purchase pieces here, or continue walking down Calle 8 Norte and buy Talavera pottery, cheaper copies of Talavera, and other local handicrafts from the dozens of small stores and street vendors along the way.

The colonial **Ex-Convento de Santa Rosa,** now a museum of native crafts, contains the intricately tiled kitchen where Puebla's renowned mole sauce is believed to have been invented by the nuns as a surprise for their demanding gourmet bishop. ⊠ *Av. 14 Pte. between Calles 3 and 5 Nte.,* ☎ *2/246–22–71.* ☞ *40¢.*

Puebla is also famous for *camote,* a popular candy made from sweet potatoes and fruit. **La Calle de las Dulces** (Sweets Street; ⊠ Av. 6 Ote. between Av. 5 de Mayo and Calle 4 Nte.) is lined with shops competing to sell a wide variety of freshly made camote.

Dining and Lodging

Puebla is noted for its cuisine—some consider it to be the best in the country. Two of Mexico's most popular dishes were created here to celebrate special occasions: mole, a sauce made with as many as 100 ingredients, the best-known mole being one with bitter chocolate. The other local specialty, believed to have been initiated by the town's nuns, is *chiles en nogada,* a green poblano chili filled with ground meats, fruits, and nuts, then covered with a sauce of chopped walnuts and cream, and topped with red pomegranate seeds; the colors represent the red, green, and white of the Mexican flag.

$$ ✕ **Las Bodegas del Molino.** In a 16th-century hacienda at the edge of town, this elegant restaurant is notable for both its setting and its fine cuisine. ⊠ *Molino de San José del Puente,* ☎ *22/49–04–83 or 22/49–06–51. No credit cards.*

$ ✕ **Fonda Santa Clara.** This popular spot is a favorite among travelers; it's only a few blocks from the Zócalo and is open for breakfast, lunch, and dinner. ⊠ *Calle 3 Pte. 307,* ☎ *22/42–26–59. AE, MC, V.*

$ ✕ **La Guadalupana.** Puebla's most talked-about restaurant is a good choice for lunch. You'll find typical Poblano dishes on the menu. ⊠ *Av. 5 Ote. 605, at Plazuela de los Sapos (Plaza of the Frogs),* ☎ *22/ 42–48–86. V.*

$$–$$$ ✕⊞ **Mesón Sacristía de la Companía.** Each room in this reconditioned 200-year-old town house is outfitted with antiques that you can purchase. The restaurant serves everything from steaks to the scrumptious "Grandma's enchiladas." ⊠ *Calle 6 Sur 304, at Callejón de los Sapos, 72000,* ☎ *22/32–45–13. 9 rooms. Restaurant, bar. AE, MC, V.*

$$$ ⊞ **Camino Real.** The accommodations are deluxe in this former 16th-century convent, with gilded antique furnishings, luminous restored fresco murals, and an exceptionally warm and professional staff. ⊠ *Av. 7 Pte. 105, 72000,* ☎ *22/29–09–09, 22/29–09–10, 800/722–6466,* 𝔽𝔸𝕏 *22/32–92–51. 83 rooms. Restaurant, bar, in-room data ports, business services. AE, DC, MC, V.*

$$$ ⊞ **El Mesón del Angel.** At the city's entrance is this quiet colonial hotel with two large gardens. It's peaceful and clean, though a bit far from the attractions. ⊠ *Av. Hermanos Serdan 807, 72100,* ☎ *22/23–83–01. 192 rooms. Restaurant, 2 bars, pool, business services. AE, MC, V.*

$$ ⊞ **Royalty.** Small and well maintained, this hotel on the main square is one of the less expensive choices in Puebla. ⊠ *Portal Hidalgo 8, 72000,* ☎ *22/42–47–40. 47 rooms. Restaurant, bar. MC, V.*

Cantona

  Puebla state is home to the fascinating Cantona—opened to the public in 1995—which has 24 ball courts where a precursor to soccer was played. It's built into a hillock that looks like a massive military fortress from afar. Larger than Teotihuacán (its archenemy), it supposedly reached its pinnacle after AD 600, and we can judge its importance from the fact that around 500 cobblestone streets and lanes crisscross its 13-square-km (5-square-mi) area. ⊠ *107 km (66 mi) northeast of Puebla: take Hwy. 150 to Hwy. 129; turn off Hwy. 129 at Oriental. In rainy season (Aug.–Oct.), you can only navigate it with 4-wheel drive.* 🖾 *$2.* ☉ *Tues.–Sun. 9–5.*

Tlaxcala

The warriors of the state of Tlaxcala (pronounced tlas-*ca*-la) played a pivotal role in the Spanish conquest by aligning themselves with Cortés against their enemy Aztecs, thus swelling the conqueror's military ranks by 5,000 men. The state capital, seat of the ancient nation with the same name, will interest both archaeology buffs and church lovers.

A former Franciscan church, now called the **Catedral de Nuestro Señora de la Asunción** (Our Lady of the Assumption Cathedral), with its adjoining **monastery** (1537–40), stands atop a hill one block from the handsome main square. This was the first permanent Catholic edifice in the New World. The most unusual feature of the church is its wood ceiling beams, carved and gilded with gold studs after the Moorish fashion. There are only three churches of this kind in Mexico. (Moorish, or mudéjar, architecture appeared in Mexico only during the very early years after the conquest, when the Moorish occupation was still recent enough to influence Spain with Arabic architectural styles.) The austere monastery, now a museum of history, displays 16th- and 18th-century religious paintings and a small collection of pre-Columbian pieces. A beautiful outdoor **chapel** near the monastery has notable Moorish and Gothic traces.

The **Palacio de Gobierno** (Government Palace), which occupies the north side of the Zócalo, was built about 1550. Inside are vivid epic murals of Tlaxcala before the conquest, painted in the 1960s by local artist Desiderio Hernández Xochitiotzin.

About 1 km (½ mi) west of Tlaxcala is the large, ornate **Santuario de la Virgen de Ocotlán** (Basílica of Our Lady of Ocotlán). The legend of the Virgin dates from 1541, when, during a severe epidemic, she appeared to a poor Indian and told him to take the water from a stream, which had miraculously appeared, to his people to cure them. The villagers recovered. The Virgin then asked for the Franciscan monks from a nearby monastery. When they arrived in her forest, they were temporarily blinded by the raging flames of a fire that didn't harm the trees. They returned the next day with an axe to cut open one particular pine (*ocotlán*) tree that had caught their attention. When they split it open, they discovered the wooden image of the Virgin, which they installed in the present basilica. Many miracles have been attributed to the Virgin since then. Noteworthy sights of the church are the churrigueresque white-plaster facade, which conjures up images of a wedding cake; the two white Poblano towers adorned with the apostles; and, inside, the brilliantly painted and gilded **Camarín de la Virgen** (Virgin's Dressing Room) with figures on each of its eight sides portraying the history of the Lady of Ocotlán.

Cacaxtla

 The archaeological site at Cacaxtla, accidentally discovered in 1975 by a peasant working the land, contains a breathtaking series of murals (AD 650–700) depicting scenes of a fierce battle between Maya and Central Mexican warriors. It's considered a major breakthrough in tracing the immigration and trade patterns of pre-Hispanic Mexico. The site was settled around 2000 BC by the Olmeca-Xicalancas, a transition culture between the Olmecs and the peoples of central Mexico, researchers say. It reached its height between AD 600 and 900 and was abandoned by 1000. The vividly portrayed battle scenes with life-size figures show warriors in lofty bird headdresses and plumage being vanquished by victors wearing jaguar skins and wielding spears, obsidian knives, and lances. The murals—painted on the walls of a series of palaces built one on top of another—are protected under a huge roof. Give yourself at least three hours to see both Cacaxtla and Xochitécatl (☞ *below*). ✉ *About 19 km (12 mi) southwest of Tlaxcala.* 🖼 *$2.50 (includes Xochitécatl), free Sun.* ⊙ *Tues.–Sun. 10–5.*

Xochitécatl

 Whereas Cantona in neighboring Puebla is all military ambience (☞ *above*), little Xochitécatl is decidedly soft and feminine, having been dedicated to a bevy of important goddesses. Four Classic period pyramids are built on a hill that affords a spectacular view of the Tlaxcala and Puebla valleys. A small on-site **museum** has a good collection of sculpted stone heads and pregnant women. ✉ *Less than 1½ km (1 mi) north of Cacaxtla.* 🖼 *Free with Cacaxtla ticket.* ⊙ *Tues.–Sun. 10–5.*

Southeast of Mexico City A to Z

Getting Around

BY CAR

From Mexico City, head east on the Viaducto Miguel Aleman toward the airport and exit right onto Calzada Zaragoza, the last wide boulevard before arriving at the airport; this becomes the Puebla Highway at the tollbooth. Route 150D is the toll road straight to **Puebla**; Route 190 is the scenic free road (the trip takes about 1½ hours on the former, three hours on the latter). To go directly to **Cholula,** take the exit at San Martín Texmelucan and follow the signs. From Puebla, Cholula is 8 km (5 mi) west. To stop at the **volcanoes,** take the free road 33 km (20 mi) to Chalco. From there it's 4 km (2½ mi) to the Ame-cameca-Chalco sign, from which you continue 22 km (13½ mi) on Route 115 to Amecameca. You'll need to go to Puebla to get to **Tlaxcala**; from there, take Highway 119 north.

Contacts and Resources

E-MAIL

The **Cyberbyte Café** (✉ Calle 2 Sur 505B, between Avs. 5 and 7 Ote., Puebla, ☎ 22/17–55–23) is open daily 10–9 and charges $2.50 an hour.

VISITOR INFORMATION

The **Puebla Tourist Office** (✉ Av. 5 Ote. 3, ☎ 22/46–12–85) is open Monday–Saturday 9–8, Sunday 9–2. Ask for Jorge Estrada or Jose Luis Hernández; both speak English and love to talk up their state.

WEST OF MEXICO CITY

A good day-trip west of Mexico City would take you to Toluca, renowned for its Friday market. For a longer stay, stop over in Valle de Bravo, a lovely lakeside village popular with vacationing chilangos; it's often called Mexico's Switzerland because of its green, hilly setting. We suggest a quick trip into Parque Nacional Desierto de los Leones—a forested national park whose centerpiece is an intriguing Carmelite monastery—and making a detour from Toluca for a picnic at Parque Nacional Nevado de Toluca.

Parque Nacional Desierto de los Leones

Several walking trails crisscross this 5,000-acre national park's pine forest. Its focal point is the ruined 17th-century **ex-monastery of the Carmelites**, isolated amid an abundance of greenery. The park played a significant role in the War of Independence: in late October 1810, at a spot called **Las Cruces**, Father Hidalgo's troops trounced the Spaniards but resolved not to go on to attack Mexico City, an error that cost the insurgents 10 more years of fighting.

Toluca

The capital of the state of Mexico is an industrial town. Once famous only for its Friday market, Toluca now has much more to offer. Indians still come in from the surrounding villages on Friday to sell their produce and handicrafts at the huge municipal market, but it's hard to find any indigenous goods among the radios and CDs from Asia and the denim jackets and jeans from the United States. For local crafts, your best bet is the **Casa de Artesanías** on Paseo Tolloca.

There are three main sights: The **Jardín Botánico Cosmovitral** (Cosmovitral Botanical Garden; ✉ Calles Sebastian Lerdo de Tejada and Benito Juárez, ☎ 72/14–67–85), open 10–5 Tuesday–Sunday, is in a remodeled, Art Nouveau structure that once housed the public market. Admission is $1. The **Iglesia de la Santa Veracruz** (✉ Av. Independencia and Calle Constitución, next to Plaza Principal, ☎ 72/15–47–33) displays a rare black Christ statue. The church is open 9–8 daily, free.

The **Museo de Culturas Populares** (☎ 72/74–12–66 or 72/74–12–77), in the **Centro Cultural Mexiquense** (Mexican Cultural Center), features indigenous crafts from the state of Mexico, including ceramics, clothing, and wooden toys. The center also houses the **Museo de Antropología e Historia** and the **Museo de Arte Moderno**. ✉ *Ex-Hacienda la Pila, 8 km [5 mi] southeast of Toluca.* 🎫 *$1 for all museums or 50¢ each.* ☉ *Tues.–Sun. 10–6.*

Parque Nacional Nevado de Toluca

At 15,090 ft, the Nevado de Toluca, a now-extinct volcano, is Mexico's fourth-tallest mountain; on clear days its crater affords wonderful views of the valley. You can hire a guide at the entrance to go with your car to the top of the crater and lead you down to its sandy floor, which surrounds two lakes. Self-guided hiking trails are plentiful.

Valle de Bravo

In colonial Valle de Bravo, white stucco houses are trimmed with wrought-iron balconies and red-tile roofs, and red-potted succulents clutter the doorways. A hilly town that rises from the shores of Lake Avandaro and is surrounded by pines and mountains, Valle was founded in 1530 but has no historical monuments to speak of other than the town church. It does, however, have plenty of diversions: boating, waterskiing, and swimming in the lake and its waterfalls, and the more sociable pleasures of the Sunday market, where exceptional pottery is the draw. Although Valle and its suburb of Avandaro are enclaves for artists and the wealthy, locals like to keep a low profile.

Lodging

$$$ 🏨 **Avandaro Golf & Spa Resort.** For a weekend stay, head for this posh former country club, where all the rooms have romantic fireplaces. In addition to its 18-hole golf course, the resort has one of the best high-tech spas in Mexico, equipped with hot tubs and offering massage, facials, body toning, and aerobics classes. ⊠ *Vega del Río, Fracc. Avandaro, 52100,* ☎ *726/6–03–66, 800/223–6510,* 📠 *726/6–09–05. 74 rooms. Restaurant, bar, pool, spa, 18-hole golf course, health club. AE, MC, V.*

West of Mexico City A to Z

Getting There

By car from Mexico City, follow Paseo de la Reforma all the way west. It eventually merges with the Carretera Libre at Toluca, and after 20 km (12 mi), you'll see signs for the turnoff to the **Parque Nacional Desierto de los Leones;** it's another 10 km (6 mi) to the park. To go straight to **Toluca,** take the toll highway (expensive, but worth it); alternatively, buses depart Terminal Poniente every 20 minutes. To reach **Parque Nacional Nevado de Toluca,** make a 44-km (27-mi) detour south of Toluca on Route 130. There are two choices for getting to **Valle de Bravo:** the winding, scenic route, which you pick up 3 km (2 mi) west of Zincantepec, or Route 15. The former takes twice as much time but is worth it for the unspoiled mountain scenery.

Visitor Information

The **Mexico State Tourist Office** (⊠ Urawa 100, Gate 110, Toluca, ☎ 72/19–51–90 or 72/19–61–58) is open weekdays 9–6.

3 BAJA CALIFORNIA

Separated from mainland Mexico by the Sea of Cortés, the Baja California peninsula stretches 1,625 km (1,000 mi) from Tijuana to Los Cabos. The desert landscape harbors isolated fishing retreats, Prohibition-era gambling palaces, world-class golf courses, and one of the busiest international borders in the world. Adventurers delight in kayaking alongside migrating gray whales, diving with hammerhead sharks, and hiking to hidden cave paintings.

By Maribeth
Mellin

Updated by
Daniel Taras

BAJA (MEANING LOWER) CALIFORNIA is an arid stretch of land dipping southward from the international boundary that divides California and Mexico. The 240-km-wide (150-mi-wide) Sea of Cortés—also called the Gulf of California—separates Baja from the Mexican mainland. Both Baja and the Gulf of California are part of Mexico.

Although only 21 km (13 mi) across at one point and 193 km (120 mi) at its widest, Baja has one of the most varied and beautiful terrains on the planet. The peninsula's two coasts are separated by great mountain ranges, with one peak soaring more than 10,000 ft high. Countless bays and coves with pristine beaches indent both shores, and islands big and small—many inhabited only by sea lions—dot the 3,364 km (2,090 mi) of coastline. You'll find stretches of desert as dry as the Sahara, as well as cultivated farmlands, vineyards, and resorts lush with swaying palm trees.

Varied, too, is the demographic makeup of Baja. The border strip of northern Baja is densely populated. Tijuana, Mexico's fourth-largest city, is home to more than 2 million people, making it more populous than the entire remainder of the peninsula. La Paz, with about 170,000 residents, is the only city of any size south of Ensenada. The two towns at Los Cabos (The Capes) have yet to reach city status.

Baja is divided politically into two states—Baja California (also called Baja Norte, meaning North Baja) and Baja California Sur (South)—at the 28th parallel, about 710 km (440 mi) south of the border. Near the tip of the peninsula, a monument marks the spot where the Tropic of Cancer crosses the Transpeninsular Highway (Mexico Highway 1).

Native Baja Californians will tell you in no uncertain terms that they live in the first California, discovered by pirates, missionaries, and explorers long before the California of the United States. Most Baja travelers have that same sense of adventure, and the peninsula has become a cult destination. Back in the days of Prohibition, when Hollywood was new, the movie crowd learned the joy of having an international border so near. John Steinbeck brought attention to La Paz when he made it a setting for his novella *The Pearl*. Erle Stanley Gardner took a break from writing to battle marlin off Los Cabos. Bing Crosby is said to have put up some of the money for the first resort hotel in San José del Cabo when the only way to get there was aboard a yacht or private plane.

Today you'll fly in on commercial jets and check into thoroughly modern hotels. The rich and famous still find Baja, particularly the southern tip, an ideal escape, and you can see them in secluded hotels along the Los Cabos Corridor. But Baja is no longer the exclusive turf of adventurers and the owners of private yachts and planes. Caravans of motor homes and pickups occasionally clog the Transpeninsular Highway, and flights into Loreto, La Paz, and Los Cabos are often packed with regular folks on their first forays into Mexico. Baja's resort towns have become mainstream, but you can still find adventure and sublime solitude at the peninsula's hidden beaches and bays.

Pleasures and Pastimes

Dining

Baja's cuisine highlights food from the sea. Fresh fish, lobster, shrimp, and abalone are particularly good. In both states, scores of restaurants and kitchens serve great, authentically Mexican seafood dishes. Beef and pork are also excellent, both grilled and marinated. Imported steak, lamb, duck, and quail are popular in upscale places. Many restaurants serve regional Mexican cuisine, and plenty of spots throughout the peninsula combine U.S. and Mexican flavors in tacos, burritos, burgers, and pizza.

Two dishes originated in Baja and have become standard fare in southern California. Lobster Puerto Nuevo–style (shellfish grilled or boiled in oil and served with beans, rice, and tortillas) comes from the fishing settlement of the same name near Tijuana. Fish tacos (chunks of deep-fried fish wrapped with condiments in a corn tortilla) are said to have originated in the northern Baja town of San Felipe. Mexico's best domestic wines are nurtured in the vineyards and wineries in the Santo Tomás and Guadalupe valleys outside Ensenada, and one of the country's most popular beers, Tecate, comes from the northern Baja town of the same name.

Restaurants as a rule are low-key, except in Tijuana, Ensenada, and Los Cabos, where dining options range from *taquerías* (taco stands) to upscale Continental dining rooms. Dress is accordingly casual at nearly all Baja restaurants, and reservations are not required unless otherwise noted. Moderate prices prevail even in city restaurants—except in Los Cabos, which can be surprisingly expensive. Some places add a 15% service charge to the bill.

CATEGORY	COST*
$$$	over $20
$$	$10–$20
$	under $10

per person for a three-course meal, excluding drinks and service

Fishing

Baja is considered one of the world's great sportfishing destinations. The fishing is best in the south, with large fishing fleets in Loreto, La Paz, and Los Cabos. Although the summer months bring the most fish, anglers are sure to catch something year-round. Fishing from Ensenada and San Quintín is best in the summer and early fall.

Golf

With championship-level courses in Tijuana, Rosarito, and Ensenada, Baja is growing in popularity among golfers. Los Cabos has experienced a particular boom, with several excellent courses opening in recent years.

Kayaking

Both the Pacific Ocean and the Sea of Cortés have isolated bays and coves ideal for kayaking. Some hotels and outfitters in Ensenada, Loreto, La Paz, and Los Cabos offer kayak rentals and excursions, and some U.S. companies offer kayaking trips to the Sea of Cortés.

Lodging

Baja lodging is mostly low-key—except world-class Los Cabos. Until the 1980s, its hotels were mostly fishing lodges where die-hard sportsmen took refuge. Now Los Cabos draws golfers to deluxe hotels that front championship courses. In the rest of Baja, you can find great deals at small, one-of-a-kind hostelries.

Reservations are a must on holiday weekends for most of Baja's coastal towns; some hotels require a minimum two-night stay for a confirmed reservation. Several hotels in Baja have toll-free numbers that connect directly to the hotel; although the operator may answer in Spanish, there is usually someone who speaks English in the reservations office. Many hotels have fax numbers (a good way to confirm reservations), although you may have to ask them to turn on the fax machine when you call. A few of the out-of-the-way and budget-priced hotels do not accept credit cards; some of the more lavish places add a 10%–20% service charge to your bill. Most properties also raise their rates for the December–April high season. Rates here are based on high-season standards. Expect to pay 25% less during the off-season. Many hotels offer midweek discounts of 30%–50% off the weekend rates; always ask about special promotions.

Several agencies in the United States book reservations at Baja hotels, condos, and time-share resorts, which may actually cost less than hotel rooms if you are traveling with a group of four or more (☞ Contacts and Resources *in* Baja Norte A to Z, *below*).

CATEGORY	COST*
$$$$	over $160
$$$	$90–$160
$$	$40–$90
$	under $40

All prices are for a standard double room, excluding service charge and 12%–17% hotel occupancy tax.

Whale-Watching
Gray whales migrate to the Pacific coast of Baja from January through March. Whale-watching expeditions are available in Ensenada, Guerrero Negro, San Ignacio, Loreto, La Paz, and Los Cabos.

Exploring Baja California

The Baja Peninsula is made up of two Mexican states: Baja California, which begins at the U.S. border, and Baja California Sur.

The northern half of the peninsula contains the largest cities and highest population. Tijuana, Tecate, and Mexicali—the peninsula's border cities—are U.S. suburbs in a sense. San Felipe, the northernmost town on the Sea of Cortés, is a popular weekend escape for Arizonans and southern Californians. Similarly, Rosarito and Ensenada, on Baja's northern Pacific coast, are practically extensions of the southern California coast, offering an experience both familiar and foreign. South of Ensenada the natural side of Baja begins to appear in desolate mountain ranges and fields of cacti and boulders.

Baja California Sur is more remote, in spite of its strong American influences. The most populated areas lie on the Sea of Cortés coast. The Pacific side is more popular with migrating gray whales, who travel by the thousands every winter from the Bering Strait to isolated coves and lagoons along this coast. For those few months, people come from around the world to Guerrero Negro and a few bays and lagoons farther south. Loreto, on the Sea of Cortés, is beloved by sportfishers who find seclusion in this small, largely undiscovered town. La Paz is capital of Baja California Sur, the region's major port, and a busy center of commerce and government. Los Cabos, made up of the two towns of Cabo San Lucas and San José del Cabo, has become one of the fastest-growing resort areas in Mexico. Despite all the development and steep prices, it remains a mysteriously natural hideaway.

Numbers in the text correspond to numbers in the margin and on the Tijuana, Ensenada, La Paz, Los Cabos Coast, San José del Cabo, and Cabo San Lucas maps.

Great Itineraries
Baja aficionados will tell you that you haven't really explored the peninsula unless you've driven its entire length, stopping at small

towns and secluded beaches along the way. That's a major journey, requiring at least 10 days of travel time—one way. If you plan to drive the peninsula, certain precautions are in order. You must have Mexican auto insurance (about $18 per day), for the length of your drive. Always carry water, and make sure your vehicle is in good condition. Keep your gas tank at least half full at all times—some remote gas stations may be out of gas just when you need it. For the most part, the Transpeninsular Highway is well maintained, although you may come across areas marred by potholes or gravel and rocks. In addition, it has only two lanes, and sharing them with semis and speeding buses can be somewhat unnerving.

Even if you don't have 10 days you can still see plenty of the peninsula's attractions by focusing on the area around where you enter Baja. A full week allows a quick jaunt through the peninsula or a more leisurely exploration of northern Baja or Baja Sur. If you have five days, you can see the most interesting towns in one of the states and still be able to linger a bit. With three days you're best off staying within the immediate vicinity of your entry point.

IF YOU HAVE 3 DAYS

In northern Baja, you can explore Tijuana, Rosarito, and Ensenada. Start in **Tijuana** ①–⑪ at the **Centro Cultural** ⑧, then stroll down **Avenida Revolución** ②. Head south before nightfall to a hotel in **Rosarito** or **Puerto Nuevo.** Tour **Ensenada** ⑫–⑲ the next day, taking in the **Fish Market** ⑭, the **Riviera del Pacífico** ⑱, and the shops on **Avenida López Mateos** ⑰. Take the third day in Rosarito.

In Baja Sur, you're best off staying in **Los Cabos,** allowing time for golf, sportfishing, and snorkeling at **Bahía Santa María** or **Bahía Chileno.**

IF YOU HAVE 5 DAYS

You can do a thorough tour of northern Baja, starting with a full day and overnight in **Tijuana** ①–⑪. From there head to the small town of **Tecate,** then on to **Mexicali** and **San Felipe.** Overnight in San Felipe; then spend Day 3 checking out the beaches before driving the backcountry to **Ensenada** ⑫–⑲. Devote Day 4 to exploring **La Bufadora** and downtown Ensenada; then head up the coast for a lobster feast at **Puerto Nuevo.** On Day 5, head back to Tijuana and the border.

If you'd rather tour Baja Sur, begin in **Los Cabos,** spending the night there and starting out early the next day for **La Paz** ⑳–㉘. Spend Day 2 exploring downtown La Paz, making sure to see the **malecón** ㉑, or boardwalk, and the **Plaza Constitución** ㉕. On Day 3, head up the coast to the small mission town of **Loreto.** Spend Days 4 and 5 making your way back to Los Cabos at a leisurely pace, stopping to explore the desert and coast along the way.

IF YOU HAVE 7 DAYS

If you want to cover a lot of distance—and spend much of your time in the car—you could technically make the long drive down the entire peninsula in a week, especially if you arrange to begin your tour in the north and drop off your car in the south. But keep in mind that most rental-car agencies will charge you a whopping drop-off fee and that the terrain covered isn't always awe-inspiring. (A leisurely round-trip takes about 14 days, especially as many of Baja's treasures take some extra time and effort to reach.) Start in **Tijuana** ①–⑪ on Day 1, touring the **Centro Cultural** ⑧ and **Avenida Revolución** ②. Head south before nightfall to a hotel in **Rosarito** or **Puerto Nuevo.** On Day 2, move on to **Ensenada** ⑫–⑲ for a brief tour of the city; then head south to **San Quintín** and **Guerrero Negro.** If you're traveling between January and March, arrange for a whale-watching tour for the next day and spend Nights 2 and 3 in Guerrero Negro. If not, overnight in Guerrero Negro and then move on for a full day's trip to **Mulege** on the Sea of Cortés. The drive between the two coasts, through stark desert scenery, is one of the most beautiful and desolate in Baja. Spend Night 3 or 4 in Mulege, allowing plenty of relaxation time after the long drive. Move on to **Loreto,** stopping for a swim at **Bahía Concepción,** and spend the next night there. If you didn't stay in Guerrero Negro for whale-watching, spend an extra night in Loreto and arrange a boat tour of the Sea of Cortés. Devote Day 6 to the drive to **La Paz** ㉒–㉘, spending the evening strolling the waterfront **malecón** ㉑. On Day 7, continue on to **Los Cabos.**

When to Tour Baja

Baja's climate is extreme, thanks to its desert locale. Temperatures are less drastic in the north—temperatures in Tijuana, Ensenada, and Rosarito are similar to those in southern California. Mexicali, on the other hand, gets extremely hot in the summer months. Northern Baja's resort cities are very crowded on holiday weekends, and advance reservations are a must. Tijuana's attractions are rarely overcrowded, and you should be able to tour them easily at any time of day.

Baja Sur's winters are mild, but not warm; Loreto, La Paz, and Los Cabos can get downright chilly in the evening. Sportfishing aficionados prefer the summer months: although the temperatures are high, the fish are abundant. Loreto and La Paz tend to be crowded only on holiday weekends, but Los Cabos is crowded through much of the year, except at the height of the summer heat.

BAJA CALIFORNIA (NORTH)

The most densely populated area of the Baja California peninsula, the state of Baja California begins at the U.S. border and extends 699 km (433 mi) to the border with Baja California Sur. Tijuana, just 29 km (18 mi) south of San Diego, is Baja's largest city; in fact, with a population that has now surpassed 2 million, it is the fourth-largest city in Mexico. Tijuana's promoters like to call it "the most visited city in the world," and certainly the border crossing to Tijuana is the busiest in the United States.

By comparison, the state's capital, Mexicali, has a population of only 800,000 residents. Although it also sits on the U.S. border, Mexicali attracts few tourists. Tecate, located between Tijuana and Mexicali, is a typical village whose main claim to fame is the Tecate brewery, where one of Mexico's most popular beers originates. Those travelers who do pass through Tecate and Mexicali are usually en route to San Felipe, the northernmost town on the Sea of Cortés.

On Baja's Pacific coast, travelers stream down the Transpeninsular Highway (Highway 1) to Rosarito and Ensenada. These beach communities are like Mexican suburbs of southern California, where English is spoken as freely as Spanish and the dollar is as readily accepted as the peso. Between Baja's towns, the landscape is unlike any other, with cacti growing beside the sea, and stark mountains and plateaus rising against clear blue skies.

Highway 3 runs east from Ensenada to San Felipe through the foothills of the Sierra San Pedro Mártir. The same highway runs north from Ensenada to Tecate through the Guadalupe Valley, where you'll find many of the area's vineyards and wineries. If you're traveling south, Ensenada is the last major city you'll see for hundreds of miles on Mexico Highway 1. San Quintín, 184 km (115 mi) south of Ensenada, is

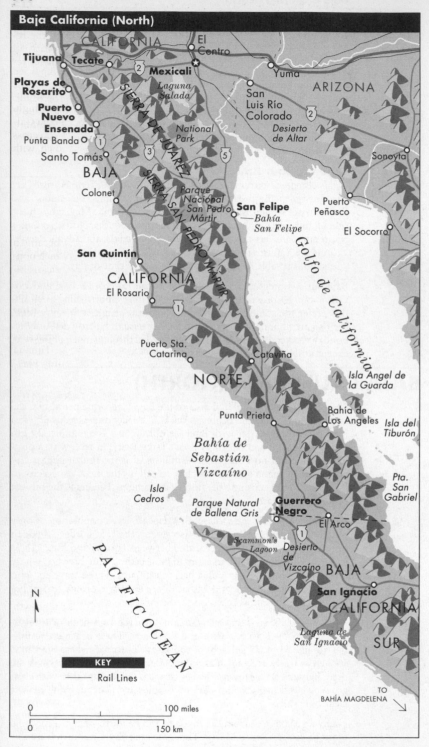

CALIFORNIA

El Centro

Tijuana   Tecate

Playas de Rosarito

Puerto Nuevo

Ensenada

Punta Banda

Santo Tomás

BAJA

Colonet

2

Mexicali

Laguna Salada

SIERRA DE JUÁREZ

National Park

3

Parque Nacional San Pedro Mártir

SIERRA SAN PEDRO MÁRTIR

Yuma

ARIZONA

San Luis Río Colorado

Desierto de Altar

Sonoyta

5

San Felipe

—Bahía San Felipe

Puerto Peñasco

El Socorro

San Quintín

CALIFORNIA

El Rosario

1

Puerto Sta. Catarina

Cataviña

NORTE

Golfo de California

Isla Angel de la Guarda

Bahía de Los Angeles

Isla del Tiburón

Punta Prieta

Bahía de Sebastián Vizcaíno

Isla Cedros

Parque Natural de Ballena Gris

Scammon's Lagoon

1

Guerrero Negro

El Arco

Desierto de Vizcaíno

BAJA

Pta. San Gabriel

San Ignacio

CALIFORNIA

Laguna de San Ignacio

SUR

N

PACIFIC OCEAN

0   100 miles

0   150 km

TO BAHÍA MAGDELENA

an agricultural community said to be the windiest spot in Baja. Sport-fishing is particularly good here, and tourism fluctuates with the reports of successful catches. Farther south are turnoffs for a dirt road to San Felipe and a paved road to Bahía de los Angeles, a formerly remote bay beloved by fishermen and naturalists.

At the end of the northern section of Baja, 595 km (370 mi) from Ensenada, stands a steel monument in the form of an eagle, 138 ft high. It marks the border between the states of Baja California and Baja California Sur, and the time changes from Pacific to Mountain as you cross that 28th parallel. Guerrero Negro, Baja Sur's northernmost town, with hotels and gas stations, is 2 km (1 mi) south.

Tijuana

29 km (18 mi) south of San Diego.

Tijuana is the only part of Mexico many people see, and it gives a distorted view of the country's many cultures. Before the city became a gigantic recreation center for southern Californians, it was a ranch populated by a few hundred Mexicans. In 1911 a group of Americans invaded the area and attempted to set up an independent republic; they were quickly driven out by Mexican soldiers. When Prohibition hit the United States in the 1920s and the Agua Caliente Racetrack and Casino opened (1929), Tijuana boomed. Americans seeking alcohol, gambling, and more fun than they could find back home flocked across the border, spending freely and fueling the region's growth. Tijuana became the entry port for what some termed a "sinful, steamy playground" frequented by Hollywood stars and the idle rich.

Then Prohibition was repealed, Mexico outlawed gambling, and Tijuana's fortunes declined. Although the flow of travelers from the north slowed to a trickle for a while, Tijuana still captivated those in search of the sort of fun that was illegal or just frowned upon at home. The ever-growing numbers of servicemen stationed in San Diego kept Tijuana's sordid reputation alive, and southern Californians continued to cross the border to explore the foreign culture and landscape. Drivers heading into Baja's wilderness passed through downtown Tijuana, stopping along Avenida Revolución and its side streets for supplies and souvenirs.

When the toll highway to Ensenada was finished in 1967, travelers bypassed the city and tourism dropped again. But Tijuana began attracting residents from throughout Latin America. The city's population mushroomed from a mere 300,000 in 1970 to more than 2 million today. The city has spread into canyons and dry riverbeds, over hillsides, and onto ocean cliffs. As the government struggles to keep up with the growth and demand for services, thousands live without electricity, running water, or adequate housing in squatters' villages along the border. Crime is now a significant problem in Tijuana. The fall of the peso caused many Mexicans from the interior to move to the border in search of work at all levels of industry. Poverty is vast, and petty crime is on the rise. Moreover, the area has become headquarters for serious drug cartels, and violent crime—reaching the highest levels of law enforcement and business—is booming. You're unlikely to witness a shooting or some other frightening situation, but be mindful of your surroundings and guard your belongings.

City leaders, realizing that tourism creates jobs and bolsters Tijuana's fragile economy, are working hard to attract visitors. Avenida Revolución, the main street that was once lined with brothels and bars, now has a lineup of shopping arcades and pseudo-Mexican restaurants and bars that cater to (often rowdy) tourists. The city has an international airport; a fine cultural center that presents professional music, dance, and theater groups from throughout the world; and deluxe high-rise hotels. The demand for high-end accommodations has increased with the growth of *maquiladoras* (foreign manufacturing plants). Casual tourists tend to visit for the day or one night. Although it's no longer considered just a bawdy border town, the city remains best known as a place for an intense, somewhat exotic day-long adventure.

Tijuana's tourist attractions have remained much the same throughout the century. The impressive El Palacio Frontón (Jai Alai Palace), where betting is allowed, draws crowds of cheering fans to its fast-paced matches. Some of Mexico's greatest bullfighters appear at the oceanfront and downtown bullrings, and an extraordinary number of places in town provide good food and drink.

And then, of course, there's shopping. From the moment you cross the border, people will approach you or call out and insist that you look at their wares. If you drive, workers will run out from auto-body shops to place bids on new paint or upholstery for your car. All along Avenida Revolución and its side streets, shops sell everything from tequila to Tiffany-style lamps. Serious shoppers can spend a full day searching and bargaining for their items of choice. If you intend to buy food in Mexico, get the U.S. customs list of articles that are illegal to bring back so that your purchases won't be confiscated.

① At the **San Ysidro Border Crossing,** locals and tourists jostle each other along the pedestrian walkway through the Viva Tijuana dining and shopping center and into the center of town. Artisans' stands line the walkway and adjoining streets, offering a quick overview of the wares to be found all over town.

② Tijuana's main tourism zone has long been the infamous **Avenida Revolución,** lined with an array of tacky shops and restaurants that cater to uninhibited travelers. Shopkeepers call out from their doorways, offering low prices for an odd assortment of garish souvenirs. Many shopping arcades open onto Avenida Revolución; inside the front doors are mazes of stands with low-priced pottery and other crafts.

③ The magnificent Moorish-style **El Palacio Frontón** (Jai Alai Palace) is an exciting place to watch and bet on fast-paced jai alai games. Next door, at a large branch of the Caliente Race Book, bettors wager on horse races and sports events broadcast from California via satellite TV (☞ Greyhound Races *in* Outdoor Activities and Sports, *below*).

④ Most of Baja's legendary wineries are in the Ensenada region, but Tijuana now has a branch of the **L.A. Cetto Winery.** You can tour the bottling plant, sample the wine, and spend as long as you like in the gift and wine shop. ✉ *Cañon Johnson 8151, at Av. Constitución,* ☎ *66/85–30–31 or 66/85–16–44.* 🎫 *$1 for tour, $2 for tour and wine tasting.* ☉ *Tues.–Sun. 10–5.*

⑤ **Mundo Divertido** is a popular family attraction in the Río zone. The amusement park includes a miniature golf course, batting cages, bumper boats, go-carts, a roller coaster, and a video-game parlor. A food court with hot dogs, burgers, and tacos will keep the kids happy. Admission is free, and the rides cost just a few pesos. ✉ *Paseo de los Héroes at Calle Velasco,* ☎ *66/34–32–13 or 66/34–32–14.* ☉ *Weekdays noon–9, weekends 11–10.*

⑥ The **Río Tijuana** area—as the section that runs along Avenida Paseo de los Héroes parallel to the dry Tijuana River is called—is one of the city's main thoroughfares, with large statues of historical figures, including

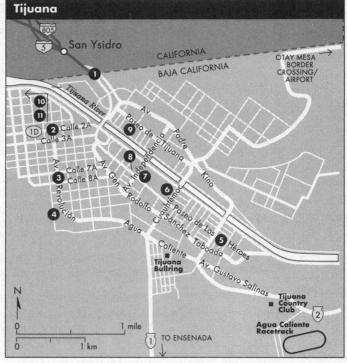

Abraham Lincoln. With its impressive ☞ **Centro Cultural**, several shopping complexes, fine restaurants, and fashionable discos, this part of town rivals Avenida Revolución for tourists' as well as locals' attention. ⊠ *Between Blvd. Agua Caliente and the border.*

⑦ Plaza Río Tijuana, the area's largest shopping complex, has good restaurants, department stores, hundreds of shops, and a multiplex theater where at least one English-language film is usually shown. Shade trees and flowers line the sidewalks that lead from the shopping complex to the Cultural Center. ⊠ *Paseo de los Héroes, across from the Centro Cultural.*

⑧ The **Centro Cultural** (Cultural Center) was designed by architects Manuel Rosen and Pedro Ramírez Vásquez, who also created Mexico City's famous Museum of Anthropology. The center's exhibits of Mexican history are a good introduction for first-time visitors to Mexico. The Omnimax Theater, with its curved 180-degree screen, shows films on a rotating schedule, often coinciding with temporary exhibits. An English-language film is usually in the lineup. Exhibits on art and culture change frequently. The center's bookstore has an excellent selection on Mexican history, culture, and arts in both Spanish and English. ⊠ *Paseo de los Héroes and Av. Independencia,* ☎ *66/84–11–11 or 66/84–11–25.* ▧ *Museum $2, museum and Omnimax Theater $3.50.* ☉ *Daily 9–8.*

⑨ The **Pueblo Amigo** entertainment center was built to resemble a colonial Mexican village, replete with stucco facades and tree-lined pathways leading to a domed gazebo. The complex includes the fanciest hotel near downtown, several restaurants and clubs, a huge grocery store, and a large branch of the Caliente Race Book, where gambling on televised races and sporting events is legal. ⊠ *Paseo Tijuana between Puente Mexico and Av. Independencia.*

⑩ **Playas Tijuana,** along the oceanfront, is a mix of modest and expensive residential neighborhoods, with a few restaurants and hotels. The isolated beaches are visited mostly by residents.

⑪ **Plaza de Toros Monumental,** the "Bullring by the Sea" (☞ Bullfighting *in* Outdoor Activities and Sports, *below*), sits at the northwest corner of the beach area near the U.S. border. The bullring is occasionally used for summer concerts.

Dining and Lodging

$$$ ✕ **Cien Años.** Mexican haute cuisine is all the rage on the mainland but has been slow to appear in Baja. This gracious Spanish colonial–style restaurant has met the need with aplomb, offering *crepas de huitlacoche* (a mushroomlike corn delicacy), beet salad, shrimp with nopal cactus, and tender beef covered with avocado and cheese. Each dish has an unusual blend of flavors—tamarind, Mexican oregano, mango, poblano chilies—that elevates the taste of even common appetizers such as *queso fundido* (melted cheese wrapped in tortillas). The soothing decor and service make for a special night out. ⊠ *Av. José María 1407, in the Zona Río,* ☎ *66/34–30–39. MC, V.*

$$ ✕ **El Faro de Mazatlán.** Fresh fish prepared simply is the hallmark of one of Tijuana's best seafood restaurants. This is the place to try ceviche, abalone, squid, and lobster without spending a fortune. Meals start with savory soup and crusty rolls. Frequented by professionals from nearby offices, the dining room is a peaceful spot for a long, leisurely lunch. Appetizers and soup are included in the price of the meal. ⊠ *Blvd. Sanchez Taboada 9542,* ☎ *66/84–88–82. MC, V.*

$$ ✕ **La Fonda de Roberto.** Roberto's is the best restaurant in Tijuana for traditional cuisine from the diverse culinary regions of Mexico. Try the *chiles en nogada* (chilies stuffed with raisins and meat and topped with cream and pomegranate seeds), meats with spicy *achiote* (a blend of seasonings) sauce, and many varieties of mole. Portions are small, so order liberally and share samples of many dishes. ⊠ *La Siesta Motel, Blvd. Cuauhtémoc Suroeste 2800 (also called Old Ensenada Hwy.), near Blvd. Agua Caliente,* ☎ *66/86–46–87. MC, V.*

$$ ✕ **La Taberna Española.** A mainstay of Plaza Fiesta's multiethnic cafés, this Spanish tapas bar attracts a youthful, sophisticated crowd. The menu is printed in Spanish, but with a bit of luck you should be able to select an interesting sampling, such as octopus basted in its own ink, spicy sausages, and Spanish tortilla with potatoes, eggs, and fava beans. The café is smoky and invariably crowded; outdoor tables have excellent people-watching. ⊠ *Plaza Fiesta, Paseo de los Héroes 10001,* ☎ *66/84–75–62. No credit cards.*

$ ✕ **Carnitas Uruapan.** You'll need to take a cab to this festive restaurant, where patrons mingle at picnic tables and toast one another to live mariachi music. The main attraction here is *carnitas* (marinated pork roasted over an open pit), sold by weight and served with homemade tortillas, salsa, cilantro, guacamole, and onions. ⊠ *Blvd. Díaz Ordaz 550,* ☎ *66/81–61–81;* ⊠ *Paseo de los Héroes at Av. Rodríguez,* ☎ *no phone. No credit cards.*

$ ✕ **La Especial.** At the foot of the stairs leading to an underground shop-
★   ping arcade, this place serves up home-style Mexican cooking at low prices. The gruff, efficient waiters, decked out in black slacks and vests, shuttle platters of *carne asada* (grilled strips of marinated meat), enchiladas, and burritos, all with a distinctive flavor found only at this busy, cavernous basement dining room. ⊠ *Av. Revolución 718,* ☎ *66/ 85–66–54. No credit cards.*

$ ✕ **Señor Frog's.** Heaping plates of barbecued chicken and ribs and buckets of ice-cold bottles of *cerveza* (beer) are the mainstay at this fun and festive formula eatery, one of many in the Carlos Anderson chain. The loud music and laughter make for a raucous atmosphere, and the food is consistently good. ⊠ *Pueblo Amigo center, Paseo Tijuana,* ☎ *66/ 82–49–64. AE, MC, V.*

$$$ 🏨 **Camino Real.** Elegant and fashionable, this branch of one of Mexico's best hotel chains opened in 1996 near the Centro Cultural—an ideal spot for walking to most attractions. Rooms are plushly decorated in browns and gold and have in-room fax lines and direct-dial phones. ⊠ *Paseo de los Héroes 10305, 22320,* ☎ *66/33–40–00, 800/ 722–6466,* FAX *66/33–40–01. 235 rooms, 15 suites. Restaurant, 2 bars, room service, laundry service. AE, MC, V.* 🕮

$$$ 🏨 **Grand Hotel.** The twin, mirrored towers of the hotel and a high-rise office building are Tijuana's most ostentatious landmarks. The hotel's atrium restaurant is a favorite lunch and Sunday brunch spot. The rooms used to be the nicest in town, but new hotels have upped the standards. Still, it's a good spot for business travelers and anyone looking for moderately priced luxury. The hotel mall has an Internet café. ⊠ *Blvd. Agua Caliente 4500, 22420,* ☎ *66/81–70–00, 01–800/02–66–007, 800/ 472–6385,* FAX *66/81–70–16. 422 rooms. Restaurant, pool, 2 tennis courts, exercise room, shops, nightclub, travel services. AE, MC, V.*

$$$ 🏨 **Holiday Inn Vita Spa Agua Caliente.** It's hard to resist this quirky hotel, despite its odd location. Set between two major boulevards on a landscaped island, the building stands beside the underground thermal spring that fed the pools at the 1920s-era Agua Caliente Spa. Today's rooms aren't as luxurious as in the past, although they're perfectly modern and sufficiently comfortable. But the true star of the property is the Vita Spa, with individual and couples' hot tubs fed from the hot, healing spring. Facials, massage, soothing mud wraps, and a cozy relaxation room make the spa a perfect weekend retreat. The Café La Faraona is good enough to attract the ladies who lunch from nearby wealthy neighborhoods. ⊠ *Paseo de los Héroes 18818, Zona Río 22320,* ☎ *66/34–69–01, 888/848–2928,* FAX *66/34–69–12. 122 rooms, 5 suites. Restaurant, pool, spa. AE, MC, V.* 🕮

$$$ 🏨 **Lucerna.** Once one of the most charming hotels in Tijuana, the Lucerna is now showing its age. Still, the lovely gardens, large pool surrounded by palms, touches of tile work, and folk art lend Mexican character to the hotel. ⊠ *Paseo de los Héroes 10902, at Av. Rodríguez, 22320,* ☎ *66/64–70–00, 01–800/02–66–300, 800/582–3762,* FAX *66/ 34–24–00. 167 rooms, 11 suites. Restaurant, coffee shop, pool, nightclub, travel services. MC, V.* 🕮

$$ 🏨 **Otay Bugambilias.** Proximity to the Tijuana airport and the Otay Mesa manufacturing plants makes this modest hotel a great find. The pink three-story building has motel-like rooms; suites have kitchenettes. The hotel offers free transportation to and from the Tijuana airport. ⊠ *Blvd. Industrial at Carretera Aeropuerto, 22450,* ☎ *66/23– 76–00, 01/800–66–426, 800/472–1153. 132 rooms, 9 suites. Restaurant, bar, pool, exercise room. AE, MC, V.*

$ 🏨 **La Villa de Zaragoza.** This brown stucco motel is such a success that the management keeps adding rooms; the newest have kitchenettes, and all offer air-conditioning and cable TV. The location, near the Jai Alai Palace and one block from Avenida Revolución, is ideal. The neighborhood can be noisy, however, and it's best to choose a room at the back. The guarded parking lot is a major plus, although you won't need a car if you stay here. The motel is used by tour groups, so book ahead for holidays and weekends. ⊠ *Av. Madero 1120, 22000,* ☎ *66/ 85–18–32,* FAX *66/85–18–37. 66 rooms. Restaurant, parking. MC, V.*

Nightlife and the Arts

Tijuana has toned down its Sin City image, but there are still plenty of raucous bars on Avenida Revolución. Locals, however, prefer the classier nightclubs in the Zona Río. Tijuana's discos usually have strict dress codes—no T-shirts, jeans, or sandals allowed.

The **Hard Rock Cafe** (⊠ Av. Revolución 520, between Calles 1 and 2, ☎ 66/85–02–06) has the same menu and decor as other branches of the ubiquitous club. This one, too, is popular with families and singles. The sophisticated disco set frequents **Como Que No** (⊠ Av. Sanchez Taboada 95, ☎ 66/84–27–91). For a change of pace from the dance-club scene, try **Dime Que Si** (☎ 66/84–27–91), a romantic piano bar. **Baby Rock** (⊠ Calle Diego Rivera 1482, Zona Río, ☎ 66/34–24–04), an offshoot of a popular Acapulco disco, attracts a young, hip crowd. **Rodeo la Media Noche** (⊠ Pueblo Amigo center, Paseo Tijuana, Zona Río, ☎ 66/82–49–67) has three levels of dance floors with a musical combination of recorded disco, live *norteño* bands, and romantic ballads. The scene includes a live indoor rodeo on weekends.

Outdoor Activities and Sports

BULLFIGHTING

Bullfights feature skilled matadors from throughout Mexico and Spain. Fights are held at **El Toreo de Tijuana** (⊠ Blvd. Agua Caliente, outside downtown, ☎ 66/85–22–10) Sunday at 4, May through October. In July and August you can see bullfights at the **Plaza de Toros Monumental** (⊠ Playas Tijuana area, Ensenada Hwy., ☎ 66/85–22–10) Sunday at 4. Admission to bullfights varies, depending on the fame of the matador and the location of your seat.

GOLF

The **Tijuana Country Club** (⊠ Blvd. Agua Caliente, east of downtown, ☎ 66/81–78–55) is open to the public and features golf pro Victor Regalado, Mexico's only two-time PGA champion. You can rent clubs, electric and hand carts, and caddies for the 18-hole course.

GREYHOUND RACES

At the **Hipódromo de Agua Caliente** (⊠ Blvd. Agua Caliente at Salinas, ☎ 66/81–78–11, 01/800–745–2252, 619/231–1910 in CA), greyhounds race nightly at 7:45 and weekend afternoons at 2. Wagering on horse races broadcast via satellite is also available.

JAI ALAI

This ancient Basque sport is played in the Moorish-style **El Palacio Frontón,** or Jai Alai Palace (⊠ Av. Revolución and Calle 8, ☎ 66/38–43–08). Matinee games start at noon Monday and Friday; night games start at 8 Tuesday through Saturday. General admission is $5.

Shopping

The Avenida Revolución shopping area spreads across Calle 1 to the pedestrian walkway leading from the border. Begin by checking out the stands along the border-crossing walkway, comparing prices as you travel toward Avenida Revolución. You may find that the best bargains are closer to the border; you can pick up your piñatas and serapes on your way out of town. The traditional shopping strip is Avenida Revolución between Calles 1 and 8; it's lined with shops and arcades that display a wide range of crafts and curios. Bargaining is expected on the streets and in the arcades, but not in the finer shops.

The shops in **Plaza Revolución** (⊠ Calle 1 and Av. Revolución) sell quality crafts. **Bazar de Mexico** (⊠ Av. Revolución at Calle 7, ☎ 66/86–52–80) is a huge complex of shops and stalls carrying the full gamut of Tijuana treasures. The **Mexicoach Termina** (⊠ Av. Revolución between Calles 6 and 7, ☎ 66/85–14–70) is a one-stop center. **La Piel** (⊠ Av. Revolución between Calles 4 and 5, ☎ 66/87–23–98) offers dependable quality in its leather jackets, backpacks, and luggage. **Ralph**

Lauren Polo Outlet (✉ Viva Tijuana Center, ☎ 66/88–76–98) is a licensed outlet for the designer's sportswear.

Sanborns (✉ Av. Revolución at Calle 8, ☎ 66/88–14–62) has beautiful crafts from throughout Mexico, an excellent bakery, and chocolates from Mexico City. **Sara's** (✉ Av. Revolución at Calle 4, ☎ 66/88–29–32), one of the best department stores in Tijuana, features a wide selection of imported perfumes and fine clothing at attractive prices. The nicest folk-art store, **Tolan** (✉ Av. Revolución between Calles 7 and 8, ☎ 66/88–36–37), carries everything from antique, carved wooden doors to tiny, ceramic miniature village scenes.

MARKET

The **Mercado Hidalgo** (✉ Av. Independencia at Av. Sanchez Taboada, 2 blocks south of Paseo de los Héroes) is Tijuana's municipal market, with rows of fresh produce, grains, herbs, some souvenirs, and the best selection of piñatas in Baja.

SHOPPING CENTERS

Plaza Fiesta (✉ Paseo de los Héroes, across from Plaza Río Tijuana) has a collection of boutiques, jewelry stores, and stained-glass shops. You can find great buys on fashionable clothing and shoes at **Plaza Río Tijuana** (✉ Paseo de los Héroes).

Playas de Rosarito

29 km (18 mi) south of Tijuana.

For better or worse, Rosarito has seen a transformation during the past few decades. The one-time small seaside community, once part of the municipality of Tijuana, had been an overlooked suburb on the way to the port city of Ensenada. But as the roads improved—and particularly after the 1973 completion of Baja's Transpeninsular Highway—Rosarito began to flower. Cityhood didn't come until 1995, when a group of residents led by Rosarito Beach Hotel owner Hugo Torres (now mayor) finally succeeded in its years-long campaign for the town's self-governance. The following year, Rosarito attracted considerable attention when 20th Century Fox built a permanent movie-production studio on the coastline south of town; the mega-success *Titanic* was shot here in 1996 and 1997. Today, much anticipation surrounds the completion of an immense pier and marina being built at the Rosarito Beach Hotel, with restaurants and shops sprouting up to meet the projected influx of tourists.

Meanwhile, Rosarito's population, now about 110,000, has been growing steadily. The city's main drag, alternately known as the Old Ensenada Highway and Boulevard Benito Juárez, reflects the unrestrained growth and speculation that have both helped and harmed Rosarito. The street is packed with restaurants, bars, and shops in a jarring juxtaposition of building styles, with some of the largest developments halted midway for lack of investors. As a result, the city has lost much of its charm; some find it downright ugly.

It nevertheless remains a relaxing place to visit—if you're here on a weekday when few tourists are in town. Southern Californians have practically made Rosarito a weekend suburb, and the crowd is far from subdued. Surfers, swimmers, and sunbathers come here to enjoy the beach, one of the longest in northern Baja; it stretches from the power plant at the north end of town to about 8 km (5 mi) south. Horseback riding, jogging, and strolling are popular along this uninterrupted strand, where whales swim within viewing distance on their winter migration and dolphins and sea lions frequent the shoreline.

Rosarito has always attracted a varied group. These days it's made up of prosperous young Californians building villas and vacation developments, retired Americans and Canadians homesteading in gated communities, and an abundance of young adults seeking cheap food, drink, and an escape from supervision. It often seems that spring break is a year-round event here, and families with small children might be offended by the rowdy behavior. The police do their best to control the revelers, but weekend nights can be outrageously noisy. If you're here to relax in peace, choose a hotel room far from any bars or restaurants.

Hedonism and health get equal billing in Rosarito. Seafood is a favorite here, especially lobster, shrimp, and abalone, and visiting Americans act as if they've been dry for months—margaritas and beer are the favored thirst quenchers. People throw off their inhibitions, at least to the degree permitted by local constables. A typical Rosarito day might begin with a breakfast of eggs, refried beans, and tortillas, followed by a few hours of horseback riding on the beach. Lying in the sun or browsing in shops takes care of midday. Siestas are imperative and are usually followed by more shopping, strolling, or sunbathing before a night of dinner and dancing.

Rosarito has few historic or cultural attractions, beaches and bars being the main draws. Sightseeing consists of strolling along the beach or down **Boulevard Benito Juárez,** which runs parallel to it. An immense Pemex gasoline installation and electric plant anchor the northern end of Boulevard Juárez, which then runs along a collection of shopping arcades, restaurants, and motels.

Dining and Lodging

$$ ✕ **Calafia.** This restaurant, a 10-minute car ride south of Rosarito, is part of a whitewashed stucco complex that houses an eclectic array of attractions—all perched above the crashing sea. The walls are a nascent museum dedicated to the missionary conquests in Baja. There's also a *Titanic* theme here, including the Titanic Dining Salon, which incorporates actual set discards from the nearby studio where the blockbuster was filmed. Featuring fresh seafood and creative Mexican cuisine, Calafia is a unique place to enjoy a meal by the sea. Or you can just have a drink on one of the cliff-side terraces. ⊠ *Old Ensenada Hwy. Km 35.5,* ☎ *661/2–15–81, 800/225–2342,* FAX *661/2–15–80. MC, V.*

$$ ✕ **La Leña.** The cornerstone restaurant of the Quinta Plaza shopping
★   center, La Leña is spacious and impeccably clean, with the tables spread far enough apart for privacy. Try any of the beef dishes, especially the tender carne asada with tortillas and guacamole. ⊠ *Quinta Plaza, Blvd. Juárez,* ☎ *661/2–08–26. MC, V.*

$$ ✕ **El Nido.** A dark, wood-paneled restaurant with leather booths and a large central fireplace, this is one of the oldest eateries in Rosarito. Diners unimpressed with newer, fancier places come here for mesquite-grilled steaks and for grilled quail from the owner's farm in the Baja wine country. ⊠ *Blvd. Juárez 67,* ☎ *661/2–14–30. No credit cards.*

$$ ✕ **El Patio.** Calm amid the bustle of the Festival Plaza complex, this tasteful, colonial-style restaurant is the best spot for a relaxed, authentic Mexican meal. Umbrella-covered tables are framed by soft blue and azure walls, and the aromas of chilies, mole, and grilled meats spark the appetite. The menu favors dishes like savory grilled quail, shrimp crepes, and chicken with poblano sauce. The bar is peaceful as well—a good place to enjoy a cocktail away from the streetside crowds. ⊠ *Festival Plaza, Blvd. Juárez,* ☎ *661/2–29–50. AE, MC, V.*

$ ✕ **La Flor de Michoacán.** Michoacán-style carnitas, served with homemade tortillas, guacamole, and salsa, are featured at this rustic Rosarito landmark, established in 1950. The tacos, *tortas* (sandwiches), and tostadas are great. Takeout is available. ✉ *Blvd. Juárez 291,* ☎ *661/ 2–18–58. No credit cards. Closed Wed.*

$$$ ▦ **Marriott Real Del Mar Residence Inn.** Golfers and escapists relish
★ their privacy at this cliffside all-suites hotel with faraway views of the
sea. Standard accommodations have living rooms with vaulted brick
ceilings, fireplaces, kitchens, and two double beds. Larger units come
with one or two bedrooms. Greens fees at the on-site golf course are
included in packages. The hotel, 19 km (12 mi) south of downtown
Tijuana and 10 km (6 mi) north of Rosarito Beach, is completely re-
moved from the action. The restaurant serves good seafood and Mex-
ican dishes. ✉ *Ensenada toll road Km 19.5, 22710,* ☎ *66/31–36–70,
800/331–3131,* 🖷 *66/31–36–77. 75 suites. Restaurant, bar, snack bar,
pool, spa, 18-hole golf course, exercise room. AE, MC, V.* ✦

$$$ ▦ **Rosarito Beach Hotel and Spa.** In the heart of Rosarito, this resort
is a piece of local history. Built during the Prohibition, it has huge ball-
rooms, tile public facilities, murals, and a glassed-in pool deck overlooking the sea. Rooms aren't as impressive. Those in the tower have
air-conditioning; some in the original building (which doesn't have air-
conditioning) are run down. Reduced midweek rates and special packages are often available. A refurbished 1930s mansion next door
houses Casa Playa Spa, with massage, beauty treatments, exercise
equipment, and hot tubs. Chabert's, the resort's French restaurant, is
as impressive for its decor as it is for the food. ✉ *Blvd. Juárez, south
end of town, 22710 (Box 430145, San Diego, CA 22710),* ☎ *661/2–
01–44, 661/2–11–26, 800/343–8582 in Mexico and the U.S.,* 🖷 *661/
2–11–25. 186 rooms, 89 suites. 3 restaurants, bar, 2 pools, spa, tennis court, exercise room, beach, playground. MC, V.* ✦

$$ ▦ **Festival Plaza.** Designed with unrestrained fun in mind, Festival Plaza
is geared toward a youthful crowd. The motel-like rooms are in an eight-
story building with a facade resembling a roller coaster. The casitas (in
the $$$ range) close to the beach are the quietest accommodations and
have small hot tubs, separate living rooms with foldout couches, and
private garages, but no kitchen facilities. The hotel also operates a complex of 13 villas just south of Rosarito; these have full kitchens. Within
the hotel complex are several bars and good restaurants—try the traditional Mexican dishes at El Patio—and the central courtyard serves
as a concert stage, children's playground, and party headquarters.
Discounted room rates are often available, especially in winter. ✉
Blvd. Juárez 11, 22710, ☎ *661/2–08–42, 661/2–29–50, 800/453–
8606,* 🖷 *661/2–01–24. 127 rooms, 5 suites, 7 casitas, 13 villas. 7 restaurants, 6 bars, pool, dance club. AE, MC, V.*

$ ▦ **Brisas del Mar.** A modern motel (built in 1992), the Brisas del Mar
is especially good for families—the large pastel rooms comfortably accommodate four people. A few of the suites on the second story have
hot tubs and ocean views; all have air-conditioning and TV. The motel
is on the inland side of Boulevard Juárez, and traffic noise can be a
problem. ✉ *Blvd. Juárez 22, 22710 (Box 18903, Coronado, CA
92178–9003),* ☎ 🖷 *661/2–25–47. 69 rooms, 2 suites. Bar, coffee
shop, pool. AE, MC, V.*

Nightlife and the Arts

Rosarito's many restaurants keep customers entertained with live
music, piano bars, or *folklórico* (folk music and dance) shows, and the
bar scene is hopping as well. Drinking-and-driving laws are stiff; the
police will fine you no matter how little you've had. If you plan to drink,
take a cab or assign a designated driver.

There's a lot going on at night at the **Rosarito Beach Hotel** (✉ Blvd.
Juárez, ☎ 661/2–01–44): live music at the ocean-view **Beachcomber
Bar** and **Hugo's**; a Mexican Fiesta on Friday night; and occasional live

bands and dances in the cavernous ballroom. **Papas and Beer** (⊠ Blvd. Juárez near Rosarito Beach Hotel, ☎ 661/2–02–44 or 661/2–04-44) draws a young, energetic crowd. The **Festival Plaza** (⊠ Blvd. Juárez 11, ☎ 661/2–08–42) has become party central for Rosarito's younger crowd and presents live concerts on the hotel's courtyard stage most weekends. In the hotel complex are **El Museo Cantina Tequila** (☎ 661/2–29–50)—locals call it the Rattlesnake Bar—dedicated to the art of imbibing tequila and stocked with more than 130 brands of the fiery drink, and **Rock & Roll Taco**—as its name suggests, a taco stand and boisterous bar all in one. A new **Señor Frog's**, (⊠ Blvd. Juárez 1 block north of the Festival Plaza) offers a raucous blend of tequila and loud music. **Rene's Sports Bar** (⊠ Carretera Transpeninsular Km 28, ☎ 661/2–74–84) draws a somewhat quieter, older crowd; the restaurant isn't great, but a few pool tables, TVs broadcasting sporting events, and a convivial gaggle of gringos make the bar a great hangout.

Outdoor Activities and Sports

GOLF

The **Real del Mar Golf Club** (⊠ 18 km [11 mi] south of the border on Ensenada toll road, ☎ 66/31–34–01) has 18 holes overlooking the ocean. Golf packages are available at some Rosarito Beach hotels.

HORSEBACK RIDING

You can hire horses at the north and south ends of Boulevard Juárez and on the beach south of the Rosarito Beach Hotel for $10 per hour. If you're a dedicated equestrian, ask about tours into the countryside, which can be arranged with the individual owners.

SURFING

The waves are particularly good at **Popotla** (Km 33), **Calafia** (Km 35.5), and **Costa Baja** (Km 36) on the Old Ensenada Highway. **Tony's Surf Shop** (⊠ Blvd. Juárez 312, ☎ 661/2–11–92) sells and rents surfing gear.

Shopping

Shopping is far better in Rosarito than in most Baja cities, especially for pottery, wood furniture, and high-end household items favored by condo-owners in nearby expat clusters. Curio stands and open-air artisans' markets line Boulevard Juárez both north and south of town. Major hotels have shopping arcades with restaurants, taco stands, and some decent crafts stores. A new shopping center being built in central Rosarito is to include Sanborns and Sara's, as well as more than 100 other stores.

You'll find an irresistible selection of Mexican folk art with a sea theme and creatively painted furnishings at **Interios del Río Casa del Arte y La Madera** (⊠ Quinta del Mar Plaza, ☎ 661/2–13–00). **Casa la Carreta** (⊠ Old Ensenada Hwy. Km 29, ☎ 661/2–05–02), one of Rosarito's best furniture shops, keeps expanding and is worth a visit just to see the wood-carvers shaping elaborate desks, dining tables, and armoires. **Don Quijote Furniture** (⊠ Blvd. Juárez s/n, across from Quinta Plaza, ☎ no phone) is a great outlet for custom furnishings and wrought iron. **The Cuban Cigar Shop** (⊠ Blvd. Juárez s/n, near the Rosarito Beach Hotel, ☎ no phone) is run by a Cubana who visits her homeland monthly, bringing back the requisite cigars along with art work, photos, and other Cuban novelties. **Pancho's Curios** (⊠ Blvd. Juárez, ☎ no phone) has a hodgepodge of blown glass, wrought iron, patio furniture, wooden masks, and pottery in the front yard and interior shop.

Casa Torres (⊠ Rosarito Beach Hotel Shopping Center, Blvd. Juárez, ☎ 661/2–10–08) carries a wide array of imported perfumes. **Margarita's**

(✉ Rosarito Beach Hotel Shopping Center, ☎ no phone) has a great selection of Guatemalan textiles and clothing. The shelves of **Taxco Curios** (✉ Quinta del Mar Plaza, ☎ 661/2–18–77) are filled with hand-blown glassware. **Apisa** (✉ Quinta del Mar Plaza, ☎ 661/2–01–25) sells state-of-the-art furnishings and iron sculpture from Guadalajara.

The **Calimax** grocery store on Boulevard Juárez is a good place to stock up on necessities.

Puerto Nuevo (Newport)

Old Ensenada Hwy. Km 44, 12 km (7½ mi) south of Rosarito.

Not so many years ago, the only way you could tell you'd reached this fishing community was by the huge mural of a 7UP bottle on the side of a building. You'd drive down the rutted dirt road to a row of restaurants, where you were served the classic Puerto Nuevo meal: grilled lobster, refried beans, rice, homemade tortillas, butter, salsa, and lime. The meal became a legend, and now at least 30 restaurants in the area offer the identical menu. An artisans' market sits at the entrance to the restaurant row, and stands selling pottery, serapes, and T-shirts line the highway. Several hotels have opened in the area, making Puerto Nuevo a self-contained destination where you can party day and night and not be concerned with the drive to hotels in Rosarito or Ensenada. Several longtime favorite inns and restaurants line the road south to Ensenada.

Dining and Lodging

Don't expect much variety in the food at any of the Puerto Nuevo restaurants: people come here for the classic lobster meal. Some places have full bars; others serve only wine and beer. **Ortega's,** with four branches in Puerto Nuevo and two in Rosarito, is the most crowded; **Ponderosa** is smaller and quieter and is run by a gracious family; **Costa Brava** is the most elegant, with tablecloths and an ocean view; and **La Casa de la Langosta** serves grilled fish along with lobster and shrimp. Lobsters in most places are priced as small, medium, and large—medium is about $15. Some of the lobster served in Puerto Nuevo comes from local waters during lobster season (October through March), although the supply can hardly keep up with the demand and most lobster is imported. There is some concern that the waters close to shore have become polluted, but the fishermen say they trap lobsters 1½ km (1 mi) or so offshore, where the waters are safe. Most places are open for lunch and dinner on a first-come, first-served basis. Some take credit cards.

$$ ✕🏠 **La Fonda.** A longtime favorite with beachgoers, La Fonda has well-★ worn rooms decorated with carved-wood furniture, old bullfighting posters, and local folk art; most rooms have great views of the ocean. There are no phones or televisions, just the sound of the surf and miles of empty beach to keep you entertained. At the restaurant you can sit on an outdoor patio and sip potent margaritas served with fresh lobster, grilled steaks, prime rib, and traditional Mexican dishes. The weekend brunch is a feast well worth a few hours of your time. The bar is packed on weekend nights, and the patrons boisterous. If you plan on getting any sleep, ask for a room as close to the sounds of the surf as possible. Credit cards are accepted at the restaurant and to reserve rooms, but accommodations have to be paid for in cash. ✉ *Old Ensenada Hwy. Km 59, 22710 (Box 430268, San Ysidro, CA 92143),* ☎ *615/5–03–07. 26 rooms. Restaurant, bar, beach. MC, V.*

$$$$ 🏠 **Sierra Plaza Bajamar.** On the grounds of the Bajamar golf resort, south of Puerto Nuevo and about halfway between Rosarito and Ensenada, this hacienda-style hotel surrounds a central courtyard. Rooms have hand-carved furnishings and French doors leading to landscaped

patios. Staying here can be peaceful except when golfers neglect to remove their shoes and clump around the brick hallways like herds of goats. Private condos (some for rent) edge the golf course and the cliffs overlooking the ocean. The rooms were refurbished in early 1999. ⊠ *Old Ensenada Hwy., Km 77.5, Ensenada 22800,* ☎ *615/5–01–51, or 619/299–1112 and 800/225–2418 in the U.S.,* ℻ *615/5–01–50. 81 rooms. Restaurant, bar, pool, 18-hole golf course, 2 tennis courts. AE, MC, V.* ✈

$$ ⛾ **Castillos Del Mar.** One of the few places with direct access to the beach, this small hotel has 34 rooms with basic amenities. Older and slightly run-down, Castillos is clean, fun, and inexpensive by local standards. Some rooms have terraces overlooking the beach. The bar gets hopping evenings, with live music most nights. ⊠ *Old Ensenada Hwy. Km 36.5, 22712,* ☎ *661/2–10–88. Restaurant, bar, pool. 34 rooms. No credit cards.*

$$ ⛾ **New Port Beach Hotel.** The closest accommodations to the lobster restaurants are in this sand-color complex with ocean views. Rooms don't have air-conditioning, but they do have heaters for chilly winter nights, along with cable TV, small balconies, and simple blue-gray and white furnishings. The hotel has dance bands in the upstairs lounge, marimba music on weekends in the lobby bar, and classical music on Sunday. ⊠ *Old Ensenada Hwy. Km 45, 22712,* ☎ *661/4–11–66, 800/ 582–1018,* ℻ *661/4–11–74. 147 rooms. Restaurant, bar, pool, 2 tennis courts, exercise room. MC, V.* ✈

$$ ⛾ **Las Rocas.** This white hotel with blue-tile domes is still the prettiest in the area, but it's beginning to look its age. The building is terraced up a hillside, giving all the rooms ocean views, but the accommodations aren't otherwise equal. The least expensive ones are small, with dripping faucets and worn furnishings. The most expensive are much larger and have fireplaces and microwaves. The pool and whirlpool seem to spill over the cliffs into the ocean. A full spa offers massage, facials, wraps, and other treatments. ⊠ *Old Ensenada Hwy. Km 37, 22710 (Box 189003 HLR, Coronado, CA 92178),* ☎ ℻ *661/ 2–21–40,* ☎ *619/234–9810 in CA, 800/733–6394 outside CA in U.S. 40 rooms, 34 suites. Restaurant, 2 bars, 2 pools, hot tub, spa, beach. AE, MC, V.* ✈

Outdoor Activities and Sports

GOLF

Bajamar (⊠ Old Ensenada Hwy. Km 77.5, ☎ 615/5–01–51, 615/5–01–61 for tee times), a 1976 course revamped and reopened in late 1993, has 18 holes of championship-level golf on the cliffs above the ocean and another nine holes near the beach.

En Route Open views of pounding surf and jagged cliffs are interspersed with one-of-a-kind hotels and restaurants along the coastline between Rosarito and Ensenada. The paved highway (Mexico Highway 1) between the two cities often cuts a path between low mountains and high oceanside cliffs. Exits lead to rural roads, oceanfront campgrounds, and an ever-increasing number of resort communities. The small fishing villages of **San Miguel** and **El Sauzal** sit off the highway to the north of Ensenada, and you can see the **Coronado Islands** clearly off the coast.

Ensenada

104 km (65 mi) south of Tijuana, 75 km (47 mi) south of Rosarito.

In 1542 Juan Rodríguez Cabrillo first discovered the seaport that Sebastián Vizcaino named Ensenada-Bahía de Todos Santos (All Saints' Bay) in 1602. Since then the town has drawn a steady stream of "discoverers" and developers. First ranchers made their homes on large plots along the coast and into the mountains. Gold miners followed, turning the area into a boomtown in the late 1800s. After mine stocks were depleted, the area settled back into a pastoral state, but the harbor gradually grew into a major port for shipping agricultural goods from the nearby ranches and farms. Today, with a population of some 300,000, it's one of Mexico's largest seaports and has a thriving fishing fleet and fish-processing industry. The smell of fish from the canneries lining the north and south sides of the city can be overpowering at times.

There are no beaches in Ensenada proper, but beaches north and south of town are satisfactory for swimming, sunning, surfing, and camping. On summer and holiday weekends the population swells, but the town rarely feels overcrowded. Whereas the hotels and resorts along the coast, especially around Rosarito, attract the bulk of the weekend escapists, Ensenada tends to draw those who want to explore a more traditional Mexican city.

In a concerted effort to attract vacationers, conventioneers, and business travelers, the waterfront area was razed and rebuilt, with taco stands replaced by shopping centers, hotels, and the massive Plaza Marina, a large shopping complex with few tenants. Cruise ships occasionally anchor in the port, bringing day-trippers for shopping and dining.

Ensenada, the third-largest city in Baja, hugs the harbor of Bahía de Todos Santos. As Alternate Highway 1 leads into town from the north, it becomes Boulevard Costero, running past shipyards filled with massive freighters.

⑫ **Parque Revolución** (Revolution Park) is the most traditional plaza in Ensenada, with a bandstand, playground, and plenty of benches in the shade. The plaza takes on a festive feeling Saturday and Sunday evenings, when neighbors congregate on the benches and children chase seagulls down the pathways. ⊠ *Av. Juárez at Av. Obregón.*

⑬ **Las Bodegas de Santo Tomás,** Baja's oldest winery, gives tours and tastings at its downtown winery and bottling plant. The restaurant in the winery, La Embotelladora Vieja (☞ Dining and Lodging, *below*), is one of Baja's finest. The winery also operates La Esquina de Bodegas (☞ Shopping, *below*), a café, shop, and gallery in a bright-blue building across Avenida Miramar. ⊠ *Av. Miramar 666,* ☎ *61/78–33–33, 619/454–7166 in the U.S.* ☎ *$2.* ☉ *Tours, tastings daily at 10, 11, noon, 1, and 3.*

The main street along the waterfront is Boulevard Costero. At its
⑭ northernmost point is an indoor-outdoor **Fish Market,** where row after row of counters displays piles of shrimp, tuna, dorado, marlin, snapper, and dozens of other species of fish caught off Baja's coasts. Outside, stands sell grilled or smoked fish, seafood cocktails, and fish tacos. Browsers can pick up some standard souvenirs, eat well for very little money, and take some great photographs. The original fish taco stands line the dirt path to the fish market. If your stomach is on the delicate side, try the fish tacos at the cleaner, quieter **Plaza de Mariscos** in the shadow of the giant beige **Plaza de Marina** that blocks the view of the traditional fish market from the street.

⑮ Fishing and whale-watching boats depart from the **Sportfishing Pier** (⊠ Blvd. Costero at Av. Alvarado). *See* Fishing *in* Outdoor Activities and Sports, *below,* for fishing and whale-watching information.

⑯ **Plaza Cívica** (⊠ Blvd. Costero at Av. Riveroll) is a block-long concrete park with sculptures of Mexican heroes Benito Juárez, Miguel Hidalgo, and Venustiano Carranza.

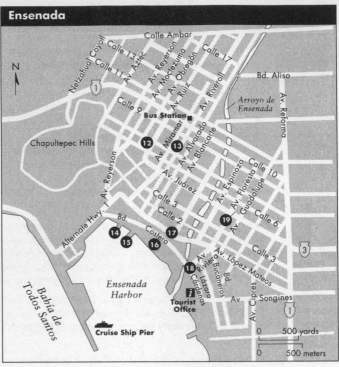

Ensenada

⑰ Ensenada's traditional tourist zone is centered along **Avenida López Mateos.** High-rise hotels, souvenir shops, restaurants, and bars line the avenue for eight blocks, from its beginning at the foot of the Chapultepec Hills to the dry channel of the Arroyo de Ensenada. Locals shop for furniture, clothing, and other necessities a few blocks inland on Avenida Juárez, in Ensenada's downtown area.

⑱ The **Riviera del Pacífico,** officially called the Centro Social, Cívico y Cultural de Ensenada (Social, Civic and Cultural Center of Ensenada), is a rambling white, hacienda-style mansion built in the 1920s with money raised on both sides of the border. An enormous gambling palace, hotel, restaurant, and bar, the glamorous Riviera was frequented by wealthy U.S. citizens and Mexicans, particularly during Prohibition. When gambling was outlawed in Mexico and Prohibition ended in the United States, the palace lost its raison d'être. You can tour some of the elegant ballrooms and halls, which occasionally host art shows and civic events. Many of the rooms are locked; check at the main office to see if there is someone available to show you around. The gardens alone are worth visiting, and the building now houses the **Museo de Historia de Ensenada,** a museum on Baja's history. ⊠ *Blvd. Costero and Av. Riviera,* ☎ *61/76–43–10, museum 61/76–05–94.* ☒ *Building and gardens free, museum $1.* ☼ *Tues.–Sun. 9–5.*

⑲ The city's largest cathedral, **Our Lady of Guadalupe** (⊠ Av. Floresta at Av. Juárez), is the heart of Ensenada for many residents.

OFF THE
BEATEN PATH

LA BUFADORA – Seawater splashes up to 75 ft in the air, spraying sightseers standing near this impressive tidal blowhole (*la bufadora* means the buffalo snort) in the coastal cliffs at **Punta Banda.** Legend has it that the blowhole was created by a whale or sea serpent trapped in an undersea cave; both these stories, and the less romantic scientific facts, are posted on a roadside plaque here. The road to La Bufadora along Punta Banda, an isolated, mountainous point that juts into the sea, is lined with stands selling olives, tamales, strands of chilies and garlic, and terra-cotta planters. The drive gives short-term visitors a sampling of Baja's wilderness and is well worth a half-day excursion. Public rest rooms are available. There is a small fee to park near the blowhole. From the lot, you file through a row of permanent vendors' stands en route to the cliff. ⊠ *Hwy. 23, 31 km (19 mi) south of Ensenada.*

Beaches
The waterfront in Ensenada proper is taken up by fishing boats, repair yards, and commercial shipping. The best swimming beaches are south of town. **Estero Beach** is long and clean, with mild waves; the Estero Beach Hotel takes up much of the oceanfront, but the beach is public. Surfers populate the beaches off Highway 1 north and south of Ensenada, particularly **San Miguel, California, Tres Marías,** and **La Joya;** scuba divers prefer **Punta Banda,** by La Bufadora. Lifeguards are rare, so swimmers should be cautious. The tourist office in Ensenada has a map that shows safe diving and surfing beaches.

Dining and Lodging
$$$ ✕ **La Embotelladora Vieja.** The most elegant restaurant in Ensenada
★ is this converted wine-aging room at the Santo Tomás winery. The decor is classic French country. The so-called Baja French menu includes appetizers of smoked tuna and French pâté; among the most sublime entrées are the grilled lobster in cabernet sauvignon sauce, beef Montpellier with green peppercorns, and quail with sauvignon blanc sauce. Teetotalers, note: Nearly every dish is prepared with wine, although much of the alcohol evaporates during cooking. You can order some dishes without alcohol-enhanced sauces. All of Baja's wineries are represented on the extensive wine list. ⊠ *Av. Miramar 666,* ☎ *61/74–08–07. MC, V. Closed Tues.*

$$$ ✕ **El Rey Sol.** From its chateaubriand *bouquetière* (garnished with a
★ bouquet of vegetables) to the savory chicken chipotle, this family-owned French restaurant sets the standard for fine dining in Baja. The decor at El Rey Sol, open since 1947, is comfortable and elegant, with Louis XIV–style furnishings, and the service is attentive. The sidewalk tables are also a perfect place to dine and enjoy the fresh air. Pastries, all made on the premises, can be bought to go from the small café in the front. ⊠ *Av. López Mateos 1000,* ☎ *61/78–17–33. AE, MC, V.*

$$ ✕ **Bronco's Steak House.** A great find near the San Nicolás Hotel, Bronco's serves exceptional steaks and Mexican specialties. Try the Boca del Rio, a New York steak stuffed with grilled onions and fiery serrano chilies. Tripe appears frequently on the menu, satisfying the cravings of the local diners gathered at many of the wood tables. Brick walls, wood-plank floors, and hanging spurs and chaps give the place a Wild West feel, but the mood is subdued and relaxed. ⊠ *Av. López Mateos 1525,* ☎ *61/72–48–92,* ꜰꜰ *61/76–49–10. MC, V.*

$$ ✕ **Casamar.** A long-standing, dependable restaurant, Casamar is known for its wide variety of excellent seafood. Lobster and shrimp are prepared in several ways but seem freshest when grilled *con mojo y ajo* (with butter and garlic). When ordering fish, always ask about the catch of the day; you might luck out and get a thick steak of fresh yellowfin tuna. ⊠ *Blvd. Lázaro Cárdenas 987,* ☎ *61/74–04–17. MC, V.*

$ ✕ **El Charro.** You can find less (and more) expensive rotisserie chicken,
★ beans, rice, and tortillas at other places downtown, but El Charro still attracts a steady stream of locals and tourists. Hungry patrons hover over platters of *chiles rellenos* (cheese-stuffed chilies deep-fried in batter), enchiladas, and fresh chips and guacamole at heavy wooden pic-

nic tables. Plump chickens slowly turn over a wood fire by the front window, and the aroma of mesquite and simmering beans fills the air. Similarly named restaurants have opened on the same block; stick with the original to avoid disappointment. ⊠ *Av. López Mateos 475,* ☎ *61/78–38–81. No credit cards.*

$ **✕ Mariscos de Bahía de Ensenada.** Red lights flicker around the front
★   door, making this popular seafood house just off the main drag easy to spot. The place is packed on weekends; tables are easier to come by weeknights. Clams, shrimp, lobster, red snapper, squid, and other fresh seafood are fried, baked, broiled, or grilled, and served with a basic iceberg-lettuce salad, white rice, and tortillas made fresh at the window-front tortilleria. A few canopied sidewalk tables allow for outdoor dining. ⊠ *Av. Riveroll 109,* ☎ *61/78–10–15. MC, V.*

$$$ **⌇ Hotel Coral & Marina.** The largest resort on the Baja Norte coast
★   features a marina with slips for 600 boats and customs-clearing facilities. The rooms in two eight-story towers are decorated in burgundy and dark green; most have waterfront balconies, seating areas, cable TV, and international phone service. Conventions, fishing and golf tournaments, and boat races fill the hotel on weekends; rates are often 30%–50% lower on winter weekdays. ⊠ *Carretera Transpeninsular Tijuana–Ensenada Km 103, No. 3421, Zona Playitas,* ☎ *61/75–00–00, 800/862–9020,* ℻ *61/75–00–05. 18 rooms, 129 suites. Restaurant, 1 indoor and 2 outdoor pools, hot tub, spa, 2 tennis courts, exercise room, dive shop, boating, fishing. MC, V.* ☙

$$$ **⌇ Punta Morro.** Just five minutes from Ensenada, this secluded all-suites
★   hotel is a great place to relax. The Punta Morro is popular with newlyweds, and, with its romantic-getaway package (which includes champagne and roses), it's known as a great place to pop the question. The restaurant, perched just above the crashing waves, features an excellent combination of Continental cuisine and fresh seafood; Continental breakfast is included and delivered to your door. All rooms have seaside terraces and fireplaces. Two- and three-bedroom suites are available for groups and families. ⊠ *Mexico Hwy. 1, 3 km (2 mi) north of town, Apdo. 2891, 22800 (Box 43-4263, San Ysidro, CA 92143),* ☎ *61/78–35–07, 800/526–6676,* ℻ *61/74–44–90. 30 suites. Restaurant, bar, pool, hot tub, beach. MC, V.* ☙

$$$ **⌇ Las Rosas.** This elegant all-suites hotel just north of Ensenada is both
★   intimate and upscale. The atrium lobby has marble floors, mint-green-and-pink couches that look out at the sea, and a glass ceiling that glows at night. All rooms face the ocean and pool; some have fireplaces and hot tubs, and even the least expensive are lovely. Las Rosas is booked solid most weekends—make reservations far in advance. *Mexico Hwy. 1 north of Ensenada (*⊠ *374 East H St., Suite A–455, Chula Vista, CA 91910),* ☎ *61/74–43–60, 800/522–1516 in AZ, CA, NV, 800/225–2786 elsewhere in the U.S. and Canada,* ℻ *61/74–45–95. 32 suites. Restaurant, bar, pool, hot tub. AE, MC, V.* ☙

$$ **⌇ Estero Beach Resort.** Families settle in for a week or more at this long-standing resort on Ensenada's best beach. The rooms (some with kitchenettes) are housed in several mint-green buildings. The best are those right by the sand; the worst (and cheapest) are in the oldest section, by the parking lot. No one expects anything fancy here, and at times it seems all the guests are attending huge wedding or birthday celebrations or family reunions. Guests spend their days swimming, fishing, riding horses, playing volleyball, and generally hanging out with friends. Nights are spent at the casual restaurant and bar. The resort is 10 km (6 mi) south of town. Midweek winter rates are a real bargain, and the resort feels almost deserted at this time. ⊠ *Mexico Hwy. 1 between Ensenada and Maneadero, 22810 (482 San Ysidro Blvd., Suite 1186, San Ysidro, CA 92173),* ☎ *61/76–62–35,* ℻ *61/76–69–*

25. 106 rooms, 2 suites. Restaurant, bar, kitchenettes, pool, 4 tennis courts, horseback riding, volleyball, shops, playground. MC, V.

$$ 🏨 **San Nicolás.** This hotel, tucked behind walls with Indian murals, was built in the early 1970s, but much of it has been refurbished since then. The suites have bedrooms with mirror ceilings, tile hot tubs, and living rooms with deep-green carpeting, mauve furnishings, and beveled-glass doors. Less extravagant rooms are comfortable and decorated with folk art. A waterfall cascades into the pool, and a good restaurant overlooks the gardens. Special rates are often available weekdays and in winter. ⊠ Av. López Mateos (also called Calle 1) and Av. Guadalupe, Apdo. 19, 22800 (Box 43706, San Diego, CA 92143), ☎ 61/76–19–01, 800/522–1516 in AZ, CA, NV, 800/225–2786 elsewhere in the U.S. and in Canada, FAX 61/76–49–30. 140 rooms and 10 suites. 2 restaurants, bar, 1 indoor and 1 outdoor pool, hot tub, dance club. AE, MC, V. ✍

$ 🏨 **Hotel del Valle.** Fishermen and budget travelers frequent the clean, basic rooms in this small hotel on a relatively quiet side street. Although the rooms lack air-conditioning, they do have fans, phones, and TVs (with local stations only). Guests have use of a coffeemaker in the lobby and parking spaces in front of the rooms. A new wing with 22 rooms was under construction at press time. Ask about rate discounts—those posted behind the front desk are about 40% higher than guests in the know normally pay. ⊠ Av. Riveroll 367, 22800, ☎ 61/78–22–24, FAX 61/74–04–66. 20 rooms. MC, V.

$ 🏨 **Joker Hotel.** A bizarre, colorful mishmash of styles makes it hard to miss the Joker, which is conveniently located for those traveling south of Ensenada. Spacious rooms have private balconies, satellite TV, and phones. Traffic noise from the highway and from guests leaving at the crack of dawn can be a problem; try to stay away from the road and the busiest parts of the parking lot. ⊠ Mexico Hwy. 1 Km 12.5, 22800, ☎ FAX 61/76–72–01. 40 rooms. Pool, hot tub. MC, V.

Nightlife and the Arts

Ensenada is a party town for college students, surfers, and other young tourists. **Hussong's Cantina** (⊠ Av. Ruíz 113, ☎ 61/74–07–20) has been an Ensenada landmark since 1892 and has changed little since then. A security guard stands by the front door to handle the often-rowdy crowd—a mix of locals and tourists of all ages over 18. The noise is usually deafening, pierced by mariachi and ranchera musicians and the whoops and hollers of the inebriated. **Papas and Beer** (⊠ Av. Ruíz at López Mateos, ☎ 61/74–01–45) attracts a collegiate crowd.

Outdoor Activities and Sports

FISHING

Boats leave the Ensenada **Sportfishing Pier** regularly. The best angling is from April through November, with bottom fishing good in the winter. Charter vessels and party boats are available from several outfitters along Avenida López Mateos and Boulevard Costero and off the sportfishing pier. Trips on group boats cost about $35 for a half day or $100 for a full day. Licenses are available at the tourist office or from charter companies.

Ensenada Clipper Fleet (⊠ Sportfishing Pier, Blvd. Costero at Av. Alvarado, ☎ 61/78–21–85) has charter and group boats. **Gordo's Sportfishing** (⊠ Sportfishing Pier, Blvd. Costero at Av. Alvarado, ☎ 61/78–35–15, FAX 61/78–23–77), one of the oldest sportfishing companies in Ensenada, has charter and group boats, and a smokehouse. You can book sportfishing packages including transportation, accommodations, and fishing through **Baja California Tours** (☎ 619/454–7166 in the U.S., FAX 619/454–2703).

The **Baja Country Club** (⊠ Mexico Hwy. 1 south of Ensenada at Maneadero, ☎ 61/73–03–03) has a secluded 18-hole course in a resort development.

Estero Beach and Punta Banda (en route to La Bufadora south of Ensenada) are both good kayaking areas, although facilities are limited. **Southwest Kayaks** (☎ 619/222–3616 in CA) offers occasional kayaking workshops at both areas.

Boats leave the Ensenada **Sportfishing Pier** for whale-watching trips from December through February. The gray whales migrating from the north to bays and lagoons in southern Baja pass through Todos Santos Bay, often close to shore. Viewers from boats usually can easily see the whales spouting and breaching not far from them. There are restrictions on how close the boats can get to the whales, so you won't be able to touch them, but you should be able to get good photos. Binoculars and telephoto camera lenses come in handy. The trips last about three hours. Vessels and tour boats are available from several outfitters, including Gordo's (☞ Fishing, *above*), along Avenida López Mateos and Boulevard Costero and off the sportfishing pier. You can book whale-watching packages, which include transportation, accommodations, and the boat trips, through **Baja California Tours** (☎ 619/454–7166 in the U.S., FAX 619/454–2703).

Shopping

Most of the tourist shops are located along Avenida López Mateos beside the hotels and restaurants. There are several two-story shopping arcades, many with empty shops. Dozens of curio shops line the street, all selling similar selections of pottery, woven blankets and serapes, embroidered dresses, and onyx chess sets.

Artes Don Quijote (⊠ Av. López Mateos 503, ☎ 61/76–94–76) has an impressive array of carved wood doors, huge terra-cotta pots, and crafts from Oaxaca. **Artesanías Castillo** (⊠ Av. López Mateos 656, ☎ 61/76–11–87) has a wide selection of silver jewelry from Taxco. **Carlos Importer** (⊠ Av. López Mateos at Alvarado, ☎ 61/78–24–63), one of the largest shops in town, sells high-quality pottery, tile, blown glassware, and iron furniture. At **Los Castillo** (⊠ Av. López Mateos 815, ☎ 61/76–11–87), the display of silver trinketry from Taxco is extensive. **Girasoles** (⊠ Av. López Mateos, ☎ no phone) stocks a great selection of dolls, pine-needle baskets, and pottery made by the Tarahumara Indians from the Copper Canyon. **La Mina de Salomón** (⊠ Av. López Mateos 1000, ☎ 61/78–28–36) carries elaborate jewelry in a tiny gallery next to El Rey Sol restaurant.

Maya Internacional (⊠ Av. López Mateos 724, ☎ 61/78–83–88) has original sculptures, jewelry, and gift items, made of pewter and silver, from various parts of Mexico. The **Centro Artesenal de Ensenada** has a smattering of galleries and shops. By far, the best shop at the Centro Artesenal is **Galería de Pérez Meillón** (⊠ Blvd. Costera 1094–39, ☎ 61/74–03–94), with its museum-quality pottery and varied folk art by indigenous northern Mexican peoples. **La Esquina de Bodegas** (⊠ Av. Miramar at Calle 6, ☎ 61/78–35–57) is an innovative gallery, shop, and café in a century-old winery building. Baja's finest wines are sold here at reasonable prices, and an upstairs gallery sells glassware, pottery, and books. The café at the back of the building serves coffee, wine, and a small menu of soups and entrées.

Tecate

32 km (20 mi) east of Tijuana, 112 km (70 mi) northeast of Ensenada.

Tecate is a quiet border community with a population of about 100,000. So incidental is the border to local life that its gates close from 10 PM until 6 AM daily. Tecate beer, one of the most popular brands in Mexico, is brewed here. Maquiladoras and agriculture are the other main industries. Tecate is also known for the vast pottery yards on the outskirts of town that line the highways to Tijuana and Ensenada. The artisans make bricks, paving tiles, roof tiles, and all sorts of planters and fountains. One of the area's largest pottery yards is at **Baja-Mex-Tile** (⊠ Blvd. Juárez 9150, Carretera Tecate a Tijuana, ☎ 665/4–02–04). Tecate's primary tourist draw is Rancho la Puerta, a fitness resort that caters to well-heeled travelers from north of the border. A bit farther south, the valleys of Guadalupe and Calafía boast some of Mexico's lushest vineyards. Olives are also grown in profusion here.

You can easily explore the town of Tecate in a few hours, lingering along the way. But you'll need a cab or car to wander the countryside and visit pottery workers, outlying ranches, and other sights. Downtown is centered on the **Parque Hidalgo.** A few cab drivers, shoe-shine boys, schoolchildren, and snuggling couples hang out here around the small gazebo, patches of lawn, and wrought-iron benches. On summer evenings, dance and band concerts are held in **Parque López Mateos,** on Highway 3 south of town.

Railroading fans enjoy the infrequent rail tours from Campo (on the U.S. side of the border), over a steel trestle bridge spanning the Campo Creek, and through the only international train tunnel to the United States and on into Tecate. **Baja California Tours** (⊠ 7734 Herschel Ave., Suite O, La Jolla, CA 92037, ☎ 619/454–7166, ℻ 619/454–2703) runs occasional rail tours.

Dining and Lodging

$$ ✕ **El Tucan.** Fancy by local standards, this motel restaurant is the current favorite for everything from hamburgers to spicy beefsteaks. The full bar and banquet facilities are favored by maquiladora executives and local bigwigs, and everyone enjoys the lively ambience in the dining room. ⊠ *Av. Juárez 1100,* ☎ *665/4–13–33. MC, V.*

$ ✕ **Panaderia de Tecate.** Open 24 hours every day except Christmas and New Year's, this simple bakery is famed throughout the region. The kitchen whips up more than 100 types of cookies, donuts, *pan dulce* (sweet bread), crunchy *bolillos* (rolls), and cakes. Snacks and burritos are served at the adjacent tile bar. ⊠ *Av. Juárez 331,* ☎ *665/4–00–40. No credit cards.*

$ ✕ **Plaza Jardin.** The setting is plain and the food simple Mexican fare, but the café tables outside have a gratifying view of the plaza. ⊠ *Callejón Libertad 274,* ☎ *665/4–34–53. No credit cards.*

$$$$ ▥ **Rancho la Puerta.** This peaceful, isolated health spa just west of Tecate is an idyllic resort—for $1,400–$2,500 a week. Spanish-style buildings with red-tile roofs and modern glass-and-wood structures are spread throughout the sprawling ranch. Hiking trails lead into scrubpine hills and on Kuchuma Mountain, and a large bright-blue pool is a central gathering spot. Guests stay in luxurious private cottages and usually check in for a week or more, taking advantage of the special diet and exercise regimen to lose weight and shape up. Transportation is available to and from the San Diego airport. ⊠ *Hwy. 2, 5 km (3 mi) west of Tecate, 21275,* ☎ *665/4–11–55; 760/744–4222; or 800/443–7565 in the U.S.; ℻ 665/4–11–08, 760/744–5007 in the U.S. 80*

rooms. Restaurant, pool, beauty salon, massage, 4 tennis courts, 3 health clubs. AE, MC, V. 🏊

$$ 🏨 **Hacienda Santa Veronica.** Billed as an off-road and dirt-racing country club, the Hacienda is a pretty countryside resort whose rooms are furnished with Mexican colonial beds, bureaus, and fireplaces. The off-road raceway is sufficiently far away from the rooms to keep the noise of revving engines from disturbing you; a number of trails for horseback riding traverse the property. Bullfighting lessons and practice fights take place here, as do "bloodless" fights, where both the matador and bull escape unscathed. ✉ *30 km (19 mi) east of Tecate off Hwy. 2,* ☎ *66/81–74–28, 800/522–1516 in CA, AZ, NV, 800/225–2786 elsewhere in the U.S. and in Canada. 87 rooms. Restaurant, bar, pool, 2 tennis courts, horseback riding. MC, V.*

Mexicali

136 km (84 mi) east of Tijuana.

Mexicali, with a population of about 850,000, shares the Imperial Valley farmland and the border crossing with Calexico, a small California city. The capital of Baja California, Mexicali sees a great deal of government activity and a steady growth of maquiladoras. Most visitors come to town on business, and the city's sights are few and far between. A tourist-oriented strip of curio shops, restaurants, and bars is located along Avenida Francisco Madero, a block south of the border. The **Museo del Estado** (State Museum), administered by the Autonomous University of Baja California (UABC), provides a comprehensive introduction to the natural and cultural history of Baja. ✉ *Av. Reforma 1998, near Calle L,* ☎ *65/52–57–17.* 🎫 *Free.* 🕐 *Tues.–Sat. 9–6, Sun. 10–2.*

Dining and Lodging

$$ ✕🏨 **La Lucerna.** The prettiest hotel in Mexicali, the colonial-style Lucerna has plenty of palms and fountains around the pools and carved wood furnishings in the dark, somber rooms. A newer section has suites with separate seating areas and more-modern furnishings. The three restaurants are pleasant, with local decor and good Mexican meals. Conventions and business meetings sometimes fill the hotel; advance reservations are advised. ✉ *Av. Benito Juárez 2151, 21270,* ☎ *65/64–70–00, 800/582–3762,* 🖷 *65/66–47–06. 175 rooms, 28 cabins, 4 suites. 3 restaurants, bar, 2 pools. MC, V.*

En Route **Parque Nacional San Pedro Mártir.** Baja's interior mountain ranges are filled with hidden caves and mountain hideaways. This park is more accessible than most, and even a short drive or hike up its rough trails offers a new perspective on Baja. As long as it hasn't been raining, a regular car can handle the dirt road into the park. ✉ *140 km (87 mi) south of Ensenada, turn off Hwy. 1 south of Colonet and drive 98 km (61 mi) east to the park.*

San Quintín

191 km (118 mi) south of Ensenada.

Agricultural fields line the highway as you enter San Quintín, the largest producer of tomatoes in Baja. The Oaxacan migrant workers who plant and pick the fertile valley's produce live in squalid camps out of the view of travelers. **Bahía de San Quintín,** which fronts a few small hotels, is among northern Baja's best fishing grounds, along with **Bahía Falsa** and **Bahía Santa María,** and the area's few hostelries tend to cater to anglers. The weather is unpredictable. High winds can kick up at almost any time, blowing sand and scrub brush across empty fields and the highway. There's little reason to come, unless the fishing is good.

Pismo clams collected at water's edge along San Quintín's bays are considered a local delicacy; roadside stands sell them fresh and cooked. Travelers often stop here for essentials en route farther south; this is the last major outpost until Guerrero Negro (a drive of about six hours). Sandy side roads lead to windswept coves and isolated hideaways. If you explore these, it's best to be in a four-wheel-drive vehicle, as the roads are rugged and the drives tend to be lengthy.

Lodging

$ ⊡ **Old Mill.** Anglers ease their boats into the sheltered bay at this longtime favorite hideaway and set up housekeeping in a variety of rooms, some with kitchens and fireplaces. Others arrive in RVs. The lodge-style bar with its huge fireplace is filled with locals and travelers on weekend nights, and the restaurant serves hearty meals, including thick steaks and generous Mexican combo plates. Credit cards are accepted only with advance reservations. ⊠ *South of San Quintín on a dirt road leading to the bay,* ☎ ℻ *619/271–0952 (CA), 877/800–4081 in the U.S. 25 rooms, 2 suites. Restaurant, bar, camping, fishing. MC, V.*

San Felipe

198 km (123 mi) south of Mexicali, 244 km (151 mi) southeast of Ensenada.

San Felipe (pop. 20,000) is the quintessential dusty fishing village with one main street (two if you count the highway into town). The **malecón** runs along a broad beach facing the Sea of Cortés and the Bahía San Felipe, with a swimming area in the middle and public changing rooms at the north end. Taco stands, bars, and restaurants line the sidewalk across the street from the beach. The only landmark in town is the **shrine of the Cerro de la Virgen** (Virgin of Guadalupe), at the north end of the malecón on a hill overlooking the sea.

In 1948 the first paved road from Mexicali was extended into town, at which point San Felipe became significant. Prior to that time only a few fishermen and their families lived along the coast; now there are impressive fishing and shrimping fleets. The **Bahía San Felipe** has dramatic changes in its tides. They crest at 20 ft, and because the beach is so shallow, the waterline can move in and out up to 1 km (about ½ mi). Local fishermen are well aware of the peculiarities of this section of the Sea of Cortés; many of them visit the shrine of the Cerro de la Virgen before setting sail.

A getaway spot for years, San Felipe used to be a place where hardy travelers in RVs and campers hid out for weeks on end. Now there are at least two dozen campgrounds and a dozen hotels in town and on the coastline both north and south of town, which fill up quickly during winter and spring holidays. At times, up to 5,000 part-time residents can be in attendance, wandering the beaches, filling the few restaurants, and enjoying the sun. On holiday weekends San Felipe can be boisterous—dune buggies, motorcycles, and off-road vehicles abound—but most of the time it's a quiet, relaxing place. The town also appeals to sportfishermen, especially in spring. Launches, bait, and supplies are readily available.

Dining and Lodging

$$ ✗ **George's.** A favorite with resident Americans, George's has comfy padded red Naugahyde booths, powerful margaritas, and very good chiles rellenos, carne asada, and seafood. ⊠ *Av. Mar de Cortés 336,* ☎ *657/7–10–57. MC, V.*

$ ✗ **Tony's Tacos.** The most popular of the many taco stands along the waterfront, Tony's is a simple spot with sidewalk picnic tables and a counter lined with condiments for the house specialty—cheap, delicious fish tacos. ⊠ *Malecón at Av. Chetumal,* ☎ *no phone. No credit cards.*

$ ✗ **El Toro.** Open for breakfast only, El Toro is renowned among locals and San Felipe regulars for its chorizo, *machaca* (marinated shredded beef), *huevos rancheros* (fried eggs served on a corn tortilla and covered with a tomato, onion, and green-pepper sauce), and American-style breakfasts. The parking lot fills with trailers hauling dune buggies and motorcycles as groups gather to fuel up before a day on the dunes. ⊠ *Hwy. 5 north of town,* ☎ *657/7–10–32. No credit cards.*

$ ✗ **Viva Mexico.** This family-run operation (formerly called Juan's Place) two blocks east of the waterfront offers consistently excellent home-style cooking at reasonable prices. The catch of the day and grilled meats come with boiled vegetables—ask for beans, rice, and the delicious homemade tortillas instead. ⊠ *Calle de Ensenada,* ☎ *no phone. No credit cards.*

$$$ ▥ **San Felipe Marina Resort.** This full-scale resort is expected to eventually include a 100-slip marina along with resort homes and hotels, although construction has been delayed. The low-slung terra-cotta building facing the sea has 60 units available as hotel rooms, time-share units, or private condos. Most rooms have kitchens, woven rugs on white-tile floors, folk-art decorations, and balconies or patios with sea views. The least expensive rooms lack kitchens and ocean views. The pool sits above the beach next to a *palapa* (thatch-roof) bar; a second, indoor pool is a delight on cold winter days. The resort is a five-minute drive south of town and has an RV campground next door. ⊠ *Carretera San Felipe Aeropuerto, Km 4.5, 21850,* ☎ *800/522–1516, 619/298–4105 (AZ, CA, NV),* ℻ *657/7–15–68. 60 rooms and 123 RV spaces. Restaurant, bar, 1 indoor and 1 outdoor pool, 2 tennis courts, exercise room, shops. AE, MC, V.*

$$ ▥ **Las Misiones.** A pretty oasis of blue pools and green palms by the beach, this resort is big with group tours. It's also a good choice if you want to get away from it all—but you'll need a car or cab to get to town. A building just down the street from the hotel contains suites that have kitchens. ⊠ *Av. Misión de Loreto 148, 21850,* ☎ *657/7–12–80, 800/298–4105,* ℻ *657/7–12–83. 185 rooms, 32 suites. Restaurant, bar, 2 pools, 2 tennis courts. AE, MC, V.*

$ ▥ **El Cortez.** Easily the most popular hotel in San Felipe, El Cortez has several types of accommodations, including moderately priced bungalows and modern hotel rooms with white walls, pastel bedspreads and drapes, and white-tile floors. The hotel's beachfront and second-story bars are both enduringly beloved, and the restaurant is the nicest water-view dining spot in town. The hotel is a five-minute walk from the malecón. ⊠ *Av. Mar de Cortés s/n, 21850 (Box 1227, Calexico, CA 92232),* ☎ *657/7–10–56,* ℻ *657/7–10–56. 102 rooms. Restaurant, 2 bars, pool. MC, V.*

Outdoor Activities and Sports

FISHING

The Sea of Cortés offers plentiful sea bass, snapper, corbina, halibut, and other game fish. Clamming is good here as well. Several companies offer sportfishing trips; among the most established are **Alex Sportfishing** (☎ 657/7–10–52), **Pelicanos** (☎ 657/7–11–88), and **San**

Felipe Sportfishing (☎ 657/7–10–55). **Del Mar Cortés Charters** (✉ Apdo. 9, San Felipe 21850, ☎ 657/7–13–03) conducts fishing trips, full- and half-day trimaran tours of the Sea of Cortés, and boat charters. It can also arrange kayak and Hobie Cat rentals through the El Dorado private community north of town.

BAJA NORTE A TO Z

Arriving and Departing

By Bus

Greyhound (☎ 619/239–3266 or 800/231–2222 in the U.S.) serves Tijuana from San Diego several times daily; the Greyhound terminal in Tijuana is at Avenida Mexico at Calle 11 (☎ 66/86–06–95). **Five Star Tours/Mexicoach** (☎ 66/85–14–70, 619/428–9517 in the U.S.) runs buses from the trolley depot on the U.S. side of the border to its depot on Avenida Revolución in Tijuana and to Rosarito. **ABC–US** (☎ 66/26–11–46) runs buses from the San Ysidro trolley stop to downtown Tijuana, Pueblo Amigo, Plaza Río Tijuana, and the Agua Caliente racetrack.

Buses connect all the towns in Baja Norte and are easy to use. Buses traveling to Rosarito no longer stop in town, but instead stop at the Rosarito exit on the toll road where taxis wait to transport passengers to town. There is no official bus station here; check at the hotels for bus-schedule information.

Autotransportes de Baja California covers the entire Baja route and connects in Mexicali with buses to Guadalajara and Mexico City. **Elite** has first-class service to mainland Mexico. **Transportes del Pacífico** goes to Mexico City and other points on the mainland from Mexicali; **Transportes Norte de Sonora** frequents border towns in Baja and on mainland Mexico.

Bus stations are in Ensenada (✉ Av. Riveroll between Calles 10 and 11, ☎ 61/78–67–70 or 61/78–66–80), Mexicali (✉ Centro Cívico, Av. Independencia, ☎ 65/57–24–22), San Felipe (✉ Av. Mar Caribe at Av. Manzanillo, ☎ 657/7–15–16), Tecate (✉ Av. Benito Juárez and Calle Abelardo Rodríguez, ☎ 665/4–12–21), and Tijuana (✉ Calzada Lázaro Cárdenas and Blvd. Arroyo Alamar, ☎ 66/21–29–82).

By Car

From San Diego, U.S. 5 and I–805 end at the San Ysidro border crossing; Highway 905 leads from I–5 and I–805 to the Tijuana border crossing at Otay Mesa. U.S. 94 from San Diego connects with U.S. 188 to the border at Tecate, 57 km (35 mi) east of San Diego. I–8 from San Diego connects with U.S. 111 at Calexico—203 km (126 mi) east—and the border crossing to Mexicali. San Felipe lies on the coast, 200 km (124 mi) south of Mexicali via Highway 5.

To head south into Baja from Tijuana, follow the signs for Ensenada Cuota, the toll road (also called Highway 1 and, on newer signs, the Scenic Highway) that runs south along the coast. There are two clearly marked exits for Rosarito, and one each for Puerto Nuevo, Bajamar, and Ensenada. The road is excellent, although it has some hair-raising curves atop the cliffs and is best driven in daylight (the stretch from Rosarito to Ensenada is one of the most scenic drives in Baja). Tollbooths accept U.S. and Mexican currency; tolls are usually about $2. Rest rooms are available near toll stations. The alternative free road—Highway 1D or Ensenada Libre—has been vastly improved, but it's difficult for the first-timer to navigate. Highway 1 continues south of

Ensenada through San Quintín to Guerrero Negro, at the border between Baja California and Baja Sur, and on to the southernmost tip of Baja; it is no longer a toll road past Ensenada, however.

Mexico Highway 2 runs east from Tijuana to Tecate and Mexicali. A toll road between Tijuana and Tecate opened in 1994, and another was completed between Tecate and Mexicali in 1995. The 134-km (83-mi) journey from Tecate east to Mexicali on La Rumorosa, as the road is known, is as exciting as a roller-coaster ride, with the highway twisting and turning down steep mountain grades and over flat, barren desert.

If you are traveling only as far as Ensenada or San Felipe, you do not need a tourist card, unless you stay longer than 72 hours. If you know you'll be traveling south of Ensenada, you can get the form at the **Mexican Customs Office** (✉ inside San Ysidro border crossing, ☎ 66/83–14–05 or 66/84–77–90). You must have Mexican auto insurance, available at agencies near the border.

Many U.S. car-rental companies do not allow their cars to be driven into Mexico (☞ Car Rental *in* Contacts and Resources, *below*).

By Plane
Tijuana's **Aeropuerto Alberado Rodriguez** is on the eastern edge of the city, near the Otay Mesa border crossing. The Tijuana airport is served from cities in Baja and mainland Mexico by **Mexicana** (☎ 66/83–28–50), **Aeroméxico** (☎ 66/85–44–01), **AeroCalifornia** (☎ 66/84–21–00 or 66/84–28–76), and **Taesa** (☎ 66/84–84–84). **Mexicana** (☎ 65/52–93–91) and **Aeroméxico** (☎ 65/57–25–51) fly to Mexicali's international airport, Aeropuerto Internacional General Rodolfo Sánchez Taboada, about 11 km (7 mi) east of town.

By Trolley
The **San Diego Trolley** (☎ 619/595–4949) travels from the Santa Fe Depot in San Diego, at Kettner Boulevard and Broadway, to within 100 ft of the border every 15 minutes from 5 AM to midnight. The 45-minute trip costs $1.75.

Getting Around

By Bus
In **Tijuana,** the downtown station for buses within the city is at Calle 1a and Avenida Madero (☎ 66/86–95–15). Most city buses at the border will take you downtown; look for the ones marked CENTRO CAMIONERA. To catch the bus back to the border from downtown, go to Calle Benito Juárez (also called Calle 2a) between Avenidas Revolución and Constitución. **Five Star Tours/Mexicoach** (☎ 619/232–5049) runs buses from the trolley depot on the U.S. side of the border to its own depot on Avenida Revolución in Tijuana. *Colectivos* (small vans often painted white with colored stripes) cover neighborhood routes in most Baja cities and towns. The destination is usually painted on the windshield; look for them on main streets.

By Car
The best way to tour Baja Norte is by car, although the driving can be difficult and confusing. If you're just visiting Tijuana, Tecate, or Mexicali, it's easiest to park on the U.S. side of the border and walk across.

The combination of overpopulation, lack of infrastructure, and heavy winter rains makes many of **Tijuana**'s streets difficult to navigate by automobile. It's always best to stick to the main thoroughfares. There are parking lots along Avenida Revolución and at most major attractions. Most of **Rosarito** proper can be explored on foot, which is a good idea on weekends, when Boulevard Juárez has bumper-to-bumper traffic. To reach **Puerto Nuevo** and other points south, continue on Boulevard Juárez (also called Old Ensenada Highway and Ensenada Libre) through town. Most of **Ensenada**'s attractions are within five blocks of the waterfront; it is easy to take a long walking tour of the city. A car is necessary to reach La Bufadora and most of the beaches. When driving farther south to **San Quintín, Guerrero Negro,** and **Baja Sur,** be sure to fill up your gas tank when it's half full. Few towns appear on the highway, and you quickly have the feeling you are headed into the unknown (unless you're following a caravan of RVs). Don't drive at night, and watch your speed. You never know when a pothole or arroyo will challenge your driving skills.

Contacts and Resources

Car Rental
Avis (☎ 800/331–1212) permits its cars to go from San Diego into Baja as far as 724 km (450 mi) south of the border. Cars must be returned by the renter to San Diego, and Mexican auto insurance is necessary. **Courtesy Rentals** (✉ 2975 Pacific Hwy., San Diego, CA 92101, ☎ 619/497–4800, 800/252–9756) allows its cars as far as Ensenada. **California Baja Rent-A-Car** (✉ 9245 Jamacha Blvd., Spring Valley, CA 91977, ☎ 619/470–8368, 888/470–7368) rents four-wheel-drive vehicles, convertibles, and sedans for use throughout Mexico (the only company to do this). If you plan to rent your car in Tijuana or San Diego and drop it in Los Cabos, be prepared to pay a hefty sum (up to $900) on top of the rental price.

ENSENADA
Fiesta Rent-a-Car (☎ 61/76–33–44) has an office in the Hotel Corona at Boulevard Costero. **Hertz** (☎ 61/78–29–82) is on Avenida Blancarte between Calles 1 and 2.

TIJUANA
The larger U.S. rental agencies have offices at the Tijuana International Airport (officially Aeropuerto Alberado Rodriguez). Offices in town include **Avis** (✉ Av. Agua Caliente 3310, ☎ 66/86–40–04 or 66/86–37–18) and **Budget** (✉ Paseo de los Héroes 77, ☎ 66/34–33–03).

Emergencies
THROUGHOUT BAJA NORTE
Police (☎ 134). **Cruz Roja** (Red Cross, ☎ 132). **Fire** (☎ 136).

TIJUANA
U.S. Consulate (☎ 66/81–74–00). The **Attorney General for the Protection of Tourists Hot Line** (☎ 66/88–05–55) takes calls weekdays to help with tourist complaints and problems.

Guided Tours
Baja California Tours (✉ 7734 Herschel Ave., Suite O, La Jolla, CA 92037, ☎ 619/454–7166, FAX 619/454–2703) has comfortable, informative bus trips throughout the Baja Peninsula. Seasonal day and overnight trips focus on whale-watching, fishing, shopping, wineries, sports, and art and cultural events in Tijuana, Rosarito, Ensenada, and San Felipe. It also offers adventure tours to Meling Ranch, a working ranch in the Sierra San Pedro Mártir about 240 km (150 mi) south of the border.

Language Classes
A great way to get to know Ensenada and improve your Spanish is to attend weekend or week-long classes at the **International Spanish Institute of Ensenada** (☎ 61/76–01–09, 818/242–5263 in California).

Reservation Agencies

Several companies specialize in arranging hotel reservations in Baja Norte, including **Baja Information** (✉ 7860 Mission Center Ct., Suite 202, San Diego, CA 92108, ☎ 619/298–4105, 800/522–1516 in CA, NV, AZ, 800/225–2786 elsewhere in the U.S. and in Canada, FAX 619/294–7366), **Baja California Tours** (✉ 7734 Herschel Ave., Suite O, La Jolla, CA 92037, ☎ 619/454–7166, FAX 619/454–2703), **Baja Lodging** (✉ Box 40285, San Diego, CA 92164, ☎ 619/491–0682), **Mexico Condo Reservations** (✉ 5801 Soledad Mountain Rd., La Jolla, CA 92037, ☎ 619/275–4500, 800/262–4500, FAX 619/456–1350), and **Mexico Resorts International** (✉ 4126 Bonita Rd., Bonita, CA 91902, ☎ 619/422–6900, 800/336–5454, FAX 619/472–6778).

Travel Club

Baja tours, Mexican auto insurance, a monthly newsletter, and workshops are available through **Discover Baja** (✉ 3089 Clairemont Dr., San Diego, CA 92117, ☎ 619/275–4225, 800/727–2252, FAX 619/275–1836).

Visitor Information

Regional tourist offices are usually open weekdays 9–7 (although some may close in early afternoon for lunch) and weekends 9–1.

Ensenada (✉ Blvd. Costera 1477, ☎ 61/72–30–22 or 61/72–30–81; ✉ Blvd. Costera at the entrance to town, ☎ 61/78–24–11). **Mexicali** (✉ Convention and Tourism Bureau, Calzada López Mateos at Calle Compresora, ☎ 65/52–23–76, ☎ FAX 65/57–25–61; ✉ State Secretary of Tourism Office, Calle Calafia at Calzada Independencia, ☎ 65/56–10–72 or 65/57–12–56). **Rosarito** (✉ Blvd. Juárez, 2nd floor of Quinta Plaza shopping center, ☎ 661/2–03–96 or 661/2–30–78). **San Felipe** (✉ Av. Mar de Cortés, ☎ 657/7–11–55 or 657/7–18–65). **Tecate** (✉ Callejón Libertad, ☎ 665/4–10–95). **Tijuana Chamber of Commerce** (✉ Av. Revolución and Calle 1, ☎ 66/88–16–85). **Tijuana Convention and Tourism Bureau** (✉ Inside San Ysidro border crossing, ☎ 66/84–04–81 or 66/84–77–90; ✉ Av. Revolución between Calles 3 and 4, ☎ 66/83–05–30 or 66/84–05–37).

BAJA CALIFORNIA SUR

With the completion in 1973 of the Transpeninsular Highway, also called Mexico Highway 1, travelers gradually started finding their way down the 1,708-km (1,059-mi) road, drawn by the wild terrain and the pristine beaches of both coastlines. Baja California Sur became Mexico's 30th state in 1974, and the population and tourism have been growing. Still, Baja Sur remains a rugged and largely undeveloped land. Many people opt to fly to the region rather than brave Highway 1. The road is in fairly good repair, but there are potholes in some stretches and services (gas, rest rooms) may not be available. Those venturing on the Transpeninsular Highway should be well prepared with water and other provisions for a long drive in desolate but beautiful country.

Whale-watching in Guerrero Negro, Scammon's Lagoon, San Ignacio Lagoon, and Magdalena Bay is a main attraction in winter. History buffs enjoy Loreto, where the first mission in the Californias was established. La Paz, today a busy governmental center and sportfishing city, was the first Spanish settlement in Baja. At the southernmost tip of the peninsula, where the Pacific Ocean and the Sea of Cortés merge, fishing aficionados, golfers, and sun worshippers gather in Los Cabos, one of Mexico's most popular and most expensive coastal resorts.

Baja California Sur

Isla Angel de la Guarda

Isla del Tiburón

Hermosillo

Mazatán

San Rafael

Tecoripa

Pta. San Gabriel

Cieneguita

El Arco

Guaymas

San Ignacio

Santa Rosalía
Mulegé

Isla Lobos

Ciudad Obregón

Navajoa

Laguna de San Ignacio

TO GUERRERO NEGRO

Pta. Concepción

Huatabampo

BAJA

Bahía Concepción

Loreto

Isla Carmen

Las Grullas Márgen Derecha

La Poza

Misión San Javier

CALIFORNIA

Topolobampo

TO LOS MOCHIS

Insurgentes

SIERRA GIGANTA

Golfo de California

Constitución

Isla San José

Bahía Magdalena

SUR

Santa Rita

Isla Partida

Isla Santa Margarita

Bahía la Paz

Pichilingue

TO MAZATLÁN

Isla Cerralvo

La Paz

Bahía los Muertos

N

El Triunfo

Punta Pescadero

PACIFIC OCEAN

Los Barriles

Buenavista

Todos Santos

La Ribera

Santiago

SIERRA DE LA LAGUNA

Cabo Pulmo

KEY

Rail Lines

Ferry Lines

San José del Cabo

Cabo San Lucas

0 —————— 100 miles

0 —————— 150 km

Guerrero Negro and Scammon's Lagoon

720 km (446 mi) south of Tijuana, 771 km (478 mi) north of La Paz.

Every December through March, thousands of gray whales swim 8,000 km (5,000 mi) south from Alaska's Bering Strait to the tip of the Baja Peninsula. Up to 6,000 whales swim past and stop close to the shore at several spots along the Baja coast—including Scammon's Lagoon near **Guerrero Negro**—to give birth to their calves. These newborns each weigh about half a ton and consume nearly 50 gallons of milk a day. In the past, Guerrero Negro was the headquarters for whale-watching trips, but many of the whale-watching operators have moved farther south, to Laguna San Ignacio and Bahía Magdalena. Still, it's easiest to spot whales from shore or to arrange for a boat in Guerrero Negro.

If it weren't for the whales and the Transpeninsular Highway, which passes near town, few would venture to Guerrero Negro, a town of 10,000. Those traveling south can easily bypass the town. The name Guerrero Negro, which means Black Warrior, was derived from a whaling ship that ran aground in Scammon's Lagoon in 1858. Near the Desierto de Vizcaíno (Vizcaíno Desert), on the Pacific Ocean, the area is best known for its salt pans, which provide work for much of the town's population and produce one third of the world's salt supply. Saltwater collects in some 780 square km (300 square mi) of sea-level ponds and evaporates quickly in the desert heat, leaving great blocks of salt. The town is dusty, windy, and generally unpleasant, but it happens to be a favored roosting spot for osprey, which build huge nests on power poles around town.

Scammon's Lagoon is about 27 km (17 mi) south of Guerrero Negro, down a rough but passable sand road that crosses the salt flats. The lagoon got its name from U.S. explorer Charles Melville Scammon of Maine, who discovered it off the coast of Baja in the mid-1800s. On his first expedition to the lagoon, Scammon and his crew collected more than 700 barrels of valuable whale oil, and the whale rush was on. Within 10 years, nearly all the whales in the lagoon had been killed, and it took almost a century for the whale population to increase to what it had been before Scammon arrived. It wasn't until the 1940s that the U.S. and Mexican governments took measures to protect the whales and banned the whalers from the lagoon.

These days, whale-watching boats—most of them *pangas* (small skiffs)—must get permission from the Mexican government to enter Scammon's Lagoon, now a national park called **Parque Natural de Ballenas Gris** (Gray Whale Natural Park). The other major whale-watching spots (also protected by the government) are farther south, at Laguna San Ignacio and Bahía Magdalena, both on the Pacific coast. If traveling on your own, you can reach Laguna San Ignacio from the town of San Ignacio (☞ *below*). Bahía Magdalena—regulars call it "Mag Bay"—is about a four-hour drive across the peninsula from La Paz. Fishermen will take you out in their boats to get closer to the whales at both places. But for a better view, and an easier stay in this rugged country, travel with an outfitter who will arrange your transportation, accommodations, and time on the water. Whales will come close to your boat, rising majestically from the water, and sometimes swim close enough to be patted on the back.

Dining and Lodging

There are several hotels in Guerrero Negro, none of which is worth visiting for its own sake. Double-occupancy rooms cost from about $25 to $70 a day; rates tend to increase during the peak whale-watching season from January through March. None of the hotels has heat, and winter nights can be downright frigid. Credit cards aren't normally accepted, but the hotels do take traveler's checks. The food in the hotel restaurants recommended below is far from haute cuisine, but it's about as good as you're going to get in the area.

$ ✕ La Espinitá. This small restaurant serves good home-style Mexican and American breakfasts, along with standard enchiladas, tacos, and fish for lunch and dinner. The market next door has cold drinks, purified water, and snacks. ⊠ *Hwy. 1 at 28th parallel next to La Pinta, Domicilio Conocido, 23940,* ☎ *no phone. No credit cards.*

$ ✕🖩 Malarrimo. This trailer park and Mexican and seafood restaurant has a 10-room motel—Cabañas San Miguelito—with private baths and TV. It fills up quickly and is one of the best deals in town. The restaurant is a favorite spot for caravans heading farther south. The grilled or steamed fresh fish, lobster, and clams are legendary, and the dining-room walls are covered with maps and photos of Baja. Whale-watching excursions from the hotel are also immensely popular and are run by knowledgeable local guides. ⊠ *Blvd. Zapata, 23940,* ☎ *115/7–02–50,* FAX *115/7–01–00. 10 rooms. Restaurant. No credit cards.*

$$ 🖩 La Pinta. A few kilometers outside of town, looking like an oasis of palms in the desert, La Pinta is the largest hotel in the area. The clean, functional rooms are dependable, the setting more attractive than that of other local lodgings, and the American–Mexican restaurant decent, but the rates are high for the area. Package deals are sometimes available if you plan to use La Pinta hotels throughout the peninsula. Whale-watching excursions can be arranged here. ⊠ *La Pinta Hwy. 1 at 28th parallel, Domicilio Conocido, 23940,* ☎ *115/7–13–01, 800/ 262–4500,* FAX *115/7–13–06. 26 rooms. Restaurant. MC, V.* 🐋

Outdoor Activities and Sports

WHALE-WATCHING

The gray whales that migrate from the Bering Strait are Guerrero Negro's biggest attraction. With a sturdy vehicle, you can drive the 24-km (15-mi) washboard dirt and sand road to Scammon's Lagoon and arrange a trip with the boat captains who await passengers there. Trips usually cost $15 per hour for a boat with up to four passengers. Start early to take advantage of the calmest water and best viewing conditions. Whale-watching from the shores of the lagoon can be disappointing without binoculars. But it is still an impressive sight to see the huge mammals spouting water high into the air, their 12-ft-wide tails flailing.

Eco-Tours Malarrimo (⊠ Blvd. Zapata, 23940, ☎ 115/7–02–50) is the best tour operator in the area. It offers four-hour trips with bus transportation to and from the lagoon (about 75% of the trip is spent in small skiffs among the whales with English-speaking guides) and lunch for $40 per person. Reserve several months in advance, especially for February, when whales appear in abundance.

San Ignacio

227 km (141 mi) southeast of Guerrero Negro.

A pleasant vestige of the missionary presence in Baja, San Ignacio is an oasis amid the Desierto de Vizcaíno. Date palms, planted by Jesuit missionaries in the late 1700s, sway gently, in sync with the town's laid-back air. San Ignacio is primarily a place to organize whale-watching and cave-painting tours or to stop and cool off in the shady *zócalo* (town square).

Lodging

$$ 🏨 **La Pinta.** This simple, functional hotel is a pleasant place to stay on your Transpeninsular journey—although you may wish for a bit more for the money. White arches frame the courtyard and pool, and the rooms are decorated with folk art and wood furnishings. Both the river and town are within walking distance. The hotel staff can set up whale-watching trips with local guides. ⊠ *2 km (1 mi) west of Hwy. 1 on an unnamed road into town, Apdo. 37, 23943,* ☎ *115/4–03–00, 800/262–4500. 28 rooms. Restaurant, bar, pool. No credit cards.* 🐢

Outdoor Activities and Sports

WHALE-WATCHING

San Ignacio is the base for trips to Laguna San Ignacio arranged through **Baja Discovery** (⊠ Box 152527, San Diego, CA 92195, ☎ 619/262–0700, 800/829–2252 in the U.S. outside San Diego). The company has a comfortable base camp at the lagoon. The tour includes round-trip transport from San Diego to San Ignacio, with an overnight at the La Pinta hotel in San Ignacio, before and after overnight camping trips at the lagoon.

Kuyima Tours (☎ 115/4–00–26) in San Ignacio offers transport between La Paz and the lagoon in San Ignacio and uses local guides as boat captains.

Santa Rosalia

77 km (48 mi) southeast of San Ignacio.

You'll find a fascinating mix of French, Mexican, and American Old West–style architecture in this dusty mining town. Santa Rosalia is known for its **Iglesia Santa Barbara,** a prefabricated iron church designed by Alexandre-Gustave Eiffel, creator of the Eiffel Tower. Be sure to stop by **El Boleo** (⊠ Av. Obregón at Calle 4), where fresh breads bring a lineup of eager bakery customers weekday mornings at 10.

Lodging

$$ 🏨 **Hotel Frances.** The former glory of this 1886 French mansion shines through despite its modest furnishings. The Frances sits on a steep hill, and many of its refurbished rooms open onto a second-story porch with views of town and the sea. There's a small pool in the courtyard and a charming restaurant. ⊠ *Av. 11 de Julio at Calle Jean M. Cousteau, 23920,* ☎ FAX *115/2–20–52. 17 rooms. Pool. No credit cards.*

$$ 🏨 **El Morro.** Santa Rosalia's best hotel is on the waterfront a bit south of town. Rooms, in a series of one-story buildings connected by rock arches and tile mosaics, are large and comfortable; some have terraces and tile bathrooms. The rooms are a bit worn, but the reasonable price and the proximity of the sea even the score. The restaurant serves bountiful Mexican combo plates, imported steak, and local seafood. The bar is a popular gathering spot for tourists. ⊠ *1½ km (1 mi) south of Santa Rosalia on Hwy. 1, 23900,* ☎ FAX *115/2–04–14. 39 rooms. Restaurant, bar, pool. No credit cards.*

Mulege

64 km (40 mi) south of Santa Rosalia.

Mulege has become a popular base for exploring the nearby mountains and for kayaking in **Bahía Concepción,** the largest protected bay in Baja. Once a mission settlement, this charming tropical town of some 3,500 residents swells in winter, when Americans and Canadians fleeing the cold arrive in motor homes. There are several campgrounds outside town and a few good hotels and restaurants in town and on the coast.

Lodging

$$$ ⌶ **Hotel Serenidad.** A Mulege mainstay for Baja aficionados since the late 1960s, the Serenidad is owned by Don and Nancy Johnson and their family, longtime Baja residents. The hotel is a delightful escape, with simple rooms in brick and stucco buildings scattered under bougainvillea vines and fruit trees. Some rooms have fireplaces and/or air-conditioning; all have private baths. The Saturday night pig roast is a Baja tradition. ✉ *2½ km (1½ mi) south of Mulege, Hwy. 1, 23900,* ☎ *115/3–05–30,* FAX *115/3–03–11. 29 rooms. Restaurant, bar, pool, private airstrip. MC, V.*

$ ⌶ **Hacienda.** Guests read and lounge in rocking chairs by the pool or along the bar at this small, comfortable hotel steps from the town plaza. Kayak trips and tours to cave paintings in the mountains can be arranged, and special fiestas are planned for groups. Rooms are spartan but work fine for a night or two. Even when other hotels in the area are nearly empty, the Hacienda is filled with Europeans attracted by the ambience and moderate room rates. ✉ *Calle Madero 3, 23900,* ☎ FAX *115/3–00–21. 20 rooms. Restaurant, bar, pool, travel services. No credit cards.*

Outdoor Activities and Sports

KAYAKING

Baja Tropicales (✉ Apdo. 60, 23900, ☎ 115/3–04–09, FAX 115/3–01–90) offers kayaks, wet suits, and other gear and several types of kayaking tours, including day trips and overnighters in the area of Mulege. Whale-watching trips on the Pacific coast are also available.

Loreto

134 km (83 mi) south of Mulege.

Loreto's setting on the Sea of Cortés is truly spectacular: the gold and green hills of the Sierra Gigante seem to tumble into the cobalt water. According to local promoters, the skies are clear 360 days of the year, and the desert climate harbors few bothersome insects.

Loreto was the site of the first California mission, founded in 1697 by Jesuit Priest Juan María Salvatierra. Seventy-two years later, a Franciscan monk from Mallorca, Spain—Father Junípero Serra—set out from here to establish a chain of missions from San Diego to San Francisco, in the land then known as Alta California. Four Indian tribes—the Kikiwa, Cochimi, Cucapa, and Kumyaii—inhabited the barren lands of Baja when Father Salvatierra arrived. Within a short time, disease and war had nearly obliterated their populations.

In 1821 Mexico achieved independence from Spain, which ordered all missionaries home. Loreto's mission was abandoned and fell into disrepair. Then in 1829, a hurricane swept through the remains, virtually destroying the settlement, capital of the Californias at the time. The capital was moved to La Paz, and Loreto languished for a century. In 1976, when oil revenue filled government coffers, the area was tapped for development. Streets were paved, and phone service, electricity, potable water, and sewage systems were installed in both the town and the surrounding area. Even an international airport was built. A luxury hotel and tennis center were opened in nearby Nopoló. Eventually, the pace of development slowed as the money dried up.

With a population of 10,000, Loreto is a good place to escape the crowds, relax, and go fishing. The fears of sports enthusiasts that the town would be spoiled have thus far been largely unfounded, although the residential trailer parks are filling up and private homes are clustered in secluded enclaves. For the most part, however, Loreto stands quietly by the sea.

The renovated **malecón,** built in 1991, turned the waterfront into a pleasant place for a stroll. A marina shelters yachts and the panga fleet; the adjoining beach is a popular gathering spot for locals, especially on Sunday afternoon, and the playground has an assortment of play equipment for children.

Loreto's only historic sight is **La Misión de Nuestra Señora de Loreto,** the first of the California missions. The stone walls, gilded altar, and primitive-style portraits of its priests are worth seeing.

El Museo de los Misiones, also called the Museum of Anthropology and History, contains religious relics, tooled leather saddles used in the 19th century, and displays of Baja's history. ✉ *Next door to La Misión de Nuestra Señora de Loreto,* ☎ *113/5–05–41.* 🎟 *$2.* 🕐 *Tues.–Sun. 9–1 and 2–6.*

Nopoló, an area being developed for luxury resorts, is about 8 km (5 mi) south of Loreto. There's a nine-court tennis complex and an 18-hole golf course, and private homes have sprung up, but the area still seems deserted.

In **Puerto Escondido,** 16 km (10 mi) down the road from Nopoló, is a marina with more than 100 boat slips. An RV park, Tripui, has a good restaurant, a few motel rooms, snack shop, bar, stores, showers, laundry, a pool, and tennis courts. A boat ramp has been completed at the marina; to pay the fee required to launch here, go to the port captain's offices (☎ 113/5–06–56, 𝔽𝔸𝕏 113/5–04–65) just south of the ramp; the offices are open weekdays 8–3.

Isla Danzante, 5 km (3 mi) southeast of Puerto Escondido, has good reefs and diving opportunities. Picnic trips to **Coronado Island,** inhabited only by sea lions, may be arranged in Loreto, Nopoló, or Puerto Escondido. The snorkeling and scuba diving on the island are excellent. Danzante and other islands off Loreto are now part of the Parque Marítimo Nacional Bahía de Loreto. Commercial fishing boats are not allowed within the 60-square-km (23-square-mi) park.

A trip to **Misión San Javier,** 32 km (20 mi) southwest of Loreto, is one of the best ways to see Baja at its most picturesque. A high-clearance vehicle is essential for the three-hour drive to the mission—and don't even try getting here if the dirt and gravel road is muddy. The road climbs past small ranches, palm groves, and the steep cliffs of the Cerro de la Giganta. Unmarked trails lead off the road to caves and remnants of **Indian cave paintings.** The mission village is a remote community of some 300 residents, many of whom come outdoors when visitors arrive. The church, built in 1699, is impressive and well preserved, set amid fruit orchards. It is often locked; ask anyone hanging about to find the person with the keys, and you'll be allowed to go inside to look at the stained-glass windows and ornate altar. Slip a few pesos into the contribution box as a courtesy to the village's inhabitants, who need all the help they can get to keep the church well maintained. Although you can drive to San Javier on your own, it helps to have a guide along to lead you to the caves and Indian paintings. Most hotels, or the tour companies listed below, can arrange tours.

Dining and Lodging

$$$ ✕ **El Nido.** If you're hungry for steak, chicken, and hearty Mexican combo plates, then this is your place. As close as you'll get to a steak house in these parts, El Nido caters to a meat-and-potatoes crowd. The wood and brass decor and courteous waiters make up for prices that seem outrageously high for the neighborhood. ✉ *Calle Salvatierra s/n,* ☎ *113/50–28–54. No credit cards.*

$$ ✕ **La Palapa.** A favorite with kayakers and travelers, this thatch-roof restaurant one block from the waterfront serves up a good combination of Mexican plates. This is the only place in town to get fried red snapper, the house specialty. Try the delicious mesquite-grilled steaks and seafood. ⊠ *Paseo Hidalgo between Calle Francisco Madero and the malecón,* ☎ *113/5–11–01. No credit cards.*

$ ✕ **Café Olé.** This local and gringo hangout is the best taquería in town, but it also serves good burgers, ice cream, and french fries. ⊠ *Calle Francisco Madero,* ☎ *113/5–04–96. No credit cards.*

$$$ ▥ **Hotel Posada de los Flores.** The overwhelming charm and attention to detail set this new hotel apart from other accommodations in the area. Exposed beams and locally crafted tile adorn every room of the remodeled colonial mansion, in Loreto's historical center. A rooftop garden provides beautiful views. Above the hotel's atrium lobby looms a crystal-bottom pool, so be sure to look up. Two restaurants serve up Loreto's finest Mexican and Italian fare. Breakfast is included. ⊠ *Calle Salvatierra at Calle Francisco Madero, 23880.* ☎ *113/5–11–62, or 877/441–6700 or 619/297–1621 in the U.S. 15 rooms. 2 restaurants, 2 bars, snack bar, pool, car rental. AE, MC, V.*

$$ ▥ **Oasis.** One of the original fishing camps, Oasis remains a favorite with those who want to spend as much time as possible on the water. Many of the rooms, set amid an oasis of palms, have a view of the water. The hotel has its own fleet of skiffs. ⊠ *Calle de la Playa at Zaragoza, Apdo. 17, 23880,* ☎ *113/5–01–12,* ℻ *113/5–07–95. 39 rooms. Pool, boating, fishing. MC, V.*

$$ ▥ **La Pinta.** Part of a Baja California hotel chain, La Pinta is a collection of pastel brick buildings right on the beach. The rooms are spacious but unremarkable, with air-conditioning and satellite TVs, and there's a large pool. ⊠ *Blvd. Misión de Loreto, 23880,* ☎ *113/5–00–25, 01–800/54–23–283, 800/522–1516 in CA, AZ, NV, 800/225–2786 elsewhere in the U.S. and in Canada,* ℻ *113/5–00–26. 48 rooms. Restaurant, bar, pool, tennis court, fishing. MC, V.* ✍

$$ ▥ **Plaza Loreto.** Since its opening in 1992, the Plaza Loreto has garnered a loyal following of Loreto regulars who appreciate the prime downtown location near the old mission. The two-story hotel has an upstairs bar overlooking the street. Rooms aren't consistently maintained—the best of the lot have TVs and huge showers. Check a few before choosing one. ⊠ *Paseo Hidalgo, 23880,* ☎ *113/5–02–80,* ℻ *113/5–08–55. 25 rooms. Bar. AE, MC, V.*

$$ ▥ **Villas de Loreto.** This is one of Loreto's nicest hideaways, just south of town. There are 10 large rooms with refrigerators and front porches, along with a large pool. An RV campground is behind the hotel buildings. Bikes are available for guests' use (free), and horseback riding, kayaking (for experienced paddlers), and fishing tours can be arranged. Smoking isn't permitted in the rooms or on the property. Continental breakfast is included in the room rate. To get here, turn right off Calle Salvatierra onto Calle Francisco Madero and drive across the dry riverbed to signs for the hotel. ⊠ *Antonio Mijares at beach, 23880,* ☎ ℻ *113/5–05–86. 10 rooms. Pool, laundry service. MC, V.*

Outdoor Activities and Sports

FISHING

Fishing put Loreto on the map, especially for American sports enthusiasts. Cabrillo and snapper are caught year-round; yellowtail in the spring; and dorado, marlin, and sailfish in the summer. If you plan to fish, bring tackle, as top-notch gear can be difficult to find, although some sportfishing fleets do update their equipment regularly. All Loreto-area hotels can arrange fishing, and many own skiffs. Local fishermen congregate with their small boats on the beach at the north and south ends of town. **Alfredo's Sportfishing** (✉ Blvd. Mateos at Juárez, across from the marina, ☎ 113/5–01–65, FAX 113/5–05–90) has good fishing guides. **Arturo's Fishing Fleet** (✉ Calle Hidalgo between the plaza and the marina, ☎ 113/5–04–09, FAX 113/5–00–22) has several types of boats and fishing packages. **The Baja Big Fish Company** (✉ Paseo Hidalgo 19, by the plaza, ☎ 113/5–00–78, 888/533–2252 in the U.S., FAX 113/5–00–78, 760/414–1855 in the U.S.) has full fishing packages from the United States, including air and hotel, as well as fishing trips if you are in Loreto. Baja Big Fish specializes in tag-and-release and in light tackle and fly-fishing.

GOLF

The 18-hole **Loreto Campo de Golf** (☎ 113/5–07–88 or 113/3–05–54) is along Nopoló Bay at the south side of the Fonatur resort. Several hotels in Loreto have golf packages and reduced or free greens fees.

KAYAKING

There are some ideal sites for kayakers off Loreto's shores. Tours and rentals can be arranged through the **Baja Outpost** (✉ Blvd. Mateos near the Oasis Hotel, ☎ 113/5–11–34, 800/789–5625). Loreto outdoor specialists for 15 years, **Las Parras Tours** (☎ 113/5–10–10, FAX 113/5–09–00) provides experienced local guides for kayaking, as well as whale-watching and scuba-diving.

SCUBA DIVING

The **Baja Outpost** (✉ Blvd. Mateos near the Oasis Hotel, ☎ 113/5–11–34, 800/789–5625), has scuba certification courses, dive trips to the islands, gear rental, and guest rooms for clients. **Las Parras Tours** (☎ 113/5–10–10, FAX 113/5–09–00) offers certification courses, guided tours, and gear rental.

TENNIS

The **Loreto Tennis Center** (☎ 113/5–07–00), 8 km (5 mi) south of town, has nine courts open to the public.

Shopping

There are few opportunities for shopping in Loreto. **El Alacran,** in the small complex behind the church on Calle Salvatierra, has remarkable folk art, jewelry, and sportswear. You can also find some nice silver shops in this complex. Groceries and ice are available on Calle Salvatierra at **El Pescador,** the town's only supermarket.

La Paz

354 km (220 mi) south of Loreto.

La Paz is one of those cities that makes you wish you'd been here 30 years ago. In the slowest of times, in late summer when the heat is oppressive, you can easily see how it must have been when it was a quiet place, living up to its name: "Peace." Today the city has a population of 175,000, with a large contingent of retirees from the United States and Canada. Travelers use La Paz as both a destination in itself and a stopping-off point en route to Los Cabos. Some call it the most traditional city on the peninsula, with the feel of a mainland community that has adapted to tourism while retaining its character. There's always excellent scuba diving and sportfishing in the gulf—La Paz is the stop-off for divers and fishermen headed for **Cerralvo, La Partida,** and the **Espíritu Santo** islands, where parrot fish, manta rays, neons, and angels blur the clear waters by the shore, and marlin, dorado, and yellowtail leap out of the sea.

Hernán Cortés and his soldiers were drawn to La Paz in 1535 by stories of magnificent pearls and women. In 1720 the Jesuits arrived to deliver their message of salvation. Instead, they inadvertently introduced smallpox, which decimated the local populace within 30 years.

A permanent settlement was established here in 1811; while the rest of Mexico was being torn apart by revolution, La Paz became a refuge for those escaping the mainland wars. La Paz became the capital of the Californias in 1829 after a hurricane nearly leveled Loreto. In 1853 a group of U.S. Southerners, led by William Walker, tried to make La Paz a slave state, but Mexicans quickly banished them. Peace reigned for the next century. In 1940 disease wiped out the oyster beds, and with the pearls gone, La Paz no longer attracted prospectors.

La Paz officially became the capital of Baja California Sur in 1974, and it is now the state's largest settlement. The city underwent considerable restoration in the late 1990s, with the main road between the airport and town enlarged to four lanes and construction of new residential areas constantly under way. It is the site of the governor's house and the state's bureaucracy, jail, and power plant, as well as the ferry port to Mazatlán.

Sights to See

⑳ At La Paz's west end is the 500-acre **Fidepaz Marina,** which includes
㉑ a luxurious resort hotel. The **malecón** is La Paz's seawall, tourist zone, and main drag rolled into one. As you enter town from the southwest (near Fidepaz Marina), Paseo Alvaro Obregón turns into the malecón at a cluster of high-rise condos. **Marina La Paz,** at the southwest end of the malecón, is an ever-growing development with condominiums, vacation homes, and a pleasant walkway lined with casual cafés.

㉒ A two-story white gazebo is the focus of the **Malecón Plaza,** a small cement square where musicians sometimes appear on weekend nights. The tourist-information center sits beside the gazebo. Across the street, Calle 16 de Septiembre leads inland to the city center. Around the plaza and all along the malecón, a steady stream of teens cruises through town, red and yellow car lights twinkling around their license plates and radios blaring.

㉓ The **Biblioteca de las Californias,** a library specializing in the history of Baja California, has reproductions of local prehistoric cave paintings, oil paintings of the missions, and the best collection of historical documents on the peninsula. Films and lectures are sometimes presented in the evening. Check the bulletin board outside the library or ask the librarian for information. ⊠ *Madero at 5 de Mayo,* ☎ *112/2–01–62.* ⊙ *Weekdays 8–6.*

La Paz's downtown is the busiest in Baja Sur, with shops crammed to-
㉔ gether on narrow streets. Downtown's big attraction is **La Catedral de Nuestra Señora de La Paz** (Our Lady of La Paz Cathedral). It was built in 1860 near the site of La Paz's first mission, which was established that same year by Jesuit Jaime Bravo. You'll see it just across from the
㉕ town's main square. The zócalo also goes by the names **Plaza Constitución** and Jardín Velazco.

㉖ La Paz's culture and heritage is well represented at the **Museum of Anthropology.** Exhibits include re-creations of Comondo and Las Palmas Indian villages, photos of cave paintings found in Baja, and copies of Cortés's writings on first sighting La Paz. Many exhibit descriptions are written only in Spanish, but the museum's staff will help translate for you. ⊠ *Altamirano and 5 de Mayo,* ☎ *112/2–01–62.* 🎫 *Donation.* ⊙ *Weekdays 8–6, Sat. 9–2.*

150

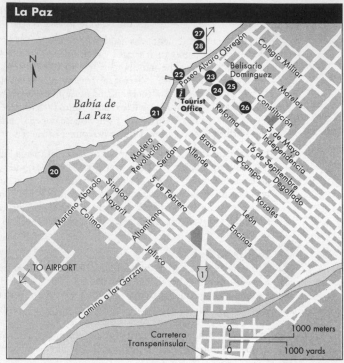

Northeast of town, Paseo Alvaro Obregón, or the malecón, becomes what is commonly known as the **Pichilingue Road.** It curves northeast along the bay about 16 km (10 mi) to the terminals where the ferries from Mazatlán and Topolobampo arrive and many of the sportfishing boats depart. At the **Ferry Terminal,** warehouses serve as waiting rooms. Roadside stands serving oysters and grilled fish line the highway across the street.

Since the time of pirate ships and Spanish invaders, **Pichilingue** was known for its preponderance of oysters bearing black pearls. In 1940 an unknown disease killed them off, leaving the beach deserted. Today Pichilingue is a pleasant place for sunbathing and watching sportfishing boats bring in their hauls. Palapa restaurants on the beach serve cold beer and oysters *diablo* (raw oysters steeped in a fiery-hot sauce), as well as some of the freshest and least expensive grilled fish in town.

Beaches

Off a dirt road just past Pichilingue, **Playa Tecolote** and **Playa Coyote** are adjacent crystal-blue coves with clean beaches. Both have restaurants, water-sports equipment rentals, and palapas for shade. This is a good place to test your kayaking skills, and rentals are available on site. Camping is allowed in the parking lots. **Playa Balandra,** on a side road between Pichilingue and Tecolote, is a peaceful cove favored by kayak and snorkeling operations from town. There are no facilities or rentals at this beach. Make arrangements in advance in town.

Dining and Lodging

$$$ ✕ **El Bismark.** You've got to go a bit out of your way for a local home-
★ style Mexican restaurant. Specialties include carne asada served with beans, guacamole, and homemade tortillas; and enormous grilled lobsters. Seafood cocktails are huge, too, and fish fillets are always fresh from the sea. You'll see families settle down for hours at long wood

tables, while waitresses divide their attention between patrons and soap operas on the TV above the bar. The desultory service is a drawback. ✉ *Santos Degollado and Av. Altamirano,* ☎ *112/2–48–54. MC, V.*

$$ ✕ **El Angél Azul.** This quiet café, gallery, and bar is a pleasant respite from the busy streets of La Paz. A short walk from *el centro* you'll find a reasonably priced menu of light Mexican and European fare and walls adorned with local artwork. Three cozy guest rooms are also available for overnights. ✉ *Independencia 518 at Guillermo Prieto,* ☎ *112/5–51–30. No credit cards. Closed Mon.*

$$ ✕ **La Paz-Lapa.** The noise level here is deafening, but this is a fun place, with a wide-screen TV in the bar and waiters so jolly you expect them to break into song. The food—basic beef, chicken, fish, and Mexican selections—is good and plentiful. Also referred to as Carlos 'n' Charlie's, La Paz-Lapa is part of the popular Carlos Anderson chain. Live bands appear weekend evenings on the back patio. ✉ *Paseo Obregón at Calle 16 de Septiembre,* ☎ *112/5–92–90. MC, V.*

$$ ✕ **La Pazta.** Locals who crave international fare rave about this trattoria with sleek black-and-white decor and excellent homemade pasta. Imported cheeses and wines, fresh herbs and vegetables, and bracing espresso and cappuccino are all welcome changes from the local seafood and taco fare. ✉ *Allende 36,* ☎ *112/5–11–95. MC, V.*

$ ✕ **El Quinto Sol Restaurante Vegetariano.** El Quinto's brightly painted exterior walls are covered with Indian snake symbols and smiling suns. The all-vegetarian menu can be a nice change of pace, and there's a wide selection of fresh juices and herbal elixirs. The four-course prix-fixe dinner (5–7 PM) is a bargain. The back half of the space is a bare-bones natural-foods store offering grains, fresh breads, soaps, oils, bulk herbs, and homeopathic remedies. ✉ *Belisario Domínguez and Independencia,* ☎ *112/2–16–92. No credit cards.*

$ ✕ **Taco Hermanos Gonzalez.** La Paz has plenty of great taco stands, but the Gonzalez brothers still corner the market with their hunks of fresh fish wrapped in corn tortillas. Bowls of condiments line the small stand, and the best fast food in town draws crowds of sidewalk munchers. ✉ *Mutualismo and Esquerro,* ☎ *no phone. No credit cards.*

$$$ ▥ **Crowne Plaza Resort.** By far the loveliest and most modern resort in La Paz, this hacienda-style inn sits beside the Fidepaz Marina. Its suites range in size and style; the largest have two bedrooms and a kitchenette. The pool flows through several levels in the courtyard, and there is a children's playground. The restaurant, with its cordial service, serene ambience, and excellent cuisine, has become a favorite among local executives. The fitness center has a sauna and steam baths and a squash court. ✉ *Lote A, Marina Fidepaz, Apdo. 482, 23000,* ☎ *112/4–08–30, 800/227–6963,* ✉ *112/4–08–37. 54 suites. Restaurant, bar, pool, health club, nightclub, business services, travel services. AE, MC, V.* ✍

$$$ ▥ **Hotel Marina.** From the lush gardens surrounding the pool and Jacuzzi to its seaside promenade along the marina walls, there are plenty of ways to spend your day at the Hotel Marina. The full-service marina offers fishing, scuba diving, and kayaking. Private charters are available. Most rooms have terraces with water views and are airy, clean, and functional. ✉ *Carretera a Pichilingue, Km 2.5, 23000,* ☎ *112/1–62–54, 01–800/68–58–800,* ✉ *112/1–21–77. 70 rooms, 18 studios, 5 suites. Restaurant, bar, pool, hot tub, tennis court. MC, V.* ✍

$$ ▥ **Los Arcos.** This is the only true colonial Mexican lodging in town. The lobby is open and bright, and leads to the central courtyard, where the rush of water in the fountain drowns out the music from the street and other noise. Most rooms have balconies. The coffee shop opens early, so you can have breakfast and pick up a box lunch if you're going fishing. The Cabañas de Los Arcos next door consists of several small brick cottages surrounded by gardens and a small hotel with a pool. ✉ *Paseo*

Obregón 498, between Rosales and Allende, 23000 (6 Jenner St., No. 120, Irvine, CA 92618), ☎ *112/2–27–44, or 714/450–9000 or 800/347–2252 in the U.S.,* FAX *112/5–43–13, 714/450–9010 in the U.S. 180 rooms at the main hotel, 30 bungalows and rooms at Cabañas. Restaurant, bar, coffee shop, 2 pools, sauna, fishing. MC, V.* ⬧

$$ ▥ **Club Hotel Cantamar.** Fernando Aguilar, the most famous scuba-diving master in the area, has expanded his operation to include this small sports lodge beside a private marina, 14 km (9 mi) north of town. Rooms have balconies that look out on the pool and the sea. The restaurant is in the clubhouse beside the dive boats. This is the ideal hangout for divers, who have easy access to some of the best diving in the Sea of Cortés. ✉ *Carretera Pichilingue (Calle Obregon 1665, Apdo. 782) 23000.* ☎ *112/2–18–26 or 112/2–70–10,* FAX *112/2–86–44. 18 rooms. Restaurant, bar, pool, dive shop, snorkeling.*

$$ ▥ **La Concha Beach Resort.** Come to La Concha for its clean private
★ beach, modern rooms, complete water-sports center, and very good restaurant. All rooms have tile floors, TVs, phones, and small refrigerators. Guests gather at the pool and the Cortez Club, a full-scale water-sports center with a bar, equipment rental, and scuba, snorkeling, kayaking, and sportfishing tours. Whale-watching trips are extremely popular in winter. The scuba operation is one of the best in La Paz, and you can arrange tours and rentals through the club even if you're not staying here. A separate building houses condos with kitchenettes, living rooms, and bedrooms ($$$), and has its own pool. Another section, in town, has six suites for long-term rental. There is a shuttle to town and back. ✉ *Carretera a Pichilingue, Km 5, 23010,* ☎ *112/1–63–44, 112/1–61–61, 800/999–2252,* FAX *112/1–62–18, 619/294–7366 in the U.S.. 107 rooms. Restaurant, 3 bars, pool, water sports, shops, travel services, car rental. AE, MC, V.* ⬧

$$ ▥ **Hotel Suites Club El Moro.** A vacation-ownership resort with suite rentals on a nightly and weekly basis, El Moro has a garden of lush palms and a densely landscaped pool area. You can recognize the building by its stark-white turrets and domes. Rooms are Mediterranean in style and decor, with arched windows, Mexican tiles, and private balconies. Some rooms have kitchens and can sleep up to five persons. A small café serves light fare. ✉ *Carretera a Pichilingue Km 2, Apdo. 357, 23010,* ☎ FAX *112/2–40–84 or 112/5–28–28. 21 suites. Restaurant, bar, pool. AE, MC, V.* ⬧

$$ ▥ **La Perla.** This brown low-rise hotel has a long-standing reputation
★ as one of the best places to stay in La Paz. Rooms have white walls and light-wood furnishings; some have king-size beds. The pool is on a second-story sundeck away from main street traffic. Noise is a factor in the oceanfront rooms; the trade-off is wonderful sunset views over the malecón. ✉ *Paseo Obregón 1570, 23010,* ☎ *112/2–07–77,* FAX *112/5–53–63. 101 rooms. Restaurant, bar, pool, shop. AE, MC, V.* ⬧

$ ▥ **Pension California.** This run-down hacienda still has clean blue-and-white rooms with baths and draws backpackers and low-budget travelers. The courtyard has picnic tables and a TV. A laid-back camaraderie prevails. ✉ *Av. Degollado 209, 23000,* ☎ *112/2–28–96. 25 rooms. No credit cards.*

Nightlife and the Arts

El Teatro de la Ciudad (✉ Av. Navarro 700, ☎ 112/5–00–04) is La Paz's cultural center. The theater seats 1,500 and is used for stage shows by visiting performers as well as by local ensembles. **La Terraza** (✉ La Perla hotel, Paseo Obregón 1570, ☎ 112/2–07–77) is the best spot for both sunset- and people-watching along the malecón.

Outdoor Activities and Sports
BOATING AND FISHING
The considerable fleet of private boats in La Paz now has room for docking at three marinas: **Fidepaz Marina** at the north end of town, and the **Marina Palmira** and **Marina La Paz** south of town. Most hotels can arrange sportfishing trips. Tournaments are held in August and November. The **Dorado Velez Fleet** (⊠ Apdo. 402, 23000, ☎ 112/2–27–44, ext. 608), operated by Jack Velez in Los Arcos hotel, has cabin cruisers; charters start around $240 per day.

SCUBA DIVING
Popular diving spots include the white coral banks off Isla Espíritu Santo, the sea lion colony off Isla Partida, and the seamount 14 km (9 mi) farther north. Conveniently, almost every hotel has arrangements with a dive outfitter. **Baja Diving & Service** (⊠ Paseo Obregón, ☎ 112/2–18–26, FAX 112/2–86–44) rents equipment and operates diving, snorkeling, and tours to Espíritu Santo, the wreck of the ferryboat *Salvatierra*, and a seamount where you can observe schools of hammerhead sharks. **Scuba Baja Joe** (⊠ Calle Obregón at Ocampo, ☎ 112/2–40–06, FAX 112/2–40–00), offers full equipment rentals and guided tours. **Baja Quest** (⊠ Sonora 174, ☎ 112/3–53–20, FAX 112/3–53–21) has day trips and live-aboard dive cruises. Two-tank dive trips run about $80. The Cortez Club at **La Concha Beach Resort** (⊠ Carretera a Pichilingue, Km 5, ☎ 112/1–63–44 or 112/1–61–61) offers dive trips.

WHALE-WATCHING
La Paz has become a center for whale-watching expeditions. Most hotels can make all the arrangements, but keep in mind that any whaling trip will entail about six hours' transportation from La Paz and back for two–three hours on the water. Serious whale fans with extra time overnight in San Ignacio, from which the ride to the coast is only about 45 minutes. In La Paz, you can arrange a trip through **Baja Quest** (⊠ Sonora 174, ☎ 112/3–53–20, FAX 112/3–53–21), **Contactours** (⊠ La Perla hotel, Paseo Obregón 1570, ☎ 112/3–22–12, FAX 112/3–50–51), or **Viajes Balandra** (⊠ Paseo Obregón at Degollado, ☎ 112/2–60–01, FAX 112/2–84–11). **Discover Baja** (☎ 800/727-2252) offers guided camping tours and whale-watching trips to Bahía Magdalena.

Shopping
Shops carrying a predictable assortment of sombreros, onyx chess sets, and painted plaster curios are scattered along Avenida Obregón across from the malecón. **Artesanías la Antigua California** (⊠ Av. Obregón 220, ☎ 112/5–52–30) has the nicest selection of Mexican folk art in La Paz, including wooden masks and lacquered boxes from Guerrero, along with a good supply of English-language books on Baja. **Artesanía Cuauhtémoc** (⊠ Av. Abasolo between Calles Nayarit and Oaxaca, ☎ no phone) is the workshop of weaver Fortunado Silva, who creates and sells cotton place mats, rugs, and tapestries. **La Tiendita** (⊠ Los Arcos hotel, Av. Obregón 498, ☎ 114/2–27–44) has embroidered guayabera shirts and dresses, tin ornaments and picture frames, and some black pottery from Oaxaca.

Los Barriles and the East Cape

105 km (65 mi) south of La Paz.

The Sea of Cortés coast north of Los Cabos has long been a favored hideaway for anglers and adventurers. The area known as the East Cape consists of a string of settlements and fishing villages between La Paz and San José del Cabo—including Los Barriles, Buena Vista, and La Ribera, all accessible from Highway 1. From Punto Pescadero in the north to Cabo Pulmo in the south, the cape is renowned for its rich fishing grounds, top-notch diving, and, when the wind kicks up, excellent windsurfing. Moderately developed but growing, the cape makes a great day trip or, if you want more time away from the glitz (and prices) of Los Cabos, a nice place to overnight. Food and lodging tend to be modest affairs; most hotels have meal plans—a good idea since fine dining is scarce.

There's an outback feel to the East Cape, with a robust group of American "settlers" making their presence known and creating a real-estate market out of thin air. For the intrepid traveler, a three-hour drive on a dirt washboard takes you along the coast to La Ribera, Punta Colorado, and Cabo Pulmo—the latter a superb dive site within a national marine reserve. (This route is *not* recommended for those bothered by dust or long stretches of precipitous driving conditions.)

Windsurfers take over the East Cape in January, when stiff breezes provide ideal conditions. Water-sports equipment and boat trips are available through area hotels, although regulars tend to bring their own gear and rent cars for getting to isolated spots. The nearest airport is at San José del Cabo, about a two-hour drive from the farthest East Cape hotels; several car rental agencies have desks at the airport. Expensive shuttle service can be arranged through most hotels, and there are plenty of cabs in the area.

Dining and Lodging

$$ ✕ **Otra Vez.** Whether you're in the mood for some simple grilled seafood, an omelet, or lobster New Orleans, this great little California-style café is sure to please. This may be the only time you see sprouts in Baja, so stock up. The clientele largely consists of expat retirees and tourists who gossip freely while listening to the Beach Boys. Live music and theme nights are featured. ⊠ *Calle 20 de Noviembre, Los Barriles,* ☎ *114/2–02–49. MC, V.*

$ ✕ **Tia Licha.** You might be able to fit a dozen friendly diners in this tiny café renowned for its home-style chiles rellenos, huevos rancheros, and fresh fish. Locals congregate here for breakfast, which is said to be the best on the Cape. ⊠ *On the road to Hotel Buena Vista Beach Resort (☞ below),* ☎ *no phone, No credit cards.*

$$$ ⊞ **Hotel Buena Vista Beach Resort.** The most pleasant surroundings on the coast are at this old-time resort built around a 1940s private mansion. Sixty tile-roof bungalows are set along flower-lined paths next to swimming pools and lawns. Some rooms have private terraces. The fishing fleet is one of the best in the area, and there are plenty of other diversions, including scuba diving, snorkeling, kayaking, horseback riding, trips to natural springs and caves, and tours into Los Cabos and La Paz. Airport shuttle service can be arranged in advance. Room rates include meals. ⊠ *Carretera Transpeninsular Km 105, Buena Vista 23500 (130 27th St., Chula Vista, CA 91911),* ☎ *114/1–00–33, 619/425–1551 (CA), 800/752–3555,* ℻ *114/1–01–33, 619/425–1832 (CA) 60 rooms. Restaurant, 2 pools, hot tub, massage, beach, dive shop, fishing. AE, MC, V.*

$$$ ⊞ **Hotel Palmas de Cortés.** A long-standing favorite with anglers, this casual lodge is often featured on sportfishing shows. It's near the famed Cortés banks, where marlin and tuna abound. The rooms and suites are sparsely furnished, with the basic comforts, and have few frills beyond powerful air-conditioners and hot showers. Caged parrots and macaws hang about the gardens among hammocks. Food is hearty and abundant and is included in your room rate. ⊠ *On the beach (take the road north through Los Barriles and continue to the beach), Los Barriles (Box 9016, Calabasas, CA 91372),* ☎ *114/1–00–50, 818/*

591–9463 in the U.S., FAX 114/1–00–46. 30 rooms, 10 suites, 10 condos. Restaurant, pool, fishing. MC, V.

$$$ 🏨 **Hotel Punta Pescadero.** Despite the vacation homes sprouting up in the area, this secluded resort is one of the most peaceful spots in Baja. Rooms have private waterfront terraces and are reserved far in advance by regulars (some 75% of the clientele is made up of returnees). They endure the half-hour drive along a hilly rock-strewn dirt road to the hotel for the sense of complete escape—miles of windswept beach, and calm coves with superb snorkeling—and the camaraderie of the staff and guests. ✉ *Camino de los Barriles a El Cardonal, Punta Pescadero 23000, 12 km (7 mi) north of Los Barriles,* ☎ FAX *114/1–01–01. 21 rooms. Restaurant, refrigerators, pool, beach, snorkeling, fishing, private airstrip. MC, V.*

$$$ 🏨 **Rancho Leonero.** Diehard anglers love this casual seaside hotel. Thatch-roof bungalows are scattered about the landscaped property. Although far from fancy, the rooms are serviceable, with tile floors, hard mattresses, and powerful showers. Meals (included in the room rate) are served family-style in the large dining room, the ambience of which depends on the guests, who can tend toward the rowdy side. In the afternoon the pool fills with sunburned boaters and their fish-story boasting. The fishing fleet, diving at nearby Cabo Pulmo's reefs, and use of kayaks are other pluses. ✉ *Carretera Transpeninsular Km 103, Buena Vista (22603 La Palma Ave., Suite 307, Yorba Linda CA 92887), 32 km (20 mi) north of San José del Cabo,* ☎ *114/1–02–16, 800/334–2252,* FAX *114/1–02–16. 27 rooms. Restaurant, pool, beach, fishing. MC, V.*

Shopping

The **Plaza Del Pueblo** (✉ Hwy. 1, Los Barriles) is just about the area's only shopping opportunity. At the **East Cape Smoke House** (☎ 114/1–02–94), you can sample and purchase freshly smoked seafood, and get a report on the local fishing conditions. The Smoke House also specializes in custom smoking and vacuum-packing your fresh catch. The small shopping center also includes an Internet shop, a tackle store, an ice cream parlor, and a bakery.

Los Cabos

195 km (121 mi) south of La Paz.

At the southern tip of the 1,625-km (1,000-mi) Baja California peninsula, the land ends in a rocky point called El Arco (The Arch), a place of stark beauty. The warm waters of the Sea of Cortés swirl into the Pacific Ocean's rugged surf as marlin and sailfish leap out of the waves. The desert ends in sandy coves, with cactus standing at their entrances like sentries under the soaring palm trees.

The conquistadores focused their attention on La Paz during expeditions from mainland Mexico in the mid-1500s, but pirates found the tip of the Baja peninsula ideal for spotting Spanish galleons traveling from the Philippines to Spain's empire in central Mexico. In their turn missionaries came to save the souls of the few thousand local Indians who lived off the sea. The Jesuits established the mission of **San José del Cabo** in the mid-1700s, but their settlements didn't last long. The missionaries (and other Europeans) had brought syphilis and smallpox along with their preachings, and, like elsewhere on the peninsula, the indigenous population was nearly wiped out after a few decades.

A different sort of explorer rediscovered this remote region in the 20th century: the angler. When pilots flew over Baja during World War II, they spotted the swirling waters and fertile fishing grounds from the air, and word soon spread. Wealthy adventurers with private planes

Los Cabos Coast

Los Pozos · 6 miles · 9 km · Los Cabos International Airport · Cabo San Lucas ③④—③⑦ · San José del Cabo ②⑨—③③ · Playa Médano · Costa Azul · Playa de Amor · Bahía Chileno · Bahía San José del Cabo · Bahía de Cabo San Lucas · Bahía Santa María · Playa Palmilla · PACIFIC OCEAN · Golfo de California

and boats created a demand for fishing lodges, airstrips, and other services, and the region became a cult destination. By the 1960s a half-dozen exclusive resorts were thriving on the cliffs and shores amid the barren landscape.

Connected by a 32-km (20-mi) stretch of highway called the **Corridor,** the two towns of Cabo San Lucas and San José del Cabo were distinct until the late 1970s, when the Mexican government's office of tourism development (Fonatur) targeted the southern tip of Baja as a major resort and dubbed the area Los Cabos. The destination now consists of three major areas: San José del Cabo, Cabo San Lucas, and the Corridor separating the two towns.

In the process Los Cabos has become one of Mexico's most popular and most expensive coastal getaways, with deluxe hotels, championship golf courses, and some of the best sportfishing in the world. Some of the world's finest hotel chains are rumored to be arriving soon. The population rate is growing faster than in any other part of Mexico, and infrastructure will soon be a problem. Despite all the development that has taken place, and the steep prices that have come along with it, the area remains a mysteriously natural hideaway.

San José del Cabo

San José del Cabo is the municipal headquarters for the two Los Cabos towns and has a population of about 25,000. The hotel zone faces a long stretch of waterfront on the Sea of Cortés; a nine-hole golf course and private residential community have been established south of the town center. The downtown area with its adobe houses and jacaranda trees still maintains the languid pace of a Mexican village, although bumper-to-bumper traffic often clogs the streets during weekday business hours. Despite the development, San José remains the more peaceful of the two towns—the one to come to for a quiet escape.

29 The **Estero de San José,** where the freshwater Río San José flows into the sea, is at the end of the tourist strip, on Paseo San José by the Presidente Inter-Continental. The estuary is now a natural preserve closed to boats. Wildlife is gradually reappearing; more than 200 species of birds can be spotted here. A building at the edge of the estuary serves as a cultural center with exhibits on Baja's indigenous people.

30 The main street in San José del Cabo is **Boulevard Mijares.** The south end of the boulevard has been designated the tourist zone, with the Los Cabos Club de Golf as its centerpiece. A few reasonably priced hotels are situated along this strip, on a beautiful long beach where the surf, unfortunately, is too dangerous for swimming.

San José del Cabo

31 Within town, Boulevard Mijares is lined with restaurants and shops. The modest yellow **City Hall** is near Avenida Zaragoza, where Boulevard Mijares ends—a spot marked by a long fountain. There is a small, shaded plaza here with a few café tables in front of small restaurants.

32 Locals and travelers mingle at the large central **plaza,** with a white wrought-iron gazebo and green benches set in the shade. The town's
33 church, the **Iglesia San José,** looms above the plaza. Be sure to walk up to the front and see the tile mural of a captured priest being dragged toward a fire by Indians.

BEACHES

Playa Hotelera is the stretch of beach that most of the finer hotels use. It's beautiful, but the current is dangerously rough, and swimming is not advised. At the east end of the beach, near the Presidente Inter-Continental, there is a freshwater lagoon filled with tropical birds and plants. If you plan to spend time here, be sure to douse yourself with insect repellent. The best swimming beach near San José is **Playa Palmilla,** which is protected by a rocky point just south of town. The northern part of the beach is cluttered with boats and shacks, but if you walk south you'll reach the Hotel Palmilla beach, a long stretch of white sand and calm sea.

DINING AND LODGING

$$$ ✕ **Damiana.** For a special night out, come to this small hacienda
★ tucked beside the plaza, past the center of town. Bougainvilleas wrap around the tall pines shading the wrought-iron tables, and the pink adobe walls glow in the candlelight. Start with fiery oysters diablo, then move on to the tender chateaubriand, charbroiled lobster, or the restaurant's signature shrimp steak, made with ground shrimp. You'll find the setting so relaxing and charming that you might want to linger well into the night. ⊠ *Blvd. Mijares 8,* ☎ *114/2–04–99. AE, MC, V.*

$$$ ✕ **Fandango.** This quirky restaurant has an excellent reputation among longtime residents, and its eclectic menu should please almost everyone. Interesting dishes include Chilean seafood stew, grilled sea bass, wild-mushroom pizza, and Thai chicken. The decor is as diverse as the menu: there's a festive mural, Chinese umbrellas, and a candlelit patio. ⊠ *Obregón 19 at Morelos,* ☎ *114/2–22–26. No credit cards.*

$$$ ✕ **Floriska.** A meal at this French-owned restaurant is sure to be a culinary highlight of your trip. The international fusion menu—which includes such savory dishes as salmon tartar, lobster in a Grand Marnier vinaigrette, and seafood casserole—is complemented by the elegant decor and fine tableware. Be sure to save room for dessert; the fruit sabayon is a divine way to end your meal. Jazz guitarists perform nightly on the outdoor patio. ⊠ *Blvd. Mijares 16-1, Col. Centro,* ☎ *114/2–46–00. AE, MC, V.*

$$$ ✕ **Hilario's.** The beautiful outdoor patio, surrounded by brick, exposed beams, and bougainvillea, and great seafood are two reasons to dine at this restaurant and bar. Hilario's has a mesquite grill and open-air kitchen, and offers a wide selection of fresh fish, including the house special for two—lobster, sea bass, shrimp, and scallops grilled and served with locally grown organic vegetables. ⊠ *Manuel Doblado 1117,* ☎ ℻ *114/2–46–55. AE, MC, V. Closed Mon.*

$$$ ✕ **Tequila Restaurante.** An old adobe home serves as the setting for the classiest restaurant in town. The lengthy tequila list gives you a chance to savor the finer brands of Mexico's national drink, and the menu challenges you to decide between excellent regional dishes and innovative Pacific Rim spring rolls, salads, and seafood with mango, ginger, and citrus sauces. Take your time and sample all you can. ⊠ *Manuel Doblado s/n,* ☎ *114/2–11–55. AE.*

$$ ✕ **Tropicana Bar and Grill.** Start the day with coffee and French toast at the sidewalk tables in front of this enduringly popular restaurant. Later, as the temperature rises, it's more comfortable to sit inside the large, air-conditioned bar over an ice-cold lemonade, watching sporting events and music videos on TV. In the evening the back patio quickly fills with a loyal clientele who enjoy the garden setting and decent cooking. The menu has grown over the years to include U.S. cuts of beef and imported seafood along with fajitas, chiles rellenos, and lobster, always in demand. The nightly dinner special is usually a good deal. ⊠ *Blvd. Mijares 30,* ☎ *114/2–15–80. AE, MC, V.*

$ ✕ **Baja Natural.** Tucked down a flight of steps away from the busy streets, this is a good place to cool off. The menu features dozens of fresh-fruit smoothies and juices, shakes, and power drinks, as well as hamburgers, hot dogs, and veggie burgers. The decor is sparse, but you're not here to be impressed with the surroundings, just refreshed. Kids will like it. ⊠ *Manuel Oblado between Morelos and Hidalgo.* ☎ *114/2–31–05. No credit cards. Closed Sun.*

$ ✕ **Restaurant La Playita.** A longtime local secret, this small, out-of-the-way restaurant has undergone several changes in owners and chefs but always draws dedicated locals and tourists. The main attraction is the seafood brought in daily by fishermen who beach their boats just a few yards away. The fish is prepared according to the whims of the cook and available ingredients; you can't go wrong if you stick with the catch of the day grilled with oil and garlic. Lunch here is a nice midday outing, especially when followed by a long walk down the largely deserted beach. ⊠ *Pueblo la Playa, 2 km (1 mi) south of San José,* ☎ *114/2–37–74. MC, V.*

$$$$ 🏨 **Casa Natalia.** Standing gracefully at the north end of San José's most charming street and public plaza is this beautiful hotel, a husband-and-wife effort opened in 1999. The bright, airy rooms, among the most private and well appointed in Los Cabos, are decorated in regional Mex-

ican motifs and have California king-size beds, European linens, re-
mote-control air-conditioning, and sliding glass doors that lead to a
private patio. From your hammock you can enjoy the view of the garden, pool, and regal palms. The restaurant, presided over by owner–
chef Luïc Tenoux, features a delicious blend of traditional Mexican and
European cuisine. ✉ *Blvd. Mijares 4, 23400,* ☎ *114/2–52–00, 888/
277–3814 in the U.S.,* ℻ *114/2–5–10. 16 rooms, 2 suites. Restaurant,
bar, pool, massage. AE, MC, V.* 🍴

$$$$ 🏨 **Presidente Inter-Continental Los Cabos.** By far the nicest—and one
of the oldest—hotels in San José, the Presidente sits amid cactus gardens next to the estuary at the end of the hotel zone. The buildings
curve around an enormous pool; the best rooms have shaded patios
and king-size beds. The hotel operates on an all-inclusive basis (rates
include all meals, drinks, and some activities)—an attractive option for
families and those happy to have a bit more quantity than quality, especially as there are few other restaurants in the immediate vicinity. A
new wing has a play area for children. ✉ *Paseo San José, at the end
of the hotel zone, 23400,* ☎ *114/2–02–11, 800/327–0200,* ℻ *114/2–
02–32. 244 rooms, 6 suites. 2 restaurants, bar, pool, 2 tennis courts,
horseback riding, beach, fishing, meeting rooms. AE, MC, V.* 🍴

$$ 🏨 **Huerta Verde.** Although far from the sea in an unlikely rural setting
just north of San José, this seven-room bed-and-breakfast is one of the
most picturesque properties in Los Cabos. A dirt road leads through
mango groves to the property's arched entryway. Brick stairs lead
through hibiscus and bougainvillea hedges to the main house and guest
rooms. Suites are in adjacent brick buildings with dome ceilings, gor-
geous handcrafted furnishings, and comfy beds and chairs. Tropical gar-
dens surround the heated pool. Hikers enjoy the trails leading to hilltops
with views of the sea. Be sure to get directions to the property, which
is south of the small town of Santa Rosa between the airport and San
José. Rates include breakfast; you can order other meals in advance.
Credit cards are accepted only with advance reservations, which are
strongly advised. ✉ *Las Animas Altas, 2 km (1 mi) off Hwy. 1, 23400,*
☎ ℻ *114/8–05–11,* ☎ *303/431–5162 in the U.S.,* ℻ *303/431–4455
in the U.S. 3 rooms, 4 suites, 1 master suite. Restaurant, bar, pool.*

$$ 🏨 **La Playita.** The small community of Pueblo la Playa just outside San
José has long been a favorite day-trip escape for those in the know. The
small hotel on the beach is the perfect hideaway if you're not interested
in shopping or bar-hopping. The rooms in the two-story building are
painted stark white and have air-conditioning, tile bathrooms, ceiling
fans, and satellite TVs; phone service is available at the front desk. There
are two penthouses—a two-bedroom and a one-bedroom—both with
kitchenettes. The restaurant is a two-minute walk away. Rates go down
about 20% in summer. ✉ *Pueblo la Playa, 2 km (1 mi) south of San
José, 23400,* ☎ ℻ *114/2–41–66, 818/962–2805 in the U.S. 24 rooms,
2 penthouses. Restaurant, bar, pool, beach, fishing. MC, V.*

$$ 🏨 **Tropicana Inn.** This small hotel is a great option if you aren't des-
perate to be on the beach. The stucco buildings decorated with tile mu-
rals of Diego Rivera paintings frame a pool and palapa bar in a quiet
enclave behind San José's main boulevard. Rooms are air-conditioned,
have satellite TV, and are maintained to look brand new. Book in ad-
vance in high season. ✉ *Blvd. Mijares 30, 23400,* ☎ *114/2–09–07,*
℻ *114/2–15–90, 510/939–2725 in the U.S. 39 rooms, 1 suite. Restau-
rant, bar, room service, pool. AE, MC, V.*

$ 🏨 **Posada Terranova.** San José's best budget hotel is a friendly place
where guests return so frequently they're almost part of the family. The
large, air-conditioned rooms are painted bright white and have two dou-
ble beds and tile bathrooms. The hotel has expanded in recent years.
Even so, when guests congregate at the front patio tables or in the restau-

rant, it still feels like a private home. ⊠ *Calle Degollado at Zaragoza, 23400,* ☎ *114/2–05–34,* 🅵🅰🆇 *114/2–09–02. 26 rooms. Restaurant, bar. AE, MC, V.* 🍴

NIGHTLIFE AND THE ARTS

The hottest nightspot in town is **Iguana Bar** (⊠ Blvd. Mijares 24, ☎ 114/2–02–66), a local hangout with live rock and roll on weekend nights during the high season. **Kitsch Café and Gallery** (⊠ Blvd. Mijares 29–1, ☎ 114/2–47–67), a gallery and coffee shop by day, draws a young crowd on weekends with open-mike poetry, tarot readings, and late-night dancing.

OUTDOOR ACTIVITIES AND SPORTS

Fishing. Most hotels in San José can arrange trips. As there is no marina in town, you'll board your boat at the marina in Cabo San Lucas—hotels will also set up transportation to the marina and prepare lunches. Pangas depart from the sand at La Playita; you can arrange trips through hotels.

Kayaking. Kayak tours and rentals are available through **Los Lobos del Mar** (⊠ Brisas del Mar RV park, on the south side of San José, ☎ 114/2–29–83). The tours paddle along the Corridor's peaceful bays and are especially fun in the winter months when gray whales pass by offshore.

Surfing. Killer Hook Surf Shop (⊠ Av. Hidalgo, ☎ 114/2–24–30) sells and rents snorkeling gear, along with surfboards and boogie boards.

SHOPPING

Shopping opportunities in San José del Cabo occur in the few streets around the main plaza and City Hall. **ADD** (⊠ Av. Zaragoza at Hidalgo, ☎ 114/3–20–55), an interior-design shop, sells gorgeous hand-painted dishes from Guanajuato and carved wood furniture from Michoacán. Across from City Hall is **Almacenes Goncanseco** (⊠ Blvd. Mijares 18, ☎ no phone), where you can get film, postcards, groceries, and liquor. **Amigos Smokeshop and Cigar Bar** (⊠ Calle Doblado and Morelos, ☎ 114/2–11–38) sells a wide selection of Cuban cigars. **Copal** (⊠ Plaza Mijares, ☎ 114/2–30–70) has a nice array of carved animals from Oaxaca, masks from Guerrero, and heavy wooden furnishings. At **Kitsch Café and Gallery** (⊠ Blvd. Mijares 29–1, ☎ 114/2–47–67), you can relax with a cappuccino or cocktail while surrounded by a wide selection of traditional crafts from around Mexico and paintings by the owner. For fresh produce, flowers, meat, fish, and a sampling of local life in San José, visit the **Mercado Municipal,** off Calle Doblado.

The Corridor

Many of the legendary fishing lodges and exclusive resorts built before the government stepped in were located along the wild cliffs between San José del Cabo and Cabo San Lucas. Since the mid-1980s, the area has developed as a destination unto itself. It has several private communities and large-scale resorts, and three championship golf courses. The highway along the Corridor has been widened to four lanes. The road is in good shape most of the time, but tends to flood during heavy rains, especially between August and November.

BEACHES

Costa Azul is the most popular surfing beach in Los Cabos. A few small campgrounds and casual restaurants line the beach facing the waves. **Playa Palmilla** is one of the Corridor's best swimming beaches.

Two bays, **Bahía Chileno** and **Bahía Santa María,** are terrific for diving and snorkeling (☞ Outdoor Activities and Sports, *below*).

DINING AND LODGING

$$$ ✕ **Pitahayas.** This elegant restaurant has found its niche in a lovely spot just above the beach at Cabo del Sol. The wide-ranging menu features Pacific Rim cuisine, blending touches of Thai, Polynesian, and Chinese cooking in unusual recipes. Lobster appears in the form of gourmet hash, duckling is served with a plum-tangerine sauce, and fresh organic vegetables are lightly stir-fried and served while still crisp. Soft jazz plays in the background, and the setting is decidedly romantic. ✉ *Hwy. 1, Km 10,* ☎ *114/5–80–10. AE, MC, V.*

$$ ✕ **Da Giorgio II.** The best sunset-watching in all of Los Cabos is at the cliffside tables outside this restaurant. Staggered along the cliffs and poised beside a small pond with a waterfall, the tables have great views of the arch at land's end. The menu focuses on pastas and pizza, and the salad bar has an abundance of fresh veggies. ✉ *Hwy. 1, Km 5,* ☎ *114/3–29–88. MC, V.*

$ ✕ **Zippers.** Home of the surfing crowd and those who like a bit of sand in their burgers, this casual palapa-roof restaurant sits on Costa Azul beach just south of San José. Burgers, ribs, and chicken are all decent, but it's the crowd that makes the place fun. ✉ *Hwy. 1, Km 18.5,* ☎ *no phone. No credit cards.*

$$$$ 🏨 **Casa Del Mar.** One of the smallest properties in the area, this hacienda-style hotel is all about luxurious privacy. An antique hand-carved wooden door leads into the courtyard-lobby with stone fountains and stairways that curve up to the rooms, spa, and library. Rooms are designed with pampering in mind—the bathrooms with whirlpool bathtubs and shower and separate toilet stalls are set a few steps above the main bedroom, where cushy beds covered in satiny soft sheets afford sea views. A series of flowing streams, fountains, and gardens leads around the pool to a wide stretch of beach where you can leave footprints in the untrammeled sand. The restaurant is excellent. ✉ *Carretera Transpeninsular Km 19.5, Cabo San Lucas 23410,* ☎ *114/4–00–30, 800/221–8808,* ℻ *114/4–00–34. 24 rooms, 32 suites. Restaurant, pool, spa, beach. AE, MC, V.* ✍

$$$$ 🏨 **Meliá Cabo Real.** This Meliá sprawls over a hilltop with a crystal-blue pool, fountains, waterfalls, white canopies shading rest areas, and a private beach created by a small jetty jutting from the rocky hillside. Maya carvings and bas-reliefs adorn the walls in the rooms, which all have landscaped terraces. The Cabo Real resort development around the hotel is ongoing, with an 18-hole golf course now open. Meliá guests can use it for a fee. The hotel shuttle runs to its sister property in Cabo San Lucas. ✉ *Carretera Transpeninsular Km 19.5, Cabo San Lucas 23400,* ☎ *114/4–00–00, 800/336–3542,* ℻ *114/4–01–01, 305/854–0660 in the U.S. 320 rooms. 4 restaurants, café, pool, 2 tennis courts, exercise room, beach, dive shop, fishing. AE, MC, V.* ✍

$$$$ 🏨 **Palmilla.** Just outside San José, the Palmilla is a gracious, sprawl-
★ ing, hacienda-style resort with a small white adobe chapel. Tile stairways lead up from flower-lined paths to large apartments with hand-carved furniture, French doors opening onto private patios, and tile baths; all rooms have TVs and phones. There's also a swimming pool with fountains, a swim-up bar, and plenty of space for serious swimmers. The buildings are spread along a hillside overlooking the beach, the service is delightfully personalized, and the hotel's La Paloma restaurant is excellent. There is a 27-hole Jack Nicklaus–designed golf course as well as a condo resort development surrounding the hotel. ✉ *Carretera Transpeninsular Km 1 (about 8 km [5 mi] from San José), 23400 (4343 Von Karman Ave., Newport Beach, CA 92660),* ☎ *114/4–50–00, 800/637–2226,* ℻ *114/4–51–00. 78 rooms, 36 suites, 1 villa. Restaurant, bar, pool, golf privileges, 2 tennis courts, beach. AE, MC, V.* ✍

$$$$ ⊡ **Twin Dolphin.** Sleek and Japanese-modern, with an austere air, the Twin Dolphin has been a hideaway for the rich and famous since 1977. Guest rooms are in low-lying casitas along a seaside cliff and are furnished in minimalist style, without TVs and phones. The hotel is worth a visit if only for the reproductions of Baja's cave paintings on the lobby wall. ⊠ *Carretera Transpeninsular Km 11.5, Cabo San Lucas 23410 (1625 W. Olympic Blvd., Suite 1005, Los Angeles, CA 90015),* ☎ *114/5–81–90, 800/421–8925,* ℻ *114/3–04–96, 213/380–1302 in the U.S. 44 rooms, 6 suites. Restaurant, bar, pool, massage, 2 tennis courts, beach, fishing. MC, V.*

$$$$ ⊡ **Las Ventanas al Paraíso.** Taking the Corridor by storm in early 1997,
★ Las Ventanas has set the standard for luxury, privacy, and amenities in Los Cabos. All suites have individual hot tubs, wood-burning fireplaces, and telescopes for viewing whales at sea and stars at night. The service is sublime—courteous staff seem to pop out of nowhere to offer anything from a beach towel to a cool drink. A sort-of handbook on contemporary seaside elegance, the hotel is filled with handcrafted lamps and doors, sculpture, and painting, and the walkways were hand laid in stone patterns. The outstanding restaurant is worth a visit for the chef's home-baked breads and innovative recipes. Guests have access to off-property golf and tennis facilities nearby. ⊠ *Carretera Transpeninsular Km 19.5, Cabo San Lucas 23400,* ☎ *114/4–03–00, 888/525–0483 in the U.S.,* ℻ *114/4–03–01, 310/824–1218 in the U.S. 61 suites. Restaurant, pool, spa, beach, fishing. AE, MC, V.*

$$$$ ⊡ **Westin Regina Resort.** The Westin is architecturally astounding, a
★ magnificent conglomeration of colors, shapes, and views. The luxurious rooms are among the best in Los Cabos, with satellite TVs, in-room safes, hair dryers, bathtubs and separate walk-in showers, and both air-conditioning and ceiling fans—a boon if you prefer open windows and sea breezes. It's a long walk from the parking lot and lobby to the rooms and pools, set above a man-made beach. The Royal Beach Club Villas are decorated with gorgeous pottery and have full kitchens and whirlpool tubs facing the sea. Two of Los Cabos's best golf courses are nearby, and the hotel is designed to keep its guests happy without their ever having to leave the grounds. ⊠ *Carretera Transpeninsular Km 22.5, Apdo. 145, San José del Cabo 23400,* ☎ *114/2–90–00, 800/228–3000,* ℻ *114/2–90–10. 243 rooms, 60 villas. 3 restaurants, 5 pools, 2 tennis courts, exercise room, beach. AE, MC, V.* ⊛

$$$ ⊡ **Hotel Cabo San Lucas.** Looking like a mountain lodge nearly buried in palms, this long-standing Corridor hotel is a favorite of Baja devotees. The rooms are furnished with sturdy, dark-wood pieces; suites and villas are more luxurious. The hacienda-style buildings are located right above Chileno Beach, one of the best diving spots in Los Cabos. ⊠ *Carretera Transpeninsular Km 14.5, Cabo San Lucas 23410,* ☎ *114/4–00–14, 800/733–2226,* ℻ *114/4–00–15, 213/655–3243 in the U.S. 89 rooms. Restaurant, pool, beach, dive shop, fishing. AE, MC, V.*

OUTDOOR ACTIVITIES AND SPORTS

Diving and Snorkeling. Bahía Chileno, an underwater preserve, teems with marine life and is a wonderful place for snorkeling and diving. You'll need to bring your own equipment. **Bahía Santa María,** a picture-perfect white-sand cove protected by towering brown cliffs, has superb snorkeling, with hundreds of colorful fish swarming through chunks of white coral. There is a concession stand on the beach with snorkeling-gear rental; its hours are erratic.

Fishing. Most Corridor hotels have excellent fishing fleets, with the boats anchored at the marina in Cabo San Lucas. Hotels typically can set up the trips and provide transportation to the marina and box lunches. **Victor's Aquatics** (☎ 114/2–10–92, ℻ 114/2–10–93) has a fleet of pangas on the Palmilla resort's beach. **Jig Stop Tours** (☎ 800/521–2281) books fishing trips for several Los Cabos fleets.

Golf. Los Cabos is a hot spot for golf, hosting tournaments including the PGA Senior Grand Slam. The courses that have brought so much attention this way are all in the Corridor and serve as the centerpieces for megaresort developments. If you aren't staying at a hotel associated with one of the courses, reserve a tee time a week in advance. Expect to pay exorbitant greens fees—$200 on average. Among the most spectacular golf courses is the 27-hole Jack Nicklaus–designed course at the **Palmilla Golf Club** (✉ Palmilla resort, Carretera Transpeninsular Km 1, ☎ 114/4–52–50, 800/386–2465). **Cabo del Sol** (☎ 114/5–82–00, 800/386–2465 in the U.S.), a resort development in the Corridor, has an 18-hole Jack Nicklaus course. Plans are for three 18-hole courses (the second designed by Tom Weiskopf). The fairly new Robert Trent Jones–designed **Cabo Real Golf Club** (✉ Meliá Cabo Real Hotel, ☎ 114/2–90–00, ext. 9205) has 36 holes.

Cabo San Lucas

Cabo San Lucas, once an unsightly fishing town with dusty streets and smelly canneries, has become Los Cabos's center of tourism activity. The sportfishing fleet is headquartered here, and cruise ships anchored off the marina disperse passengers into town. Trendy restaurants and bars line the streets, and massive hotels have risen on every available plot of waterfront turf—alas, a five-story condo-hotel complex along the bay blocks the view from the town's older hotels. Cabo San Lucas is decidedly *in*—for its rowdy nightlife, its slew of restaurants, and its shopportunities.

Highway 1 leads into the center of Cabo San Lucas, ending at Kilometer 1 on the Transpeninsular Highway. The main downtown street, **(34)** Avenida Lázaro Cárdenas, passes the pretty **Plaza San Lucas** with its white wrought-iron gazebo. Buildings around the plaza house galleries and restaurants. Most of the shops, services, and restaurants are located between Avenida Cárdenas and the waterfront.

Boulevard Marina has been transformed from a dusty main drag into a busy thoroughfare lined with hotels and cafés. Paved walkways now run from here to the hotels and beaches on the east end of town and **(35)** west to the **Handicrafts Market** at the Cabo San Lucas marina (☞ Shop-**(36)** ping, *below*). The sportfishing fleet is docked in the **Bahía de Cabo San Lucas,** and there are glass-bottom boats available at the water's edge.

(37) The most spectacular sight in Cabo San Lucas is **El Arco.** The natural rock arch is visible from the marina and from some of the hotels but is more impressive from the water. **El Faro de Cabo Falso** (Lighthouse of the False Cape), built in 1890 and set amid sand dunes, is a little bit farther on from El Arco. You need a four-wheel-drive vehicle to reach the lighthouse by land. If you don't take at least a short boat ride out to the arch and Playa de Amor, the beach underneath, you haven't fully appreciated Cabo.

BEACHES

Playa de Amor consists of a secluded cove at the very end of the peninsula, with the Sea of Cortés on one side and the Pacific Ocean on the other. The contrast between the peaceful azure cove on the Sea of Cortés and the pounding white surf of the Pacific is dramatic. **Playa Hacienda,** in the inner harbor by the Hacienda Hotel, has the calmest waters of any beach in town and good snorkeling around the rocky point. **Playa Médano,** just north of Cabo San Lucas, is the most popular stretch in Los Cabos (and possibly in all Baja) for sunbathing and people-watching. The 3-km (2-mi) span of white sand is always crowded, especially

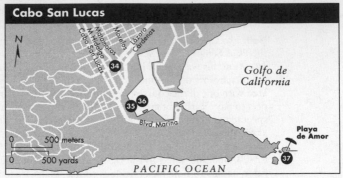

on weekends. **Playa Solmar,** fringing the Solmar Hotel, is a beautiful wide beach at the base of the mountains leading into the Pacific, but it has dangerous surf with a swift undertow. Stick to sunbathing here.

DINING AND LODGING

$$$ ✕ **El Galeón.** Considered by some the most distinguished dining room in town, El Galeón is across from the marina. The choice seats are on the outside terraces facing the water; the inside is decorated with heavy wooden furniture. Traditional Italian, Mexican, and American dishes are prepared expertly, with an emphasis on thick, tender cuts of beef. The piano bar is a nice setting for a late-night brandy. ⊠ *across from the marina by the road to Finisterra Hotel,* ☎ 114/3–04–43. AE, MC, V.

$$$ ✕ **Mi Casa.** One of Cabo's best restaurants is in a cobalt-blue build-
★ ing painted with a mural of a burro, just across the street from the main plaza. Mexican cuisine reaches gourmet status here with fresh tuna and dorado served with tomatillo salsa or Yucatecan achiote, or with so-phisticated dishes such as chili en nogada. The restaurant quickly out-grew its small dining room and has spread into a large back courtyard. It's especially nice at night, illuminated by candlelight and the moon. ⊠ *Av. Cabo San Lucas,* ☎ 114/3–19–33. MC, V.

$$$ ✕ **Peacocks.** The ubiquitous fresh-fish dinner achieves gustatory em-
★ inence when prepared by Bernard Voll. His dorado is coated with a crust of chopped pecans, and his shrimp masterfully tossed with spinach fettuccine. This chef is known for his incredible desserts—if you miss dinner, be sure to stop by for a cappuccino and a tequila mousse. The candlelit two-level dining room has an open kitchen and is topped by an enormous palapa; you can also dine on an outdoor patio. ⊠ *Paseo Pescador near Playa Médano,* ☎ 114/3–18–58. AE, MC, V.

$$ ✕ **Edith's Café.** Calm and romantic by local standards, this small café starts out with live jazz and blues in the background and views of the sea. Lobster and other seafood, an excellent wine list, and good cof-fees and desserts fill out the picture of a long, romantic dinner here. ⊠ *Paseo del Pescador near Playa Médano,* ☎ 114/3–08–01. MC, V.

$$ ✕ **Pancho's.** This festive restaurant, a favorite among locals in the know, has an enormous collection of tequilas (almost 500 labels); take ad-vantage of owner John Bragg's encyclopedic knowledge of tequila and sample a few. Oaxacan tablecloths, murals, painted chairs, and stream-ers add to the fun atmosphere. The menu offers a variety of delicious seafood and regional Mexican specialties; try the tortilla soup, chiles rellenos, or stuffed bacon-wrapped shrimp. Pancho's is also open for breakfast. ⊠ *Hidalgo between Zapata and Serdan,* ☎ 114/3–09–73, ℻ 114/3–50–95. AE, MC, V.

$$ ✕ **El Shrimp Bucket.** This is the calmest of the three Carlos Anderson restaurants in Cabo San Lucas. A few tables are set out on the walk-way that runs along the marina in front of the Marina Fiesta Hotel, a good spot to relax and watch the boats rock on the water. The indoor dining room has the chain's typical mishmash decor and quirky adornments. The food—barbecued ribs and chicken, burgers, piles of fried shrimp—is dependable and abundant. ✉ *Blvd. Marina in Marina Fiesta complex,* ☎ *114/3–25–98. AE, MC, V.*

$ ✕ **Fish Company.** It's easy to overlook this small seafood joint surrounded by flashier restaurants, but don't: the owner has perfected the art of preparing flavorful meals at reasonable prices. Nine tables covered with blue-and-white cloths sit just in from the sidewalk in the narrow dining room, and the aroma of fresh grilled fish fills the air. Breakfast specialties include a great chorizo-and-cheese omelet. Among lunch and dinner choices are shrimp with oyster sauce and fresh fish smothered in garlic. For a low-cost feast, bring your own catch here to have it prepared. ✉ *Av. Guerrero between Blvd. Marina and Zapata,* ☎ *114/ 3–14–05. No credit cards.*

$ ✕ **The Office.** Playa Médano is lined with cafés on the sand, some with lounge chairs, others with more-formal settings. All serve the same basics—cold beer, snacks, fish tacos, french fries—and most accompany the meal with loud American rock. The Office, which has provided perfect vacation photo opportunities for more than a decade, has grown like its neighbors but remains a locals' hangout. ✉ *Playa Médano,* ☎ *114/3–34–64. No credit cards.*

$ ✕ **Señor Greenberg's Mexicatessen.** Pastrami, chopped liver, knishes, bagels, lox, cheesecake—such wonders one finds behind the glass counters at this decent Mexican incarnation of a New York deli. It's open 24 hours; the tables, air-conditioning, stacks of newspapers, and soft music encourage frequent visits. ✉ *Plaza Nautical on Blvd. Marina,* ☎ *114/3–56–30. AE, MC, V.*

$$$$ ▦ **Finisterra.** One of the oldest hotels in Cabo, the Finisterra is now also one of the most modern, thanks to the two towers rising directly from the beach. An eight-story-high palapa covers the restaurant and bar on the beach next to two free-form swimming pools. Rooms in the new buildings, with oceanfront balconies, are by far the nicest; some have king-size beds. Longtime guests favor the less-expensive older section of the hotel, with its stone buildings that have a fishing-lodge feel. The restaurant is only fair, but the Whale Watcher bar atop a high cliff has the best view in town. ✉ *Blvd. Marina, 23410 (6 Jenner St., No. 120, Irvine, CA 92618),* ☎ *114/3–33–33, 714/450–9000 or 800/347– 2252 in the U.S.,* ⅏ *114/3–05–90, 714/450–9010 in the U.S. 237 rooms. 2 restaurants, 2 bars, 3 pools, travel services. AE, MC, V.* ☙

$$$$ ▦ **Hotel Hacienda.** Set on the tip of a tree-filled point jutting into Bahía San Lucas, the Hacienda resembles a Spanish colonial inn with its white arches and bell towers, stone fountains, and statues of Indian gods set amid scarlet hibiscus and bougainvillea. The bar is a veritable museum of Indian artifacts. The white rooms have red-tile floors, tile baths, and folk art on the walls. The water-sports center is on the calmest beach in town and has kayaks, Jet Skis, snorkeling equipment, and any other gear you might need. The hotel has a three-night minimum stay on weekdays, and a four-night minimum on weekends in the high season. ✉ *Playa Médano, 23410,* ☎ *114/3–20–62, 114/3–01–22, 800/733–2226. 51 rooms, 12 suites, 10 town houses, 9 garden patio rooms, 30 beachfront cabañas. Restaurant, bar, pool, beach, dive shop. MC, V.*

$$$$ ▦ **Meliá San Lucas.** From the moment you enter the Meliá and spot El ★ Arco framed by the lobby's arches, you know you're at a hotel where details are important. The blue walls and linens in the rooms complement the views of the aquamarine sea; the outer adobe walls of the terraced hotel buildings glow orange and gold with the changing sunlight. The Meliá has a long beach with calm waters, a spacious hot tub under the palms, and all the equipment you could need for playing on and in

the water. Early reservations are essential. ⌷ *Playa Médano, 23410,* ☎ *114/3–44–44, 800/336–3542,* FAX *114/3–04–18. 142 rooms, 6 suites. 3 restaurants, 2 pools, hot tub, beach. AE, MC, V.*

$$$$ 🄴 **Pueblo Bonito Rosé.** Soft pink Mediterranean-style buildings surround lush gardens populated with strolling peacocks at this Playa Médano resort. Waterfalls, fountains, and a hot tub separate the pool area into several sections so serious swimmers have room for laps while kids have their own area for splashing about. Many of the commodious suites have kitchenettes, and the restaurants are worth checking out. ⌷ *Playa Médano, 23410,* ☎ *114/3–55–00, 800/940–8250,* FAX *114/3–59–79. 260 suites. 2 restaurants, pool, beach, snorkeling, jet skiing. MC, V.*

$$$$ 🄴 **Solmar Suites.** From afar, the Solmar looks like a space colony, set
★ against granite cliffs at the tip of Land's End, facing the wild Pacific. The rooms, decorated in Mexico–Santa Fe style, have separate sitting areas and tile baths; the best ones are set up against the rocks right over the beach. The adjacent time-share and condo units have kitchenettes and a private pool area. The surf here is far too dangerous for swimming, but don't miss a stroll along the wide strip of beach. Most visitors hang out around the two additional pools and swim-up bars, joining in with the ever-present musicians. The Solmar's sportfishing fleet is first-rate. The good restaurant hosts a Saturday night Mexican fiesta and buffet dinner. ⌷ *Blvd. Marina, Apdo. 8, 23410 (Box 383, Pacific Palisades, CA 90272),* ☎ *114/3–35–35, 310/459–9861 or 800/ 344–3349 in the U.S.,* FAX *114/3–04–10, 310/454–1686 in the U.S. 86 rooms, 4 suites, 68 condos. Restaurant, bar, 3 pools, beach, dive shop, fishing. AE, MC, V.*

$$$ 🄴 **Casa Rafael's.** This intimate boutique hotel is the perfect spot if you are looking for privacy rather than recreational diversions. Rooms are individually decorated with an eclectic collection of antiques and modern furnishings; all have air-conditioning and private baths. A lap pool on the terrace behind the house is surrounded by plants, and there's a small exercise room and hot tub. ⌷ *Calle Médano at Camino Pescador, between Hotel Hacienda and Marina Sol condos, 23410,* ☎ FAX *114/ 3–07–39,* FAX *114/3–16–79. 12 rooms. Restaurant, pool, hot tub, exercise room. AE, MC, V.*

$$ 🄴 **The Bungalows Breakfast Inn.** If solitude and a reasonable room rate are more important than being in the center of the action, this is your place, 10 blocks from the beach. Several two-story buildings frame a small, heated pool. Rooms are beautifully decorated with Mexican textiles and art. Breakfast is included in the rates; smoking is not permitted. ⌷ *Calle Constitución (5 blocks from main plaza), 23410,* ☎ FAX *114/ 3–50–35. 16 suites. Breakfast room, pool. No credit cards.*

$$ 🄴 **Siesta Suites.** You'll have to forgo air-conditioning to remain in the inexpensive range, but you'll get a large, immaculate room with kitchenette. The three-story hotel sits just two blocks from the marina, and the proprietors are the friendliest in town. Music from nearby bars might bother some. ⌷ *Calle Zapata, Apdo. 310, 23410,* ☎ FAX *114/3–64– 94, 602/331–1354 in the U.S. 5 rooms, 15 suites. Kitchenettes. No credit cards.* 🐾

$ 🄴 **Las Villas Turismo Juvenil.** Cabo's youth hostel is about 10 blocks from the waterfront in a quiet neighborhood. Two dormitory rooms have bunk beds and shelves, and there are several private rooms with shared baths. In the courtyard, you can use sinks and counters to fix meals and wash clothes. ⌷ *Av. de la Juventud, 23410,* ☎ *114/3–01– 48. 2 dorms, 11 private rooms. No credit cards.*

NIGHTLIFE AND THE ARTS

Some travelers choose Cabo San Lucas for its nightlife, which consists mainly of noisy bars with blaring music and plenty of dancing, flirting, and imbibing. The latest U.S. bands play over an excellent sound system at **Cabo Wabo** (⊠ Calle Guerrero, ☎ 114/3–11–98), but the impromptu jam sessions with appearances by Sammy Hagar—an owner—and his many music-business friends are the real highlight. **Squid Roe** (⊠ Av. Cárdenas, ☎ 114/3–06–55) is the rowdiest spot in town, packed with young foreigners who work in the local tourist industry and know how to party. **The Nowhere Bar** (⊠ Plaza Bonita, Blvd. Marina, ☎ 114/3–44–93) is the place to be Tuesday for Ladies' Night. **Giggling Marlin** (⊠ Blvd. Marina, ☎ 114/3–11–82) seems to have been around forever as the favorite watering hole for fishermen and their girlfriends. **El Galeón** (⊠ Blvd. Marina, ☎ 114/3–04–43) is a welcome refuge for the quieter crowd, who sip brandy by the piano bar. **Edith's** (⊠ Paseo del Pescador at Playa Médano, ☎ 114/3–08–01) presents live jazz in a tasteful garden setting.

OUTDOOR ACTIVITIES AND SPORTS

Diving. El Arco is a prime diving and snorkeling area, as are several rocky points off the coast. Most hotels offer diving trips and equipment rental. The oldest and most complete dive shop in the area is **Amigos del Mar** (⊠ near the sportfishing docks at the harbor, ☎ 114/3–05–05, 800/344–3349, FAX 114/3–08–87). **Cabo Acuadeportes** (⊠ Hotel Hacienda, Playa Médano, ☎ 114/3–01–17) offers diving trips along with all other imaginable water sports. The **Solmar V** (⊠ Solmar Suites Hotel, Blvd. Marina, ☎ 114/3–00–22, 800/344–3349), a live-aboard dive boat, takes weeklong trips to the islands of Socorro, San Benedicto, and Clarion, and the coral reefs at Cabo Pulmo. It has 12 cabins with private baths (maximum, 24 passengers).

Fishing. There are more than 800 species of fish in the waters off Los Cabos. Most hotels will arrange fishing charters, which include a captain and mate, tackle, bait, licenses, and drinks. Prices start at $250 per day for a 25-ft cruiser. Some charters provide lunch, and most can arrange to have your catch mounted, frozen, or smoked. Most of the boats leave from the sportfishing docks in the Cabo San Lucas marina. Usually there are a fair number of pangas for rent at about $30 per hour with a five-hour minimum. Dependable companies include the following: **Gaviota Fleet** (⊠ at the marina, ☎ 114/3–04–30, 800/521–2281); **Minerva's** (⊠ at the marina and on Madero between Blvd. Marina and Guerrero, ☎ 114/3–12–82, FAX 114/3–04–40); **Pisces Sportfishing Fleet** (⊠ at the marina, ☎ 114/3–12–88); and **Solmar Fleet** (⊠ Solmar Suites Hotel, Blvd. Marina, ☎ 114/3–35–35, 114/3–00–22, 800/344–3349, FAX 114/3–04–10, 310/454–1686 in the U.S.).

Horseback Riding. Cantering down an isolated beach or up a desert trail is one of the great pleasures of Baja (as long as the sun isn't beating down on your head). Horses are available for rent in a shady grove in front of the Playa Médano hotels; contact **Rancho Collins Horses** (☎ 114/3–36–52). **Red Rose Riding Stables** (⊠ Hwy. 1, Km 4, ☎ 114/3–48–26) has healthy horses for all levels of riders and an impressive array of tack. The **Cuadra San Francisco Equestrian Center** (⊠ on Corridor highway across from Cabo Real development, ☎ no phone, arrange at your hotel desk) is a professional center with training and trail rides.

Whale-Watching. The gray whale migration doesn't end at Baja's Pacific lagoons. Plenty of whales of all sizes make it down to the warmer waters off Los Cabos and into the Sea of Cortés. Several companies run whale-watching trips from Cabo San Lucas. Check with **Cabo Acuadeportes** (☞ Diving, *above*) or any of the fishing companies. To watch whales from shore, go to the beach at the Solmar Suites or any Corridor hotel, or the lookout points along the Corridor highway.

SHOPPING

Some of the nicest shops in Cabo San Lucas are in **Plaza Bonita** on the waterfront at the beginning of Boulevard Marina. **Cartes** (⊠ Plaza Bonita, Blvd. Marina, ☎ 114/3–17–70) is the best of Los Cabos's many home-furnishing stores, with an irresistible array of hand-painted pottery and tableware, pewter frames, handblown glass, and carved furniture. **Libros** (⊠ Plaza Bonita, Blvd. Marina, ☎ 114/3–17–70) carries a vast number of English-language novels and magazines. **Dos Lunas** (⊠ Plaza Bonita, Blvd. Marina, ☎ 114/3–19–69) has a trendy selection of colorful sportswear. **Francisco's Café del Mundo** (⊠ Plaza Bonita, Blvd. Marina, ☎ 114/3–23–66) is the place to take an espresso or cappuccino break.

Boulevard Marina and the side streets between the waterfront and the main plaza are filled with an ever-changing parade of small shops. **Necri** (⊠ Blvd. Marina between Madero and Ocampo, ☎ 114/3–02–83) has an excellent selection of folk art and furnishings. **El Callejon** (⊠ Guerrero between Cárdenas and Madero, ☎ 114/3–11–39) has multiple showrooms with gorgeous furniture, lamps, dishes, and pottery. **Cuca's Blanket Factory** (⊠ Cárdenas at Matamoros, ☎ 114/3–19–13) sells the typical array of serapes and cotton blankets with a twist: you can design your own and have it ready the next day. **Mama Eli's** (⊠ Av. San Lucas, ☎ 114/3–16–16) is a three-story gallery with fine furnishings, ceramics, appliquéd clothing, and children's toys. **Galeria Gatemelatta** (⊠ on the dirt road to Hotel Hacienda, ☎ 114/3–11–66) specializes in colonial furniture and antiques.

At the **Handicrafts Market** in the marina, you can pose for a photo with an iguana, plan a ride in a glass-bottom boat, or browse to your heart's content through stalls packed with blankets, sombreros, and pottery.

Todos Santos

30 km (19 mi) north of Cabo San Lucas.

The Pacific side of the tip of Baja has remained largely undeveloped. The exception is the small agricultural town of Todos Santos, which has become a haven for artists, architects, and speculators who have contributed to a rapid rise in real-estate prices. The town sits a bit inland from the rugged coast and is classically charming with its 19th-century brick-and-stucco buildings and small central plaza. It's an ideal retirement haven for those who deplore the overdevelopment of Baja's tip, since both Los Cabos and La Paz are within easy driving distance. Todos Santos also benefits from cooling breezes from the Pacific and fresh water from underground springs. New neighborhoods are rising in the outskirts of town, usually before electricity, telephone lines, and water pipes are installed. Stop lights have appeared in abundance, along with NO PARKING signs. Entrepreneurs have turned some of the plaza-front buildings into galleries and cafés with erratic hours determined by the presence of tourists.

Los Cabos regulars typically drive up the coast to Todos Santos on day trips, eyeing the latest billboards announcing housing developments and stopping to watch surfers at Playa Migrio, Playa los Cerritos, and Punta Gaspareo, where a few solitary villas and motor homes sit on idyllic, although windy, beaches. El Pescadero is the largest settlement before Todos Santos, populated by ranchers and farmers who grow herbs and vegetables for the restaurants in Los Cabos. Seasonal produce is sold at small stands by the side of the road. Dirt roads intersect the highway at several points along the way to Todos Santos, but you should attempt these roads only with four-wheel-drive vehicles—sands on the beach or in the desert will stop conventional vehicles in their tracks.

During high season, you might be surprised to find tour buses clogging the streets around the plaza in Todos Santos; it is a pit stop on tours between Cabo San Lucas and La Paz. When the buses leave, the town is a pleasant and peaceful place to wander before and after a lunch at the Cafe Santa Fe. If you drive to Todos Santos on your own, head back to Cabo before dark; Highway 19 between the two towns is unlit and is prone to high winds and flooding. When you get to town, be sure to pick up *El Calendario de Todos Santos,* a free monthly guide with the most current happenings and developments.

Dining and Lodging

$$ ✗ **Cafe Santa Fe.** Owners Paula and Ezio Colombo can be credited with much of their town's popularity since their Italian restaurant is a destination in its own right. And many Cabo residents lunch here weekly. The setting, with tables amid herb gardens in an overgrown courtyard, is part of the appeal, but the reason you can't get a table on weekends is the food—salads and soups made from homegrown organic vegetables and herbs, homemade pastas and calzone, and fresh fish with light herbal sauces. It's tempting to linger for hours over a bottle of Chianti, but make sure you've got an alert designated driver to get you home. ⊠ *Calle Centenario,* ☎ *114/5–03–40. No credit cards. Closed Tues., parts of Sept. and Oct.*

$$ ✗ **Caffé Todos Santos.** Omelets, bagels, granola, and delicious wholegrain breads delight the breakfast crowd at this small café, known to have the best Mexican food in town; deli sandwiches, fresh salads, and an array of tamales, *flautas* (tortillas rolled around savory fillings), and combo plates are lunch and dinner highlights. Check for fresh seafood on the daily specials board, and pick up a loaf of bread for the road. You'll enjoy the high ceilings and quirky charm of the main dining room or the shady calm of the outdoor patio. ⊠ *Calle Centenario 33,* ☎ *no phone. No credit cards.*

$$$ ▥ **Todos Santos Inn.** The four guest rooms in this converted 19th-cen-
★ tury house are unparalleled in design and comfort. Gorgeous antiques are set against stone walls under brick ceilings. Ceiling fans and the shade from garden trees keep the rooms cool and breezy. The absence of telephones and TVs makes a perfect foil for the conceits of Los Cabos. And good restaurants are within easy walking distance. The whole house can be booked by vacationing families. ⊠ *Calle Legaspi, 23300,* ☎ FAX *114/5–00–40. 4 rooms. No credit cards.*

$$ ▥ **Hosteria Casitas.** If the Cabos have got you feeling like turning down the volume (and the cash flow), this B&B in a lush garden setting might give you the quiet you're looking for—and great breakfasts to start the day. The buildings' traditional Mexican architecture makes for cool accommodations. Owner Wendy Faith's art-glass studio is also on site. ⊠ *Calle Rangel at Obregón and Hidalgo, A.P. 73, 23300,* ☎ FAX *114/5–02–55. 3 rooms with private ½ bath and shared showers, 2 suites with bath. No credit cards.*

$ ▥ **Hotel Misión del Pilar.** Offering comfortable but spartan accommodations, this hotel is fine for those who don't mind close quarters with no frills. The hotel is down the street from Pilar's Taco Stand, the town bus stop. ⊠ *Colegio Militar and Hidalgo, 23300,* ☎ *114/5–01–14. 12 rooms. No credit cards.*

BAJA SUR A TO Z

Arriving and Departing

By Boat

Cruise lines that use Cabo San Lucas as a port of call include the following: **Carnival** (☎ 800/327–9501), **Princess** (☎ 800/421–0522), and **Royal Caribbean** (☎ 800/327–0271).

By Bus

The **Autotransportes de Baja California** bus line runs the length of the peninsula from Tijuana to Los Cabos, stopping at towns en route; the peninsula-long trip takes 22 hours. The **Aguila** bus line runs from Santa Rosalia to Los Cabos.

GUERRERO NEGRO

Autotransportes de Baja California (☎ 112/2–64–76) runs buses from La Paz to Guerrero Negro; the bus stops at the highway entrance to town.

LA PAZ

Autotransportes de Baja California (☎ 112/2–70–94) and **Aguila** (☎ 112/2–42–70) run along the Transpeninsular Highway to the border and to Los Cabos.

LORETO

Loreto is serviced by **Autotransportes de Baja California** and **Aguila**. The **Loreto bus terminal** (✉ Salvatierra and Tamaral, ☎ 113/5–07–67) sits at the entrance to town.

LOS CABOS

Autotransportes de Baja California (☎ 114/2–02–00) travels from Tijuana to Los Cabos and between Cabo San Lucas and San José daily.

By Car

Mexico Highway 1, also known as the Transpeninsular Highway, runs the entire 1,700 km (1,060 mi) from Tijuana to Cabo San Lucas. The highway's condition varies depending on the weather and intervals between road repairs. Do not drive it at high speeds or at night—it is not lighted. There are exits for all the principal towns in Baja Sur.

The road between San José del Cabo and Cabo San Lucas was widened to four lanes and is in good condition, although dips and bridges become flooded in heavy rains.

By Ferry

LA PAZ

The ferry system connecting Baja to mainland Mexico has been privatized and is constantly undergoing changes in rates and schedules. Currently there are **Sematur** ferries from La Paz to Mazatlán (an 18-hour trip) five days a week. Tickets are available at the **ferry office** (☎ 112/5–38–33 or 112/5–46–66, 𝔽𝔸𝕏 112/5–65–88) at the dock on the road to Pichilingue and at the **Sematur downtown office** (✉ Av. 5 de Mayo 502, ☎ 112/5–38–33, 𝔽𝔸𝕏 112/5–46–66). The Sematur Web site (www.ferrysematur.com.mx) *should* have the most up-to-date information, but isn't always accurate. Purchase your ticket in advance of your trip—it's probably best to use a Mexican travel agent for this—and expect confusion. Continuous changes in Sematur procedure and pricing make it difficult for even ferry personnel to keep up with the latest policy. If you plan to take a car or a motor home on the ferry to the mainland, you must obtain a vehicle permit before boarding the ferry and must have Mexican auto-insurance papers; everyone crossing to the mainland also needs a tourist card. Tourism officials in La

Paz strongly suggest that you obtain the vehicle permit when crossing the U.S. border into Baja; although permits are not needed in Baja, offices at the border are better equipped to handle the paperwork than those in La Paz. Tourist cards also are available at the border. It would be wise to take copies of the following, in triplicate, plus the original: passport, tourist card, birth certificate, and vehicle registration.

SANTA ROSALIA

Ferries travel from Santa Rosalia to Guaymas on the mainland Pacific coast. They depart for the seven-hour trip to the mainland at 11 PM on Wednesday and Sunday and arrive in Santa Rosalia at 4 PM Tuesday and Sunday. Buy tickets in advance at the **Santa Rosalia ferry terminal** (☎ 115/2–00–14, FAX 115/2–00–13), just south of town on Highway 1. Schedules are often erratic.

By Plane

LA PAZ

The La Paz airport, about 16 km (10 mi) north of town, is served by **AeroCalifornia** (☎ 112/5–10–23) from Tijuana and Loreto and **Aeroméxico** (☎ 112/2–00–91) from Los Angeles, Tucson, Tijuana, Mexico City, and other cities within Mexico.

LORETO

AeroCalifornia (☎ 113/5–00–50, 113/5–05–55, 800/237–6225 in the U.S.) has daily flights from Los Angeles and La Paz to Loreto's airport, which is 7 km (4½ mi) southwest of town.

LOS CABOS

The **Los Cabos International Airport** (☎ 114/2–03–41) is about 11 km (7 mi) north of San José del Cabo and about 48 km (30 mi) from Cabo San Lucas. **AeroCalifornia** (☎ 114/6–52–52, 800/237–6225) flies to Los Cabos from Los Angeles and Tijuana; **Mexicana** (☎ 114/6–50–01) from Guadalajara, Mexico City, and Los Angeles; **Aeroméxico** (☎ 114/6–50–97, 800/237–6639) from San Diego and Mexico City; **Alaska Airlines** (☎ 114/6–51–01, 800/426–0333) from Anchorage, Fairbanks, Portland, Phoenix, San Francisco, San Diego, Los Angeles, and Seattle; **America West** (☎ 114/2–28–82, 114/2–28–80, 800/235–9292) from Phoenix; **Continental** (☎ 114/2–38–80, 114/2–09–59, 800/525–0280) from Houston. Other international airlines may have service in winter.

Getting Around

Loreto

Taxis are in good supply and fares are inexpensive. There are two gas stations in Loreto; be sure to fill your tank before heading out on any long jaunts.

La Paz

A car isn't necessary if you plan to stay in town; taxis are readily available and inexpensive. It's also fairly easy to get around by bus in La Paz: city buses run along the malecón and into downtown. If you'd like to explore the remote beaches, *see* Car and Jeep Rental *in* Contacts and Resources, *below.*

Los Cabos

The best way to see the sights is on foot. Downtown San José and Cabo San Lucas are compact, with the plaza, church, shops, and restaurants within a few blocks of one another. Bus service runs between the towns, although buses might not stop along the Corridor. If you plan to dine at the Corridor hotels or travel frequently between the two towns, it's a good idea to rent a car for a few days. Taxi fares are steep here.

Contacts and Resources

Car and Jeep Rental

Thrifty (✉ Blvd. Misiones s/n, ☎ 113/3–07–00).

Avis (✉ at the airport, ☎ 112/2–18–13 or 112/2–26–51), **Budget** (✉ Paseo Obregón at Hidalgo, ☎ 112/2–10–97 or 112/2–76–55), **Hertz** (✉ at the airport, ☎ 112/2–09–19).

California Baja Rent-A-Car (✉ 9245 Jamacha Blvd., Spring Valley, CA 91977, ☎ 619/470–8368, 888/470–7368 in the U.S.) rents four-wheel-drive vehicles, convertibles, and sedans for use throughout Mexico; you can pick up a car in Tijuana and drop it off in Los Cabos, but expect to pay a hefty additional charge.

The following car-rental agencies have desks at the airport and in San José or Cabo San Lucas: **Avis** (☎ 114/6–03–88), **Dollar** (☎ 114/2–01–00 or 114/3–12–50), **National** (☎ 114/2–24–22 or 114/3–14–14), and **Thrifty** (☎ 114/6–50–30 or 114/3–16–66).

E-Mail

Dr. Z's Internet Café and Bar (✉ Blvd. Cárdenas across from Pemex, Cabo San Lucas, ☎ 114/3–53–90) has a full bar and casual menu, and charges $9 an hour for Internet access. **Cabocafe** (✉ Plaza José Green, Suite 3, Blvd. Mijares, San José del Cabo, ☎ 114/2–52–50) offers access for $9 an hour.

Emergencies

Police (☎ 112/2–66–10), **Fire** (☎ 112/2–74–74), and **Red Cross** (☎ 112/2–11–11).

Police: Cabo San Lucas (☎ 114/3–39–77) and San José del Cabo (☎ 114/2–03–61). **Hospital:** Cabo San Lucas (☎ 114/3–15–94) and San José del Cabo (☎ 114/2–00–13). **Red Cross:** Cabo San Lucas (☎ 114/3–33–00) and San José del Cabo (☎ 114/2–03–16).

Guided Tours

Eco-Tours Malarrimo (✉ Blvd. Zapata, 23940, ☎ 115/7–02–50) is the best tour operator on the top end of Baja Sur. The company runs four-hour tours ($40 per person) by bus to and from Scammon's Lagoon, three hours in small skiffs among whales with English-speaking guides, and lunch. Reserve several months in advance, especially for February, when whales appear in abundance.

Picnic cruises to Isla Coronado and trips inland to Misión San Javier and prehistoric rock paintings, as well as kayaking, sportfishing, diving, and day trips north to Mulege, can be arranged through hotels and the following agencies: **Alfredo's Sportfishing** (✉ on the malecón, Apdo. 39, Loreto 23880, ☎ 113/5–01–65 or 113/5–0–32, FAX 113/5–05–90), for general local information and tours, and **Las Parras Tours** (✉ Salvatierra at Madero, ☎ 113/5–10–10, FAX 113/5–09–00), for local-guided adventure tours focusing on natural history and conservation.

LA PAZ

The **Cortez Club** at La Concha Beach Resort (☞ Dining and Lodging *in* La Paz, *above*) has diving, fishing, whale-watching, and cruising tours and is the most complete tour facility in La Paz.

Several U.S. companies have whale-watching and kayaking tours that begin in La Paz. **Baja Expeditions** (⊠ 2625 Garnet Ave., San Diego, CA 92109, ☎ 619/581–3311, 800/843–6967 in the U.S. and Canada, ⅉ 619/581–6542) has hotel and diving packages and live-aboard dive-boat trips to the islands, seamount, and wrecks; whale-watching trips on boats and kayaks; and trips to Mulege and Bahía Concepción, which are especially popular for paddling. **Baja California Tours** (⊠ 7734 Herschel Ave., Suite O, La Jolla, CA 92037, ☎ 619/454–7166, ⅉ 619/454–2703) has information on and makes reservations with several companies offering whale-watching tours. **Discover Baja** (⊠ 3089 Clairemont Dr., San Diego, CA 92117, ☎ 619/275–4225, 800/727–2252, ⅉ 619/275–1836) has whale-watching trips to San Ignacio Lagoon. **Holiday Expeditions** (⊠ 544 E. 3900 S., Salt Lake City, UT 98410, ☎ 801/266–2087, 800/624–6323 in the U.S. outside UT, ⅉ 801/266–1448) runs whale-watching and kayak excursions out of La Paz. **Linblad Special Expeditions** (⊠ 720 Fifth Ave., New York, NY 10019, ☎ 212/765–7740, 800/397–3348) runs live-aboard whale-watching trips from La Paz to Magdalena Bay.

LOS CABOS

With the water as the main attraction, most tours involve getting into a boat and diving or fishing. It's a must to take a ride to El Arco, the natural rock arches at Land's End, and Playa de Amor (Lover's Beach), where the Sea of Cortés merges with the Pacific. Nearly all hotels have frequent boat trips to these destinations; the fare depends on how far your hotel is from the point. Tour boats dock by the arts-and-crafts market in the Cabo San Lucas marina, and the sidewalk along the water is lined with salesmen offering boat rides. Check out the boat before you pay, and make sure there are life jackets on board.

Contactours (⊠ Finisterra Hotel, Blvd. Marina, ☎ 114/3–33–33 or 114/3–24–39; also at several other hotels) and **TourCabos** (⊠ Plaza los Cabos, Paseo San José, ☎ 114/2–09–82, ⅉ 114/2–07–82) run boat trips, offer horseback riding, and can provide information on water sports. **Baja Travel Adventures** (☎ 114/3–19–34 or 114/3–44–74) has trips to Todos Santos and La Paz and will individually design tours; ask at hotel tour desks if there's no answer when you phone the company's office.

Pez Gato (⊠ on the marina near Plaza Las Glorias hotel, ☎ 114/3–37–97) has sailing and sunset cruises on a 46-ft catamaran, with live music ($35 per person, including drinks), as well as snorkeling and sailing tours ($30 per person). All trips depart from the marina in Cabo San Lucas; call or stop by the booth at the marina for further information.

Visitor Information

La Paz (⊠ Mariano Abasolo s/n, ☎ 112/4–01–00, ⅉ 112/4–07–22; ⊠ on the malecón near Calle 16 de Septiembre, ☎ 112/2–59–39).

There are no official tourist-information offices in **Los Cabos;** hotel tour desks are the best sources of information. Avoid tour stands on the streets; they are usually associated with time-share operations.

4   SONORA

Cowboys still ride the range in Mexican ranch country, but beaches have upstaged beef as this northwestern state's economic indicator. Along with relatively unspoiled and inexpensive coastal towns such as Bahía Kino and San Carlos, Sonora's lures include colonial Alamos, a sprinkling of Spanish missions, and an immaculate former silver-mining center with cobblestone streets and restored haciendas that evoke the spirit of Old Mexico.

Sonora, Mexico's second-largest, second-richest state, is a vacationland with its own band of devoted followers. Many are from Arizona, for whom the beaches of Sonora, its sister state, are closer, cheaper, and more interesting than those of southern California; and this stretch of the Mexican northwest is reminiscent of the old Wild West in the United States. *Rancheras,* ballads not unlike country-and-western songs, blare from saloons and radios. Irrigated ranch lands feed Mexico's finest beef cattle, and rivers flowing westward from the Sierra Madre are diverted by giant dams to irrigate a low rainfall area that now produces cotton, sugarcane, and vegetables. Hermosillo, Sonora's capital, bustles with agricultural commerce in the midst of the fertile lands that turn dry again toward the coast.

Mexico Highway 15 begins at the border town of Nogales, Sonora, adjacent to the U.S. town of Nogales, Arizona. It passes south through Hermosillo and reaches the Sea of Cortés (also called the Gulf of California) at Guaymas, 418 km (259 mi) from the Arizona border. The Sonoran desert dominates the landscape through northern Sonora, as it does in southern Arizona. Long stretches of flat scrub are punctuated by brown hills and mountains, towering saguaros, and organ-pipe cacti. Highway 15 continues southward after Guaymas, as the landscape gradually takes on a more tropical aspect, and finally enters the state of Sinaloa just north of the city of Los Mochis. Except in the mountains, the entire region is uncomfortably warm between May and late September, with afternoon temperatures sometimes exceeding 120°F.

In 1540 Francisco Vázquez de Coronado, governor of the provinces to the south, became the first Spanish leader to walk the plains of Sonora. More than a century later, Father Eusebio Francisco Kino led a missionary expedition to Sonora and what is now southern Arizona—an area referred to historically as the Pimeria Alta—founding several towns and missions there. Although Alamos, in the south of Sonora, boomed with silver-mining wealth in the late 17th century, no one paid much attention to the northern part of the region for the next three centuries. It was not part of the Mexican territory ceded to the U.S. after the War of 1847. Sonora became a haven for Arizona outlaws, and international squabbles bloomed and faded over the next decades as officials argued over issues such as the right to pursue criminals across the border. During the last quarter of the 19th century, Porfirio Díaz, dictator of Mexico for most of the years between 1876 and 1911, finally moved to secure the state by settling it.

For Don Porfirio, however, developing Sonora may have been a mistake: the revolutionaries who later overthrew him came from here. In fact, Mexico was ruled by the Sonora dynasty for nearly a quarter century and, until the 1994 assassination of Sonora native son Luis Donaldo Colosio, the ruling-party candidate for president, it appeared likely that a Sonoran would control the destiny of the country again. The Mexican Revolution brought prosperity to the state. With irrigation from the state's dams, inhabitants have been able to grow enough wheat not only for Mexico but also for export.

Pleasures and Pastimes

Beaches
Lively hotels and restaurants line the coastal areas around San Carlos, Guaymas, and Puerto Peñasco, but if you are willing to take more time for travel and forgo facilities, you'll find miles and miles of more-secluded beaches that run along the Sea of Cortés. Most of Sonora's main

beaches have paved access roads, but some of the best—like pristine Playa San Nicolás just south of Bahía Kino (Kino Bay)—await the adventurous at the end of rutted, washed-out dirt tracks.

Dining

Sonoran cuisine is distinguished by the high quality of its steaks and the freshness of its fish. Sonora is also the home of the giant flour tortilla and bean burritos. There are no five-star restaurants in the state, but shrimp lovers will find plenty to like in Sonora, especially in Guaymas. Traditional-Mexican foodies will be contented as well, with an abundance of dishes such as enchiladas, tamales, and some of the best *carne asada* (grilled marinated meat) in Mexico. Indeed, the style of Mexican cooking with which most Americans are familiar derives from this region. Casual dress (but not beachwear) is always acceptable, and reservations are rarely needed.

CATEGORY	COST*
$$$$	over $35
$$$	$25–$35
$$	$15–$25
$	under $15

*per person for a three-course meal, excluding drinks, service, and tax

Lodging

In Sonora you might find yourself sleeping in a converted convent in fashionable Alamos, growing a Hemingway beard in a beach bungalow at Bahía Kino, or luxuriating in a five-star resort in San Carlos. Lodging in Sonora is no longer the bargain it once was, but prices are still lower here than for comparable accommodations in the better-known vacation spots in other parts of Mexico.

CATEGORY	COST*
$$$$	over $100
$$$	$70–$100
$$	$35–$70
$	under $35

*All prices are for a standard double room, excluding tax.

Missions

Nestled among Sonora's hills and river valleys are a handful of almost forgotten missions that were founded by Jesuit fathers in the 17th and early 18th centuries and completed by the Franciscans in the late-18th and 19th centuries. Some of the churches, such as San Ignacio, still serve the small agricultural communities around them, whereas others, like Cocospera, are mostly shadows of their remarkable past.

Exploring Sonora

Sonoran landscapes are as varied as the state is vast. From the seemingly endless tracts of desert that tumble into the Sea of Cortés to the mountains of the Sierra Madre and the fields and valleys that nurture its produce and livestock, Sonora is a place of dramatic contrasts.

Mexico Highway 2 enters Sonora's far northwest from Baja California, paralleling the U.S. border. There are several crossing points, but most people entering Sonora from the United States do so at Nogales, south of Tucson, Arizona. It is also a point of entry for winter fruit and vegetables exported to the United States.

Numbers in the text correspond to numbers in the margin and on the Sonora map.

Great Itineraries

Because it is so diverse, the state of Sonora demands eight days or more to really do it justice. With less time, you'll have to decide whether seashore, mountains, or missions are most important.

IF YOU HAVE 3 DAYS

Take Highway 15 south from Nogales to **Magdalena** ⑤ and stop to see the plaza and church, and the bones of missionary explorer Eusebio Francisco Kino. If you're interested in churches, you might spend the night in this area—nine missions founded by Father Kino are accessible from here by car. Then continue south on the same highway to the state capital, **Hermosillo** ⑥, where you will find a variety of good hotels and restaurants. Overnight here and spend the next morning touring the city or browsing through the Centro Ecologico, which is of special interest to children. After lunch, drive west on Highway 16 to **Bahía Kino** ⑦, a perfect beach for a one- or two-night retreat. The drive back to the Arizona border from Kino Bay is about six hours.

An alternative three-day itinerary is to cross the U.S. border at Lukeville-Sonoyta, explore the lunarlike regions of the **Sierra del Pinacate** ②, and then cool off on the beaches of **Puerto Peñasco** ③ for the rest of the first day and the next. Then take Highway 2 about 2¾ hours to **Magdalena** ⑤ and stop for lunch and a visit to the Kino shrine before heading north on Highway 15 to **Nogales** ①. Spend an afternoon shopping there before you cross the U.S. border.

IF YOU HAVE 5 DAYS

Take Highway 15 from **Nogales** ① to **Guaymas** ⑨; the drive will take six or seven hours. Exploring the town of Guaymas and the adjacent resort area of **San Carlos** ⑩ will give you plenty to do for two days and nights. Continue south and then east for 3½ hours to charming colonial **Alamos** ⑪, in the foothills of the Sierra Madre. After one or two nights in Alamos, head back north. You might consider spending the night along the tranquil shores of **Bahía Kino** ⑦ on your way home.

IF YOU HAVE 8 DAYS

Combine the second of the three-day itineraries with the five-day itinerary, but stop off at **Hermosillo** ⑥ on the way down to **Guaymas** ⑨. If you have extra time, you might want to take a short side trip from Alamos to **Aduana** ⑫, former site of a thriving silver mine and current location of a thriving gourmet restaurant.

When to Tour

Summer temperatures in Sonora are as high as they are in southern Arizona, so unless you are prepared to broil, plan your trip for sometime between October and April.

Nogales

❶ *100 km (62 mi) south of Tucson via Highway 19, on the Arizona-Mexico border.*

Bustling Nogales can become fairly rowdy on weekend evenings, when under-age Tucsonans head south of the border to drink. It has some good restaurants, however, and visitors can find fine-quality crafts and furnishings in addition to the usual made-for-tourists souvenirs. If you're just coming for the day, it's best to park on the Arizona side of the border—you'll see many guarded lots that cost about $8 for the day—and walk across. Most of the good shopping is within easy strolling distance of the border.

The shopping area centers mainly on Avenida Obregón, which begins a few blocks west of the border entrance and runs north–south; just

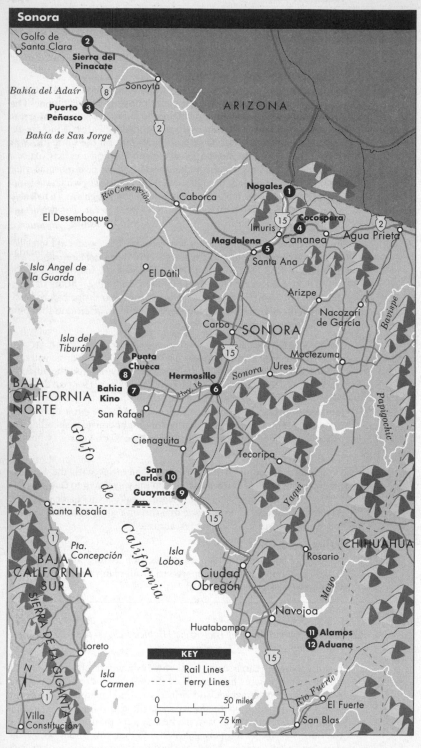

Sonora

follow the crowds. Most of the good restaurants near the border are also on Obregón. Take Obregón as far south as you like; you'll know you have entered workaday Mexico when the shops are no longer fronted by smiling, English-speaking hucksters trying to hustle you in the door ("What you need? I got the best! Cheap! Take a look!").

Dining

$$ ✕ **El Cid.** This clean, festive restaurant has something for everyone. The menu features a variety of sandwiches, burgers, fresh seafood, and traditional Mexican specialties such as *camarones ajo,* (grilled garlic shrimp) and carne asada. Be sure to wash it all down with a house-special margarita. ⊠ *Av. Obregón 124,* ☎ *631/2–19–00. MC, V.*

$$ ✕ **La Roca.** This elegant restaurant on the sprawling second floor of a
★ stately old stone house has great beamed ceilings, fireplaces, and a variety of dining rooms. The best place for a margarita is on the balcony overlooking a charming patio with magnolia trees and a gurgling fountain. Among the excellent meat and seafood dishes is *carne tampiqueña,* an assortment of grilled meats that comes with a *chile relleno* (a chili pepper stuffed with cheese, batter-dipped, and fried) and an enchilada. The *queso la Roca* (seasoned potato slices covered with melted cheese) makes a fine starter. ⊠ *Calle Elias 91,* ☎ *631/2–08–91. MC, V.*

$ ✕ **Elvira.** The free shot of tequila that comes with each meal complements Elvira's fine fish dishes, chicken mole, or chiles rellenos. This large, friendly restaurant, which is divided into intimate dining areas, is at the very end of Avenida Obregón, next to the border. It is popular with frequent visitors to Nogales. ⊠ *Av. Obregón 1,* ☎ *631/2–47–73. MC, V.*

Shopping

Nogales's wide selection of handicrafts, furnishings, and jewelry makes for some of Sonora's best shopping. At more-informal shops, bargaining is not only acceptable but expected. The following shops tend to have fixed prices: **El Sarape** (⊠ Av. Obregón 161, ☎ 631/2–03–09) specializes in sterling-silver jewelry from Taxco and designer clothing for women. **Mickey** (⊠ Av. Obregón 128–130, ☎ 631/2–22–99) has two floors of handcrafted Mexican treasures, *equipale* (pigskin) furniture, Talavera ceramic dishes, pottery, glassware, and liquors. East of the railroad tracks and off the beaten tourist path, **El Changarro** (⊠ Calle Elias 93, ☎ 631/2–05–45) carries high-quality furniture, antiques, pottery, and handwoven rugs.

Sierra del Pinacate

❷ *50 km (31 mi) west of Lukeville-Sonoyta.*

Midway between the Arizona border and the beach town of Puerto Peñasco, Sierra del Pinacate is a Biosphere Reserve International Park best known for its volcanic rock formations and craters so moonlike that they were used for training the Apollo astronauts. The diversity of the lava flows makes Pinacate unique, as does the striking combination of Sonoran desert and volcanic field. Highlights of the area include **Santa Clara peak,** a little more than 4,000 ft high and 2.5 million years old, and **El Elegante crater,** 1½ km (1 mi) across and 750 ft deep, created by a giant steam eruption 150,000 years ago.

There are no facilities of any kind at Pinacate. You'll need to bring your own water—take plenty of it—food, and extra gasoline, as well as a good map, which you can get in Arizona at Si Como No bookstore in Ajo or at Tucson's Map and Flag Center, or in Mexico at the Desert and Ocean Studies Center (CEDO; ☞ Puerto Peñasco, *below*). A high-clearance vehicle is strongly advised, and four-wheel drive is recommended. Camping is allowed with a permit obtainable from the Oficina

Sierra del Pinacate in Sonoyta, a block south of the border crossing on the west side of the street. You must register at the park entrance.

Summer temperatures can be blistering. The best time to visit is between November and March, when daytime temperatures range between 60°F and 90°F. Tours can be arranged through the tourism office in Puerto Peñasco. An excellent naturalist-led tour in English is available from Ajo Stage Lines (✉ 1041 Solana St., Ajo, AZ 85321, ☎ 520/387–6559 or 800/942–1981).

Puerto Peñasco

❸ *104 km (65 mi) south of the Arizona border at Lukeville on Mexico Highway 8.*

The real appeal of Puerto Peñasco, at the north end of the Sea of Cortés, is the miles of sandy beaches, often punctuated by stretches of black, volcanic rock that get inundated at high tide. Puerto Peñasco, or Rocky Point, has a remarkably high tide change—as much as 23 ft, depending on the season. At low tide the cragged stretches of coastline are great for poking among countless shallow tidal pools inhabited by such local marine life as octopus, shrimp, and starfish.

This coastline is rapidly changing. A number of major projects have been under construction—including a complex with a shopping center, luxury hotel, condos and villas, a yacht club, a golf course, and a marina—all designed to attract an upscale clientele.

The town was established about 1927, when Mexican fishermen found abundant shrimp beds in the area and American John Stone built the first hotel; Al Capone was a frequent visitor during the Prohibition era, when he was hiding from U.S. law. Puerto Peñasco is rather faceless, but the "old town" has a number of interesting shopping stalls, fish markets, and restaurants.

Puerto Peñasco was dubbed Rocky Point by British explorers in the 18th century, and that's the name most Americans know it by today. For now it is a popular wintering spot for American RVers and retirees, and a favorite weekend getaway for beach-seeking Arizonans—especially college kids during spring break. Thanks to a special program, Mexican immigration laws—as well as vehicle-import laws—are relaxed for tourists crossing into this so-called free zone. Simply tell the border guards that you are heading for Puerto Peñasco as you drive through—but don't neglect to get Mexican auto insurance.

The northern Gulf area forms a desert-coast ecosystem unmatched in the Western Hemisphere, and scientists from both the United States and Mexico conduct research programs at the **Intercultural Center for the Study of Desert and Oceans** (known as CEDO, its acronym in Spanish), about 3 km (2 mi) east of town on Fremont Boulevard, in the Las Conchas housing development. You can take a tour of the facility (Tuesday at 2, Saturday at 4) to learn about its history and current projects, or just pick up a tide calendar—useful if you're planning beach activities—or field guide from the gift shop. Don't forget to stop in at the small **CETMAR Aquarium** (☎ 638/2–00–10) next door, which is an especially kid-friendly, hands-on experience. Talks are offered sporadically on a wide range of topics. The aquarium charges $2 admission and is open weekdays 10–2:30 and weekends 10:30–7. ✉ *Turn east at municipal building and follow signs for Caborca Rd., where there will be signs for Las Conchas Beach and CEDO,* ☎ *638/2–01–13.* ▣ *Free.* ⊙ *Daily 9–5.*

Dining and Lodging

$$$ ✕ **Puesta del Sol.** As the name ("setting of the sun") implies, this is a
★ perfect place to see the sun set, with plenty of outdoor seating on a
patio overlooking the beach. Puesta del Sol serves many seafood dishes
and soups, with appetizers to appeal to American tastes. The fish Mor-
nay (with a creamy cheese sauce) is good, as is the grilled lobster—and
the margaritas are to die for. ✉ *Hotel Playa Bonita, Paseo Balboa,* ☎
638/3–25–86. MC, V.

$$–$$$ ✕ **Costa Brava.** In town, this small, split-level restaurant has excellent
service and a great view of the Gulf. For four, try the excellent *marinera
de la casa,* a combination of octopus, shrimp, sea snails, and clams.
The house specialty is a dish of succulent prawns, done any way you
like, and the seafood soup is also good. Hundreds of business cards
on the wall testify to this place's popularity with Americans. ✉ *Blvd.
Kino 41, at Paseo Estrella,* ☎ *638/3–31–30. MC, V.*

$$ ✕ **La Casa del Capitán.** Perched atop Rocky Point's tallest "rock," this
restaurant has the best views over the bay and the town below. There's
inside dining, but the long outdoor porch overlooking the sea is the
place to be. A wide-ranging menu includes everything from nachos and
quesadillas to flaming brandied jumbo shrimp. ✉ *Follow Blvd. Benito Juárez to* LA CASA DEL CAPITÁN *sign and head up the steep hill,* ☎
638/3–60–27. MC, V.

$$ ✕ **Friendly Dolphin.** You'll recognize this charming downtown spot
by the bright blue dolphins on its doorway. Inside, the place feels
like a wealthy Mexican family home, with nicely stuccoed ceilings,
wood-paneled windows, and exquisite hand-painted tiles. Interest-
ing old photographs, including some of Emiliano Zapata and Pan-
cho Villa, line the hallways. Gaston, the owner, can often be found
on the premises singing in an operatic baritone as rich and robust
as the food he serves. Unique family recipes include foil-wrapped
shrimp or fish prepared *estilo delfín*—steamed in orange juice, herbs,
and spices. An upstairs porch overlooks the harbor. ✉ *Av. Alcantar
44,* ☎ *638/3–26–08. MC, V.*

$ ✕ **La Curva.** This friendly family restaurant with great Mexican food
is easy to spot if you look for the mermaid on the sign. The menu lists
more than 100 items (including shrimp cooked 20 ways). Turn east
where the railroad tracks cross the main road into town. ✉ *Blvd. Kino
and Comonfort,* ☎ *638/3–34–70. MC, V.*

$$$–$$$$ 🏨 **Plaza Las Glorias.** One of a chain of hotels in Mexico, Plaza Las
Glorias is the first lodging of its kind at Puerto Peñasco. Changing the
face of the town, this soaring monument to Mexico's desire to pro-
mote tourism at any cost sits like a sand-color fortress overlooking the
beach. The open, marble-floor lobby with its towering quadrangular
ceiling and bamboo-covered skylights draws gasps of admiration from
the busloads of tourists who flock to the hotel. Rooms are well ap-
pointed, many of them with kitchenettes; all offer ocean views. ✉ *Paseo
Las Glorias, Las Explanadas 83550,* ☎ *638/3–60–10, 01–800/342–
2644, 800/515–4321,* ℻ *638/3–60–15. 210 rooms. 2 restaurants, bar,
pool, hot tub, beach, snorkeling, shops. AE, MC, V.*

$$$ 🏨 **Playa Bonita.** One of the first three hotels in Rocky Point, Playa Bonita
offers clean, comfortable rooms; ask for one facing the hotel's broad,
sandy beach. This place is very popular with Americans, who also enjoy
the Puesta del Sol restaurant (☞ *above*). An RV park offers 200
hookups at $16 a day. ✉ *Paseo Balboa 100, 85550,* ☎ *638/3–25–86,
520/393–0468 in the U.S. 120 rooms, 6 suites. Restaurant, bar, hot
tub, pool, beach. MC, V.*

$$ 🏨 **Costa Brava.** All the rooms in this small, clean, and economical down-
town hotel overlook the Gulf. Down the street are the fish markets,
popular with those who bring the catch of the day back across the bor-

der. ✉ *Malecón Kino and Paseo Estrella, 83550,* ☎ *638/3–41–00 or 638/3–41–01,* 𝙵𝘼𝙓 *638/3–36–21. 25 rooms. Restaurant, bar. MC, V.*

Nightlife and the Arts

Nightlife tends to be spontaneous and informal in Puerto Peñasco. All ages congregate along the beaches near **Manny's Beach Club** (✉ Avs. Coahuila and Primera, ☎ 638/3–36–05), where recorded music is always blaring. Manny's is the place for those who don't want to put too much distance between the water's edge and their next margarita; it's right on the beach, with signs like NO SHOES, NO SHIRT, NO PROBLEM. The food is nothing special, but as the quintessential beach hangout, Manny's is not to be missed.

Outdoor Activities and Sports

WATER SPORTS

At **Sun and Fun Dive Shop** (✉ Av. Benito Juárez and Parque Industrial, ☎ 638/3–54–50) you can rent diving or snorkeling equipment or receive PADI and NAUI scuba instruction. Sunset cruises, fishing charters, and snorkeling trips can all be booked here.

Cocospera

❹ *104 km (65 mi) southeast of Nogales, between Imuris and Cananea.*

Cocospera is one of the two dozen churches established in the state of Sonora and Arizona by Father Eusebio Francisco Kino between 1687 and 1711; the crumbling adobe mission sits on a bluff above an oak forest and farmlands in a mountain pass in the Sierra Madre Occidental. To get here from Nogales, take Highway 15 Libre to Highway 2.

Magdalena

❺ *25 km (16 mi) south of Imuris, 96 km (60 mi) from Nogales.*

The grave of Father Eusebio Francisco Kino was discovered in Magdalena in 1966. His remains are in a mausoleum across the plaza from **Santa Maria Magdalena de Buquivaba,** the cathedral that stands on one of the missions he founded. A $1 million monument to the memory of this pioneer priest also stands here. A number of shops surround the plaza, selling curios, blankets, and religious artifacts; stop in at the bakery for some excellent sweet rolls and bread. Magdalena is now also known as the final resting place of its beloved native son, slain presidential candidate Luis Donaldo Colosio, whose statue also presides over the plaza.

If you're really interested in Spanish missions and in rural Mexican life as it has been lived for centuries, drive just a few kilometers north of Magdalena on a clearly marked dirt road to **San Ignacio,** another of Father Kino's churches, still in use in a tiny Mexican farming village.

Hermosillo

❻ *185 km (115 mi) south of Magdalena on Highway 15.*

Hermosillo (pop. 850,000) is the capital of Sonora, a status it has held on and off since 1831. It is the seat of the state university and benefits from that institution's cultural activities. If you know a bit of Spanish, you might think the city's name means "little beauty." In fact, it honors José Mariá González Hermosillo, one of the leaders in Mexico's War of Independence.

Settled in 1742 by Captain Augustín de Vildosola and a contingent of 50 soldiers, Hermosillo was originally called Pitic, the Pima Indian name for "the place where two rivers meet." The city's most prestigious neighborhood—home to the governor and U.S. consul, among other prominent citizens—still bears the name Pitic. Located immediately north of the highway into town and just behind the Hotel Bugambilia, the area is worth an hour's stroll to view the creative handling of concrete, tile, and other materials in the homes of Hermosillo's affluent residents.

A business center for the state of Sonora, Hermosillo is largely modern, but some lovely plazas and parks hark back to a more graceful past. Although Hermosillo is usually just considered a jumping-off point for Bahía Kino or Guaymas, it has a number of attractions in its own right, as well as the best accommodations and restaurants until you reach Guaymas or San Carlos.

The city's main boulevard is lined with monuments to Sonora's famous sons: Adolfo de la Huerta, Alvaro Obregón, Plutarco Elías Calles, and Abelardo Rodríguez (after whom the boulevard is named)—all presidents of the country after the revolution (Rodríguez also served as governor of Sonora). At the center of town, look for the **Plaza Zaragoza** and the standout **Catedral de San Agustín** (1878), which had been regilded at great expense. Across from the cathedral is the **Palacio de Gobierno del Estado,** its graceful courtyard surrounded by somewhat disjunctive modern murals depicting Sonoran history. Between the two buildings sits an ornate Victorian gazebo. On the south edge of town, the **Plaza de los Tres Pueblos** marks the original settlement.

Overlooking the city on the Cerro la Campana (Hill of Bells), the **Museo de Sonora,** a former penitentiary, has regional history displays; you can also tour the tiny, dark prison cells. ⊠ *Calle California,* ☎ *62/13–12–34.* ☜ *$1.50, free Sun.* ☉ *Wed.–Sat. 10–5, Sun. 9–4.*

The **Museo de la Universidad de Sonora** has interesting exhibits of pre-Columbian artifacts, including 500-year-old Pima mummies. ⊠ *Blvds. Luis Encinas and Rosales,* ☎ *no phone.* ☜ *Free.* ☉ *Weekdays 9–1 and 4–6, Sat. 9–1.*

On the highway south of town, stop at the **Centro Ecologico,** an environmental and ecological park (read: zoo) where more than 500 species of plants and animals—both native to Sonora as well as exotic—can be found. It is modeled after the Arizona–Sonora Desert Museum in Tucson and is best visited November through March because of the heat and lack of shade the rest of the year. ⊠ *Hwy. 15, 5 km (3 mi) south of Hermosillo,* ☎ *62/50–11–37.* ☜ *$1.* ☉ *Tues.–Sat. 8–5.*

Dining and Lodging

$$$ ✕ **Xochimilco.** This large and friendly place, which offers indoor and outdoor dining, is deeply shaded by large fiddle-leaf figs and yucateca trees on a narrow side street in the southern part of town (from Blvd. Rosales, follow the sign near the Oxxo store). Popular with locals and regulars from across the border, Xochimilco serves well-prepared typical Sonoran dishes. ⊠ *Av. Obregón 51,* ☎ *62/50–40–89. MC, V.*

$$ ✕ **Sonora Steak.** Here in a restored old house you can enjoy the finest cuts of the famous Sonoran beef at reasonable prices. An organist plays mellow music to help digest that steak. The restaurant also serves seafood and is a good spot for a late-night meal—it's open until midnight. ⊠ *Blvd. Kino 914,* ☎ *62/10–03–13. MC, V.*

$$$$ ▥ **Fiesta Americana.** Hermosillo's only five-star hotel, this full-service property is the largest in town and popular among business travelers. The decor is predictable, but some rooms have excellent views, and the beds are large and firm. ⊠ *Blvd. Kino 369, 83010,* ☎ *62/59–60–00, 800/648–5540,* ☒ *62/59–60–60. 221 rooms. Restaurant, cafeteria, lobby lounge, pool, tennis court, health club, dance club, business services, travel services. AE, MC, V.* ☙

$$$$ 🛏 **Holiday Inn Hermosillo.** Two-thirds of the attractive rooms in this contemporary Spanish-style hotel look out on extensive, well-kept gardens and a good-size pool. The staff is geared toward accommodating the many Mexican business travelers who stay here. ⊠ *Blvd. Kino and Ramón Corral 1110, 83010,* ☎ *62/14–45–70, 800/65–4329,* 𝔽𝔸𝕏 *62/14–64–73. 132 rooms. Restaurant, bar, pool, exercise room. AE, MC, V.* 🏊

$$$ 🛏 **Hotel Bugambilia.** This green oasis on the boulevard into Hermosillo is one of the first motels in town. Here you will find a more personal atmosphere than at some of the faceless chain hotels around it. Rates include breakfast. ⊠ *Blvd. Kino 712, 83010,* ☎ *62/14–50–50,* 𝔽𝔸𝕏 *62/14–52–52. 103 rooms. Restaurant, pool. AE, MC, V.*

$$ 🛏 **Hotel Gandara.** One of the old traditional spots in Hermosillo, this hotel, with its palm trees, gardens, and colonnades, has the charm of Old Spain. You can stay in bungalows or in conventional-style hotel rooms; all offer cable TV and coffeemakers. ⊠ *Blvd. E. Kino 1000, 83150,* ☎ *62/14–44–14 or 01–800/6–23–44,* 𝔽𝔸𝕏 *62/14–99–26. 141 rooms, 7 suites. Restaurant, bar, coffee shop, pool. AE, MC, V.*

Nightlife and the Arts

Hermosillo is home to several lively night spots. **La Trova** (⊠ Calle Guerrero and Tamaulipas, ☎ 62/14–28–61) has live Latin-style music and dancing Wednesday through Saturday. **Bar Freedom** (⊠ Blvd. Kino 1012, ☎ 62/15–13–40) is a popular upscale bar and restaurant, as is **Joy's** (⊠ Fiesta Americana, Blvd. Kino 369, ☎ 62/59–60–00). **Marco n' Charlie's** (⊠ corner of Blvd. Rodríguez and Calle San Luis Potosí, ☎ 62/15–30–61) is a watering hole for young, middle-class locals.

Shopping

In the downtown markets of Hermosillo, particularly along Avenidas Serdán and Monterrey, you can buy anything from blankets and candles to wedding attire, as well as a variety of *charro* (Mexican cowboy) items; the variety of goods concentrated in this area equals what you'll find in Nogales, and the prices are better.

Bahía Kino

❼ *116 km (72 mi) west of Hermosillo on Highway 16.*

On the shore of the Sea of Cortés lies Bahía Kino, home to some of the prettiest beaches in northwest Mexico. For many years, Bahía Kino was undiscovered except by RV owners and other aficionados of the unspoiled. In the past decade or so, great change has come at the hands of North Americans who have been plopping down trailers and building condos and beach houses here. Bahía Kino itself is divided into Kino Viejo (Old Kino, the Mexican village) and Kino Nuevo (New Kino), where the beaches, condos, RV sites, and other tourist facilities are.

Consider taking a run across the narrow channel to **Isla del Tiburón** (Shark Island), which is being developed into one of the finest wildlife and game refuges in North America. Permission to visit Tiburón may be obtained from the Port Captain, at the end of the main street in Kino Viejo. Ask at any of the area hotels or RV parks where to find a reliable guide. Only the Seri Indians, for whom Isla del Tiburón is a traditional fishing ground, need no permit. For a crash ethnography of the Seri, poke around the hodgepodge of a collection in the **Museo de los Seris.** You can buy their fine ironwood animal carvings, tightly woven and prized baskets, as well as other crafts in the gift shop. ⊠ *Blvd. Mar de Cortés at Calle Progreso.* 🎫 *30¢.* ☉ *Wed.–Sun. 9–4.*

Note: The Seri are sensitive about having their picture taken. Be sure to ask permission before snapping.

Dining and Lodging

$$ ✕ **La Palapa.** This thatch-roof restaurant, with a casual interior and a small balcony overlooking the beach, has great seafood. The shrimp brochette with green chilies is memorable, especially with a glass of some very palatable Mexican wine. ⊠ *Blvd. Mar de Cortés and Wellington, on the way into Kino Nuevo,* ☎ *624/2–02–10. MC, V.*

$$ ✕ **El Pargo Rojo.** The best-known restaurant in town has fish and fishnets decorating its two rooms (with a small bandstand for musicians). The catch of the day varies, but you can depend on consistent quality, including such classics as a brimming shrimp cocktail for starters and fresh lobster any way you want it. Fine cuts of meat are available and, depending on your luck, you'll either be serenaded by Mexican musicians or by the ceaseless wailing of recorded, polkalike *norteña* music. ⊠ *Blvd. Mar de Cortés 1426, Kino Nuevo,* ☎ *624/ 2–02–05. MC, V.*

$ ✕ **Restaurant Kino Bay.** Owned by an American, this clean, comfortable family restaurant overlooks the bay. One of the few places serving breakfast, lunch, and dinner, it's a perfect spot for coffee, morning pancakes, and pelican viewing. ⊠ *Near the end of Blvd. Mar de Cortés at Alecantres,* ☎ *624/2–00–49. No credit cards.*

$ ✕ **Restaurant Marlin.** This restaurant in Kino Viejo is only hard to find the first time; after that, you will return frequently, drawn by the clean, unpretentious atmosphere and congenial service—not to mention margaritas as big as fishbowls. After serving you superb seafood dishes such as *sopa de siete mares* (soup of the seven seas) or *jaiba a la diabla* (deviled crab), your waiter might produce a guitar and serenade you free of charge. ⊠ *Calles Tastiota and Guaymas,* ☎ *624/2–01–11. Reservations not accepted. MC, V.*

$$$ ⊡ **Anchor House.** Opened in 1996, this bed-and-breakfast is a spacious, beachfront home away from home for travelers who want a warm American welcome. The owners have lived in Kino for years and are knowledgeable about every facet of life in this growing community. Coffee is always brewing, and the breakfasts are hearty. Children and pets are not allowed, and there is a two-night minimum. ⊠ *Blvd. Mar de Cortés 3525, Kino Nuevo 83340,* ☎ *624/2–01–41. 5 rooms. No credit cards.*

$$$ ⊡ **Posada Santa Gemma.** On a beautiful strip of beach, these eclectically furnished two-story bungalows with kitchenettes, fireplaces, and spectacular views of the sea are ideal for families. Each has two bedrooms and sleeps four or five comfortably. Bring your own cooking utensils and settle in. ⊠ *Blvd. Mar de Cortés, Kino Nuevo 83340,* ☎ *624/2–00–26,* ℻ *624/14–55–79. 14 bungalows. Beach. MC, V.*

$$ ⊡ **Posada del Mar.** Across the street from the beach and set back from a rambling garden with a small swimming pool and winding walkways hewn from rock, this mission-style hotel was one of the first in Kino Nuevo. Antiques and Mexican art lend an old-world charm. ⊠ *Blvd. Mar de Cortés and Creta, Apdo. 132, Kino Nuevo 83340,* ☎ *624/2–01–55. 42 rooms, 2 suites, 4 bungalows. Restaurant, bar, pool. MC, V.*

Punta Chueca

⑧ *27 km (17 mi) north of Bahía Kino.*

This rustic Scri fishing village perches at the end of a bumpy, winding dirt road. You'll pass exquisite vistas of the bay, distant empty beaches, and rolling mountains. The inhabitants of this community live a subsistence lifestyle, relying on the sea and desert much as they have for hundreds of years.

With fewer than 1,000 Seris in existence, this tribe represents an ancient culture on the verge of extinction. The Seris' love for their natu-

ral surroundings is evident in the necklaces that they have traditionally worn and now create to sell. Pretty little shells are wound into the
shape of flowers and strung with wild desert seeds and tiny bleached
snake vertebrae to result in delicate necklaces. Seri women weave elaborate *canastas* (baskets) of torote grass, which have become highly prized
and expensive.

As you get out of your car and head toward the only "store" in town,
be prepared to encounter an entourage of Seri women dressed in colorful ankle-length skirts, their heads covered with scarves and their eager
outstretched arms laden with necklaces for sale. The Seri are also
known for their carved ironwood figurines that represent the animal
world around them, including dolphins, turtles, and pelicans. Note:
In recent years, many Mexican merchants have taken to machine-
making large figures out of ironwood for the tourist trade, thereby se-
riously depleting the supply of the unique tree that grows only in the
Sonoran desert. Make sure the ones you buy are made by the Seri.

Guaymas

9 *128 km (79 mi) south of Hermosillo.*

The buzz and bustle of Guaymas—Mexico's seventh-largest port—has
a pleasant backdrop of rusty red, saguaro-speckled mountains that nudge
the deep-blue waters of a sprawling bay on the Sea of Cortés. The Spanish arrived in this "port of ports" as early as the mid-16th century. In
1701, two Jesuit priests, Father Francisco Eusebio Kino and his col-
league Juan María Salvatierra, erected a mission base here intended to
convert the native Guaimas, Seri, and Yaqui Indians.

Guaymas was officially declared a port in 1814 and became an important center of trade with Europe as well as within Mexico. In 1847,
during the Mexican–American War, U.S. naval forces attacked and occupied the town for a year. Bumbling filibuster William Walker also
managed to take Guaymas for a short time in 1853, and, in 1866, during Maximilian's brief reign, the French took control. Today, foreign
invaders in Guaymas are mostly travelers passing through on their way
somewhere else. Given its proximity to the beaches of San Carlos and
Mazatlán, as well as the twice-weekly ferry that travels between Guaymas and Santa Rosalía on the Baja peninsula, modern Guaymas is more
a stepping stone than a destination. That said, there is plenty to do here
to put together a pleasant day in this congenial seaside town.

After the throngs at the *mercado,* a daily municipal market, you'll find
quiet at the 19th-century **Catedral de San Fernando.** Or you might relax
in the typical Mexican park across the street from the church, **Plaza
13 de Julio,** with its white, Moorish-style, lacy wrought-iron bandstand
and time-worn, tree-shaded benches. **Plaza de los Tres Presidentes** is
within walking distance of Plaza 13 de Julio. In front of the 1899 **Palacio Municipal** (City Hall) loom imposing statues of the three Sonora-
born presidents of Mexico: Plutarco Elías Calles, Adolfo de la Huerta,
and Abelardo Rodríguez.

Dining and Lodging

$$ ✕ **Los Barcos.** Across the street from the harbor, Los Barcos offers a
predictable seafood-and-steak menu. The main room is large and
pseudo-beach casual, with picnic tables and overhead palm fronds and
nets; there are also two smaller, more traditional dining rooms. The
crab tostadas are especially good. ⊠ *Calle 22 and Malecón,* ☎ *622/
2–76–50. MC, V.*

$ ✕ **Los Delfines.** At the end of the harbor, this spacious restaurant offers a variety of no-frills fresh seafood and a postcard-perfect view of the water. Popular with the locals, who enjoy the *ambiente familiar* (family atmosphere), Los Delfines has a festive air; a band plays weekend afternoons. ⊠ *At end of Blvd. Sanchez Taboada,* ☎ *622/2–92– 30. Reservations not accepted. No credit cards.*

$$$ ⊞ **Hotel Armida.** Close to the shops and restaurants of downtown Guaymas, this sand-color hotel has a large, well-kept pool; a good coffee shop where locals gather for power breakfasts; and an excellent steak house, El Oeste. Rooms in the hotel's old section are dark, with ill-matched furnishings. The larger, brighter accommodations in the newest section, done in light wood, are worth the higher rates; many have balconies overlooking the pool. ⊠ *Carretera Internacional, Salida Norte, Apdo. 296, 85400,* ☎ *622/4–30–35, 800/732–0780,* ℻ *622/ 2–04–48. 80 rooms, 45 suites. Restaurant, bar, coffee shop, room service, pool, laundry service. AE, MC, V.*

$$$ ⊞ **Playa de Cortés.** This fine, sprawling old hotel overlooking the Bacochibampo Bay is built and decorated like a Spanish colonial hacienda, with towering wooden beam ceilings and a lavish fireplace in the reception room. With tropical landscaping and a sweeping view of the bay, this hotel evokes its genteel past before condos and time-shares. The rooms are furnished with hand-carved antiques; many have fireplaces and balconies. Some private casitas are available, too. To get here from the highway, take the turnoff for Colonia Miramar. ⊠ *Bahía Bacochibampo, San Carlos 85506 (A.P. 66, Guaymas 85400),* ☎ *622/ 1–12–24 or 622/1–10–47,* ℻ *622/1–01–35. 120 rooms. Restaurant, bar, pool, tennis court, beach. AE, MC, V.*

Nightlife and the Arts

Gathering spots in the area include the disco **Xanadu** (⊠ Malecón Malpica, ☎ 622/2–83–88). The younger set heads to **Charles Baby** (⊠ Av. Serdán and Malecón, ☎ no phone).

Shopping

Plaza el Vigía, a huge shopping center on the main road from the north into Guaymas, has everything from groceries, film, toiletries, and clothes to household wares. In Guaymas, the **Mercado Publico** is the best place for *artesanías* (crafts) such as baskets, hats, necklaces, and other trinkets. Visit the **Casa de las Conchas** (⊠ Calle 24 No. 3, across from Plaza de la Madre, ☎ 622/2–01–99) and admire beautiful seashell handicrafts, as well as 400–500 types of seashells; right next door is a great little ice-cream parlor.

San Carlos

⑩ *32 km (20 mi) northwest of Guaymas.*

Long considered an extension of Guaymas, this resort town—on the other side of the rocky peninsula that separates Bacochibampo Bay from San Carlos Bay—has a personality of its own. Whitewashed houses with red-tile roofs snuggle together along the water where countless yachts and motorboats are docked. The town is a laid-back favorite among professional anglers, North American tourists, and the time-share crowd, as well as wealthy Mexican families from Guaymas. There is a growing assortment of hotels, motels, and condominiums, as well as a country club with an 18-hole golf course.

The overlapping of desert and tropical flora and fauna has created a fascinating diversity of species along this coast. Among marine life, more than 650 species of fish exist here; red snapper, marlin, corbina, yellowtail, sea bass, and flounder are commonly caught. Whales have been spotted in San Carlos Bay, and there is an abundance of dolphins and pelicans. The water is calm and warm enough through October for the whole family to enjoy excellent swimming. Scuba, snorkeling, fishing, and boat excursions are popular, too.

The quiet 5-km (3-mi) stretch of sandy beach at **Los Algodones,** where the San Carlos Plaza Hotel and Club Med are now, was in the 1960s a location site for the film *Catch 22*. Mexico's first man-made marina lies in the shadow of the jagged twin-peak **Tetakawi mountain,** once a sacred site where Indian warriors gathered to gain spiritual strength. An interesting day trip can be made by boat out to the pristine **San Pedro Island,** where sea lions frolic on the rocks.

To reach San Carlos from Guaymas, take Mexico 15 north for about 8 km (5 mi) to the well-marked turnoff for San Carlos. Continue for 24 km (15 mi) on the four-lane **Corredor Escénico** (Scenic Corridor), which was completed in 1995 to replace an infamously bumpy road.

Dining and Lodging

$$ ✕ **Bananas.** American food (BLTs, burgers, fries), Mexican fare—try "shrimp bananas," wrapped in bacon with barbecue sauce—and even sushi are served in a single large room with a peaked ceiling lined with palm fronds. There are a few seats in the entrance patio as well. A copy of Charlie Chaplin's 1924 marriage license hangs on the wall by the rest rooms. ⊠ *Av. San Carlos 345,* ☎ *622/6–06–10. Reservations not accepted. MC, V.*

$$ ✕ **Rosa's Cantina.** Bearing little resemblance to the saloon in M. Robins's song, "El Paso," this cozy, pink, laid-back restaurant has picnic tables that fill two large dining rooms. Come to feast on ample breakfasts of *huevos rancheros* (eggs with chorizo). The tortilla soup is great for lunch or dinner, and the homemade salsa is divine. ⊠ *Calle Aurora 297,* ☎ *622/6–10–00. Reservations not accepted. MC, V.*

$–$$ ✕ **El Pueblito.** This is San Carlos's most sophisticated eatery, although all the "authentic" Mexican decor is a bit excessive. You'll be treated to creative international cuisine, as well as regional favorites. The Tetakawi prawns, stuffed with other shellfish and served in a rich and creamy béchamel sauce, are a heavenly indulgence. ⊠ *San Carlos Plaza Hotel, Paseo Mar Barmejo Nte., Los Algodones, Apdo. 441,* ☎ *622/6–07–77. AE, MC, V.*

$$$$ 🛏 **Club Med Sonora Bay.** Although San Carlos is expanding rapidly in its direction, this Club Med is still secluded from the main tourist area, its verdant 42-acre complex spreading fortresslike behind a large gate fronted by saguaros. Accommodations are characteristically tasteful but plain, and the range of available activities is as great as one would expect from the chain. All meals, soft drinks, and tips—and many sports, such as sailing and scuba diving—are included. It's worth paying extra for the dawn horseback ride to the foothills of the nearby Sierra Madre. ⊠ *Playa de los Algodones, 85400,* ☎ *622/7–00–09, 800/258–2633,* 𝔽𝔸𝕏 *622/7–00–02. 375 rooms. 3 restaurants, bar, pool, sauna, golf course, 28 tennis courts, horseback riding, beach, windsurfing, boating. AE, MC, V. Closed Oct. 31–mid-Mar.* ✑

$$$$ 🛏 **Plaza Las Glorias.** This condo-hotel complex overlooks the San Carlos marina. It's smaller than the San Carlos Plaza Hotel but nearly as impressive. Subtle pastels set a tasteful tone in the comfortable modern rooms. Most accommodations have a tiny kitchenette; a few have private hot tubs. ⊠ *Plaza Comercial San Carlos 10, Planta Baja, 85006,* ☎ *622/6–10–21 or 622/6–10–34,* 𝔽𝔸𝕏 *622/6–10–35. 87 rooms, 18 suites. Restaurant, snack bar, 2 pools, baby-sitting, travel services, car rental. AE, MC, V.*

$$$$ ⊞ **San Carlos Plaza Hotel and Resort.** Rising from San Carlos Bay en route to Club Med, this huge structure is thoroughly and strikingly pink. It's the most luxurious hotel in Sonora, with a marble-floor atrium lobby that opens onto a large pool and beach. Rooms are done in an attractive contemporary style. All have safes and minibars, and rooms on the first two floors have balconies overlooking the sea. Children love the swimming-pool slide and horseback riding on the beautiful beach. ⊠ *Paseo Mar Barmejo Nte. 4, Los Algodones, Apdo. 441, 85506,* ☎ *622/7–00–77, 800/854–2320,* FAX *622/7–00–98. 148 rooms, 25 suites. 3 restaurants, 2 bars, snack bar, 2 pools, hot tub, 2 tennis courts, exercise room, horseback riding, volleyball, beach, travel services, car rental. AE, MC, V.*

$$ ⊞ **Fiesta San Carlos.** This small hotel on the bay has a lot of charm and is clean and comfortable. Accommodations with kitchens are available. ⊠ *Carretera Escénico San Carlos Km 8.5, 85506,* ☎ *622/ 6–02–29. 32 rooms. Restaurant, bar, pool. AE, MC, V.*

$$ ⊞ **Hacienda Tetakawi.** This hotel and trailer park across from the beach on the main street of town is a Best Western. Rooms are generic but clean, and each has a balcony with a view of the sea. ⊠ *Carretera Escénico San Carlos Km 10, 85000,* ☎ *622/6–02–48. 22 rooms. Restaurant, bar. AE, MC, V.*

Nightlife and the Arts

One favorite gathering spot in the area is **Ranas Ranas** (⊠ Carretera San Carlos Km 9.5, ☎ 622/6–07–27), from which you can enjoy a view of the beach. For a feast of artwork by a variety of Mexican and foreign artists, stop by the two floors at the **Galería Bellas Artes** (⊠ Villa Hermosa 111, ☎ 622/60–07–3), where their work is for sale. It's open Monday–Saturday 9:30–5.

Outdoor Activities and Sports

GOLF

Most hotels in the Guaymas–San Carlos area can arrange for temporary membership at the **San Carlos Country Club,** which has an 18-hole golf course.

HORSEBACK RIDING

You can inquire at the **San Carlos Plaza Hotel** (⊠ Paseo Mar Barmejo Nte. 4, Los Algodones, Apdo. 441, ☎ 622/7–00–77, 800/854–2320 in the U.S.) about horses for hire.

WATER SPORTS

Gary's Dive Shop (⊠ Blvd. Beltrones Km 10, San Carlos, ☎ 622/6–00–49, 622/6–00–24 after hours, www.garysdivemexico.com) runs fishing, snorkeling, and PADI-certified diving excursions. You can also book sunset cruises, and whale-watching and customized expeditions.

Shopping

Sagitario's Gift Shop (⊠ Carretera San Carlos 132, ☎ 622/6–00–90), across from the entrance to the San Carlos Country Club, features clothing and a variety of crafts, including wood carvings, baskets, high-quality rugs, and Talavera tile. **Kiamy's Gift Shop** (⊠ Carretera San Carlos Km 10, ☎ 622/6–04–00) is like a bazaar, with something for everyone, at a reasonable price; silver jewelry, earrings, leather bags, Yaqui Indian masks, T-shirts, and caps, as well as a variety of ceramics, can be found here.

Alamos

⓫ *257 km (160 mi) southeast of Guaymas.*

With its cobblestone streets, charming central plaza, 200-year-old mission church, and a large number of thoughtfully restored haciendas, Alamos is the most authentic colonial-style town in Sonora. Set in the ecologically rich zone where the Sonoran desert meets a dry tropical forest (also called the thorn forest) in the foothills of the Sierra Madre, the entire town is designated a national monument, and it manages to consistently maintain the dignified side of the early days of Mexico.

Coronado camped here in 1540, and a Jesuit mission was established in 1630, but the town really boomed when silver was discovered in the area during the 1680s. Wealth from the mines financed Spanish expeditions to the north—as far as Los Angeles and San Francisco during the 1770s and '80s—and the town became the capital of the state of Occidente, which combined the provinces of Sinaloa and Sonora, from 1827 to 1832. A government mint was established here in 1864. The mines closed by the end of the 19th century, and the town went into decline.

These days, Alamos is reinventing itself as a tourist spot. Leading the movement are a growing number of expats who have been buying and restoring sprawling haciendas near the center of town, turning some into hotels. So far, the foreigners' efforts to keep the town producing magical, postcard moments seem to be successful.

Points of interest include the impressive **cathedral** on the central Plaza las Armas, begun in 1787 on the site of a 17th-century Jesuit adobe church and completed in 1894. It is fronted by an ornate Moorish-style wrought-iron gazebo, brought from Mazatlán in 1904. To the west of the square, on Guadalupe Hill, is the old Alamos **jail,** built around the turn of the 20th century; it is now a private home, but visitors may tour the structure on occasional Saturdays when tours of the many beautiful **restored colonial houses** in town are also held. The tourist office and all the local hotels have listings of the times and rates.

Not to be missed, the **Museo Costumbrista de Sonora** gives an excellent overview of the cultural history of the entire state of Sonora. The numerous well-marked (but only in Spanish) displays include artifacts from the nearby silver mines and coins from the mints of Alamos and Hermosillo, as well as typical examples of the clothing and furnishings of prominent local families. ☒ *Calle Guadalupe Victoria 1, on Plaza las Armas,* ☎ *642/8–00–53.* ☒ *$1.* ☉ *Wed.–Sun. 9–6.*

Dining and Lodging

$ ✕ **Las Palmeras.** This Mexican family restaurant is crammed onto the
★ sidewalk across the street from the Museo Costumbrista de Sonora and right on the main square. Here you might get homemade *rosca* bread (a sweet, round loaf) with your coffee and an assortment of daily specials. The corn tamales are hard to beat. The other specialities are the chile relleno and the carne Milanese. ☒ *Lázaro Cárdenas 9,* ☎ *642/ 8–00–65. Reservations not accepted. No credit cards.*

$ ✕ **Polo's.** One of the few hangouts for locals, this place is not unfriendly to the many gringos who flock to this beautiful colonial town—but it's not the most welcoming either. That said, Polo's does have many loyal gringo customers. The food is simple but very good: sandwiches and shish kebab. Sonoran steaks are the speciality. ☒ *Calle Zaragosa 4,* ☎ *642/8–00–01. No credit cards.*

$ ✕ **Los Sabinos.** This small, unpretentious café, with indoor and outdoor seating, offers house specials of beef tips and ranch-style shrimp, along with fried fillet of sole in garlic butter as well as several types of tacos and hamburgers. ☒ *Calle 2 de Abril No. 5,* ☎ *642/8–05–98. Reservations not accepted. No credit cards.*

$$$$ ☒ **Hacienda de los Santos.** Owned by a Californian couple, Alamos's
★ most opulent hotel rambles across the lushly landscaped grounds of
four restored and linked colonial mansions. Filling every room and lining the long porticos around the many courtyards are centuries-old *santos, retablos,* and other religious art; hand-carved antique wooden
furniture; huge and inviting leather sofas; and scores of other old Mexican and Southwest treasures. Spacious bedrooms are appointed with
beautiful Spanish Colonial furnishings, gigantic tile baths, and fireplaces.
The attentive, sometimes bubbly staff knows how to pamper. ☒ *Calle
Molina 8, 85763,* ☎ *642/8–02–22,* ℻ *642/8–03–67. 11 rooms, 3
suites. Restaurant, bar, 3 pools, spa, private airstrip. MC, V.*

$$$ ☒ **Casa de los Tesoros.** This hotel, the House of Treasures, is a pic-
turesque and romantic converted 18th-century convent. The rooms
are former nuns' cells and have fireplaces, tile baths, antique furnishings,
and high-quality handicrafts on the walls. Room rates include break-
fast, and the restaurant is excellent. ☒ *Av. Obregón 10, Apdo. 12,
85763,* ☎ *642/8–00–10,* ℻ *642/8–04–00. 15 rooms, 2 suites. Restau-
rant, bar, pool. MC, V.*

$$$ ☒ **Casa Encantada.** Just off the main square, this lovely B&B owned
by a California couple is the converted 250-year-old mansion of one
of Alamos's former Spanish mine owners. Rooms retain a colonial character, with high-beamed ceilings, fireplaces, and carved-wood furnishings; all have tile baths and good lighting. ☒ *Calle Juárez 20, 85760,*
☎ *642/8–04–82,* ℻ *642/8–00–04. 10 rooms. Pool. MC, V.*

$$$ ☒ **Casa Obregón Dieciocho.** This sprawling 275-year-old casa owned
by artist and chef Roberto Bloor has two suites, both with a bedroom,
sitting room, fireplace, coffeemaker, bath, and private patio. Guests
can sit out in a lovely, lush garden; inside, colorful crafts and paint-
ings abound. Write for reservations or (at a slightly extra expense) book
almost any accommodation in town through Fraser & Pratt Real Es-
tate in Alamos (☎ 642/8–07–90 or 642/8–01–18). ☒ *Av. Obregón 18,
85760. 2 suites. No credit cards.*

Shopping

It's worth a peek into the three crowded rooms of **El Nicho Curios** (☒
Calle Juárez 15, ☎ 642/8–02–13), filled with treasures ranging from
Mexican religious paintings to old jewelry and regional pottery. In ad-
dition, small stores lining **Plaza Alameda** (northwest of the central plaza)
sell Mexican sweets, fabrics, belts, and hats, among other items.

Aduana

⑫ *8 km (5 mi) west of Alamos.*

Aduana was formerly the site of one of the richest mines in the dis-
trict. Today it is the unlikely location of one of Sonora's best restau-
rants, **Casa la Aduana.** Mexican tourists and expats living in Alamos
spill from the nondescript dining room onto the patio of this gourmet
eatery run by California exile Samuel Beardsley. A four-course, prix-
fixe menu ($12 or $16) is served at both lunch and dinner, and entrée
selections might include chicken in apple–chipotle cream or grilled Nor-
wegian salmon. Call ahead for reservations (☎ 648/2–25–25).

Across the plaza from Casa la Aduana is the **Iglesia de Nuestra Señora
de Balvanere.** A cactus that grows out of one of the church's walls is
said to mark the spot where the Virgin appeared to the Yaqui Indi-
ans in the late 17th century, an event that is celebrated by a proces-
sion every November 21.

SONORA A TO Z

Arriving and Departing

By Bus

Frequent buses travel to Hermosillo and Guaymas from Nogales, Tijuana, and Mexicali via **Tres Estrellas de Oro** (☎ 655/7–24–10). **Golden State Buses** (☎ 642/8–01–75, 520/624–9434) makes daily trips between Tucson, Arizona, and Alamos, with stops at major points along the way. **ABC Bus Service** (☎ 01–800/621–3623) travels between Puerto Peñasco and Cabo San Lucas, with plenty of stops en route.

By Car

Many visitors to Sonora travel by car from Tucson via I–19 to the border in Nogales, Arizona, and then pick up Mexico's Highway 15, which begins in Nogales, Sonora. Highway 15 is now a divided four-lane road, making the ride much quicker and easier than it used to be. This convenience, however, comes at a cost: drivers heading south to Alamos can expect to pay approximately $35 in tolls. The alternative "Libre" (free) routes are much slower and often poorly maintained.

There are two points of entry into Nogales. Most drivers take U.S. I–19 to the end and then follow the signs to the border crossing. This route, however, will take you through the busiest streets of Nogales. It's better to take the Mariposa exit west from I–19, which leads to the international truck crossing and joins a small periphery highway that connects with Highway 15 after skirting the worst traffic.

The official checkpoint for entering Mexico is 21 km (13 mi) south of Nogales. It is here that you have to buy insurance and complete paperwork to bring in your car if you haven't already done so in Tucson at either **Sanborn's Mexico Insurance** (✉ 105 W. Grant, Tucson, ☎ 520/327–1255) or the **Arizona Automobile Association** (✉ 8204 E. Broadway, Tucson, ☎ 520/296–7461; ✉ 6950 N. Oracle Rd., Phoenix, ☎ 520/885–0694 or 800/352–5382). *See* Car Travel *in* Smart Travel Tips A to Z, at the end of the book, regarding requirements for driving into Mexico.

As a result of the **Sonora Only** program, if you are not planning to go farther into Mexico, you do not have to leave a credit-card imprint or pay a deposit (though insurance is still required). Stop at the "Sonora Only" booth at the Km 21 checkpoint.

By Ferry

Ferries from Guaymas to Santa Rosalía on the Baja coast leave Wednesday and Friday at 8 AM and are scheduled to arrive at 3 PM. You can buy tickets the day before or the morning of the day you plan to travel unless you have a car, for which you must make reservations three weeks in advance. Fares are about $20 for a reclining seat and $40 for a cabin. Car transportation is priced by car size, with the smallest cars costing at least $200. Purchase tickets at the **Sematur ferry terminal** (✉ Av. Serdán, ☎ 622/2–23–24 or 01–800/69–69–600), just east of the center of Guaymas. Check with the Guaymas tourist office (☞ Visitor Information *in* Contacts and Resources, *below*) for the latest information and schedules.

By Plane

AeroCalifornia (☎ 62/60–25–55, 800/237–6225) offers daily nonstop jet service from Los Angeles and Tucson to Hermosillo. **Aeroméxico** and its subsidiary Aero Litoral (☎ 622/2–01–23, 01–800/02–14–000, 800/237–6639 in the U.S.) has daily flights to Hermosillo from Tucson, and flights from Los Angeles to Hermosillo. Aeroméxico has direct flights to Hermosillo from many cities in Mexico—including

Mexico City, Tijuana, Chihuahua, and Guadalajara—and from La Paz and Mexico City to Guaymas; connections to other U.S. cities can be made from these points. **America West Express** (☎ 01–800/23–59–292, 800/363–2597) has daily flights to Hermosillo from Phoenix.

Getting Around

By far the easiest way to get around is by automobile—Guaymas and San Carlos are particularly spread out. Most hotels have car-rental agencies. Buses between towns are frequent and inexpensive.

Contacts and Resources

Car Rental

In **Guaymas,** the agencies to contact are **Budget** (☎ 622/2–14–50) and **Hertz** (☎ 622/2–10–00), both on the main highway.

Rental agencies in **Hermosillo** include **Budget** (✉ Carmendia 46, at Tamaulipas, ☎ 62/14–30–33) and **Hertz** (✉ Blvds. Rodríguez and Guerrero, ☎ 62/14–85–00).

Consulate

There is a **U.S. consulate** (✉ Calle Monterrey 140, ☎ 62/17–23–75) in Hermosillo, in back of Hotel Calinda near downtown.

Emergencies

Guaymas: Police (☎ 622/4–01–05), **Red Cross** (☎ 622/3–05–87), **hospital** (☎ 622/2–01–22).

Hermosillo: Police (☎ 62/12–59–05 or 13–27–01), **Red Cross** (☎ 62/14–07–69), **hospital** (☎ 62/13–25–56). The **Green Angels** (☎ 62/69–27–14) is a very helpful state-run road service for travelers.

Puerto Peñasco: Red Cross (☎ 638/3–22–66).

Guided Tours

Arizona Coach Tours (✉ 200 E. 35th St., Tucson, AZ, ☎ 520/791–0210) runs mostly senior-citizen package tours to Alamos, San Carlos, Puerto Peñasco and the Copper Canyon. **Mexico Tours** (✉ 1604 E. Seneca, Tucson, AZ, ☎ 520/325–3284, 800/347–4731) offers package tours to San Carlos and Puerto Peñasco.

Visitor Information

In addition to the tourism offices listed below—which are better to visit than to try to reach by phone—the **Sonora Department of Tourism** (☎ 800/476–6672) will send you mounds of information and a helpful, full-color magazine.

Alamos (✉ Main Plaza, Calle Juárez 6, ☎ 642/8–04–50); **Guaymas** (✉ Calle 19 and Av. 6, ☎ 622/4–41–14); **San Carlos** (✉ Corredor Escénico San Carlos, Edificio Bella Mar, ☎ 622/6–12–22); **Hermosillo** (✉ Centro de Gobierno, 3rd floor, Paseo Canal and Comonfort, ☎ 62/13–18–61 or 01–800/71–62–555); **Puerto Peñasco** (✉ Blvds. Juárez and V. Estrella, ☎ 638/3–50–10 or 01–888/50–81–22 in Mexico).

5 THE COPPER CANYON: FROM LOS MOCHIS TO CHIHUAHUA CITY

In the heart of the scenic, rugged Sierra Madre, the Copper Canyon—a series of gorges, some deeper than the Grand Canyon in the United States—is known for hikes that range from pleasant walks to thigh-busting descents to the canyon floor. These gorges are home to the largely reclusive Tarahumara Indians. One of North America's most spectacular train trips snakes its way through this magnificent, mostly uncharted region, usually beginning or ending in the lively city of Chihuahua.

Updated by
Charles
Runnette

T HE MAGNIFICENT series of gorges known collectively as Barranca del Cobre—the Copper Canyon—is the real hidden treasure of the Sierra Madre. Inaccessible to the casual visitor until the early 1960s and still largely uncharted, the canyons may now be explored by taking one of the most breathtaking rides in North America: the Chihuahua al Pacífico railroad whistles down 661 km (410 mi) of track, passing through 87 tunnels and crossing 35 bridges through rugged country as rich in history and culture as in physical beauty.

The *barrancas* (canyons) of the Sierra Tarahumara, as this portion of the Sierra Madre Occidental is known, are on the eastern edge of the Pacific "Ring of Fire." Seismic and volcanic activity set the stage, in the process hurling a good quantity of the earth's buried mineral wealth to the surface. The canyons were then carved over eons by the Urique, Septentrión, Batopilas, and Chínipas rivers and further defined by wind erosion. Totaling more than 1,452 km (900 mi) in length and capable of enveloping four times the area of the Arizona Grand Canyon, the gorges are nearly a mile deep and wide in places. The average height of the peaks is 8,000 ft, and some rise to more than 12,000 ft. Four of the major barrancas—Copper, Urique, Sinforosa, and Batopilas— descend deeper than the Grand Canyon, Urique by nearly 1,500 ft.

The idea of building a rail line to cross this region was first conceived in 1872 by Albert Kinsey Owen, an idealistic American socialist. Owen met with some success initially. More than 1,500 people came from the states to join him in Topolobampo, his utopian colony on the Mexican west coast, and in 1881 he obtained a concession from Mexican president General Manuel Gonzáles to build the railroad. Construction on the flat stretches near Los Mochis and Chihuahua presented no difficulties, but eventually the huge mountains of the Sierra Madre got in the way of Owen's dream, along with the twin scourges of typhoid and disillusionment within the community.

After Owen abandoned the project in 1893, it was taken up in 1900 by American railroad magnate and spiritualist Edward Arthur Stilwell. One of Stilwell's contractors in western Chihuahua was Pancho Villa, who ended up tearing up his own work during the Mexican Revolution in order to impede the movement of government troops. By 1910, when the Mexican Revolution started, the Mexican government had taken charge of building the railroad line. But progress was very slow until 1940, when surveying the difficult Sierra Madre stretch finally began in earnest. Some 90 years and more than $100 million after it was started, the Ferrocarril Chihuahua al Pacífico was dedicated on November 23, 1961.

The railroad no longer starts at Topolobampo but at nearby Los Mochis, and Chihuahua City—capital of the eponymous state—is at the other end of the line. The city was established in 1709, after the Spanish discovered silver in the area around 1649. Chihuahua still derives its wealth from mining, as well as ranching, agriculture, and lumber.

Closely related to the Pima Indians of southern Arizona, the Tarahumara Indians once occupied the entire state of Chihuahua. They are renowned for their running ability—Tarahumara is a Spanish corruption of their word Rarámuri, which means "running people"; it's said that in earlier times the Tarahumara hunted deer by chasing them to the point of collapse. Like so many native groups, the Tarahumara were totally disrupted by the European arrival in the area. The Spanish made them serve in the mines, then the Mexicans and Americans put them to work on the railroads. The threat of slavery and the series of wars that began in the 1600s and continued until the 20th century forced them to retreat deeper into the canyons, where they are still subject to having their lands taken over by loggers and drug lords. Many are semi-nomadic, roaming the high plateaus of the Sierra Madre in summer and moving down to the warmer canyon floor in winter. Their population, ravaged over the years by disease, drought, and poverty, is estimated at around 50,000.

Pleasures and Pastimes

Dining

Throughout the canyons you'll encounter relatively undeveloped areas where there are few eateries besides those connected with lodges. In Los Mochis and Topolobampo your best bet is seafood. At the hotels in Cerocahui, Divisadero, and Posada Barrancas, hearty meals are generally included in room rates. There are a few more dining options in Creel, where, in addition to hotel dining rooms, you'll find small cafés along the town's main street, Avenida López Mateos.

You'll have the greatest choice of restaurants in Chihuahua City. The state is a large producer of beef, so upscale steak houses and places serving *carne asada* (charbroiled strips of marinated beef) abound, but Mexican specialties and seafood flown in from the coast are also available. Many of Chihuahua's well-appointed international restaurants are in the Zona Dorada, on Calle Juárez starting at its intersection with Calle Colón.

Dress is casual everywhere except at some of Chihuahua's pricier restaurants. Unless otherwise indicated, reservations aren't necessary.

CATEGORY	COST*
$$$$	over $20
$$$	$15–$20
$$	$8–$15
$	under $8

per person for a three-course meal, excluding drinks and service, but including 15% sales tax

Hiking

Hiking in the Copper Canyon is fantastic if you take the proper precautions. *Mexico's Copper Canyon Country,* by M. John Fayhee, is a good source of information. But even the most experienced trekkers should enlist the help of local guides, who can be contacted through all the hotels in the area or through travel agents in Los Mochis and Chihuahua. Few adequate maps are available for even the so-called marked trails, and many of the better-worn routes into the canyon are made by the Tarahumara, whose prime concern is getting from one habitable area to the next rather than getting to the bottom.

Urique Canyon is most easily reached from Cerocahui. The Copper Canyon proper is most accessible from Divisadero. Trails range from easy rim walks to a 27-km (17-mi) descent to the bottom. If you're in Creel, a gentle and rewarding hike is the 6-km (4-mi) walk from the Copper Canyon Lodge to 100-ft-high Cusárare Falls. More difficult but equally scenic is the trek to the base of Basaseachi Falls—a full-day outing. The descent into Batopilas Canyon from Creel—a not-for-the-faint-of-heart affair—requires an overnight stay.

Horseback Riding

Most hotels in the canyon area can arrange for local guides with gentle horses, but most trips aren't for couch potatoes. The trails into the canyon are badly defined and can be rocky as well as slippery. At rough spots you might be asked to dismount and walk part of the way. A fairly easy and inexpensive ride is to Wicochic Falls at Cerocahui, about two hours round-trip, including a half-hour hike at the end, where the trail is too narrow for the horses. From Divisadero, the four-hour round-trip to Bacajipare, a Tarahumara village in the Copper Canyon, has stunning vistas, but it's not for the fainthearted.

Lodging

Accommodations in this area tend to fall into two categories: comfortable but characterless in the cities, and charming but rustic in the villages. In Cerocahui, Divisadero, Posada Barrancas (*posada* means "inn"), and Creel, all the hotels send buses or cars to meet the train. If you don't have a reservation, you'll have to make a quick decision and then hop on the hotel vehicle of your choice. In summer, October, and around Christmas and Easter, it's important to book in advance. Where indicated, rates for hotels include meals.

CATEGORY	COST*
$$$$	over $90
$$$	$60–$90
$$	$25–$60
$	under $25

All prices are for a standard double room, excluding 15% tax.

Nightlife

Conversing with fellow guests in your lodge or stargazing from a rooftop balcony are about the extent of nighttime activities in the heart of Sierra country, although occasionally one of the larger hotels will have performances in the evening by Tarahumara dancers or Mexican musicians. Entertainment is considerably less rural in Los Mochis, and Chihuahua is a typically bustling, late-night Mexican city.

Shopping

A main source of cash income for the Tarahumara is their crafts, including lovely handwoven baskets made from sotol (an agavelike plant) or pine needles, carved wooden dolls, rustic pottery, roughly carved wooden masks, brightly colored woven belts and sashes made on back-strap looms, and wooden fiddles decorated with faces from which the men produce haunting music. The Tarahumara women, who are generally shy about talking with tourists, sell their wares throughout the Copper Canyon area. Their prices are fair, so bargaining is unnecessary. Tarahumara wares are sold at the Divisadero train station and at shops in Creel and Chihuahua. Chihuahua is known for affordable cowboy boots, and *bota* (boot) shops proliferate downtown.

Exploring the Copper Canyon

Imagine visiting the Grand Canyon in the days before it was tamed by tourist facilities and you'll have some sense of what a trip through the Copper Canyon will be like—for better and for worse. That is, with the opportunity to encounter a relatively untouched natural site come some of the discomforts of the rustic experience. But if you are careful in your choice of time to visit and are properly prepared, the trip's myriad rewards should far outstrip any temporary inconveniences.

Numbers in the text correspond to numbers in the margin and on the Copper Canyon map.

Great Itineraries

You'll see some beautiful scenery even if you only ride the railroad—including a panoramic look into the canyons during a 15-minute stop at Divisadero—but you'll take in only a fraction of what the canyons have to offer if you don't get off the train. If possible, plan on a night in Cerocahui (Bahuichivo stop), one at Posada Barrancas or Divisadero (the train stations are five minutes apart), and one or two at Creel.

Most people make their way into the Copper Canyon via Los Mochis, which is the easiest route if you're coming from California or Arizona. On top of that, some of the best scenery is at the western end of the ride, and you're likely to miss it if you approach Los Mochis in the evening. Train delays of three hours or more are not unusual, so even during the extended daylight hours of summer, you can't count on reaching the scenic end of the route before dark.

Even if you drive down to either Los Mochis or Chihuahua, your itinerary will be largely dependent on the schedule of the Chihuahua al Pacífico train: it runs in each direction only once a day, so you must plan the time spent in each stop accordingly. The following itineraries assume you will add on a day's train ride to return to your starting point—unless you catch one of the Aerolitoral flights between Los Mochis and Chihuahua. The small turboprops fly low over the mountains and canyons, providing magnificent views.

Note: The Sinaloa-Chihuahua state border divides two time zones: Mountain Time to the west and Central Time to the east.

IF YOU HAVE 3 DAYS

Departing from **Los Mochis** ①, take the 6 AM Chihuahua al Pacífico train and get off at Bahuichivo, where you can explore the mission at **Cerocahui** ③ and the overlook into Urique Canyon. The next day, continue to **Divisadero** ④, where it's practically impossible not to get a room with a view. Spend your last day exploring **Creel** ⑤ and taking a short hike to the falls near Cusárare. If you begin the trip in **Chihuahua City** ⑧, make Cerocahui your final stop.

IF YOU HAVE 5 DAYS

Starting in the west, consider spending a day in the old colonial town of **El Fuerte** ②, then catching the train through the canyons at 7:30 the next morning. Follow the three-day itinerary, above, and use the last day and night to extend your time in **Creel** ⑤, with a visit to the Tarahumara community of San Ignacio or a drive to Basaseachi Falls. If you start in the east, you might take the extra day to explore **Chihuahua City** ⑧. Don't miss Pancho Villa's home, now a museum.

IF YOU HAVE 8 OR MORE DAYS

Spend a day each in **El Fuerte** ②, **Cerocahui** ③, and **Divisadero** ④, then extend your stay in **Creel** ⑤ to include a trip down to the former silver mining town of **Batopilas** ⑥. It's six to eight hours each way by car (preferably four-wheel drive) or bus, so you'll want to spend at least two nights. You'll be ready for modern conveniences after that, so plan to enjoy the restaurants and museums of **Chihuahua City** ⑧ for an additional day. Another option would be to visit the Mennonite community near **Cuauhtémoc** ⑦ before going on to Chihuahua.

When to Tour

Unless you're planning to head deep into the barrancas, winter—December through February—is not the best time to come. Some of the hotels in the region are inadequately prepared for the cold, and the minor rainy season in January renders some of the roads for side excursions impassable. The warm months are May through September. The rainy season, late June through September, brings precipitation for a short period every day, but this shouldn't interfere with your enjoyment in any way. It's temperate in the highlands during the summer. If you're planning to hike down into the canyons, however, remember that the deeper you go, the hotter it will get. The best months to visit are Oc-

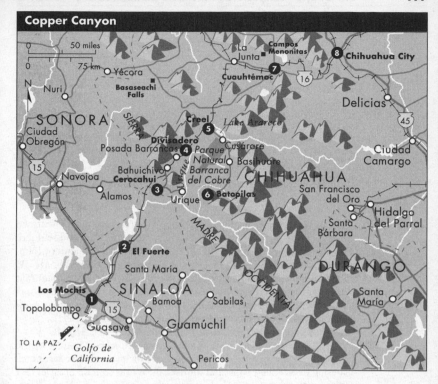

Copper Canyon

tober and November, when the weather is still warm and rains have brought out all the colors in the Sierra Tarahumara.

Many people come during Easter and Christmas, specifically to see the Tarahumaras' colorful take on church holidays. On these and other religious feast days, Tarahumara villages challenge one another in races that can go for days. The men run in small groups, upward of 161 km (100 mi) or more, all the while kicking a wooden ball. It's not *just* fun and games—each village places a huge communal wager for this winner-take-all event.

Los Mochis

❶ *763 km (473 mi) south of Nogales on the Arizona-Mexico border.*

At the western end of the rail line, Los Mochis (population 331,000) is an agricultural boomtown. The rail terminus and the city's location about 19 km (12 mi) from the harbor at Topolobampo make it the export center of the state of Sinaloa. You can tour Benjamin Johnston's sugar refinery, the **Ingenio Azucarero,** around which the town grew. Near Johnston's estate you can still see the American colony—the group of brick bungalows that housed his associates.

The **Museo Regional del Valle del Fuerte** rotates work by local, regional, national, and international artists, and has a didactic exhibit on the area's history. A replica of a railroad steam engine is on permanent display. Labels are in Spanish only. ⊠ *Obregón and Mina,* ☎ *68/12–46–92.* ☜ *$1.* ◷ *Tues.–Sun. 10–1 and 4–7.*

Cottonwood trees and bougainvillea line the highway from Los Mochis to **Topolobampo.** Fields en route are planted with crops ranging from sugarcane to marigolds and mangoes. Once the site of Albert Owen's utopian colony and the center of the railroad-building activity in the area, it is now a suburb of Los Mochis. **Isla El Farallón,** off the coast, is a breeding ground for the sea lions that gave the town its name: in the language of the Mayo Indians who once dominated the area, *Topolobampo* means "watering place of the sea lions."

Dining and Lodging

$$ ✕ El Farallón. Nautical decor and murals set the tone for the excellent fish served at this simple restaurant. Sushi and sashimi are especially good, as is the *pitalla* (cactus fruit with brightly colored flesh) ice cream. ✉ *Obregón 593, at Ángel Flores,* ☎ *68/12–14–28 or 68/12–12–73. AE, MC, V.*

$$ ✕ Las Fuentes. This unpretentious, colonial-style restaurant specializes in Sinaloan and U.S. beef cuts. Try the local favorite, *cabreria*—a thinly cut fillet. ✉ *Calzada López Mateos 1070 Nte., at Jiquilpan,* ☎ *68/12–47–70. AE, MC, V.*

$$ ✕ Restaurante España. This slightly upscale restaurant in downtown Los Mochis is popular with the local business crowd. Good seafood, U.S. cuts of beef, and Spanish dishes are served around an indoor fountain. ✉ *Obregón 525,* ☎ *68/12–22–21 or 68/12–23–35. AE, MC, V.*

$ ✕ El Taquito. In the very center of Los Mochis, this diner-style restaurant serves well-prepared and reasonably priced Mexican standards 24 hours a day, every day. For a hearty meal try the *carne tampiqueña*—a tasty steak with enchiladas, guacamole, and *frijoles* (beans) on the side. ✉ *Av. Leyva between Hidalgo and Independencia,* ☎ *68/12–81–19. AE, MC, V.*

$$$ ✕▦ Hotel Plaza Inn. This one-time 40-room motel was bought by the Balderrama family in 1986 and is now Los Mochis's only five-star hotel. Catering to businesspeople and tourists, the rooms contain luxuries that you won't necessarily find elsewhere: three phones (one in the bathroom), tubs, card keys, and locks and security safes. Furniture is sturdy but rather standard; beds are covered with floral spreads. There's a small club for duck hunters and fishermen. The restaurant here, Mr. Owen's, on the ground floor, is reliable. ✉ *Av. Leyva and Cárdenas, 81200,* ☎ *68/18–10–42, 800/862–9026,* ℻ *68/12–15–90. 100 rooms, 25 suites. Restaurant, bar, nightclub, travel services. AE, DC, MC, V.*

$$$ ✕▦ Hotel Santa Anita. The central reservations link of the Balderrama chain, this downtown hotel is also an informal information center for what's happening along the Chihuahua al Pacífico route and a place to book tours. Built in 1959, the property has midsize rooms fitted with tasteful and comfortable modern furniture. All have cable TVs, and many have hair dryers and scalloped onyx sinks. The restaurant is one of the best in town. ✉ *Av. Leyva and Hidalgo, 81200,* ☎ *68/18–70–46, 800/862–9026,* ℻ *68/12–00–46. 133 rooms. Restaurant, bar, travel services. AE, DC, MC, V.*

$$ ▦ Corintios Hotel. This modern-style dwelling with a dark-glass facade has a bit more class than the other reasonable hotels in town. Rooms have diffused lighting, with both carpeted and tile floors. The hotel has no elevator. ✉ *Obregón 580 Pte., 82000,* ☎ *68/18–23–00,* ℻ *68/18–22–24. 34 rooms, 1 suite, 6 junior suites. Restaurant, bar, hot tub, exercise room, travel services. AE, DC, MC, V.*

$$ ▦ Villa Cahita. The main attraction to this rustic hotel two blocks from El Dorado is its expansive lobby and restaurant area with comfortable *equipale* (tree-branch-and-pigskin) chairs and high ceilings. The junior suites are a good buy, and secure parking is available. ✉ *Ignacio Ramirez 400 Pte., 81200,* ☎ *68/12–12–00,* ℻ *68/12–63–35. 50 rooms, 16 junior suites. Restaurant, bar, travel services. AE, DC, MC, V.*

Nightlife

Locals kick up their heels at **Fantasy Laser Club** (✉ Hotel Plaza Inn, Av. Leyva and Cárdenas, ☎ 68/18–70–46). **Morocco** (✉ Av. Leyva and

Rendon, ☎ 68/12–13–88) is a disco downtown. **Yesterday** (✉ Obregón and Guerrero, ☎ 68/15–38–10) has live bands for an over-30 audience.

Shopping

If you're headed to Divisadero, Creel, or beyond, snacks and reading material can help pass the nine-hour-plus journey. **Librería Los Mochis** (✉ Calle Madero Pte. 402, at Av. Leyva) has English-language best-sellers and magazines and Spanish-language daily newspapers. **La Cava Deli** (✉ Av. Leyva 425, ☎ 14/18–06–36) sells American and Mexican beers, a good selection of wines and liquors, Cuban cigars, and snack foods. If a celebration is in order, you can pick up **piñatas** for $5–$10 at the small family business at Callejón Guadalupe Victoria 43.

El Fuerte

❷ *80 km (50 mi) northeast of Los Mochis.*

If you're ready for old Mexico, take a bus to El Fuerte (instead of the train that leaves at the crack of dawn), stay the night, and sleep in an hour longer before grabbing the 7:30 train to points east. A bus with comfortable seats leaves from **Mercado Independencia** (✉ corner of Avs. Independencia and Degollado), every half hour 7:30 AM–8:30 PM for the two-hour trip. Fresh foods are available at the mercado.

The small colonial town of El Fuerte was named after the 17th-century fort built by the Spaniards to protect against attacks by the local Mayo, Sinaloa, Zuaque, and Tehueco Indians. Conquistador Don Francisco de Ibarra and a small group of soldiers founded it in 1564, and they called their town San Juan de Carapoa. Located on the central El Camino Real route, El Fuerte was at one time the frontier outpost from which the Spanish set out to explore and settle New Mexico and California. For three centuries, it was a major trading post for gold and silver miners from the nearby Sierras and the most important commercial and farming center of the area. It was chosen as Sinaloa's capital in 1824 and remained so for several years.

El Fuerte, now a rather sleepy town of 25,000, has intact colonial mansions, one of the best being the Posada del Hidalgo (☞ Dining and Lodging, *below*). Most of the historic houses are set off the cobblestone streets leading from the central plaza.

Dining and Lodging

$$ ✕ **El Mesón del General.** Just a block off the main plaza, this is the best bet in town for good freshwater fish and crayfish caught in a nearby lake. A varied menu includes Mexican fare, *langostino caque* (local river crawfish) and *lobina* (black bass), and tasty steaks. ✉ *Benito Juárez 202,* ☎ *68/93–02–60. No credit cards.*

$$$$ 🛏 **El Fuerte Lodge.** Long-time hunting guide Robert Brand expanded
★   his lodge in the restored 380-year-old mansion of Spanish explorer Francisco Ibarra situated on the old Camino Real—two blocks off the town square—and now offers it to canyon travelers. A flower-filled courtyard has been fitted with a waterfall and hidden Jacuzzi, and some of Mexico's best *artesanía* (folk art) adorns the rooms and common areas. ✉ *Montesclaro 37, 81820,* ☎ *68/93–02–26. 25 rooms. Bar, dining room, air-conditioning, pool. MC, V.*

$$$ 🛏 **Posada del Hidalgo.** You'll be transported back to a more gracious
★   era at this restored hacienda, with its gardens and cobblestone paths, built in 1895 by Rafael Almada, the richest man in nearby Alamos. It's difficult to choose between the larger rooms with balconies, set off a lobby filled with period artifacts, and those that open onto the gardens. All are decorated with rough-hewn handcrafted furniture. *Langostino* (crawfish) is a specialty of the dining room. ✉ *Hidalgo 101,*

☎ 68/93–02–42 (*Reservations: Hotel Santa Anita, Av. Leyva and Hidalgo, Apdo. 159, Los Mochis 81200,* ☎ *68/18–70–46, 800/862–9026,* FAX *68/18–15–90*). *50 rooms, 3 suites. Bar, dining room, air-conditioning, pool, dance club. AE, MC, V.*

$$ 🏨 **Mirador de Montesclaros.** On the Cerro de las Pilas, the highest spot
★ in El Fuerte, with a commanding view, is this small, adobe-and-wood posada owned by local guide Eleazar Gamez. Rooms are rustic but very creatively decorated with family heirlooms and antiques from friends in town, each piece with its own story that the owner gladly shares. Continental breakfast and a tour of El Fuerte are included in the room price. ⊠ *Cerro de las Pilas,* ☎ *68/93–10–05. 5 rooms. Bar. No credit cards.*

En Route   As the train ascends almost 5,906 ft from El Fuerte to Bahuichivo, it passes through 87 tunnels and over 24 bridges, including the longest and highest ones of the rail system. The scenery shifts from Sinaloan thorn forest, with cactus and scrublike vegetation; to the pools, cascades, and tropical trees of the Río Septentrión canyon; to the oak and pine forest that begins to take over past Temoris, where a plaque marks the 1961 dedication of the railroad by President López Mateos.

Cerocahui

❸ *160 km (100 mi) northeast of El Fuerte.*

The quiet mountain village of Cerocahui, just inside the Sinaloa state border, is a good place to get a sense of how people live in the canyon area. Next door to the Hotel Misión is a **Jesuit mission,** established around 1680 by Juan María de Salvatierra, who proselytized widely in the region. It is said that because the Tarahumara were the most difficult Indians to convert, he considered this mission his favorite among the many he founded. Nearby, the church operates a boarding school for Tarahumara children. From the train station at Bahuichivo, two hotels have buses that make the 45-minute ride up the bumpy, unpaved road to Cerocahui.

The prime reason to come to Cerocahui is its accessibility to **Urique Canyon.** It's a kidney-crunching ride to the **Cerro del Gallego lookout,** where amid mountains spread against the horizon you can make out the slim thread of the Urique River and the old mining town of Urique, a dot on the distant canyon bottom. On the way up you'll pass a Tarahumara cave where women sell baskets. Nearby, a shrine to the Virgin of Fatima is strikingly set against a spring in the mountainside. From Cerro del Gallego the road continues down the canyon into Urique, which has a few basic hotels and restaurants. A public bus makes the trip from Cerocahui a few times a week, but many people opt for the local hotels' round-trip, full-day tours.

Dining and Lodging

$$$$ ✕🏨 **Hotel Misión.** Part of the Balderrama chain—the Copper Canyon's equivalent of the Grand Canyon's Fred Harvey hotel empire—this is the only accommodation in Cerocahui itself. The main house, which looks like a combination ski lodge and hacienda, contains the hotel's office, small shops, and a dining room, bar, and lounge. There are two large fireplaces around which to huddle in winter: Cerocahui isn't wired for electricity, and the hotel uses its generator for only a few hours. The plain rooms have beam ceilings, Spanish colonial–style furnishings, wood-burning stoves, and kerosene lamps. Rates include meals. ⊠ *Cerocahui. Reservations: Hotel Santa Anita, Av. Leyva and Hidalgo, Apdo. 159, Los Mochis 81200,* ☎ *68/18–70–46 ext. 432, 800/896–8196,* FAX *68/12–00–46. 38 rooms. Restaurant, bar. AE, DC, MC, V.*

$$$$ XⓂ **Paraíso del Oso Lodge.** Doug "Diego" Rhodes runs a lodge near
★   Cerocahui that's known as a base camp for the great horseback rides
        he leads through the Urique Canyon to Batopilas and beyond. The rooms
        are plain, with simple handmade wood furniture. You have to stoke
        the wood-burning stove for heat at night, as there is no electricity here.
        A huge window-filled lobby affords excellent views of the cliffs above
        the lodge. A gift shop carries local crafts as well as wares from other
        parts of Mexico. Rates include meals. *5 km (3 mi) outside of Ceroc-
        ahui. Reservations:* ✉ *Box 31089, El Paso, TX 79931,* ☎ FAX *14/21–
        33–72, in Chihuahua City. 16 rooms. Dining room. MC, V.*

Divisadero

❹   *80 km (50 mi) northeast of Cerocahui, in the state of Chihuahua.*

There's little to do in Divisadero, a postage stamp of a place on the
Continental Divide, but it's impossible to be unmoved by its Copper
Canyon vistas—don't miss the canyon at sunset. You can also glimpse
a bit of the distant Urique and Tararecua canyons from here. A popular excursion (the Hotel Cabañas Divisadero-Barrancas has a $65
guided trip) that takes about five hours round-trip on foot or on horseback is to Bacajipare, a Tarahumara village in the canyon.

Dining and Lodging

$$$$ XⓂ **Hotel Cabañas Divisadero-Barrancas.** The dining room and Rooms
        1–10 in the old section and 35–52 in the newer section of this canyon-
        rim hotel have panoramic views. Food and service get mixed reviews
        from the international visitors who sign the guest log, but you're not
        likely to notice what you're eating when you look out the window. The
        Sandoval family has owned the vast tract of land surrounding the
        hotel since the former mayor of Batopilas, Indalecio Sandoval, bought
        it to escape the summer heat of that town, and later to hide himself
        and his family from Pancho Villa's revolutionaries. Rates include
        meals. *Divisadero stop on Chihuahua al Pacífico train. Reservations:*
        ✉ *Av. Mirador 4516, Apdo. 661, Col. Residencial Campestre, Chi-
        huahua, Chihuahua 31000,* ☎ *14/15–11–99,* FAX *14/15–65–75. 48
        rooms with shower. Restaurant, bar. AE, MC, V.*

$$$$ XⓂ **Hotel Posada Barrancas Mirador.** This beautiful pink hotel—an-
★   other link in the Balderrama chain—is perched on the edge of the Cop-
        per Canyon. The dining room and all the guest rooms have spectacular
        views; balconies seem to hang right over the abyss. Accommodations
        are bright, with custom-made furniture, hand-loomed textiles, and
        heat from fireplaces. The copious meals are good. The hotel can or-
        ganize day trips to Creel and the surrounding area. Rates include
        meals. *Posada Barrancas stop on Chihuahua al Pacífico train. Reser-
        vations:* ✉ *Hotel Santa Anita, Av. Leyva and Hidalgo, Apdo. 159, Los
        Mochis 81200,* ☎ *68/18–70–46, 800/862–9026,* FAX *68/12–00–46. 46
        rooms. Restaurant, bar, meeting rooms. AE, MC, V.*

$$$$ XⓂ **Rancho Posada Hotel.** This is a good base from which to explore
        the Barranca del Cobre. The 14 remodeled rooms have ocher stucco
        walls, ceramic-tile floors, and colonial-style, hand-painted furniture;
        all but six have cozy fireplaces. The older accommodations, also slated
        for remodeling, have plain, contemporary-style furnishings of dark wood.
        The redecorated lobby–dining room has a massive stone fireplace,
        beamed ceiling, and new wood furniture. Rates include meals. *Posada
        Barrancas stop on Chihuahua al Pacífico train. Reservations:* ✉ *Hotel
        Santa Anita, Av. Leyva and Hidalgo, Apdo. 159, Los Mochis 81200,*
        ☎ *68/18–70–46, 800/862–9026,* FAX *68/12–00–46. 34 rooms, 1 suite.
        Restaurant, bar. AE, MC, V.*

$$$ ✕🖬 **Hotel Mansion Tarahumara.** It's a bit disconcerting to come across
★ a red-turreted, medieval-style "castle" out in barranca country, but some-
how this whimsical fancy works. All rooms (15 in separate cabins) have
Spanish contemporary-style light-pine furniture, plus fireplaces and in-
dividual heaters. The newest units have pine-log walls. Older rooms
have gray cobblestone walls that match the lodge's exterior. The large
dining hall is hard to keep warm in winter but has wonderful views of
the Sierra Madre. All meals are included. ✉ *Posada Barrancas. Reser-
vations: Av. Juárez 1602-A, Col. Centro, Chihuahua, Chihuahua
31000,* ☎ *14/15–47–21,* 🖷 *14/16–54–44. 57 rooms, 1 suite. Restau-
rant, bar, pool, tennis court, dance club, meeting rooms, travel services.
AE, DC, MC, V.*

Creel

⑤ *60 km (37 mi) northeast of Divisadero.*

Nestled in pine-covered mountains, Creel is a rugged mining, ranch-
ing, and logging town that grew up around the railroad station. The
largest settlement in the area, it's also a gathering place for Tarahu-
mara Indians seeking supplies and markets for their crafts. It's easy to
imagine American frontier towns at the turn of the 20th century look-
ing like Creel—without, of course, the international backpacking con-
tingent that makes this town its base.

It's 19 km (12 mi) from Creel to **Cusárare,** a Tarahumara village with
a 300-year-old Jesuit mission. En route you'll pass limpid-blue Lake
Arareco and the turnoff for the strange volcanic-rock formations of
the Valley of the Mushrooms. An impressive waterfall can be reached
by an easy 6-km (4-mi) hike from town through a lovely piñon forest.

If the unpaved roads are passable, consider taking the longer trips to
the **Recohuata Hot Springs,** a fairly strenuous hike down from the rim
of the Tararecua Canyon, and to **El Tejaban,** a spectacular overlook
at the Copper Canyon. Among several worthwhile day trips along the
way to the colonial town of Batopilas (☞ *below*) are **Basihuare,** where
wide horizontal bands of color cross huge vertical outcroppings of rock;
the **Urique Canyon overlook,** a perspective that differs from the one
at Divisadero; and **La Bufa,** site of a former Spanish silver mine. Sev-
enty-three kilometers (45 mi) northwest of Creel, along an unpaved,
winding road, the 806-ft **Basaseachi Falls** are among the highest cas-
cades in North America.

Dining and Lodging

$ ✕ **Tío Molcas.** Furnished with chunky wooden tables and chairs, this
small, cheerful restaurant dishes up delicious Mexican food, especially
the cheese enchiladas topped with a zesty red-pepper sauce. ✉ *Av. López
Mateos 35,* ☎ *145/6–00–33. No credit cards.*

$ ✕ **Veronica's.** This clean, simple eatery on the main street is popular
with locals and tourists for its variety of tasty and economical meals.
Comidas corridas—set meals with soup, main course, and dessert—
are available, or you can order à la carte. Try the *sopa de verduras* (veg-
etable soup), or the vegetarian tacos. The salsa is sublime. ✉ *Av.
López Mateos 34,* ☎ *no phone. No credit cards.*

$$$$ 🖬 **Copper Canyon Sierra Lodge.** About 24 km (15 mi) from Creel, set
★ in a peaceful piñon forest near Cusárare Falls, this hotel is an incred-
ibly successful blend of elegant and rustic. Adjacent to a Tarahumara
village, the lodge gives guests a closer look at the daily lives of these
very private cave-dwelling natives. There's no electricity in the lodge
itself, but the pine-paneled rooms with antique furnishings and tile,
hot-water baths are romantically equipped with kerosene lamps and

wood stoves. People usually book rooms here as part of an all-inclusive package deal with a sister lodge in Batopilas, but the lodge will accept walk-ins if space permits. ⊠ *Cusárare.* ⊠ *Reservations: Copper Canyon Lodges, 2741 Paldan, Auburn Hills, MI 48326,* ☎ *248/340–7230, 800/776–3942 in the U.S. and Canada. 14 rooms. Restaurant, bar. AE, D, MC, V.* ✎

$$$ 🏨 **Best Western: The Lodge at Creel.** At the other end of town from the plaza, this lodge is actually several log buildings with four rooms each. The spacious, well-lighted, comfortable quarters exude rustic-chic charm with their pine floors and walls, high double beds with thick coverlets, Tarahumara artifacts, and old-fashioned "wood stoves" that are really gas-log heaters controlled by wall thermostats. The main lodge building has a small bar–dining area with leather-and-wood furniture. ⊠ *Av. López Mateos 61, 33200,* ☎ *145/6–00–71,* 𝙵𝙰𝚇 *145/6–00–82. 29 rooms. Restaurant, bar. AE, MC, V.*

$$ 🏨 **Margarita's Plaza Mexicana.** This pretty hotel with two floors of rooms around a private courtyard is one of the town bargains, serving up solid meals and honest hospitality at low prices. The rooms, with private baths, individual heat, and plenty of hot water, are decorated with locally crafted pine furniture and charming murals depicting Tarahumara activities. Two complaints often heard about the Plaza Mexicana are that it's too aggressive in soliciting guests to go on its tours and that the nightly tequila parties it throws for its two properties— Margarita's is the other one (☞ below)—can get quite noisy. Rates include breakfast and dinner. ⊠ *Calle Chapultepec, 1 block off Av. López Mateos, 33200,* ☎ *145/6–02–45 or 145/6–00–45. 26 rooms. Restaurant, bar. AE, MC, V.*

$$ 🏨 **Motel Parador de la Montaña.** This clean, well-run motel has large, comfortable, no-frills rooms with private, hot-water baths; a secure parking area; and a cozy wood-paneled lounge where the warmth radiating from the huge stone fireplace beckons you to plop down on the funky, handmade pine furniture and relax. ⊠ *Av. López Mateos 41, 33200,* ☎ *145/6–00–75. 50 rooms. Restaurant, bar. AE, MC, V.*

$ 🏨 **Margarita's.** If a small boy at the train station offers to take you to
★ Margarita's, and the prospect of hanging out with a motley neo-beatnik crowd appeals, go with him for one of the best deals in town. There's no sign on the door, and even if you follow directions (it's between the two churches facing the plaza), you may think you're walking into a private kitchen when you enter. At this gathering spot for backpackers, you can get anything from a bunk bed in a dorm room (less than $6) to a double room with two beds and a private bathroom (around $11 per person). Prices include breakfast and dinner. The rooms—with wrought-iron lamps, light-wood furnishings, and clean, modern baths— are as pleasant as anything you'll find for three times the price. ⊠ *Av. López Mateos 11, 33200,* ☎ *145/6–00–45 or 145/6–02–45. 21 rooms, 15 with bath. Restaurant. No credit cards.*

Nightlife

When the sun goes down in Creel, head to **Laylo's Lounge** (⊠ Av. López Mateos, at the west end of town, ☎ no phone), next to El Caballo Bayo restaurant. Although it stays open only until 9 PM, the **Sierra Tropico** ice-cream parlor (⊠ Av. López Mateos 27, ☎ no phone), in the middle of town, is worth a visit.

Shopping

For Tarahumara dolls and handiwork, check out **Artesanías Misión,** on the town plaza. The gift shop in **Casa de las Artesanías,** an excellent museum (on the plaza) focusing on traditional Tarahumara life, including a beautiful exhibit of black-and-white photographs, has Tarahumara crafts and dolls. At the west end of Avenida López Mateos, **Artesanías Victoria** sells huge Tarahumara pots and handmade wood furniture.

Batopilas

6 *80 km (50 mi) southeast of Creel.*

This remote village of about 800 people was once one of the wealthiest towns in Mexico because of the nearby veins of silver mined on and off from the time of the conquistadores. At one time it was the only place in the country besides Mexico City that had electricity. The hair-raising, 80-km (50-mi) ride down dusty, unpaved roads to the now-sleepy town at the bottom of Batopilas Canyon takes about 5½ hours by car from Creel (closer to seven hours on the local bus, which runs back and forth every day except Sunday). Sights in this lush, flower-filled oasis include the ruined **hacienda of Alexander Shepherd,** built in the late 1800s by one of the town's wealthiest mine owners; the original **aqueduct,** which still services the town (it's set along the Camino Real); and a triple-dome 17th-century **cathedral,** mysteriously isolated in the Satevo Valley on a scenic 6½-km (4-mi) hike from town. Because it takes much of a day to get down to Batopilas, you'll need to stay overnight at one of the town's modest posadas or at the quirkily opulent Copper Canyon Riverside Lodge.

Lodging

$$$$ ⊞ **Copper Canyon Riverside Lodge.** The sprawling grounds of three
★   connected and restored late-19th-century haciendas are filled with all sorts of delicious nooks and crannies to explore. Each of the high-ceiling rooms is individually decorated, but all have spacious private baths and huge feather duvets. Only partially wired for electricity, the accommodations have an odd mix of kerosene reading lamps and electrical outlets for hair dryers. The gourmet meals are excellent. Rooms are usually booked as part of an all-inclusive package deal with a sister lodge in Cusárare (☞ Creel, *above*), but walk-ins are welcome when space permits. Rates include all meals. ⊠ *Batopilas. Reservations: Copper Canyon Lodges, 2741 Paldan, Auburn Hills, MI 48326,* ☎ *248/340–7230, 800/776–3942 in the U.S. and Canada. 14 rooms. Restaurant. AE, D, MC, V.*☻

Cuauhtémoc

7 *128 km (79 mi) northeast of Creel, 105 km (65 mi) southwest of Chihuahua.*

A rather anomalous experience in Mexico is a visit to **Campos Menonitas,** a large Mennonite community in Cuauhtémoc. Some 20,000 Mennonites came to the San Antonio Valley in 1922 at the invitation of President Alvaro Obregón, who gave them the right to live freely and autonomously in return for farming the 247,000 acres of land.

You can set up a tour in Cuauhtémoc at the Tarahumara Inn (⊠ Av. Allende and Calle 5A, ☎ 158/1–19–19), or Mennonite David Friesen's travel agency Cumbres Friesen (⊠ Calle 3A No. 466, ☎ 158/2–54–57, ☒ 158/2–40–60), or in Chihuahua (☞ Contacts and Resources *in* Copper Canyon/Chihuahua A to Z, *below*).

Chihuahua City

8 *375 km (233 mi) south of the El Paso–Ciudad Juárez border, 1,440 km (893 mi) northwest of Mexico City.*

If you're arriving from the peaceful Copper Canyon, the sprawling city of Chihuahua with nearly 1 million inhabitants might come as a bit of a jolt. But then, the city is known for its jolting nature—two of Mexico's most famous revolutionaries are closely tied to Chihuahua. The father of Mexican independence, Father Miguel Hidalgo, and his co-conspirators were executed here by the Spanish in 1811. And Chihuahua was home to General Pancho Villa. His revolutionary army, the División del Norte (Army of the North), was decisive in overthrowing dictator Porfirio Díaz in 1910 and securing victory in the ensuing civil war. A half-century earlier, Benito Juárez, known as the Abraham Lincoln of Mexico, made Chihuahua his base when the French invaded the country in 1865.

Whatever you do, don't miss the Museo Histórico de la Revolución en el Estado de Chihuahua, better known as **Pancho Villa's House.** Villa lived in this 1909 mansion, also called the "Quinta Luz" (*quinta* can mean "mansion"), with his second wife, Luz Corral. She stayed here until her death on June 6, 1981, willing the residence to the government. The 50 small rooms that used to board Villa's bodyguards now house a vast array of artifacts of Chihuahua's cultural and revolutionary history. Parked in the museum's courtyard is the bullet-ridden 1919 Dodge in which Villa was assassinated in 1923 at the age of 45. ⊠ *Calle Décima 3014,* ☎ *14/ 16–29–58.* ▣ *$1.* ☉ *Tues.–Sat. 9–1 and 3–7, Sun. 9–5.*

The **Catedral,** on the town's central square, is also worth a visit. Construction on this beautiful Baroque structure was started by the Jesuits in 1726 and not completed until 1825 because of local Indian uprisings. The opulent church has Carrara marble altars, a 24-karat solid-gold ceiling, a cedar-and-brass depiction of Saints Peter and Paul, and a huge German-made organ. In the back of the cathedral, the **Museum of Sacred Art** displays the work of seven local artists of the 18th-century Mexican Baroque tradition. ⊠ *Plaza de la Constitución,* ☎ *no phone.* ▣ *50¢.* ☉ *Weekdays 10–2 and 4–6.*

The **Palacio de Gobierno** (State Capitol) was built by the Jesuits as a convent in 1882. Converted into government offices in 1891, it was destroyed by a fire in the early 1940s and rebuilt in 1947. Murals around the patio depict famous episodes from the history of the state of Chihuahua. A plaque commemorates the spot where Father Hidalgo was executed on the morning of July 30, 1811. ⊠ *Plaza Hidalgo,* ☎ *14/ 10–63–24.* ▣ *Free.* ☉ *Daily 8–8.*

The **Palacio Federal** (Federal Building) houses the city's main post office and telegraph office, as well as the dungeon where Hidalgo was imprisoned before he was executed by the Spanish. His pistols, traveler's trunk, crucifix, and reproductions of his letters are on display here. ⊠ *Calle Libertad around the corner from Plaza Hidalgo,* ☎ *14/ 10–35–95.* ▣ *Free.* ☉ *Tues.–Sun. 9–7.*

The 1721 **Iglesia de San Francisco** (San Francisco Church) is the oldest church built in Chihuahua that is still standing. Father Hidalgo's decapitated body was interred in the chapel of this simple church from 1811 to 1827, when it was sent to Mexico City. His head was publicly displayed for 10 years by Spanish Royalists in Guanajuato on the Alhóndiga de Granaditas (☞ Guanajuato *in* Chapter 7). ⊠ *Av. Libertad at Calle 15,* ☎ *no phone.* ▣ *Free.* ☉ *Daily 7–7.*

Slightly outside the center of town but well worth a visit is the Cultural Center of the University of Chihuahua, known as **Quinta Gameros.** This hybrid French Second Empire–Art Nouveau mansion, with stained-glass windows, ornate wooden staircases, rococo plaster wall panels, and lavish ironwork, was built in 1910 by Julio Corredor, a Colombian architect, for Manuel Gameros, a wealthy mining engineer. Here you'll see European art of the past two centuries as well as changing exhibitions ranging from Mennonite crafts to contemporary art. ⊠ *Calle Bolívar 401,* ☎ *14/16–66–84.* ⊠ *$1.* ☉ *Tue.–Sun. 10–2 and 4–7.*

Not to be confused with the University Cultural Center, the **Chihuahua Cultural Center** displays exquisite Paquimé ceramics from the pre-Columbian settlement of Casas Grandes northwest of Chihuahua. ⊠ *Aldama and Ocampo,* ☎ *14/16–13–36.* ⊠ *Free.* ☉ *Tues.–Sun. 10–2 and 4–7.*

A restoration project has made the site of the town's original settlement, **Santa Eulalia,** particularly appealing. The 30-minute drive southeast of town, about $10 one-way by taxi (less by bus), is repaid by the colonial architecture and cobblestone streets of this village, which was founded in 1652. Tours of local silver mines can be arranged by guides in town. The religious artwork in the 18th-century cathedral is noteworthy, and the **Mesón de Santa Eulalia** restaurant (☎ 14/11–14–27), near the plaza, has a lovely courtyard, open weekends 1:30–7.

OFF THE
BEATEN PATH

Casas Grandes. Some 350 km (161 mi) northwest of Chihuahua, the twin towns of Nuevo Casas Grandes and Casas Grandes are the gateways to the ancient area known as Paquimé, recently declared a UNESCO World Heritage site. Nuevo Casas Grandes, a two-horse town with wide, dusty streets and cowboys en regalia, has the hotels and most of the local restaurants. Sleepy Casas Grandes, 8 km (5 mi) away, occupies a single square block.

Near the aspen-lined Casas Grandes River, sheltered by the burnt-sienna peaks of the Sierra Madre Occidental, Paquimé was inhabited by Pima, Concho, and Tolima peoples between AD 700 and 1500. A key site poised between the Pueblo cultures of the now-American southwest and their Mesoamerican neighbors—with architecture borrowed from each—Paquimé was a cosmopolitan center for trade whose residents raised fowl and manufactured jewelry. Evidence of their worldliness still stands, in the form of heat-shielding walls and intricate indoor plumbing systems. The high-tech museum on site houses Paquimé artifacts and ceramics and has bilingual descriptions of local cultural, religious, and economic practices. ⊠ *Museum $1.* ☉ *Tues.–Sat. 10–6, Sun. 11–5.*

In Nuevo Casas Grandes, Restaurante Constantino (⊠ Juárez, across from Hotel Paquimé, ☎ 169/4–10–05) makes great enchiladas and has a full breakfast menu. In Casas Grandes, El Pueblo (⊠ off Juárez, ☎ 169/2–41–22) draws residents from all around with great food (no breakfast) and a full bar. Motel Piñon (⊠ Juárez 605, Nuevo Casas Grandes, ☎ 169/4–06–55) has a swimming pool and a private collection of ancient *ollas* (clay pots) from Paquimé. Motel Hacienda (⊠ Juárez 2603, Nuevo Casas Grandes, ☎ 169/4–10–46) has 124 rooms and is considered one of the best places to stay in the city. Omnibus de México makes the 5½-hour trip from Chihuahua (☞ Arriving and Departing *in* Copper Canyon/Chihuahua A to Z, *below*) to Nuevo Casas Grandes (about $15). To get to the ruins, hop a blue-and-gold CASAS GRANDES bus (30¢) at Constitución and 16 de Septiembre. After 15 minutes, get off at Casas Grandes' *zócalo* (main square). Paquimé is a 10-minute walk from town—follow the PAQUIMÉ sign on Constitución. The last bus returns to Nuevo Casas Grandes at 9 PM.

Dining and Lodging

$$ ✕ **La Calesa.** A large, dimly lit room with wood paneling and red tablecloths and curtains, this looks like the classic steak house it is. The filet mignon and rib-eye steaks from the area are particularly recommended as entrées; try the former cooked with mushrooms. ⊠ *Av. Juárez 3300,* ☎ *14/10–10–38 or 14/16–02–22. AE, MC, V.*

$$ ✕ **Club de Los Parados.** Almost four decades of Chihuahua's history
★ have passed through the doors of this landmark restaurant in an adobe-style house. It was started by Tony Vega, a wealthy cattle rancher who died in 1991, as a place to socialize with his fellow ranchers. The story goes that when they went out drinking, the one who sat (or fell) down first had to pick up the tab; Los Parados means "the standing ones." Excellently grilled steaks and chicken as well as tasty Mexican specialties are served in a large room with a wood-burning kiva fireplace. ✉ *Av. Juárez 3901,* ☎ *14/15–35–04 or 14/10–35–59. AE, MC, V.*

$$ ✕ **Rincon Mexicano.** The folks who run the Mesón de Santa Eulalia restaurant in Santa Eulalia also serve some of the best Mexican food in Chihuahua and always have mariachi musicians to serenade you. ✉ *Av. Cuauhtémoc 224,* ☎ *14/11–14–27. AE, MC, V.*

$–$$ ✕ **La Casa de Los Milagros.** According to locals, this blue house with frilly white trim was once the favorite "Casa de Muñecas" (dollhouse) of Pancho Villa and his compañeros. Today it's the happening place for light Mexican snacks, drinks, and music after 9 PM, when the courtyard and rooms of this rambling abode start to fill with well-heeled, twentysomething Chihuahuans. ✉ *Victoria 812, near Ocampo,* ☎ *14/ 37–06–93. AE, MC, V.*

$ ✕ **Ah Chiles.** If you like it hot, this is the spot. A block from Plaza Hidalgo, this Chihuahua chain serves *norteño* (northern Mexican) food and dishes out a dozen different salsas. It also has foot-long hot dogs, hot wings, stuffed baked potatoes, and shrimp burgers. Ah Chiles is next to three other worthy, modestly priced restaurants: Ricky's Tacos, 1000 Tortas, and El Burro Seguido. ✉ *Aldama 712, corner of Guerrero,* ☎ *14/37–09–77. No credit cards.*

$$$$ ⌅ **Westin Soberano Chihuahua.** At the edge of town atop a rise that has magnificent views of the city and surrounding mountains, Chihuahua's first *gran turismo* (Mexico's highest quality level) hotel sparkles with fountains and marble. Designed around an atrium with a several-story waterfall cascading down one wall, the hotel is a contemporary palace of sorts in contrast to the rustic accommodations of the Copper Canyon. Rooms are plush, with richly patterned textiles, comfortable furniture, TV in a tall chest, and bath with both tub and shower. ✉ *Barranca del Cobre 3211, Fracc. Barrancas, 31125,* ☎ *14/29–29–29 or 01–800–711– 4099,* 🖷 *14/29–29–00. 194 rooms, 10 suites. 2 restaurants, bar, pool, health club, meeting rooms, car rental. AE, DC, MC, V.*

$$$ ⌅ **Holiday Inn Hotel & Suites.** This appealing property combines com-
★ fort, style, and convenience: 10 minutes from the downtown sights, Chihuahua's first all-suites hotel is decorated in contemporary style. Each room has a kitchenette with stove, dishwasher, and coffeemaker, as well as a VCR. A complimentary Continental breakfast buffet is served at the Clubhouse. The English-speaking staff is friendly and helpful. ✉ *Escudero 702, 31000,* ☎ *14/39–00–00 or 01–800/009–9900,* 🖷 *14/14–33–13. 74 suites. Restaurant, 2 pools, spa, basketball, exercise room. AE, DC, MC, V.*

$$$ ⌅ **Hotel San Francisco.** A favorite of Mexican business travelers, this modern five-story hotel has a prime location right next to the Cathedral and Plaza de Armas. Its clean and comfortable if somewhat bland rooms are equipped with color TVs and phones. The lobby, somewhat gloomy during the day, can be lively at night. ✉ *Victoria 409, 31000,* ☎ *14/16–75–50, 01–800/71–41–107, 800/847–2546,* 🖷 *14/15–35– 38. 111 rooms, 20 suites. Restaurant, bar. AE, MC, V.*

$$$ ⌅ **Palacio del Sol.** This five-star hotel, just two blocks from the cathe-
★ dral, is set up for businesspeople staying long term: some rooms include such luxuries as computer ports and a radio. Although convenient to downtown and very comfortable, it lacks the Mexican charm of some lesser quality hotels. ✉ *Independencia 116,* ☎ *14/16–60–00, 01–800/*

71–14–007, 800/852–4049, FAX 14/16–08–66. *152 rooms, 31 suites. 2 restaurants, lobby bar, exercise room, billiards, coin laundry, laundry service, meeting rooms, car rental. AE, DC, MC, V.*

$$ 🖭 **Posada Tierra Blanca.** Across the street from the Palacio del Sol but considerably less expensive, this modern motel-style property is convenient to downtown sights. Rooms, decorated in red and black with pseudo-antique furnishings, are large and well heated in winter; all have TVs. ⊠ *Niños Heroes 102,* ☎ 14/15–00–00, FAX 14/16–00–63. *98 rooms, 5 suites. Restaurant, piano bar, pool. AE, MC, V.*

Nightlife and the Arts

Chihuahua has the most nightlife options in the Copper Canyon area. **La Casa de Los Milagros** (☞ Dining and Lodging, *above*) starts to groove after 9 PM. **La Reggae** (⊠ Blvd. Ortiz Mena and Bosque de la Reina, ☎ 14/15–47–55) draws a dancing crowd with its rock-and-roll bands. **Taberna La Cerveceria** (⊠ Av. Juárez 3333, ☎ 14/15–83–80) is a glass-encased, neon-laced restaurant and bar in a four-story former brewery where you can play pool or dance to a DJ.

The **Hotel San Francisco** (☞ Dining and Lodging, *above*) has a piano bar. At **Hotel Sicomoro** (⊠ Blvd. Ortiz Mena 411, ☎ 14/13–54–45), there's live entertainment nightly in the lobby bar. Compared with dance clubs, **El Leñador** (⊠ Avs. Tecnologico and Pascual Orozco) offers a more tranquil scene, with Mexican and Cuban folksingers.

Shopping

Mercado de Artesanías (⊠ Calle Victoria 506 and Aldama 511, ☎ 14/15–34–62), a block wide with two entrances, sells everything from jewelry, candy, and T-shirts to crafts from all over the region. Across the street from the *calabozo* (calaboose) where Father Hidalgo was jailed, the **Casa de las Artesanías del Estado de Chihuahua** (⊠ Av. Juárez 705, ☎ 14/37–12–92) carries the best selection of Tarahumara and regional crafts in the state. In addition to selling gems and geodes from the area, the **Rock Shop** (⊠ Calle Décima, directly across from Pancho Villa's home, ☎ 14/15–28–82) carries a wide variety of crafts.

COPPER CANYON/CHIHUAHUA A TO Z

Arriving and Departing

By Boat

The Sematur **car ferry** runs daily from La Paz to Topolobampo, depending on the weather. It leaves La Paz at 11 AM and arrives in Topolobampo at approximately 8 PM. The return trip leaves at 10 PM and arrives in La Paz at 7 AM. In Los Mochis, contact the travel agency Festival Tour (⊠ Allende Sur 655, below Hotel Americas, Los Mochis, ☎ 68/18–39–86) for information and reservations. In Topolobampo, contact **Sematur** (☎ 68/62–01–41, FAX 68/62–00–35).

By Bus

Chihuahua: The **Chihuahuenses** (☎ 14/29–02–42 or 14/29–02–40) and **Omnibus de México** (☎ 14/10–30–90 or 14/20–15–80) lines run clean, air-conditioned buses from Ciudad Juárez to Chihuahua. These leave approximately every 30 minutes from 7 AM to 8 PM. The cost of the 4½-hour trip is approximately $20 for first class. Buses shuttle between El Paso and Ciudad Juárez every two hours; the price is $5.

Los Mochis: The **Elite** (☎ 63/13–54–01 in Nogales, 68/12–17–57 in Los Mochis), **Transportes del Pacifico** (☎ 63/13–16–06 in Nogales, 68/12–03–41 in Los Mochis), **Transport Norte de Sonora** (☎ 63/12–54–54 in Nogales, 68/12–04–11 in Los Mochis), and **TUFESA** (☎ 63/13–38–

62 in Nogales) bus lines all leave every hour from Nogales, Sonora, to Los Mochis. With luck, the $30 trip should take about 12 hours.

By Car

Most U.S. and Canadian visitors drive to **Chihuahua** via Mexico Highway 45 from the El Paso–Ciudad Juárez border, a distance of 375 km (233 mi), or up from Mexico City, 1,440 km (893 mi). The drive down to **Los Mochis** from Nogales on the Arizona border via Mexico Highway 15, four lanes much of the way, is 763 km (473 mi).

Paved roads connect Chihuahua to **Creel** and **Divisadero:** take Mexico Highway 16 west to San Pedro, then State Highway 127 south to Creel. The 300-km (186-mi) trip takes 3½–4 hours in good weather. This drive, through the pine forests of the Sierra Madre foothills, is more scenic than the railroad route via the plains area. Driving is a good option if you have a four-wheel-drive vehicle, because there are many worthwhile, if difficult, excursions into the canyons from Creel. From Divisadero to **Bahuichivo,** the dirt road is full of potholes and especially dangerous in rain or snow.

By Plane

To Chihuahua: Aeroméxico and its feeder airline, Aerolitoral (⊠ Paseo Bolívar 405, next to Quinta Gameros, ☎ 01–800/9–09–99), have daily flights from Los Angeles, Phoenix, and Tucson, and from San Antonio and El Paso. Within Mexico, the airlines have daily flights from Mexico City, Monterrey, Guadalajara, and Tijuana. **AeroCalifornia** (☎ 14/37–10–22 in Chihuahua) has flights from Mexico City and Tijuana. Of the major U.S. carriers, only **Continental** (☎ 01–800/900–5000) serves Chihuahua with daily flights from its hub in Houston.

To Los Mochis: AeroCalifornia (☎ 68/18–16–16 in Los Mochis) has daily flights from Los Angeles, Tucson, Tijuana, Mexico City, and Guadalajara. **Aeroméxico** and Aerolitoral (☎ 68/15–29–50 in Los Mochis) fly from Los Angeles, Phoenix, Tucson, San Antonio, El Paso, Mexico City, La Paz, and Chihuahua.

By Train

There is no first-class service from any U.S. border city to either Los Mochis or Chihuahua. Some luxury trains go directly from the United States to the Copper Canyon (☞ Guided Tours *in* Contacts and Resources, *below*).

Getting Around

By Taxi

In **Chihuahua** and **Los Mochis,** taxis are easy to find and can be engaged at hotels or hailed on the street. The trip from the airport into town costs about $6 in Chihuahua and $12 in Los Mochis. Always agree on a price before getting into the cab.

By Train

The **Ferrocarril Chihuahua al Pacífico** line (*Che'Pa'*, as it is affectionately called by locals) runs a first-class and a second-class train daily in each direction from Chihuahua and Los Mochis through the Copper Canyon. For long-term reservations and price information, your best bet may be using one of the private train companies or tour operators (☞ Guided Tours *in* Contacts and Resources, *below*).

The first-class train departs from Los Mochis at 6 AM (sit on the right side of the train for the best views) and arrives in Chihuahua 15 hours later. Westbound, it departs from Chihuahua at 6 AM and arrives in Los Mochis around 8 PM (most of the time, but delays of three hours or more are not unusual). You can buy tickets at the train station or at almost any hotel in Los Mochis or Chihuahua. The price is about $40 each way, plus a 15% charge for up to two stopovers en route, which you should arrange when you buy tickets. Make reservations (☎ 14/15–77–56 in Chihuahua, 68/12–08–53 in Los Mochis, FAX 14/10–90–59 in Chihuahua, 68/15–77–75 in Los Mochis) at least a week in advance during the busy months of July, August, and October, and around Christmas and Easter. It's best to book through a hotel, tour company, or travel agency, as the phones in the local train stations are rarely answered. Keep in mind that it's the scenery, not the vehicle, that continues to draw passengers. Guards armed with automatic weapons often patrol the passenger cars to discourage robberies. Exercise caution by carrying passports and cash in a money belt and leaving your jewelry at home. Bring your own food and drink, as there is no guarantee that even on the first-class train there will be any for sale.

The second-class train, *El Pollero,* leaves an hour later from each terminus but makes many stops and is scheduled to arrive 3½ hours later in both directions than the first-class train. Although it is less comfortable, this train is a good way to meet local residents and their poultry. No reservations are needed; prices are approximately $9 each way.

If you're driving down to Los Mochis, you're better off leaving your car there and taking the train round-trip. If you're coming via Chihuahua, however, consider driving to Creel or Divisadero and doing a round-trip from there.

Contacts and Resources

Car Rental
CHIHUAHUA

Avis (⊠ Av. Universidad 1703, ☎ 14/14–19–99), **Budget** (⊠ Ortiz Mena 3322, ☎ 14/14–21–71), and **Hertz** (⊠ Av. Revolución 514, ☎ 14/16–64–73) all have offices at the airport.

LOS MOCHIS

Car companies at the airport and in town include **AGA** (⊠ Av. Leyva and Callejón Municipal, ☎ 68/12–53–60), **Budget** (⊠ G. Prieto 850 Nte., ☎ 68/15–83–00, FAX 68/15–84–00), and **Hertz** (⊠ Av. Leyva 171 Nte., ☎ 68/12–11–22, FAX 68/15–19–29).

Emergencies
CHIHUAHUA

Police (☎ 06), **Cruz Roja** (Red Cross; ☎ 14/11–14–84 or 14/11–22–11), and **Bomberos** (Fire Dept.; ☎ 14/10–07–70). Two facilities for handling the injured or sick are **Clínica del Parque** (⊠ Calle de la Llave and Leal Rodriguez, ☎ 14/15–74–11 or 14/15–73–39) and **Hospital del Centro del Estado** (⊠ Calle 33 and Rosales, ☎ 14/15–47–20 or 14/15–90–00).

LOS MOCHIS

Police (☎ 06), **Cruz Roja** (Red Cross; ⊠ Guillermo Prieto and Tenochtitlán, ☎ 68/15–08–08 or 68/18–64–64), and **Bomberos** (Fire Dept.; ☎ 68/12–01–00).

Guided Tours
Most large hotels in Los Mochis and Chihuahua have in-house travel agencies that arrange city tours and tours of the Copper Canyon area, as well as hiking, hunting, and fishing expeditions. In **Los Mochis,** the Hotel Santa Anita offers city tours for about $29 per person. In **Chihuahua,** independent travel agencies include the American Express agent, **Rojo y Casavantes** (⊠ Calle Vincent Guerrero 1207, ☎ 14/15–58–58 or 14/15–74–70, FAX 14/15–53–84), and, particularly recommended,

Turismo Al Mar (⊠ Calle Verna 2202, ☎ FAX 14/16–65–89, ☎ 14/16–59–50). In Cuauhtémoc, **Cumbres Friesen** (⊠ Calle 3A No. 466, Cuauhtémoc, ☎ 158/2–54–57, FAX 158/2–40–60), owned by Mennonite David Friesen, can arrange Mennonite tours.

From the United States, the oldest operator in the area is **Pan American Tours** (⊠ Box 9401, El Paso, TX 79984, ☎ 915/778–5395 or 800/876–3942). Prices for tailor-made tours between Los Mochis and Chihuahua range from about $300 to $700 per person, depending on length of stay and number of stops made. **Synergy Tours** (⊠ 7336 E. Shoeman La., Suite 120, Scottsdale, AZ 85251, ☎ 800/569–1797, FAX 602/994–4439) runs individual and group trips about 10 times a year, including off-the-beaten-path treks. **California Native** (⊠ 6701 W. 87th Pl., Los Angeles, CA 90045, ☎ 800/926–1140) runs a seven-day escorted trip through the Copper Canyon every month that starts at $1,650, and also has backpacking, mountain-biking, and deluxe excursions. A good tour operator who will book horseback-riding tours through the Copper Canyon is **Native Trails** (⊠ 6440 Airport Rd., Suite C, El Paso, TX 79925, ☎ 800/884–3107).

TRAIN TOURS

Sierra Madre Express of Tucson (⊠ Box 26381, Tucson, AZ 85726, ☎ 520/747–0346 or 800/666–0346) runs its own deluxe trains (with dome/dining and Pullman cars) to the Copper Canyon from Tucson on eight-day, seven-night trips about four times a year. Its trips combine the charm of sleeping on the train with first-class accommodations. The luxury train **South Orient Express** (⊠ 16800 Greenspoint Park Dr., Suite 245 N, Houston, TX 77060, ☎ 800/659–7602) offers all-inclusive "rail cruises"—in dome, dining/lounge, and Pullman cars—from Chihuahua and Los Mochis spring and fall (and from Fort Worth twice a year), starting at $1,549 per person for a five-day trip. The company also has individual trips year-round on its slightly less luxurious "VSP" train, ranging from transportation only ($198 one-way between Chihuahua and Los Mochis with unlimited stops) to packages with lodging, meals, and sight-seeing.

Late-Night Pharmacies

CHIHUAHUA

Chihuahua has an abundance of pharmacies with late-night service in the city center. **Farmacia Mendoza** (⊠ Calle Aldama 1901, ☎ 14/16–44–14 or 14/10–27–96) is open 24 hours.

LOS MOCHIS

Farmacia San Jorge (⊠ Av. Independencia and Angel Flores, ☎ 68/15–74–74; ⊠ corner of Degollado and Juárez, ☎ 68/18–18–19) has two stores in Los Mochis that are open 24 hours.

Money Exchange

Be sure to change money before you get into real barranca country: there are no banks in Cerocahui, Divisadero, or Posada Barrancas, and no guarantee that the hotels in those places will have enough cash to accommodate you. A bank in the main plaza at Creel transacts foreign exchanges from 10:30 to noon only. In Los Mochis, most banking hours are weekdays between 8:30 and 4:30; some banks open Saturday morning. In Chihuahua, most banks open weekdays from 9 to 1:30 and from 3:30 to 7:30, and Saturday from 9 to 1:30. **Banco Bital** in downtown Chihuahua (⊠ Libertad 1922, ☎ 14/16–08–80) is open Monday through Saturday 8–8. The **Casa de Cambio Rachasa** (⊠ Av. Ocampo and Niños Heroes, ☎ 14/10–03–33), open Monday through Saturday 9–9, Sunday 9–2, has good exchange rates and quick service. In El Fuerte, **Bancomer** (⊠ corner of Constitución and Juárez) is open Monday

5 THE COPPER CANYON: FROM LOS MOCHIS TO CHIHUAHUA CITY

In the heart of the scenic, rugged Sierra Madre, the Copper Canyon—a series of gorges, some deeper than the Grand Canyon in the United States—is known for hikes that range from pleasant walks to thigh-busting descents to the canyon floor. These gorges are home to the largely reclusive Tarahumara Indians. One of North America's most spectacular train trips snakes its way through this magnificent, mostly uncharted region, usually beginning or ending in the lively city of Chihuahua.

GUADALAJARA

*Including Tlaquepaque, Tonalá,
and Lake Chapala*

Colonial architecture that dates to the city's heyday as the center of regional commerce is among the lures of Guadalajara, which introduced the world to mariachis, tequila, *charreadas* (rodeos), and the Mexican hat dance. On the city's outskirts, Tlaquepaque has some of Mexico's finest crafts, as does Tonalá. A near-perfect semitropical climate and proximity to the Pacific Ocean—240 km (149 mi) away—ensure warm, sunny days with just a hint of humidity and cool, clear nights.

Updated by
Shane
Christensen

T RADITIONS ARE PRESERVED and customs perpetuated in Guadalajara; it's a place where the siesta is an institution and the fiesta
an art form. Mexico's second-largest city, and the capital of the
state of Jalisco, Guadalajara is engaged in a struggle to retain its
provincial ambience and colonial charm as its population surpasses 7
million. Émigrés from Mexico City after the devastating 1985 earthquake and staggering numbers of the rural poor seeking employment
created a population explosion that continues to strain public services
and the city's often outdated infrastructure. Visitors can enjoy the
tree-lined boulevards, parks, plazas, and stately churrigueresque architecture, but recent years have brought traffic jams and increasingly
heavy pollution.

Guadalajara has always been one of the most socially traditional and
politically conservative cities in Mexico. It has also been the seat of
Christian fundamentalism and was one of the strategic areas of the Cris-
teros, a movement of right-wing Catholic zealots in western Mexico
in the 1920s. Tapatíos, as the city's residents are called (the name comes
from *tlapatiotl,* three units or purses of cacao or other commodities
used as currency by the Indians of the area), even seem to take a certain amount of pride in their straight and narrow outlook.

Still, Tapatíos are historically accustomed to challenge and change. Within
10 years of its founding in 1531, the location of the city changed three
times. In 1542 the City Council followed the advice of Doña Beatriz
Hernández to build the city in the center of the Atemajac Valley, where
it could expand. Thus Guadalajara was placed on a mile-high plain of
the Sierra Madre, bounded on three sides by rugged cliffs and on the
fourth by the spectacular Barranca de Oblatos (Oblatos Canyon).

Geographically remote from the rest of the republic during the nearly
300 years of Spanish rule, the city cultivated and maintained a political and cultural autonomy. By the end of the 16th century, money was
flowing into Guadalajara from the rich farms and silver mines in the
region, creating the first millionaires of what was then known as New
Galicia. Under orders from Spain, much of the wealth was lavished on
magnificent churches, residences, and monuments. Many of these reminders of the golden era still stand in downtown Guadalajara.

The suburbs of Tlaquepaque (pronounced tla-kay-*pah*-kay) and Tonalá
(pronounced toe-na-*la*) produce some of Mexico's finest and most
popular traditional crafts and folk art. Lake Chapala—Mexico's largest
body of fresh water—and the nearby towns Chapala and Ajijic have
lured retirees from the United States and Canada, who enjoy most of
the amenities they were accustomed to north of the border.

Pleasures and Pastimes

Arts and Architecture

You can find all kinds of Mexican and international arts in Guadalajara—from the traditional Ballet Folklórico at the Teatro Degollado
to rock groups at the Instituto Cultural Cabañas. Galleries and museums around town also offer the best of modern and traditional work.
Numerous 16th-century colonial buildings fill the downtown area, connected by a series of large, Spanish-style plazas.

Churches

Guadalajara seems to have a church every block or two—there are 15
in the downtown area alone, all dating from the colonial era. Some

have elaborately carved facades, and others conceal ornate Baroque altars and priceless colonial oil paintings behind sober stone exteriors.

Dining

The variety of Guadalajara's restaurants includes classic Mexican dishes, Continental delicacies, Argentine-style steaks, and fresh seafood. Savory regional specialties—often served in simpler places—include *birria,* a spicy stew prepared with goat, lamb, or beef in a light tomato broth; *pozole,* a thick pork and hominy soup; and *carne en su jugo,* consisting of steak bits in a clear spicy broth with bacon, beans, and cilantro, usually served with a side of tiny, grilled whole onions.

Lodging

Hotels run the gamut from older establishments in the downtown historic district—including one finely restored building that has been a hotel since 1610—to representatives of the large chains, most of which are on or near Avenida López Mateos Sur, a 16-km (10-mi) strip extending from the Minerva Fountain to the Plaza del Sol shopping center. In the mid-1990s several hotels were built close to the Expo-Guadalajara convention center, which opened in 1987.

Shopping

Blown glass, hand-carved wood furniture, fine leatherwork, and hand-glazed pottery are local traditions. Two of the most common ceramic techniques are *barro bruñido,* in which the pieces are hand-burnished to a soft sheen, and *petatillo,* in which glaze is applied to earthenware in a fine crosshatch pattern. Guadalajara is also home to a thriving shoe industry. At sprawling markets you can bargain for anything from embroidered shirts to huaraches, and sleek shopping malls have full-service department stores and trendy boutiques.

Sports

Highly stylized *charreadas,* traditional Mexican rodeos, are presented weekly, and there are bullfights in October and November. Late August through May, soccer fans crowd Estadio Jalisco (Jalisco Stadium).

EXPLORING GUADALAJARA

Metropolitan Guadalajara consists of a historic city center and nearby urban districts, as well as neighboring Tlaquepaque, Tonalá, and Zapopan, and the tranquil villages on Lake Chapala's shores.

Numbers in the text correspond to numbers in the margin and on the Downtown Guadalajara, Tlaquepaque, Tonalá, and Lake Chapala Area maps.

Great Itineraries

It's not surprising that Guadalajara has been described as *señorial y moderna* (lordly and modern). Along with the graciousness of colonial Mexico, you can take in as much as you want of the 20th century. And nearby pueblos are an eye on traditional rural life. Ten days would allow you to fully explore the city and surrounding villages, as well as to take an excursion or two to points farther afield. With five days to spend, you'll have time to see most of the city's highlights and to get to know Tlaquepaque, Tonalá, and the Lake Chapala area. In three days, you can take in the historic city center and make day trips to Tlaquepaque, Tonalá, and Lake Chapala.

IF YOU HAVE 3 DAYS

Spend your first day in the historic **el centro** ①–⑩ (town center). The next day, spend the morning and have lunch in **Tlaquepaque** ⑳–㉚, and visit **Tonalá** ㉛–㊲ in the afternoon. On your third day, head for **Lake**

Chapala ⑧–⑭; stroll and shop, take a boat trip on the lake, and enjoy lunch or dinner in one of the area's fine restaurants.

IF YOU HAVE 5 DAYS

See **el centro** ①–⑩ on your first day, and then consider your interests. If traditional crafts lure you, devote a day to **Tlaquepaque** ⑳–㉚ and Day 3 to **Tonalá** ㉛–㊲. Or explore the two towns in one day, and leave a day to spend around **Lake Chapala** ⑧–⑭. Spend your final day back in Guadalajara in additional museums and the **Basílica de la Virgen de Zapopan** ⑯, for which you'll need several hours, or even the **Zoológico Guadalajara** ⑭. Plan an afternoon of strolling past the mansions that were built by Guadalajara's upper classes in the glorious twilight before the 1910 revolution; the best area is in a six-block radius around Avenida Vallarta west of Avenida Chapultepec. If you'd like to get your feet on the ground in more-natural surroundings, hike in the nearby **Barranca de Oblatos.**

IF YOU HAVE 7 DAYS

You will be able to cover all of **el centro** ①–⑩ plus the other city sights, and **Tlaquepaque** ⑳–㉚, **Tonalá** ㉛–㊲, and the **Lake Chapala** ⑧–⑭ area. Fill in the gaps with a visit to Tequila and a soak in the soothing thermal waters of **San Juan Cosalá** or **Río Caliente.**

Guadalajara

Beginning around 1960, 20th-century architecture started to threaten the historical integrity of this provincial state capital. In the early 1980s the city declared a 30-square-block area in the heart of downtown a cultural sanctuary, and in the late 1990s private-sector groups formed a trust to continue spiffing up **el centro.** The 16th-century buildings here are connected by a series of large Spanish-style plazas where children chase balloons, young lovers coo on tree-shaded park benches, and grandparents stroll hand in hand past vendors and marble fountains. At nearby **Plaza de los Mariachis,** the nostalgic songs and music of sombrero-topped troubadours fill the air.

Outside the city center, most tourist sights and large hotels are located in three areas: near Avenida Chapultepec, near the Minerva Fountain and Los Arcos monument, and in the Plaza del Sol shopping area (several miles southwest of downtown).

A Good Walk

Guadalajara's 17th-century **Catedral** ①, on the north side of Plaza de Armas, is the place to start exploring downtown. After you've marveled at the interior, exit through the main doors and cross Avenida Alcalde to Plaza de la Ciudad de Guadalajara, with its large fountain, outdoor café, and benches scattered beneath square-cut laurel trees. To your right (with your back toward the cathedral) across Avenida Hidalgo is the deceptive facade of the **Palacio Municipal** ②.

From the corner of Avenidas Alcalde and Hidalgo, head one block east to Calle Liceo, where you'll see the **Museo Regional de Guadalajara** ③. You'll pass the Rotonda de Hombres Ilustres de Jalisco, a tree-shaded square whose central colonnaded rotunda covers a mausoleum containing the remains of 17 of the state of Jalisco's favorite sons and one daughter.

After you leave the museum, you can turn either way on Calle Liceo: three blocks to your right is the **Casa-Museo López Portillo** ④ and, north and west of that, on Avenida Alcalde, the **Museo del Periodismo y de las Artes Gráficas** ⑤. Around the corner to the left of the Museo Regional, on Avenida Hidalgo, are the Palacio Legislativo—a former

Downtown Guadalajara

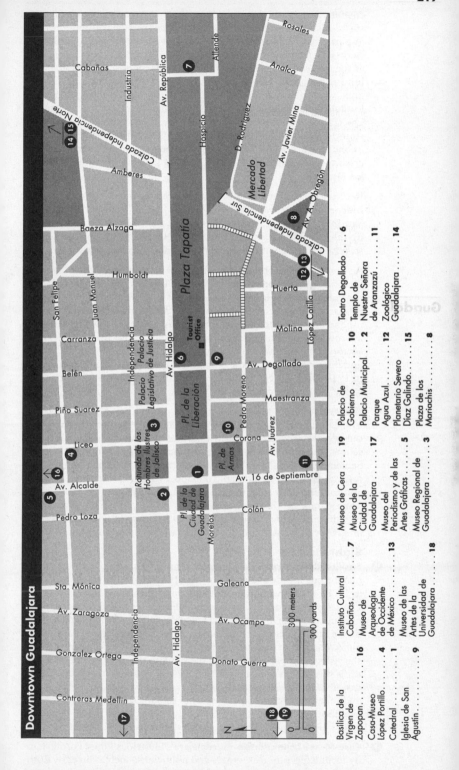

customs house, tobacco warehouse, and inn that today houses Jalisco's state legislature—and the Palacio de Justicia, which was built in 1588 as part of Guadalajara's first convent and now is the state courthouse. Across Avenida Hidalgo on your right sprawls the Plaza de la Liberación, at the east end of which rises the spectacular **Teatro Degollado** ⑥. Behind it begins the Plaza Tapatía, a five-block-long pedestrian mall lined with shops, trees, and whimsical sculpture. At the end, visit the **Instituto Cultural Cabañas** ⑦. Then proceed back west to the modernistic Quetzalcóatl Fountain in the center. Turn left and walk down the stairs to the sprawling **Mercado Libertad** (☞ Markets and Handicrafts *in* Shopping, *below*). Turn left again when you leave the market and cross the pedestrian bridge over Avenida Javier Mina to the **Plaza de los Mariachis** ⑧.

Return to Plaza Tapatía by heading right to the intersection of Calzada Independencia Sur and Avenida Javier Mina, in front of the Iglesia de San Juan de Dios. Continue two blocks past the church and go back up the stairs. Turn left and walk west four blocks (so you can see the stores on this side of the plaza) to the **Iglesia de San Agustín** ⑨.

As you leave the church, turn left down Calle Morelos to Avenida Corona. Turn left again and walk a half block to the main entrance of the **Palacio de Gobierno** ⑩ to see two of José Clemente Orozco's murals. Exit the palacio back onto Avenida Corona (the way you came in) and cross the street to the Plaza de Armas, where you can rest on a wrought-iron bench, imagining yourself in the Porfiriato—Mexico's Victorian period—when gracious *dons* and *doñas* strolled amid the trees and flower beds around the ornately sculpted kiosk, a gift from France in 1910. With the cathedral to your right, you've come full circle back to the north side of the plaza.

TIMING

You can take in most of downtown Guadalajara in a day. The sights outside of the center can easily take a half or full day each. Most museums, the zoo, and the planetarium are closed Monday. In early September Guadalajara hosts the international mariachi and tequila festival, bringing traditional troubadours from as far away as Japan and running daily train trips to Tequila, home of the fiery elixir of the same name. In October the city puts on the Fiestas de Octubre, a monthlong cultural festival that exudes a county fair–like atmosphere and is sprinkled with top-flight international entertainment.

Sights to See

⑯ Basílica de la Virgen de Zapopan. This vast church, with an ornate plateresque facade and *mudéjar* (Moorish) tile dome, was consecrated in 1730. It is known throughout Mexico as the home of La Zapopanita, Our Lady of Zapopan. The 10-inch-high statue is venerated as the source of many miracles in and around Guadalajara. Every October 12, more than a million people crowd the streets leading to Zapopan as the Virgin is returned to the basilica after a five-month absence, during which she visits every parish church in the state. In the right side of the basilica is the **Museo Huichol** (✉ Avs. Avila Camacho and de las Américas, ☎ 3/36–44–30), a small gallery and shop with exquisite beadwork and other handicrafts by the Huichol Indians of northern Jalisco and neighboring states Zacatecas and Nayarit; it's open Tues.–Sun. 9–2, 4–7. The basilica is 7 km (4½ mi) west–northwest of downtown.

④ Casa-Museo López Portillo. Guadalajara's illustrious López Portillo family included prominent writers and politicians, such as an early 20th-century Jalisco governor and his Mexico City–born grandson, José López Portillo, president of Mexico in 1976–82. As is typical of homes built by Mexico's 19th-century upper class, the plain stucco exterior belies the rich interior, where French Baroque–style rooms ring a spacious interior patio. ✉ *Liceo 177, at San Felipe,* ☎ *3/613–2411.* 🖃 *Free.* ⊙ *Weekdays 9–8, Sat. 9–1.*

★ **❶ Catedral.** Consecrated in 1618, this focal point of downtown is an intriguing mélange of Baroque, Gothic, and other styles, the result of design and structural modifications during its 57 years of construction. Its emblematic twin towers replaced the originals, which fell in the earthquake of 1818. Ten of the silver-and-gilt altars were gifts from King Fernando VII, in appreciation of Guadalajara's financial support of Spain during the Napoleonic Wars; the 11th, of white marble, was carved in Italy in 1863. On the walls of the cathedral hang some of the world's most beautiful *retablos* (altarpieces); above the sacristy is the priceless 17th-century painting by Bartolomé Esteban Murillo, *The Assumption of the Virgin.* In a loft high above the main entrance is a magnificent late-19th-century French organ, featured in an organ festival usually held every May. ✉ *Av. Alcalde between Av. Hidalgo and Calle Morelos.* ⊙ *Daily 8–7.*

❾ Iglesia de San Agustín. The venerable St. Augustine Church is one of the oldest churches in the city. It has been remodeled many times since its consecration in 1574, but the sacristy is preserved in its original form. The building to the left of the church, originally an Augustinian cloister, is now the **Escuela de Música** (School of Music) of the University of Guadalajara. Free recitals and concerts are held on its patio. ✉ *Calle Morelos at Av. Degollado,* ☎ *3/614–5365.* ⊙ *Daily 8–8.*

★ **❼ Instituto Cultural Cabañas.** This landmark neoclassical-style cultural center was designed by the famous Spanish architect–sculptor Manuel Tolsá. Originally an orphanage, the building served as home for 400 orphans and indigent children until the 1970s, when the orphanage moved. The rooms, which surround 23 flower-filled patios, contain permanent and revolving art exhibits. The central dome and walls of the main chapel display a series of murals painted by José Clemente Orozco in 1938–39. *The Man of Fire,* which depicts a man enveloped in flames who is ascending toward infinity and yet not consumed by the fire, represents the spirit of humankind. It is widely considered to be his finest work. Room 33 has a permanent exhibit of Orozco's paintings, cartoons, and drawings. Ask the attendant at the front desk for an English-speaking guide. ✉ *Calle Cabañas 8, at Plaza Tapatía,* ☎ *3/617–4322, 3/617–4440.* 🖃 *About $1, free Sun.* ⊙ *Tues.–Sat. 10–6, Sun. 10–3.*

⓭ Museo de Arqueología de Occidente de México. The Archaeological Museum of Western Mexico houses pottery and other artifacts used by ancient peoples of what are now the states of Colima, Jalisco, and Nayarit. It's across from the entrance to Parque Agua Azul. ✉ *Calzada Independencia Sur and Av. del Campesino,* ☎ *no phone.* 🖃 *40¢.* ⊙ *Tues.–Sun. 10–2 and 4–7.*

⓲ Museo de las Artes de la Universidad de Guadalajara. This impressive contemporary-art museum and its exquisite early 20th-century building belong to the University of Guadalajara. It has a permanent collection of 20th-century drawings and paintings and revolving exhibits of modern Latin American, U.S., and European work. Look for the murals Orozco painted upon returning to Guadalajara at age 53. The *paraninfo*—a round theater in the museum's center—frequently hosts chamber-music groups. There is also a charming café.

Behind the museum, on Avenida Lopez Cotilla, the **Templo Expiatorio** is a striking Gothic church modeled after the Orvieto Cathedral in

Italy. ⊠ *Av. Juárez at Av. Enrique Díaz de León,* ☎ *3/825–6114, 3/ 825–7553, ext. 66.* 🎫 *About $1.* ⊙ *Weekdays 9–9.*

🔵 ⑲ **Museo de Cera.** At Guadalajara's 120-figure wax museum, now in the historic downtown area across from Plaza de la Liberación, go eye-to-eye with Madonna, Mahatma Gandhi, beloved Mexican comic Cantinflas, and a host of other Mexican and international political and artistic luminaries. Visit the underground Aztec sacrificial chamber and a chamber of horrors. A wax mariachi, playing "Guadalajara Guadalajara," greets you at the door. ⊠ *Calle Morelos 217,* ☎ *3/614–8487.* 🎫 *$1.50.* ⊙ *Daily 11–8:30.*

⑰ **Museo de la Ciudad de Guadalajara.** In a series of rooms surrounding the tranquil interior patio of this spacious remodeled colonial home, you'll find informative artwork, artifacts, and reproductions of documents about the city's development from pre-Hispanic times through the 20th century. ⊠ *Calle Independencia 684, between Contreras Medellín and Mariano Bárcenas,* ☎ *3/658–2531, 3/658–3706.* 🎫 *30¢, free Sun.* ⊙ *Wed.–Sat. 10–5:30, Sun. 10–2:30.*

⑤ **Museo del Periodismo y de las Artes Gráficas.** In 1792 Guadalajara's first printing press was set up on this site, where today you can see displays of historic newspapers, printing presses, recording equipment, and a complete television studio. The building has long been known as the Casa de los Perros because of the two wrought-iron dogs (*perros*) "guarding" the roof. ⊠ *Av. Alcalde 225, between Reforma and San Felipe,* ☎ *3/613–9286.* 🎫 *About 50¢.* ⊙ *Weekdays 9–3.*

★ ③ **Museo Regional de Guadalajara.** Constructed as a seminary in 1701, this distinguished building has been home to the Regional Museum (also known as the State Museum) since 1918. The first-floor galleries, which surround a garden courtyard, contain artifacts and memorabilia that trace the history of western Mexico from prehistoric times through the Spanish conquest; there are also revolving arts and crafts exhibits. On the second-floor balcony are five 19th-century carriages; the galleries offer an impressive collection of paintings by European and Mexican artists, including Bartolomé Esteban Murillo. ⊠ *Liceo 60,* ☎ *3/614–9957.* 🎫 *About $1.60, free Tues.* ⊙ *Tues.–Sun. 9–3:45.*

⑩ **Palacio de Gobierno.** Built in 1643, this churrigueresque and neoclassical structure houses Jalisco's state government offices and two of José Clemente Orozco's most passionate murals. You'll see the first one in the stairwell to the right after you enter: a gigantic Father Miguel Hidalgo looming amid shadowy figures representing oppression and slavery. The second, in the former state-legislature quarters on the upper level, depicts Juárez and other figures of the 1850s Reform era. ⊠ *Av. Corona between Calle Morelos and Pedro Moreno.* ⊙ *Daily 9–8:45.*

② **Palacio Municipal.** Guadalajara's city hall is a clever, colonial-style fake: it was built in 1952 with an arched facade and interior patio to fit in with neighboring buildings. Inside is a colorful, if frightening, mural depicting scenes from Judgment Day. ⊠ *Av. Hidalgo at Av. Alcalde.* ⊙ *Daily 9–8.*

🔵 ⑫ **Parque Agua Azul.** Amid acres of trees and flowers, this popular park has carnival rides, tropical birds in cages, an orchid house, and a geodesic dome covering a tropical garden. Next to the park entrance, the small **Teatro Experimental** (☎ 3/619–1176) presents many Spanish-language children's plays. Dramas and chamber music are also performed here. The **Museo de la Paleontología** (☎ 3/619–7043), on the southeast side of the park, has hands-on geography, outer-space, and natural-history displays for kids. ⊠ *Calzada Independencia Sur and Av. del Campesino 973,* ☎ *3/619–0328, 3/619–0332.* ☞ *40¢.* ⊘ *Tues.–Sun. 10–6:30.*

☻ ⑮ **Planetario Severo Díaz Galindo.** A modern facility with astronomy shows and aeronautical displays, the planetarium also has exhibits that allow children to test the forces and laws of nature. It's 6 km (4 mi) northeast of downtown. ⊠ *Anillo Periférico Manuel Gomez Morin 401, east of Calzada Independencia,* ☎ *3/674–4106, 3/674–3978.* ☞ *Museum 20¢, astronomy show and movie 40¢.* ⊘ *Tues.–Sun. 9–7.*

★ ⑧ **Plaza de los Mariachis.** Experience the most Mexican of music in this picturesque little plaza complete with cafés, where strolling mariachi groups perform. Although the action lasts all night, it's much safer to visit in daytime. Use the pedestrian overpass from the Mercado Libertad to avoid the heavy traffic. ⊠ *Calzada Independencia Sur, between Av. Javier Mina and Alvaro Obregón.* ☞ *Mariachi serenade about $4 a song.*

★ ⑥ **Teatro Degollado.** Inaugurated in 1866, this magnificent theater was modeled after Milan's La Scala. Above the Corinthian columns gracing the entrance is a relief depicting Apollo and the nine Muses. Inside, the recently refurbished theater has kept its traditional red-and-gold color scheme, but it now has alternating seats, so that in orchestra seats you will no longer have to stare at the head of the person in front of you. The balconies ascend to a multitier dome adorned with Gerardo Suárez's depiction of Dante's *Divine Comedy.* The theater is the permanent home for the Jalisco Philharmonic and the Ballet Folklórico of the University of Guadalajara and also hosts visiting orchestras, plays, and numerous other performances.

According to tradition, Guadalajara was founded on the site of what is now the **Plaza de los Fundadores,** which flanks the east side of the theater. A sculpted frieze on the rear wall of the Teatro Degollado depicts the historic event. ⊠ *Av. Degollado, between Av. Hidalgo and Calle Morelos,* ☎ *3/614–4773, 3/613–1115.* ⊘ *Mon.–Sat. 10–2 and during performances.*

NEED A
BREAK?
A signature pink-and-white color scheme heralds the city's most popular ice-cream chain. A stop at **Helados Bing** (⊠ on the north side of Plaza Tapatía, east of the Quetzalcóatl Fountain) provides a welcome respite from an afternoon of sight-seeing. Choose from more than 20 flavors of pasteurized ice cream and ices, and relax on a shaded bench.

⑪ **Templo de Nuestra Señora de Aranzazú.** Don't be fooled by Our Lady of Aranzazú's drab brown stone exterior: inside is a spectacular Baroque gilt altar whose 14 niches contain life-size statues of saints. The walls' and ceilings' intricate floral details are painted in bright shades of turquoise, rose, and rust. The church is on the west side of Parque San Francisco, a small green oasis that draws food vendors, families, and senior citizens. ⊠ *Av. 16 de Septiembre and Prisciliano Sánchez,* ☎ *3/614–4083.* ⊘ *Weekdays 10–2 and 4–7, Sat. 10–2, Sun. 11:30–8:30.*

☻ ⑭ **Zoológico Guadalajara.** On the edge of the jagged Barranca Huentitán (Huentitán Canyon), the impressive zoo has more than 1,500 animals representing some 300 species. For 50¢ a train gives guided tours. The adjacent **Selva Mágica,** or Magic Jungle amusement park, has carnival rides and attractions for about $1.30. The complex is 6 km (nearly 4 mi) northeast of downtown, near the planetarium. ⊠ *Paseo del Zoológico 600,* ☎ *3/674–4488.* ☞ *$1.80.* ⊘ *Daily 10–6.*

OFF THE
BEATEN PATH   **BARRANCA DE OBLATOS –** A spectacular 2,000-ft-deep gorge, Oblatos Canyon also has hiking trails and the narrow Cola de Caballo waterfall, named for its horse-tail shape. For the best view, go to the lookout area, or Parque Mirador, at the top. ⌧ *10 km (6 mi) northeast of downtown Guadalajara via Calzada Independencia Nte.*

DINING

Guadalajara eateries continue to be very affordable. Most are open throughout the evening, although seafood restaurants often close earlier. A number of places listed below have branches elsewhere in the city; our choices are either the most colorful, original locations or those most convenient to the hotel areas. Because Guadalajara is a big, business-oriented city, it is advisable to dress well for $$$ restaurants.

CATEGORY	COST*
$$$	$15–$25
$$	$10–$15
$	under $10

*per person for a three-course meal, excluding drinks, service, and 15% sales tax

$$$ ✕ **Santo Coyote.** Located in the former U.S. Consul General's residence,
★ this *nuevo* Mexican eatery remains the talk of the town. Murals of goddesses adorn one dining area, waterfalls flow, and candles burn at a huge shrine to Mexico's patron saint—the Virgin of Guadalupe. Look on the menu for wood-fired roast or grilled *cabrito* (goat)—a house specialty—or baby back ribs topped with a tamarind and pepper sauce, or marrow soup. Service and presentation are excellent. ⌧ *Lerdo de Tejada 2379*, ☎ *3/616–6978. AE, MC, V.*

$$–$$$ ✕ **La Rinconada.** One of the finest restaurants in the historic center,
★ La Rinconada has appeared in numerous Mexican movies and TV comedies—a favorite setting for its old Guadalajara charm. The colonial dining room, with its arched pillars and high vault, was the original centerpiece of an 1897 farm; today it is the first choice for local businesspeople in search of excellent steak and seafood dishes. The *pescado* Veracruzana is a white-wine-marinated white fish with tomato sauce; the *plato Mexicano* includes chopped steak in a mild red sauce served with an enchilada, quesadilla, guacamole, rice, and beans. There is live piano music between 2 and 6:30 daily. ⌧ *Calle Morelos 86, at Plaza Tapatía*, ☎ *3/613–9914, 3/613–9925. AE, MC, V.*

$$–$$$ ✕ **La Trattoria.** Guadalajara's top Italian restaurant has retained its reputation as a family place committed to good value. Pictures of Italian piazzas decorate the dining room, which has closely spaced tables. The menu's best options include *spaghetti frutti di mari* (seafood spaghetti) and *scaloppine alla Marsala* (beef medallions with Marsala and mushrooms). The homemade bread is delicious, and all meals include the salad bar. ⌧ *Av. Niños Héroes 3051*, ☎ *3/122–1817. AE, MC, V.*

$$ ✕ **Casa Bariachi.** This grand mariachi restaurant and bar is a favorite among locals, a place to celebrate with friends and enjoy some of Guadalajara's finest mariachi bands. Expect waiters as well as diners to sing along. The menu highlights steaks and alcoholic drinks, and the fiesta continues until 3 AM. ⌧ *Av. Vallarta 2221*, ☎ *3/615–0029, 3/616–9900. AE, MC, V. Closed Sun.*

$$ ✕ **C77.** Decorative tilework by Tonalá artisan Jorge Wilmot covers the walls here, where the signature dish is paella. Since 1952, C77—originally known as the Copenhagen—has served up the famous dish of Valencia, Spain, as well as beef and seafood entrées, pastas, and Spanish-style tortillas. C77 is also the unofficial headquarters for Guadala-

jara's jazz aficionados; some of the city's best jazz musicians play everything from Brubeck to Count Basie here at night. ⊠ *Marcos Castellanos 136-Z,* ☎ *3/141–0603. AE. Closed Sun.*

$$ ✕ **La Destilería.** If you can't make it to the village of Tequila, here's the next best thing: a restaurant-cum-tequila-museum that serves novel Mexican specialties and 240 varieties of the fiery liquor. Antique photos of tequila distilleries and bilingual plaques explaining tequila's history line the brick walls. ⊠ *Av. México 2916,* ☎ *3/640–3110. AE, MC, V.*

$$ ✕ **La Estancia Gaucha.** In a town that loves Argentine cuisine, this nononsense steak establishment is considered by many to be the cream of the crop. Among the best cuts here are the *churrasco estancia* (rib eye) and the *bife de chorizo* (essentially New York strip). The empanadas and the *parillada* (a mixed grill that often includes beef, sausages, and selected organ meats) are also delicious. Piano music accompanies dinner Wednesday through Saturday. ⊠ *Av. Niños Héroes 2860,* ☎ *3/122–6565. AE, MC, V.*

$$ ✕ **El Farallón de Tepic.** Set underneath a bright blue awning, this open-air establishment is reminiscent of beach restaurants in the nearby state of Nayarit. Order fresh pescado—usually red snapper or an equally mild fish—grilled with garlic or butter, in classic tomato sauce, breaded, or stuffed with seafood and cheese. Pescado *sarandeado* (whole barbecued fish, stuffed with vegetables) is worth every second of the 30-minute wait. Try the homemade flan for dessert. ⊠ *Av. Niño Obrero 560,* ☎ *3/121–2616, 3/121–9616. AE, MC, V. No dinner.*

$$ ✕ **La Feria.** Boasting the most festive atmosphere of any restaurant down-
★ town, La Feria offers spectacular entertainment: mariachis, *charros* (cowboys), and traditional Mexican folkloric dances. Come for a late lunch or appetizers to catch the afternoon show, or for a late-night dinner to catch the evening shows. The shrimp tacos are scrumptious, and meat lovers will want to share the parillada for two; the version here includes tender flank steak, roast pork leg and chicken, and spicy Mexican chorizo. After the show, play *lotteria* (a type of bingo) for a bottle of tequila or have a parakeet choose your fortune. ⊠ *Av. Corona 291,* ☎ *3/613–1812, 3/613–1839. AE, MC, V.*

$$ ✕ **Formosa Gardens.** For a taste of home, it's no wonder Guadalajara's Asian residents visit Formosa Gardens, which has sister restaurants in Beijing and Taiwan. Peking duck is crisp and tasty here, but go for the deep-fried orange beef—sweet and tangy. This beautiful mansion opens onto a garden dining area, where each table is set with crisp linens. Formosa Gardens is open for three meals a day. ⊠ *Av. Union 322,* ☎ *3/615–7415. AE, MC, V.*

$$ ✕ **Pierrot.** This quiet French dining room offers mouth-watering pâtés
★ followed by seafood, chicken, and beef entrées—among them trout almondine, osso buco, and pâté-stuffed chicken breast in tarragon sauce. Wall-mounted lamps with fringed velvet shades and fresh flowers on each table lend a gracious touch. ⊠ *Justo Sierra 2355,* ☎ *3/630–2087, 3/615–4758. AE, MC, V. Closed Sun.*

$ ✕ **La Chata.** Sombreros, gaily striped serapes, and exquisitely glazed plates adorn the white walls of this popular downtown eatery. Start off with guacamole and then savor the zesty *chiles rellenos* (stuffed peppers). Or try one of the spicy roasted meat dishes, such as *carne tampiqueña,* served with rice, beans, and enchiladas. Complement your meal with a cool, sweet *horchata,* a drink made from rice and brown sugar simmered in milk, then chilled. ⊠ *Av. Corona 126, between Avs. López Cotilla and Juárez,* ☎ *3/613–0588. AE, MC, V.*

$ ✕ **Karne Garibaldi.** According to the *Guinness Book of World Records,* this Tapatío institution has the fastest service in the world. Seconds after you arrive, grilled onions, tortillas, and refried beans mixed with corn

Guadalajara Dining & Lodging

Plaza Bonita

Plaza México

Plaza México

Av. Golfo de Cortés

Romero

Fideas

Arias

Av. Vallarta

Av. López Mateos

Azuela

S. Díaz

Gran Plaza Guadalajara

San Martín de Porres

P.P. Velázquez

Calz. Lázaro Cárdenas

San Francisco

Av. López Mateos Sur

San Vicente de Paul el Carmen

San Ernesto

San Juan Bosco

La Reyna

San Agustín

Sta. Beatriz

San Enrique

Av. Guadalupe

Av. Niños Héroes

La Luna

Nebulosa

Noche

Hércule

Del Parque

Atmósfera

Día

Sol

Centro Cultural las Colas

Av. La Aurora

Juan de Tepeyac

Valeriano

Av. de Zumárraga

Av. Chapalita

Merced

Eclipse

Hayo

Cosmos

Cuauhtémoc

Av. del Niño Obrero

Ubilete

12 de Diciembre

Av. de las Rosas

Parque de las Estrellas

Tonallan

Av. del Árbol

Aztlan

Plancarte

Plaza del Ángel

Tlahuac

Av. Xochitl

Tezozomoc

Tizoc

Av. López Mateos Sur

Av. Faro

La Pradera

Los Estrellas

Av. Arboleda

KEY

— Rail Lines

Av. Plaza del Sol

Av. Mariano Otero

Club Hípico

0   600 meters

0   600 yards

Av. Moctezuma

Mixcoatl

Turquesa

Av. Topacio

Diamante

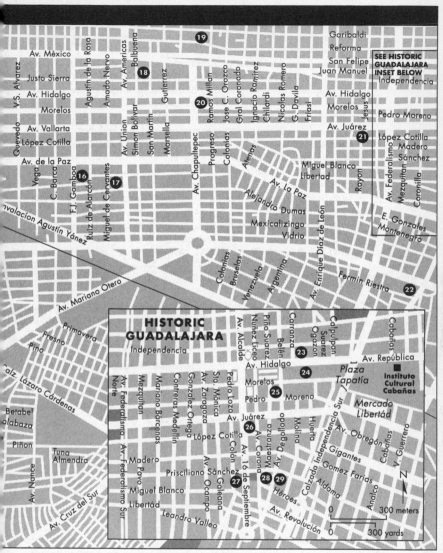

HISTORIC GUADALAJARA

Garibaldi
Reforma
San Felipe
Juan Manuel

SEE HISTORIC GUADALAJARA INSET BELOW

Independencia

Av. México
Justo Sierra
Av. Hidalgo
Morelos
Av. Vallarta
López Cotilla
Av. de la Paz

Av. Hidalgo
Morelos
Jesús
Av. Juárez

Pedro Moreno
López Cotilla
Madero
Sánchez

Miguel Blanco
Libertad

Av. La Paz
Alejandro Dumas
Mexicalizingo
Vidrio

E. Gonzales
Montenegro

Colonias
Bruselas
Venezuela
Argentina

Av. Enrique Díaz de León

Fermín Riestra

Av. Mariano Otero

Primavera
Fresno
Pino

Calz. Lázaro Cárdenas

Betabel
Calabaza
Piñon

Tuna
Almendra

Av. Nance

Av. Cruz del Sur

Independencia

Av. Alcalde
Núñez Liceo
Pino Suárez
Belén
Carranza

Av. Federalismo Norte
Mezquitan
Mariano Bárcenas
González Ortega
Contreras Medellín
Santa Mónica
Av. Zaragoza

Av. Hidalgo
Morelos
Pedro

Pedro Loza
Colón

Av. Juárez
López Cotilla

Priscilano Sánchez
Madero
Pavo
Miguel Blanco
Libertad

Av. Federalismo Sur

Leandro Valleo

Av. 16 de Septiembre

Galeana
Av. Ocampo

Av. Corona
Maestranza
Av. Degollado

Héroes
Av. Revolución

Plaza Tapatía

Av. República
Cabañas

Instituto Cultural Cabañas

Mercado Libertad

Av. Obregón

Gigantes
Gomez Farias
Aldama

Cabañas
V. Guerrero
Analco

Calzada Independencia Sur
Huerta
Molina

Capulupan
Suárez
Ogazon

0   300 meters

0   300 yards

Lodging

bid you to dig in. The only dish is carne in su jugo, a tasty combination of finely diced beef and bacon simmered in a rich beef broth, which takes less than a minute to arrive. With a beer or a soda, this is a great down-home meal. ⊠ *Garibaldi 1306,* ☎ *3/826–1286. AE, MC, V.*

$ ✕ **Mondo Cafe.** The alluring fragrance from Mondo's coffee roaster wafts into wide, tree-lined Avenida Chapultepec. Foreign and local students frequent this favorite coffee house for its large picture-window views onto the busy avenue and for various blends of fresh-roasted coffee. Breakfasts are hearty, and the mixed fruit and vegetable juices and flavored coffees are the perfect way to start the day. The American owner is a former manager of Starbucks in Seattle. ⊠ *Av. Chapultepec and Pedro Moreno,* ☎ *3/616–2709. MC, V.*

$ ✕ **La Pianola.** The entrance—through what looks like an open-air
★ kitchen where costumed women are making tortillas—may be misleading to first-timers: in back is a large restaurant and garden with an excellent, varied Mexican menu. Specialties include pozole and chilies *en nogada,* spicy stuffed chili peppers in a walnut cream sauce. The signature player-piano music accompanies the meal. ⊠ *Av. México 3220,* ☎ *3/813–1385 or 3/813–2412. AE, MC, V.*

LODGING

Guadalajara has a variety of hotels in all price ranges. Call ahead if you're apprehensive about noise levels outside your hotel room; many hotels are on busy intersections, and you'd be well advised to consult the reservation clerk on the matter of a room away from the hubbub.

The rates given are based on the year-round or peak-season price; off-peak (summer) or promotional rates may be lower. You can expect hotels in the $$$ and $$$$ categories to have purified-water systems and English-language TV channels. Many hotels have begun to install in-room data ports, so ask when you reserve.

CATEGORY	COST*
$$$$	over $160
$$$	$90–$160
$$	$40–$90
$	under $40

All prices are for a standard double room, excluding 15% VAT and 2% hotel tax.

$$$$ 🏨 **Quinta Real.** Stone and brick walls, colonial arches, and objets
★ d'art highlight public areas of this luxury hotel on the city's west side. Suites are plush and intimate, with select neocolonial furnishings, including glass-top writing tables with carved-stone pedestals and fireplaces with marble mantelpieces. Tile bathrooms have marble sinks and bronze fixtures; some suites have sunken hot tubs. Deluxe tower accommodations are more lavish, although removed from the gardens below. ⊠ *Av. México 2727, at Av. López Mateos Sur, 44680,* ☎ *3/615–0000, 01–800/713–1966, 800/445–4565,* 🅵🅰🆇 *3/630–1797. 76 suites. Restaurant, no-smoking floor, pool, baby-sitting, concierge, free parking. AE, DC, MC, V.* 🍃

$$$–$$$$ 🏨 **Hilton.** Adjacent to the Guadalajara World Trade Center and Expo, the Hilton is a premier business destination. Although the hotel lacks character, it has modern furnishings and considerable business services, including a multilingual staff, a private executive floor, and a well-equipped business center. The hotel caters to convention goers. ⊠ *Av. de las Rosas 2933, 44540,* ☎ *3/678–0505, 3/678–0510, 01–800/003–1400, 800/445–8667 in the U.S. and Canada,* 🅵🅰🆇 *3/678–0511. 402 rooms, 20 suites. 2 restaurants, bar, in-room data ports, no-smoking*

rooms, pool, beauty salon, massage, exercise room, concierge floor, business services, meeting rooms, car rental. AE, DC, MC, V. ✧

$$$–$$$$ 🏨 **Presidente Inter-Continental.** A modern hotel with a 12-story atrium lobby, this Inter-Continental attracts a sophisticated business clientele. For the best city view, request a room on an upper floor facing the Plaza del Sol shopping center. There's a Tane silver shop on the premises, and guests can use nearby golf and tennis facilities. The hotel's health club is the best in the city. ✉ *Av. López Mateos Sur and Moctezuma, 45050,* ☎ *3/678–1234, 01–800/904–4400, 800/327–0200,* Ⅸ *3/678–1222. 266 rooms, 145 suites. Restaurant, bar, coffee shop, in-room data ports, pool, spa, health club, shops, baby-sitting, concierge floor, business services, meeting rooms, airport shuttle, car rental, free parking. AE, DC, MC, V.* ✧

$$$ 🏨 **Camino Real.** A 15-minute cab ride from downtown will bring you to the first of Guadalajara's luxury hotels. Although its five stars are likely posted more for reasons of tradition than for overall quality, guest rooms are large and well-decorated, with many surrounding the pool and hotel lawns. Those in the rear face noisy Avenida Vallarta. ✉ *Av. Vallarta 5005, 45040,* ☎ *3/121–8000, 01–800/947–7325, 800/996–7325,* Ⅸ *3/121–8070. 195 rooms, 10 suites. Restaurant, bar, coffee shop, in-room data ports, no-smoking rooms, 5 pools, tennis court, health club, baby-sitting, concierge, free parking. AE, DC, MC, V.*

$$$ 🏨 **Crowne Plaza Guadalajara.** Those who come to Guadalajara for
★ its eternally springlike climate will enjoy this hotel's expansive, shaded, well-tended gardens surrounding a large pool and sunbathing area. Rooms have marble baths, upholstered furniture, carpeting, and lots of natural light. Tower rooms have mountain views, although the Plaza Club rooms surrounding the pool have better furnishings and amenities. Service is excellent. ✉ *Av. López Mateos Sur 2500, 45050,* ☎ *3/634–1034, 01–800/365–5500, 800/227–6963 in the U.S. and Canada,* Ⅸ *3/631–9393. 288 rooms, 4 suites. 3 restaurants, bar, in-room data ports, no-smoking floor, pool, beauty salon, massage, miniature golf, 2 tennis courts, exercise room, shops, baby-sitting, concierge floor, airport shuttle, car rental, free parking. AE, DC, MC, V.*

$$$ 🏨 **Fiesta Americana.** The dramatic glass facade of this luxury high-rise
★ faces the Minerva Fountain, on the city's west side. Four glass-enclosed elevators ascend above the 14-story atrium lobby to the city's largest guest rooms, boasting modern furnishings, marble bathrooms, and panoramic views. The business center is the best-equipped in the city. ✉ *Aurelio Aceves 225, 44110,* ☎ *3/825–3434, 01–800/504–5000, 800/343–7821,* Ⅸ *3/630–3725. 389 rooms, 25 suites. Restaurant, bar, coffee shop, in-room data ports, no-smoking floors, pool, beauty salon, 2 tennis courts, exercise room, shops, baby-sitting, concierge, business services, meeting rooms, car rental, free parking. AE, DC, MC, V.*

$$ 🏨 **De Mendoza.** The convenience of this downtown hotel—on a quiet
★ side street a block from the Teatro Degollado—combined with its impressive postcolonial architecture and refined atmosphere make it an easy choice. Beam ceilings, hand-carved furniture and doors, and wrought-iron railings decorate public areas and rooms. An inviting courtyard pool lies just outside the hotel's acclaimed international restaurant, and service is commendable. ✉ *Calle Venustiano Carranza 16, 44100,* ☎ *3/613–4646, 3/614–2621, 01–800/361–2600,* Ⅸ *3/613–7310. 87 rooms, 17 suites. Restaurant, in-room data ports, no-smoking rooms, pool. AE, DC, MC, V.* ✧

$$ 🏨 **Diana.** Mexican and European travelers favor this six-story hotel two blocks from the Minerva Fountain. The white stucco lobby adjoins a small lounge and busy restaurant. Standard-size rooms have white-on-white walls and ceilings with brightly patterned curtains and bedspreads. The quietest rooms are on the upper floors in the rear; some suites have private saunas. ⊠ *Circunvalación Agustín Yáñez 2760, 44100,* ☎ *3/615–5510, 3/615–6428, 01–800/253–6789,* 𝔽𝔸𝕏 *3/630– 3685. 110 rooms, 20 suites. Restaurant, bar, coffee shop, pool, airport shuttle, free parking. AE, DC, MC, V.*

$$ 🏨 **Francés.** Guadalajara's oldest hotel, dating from 1610, was de-
★ clared a national monument in 1981 following extensive restoration. Stone columns and colonial arches surround a three-story enclosed atrium lobby with a polished marble fountain and cut-crystal chandeliers. On Friday, loud live music is played at the lobby bar until midnight. Although room sizes vary, all have colonial ambience, with white stucco walls, polished wood floors, and high beam ceilings. For the best city views (although there's a slight noise trade-off), ask for a room facing Calle Maestranza. ⊠ *Calle Maestranza 35, 44100,* ☎ *3/613–1190, 3/ 613–0936, 01–800/718–5309,* 𝔽𝔸𝕏 *3/658–2831. 50 rooms, 10 suites. Restaurant, bar, fans, dance club, car rental, free parking. AE, MC, V.*

$$ 🏨 **Misión Carlton.** This modern 20-story tower hotel on the edge of downtown offers oversize rooms. Ivy-draped walls surround the rear gardens and fountain. Although the hotel is convenient for tourists, it caters to the business traveler. The upper floors provide a spectacular city view and a retreat from the horrendous street noise. ⊠ *Av. Niños Héroes 125, at Av. 16 de Septiembre, 44100,* ☎ *3/614–7272,* 𝔽𝔸𝕏 *3/ 613–5539. 207 rooms, 8 suites. Restaurant, 2 bars, no-smoking floor, pool, health club, free parking. AE, MC, V.*

$$ 🏨 **Plaza Del Sol.** Location and price bring families, young adults, and tour groups to this two-building hotel at the south end of the Plaza del Sol shopping center. Rooms—all modern and carpeted—and public areas are painted glossy white. Accommodations in the cylindrical tower are a bit larger and have views of Plaza del Sol. ⊠ *Avs. López Mateos and Mariano Otero, 45050,* ☎ *3/647–8790, 01–800/368–8000,* 𝔽𝔸𝕏 *3/ 122–9685. 341 rooms, 16 suites. Restaurant, bar, coffee shop, pool, baby-sitting, concierge floor, free parking. AE, DC, MC, V.*

$$ 🏨 **Posada Guadalajara.** Rooms in this colonial-style hotel open onto airy, wrought-iron–railed hallways overlooking the small patio and its enormous stone fountain. Accommodations are clean and comfortable and have carved wood furniture. In addition to its loyal international patrons, the Posada welcomes visiting sports teams, so evenings here can seem either festive or raucous. The hotel is south of Calzada Lázaro Cárdenas, about 1½ km (1 mi) northeast of Plaza del Sol. ⊠ *Av. López Mateos Sur 1280, 45040,* ☎ *3/121–2022, 3/121–2904,* 𝔽𝔸𝕏 *3/122–1834. 170 rooms, 3 suites. Restaurant, bar, pool, baby-sitting, free parking. AE, DC, MC, V.*

$$ 🏨 **Santiago de Compostela.** This cozy downtown hotel in a converted 19th-century building is across from the Parque San Francisco and offers modern, carpeted accommodations. Rooms overlooking the park— where you can watch worshipers file into the two colonial churches—have tall, narrow windows with iron balconies. Inside rooms open onto an atrium. In contrast to many hotels, all the bathrooms here have tubs, and the suites have Jacuzzis. The open-air pool and sunning area on the fifth floor overlook the park. A drawback is that there is one small elevator to service the six floors. ⊠ *Colón 272, 44100,* ☎ *3/613–8880, 01–800/365–5300,* 𝔽𝔸𝕏 *3/658–1925. 91 rooms, 4 suites. Restaurant, bar, pool, free parking. AE, DC, MC, V.*

$ 🏨 **San Francisco.** Once on its quiet downtown side street, you can't miss this attractive two-story colonial-style building. The lushly planted courtyard makes a pleasant sitting area, and brightly polished copper lamps lend a delightful sparkle to the simply furnished rooms. ⊠ *Calle Degollado 267, 44100,* ☎ *3/613–8954,* 𝔽𝔸𝕏 *3/613–3257. 74 rooms, 2 suites. Restaurant, baby-sitting, laundry service, free parking. AE, MC, V.*

NIGHTLIFE AND THE ARTS

Guadalajara is an active cultural and performing-arts center, offering excellent local talent and well-known artists and entertainers from abroad. The U.S. and Canadian communities have also developed a schedule of English-language cultural events. During the afternoon and evening, many cafés along Avenida Chapultepec also have live music.

The Arts

DANCE

Ballet Folklórico of the University of Guadalajara. The university's internationally acclaimed troupe offers traditional Mexican folkloric dances and music in the Teatro Degollado(☞ *below*) every Sunday at 10 AM. ☎ *$2.50–$11.*

PERFORMANCE VENUES

Cine Cinematógrafo I, II, and III. Founded by two Guadalajara-area movie buffs, these theaters often present English-language and other foreign films—of the art-house variety—with Spanish subtitles. ⊠ *Av. Vallarta 1102,* ☎ *3/825–0514;* ⊠ *Av. México 2222,* ☎ *3/630–1208;* ⊠ *Av. Patria 600,* ☎ *3/629–4780.*

Ex-Convento del Carmen. Music groups of all types perform on the spacious patio of the former convent of Our Lady of Mt. Carmel. There's also a café, spacious art gallery, and bookshop. It's 6½ blocks west of Avenida 16 de Septiembre. ⊠ *Av. Juárez 638,* ☎ *3/614–7184.*

Instituto Cultural Cabañas. Large-scale theater, dance, and musical performances take place on a patio within the institute. The Tolsá Chapel hosts more-intimate events, and subtitled English-language films are often shown in a movie theater here. Exhibits of both Mexican and foreign art are on display, and free art classes are taught. ⊠ *Calle Cabañas 8, at Plaza Tapatía,* ☎ *3/617–4322, 3/617–4440.*

Plaza de Armas. The State Band of Jalisco plays here Thursday and Sunday evenings at 6:30. Tuesday evening, the Municipal Band of Guadalajara performs at 6:30. ⊠ *Av. Corona between Calle Morelos and Pedro Moreno, across from Palacio de Gobierno.*

Teatro Degollado. Nationally and internationally famous artists perform here year-round. The refurbished velvet seats are comfortable, the acoustics are excellent, and the central air-conditioning can be a treat. ⊠ *Calle Degollado, between Av. Hidalgo and Calle Morelos,* ☎ *3/614–4773, 3/613–1115.* ☎ *$3–$10 per performance.*

SYMPHONY

Orquesta Filarmónica de Jalisco. Conducted by Maestro Guillermo Salvador, performances take place Sunday and Friday at the Teatro Degollado (☞ *Performance Venues, above*). ☎ *3/658–3812, 3/658–3819.* ☎ *$2–$20.*

Nightlife

A string of Guadalajara night spots generally geared to the under-30 crowd lines Avenida Vallarta and the centro area, but there are alternatives. The best salsa spot is **Cubilete** (⊠ General Río Seco 9, in the nine-corners area of downtown, ☎ 3/613–2096), where Rosalia—a younger version of Celia Cruz—belts out tunes that keep you dancing between the tables Friday and Saturday. For a bit of local color, stop downtown at **La Maestranza** (⊠ Calle Maestranza 179, ☎ 3/613–5878), a renovated 1940s cantina chock-full of bullfighting memorabilia.

The best hotel clubs include the Fiesta Americana's sleek **Lobby Bar,** for pop and mariachi-style music, and the **Caballo Negro** dance club (⊠ Aurelio Aceves 225, ☎ 3/825–3434, 01–800/504–5000), with live entertainment. **La Diligencia** (⊠ Av. Vallarta 5005, ☎ 3/121–8000, 01–

800/947–7325), a romantic spot in the Camino Real, features tropical and other music for dancing. The Crowne Plaza's jungle-theme **Manglar** (⊠ Av. López Mateos Sur 2500, ☎ 3/634–1034, 01–800/365–5500) has a game room and large-screen TV, in addition to live Latin music.

As at 1960s coffeehouses, patrons sit around a small stage at **La Peña Cuicacalli** (⊠ Av. Niños Héroes 1988, on the traffic circle, ☎ 3/825–4690) to listen nightly to folk music from Mexico, Latin America, and Spain; call for performance times. **Despeñadaro** (⊠ Av. Vallarta 1110, ☎ 3/825–5853) has folk music Tuesday through Saturday at 9 PM and Sunday at 6:30 PM in an airy patio setting. Jazz combos hold court at the intimate **C77** (⊠ Marcos Castellanos 136-Z, ☎ 3/141–0603) Monday through Saturday after 8 PM in winter, 9 PM in summer.

DANCE CLUBS AND DISCOS

A hot spot in town is the 94th **Hard Rock Cafe** (⊠ Av. Vallarta 2125, ☎ 3/616–4560), in the Centro Magno mall. Live bands play from 10 PM on. You can dance most of the night to popular Latin and European music at the multilevel **Tropigala** (⊠ Av. López Mateos Sur and Iztaccíhuatl, across from Plaza del Sol shopping center, ☎ 3/122–5553, 3/122–7903). **Co-Co & Co-Co** (⊠ Av. Corona 160, ☎ 3/614–5714), at the Fenix hotel downtown, is an option if you feel like dancing.

Salón Veracruz (⊠ Manzano 486, behind the Hotel Carlton, ☎ 3/613–4422), is a spartan, old-style dance hall where a 15-piece tropical band keeps hundreds of hoofers moving to *cumbias* (Colombian dances), merengue, and danzón. It's open Wednesday through Sunday, 9:30 PM–3:30 AM. Another good dance club with a live Latin beat is the **Copacabana** (⊠ Av. López Mateos Sur and Las Aguilas, ☎ 3/631–4596).

Good downtown discos include **Maxim's** (⊠ Calle Maestranza 35, ☎ 3/613–1190, 3/613–0936, 01–800/718–5309) in the Francés. The Plaza Del Sol has its own dance club, the **Factory** (⊠ Avs. López Mateos and Mariano Otero, ☎ 3/647–8790, 01–800/368–8000).

OUTDOOR ACTIVITIES AND SPORTS

Participant Sports

Amusement Park

If you're with teenagers, the **Go Kartmania** go-cart racetrack park will please them. Four tracks are available inside a tree-lined former city park. Budding Mario Andrettis from 8 to 80 can race around in quality go-carts on well-designed tracks that have banked curves, trees, and landscaping. A cafeteria and amusement arcade are also on site. ⊠ *Av. Avila Camacho 2700, ☎ 3/854–3193, 3/854–2894. ▣ Entrance 30¢. ☉ Daily 10–10.*

Fitness Clubs

The health club at the **Presidente Inter-Continental** (☎ 3/678–1227) is open to nonguests for about $12 a day. It includes a fitness center, heated pool, massage, and spa. Celebrities visit **Gold's Gym** (⊠ Av. Xóchitl 4203, near Plaza del Sol shopping center, ☎ 3/647–0420) for its unique amenities, such as a climbing wall, a full basketball court, and boxing, kickboxing, and Tae Kwon Do lessons. Guest passes are available for about $10 a day.

Golf

Several golf clubs admit nonmembers upon payment of a greens fee of $40–$100. **El Palomar** (⊠ Paseo de la Cima 437, ☎ 3/684–4434, 3/684–4436), is the most exclusive country club in Guadalajara. Across from Montenegro Park is the **Atlas Chapalita Golf Club** (⊠ Carretera

Guadalajara-Chapala, ☎ 3/689–2620, 3/689–0240). Tuesday and Thursday are the least crowded at **Las Cañadas Country Club** (⊠ Av. Bosques San Isidro 777, ☎ 3/685–0285, 3/685–0412). **Club de Golf Santa Anita** (⊠ Carretera a Morelia Km 6.5, ☎ 3/686–0321) is another option for visiting golfers.

Ice-Skating

The **Iceland Pista de Hielo** has daily one-hour public ice-skating sessions. There's also a restaurant and ice-cream parlor. ⊠ *Av. México 2582,* ☎ *3/615–4438, 3/615–7876.* ☜ *$4 an hour, including skates.* ⊙ 9:20 AM–9:40 PM.

Tennis

The **Crowne Plaza Guadalajara** (⊠ Av. López Mateos Sur 2500, ☎ 3/634–1034) allows nonguests to use its two courts, open 7–7, for a fee. Nonguests are allowed to use the **Camino Real** court (⊠ Av. Vallarta 5005, ☎ 3/134–2424) for a fee. It's open 7 AM–10 PM. English is spoken at the **Club de Tenis Royal** (⊠ San Ignacio 316, ☎ 3/647–5348), where you can take lessons. It's open 7 AM–11 PM.

Spectator Sports

Bullfighting

Corridas (bullfights) begin at 4:30 PM at **Plaza Nuevo Progreso** on Sunday, weekly in October, November, and early December, and every other week from mid-January through March. *Novilleros* (apprentice matadors) work the cape each Sunday in April and May. You can buy tickets for either the *sol* (sunny) or *sombra* (shady) side of the bullring. Since the action begins in the late afternoon, take cheaper seats on the sunny side. You can buy tickets at the bullring (about 5 km [3 mi] northeast of downtown) or at the bullring's booth in Plaza México. ⊠ *M. Pirineos 1930 and Calzada Independencia Nte., across from Estadio Jalisco,* ☎ *3/637–9982, 3/651–8378.* ☜ *$5–$38.*

Charreadas

Charreadas take place at the **Lienzo Charros de Jalisco** every Sunday at noon. The cowboys compete in 10 events; mariachis or *bandas* (brass bands) perform during breaks; and food and alcoholic beverages are available. ⊠ *Av. Dr. R. Michel 577, next to Parque Agua Azul,* ☎ *3/619–3232.* ☜ *About $2.*

Soccer

You can see afternoon and evening professional soccer matches at **Estadio Jalisco.** Schedules and admission vary with the team. ⊠ *Siete Colinas 1772 and Calzada Independencia Nte., across from bullring,* ☎ *3/637–0563, 3/637–0301, 3/637–0299.* ☜ *90¢–$15.*

SHOPPING

Guadalajara has a great variety of high-quality merchandise at low prices, although you also can find high-priced low-quality items. Store hours tend to be Monday through Saturday 9–8, Sunday 10–2; shopping-mall stores generally stay open at lunch. *Tianguis* (street markets) run every day throughout the Guadalajara area; you never know what you'll find. If you are interested in traditional arts and crafts, don't miss Tlaquepaque and Tonalá (☞ Side Trips from Guadalajara, *below*).

Malls

In Guadalajara, as in all other major cities, shopping malls are springing up everywhere. The metropolitan area now has more than 30. **El Charro,** an excellent leather-goods store, has branches in La Gran Plaza and Plaza del Sol as well as downtown.

Centro Magno. This three-story mall opened with great fanfare just a few blocks from the Minerva. A number of upscale boutiques and bistros, along with a Hard Rock Cafe, make this a trendy shopping and dining spot. There's a large cineplex on the top floor. ⊠ *Av. Vallarta 2125.* ☉ *Daily 10–10.*

Galería del Calzado. The 60 stores in this westside complex all sell shoes. Guadalajara is one of Mexico's leading shoe centers, and high-quality footwear and accessories are available here, many at lower prices than in the States. ⊠ *Avs. México and Yaquis,* ☎ *3/647–6422.* ☉ *Mon.–Sat. 11–9, Sun. 11–8:30.*

La Gran Plaza. A sleek three-story glass-and-steel exterior houses 334 commercial spaces and a 14-plex cinema, surrounded by a large food court and some quality restaurants. It's east of the Guadalajara Chamber of Commerce and the Camino Real hotel. ⊠ *Av. Vallarta 3959,* ☎ *3/122–3004.* ☉ *Daily 10–9:30.*

Plaza del Sol. The city's largest mall sprawls like a park, with 270 commercial spaces, outdoor patios, trees and garden areas, and parking for 2,100 cars. It's across from the Presidente Inter-Continental hotel. ⊠ *Avs. López Mateos Sur and Mariano Otero,* ☎ *3/121–5950.* ☉ *Weekdays 10–8, Sat. 10–9, Sun. 10–7.*

Plaza México. There are about 120 stores in the city's second most popular shopping mall, seven blocks west of the Plaza Galería del Calzado. ⊠ *Av. México 3300,* ☎ *3/813–2488.* ☉ *Daily 10–8.*

Markets and Handicrafts

El Baratillo. This is one of the world's largest flea markets. Thirty city blocks are lined with stalls, tents, and blankets piled high with new, used, and antique merchandise. ⊠ *On and around Calle Esteban Loera, some 15 blocks east of Mercado Libertad.* ☉ *Sun. 7–5.*

Bazar Capitán. Serious art, crafts, and antiques lovers may want to consult an expert if time is limited. Bazar Capitán's Robert Alvarado, who has 30 years in the art and antiques business, runs personalized buying tours for small groups. His bilingual *El Antiquario* magazine promotes local antiquities dealers. ⊠ *Argentina 73, ½ block off Av. Vallarta,* ☎ *3/827–1990.* ☉ *Weekdays noon–6.*

Calle Esteban Alatorre. Several blocks of shoe stores—all reasonably priced—line this street. ⊠ *East of Calzada Independencia Nte. and 4 blocks north of Av. Hidalgo.*

Instituto de Artesanías Jaliscienses. Run by the state government, this store has a wide selection of the exquisite blown glass and hand-glazed pottery typical of Jalisco artisans. There are also fine crafts from other parts of Mexico. Everything is sold at fixed prices. ⊠ *Calzadas González Gallo 20 and Independencia Sur, next to Parque Agua Azul,* ☎ *3/619–4664.* ☉ *Weekdays 10–6, Sat. 10–5, Sun. 10–3.*

Mercado Libertad. Also known as the Mercado San Juan de Dios, the Liberty Market is one of Latin America's largest enclosed markets. Within a three-square-block area, you can browse through more than 1,000 privately owned stalls selling everything from clothing and crafts to live animals and gold watches. ⊠ *Calzada Independencia Sur between Dionísio Rodríguez and Av. Javier Mina.* ☉ *Daily 10–8.*

SIDE TRIPS FROM GUADALAJARA

No trip to Guadalajara is complete without an excursion out of the city, whether you're into shopping for crafts in Tlaquepaque and Tonalá, taking in the freshwater breezes of Lake Chapala, or unlocking the secrets of Mexican fire water in Tequila.

Tlaquepaque and Tonalá

For inveterate shoppers, a combined visit to the crafts meccas of Tlaquepaque and Tonalá makes a perfect day trip from Guadalajara. There's at least one bed-and-breakfast in Tlaquepaque if you really want to shop until you drop, but it's easy enough to return to the wider selection of lodgings in Guadalajara.

Tlaquepaque

7 km (4½ mi) southeast of downtown Guadalajara.

Tlaquepaque is known throughout Mexico as an arts-and-crafts center. Among its offerings are intricate blown-glass miniatures; exquisite pottery; jewelry, silver, and copperware; leather and hand-carved wood furniture; and handwoven clothing. More than 300 shops line pedestrian malls and plazas in this charming town.

Distinctive decorated pottery, sold in stores throughout the town, was first fashioned by nearby Tonaltecan Indians in the mid-16th century. The small village remained virtually isolated until June 13, 1821, when local authorities met here to sign a regional proclamation of independence from Spain. Soon after, wealthy Guadalajara residents began to build palatial summer houses. Many of these magnificent buildings have been restored, and today they house shops and restaurants.

In 1870 the art of glass-blowing was introduced from Europe. As people started coming to purchase the pottery and intricate glass creations, more artisans—weavers, jewelers, and wood-carvers—arrived and built workshops. In 1973 downtown Tlaquepaque underwent a major renovation, the highlight of which was the creation of a wide pedestrian mall, Calle Independencia. More shops line Calle Juárez, a block south, as well as the many side streets.

The following are some of the highlights you'll come across if you start walking from the west end of Calle Independencia.

20 Color seems to explode in the more than 10 rooms of **La Casa Canela,** exquisitely decorated with vivid papier-mâché flowers, finely glazed pottery, and elegant furniture. All surround a courtyard blooming with tropical plants. Free tequila and snacks are served on Saturday. ⊠ *Calle Independencia 258,* ☎ *3/635–3717, 3/657–1343.* ☉ *Weekdays 10–2 and 3–7, Sat. 10–6, Sun. 11–3.*

★ **21** Housed in a colonial mansion, **Museo Regional de la Cerámica** (Regional Museum of Ceramics) covers the evolution of ceramic wares in the Atemajac Valley during the past century. ⊠ *Calle Independencia 237,* ☎ *3/635–5404.* ☺ *Free.* ☉ *Tues.–Sat. 10–6, Sun. 10–3.*

22 Sergio Bustamante's work is found in galleries throughout the world, but you can purchase his whimsical sculpture or silver- and gold-plated jewelry for considerably less at **Galería Sergio Bustamante.** At the back is an art gallery featuring work by Mexican artists. The flamingos under the waterfall in the rear are real. ⊠ *Calle Independencia 236,* ☎ *3/639–5519.* ☉ *Mon.–Sat. 10–7, Sun. 11–3.*

23 Ceramic works from across Mexico are displayed at the **Museo Municipal del Premio Nacional de la Cerámica.** This museum has won numerous prizes for its collection, which includes life-size ceramic sculptures in the courtyard. ⊠ *Prisciliano Sánchez 191,* ☎ *3/639–5646.* ☺ *Free.* ☉ *Tues.–Sun. 10–6.*

24 Step through the doors of **Agustín Parra Diseño Barroco** to arrive in a mystical 18th-century land. Spiritual music guides you through the immense store, overflowing with exquisite Baroque-style statues, wood-

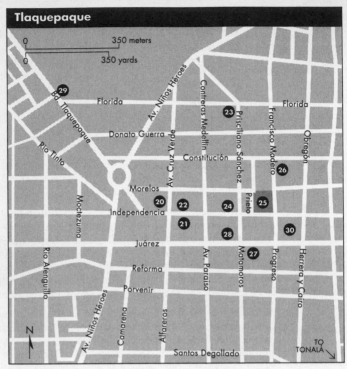

Tlaquepaque

and-gilt altarpieces, and sculptures of virgins, angels, saints, and cherubs. ⊠ *Calle Independencia 158,* ☎ *3/657–8530, 3/657–0316.* ☉ *Weekdays 10–2 and 3–7, Sat. 10–7:30, Sun. 10–5.*

㉕ Franciscan friars founded the **Templo Parroquial de San Pedro** during the Spanish conquest, naming the parish church in honor of San Pedro de Analco. In line with the custom of naming a town after its principal church, in 1915 the town's name was officially changed to San Pedro Tlaquepaque. The altars of Our Lady of Guadalupe and the Sacred Heart of Jesus are intricately carved in silver and gilt. ⊠ *In square at Calles Guillermo Prieto and Morelos.* ☉ *Daily 7 AM–9 PM.*

In 1959 Ken Edwards introduced more-durable stoneware (which is by nature lead-free) into the Tonalá pottery vernacular—the original local earthenware is more fragile. His store, **Cerámica de Ken Edwards,** is filled with brightly colored, hand-decorated plates, cups, and vases. Ask to see the seconds; some are real bargains. Edwards also has a workshop in Tonalá (☞ *Tonalá, below*). ⊠ *Francisco Madero 70,* ☎ *3/635–5456.* ☉ *Mon.–Sat. 10:30–7.*

㉗ At the **Plaza de Artesanías,** browse through boutiques selling high-quality leather goods, embroidered clothing, ceramics, and blown glass. Some shops close on weekends. ⊠ *Juárez 145.*

㉘ Hacienda-style furniture and antiques fill the two-story **Bazar Hecht.** The Hecht family is known throughout Mexico for its high-quality, ornately sculpted tables, armoires, and chairs. ⊠ *Juárez 162,* ☎ *3/659–0205.* ☉ *Weekdays 10–2:30 and 3:30–7, Sat. 10:30–3 and 4–7.*

㉙ Vibrantly painted hand-carved wood furniture is created at **Cerámica El Palomar.** The Velasco family has been known for decades for its decorative ceramics as well. Michoacán hand-sewn table linens and Tonalá blown glass are also available. ⊠ *Av. Marcelino Garcia Barragán 1905*, ☎ *3/635–8098*. ⊙ *Weekdays 10–7, Sat. 10–2.*

③⓪ When you're ready for lunch or simply a drink, head for **El Parián**, a 120-year-old former handicrafts market south of Calle Independencia that's now an enormous cantina (some say the biggest in Mexico). Mariachis stroll through in the afternoons and—although the food is only average—the margaritas slide down well. Use the arcade shops here only to compare prices; *shop* on Calle Independencia or another main street. ⊠ *Jardín Hidalgo*, ☎ *3/659–2362.*

DINING

$$ ✕ **Casa Fuerte.** Dine on such gourmet Mexican dishes as chicken stuffed with *huitlacoche* (a corn fungus known as Mexico's answer to the truffle) and shrimp in tamarind sauce. There are tables on the front sidewalk or in the verdant patio garden, decorated with palms and a fountain. ⊠ *Calle Independencia 224*, ☎ *3/639–6481. AE, MC, V.*

$$ ✕ **Restaurant sin Nombre.** The "Restaurant with No Name" serves Span-
★ ish nouvelle cuisine, a combination of pre-Hispanic and modern recipes. High adobe walls surround the 17th-century colonial building and extensive gardens. Afternoon entertainment includes jazz and traditional Mexican music. ⊠ *Francisco Madero 80*, ☎ *3/635–4520. AE, MC, V.*

$ ✕ **El Abajeño.** At this branch of the local chain that serves quality Mexican specialties, look for the *carnitas* (pork) or *filete tapado* (cheese-topped fillet of beef) for two. Traditional Mexican dance performances take place weekends at 4:30. ⊠ *Juárez 231*, ☎ *3/635–9015. MC, V.*

Tonalá
8 km (5 mi) east of Tlaquepaque.

Tonalá is 10 minutes away but centuries removed from its commercial neighbor, Tlaquepaque. One of Mexico's oldest pueblos, Tonalá is a quiet village with dusty, cobblestone streets and adobe houses. The village was both the pre-Hispanic capital of the Atemajac Valley Indians and the capital of New Spain when Captain Juan de Oñate moved Guadalajara here in 1532. Within three years, however, unfriendly Indians and a lack of water forced the Spaniards out.

Today, municipal officials say more than 6,000 artisans live and work here. Indeed, much of the ceramics and pottery sold in Tlaquepaque (and in many other parts of the world) are made in Tonalá. In small home studios, families create the lovely pieces, cobalt-blue glassware, and playful animals with the same materials and techniques their ancestors used. It's possible to visit many home studios on free tours offered by the Tonalá municipal tourist office (☞ Visitor Information *in* Tlaquepaque and Tonalá, *below*), beginning from the Casa de Artesanos, with one-day advance notice.

On Thursday, much Tonalá merchandise is sold at bargain prices at one of the best tianguis in all of Mexico (avoid Sunday). Most stores are open Monday through Saturday 10–2 and 4–7, Sunday 10–2.

Below are some of the highlights of a walk north and generally east of Avenida de los Tonaltecas, a main drag lined with shops and cafés.

③① A virtual department store of Mexican folk art and crafts, the **Casa de los Artesanos** displays an excellent selection of works by the best of Tonalá's artisans. The work of generations is here, including items made from wood, glass, wrought iron, brass, and of course clay. More than 20 techniques of producing barro are used in the village. Prices are reasonable, and the staff here can direct you to local artisans' studios. ⊠ *Av. de los Tonaltecas Sur 140*, ☎ *3/683–0590.* ⊙ *Weekdays 9–7, weekends 9–3.*

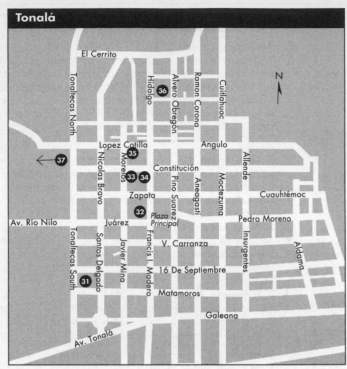

Tonalá

El Cerrito

Tonallecas North

Hidalgo

Alvero Obregón

Ramon Corona

Curitlahuac

N

Lopez Cotilla

Nicolas Bravo

Morelos

Constitución

Angulo

Allende

Moctezuma

Cuauhtémoc

Zapata

Pino Suárez

Aneogasi

Av. Río Nilo

Juárez

Plaza
Principal

Pedro Moreno

Tonallecas South

Santos Delgado

Javier Mina

Francis I. Madero

V. Carranza

Insurgentes

Aldama

16 De Septiembre

Matamoros

Galeana

Av. Tonalá

---

32 In the **Santuário,** or parish church, paintings of the 14 stations of the cross fill the walls. Next door is the simple **Palacio Municipal,** or City Hall. The **Plaza Principal** is across the street. ⊠ *Juárez at Hidalgo.*

33 One of Tonalá's largest exporters of hand-painted ceramics abroad is **Erandi.** Its new exhibition center is in founder Jorge Wilmot's former workshop. To see artisans in action, stop by their factory three blocks away. ⊠ *Calle Morelos 86,* ☎ *3/812–1603.* ⊙ *Tues.–Sat. 9–6, Sun. 9–2. Factory:* ⊠ *Lopez Cotilla 118,* ☎ *3/683–0253.* ⊙ *Weekdays 9–6, Sat. 9–2.*

34 The Bernabe family has made exquisite petatillo ceramics for generations, as well as simpler stoneware. The sprawling workshop in back of the **Galería José Bernabe** is open to visitors. ⊠ *Hidalgo 83, between Zapata and Constitución,* ☎ *3/683–0040.* ⊙ *Weekdays 10–3 and 4–7, weekends 10–3. Workshop closed weekends.*

35 At the **Cerámica de Ken Edwards** workshop, you can view Edwards's trademark lead-free stoneware, which revolutionized centuries-old techniques. Although Edwards has moved on to Guatemala, his quality ceramics live on. ⊠ *Calle Morelos 184,* ☎ *3/683–0313.* ⊙ *Weekdays 9–6, Sat. 9–1.*

36 Tonalá native J. Cruz Coldívar, who signs his work and named his shop **El 7** (el see-*ey*-tey), makes striking hand-painted masks, as well as decorative plates and other wall hangings. He has exhibited throughout Mexico, and also in North and South America and Europe. The Spanish Crown owns a number of his works. ⊠ *Privado Obregón 28, north of town center,* ☎ *3/683–0873.* ⊙ *Weekdays 9–6, Sat. 9–1.*

37 On a small patio behind his home, **Salvador Vásquez Carmona** molds enormous ceramic pots and glazes them with intricate and fanciful designs. Numerous awards certificates hang in his living room. Call before visiting. ⊠ *Av. de los Maestros 328, west of Av. de los Tonaltecas,* ☎ *3/683–2896.*

DINING

$–$$ ✕ **El Rincón del Sol.** A peaceful covered patio invites you to sip margaritas while listening to live guitar music. Try the chilies en nogada or one of the steak or chicken dishes. ⊠ *Av. 16 de Septiembre 61,* ☎ *3/683–1989. AE, MC, V.*

$ ✕ **Restaurant Jalepeños.** Steaks are the house specialty in this small but tastefully appointed restaurant. ⊠ *Madero 23, ½ block from town hall,* ☎ *3/683–0344. MC, V.*

$ ✕ **Restaurant Trópico de Tonalá.** This popular six-table luncheonette with counter area serves tasty, fresh sandwiches, soups, and chicken and meat dishes. ⊠ *Madero 15,* ☎ *3/683–0689. No credit cards.*

Tlaquepaque and Tonalá A to Z

ARRIVING AND DEPARTING

By Bus. There is frequent public bus service from downtown Guadalajara and the Plaza del Sol shopping center to Tlaquepaque and Tonalá. The trips take around 30 and 45 minutes, respectively.

By Car. From Guadalajara, take Avenida Revolución southeast. At the Plaza de la Bandera, jog right onto Boulevard General Marcelino García Barragán, which becomes Boulevard Tlaquepaque as it leads into town. When you reach the *glorieta* (traffic circle), follow the circle around to Avenida Niños Héroes. The first intersection is Calle Independencia, the pedestrian mall. From the Plaza del Sol area, take Calzada Lázaro Cárdenas southeast to the Alamo traffic circle. Fork off to the north onto Avenida Niños Héroes. Both routes take around 20 minutes.

To get from Tlaquepaque to Tonalá, take Avenida Río Nilo southeast directly into town, to the intersection of Avenida de los Tonaltecas.

By Taxi. The fare from downtown Guadalajara to Tlaquepaque is about $6. The cab ride to Tonalá from downtown Guadalajara costs about $8. A cab from Tlaquepaque to Tonalá runs about $4.

VISITOR INFORMATION

The **Tlaquepaque municipal tourist office** (⊠ Pila Seca 15-16, in front of the arches, Tlaquepaque, ☎ 3/635–5756 or 3/657–3846), open weekdays 9–7, is in the Centro Cultural.

The **Tonalá municipal tourist office** (⊠ Av. Hidalgo 21, Tonalá, ☎ 3/683–0047 or 3/683–0048) is open weekdays 9–3 and Saturday 9–1.

Around Lake Chapala

Could it be the area's Mexican arts and culture? Or perhaps the favorable exchange rate? Or even the springlike climate? Whatever the reason, more than 35,000 U.S. and Canadian citizens have retired in and around Guadalajara. The majority reside along the shores of Lake Chapala, Mexico's largest inland lake.

The jagged mountains that ring the lake make it seem a world away from Guadalajara; the tranquility offers a welcome contrast to the bustling city. Sunsets are spectacular, and there's just enough humidity to keep the abundant bougainvillea blooming and ensure no drastic temperature fluctuations. Unfortunately, the lake is polluted and fighting a battle with *lirio* (water hyacinth), a succulent plant that threatens to cover much of the water's surface. For years the lake has also been threatened by dangerously low water levels caused by overconsumption from Guadalajara and surrounding states. But Chapala has been declared part of Mexico's national heritage, and steps are being taken to find alternative water sources and to protect the lake from further industrial dumping from Río Lerma, which feeds it.

Spanish settlement in the area dates from 1538, when Franciscan friar Miguel de Bolonio arrived and began to convert the Taltica Indians to Christianity. Their chief was named Chapalac, from which the name Chapala is said to have originated. Today, Chapala is the area's largest settlement. Eight kilometers (5 mi) to the west, the more tranquil village of Ajijic has been home to expatriate artists and writers since the 1920s. The towns and villages along the lake are linked by one highway with multiple names, such as Carretera Chapala-Ajijic or Carretera Ajijic-Jocotepec.

Chapala
45 km (28 mi) south of Guadalajara.

With Chapala's proximity to rapidly growing Guadalajara, as well as its comfortable climate, it is surprising that tourists didn't frequent the area until the late 19th century. Then-president Porfirio Díaz heard that aristocrats had discovered this ideal place for weekend getaways, and he began spending holidays here in 1904. Soon summer homes were built, and in 1910 the Chapala Yacht Club opened. Word of the town, with its lavish lawn parties and magnificent estates, spread quickly to the United States and Europe.

Nowadays the town of Chapala has a population of some 35,000 and attracts a less influential but equally fun-loving assortment of visitors. On weekends the streets are filled with Mexican families. Throughout the week American and Canadian retirees stroll along the lakeside promenade, play golf, and relax on the verandas of downtown restaurants.

Avenida Madero, lined with pleasant restaurants, shops, and cafés, is the town's main drag. On Madero, four blocks north of the lake, the
㊳ **plaza,** at the corner of López Cotilla, is a relaxing spot to sit and read
㊴ the paper. Two blocks south of the plaza, the **Iglesia de San Francisco** is easy to spot by the blue neon crosses on its twin steeples. The church was built in 1528 and reconstructed in 1580. On weekends, the tran-
㊵ quil lakeside **Parque la Cristianía,** on the south side of the *malecón* (boardwalk), fills with Tapatíos taking a respite from the city and browsing the ever-present souvenir booths. At the end of the park are a small handicrafts market and a number of open-air cafés featuring *pescado blanco,* the white fish native to the lake. Because of pollution, we cannot recommend that you partake of this regional delicacy, although other food is fine.

㊶ A visit to **Isla de los Alacranes** (Scorpion Island) is a popular excursion from the Chapala pier at the end of Avenida Madero. The view
㊷ of the shore area is enchanting. You can take a trip to **Isla de Mezcala,** about 12 km (7½ mi) northeast of Isla de los Alacranes, and explore the ruins of a fortress that housed a band of rebels during the early 19th-century war of independence with Spain. Depending on the duration of the trip, the price ranges from about $15 to $60 for a launch (leaving from the Chapala pier at the end of Avenida Madero) with a capacity of eight adults.

DINING AND LODGING
$$ ✕ **Beer Garden.** The roofed terrace here has been a favorite watering hole and lunch spot since 1929. Enjoy the expansive lake view while you eat one of the tasty seafood, chicken, or beef specialties. ✉ *Paseo Ramón Corona at northwest corner of Av. Madero,* ☎ *376/5–44–27. AE, MC, V. Closed Tues.–Wed.*

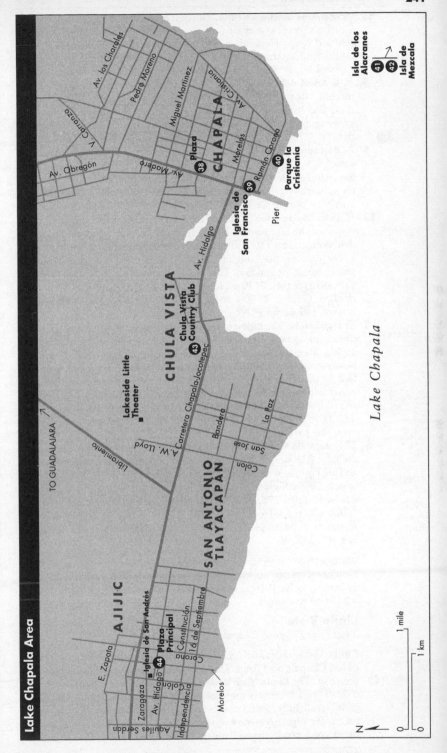

Lake Chapala Area

TO GUADALAJARA

AJIJIC

E. Zapata

Zaragoza

Aquiles Serdán

Av. Hidalgo

Colón

Independencia

Constitución

16 de Septiembre

Morelos

Iglesia de San Andrés

Plaza Principal
44

Libramiento

A.W. Lloyd

SAN ANTONIO TLAYACAPÁN

Colón

San José

Bandera

La Paz

Carretera Chapala-Jocotepec

CHULA VISTA

Lakeside Little Theater

Chula Vista Country Club
43

Av. Hidalgo

Iglesia de San Francisco

Pier

39

Ramón Corona

Parque la Cristianía
40

Morelos

CHAPALA

Plaza
38

Av. Madero

Av. Obregón

V. Carranza

Av. los Charales

Pedro Moreno

Miguel Martínez

Av. Cristanía

Isla de los Alacranes
41

Isla de Mezcala
42

Lake Chapala

1 mile

1 km

N

$$ ✕ **Mariscos Guicho's e Hijos.** The best of the waterfront seafood joints, Guicho's serves savory caviar tacos, frog legs, garlic shrimp, and spicy seafood soup. The audacious lime-green walls and cheery red table-cloths lend a particularly authentic Mexican charm. ⊠ *Paseo Ramón Corona 20,* ☎ *376/5–32–32. No credit cards. Closed Tues.*

$ ✕ **El Arbol del Café** (The Coffee Tree). Local expatriates cherish this modest café for its roasted-on-the-premises specialty coffee, imported teas, and homemade cakes. Sip a decaffeinated cappuccino (which you won't often find in Mexico) and peruse the day's English-language papers. ⊠ *Av. Hidalgo 236,* ☎ *no phone. No credit cards. Closed Sun.*

$ ✕ **Restaurant Cazadores.** This grandly turreted building was once the summer home of the Braniff family, owners of the now-defunct air-line. The food is nothing special—just come for a cool drink and watch the action along the malecón. ⊠ *Av. Madero and Paseo Ramón Corona, northeast corner,* ☎ *376/5–21–62. AE, MC, V. Closed Mon.*

$$ 🛏 **Lake Chapala Inn.** Three of the four rooms in this renovated man-sion face the lake and all have whitewashed oak furniture, large gar-den terraces, and TVs and phones. A dining room, library, and gourmet kitchen are on site, and an English-style breakfast is included in the rates (except for Sunday). The family-run hotel caters to American and Canadian tourists. ⊠ *Paseo Ramón Corona 23, down the malecón from the Beer Garden, 45900,* ☎ *FAX 376/5–47–86. 4 rooms. Pool, laundry service, free parking. No credit cards.* 🐾

$ 🛏 **Hotel Nido.** The oldest hotel on the lake was built in the early 1900s to accommodate President Porfirio Díaz and his entourage. In the 1940s, Mexican film star María Félix spent the first of her numerous honeymoons here, and the whitewashed high-ceiling lobby still feels like the scene of a melodrama waiting to happen. There's a picturesque patio and garden in the rear. However, the building's exterior is a shambles, and guest rooms are strictly functional. ⊠ *Av. Madero 202, 45900,* ☎ *376/5–21–16. 30 rooms. Restaurant, bar, pool, laundry ser-vice, free parking. MC, V.*

$ 🛏 **Hotel Villa Montecarlo.** Look out on spacious lawns on a hill above the lake. The simple rooms are housed in three-story contiguous units and are popular with Mexican families. One of the two swimming pools, which are the biggest in the area, is filled with natural thermal water. ⊠ *Av. Hidalgo 296, about 1 km (½ mi) west of Av. Madero, 45900,* ☎ *FAX 376/5–22–16, 376/5–21–20, 376/5–33–66. 46 rooms, 2 suites. Restaurant, bar, 2 pools, 2 tennis courts, laundry service, free park-ing. AE, MC, V.*

OUTDOOR ACTIVITIES AND SPORTS

Nonmembers can golf at the **Chapala Country Club** (⊠ Vista del Lago 1, San Nicholás Ibarra, ☎ 376/3–51–36), except for Tuesday, when it's closed to visitors.

Chula Vista

3 km (2 mi) west of Chapala.

Chula Vista, the most American neighborhood in Mexico, lies be-tween Chapala and Ajijic. Dozens of condos dot the hillside north of
④③ the road. The **Chula Vista Country Club** (⊠ Paseo de Golf 5, ☎ 376/6–25–15) is a favorite of the local *norteamericano* community. The "billy-goat" (read: hilly) golf course here—open to nonmembers who pay the greens fee—has great views of the lake and offers a real workout, as the rugged terrain cannot be negotiated by golf cart.

DINING

$ ✕ **Chicken Little.** As its name suggests, this place serves roast chicken, but you'll also find soups, salads, sandwiches, and American-style pies and cakes. ⊠ *Av. Hidalgo 101-B, in Riberas del Pilar,* ☎ *376/5–43–99. No credit cards. Closed Sun. No dinner.*

NIGHTLIFE AND THE ARTS

Just west of Chula Vista, above the PAL Trailer Park and next to Oak Hill High School, the 112-seat **Lakeside Little Theater** (☎ 376/5–34–79) stages English-language musicals and plays throughout the year. Box-office hours are 10 AM–1 PM starting three days before performances and one hour before curtain. To find out what's playing, look in *The Guadalajara Reporter* or the *Lake Chapala Review.*

Banana's Night Club has a live house band weekends and has become a favorite of North Americans and locals who count a beer mug with their name at the bar. There is line dancing Wednesday to country favorites, and the avocado and pork burritos are delicious. ⊠ *Carretera Chapala-Jocotepec 159, San Antonio Tlayacapán,* ☎ *376/6–09–35. No credit cards. Closed Sun.–Tues.*

Ajijic
8 km (5 mi) west of Chapala.

Despite blocks of galleries and crafts shops, Ajijic's small-town ambience is still defined by its narrow cobblestone streets, whitewashed buildings, and gentle pace. Still, the foreign influence is unmistakable: English is spoken almost as widely here as Spanish, and license plates run the gamut from Alaska to Texas. A recent building boom is straining the pueblo's traffic capacity.

④ Some visitors park near the **Plaza Principal** (also called the Plaza de Armas or Jardín), the tree- and flower-filled central square at the corner of Avenidas Colón and Hidalgo, although it may be easier to find space a few blocks farther on at the edge of the pier. The **Iglesia de San Andrés** (Church of St. Andrew) sits on the Jardín's north side. In late November the plaza fills for the saint's nine-day fiesta.

Walk down Calle Morelos (the continuation of Avenida Colón) toward the lake and you'll find stores and boutiques that sell everything from designer fashions to traditional arts and crafts. Turn left onto Independencia to find about a dozen art galleries and studios.

DINING AND LODGING

In addition to the establishments listed below, there are other good-quality lodgings in the area. Consult the tourist office in Chapala, the *Ojo del Lago* newspaper, or *The Guadalajara Colony Reporter.* Note that restaurants in Ajijic seem to come and go yearly.

$$ ★ ✕ **Ajijic Grill.** Savor Japanese specialties prepared table-side, along with grilled meats, seafood, and fresh salads. The wonderful patio is surrounded by small white lights, and a sushi bar has been added. ⊠ *Calle Morelos 5,* ☎ *376/6–24–58. MC, V. Closed Tues.*

$$ ✕ **Johanna's German Restaurant.** This small, intimate bit of Bavaria on the lake serves up a variety of excellent sausages and authentic German cuisine. ⊠ *Blvd. Ajijic 118A, in front of the La Floresta Auditorium,* ☎ *376/6–04–37. No credit cards. Closed Mon.*

$$ ✕ **La Luz de La Luna.** In the expansive gardens of La Colección Moon (☞ Shopping, *below*), high style and presentation and a Spanish influence on the menu make this a worthy stop. Among the weekly specials are stuffed chicken, beef fajitas, veal, and seafood. ⊠ *Río Zula 4,* ☎ *376/6–20–92. MC, V. Closed Mon.*

$ ✕ **La Casa del Waffle.** Stop in this bright cheery spot for breakfast and choose from 12 varieties of waffles and numerous other favorites. ⊠ *Carretera Chapala–Jocotepec Pte. 75, on the highway west of Ajijic,* ☎ *376/6–23–01. No credit cards. Closed Tues. No dinner.*

$ ✕ **Salvador's.** An afternoon hangout for local expatriates, this restaurant has a well-kept salad bar and specialties from both south and north of the border. ✉ *Carretera Chapala–Jocotepec 56, in Plaza Bugambilias,* ☎ *376/6–23–01. No credit cards.*

$$ ✕▥ **La Nueva Posada.** Luxuriant gardens framed in bougainvillea over-
★ look the lake at this charming inn, run by a gracious Canadian family. The spacious, well-lighted rooms have warm pastel color schemes and original watercolors. Chef Lorraine Rousseau's eclectic menu is delicious, and there is fine entertainment most evenings, typically an American jazz trio or tropical music. ✉ *Donato Guerra 9, Apdo. 30, 45920,* ☎ *376/6–14–44,* ℻ *376/6–20–49. 19 rooms, 4 suites. Restaurant, bar, fans, pool, laundry service, free parking. MC, V.* ✎

$$ ▥ **Los Artistas.** One of Ajijic's elegant walled-in homes, this friendly inn is surrounded by an acre of splendidly landscaped gardens. Each room is uniquely decorated with colorful handwoven Mexican bedspreads and fresh-cut tropical bouquets. Rates include a breakfast buffet of local fruits, yogurt, granola, and fresh homemade breads. ✉ *Constitución 105, 45920,* ☎ *376/6–10–27,* ℻ *376/6–17–62. 6 rooms. Pool, free parking. No credit cards.*

$$ ▥ **Inn at San Andres.** This small B and B integrates hand-painted tiles and rustic furniture in each one-of-a-kind suite. ✉ *Galeana 22-A, 1 block off plaza, 45920,* ☎ *376/6–12–50, 703/830–8398 in the U.S. (with Denise Clark),* ℻ *376/6–12–50. 5 suites. Pool. No credit cards.*

$$ ▥ **Real de Chapala.** Rooms at this lakeside hotel are airy and ample, and all suites have small individual swimming pools. The Sunday mariachi lunch is popular with weekend visitors from Guadalajara. ✉ *Paseo del Prado 20, 45920,* ☎ *376/6–00–14, 376/6–00–21,* ℻ *376/ 6–00–25. For reservations in Guadalajara:* ✉ *Hoteles Real, Rubén Darío 1262, 44630,* ☎ *3/641–9097, 3/641–9093,* ℻ *3/642–8878. 76 rooms, 5 suites. Restaurant, bar, fans, pool, wading pool, 2 tennis courts, volleyball, laundry service, free parking. AE, MC, V.*

NIGHTLIFE AND THE ARTS

The rambling, hacienda-style **Posada Ajijic** (✉ Calle Morelos, facing the lake, ☎ 376/6–07–44, 376/6–04–30) is a restaurant, bar, and popular weekend dance place with a spectacular water view. A cozy, candlelit nightclub, **Viva Maria** (✉ Donato Guerra 20, ☎ 376/6–09–84) presents an eclectic range of live musical offerings. Dance clubs and night spots come and go quickly here; ask about the latest craze at your hotel or the tourist office.

SHOPPING

The shores of Lake Chapala are teaming with artisan workshops, many of which have replaced Tonalá as the region's source of export-quality crafts. Although Ajijic doesn't have as many boutiques and crafts shops as inhabitants, it sometimes seems that way. **Casa de las Artesanías Ajijik** (✉ Carretera Chapala-Jocotepec, Km 6.5, ☎ 376/6–05–48) is a branch of the state-run Instituto de Artesanías Jaliscienses crafts shop (☞ Shopping *under* Exploring Guadalajara, *above*). It's open weekdays 10–6, Saturday 10–4, and Sunday 10–2. **La Colección Bárbara** (✉ Av. Independencia 7A–9A, ☎ 376/6–18–24), open Monday–Saturday 10–5, sells traditional crafts, antiques, and fine furniture. **La Colección Moon** (✉ Río Zula 4, south of Ocampo, ☎ 376/6–10–00) carries a selection of owner Billy Moon's high-end lamps, wrought-iron furniture, and other decorative items. It's open weekdays 8–1 and 4–6, weekends 9–6. You can find exhibits of sculpture, paintings, prints, photography, pottery, and other art mediums by local artists at **Galería Americas** (✉ Paseo Ramón Corona 11, across from the Lake Chapala Society, ☎ 376/6–12–92). Local artists' works are on offer at **Galeria**

Daniel Palma (✉ Ocampo 30, ☎ 376/6–16–88). Open Monday–Saturday 10–2 and 3–6, and Sunday 11–3, the **Mi México** (✉ Calle Morelos 8, ☎ 376/6–01–33) boutique sells pottery, blown glass, women's clothing, and other crafts and gifts. **Opus Boutique and Galería** (✉ Calle Morelos 15, ☎ 376/6–17–90) sells masks, folk art, jewelry, and women's clothing.

For Cuban and Mexican cigars, go to **La Antigua Axixic Tobacco and Gift Shop** (✉ Constitución 71A, ☎ no phone), open weekdays 10–5, weekends 10–2.

WATER PARK
Take a break with the children—or pretend you are one again—and explore the **Tobolandia** water park. ✉ *Blvd. Ajijic 57,* ☎ *376/6–21–20.* 🎫 *$3.50.* ☉ *Daily 10–6.*

San Juan Cosalá
10 km (6 mi) west of Chapala.

San Juan Cosalá is known for its natural thermal-water spas on the shores of Lake Chapala, with the mountains rising to the north. The **Hotel Balneario San Juan Cosalá** (☎ 376/1–02–22) welcomes both daytrippers and overnight guests to its four large swimming pools and two wading pools. A restaurant with international fare is on the premises. The **Villas Buenaventura Cosalá** (☎ 376/1–02–02) has a two-night minimum on weekends. Facilities include six one-bedroom suites and 11 with two bedrooms, all with kitchenettes, TVs, and thermal-water bathtubs. There are also thermal hot tubs and swimming pools.

Lake Chapala A to Z
ARRIVING AND DEPARTING
By Bus. There is frequent bus service to Chapala, Ajijic, and other lakeside towns from both Guadalajara's Antigua Central Camionera (Old Bus Station) and Central Camionera Nueva for about $3. Make sure you ask for the *directo* (direct) as opposed to *clase segunda* (second class), which stops at every little pueblo en route.

By Car. From downtown Guadalajara take Avenida Federalismo south to Calzada Lázaro Cárdenas, turn left, and continue southeast. Follow the signs as Lázaro Cárdenas converges with the Carretera a Chapala, whose route number is both 23 and 44. The trip takes 50 minutes.

ENGLISH-LANGUAGE PUBLICATIONS
The *Ojo del Lago* monthly newspaper is available free throughout Chapala and Ajijic. The monthly *Lake Chapala Review* sells for less than a dollar. The *Guadalajara Reporter* weekly newspaper (☞ Contacts and Resources *in* Guadalajara A to Z, *below*) devotes a section to lakeside news and events. **Libros de Chapala** (✉ Av. Madero, across from the plaza, Chapala), open daily 9–2 and 3–6, has an extensive range of English-language magazines, U.S. and Canadian newspapers, and a large selection of books on Mexico in English. **Portalibros** (✉ Constitución 2A, Ajijic, ☎ 376/6–19–98) carries a wide selection of used books in English. It's open Monday–Saturday 9:30–5.

VISITOR INFORMATION
The **Jalisco state tourism office** (✉ Madero 407-A, 2nd floor, ☎ FAX 376/5–31–41) in Chapala is open weekdays 9–7, weekends 9–5.

In Ajijic, the nonprofit **Lake Chapala Society** (✉ Av. 16 de Septiembre 16A, ☎ no phone), open Monday–Saturday 10–1, provides information about the area.

Tequila

56 km (35 mi) northwest of Guadalajara.

For a close look at how Mexico's most famous liquor is made from the spiny blue agave plant that grows in the fields alongside the highway, spend part or all of a day in this tidy village. It's said that centuries ago, the Tiquilas, a small Nahuatl-speaking tribe, discovered the heart of the agave produced a juice that could be fermented to make various intoxicating drinks. When distilled (an innovation introduced after the arrival of the Spanish in the 16th century), the fermented liquid turns into the heady liquor. You can tour the famous Sauza Distillery or one of the other modern tequila distilleries here. Follow the signs, and plan to arrive on a weekday between 10 AM and 1 PM. Frequent bus service is available from Guadalajara's Old Bus Station, and various Guadalajara tour companies offer guided excursions (☞ Contacts and Resources *in* Guadalajara A to Z, *below*). Each Saturday the Tequila Express leaves Guadalajara on a 10-hour trip that includes the Herradura Distillery, a satisfying lunch, a folkloric ballet performance, serenades by mariachis, and an unlimited supply of Mexico's most famous liquor.

GUADALAJARA A TO Z

Arriving and Departing

By Bus

First-class, air-conditioned buses with rest rooms run daily to Guadalajara from most major cities on the border. **Greyhound** (☎ 01–800/712–8819) has schedule and fare information for service into Mexico, although you will have to change to a Mexican carrier at the border. Guadalajara's **Nueva Central Camionera** (New Bus Station) is 10 km (6 mi) southeast of downtown Guadalajara on the highway to Zapotlanejo. First-class bus companies that serve Guadalajara from within Mexico include **Elite** (☎ 3/679–0404); **ETN** (☎ 3/600–0775, 01–800/360–4200); **Primera Plus** (☎ 3/600–0398); and **Omnibus de México** (☎ 3/600–0469). Of these, ETN is generally considered the most pleasant to travel with.

By Car

Major routes include Highway 54, which leads south to Colima (220 km [136 mi]) and north to Zacatecas (320 km [198 mi]). Highway 15D goes southeast to Morelia (255 km [58 mi]), continuing to Mexico City (209 km [130 mi]). The Plan de Barrancas Highway 15 heads north through some of the most beautiful country in Jalisco and neighboring Nayarit state. If you have a choice between a free or toll road, remember that the latter tend to be quite expensive but are in far better condition than their free counterparts.

By Plane

Libertador Miguel Hidalgo International Airport (☎ 3/688–5248, 3/688–5127) is 16½ km (10 mi) south of Guadalajara. A new international terminal is planned in the next decade to help meet the demands of increased air service to the area.

Aeroméxico (☎ 01–800/021–4000) has nonstop service to Guadalajara from Los Angeles. **Mexicana** (☎ 3/678–7676, 01–800/502–2000) has direct flights from Chicago, Los Angeles, San Francisco, and San José. **Taesa** (☎ 3/688–5858, 01–800/904–6300) flies direct from Chicago and Oakland. Through Dallas, **American Airlines** (☎ 3/616–4090) provides service to Guadalajara from all cities in its system. **Con-**

tinental (☎ 3/688–5141, 01–800/900–5000) provides the same service through Houston. **Delta Air Lines** (☎ 3/630–3530, 01–800/902–2100) flies direct from Los Angeles.

FROM THE AIRPORT TO DOWNTOWN

By Car. The Chapala Highway 23 (also numbered 44)—a well-paved four-lane thoroughfare—stretches north from the airport to the city. The 30-minute trip can be delayed by slow-moving caravans of trucks and weekend recreational traffic.

By Taxi or Van. Autotransportaciones Aeropuerto (☎ 3/812–4278 or 3/812–4308) is a *combi* (VW minibus) and 24-hour taxi service to and from anywhere in the Guadalajara area. Fares, based on distance, range from $8 to $12 for up to three people going to the same destination. At the airport, buy a ticket from the booth outside the terminal exit. Going to the airport, a regular city taxi should charge similar fares (they aren't allowed to pick up passengers at the airport).

By Train

The Mexican train system has been privatized, and most passenger service in the country has been suspended, except for a couple of tourist trips, including an excursion day trip each Saturday from Guadalajara to Tequila and back. Tickets are only available from the **Camera de Comercio** (Chamber of Commerce, ☎ 3/122–9020) for $40. The trip runs from 10:30 AM to 8:30 PM. Weekly service to the interior of Jalisco is slowly being added. Guadalajara's **Estación de Ferrocarriles** (train station; ☎ 3/650–0826, 3/650–1082) is at the south end of Avenida 16 de Septiembre, past Parque Agua Azul.

Getting Around

Guadalajara's major attractions are best seen on foot. For points outside the city center, Guadalajara has an inexpensive, well-organized public-transportation system.

By Bus

This is without a doubt the most economical and efficient—but sometimes least comfortable—means of traversing the city. Buses run every few minutes between 6 AM and 11 PM to all local attractions, including Tlaquepaque, Tonalá, and Zapopan. Fares are roughly 30¢, making buses the preferred mode of transportation for Guadalajara natives, so expect to stand during daytime. Various "luxury" buses—which run on some of the main routes through the city, including out to Tlaquepaque and Tonalá—cost 55¢ and are much less crowded and vastly more comfortable.

Buses to and from such nearby destinations as Chapala, Ajijic, and Tequila depart from the **Antigua Central Camionera,** just northeast of the Parque Agua Azul on Avenida Dr. R. Michel, between Calles Los Angeles and 5 de Febrero.

By Car

Beware of heavy traffic and *topes* (speed bumps). Traffic circles are common at many busy intersections. Parking in the city center can be scarce, so take a taxi or bus if you're not staying nearby; otherwise, try the underground lots across from the Palacio Municipal (⊠ Av. Hidalgo and Calle Pedro Loza) and below the Plaza de la Liberación (⊠ Av. Hidalgo and Calle Belén, in front of the Teatro Degollado). If you park illegally, the police may tow your vehicle and you'll have to go to the municipal transit office to pay a fine as well as to one of the *correlones* (holding areas) to pay the tow charge (around $15) and retrieve your car.

By Subway

Guadalajara's underground *tren ligero* (light train) system is clean, safe, and efficient. Line 1 runs along Avenida Federalismo from the Periférico (city beltway) Sur to Periférico Norte, near the Benito Juárez Auditorium. Line 2 runs east–west along Avenida Javier Mina (which becomes Avenida Juárez at Calzada Independencia) from Tetlán in eastern Guadalajara to Avenida Federalismo. Line 3 makes its way along Avenida Revolución. Trains run about every 15 minutes from 6 AM to 11 PM; a token for one trip costs about 30¢. **Juárez Station,** where Lines 1 and 2 meet, serves as a public art gallery, with changing exhibits of works by Mexican artists.

By Taxi

Taxis are readily available and reasonably economical. Tell the driver where you are going and agree on a fare *before* you enter the cab. Fare schedules listing prices to downtown and all major attractions are posted in most hotel lobbies. *Sitios* (cab stands) are near all hotels and attractions. Fares go up about 25% at night.

Contacts and Resources

Car Rental

Car rental agencies with offices at the Guadalajara airport include **Avis** (☎ 3/688–5528, 3/688–5656), **Budget** (☎ 3/613–0286; also ✉ Av. Niños Héroes 934, at Av. 16 de Septiembre, ☎ 3/613–0027), **Dollar** (☎ 3/688–5659; also ✉ Av. Federalismo Sur 540A, ☎ 3/826–7959), **Hertz** (☎ 3/688–5403; also ✉ Av. 16 de Septiembre 738-B, ☎ 3/614–6162), **National** (☎ 3/614–7175; also ✉ Av. Niños Héroes 961-C, ☎ 01–800/003–9500), and **Thrifty** (☎ 3/688–6346; also ✉ Av. Niños Héroes 963-2, ☎ 01–800/021–2277).

Consulates

For information about consulates other than those listed below, call **Guadalajara's consular association** (☎ 3/616–0629), open weekdays 9–3 and 5–8.

The **U.S. Consulate** (✉ Progreso 175, between Av. López Cotilla and Libertad, ☎ 3/825–2700, 3/825–2998, 3/826–5553 after-hours emergency) is open weekdays 8–4:30; the American Citizens Services office is open weekday mornings 8:30–11:30. The **Canadian Consulate** (✉ Fiesta Americana, Aurelio Aceves 225, ☎ 3/616–5642, 01–800/706–2900 after-hours emergency) is open weekdays 8:30–2 and 3–5. The **U.K. Consulate** (✉ Eulogio Parra 2539, ☎ 3/636–6118) is open only by appointment.

Doctors and Dentists

The U.S. Consulate (☞ Consulates, *above*) maintains a list of English-speaking doctors and dentists. All major hotels have the names of doctors who are on 24-hour call.

Emergencies

Dialing 080 will connect you with a central emergency system (for all of the organizations listed below and other metro-area police stations). Ask for an English-speaking operator. **Guadalajara City police** (☎ 3/618–0260). **State police** (☎ 3/617–5828, 3/617–5538). **Highway patrol** (☎ 3/629–5082, 3/629–5085). **Fire department** (☎ 3/619–0794, 3/619–0510). **Cruz Roja** (Red Cross; ☎ 3/614–5600, 3/614–2707). **Cruz Verde** (Green Cross municipal emergency medical service; ☎ 3/812–5143, 3/812–0472).

English-Language Bookstores and Publications
Sandi Bookstore (✉ Av. Tepeyac 718, in Chapalita district, ☎ 3/121–0863), open weekdays 9:30–2:30 and 3:30–7, Saturday 9:30–2, sells many newspapers, magazines, and books.

The Guadalajara Reporter, a weekly newspaper sold for 80¢ at newsstands and hotels, includes excellent community and cultural listings. Another excellent source of information on the Lake Chapala area and other excursions in the states of Jalisco, Colima, Nayarit, and Michoacán is *Outdoors in Western Mexico* by John and Susana Pint (Editoriales Agata, 1998). The monthly newspapers *Ojo del Lago* and *Lake Chapala Review* cover the Lake Chapala area (☞ Around Lake Chapala *in* Side Trips from Guadalajara, *above*).

Guided Tours
Most tour operators in Guadalajara have guided city tours and excursions to Tequila, Lake Chapala, Tlaquepaque, and Tonalá.

CALANDRIAS
You can hire a horse-drawn carriage in front of the Museo Regional, the Mercado Libertad, or Parque San Francisco. The charge is about $12 for an hour-long tour for up to four passengers. Few drivers speak English.

TOUR OPERATORS
Copenhagen Tours (✉ Av. J. Manuel Clouthier 152, Col. Prados Vallarta, ☎ 3/629–7957, 3/629–4758). **Panoramex** (✉ Av. Federalismo Sur 944, ☎ 3/810–5109, 3/810–5005; ✉ Av. Mariano Otero 2407-3, on the traffic circle, ☎ 3/647–0972).

Charter Club Tours (✉ Carretera Chapala–Jalisco Ote. 1, Ajijic, ☎ 376/6–17–77).

Hospitals
Hospital del Carmen (✉ Tarascos 3435, near Plaza México mall, ☎ 3/813–0128, 3/813–0025); **Hospital México-Americano** (✉ Colomos 2110, ☎ 3/641–3141, 3/642–4520); **Hospital San Javier** (✉ Av. Pablo Casals 640, Col. Providencia, ☎ 3/669–0222); and **Hospital Santa María Chapalita** (✉ Av. Niño Obrero 1666, in Chapalita district, ☎ 3/678–1400).

Letters and E-Mail
The main **post office** (✉ Administración de Correos 1, ☎ 3/614–8125) is open weekdays 8–7.

Internet cafés increasingly are becoming an option to slow postal service in Mexico. The rates at **CCCP** (✉ Av. Alcade 159, ☎ 3/614–5311) are inexpensive.

Money Exchange
The most convenient places to change dollars are *casas de cambio,* generally open weekdays 9–6 and Saturday until 1 PM. Many of them are on Calle López Cotilla downtown and in the Plaza del Sol area. Banks tend to have more-limited hours, longer waits, and a poorer exchange rates.

Pharmacies
Farmacias Guadalajara (✉ Av. Las Americas 2, ☎ 3/615–8516; ✉ Av. Javier Mina 221, between Calle Cabañas and Vicente Guerrero, ☎ 3/617–8555; ✉ Av. Tepeyac 646, in Chapalita district, ☎ 3/121–2581; ✉ Plaza México, ☎ 3/813–2698) has several branches that are open 24 hours.

Travel Agencies

Many of the city's 100-plus travel agencies are in the two hotel zones, el centro and Avenida López Mateos Sur, on the city's southwest side. Near the Minerva Fountain you'll find **American Express** (✉ Av. Vallarta 2440, ☎ 3/818–2323, 3/818–2325).

Visitor Information

The **Jalisco state tourist offices** have information about Guadalajara and other parts of Mexico. ✉ *Calle Morelos 102, in Plaza Tapatía,* ☎ *3/668–1600, 01–800/363–2200.* ✆ *Weekdays 9–8, weekends 9–1;* ✉ *Palacio de Gobierno.* ✆ *Weekdays 10–3 and 4–8, Sat. 9:30–1.*

Guadalajara has **tourist-information booths** (☎ 3/616–3333, 3/616–3335, ☎ FAX 3/616–3332), open Monday through Saturday 9–7, which are staffed by city tourist police. Locations are downtown in the Plaza Guadalajara, in Los Arcos monument on Avenida Vallarta just east of the Minerva Fountain, in Parque San Francisco, in front of the Instituto Cultural Cabañas, in front of Mercado Libertad, at Vicente Guerrero 233 (open weekdays only), and at the airport. English-language tours can be arranged via written request; fax the request to the Director General de Turismo y Promoción Económica.

7 THE HEARTLAND

Rich with the history of Mexico's revolution, the heartland is a treasury of colonial towns—Guanajuato, Zacatecas, Querétaro, Morelia, and Pátzcuaro, among others—whose residents lead quiet, largely traditional lives. Even in San Miguel de Allende, an American art colony and home to a well-known language institute, women wash their clothes and gossip at the local lavandería as they have for hundreds of years.

Updated by
Gina Hyams

MEXICO'S HEARTLAND, so named for its central position in the country, is known for its well-preserved colonial architecture, its fertile farmland and surrounding mountains, and its leading role in Mexican history, particularly during the War of Independence (1810–21). The Bajío (ba-*hee*-o), as it is also called, corresponds roughly to the states of Guanajuato and parts of Querétaro and Michoacán. In the hills surrounding the cities of Guanajuato, Zacatecas, Querétaro, and San Miguel de Allende, the Spanish found silver in the 1500s, leading them to colonize the area heavily.

Three centuries later, wealthy Creoles (Mexicans of Spanish descent) in Querétaro and San Miguel took the first audacious steps toward independence from Spain. When their clandestine efforts were discovered, two of the early insurgents, Ignacio Allende and Father Miguel Hidalgo, began in earnest the War of Independence.

When Allende and Hidalgo were executed in 1811, another native son, José María Morelos, picked up the independence banner. This mestizo (mixed race) mule skinner–turned–priest–turned–soldier, with his army of 9,000, came close to gaining control of the land before he was killed in 1815. Thirteen years later, the city of Valladolid was renamed Morelia in his honor.

Long after the War of Independence ended in 1821, the cities of the Bajío continued to play a prominent role in Mexico's history. Three major events took place in Querétaro alone: in 1848 the Mexican-American War ended with the signing of the Treaty of Guadalupe Hidalgo; in 1867 Austrian Maximilian of Hapsburg, crowned Emperor of Mexico by Napoleon III of France, was executed in the hills north of town; and in 1917 the Mexican Constitution was signed here.

The heartland honors the events and people that helped shape modern Mexico. In ornate cathedrals or bucolic plazas, down narrow alleyways or atop high hillsides, you'll find monuments—and remnants—of a heroic past. During numerous fiestas, you can savor the region's historic spirit. On a night filled with fireworks, off-key music, and tireless celebrants, it's hard not to be caught up in the vital expression of national pride.

Tourism is welcomed in the heartland, especially in these hard economic times, and, for the most part, it doesn't disrupt the normal routines of residents. Families visit parks for Sunday picnics, youngsters tussle in school courtyards, old men chat in shaded plazas, and Purépecha women in traditional garb sell their wares in crowded *mercados* (markets). Unlike areas where attractions have been specifically designed for tourism, the Bajío relies on its historic ties and the architectural integrity of its cities to appeal to travelers. Although this is an interesting area to tour by car, there is frequent inexpensive bus service from one city to the next throughout the Bajío.

Pleasures and Pastimes

Architecture

Financed largely by the region's fabulously wealthy silver mines, the cities of the heartland are architectural masterpieces full of buildings richly worked with curvaceous lines, human, animal, plant, and geometric motifs, and sculptural depth that accents the play of light and shadow. From the stately, almost European grandeur of Morelia to the steep, labyrinthine allure of Guanajuato and the sandstone pink splendor of Zacatecas, no two towns are alike. San Miguel de Allende's Gothic-style parish church puts a Gallic touch on an otherwise very

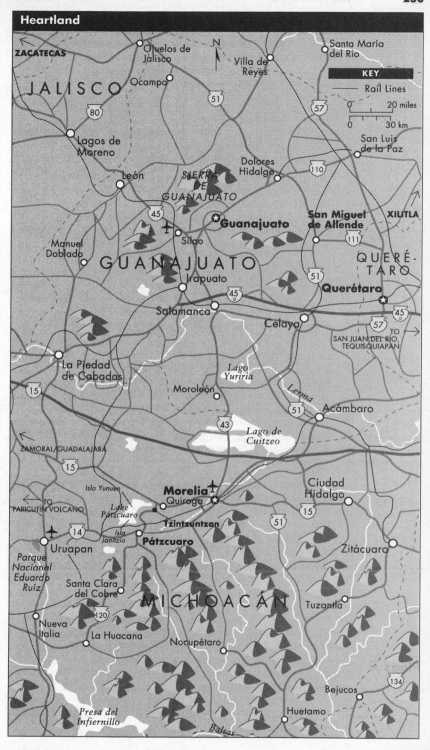

Mexican skyline. And in Pátzcuaro and Querétaro, the ornate 16th-century colonial mansions surrounding the city squares have been converted into hotels and government offices, making their interior patios accessible to the public.

Dining

It's no surprise that culinary tastes vary widely in the heartland, which spans a large area across central Mexico. In the state of Michoacán, Purépecha Indian influences predominate. The tomato-based *sopa tarasca* (a soup with cheese, cream, and tortillas) is one of the best-known regional specialties. Because of the numerous lakes and rivers in the state, several types of freshwater fish are often served in Michoacán restaurants.

At the northern end of the heartland, in Zacatecas, the hearty, meat-eating tastes of the *norteños* (northerners) rule the dinner table. Although beef is the favored dish, other specialties include *asado de boda* (wedding barbecue), pork in a spicy but semisweet sauce. The region is also known for its cheese and wine. And because of San Miguel's expatriate community, the city has a wealth of worthy eateries.

CATEGORY	COST*
$$$$	over $15
$$$	$10–$15
$$	$5–$10
$	under $5

per person for a three-course meal, excluding drinks and service

Hiking and Walking

With its rolling farmland, lofty volcanoes, lakes, and Indian villages, Michoacán is a perfect area for day hikes. Trails near Pátzcuaro wind up to nearby hilltops for great views across town and the surrounding countryside, and in Uruapan—64 km (40 mi) away and 2,000 ft lower in elevation—you can walk along a lush river valley. And no tour of the heartland would be complete without a few days of leisurely strolling on the avenues and back streets of colonial cities and towns.

Lodging

In many of the heartland's colonial cities, restored haciendas of the fabulously rich residents of centuries past make the best lodgings. Often near the center of town, sometimes facing directly onto plazas, some of these mansions date from the 16th century. There are also deluxe modern high-rises and functional, low-cost hotels. Except for five-star hotels, most properties in the region aren't heated; you may want to bring warm, comfortable clothes for indoor wear, or to inquire in advance if heating is important to you. In restored colonial properties, rooms often vary dramatically as to size and furnishings, so if you aren't satisfied with the one you are shown, ask to see another. High season, for the most part, is limited to specific dates surrounding Christmas, Easter, and regional festivals. Most moderate and inexpensive hotels quote prices with 15% value-added tax already included.

CATEGORY	COST*
$$$$	over $90
$$$	$50–$90
$$	$25–$50
$	under $25

All prices are for a standard double room, including 15% tax.

Exploring the Heartland

Many travelers barrel past the heartland to points north or west of Mexico City, but there are plenty of reasons to stop here: browsing in the shops of San Miguel or Guanajuato for bargains in silver and other local crafts, or heading to the state of Michoacán, renowned for its folklore and folk crafts, especially ceramics and lacquerware. Stay longer to linger over the wealth of architectural styles that each of the colonial cities has to offer.

Numbers in the text correspond to numbers in the margin and on the San Miguel de Allende, Guanajuato, Zacatecas, Querétaro, Morelia, and Pátzcuaro maps.

Great Itineraries

If you have only a couple of days to spare, stop in any of several colonial cities for a taste of life in the heartland—each one has its own particular flavor. If you happen to fall under the heartland's peaceful, friendly spell, you'll want a week to 10 days to give yourself time to drink in the atmosphere of two or three of the region's cities.

IF YOU HAVE 3 DAYS

Head to **Guanajuato** ⑫–㉒ (365 km [226 mi] from Mexico City), the most architecturally dramatic of the heartland cities. Make a day trip from here to the picturesque town of **San Miguel de Allende** ①–⑪, 90 minutes away by car or bus, to shop for crafts.

Another option is to go from Mexico City to the Michoacán capital of **Morelia** ㊵–㊾ (about four hours by car) and spend a day taking in its stately architecture and café-lined plaza. The next day, drive on to **Pátzcuaro** ㊿–㊽, set among volcanoes in the center of Purépecha Indian country. Spend the morning in the bustling market or strolling in the surrounding countryside before making a late-afternoon return to Mexico City.

IF YOU HAVE 5 DAYS

Make **Guanajuato** ⑫–㉒ your base and allow an extra day to see its churches and museums—perhaps even the gruesome Mummy Museum. Stop off at the town of Dolores Hidalgo, home of Mexican independence, on your way to a day of shopping in San Miguel. Overnight in San Miguel and the next morning head for **Querétaro** ㉜–㊴, 63 km (39 mi) away. This quiet colonial city is considered the capital of the Bajío. After a night in a downtown hotel, return to Mexico City (three hours) or to the airport outside Guanajuato (2½ hours).

If you decide to spend several days in Michoacán, you can easily fill your time exploring the state's colonial towns and enjoying the lush, mountainous countryside. After three days in **Morelia** ㊵–㊾ and **Pátzcuaro** ㊿–㊽, take a day trip to explore the crater on an extinct volcano in **San Juan Parangaricútiro** or the ruins of an ancient Purépecha Indian capital, **Tzintzuntzan** (both are easy day trips from Pátzcuaro), before returning on the final day to Morelia and Mexico City.

IF YOU HAVE 7 DAYS

From your base in **Guanajuato** ⑫–㉒, consider adding to the first of the five-day itineraries a round-trip flight from León's Guanajuato International Airport to **Zacatecas** ㉓–㉛. This would give you a day and a half to explore the northern colonial mining city. Because it lies off the main tourist track, Zacatecas has a refreshingly unself-conscious mood. Another possibility for a week in the heartland would be to make a loop from Mexico City that includes both Morelia and Guanajuato. You'd have time for leisurely side trips to **Pátzcuaro** ㊿–㊽ and **San Miguel de Allende** ①–⑪ and a stop in **Querétaro** ㉜–㊴. When in Pátzcuaro, be sure to take a boat out to the island town of **Janitzio** on nearby Lake Pátzcuaro, home of Mexico's most famous Day of the Dead festival (lasting up to two days), or to the island of **Yunuen,** which isn't as yet besieged by tourists.

When to Tour the Heartland

One of the most pleasing aspects of the heartland is its superb climate—it rarely gets overly hot, even in the middle of summer, and although winter days can get nippy, especially in northern Zacatecas, they are generally temperate. Average temperatures in the southern city of Morelia range from 20°C (68°F) in May to just under 10°C (49°F) in January. Zacatecas is more extreme, with winter temperatures as low as 0°C (32°F) and snow flurries every several years, and summer highs of 28°C–30°C (81°F–85°F). Nights are cool all year in most of the region's cities. The rainy season across the heartland hits between June and October and is generally strongest in July and August.

Consider going to the heartland for cultural festivals or religious events: in October Guanajuato's three-week-long International Cervantes Festival, which brings actors, musicians, painters, and hundreds of thousands of visitors to town; in late November San Miguel's Jazz Festival International; and November 1–2 on the island of Janítzio, where local Purépecha (also called Tarascan) Indians hold a Day of the Dead in honor of their ancestors. Of ecological interest is the arrival of millions of monarch butterflies near Morelia between early November and early March.

SAN MIGUEL DE ALLENDE

San Miguel de Allende first began luring foreigners in the late 1930s when American Stirling Dickinson and prominent local residents founded an art school in this mountainous settlement. The school, now called the Instituto Allende, has grown in stature over the years—as has the city's reputation as a writers' and artists' colony. Walk down any cobblestone street and you're likely to see residents of a variety of national origins. Some come to study at the Instituto Allende or the Academia Hispano-Americana, some to escape the harsh northern winters, and still others to retire.

Cultural offerings in this town of about 110,000 reflect its large American and Canadian community. There are literary readings, art shows, a yearly jazz festival, psychic fairs, aerobics and past-life regression classes, and a lending library. International influence notwithstanding, San Miguel, declared a national monument in 1926, retains its Mexican characteristics. Wandering down streets lined with 18th-century mansions, you'll also discover fountains, monuments, and churches—all reminders of the city's illustrious, and sometimes notorious, past. The onetime headquarters of the Spanish Inquisition in New Spain, for example, is located at the corner of Calles Hernández Macías and Pila Seca. The former Inquisition jail stands across the way. Independence Day is celebrated with exceptional fervor in San Miguel, with fireworks, dances, and parades September 15 and 16, and bullfights and cultural events for the remainder of the month, including the running of the bulls.

Exploring San Miguel de Allende

You'll find most of San Miguel's sights in a cluster downtown, which you can visit in a couple of hours.

A Good Walk

Begin at the main plaza, otherwise known as **El Jardín** ①. After you get a feel for the square, stop into **La Parroquia** ②, the sandstone church on its south side. Three blocks northeast of La Parroquia (take Calle San Francisco, on the north side of El Jardín, to Calle Juárez) is the **Iglesia de San Francisco** ③, with a fine churrigueresque (heavily ornamented) facade. Take a few steps north on Calle Juárez to Calle

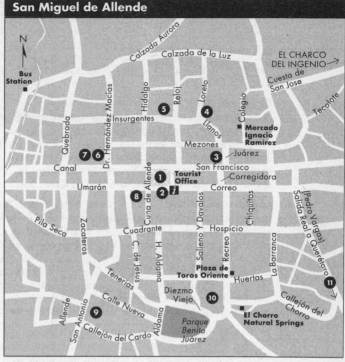

San Miguel de Allende

Mesones, then east to Calle Colegio, where the colorful **Mercado Ig-nacio Ramírez** (☞ Markets *in* Shopping, *below*) occupies a cavernous structure off the west side of the street. The dome of the **Oratorio de San Felipe Neri** ④ is visible just before the market.

A block west of the church on Calle Insurgentes, **La Biblioteca Públi-ca** ⑤ is a great place to catch up on town events. Continue west from the library two blocks to Calle Hernández Macías, then head south to the **Bellas Artes** ⑥ cultural center at No. 75 and the ornate **Iglesia de la Concepción** ⑦ behind it. Take Hernández Macías south for a block and turn left on Calle Umarán to reach the **Casa de Ignacio Allende** ⑧, birthplace of the Mexican national hero. You've circled back to the southwest corner of El Jardín.

After making your way around the center of town, consider a leisurely stroll to sights a bit farther afield. From the south side of the plaza (by La Parroquia), head west four blocks on Calle Umarán until you reach Calle Zacateros. Turn south on this narrow cobblestone street for some of the town's most interesting crafts shops—stocked with every-thing from silver jewelry to Mexican ceremonial masks.

Past the shops, Calle Zacateros becomes Ancha de San Antonio. On your left at No. 20 is the renowned **Instituto Allende** ⑨, where many of San Miguel's foreign visitors come to study. From the institute, continue south on Ancha de San Antonio until you reach Callejón del Cardo on your left. Continue past St. Paul's Episcopal Church, an expat house of worship, until you arrive at the cobblestone Calle Aldama on your left. Head downhill and walk briefly through a neighborhood of whitewashed houses before reaching the north en-trance to the 5-acre Parque Benito Juárez, an oasis of evergreens, palm trees, and gardens.

From the north edge of the park, follow Calle Diezmo Viejo to the terra-cotta–color mansion known as La Huerta Santa Elena. From here turn left and walk one block uphill to the **Lavandería** ⑩, San Miguel's out-door laundry and a favorite gathering spot for local women. Calle Recreo, above the Lavandería, heads north back toward the plaza: fol-low Recreo until reaching Calle Correo, turn left, and walk three blocks to return to El Jardín.

Sights to See

⑥ **Bellas Artes.** This impressive cloister across the street from the U.S. Con-sulate was once the Royal Convent of the Conception. Since 1938 it has been an institute for the study of music, dance, and the visual arts. There are rotating exhibits and a cafeteria on the patio. A bulletin board at the entrance lists cultural events. ⊠ *Calle Hernández Macías 75,* ☎ *4/152–0289.* ☞ *Free.* ۰ *Mon.–Sat. 9–8, Sun. 10–2.*

⑤ **La Biblioteca Pública.** Notices—about such things as literary readings or yoga and aerobics classes—are posted on the bulletin board in the entranceway to the library. There is a lovely courtyard café inside, as well as the offices of the English-language newspaper *Atención San Miguel* and reading rooms with back issues of popular publications and books in English. It's a great place to take a breather from sight-seeing. On Sunday a two-hour house-and-garden tour (about $15) of San Miguel leaves the library at noon. ⊠ *Calle Insurgentes 25,* ☎ *4/152–0293,* 𝔽𝔸𝕏 *4/152–3770.* ۰ *Weekdays 10–2 and 4–7, Sat. 10–2.*

⑧ **Casa de Ignacio Allende.** Now housing a museum and gallery, this is the birthplace of Ignacio Allende, one of Mexico's great independence heroes. Allende was a Creole aristocrat who, along with Father Miguel Hidalgo, plotted in the early 1800s to overthrow the Spanish regime. At clandestine meetings held in San Miguel and nearby Querétaro, the two discussed strategies, organized an army, gathered weapons, and enlisted the support of clerics for the struggle ahead.

Spanish Royalists learned of their plot and began arresting conspira-tors in Querétaro on September 13, 1810. Allende and Hidalgo received word of these actions and hastened their plans. At dawn on Septem-ber 16, they rang out the cry for independence, and the fighting began. Allende was captured and executed by the Royalists the following year. As a tribute to his brave efforts, San Miguel El Grande was re-named San Miguel de Allende in the 20th century. ⊠ *Calle Cuna de Allende 1,* ☎ *4/152–2499.* ☞ *$2.* ۰ *Tues.–Sun. 10–4.*

El Charco del Ingenio. Founded in 1991 northeast of the city center, San Miguel's botanical garden is an enjoyable place to walk, particu-larly in the early morning or late afternoon. Its five-odd miles of path-ways wind past more than 1,500 species of cacti and succulents. ⊠ *1½ km (1 mi) northeast of El Jardín (*☞ *below); signs point the way off Cuesta de San Jose.* ☞ *$1.* ۰ *Sunrise–sunset.*

⑦ **Iglesia de la Concepción.** Just behind the Bellas Artes cultural center, this church has one of the largest domes in Mexico. The two-story dome (completed in 1891) and the elegant Corinthian columns and pilasters gracing its drum are said to have been inspired by the dome of the Hôtel des Invalides in Paris. Ceferino Gutiérrez (of La Parroquia fame) is cred-ited with its design. ⊠ *Calle Canal between Calles Hernández Macías and Zacateros.*

③ **Iglesia de San Francisco.** The San Francisco Church has one of the finest churrigueresque facades in the state of Guanajuato. This term for the style refers to José Churriguera, a 17th-century (Baroque) Spanish ar-chitect, noted for his extravagant surface decoration. Built in the late

18th century, it was financed by donations from wealthy patrons and by revenue from bullfights. Topping the elaborately carved exterior is the image of Saint Francis of Assisi. Below, along with a crucifix, are sculptures of Saint John and Our Lady of Sorrows. ⊠ *Calle Juárez between Calles San Francisco and Mesones.*

❾ Instituto Allende. The school is set in the former country estate of the Count of Canal. Since its founding in 1951, thousands of students from around the world have come to learn Spanish and to take classes in social studies and the arts here. Courses last from a couple of weeks to a month or longer. Lush with bougainvillea, rosebushes, and ivy vines, the grounds provide a quiet refuge for students and visitors alike. ⊠ *Ancha de San Antonio 20,* ☎ *4/152–0190,* ℻ *4/152–4538.* ☉ *Weekdays 8–6, Sat. 9–1.*

❶ El Jardín (The Garden). The heart of San Miguel is the plaza commonly known as El Jardín. Seated on one of its wrought-iron benches, you'll quickly get a feel for the town: old men with canes exchange tales, young lovers smooch, fruit vendors hawk their wares, and bells from nearby La Parroquia pierce the thin mountain air at each quarter hour. At dusk thousands of grackles make a fantastic ruckus as they return to roost in the laurel trees. ⊠ *Bounded by Calle Correo on the south, Calle San Francisco on the north, Portal Allende on the west, and Portal Guadalupe on the east.*

NEED A BREAK? On the southwest corner of the main plaza is **Café del Jardín** (⊠ Portal Allende 2, ☎ 4/152–5006). This unassuming little café has excellent coffee, cappuccino, hot chocolate, and, in the evening, pizza. Breakfasts are tasty and inexpensive. There's friendly service and, best of all—it's that American influence—free coffee refills.

❿ Lavandería. At this outdoor public laundry—a collection of red cement tubs set above Parque Benito Juárez—local women gather daily to wash clothes and chat as their predecessors have done for centuries. Although some women claim to have more-efficient washing facilities at home, the lure of the spring-fed troughs—not to mention the chance to catch up on the news—brings them to this shaded courtyard. ⊠ *Calle Diezmo Viejo at Calle Recreo.*

⓫ El Mirador. Climb El Mirador (The Lookout) for a panorama of the city, mountains, and reservoir below. The vista is great at sunset, and chances are you won't be alone. Locals and tourists like to join Ignacio Allende, whose bronze image commands this spot. ⊠ *1 block before town turn right off Calle Recreo onto Calle Hospicio, follow Hospicio 3 blocks to Calle Pedro Vargas, turn right, and head uphill to the overlook.*

❹ Oratorio de San Felipe Neri. Built by local Indians in 1712, the original chapel can still be glimpsed in the eastern facade, made of pink stone and adorned with a figure of Our Lady of Solitude. The newer, southern front was built in an ornate Baroque style. In 1734 the wealthy Count of Canal paid for an addition to the Oratorio. His **Templo de Santa Casa de Loreto,** dedicated to the Virgin of Loreto, is just behind the Oratorio. Its main entrance, now blocked by a grille, is on the Oratorio's left rear side. Peer through the grille to see the heavily gilded altars and effigies of the count and his wife, under which they are buried. ⊠ *Calles Insurgentes and Loreto.*

❷ La Parroquia. This towering Gothic Revival parish church, made of local *cantera* sandstone, was designed in the late 19th century by self-trained Indian mason Ceferino Gutiérrez, who sketched his designs in the sand with a stick. Gutiérrez was purportedly inspired by postcards of European Gothic cathedrals. Since the postcards gave no hint of what the back of those cathedrals looked like, the posterior of La Parroquia was done in quintessential Mexican style.

La Parroquia still functions as a house of worship, although its interior has been changed over the years. Gilded wood altars, for example, were replaced with neoclassical stone altars. The original bell, cast in 1732, still calls parishioners to mass several times daily. ⊠ *South side of El Jardín on Calle Correo.*

Dining

For its size, San Miguel has a surprisingly large number of international restaurants. The recent influx of Americans and Canadians has given rise to new Tex-Mex and health-food places. A European influence has contributed to variations on French, Italian, and Spanish themes.

$$$ ✕ **La Antigua Restaurant y Tapa Bar.** A cheerful room with fewer than a dozen tables and a long, polished wood bar, La Antigua puts you in the mood for a large variety of tapas with its European café furniture and Spanish bolero music. Among its specialties are *queso antiguo* (baked cheese with chilies), *chisterra* (a sliced and fried Spanish-style sausage), *camarones con tocineta* (jumbo shrimp fried with bacon), and *pulpo antiguo* (octopus sautéed in garlic and herbs). ⊠ *Calle Canal 9,* ☎ *4/152–2586. AE, MC, V.*

$$$ ✕ **Bugambilia.** Founded in 1945, Mercedes Arteaga Tovar's restaurant
★ has a well-earned reputation for serving fine traditional Mexican cuisine. Try such classic specialties as *pollo en pulque* (chicken stewed in pulque—the fermented juice of the agave plant) and *tinga* (shredded pork loin, chorizo, and potatoes in a tomato, onion, and chipotle chili sauce). The candlelit, tree-filled colonial courtyard and live classical guitarist make for a romantic setting. ⊠ *Calle Hidalgo 42,* ☎ *4/152–0127. AE, MC, V.*

$$ ✕ **Fonda Mesón de San José.** On an umbrella-shaded cobblestone
★ patio inside a complex of small shops, this well-established restaurant serves German, Mexican, and vegetarian dishes. Locals wax enthusiastic about owner-chef Angela Merkel's roulade, potato pancakes, and German chocolate cake, as well as her *chile en nogada*, a mild chili stuffed with ground meat and raisins and topped with cream sauce and pomegranate seeds. The sunny patio is great for lunch, less popular for dinner. ⊠ *Calle Mesones 38,* ☎ *4/152–3848. MC, V.*

$$ ✕ **Mama Mia.** If you want a change from Mexican food you will enjoy Mama Mia's satisfying assortment of pastas and pizzas. Try the house special: fettuccine Alex, with white wine, ham, cream, and mushrooms. Folk musicians entertain on the lush outdoor patio come dusk. ⊠ *Calle Umarán 8,* ☎ *4/152–2063. AE, MC, V.*

$$ ✕ **Rincón Español.** The soft pink walls of this pleasant Spanish restaurant are covered with reproductions of the works of famous Spanish artists, and its nickname, La Casa de la Paella, reveals its specialty. Not a little of Rincón's charm derives from the evening guitar music and flamenco dancing, pleasing adjuncts to dessert. ⊠ *Calle Correo 29,* ☎ *4/152–2984. MC, V.*

$ ✕ **La Buena Vida.** Don't miss this fabulous bakery and tiny coffee shop and its mouthwatering orange scones, chocolate-chip cookies, and light breakfasts. If the few patio tables are full, take your treats to the plaza. ⊠ *Hernández Macías 72–5,* ☎ *4/152–2211. No credit cards.*

$ ✕ **Café de la Parroquia.** Stop in for breakfast or lunch, both served either outside on the charming patio or indoors. Economical daily lunch menus include soup, main dish, beverage, dessert, and coffee. ⊠ *Calle Jesús 11,* ☎ *4/152–3161. No credit cards. Closed Mon. No dinner.*

Lodging

San Miguel has a wide selection of lodging, from cozy bed-and-breakfasts to elegant all-suites properties. Rooms fill up quickly during summer and winter seasons, when northern tourists migrate here in droves. Make reservations several months in advance if you plan to visit at these times or during the September Independence Day festivities.

$$$$ ★ 🏨 **Casa de Sierra Nevada.** Built in 1580 as the residence of the archbishop of Guanajuato, this elegant country-style inn still attracts ambassadors, diplomats, film stars, and other luminaries; children under 16 aren't admitted, however. Its complex of eight colonial buildings, all located within a few blocks of the main plaza, contains 20 individually decorated suites and 17 deluxe rooms. Lace curtains, handwoven rugs, and chandeliers adorn some rooms; fireplaces, cozy private terraces, and skylights enhance others. The international cuisine at the hotel's original restaurant is delicately prepared and beautifully presented. Jazz enlivens the formal dining room Wednesday evenings, and classical duets play during weekend lunch. In 1997, the hotel opened **Casa de Sierra Nevada en el Parque** (✉ Santa Elena 2), an exquisitely restored 18th-century ex-hacienda with just five guest rooms. Its restaurant serves refined versions of traditional Mexican dishes and has a wonderful view of Parque Benito Juárez. ✉ *Calle Hospicio 35, 37700,* ☎ *4/152–7040,* FAX *4/152–2337. 17 rooms, 20 suites. 2 restaurants, bar, pool, massage, spa, horseback riding. AE, MC, V.* ❧

$$$$ 🏨 **La Puertecita Boutique Hotel.** Set in a secluded, wooded canyon in the tony Atascadero neighborhood, this luxury no-smoking hotel has uniquely decorated rooms with rustic Mexican furnishings, domed vaulted ceilings, and in many cases private patios, fireplaces, and bathrooms with small indoor gardens. Customized vacation packages including room, meals, mountain biking, horseback riding, hot-springs excursions, and yoga, cooking, art, or Spanish classes are available. The hotel has a membership at Club Malanquin so guests can use the golf and tennis facilities. ✉ *Santo Domingo 75, 37740,* ☎ *4/152–5011, 4/152–2250,* FAX *4/152–5505. 18 rooms, 6 suites. Restaurant, bar, 2 pools, massage, billiards. AE, MC, V.* ❧

$$$$ 🏨 **Villa Jacaranda.** Near the Parque Benito Juárez, the Villa Jacaranda has a full range of amenities. Rooms, although unimaginatively decorated, have space heaters (not something to be taken for granted in these parts) and cable TV. The hotel's Cine/Bar shows American movies daily at 7:30 PM and live sports events on a giant screen. The price of admission—roughly $4.50—includes a drink. The restaurant serves international and Mexican cuisine in the homey dining room or in a stained-glass gazebo, and there's a delicious Sunday champagne brunch for about $8. ✉ *Calle Aldama 53, 37700,* ☎ *4/152–1015, 4/152–0811, 800/310–9688,* FAX *4/152–0883. 5 rooms, 11 suites. Restaurant, bar, hot tub, cinema, free parking. AE, MC, V.* ❧

$$$ 🏨 **Casa Carmen.** Run by a friendly San Miguel family, this pension is an oasis of peace in the center of town. The 200-year-old house two blocks from El Jardín has large, clean rooms, each with desk or writing table and portable gas heater, and two small patios. The large suite on the top floor has a great view of the city for the same price, but is often booked far in advance. Rates include breakfast and lunch. ✉ *Calle Correo 31, 37700,* ☎ *4/152–0844. 12 rooms. Dining room. No credit cards.*

$$$ ★ 🏨 **Casa Luna.** In a restored 300-year-old Spanish colonial house, this lovely B&B has 2-ft-thick walls, 20-ft-high ceilings, and tranquil fountain- and flower-filled patios. The luxurious rooms have antiques, fireplaces, featherbeds, and bathtubs. The rooftop honor bar is spectacular at night, lighted by some two dozen miniature tin star lights. A three-night minimum stay is required; children are allowed only when the entire house is rented to one party. ⊠ *Pila Seca 11, 37700,* ☎ ℻ *4/152–1117. 8 rooms, 1 suite. Dining room. AE, MC, V.*

$$$ 🖬 **Villa Mirasol.** Each of this lodge's rooms is tastefully decorated with original prints, oil paintings, pastels, or small sculptures. Most rooms are flooded with sunlight during the day. All have either a private or shared terrace. In 1999, the owner opened a second branch in a cozy house near the Mercado Ignacio Ramírez (⊠ Callejón del Pueblito 4–A). Both locations are on quiet streets, each about a 10-minute walk from the main plaza. Villa Mirasol includes in its price a rich breakfast. Children under age 12 aren't permitted. ⊠ *Pila Seca 35 (Apdo. 409), 37700,* ☎ *4/152–6685, 4/154–5113,* ℻ *4/152–1564. 13 rooms, 6 suites. Dining room. AE, MC, V.* ☜

$$ 🖬 **La Mansión del Bosque.** On a quiet side street across from the Parque Benito Juárez, this cozy guest house caters to long-term guests, especially in winter. The hotel, which operates on a Modified American Plan that includes breakfast and dinner, is an attractive red-stucco building of many levels, resembling a Taos pueblo dwelling. Some rooms have motel-like furnishings and day beds, others are more pleasingly decorated. Many have working fireplaces; all have private or shared plant-filled terraces. The lounge invites mingling with other guests and has books, magazines, cable TV, and a phone for long-distance calls. ⊠ *Calle Aldama 65, 37700,* ☎ ℻ *4/152–0277. 23 rooms. Restaurant, bar, lounge. No credit cards.*

$$ 🖬 **Posada de las Monjas.** This 19th-century inn has been operating as a hotel for more than 50 years. Rooms are simply furnished in a colonial style. Some in the old wing are uncomfortably dark and cramped. The rooftop public terrace has tables and lounge chairs and offers commanding views of mountains and city. Some rooms have fireplaces, and there's a communal TV in the lobby, which looks like a formal Mexican living room. ⊠ *Calle Canal 37, 37700,* ☎ *4/152–0171,* ℻ *4/152–6227. 65 rooms. Restaurant, bar, laundry service, free parking. AE, MC, V.*

$$ 🖬 **Quinta Loreto.** Clean, plain, comfortable rooms, shady and pleasantly kept grounds, and excellent *comida casera* (home cooking) make this inexpensive hotel a favorite with snowbirds and other San Miguel aficionados. Each room has a gas heater, TV, and phone. There is a dilapidated tennis court and an unheated pool, which is uninvitingly dirty. The hotel is about a 10-minute walk north of the main plaza, near the market. Many nonguests take their meals in the unpretentious dining room, especially the diet-defying *comida corrida* (fixed-menu lunch), served daily. ⊠ *Calle Loreto 15, 37700,* ☎ *4/152–0042,* ℻ *4/152–3616. 40 rooms. Restaurant, pool, tennis court. AE, MC, V.*

Nightlife and the Arts

The Arts

San Miguel, long known as an artists' colony, continues to nurture that image today. Galleries, museums, and arty shops line the streets near El Jardín, and two government-run salons—at **Bellas Artes** and **Instituto Allende** (☞ Sights to See *in* Exploring San Miguel de Allende, *above*, for both)—feature the work of Mexican artists. For a sampling of both regional and international talent, visit **Galería San Miguel** (⊠ Plaza Principal 14, ☎ 4/152–0454, 4/152–1046), **Galería Atenea** (⊠ Calle Cuna de Allende 15, ☎ 4/152–0785), **Kligerman Gallery** (⊠ Calle San Francisco 11, ☎ 4/152–0951), **Galería del Pueblo** (⊠ Calle Correo 12A, ☎ 4/152–1448), **Galería Duo Duo** (⊠ Pila Seca 3, ☎ 4/152–6211), or **Galería de Arte Contemporáneo** (⊠ Cuadrante 2-A, ☎ 4/154–4594). Most close weekdays between 2 and 4 and are open Sunday 10 or 11 to 2 or 3.

For more than 20 years, San Miguel has played host to the world-class **Festival de Musica de Camara** in August, a feast of classical chamber music that in past years has included the illustrious Tokyo String Quartet. The **Jazz Festival International** takes place around the last week in November. There is live jazz, workshops, and after-hour jam sessions. Tickets may be purchased individually or for the series. Call the tourist office (☞ Contacts and Resources *in* San Miguel de Allende A to Z, *below*) for dates and details.

Nightlife

On most evenings in San Miguel you can readily satisfy a whim for a literary reading, an American movie, a theatrical production, or a turn on a disco dance floor. The most up-to-date listings of events can be found in the English-language paper *Atención San Miguel,* published every Sunday. The bulletin board at the public library (⊠ Calle Insurgentes 25) is also a good source of current events.

La Fragua (⊠ Calle Cuna de Allende 3, ☎ 4/152–1144), just a couple of doors off El Jardín, often has traditional Mexican soloists or bands. Mobbed with upscale Mexican twentysomethings on the weekends, **El Grito** (⊠ Calle Umarán 15, ☎ 4/152–0048) tries hard to imitate a trendy New York nightclub—complete with a doorman who decides who's fashionable enough to get in. **Mama Mia** (⊠ Calle Umarán 8, ☎ 4/152–2063) offers everything from Peruvian folk music, classical guitar, and flamenco to salsa and rock. You can hear live music at **Pancho and Lefty's** (⊠ Calle Mesones 99, ☎ 4/152–1958), from rock, jazz, or blues bands, depending on the night. Jazz and blues reign every night at **Tío Lucas** (⊠ Calle Mesones 103, ☎ 4/152–4996), a favorite hangout of Instituto Allende art students.

Outdoor Activities and Sports

Taboada (⊠ Dolores Hidalgo Hwy., Km 8) has three outdoor geothermally heated pools, one of which is Olympic-size and good for doing laps. They are open to the public for $3.50; closed Tuesday. The more exclusive **Hotel Hacienda Taboada** (⊠ Dolores Hidalgo Hwy., Km 8, ☎ 4/152–0888, 4/152–0850, ℻ 4/152–1798) has several geothermal pools, manicured grounds, and tennis courts. It's open to the public for about $15, which includes lunch; closed Wednesday. The **Club de Golf Malanquin** (⊠ Celaya Hwy., Km 3, ☎ 4/152–0516) has a heated pool, steam baths, tennis courts, and nine holes of golf, all of which are open to the public for a guest fee of $15 on weekdays or $20 on weekends; it's closed Monday.

Ballooning

Gone with the Wind Balloon Adventures (⊠ Calle Recreo 68, ☎ 4/152–6735) offers hot-air balloon rides over town and the surrounding countryside with licensed/certified pilots from Napa Valley, California. The one-hour flights depart at 6 or 7 AM, depending on the season. The $125 cost includes breakfast upon landing.

Biking

Aventuras San Miguel (⊠ Calle Recreo 10, ☎ ℻ 4/152–6406) rents bicycles at reasonable prices. **Bici-Burro** (⊠ Calle Hospicio 1, csq. Barranca, ☎ 4/152–1526) rents and services bikes for exploring San Miguel and environs.

Horseback Riding

Aventuras San Miguel (☞ Biking, *above*) rents horses at reasonable rates. The equestrian center of the **Casa de Sierra Nevada** (☞ Lodging, *above*) offers riding lessons, carriage rides, and horse rental at its 500-acre ranch for about $30 per hour.

Spectator Sports

To witness the pageantry of a traditional Mexican bullfight, go to the **Plaza de Toros Oriente** (⊠ off Calle Recreo), which has events several times a year. The most important contest takes place in the last week of September during *la fiesta de San Miguel*. Call the tourist office (☞ Contacts and Resources *in* San Miguel de Allende A to Z, *below*) for more information.

Shopping

For centuries San Miguel's artisans have been creating crafts ranging from straw products to metalwork. Although some boutiques in town may be a bit pricey, you can find good buys on silver, brass, tin, woven-cotton goods, and folk art. Store hours tend to be erratic, but most stores open daily at around 9, shut their doors for the traditional afternoon siesta (2 to 4 or 5), then reopen in the afternoon until 7 or 8, and open for just a half day on Sunday. Most San Miguel shops accept MasterCard and Visa.

Markets

Mercado Ignacio Ramírez, a traditional Mexican covered market off Calle Colegio, one block north of Calle Mesones, is a colorful jumble of fresh fruits and vegetables, flowers, bloody butchers' counters, inexpensive plastic toys, taco stands, and Mexican-made cassettes. Spilling out for several blocks behind the Mercado Ignacio Ramírez, the **Mercado de Artesanías** (artisans' market) is where you'll find vendors of local work—glass, tin, and papier mâché—as well as some of the best prices on silver jewelry in town.

Specialty Shops

FOLK ART

Artes de México (⊠ Calzada Aurora 47, at Dolores Hidalgo exit, ☎ 4/152–0764) has been producing and selling traditional crafts, including furniture, metalwork, and ceramics, for more than 40 years. Although the inventory at the **Casa Maxwell** (⊠ Calle Canal 14, ☎ 4/152–0247) has slipped in quality, there is still a reasonable selection of folk art. **La Calaca** (⊠ Calle Mesones 93, ☎ 4/152–3954) focuses on quality antique folk art from the Americas, mainly Mexico, Guatemala, and Peru. **Tonatiu Metzli** (⊠ Calle Juárez 7, ☎ 4/152–0869) has a wonderful selection of both antique and contemporary masks from all over Mexico. **Veryka** (⊠ Zacateros 6-A, ☎ 4/152–2114), whose emphasis is on Latin American folk art, has a particularly fine selection of *muertos* (skeleton figurines for the Day of the Dead) from Puebla. **La Guadalupana** (⊠ Calle Codo 1B, ☎ no phone) sells all manner of items adorned with images of Mexico's beloved Virgin of Guadalupe—from temporary tattoos to coffee mugs. **Talisman Boutique** (⊠ Calle Mesones 38, ☎ 4/152–2593) sells beautiful embroidered *huipiles* (tunics or blouses) from southern Mexico and Guatemala.

HOUSEWARES

Casa Canal (⊠ Calle Canal 3, ☎ 4/152–0479), in a beautiful old hacienda, sells new furniture, much of it in traditional styles. **Casa María Luisa** (⊠ Calle Canal 40, ☎ 4/152–0130) has a fantastic jumble of furniture, glassware, wall hangings, and lamps, as well as an enormous selection of collectibles made of tin, iron, wood, and glass. **Casa Vieja** (⊠ Calle Mesones 83, ☎ 4/152–1284) has tons of glassware and ceramics, decorative and functional housewares, picture frames, furniture, and more. **México Lindo** (⊠ Calle Mesones 85, ☎ 4/152–0730) sells a good selection of hand-painted tiles and ceramics from Dolores Hidalgo. **La Zandunga** (⊠ Calle Hernández Macías 129, ☎ 4/152–4608) sells high-quality, 100% wool rugs from Oaxaca.

MÉXICO: HECHO A MANO

HANDMADE IN MEXICO: Some of the world's finest *artesanías* (handicrafts) come from this country. Artisanal work is varied, original, colorful, and inexpensive, and it supports millions of families who are carrying on ancient and more recent traditions. Although cheap, shoddy items masquerading as "native crafts" are certainly common, careful shoppers who take their time can come away with real works of folk art. Also keep in mind that many items are exempt from duty.

The crafts to look for are ceramics, woodwork, lacquerware, leather, weaving and textiles, and silver, gold, and semiprecious stone jewelry. Each region has its specialty. Cities that are noted for the quality of their crafts are Puebla (Chapter 2); Nogales in Sonora (Chapter 4); Guadalajara, Tlaquepaque, and Tonalá in Jalisco (Chapter 6); San Miguel de Allende, Guanajuato, and Pátzcuaro in the heartland (Chapter 7); Taxco in Morelos (Chapter 9); Oaxaca City in Oaxaca (Chapter 10); San Cristóbal de las Casas in Chiapas (Chapter 11); and Mérida in Yucatán (Chapter 13).

Ceramics. Talavera-style tiles (blue majolica) and other ceramic ware are at their best in Puebla. Oaxaca state is known for its unglazed, burnished black pottery. Inventive masks and figurines come from Valle de Bravo, Pátzcuaro in the state of Michoacán, Tonalá outside of Guadalajara, Taxco, and Chiapas.

Jewelry. Silver is best in Taxco, San Miguel de Allende, and Oaxaca; be sure purchases are stamped "925," which means 92.5% pure silver. You can find gold filigree in Guanajuato and Oaxaca. Oaxaca and Chiapas are also known for their amber, but be aware that much of what is sold as amber is in fact glass or plastic. Good rules of thumb: don't buy amber off the street; and if it seems like

a great bargain, it's probably fake. For semiprecious stones, go to jewelers' shops in Puebla and Querétaro. Coral jewelry is sold in the Yucatán and other coastal areas, but because of the massive ecological damage caused by coral harvesting, the practice around it is environmentally unsensible.

Leather. The key places to find quality leatherwork are Guadalajara, Oaxaca (for sandals), Chiapas (for belts and purses), and the Yucatán (for bags).

Metalwork. Look for copper in Santa Clara del Cobre in Michoacán, and tin in San Miguel de Allende and Oaxaca.

Weavings and Textiles. Fabric work is quite varied: you'll find *rebozos* (shawls) and blankets around Oaxaca, Guadalajara, Jalapa, and Pátzcuaro; *huipiles* (heavily embroidered tunics worn by Indian women) and other embroidered clothing in Michoacán, Oaxaca state, Chiapas, and the Yucatán; masterfully woven rugs, some colored with natural dyes, in Oaxaca; hammocks and baskets in Oaxaca and the Yucatán; lace in the colonial cities of the heartland area; *guayaberas* (comfortable, embroidered and/or pleated men's dress shirts, now usually mass-produced) along the Gulf coast; and reed mats in Oaxaca and Valle de Bravo. The Mezquital region east of Querétaro can also be rewarding, as can shopping for Huichol Indian yarn paintings and embroidery near Puerto Vallarta.

Woodwork. Look for masks in Mexico City; *alebrijes* (painted wooden animals) in Oaxaca; furniture in Cuernavaca, Guadalajara, San Miguel de Allende, Querétaro, Tequisquiapan, and Pátzcuaro; lacquerware in Uruapan and Pátzcuaro in Michoacán, Chiapa de Corzo in Chiapas, and Puerto Vallarta for pieces from Olinalá in Guerrero state; and guitars in Paracho, Michoacán.

JEWELRY

Established in 1963, **Joyería David** (⊠ Calle Zacateros 53, ☎ 4/152–0056) has an extensive selection of gold, silver, copper, and brass jewelry, all made on the premises. A number of pieces contain Mexican opals, amethysts, topaz, malachite, and turquoise. The reputable **Beckmann Joyería** (⊠ Calle Hernández Macías 105, ☎ 4/152–1613) designs its own gold and silver pieces. **Platería Cerroblanco** (⊠ Calle Canal 17, ☎ 4/152–0502) creates and crafts its own silver and gold jewelry and will arrange a visit to its *taller* (workshop) on request. **Joyería Precolombina** (⊠ Calle Hidalgo 13, ☎ no phone) sells quality reproductions of pre-Columbian jewelry in silver, copper, and gold.

Side Trip to Dolores Hidalgo

50 km (31 mi) north of San Miguel via Rte. 51.

Dolores Hidalgo played an important role in the fight for independence. It was here, before dawn on September 16, 1810, that Father Miguel Hidalgo—the local priest—gave an impassioned sermon to his clergy that ended with the *grito* (cry), "Viva Ferdinand VII (king of Spain at the time)! Death to bad government!" At 11 PM on September 15, politicians throughout the land repeat a revised version of the grito—"Viva Mexico! Viva Mexico! Viva Mexico!"—signaling the start of Independence Day celebrations. On September 16 (and only on this day), the bell in Hidalgo's parish church is rung.

Casa Hidalgo, the house where Father Hidalgo lived, is now a museum. It contains copies of important letters Hidalgo sent or received, and other independence memorabilia. ⊠ *Calle Morelos 1, ☎ 4/182–0171.* ▩ *About $2, free Sun.* ☉ *Tues.–Sat. 10–5:45, Sun. 10–4:45.*

Dolores Hidalgo is famous for its lovely hand-glazed Talavera-style ceramics, most notably tiles and tableware. There are good prices at the town's many stores and factories. After shopping, head for the plaza for some of the most exotic ice creams you'll taste—flavors such as mole, avocado, beer, and corn. The town is an easy one-hour bus ride from San Miguel de Allende's Central de Autobuses.

San Miguel de Allende A to Z

Arriving and Departing

BY BUS

Daily buses run direct from Mexico City's Central del Norte (North Bus Station) to the Central de Autobuses in San Miguel. Several major lines have frequent service. They include **ETN** (☎ 4/152–0078, 4/152–3104), for which you can buy tickets through The Travel Institute of San Miguel (☞ Guided Tours *in* Contacts and Resources, *below*); **Flecha Amarilla** (☎ 4/152–7323); **Primera Plus** (☎ 4/152–5043); **Herradura de Plata** (☎ 4/152–0725); and **Pegasso Plus** (☎ 4/152–0725). Travel time is about four hours.

BY CAR

Driving time from Mexico City to San Miguel is roughly four hours via Route 57 (to Querétaro) then Route 111. Traveling on Route 45 from Mexico City, a road connecting to Routes 57 and 111 bypasses Querétaro, saving a half hour. Guanajuato is 100 km (62 mi), about 1½ hours, west of San Miguel.

BY PLANE

International airlines that fly into León's Guanajuato International Airport, which is about 1½ hours from San Miguel, include **Aeroméxico** (☎ 47/14–05–74) from Los Angeles; **American** (☎ 47/16–05–02) from

Dallas–Fort Worth; **Continental** (☎ 47/14–71–10) from Houston; and **Mexicana** (☎ 47/13–45–50) from Chicago.

Taxis from León's Guanajuato International Airport to downtown San Miguel take 1½ hours and cost about $60.

Getting Around

San Miguel de Allende is best covered on foot, keeping in mind two pieces of advice. The city is more than a mile above sea level, so you might tire quickly during your first few days here if you aren't accustomed to high altitudes. Streets are paved with rugged cobblestones, and some have no sidewalks. Sturdy footwear, such as athletic or other rubber-sole walking shoes, is recommended.

BY TAXI

You can easily hail a taxi on the street or find one at taxi stands such as **Sitio Allende** in the main plaza (☎ 4/152–0550, 4/152–0192), **Sitio San Francisco** on Calle Mesones (☎ no phone), or **Sitio San Felipe** on Calle Juárez (☎ no phone). Flat rates to the bus terminal, train station, and other parts of the city apply.

Contacts and Resources

BUSINESS SERVICES

La Conexión (✉ Calle Aldama 1, ☎ FAX 4/152–1687, 4/152–1599) has 24-hour answering and fax service, a Mexico address for receiving mail, lockboxes, packing and shipping, e-mail, and other services. **Unísono Net** (✉ Calle Hernández Macías 72B, upstairs, ☎ 4/152–6331, FAX 4/152–4958) charges $6 an hour for Internet access and has PCs and Mac computers available.

CAR RENTAL

Hola Rent a Car (✉ Plaza Principal 2, Int. 5, ☎ 4/152–0198) has a limited selection of manual-transmission compacts available.

CONSULATE

The **U.S. Consulate** (✉ Calle Hernández Macías 72, ☎ 4/152–2357 during office hours, 4/152–0068 and 4/152–0653 for emergencies) is open weekdays 9–1.

EMERGENCIES

Police (☎ 4/152–0022). **Traffic Police** (☎ 4/152–0538). **Fire Department** (☎ 4/152–2888). **Ambulance–Red Cross** (☎ 4/152–4121, 4/152–4225).

Hospital. The staff at **Hospital de la Fé** (✉ Libramiento a Dolores Hidalgo 43, ☎ 4/152–2233, 4/152–2320) can refer you to an English-speaking doctor.

Pharmacies. San Miguel has many pharmacies. American residents recommend **Botica Agundis** (✉ Calle Canal 26, ☎ 4/152–1198), where English speakers are often on hand. It's open daily 10:30 AM–11 PM.

ENGLISH-LANGUAGE BOOKSTORES

El Colibrí (✉ Sollano 30, ☎ 4/152–0751) has a good selection of paperback novels, magazines, and a few art supplies. **Libros el Tecolote** (✉ Calle Jesús 11, ☎ FAX 4/152–7395) has a great selection of new and used books on Mexican art, history, literature, and cooking.

GUIDED TOURS

Aventuras San Miguel (✉ Calle Recreo 10, ☎ FAX 4/152–6406) has off-the-beaten-track mountain-bike treks, "ghost town" trips, even nighttime full-moon excursions. **Colonial México Tours** (✉ Plaza Portal Allende 4, 2nd floor, ☎ FAX 4/152–5794) runs historical tours to Guanajuato, Querétaro, and Dolores Hidalgo. Recommended for local tours

268

Guanajuato

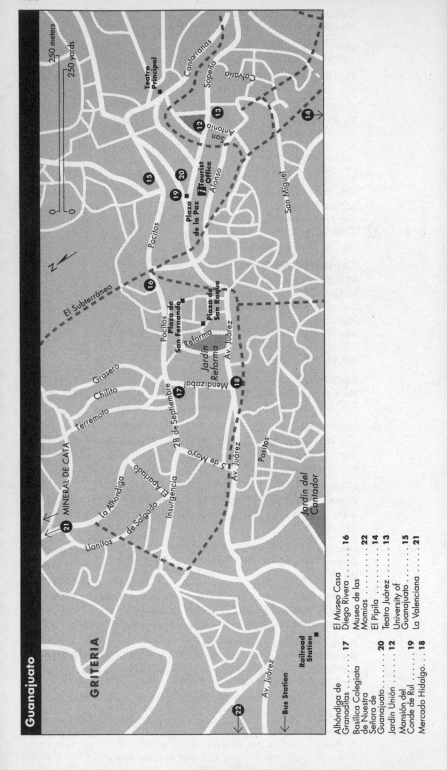

is **The Travel Institute of San Miguel** (✉ Calle Cuna de Allende 11, ☎ 4/152–0078, 4/152–3104, ℻ 4/152–0121).

MONEY EXCHANGE
A better bet for money exchange than the slow-moving bank lines is **Deal Casa de Cambio** (✉ Calles San Francisco 4, Correo 15, or Juárez 27, ☎ 4/152–2932), open weekdays 9–6, Saturday 9–2.

TRAVEL AGENCY
Viajes Vértiz (✉ Calle Hidalgo 1A, ☎ 4/152–1856, 4/152–1695, ℻ 4/152–0499) is the American Express representative.

VISITOR INFORMATION
Delegación de Turismo (✉ southeast corner of El Jardín, in a glassed-in office next to la Terraza restaurant, ☎ 4/152–6565) is open weekdays 10–3 and 5–7, Saturday 10–2.

GUANAJUATO

100 km (62 mi) west of San Miguel de Allende, 365 km (226 mi) northwest of Mexico City.

Once Mexico's most prominent silver-mining city, Guanajuato is a colonial gem, tucked into the mountains at 6,700 ft. This provincial state capital is distinguished by twisting cobblestone alleyways, colorful houses, 15 shaded plazas, and a vast subterranean roadway where a rushing river once coursed. In the center of town is **Alhóndiga de Granaditas,** an 18th-century grain-storage facility that was the site of Mexico's first major victory in its War of Independence from Spain.

The city fills to overflowing in mid-October with the International Cervantes Festival, a three-week celebration of the arts. During the rest of the year, things regain a semblance of normalcy. Students rush to class with books tucked under their arms, women eye fresh produce at the Mercado Hidalgo, and old men utter greetings from behind whitewashed doorways. On weekend nights, *estudiantinas* (student minstrels dressed as medieval troubadours) serenade the public in the city squares.

Exploring Guanajuato

Although Guanajuato's many plazas and labyrinthine streets may seem confusing at first, this is not a bad city in which to get lost. The center is small, and there are wonderful surprises around every corner. Remember that the top of the Alhóndiga (which you can see from many spots in town) points north, and the spires of the Basílica Colegiata Nuestra Señora de Guanajuato, at Plaza de la Paz, point south.

A Good Walk

The tourist office, at Plaza de la Paz 14, is a good place to begin a walking tour. Turn right and walk up Avenida Juárez to reach **Jardín Unión** ⑫, Guanajuato's central square. The ornate **Teatro Juárez** ⑬ is just past the Jardín to your right on Calle Sopeña. The hardy might want to make a detour and take a half-hour climb to **El Pípila** ⑭, a monument to a hero of the War of Independence of 1810 that looms over the center of the city. If you're interested, bear right on Calle Sopeña just past the Teatro Juárez. A sign marked EL PÍPILA will direct you onto Callejón de Calvario, which eventually leads to the hillside memorial.

Head back into town on Calle Cantarranas, a main street that winds down the hill and around the Jardín Unión. Just before Calle Cantarranas changes its name to Calle Pocitos, you'll see the **University of Guanajuato** ⑮. A short way down from where Calle Cantarranas becomes

Calle Pocitos is **El Museo Casa Diego Rivera** ⑯, birthplace of Mexico's famous muralist. Calle Pocitos weaves past more residences and eventually becomes Calle 28 de Septiembre. On the left, just past the junction with Mendizabal, is the **Alhóndiga de Granaditas** ⑰, a former fortress converted into a state museum. Head one block south to return to Avenida Juárez and the glassed-in **Mercado Hidalgo** ⑱.

Turn right on Juárez as you leave the market and continue until the road splits near the Jardín Reforma. Bear left and cut down Calle Reforma, a short alleyway lined with shops. Keep right at the end of the street and you'll come to two pleasant courtyards: Plaza San Roque, which hosts outdoor performances during the Cervantes Festival, and Plaza San Fernando, a shady square where many book fairs are held. This short detour will return you to Avenida Juárez, where it's a slight climb up to Plaza de la Paz, a square built from 1895 to 1898 and surrounded by some of the city's finest colonial buildings, including the 18th-century **Mansión del Conde de Rul** ⑲. The bright-yellow 17th-century Baroque **Basílica Colegiata de Nuestra Señora de Guanajuato** ⑳ dominates the plaza. If you continue up Avenida Juárez about half a block past the plaza, you'll pass the tourist office again and arrive back at the Jardín Unión.

Sights to See

⑰ **Alhóndiga de Granaditas.** A massive stone structure with horizontal slit windows, this 18th-century grain-storage facility served as a jail under Emperor Maximilian and as a fortress during the War of Independence, where El Pípila committed his courageous act. It is now a state museum with exhibits on local history, archaeology, and crafts. The hooks on which the Spanish Royalists hung the severed heads of Father Hidalgo, Ignacio Allende, and two other independence leaders still dangle on the exterior. ⊠ *Calle 28 de Septiembre 6,* ☎ *4/732–1112.* ☞ *About $2, free Sun.* ☉ *Tues.–Sat. 10–1:30 and 4–5:30, Sun. 10–2:30.*

⑳ **Basílica Colegiata de Nuestra Señora de Guanajuato.** A 17th-century Baroque church painted a striking shade of yellow, the Basílica dominates Plaza de la Paz. Inside is the oldest Christian statue in Mexico, a bejeweled 8th-century statue of the Virgin. The highly venerated figure was a gift from King Philip II of Spain in 1557. On the Friday preceding Good Friday, miners, accompanied by floats and mariachi bands, parade to the Basílica to pay homage to the Lady of Guanajuato. ⊠ *Plaza de la Paz.* ☉ *Daily 9–8.*

⑫ **Jardín Unión.** This tree-lined, wedge-shape plaza is Guanajuato's central square. All three sides of the wedge are pedestrian walkways. Tuesday, Thursday, and Sunday evenings, musical performances take place in the band shell here; at other times, groups of musicians break into impromptu song along the plaza's shaded tile walkways.

NEED A BREAK?

For alfresco dining at the Jardín, try the terrace at the **Hotel Museo Posada Santa Fé** (⊠ Jardín Unión 12, ☎ 4/732–0084). You can order a cappuccino and a slice of cake, or a full meal. Try the *pozole estilo Guanajuato* (hominy soup into which you spoon, or squeeze, the desired amounts of onions, radishes, lettuce, lime, and chili peppers). **Rincón del Arte** (⊠ Calle Sopeña 10, ☎ 4/732–2566) has indoor and outdoor tables next to Teatro Juárez and serves good soups and sandwiches, as well as an interesting assortment of spiked specialty coffees—among them *cafe diable* (coffee, rum, and lemon juice).

⑲ **Mansión del Conde de Rul.** This 18th-century residence, now a government office, housed the count of Rul and Valenciana, who owned ☞ La Valenciana, which was then the country's richest silver mine. The two-story structure was designed by famed Mexican architect Eduardo Tresguerras. ⊠ *Plaza de la Paz at Av. Juárez and Callejón del Estudiante,* ☎ *no phone.* 🖼 *Free.* ⊙ *Weekdays 8–3.*

⑱ Mercado Hidalgo. You can't miss this 1910 cast-iron-and-glass structure, designed by the one-and-only Gustave Eiffel. Though the balcony stalls are filled with T-shirts and cheap plastic toys, the lower level is full of authentic local wares and colorful basketry, as well as fresh produce, peanuts, and honey-drenched nut candies shaped like mummies. ⊠ *Calle Juárez near Mendizabal.* ⊙ *Daily 8–8.*

⑯ El Museo Casa Diego Rivera. This museum, birthplace of Mexico's best-known muralist, Diego Rivera, contains family portraits and furniture as well as works by the master, among them his studies for the controversial mural commissioned for New York City's Rockefeller Center. Completed in 1933, the mural contained a portrait of Lenin and had a decidedly Communist bent, which caused it to be removed immediately after it was displayed. The museum's upper galleries show revolving contemporary-art exhibits. ⊠ *Calle Pocitos 47,* ☎ *4/732–1197.* 🖼 *$1.* ⊙ *Tues.–Sat. 10–6:30, Sun. 10–2:30.*

㉒ Museo de las Momias. For a macabre thrill, check out this unique museum located at the municipal cemetery off Calzada del Panteón, at the west end of town. In the museum, mummified human corpses—once buried in the cemetery—are on display. Until the law was amended in 1858, if a grave site hadn't been paid for after five years, the corpse was removed to make room for new arrivals. Because of the mineral properties of the local soil, these cadavers (the oldest is more than 130 years old) were in astonishingly good condition upon exhumation. The most gruesome are exhibited in glass cases. ⊠ *Panteón Municipal,* ☎ *4/732–0639.* 🖼 *$2.* ⊙ *Daily 9–6.*

⑭ El Pípila. A half hour's climb from downtown is the monument to Juan José de los Reyes Martínez, a young miner and hero of the War of Independence of 1810. Nicknamed El Pípila, De los Reyes crept into the ☞ **Alhóndiga de Granaditas,** where Spanish Royalists were hiding. With a stone shield strapped to his back, he set the front door ablaze. The Spanish troops were captured by Father Hidalgo's army in this early battle, giving the independence forces their first major military victory. There's a splendid view of the city from the monument. It's easiest to take a taxi or a bus (marked PÍPILA) from the Jardín. ⊠ *Carretera Panorámica, on bluff above south side of Jardín Unión.*

⑬ Teatro Juárez. Adorned with bronze lion sculptures and a line of large Greek muses overlooking the Jardín Unión from the roof, the theater was inaugurated by Mexican dictator Porfirio Díaz in 1903 with a performance of *Aïda.* It now serves as the principal venue of the annual International Cervantes Festival (☞ Nightlife and the Arts, *below*). A brief tour of the Art Deco interior is available. ⊠ *Calle Sopeña s/n,* ☎ *4/732–0183.* 🖼 *Tour 50¢.* ⊙ *Tues.–Sun. 9–1:45 and 5–7:45.*

⑮ University of Guanajuato. Founded in 1732, the university was formerly a Jesuit seminary. The original churrigueresque church, **La Compañía,** still stands next door. The facade of the university building, built in 1955, was designed to blend in with the town's architecture. If you do wander inside, check out the bulletin boards for notices of cultural events in town. ⊠ *Calle Lascurain de Retana 5, ½ block north of Plaza de la Paz,* ☎ *4/732–0006.* ⊙ *Weekdays 8–3:30.*

㉑ La Valenciana. Officially called La Iglesia de San Cayetano, this is one of the best-known colonial churches in all of Mexico. The mid- to late-18th-century pink stone facade is brilliantly ornate. Inside are three altars, each hand-carved in wood and gilded, in different styles: plateresque, churrigueresque, and Baroque. There are also fine examples of religious painting from the viceregal period. The silver mine near the church, also called La Valenciana, was discovered in 1760 and is still in operation today. Although you can't descend into the 1,650-ft-deep mine shaft, if the caretaker is around he'll usually let you take a peek down. The mine and the church are included in any guided tour of Guanajuato, and there are also frequent buses (marked LA VALENCIANA) from the city center. ⊠ *Carretera Guanajuato–Dolores Hidalgo, Km 2.* ☉ *Daily 9–6.*

OFF THE
BEATEN PATH **MINERAL DE CATA –** The modest church at Mineral de Cata, officially called Señor de Villaseca, is a moving testament to religious faith. Since its founding in 1725, silver miners and their families have come here to offer heartfelt *ex-votos* (sometimes called *retablos*)—folk paintings with text about prayer and gratitude. The church is now covered floor to ceiling with these remarkable offerings. Those near the ceiling are a couple hundred years old, painted on tin. The recent, lower ones deal with contemporary issues, such as immigration. It is best to take a taxi here and have the driver wait (which will run you about $8 an hour) while you look inside. ⊠ *Callejón del Quijote.*

Dining

Guanajuato's better restaurants are located in hotels near the Jardín Unión and on the highway to Dolores Hidalgo. For simpler fare, private eateries around town offer a good variety of Mexican and international dishes. Dress tends to be casual.

$$$ ✕ **Casa del Conde de la Valenciana.** Come to this refurbished 18th-
★ century home across the street from La Iglesia de San Cayetano (La Valenciana) for superbly prepared traditional Mexican and international fare. Fresh gazpacho comes in a bowl made of ice, and the tender *lomo en salsa de ciruela pasa* (pork shoulder in prune sauce) and *pollo a la flor de calabaza* (chicken with poblano chili slices and squash-blossom sauce) are delicious. ⊠ *Carretera Guanajuato–Dolores Hidalgo, Km 5,* ☎ *4/732–2550. MC, V. Closed Sun. No dinner.*

$$$ ✕ **El Comedor Real.** Continental cuisine served in a medieval environment
★ defines this bright whitewashed restaurant in the Hotel Castillo Santa Cecilia. It serves such specialties as *filete pimienta* (steak with peppercorns) and fish soup with vegetables. Troubadours perform every Friday and Saturday at 10:30 PM at La Cava, the bar next door. ⊠ *Camino a la Valenciana s/n, Km 1,* ☎ *4/732–0485. AE, MC, V.*

$$$ ✕ **Tasca de los Santos.** This cozy restaurant, across the street from the Basílica, specializes in Spanish and international fare. Recommended dishes include the *sopa de mariscos* (a rich broth with shrimp, mussels, clams, and crabs, all in their shells) and *filete parrilla* (grilled beef with baked potatoes and spinach). Dine inside or out under umbrellas on the plaza, with a view of the fountain. A variety of music, ranging from French to Russian, enhances the cosmopolitan mood. ⊠ *Plaza de la Paz 28,* ☎ *4/732–2320. AE, MC, V.*

$$ ✕ **El Retiro.** This traditional Mexican restaurant up the street from the Teatro Juárez is often crowded for the main midday meal. At other times you can relax with a steaming cappuccino. Although local residents swear by El Retiro's reputation, it's hardly the "retreat" that its name implies. The food is good, but the waiters are often mesmerized by televised soccer games, and pop music sometimes replaces the classical fare that prevailed in gentler times. A full comida corrida runs about $3; try the broiled steak with mushroom sauce, a Spanish omelet, or *mole poblano* (a complex sauce made with poblano chilies and chocolate) with chicken. ⊠ *Calle Sopeña 12,* ☎ *4/732–0622. MC, V.*

$ ✕ **El Pingüis Cafeteria.** Cheap and plentiful food attracts the university crowd to this spartan eatery decorated with Mexican art posters. For about $2.50, a midday meal consists of soup, Mexican rice, a chicken or beef dish, dessert, and coffee. *Consumé de verduras* (vegetable soup) is good, as is the *café americano*. Service can be slow, but vibrant music and a lively crowd will keep you entertained. ✉ *Jardín Unión at Allende 3,* ☎ 4/732–1414. *No credit cards.*

$ ✕ **Truco 7.** Red tile floors, *equipale* (pigskin) chairs, and original art
★ enliven this cozy coffeehouse and restaurant. In the morning, serious students hunch over coffee and textbooks. Later in the day locals and savvy tourists pile in for the inexpensive comida corrida, sandwiches, or grilled chicken. The atmosphere is also lively at night, when Mexican wines are served by the glass. ✉ *Calle Truco 7,* ☎ 4/732–8374. *No credit cards.*

$ ✕ **El Unicorno Azul.** If you are growing weary of heavy meat dishes, stop by this food counter just behind Jardín Unión: it serves fruit drinks, yogurt, and vegetarian burgers and sandwiches. The owner will cheerfully recommend other health-food places and yoga classes. ✉ *Plaza del Baratillo 2,* ☎ 4/732–0700. *No credit cards. Closed Sun.*

Lodging

Guanajuato's less expensive hotels are along Avenida Juárez and Calle de la Alhóndiga. Moderately priced and upscale properties are near the Jardín Unión and on the outskirts of town. It's best to secure reservations at least six months in advance if you plan to attend the Cervantes Festival, which usually runs from mid- to late October.

$$$$ ☷ **La Casa de Espíritus Alegres Bed and Breakfast.** A paradise for folk-
★ art lovers, this "house of good spirits" is filled with extraordinary crafts from every state in Mexico. Owned by a California artist, the lovingly restored hacienda (circa 1700) has thick stone walls and serene grounds lush with bougainvillea, banana trees, and calla lilies. All rooms have hand-glazed tile baths, fireplaces, and a private terrace, patio, or balcony. Rates include a sumptuous breakfast served in a glassed-in atrium overlooking the garden. Children are not admitted. Marfil is about a 15-minute drive from the center of town—frequent bus service is available. ✉ *La Ex-Hacienda La Trinidad 1, Marfil 36250,* ☎ FAX 4/733–1013. *5 rooms, 3 suites. Bar, free parking. No credit cards.*

$$$ ☷ **Hostería del Frayle.** A half block off Jardín Unión, this quiet four-story lodging was once the Casa de Moneda, where ore was taken to be refined after it was brought out of the mines. Built in 1673 and turned into a hotel in the mid-1960s, it has whitewashed plaster and wood-beam rooms (which nonetheless are somewhat dark), arranged around a small maze of stairways, landings, and courtyards. All have phones and TVs (local channels only), and some have excellent views of the Pípila, Teatro Juárez, and Jardín Unión. The staff is extremely friendly and helpful. ✉ *Calle Sopeña 3, 36000,* ☎ FAX 4/732–1179. *32 rooms, 5 suites. Restaurant, bar. MC, V.*

$$$ ☷ **Hotel Museo Posada Santa Fé.** This colonial-style inn, at the Jardín Unión, has been in operation since 1862. Large historic paintings by local artist Don Manuel Leal hang in the wood-paneled lobby. A sweeping, if tattered, carpeted stairway leads to second-floor quarters. Each room has cable TV and a phone. Rooms facing the plaza can be noisy; quieter rooms face narrow alleyways. ✉ *Plaza Principal at Jardín Unión 12, 36000,* ☎ 4/732–0084, FAX 4/732–4653. *47 rooms, 9 suites. 2 restaurants, bar. AE, MC, V.*

$$$ ☷ **Parador San Javier.** This immaculately restored hacienda was con-
★ verted into a hotel in 1971. A safe from the Hacienda San Javier and old wood trunks still decorate the large, plant-filled lobby. Rooms are

clean and have attractive appointments: lace curtains, crisp coverlets, and blue-and-white-tile baths. A few of the 16 colonial-style rooms reached via a stone archway have fireplaces. Newer rooms in the adjoining high-rise have satellite TVs. A word of caution: large convention groups sometimes crowd the facility. ⊠ *Plaza Aldama 92, 36000,* ☎ *4/732–0626,* FAX *4/732–3114. 100 rooms, 12 suites. 2 restaurants, bar, café, pool, dance club, free parking. AE, MC, V.*

$ ⊡ **Hotel Socavón.** One of Guanajuato's newer hotels, this modest five-story property was built in 1981. Don't be put off by the gloomy, tunnel-like entrance: open-air walkways, with views of surrounding mountains, lead to guest quarters. Each small room—simply furnished with a bed, desk, and tiny TV—has a wood-beam ceiling and a modern bath. Fourth-floor corner rooms have some good views. ⊠ *Calle de la Alhóndiga 41A, 36000,* ☎ *4/732–6666,* ☎ FAX *4/732–4885. 40 rooms. Restaurant, bar. AE, MC, V.*

Nightlife and the Arts

Guanajuato, on most nights a somnolent provincial capital, awakens each fall for the **International Cervantes Festival.** For three weeks in October world-renowned actors, musicians, and dance troupes (which have included the Bolshoi Ballet) perform nightly at the Teatro Juárez and other venues in town. Plaza San Roque, a small square near the Jardín Reforma, hosts a series of *Entremeses Cervantinos*—swashbuckling one-act farces by classical Spanish writers. Grandstand seats require advance tickets, but crowds often gather by the edge of the plaza and watch for free. An estimated 450,000 people attended the 1999 festivities, a fact that those who abhor crowds should take into account. If you plan to be in Guanajuato for the festival, contact the Festival Internacional Cervantino office (⊠ Plaza de San Francisquito 1, ☎ 4/731–1150, 4/731–1161, FAX 4/732–6775) or Ticketmaster (☎ 5/325–9000) at least six months in advance for top-billed events.

At other times of the year, nightlife in Guanajuato mostly consists of dramatic, dance, and musical performances at the **Teatro Juárez** (⊠ Calle de Sopeña s/n, ☎ 4/732–0183). Friday and Saturday at 8 PM, *callejoneadas* (mobile musical parties) begin in front of the Teatro Juárez and meander through town (don't forget to tip the musicians). The **Teatro Principal** (⊠ Calle Hidalgo, ☎ 4/732–1523) shows American movies several times a week, and some hotels, including the **Parador San Javier** (☞ Lodging, *above*) and the **Castillo Santa Cecilia** (⊠ Camino a la Valenciana s/n, Km 1, ☎ 4/732–0485), provide evening musical entertainment. You'll find several nightclubs in or near the downtown area, including **Discoteque El Pequeño Juan** (⊠ Panorámica Al Pípila at Callejón de Guadalupe, ☎ 4/732–2308). Its panoramic view of the city at night is stunning.

Shopping

You'll find painterly, old-style majolica ceramics at **Capelo** (⊠ Cerro de la Cruz s/n, a dirt road off the Guanajuato–Dolores Hidalgo Hwy., past La Valenciana, ☎ 4/732–8964) and at the **Gorky González Workshop** (⊠ Pastita Ex-huerta de Montenegro s/n, past the baseball stadium, ☎ 4/731–0389). Both venerable studios now use lead-safe glazes. Next to the Casa del Conde de la Valenciana restaurant, **Casa del Conde de la Valenciana** (⊠ Carretera Guanajuato–Dolores Hidalgo, Km 5, ☎ 4/732–2550) specializes in brass, tin, ceramic, and wrought-iron home decorations from Mexico and Africa. Some jewelry and regional knickknacks are sold at the **Mercado Hidalgo** (☞ Sights to See *in* Exploring Guanajuato, *above*). **Artesanías Vázques** (⊠ Cantarranas 8, ☎ FAX 4/732–5231) carries Talavera ceramics from Dolores Hidalgo. There are other shops that sell ceramics and woolen shawls and sweaters around Plaza de la Paz and Jardín Unión. Silver is available from street vendors and shops clustered near La Valenciana and El Pípila.

Side Trip

León
56 km (35 mi) northwest of Guanajuato.

Best known as the shoemaking capital of Mexico, León is also an important center for industry and commerce. With more than 1 million people, it is the state's most populous urban area.

If you know footwear and have the time (and patience) to browse through the downtown shops, you might find some good buys in León. First try the **Plaza del Zapato,** a mall with 70 stores on Boulevard Adolfo López Mateos, roughly one block from the bus station. From here take a taxi west (about a 10-minute ride) to the **Zona Peatonal,** a pedestrian zone with several shoe stores. On **Calle Praxedis Guerrero,** various artisans' stands sell leather goods.

Flecha Amarilla **buses** leave Guanajuato's Central Camionera every 15 minutes for León; the ride takes about 45 minutes and costs less than $1. **Taxis** cost about $17 one way. Pick up a map of León at the tourist office in Guanajuato.

Guanajuato A to Z

Arriving and Departing
BY BUS
Direct bus service is available between the Central del Norte (North Bus Station) in Mexico City and Guanajuato's **Central Camionera** (on the southwestern outskirts of town). **Taxis** to downtown from the Camionera cost $2–$3. Several lines—including **Flecha Amarilla** (☎ 4/733–1332, 4/733–1333) and **Estrella Blanca** (☎ 4/733–1344)—have hourly service. Travel time is about five hours. Deluxe buses, including those of **ETN** (☎ 4/733–1579, 4/733–0289) and **Primera Plus** (☎ 4/733–1332, 4/733–1333) connect Guanajuato to Mexico City, San Miguel, and Guadalajara. There are several departures daily.

BY CAR
Guanajuato is 365 km (226 mi), about five hours, northwest of Mexico City via Route 57 (to Querétaro), then via Route 45.

BY PLANE
León's Guanajuato International Airport is 40 km (25 mi) west of the city of Guanajuato. (☞ *See* Arriving and Departing *in* San Miguel de Allende A to Z, *above,* for international carriers that serve this airport.) The taxi ride from the airport to Guanajuato costs about $17 and takes around 45 minutes.

Getting Around
Don't bother with a car in Guanajuato. Many of the attractions are within strolling distance of one another and located between Avenida Juárez and Calle Pocitos, the city's two major north–south arteries. The twisting subterranean roadway—El Subterráneo—also has a primarily north–south orientation.

BY TAXI
You can find taxis at *sitios* (taxi stands) near the Jardín Unión, Plaza de la Paz, and Mercado Hidalgo.

Contacts and Resources

CAR RENTAL

Avis (✉ Hotel Fiesta Americana, Los Gabilanes, León, ☎ FAX 47/13–60–40) will drop a car at your hotel in Guanajuato.

E-MAIL

Redes Internet (✉ Alonso 70, ☎ 4/732–0611), open weekdays 9:30–8 and Saturday 10–3, charges $3 an hour for Internet access.

EMERGENCIES

Few people in Guanajuato have a good command of English, so in an emergency it's best to contact your hotel manager or the tourist office.

Police (☎ 4/732–0266). **Ambulance–Red Cross** (☎ 4/732–0487). **Hospital General** (☎ 4/733–1577).

GUIDED TOURS

The following tour operators give half- and full-day tours with English-speaking guides. These tours typically include the Museum of Mummies, the church and mines of Valenciana, the monument to Pípila, the Panoramic Highway, subterranean streets, and residential neighborhoods. Night tours often begin at the Pípila Monument for a nighttime city view and end at a dance club. Estudiantinas usually perform during the weekend tours.

Transporte Exclusivo de Turismo (✉ Av. Juárez and Calle 5 de Mayo, ☎ 4/732–5968) has several tours of Guanajuato and its environs.

Transporte Turísticos de Guanajuato (✉ Plaza de la Paz 2, by Basílica de Guanajuato, ☎ 4/732–2134, 4/732–2838) also has a kiosk at the main bus terminal (no phone).

PHARMACY

El Fénix (✉ Av. Juárez 104, ☎ 4/732–6140) is open Monday–Saturday 8 AM–9:45 PM, Sunday 9–9.

TRAVEL AGENCIES

Viajes Georama (✉ Plaza de la Paz 34, ☎ 4/732–5909, FAX 4/732–1954) is the local American Express representative. **Viajes Frausto** (✉ Calle González Obregón 10, ☎ 4/732–3580, FAX 4/732–6620) is reliable for hotel and airline reservations.

VISITOR INFORMATION

The **Guanajuato tourist office** (✉ Plaza de la Paz 14, ☎ 4/732–1574, 4/732–1982, FAX 4/732–4251) is open daily 9–7.

ZACATECAS

In colonial days Zacatecas was the largest silver-producing city in the world, sending great treasures of the precious metal to the king of Spain. Still a large silver-mining center, with factories producing silver jewelry and trade schools training apprentices in the fine art of handmade silver craft, Zacatecas is relatively undiscovered by foreigners. Although it is a state capital with a population of some 300,000, it has the feel of a much smaller place. Zacatecas is kept spotlessly clean, thanks to civic pride and a mandate by the governor of the state of Zacatecas. This city is rightly famous for its historic role as the scene of one of Pancho Villa's most spectacular battles and for its 18th-century colonial architecture.

One of the town's unique charms is the *tambora,* a musical walk up and down the streets and alleyways led by a *tamborazo,* a typical local band that shatters the evening quiet with merriment. Also known as a callejoneada (*callejón* means "alley"), the tambora is a popular free-for-all, in which everyone along the way either joins in the procession

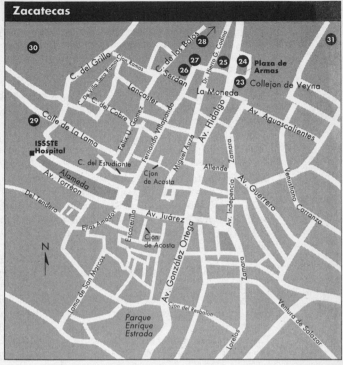

or leans from balconies and doorways to cheer the group on. During the December *feria* (festival), the tamborazos play night and day as they serenade the Virgin of Zacatecas.

Exploring Zacatecas

Most of Zacatecas's colonial sights are near the city center, making it an easy place to explore on foot—and there is rarely much traffic in town. For an overview of Zacatecas, you can walk or taxi up to the mine, catch an elevator to a nearby hilltop, take the cable car across the city, then return to your starting point below by taxi or bus.

A Good Walk

Start your tour at the Plaza de Armas, in the center of the city. Here you'll find the stunning **Catedral de Zacatecas** ㉓ and the **Palacio del Gobierno** ㉔. Across the street from the plaza are two beautiful colonial buildings worth exploring; one is known as the **Palacio de la Mala Noche** ㉕ because of a local legend. Go to the Plaza Santo Domingo, two blocks west of the cathedral, to see the art in the **Pedro Coronel Museum** ㉖ and the Baroque **Templo de Santo Domingo** ㉗ right next door. To visit the museum of the other Coronel brother—both were equally fanatical art collectors—return to the cathedral, turn left on Avenida Hidalgo, and walk about 1 km (½ mi) north of the plaza to the **Rafael Coronel Museum** ㉘.

For a longer walk, head south on Avenida Hidalgo until you come to Juárez, then go right (roughly west) up the hill, passing the several-block-long Alameda park and the Social Security Hospital to get to **La Mina Eden** ㉙. After touring the mine, you can take an elevator up to Cerro del Grillo (Cricket Hill) and catch the **Teleférico** ㉚ cable car across the city to **Cerro de la Bufa** ㉛, site of Pancho Villa's famous battle.

Sights to See

㉓ Catedral de Zacatecas. This is one of Mexico's finest interpretations of Baroque style. Each of the facades tells a different legend. According to one of them, an anticlerical governor of the state used the cathedral's silver cross and baptismal font to mint Zacatecas's first silver coins. ⊠ *South side of Plaza de Armas on Av. Hidalgo.*

<table>
<tr><td>NEED A
BREAK?</td><td>The Café y Nevería Acrópolis (⊠ Av. Hidalgo at Plazuela Candelario Huizar, ☎ 4/922–1284), alongside the cathedral, is a quaint diner where locals talk shop over strong Turkish coffee ($1.20). The café, open daily 8 AM–10 PM, sells lots of homemade pastries and cakes, as well as a variety of Mexican snacks.</td></tr>
</table>

㉛ Cerro de la Bufa. The city trademark, this rugged hill is the site of Pancho Villa's definitive battle against dictator Victoriano Huerta in June 1914. The spacious **Plaza de la Revolución,** paved with the three shades of pink Zacatecan stone, is crowned with three huge equestrian statues of Villa and two other heroes, Felipe Angeles and Panfilo Natera. Also on the site are the **Sanctuary of the Virgin of Patrocinio,** a chapel dedicated to the patron of the city, and the **Museo de la Toma de Zacatecas,** which has nine rooms filled with historic objects such as guns, newspapers, furniture, and clothing from the days of Pancho Villa. ⊠ *If driving, follow Av. Hidalgo north from town to Av. Juan de Tolosa; turn right and continue until you come to a fountain; take 1st immediate right off retorno (crossover) onto Calle Mexicapan, which leads to Carretera Panorámica. Turn right to signposted Carretera La Bufa, which leads to top of hill.* ☎ *Museum 4/922–8066.* 🎟 *$1.* ☉ *Tues.–Sun. 10–4:30.*

㉙ La Mina Eden. Now a tourist attraction, the Eden Mine supplied most of Zacatecas's silver from 1586 until 1960. An open mine train runs down into the underground tunnels. The tour is in Spanish, but you'll have no trouble imagining what the life of the miners was like. Be sure to wear sturdy shoes. Remember that mines are dark; through much of the tour, your only light may be the guide's flashlight. Farther down the train track there is another stop at, of all places, a discotheque (☞ Nightlife and the Arts, *below*). There's a small gift shop at the entrance. ⊠ *Entrance on Antonio Dovali off Av. Torreon beyond Alameda García de la Cadena,* ☎ *4/922–3002.* 🎟 *$1.50.* ☉ *Daily 11–6.*

㉕ Palacio de la Mala Noche. The Palace of the Bad Night is one of two beautiful 18th-century colonial buildings across from the downtown plaza. Both declared national monuments, they are built from native pink stone and have lacy ironwork balconies. One of them now houses the Continental Plaza hotel (☞ Dining and Lodging, *below*), and the other is a municipal building known as El Palacio de la Mala Noche. Legend has it that this was the home of a silver-mine owner who was called upon so often to help the needy that he built a hidden door from which he could enter and leave the palace undisturbed. Up the hill along the side of the palace, you will find the so-called hidden door. ⊠ *Av. Hidalgo 639.* 🎟 *Free.* ☉ *Weekdays 10–2 and 4–7.*

㉔ Palacio del Gobierno. The Governor's Palace is an 18th-century mansion with flower-filled courtyards and, on the main staircase, a powerful mural painted in 1970 by Antónío Pintor Rodríguez that depicts the history of Zacatecas. ⊠ *East side of Plaza de Armas.* 🎟 *Free.* ☉ *Weekdays 9–2 and 5–8, Sat. 9–1.*

★ **㉖ Pedro Coronel Museum.** Originally a Jesuit monastery, this building was used as a jail in the 18th century. The museum houses the work of Zacatecan artist and sculptor Pedro Coronel and his extensive collection of works by Picasso, Dalí, Miró, Braque, and Chagall, among others, as well as art from Africa, China, Japan, India, Tibet, Greece, and Egypt. ⊠ *Av. Fernando Villalpando at Plaza Santo Domingo,* ☎ *4/922–8021.* ⊡ *About $1.50.* ◐ *Fri.–Wed. 9:30–5.*

★ ㉘ **Rafael Coronel Museum.** The museum is in the Ex-Convento de San Francisco, northeast of the town center toward Lomas del Calvario. Its mellowed pink 18th-century facade conceals a rambling structure of open, arched corridors, all leading through garden patios to rooms that contain an amazing collection of some 4,500 *máscaras* (masks)— saints and devils, wise men and fools, animals and humans—used in regional festivals all over Mexico. There is also an outstanding display of puppets. ⊠ *Off Vergel Nuevo between Chaveño and Garcia Salinas,* ☎ *4/922–8116.* ⊡ *About $1.50.* ◐ *Thurs.–Tues. 10–5.*

㉚ **Teleférico.** The only cable car in the world that crosses an entire city, the Teleférico runs from **Cerro del Grillo** (Cricket Hill) above the Eden Mine to ☞ **Cerro de la Bufa** and operates daily from 10 until dusk, except when there are high winds. True, it crosses at the narrowest point, but it presents a magnificent panoramic view of the city and its many Baroque church domes and spires. It's also well worth the cost to get the ride up to Cerro de la Bufa, which is quite a climb otherwise. ⊠ *Cerro del Grillo station is just off Paseo Díaz Ordaz, a steep walk from Plaza de Armas,* ☎ *4/922–5694.* ⊡ *About $2.* ◐ *Daily 10–6.*

㉗ **Templo de Santo Domingo.** This 18th-century Jesuit church has an ornamented facade and a rich interior that includes gold-leaf religious paintings. The sacristy also contains an impressive collection of religious art. ⊠ *Av. Fernando Villalpando at Plaza Santo Domingo.* ◐ *Daily 8–2 and 5–9.*

Dining and Lodging

Several of Zacatecas's better restaurants are in hotels, and many of the best lodgings are in beautiful, well-preserved 18th- and 19th-century buildings. Other popular restaurants are on Avenida Juárez, which intersects Avenida Hidalgo.

$$$ ✕ **La Cuija.** Regional food is the strength of this large restaurant, ★ whose name means "the gecko." Start off with an appetizer of three quesadillas: one each of squash blossoms, cheese, and *huitlacoche* (a corn fungus delicacy). Also recommended are the *sopa campera* (a cream soup with corn and squash blossoms), and asado de boda (pork in a semisweet and spicy sauce). The decor approximates a wine cellar, and in addition to fine food, the restaurant serves wine from the owner's Cachola Vineyards in Valle de las Arsinas. A traditional Mexican trio plays Thursday–Sunday afternoons. ⊠ *Centro Commercial El Mercado, bottom level,* ☎ *4/922–8275. AE, V.*

$$ ✕ **Cenaduría Los Dorados.** Hidden on a small square adjacent to the Ex-Convent of San Francisco, this small, cheery restaurant is packed with memorabilia from the War of Independence. There is a no-smoking section, and the food is tasty and wholesome, if perhaps a bit toned down for foreigners' palates. Dinner is the most popular meal here. ⊠ *Plazuela de García 1314,* ☎ *4/922–5722. No credit cards.*

$ ✕ **Mesón la Mina.** Popular with local small-business men, this no-frills restaurant near the Jardín Independencia is a study in contrasts: waiters in crisp black and white hurry attentively to your Formica table, bringing appetizing meals in extra-large portions on institution-style plastic plates. There are meats, burgers, sandwiches, enchiladas, and a huge fixed-price midday meal of soup, rice, main dish, vegetable, beans, dessert, and coffee—for about $3. ⊠ *Juárez 15,* ☎ *no phone. No credit cards.*

$$$$ ✕🏨 **Continental Plaza.** This beautiful old colonial building faces the
Plaza de Armas and the cathedral in the heart of the city. The pink-
stone facade dates from the 18th century; unfortunately the modern
interior is rather stark and charmless. Rooms are fitted with new but
unexceptional furniture. Those facing the plaza are within earshot of
late-night and early morning tamborazo music during festivals. That
said, you'll get a great view of the goings-on from your small balcony.
The hotel's restaurant, Candiles, is one of the best in Zacatecas. The
menu includes both Continental and regional dishes, and there is a
daily breakfast buffet. ✉ *Av. Hidalgo 703, 98000,* ☎ *4/922–6183,*
FAX *4/922–6245. 86 rooms, 13 suites. Restaurant, bar, convention
center, free parking. AE, MC, V.*

$$$$ 🏨 **Quinta Real.** This hotel must be one of the most unusual in the
★   world: it is built around Mexico's oldest bullring, the second one constructed in the Western Hemisphere. The terrazzo-paved ring provides a unique view for the guest rooms, each with a balcony
overlooking the *plaza de toro* (bullring) itself. Large and bright, the
plush rooms are decorated in pastel fabrics that complement the dark
traditional furniture. The bar occupies some of the former bull pens,
and an outdoor café with bright-white umbrella tables takes up two
levels of the spectator area. Fine Continental cuisine is served in the
elaborate, formal restaurant, with an awesome view of the bullring
and the aqueduct beyond. ✉ *Av. Rayon 434, 98000,* ☎ *4/922–
9104,* FAX *4/922–8440. 36 rooms, 11 suites. Restaurant, bar, café, free
parking. AE, MC, V.*

$$$ 🏨 **Holiday Inn.** One of the most modern hotels in Zacatecas, this
pleasant property is only three blocks from the historic town center.
From the bay windows of its front rooms you can see over the rooftops
of the whitewashed dome of the beautiful Templo San José. Furnish-
ings in rooms—all with satellite TVs, individual climate control, and
marble baths—include Mexican chests and ironwork headboards. ✉
Blvd. López Matéos and Callejón del Barro, 98000, ☎ *4/922–3311,*
FAX *4/922–3415. 111 rooms, 15 suites. 2 restaurants, bar, coffee shop,
pool, nightclub, playground, free parking. AE, MC, V.*

$$$ 🏨 **Mesón de Jobito.** This early 19th-century apartment building stood
★   for well over a hundred years before its recent conversion to a four-
star hotel. The two levels of guest rooms are done in tasteful modern
decor, with wall-to-wall carpet and striped drapes. All rooms have cable
TVs and phones. The restful atmosphere is enhanced by the Mesón's
perfect location on a blissfully quiet little plaza a few blocks from the
cathedral. ✉ *Jardín Juárez 143, 98000,* ☎ FAX *4/924–1722. 25 rooms,
6 suites. Restaurant, bar. AE, MC, V.*

$$ 🏨 **Posada de la Moneda.** This very Mexican hotel in the middle of down-
town is adequate if you're on a budget. Everything is highly polished,
especially the lobby's marble floor. If the room furnishings are a bit thread-
bare, they are clean, and the carpet is relatively new. Each room has a
phone and TV (local channels only). ✉ *Av. Hidalgo 413, 98000,* ☎ FAX
4/922–0881. 34 rooms, 2 suites. Restaurant, bar. AE, MC, V.

Nightlife and the Arts

A must-see if only for its uniqueness, **El Malacate** (✉ La Mina Eden,
☎ 4/922–3002), the discotheque in the Eden Mine, is more than 1,000
ft underground. It's best to make reservations at this popular place, which
is both crowded and noisy. It's open Thursday–Saturday night; the
cover charge is $7. There's live music in the lobby bar of the **Continental
Plaza** (☞ Dining and Lodging, *above*); the **Holiday Inn** (☞ Dining and
Lodging, *above*) has a nightclub with live entertainment.

Shopping

Don't expect to find quality crafts in Zacatecas; souvenirs are more along the line of tacky knickknacks than handicrafts. There is some decent silver jewelry, although not as much as one would expect.

Crafts

Opposite the east end of Plaza de Armas is **La Cazzorra** (⊠ Av. Hidalgo 713, ☎ 4/924–0484), a collectibles shop with authentic antiques, books about Zacatecas, wood furniture, Huichol art, and ceramics. The owners are a good source of information about the city.

Silver

The **Centro Comercial El Mercado** (⊠ Calle Hidalgo, next to cathedral) has a few shops with silver goods. Centro Platero Zacatecas (☎ 4/923–1007) sells silver jewelry with regional designs, made in its factory in nearby Guadalupe. Yohuatl (☎ no phone) sells a large selection of silver jewelry and accessories for women and men.

Side Trips

Guadalupe

7 km (4½ mi) southeast of Zacatecas.

If you are interested in colonial art and architecture, don't miss this small town. Its centerpiece is the **Ex-Convento de Guadalupe,** founded by Franciscan monks in 1707. It currently houses the **Museo de Arte Virreinal** (*virreinal* means "viceregal," or "colonial"), run by the Instituto Nacional de Antropología e Historia. The convent is itself a work of art, with its Baroque **Templo de Guadalupe** and the **Capilla de Nápoles,** but even more impressive is the stunning collection of religious art under its roof. Works by Miguel Cabrera, Nicolás Rodríguez Juárez, Cristóbal de Villalpando, and Andrés López are included. ⊠ *Jardín Juárez s/n,* ☎ 4/923–2386. 🎫 *$2, free Sun.* ☉ *Daily 10–4:30.*

In the 18th-century mansion of don Ignacio de Bernárdez, the **Centro Platero Zacatecas** is a school and factory for handmade silver jewelry and other items. Stop in to watch student silversmiths master this fine tradition. ⊠ *Casco de la Ex-Hacienda Bernárdez,* ☎ 4/923–1007. ☉ *Weekdays 10–6, Sat. 10–2.*

Zona Arqueológica La Quemada

50 km (31 mi) southwest of Zacatecas on Hwy. 54, 3 km (2 mi) off highway.

This ancient city was already a ruin before the Spaniards arrived in the 16th century. The site's original name, "Chicomostoc," means "place of the seven tribes." Although it was once believed that seven different Indian cultures built here, one community atop the other, this theory is currently under scrutiny. The remaining edifices appear to be constructed of thin slabs of stone wedged into place. The principal draw is a group of rose-color ruins containing 11 large, round columns built entirely of the same small slabs of rock seen in the rest of the ruins. An impressive site museum has a scale model of the ruins and some interesting artifacts. To get here, take a bus toward Villanueva, get off at the entrance to La Quemada, and walk in 3 km (2 mi). The bus ride takes about an hour. Alternatively, take a taxi or guided tour. ☎ *No phone.* 🎫 *$2, free Sun.* ☉ *Site and museum daily 10–4:30.*

Zacatecas A to Z

Arriving and Departing

BY BUS

Omnibus de México (☎ 4/922–0274) and **Turistar** and **Futura** (☎ 4/922–0042) run several first- and second-class buses daily from Mexico City to Zacatecas. The trip takes eight to nine hours.

BY CAR

Zacatecas is 603 km (375 mi), about 7½–8 hours, northwest of Mexico City via Route 57 (to Querétaro and San Luis Potosí) and Route 49.

BY PLANE

Mexicana (☎ 4/922–7470, 4/922–3248) has direct service to Zacatecas from Chicago, Denver, and Los Angeles. In Zacatecas, the Mexicana office is at Av. Hidalgo 406. The airport is 29 km (18 mi) north of town. **Aerotransportes** (☎ 4/922–5946) makes the trip for about $5; private taxis cost about $15.

Getting Around

You can get to most of the town-center attractions on foot, although you might want to hire a taxi if you want to tour a mine or take a ride on the Teleférico (cable car) to the top of Cerro de la Bufa. The city has an excellent and inexpensive bus system.

Contacts and Resources

E-MAIL

Cronos (✉ Av. Rayon 212, ☎ 4/922–1548), open Monday–Saturday 9–9, Sunday 10–9, charges $2 an hour for Internet access.

EMERGENCIES

Police (☎ 4/922–0180). **Red Cross** (☎ 4/922–3005). **Hospital General** (☎ 4/923–3004). **Emergency Service** (☎ 06). English is not generally spoken in Zacatecas, so it's best to contact your hotel manager or the tourist office in case of an emergency.

GUIDED TOURS

Viajes Mazzoco (✉ Calle Satima 115, ☎ FAX 4/922–0859), a well-established travel agency and the local American Express representative, gives a four-hour tour of the city center, the Eden Mine, the Teleférico, and La Bufa for about $12 a person. There are also tours to La Quemada ruins and environs ($16).

Operadora Zacatecas (✉ Av. Hidalgo 630, ☎ 4/924–0050) is recommended by the tourism office, and offers tours of the city center and elsewhere in the area.

PHARMACY

Farmacia Isstezac (✉ Tacuba 153, ☎ 4/924–0690) is open daily 8 AM–10 PM.

VISITOR INFORMATION

The **tourist information office** (✉ Av. Hidalgo 403, 2nd floor, ☎ 4/924–4047, 4/924–0552), is open weekdays 9–8, weekends 9–7.

QUERÉTARO

In 1810 the first plans for independence were hatched at the Querétaro home of Josefa Ortiz de Domínguez—known as La Corregidora, wife of El Corregidor, Querétaro's mayor of the time. She was a heroine of the independence movement. In 1848 the Mexican–American War was concluded in this city with the signing of the Treaty of Guadalupe Hidalgo. Emperor Maximilian made his last stand here in 1867 and was

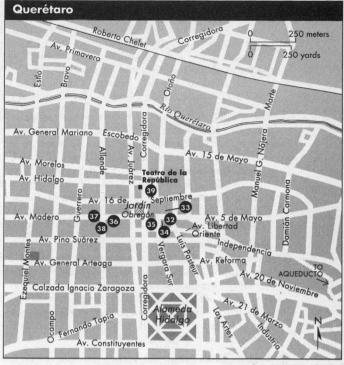

executed by firing squad on the *Cerro de las Campanas* (Hill of the Church
Bells), north of town. A small memorial chapel, built by the Austrian
government, marks the spot. A gigantic statue of Benito Juárez crowns
a park on the crest of the hill just above it. Also, in 1917, the Mexican
Constitution, which is still in force, was signed here. Now Querétaro is
a state capital and an industrial center of nearly 1 million people.

Throughout Querétaro are markers, museums, churches, and monuments
that commemorate the city's heroes and historic moments. A prevailing
sense of civic pride is evident in the impeccably renovated mansions, the
flower-draped cobblestone pedestrian walkways, and the hospitable
plazas, which are softly lighted at night. On Sunday evening couples dance
to live *danzón* music in the main plaza, or simply chat and enjoy the company of their friends. The people are among the most congenial in central Mexico and are quick to share their favorite sites and tales with travelers.

Querétaro is also renowned for opals—red, green, honey, and fire
stones. Caveat emptor: some street vendors sell opals so full of water
that they crumble shortly after purchase. Buy from reputable dealers
(☞ Shopping, *below*).

Exploring Querétaro

Although Querétaro extends for some distance, the historic district is
in the heart of town. You can easily spend a day or two here visiting
museums, admiring architecture, and taking in local history.

A Good Walk

Most sights are near the **Plaza de la Independencia** ㉜. The **Palacio del
Gobierno del Estado** ㉝ is on the plaza's northwest corner. If you walk
around the square counterclockwise, you'll come to the Palacio de Jus-

ticia, originally built as a mansion for the wealthy Domingo Iglesia and, beside it, the **Casa de Ecala** ㉞. Just past the Casa de Ecala is Avenida Libertad Oriente, one of the city's bougainvillea-draped pedestrian walkways. Turn west here and walk two blocks to reach Calle Corregidora. Bear right again, and in the middle of a long block you'll find the entrance to the **Museo Regional de Querétaro** ㉟. Cross the street to Avenida Madero, another "pedway," this one lined with shops. The city's main square, Jardín Obregón, will be on your right.

One block past Avenida Juárez on the corner of Calle Allende Sur and Madero you'll see the former **Casa de la Marquesa** ㊱, an 18th-century mansion converted into a hotel (☞ Sights to See *and* Lodging, *below*). Across Allende, next to the Church of Santa Clara, is the neoclassical **Fountain of Neptune** ㊲. From the fountain, make a left on Calle Allende and walk almost a block to a fine example of Baroque architecture, the **Museo de Arte de Querétaro** ㊳. Retrace your steps to Calle Corregidora. Make a left and walk one block to Calle 16 de Septiembre. Across the street is the **Jardín de la Corregidora** ㊴.

Sights to See

㉞ **Casa de Ecala.** Currently housing the offices of DIF, a family-services organization, this Mexican Baroque palace has its original facade. As the story goes, its 18th-century owner adorned his home elaborately in order to outdo his neighbor, starting a remodeling war in which the Casa de Ecala eventually triumphed. Visitors are welcome to walk around the courtyard when the offices are open. ⊠ *Pasteur Sur 6, Plaza de la Independencia.* ⊙ *Weekdays 9–7.*

㊱ **Casa de la Marquesa.** Today a five-star hotel (☞ Lodging, *below*), this beautifully restored 18th-century house was built by the second Marqués de la Villa del Villar del Aguila. Most of the legends about the house's construction suggest that it was built to impress a nun with whom the marquis was terribly smitten. But he didn't live to see the casa completed in 1756, and its first resident was his widow, who had a penchant for things Arabic. The interior is *mudéjar* (Moorish) style, with lovely tilework. Stop in for a drink and the elegant atmosphere of **Don Porfirio's Bar.** ⊠ *Madero 41.*

㊲ **Fountain of Neptune.** Built in 1797 by Eduardo Tresguerras, the renowned Mexican architect and a native of the Bajío, the fountain originally stood in the orchard of the Monastery of San Antonio. According to one story, when the monks faced serious economic problems, they sold part of their land and the fountain along with it. It now stands next to the Church of Santa Clara. ⊠ *Calle Allende at Madero.*

㊴ **Jardín de la Corregidora.** This plaza is prominently marked by a statue of the War of Independence heroine—Josefa Ortiz de Domínguez—whose moniker it bears. Behind the monument stands the **Arbol de la Amistad** (Tree of Friendship). Planted in 1977 in a mixture of soils from around the world, the tree symbolizes Querétaro's hospitality to all travelers. This is the calmest square in town, with plenty of choices for patio dining. ⊠ *Calle Corregidora and Andador 16 de Septiembre.* ☒ *Free.*

㊳ **Museo de Arte de Querétaro.** A fine example of Baroque architecture, the museum is housed in an 18th-century Augustinian monastery. Its collection focuses on European and Mexican paintings from the 17th through 19th centuries, and there are rotating exhibits of 20th-century art. Note the elegant and fascinating Baroque patio, and ask for an explanation of the symbolism of its columns and the figures in the conch shells at the top of each arch. ⊠ *Calle Allende 14 Sur,* ☎ *4/212–2357.* ☒ *About $1, free Tues.* ⊙ *Tues.–Sun. 11–6.*

③⑤ **Museo Regional de Querétaro.** This bright yellow, 17th-century Franciscan monastery displays the works of colonial and European artists in addition to historic memorabilia, including early copies of the Mexican Constitution and the table on which the Treaty of Guadalupé Hidalgo was signed. ⊠ *Calle Corregidora 3, at Av. Libertad,* ☎ *4/212–2031.* ☒ *About $2, free Sun.* ⊘ *Tues.–Sun. 10–7.*

③③ **Palacio del Gobierno del Estado.** Also known as La Casa de la Corregidora, in 1810 this was the home of Querétaro's mayor-magistrate (El Corregidor) and his wife, Josefa Ortiz de Domínguez (La Corregidora). On many evenings, conspirators—including Ignacio Allende and Father Miguel Hidalgo—came here under the guise of participating in La Corregidora's literary salon. When El Corregidor learned that they were actually plotting the course for independence, he imprisoned his wife in her room. La Corregidora managed to whisper a warning to a coconspirator, who notified Allende and Hidalgo. A few days later, on September 16, Father Hidalgo tolled the bell of his church to signal the beginning of the fight for freedom. A replica of the bell can be seen atop the building. Now the Palacio houses municipal government offices. ⊠ *Northwest corner of Plaza de la Independencia.* ☒ *Free.* ⊘ *Weekdays 9–8, Sat. 9–2.*

③② **Plaza de la Independencia.** Bordered by carefully restored colonial mansions, this immaculate square, also known as Plaza de Armas, is especially lovely at night, when the central fountain is lighted. Built in 1842, the fountain is dedicated to the Marqués de la Villa del Villar, who constructed Querétaro's elegant aqueduct and provided the city with drinking water. The old stone aqueduct with its 74 towering arches still stands at the east end of town. ⊠ *Bounded by Av. 5 de Mayo on the north, Av. Libertad on the south, Luis Pasteur on the east, and Vergara Sur on the west.*

Dining

Many of Querétaro's dining spots are near the main plaza (Jardín Obregón), along Calle Corregidora, near the Teatro de la República, and particularly in the Jardín de la Corregidora. There are more-upscale restaurants in hotels on the Plaza de la Independencia and off Route 57, north of the city.

$$$ ✕ **Fonda del Refugio.** Situated in the Jardín de la Corregidora, this restaurant offers intimate indoor and outdoor dining. Inside, fresh flowers adorn white-clothed tables; outside, comfortable leather chairs face the surrounding gardens. Seafood and beef fillets are the specialties; consider ordering the fillet of beef cooked in red wine, lemon, mustard, and peppers, or the scallops prepared in marsala. Cocktails are served on the terrace at night, when diners are often serenaded by guitar-playing trios. ⊠ *Jardín de la Corregidora 26,* ☎ *4/212–0755. AE, MC, V.*

$$$ ✕ **Restaurante Josecho.** Bullfight aficionados and other sports fans fre-
★ quent this highway road stop next to the bullring at the southwest end of town as much for the lively atmosphere as for the food. Wood-paneled walls are hung with hunting trophies, including geese, elk, bears, and leopards; waiters celebrate patrons' birthdays by banging on pewter plates and blasting a red siren. The place quiets down at night, when a classical guitarist or pianist performs. House specialties include *filete Josecho* (steak with cheese and mushrooms) and *filete Chemita* (steak sautéed in butter with onions). ⊠ *Dalia 1, next to Plaza de Toros Santa María,* ☎ *4/216–0229, 4/216–0201. AE, MC, V.*

$$ ✕ **El Mesón de Chucho el Roto.** Named after Querétaro's version of Robin Hood, this restaurant is on the quiet Plaza de Armas. It has an interesting menu that highlights regional cooking, including exotic tacos of either steamed goat, shrimp with nopal cactus, or squash blossoms. You can enjoy a variety of breakfast foods here as well, either overlooking the plaza from the café tables outside, indoors, or on the back patio. ⊠ *Plaza de Armas,* ☎ *4/212–4295. AE, MC, V.*

$ ✕ **Bisquets Bisquets.** Mexican families flock to this friendly spot after church for good and hearty inexpensive food. The specialty of the house is—you guessed it—biscuits, made fresh on the premises, with such traditional toppings as butter and jelly or with more unusual ones such as mole or tuna. There are good enchiladas *Queretanas,* with cheese, potatoes, carrots, and cream, and *huevos al albañil* (eggs with red sauce and beans). ⊠ *Plaza de la Constitución, near Calle Corregidora at Calle Madero,* ☎ *4/214–1481. No credit cards.*

$ ✕ **La Mariposa.** Celebrating more than 50 years in business, La Mariposa is easily recognized by the wrought-iron butterfly (*mariposa*) over the entrance. This is the place for coffee and cake or a light Mexican lunch: enchiladas, tacos, tamales, and *tortas* (sandwiches). It's a favorite among locals despite its very plain, cafeteria-like appearance; some visitors describe it as "sterile." ⊠ *Angela Peralta 7,* ☎ *4/212–1166, 4/212–4849. No credit cards.*

Lodging

Several new hotels in various price ranges have opened in Querétaro in the past 10 years. Lower-priced hotels are located near the main plaza and thus tend to be noisy; restored colonial mansions are on or near the city's many plazas in the heart of town; and deluxe properties are on the outskirts of town.

$$$$ 🏨 **Casa de la Marquesa.** This beautifully restored property, originally
★   an 18th-century private home (☞ Sights to See *in* Exploring Querétaro, *above*), is perfectly situated in the heart of Querétaro. The central courtyard of the main building is a beautifully decorated sitting room. Each large guest room is furnished differently with antique furniture, tasteful art, parquet floors, and area rugs, and each has a direct-dial telephone. Rooms in the main building are more elegant and expensive than those in La Casa Azul (children under 12 are not admitted in the main building). The property's award-winning restaurant, Comedor de la Marquesa, is elegant and a bit austere. It specializes in such regional rarities as boar, venison, and *escamole* (ant eggs) in season, as well as more-traditional international cookery. ⊠ *Madero 41, 76000,* ☎ *4/212–0092,* ℻ *4/212–0098. 6 rooms, 19 suites. 2 restaurants, bar, room service, shops. AE, MC, V.*

$$$$ 🏨 **Hacienda Jurica.** A favorite getaway for Mexico City families, this
★   sprawling 16th-century ex-hacienda has nearly 30 acres of grassy sports fields, topiary gardens, a horse stable, and heated pool, and you can play golf at a nearby course. The grounds and courtyards are dotted with antique horse-drawn carriages, and the spacious earth-tone rooms have substantial dark wood furniture, satellite TVs, and minibars. The hacienda is in Jurica, an upscale residential neighborhood 13 km (8 mi) northwest of the city off Highway 57 and is easiest to reach by car. ⊠ *Carretera Mexico–San Luis Potosí, Km 229 (Apdo. 338), 76100,* ☎ *4/218–0022,* ℻ *4/218–0136. 176 rooms, 6 suites. Restaurant, bar, minibars, pool, 2 tennis courts, horseback riding, billiards, travel services, free parking. AE, MC, V.*

$$$$ 🏨 **Holiday Inn Querétaro.** This gracious, well-run establishment has a lot more charm than others in the chain. Located 3 km (about 2 mi) west of the historic district off Highway 57, the contemporary building incorporates many colonial touches such as stone archways and domed *boveda* (vaulted) ceilings. Sunny, ample rooms are comfortably appointed with rustic Mexican furnishings, cheery pastel bedspreads,

satellite TVs, and minibars. ⊠ *Av. 5 de Febrero 110, 76000,* ☎ *4/216–0202,* 𝔽𝔸𝕏 *4/216–8902. 171 rooms, 4 suites. 2 restaurants, piano bar, minibars, no-smoking rooms, pool, exercise room, baby-sitting, travel services, free parking. AE, MC, V.*

$$$ 🖫 **Hotel Mirabel.** A favorite among business travelers and conventioneers, this modern high-rise hums with activity. Its carpeted rooms are insulated and quiet and have cable TVs, telephones, wooden desks, and air-conditioning. Some double rooms have views of the Alameda Hidalgo park; some singles overlook a soccer stadium. ⊠ *Av. Constituyentes Ote. 2, 76000,* ☎ *4/214–3099 or 4/214–3444,* 𝔽𝔸𝕏 *4/214–3585. 170 rooms, 10 suites. Restaurant, bar. AE, MC, V.*

$$$ 🖫 **Mesón de Santa Rosa.** Located on the quiet Plaza de la Independencia, this elegant property was used almost 300 years ago as a
★ stopover for travelers to the north. Rooms are clustered around a quiet courtyard; lace-hung glass doors and wood-beam ceilings maintain the colonial charm. Amenities such as satellite TVs, minibars, and a heated pool make this lovely hotel comfortable as well. ⊠ *Pasteur Sur 17, 76000,* ☎ *4/224–2623,* 𝔽𝔸𝕏 *4/212–5522. 5 rooms, 17 suites. Restaurant, bar, minibars, pool. AE, MC, V.*

$$ 🖫 **Hotel Señorial.** This sprawling four-story property has plain but clean, large, and modern rooms with telephones and cable TVs. Rooms in front face a narrow, busy street, but traffic slows in the evening. There are purified-water dispensers in the hallways. The restaurant serves a Sunday buffet lunch. ⊠ *Guerrero Nte. 10-A, 76000,* ☎ *4/214–3700,* 𝔽𝔸𝕏 *4/214–1945. 54 rooms. Restaurant. V.*

Nightlife and the Arts

Band concerts are held in the **Jardín Obregón,** Querétaro's main square, every Sunday evening at 6. A monthly publication called *Tesoro Turístico,* available at the tourist office, provides information about current festivals, concerts, and other cultural events.

Shopping

A number of stores around town sell opals (not milky white, like Australian opals, but beautiful nonetheless) and other locally mined gems. If you're in the market for loose stones or opal jewelry, do some comparison shopping, as you're apt to find better prices here than in the United States. Two reputable dealers are **Villalone y Artesanos** (⊠ Av. Libertad 24, ☎ 4/212–8414) and **Lapidaria Querétaro** (⊠ Corregedora 149 Nte., ☎ 4/212–0030).

Side Trips from Querétaro

San Juan del Río and Tequisquiapan are both within an hour's drive of Querétaro. The highway between Querétaro and San Juan del Río is paved with factories, and San Juan is a bustling manufacturing center whose only real appeal is the semiprecious stones—especially opals, topaz, and amethyst—sold here, both loose or in settings. Tequisquiapan, on the other hand, is a tranquil and pretty *pueblo* (town) drenched in sun and bougainvilleas and flowering trees, and known as a producer of wicker and other handicrafts. Once frequented by harried Mexican urbanites who came to soak in the area's thermal waters, Tequis (as the locals call it) now suffers a dearth of hot water.

A car is the best means to get around. Buses serve both towns from Querétaro, but the trip is longer. If you go to both towns, shop first in San Juan del Río, then head to Tequisquiapan to look around, shop a bit, and perhaps have a meal or a snack. A taxi between the two towns costs about $4.50.

San Juan del Río
51 km (32 mi) southeast of Querétaro via Rte. 57.

Most of San Juan's gem shops are located near the main plaza downtown, and along Avenida Juárez and Calle 16 de Septiembre. **Lapidaria Guerrero** (⊠ Av. Juárez Pte. 4, ☎ 4/272–1481) has an exceptionally large collection of opal, amethyst, turquoise, and topaz jewelry. The store is open daily 10–2 and 3–7:30.

Tequisquiapan
19 km (12 mi) east of San Juan del Río, off Rte. 120.

This town, famous for centuries for its restorative thermal waters, has in recent years lost much of its thermal flow, reportedly due to the extraordinary water consumption of a paper mill in the area. Many spas struggle on as simple swimming pools/recreation areas, but as the main tourist draw has receded with the once-warm waters, most are deserted midweek. Things do liven up on hot weekends, however. The **tourist office** (⊠ Andador Independencia 1, Plaza Miguel Hidalgo, ☎ 4/273–0295), open daily 9–7, will cheerfully direct you to one or more of the spas, most of which are outside of town.

After lunch or a snack, head to the shops or to the **Mercado de Artesanías** (⊠ Calzado de los Misterios s/n, ☎ no phone), where woven goods, jewelry, and locally made furniture are sold. The **Templo de Santa Maria de la Asunción,** on the main plaza, was begun in 1874 in the neoclassical style, but not completed until the beginning of the 20th century. In late May or early June, the city hosts an annual, weeklong **wine and cheese festival.**

Xilitla
Approximately 320 km (198 mi) northeast of Querétaro.

Feel the ordinary world fade away with a trip to the decidedly off-the-beaten-path **Las Pozas** (The Pools), the extraordinary sculpture garden of the late, eccentric English millionaire Edward James (1907–84). Friend of artists Dalí and Picasso and rumored to be the illegitimate son of King Edward VII, James spent 20 years building 36 surrealist concrete structures deep in the waterfall-filled Xilitla jungle. These amazing structures are half-finished fantasy castles, gradually falling to ruin as the rain forest slithers in to claim them. It's like the ultimate child's fort. The castles don't have walls—just vine-entwined pillars, secret passageways, and operatic staircases leading nowhere.

It is a six- to seven-hour thrilling but exhausting mountainous drive to Xilitla, with hairpin turns and spectacular desert, forest, and jungle vistas. Plan on staying at least two nights, as you'll want time to soak up the jungle magic. If you choose not to drive, you can take a bus to Ciudad Valles (1½-hour drive from Xilitla) or fly to Tampico (3½-hour drive from Xilitla), and arrange ahead for the staff of Posada El Castillo (☞ Lodging, *below*) to pick you up. ⊠ *From Querétaro, head north on Hwy. 57 (Carretera Mexico–San Luis Potosí). Not far from the city, take the* PEÑA DE BERNAL *turnoff, marked on a bridge overpass and also on a smaller sign at the Cadareyta exit. Continue north through Bernal, after which the road will join Rte. 120. Take 120 through Jalpan and then on to Xilitla, just across the border in the state of San Luis Potosí. The turnoff to Las Pozas is just beyond Xilitla on the left after passing a small bridge.* ☎ *$1.50.* ☉ *Daily dawn–dusk.*

LODGING

$$ ▥ **Posada El Castillo.** When he wasn't living in his jungle hut, the eccentric English millionaire Edward James stayed in town (a 10-minute drive away) in a whimsical house that feels like an extension of the garden structures at Las Pozas—except that it has walls. That house, El Castillo (the castle), is now a quirky inn run by Lenore and Avery Danziger, who have made an award-winning documentary film about James that they happily screen for guests. Rooms are adorned with simple wooden furnishings; the best rooms have huge Gothic windows and panoramic mountain views. You can arrange to have meals here; otherwise there are few dining options in the area. ⊠ *Ocampo 105, San Luis Potosí 79900,* ☎ *136/5–00–38,* 𝖥𝖠𝖷 *136/5–00–55. 7 rooms. Pool. No credit cards.* ✎

Querétaro A to Z

Arriving and Departing

BY BUS

Daily buses run direct between Mexico City's Central del Norte (North Bus Station) and Querétaro's Central de Autobuses. Major lines—including **Flecha Amarilla** (☎ 4/211–4001), **Omnibus de México** (☎ 4/229–0029, 4/229–0329), **ETN** (☎ 4/229–0078, 4/229–0019), and **Futura** (☎ 4/229–0022)—have frequent service; travel time is about three hours. Buses also leave several times a day for Guanajuato, San Miguel de Allende, and Morelia.

BY CAR

Querétaro is 220 km (136 mi) northwest of Mexico City, a three-hour drive on Route 57.

Getting Around

Most of Querétaro's historic sites are within walking distance of one another in the downtown district and can be reached by a series of walkways that are closed to automobile traffic most of the day. If you want to venture farther afield, you will find that buses and taxis run frequently along the main streets and are inexpensive.

Contacts and Resources

CAR RENTAL

Budget (⊠ Av. Constituyentes Ote. 73, ☎ 𝖥𝖠𝖷 4/213–4498). **Avis** (⊠ Prol. Corregidora Nte. 318, Col. Alamos, 3a sección, ☎ 4/224–1785, 4/224–3351, 𝖥𝖠𝖷 4/224–1786).

E-MAIL

Web Café (⊠ Ezequiel Montes Sur 67, ☎ 4/216–0250, 4/216–7272), open Monday–Saturday 10–10, Sunday 2–10, charges $3 an hour for Internet access.

EMERGENCIES

Police (☎ 4/220–8383, 4/220–8503). **Ambulance–Red Cross** (☎ 4/229–0545, 4/229–0665). **Fire Department** (☎ 4/212–3939). **Traffic Police** (☎ 4/213–8424).

Hospital. Sanatorio Alcocer Pozo (⊠ Calle Reforma 23, ☎ 4/212–0149, 4/212–1787).

GUIDED TOURS

The tourist office conducts hour-long trolley tours of the city's historic landmarks at 9, 10, and 11 AM and at 4, 5, and 6 PM Tuesday–Sunday. To arrange a city tour in English, call the office (☞ Visitor Information, *below*)—one day in advance if possible. The cost is about $1.50.

MONEY EXCHANGE

Casa de Cambio Acueducto (⊠ Av. Juárez Sur 58, ☎ 4/212–9304) is open weekdays 9–2 and 4–6, Saturday 9–1.

TRAVEL AGENCY

Turismo Beverly (⊠ Av. Tecnologia 118, ☎ 4/216–1500, 4/216–1260, 𝖥𝖠𝖷 4/216–8524).

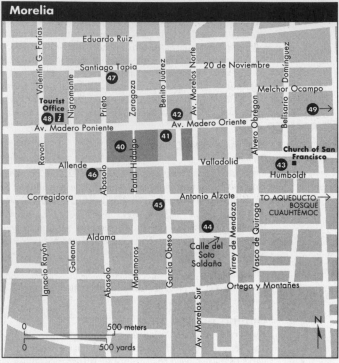

VISITOR INFORMATION

Dirección de Turismo del Estado (✉ Plaza de la Independencia at Pasteur 4 Nte., ☎ 4/212–1412, 4/212–0907, ℻ 4/212–1004) is open weekdays 8–8, weekends 9–8.

MORELIA

With its long, wide boulevards and earth-tone colonial mansions, Morelia is the gracious capital of the state of Michoacán. Founded in 1541 as Valladolid (after the Spanish city), it changed its name in 1828 to honor José María Morelos, the town's most famous son. The legendary mule skinner–turned–priest took up the battle for independence after its early leaders were executed in 1811.

Morelos began with an ill-equipped army of 25 but soon organized a contingent of 9,000 that nearly gained control of the country. Although he was defeated and executed in 1815, he left behind a long-standing reformist legacy that called for universal suffrage, racial equality, and the demise of the hacienda system. The city today still pays tribute to Morelos—his former home has been turned into a museum, and his birthplace is now a library.

Morelianos love music, and several annual festivals are designed to indulge them. Each May the city celebrates the International Organ Festival in the cathedral, giving voice to its outstanding 4,600-pipe organ. The last two weeks in July are given to the Festival International de Música, featuring baroque and chamber music, with orchestras participating from throughout Mexico.

Morelia has the delicious distinction of being the candy capital of Mexico. So strong is the sweet-eating tradition that the city has a **Mercado de**

Dulces—a sweets market. Morelia is also the home of writers, artists, philosophers, and poets, as well as American retirees.

Exploring Morelia

To explore Morelia and its surrounding hillside neighborhoods thoroughly would take some time. However, if you stroll through the historic plazas and frequent the cafés (as many locals do), you will begin to feel the city's vitality. Although the vehicle and sidewalk traffic can get a little heavy at times, Morelia is a pedestrian-friendly city.

A Good Walk

Begin your walk in Morelia's tree-lined downtown **Plaza de Armas** ⑩, on the east side of which is the city's famed **Catedral** ㊶. As you leave the cathedral, cross Avenida Madero to the **Palacio de Gobierno** ㊷, a former seminary. From the palace it's four blocks east along Avenida Madero to Calle de Belisario Domínguez. Make a right and walk one block south to the Church of San Francisco. To the rear of the church, in the former convent of San Francisco, is the entrance to the **Casa de las Artesanías del Estado de Michoacán** ㊸, a virtual cornucopia of crafts from around the state.

Walk two blocks south on Calle Vasco de Quiroga, a street lined with vendors, until you come to Calle del Soto Saldaña. Head west another two blocks to Avenida Morelos Sur. The corner building on the right is the **Casa Museo de Morelos** ㊹, which displays memorabilia of the independence leader. It's one block north from the museum to Calle Antonio Alzate and then one block west (where the street name changes to Calle Corregidora) to Calle García Obeso. On this corner stands the **Museo Casa Natal de Morelos** ㊺, Morelos's birthplace. Continue west on Calle Corregidora until you reach Calle Abasolo. On Calle Allende, one block to the north, you'll find the **Museo Regional Michoacano** ㊻.

After leaving the museum take Calle Abasolo back to the plaza; 2½ blocks to the north, you'll see the **Museo del Estado** ㊼ on the right side of the street (which changes to Calle Guillermo Prieto at Avenida Madero). Return to Avenida Madero, and then go two blocks to the right to the corner of the Valentín Gómez Farias, to the **Mercado de Dulces** ㊽.

For a longer stroll, take Avenida Madero east a dozen blocks or so to where it forks. Stay to the right; you'll see the **Fountain of the Tarascans** on a traffic island to your left. Just past the fountain, Morelia's mile-long **aqueduct** begins. This 1875 structure, which consists of 253 arches, once carried the city's main source of drinking water. It's particularly beautiful at night when its arches—some rising to 30 ft—are illuminated. Two blocks farther along (Madero is now called Avenida Acueducto) is the entrance to **Bosque Cuauhtémoc,** Morelia's largest park. If you happen by during the week, you may encounter university students studying (or lounging) beneath the palms and evergreens. On weekends, especially Sunday, families on outings take over. Two blocks past the park entrance, you'll see the **Museo de Arte Contemporáneo** ㊾, also on the right side of the street.

Sights to See

㊸ **Casa de las Artesanías del Estado de Michoacán.** In the 16th century, Vasco de Quiroga, the bishop of Michoacán, helped the Purépecha Indians develop artistic specialties so they could be self-supporting. At this two-story museum and store, you can see the work that the Purépechas still produce: copper goods from Santa Clara del Cobre, lacquerware from Uruapan, straw items and pottery from Pátzcuaro, guitars from Paracho, fanciful ceramic devil figures from Ocumicho. At the **Museo Michoacana de las Artesanías** in the two main floors around the courtyard, some of these items are showcased behind glass while artists demonstrate how they are made. ☒ *Calle Fray Juan de San Miguel 129,* ☎ *museum 4/312–2486, store 4/312–1248.* ☒ *Free.* ⊙ *Mon.–Sat. 10–3 and 5–8, Sun. 10–4:30.*

44 **Casa Museo de Morelos.** What is now a two-story museum was acquired in 1801 by José María Morelos and served as home to generations of the Mexican independence leader's family until 1934. Owned by the Mexican government, it contains family portraits, a copy of Morelos's birth certificate, various artifacts from the independence movement (such as a camp bed used by Ignacio Allende), and the blindfold Morelos wore for his execution. The excellent free tour is in Spanish only. ☒ *Av. Morelos Sur 323,* ☎ *4/313–2651.* ☒ *About $1.50.* ⊙ *Daily 9–7.*

41 **Catedral.** Morelia's cathedral is a majestic structure built between 1640 and 1744. It is known throughout Mexico for its 200-ft Baroque towers, among the tallest in the land, and for its 4,600-pipe organ, one of the finest in the world. The organ is the vehicle for the international organ festival held here each May. ☒ *Av. Madero between Plaza de Armas and Av. Morelos.*

48 **Mercado de Dulces.** If you have a sweet tooth, don't miss Morelia's famous candy market, just behind the tourist office. All sorts of local sweets are for sale, such as *ate* (a candied fruit) and *cajeta* (heavenly caramel sauce made from goat's milk). ☒ *Av. Madero Pte. and Valentín Gómez Farías.* ⊙ *Daily 10–9.*

45 **Museo Casa Natal de Morelos.** José María Morelos's birthplace is now a library and national monument housing mostly literature and history books (as well as two murals by Moreliano Alfredo Zalce). Be sure to visit the courtyard in back: it's a tranquil square, adjacent to the Church of San Agustín; a marker and an eternal flame honor the fallen hero. ☒ *Calle Corregidora 113,* ☎ *4/312–2793.* ☒ *Free.* ⊙ *Weekdays 9–7, Sat. 9–1.*

49 **Museo de Arte Contemporáneo.** The works of contemporary Mexican and international artists are on view at this well-lighted museum near the Bosque Cuauhtémoc. ☒ *Av. Acueducto 18,* ☎ *4/312–5404.* ☒ *Free.* ⊙ *Tues.–Sun. 10–2 and 4–8.*

47 **Museo del Estado.** Just across from a small plaza with statues of Bishop Vasco de Quiroga and Spanish writer Miguel de Cervantes, this history museum is located in a stately mansion that was once the home of the wife of Agustín de Iturbide, Mexico's only native-born emperor. A highlight of the collection is a complete Morelia pharmacy dating from 1868. ☒ *Guillermo Prieto 176,* ☎ *4/313–0629.* ☒ *Free.* ⊙ *Weekdays 9–2 and 4–8, weekends 9–2 and 4–7.*

46 **Museo Regional Michoacano.** An 18th-century former palace, the museum traces the history of Mexico from its pre-Hispanic days through the Cardenista period, which ended in 1940. President Lázaro Cárdenas, a native of Michoacán, was one of Mexico's most popular leaders because of his nationalization of the oil industry and his support of other populist reforms. The ground floor contains an art gallery, plus archaeological exhibits from Michoacán. Upstairs is an assortment of colonial objects, including furniture, weapons, and religious paintings. ☒ *Calle Allende 305,* ☎ *4/312–0407.* ☒ *About $2, free Sun.* ⊙ *Tues.–Sat. 9–7, Sun. 9–3.*

NEED A BREAK?   When you've finished your tour of the Museo Regional Michoacana, walk across the street to the colonial stone *portales* (arcades). The portales on one side of the square contain popular sidewalk cafés. For a sandwich or a fruit cocktail, or a good selection of juices, coffees, and teas, try **Café Catedral** (✉ Portal Hidalgo 213, ☎ 4/312–3289). No one will mind if you linger over a book or newspaper for the better part of an hour sipping an excellent café americano—in fact, you might have to wait that long just to get the bill.

42 **Palacio de Gobierno.** This former Tridentine seminary, built in 1770, has had such notable graduates as independence hero José María Morelos, social reformer Melchor Ocampo, and the first emperor of Mexico, Agustín de Iturbide. Striking murals decorate the stairway and second floor. Painted by local artist Alfredo Zalce in the early 1960s, they depict dramatic, often bloody scenes from Mexico's history. ✉ *Av. Madero 63,* ☎ *4/312–7872.* *Free.* *Weekdays 9–3 and 6–9.*

40 **Plaza de Armas.** During the War of Independence, several rebel priests were brutally murdered on this site, and the plaza, known as Plaza de los Mártires, is named after them. Today, however, the square belies its violent past: sweethearts stroll along the tree-lined walks, vendors sell mounds of roasted peanuts, placards announce cultural events, and lively recorded music blasts from a silver-dome band shell. ✉ *Bounded on the north by Av. Madero, on the south by Calle Allende, on the west by Calle Abasolo, and on the east by the cathedral.*

Dining

Some of Michoacán's tastiest dishes—tomato-based Tarascan soup, corn products such as *huchepos* (sweet tamales) and *corundas* (savory triangular tamales), and game (rabbit and quail)—are served at Morelia restaurants. Traditional chicken and beef fare are also available, as are international dishes. As a rule, more-upscale restaurants are in hotels near the plaza and on the outskirts of town.

$$$ ★ ✕ **Fonda Las Mercedes.** This delightful restaurant's arty, modern furnishings somehow fit perfectly in the plant-filled stone patio of this restored colonial mansion. The ambience is intimate yet airy, with a lovely soft natural light during the day. The inside dining room, which is equally pleasant, may be cozier on chilly days or evenings. Offerings from the eclectic menu include lots of soups and six kinds of crepes. If you dare, try the sinfully rich pasta with pistachios and pine nuts in cream sauce. ✉ *León Guzmán 47,* ☎ *4/312–6113. AE, MC, V. No dinner Sun.*

$$ ✕ **Boca del Río.** Large picture windows opening onto a busy intersection provide ample light for this cheerful yet cafeteria-like restaurant, which claims to have fresh fish and seafood trucked in daily from Sinaloa and Veracruz. There are light snacks such as *coctel de camarones* (shrimp cocktail), along with heartier fare, such as the *jaiba rellena* (mushroom-and-cheese-stuffed crabs liberally seasoned with garlic). Beef and chicken dishes and a vegetarian sandwich are also offered. After lunch, head to the sprawling Mercado de Dulces, just across the street, for dessert. ✉ *Valentín Gómez Farías 185,* ☎ *4/312–9974. AE, MC, V.*

$$ ★ ✕ **Cenaduría Lupita II.** This restaurant is outside the city center in the financial district near the Gigante supermarket and cinema. Although the name labels it a dinner spot (*cena* means dinner), enormous buffets are served for all three meals. The lunch buffet offers unlimited access to salads, soup, meats, desserts, coffee, juices, and beer or tequila. Dinner is built around *antojitos* (appetizers), but it's still a huge amount and assortment of foods. Eating here is a great way to try different regional specialties and find your favorites. ✉ *Av. Camelinas 3100, Col. Jardines del Rincón,* ☎ *4/324–4067. AE, MC, V.*

$ ✕ **Taquería Pioneros.** There's a reason the tables are full at lunch at this
★ positively plain taco shop: it has delicious grilled meats, served Michoacán
style with salsas and mountains of fresh, hot tortillas made on site. The
pionero (beef, ham, bacon, onions, and cheese, all grilled) is the only style
served in a half portion, which is plenty for most appetites. Quesadillas,
sincronizadas (quesadillas with ham), and beans are also served, as is beer
and soda. ⊠ *A. Serdán 7, at Ocampo,* ☎ *no phone. No credit cards.*

Lodging

Morelia offers a number of pleasant colonial-style hotels both in the
downtown and outlying areas. Generally, the cheapest properties are
near the bus station, moderately priced selections are clustered around
the plaza (or on nearby side streets), and deluxe resort hotels are in or
near the Santa María hills.

$$$$ ▦ **Villa Montaña.** French count Philippe de Reiset has fitted this villa with
★ all the trappings of a wealthy Mexican estate. High above Morelia in the
Santa María hills, its five impeccably groomed acres are dotted with a
pool, tennis court, and stone sculptures. Each individually decorated
unit has at least one piece of antique furniture, and most have a fireplace
and private patio. The hotel's renowned restaurant serves North American, French, and Mexican cuisine, and huge windows afford a marvelous
view of Morelia, especially at night. Children under age eight are discouraged
from dining in the restaurant, but the hotel can provide baby-sitters if re-
quested a day in advance. ⊠ *Calle Patzimba 201, 58000,* ☎ *4/314–0231,
4/314–0179,* 🆁🆇 *4/315–1423. 15 rooms, 25 suites. Restaurant, piano bar,
in-room safes, pool, tennis court, baby-sitting, laundry service, meeting
room, business services, free parking. AE, MC, V.*✆

$$$ ▦ **Hotel Catedral.** Located in a restored colonial mansion, this three-
story property began operating as a hotel some 30 years ago. Its mod-
ern rooms are clustered around a skylighted courtyard; eight of them
overlook the main plaza and cathedral on Avenida Madero. Interior
quarters have less dramatic views but are less noisy. All rooms have
dark wood furnishings, telephones, and cable TVs. The beds are rather
soft. Rates include Continental breakfast. ⊠ *Calle Zaragoza 37, 58000,*
☎ *4/313–0783, 4/313–0467,* 🆁🆇 *4/313–0406. 43 rooms, 2 suites.
Restaurant, bar, baby-sitting, dry cleaning. AE, MC, V.*

$$$ ▦ **Hotel Mansión Acueducto.** An elaborate wood and wrought-iron stair-
case leads from the elegant lobby to more-modest quarters upstairs.
Rooms have dark, colonial-style furniture, telephones, and color cable
TVs. Older rooms overlook the aqueduct and nearby park. Rooms in
the motel-like wing have views of the garden, pool, and surrounding
city. At times, student groups book the entire property. ⊠ *Av. Acueducto 25, 58000,* ☎ *4/312–3301,* 🆁🆇 *4/312–2020. 36 rooms, 1 suite.
Restaurant, bar, pool, free parking. AE, MC, V.*

$$$ ▦ **Hotel Virrey de Mendoza.** Built in 1565 to house a Spanish noble-
★ man, this downtown hotel still radiates plenty of Old World atmosphere.
The elegant lobby lounge is fitted with an enormous stone fireplace
and cushy black leather couches. Guest rooms have dark colonial-style
furnishings, lace curtains, soaring ceilings, and creaking hardwood floors,
as well as cable TVs and telephones. The bathrooms have porcelain
tubs. ⊠ *Av. Madero Pte. 310, 58000,* ☎ *4/312–0633, 4/312–4940,*
🆁🆇 *4/312–6719. 48 rooms, 9 suites. Restaurant, bar, coffee shop, laun-
dry service, free parking. AE, MC, V.*✆

$$ ▦ **Hotel Posada de la Soledad.** Set in a restored private mansion built
★ in the late 17th century, the Posada de la Soledad is conveniently located
one block from the Plaza de Armas. All rooms have cable TVs, but otherwise vary in size, decoration, amenities, and price. The rooms in the original section surround an elegant patio with a large fountain and massive

bougainvilleas. Rooms in a newer section are smaller and plainly furnished but quiet; rooms on Calle Ocampo get loud traffic noise from the street. If you're not impressed with the room you are shown, ask to see another. ⊠ *Ignacio Zaragoza 90, 58000,* ☎ *4/312–1888,* FAX *4/312–2111. 48 rooms, 9 suites. Restaurant, bar. AE, MC, V.*

$ 🖫 **Hotel Valladolid.** Right on the Plaza de Armas, this sister property of the slightly more impressive Hotel Catedral has plain but clean rooms with brick floors and striped bedspreads. Twenty of the rooms have cable TV (none have phones), and the price includes a Continental breakfast. ⊠ *Portal Hidalgo 245, 58000,* ☎ *4/312–0027,* FAX *4/312–4663. 25 rooms. Restaurant. AE, MC, V.*

Nightlife and the Arts

Morelia has two lively folk-music clubs, both in beautiful colonial courtyards downtown. Named after the army of Mexican Revolutionary hero General Emiliano Zapata, **Bola Suriana** (⊠ Allende 355, ☎ 4/312–4141) presents traditional Mexican music Monday–Saturday from 9 PM to 1 AM. **Colibri** (⊠ Galeana 36, ☎ 4/312–2261) has folk music from throughout Latin America every night from 9:30 PM to 1 AM.

Side Trip to Santuario de Mariposas el Rosario

Approximately 115 km (71 mi) east of Morelia.

Every year 100 million monarch butterflies migrate from the United States and Canada to winter in the easternmost part of Michoacán, near the border of México state. A visit to the **Santuario de Mariposas el Rosario** (El Rosario Monarch Butterfly Sanctuary) between early November and early March is an awesome sensory experience. Caked with orange and black butterflies, the pine forest looks like it's on fire. Listen closely and you'll hear the rustle of nearly a billion wings beating. The hike to the groves is a steep climb, and the high altitude (10,400 ft) will require that you take it slowly.

This day trip takes about 10 hours, but it's well worth the effort. If you choose not to drive the rough roads, catch a guided tour in Morelia (☞ Contacts and Resources *in* Morelia A to Z, *below*). ⊠ *Hwy. 15 east to Zitácuaro, then take marked but unnumbered road north to Angangueo, and on to sanctuary entrance.* 🖾 *$3 (plus tip for guide).* ☉ *Daily 10–5.*

Morelia A to Z

Arriving and Departing

BY BUS

Direct bus service is available daily between the Terminal Poniente (West Terminal, commonly referred to as the Observatorio) in Mexico City and Morelia's **Central de Autobuses** (⊠ Eduardo Ruiz, between Valentín Gómez Farías and Guzmán, ☎ 4/312–5664). Several bus lines have frequent service; the most direct trip ($18) takes four hours on either **ETN** (☎ 4/313–7440 or 4/313–4137) or **Herradura de Plata** (☎ 4/312–2988). Buses leave every hour or two around the clock.

BY CAR

The drive from Mexico City to Morelia (302 km [187 mi]) on the toll road through Toluca, Atlacamulco, Contepec, and Maravatio takes about four hours.

BY PLANE

There are daily flights between **Francisco Mujica International Airport,** 24 km (15 mi) north of Morelia, and Mexico City's International Airport on Aeroméxico (☎ 01–800/021–4000). Mexicana (☎ 4/324–3808,

4/324–3818) has direct flights to and from Los Angeles, San Francisco, and Chicago. Flights are subject to cancellation; flight times change often and must be confirmed one day in advance. The 45-minute taxi ride from the airport to Morelia costs about $20.

Getting Around

As in many heartland cities, Morelia's major sights are near the center of town and easy to get to on foot. Street names in Morelia change frequently, especially on either side of Avenida Madero, the city's main east–west artery. Taxis in Morelia can be hailed on the street or found near the main plaza. Buses run the length of Avenida Madero.

Contacts and Resources

CAR RENTAL

Budget (⊠ Francisco Mujica International Airport, ☎ 4/313–3399). **National** (⊠ Francisco Mujica International Airport and Av. Acueducto 3891, ☎ 4/324–6747).

E-MAIL

Chat Room Cyber Café (⊠ Nigromante 132-A, ☎ 4/312–9222), open Monday–Saturday 9 AM–10 PM and Sunday noon–9, charges about $3 an hour for Internet access.

EMERGENCIES

Police (☎ 4/326–8522). **Ambulance–Red Cross** (Cruz Roja, ☎ 4/314–5151). **Hospital de la Cruz Roja** (☎ 4/314–5025). **Consumer Protection Office** (☎ 4/315–6202). **Fire Department** (☎ 4/312–1235). **Hospital Memorial** (☎ 4/315–1047, 4/315–1099). **Green Angels** (☎ 4/312–7777).

GUIDED TOURS

The following operators offer tours of Morelia and the butterfly sanctuary: **Ayangupani** (⊠ contact through David Saucedo Ortega at the Villa Montaña front desk, Calle Patzimba 201, ☎ FAX 4/315–4045), **Explora Viajes** (⊠ Av. Madero Ote. 493B, ☎ 4/312–7766, FAX 4/312–7660), and **Morelia Operadores de Viajes** (⊠ Valentín Gómez Farías 131, ☎ 4/312–8723, 4/312–8747, FAX 4/312–9591).

MONEY EXCHANGES

Casa Cambio Valladolid (⊠ Portal Matamoros 86, ☎ 4/312–8586) is open weekdays 9–6, Saturday 9–1:30.

TRAVEL AGENCIES

Gran Turismo (⊠ Edificio Ejecutivo Camelinas, Av. Camelinas 3233, Int. 102–103, ☎ 4/324–0484, FAX 4/324–0495) is the American Express representative.

VISITOR INFORMATION

Secretaría Estatal de Turismo (⊠ Palacio Clavijero, Calle Nigromante 79, ☎ 4/317–2371, FAX 4/312–9816) is open weekdays 9–8, weekends 9–7.

PÁTZCUARO

Pátzcuaro, the 16th-century capital of Michoacán, exists in a time warp. A bit more than an hour by car from Morelia, this beautiful lakeside community set at 7,250 ft in the Sierra Madre is home to the Purépecha Indians, who fish, farm, and ply their crafts as they have for centuries. Women wrapped tightly in their striped wool *rebozos* (shawls) hurry to market in the chilly morning air. Men in traditional straw hats wheel overburdened carts down crooked, dusty backstreets.

The architecture, too, has remained largely unchanged over the years. In the 16th century, under kindly Bishop Vasco de Quiroga, Pátzcuaro underwent a building boom. After he died in 1565, the state capital was

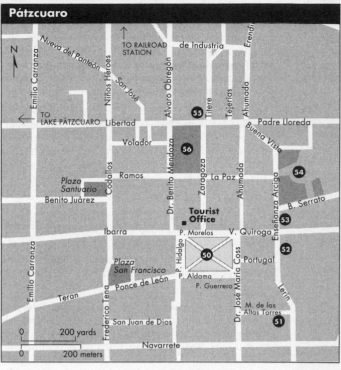

moved to Morelia, and the town became a cultural (and architectural) backwater for hundreds of years. These days 16th-century mansions surround the downtown plazas; one-story whitewashed houses with sloping red tile roofs line the side streets and hills.

Despite the altitude, the weather in Pátzcuaro is temperate year-round. (Autumn and winter nights, however, are cold; sweaters and jackets are a must.) On November 1—the night preceding the Day of the Dead—the town is inundated with tourists en route to Janítzio, an island in Lake Pátzcuaro, where one of the most elaborate graveyard ceremonies in all of Mexico takes place. Go to the island of Yunuen for an authentic glimpse of daily island life, and you can stay overnight. At numerous small towns around the lake you can buy craft items from their makers, in the process absorbing a bit of small-town rural Mexico. These towns are just beginning to attract tourism, and several new dining and lodging venues are opening up outside Pátzcuaro. The Delegación de Turismo can share suggestions for adventures outside Pátzcuaro, as can expert local tour guides Francisco Castilleja and Marilyn Mayo (☞ Contacts and Resources *in* Pátzcuaro A to Z, *below*).

Exploring Pátzcuaro

Most of Pátzcuaro's sights can be seen in a few hours, but the town and outlying areas deserve to be explored at a leisurely pace. There can be some traffic in the Plaza Bocanegra and on the main road coming into town, but elsewhere it is blissfully quiet.

A Good Walk

Start your stroll at the **tourist office** (Plaza Vasco de Quiroga 50A), where you can pick up maps and brochures. Walk across the large **Plaza Vasco de Quiroga** ⑤ to the east side of the square and turn right on Calle Dr.

José María Coss; in less than a block you'll see a long cobblestone walkway leading to **La Casa de los 11 Patios** ⑤, a former convent now housing a number of crafts shops. As you leave the complex, continue up a stone walkway to Calle Lerín. To the north (past Calle Portugal) is the **Templo de la Compañía** ⑤, the state's first cathedral. After visiting the church, continue another half block along Calle Lerín to the **Museo de Artes Populares** ⑤ on your right.

Directly down Calle Lerín and across a cobblestone courtyard is **La Basílica de Nuestra Señora de la Salud** ⑤. Walk downhill from the basilica (take Buenavista to Libertad and turn left) to reach the **Biblioteca Pública Gertrudis Bocanegra** ⑤. For a nice detour from the library, continue for a half block to the large outdoor **mercado** sprawled along Calle Libertad and its side streets. At times the road is so crowded with people and their wares—fruit, vegetables, beans, rice, herbs, and other necessities of daily life—that it is difficult to walk. If you press on for about a block, you'll see an indoor market to your left, filled with more produce, large hanging slabs of meat, hot food, and a variety of cheap trinkets. When you're done with your market tour, retrace your steps down Calle Libertad. Across the street from the library, you can rest at **Plaza Bocanegra** ⑤, just one block north of your starting point, Plaza Vasco de Quiroga.

Sights to See

⑤ **La Basílica de Nuestra Señora de la Salud** (Basilica of our Lady of Health). The church was begun in 1554 by Vasco de Quiroga, and throughout the centuries others—undaunted by earthquakes and fires—took up the cause and constructed the church in honor of the Virgin of Health. Near the main altar is a statue of the Virgin made of derivatives of cornstalks and orchids. Several masses are still held here daily; the earliest begins shortly after dawn. Out front, Purépecha women sell hot tortillas, herbal mixtures for teas, and religious objects. You can glimpse Lake Pátzcuaro in the distance. ⊠ *Calle Lerín s/n, near Calle Benigno Serrato.*

⑤ **Biblioteca Pública Gertrudis Bocanegra.** In the back of this library, a vast mural painted by Juan O'Gorman in 1942 depicts in great detail the history of the region and of the Purépecha people. In the bottom right of the mural, you can see Gertrudis Bocanegra, a local heroine who was shot in 1814 for refusing to divulge the revolutionaries' secrets to the Spaniards. ⊠ *North side of Plaza Bocanegra.* ☉ *Weekdays 9–7.*

⑤ **La Casa de los 11 Patios.** An 18th-century convent, 11 Patios houses a number of high-quality shops featuring Purépecha handiwork. As you meander through the shops and courtyards, you'll encounter weavers producing large bolts of cloth, artists trimming black lacquerware with gold, and seamstresses embroidering blouses. If you plan to shop in Pátzcuaro, this is a good place to start. You can view the selection of regional goods and begin to compare prices. ⊠ *Calle Madrigal de las Altas Torres s/n.* ☉ *Daily 10–2 and 4–8.*

⑤ **Museo de Artes Populares.** Home to the Colegio de San Nicolás Obispo in the 16th century, the building today houses displays of colonial and contemporary crafts, such as ceramics, masks, lacquerware, paintings, and ex-votos in its many rooms. Behind this building is a *troje* (traditional Purépecha wooden house) braced atop a stone platform. ⊠ *Calle Lerín,* ☎ *434/2–10–29.* ☷ *About $2, free Sun.* ☉ *Tues.–Sat. 9–7, Sun. 9–2:30.*

⑤ **Plaza Bocanegra.** The smaller of the city's two squares (it's also called Plaza Chica), this is the center of Pátzcuaro's commercial life. Bootblacks, pushcart vendors, and bus and taxi stands are all in the plaza, which is embellished by a statue of the local heroine, Gertrudis Bocanegra.

⊠ *Bounded by Av. Libertad on the north, Portal Regules on the south, Dr. Benito Mendoza on the west, and Calle Zaragoza on the east.*

50 Plaza Vasco de Quiroga. A tranquil courtyard surrounded by ash and pine trees and 16th-century mansions (since converted into hotels and shops), the larger of the two downtown plazas commemorates the bishop who restored dignity to the Purépecha people. During the Spanish conquest, Nuño de Guzmán, a lieutenant in Hernán Cortés's army, committed atrocities on the local population in his efforts to conquer western Mexico. He was eventually arrested by the Spanish authorities, and in 1537 Vasco de Quiroga was appointed bishop of Michoacán. Attempting to regain the trust of the indigenous people, he established a number of model villages in the area and promoted the development of artesanía commerce among the Purépechas. Quiroga died in 1565, and his remains were consecrated in the ☞ **Basílica de Nuestra Señora de la Salud.** ⊠ *Bounded by Calle Quiroga on the north, Av. Ponce de León on the south, Portal Hidalgo on the west, and Dr. José María Coss on the east.*

NEED A
BREAK?

Before heading to Lake Pátzcuaro, sit in **Plaza Vasco de Quiroga** for a moment and enjoy a rich Michoacán ice cream you can buy under the portals on the west side of the plaza. Or sip a warming Doña Paca cappuccino spiked with *rompope* (egg liqueur) at the sidewalk café in front of **Mansión Iturbe** (☞ Lodging, *below*).

52 Templo de la Compañia. Michoacán's first cathedral was begun in 1540 by order of Vasco de Quiroga and completed in 1546. When the state capital was moved to Morelia some 20 years later, the church was taken over by the Jesuits. Today it remains much as it was in the 16th century. Moss has grown over the crumbling stone steps outside; the dank interior is planked with thick wood floors and lined with bare wood benches. ⊠ *Calle Lerín s/n, near Calle Alcantaría.*

OFF THE
BEATEN PATH

LAKE PÁTZCUARO – Just a 10-minute taxi ride from downtown are the tranquil shores of Lake Pátzcuaro. There are a few lakeside restaurants here that serve fresh whitefish and other local catches. Amble along the dock or peek into the waterfront crafts shops. A boat trip to Janitzio (the largest of Lake Pátzcuaro's five islands), or to tiny Yunuen, is recommended. Wooden launches, with room for 25 people, depart for Janitzio and the other islands daily 9–6. Purchase round-trip tickets for $3 at a dockside office (prices are controlled by the tourist department). The ride to Janítzio takes about 30 minutes and is particularly beautiful in late afternoon, when the sun is low in the sky. Once you're out on the lake, fishermen with butterfly nets may approach your boat. The nets are no longer used for fishing, but for a small donation these locals will let you take their picture.

On most days (November 1 being the exception), Janítzio is a quiet albeit touristy island inhabited by Purépecha Indians. It is crowned by a huge statue of independence hero José María Morelos, which is accessible by a cobblestone stairway. Although the road twists past many souvenir stands as it ascends, don't be discouraged. The view from the summit—of the lake, the town, and the surrounding hills—is well worth the climb. Inside the statue are some remarkable murals that spiral up from the base to the tip of the monument.

Although Janítzio has succumbed to tourism, the small island of Yunuen is just beginning to attract visitors. This tranquil town has just 21 families, and provides a more accurate picture of island life than does Janítzio. You can get a boat to here from the ferry landing, or arrange to stay overnight in simple yet clean cabins available for visitors. The office of tourism can provide information.

Dining

Many restaurants in Pátzcuaro specialize in seafood. In addition to white-fish, look for *trucha* (trout) and *charales* and *boquerones* (two small, locally caught fish served as appetizers). Purépecha dishes, such as sopa tarasca, are also common. As a rule, restaurants are located around the two plazas and in hotels. Since the large meal is served at midday, many dining establishments are shuttered by 9.

Note: Many Pátzcuaro restaurants and hotels do not accept traveler's checks, although some will take major credit cards.

$$$ ✕ **El Primer Piso.** This second-floor restaurant overlooks Plaza Vasco de
★ Quiroga, and on warm nights you can watch the comings and goings from a balcony table. There's plenty to look at inside as well; the restaurant doubles as an art gallery. The eclectic menu provides a break from the rather monotonous Pátzcuaro fare: try the pear salad with goat cheese, walnuts, and watercress, or the white-chocolate mousse with black-berries and melon cream. ⊠ *Plaza Vasco de Quiroga 29,* ☎ *434/2–01–22. AE. Closed Tues.*

$$ ✕ **El Patio.** Although this low-key restaurant features mouthwatering whitefish platters (including salsa, vegetables, and french fries), it's possible to duck in at midday for just a strong cappuccino or glass of Mexican wine. For a late-afternoon snack, a plate of quesadillas with a side order of guacamole is highly recommended, and the sopa tarasca is superb. ⊠ *Plaza Vasco de Quiroga 19,* ☎ *434/2–04–84. MC, V.*

$ ✕ **Restaurante Gran Hotel.** Although this one-room restaurant is connected to the Gran Hotel, it is independently owned and attracts a mix of locals and tourists to its midday meal. The tables on the sidewalk are a fun spot to take in the Plaza Chica hubbub. The food is good and wholesome. Specialties include lightly breaded whitefish, chicken with mole sauce, and Tarascan soup. ⊠ *Portal Regules 6,* ☎ *434/2–04–43. No credit cards.*

Lodging

Although Pátzcuaro has no deluxe hotels, there is an ample number of clean, moderately priced properties. Most are on or within a few blocks of the Plaza Vasco de Quiroga. Several more-expensive hotels are on Avenida Lázaro Cárdenas, the road to Lake Pátzcuaro. If you're planning to be in town on or near November 1–2, the Mexican Day of the Dead, make hotel reservations at least six months in advance.

$$$ 🏨 **Hotel Posada de Don Vasco.** Located several minutes out of town on the road to Lake Pátzcuaro, this sprawling resort hotel offers a wide range of amenities, including satellite TV. Its 30 newer rooms are thickly carpeted and have either balconies or patios; the older quarters, which are oddly decorated with gold and brown patterned rugs and bright checkered bedspreads, are smaller and open onto a courtyard. The lovely, manicured grounds are relatively quiet despite the occasional rumbling of a passing bus or truck. The restaurant is decorated like a prosperous country estate, with a large fireplace that blazes on cold nights. At the Saturday buffet dinner, the regional Dance of the Old Men is performed at 8:30 PM. Unfortunately, the food is uninspired. ⊠ *Av. Las Americas 450, 61600,* ☎ *434/2–39–71, 434/2–24–90,* FAX *434/2–02–62. 99 rooms, 4 suites. Restaurant, pool, tennis court, badminton, bowling, billiards. AE, MC, V.*

$$ 🏨 **Cabañas Yunuen.** This complex was built in 1993 on the island of Yunuen in collaboration with the Department of Tourism to promote visits to some of the area's more authentic communities. There are six cabins in all: two each for 2, 4, and 16 people; each has a kitchenette with small refrigerator and satellite TV. Breakfast or dinner and round-trip transportation by boat is included in the price, about $28 for two people. ✉ *Domicilio Conocido, Isla de Yunuen,* ☎ *434/2–44–73, 4/311–76–80 in Morelia. 6 cabins. Dining room, kitchenettes. No credit cards.*

$$ 🏨 **Los Escudos.** Today a cozy hotel, this property was originally a 16th-century home. Its courtyards bloom with potted plants, and some guest rooms contain small murals of Purépecha Indian scenes. Ten rooms situated in back and shielded from street noise open onto an outdoor patio. All rooms have color cable TVs and telephones; five have fireplaces. The adjoining restaurant has a varied menu, ranging from club sandwiches to multicourse midday meals. Particularly tempting is the *pollo especial Los Escudos* (chicken sautéed in tomato sauce and vegetables). ✉ *Portal Hidalgo 73, 61600,* ☎ *434/2–01–38, 434/2–12–90,* ℻ *434/2–06–49. 31 rooms, 2 suites. Restaurant. MC, V.*

$$ 🏨 **Mansión Iturbe.** This hotel, housed in a 17th-century mansion, still
★ retains much of its colonial charm. Both the rooms and corridors are frailly lighted, giving the impression of a true 17th-century home. Plant-filled courtyards are ringed by stone archways. Rooms, with large wood-and-glass doors, are partially carpeted. Bicycles are lent to guests for a few hours per stay, and every fourth night is free. Breakfast is included in the room rate. There are several restaurants, the most lively being El Viejo Gaucho, where pizzas, meats, and *empanadas* (meat-filled pastries) are served and live music is performed Wednesday–Sunday nights. ✉ *Portal Morelos 59, 61600,* ☎ *434/2–03–68, 434/2–36–28,* ℻ *4/313–45–93 in Morelia. 10 rooms, 4 suites. 3 restaurants, bicycles. AE, MC, V.* ✆

$ 🏨 **Hotel Posada La Basílica.** This colonial-style inn, housed in a
★ 17th-century building, faces the Basílica de Nuestra Señora de la Salud, and on some mornings strains from a postdawn mass filter softly into the hotel. The property has comfortable, individually decorated rooms, some with fireplaces. Thick wood shutters cover floor-to-ceiling windows, and walls are trimmed in hand-painted colonial designs. The restaurant has views of the mountains, the lake, and tile-roof homes. Open for breakfast and lunch only, it offers such regional specialties as broiled trout with garlic and tamales with sweet cream. Service can be slow, as the waiter tends to hide in the kitchen. ✉ *Calle Arciga 6, 61600,* ☎ *434/2–11–08,* ℻ *434/2–06–59. 12 rooms. Restaurant. MC, V.*

$ 🏨 **Mesón del Gallo.** On a fairly quiet side street near the Casa de los 11 Patios, this two-story property is beginning to look a bit shabby. Beds have wood-and-tile headboards and magenta spreads and curtains. Suites, complete with minibars, are furnished in more subdued hues. All rooms have telephones but no TV. There is a grassy patio encircled by bougainvillea and fruit trees with a lonely umbrella table in the middle. Rates include breakfast. ✉ *Calle Dr. Coss 20, 61600,* ☎ *434/2–14–74,* ℻ *434/2–15–11. 20 rooms, 5 suites. Restaurant, bar. AE, MC, V.*

Nightlife and the Arts

The **Danza de los Viejitos** (Dance of the Little Old Men), a widely known regional dance, is performed during Saturday dinner at Hotel Posada de Don Vasco (☞ Lodging, *above*) for approximately $12 (includes dinner). The dance is also performed Saturday night at 8 PM at Los Escudos (☞ Lodging, *above*), on Plaza de Quiroga.

Shopping

Pátzcuaro has some of Mexico's finest folk-art shopping. **Mantas Tipicas** (✉ Calle Dr. Coss 5, ☎ 434/2–13–24) sells hand-loomed tablecloths and more. **Bordados Santa Cruz** (✉ Calle Dr. Coss 3, ☎ no phone) is a women's embroidery collective. High-quality ceramics, furniture, and silver jewelry can be found at **Galería del Arcángel** (⊠ Arciga 30, ☎ 434/ 2–17–74). And don't miss the stands in front of the basilica and at the daily mercado west of Plaza Chica. **Galería Iturbe** (⊠ Portal Morelos 59), at Mansión Iturbe, has a whimsical assortment of Ocumicho devil figures, copper jewelry, and the work of local painters. Ask the hotel desk clerk to open the store for you as it's often closed. Since 1898, the family-run **Chocolate Casero Joaquinita** (⊠ Enseñanza 38, ☎ 434/2–45–14) has been concocting delectable homemade cinnamon-spiced hot-chocolate tablets. **Santa Teresa Velas y Cirios** (⊠ Portal Hidalgo 71, ☎ 434/ 2–02–14) sells handsome handmade candles in a rainbow of colors.

Side Trips

Tzintzuntzan

 17 km (10½ mi) northeast of Pátzcuaro.

When the Spanish came to colonize the region in the 16th century, some 40,000 Purépechas lived and worshiped in this lakeshore village, which they called "place of the hummingbirds." The ruins of the pyramid-shape temples, or *yacatas,* found in the ancient capital of the Purépecha kingdom still stand today and are open to the public for $2. There are also vestiges of a 16th-century Franciscan monastery where Spanish friars attempted to convert the Indians to Christianity. Although Tzintzuntzan lost some prominence when Bishop Vasco de Quiroga moved the seat of his diocese to Pátzcuaro in 1540, the village is still well known for the straw and ceramic handicrafts made by the Purépecha Indians and sold in numerous shops along the main street of town. The bus marked QUIROGA takes a half hour to get from Pátzcuaro's Central Camionera to Tzintzuntzan.

Santa Clara del Cobre
20 km (12½ mi) south of Pátzcuaro.

Since before the conquest, Santa Clara del Cobre has been a center for copper arts. Now the local copper mines are empty, but the artisans still make gorgeous vessels, plates, napkin rings, and jewelry using the traditional method of pounding out each piece of metal by hand. For an introduction to quality and range of styles available, visit the **Museo del Cobre** (⊠ Calles Morelos and Pino Suárez, near the plaza), open Tuesday–Sunday 10–3 and 5–7. Admission is 25¢. Then explore the 50-some little shops and factories in town. The bus to Santa Clara del Cobre from Pátzcuaro's Central Camionera takes 40 minutes.

Uruapan
64 km (40 mi) west of Pátzcuaro.

The subtropical town of Uruapan is distinctly different from its lakeside neighbor: some 2,000 ft lower than Pátzcuaro, although still at an elevation of 5,300 ft, it is a populous commercial center with a warm climate and lush vegetation. The town's name is derived from the Purépecha word *urupan,* meaning "where the flowers bloom." Uruapan celebrates Palm Sunday with a lively procession through the streets, brass bands, and a spectacular, bargain-filled crafts market in the central plaza—one of the best in all of Mexico.

You can get to Uruapan from Pátzcuaro by car or bus. Route 14 and the new toll road are the most direct routes between the two cities. There is also frequent bus service on the Flecha Amarilla and other major lines; travel time is about 70 minutes.

You can see several points of interest within a few hours. The **Mercado de Antojitos,** an immense, sprawling market, begins in back of the Museo Regional de Arte Popular and extends quite a distance north along Calle

Constitución. Along the road, Purépecha Indians sell large mounds of produce, fresh fish, beans, homemade cheese, and a variety of cheap manufactured goods. If you travel south along Calle Constitución, you'll come to a courtyard where vendors sell hot food.

The **Museo Regional de Arte Popular,** opposite the north side of Uruapan's Plaza Principal, was a 16th-century hospital known as La Huatápera before its conversion. It houses a collection of crafts from the state of Michoacán, including an excellent display of lacquerware made in Uruapan. ☎ 4/524–3434. ☒ *Free.* ◎ *Tues.–Sun. 9:30–1:30 and 3:30–6.*

★ **Parque Nacional Eduardo Ruiz** (about six long blocks from the Plaza Principal off Calle Independencia) is a gem of an urban park. Its paved paths meander through verdant tropical acreage past abundant waterfalls, fountains, and springs to the source of the Río Cupatitzio. There also is a trout farm here and a popular playground.

Eleven kilometers (7 mi) south along the Río Cupatitzio is the magnificent waterfall at **Tzaráracua.** At this point the river plunges 150 ft off a sheer rock cliff into a riverbed below; a rainbow seems to hang perpetually over the site. Buses marked TZARÁRACUA leave sporadically from the Plaza Principal in Uruapan. You can also take a taxi for about $3, or drive there via Avenida Lázaro Cárdenas.

Farther afield, about 32 km (20 mi) north of Uruapan, lies the dormant **Paricutín volcano.** Its initial burst of lava and ashes wiped out the nearby village of San Juan Parangaricútiro in 1943. Today travelers can visit this buried site by hiring gentle mountain ponies and a Purépecha guide in the town of Angahuan. To reach Angahuan, take the Los Reyes bus from Uruapan's Central Camionera or go by car via the Uruapan–Carapan highway.

DINING
For good comida casera, try **El Rincón del Burrito** (☒ Portal Matamorros 7, ☎ no phone) or the restaurant at **Mansión de Cupatitzio,** in the national park at the mouth of the Río Cupatitzio (☒ Parque Nacional s/n, ☎ 4/523–2070, 4/523–2100).

Pátzcuaro A to Z

Arriving and Departing

BY BUS
Buses run daily between the Terminal Poniente (West Terminal, commonly referred to as the Observatorio) in Mexico City and Pátzcuaro's **Central Camionera** (☒ El Libramiento, on the southwestern outskirts of town). Several lines offer frequent service; the most direct trip, which takes five hours, is on either Herradura de Plata or Pegasso Plus (☎ 434/2–10–45 for both lines), or ETN (☎ 434/2–10–60). Transportation coming from most heartland cities goes to Morelia; buses leave about every 15 minutes from there on the 45-minute trip to Pátzcuaro.

BY CAR
The Mexico City–Guadalajara tollway cuts driving time to Pátzcuaro to 4½ or 5 hours, and the trip on to Guadalajara to four hours by car. From Morelia, the excellent free road to Pátzcuaro takes just over an hour. You'll have to rent a car in Mexico City or Morelia, as there are no rental outlets in Pátzcuaro.

Getting Around
Many of Pátzcuaro's principal sights are near the Plaza Vasco de Quiroga and Plaza Bocanegra in the center of town. Taxis and buses to the lake can also be found at the latter square. If you want to visit

surrounding villages, taxi drivers will drive you for a reasonable rate. Be sure to agree on a fee before setting out.

Contacts and Resources

E-MAIL

Informatica Integral de Pátzcuaro (✉ Plaza Vasco de Quiroga 64), open daily 9–9, charges $2 an hour for Internet access.

EMERGENCIES

Police (☎ 434/2–00–04). **Traffic Police** (☎ 434/2–05–65). **Rescue** (☎ 434/2–02–09).

Hospital Civil (Romero 10, ☎ 434/2–02–85).

Pharmacy. Farmacia La Paz (✉ La Paz and Bocanegra in Plaza Bocanegra, ☎ 434/2–08–10).

GUIDED TOURS

Marilyn Mayo (✉ Apdo. 416, 61600, ☎ 434/2–23–01, FAX 434/2–27–56) designs custom tours based on your interests. She can take you to exuberant fiestas in tiny villages, to the home studios of master artisans, to the butterfly sanctuary, or any other place you want to go. Guide **Francisco Castilleja** (✉ Centro Eronga, Profr. Urueta 105, ☎ 434/4–01–67) is highly knowledgeable about pre-Hispanic philosophy, history, archaeology, and medicinal herbs. He speaks fluent English, German, French, and Spanish.

MONEY EXCHANGE

Banca Promex (✉ Portal Regules 9, ☎ 434/2–24–66). **Banamex** (✉ Portal Juárez 32, ☎ 434/2–15–50, 434/2–10–31). **Bancomer** (✉ Zaragoza 23, ☎ 434/2–03–34). A **Banamex Caja Permanente ATM** is located on Dr. Benito Mendoza, between the two plazas.

VISITOR INFORMATION

Delegación de Turismo (✉ Plaza Vasco de Quiroga 50A, ☎ FAX 434/2–12–14) is the official tourism office and, although you may not find anyone here who speaks English, it will do its best to provide information regarding excursions outside Pátzcuaro. It's open Monday–Saturday 9–2 and 4–7, Sunday 9–2.

Dirección de Orientación y Fomento al Turismo (✉ Portal Hidalgo 1, on Plaza de Quiroga, ☎ 434/2–02–15, 434/2–02–16, FAX 434/32–09–67) offers maps and can answer basic questions about tourist facilities in Pátzcuaro. It's open daily 9–3 and 5–7.

8 PACIFIC COAST RESORTS

Hollywood introduced us to two of the Mexican Riviera's most popular towns: Ava Gardner and Richard Burton's sleepy, steamy Puerto Vallarta in *The Night of the Iguana* and the sparkling Manzanillo coast that served as the backdrop to Bo Derek—and Dudley Moore's antics—in *10*. These days both places are prime cruise-ship stops, as is Mazatlán, a bustling port that attracts sportfishing enthusiasts and surfers. Ixtapa/Zihuatanejo has two-for-one appeal, one of Mexico's most charming fishing villages adjoining a pristine resort.

Updated by
Shane
Christensen

A CROSS THE GULF OF CALIFORNIA from the Baja California
Peninsula lies Mazatlán, Mexico's largest Pacific port and the
major Mexican resort closest to the United States, some 1,200
km (745 mi) south of the Arizona border. This is the beginning of what
cruise-ship operators now call the Mexican Riviera, or the Gold Coast.
The coastline for the next 1,400 km (870 mi) is Mexico's tropical paradise. The Gulf of California, or the Sea of Cortés, as it is also called,
ends just below the Tropic of Cancer, leaving the Pacific coastline
open to fresh sea breezes. The coast's resorts—Mazatlán, Puerto Vallarta, Manzanillo, Ixtapa/Zihuatanejo, and Acapulco—are therefore
less muggy than gulf towns to the north. The water is colder, too, and
waves can get very rough.

The Pacific Coast doesn't have the rich cultural heritage of Mexico's
inland colonial villages and silver cities, and the history is sketchy at
best. It's not the place to see ruins, museums, and cathedrals; it's a gathering spot for sun worshipers, sportfishing enthusiasts, surfers, and swimmers. Not far from the resort regions are jungle streams and ocean coves,
but the majority of visitors never venture to these isolated sites, preferring instead to immerse themselves in the simultaneously bustling
and restful resort lifestyle, where great dining, shopping, and sunbathing are the major draws.

Mazatlán is first and foremost a busy commercial center, thanks to an
excellent port and the fertility of the surrounding countryside. More than
600,000 acres of farmland near Mazatlán produce tomatoes, melons,
cantaloupes, wheat, and cotton, much of which is shipped to the United
States. And nearly all of the 150,000 tons of shrimp hauled in annually is processed and frozen for the American and Japanese markets.

Sportfishing accounts for Mazatlán's resort status. The port sits at the
juncture of the Pacific and the Sea of Cortés, forming what has been
called the world's greatest natural fish trap. Hunters are drawn to the
quail, duck, and dove that thrive in the hillsides, and surfers find great
waves on nearby beaches. Another draw is that accommodations are
about half the cost of those in Cancún.

Tepic, capital of the state of Nayarit, lies between Mazatlán and Puerto
Vallarta. From here, travelers coming down from the border by bus
change buses to head to the coast. Budgeteers and those who shun
megaresorts often head straight for San Blas, a small seaside village about
37 km (23 mi) northwest of Tepic through the jungle.

Some 323 km (200 mi) south of Mazatlán is **Puerto Vallarta,** by far
the best-known resort on the upper Pacific Coast. The late film director and sometime resident John Huston put the town on the map
when he filmed Tennessee Williams's *The Night of the Iguana* on the
outskirts of the village in 1963. Elizabeth Taylor came to keep Richard
Burton company during the filming, and the gossip about their romance—both were married at the time, but not to each other—brought
this quaint Mexican fishing village with its cobblestone lanes and
whitewashed, tile-roof houses to the public's attention. Before long,
travel agents were deluged with queries about Puerto Vallarta.

The fabled cobblestone streets are clogged with bumper-to-bumper traffic during the holiday season, but, despite the city's resort status, parts
of Puerto Vallarta are still picturesque. For a sense of the Eden that
once was, travel south of town to the lush green mountains where the
Río Tomatlán tumbles over boulders into the sea, or north to Punta

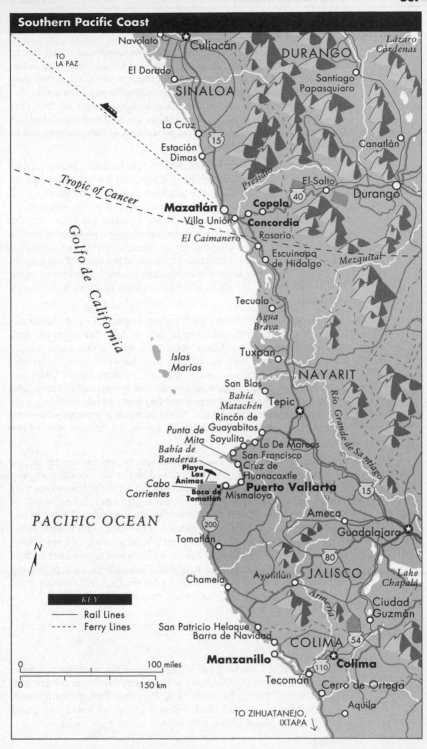

Southern Pacific Coast

Mita on the northern tip of Bahía de Banderas (Bay of Flags), where the exclusive Four Seasons resort lies.

Conquistador Hernán Cortés envisioned **Manzanillo** as a gateway to the Orient: from these shores, Spanish galleons would bring in the riches of Cathay to be trekked across the continent to Veracruz, where they would fill vessels headed for Spain. But Acapulco, not Manzanillo, became the port of call for the Manila galleons that arrived each year with riches from beyond the seas. Pirates are said to have staked out Manzanillo during the colonial era, and chests of loot are rumored to be buried beneath the sands.

With the coming of the railroads, Manzanillo became a major port of entry. It is now Mexico's second busiest port, and the lights of freighters at anchor can be seen along the southern beaches. Fifty years ago, a few seaside hotels opened up on the outskirts of town, which vacationers reached by train. The jet age, however, seemed to doom the port as a sunny vacation spot. Then Bolivian tin magnate Antenor Patiño built **Las Hadas** (The Fairies), a lavish Moorish-style resort complex inaugurated in 1974. It attracted the beautiful people, and for a while Las Hadas was better known than Manzanillo itself. The film *10* made a star of the resort as well as household names of its stars, Bo Derek and Dudley Moore.

In recent years there's been a push to turn Manzanillo and coastal villages to the north in neighboring Jalisco, such as Barra de Navidad, Melaque, Tenacatita, and Costa de Careyes, into a tourist zone. A four-lane toll road now cuts the driving time between Manzanillo and Guadalajara, Mexico's second-largest city, to three hours. Older hotels have been spruced up, and all-inclusive resorts constructed. The best hotel in Manzanillo is the **Grand Bay hotel** in Isla Navidad, a resort complex spread over some 1,200 acres on a peninsula between the Pacific Ocean and the Navidad Lagoon, 20 minutes west of the Manzanillo airport.

The southernmost of the Pacific Coast resorts and the newest kid on the scene—like Cancún, it was developed by the Mexican government in the early 1970s—**Ixtapa/Zihuatanejo** lies on the northwestern part of the state of Guerrero's coastline, some 500 km (300 mi) south of Manzanillo. It comprises two distinct destinations only 7 km (4½ mi) from each other. Ixtapa is the glitzier of the two, with international chain hotels lining its hotel zone, but it's far smaller and more low-key than older resorts such as Puerto Vallarta and newer ones such as Cancún. Its development put neighbor Zihuatanejo, a sleepy fishing village virtually unknown even among Mexicans, on the tourist map. In Zihuatanejo, La Casa Que Canta is one of the finest small hotels in the world.

Pleasures and Pastimes

Beaches

Mexico's Pacific Coast doubtless has some of North America's most inviting beaches, with deliciously warm waters and spectacular sunsets. There are beaches for every taste: long stretches of creamy sand, crescents of soft gold and black volcanic grains, secluded coves, and pristine shores accessible only by boat.

Dining

The emphasis in Mazatlán is on casual, bountiful dining, and the prices are reasonable. Shrimp, octopus, oysters, and fresh fish are the highlights; be sure to have a seafood cocktail along the beach. Dress is generally casual, too, with shorts, sundresses, and T-shirts commonplace. Puerto Vallarta has the widest array of restaurants, some with spectacular views, others hidden in the small, romantic patios of former homes, and still others—especially those on the *malecón* (seaside walkway or boardwalk)—as popular for people-watching as they are for their great seafood. Several Manzanillo dining spots have scenic views of the jungle and water that compensate for their lack of culinary excitement. In Ixtapa/Zihuatanejo, restaurants range from simple beach eateries to deluxe establishments with international chefs.

Some hotel restaurants add a 10%–15% service charge to your tab.

CATEGORY	COST*
$$$$	over $35
$$$	$25–$35
$$	$15–$25
$	under $15

*per person for a three-course meal including 15% sales tax, and excluding drinks and service

Fishing

Mazatlán is tops in the Mexican Pacific for billfishing. Sailfish run March to December, blue and black marlin May to December, and swordfish and striped marlin December to April. Other sportfish include roosterfish, wahoo, yellowfin tuna, bonita, mahimahi, and shark. Light-tackle fishing in the lagoons and just off the beach in *pangas* (small boats) for *huachinango* (red snapper) is also popular. Bass anglers will be pleased with the freshwater lakes in the local foothills of the Sierra Madre.

Sportfishing is good off Puerto Vallarta most of the year, particularly for billfish, rooster fish, mahimahi, yellowtail, and bonito. Manzanillo claims to be the sailfish capital of the world; the season runs from mid-October through March. Blue marlin and dorado are also abundant. Ixtapa/Zihuatanejo is becoming Mexico's new sportfishing destination. Anglers revel in the profusion of sailfish (November through March), black and blue marlin (February through May), yellowfin tuna (November through June), and mahimahi (November through January). In November, Mazatlán, Puerto Vallarta, and Manzanillo host international fishing tournaments. If you're not after a memento, most operations have a catch-and-release option.

Horseback Riding

In most Pacific Coast resorts, horseback riding along the shore is popular, and horses can be rented by the hour at major beaches. In Puerto Vallarta, several stables offer sunset rides, three-hour mountain trips, and rides to colonial villages in the Sierra Madre.

Lodging

Although not known for its upscale resorts, Mazatlán now has its share of luxury properties, along with comfortable beachfront hotels. It also has one of the highest concentrations of trailer parks in the country. In Puerto Vallarta, accommodations range from tiny inns to luxury waterfront hotels and spectacular resorts tucked away on hidden coves. The choices in Ixtapa/Zihuatanejo run the lodging gamut—big beachfront properties are the norm in Ixtapa; Zihuatanejo has budget hotels and two of the most exclusive small hotels in Mexico.

Most hotels raise their rates for the high season (December 15 through Easter Week); rates are lowest in May and June, the beginning of the rainy season (which lasts from late May to early October), and in September and October when hurricanes sweep the coast. Rates rise somewhat during July and August when most Mexican families take advantage of the warm waters and swarm the beaches for their sum-

mer vacations. Price categories are based on high-season rates; expect
to pay 25% less during the off-season.

CATEGORY	COST*
$$$$	over $200
$$$	$100–$200
$$	$50–$100
$	under $50

*All prices are for a standard double room, excluding 15% VAT (17% in the
state of Jalisco).*

Shopping

You can spend as much time shopping in Puerto Vallarta as you can
lazing in the sun. Shops selling excellent crafts from around the country vie with upscale art galleries and clothing and jewelry boutiques
for buyers' attention, especially in the downtown area. The selection
of Mexican crafts in Mazatlán is almost as good. Zihuatanejo has some
colorful crafts markets. The unique ceramics and masks from the state
of Guerrero, where the little fishing town is located, are especially plentiful.

Water Sports

Parasailing, swimming, windsurfing, sailing, kayaking, and waterskiing are popular at Pacific Coast resorts. Manzanillo and Mazatlán have
some of the finest surfing in Mexico, and the best diving spots in this
area are found around the islands off Puerto Vallarta, Ixtapa, and
Mazatlán. Puerto Vallarta hosts Mexico's annual boat show each
November, as well as various sailing regattas in winter.

Exploring the Pacific Coast Resorts

Resorts on this coastal stretch are at their best in winter, with temperatures in the 70s and 80s (a bit higher in Ixtapa/Zihuatanejo). The
off-season brings humidity, mosquitoes, and higher temperatures
(northernmost Mazatlán remains coolest), but also emptier beaches,
warmer water (well into the 70s), and less-crowded streets—plus 25%–
35% lower room rates and cheaper rental-car costs. Toward the end
of the rainy season, which involves mostly brief daily showers, the countryside and the mountainous backdrop of the Sierra Madre del Sur turn
brilliantly green with multicolor blossoms.

MAZATLÁN

Mazatlán is the Aztec word for "place of the deer," and long ago its
islands and shores sheltered far more deer than humans. Today it is a
city of some 500,000 residents and draws about 1 million tourists a
year, although it seems to be losing some of its clientele to such glitzier
resorts as Cancún. Sunning, surfing, fishing, and sailing are the primary attractions, and in the winter months visitors from inland Mexico, the United States, and Canada flock to Mazatlán for a break in
the sun. Hotel and restaurant prices are lower than elsewhere on the
coast, and the ambience is more that of a fishing town than a tourist
haven. Upscale resorts and ritzy restaurants aren't part of Mazatlán's
repertoire, although there is a fair dose of luxury at the Marina El Cid
Hotel and Yacht Club, Royal Villas, and Pueblo Bonito resorts.

Hunting and fishing were the original draw for visitors. At one time,
duck, quail, pheasant, and other wildfowl fed in the lagoons, and
jaguars, mountain lions, rabbits, and coyotes roamed the surrounding
hills. Hunters have to search a little harder and farther for their prey
these days, but there's still plenty of wildlife near Mazatlán. The city

is the base for Mexico's largest sportfishing fleet; fishermen haul the biggest catches (in size and number) on the coast. The average annual haul is 10,000 sailfish and 5,000 marlin. A record 988-pound marlin and 203-pound sailfish were pulled from these waters.

The Spanish settled in the Mazatlán region in 1531 and used the indigenous people as a labor force to create the port and village. In the ensuing centuries, the center of Mazatlán gradually moved north. The original site is now the village of Villa Union, 24 km (15 mi) southeast of the harbor.

In the early 1600s, the colonial government built a small fort and watchtowers atop the hills in the city to control the English and French pirates who used the harbor as a place from which to attack the rich Spanish galleons that plied the coast. Pirates were gone by 1800, but legends of buried treasure in the caves along the coast still circulate.

The port has a history of blockades. In 1847, during the Mexican War, U.S. forces marched down from the border through northeast Mexico and closed it. In 1864, the French bombarded the city and then controlled it for several years. The British occupied the port for a short period in 1871. Mexico's own internal warring factions took over from time to time. And after the Civil War in the United States, a group of Southerners tried to turn Mazatlán into a slave city.

Mazatlán has the country's largest shrimping fleet. Sinaloa, one of Mexico's richest states, uses the port to ship its agricultural products.

Exploring Mazatlán

Mazatlán's highlights are spread far and wide, and walking from one section of town to the other can take hours. The best way to travel is via *pulmonías* (open-air jitneys, literally "pneumonias") so you can sunbathe and take pictures as you cruise along, although you won't be able to roll up any windows to protect yourself from automobile fumes. If you choose to rent a car and drive, you can tour at your own pace. There are no traffic jams in Mazatlán, except near the market in downtown, where parking can also be a major problem. Downtown is virtually the only area of Mazatlán that can be walked; many visitors never see it, but it's worth spending a morning here.

Numbers in the text correspond to numbers in the margin and on the Mazatlán map.

A Good Tour

Start from the **Zona Dorada** (Golden Zone) ①, Mazatlán's central tourist area, which begins at Punta Camarón (Shrimp Point). If you travel north from here along the coast on Avenida Camarón Sábalo, you'll pass some of the city's most luxurious and priciest hotels. This route affords a good view of Mazatlán's three Pacific islands—Isla de los Pájaros, Isla de los Venados, and Isla de los Chivos. Just past the Camino Real resort, Avenida Camarón Sábalo becomes Avenida Sábalo Cerritos and crosses over the Estero del Sábalo, a long lagoon popular with bird-watchers. The area north of here is developing as an exclusive touring and resort area; towering condos are already being built.

South of the Zona Dorada, the main road changes names frequently. The 16-km (10-mi) malecón, Mazatlán's version of a main highway and beachfront boardwalk, begins at Punta Camarón and is here called Avenida del Mar. In a few blocks, you'll come to the city's highly recommended aquarium, **Acuario Mazatlán** ②, down Avenida de los Deportes. Avenida del Mar continues past beaches popular with residents and travelers staying at the budget hotels across the street. You're sure

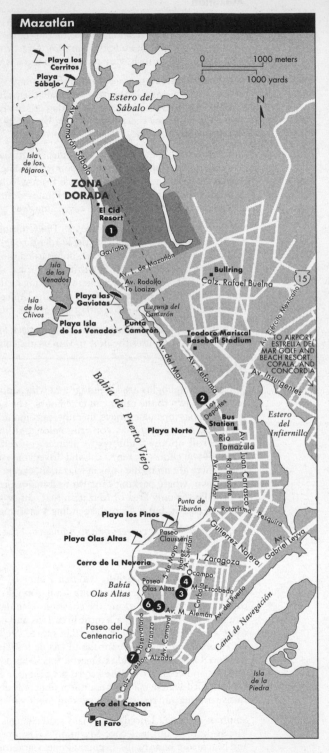

to notice the avenue's main landmark, the Monumento al Pescador: an enormous statue of a voluptuous, nude woman reclining on an anchor, her hand extended toward a nude fisherman dragging his nets.

Calles Juárez and Cinco de Mayo intersect with Avenida del Mar and lead to Mazatlán's real downtown, where the streets are filled with buses and people rushing to and from work and the market. The heart of the city is the **Plaza República** ③ or *zócalo* (main square); just across the street you'll see the twin-spire **Mazatlán Catedral** ④. On the streets facing the zócalo are the City Hall, banks, post office, and telegraph office. About three blocks southeast of the zócalo, a school for the arts and the Teatro Angela Peralta, both built in 1860 and now beautifully restored, were declared historic monuments in 1990. Stop for a drink or a bite at any one of the establishments in front of the nearby Plaza Machado, where neighborhood fiestas are held on special occasions. Head three blocks west to the **Museo de Arte de Mazatlán** ⑤, as well as the simple **Instituto Nacional de Antropología y Historia** ⑥.

Back along the waterfront, Avenida del Mar turns into Paseo Claussen as it heads south. If you continue along the malecón, you'll pass El Fuerte Carranza, an old Spanish fort built to defend the city against the French; Casa del Marino, a shelter for sailors; Playa Olas Altas (☞ Beaches, *below*); High-Divers Park, where young men climb to a white platform and plunge into the sea—spectacular at night, when the divers leap carrying flaming torches; and La Mazatleca, a bronze nymph. Across the street is a small bronze deer, Mazatlán's mascot. Just south is the Monument to the Continuity of Life, a large fountain with a handsome couple on top of a large conch shell and a school of porpoises leaping from the water. Paseo Claussen leads to Olas Altas, site of Old Mazatlán, the center for tourism in the 1940s. Olas Altas ("high waves") ends at a small traffic circle. A plaque at the circle bears the state symbol of Sinaloa. Above Olas Altas is **Cerro de Vigía** ⑦ (Lookout Hill).

Sights to See

⑫ ❷ **Acuario Mazatlán.** A perfect child-pleaser, Mazatlán's aquarium features tanks of sharks, sea horses, eels, lobsters, and multicolor salt- and freshwater fish. A fanciful bronze fountain and sculpture of two boys feeding a dolphin marks the aquarium's entrance, and an aviary sits amid the trees in the adjacent botanical garden. Bird and sea-lion shows, along with diving exhibitions, are performed throughout the day. ⊠ *Av. de los Deportes 111,* ☎ *69/81–78–15.* ☜ *$4.* ☉ *Daily 9:30–6.*

❼ **Cerro de Vigía** (Lookout Hill). The view from this windy hill above Olas Altas is fantastic: you can see both sides of Mazatlán, the harbor, and the Pacific. It's a steep climb up, better done by taxi than on foot. If you decide to hike it, do it early in the morning before the sun is at its hottest, and although a shop at the top frequently sells soft drinks, you should bring some water. At the top of the hill you'll see a weather station, along with a rusty cannon and the **Centenario Pérgola,** built in 1848 to celebrate the end of the U.S. invasion.

❻ **Instituto Nacional de Antropología y Historia.** The town's archaeological museum houses a small but fairly interesting collection of artifacts from the region. Particularly interesting is an exhibit of exquisite polychrome pottery with elaborate black and red designs left behind by the Totorames, an indigenous tribe that inhabited the area up until 200 years before the Spanish arrived. ⊠ *Sixto Osuna 76, off Paseo Olas Altas,* ☎ *69/81–14–55.* ☜ *Free.* ☉ *Weekdays 9–4.*

NEED A
BREAK?

The sidewalk tables at **Copa de Leche and Fonda Santa Clara** (⊠ Paseo Olas Altas, near Sixto Osuna) are perfect for watching sunsets.

❹ Mazatlán Catedral. The blue-and-gold spires of the downtown cathedral are a city landmark. Built in 1890 and made a basilica in 1935, this church has a gilded and ornate triple altar, with murals of angels overhead and many small altars along the sides. A sign at the entrance requests that visitors be appropriately attired (no shorts or tank tops inside). ⊠ *Calles Juárez and Plazuela República.*

❺ Museo de Arte de Mazatlán. This small museum shows the work of local, regional, and national artists, including Gerardo Santamarino, Jose Luis Cuevas, and Armando Nava. Daily painting classes are offered here. ⊠ *Sixto Osuna and Venustiano Carranza,* ☎ 🅕🅐🅧 *69/85–35–02.* 🎟 *75¢.* ☉ *Tues.–Sat. 10–2 and 5–8, Sun. 10–1.*

❸ Plaza República. At the center of downtown, this city square hosts one of the most fascinating gazebos in Mexico—what looks like a '50s diner inside the lower level and a wrought-iron bandstand on top. The green-and-orange tile on the walls, ancient jukebox, and soda fountain serving shakes, burgers, and hot dogs couldn't make a more surprising sight. Tourists and locals fill the plaza Sunday afternoon to hear local musicians play from the bandstand. ⊠ *Bounded by 21 de Marzo to the north, Flores to the south, Benito Juárez to the east, and Nelson to the west.*

❶ Zona Dorada. Marking the beginning of Mazatlán's tourist zone is **Punta Camarón,** the rocky outcropping on which Valentino's disco sits, resembling a Moorish palace perched above the sea. To the north, Avenida Camarón Sábalo forms the eastern border of the zone, whereas Avenida Rodolfo T. Loaiza runs closer to the beach. In this four-block pocket are many of the hotels, shops, and restaurants—and the majority of visitors intent on having a good time sunning, shopping, and partying. This is the place to souvenir-shop, hit the discos, and check out the hotel bars.

NEED A
BREAK?

No Name Café (⊠ Av. Rodolfo T. Loaiza 417, ☎ 69/13–20–31), in the Mazatlán Arts and Crafts Center, is a good spot for barbecued ribs and beer. **Helados Bing** (⊠ Avs. Camarón Sábalo and Gaviotas, ☎ 69/13–55–10) has good hot-fudge sundaes and ice-cream cones. At the **Panadería Panamá** (⊠ Av. Camarón Sábalo across from Las Palmas hotel, ☎ 69/13–69–77), you can sit at a table and enjoy fragrant cinnamon-flavored coffee with fresh-baked pastries.

Around Mazatlán

CONCORDIA

48 km (30 mi) east of Mazatlán.

Concordia is known for its furniture makers (a huge wood chair marks the entrance to the small town), its 18th-century church, and its brown clay pottery. The trip, over a spectacular road, makes a nice change of pace from Mazatlán.

COPALA

25 km (15 mi) east of Concordia.

A scenic colonial mining town at the foot of the Sierra Madre Occidental, Copala features a charming zócalo, cobblestone streets, colorful facades, and beautiful ironwork balconies and windows. Stop into Daniel's restaurant on the square for a slice of delicious cream pie.

TEACAPAN
25 km (15 mi) south of Mazatlán.

A serene drive into cattle and coconut country, with a stop in the pueblo of Esquinapa to see its interesting church, is topped off with a cruise on the large estuary spanning the border of Sinaloa and Nayarit states for bird-watching—and a seaside meal of shrimp empanadas. Let Marlin Tours (☞ Contacts and Resources *in* Mazatlán A to Z, *below*) handle this one for you.

Beaches

Playa los Cerritos. The northernmost beach on the outskirts of town, which runs from the Camino Real to Punta Cerritos, is also the cleanest and least populated. The waves can be too rough for swimming, but they're great for surfing, and Mazatlán's local surf club frequently uses the area to train its members for competitions throughout Mexico. A decent *palapa* (thatch-roof hut) restaurant/bar on the north end of the beach is a good place to meet local surfers.

Playa Isla de la Piedra. Sixteen kilometers (10 mi) of unspoiled beaches allow enough room for all visitors to spread out and claim their own space. This is the place to rent a horse for a good long ride on the beach—there's nothing but sand and coconut palms. Look for the numerous sand dollars that cover the southern end of the peninsula. On Sunday, the beach looks like a small village, with lots of music and fun. Many of the small palapas set up along the north end of the beach serve a tasty smoked marlin. The palapas near the launches to Isla de la Piedra (Stone Island) sell sugarcane sticks, which look like bamboo and are good for quenching your thirst.

Playa Isla de los Venados. Boats make frequent departures from the Zona Dorada hotels for this beach on Deer Island. It's only a 10-minute ride, but the difference in ambience is striking. The beach is pretty, uncluttered, and clean, and you can hike around the southern point of the island to small, secluded coves covered with shells. El Cid hotel employs a 1964 army surplus Lark-5 amphibious vehicle, affectionately known as "the shark," to take you to the island and back.

Playa Norte. This strand begins at Punta Camarón (Valentino's is a landmark) along Avenida del Mar and the malecón and runs to the Fisherman's Monument. The dark brown sand is dirty and rocky at some points, but clean at others, and is popular with those staying at hotels that don't have beach access. It is also a favorite area for runners at dawn and dusk. Palapas selling cold drinks, tacos, and fresh fish line the beach. Consider trying the fresh coconut milk.

Playa Olas Altas. This beach, whose name means "high waves," was the first tourist beach in Mazatlán, running south along the malecón from the Fisherman's Monument. Surfers congregate here during the summer months, when the waves are at their highest.

Playa Sábalo and Playa las Gaviotas. Mazatlán's two most popular beaches are at either end of the Zona Dorada. There are as many vendors selling blankets, pottery, lace tablecloths, and silver jewelry as there are sunbathers. Boats, windsurfers, and parasailers line the shores. The beach is protected from heavy surf by the three islands—Venados, Pájaros, and Chivos. You can safely stroll these beaches until midnight and eavesdrop on the social action in the hotels while enjoying a few romantic moments without vendors and crowds.

Dining

$$$ ✕ **Angelo's.** With its fresh flowers, cream-and-beige decor, gentle
★ piano music, and soft candlelight, this is by far the most elegant restaurant in Mazatlán. The Italian and Continental cuisine is outstanding—try the veal scallopini with mushrooms or shrimp marinara on pasta—and the service is impeccable. ✉ *Pueblo Bonito, Av. Camarón Sábalo 2121,* ☎ *69/14–37–00. AE, DC, MC, V. No lunch.*

$$$ ✕ **La Costa Marinera.** It's always a party at this seafood restaurant with a live mariachi band. Pacific lobster is the house specialty, and the local seafood is as fresh as it gets. ✉ *Priv. Camarón and Priv. Florida,* ☎ *69/14–19–28. No credit cards.*

$$$ ✕ **Sr. Peppers.** Elegant yet unpretentious, with ceiling fans, lush foliage, and candlelit tables, Sr. Peppers serves choice steaks and lobsters cooked over a mesquite grill. Enjoy the dance floor and live music. ✉ *Av. Camarón Sábalo across from Camino Real,* ☎ *69/14–01–20. AE, MC, V. No lunch.*

$$ ✕ **La Casa Country.** This festive restaurant in front of El Quijote Inn serves a variety of steaks and Mexican dishes to a country-loving crowd. Steaks are grilled over charcoal or fire wood—the *arrachera* (skirt steak) served with kettle beans and guacamole is a good bet, as is the rib-eye with baked potato. Margaritas and piña coladas are served by the pitcher; at night, country-music fans are brought to their feet for dancin' and carousin'. ✉ *Av. Camarón Sábalo s/n,* ☎ *69/16–53–00. AE, MC, V.*

$$ ✕ **La Concha.** One of the prettiest waterside dining spots, La Concha
★ is a large enclosed palapa with three levels of seating, including a spacious dance floor adorned with twinkling lights and outdoor tables by the sand. Adventurous types might attempt the stingray with black butter or calamari in its ink, and the more conservative can try a thick filet mignon cooked to perfection. During the winter season there's live music. La Concha is also open for breakfast and lunch; there's a fabulous Sunday champagne brunch. ✉ *El Cid, Av. Camarón Sábalo s/n,* ☎ *69/13–33–33. AE, DC, MC, V.*

$$ ✕ **Pedro & Lola.** Authentic Mexican seafood is served in this 19th-cen-
★ tury building in the heart of the historic center, decorated with neo-Mexican art. Try the *papillot,* the day's fresh catch cooked in foil with white wine, shrimp, and mushrooms. Named after Mexican *ranchera* singers Pedro Infarte and Lola Beltran, the restaurant hosts excellent live music in the evening. ✉ *Carnaval 1303, next to Plaza Machado,* ☎ *69/82–25–89. AE, MC, V. No lunch.*

$$ ✕ **Señor Frog.** Another member of the Carlos Anderson chain, Señor Frog is Mazatlán's tourist mecca. Bandidos carry tequila bottles and shot glasses in their bandoliers, leather belts that held ammunition in the old Westerns. Barbecued ribs and chicken, served with corn on the cob, and heaping portions of standard Mexican dishes are the specialty. The drinking, dancing, and carousing go on well into the night. ✉ *Av. del Mar,* ☎ *69/82–19–25. AE, MC, V.*

$$ ✕ **El Shrimp Bucket.** In Old Mazatlán, facing the water, this was the original Carlos 'n' Charlie's. The garden patio restaurant (part of the inexpensive Hotel Siesta) is much quieter than its predecessors—some would call it respectable. This is the in spot for Mazatlán businessmen and social mavens at breakfast (from 6 AM). For lunch or dinner, best bets are fried shrimp served in clay buckets and barbecued ribs. Portions are large, and there's live music at night. ✉ *Paseo Olas Altas 11–126,* ☎ *69/81–63–50. AE, MC, V.*

$–$$ ✕ **El Paraíso Tres Islas.** A wonderful palapa on the beach, across from Sea Shell City (☞ Zona Dorada *in* Shopping, *below*), Tres Islas is a favorite with families who spend all Sunday afternoon feasting on fresh fish. Try smoked marlin, oysters diablo, octopus, or the seafood platter. The setting is the nicest in town, close to the water with a good view of the three islands. The waiters are friendly and eager to help. ⊠ *Av. Rodolfo T. Loaiza 404,* ☎ *69/14–28–12. MC, V.*

$ ✕ **Karnes en Su Jugo.** A small family-run café on the malecón, with a few outdoor tables and a large indoor restaurant, this establishment specializes in *karnes en su jugo* (literally, "beef in its juice"), a Mexican stew with chopped beef, onions, beans, and bacon. It's a satisfying meal, especially when eaten with a basket of homemade tortillas. ⊠ *Av. del Mar 550,* ☎ *69/82–13–22. No credit cards.*

$ ✕ **Pepe's & Joe.** This restaurant in the Fiesta Land complex (☞ Nightlife,
★ *below*) is nirvana for beer lovers—the brew is made on the premises. There are also good hamburgers, hot dogs, club sandwiches, and the like. Grab a quick bite here before heading to the discos next door. ⊠ *Punta Camarón,* ☎ *69/84–16–66 ext. 209. AE, MC, V. Closed lunch.*

Lodging

Most of Mazatlán's hotels are in the Zona Dorada, along the beaches. Less expensive places are in Old Mazatlán, the original tourist zone along the malecón on the south side of downtown.

$$$–$$$$ 🏨 **El Cid.** The largest resort in Mazatlán, and perhaps in Mexico, El Cid
★ has 1,320 rooms on four different properties, three of which are here. The fourth, the upscale Marina El Cid Hotel and Yacht Club, is at the north end of town and has 210 suites and a 100-slip marina. A free shuttle connects the properties. If you want to be part of the action, ask for a suite in the El Moro tower overlooking the ocean (much nicer than rooms in the older Castilla tower). Other perks include a full-service spa and fitness center, America's Favorite Golf Schools and attendant 27-hole course, and a megatravel service with a deep-sea fishing fleet. The spacious rooms overlook the pool and beach (one of the longest and cleanest in the area), and the hotel is popular with convention groups as well as individual travelers. The glass-enclosed arcade has nice boutiques, and La Concha (☞ Dining, *above*) is one of the most romantic spots on the beach. ⊠ *Av. Camarón Sábalo s/n, 82110,* ☎ *69/13–33–33, 800/525–1925,* 🅵🅰🆇 *69/14–13–11. 720 rooms, 600 suites. 5 restaurants, 4 bars, 8 pools, 27-hole golf course, 17 tennis courts, health club, beach, shops, dance club, children's programs (ages 4–12), concierge, business services, travel services, car rental. AE, DC, MC, V.* 🐾

$$$ 🏨 **Holiday Inn Sunspree Resort.** A consistently good hotel, the Holiday Inn has been drastically improved in recent years. Tour and convention groups fill the rooms and create a party mood by the pool and on the beach. The Kid's Spree program provides activities to keep children busy and parents relaxed. All rooms are done in whites and pastels, with large sliding doors that open to pretty views of the islands. Standard amenities now include remote-control cable TV, hair dryer, refrigerator, and coffeemaker. ⊠ *Av. Camarón Sábalo 696, 82110,* ☎ *69/13–22–22, 800/465–4329,* 🅵🅰🆇 *69/14–12–87. 137 rooms, 23 suites. 2 restaurants, 2 bars, pool, tennis court, exercise room, volleyball, beach, children's programs (ages 6–15). AE, MC, V.*

$$$ 🏨 **Pueblo Bonito.** One of the most beautiful properties in Mazatlán, this
★ all-suites hotel and time-share resort has an enormous lobby with chandeliers, beveled-glass doors, and gleaming red-and-white tile floors. The pink terra-cotta rooms have dome ceilings. An arched doorway leads from the tile kitchen into the elegant seating area, which is furnished with pale pink and beige couches and glass tables. Pink flamingos stroll on the manicured lawns, golden koi swim in small ponds, and bronzed sunbathers repose on padded white lounge chairs by the crystal-blue pool. One drawback to staying here: you're likely to be approached by

time-share solicitors. Angelo's (☞ Dining, *above*) is a dining must—as elegant as Mazatlán gets. ⊠ *Av. Camarón Sábalo 2121, 82110,* ☎ *69/ 14–37–00, 800/990–8250,* ፎ፟ᐧ *69/14–17–23. 250 suites. 3 restaurants, bar, 2 pools, exercise room, beach. AE, MC, V.* ❦

$$$ ⊞ **Royal Villas Resort.** This pyramid-shape 12-story structure is decidedly
★ more attractive on the inside. Panoramic elevators transport you from the cool marble atrium lobby to the upper floors. The large guest rooms with tile floors are decorated in cool colors; all have two double beds, ocean views, remote-control TVs, balconies, and kitchenettes. Access to the inviting pool is by a bridge that crosses over a tropical fish–filled pond. ⊠ *Av. Camarón Sábalo 500, 82110,* ☎ *69/16–61– 61, 800/898–3564,* ፎ፟ᐧ *69/14–07–77. 125 rooms. 2 restaurants, bar, pool, hot tub, exercise room, beach, business services. AE, MC, V.* ❦

$$$ ⊞ **Los Sábalos.** The location of this white high-rise, in the center of the Zona Dorada, is great, and there's a long clean beach. You feel as though you're in the thick of the action, amid the flight attendants who lay over at Los Sábalos; it's the home of Joe's Oyster Bar, one of the most popular discos in town. ⊠ *Av. Rodolfo T. Loaiza 100, 82110,* ☎ *69/83–53–33, 800/528–8760, 877/756–7532 in Canada,* ፎ፟ᐧ *69/83– 81–56. 185 rooms. 4 restaurants, 2 bars, pool, 2 tennis courts, health club, beach, dance club. AE, DC, MC, V.* ❦

$$ ⊞ **Casa Contenta.** A small surprise on the beach one block north of
★ Las Flores, this property has seven one-bedroom apartments in a colonial-style building, as well as a large beachfront house with three bedrooms, three baths, living and dining room, and even servants' quarters; the house accommodates eight people. All units have equipped kitchens, but there are no TVs or phones in the rooms. Casa Contenta has many longtime repeat clients who book years in advance. ⊠ *Av. Rodolfo T. Loaiza 224, 82110,* ☎ *69/13–49–76,* ፎ፟ᐧ *69/13–99–86. 8 units. Kitchenettes, pool. MC, V.*

$$ ⊞ **Fiesta Inn.** One of Mazatlán's newest hotels, the Fiesta Inn is operated by Posadas, a large Mexican hotel chain. The sleek nine-story tower is on the beach between the Holiday Inn and Doubletree hotels. Guest rooms are nicely decorated with marble floors, light-wood furniture, and pleasing pastels. ⊠ *Av. Camarón Sábalo 1927, 82110,* ☎ *69/89– 01–00, 01–800/504–5000, 800/343–7821,* ፎ፟ᐧ *69/89–01–30. 117 rooms. 2 restaurants, bar, pool, exercise room, business services. AE, DC, MC, V.*

$$ ⊞ **Hotel Plaza Marina.** Near the Fisherman's Monument downtown, all suites at this hotel—one of Mazatlán's newer lodging choices—have ocean views. Rooms face the pool and have pastel color schemes. For children, the pool has a 12-ft-long underwater tunnel. Don't be frightened by the lifelike, 4-ft-tall wooden cobra in the lobby. ⊠ *Av. del Mar 73, 82110,* ☎ *69/82–36–22, 01–800/711–9465,* ፎ፟ᐧ *69/82–34–99. 56 rooms, 43 suites. 2 restaurants, 2 bars, pool, exercise room, travel services. AE, MC, V.*

$$ ⊞ **Playa Mazatlán.** Palapas are set up on the patios by the rooms in
★ this casual hotel, which is popular with Mexican families and laid-back singles more concerned with comfort than style. The bright, sunny rooms have tile headboards and tile tables by the windows. There's a volleyball net on the beach, and two small stands sell good, inexpensive snacks. Don't miss the Mexican Fiesta Night, without a doubt the best in town. ⊠ *Av. Rodolfo T. Loaiza 202, 82110,* ☎ *69/89–05–55, 800/762– 5816,* ፎ፟ᐧ *69/14–03–66. 425 rooms. 2 restaurants, bar, 3 pools, hot tub, exercise room, beach. AE, MC, V.* ❦

$$ ⊞ **El Quijote Inn.** On the beach, in the midst of the hotel zone, this five-story inn is a tranquil alternative to some of the more frenzied facilities. Accommodations include studios and one- or two-bedroom suites

Fodor's Mexico   20.00
0679005471

SUB TOTAL   20.00
SALES TAX   1.40
TOTAL   21.40
AMOUNT TENDERED
CASH   21.40

TOTAL PAYMENT   21.45
CHANGE   .05
Thanks for shopping at Barnes & Noble!
#43538 11-10-00 12:49P MIR

Full refund issued for new and unread books and unopened music within 14 days with a receipt from any Barnes & Noble store.
Store Credit issued for new and unread books and unopened music after 14 days or without a sales receipt. Credit issued at lowest sale price.

Full refund issued for new and unread books and unopened music within 14 days with a receipt from any Barnes & Noble store.
Store Credit issued for new and unread books and unopened music after 14 days or without a sales receipt. Credit issued at lowest sale price.

(suites have full kitchens). All units have tile floors, rattan furnishings, satellite TV, and patios or balconies. ⊠ *Avs. Camarón Sábalo and Tiburón, 82110,* ☎ *69/14–11–34,* FAX *69/14–33–44. 67 suites. Restaurant, bar, pool, hot tub. AE, MC, V.*

$ ⌸ **Azteca Inn.** This hotel across the street from the Playa Mazatlán hotel is a great find for budget travelers who like to be in the center of things. The brown-and-white exterior color scheme isn't carried over into the rooms, which are decorated in reds and yellows. Most of the accommodations have two double beds, and all have satellite TV. The staff couldn't be friendlier. ⊠ *Av. Rodolfo T. Loaiza 307, 82110,* ☎ *69/13–44–77,* FAX *69/13–74–76. 74 rooms. Restaurant, bar, pool, hot tub. AE, MC, V.* ✑

$ ⌸ **Hotel Siesta.** The rooms are comfortable at this traditional, unpretentious budget hotel in the downtown area, with cable TV and air-conditioning. Interior-facing rooms line a balcony that overlooks the courtyard and the Shrimp Bucket restaurant, where live music is played nightly in winter until 11 PM. ⊠ *Paseo Olas Altas 11 Sur, 82110,* ☎ *69/81–26–40, 01–800/711–5229,* FAX *69/82–26–33. 57 rooms. Restaurant, room service, laundry service and dry cleaning, travel services, car rental. AE, MC, V.* ✑

$ ⌸ **Plaza Gaviotas.** Most of the salmon-color rooms in this clean, colonial-style budget hotel, across the street from Playa Mazatlán, have balconies. All have showers. ⊠ *Av. Rodolfo T. Loaiza and Bugambilias 100, 82110,* ☎ *69/13–43–22,* FAX *69/13–66–85. 67 rooms. Restaurant, bar, pool. AE, MC, V.*

Nightlife

Valentino's, Bora Bora, Pepe's & Joe, and Sheik are all part of the complex known as **Fiesta Land** (☎ 69/84–17–22, 69/84–16–66, 69/84–17–77). Valentino's, with its stark white towers rising on Punta Camarón, draws a glitzy crowd for rocking on the dance floor or karaoke in a separate room. Bora Bora, a casual palapa bar on the beach, is alive with music and dancing 9–4. Pepe's & Joe (☞ Dining, *above*) is a microbrew-beer factory with good eats. Sheik is a restaurant extravaganza complete with waterfalls, ocean views, Moorish-inspired stained-glass windows, marble floors, and a central domed skylight; this place shouldn't be missed, at least for an early evening drink. **El Caracol Disco Club** (⊠ Av. Camarón Sábalo s/n, ☎ 69/13–33–33), at El Cid resort complex, has a high-tech disco, billiards, board and arcade games, and different theme nights throughout the week. A hefty $20 cover includes all drinks and games. **Joe's Oyster Bar** (⊠ Los Sábalos hotel, Av. Rodolfo T. Loaiza 100, ☎ 69/83–53–33) is a popular beachfront spot where the dancing starts at noon and lasts until 2 AM. **Copa Cubana** (⊠ Paseo Olas Altas 1220-B Sur, ☎ 69/82–61–66) features Cuban dance music Thursday–Saturday 9:30–4 and Sunday until 2 for a $10 cover. Also in the historic center, **Cafe Pacífico** (⊠ Constitution 501, ☎ 69/81–39–72) has live jazz Thursday–Saturday nights.

The **Mexican Fiesta,** held Tuesday, Thursday, and Saturday 7–10:30 at the Playa Mazatlán (☞ Lodging, *above*), is a good entertainment bet. The $20 fee includes a lavish Mexican buffet, open bar, folk dances, and live music for dancing. **El Cid** (☞ Lodging, *above*) also has excellent theme nights throughout the week. Almost all hotel travel desks can provide you with information on days and times.

Outdoor Activities and Sports

Participant Sports

ECOTOURS

The **Mazatleco Sport Center** (⊠ Av. Rodolfo T. Loaiza 408–1B, ☎ 69/16–77–20) in the Zona Dorada offers mangrove-kayaking, snorkeling, bird-watching, mountain-biking, and sailing tours and equipment rentals.

FISHING

More than a dozen sportfishing fleets operate from the docks south of the lighthouse. Hotels can arrange charters, or you can contact the companies directly. Charters include a full day of fishing, bait, and tackle. Prices range from $70 to $100 per person on a party boat, or from $200 to $300 to charter an entire boat. Charter companies include **Bill Heimpel's Star Fleet** (☎ 69/82–26–65), **Flota Faro** (☎ 69/81–28–24), **Flota Bibi** (☎ 69/81–36–40), and **De Oro** (☎ 69/82–31–30).

GOLF

Arthur Martori and Merv Griffin are two of the investors in the **Estrella del Mar and Beach Resort Complex** (☎ 69/82–33–00, ℻ 69/82–33–69) south of Mazatlán proper, off the airport highway on the road to Isla de la Piedra. Here you'll find a championship 18-hole Robert Trent Jones golf course open to the public for $85. The spectacular 27-hole course at **El Cid** (☎ 69/13–33–33), designed by Lee Trevino, is reserved for members of the resort, hotel guests, and their guests.

HORSEBACK RIDING

You can rent horses on **Isla de la Piedra** for about $3 per hour, guide included, unless you ask to go it alone.

TENNIS

Many of the hotels have courts, some of which are open to the public, and there are a few public courts not connected to the hotels. Call in advance for reservations at **El Cid** (☎ 69/13–33–33), which has 17 courts; the **Racket Club** (☎ 69/13–59–39), with 6 courts; **Costa de Oro** (☎ 69/13–53–44), with 3 courts; and **Camino Real** (☎ 69/13–11–11), with 2 courts.

WATER SPORTS

Jet Skis, Hobie Cats (a two-person catamaran), and windsurfers are available for rent at most hotels, and parasailing is popular along the Zona Dorada. Scuba diving and snorkeling are catching on, but there are no really great diving spots. The best are around Isla de los Venados. For rentals and trips, contact the following operators: **Doubletree** (⊠ Av. Camarón Sábalo, ☎ 69/13–02–00), **El Cid Resort Aqua Sport Center** (⊠ Av. Camarón Sábalo s/n, ☎ 69/13–33–33), **Los Sábalos** (⊠ Av. Rodolfo T. Loaiza 100, ☎ 69/83–53–33), and **Camino Real Sports Center** (⊠ Punta del Sábalo s/n, ☎ 69/13–11–11).

Parque Acuático Mazaguas (⊠ Av. Sábalo Cerritos and Entronque Habal Cerritos, ☎ 69/88–00–41) has water slides, wading pools, and a pool with man-made waves—a total of 20 water activities on 4 acres.

Spectator Sports

BASEBALL

The people of Mazatlán loyally support their team, **Los Venados** (☎ 69/83–79–33), a Pacific League Triple A team. Games are played at the Teodoro Mariscal Baseball Stadium (⊠ Blvd. Justo Sierra) October through April.

BULLFIGHTS AND CHARREADAS

Bullfights are held most Sunday afternoons at 3:30 December to May at the bullring on Calzada Rafael Buelna. *Charreadas* (rodeos) take place

When it Comes to Getting Local Currency at an ATM, Same Thing.

Whether you're in Yosemite or Yemen, using your Visa® card or ATM card with the PLUS symbol is the easiest and most convenient way to get local currency. For example, let's say you're in France. When you make a withdrawal, using your secured PIN, it's dispensed in francs, but is debited from your account in U.S. dollars. This makes it easy to take advantage of favorable exchange rates. And if you need help finding one of Visa's 627,000 ATMs in 127 countries worldwide, visit **visa.com/pd/atm**. We'll make finding an ATM as easy as finding the Eiffel Tower, the Pyramids or even the Grand Canyon.

It's Everywhere You Want To Be.®

SEE THE WORLD
IN FULL COLOR

Fodor's Exploring Guides bring all the great sights vividly to life with hundreds of photographs, fascinating historical background, and colorful anecdotes. Detailed maps and practical information keep you headed in the right direction.

Pair a **Fodor's** Exploring Guide with your trusted Gold Guide for a complete planning package.

year-round. Tickets (about $20) are available at the **bullring** (☎ 69/86–91–55, 69/86–86–33), through most hotels and travel agencies, and from Valentino's (☞ Nightlife, *above*).

Shopping

Zona Dorada

In the Zona Dorada, particularly along Avenidas Camarón Sábalo and Rodolfo T. Loaiza, you can buy everything from piñatas to designer clothing. Leather shops are clustered in the southern end of the Zona Dorada.

CLOTHING

For sportswear, visit **Aca Joe** (⊠ Avs. Camarón Sábalo and Gaviotas, ☎ 69/13–33–00), whose line of well-designed casual clothes for men is popular throughout Mexico and the United States.

Designer's Bazaar (⊠ Av. Rodolfo T. Loaiza 217, ☎ 69/83–60–39), a two-story shop near Los Sábalos hotel, has a nice selection of arts and crafts, jewelry, and hand-embroidered clothing.

Señor Frog's Official Store (⊠ Av. del Mar, ☎ 69/82–19–25), attached to the popular restaurant of the same name (☞ Dining, *above*), carries its own fun line of souvenirs, sports equipment, and beachwear.

CRAFTS

La Carreta (⊠ Playa Mazatlán, ☎ 69/13–83–20), open daily 10–6, has the finest selection of high-quality Mexican folk art in town.

Madonna (⊠ Av. Las Garzas, ☎ 69/14–23–89) displays an extensive collection of silver and gold jewelry as well as masks and handicrafts; it's open daily 9–8.

The best place for browsing is the **Mazatlán Arts and Crafts Center** (⊠ Av. Rodolfo T. Loaiza 417, ☎ 69/13–21–20), which originally was designed as a place to view artisans at work and buy their wares. The center has a good sampling of the city's souvenir selection—onyx chess sets, straw sombreros, leather jackets, sandals, coconut masks, and Mickey Mouse piñatas. The center is open 9–6.

Dealers Ron and Teresa Tammekand represent a number of top artists at **Mazatlán Art Gallery** (⊠ Plaza Balboa, Av. Camarón Sábalo 4480, ☎ 69/14–36–12) and hold one-person shows in winter.

Sea Shell City (⊠ Av. Rodolfo T. Loaiza 407, ☎ 69/13–13–01) is a must-see. It has two floors packed with shells from around the world that have been glued, strung, and molded into every imaginable shape from lamps to necklaces. Check out the enormous fountain upstairs. Sea Shell City is open Monday–Saturday 9–7:30, Sunday 9–6:30.

JEWELRY

Rubio Jewelers (⊠ Costa de Oro hotel, Av. Camarón Sábalo s/n, ☎ 69/14–31–67) carries fine gold and silver jewelry as well as ceramics. It's also Mazatlán's exclusive distributor of Sergio Bustamante's whimsical papier-mâché sculptures.

Downtown

The gigantic **Mercado Central,** between Calles Juárez and Serdán, is open daily and filled with produce, meat, fish, and handicrafts that are sold at the lowest prices in town. It takes some searching to find quality handicrafts, but that's part of the fun.

At **Nidart** gallery and workshop (⊠ Libertad and Carnaval, ☎ 69/81–00–02), handcrafted leather masks and figures and other Mexican arts and crafts are displayed in a beautiful setting.

Mazatlán A to Z

Arriving and Departing

BY BUS

Transportes Norte de Sonora, Estrella Blanca, Elite, and Trans-Pacífico
(☎ 69/82–05–77, 69/82–19–49) have service to Mazatlán from Nogales, Arizona, and from Sonora, and connect the coast with inland
Mexico. The Mazatlán bus terminal is on Carretera Internacional
1203, three blocks behind the Sands Hotel.

BY CAR

Mazatlán is 1,212 km (751 mi) from the border city of Nogales, Arizona, via Mexico Route 15, either on the excellent but quite expensive toll road or on the federal highway. An overnight stop is
recommended as driving at night in Mexico can be hazardous.

BY FERRY

Ferry service (☎ 01–800/696–9600) between La Paz and Mazatlán was
privatized a few years back, and the service is now fairly reliable. The
ferry departs daily from Mazatlán's Playa Sur terminal at 3 PM and takes
about 18 hours to reach La Paz. The one-way fare is about $25 for
regular passage and $60 per person for a private cabin for two with
bed and bath.

BY PLANE

Mazatlán's **Rafael Buelna International Airport** (☎ 69/82–21–77) is serviced by several airlines. **Aeroméxico** (☎ 69/14–16–21) has flights from
multiple U.S. and Mexican cities. **Alaska Airlines** (☎ 69/85–27–30) flies
in from Los Angeles, San Diego, Portland, and Seattle. **Continental** (☎
01–800/900–5000) flies from Houston. **AeroCalifornia** (☎ 69/13–20–
42) has flights from Los Angeles; **Mexicana** (☎ 69/82–56–66) flies in
from Denver, Los Angeles, and several Mexican cities. **America West**
(☎ 01–800/363–2597) links Mazatlán with Phoenix.

The airport is a good 40-minute drive from town. **Autotransportes Aeropuerto** (☎ 69/81–55–54) provides Volkswagen van shuttles to Mazatlán.
The cost is $6 per person for *colectivo* (shared) service, $22 for a private car.

BY SHIP

Carnival Cruise Line, Celebrity Cruises, Cunard, Holland America Line,
and **Krystal P&O,** among other cruise lines, include Mazatlán on their
winter itineraries.

BY TRAIN

The railroads were privatized in January 1998, and the previously subsidized passenger service along Mexico's Pacific corridor (and elsewhere
in the country) has been suspended.

Getting Around

BY BUS

There are several bus lines, which run frequently along all major avenues. Routes are clearly marked. Fares start at about 30¢ and increase
slightly depending on the destination.

Mazatlán's minibuses will take you from the downtown market area
all the way to the Zona Dorada for 25¢; just flag one down.

BY CAR

A car isn't necessary in town since public transportation is good, but
you might want one for a self-guided tour of the area. Rentals usually
include free mileage. A Volkswagen Beetle costs about $50 per day with
insurance; a sedan with air-conditioning and automatic transmission
is about $90 per day.

Most tourist hotels are located in the Zona Dorada, about 3 km (2 mi) north of downtown, but taxis cruise the strip regularly. Fares start at $3. A fun way to get around is on the pulmonías. The fare, for up to three passengers, starts at about $3 and increases according to the distance of the trip. Complaints have been registered, however, about susceptibility to fumes from other vehicles.

Contacts and Resources

CAR RENTAL

The following rental firms have desks at Rafael Buelna International Airport: **Hertz** (⊠ Av. Camarón Sábalo 314, ☎ 69/13–60–60), **Budget** (⊠ Av. Camarón Sábalo 402, ☎ 69/13–20–00), and **National** (⊠ Plaza el Camarón, Av. Camarón Sábalo, ☎ 69/13–60–00).

CONSULATES

U.S. Consulate (⊠ Av. Rodolfo T. Loaiza 202, ☎ 69/16–58–89). **Canadian Consulate** (⊠ Av. Rodolfo T. Loaiza 202, ☎ 69/13–73–20).

EMERGENCIES

Dial 060 for all emergencies involving the **police department, fire department, or Red Cross. Toll-free medical or travel advice** (☎ 01–800/903–9200). **Sharp Hospital** (☎ 69/86–56–76, 69/83–63–41).

ENGLISH-LANGUAGE BOOKSTORES AND PUBLICATIONS

The best place for new releases, dictionaries, and maps is **Mazatlán Book and Coffee Company** (☎ 69/16–78–99), across from the Costa de Oro Hotel behind Banco Santanger Mexicano. The store is open daily 9–7 and has copies of Mazatlán's English newspaper, *Pacific Pearl.*

GUIDED TOURS

Note: Formerly ubiquitous sidewalk stands staffed by persuasive hawkers of free tours of the area along with free drinks and meals—whose true goal is to sell time-shares and condos—have been limited to areas in front of these properties.

The three-hour **city tour,** which should cost around $16, is a good way to get the lay of the land, particularly downtown, which can be a bit confusing.

Three-hour cruises aboard *Costalegre* (☎ 69/16–57–47) cost about $10 and navigate the bay and harbor, past the islands and sportfishing fleet. A day tour on the square rigger *Chemainus* (☎ 69/87–07–89) includes boom netting. Sunset tours are also available. These and other harbor cruises generally last about three hours and feature music and dancing. **Viajes el Sábalo** (☞ Travel Agencies, *below*) runs a five-hour tour to see the seals at Isla de la Piedra, with time for lunch and a swim. The cost is about $23.

Also available are all-day **country tours,** which go to Concordia and Copala (about $35) and include lunch. **Marlin Tours** (☞ Travel Agencies, *below*) runs a trip to Teacapan, an ecological reserve. The nine-hour excursion costs $45 and includes Continental breakfast served on the bus, a stop at Rosario, and a seafood lunch at almost-deserted La Tambora beach. The tour companies also offer individual guided tours and sportfishing outings.

LETTERS AND E-MAIL

The main post office is downtown, across from the main plaza. However, if you are in the Zona Dorada, it's easier to go to **Mail Boxes Etc.** (⊠ Av. Camarón Sábalo 310), which offers fax and e-mail services, in addition to regular postal services.

American Express (⊠ Plaza Balboa, Locale 4/16, ☎ 69/13–06–00), **Marlin Tours** (⊠ Calle Laguna 300, ☎ 69/13–53–01), **Viajes el Sábalo** (⊠ Los Sábalos shopping center, ☎ 69/83–19–33; ⊠ Camino Real, Punta del Sábalo s/n, ☎ 69/13–11–11). Agencies are open weekdays 10–2 and 4–7, Saturday 10–2.

The **State Tourism Office** (⊠ Av. Camarón Sábalo, Banrural Bldg., 4th floor, ☎ 69/16–51–60 to –67) is open weekdays 9–5.

PUERTO VALLARTA

On the edge of the Sierra Madre range sits one of the most popular vacation spots in Mexico. When Puerto Vallarta first entered the public's consciousness, with John Huston's 1964 movie *The Night of the Iguana,* it seemed an almost mythical tropical paradise. At the time it was a quiet fishing and farming community in an exquisite setting.

Puerto Vallarta's Bahía de Banderas attracted pirates and explorers as early as the 1500s; it was used as a stopover on long sailings as a place for the crew to relax (or maybe plunder and pillage). Sir Francis Drake apparently stopped here. In the mid-1850s, Don Guadalupe Sánchez Carrillo developed the bay as a port for the silver mines by the Río Cuale. Then it was known as Puerto de Peñas and had about 1,500 inhabitants. It remained a village until 1918, when it was made a municipality by the state of Jalisco and named after Ignacio L. Vallarta, a governor of Jalisco.

In the 1950s Puerto Vallarta was essentially a pretty hideaway for those in the know—the wealthy and some hardy escapists. After the publicity brought on by *The Night of the Iguana,* tourism began to boom. PV—as the former fishing village is called these days—is now a city with more than 300,000 residents. Airports, hotels, and highways have supplanted palm groves and fishing shacks. About 1.5 million people visit each year, and from November through April cobblestone streets are clogged with pedestrians and cars. There are now more than 9,000 hotel rooms in Puerto Vallarta.

Despite the transformation, every attempt has been made to keep the town's character and image intact. Even the parking lot at the local Gigante supermarket is cobblestone, and by law any house built in town must be painted white. When you visit, you'll still see houses with red-tile roofs on palm-covered hills overlooking glistening blue water. Pack mules clop down the steep cobblestone streets. Within 16 km (10 mi) of town are peaceful coves, rushing rivers, and steep mountain roads that curve and twist through jungles of pines and palms.

Exploring Puerto Vallarta

Central Puerto Vallarta has three major components: the northern hotel and resort region, the downtown area, and the area encompassing the Río Cuale—where you'll find a sliver of an island that's home to a language-and-arts school, the Anthropology Museum, restaurants, and shops—and Playa de los Muertos, the region's most popular beach. A cab or rental car is necessary to explore the hotel zone, which is basically a long stretch of shopping centers, restaurants, and hotels, but you don't want to have a car downtown and in the Río Cuale area. Most of the interesting sights can be covered on foot—just be sure you wear comfortable shoes for the cobblestone streets.

Numbers in the text correspond to numbers in the margin and on the Puerto Vallarta map.

A Good Walk

When you start seeing cobblestone streets, you're in the downtown area, also known as **Old Town.** This is the heart of PV, a vestige of old Puerto Vallarta. Start your walk at the northern end of the delightful **malecón** ⑧, which runs parallel to Díaz Ordáz beginning at 31 de Octubre. Two and a half blocks south on Díaz Ordáz, where it merges with Calle Morelos at the old lighthouse tower, is the town's main zócalo, Plaza de Armas. On the northern side of the busy tree-shaded plaza you'll see **City Hall** ⑨, uninteresting but for a charming Manuel Lepe mural depicting his vision of life in Puerto Vallarta. Dominating the square from a block east is **La Iglesia de Nuestra Señora de Guadalupe** ⑩, which is topped by a distinctive crown. Los Arcos Amphitheater, across the street from the plaza on the malecón, is host to a number of concerts and other performances. Local artists show their wares here in the evenings.

Head south a few blocks and you'll come to the bustling **Mercado Municipal** (☞ Markets *in* Shopping, *below*); it's at the foot of the upper bridge over the Río Cuale, which runs into the bay just past Plaza Serdán. The steep hillside above, dotted with charming villas, is called **Gringo Gulch** ⑪. Reach it by climbing the steps on Calle Zaragoza. In the middle of the Río Cuale lies the **Isla Río Cuale** ⑫, an inviting place for dining and browsing, reachable via steps leading under the two bridges.

Sights to See

⑨ **City Hall.** The late Manuel Lepe's 1981 mural depicting Puerto Vallarta as a fanciful seaside fishing and farming village hangs above the stairs on city hall's second floor. Lepe, known for his blissful, primitive-style scenes of the city, filled with smiling angels, is Puerto Vallarta's most famous—and most copied—artist. The tourism office is on the first floor. ⊠ *Av. Juárez by zócalo.* ⊙ *Weekdays 9–5.*

⑪ **Gringo Gulch.** Named after the hundreds of expatriates from the United States who settled here in the 1950s, this neighborhood's most famous attraction is Elizabeth Taylor's former home, **Casa Kimberly.** It's connected to Richard Burton's former home across the street by the "love bridge" he had constructed. The house has been converted into a bed-and-breakfast (☞ Lodging, *below*), but tours are offered to the general public daily 9–6 in season and Monday–Saturday 10–2 off-season. Burton bought the 24,000-square-ft home for Taylor's 32nd birthday after they'd filmed *The Night of the Iguana* together. Taylor owned the house for 26 years, and left 98% of her possessions behind (all on display) when she sold it in 1990. ⊠ *Calle Zaragoza 445,* ☎ ℻ *322/ 2–13–36.* ☞ *$6.*

⑩ **La Iglesia de Nuestra Señora de Guadalupe** (Church of Our Lady of Guadalupe). The town's main church is topped by an ornate crown that replicates the one worn by Carlota, the empress of Mexico in the late 1860s. The crown toppled during the earthquake that shook this area of the Pacific Coast in October 1995, and was quickly replaced with a fiberglass version in time for the celebration of the Feast of the Virgin of Guadalupe (December 12). Sculptor Octavio Gonzalez was commissioned to build a new crown out of brass, and it's still in the works. Signs posted at the entrances to the church ask that you not visit wearing shorts, miniskirts, or sleeveless shirts. ⊠ *Calle Hidalgo, 1 block east of zócalo.* ⊙ *Weekdays 7:30 AM–8 PM, Sat. 7:30 AM–8:30 PM, Sun. 6:30 AM–8:30 PM.*

⑫ **Isla Río Cuale** (Cuale River Island). Surrounded by two arms of the Río Cuale, this island effectively slices the downtown in two. It has an out-

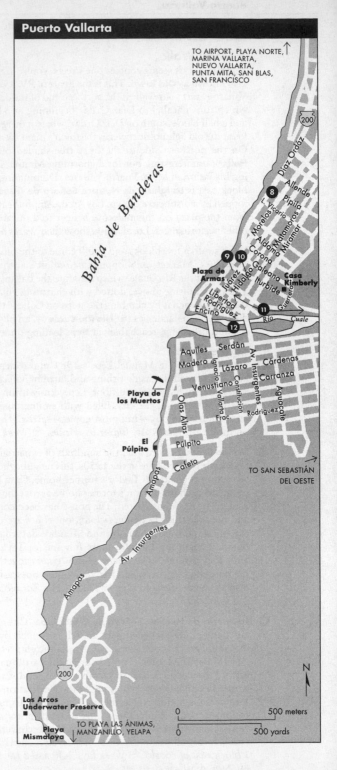

Puerto Vallarta

TO AIRPORT, PLAYA NORTE,
MARINA VALLARTA,
NUEVO VALLARTA,
PUNTA MITA, SAN BLAS,
SAN FRANCISCO

200

Bahía de Banderas

Díaz Ordáz

Allende

Pipila

I. Vicario

Morelos

Aldama

Matamoros

Miramar

Corona

Galeana

8

9   10

Plaza de
Armas

Juárez

Hidalgo

Iturbide

Casa
Kimberly

Libertad

Rodríguez

Guerrero

Encino

11

Río   Cuale

12

Aquiles   Serdán

Madero

Ignacio
Vallarta

Lázaro

Av. Insurgentes

Cárdenas

Constitución

Carranza

Venustiano

Frac.

Rodríguez

Aguacate

Playa de
los Muertos

Olas Altas

El
Púlpito

Pulpito

Cafeto

TO SAN SEBASTIÁN
DEL OESTE

Amapas

Av. Insurgentes

Amapas

200

N

Las Arcos
Underwater Preserve

Playa
Mismaloya

TO PLAYA LAS ÁNIMAS,
MANZANILLO, YELAPA

0   500 meters

0   500 yards

door marketplace with boutiques, souvenir stands, trendy restaurants, and inexpensive cafés; a bronze statue of film director John Huston dominates the main square. The **Museo Arqueológico** (⊠ western tip of island, ☎ no phone) hosts a nice collection of pre-Columbian figures and Indian artifacts. The museum is open daily 10–2 and 4–6. The large patio on the east end of the island often hosts rehearsals of the local ballet folklórico and other cultural events. ⊠ *To reach Isla Río Cuale from north side of town, cross bridge at Encino and Juárez or at Libertad and Miramar. From the south, cross at Ignacio L. Vallarta and Aquiles Serdán, or at Insurgentes and Aquiles Serdán.*

⑧ **Malecón.** The malecón is downtown's main drag, a nice place to rest on a white wrought-iron bench. A seawall and sidewalk run along the bay, and restaurants, cafés, and shops are across the street. You'll see some interesting sculpture along the walkway—among other pieces, the bronze sea horse that has become Puerto Vallarta's trademark, as well as the recent addition of a **Rotunda del Mar,** a collection of whimsical statues by artist Alejandro Colunga. ⊠ *Parallel to Díaz Ordáz for approximately 16 blocks, extending from Río Cuale northeast to 31 de Octubre.*

Beaches

Puerto Vallarta's stellar attraction is its amazing beaches: crescents of golden sand, fringed with palms, along the hotel zone; endless stretches of gloriously unpopulated beaches to the north; and soft creamy beaches on craggy coves to the south.

Boca de Tomatlán. This small village at the mouth of the Río Tomatlán (Tomatlán River) is about 17 km (10½ mi) south of Puerto Vallarta and 4 km (2½ mi) south of Mismaloya (☞ *below*). It's a beautiful spot away from the crowds and popular with the locals. Just before you reach the dirt road to the beach, there are several large palapa restaurants. Chee Chee's, a massive restaurant, shopping, and swimming-pool complex, spreads down a steep hillside like a small village. Farther along the main road, through Boca, is Chico's Paradise (☞ Dining, *below*). Just a bit farther is Las Orquidias, a riverfront restaurant 1 km (½ mi) down a dirt road, where you can swim in clear river pools and delight in the orchids blooming there in the summer. Tour boats leave from Boca to Los Arcos and the more secluded beaches of Playa Las Ánimas and Yelapa (☞ *below*).

Nayarit. North of Puerto Vallarta on the coast of Nayarit is a string of beautiful, unpopulated beach areas. **Lo de Marcos,** about 40 km (25 mi) away, is one of the most attractive. **Sayulita,** about 45 minutes away, has a great beach hidden behind a hill only 10 minutes on foot north of the town center, excellent surfing, and some good eating spots. People have described it as being like Puerto Vallarta 40 years ago. Fifteen minutes north of Sayulita is the interesting town of **San Francisco,** unofficially known as San Pancho, with modest rental bungalows and eateries and a 1½-km- (1-mi-) long, barely developed stretch of beach.

Playa Las Ánimas and Yelapa. Playa Las Ánimas and Yelapa are secluded fishing villages accessible only by boat. The former is about 25 minutes southeast of Puerto Vallarta, the latter approximately an hour away in the same direction. Both villages have small communities of hardy isolationists; of late, Yelapa has attracted more and more foreigners who settle in permanently. At Yelapa, take a 20-minute hike from the beach into the jungle to see the waterfalls. At Quimixto (another beautiful beach with calm, clear waters to the south of Mismaloya) mount a horse for a 15-minute ride up to a spectacular large clear pool under a waterfall for swimming and a light seafood lunch. Tour groups arriving on cruise ships visit the beaches daily, and motor launches leave from Tomatlán and the pier at Los Muertos for Las Ánimas, Quimixto, and Yelapa (☞ Contacts and Resources *in* Puerto Vallarta A to Z, *below*); the cost is $10–$20 per person.

Playa de los Muertos. This beach on the south side of the Río Cuale has long been a budget traveler's domain, although it has some of the more expensive restaurants and shops; it's by far the most popular and most crowded beach in Puerto Vallarta. Long ago, the beach was the site of a battle between pirates and Indians. The town's boosters tried for years to change the name Playa de los Muertos (Beach of the Dead) to Playa del Sol (Beach of the Sun), but they weren't successful. The area around the beach is now promoted as the Zona Romantica, but locals still call it Los Muertos. Strolling vendors selling lace tablecloths, wooden statues, kites, and jewelry are almost as abundant as sunbathers. Beach toys for rent include everything from rubber inner tubes to windsurfers. Plaza Lázaro Cárdenas is a pretty spot at the north end of the beach; to the south, Playa de los Muertos ends at a rocky point called El Púlpito.

Playa Mismaloya. A visit to Puerto Vallarta without a side trip to Playa Mismaloya is nearly unthinkable, since this is where "the movie" was made. The 13-km (8-mi) drive south from the center of town on Highway 200 (you can take a taxi or a bus) passes spectacular houses, some of PV's oldest and quietest resorts, and a slew of condo and time-share developments. A pretty cove, somewhat spoiled by La Jolla de Mismaloya—a huge hotel complex built on its shores—Mismaloya is backed by rugged, rocky hills and affords a good view of Los Arcos, a rock formation in the water. Catamaran cruises, which can be booked through Vallarta Adventures (☎ 322/1–06–57), leave the Cruise Ship Terminal nightly at 6 for dinner and dancing on the terraces of John Huston's former home, set at the edge of the jungle on a private bay in Las Caletas, southeast of Mismaloya Beach (and accessible only by boat). Or hoist the skull and crossbones and depart on the *Marigalante* (☎ 322/31–03–09), a replica of a 15th-century caravel that sails to the Marietas Islands during the day and passes Los Arcos on a sunset cruise that includes fireworks and a barbecue dinner.

Playa Norte. Also known as Playa de Oro, this is Puerto Vallarta's northernmost beach, stretching from the marina and cruise-ship terminal to downtown. The beach changes a bit with the character of each hotel it fronts, but it is particularly nice by the Fiesta Americana and the Krystal hotels.

Punta Mita. Twelve kilometers (7 mi) north of Nuevo Vallarta, on yet another beautiful beach, is the town of Bucerias. From here, you follow the bend of Bahía de Banderas past several small and pristine beaches—including Cruz de Huanacaxtle and Anclote—to Punta Mita, on the northern tip of the Bahía de Banderas. A four-lane highway links Punta Mita, home of the posh Four Seasons Resort (☞ Lodging, *below*), to the Puerto Vallarta airport. Punta Mita has blue bay water that's perfect for swimming, and around the bend there are waves for surfing. Here, the views of the bay and of the Sierra Madre are fantastic. This is a prime spot for viewing a sunset and, during the winter months, the whales that come here to mate in the warm waters of the Mexican Pacific. Scuba divers like the fairly clear waters and abundance of tropical fish and coral on the bay side of the Isla Marietas, offshore.

Dining

$$$$ ✕ **Café des Artistes.** With a breathtaking view of the Pacific, this is Puerto Vallarta's most sophisticated—and expensive—dining spot. Owner/chef Thierry Blouet combines Mexican ingredients with European techniques to produce such interesting combinations as cream of prawn and pumpkin soup, mussels in a scallop mousse, and roast duck with soy and honey. A piano/flute duo provides musical accompaniment. ⊠ *Guadalupe Sánchez 740,* ☎ *322/2-32–28. Reservations essential. AE, DC, MC, V. No lunch.*

$$$$ ✕ **River Cafe.** Candles flicker at romantic tables lining the river bank, and tiny white lights wrap the palm trees surrounding the restaurant's multilevel terrace. Attentive waiters serve such international dishes as steak, lobster, and pasta to a well-dressed crowd. There's a small bar area if you want to stop by for just a drink. ⊠ *Isla Río Cuale, Local 4,* ☎ *322/3–07–88. AE, MC, V.*

$$$ ✕ **Adobe Café.** Shades of white and earth tones, stark trees, fresh flowers, and an interesting menu make for a delightful dining experience. Specialties include cream of coriander soup with clams, pork tenderloin in rum, and one of the best desserts in town: a sinfully rich chocolate mousse between two layers of chocolate cake and chocolate icing. ⊠ *Basilio Badillo 252,* ☎ *322/2–67–20. MC, V. No lunch.*

$$$ ✕ **Bombo's.** This place is elegant and romantic, with a serene orchid-and-white decor, and a sweeping view of Puerto Vallarta. An exceptionally creative international menu includes smoked-salmon mousse, kiwi margaritas, and cream of artichoke soup with pistachios. ⊠ *Corona 327, at Matamoros,* ☎ *322/2–51–64. AE, MC, V. No lunch.*

$$$ ✕ **Café Maximilian.** Efficient and fluid service accompanied by genuine smiles from both diners and staff make this a top spot to eat out at in Los Muertos. Viennese and other European entrées dominate the menu, including braised baby lamb strips with rosemary and an excellent pork loin escallop with homemade noodles. An espresso and dessert bar shares sidewalk space with a dozen tables. ⊠ *Olas Altas 380,* ☎ *322/3–07–60. AE, MC, V. Closed Fri. No lunch.*

$$$ ✕ **Chef Roger.** The cozy patio of a typical Puerto Vallarta house is the
★ unpretentious setting for one of the best restaurants in town. Roger Dreier, the Swiss owner and chef, combines his European training with Mexican ingredients, and the results are superb. Don't leave town without trying the coconut breaded shrimp with pineapple sauce, and for dessert, the fried apples with vanilla sauce. ⊠ *Basilio Badillo 180,* ☎ *322/2–59–00. Reservations essential. AE, DC, MC, V. No lunch.*

$$$ ✕ **Daiquiri Dick's.** The beachside patio dining room of this long-time *vallartense* favorite for Sunday brunch frames one of the best views of the bay. The Caesar salad explodes with flavor. The medallions of beef tenderloin demi-glacé and the lobster tacos are superb. Finish off with a hazelnut daiquiri. ⊠ *Olas Altas 314,* ☎ *322/2–05–66. MC, V.*

$$$ ✕ **Trio.** Two young German chefs, Bernhard Guth and Peter Lodes, have
★ become the favorites of local diners with their avant-garde creations—such as orange-crusted sea bass with a sweet purée of garbanzo, dates, olives, and cider, or the rack of lamb and ravioli with lamb ragout, vegetables, and mint sauce. The artsy crowd and professional staff make for a wonderful dining experience. The kitchen stays open a bit later than most in Vallarta (usually until midnight), and there's a rooftop terrace on which to dine or have drinks. ⊠ *Guerrero 264,* ☎ *322/2–21–96. AE, DC, MC, V.*

$$ ✕ **Don Pedro's.** Everything is a treat at this giant beachfront palapa
★ in Sayulita, a half hour north of the airport, where European-trained chef and co-owner Nicholas Parrillo serves an array of fish, seafood, and poultry sprinkled with herbs and grilled over mesquite. Everything

is fresh as can be and made on the premises, from the crusty herbed breads and pizzas to the rich mango ice cream. ⊠ *Calle Marlin 2, midway along Sayulita town beach, 35 km (22 mi) north of Puerto Vallarta airport,* ☎ *327/5–02–29. MC, V. Closed July–Oct.*

$$ ✕ **Felipe's.** Sitting high on a hill, Felipe Palacio's gracious family home has the charm of old Vallarta mixed with spectacular views of the bay and town from its multilevel terraces. Grilled seafood and steaks are superbly prepared. ⊠ *Av. Insurgentes 466,* ☎ *322/2–38–20. AE, MC, V. No lunch.*

$$ ✕ **Flaming Sombrero.** Grill your own marinated beef, lamb, chicken, pork, marlin, or prawns on a huge searing brass sombrero at the table with vegetables sizzling on the rim. The drink of the house is a Nicholashka: chew a slice of lime with ground coffee and sugar and take a shot of vodka. ⊠ *31 de Octubre 380,* ☎ *322/2–55–95. MC, V. Closed Mon.*

$–$$ ✕ **Chico's Paradise.** It's easy to while away hours—or even the day—
★ under the huge palapa, enjoying the sound of the waterfall, taking a dip in the river, or watching tortillas being made by hand. Three parrots will keep you occupied with their antics. Seafood, including fresh jumbo shrimp or stuffed crab, is a specialty, but *chiles rellenos* (stuffed chili peppers) and chicken burritos are also popular. Or just come for some of the huge tropical drinks—take the bus marked MISMALOYA (they run about every 15 minutes from the corner of Av. Insurgentes and Basilio Badillo to Boca de Tomatlán and back). In the off season, the place closes just after sunset. ⊠ *Carretera a Manzanillo Km 20,* ☎ *322/2–07–47. No credit cards.*

$ ✕ **Andale.** A Playa de los Muertos hangout and a good spot for an afternoon beer with locals, this restaurant serves giant shrimp, great herb–garlic bread, and delicious black-bean soup. ⊠ *Olas Altas 425,* ☎ *322/2–10–54. DC, MC, V.*

$ ✕ **Cafe de Olla.** This is the place for cheap, down-to-earth, authentic
★ Mexican food, from enchiladas to *carne asada* (grilled strips of marinated meat) to chiles rellenos. Service is excellent and the atmosphere inviting: trees extend from the dining-room floor through the roof, local artwork adorns the walls, and salsa music often plays in the background. The restaurant is hugely popular and you may need to wait a short while for a table. ⊠ *Basilio Badillo 168-A,* ☎ *322/3–16–26. No credit cards. Closed Tues.*

$ ✕ **Really Rosie's.** This is where to go if you want a taste of home. With a menu listing homemade corned-beef hash, biscuits and gravy, and cheese blintzes for breakfast—and meat loaf and country-fried steak and mashed potatoes among other dinner favorites—Rosie Sorrenson's food will soothe you if you're wearying of the exotic. Don't feel like going out? Rosie's delivers. ⊠ *31 de Octubre 149,* ☎ *322/2–44–27. DC, MC, V.*

Lodging

Most of PV's deluxe resorts are to the north of downtown. Many are concentrated in the Marina Vallarta complex, practically a town unto itself with a marina, hundreds of condominiums, shopping centers, an 18-hole golf course, and the Royal Pacific Yacht Club. Farther north is Nuevo Vallarta, just over the Jalisco state line in Nayarit, at the mouth of the Río Ameca. This beautiful community with beachfront houses and condos on canals with direct access to the bay is home to several all-inclusive resorts, among them the Sierra Puerto Vallarta and two Diamond Resort hotels. South of downtown and the Río Cuale, in the Playa de los Muertos and Olas Altas areas, the rates are lower. If you head farther south still, the prices go up again: some spectacular properties are tucked away on hidden coves on the road to Manzanillo.

Rates at most hotels usually go down 25%–30% just after Easter week through December 15, although they rebound during July and August when most nationals take a two-week vacation. Reservations are a must at Christmas, New Year's, Easter, and in July and August. Hotels in the state of Jalisco charge a 2% room tax in addition to the 15% VAT.

$$$$
★ ⛟ **Camino Real.** One of PV's first hotels, this property sits on a lovely small bay south of town. The rooms have cool marble floors with white furniture and bright pink, yellow, and purple highlights against stark white walls. The hotel has all the five-star touches—from plush robes in the rooms to the palapas on the beach and the fragrant white jasmine blooming along the natural waterfall. La Brisa restaurant, on the northern end of the beach, serves superb seafood lunches. Even nicer is La Perla, with excellent international food accompanied by a concert pianist. A newer 11-story tower houses the Camino Real Club, where guests receive upgraded amenities and breakfast on a picturesque terrace over the ocean; the club's upper floors have whirlpool baths. The hotel is also involved in an extensive marine turtle–conservation program. ⊠ *Playa Las Estacas, 48300,* ☎ *322/1–50–00, 800/722–6466,* ℻ *322/1–60–00. 326 rooms, 11 suites. 5 restaurants, 3 bars, 2 pools, wading pool, 2 tennis courts, exercise room, health club, beach, travel services, car rental. AE, DC, MC, V.* ⊗

$$$$
★ ⛟ **Four Seasons Resort.** This secluded, private resort community at Punta Mita, a 40-minute drive northwest of the Puerto Vallarta International Airport, is destined to be one of the world's most exclusive hotels (standard rooms start at $500 here). Rooms are housed in quaint red-tile-roof Mexican-style casitas of one, two, and three stories. Furnished like luxurious Mexican homes and fitted with traditional Four Seasons amenities, rooms are spacious and feature private terraces or balconies with sweeping beach and sea views. Most of the suites have private plunge pools as well as fax machines. Sports facilities include a Jack Nicklaus-designed 18-hole championship golf course with a unique island hole (No. 3B), tennis courts, a beautiful health club, and beach activities. The pool is gorgeous, and service is impeccable. ⊠ *Punta Mita, Nayarit 63732,* ☎ *322/1–24–81, 800/819–5053 in the U.S. and Canada,* ℻ *322/1–24–88. 82 rooms, 18 suites. 3 restaurants, bar, in-room data ports, pool, wading pool, hot tub, spa, 18-hole golf course, 4 tennis courts, health club, horseback riding, snorkeling, windsurfing, children's programs (ages 5–12), concierge, car rental. AE, DC, MC, V.* ⊗

$$$$ ⛟ **La Jolla de Mismaloya.** Despite the fact that the overpowering design of this hotel has ruined the view of beautiful Mismaloya Bay, the lucky guests here literally have half the bay to themselves, as well as a fabulous view of Puerto Vallarta's famous arches (rock formations jutting out of the sea). The hotel's huge one- and two-bedroom suites have terraces, and the many activities for children make it an ideal family getaway. This hotel consistently gets high marks from guests. ⊠ *Off Hwy. 200 at Mismaloya Bay, 48300,* ☎ *322/8–06–60, 800/322–2343,* ℻ *322/8–05–00. 303 suites. 5 restaurants, bar, 4 pools, hot tub, spa, 2 tennis courts, exercise room, beach, dive shop, snorkeling, children's programs (ages 5–11), concierge, travel services, car rental. AE, DC, MC, V.* ⊗

$$$$ ⛟ **Meliá Puerto Vallarta.** On the beach in Marina Vallarta, this Sol Meliá hotel is a top-of-the-line all-inclusive resort only three blocks from the marina's 18-hole golf course. The exterior is an off-putting institutional style, but the lobby is a pleasing blend of textures and colors, with marble and tile floors contrasting with colorful Mexican crafts and cozy wicker furniture. The large rooms are decorated in soft natural tones of cream and sand, with colorful accents. Amenities include hair dryers and in-room safes, the largest pool in the area, the Mini Club, an outdoor theater, and nightly shows. Two children under age seven can stay free (including meals and activities) if they share a room with their parents. ⊠ *Paseo de la Marina Sur 7, 48354,* ☎ *322/1–02–00, 800/336–3542,* 𝔽𝔸𝕏 *322/1–01–18. 370 rooms and suites. 3 restaurants, 3 bars, pool, 2 tennis courts, archery, exercise room, beach, shops, video games, children's programs (ages 4–12), meeting rooms. AE, DC, MC, V.*

$$$$ **⊡ Paradise Village.** Built like an Aztec pyramid, this Nuevo Vallarta hotel and time-share property has its own marina and zoo (with a pair of tigers, a crocodile, deer, and various birds). All suites have tile floors and balconies with either marina or ocean views. Sofa-beds and a full kitchen—including stove, microwave, refrigerator, and good cookware—are de rigueur. Locals come by to use the spa, which is noted for its massages and facials. Paradise Village is the top hotel in Nuevo Vallarta. ⊠ *Paseo de los Cocoteros 18, Nuevo Vallarta, 63732,* ☎ *322/6–67–07,* 𝔽𝔸𝕏 *329/6–67–13. 480 suites. 2 restaurants, 2 bars, 2 snack bars, 3 pools, spa, 4 tennis courts, aerobics, volleyball, beach, windsurfing, jet skiing, travel services, car rental. AE, DC, MC, V.*

$$$$ **⊡ Sierra Hotel Nuevo Vallarta.** Situated on a long, wide expanse of creamy sand beach in Nuevo Vallarta, the Sierra is a deluxe all-inclusive property. The rooms are light and airy, with tile floors, light-wood and wicker furniture, and the ubiquitous pastel bedspreads. Activities are nonstop: cookouts, beach parties, Mexican fiestas, disco blasts, theme nights, musicals, karaoke, restaurants, and bars. Daytime activities include aerobics, beach and pool volleyball, tennis, minigolf, windsurfing, kayaking, and water biking, as well as jungle and city tours. A golf course is minutes away. ⊠ *Paseo de los Cocoteros 19, Nuevo Vallarta, 63732,* ☎ *329/7–13–00, 800/515–4321,* 𝔽𝔸𝕏 *329/7–11–62. 350 rooms and suites. 3 restaurants, 3 bars, 3 pools, tennis court, aerobics, volleyball, beach, windsurfing. AE, DC, MC, V.*

$$$$ **⊡ Westin Regina.** This attractive hotel sits on a choice 21-acre site in
★   Marina Vallarta. In addition to four pools, a long stretch of beach, and a full range of facilities and activities (including an excellent kid's club), the Westin has spacious balconied rooms with marble bathrooms and brightly colored, handwoven spreads and drapes. Rooms above the fourth floor have ocean views, whereas those below face the 600 palm trees surrounding the beautiful pools. Most of the suites have Jacuzzis. The hotel also has a turtle nursery; you can help release baby turtles into the sea. ⊠ *Paseo de la Marina Sur 205, 48321,* ☎ *322/1–11–00, 800/228–3000 in the U.S.,* 𝔽𝔸𝕏 *322/1–11–21. 266 rooms, 14 suites. 2 restaurants, 3 bars, 4 pools, spa, 3 tennis courts, health club, beach, baby-sitting, children's programs (ages 3–7), concierge, car rental. AE, DC, MC, V.* ✍

$$$–$$$$ **⊡ Krystal Vallarta.** A full-service resort that sprawls over acreage equivalent to that of a small town, the Krystal has hotel rooms and villas, many with private pools. The accommodations exude Mexican character, with tile floors and Spanish colonial-style furnishings. Not all rooms are by the ocean, but the secluded beach can accommodate all sunseekers. ⊠ *Carretera Aeropuerto, 48300,* ☎ *322/4–01–11, 800/231–9860,* 𝔽𝔸𝕏 *322/4–01–11. 291 rooms, 114 villas. 3 restaurants, 3 bars, 4 pools, 2 tennis courts, beach, dance club, travel services. AE, DC, MC, V.*

$$$–$$$$ **⊡ Marriott Casa Magna.** Located in Marina Vallarta, with El Salado beach to the front and the marina's 18-hole, Joe Finger–designed golf course to the rear, the Marriott Casa Magna is one of Vallarta's newest, largest, and most glamorous hotels. The vast, plant-filled marble lobbies that open onto the huge pool area are hung with chandeliers. The rooms are decorated with light woods and cream colors. All have at least a partial view of the bay. And if the water sports, tennis, restaurants, nightclubs, kid's club, and other hotel amenities aren't enough, you also have access to the facilities of the Marina Vallarta complex, including a huge shopping center, a yacht club, and yet more restaurants. ⊠ *Paseo de la Marina 5, 48354,* ☎ *322/1–00–04, 800/228–9290,* FAX *322/1–07–60. 433 rooms, 29 suites. 4 restaurants, 3 bars, pool, 3 tennis courts, exercise room, beach, dance club, baby-sitting, children's programs (ages 5–12). AE, DC, MC, V.*

$$$ 🏨 **Continental Plaza Puerto Vallarta.** Ideal for tennis lovers, this Mexican colonial complex has a tennis club with eight courts and daily tennis clinics. The resort has a shopping plaza, several restaurants and bars, a large swimming pool, and a nice beach. ⊠ *Carretera Aeropuerto Km 0.5, Zona Hotelera Las Glorias, 48300,* ☎ *322/4–01–23, 800/515–4321,* FAX *322/4–39–32. 309 rooms. 3 restaurants, 2 bars, pool, 8 tennis courts, beach. AE, DC, MC, V.*

$$$ 🏨 **Fiesta Americana.** A seven-story palapa covers the lobby and a
★ large round bar. The dramatically designed terra-cotta building rises above a deep-blue pool that flows under bridges, palm oases, and palapa restaurants set on platforms over the water. The ocean-view rooms have a modern pink and terra-cotta color scheme; each has beige marble floors, tile bath with powerful shower, and balcony. The beach bustles with activity—parasailing, snorkeling, and, of course, sunbathing. The restaurants are excellent, especially the breakfast buffet by the pool. ⊠ *Blvd. Francisco Medina Ascencío Km 2.5, 48300,* ☎ *322/4–20–10, 01–800/504–5000, 800/345—5094,* FAX *322/4–21–08. 255 rooms, 36 suites. 3 restaurants, 4 bars, room service, pool, beauty salon, beach, concierge, travel services, car rental. AE, DC, MC, V.*

$$–$$$ 🏨 **Casa Kimberly.** The former homes of Elizabeth Taylor and Richard
★ Burton, located on opposite sides of the street but joined by a footbridge (in a part of town now called Gringo Gulch), have been converted into a B&B. Both houses are surprisingly unpretentious; only Richard's had a pool. The current owner, naturally enough, exploits the Liz and Dick legend and has added on a museum devoted to them. So if you stay here, be prepared to have tour groups wandering through the property during the day. Lavender (supposedly Elizabeth's favorite color, at least during her Puerto Vallarta days) prevails, and tables and walls are adorned with photos of the famous lovers. Rates include a full breakfast, except Sunday. ⊠ *Calle Zaragoza 445, 48300,* ☎ FAX *322/2–13–36. 8 rooms. Pool. No credit cards.*

$$–$$$ 🏨 **Villa Amor.** Tarzan never had it so good. What began as a home on top of a hill migrated into luxury palapa suites among the trees, with more outdoor than indoor living and beautiful views of Sayulita's coast. The larger suites have plunge pools on their terraces—but leave the younger children at home, as the pools definitely are not childproof. The restaurant is good and has live music on weekends. A beautiful beach is just a two-minute walk away. ⊠ *Playa Sayulita, Nayarit,* ☎ FAX *327/ 5–01–96. 12 villas. Restaurant, snorkeling, surfing. No credit cards.*

$$ 🏨 **Buenaventura.** This hotel's location is ideal, on the edge of down-
★ town, within walking distance (10 blocks or so) of the Río Cuale and, in the opposite direction, of the shops, hotels, and restaurants on the airport highway. From the street it looks rather austere, but just inside the door is an enormous five-story open lobby and bar. The bright, cheerful rooms have beam ceilings and pale-wood furnishings; most have ocean views. A new seven-story luxury tower recently opened, with six different styles of suites, many with Jacuzzis. ⊠ *Av. México 1301, 48350,* ☎ *322/2–37–37,* FAX *322/2–35–46. 199 rooms, 37 suites. 2 restaurants, 2 bars, 2 pools, massage, hot tub, exercise room, beach, travel services, car rental. AE, DC, MC, V.* 🐾

$$ 🏨 **Playa Los Arcos.** By far the most popular hotel on the beach by the Río Cuale, Los Arcos has a pretty central courtyard and pool and a friendly air. A glass elevator rises by the pool to the rooms, which are

fitted with light-wood and pastel furnishings and have small balconies. ✉ *Olas Altas 380, 48380,* ☎ *322/2–05–83,* FAX *322/2–24–18. 162 rooms, 13 suites. Restaurant, bar, pool, beach. AE, MC, V.*

$–$$ ⊞ **Dulce Vida.** Popular with family groups as well as solo travelers, ★ this hidden villa four blocks off the bustling malecón has six suites of various sizes decorated with Mexican art and comfortable furniture. All have well-equipped kitchens and most have ocean-view terraces; the largest has two bedrooms, two baths, and a separate dining room. There's a red-tile pool, tropical gardens, and Continental breakfast daily. ✉ *Calle Aldama 295, 48300,* ☎ *322/2–10–08, 800/600–6026,* FAX *322/ 2–58–15. 6 suites. Pool. AE, MC, V.*✍

$ ⊞ **Hotel Rosita.** The city's first official hotel opened its doors in 1948. Since then, this family-run business has served many repeat guests. On the northern edge of the malecón, it's a great spot for budget travelers who want to be close to the action. All rooms have air-conditioning. ✉ *Paseo Díaz Ordaz 901, 48380,* ☎ FAX *322/3–20–00, 322/2–10– 33. 112 rooms. Restaurant, pool. AE, MC, V.*✍

$ ⊞ **Posada de Roger.** One of PV's least expensive hotels, the Posada ★ de Roger is in many ways the most enjoyable, if you like the company of Europeans and Canadians who are savvy about budget traveling. The rooms have telephones, TVs, and air-conditioning; the showers are hot, the beds comfortable, and the pool is an international meeting spot. You can have your mail held here, and the desk clerks are knowledgeable about other budget hotels and restaurants. ✉ *Basilio Badillo 237, 48380,* ☎ *322/2–08–36,* FAX *322/3–04–82. 48 rooms. Restaurant, bar, pool. AE, MC, V.*✍

En Route to Manzanillo

The coastline south of Puerto Vallarta is sprinkled with some of the Mexican Riviera's most exclusive and secluded one-of-a-kind resorts. But you'll never see them from Highway 200 as you head south—it's a rugged, twisting road a short distance from the coast that runs through a tropical forest of pines and palms. Most resorts are on unpaved roads. To get down here, fly to Puerto Vallarta or Manzanillo and take a taxi or hotel van to your resort (which can run well over $100). Having arrived, you're likely to stay put for a week or more, leaving only for the requisite shopping spree in PV. South of PV, the best resorts are in Cihuatlán, Costa de Careyes, and San Patricio Melaque.

Lodging

$$$$ ⊞ **Las Alamandas.** One of Mexico's most exclusive—and expensive— ★ resorts, Las Alamandas is low key rather than glitzy. Surrounded by a natural preserve with abundant wildlife, the property's villas and one casita are decorated with folk art and traditional Mexican furnishings (some also have TVs and VCRs). Among the outdoor activities are golf, horseback riding, fishing, hot-air balloon rides, and boat rides along the Río San Nicolás. Many guests fly into the hotel's private helipad; others take the hotel's limo from either the Puerto Vallarta airport (1¾ hours) or the Manzanillo airport (1½ hours). There's a two-night-stay minimum; meal packages are available. ✉ *A.P. 201, San Patricio Melaque, Jalisco 48980 (3525 Sage Rd., Houston, TX 77056),* ☎ *328/ 5–55–00, or 713/961–3117 or 800/223–6510 in the U.S.,* FAX *328/5– 50–27, 713/961–3411 in the U.S. 8 suites, 4 villas. Restaurant, pool, tennis court, croquet, exercise room, Ping-Pong, volleyball, beach, snorkeling, mountain bikes. AE, MC, V.*

$$$$ ⊞ **The Careyes.** Resembling a Hispanic village nestled on a peaceful bay, this exquisitely understated luxury resort is situated on Mexico's "Turtle Coast," 98 km (60 mi) north of Manzanillo airport and 172 km (107 mi) south of Puerto Vallarta. There are 51 recently renovated intimate rooms and suites (some with private plunge pools) decorated in warm Mediterranean colors, pool, tennis, golf nearby at The Tamarindo, and a full-service spa featuring European beauty and body treatments. There's also a full range of water sports and excursions to nearby lagoons, tropical forests, and Teapa Beach to see turtles breeding between July and October. ☒ *Barra de Navidad Hwy. Km 53.5, Careyes, Jalisco 48970,* ☎ *335/1–00–00,* FAX *335/1–10–00. 51 rooms and suites. Restaurant, bar, pool, spa, 2 tennis courts, health club, beach, snorkeling, boating, fishing. AE, DC, MC, V.* ☜

$$$$ 🏨 **The Tamarindo.** This magical resort, nestled in palm groves and sur-
★ rounded by more than 2,000 acres of ecological reserve and jungle, lies on 16 km (10 mi) of private coast. The 28 secluded villas, all with private plunge pools and outdoor living rooms, have been designed of natural regional materials and textures. Meals are served under an awning on the beach in a casual rustic setting. Activities include an oceanfront 18-hole golf course, a tennis club, and three secluded beaches. At night, the gracious staff lights more than 1,500 candles around the villas to create a truly enchanting setting. ☒ *Melaque–Puerto Vallarta Hwy. Km 7.5, Cihuatlán, Jalisco 48970,* ☎ *335/1–50–31,* FAX *335/1–50–32. 28 villas. Restaurant, bar, pool, 18-hole golf course, 2 tennis courts, beach, dive shop, snorkeling, boating. AE, DC, MC, V.* ☜

$$$ 🏨 **Playa Blanca.** This Club Med has all the services the pioneer all-inclusive chain is known for—diving, fishing, pool bars, horseback riding, even a trapeze and circus school. The food, usually served buffet style, is ample and good, and there's a dinner-only restaurant with waiter service. The resort doesn't exactly feel isolated: with 300 rooms, a disco, and aerobics classes, the ambience is more celebratory than somnolent. Guests here tend to be earthy, active couples and singles in their late twenties to early forties. Playa Blanca has a rock-climbing wall and offers mountain biking. The staff comes from around the world. ☒ *Off Hwy. 200, Playa Blanca, Costa de Careyes 48980,* ☎ *335/1–00–01, 335/1–00–02, 800/258–2633,* FAX *335/1–00–04. 295 rooms. 2 restaurants, 3 bars, pool, 6 tennis courts, exercise room, horseback riding, beach, kayaking, snorkeling, sailing, windsurfing. AE, MC, V.*

Nightlife and the Arts

Puerto Vallarta is a party town, where the discos open at 10 PM and stay open until 3 or 4 AM. A minimum $20 cover charge is common in the popular discos, many of which are at hotels. The Krystal Vallarta hotel has **Christine's** (☎ 322/4–02–02), which features a spectacular light show set to music from disco to techno nightly at 11:30. **Champions** (☒ Paseo de la Marina 5, ☎ 322/1–00–04), at the Marriott Casa Magna, has music for almost all ages. **Friday López** (☎ 322/4–20–10), at the Fiesta Americana, has karaoke and dancing. **The Zoo** (☒ Paseo Díaz Ordaz 630, ☎ 322/2–49–45) and **Cactus Club** (☒ Ignacio L. Vallarta 399, ☎ 322/2–60–37) attract a young crowd. Motorcycle fans can let loose at **The American Legend Bar** (☒ Ignacio L. Vallarta 237, ☎ 322/2–24–00), where live rock mixes with Harley Davidsons. Harley rentals and clothing are available.

Everything its name implies and more, **Collage** (☎ 322/1–05–05), on the highway at the Marina Vallarta complex, has several restaurants, a bowling alley, billiards, two bars, shuffleboard, a video arcade, and a disco. The **Kit Kat** (☒ Pulpita 120, ☎ 322/3–03–93), somewhere between Art Deco and a Santa Monica fern bar, has the best martinis in town. **Cuiza** (☒ Isla Río Cuale 3, ☎ 322/2–56–46) has the best live jazz in the hands of Beverly and Willow, and an excellent bar and cigar shop. **El Faro** (The Lighthouse; ☒ Royal Pacific Yacht Club, Marina Vallarta, ☎ 322/1–05–41) is a romantic spot from which to watch a lightning storm roll into the bay at night in hurricane season, or just to see a good piece of the bay and marina from on high.

Mexican fiestas are popular at the hotels and can be lavish affairs with buffet dinners, folk dances, and fireworks. Reservations may be made with the hotels or travel agencies. Some of the more spectacular shows are at La Iguana Tourist Center (☎ 322/2–01–05), the Krystal Vallarta (☎ 322/4–01–11), and the Sheraton (☎ 322/6–04–04). The **Camino Real** (☎ 322/1–50–00) hosts cultural events, such as music concerts or folkloric dances, on the first Thursday of every month at 9 PM.

Outdoor Activities and Sports

Swimming, sailing, windsurfing, and parasailing are popular sports at the beachfront hotels, which have stands on the beach offering boat trips and equipment. You needn't be a guest to buy these services.

Biking

Bike Mexico (✉ Guerrero 361, ☎ 322/3–16–80) provides the gear (21-speed mountain bikes, helmets, lunch, and refreshments) for four- to six-hour bike tours to rivers, mountains, and jungles; these jaunts are tailored to each rider's experience and fitness level.

B-B-Bobby's Bikes (✉ Miramar 399, ☎ 322/3–00–08) rents all types of bikes and equipment by the day or week and runs tours.

Fishing

The Progreso Fishermen's Cooperative offers a variety of fishing trips from its shack on the north end of the malecón; most hotels can arrange your reservations. Large group boats cost about $60 per person for a day's fishing. Other cruisers may be chartered for $150–$350 a day, depending on the size of the boat and the length of the trip. Charters include a skipper, license, bait, and tackle; some also include lunch. Canadian Candice Shaw runs a bilingual-crewed boat, **Fishing with Carolina,** (☎ 322/4–72–50, 329/2–29–53), with three chairs; an all-day trip runs $300.

Golf

There is a Joe Finger–designed 18-hole course at the **Marina Vallarta** complex (☎ 322/1–01–73). The 18-hole course at **Los Flamingos Country Club** (✉ 12 km [8 mi] south of airport, ☎ 329/8–02–80) was designed by Percy Clifford. Reservations should be made through your hotel a day in advance.

Horseback Riding

Horseback riding along the shore is popular, and horses can be rented by the hour at major beaches. Several stables, including **Rancho Charro** (✉ Poblano de Playa Grande, ☎ 322/4–01–14) and **Rancho El Ojo de Agua** (✉ Cerrada de Cardenal 227, ☎ 322/4–82–40), run three-hour trips into the mountains, sunset rides, and longer excursions to charming colonial villages in the Sierra Madre. Time is allotted for lunch and a swim in a mountain stream or lake.

Swim with Dolphins

A magical experience awaits those at **Dolfin Adventure park,** where you can touch, feel, talk to, and even kiss one of the Pacific bottlenose dolphins. The center has a program for children with special needs. Reservations for any of the three daily programs (10, noon, and 3) are a must. ✉ *Marina Nueva Vallarta,* ☎ 322/1–06–57, 329/7–07–07. ⌚ *About $13 to swim with dolphins.*

Tennis

Most of the larger hotels have tennis courts. Nonmembers can play at the **Continental Plaza Tennis Club** (☎ 322/4–01–23 ext. 500), which offers private lessons and group clinics, or at the **Iguana Tennis Club** (☎ 322/1–06–83).

Ultra-Light Planes

See and photograph Vallarta from a bird's-eye view while certified pilots from **Wings Air Tours** (✉ Blvd. Francisco Medina Ascencío 2333, ☎ 322/4–96–40) take you on any number of tours for up to an hour.

Water Sports

Snorkeling and diving are most common at Los Arcos, a natural underwater preserve on the way to Mismaloya. Punta Mita, about 80 km (50 mi) north of Puerto Vallarta, has some good diving spots, as does Quimixto Bay, about 32 km (20 mi) south and accessible only by boat. Experienced divers prefer Las Marietas, Chimo, and El Morro, a group of islands off the coast.

Some hotels rent out snorkeling and diving equipment and have short diving courses at their pools. For intensive certification courses, dive trips, and rentals, contact **Chico's Dive Shop** (✉ Paseo Díaz Ordaz 772, ☎ 322/2–18–95) or **Pacific Scuba** (✉ Juárez 722, ☎ 322/2–47–41).

Shopping

Puerto Vallarta has been described as one huge shopping mall interspersed with hotels and beaches. This is an exaggeration, but PV can definitely get into a shopper's blood. There are dozens of excellent shops stocked with some of the best crafts from all around Mexico, as well as several fine-art galleries. Prices in the shops are fixed, and U.S. dollars and credit cards are accepted. Bargaining is expected in the markets and by the vendors on the beach, who also freely accept American money. Most stores are open 10–8. A few close for siesta at 1 or 2, then reopen at 4.

Art

The late Manuel Lepe is perhaps Puerto Vallarta's most famous artist. His primitive style can be seen in the prints and posters that are still available at several of the galleries and shops around town. Sergio Bustamante, the creator of life-size brass, copper, and papier-mâché animals, has his own galleries: **Sergio Bustamante** (✉ Av. Juárez 275, ☎ 322/2–11–29; ✉ Paseo Díaz Ordaz 716, ☎ 322/3–14–07; ✉ Paseo Díaz Ordaz 542, ☎ 322/2–54–80). Many collectors of Mexican art come to Vallarta to find a good buy. **Galería Uno** (✉ Calle Morelos 561, ☎ 322/2–09–08) specializes in paintings, sculptures, and silkscreens from all over Mexico, but owners Jan Lavender and Martina Goldberg are especially enthusiastic about promoting local talent. Contemporary art and sculpture are displayed in one of Mexico's finest galleries, **Galería Pacífico** (✉ Calle Aldama 174, ☎ 322/2–19–82). **Galería Rosas Blancas** (✉ Juárez 523, ☎ 322/2–11–68) combines a gallery featuring local and other Mexican artists with an artist's store. The very well-run **Galería Arte Latinoamericano** (✉ Josefa Ortiz Dominguez 155, ☎ 322/2–44–06) is the area's newest gallery, featuring contemporary art, sculptures, and lithographs. On the promenade in Marina Vallarta, **Arte de las Américas** (✉ Marina las Palmas II–16, ☎ 322/1–19–85) displays the work of celebrated and emerging contemporary artists.

Clothing

Most of the brand-name sportswear shops are located along the malecón and down its side streets. Many of these stores also have branches in the shopping centers or along Carretera Aeropuerto. **Aca**

Joe (✉ Paseo Díaz Ordaz 588, ☎ 322/3–04–24) sells excellent quality pants, T-shirts, shorts, jackets, and sweats in smashing colors, all neatly displayed. **Express–Guess** (✉ Paseo Díaz Ordaz 660, ☎ 322/ 2–64–70) carries its own line of well-designed quality sportswear.

More-elegant, dressier clothes, made of soft flowing fabrics in tropical prints, can be found at **Sucesos Boutique** (✉ Libertad and Hidalgo, ☎ 322/2–10–02), which features hand-painted fabrics and fashionable gauze resortwear. **La Bohemia** (✉ Juárez 479, ☎ 322/2–63–76; ✉ Marina Las Iguanas H-7, ☎ 322/1–21–60) displays contemporary resortwear, original designer artwear, unique jewelry, and accessories. **Gueros** (✉ Calle Zaragoza 160, ☎ 322/2–06–33) carries outfits with a Mexican accent, designed by Alejandro Julián and hand-embroidered with Huichol Indian motifs.

Lina (✉ Calles Zaragoza and Morelos, ☎ 322/2–47–85) carries handmade and embroidered clothes from Chiapas. **María de Guadalajara** (✉ Puesta del Sol condominiums in Marina Vallarta, ☎ 322/1–02–62 ext. 1015; ✉ Calle Morelos 550, ☎ 322/2–23–87; ✉ Plaza Malecón and Paseo Díaz Ordaz, ☎ 322/2–47–35) carries easy-to-wear clothing for women in gauzy cotton fabrics dyed in luscious colors. **Nina & June** (✉ Hidalgo 227–8, ☎ 322/2–30–99) specializes in Nina's handwoven originally designed fashions, fanciful accessories, and June's silver jewelry.

Folk Art

Few cities in Mexico have a collection of the country's fine folk art that is as representative as the one in Puerto Vallarta. Masks, pottery, lacquerware, clothing, mirrors, glass dishes, windows and lamps, carved-wood animals and doors, antiques and modern art, hand-dyed woven rugs, and embroidered clothing are all available in the markets and from vendors. **Alfarería Tlaquepaque** (✉ Av. México 1100, ☎ 322/3–21–21) stocks a varied selection of baked earthenware suns, carved-wood figures, blown glass, baskets, ceramics, and painted animals from all over Mexico. **Talavera Etc.** (✉ Ignacio L. Vallarta 266, ☎ 322/2–41–00) has fine, handcrafted majolica ceramics and antique Mexican jewelry. **Mundo de Azulejos** (✉ Carranza 374, ☎ 322/2–26–75) sells a line of Talavera tiles and will create tile replicas of your favorite scene or work of art in 24 to 48 hours. **Puerco Azul** (✉ Marina Las Palmas II promenade, ☎ 322/1–19–85) carries one-of-a-kind items for the home, including furniture, ceramics, antiques, glassware, and whimsical pig and other animal figurines. **Olinalá** (✉ Lázaro Cárdenas 274, ☎ 322/2–49–95) is a two-story gallery and shop filled with masks from all over Mexico, as well as colonial-inspired carvings, lacquered boxes, and trays from Michoacán. **Galería de Ollas** (✉ Calle Morelos 101, ☎ 322/3–10–45) has the wondrous pottery of Mata Ortiz exclusively. Original hand-loomed rugs, fabrics, and hand-painted furniture are on display at **Tamacani** (✉ Plaza Marina D-2, ☎ 322/1–09–82). **Mundo de Cristal** (✉ Av. Insurgentes 333, ☎ 322/2–41–57) is a glass factory where glassblowers create both avant-garde and classic designs.

Jewelry

There is a good selection of Mexican silver in Puerto Vallarta, but watch out for fake silver made with alloys, which is known as *chapa*. Real silver carries the 925 silver stamp required by the government. It is best to visit a reputable jeweler, such as **Pladi** (✉ Hidalgo 168, ☎ 322/2–56–06), which displays the creative silver jewelry designs of Rocio Guardia and Martha García. At **Ric Taxco** (✉ Pueblo Viejo shopping center, ☎ 322/3–01–43; ✉ Villa Vallarta shopping center, ☎ 322/4–45–98), much of the sterling silver and gold jewelry is inspired by pre-Hispanic designs. **Joyas Finas Suneson** (✉ Calle Morelos 593, ☎ 322/

2–57–15) specializes in nice silver jewelry and objets d'art by some of Mexico's finest designers.

Markets

The **Mercado Municipal,** at Avenida Miramar and Libertad, is a typical market plopped down in the busiest part of town. Flowers, piñatas, produce, and plastics are all shoved together in indoor and outdoor stands that cover a full city block. The strip of **shops along Isla Río Cuale** is an outdoor market of sorts, with souvenir stands and exclusive boutiques interspersed with restaurants and cafés. Bargaining at the stalls in the market and on the island is expected.

Shopping Centers

The highway on the north side of town is lined with small arcades and large shopping centers that are occupied by handicrafts and sportswear shops. The best selections are at **Plaza Malecón,** at the beginning of Paseo Díaz Ordaz; **Plaza Marina,** on the highway at Marina Vallarta; the **Gigante Plaza,** by the Fiesta Americana hotel; and **Villa Vallarta,** by the Plaza las Glorias hotel.

Puerto Vallarta A to Z

Arriving and Departing

BY BUS

A kilometer (½ mi) north of the airport is PV's new **Central Camionero** (✉ Puerto Vallarta–Tepic Hwy. Km 9, ☎ 322/1–07–39), or central bus station. **ETN** (☎ 322/1–05–50) has the most luxurious service to Guadalajara and Mexico City, with reclining seats that rival first-class airline seats in their roominess. Three other major bus lines, **Transportes del Pacífico** (☎ 322/1–00–21), **Elite** (☎ 322/1–08–48), and **Primera Plus** (☎ 322/ 1–00–95) service the area. Elite, which incorporates three lines (Estrella Blanca, Tres Estrellas de Oro, and Norte de Sonora), has excellent first-class service (reclining seats, air-conditioning, refreshment service, functioning bathroom) to Guadalajara, Aguascalientes, and Mexico City.

BY CAR

Puerto Vallarta is about 1,900 km (1,200 mi) south of Nogales, Arizona, at the U.S.–Mexico border, 354 km (220 mi) from Guadalajara, and 167 km (104 mi) from Tepic. Driving to Puerto Vallarta is not difficult, but driving in the city can be horrid.

BY PLANE

Puerto Vallarta's **Gustavo Díaz Ordaz International Airport** (☎ 322/ 1–12–98) is 6½ km (4 mi) north of town, not far from the major resorts. The Mexican airlines have daily flights from Mexico City, Guadalajara, Monterrey, Manzanillo, Tampico, and Tepic. **Mexicana** (☎ 322/1–12–66, 01–800/366–5400) has direct service from Chicago, Los Angeles, and Denver via Mazatlán. **Aeroméxico** (☎ 322/1–19–10) has flights from multiple U.S. and Mexican cities. Several U.S. carriers also serve Puerto Vallarta, including **Alaska Airlines** (☎ 322/1–13– 53), **American** (☎ 322/1–17–99), and **Continental** (☎ 01–800/900– 5000). **America West** (☎ 01–800/363–2597 flies in from Phoenix.

Volkswagen vans provide economical transportation from the airport to hotels.

BY SHIP

Several cruise lines, including **Carnival, Celebrity, Crystal P&O, Cunard, Holland America Line, Krystal, Princess Cruises, Royal Caribbean Cruises,** and **Royal Cruise Line,** sail to Puerto Vallarta from Los Angeles during the winter months.

Getting Around

BY BUS

City buses serve downtown, the northern hotel zone, and the southern beaches. Bus stops—marked by blue-and-white signs—are located every two or three blocks along the highway (Carretera Aeropuerto) and in town. *Combis* (Volkswagen vans) are used as shared economical taxis in Nayarit and will drop off passengers in Puerto Vallarta along the main road as far south as the malecón.

BY CAR

Several agencies in Puerto Vallarta rent Jeeps, open-air Volkswagen Beetles, and automatic-transmission sedans (☞ Car Rental *in* Contacts and Resources, *below*).

Note: Driving in the city can be very unpleasant. From December through April—peak tourist season—traffic clogs the small cobblestone streets. During the rainy season, from July through October, the streets become flooded and the hills are muddy and slippery.

BY TAXI

Many hotels post fares to common destinations; be sure to agree on a fare before the cab takes off. The ride from the north-side hotels to downtown costs about $2.50, plus 50¢ to cross the bridge.

Contacts and Resources

CAR RENTAL

During the high season, rentals start at $60 per day, including insurance and mileage; off-season, they start at $45 per day. Be certain to ask about special promotions, even during the high season. All the car-rental agencies below have desks at the airport; some have offices along the highway, but they are spread out, so compare prices at the airport or call from your hotel.

Agencies include **Alamo** (✉ Blvd. Francisco Medina Ascencio, in front of Gustavo Díaz Ordaz International Airport, ☎ 322/1–30–30), **Avis** (✉ Gustavo Díaz Ordaz International Airport, ☎ 322/1–11–12), **Budget** (✉ Carretera Aeropuerto Km 7.5, ☎ 322/2–29–80), **Hertz** (✉ Blvd. Francisco Medina Ascencio, ☎ 322/2–00–24), and **National** (✉ Carretera Aeropuerto Km 1.5, ☎ 322/2–05–15).

CONSULATES

U.S. Consulate (✉ Calle Zaragoza 160, 2nd floor, ☎ 322/2–00–69). **Canadian Consulate** (✉ Calle Zaragoza 160, ☎ 322/2–53–98).

EMERGENCIES

Police (✉ City Hall, Calles Morelos and Iturbide, ☎ 322/1–25–86). **Fire Department** (*Bomberos;* ☎ 322/4–77–01). **Red Cross** (☎ 322/2–15–33). **Hospital** (✉ Plaza Neptuno, Marina Vallarta, ☎ 322/1–00–23, 01–800/815–1921).

GUIDED TOURS

The five-hour **city tour** is a good way to get the lay of the land, from Marina Vallarta and Gringo Gulch to the Río Cuale and Playa Mismaloya, where *The Night of the Iguana* was filmed. Almost everyone goes on at least one daytime or sunset cruise around the bay, sighting scenic isolated coves and barren beaches from the deck of a sailboat or yacht. A full-day excursion to Yelapa or Las Ánimas, seaside communities that can be reached only by boat, gives you a feeling of what life is like in a secluded tropical paradise.

Daytime cruises go to Los Arcos, Yelapa, Quimixto, and Playa Las Ánimas, and to Isla Marietas for whale-watching (during winter months), snorkeling, swimming, and lunch. **Intermar Vallarta**

(☞ Travel Agencies, *below*) offers a dinner cruise to movie director John Huston's former home, on a private bay south of the city, with dancing on the return trip. Charter **airline tours** fly to San Sebastián del Oeste, an interesting old mining town in the Sierra Madre, 62 km (38 mi) from Puerto Vallarta.

Tropical tours visit mango and banana plantations in Nayarit and include stops in Nayarit's capital, Tepic, and the small seaside town of San Blas for a boat ride on the Río Tovara, through jungle thick with tropical plants and birds, with a stop for a refreshing swim in a natural spring. Other trips head south to Boca de Tomatlán, the mouth of the river that flows from the mountains into the sea.

Tours may be arranged through your hotel or one of the many tour operators with offices at hotels and in town. **Harris Tours** (☎ 322/3-29-72) is the main operator of guided tours in the area. City tours run about $16; tours to Yelapa run about $30; and tours to Las Ánimas and Quimixto cost approximately $40. It's worth the few extra dollars to go on a private tour (small groups) in a van rather than with a large group on a tour bus.

LETTERS AND E-MAIL

The best place for postal services is **Mail Boxes Etc.** (✉ Blvd. Francisco Medina Ascencio, Edificio Andrea Mar Local 7, ☎ 322/4-94-34), which also offers fax and e-mail services. Inexpensive Internet access is offered at **The Net House** (✉ Ignacio L. Vallarta 232, ☎ 322/2-69-53).

TRAVEL AGENCIES

American Express (✉ Morelos 660, ☎ 322/3-29-55). **Intermar Vallarta** (✉ Paseo de la Marina s/n, Condominio Via Golf, ☎ 322/1-07-34).

VISITOR INFORMATION

The **municipal tourist office** (✉ Independencia 123, ☎ 322/3-25-00, ext. 230 or 231), open weekdays 9–5, is on the Plaza Principal.

The **State Tourism Office** (✉ Plaza Marina, ☎ 322/1-26-76, 322/1-26-77) is open weekdays 9–7, Saturday 9–1. Dial ☎ 01–800/492–9832 for the toll-free tourist-information help line.

MANZANILLO

Nature is undoubtedly Manzanillo's best attraction. Its twin bahías, Manzanillo and Santiago, where crystal blue waters lap the black and gold volcanic sand, have caught outsiders' eyes since Cortés conquered Mexico. In the July–September rainy season, rivers and lagoons swell, forming waterfalls and ponds. White herons and pink flamingos flock to the fertile waters, and white butterflies flutter above the flowers in the chamomile fields—*manzanillo* is Spanish for chamomile.

Península de Santiago, which separates Bahía Santiago and Bahía Manzanillo, is the site of Las Hadas resort. From the water or points above the beach, the resort seems a mirage, a mass of white domes and peaks that radiate in the midday heat. When Bolivian tin magnate Antenor Patiño conceived of this white palace in the early 1960s, Manzanillo was easier to reach by sea than land, a rugged, primitive port that attracted the hardy who didn't mind creating their own tropical paradise. In 1974 when Patiño's retreat was complete, the international social set began to visit Manzanillo, thus putting the city in magazines and on television screens around the world. Even then, Manzanillo remained essentially a port city with only a few tourist attractions.

The October 1995 earthquake did considerable damage to the area. It leveled one of the hotels as well as the headquarters of the state at-

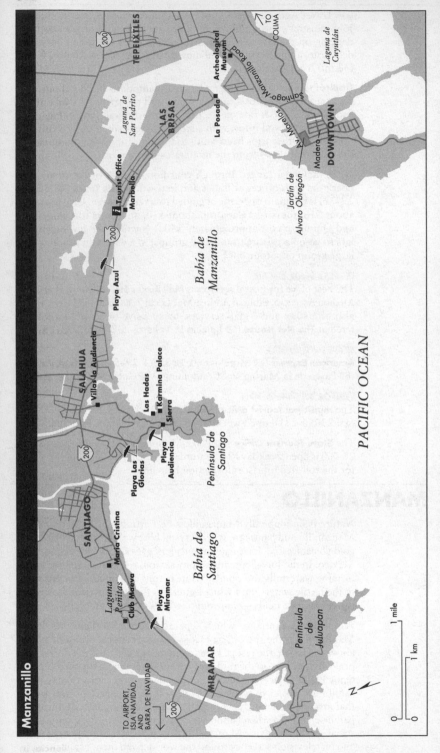

Manzanillo

torney general and caused a great deal of damage to the golf courses. With typical Mexican resilience, however, most everything was back in shape by the start of that winter season.

Manzanillo is still relatively undeveloped, a sleeper compared with other Pacific Coast resorts. Investors have plenty of land to divvy up for their financially rewarding havens, and existing resorts are spread out. The latest of these, Isla Navidad, is on 1,230 acres on a peninsula about 20 minutes north of the Manzanillo airport. Robert Von Hagge designed the 27-hole golf course, and other amenities include a full-service marina. Many shops and hotel desks close for afternoon siesta, and on Sunday most businesses (including restaurants) shut down and everyone heads for the beach.

Exploring Manzanillo

A vacation in Manzanillo is not spent shopping and sightseeing. You stay put, relax on the beach, and maybe take a few hours' break from the sun and sand to survey the local scene casually.

A Good Tour

The **Santiago** area, on Santiago Bay between the Santiago and Juluapan peninsulas, is tourist-oriented, with clusters of shops and restaurants by the beach. The next area to the east, **Salahua,** is residential, with a baseball field and restaurants. Farther southeast on Manzanillo Bay, past the traffic circle and Avenida Morelos, you'll see **Las Brisas** beach, where some of the more reasonably priced hotels are located.

Downtown is busy and jam-packed, but of little tourist interest, except for the bustling seaport and, just north of downtown, the **Archeological Museum,** which is at the San Pedrito campus of the University of Colima. A happy surprise in this otherwise culturally bereft region, the museum displays 5,000 of its more than 18,000 artifacts, which come from the immediate region, the state of Colima, and Mesoamerica. ⊠ *San Pedrito traffic circle,* ☎ *333/2–22–56.* ⊡ *$1.* ⊙ *Tues.–Sat. 10–2 and 5–8, Sun. 10–1.*

At the beginning of the harbor, Highway 200 jogs around downtown and intersects with Highway 110 to Colima. Avenida Morelos leads past the shipyards and into town. Just before you reach the port, stop at **Laguna de San Pedrito,** where graceful white herons and vivid pink flamingos assemble at sunset. The zócalo, or **Jardín Obregón,** is right on the main road by the waterfront. It's small but quite lively in the evening.

Beaches

Manzanillo's biggest attraction is its beaches. Every day is a beach day, and Sundays are downright festive, with half the town gathered to play onshore. The volcanic sand is a mix of black, white, and brown, with the southernmost beaches the blackest. Most beaches post warning flags if the conditions are dangerous or if jellyfish have been sighted.

Playa Miramar, at the north end of Santiago Bay, is populated by windsurfers and boogie-boarders. The beach in front of Club Santiago, once the favored hangout for locals, is now accessible only by walking north along the beach from the highway or by passing the guards at the club gates. The main stretch of beach is across the highway from Club Maeva. Manzanillo's best beach is probably **Playa Audiencia,** in a cove along the north side of Santiago Peninsula. The local Indians supposedly granted Cortés an audience here—thus the name. Located between two rock outcroppings, it's a good spot for snorkeling. The

Sierra hotel is located in the middle of the beach, making public access limited. **Playa Azul,** also called Playa Santiago, is a long strand that runs from Santiago Peninsula along Manzanillo Bay to Playa Las Brisas. The surf gets rough along the north end; swimming is better toward Las Brisas. South of town is **Playa Cuyutlán,** a black-sand beach on the open sea. Legend has it that the great *ola verde* (green wave) rises some 30 ft each spring during the full moon. In reality, the surf is high in spring but not quite as big as the original ola verde, which took the tiny town of Cuyutlán by surprise in 1959.

Barra de Navidad and **San Patricio Melaque,** to the north, have popular beaches that are good for surfing in the fall months. Palapa restaurants along the beach serve fresh fish. In Barra de Navidad, there are panga trips to a small island just offshore, where unbroken seashells are abundant. When the tide is low, it is possible to walk along the beach from Barra to Melaque, a distance of about 6 km (almost 4 mi).

Dining

$$$ ✕ **Legazpi.** This international restaurant is at Las Hadas, and it is beautiful. The service is white-glove perfection, but friendly rather than pretentious, and the food is decidedly elegant. The emphasis is on Continental cuisine with a Mexican touch, including Tulum salad (lettuce with crabmeat, avocado, and quail eggs) and grilled salmon with Jamaica sauce. The only drawback is finding a day when the restaurant is open. ✉ *Camino Real Las Hadas, Av. de los Riscos,* ☎ *333/4–01–01. AE, DC, MC, V. Closed Wed., Fri., Sun. No lunch.*

$$–$$$ ✕ **L' Recif.** With a huge palapa set on a cliff with waves crashing on
★ the rocks below, and a pool/bar to one side, this is undoubtedly the best dinner-with-a-view in the area. If you see a whale in the bay and tell the waiters, they will charge you a 15% "whale tax." Seafood is the specialty, but all the food is gourmet quality. ✉ *Cerro del Cenicero s/n, El Naranjo, Condominio Vida del Mar,* ☎ *333/5–09–00. MC, V. Closed Sept.–Oct. Closed Mon. May–Aug.*

$$–$$$ ✕ **Toscana.** Most tables at this French-Italian restaurant sit on the charming outdoor terrace adjacent to the beach. Specialties include smoked-salmon quiche, the San Remo salad (with tomatoes, onions, black olives, and Italian dressing), shrimp tempura, and a seafood assortment with scallop ceviche, shrimp, clams, and calamari. Live music is offered nightly. ✉ *Blvd. Costero Miguel de la Madrid 3177,* ☎ *333/3–25–15. MC, V. No lunch.*

$$–$$$ ✕ **Willy's.** Some people have been known to dine at Willy's every
★ night of their stay in Manzanillo. The French-inspired food is the best in the city, and the owner, Jean François, is personable and gracious. The best choices include crab-and-shrimp terrine, sea bass with mango and ginger, and duck with blackberries. A guitarist enlivens the informal beachfront setting. ✉ *Crucero Las Brisas,* ☎ *333/3–17–94. AE, MC, V. No lunch.*

$$ ✕ **El Bigotes.** Good seafood is served in this chain's two separate restaurants at a very leisurely pace, under a delightful palapa on the beach. The house specialty is a spicy *pescado sarandeado* (whole fish marinated and grilled over hot coals). The flan *napolitano* is a good choice for dessert. ✉ *Blvd. Costero Miguel de la Madrid 3157,* ☎ *333/4–08–31;* ✉ *Puesta del Sol 3,* ☎ *333/3–12–36. AE, DC, MC, V.*

$$ ✕ **Guadalajara Grill.** The liveliest restaurant in town doubles as a bar-disco, since it is attached to Carlos 'n' Charlies. Very popular with English-speaking tourists, Guadalajara Grill even has its own line of clothing. Mexican plates include enchiladas, chiles rellenos, fajitas, and a variety of fish dishes. People congregate here to watch sports, and the restaurant usually starts rocking with music and dancing after

10:30 PM. Mariachi singers come on Tuesday and Thursday. ⊠ *Av. Audiencia Plaza Pacifico,* ☎ *333/4–12–72. AE, MC, V.*

$$ ✕ **El Meson Español.** Paella, roast leg of lamb, and a superb Caesar salad prepared tableside are just a few of the specialties at this new family-run restaurant. There is a nightly buffet, and live music 8–11:30. ⊠ *Santiago–Manzanillo Rd. s/n,* ☎ *no phone. AE, MC, V.*

$$ ✕ **Porto Fino's.** If local food is starting to weigh you down, come here for the city's best all around Italian menu and wood-fired pizzas—or have Porto Fino's deliver to your hotel. ⊠ *Blvd. Costero Miguel de la Madrid Km 10,* ☎ *333/3–13–33. MC, V. Closed Mon.*

$$ ✕ **El Vaquero Campestre.** *Vaquero* means "cowboy," so it's no surprise to find a setting reminiscent of a ranchers' saloon and a menu emphasizing beef. The selections are prepared either marinated and seasoned as carne asada or simply grilled. ⊠ *Av. la Audiencia Lote 2,* ☎ *333/4–15–48. MC, V.*

$ ✕ **Juanito's.** This gringo hangout is owned by an American who married a local woman and settled in Manzanillo in 1976. It's the most popular spot in town for breakfast, and also specializes in great burgers, malts, fries, barbecued ribs, and fried chicken. Juanito's is the spot to watch U.S. football in good company. It's also one of Manzanillo's only Internet cafés, in case you need a 'net fix. Expect quick service and good coffee. ⊠ *Blvd. Costero Miguel de la Madrid Km 14,* ☎ *333/3–13–88. Reservations not accepted. AE, MC, V.*

Lodging

Lodging in Manzanillo was at one time a bargain, and although the $10 room is a thing of the past, there are still several decent places where you can lay your head for less than $40. Travelers on a tighter budget usually head to the towns of Barra de Navidad and Melaque. As with the rest of the Pacific Coast, Manzanillo is in the midst of a building boom, mainly condominiums, to accommodate the growing number of people from Guadalajara buying vacation homes here. The resorts are spread out along the Santiago–Manzanillo Road.

$$$$ 🏨 **Camino Real Las Hadas.** Las Hadas for many years was Manzanillo's premier resort, and its exotic Moorish buildings with white spires remain architectural wonders. The setting and grounds are still beautiful, but the upscale services of yesteryear have been allowed to wane. The hotel boasts its own golf course and looks over a gorgeous bay, and Legazpi restaurant is the city's most elegant. ⊠ *Av. de los Riscos, Fracc. la Audencia, 28200,* ☎ *333/4–00–00, 800/722–6466,* FAX *333/4–19–50. 184 rooms, 36 suites. 4 restaurants, 3 bars, 2 pools, beauty salon, massage, 18-hole golf course, 10 tennis courts, beach, shops, babysitting, laundry service, travel services. AE, DC, MC, V.* 🏊

$$$$ 🏨 **Grand Bay.** Set on a 1,200-acre peninsula between the Pacific and
★ the Navidad lagoon, 30 minutes north of Manzanillo airport, this no-holds-barred resort cascades down a hill to a delightful stretch of private beach. Rooms in this luxurious Mexican-style hotel, with Spanish arches, shady patios, fountains, and lush gardens, have mountain or sea views, imported marble baths, original art, and deluxe amenities. Two beautiful tiered pools wind their way through the gardens; another pool lies on the 10th floor, where most of the suites are located. Guests may play the adjacent 27-hole Robert Von Hagge–designed golf course. ⊠ *Isla Navidad (A.P. 20), Jalisco 48987,* ☎ *335/5–50–50, 888/804–7263 in the U.S.,* FAX *335/5–60–71. 158 rooms, 41 suites. 3 restaurants, 3 bars, 3 pools, golf privileges, 3 tennis courts, health club, volleyball, beach, dive shop, snorkeling, jet skiing, waterskiing, fishing, baby-sitting, children's programs (ages 4–12), concierge. AE, DC, MC, V.* 🏊

$$$$ ▥ **Karmina Palace.** Manzanillo's newest all-inclusive hotel is just across the hill from Las Hadas. Suites here face either the ocean, pool, or Las Hadas's golf course. In fact, the 18th hole is on Karmina's spacious lawns, which have cascades, fountains, eight multitier lagoon-pools, and a beautiful palapa restaurant at the ocean's edge. Junior suites have two TVs, marble floors, refrigerator, air-conditioning and fans, balcony or terrace, and large tubs with separate shower facilities and double vanities in the bathrooms. Complimentary soda, water, and upscale beauty products come in all rooms. The resort has 24-hour concierge service and a well-equipped business center. Despite the hotel's impressive facilities, service is average. ⊠ *Av. Vista Hermosa 13, Fracc. Península de Santiago, Santiago, Colima 28200,* ☎ *333/4–13–13,* 𝔽𝔸𝕏 *333/4–19–15. 325 suites. 3 restaurants, 8 pools, 18-hole golf course, 10 tennis courts, health club, beach, video games, baby-sitting. AE, V.*

$$$$ ▥ **Sierra.** This 19-story white stucco giant is popular with families (up to two children under age six stay free in their parents' room) and conventioneers. Most of the 317 inviting rooms and suites have private balconies and a view of the bay. A large free-form pool, four tennis courts, and several bars and restaurants round out the property. Light-wood and pastel colors dominate the pleasant decor. The all-inclusive resort includes buffet meals, snacks, dinners at a gourmet restaurant, drinks, tennis, and water sports such as kayaking and windsurfing. ⊠ *Av. de la Audiencia 1, 28200,* ☎ *333/3–20–00,* 𝔽𝔸𝕏 *333/3–22–72. 317 rooms and suites. 3 restaurants, 4 bars, pool, 4 tennis courts, beach, children's programs (ages 4–12). AE, DC, MC, V.*

$$$ ▥ **Marina Puerto Dorado.** There are excellent views of the bay and har-
★   bor from this family hotel, which looks a lot like condos. With 40 suites, 10 of them penthouse suites with Jacuzzis and wet bars, this is a good bet for large families. ⊠ *Av. Lázaro Cárdenas 101, Fracc. Las Brisas Playa Azul, 28200,* ☎ *333/4–14–80,* 𝔽𝔸𝕏 *3/647–98–50. 40 suites. Restaurant, 2 bars, pool, beach. AE, MC, V.*

$$ ▥ **La Posada.** This "passionate pink" hotel has been a favorite for North
★   Americans since 1957. With only 24 rooms, most guests get to know each other well, mingling in the sala, a large living-dining room with a communal coffeepot. Rooms are comfortable and simple; there's one on the beach. Old iron keys work the antique locks. The room rate includes a complete breakfast. The beer and soft-drink service is on an honor system. ⊠ *Las Brisas, 28200,* ☎ 𝔽𝔸𝕏 *333/3–18–99. 24 rooms. Bar, snack bar, pool, beach. MC, V.*

$$ ▥ **Villas la Audiencia.** Well located—it's a block from the Las Hadas turnoff and about 1 km (½ mi) from the beach—this small white-and-red hotel and villa complex overlooks the Mantarraya golf course. Everything is spotless, and the simple air-conditioned rooms and villas (villas have kitchenettes) are pleasantly decorated and quite comfortable. Free transportation is provided to the beach. ⊠ *Av. de la Audiencia and Las Palmas, off Santiago–Manzanillo Rd., 28860,* ☎ *333/3–08–61,* 𝔽𝔸𝕏 *333/ 3–26–53. 20 rooms, 26 villas. Restaurant, pool. AE, MC, V.*

$ ▥ **Marbella.** This hotel is one of the few reasonably priced places on the beach. The best rooms are on the ocean; each has a tiny balcony under the palms. The accommodations are color-coordinated and have air-conditioning and TV. The Marbella has a good Spanish/seafood restaurant, El Marinero. ⊠ *Santiago–Manzanillo Rd. Km 9.5, 28869,* ☎ *333/3–11–03,* 𝔽𝔸𝕏 *333/3–12–22. 92 rooms. Restaurant, bar, pool. AE, MC, V.*

$ ▥ **María Cristina.** This clean but drab two-story motel is in the Santiago area, five blocks from the beach. All rooms have TVs, but only three—they call them "bungalows"—are air-conditioned; they're well worth the small difference in price. ⊠ *Calle 28 de Agosto 36, 28860,* ☎ *333/3–09–66,* 𝔽𝔸𝕏 *333/4–14–30. 21 rooms. Pool. MC, V.*

Nightlife and the Arts

For a rowdy drinking and dancing scene, head for **Carlos 'n' Charlies** (✉ Av. Audencia Plaza Pacífico, ☎ 333/4–12–72). **VOG** (✉ Santiago–Manzanillo Rd. Km 9.2, ☎ 333/3–18–75) is a popular place to boogie. **Olas** (✉ Blvd. Costero Miguel de la Madrid Km 7.5, ☎ 333/4–03–83) is a good spot for shooting pool and listening to oldies rock and roll. The **Lobby** piano bar (✉ Las Hadas, ☎ 333/1–01–01) is a relaxing, romantic spot for a nightcap.

Outdoor Activities and Sports

Fishing

Sportfishing charters ($50–$500) are available at major hotels and through tour agencies.

Golf

La Mantarraya (☎ 333/4–00–00), the 18-hole golf course at Las Hadas, designed by Roy Dye, has been rated among the world's 100 best courses by *Golf Digest*. **Club Santiago** (☎ 333/5–04–10) has a nine-hole course designed by Larry Hughes. Robert Von Hagge mapped out the 27-hole course on **Isla Navidad** (☎ 333/5–63–90).

Water Sports

Windsurfing has become quite popular on Manzanillo's beaches, and Jet Skis roar about, but there isn't much in the way of parasailing. The rocky points off Manzanillo's peninsulas and coves make good spots for snorkeling and scuba diving. Pangas can be rented on some beaches so you can reach the better spots.

Shopping

Most of the hotels offer a small selection of folk art and beachwear, but, in general, shops selling items that might interest tourists don't fare well in Manzanillo, probably because most visitors are more interested in activities involving the sun and sea. There are some fairly uninteresting shops around Manzanillo's main square, hardly worth the trip downtown, and there are some shops at Plaza Manzanillo, a shopping center at Km 7.5 on the Santiago–Manzanillo Road. Most of the shops are closed 2–4; many are open Sunday 10–2. **Centro Artesenal Las Primaveras** (✉ Juárez 40, Santiago, ☎ 333/3–16–99) is about the best bet for handcrafted folk art.

Side Trip

Colima

98 km (61 mi) northeast of Manzanillo.

Colima, the capital of the eponymous state, is about an hour from Manzanillo via an excellent toll road that continues on to Guadalajara. An easygoing provincial city with well-maintained colonial buildings, Colima is most famous for the pre-Hispanic "Colima Dog" figurines, which originated in this state and which are on display—along with other archaeological pieces—at the **Museo de las Culturas del Occidente** (Museum of Western Cultures; ✉ Casa de la Cultura, Calzada Galván and Av. Ejército Nacional, ☎ 331/2–31–55). The **Museo de Artes Populares María Teresa Pomar** (María Teresa Pomar Handicrafts Museum; ✉ Calle Gabino Barreda and Manuel Gallardo, ☎ 331/2–68–69) has a large collection of pre-Hispanic and contemporary Indian costumes, masks, instruments, and other artifacts. Entry to the museum, open daily 10–2 and 5–8, is free.

The town of **Comala,** a 15-minute ride north of Colima, is noted for hand-painted colonial furniture and ironwork. Imposing twin volcano peaks rise up from the **Volcán de Colima National Park,** about 30 km (18 mi) north of Comala.

Manzanillo A to Z

Arriving and Departing

BY BUS

Elite and **Estrella Blanca** (☎ 333/2–04–32 for both) and **Primera Plus** (☎ 333/2–14–31) have first-class service (lavatory, TV, and air-conditioning) to and from Puerto Vallarta, Guadalajara, Tijuana, Acapulco, and Mexico City. Service is also available to coastal towns. Many of the resorts in the Manzanillo area are 1–2 km (½–1 mi) from the bus stop on the highway. **ETN** (✉ Blvd. Costero Miguel de la Madrid Km 13.5, ☎ 333/4–10–50) has by far the most-comfortable buses, with wide, almost totally reclining seats, to Guadalajara and Mexico City.

BY CAR

The trip south from the Arizona border to Manzanillo is about 2,419 km (1,500 mi); from Guadalajara, it is 332 km (200 mi) over mostly well-kept highways; from Puerto Vallarta, 242 km (150 mi) over winding mountain roads. Highway 200 runs along the coast from Tepic, in the state of Nayarit, to Manzanillo. The road is quite narrow but well maintained. However, drivers should constantly be on the alert for an unexpected cow, burro, dog—or drunk—on the road. Detours are frequent, especially during the rainy season. If you are stopped by federal police or army soldiers at periodic check stations, you have nothing to fear unless you are carrying weapons or drugs. They generally wave tourists on without going through their belongings.

BY PLANE

Manzanillo's **Aeropuerto Internacional Playa de Oro** (☎ 333/3–25–25) is 32 km (20 mi) north of town, on the way to Barra de Navidad. **Aeroméxico** (☎ 01–800/3–62–02) and **Mexicana** (☎ 333/3–23–23) serve most major cities via Mexico City. **Alaska Airlines** (☎ 800/426–0333) flies from Los Angeles, Portland, San Diego, and Seattle. **America West** (☎ 01–800/363–2597) flies in twice a week from Phoenix; **AeroCalifornia** (☎ 333/4–14–14) flies in from Los Angeles daily.

Volkswagen vans transport passengers from the airport to major resorts; these shuttles are less expensive than taxis.

Getting Around

A car is almost essential for exploring the area on your own. The highway from Santiago to Manzanillo is commonly called Carretera Santiago–Manzanillo, Manzanillo–Aeropuerto, Salahua–Santiago, or any number of things depending on the closest landmark. It's called the Santiago–Manzanillo Road throughout this chapter to lessen confusion. Highway 200 runs north along the coast past Manzanillo and Santiago bays to Barra de Navidad and Melaque; Highway 110 goes east to Colima.

Avenida Morelos, the main drag in town, runs from Manzanillo Bay past the port and shipyards to the plaza. If you plan to explore the downtown, park along the waterfront across from the plaza and walk—all the shops and hotels are within a few blocks.

Street addresses aren't often used in Manzanillo; instead, locations are designated by neighborhood—the Las Brisas area, Santiago Peninsula (also known as the Las Hadas Road), and so on. Maps with actual street names are rare (or inaccurate).

Contacts and Resources

CAR RENTAL

Rates vary depending on where you rent your car, but rentals are fairly costly ($50 per day for a standard shift without air-conditioning to $70 for a model with automatic transmission and air-conditioning). Most offer 200 km (120 mi) free, which should give you enough roaming room for one day.

Hertz (Blvd. Costero Miguel de la Madrid 1246-B, ☎ 333/3–31–41), **Dollar** (Paseo de las Palmas, ☎ 333/3–14–32) and **National** (Blvd. Costero Miguel de la Madrid 1070, ☎ 333/3–06–11, 333/3–11–40) also have offices at the airport, and most large hotels have at least one company represented.

EMERGENCIES

Police (☎ 333/4–05–57). **Fire Department** (*Bomberos*; ☎ 333/2–39–34). **Red Cross** (☎ 333/6–56–51). **Hospital** (☎ 333/6–72–72).

GUIDED TOURS

Manzanillo is so spread out that if you want to get the lay of the land, it's best to go on a guided tour. More appealing, though, than the city tours are the sportfishing trips, sunset cruises, horseback outings, and excursions to Colima, Comala, and the volcanoes that can be arranged through a travel agency.

TRAVEL AGENCIES

Most hotels offer at least one agency's services. Agencies include **Avitesa** (⊠ Blvd. Costero Miguel de la Madrid Km 11.5, ☎ 333/3–29–99), **Aeroviajes Manzanillo** (⊠ Av. México 69, ☎ 333/4–24–24), **Bahías Gemelas Agencia de Viajes** (⊠ Blvd. Costero Miguel de la Madrid 1506, ☎ 333/3–10–00), and **Viajes Héctur** (⊠ Blvd. Costero Miguel de la Madrid 3147, ☎ 333/3–17–07).

VISITOR INFORMATION

The **State Tourism Office** (⊠ Blvd. Costero Miguel de la Madrid Km 9.5, ☎ 333/3–22–77) is open weekdays 9–7:30.

IXTAPA/ZIHUATANEJO

One of the most appealing of the Pacific Coast destinations, Ixtapa/Zihuatanejo is a taste of Mexico present and past. Ixtapa (pronounced eeks-*tah*-pa), where most Americans stay—probably because they can't pronounce Zihuatanejo (see-wa-ta-*nay*-ho)—is young and glitzy. Exclusively a vacation resort, it was created in the early 1970s by Fonatur, Mexico's National Fund for Tourism Development, which also brought us Cancún, Huatulco, and San José del Cabo. Large chain hotels cluster in the hotel zone around Palmar Bay, where conditions are ideal for swimming and water sports; across the road are clusters of shopping plazas. The hotels are well spaced, there's always plenty of room on the beach, and the pace is leisurely.

Zihuatanejo, only 7 km (4 mi) down the coast (southeast) from Ixtapa, is an old fishing village on a picturesque sheltered bay. Until the advent of Ixtapa, it was hardly known. But long before Columbus sailed to America, Zihuatanejo was a sanctuary for indigenous nobility. Figurines, ceramics, stone carvings, and stelac still being found in the area verify the presence of civilizations dating as far back as the Olmecs (3000 BC). The original name, Cihuatlán, means "place of women" in the Nahuatl language. Weaving was likely the dominant industry in this matriarchal society, as evidenced by pre-Hispanic figurines, bobbins, and other related artifacts found in the area.

In 1527, Spanish conquistadors launched a trade route from Zihuatanejo Bay to the Orient. Galleons returned with silks, spices, and, according to some historians, the first coconut palms to arrive in the Americas, brought from the Philippines. But the Spaniards did little colonizing here. A scout sent by Cortés reported back to the conquistador that the place was nothing great, tagging the name Cihuatlán with the demeaning Spanish suffix "nejo"—hence "Zihuatanejo."

With the advent of Ixtapa, Zihuatanejo began to grow, and the little dirt streets were paved with decorative brick. The place has managed to retain its charm, even if its malecón and narrow streets are lined with hotels, restaurants, and shops. Zihuatanejo is also home to some of Mexico's most exclusive boutique hotels, and many people who know both Ixtapa and this authentic Mexican village prefer to stay here.

Exploring Ixtapa/Zihuatanejo

Ixtapa and Zihuatanejo have few sights per se, but they're both pleasant places to stroll—the former especially if you enjoy a modern beach ambience and shops, the latter if you like local color.

A Good Tour
The entire hotel zone in **Ixtapa** extends along a 3-km (2-mi) strip of wide sandy beach called Playa del Palmar, on the open Pacific. It's fun to walk along the beach to check out the various hotel scenes and watersports activities. Alternatively, you can stroll the length of the zone on Boulevard Ixtapa, a nicely landscaped and immaculate thoroughfare; a series of Mexican village–style shopping malls line the boulevard across the street from the hotels. At one end of the hotel zone (when you enter from Zihuatanejo) is the 18-hole Ixtapa Golf Club, while on the other (generally described as being "up the coast," but actually lying to the northwest) you'll come to the Marina Ixtapa development, which includes a 600-slip yacht marina, a promenade with restaurants and shops, and the 18-hole Marina Golf Course. If you want to venture out of this compact resort area, take a taxi 15 minutes up the coast to **Playa Linda**. It's a 10-minute boat ride from here to **Ixtapa Island**, where you can spend the day eating, sunning, and swimming.

Zihuatanejo flanks a charming enclosed bay with calm beaches. A simple way to tour the town is to take a taxi to the municipal pier (*muelle*), from which skiffs continually depart for the 10-minute ride to **Playa las Gatas**, accessible only by water. The sportfishing boats depart from this pier, too, and it's the beginning of the **Paseo del Pescador** (Fisherman's Walk), or malecón, which runs along the municipal beach, the most picturesque part of town. The brick-paved seaside path, only ½ km (⅓ mi) long, is lined with small restaurants and overflowing shops; you'll pass a basketball court that doubles as the town square. The malecón ends at the **Museo Arqueológico** (✉ east end of Paseo del Pescador, ☎ 755/3–25–52), where 311 pre-Hispanic pieces as well as murals and maps are on permanent display; it's open Tuesday–Sunday 10–6. If you continue beyond the museum, you can take a footpath cut into the rocks to **Playa la Madera**.

Beaches

Ixtapa
Ixtapa Island. The most popular beach on Ixtapa Island is Playa Cuachalalate, named for a local tree whose bark has been used as a remedy for kidney ailments since ancient times. This beach is lined with good seafood eateries and is excellent for swimming. A short walk across to the other side of the island takes you to the gorgeous sandy Varadero

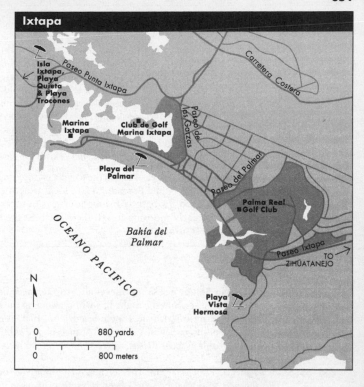

Beach. It's also lined with small restaurants, and there are water-sports facilities. Just behind the restaurants is Playa Coral, with crystal-clear water that's ideal for snorkeling. Playa Carey, toward the south end of the island, is small and isolated. Pangas run between the boat landings at both Cuachalalate and Varadero beaches and Playa Linda (☞ *below*) on the mainland.

Playa del Palmar. Ixtapa's main beach, this 3-km- (2-mi-) long broad sandy stretch runs along the hotel zone. Water-sports facilities are available all along the shore. Since this is essentially open sea, the surf can be quite strong.

Playa Linda. About 10 minutes beyond the Ixtapa hotel zone, the long, pristine Playa Linda has a handicraft mart at its edge, as well as a rock jetty from which covered pangas make the 10-minute trip to Ixtapa Island (☞ *above*). Boats run continuously from early morning until 5 PM, and cost about $4 round-trip. The beach provides an excellent setting for horseback riding and jogging.

Zihuatanejo

Playa la Madera. Across Zihuatanejo Bay from Playa Municipal (☞ *below*), Playa la Madera may be reached via a seaside footpath cut into the rocks. Also accessible by car, this pancake-flat beach has a sprinkling of small hotels and restaurants. It was named madera, or "wood," beach because it was a Spanish port for shipping oak, pine, cedar, and mahogany cut from the nearby Sierra Madre Sur.

Playa la Ropa. On the other side of a rocky point, Playa la Ropa is the most beautiful beach in the area; it's a five-minute taxi ride from town. Along this 1-km (½-mi) stretch of soft sand are water-sports facilities, open-air restaurants, and a few hotels. It got its name ("clothes beach") when a Spanish galleon returning from the Orient ran aground here, strewing its cargo of silks and clothing.

Playa las Gatas. Named for the *gatas* (docile nurse sharks) that used to linger here, this beach has a mysterious long row of hewn rocks just off-shore that serves as a breakwater. Legend has it that a Tarascan king built it to shelter his royal daughter's private beach. It is now lined with simple seafood eateries that have lounge chairs for sunning, and the waters are ideal for swimming and snorkeling. Las Gatas is accessible only by boat; pangas run continuously to and from the municipal pier until 5 PM. Purchase your round-trip ticket (about $3) at the Cooperativa office at the beginning of the pier. Keep the ticket stub for your return trip.

Playa Municipal. At the edge of town, the town's picturesque main beach is rimmed by the Paseo del Pescador. Here local fishermen keep their skiffs and gear, used for nightly fishing journeys out to sea. They return here in the early morning to sell their catch to the local townspeople and to restaurateurs.

Dining

Ixtapa

$$$$ ✕ **Villa de la Selva.** These multilevel cliff-top terraces have views of the sunset, the stars, and the night-lit surf breaking on the rocks below. Excellent international dishes include ceviche, filet mignon with a caramelized-onion red-wine sauce, and orange-glazed salmon. ⊠ *Paseo la Roca, beyond Westin Brisas,* ☎ *755/3–03–62. Reservations essential. AE, DC, MC, V. No lunch.*

$$$-$$$$ ✕ **Bogart's.** Play it again: the setting is strikingly Moroccan, à la *Casablanca,* and anyone who's been to any of the links in the Krystal hotel chain is familiar with this exotic (and expensive) eatery. A Moorish fountain and piano music add to the movie-theme atmosphere. The largely international menu includes Suprema Casablanca, breaded chicken breasts stuffed with lobster. ⊠ *Krystal Ixtapa, Blvd. Ixtapa,* ☎ *755/3–03–03. Reservations essential. AE, DC, MC, V. No lunch.*

$$$ ✕ **Beccofino.** This marina-side restaurant is always crowded, even when
★   its neighbors are empty. Among the best dishes on the Northern Italian menu are minestrone soup, *caprese* salad (with tomatoes, basil, and mozzarella), fish fillet (usually red snapper or mahimahi) with a champagne sauce, salmon ravioli in cream, and chicken cacciatore. There's alfresco seating on a canopied deck adjacent to the water. ⊠ *Plaza Marina Ixtapa,* ☎ *755/3–17–70. Reservations essential. AE, MC, V.*

$$$ ✕ **El Galeón.** Seafood lovers and people-watchers like to settle in at Marina Ixtapa's nautical-decor bar and outdoor terrace; there's additional seating on a simulated galleon right on the water. The fresh tuna steak is outstanding, as are the pastas; upscale Mexican fare is also available. ⊠ *Plaza Marina Ixtapa,* ☎ *755/3–21–50. AE, MC, V.*

$$ ✕ **Casa Morelos.** You wouldn't expect a refined restaurant to be positioned next to Señor Frog and its ever-partying crowd, but Casa Morelos is just that—calm patio dining with excellent Mexican seafood selections. The chile relleno *de mariscos* (roasted chili stuffed with seafood), fish and octopus fajitas, and tuna steak topped with seven kinds of dry chilies are all filling and delicious. Save a little room after for a margarita and a dance next door. ⊠ *La Puerta shopping center,* ☎ *755/9–10–18. AE, MC, V.*

$$ ✕ **El Infierno y la Gloria.** "Hell and Glory" is a Mexican cantina-bar and restaurant, serving an array of typical dishes. The food is good, and you'll enjoy looking at the walls, hand-painted with Mexican scenes and allegories. ⊠ *La Puerta shopping center,* ☎ *755/3–03–04. AE, MC, V.*

$$ ✕ **La Valentina.** This addition to Ixtapa's dining scene is part of a rel-
★ atively new and highly successful group of restaurants that have opened
in Mexico City and Dallas. The team of PR whizzes behind these ven-
tures has access to some of the finest Mexican gourmet recipes, many
from celebrities such as artist Martha Chapa. Truly memorable is the
pollo en mole de tamarindo (chicken in a spicy sauce flavored with
tamarind and chocolate). The decor is as Mexican as the menu. Also
on the premises are a video bar and disco. ✉ *Blvd. Ixtapa next to Dou-
bletree hotel,* ☎ *755/3–11–90. AE, MC, V. No lunch.*

$-$$ ✕ **Mamma Norma y J. J. Cuisine.** You can dine indoors or alfresco at
this casual eatery, which has the best pizzas in town as well as tasty
grilled tuna steaks, shrimp, lobster, and wholesome salads. ✉ *La
Puerta shopping center,* ☎ *755/3–02–74. MC, V.*

$ ✕ **Nueva Zelanda.** Although open all day, this sparkling little coffee
shop is best known for its tasty breakfasts. Nueva Zelanda also serves
tortas and an array of fresh tropical fruit juices and fruit salads. ✉ *Los
Patios shopping center, behind bandstand,* ☎ *755/3–08–38;* ✉ *Calle
Cuauhtémoc 23, Zihuatanejo,* ☎ *755/4–23–40. Reservations not accepted. No credit cards.*

Zihuatanejo

$$-$$$ ✕ **Coconuts.** Originally a weigh-in station for a coconut plantation, Co-
conuts has become one of the top restaurants in Zihuatanejo. Under
the direction of Chef Patricia Cummings and her American colleagues,
Coconuts serves a variety of dishes, including roast pork loin, seafood
tacos, coconut shrimp, and a number of vegetarian items. Dessert cof-
fees are served flaming at your table. ✉ *Austín Ramírez 1,* ☎ *755/4–
25–18. AE, DC, MC, V. Closed lunch May–early Oct.*

$$-$$$ ✕ **Paul's.** This no-nonsense eatery doesn't open until 2 PM, but it's got
some of the best food in town. The zany Swiss-German owner seems
to have created an eclectic lifestyle here, and he may well greet you
dressed in shorts and an unbuttoned Hawaiian shirt. Notwithstanding his fashion choices, Paul has crafted a small international menu of
wonderful dishes. Start with the lentil soup, fresh artichoke, or escar-
got, followed by quail, pork chops, or poached mahimahi served with
a dill sauce. After dinner, retreat to the small piano bar next door. ✉
Benito Juárez 23, ☎ *755/4–65–28. MC, V.*

$$ ✕ **Casa Elvira.** Opened in 1956, this Zihuatanejo institution near the
town pier has a pleasant dining room and serves a wide variety of seafood
and Mexican dishes. Lobster is the house specialty. The restaurant gets
crowded during high season. ✉ *Paseo del Pescador 8,* ☎ *755/4–20–
61. MC, V.*

$$ ✕ **Kau-Kan.** Opened in the mid-1990s, this restaurant immediately became a local favorite. Owner-chef Ricardo Rodriguez, previously the
chef at the nearby Casa Que Canta and, before then, at Mexico City's
Champs-Élysées restaurant, serves imaginative, exquisitely prepared
seafood, from fillet of sea bass to potato stuffed with shrimp and lobster in a basil and garlic sauce. Kau-Kan enjoys a gorgeous location
overlooking Zihuatanejo Bay and is probably the most elegant restaurant in town. ✉ *Carretera Escénica Lote 7,* ☎ *755/4–84–46. AE, MC,
V. No lunch during winter.*

$-$$ ✕ **Rossy.** A local favorite for dining on the roof terrace or right on the
beach, Rossy features seafood, including a tempting shrimp-and-
pineapple brochette. Musicians usually serenade diners on weekends.
✉ *South end of Playa la Ropa,* ☎ *755/4–40–04. MC, V.*

$-$$ ✕ **La Sirena Gorda.** Oil paintings and a bronze statue depict the name-
sake "fat mermaid," and a small boutique sells logo T-shirts and memorabilia. Specialties at this friendly restaurant near the pier include
seafood tacos and octopus kebab. The setting is casual, with an out-

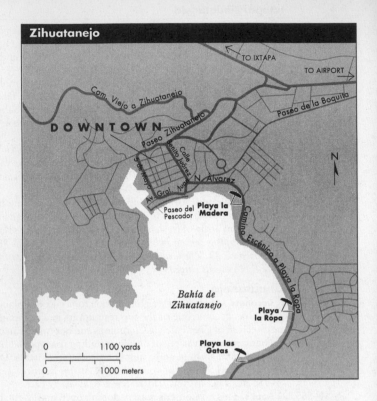

Zihuatanejo

TO IXTAPA

TO AIRPORT

Cam. Viejo a Zihuatanejo

Paseo de la Boquita

DOWNTOWN

Paseo Zihuatanejo

Calle Benito Juárez

Calle 5 de Mayo

Av. Gral. Aurora

N. Álvarez

Paseo del Pescador

Playa la Madera

Camino Escénico a Playa la Ropa

Bahía de Zihuatanejo

Playa la Ropa

Playa las Gatas

N

0   1100 yards

0   1000 meters

door patio. ⊠ *Paseo del Pescador 20,* ☎ *755/4–26–87. Reservations not accepted. MC, V. Closed Wed.*

$ ✕ **Casa Puntarenas.** Talk about homey restaurants: Casa Puntarenas is not only family-owned and -operated, but it's also run out of the family residence. You'll select from a menu of seafood specialties and write your order on a piece of paper, which later becomes your check. To get here, cross the footbridge over the lagoon at the west end of town near the pier (or take a taxi). ⊠ *Noria 12,* ☎ *755/4–21–09. Reservations not accepted. No credit cards. Closed mid-Mar.–mid-Dec. No lunch.*

$ ✕ **La Mordida.** Join the throngs at this simple, very popular eatery for pizza and tasty charcoal-broiled burgers. ⊠ *Paseo de la Boquita 20,* ☎ *755/4–82–16. No credit cards. No lunch.*

$ ✕ **La Perla.** Eat indoors if you want sports-bar action, or outdoors on Playa la Ropa. Among the seafood specialties, *filete La Perla* (baked with cheese) is a favorite. ⊠ *Playa la Ropa,* ☎ *755/4–27–00. AE, MC, V.*

Dining and Lodging

Zihuatanejo

$$$$ ✕☐ **Casa Cuitlateca.** The smallest (and newest) of Zihuatanejo's boutique hotels opened high above the bay, with spectacular views from three of the four individually decorated suites. Rooms have handmade furnishings and arts and crafts from four Mexican states; all artwork on the premises is available for purchase. A beautiful infinity pool is surrounded by a small fish pond, and there's a cool-water whirlpool on the villa's rooftop. The patio restaurant, which is open to the public, serves a fixed, multicourse dinner each night for $50. The hotel's small staff offers personalized attention and will arrange nearly any excursion you can think of. Children under 16 are not allowed at the hotel. ⊠ *Calle Playa la Ropa (Apdo. 124), 40880,* ☎ *755/4–24–48,*

877/541–1234, 🕾 *755/4–21–57. 4 suites. Restaurant, pool, hot tub. AE, MC, V.* ❧

$$$$ ✕🏨 **La Casa Que Canta.** One of the loveliest small hotels in the world,
★ "The House That Sings" is perched on a cliffside above Zihuatanejo Bay. The multilevel palapa-topped lobby is adorned with folk-art furnishings, including hand-painted chairs with Frida Kahlo motifs. The individually designed suites, named for Mexican songs, boast gorgeous ocean views from both the bedroom balcony and living-room terrace; 10 have private infinity pools. Fresh flower petals are arranged into beautiful designs on your bed each day. Because of the stepped architecture, the main swimming pool seems to be airborne; below, a saltwater pool features a sea Jacuzzi (the beach is just a two-minute walk away). The romantic outdoor restaurant serves authentic Mexican dishes and opens to the public after 6 PM (reservations required). Children under 16 are not accepted at the hotel. ⊠ *Camino Escénico a Playa la Ropa, 40880,* 🕾 *755/4–65–29, 01–800/71–09–345, 888/ 523–5050,* 🕾 *755/4–79–00. 24 suites. Restaurant, 2 pools, exercise room. AE, DC, MC, V.* ❧

$$$$ ✕🏨 **Villa del Sol.** Zihuatanejo's first luxury hotel sits on 6 acres of coconut palms, lush tropical gardens, fountains, and meandering paths leading to Playa la Ropa, one of the loveliest beaches on the Pacific coast. Because the property is German-owned and -run, it is popular with European, as well as North American, travelers. Rooms and baths are artistically designed, with canopied king-size beds, colorful folk-art furnishings, and terraces or balconies; beachfront and lagoon suites are considerably nicer than lower-priced rooms. In the evening, the European and Mexican chefs prepare fine international and local dishes—try resisting Chef Fabrice's apple-and-cinnamon tacos—using the freshest of ingredients. Children under 14 are not accepted during high season. ⊠ *Playa la Ropa (Apdo. 84), 40880,* 🕾 *755/4–22–39, 888/389–2645,* 🕾 *755/4–27–58. 54 suites. 2 restaurants, 4 pools, 2 tennis courts, beach. AE, MC, V.* ❧

Lodging

There is a wide range of hotel accommodations in Ixtapa and in Zihuatanejo. Pricier Ixtapa has almost exclusively deluxe, beachfront properties, and almost all are located along the Zona Hotelera, a 3-km (2-mi) stretch of Playa del Palmar. Their quality, however, doesn't always match that of the other properties of international chains whose names they bear. Most of the budget accommodations are in Zihuatanejo, where the best hotels are on or overlooking La Madera or La Ropa beach, and the least expensive are downtown. There are also a few choices in Troncones, a tiny beach about 30 minutes northwest of Zihuatanejo by car.

Elizabeth Williams (⊠ Apdo. 169, Zihuatanejo, Guerrero, 🕾 755/4– 26–06, 775/3–11–08, 🕾 755/4–47–62) specializes in apartment, home, and villa rentals and sales. She is also the U.S. Consular Agent in the area, with an office in Ixtapa (🕾 755/4–26–06, 775/3–11–08).

Ixtapa

$$$$ 🏨 **Presidente Inter-Continental Ixtapa.** A member of the Inter-Continental chain, this is one of Ixtapa's best all-inclusive properties. Rooms are attractively decorated in creams and whites, and rates include all meals, 24-hour beverage service, and various recreational activities— most of them centered on the pool. If you want tranquility, request a room near the east pool, away from where the action is. ⊠ *Blvd. Ixtapa s/n, 40880,* 🕾 *755/3–00–18, 800/327–0200,* 🕾 *755/3–23–12. 438 rooms and suites. 4 restaurants, bar, 2 pools, wading pool, sauna, steam room, golf privileges, 2 tennis courts, basketball, exercise room,*

volleyball, beach, snorkeling, dance club, children's programs (ages 3–10). AE, DC, MC, V. 🏊

$$$$ ⊞ **Westin Brisas Ixtapa.** This immense, pyramid-shape architectural
★   wonder slopes down a hillside to its own secluded cove and beach, Playa
Vista Hermosa. The grounds are lush with jungle vegetation; fresh flowers decorate your room. Every unit has a private balcony with a hammock, ocean view, and a table for room-service dining; junior suites
have larger balconies with hot tubs. (Although this is Ixtapa's top hotel,
accommodations are not as luxurious as what you might find at a Westin
elsewhere.) Guests and nonguests enjoy the hotel's excellent Portofino
and El Mexicano restaurants. ⊠ *Playa Vista Hermosa, Apdo. 87,
40880,* ☎ *755/3–21–21, 800/228–3000,* 🅵🅰🅇 *755/3–07–51. 447 rooms
and suites. 4 restaurants, 2 bars, 3 pools, wading pool, beauty salon,
4 tennis courts, exercise room, laundry service, concierge floor, business services, travel services, car rental. AE, DC, MC, V.*

$$$–$$$$ ⊞ **Krystal Ixtapa.** Shaped like a boat with its bow pointing to the sea,
this beachfront hotel along the Zona Hotelera is comfortable if lacking
in charm. Rooms are standard contemporary style with a view to the
ocean, and there is a no-smoking floor. The Club Krystalito provides recre-
ational activities for children, and because of its meeting facilities, the
hotel is often filled with conventioneers. The Krystal is home to Chris-
tine, Ixtapa's most popular disco, and Bogart's (☞ Ixtapa *in* Dining, *above*).
⊠ *Blvd. Ixtapa, 40880,* ☎ *755/3–03–33, 800/231–9860,* 🅵🅰🅇 *755/3–02–
16. 254 rooms and 20 suites. 4 restaurants, coffee shop, no-smoking floor,
pool, beauty salon, massage, sauna, 2 tennis courts, exercise room,
dance club, children's programs (ages 3–10), laundry service, meeting
rooms, travel services, car rental. AE, DC, MC, V.*

$$$ ⊞ **Dorado Pacífico.** This privately owned beachfront hotel is known
for its fine food and good service. The huge pool, with two water slides,
makes it a favorite with youngsters. Modern rooms are decorated in
soft colors, and all have ocean views. Glass elevators look out on the
dramatic atrium lobby. Try the beachside Cebolla Roja restaurant for
dinner. ⊠ *Blvd. Ixtapa, 40880,* ☎ *755/3–20–25, 800/448–8355,* 🅵🅰🅇
*755/3–01–26. 285 rooms and suites. 3 restaurants, bar, pool, massage,
4 tennis courts, children's programs (ages 10+). AE, DC, MC, V.*

$$$ ⊞ **Villa del Lago.** In a modern colonial-style house that was totally re-
modeled in 1997, this B&B is the only listed Ixtapa property not on
the beach. It is, however, a golfer's dream, facing the sixth-hole tee of
the Palma Real Golf Club (designed by Robert Trent Jones Jr.). The
two-level master suite, terrace, and swimming pool have views of the
lush green course and the mountains beyond. Golf packages are avail-
able for this course as well as for the Robert Von Hagge–designed 18-
hole course at Marina Ixtapa. The hotel provides free transportation
to the beaches and commercial center of Ixtapa. Rooms have phones
but no TVs, and rates include breakfast. ⊠ *Retorno Alondras 244,
40880,* ☎ *755/3–14–82,* 🅵🅰🅇 *755/3–14–22, 619/575–1766 in the U.S.
7 suites. Restaurant, pool, library. AE, MC, V.*

$$ ⊞ **Posada Real.** Smaller and more intimate than most of the other Ixtapa hotels, this member of the Best Western chain sits on Playa del
Palmar, has lots of charm, and is a good value. ⊠ *Blvd. Ixtapa, 40880,*
☎ *755/3–16–85, 800/528–1234,* 🅵🅰🅇 *755/3–18–05. 110 rooms. Restaurant, bar, 2 pools, wading pool. AE, DC, MC, V.*

Troncones

$$ ⊞ **El Burro Borracho.** For out-of-the-way seclusion, you can venture
northwest about 30 minutes to Troncones. Six comfortable stone cot-
tages and a congenial restaurant-bar sit right on the 5-km- (3-mi-) long
beach. The menu ranges from cheeseburgers to fresh lobster. Lie in a
hammock or go beachcombing, boogie-boarding, hiking, or cave ex-

ploring. Owners Dewey and Carolyn are also known for their Casa de la Tortuga B&B, just up the beach. Trailer spaces are also available. ⊠ *Troncones Beach (Apdo. 277, Zihuatanejo 40880),* ☎ *755/3–28–00,* ℻ *755/3–28–07. 6 bungalows. Restaurant, hiking, beach. No credit cards. Closed Aug. 30–Oct. 15.*

$$ ⊞ **Casa Ki.** These bungalows, overseen by Ed and Ellen Weston, are a homey haven in the wilds of Troncones. A fully equipped kitchen and barbecue are available to guests, and breakfast is included in the rates. ⊠ *Troncones Beach (Apdo. 405, Zihuatanejo 40880),* ☎ *755/3–28–15,* ℻ *755/3–24–17. 3 bungalows, 1 house. Beach. No credit cards.*

Zihuatanejo

$$$$ ⊞ **Puerto Mío.** This upscale hotel is spread over a hill on the northwest corner of Zihuatanejo Bay. Most guest rooms are in the hilltop Casa del Mar (house of the sea), with an infinity pool and great view of the bay. Arrangements of fresh flower petals are left on your bed on arrival, and terrace suites use their verandas as living rooms. Below, the hotel has a number of seaside-level facilities, including a romantic international restaurant, terrace bar, pool, two junior suites, and a marina where the Zihuatanejo Scuba Center is based; the beach here is rocky. Children under 16 are not accepted during the high season. ⊠ *Playa del Almacén, 40880,* ☎ *755/4–33–44, 01–800/711–2080, 888/369–2645,* ℻ *755/4–35–35. 25 rooms and suites. Restaurant, bar, 2 pools, dive shop. AE, MC, V. Closed Sept.* ✫

$$–$$$ ⊞ **Irma.** One of Zihuatanejo's originals, this simple colonial-style hotel sits on a bluff overlooking Madera Beach (accessible by a stairway). Rooms are stark but clean—some have ocean views and air-conditioners (rooms on the renovated sixth floor are nicer than others). ⊠ *Playa la Madera s/n, Apdo. 4, 40880,* ☎ *755/4–21–05,* ℻ *755/4–37–38. 73 rooms. Restaurant, bar, pool. AE, MC, V.* ✫

$$ ⊞ **Bungalows Pacíficos.** Terraced down a cliffside above Playa la Madera, each of the spacious bungalows has its own large veranda with a sweeping view of Zihuatanejo Bay as well as a fully equipped kitchen. The owner speaks Spanish, English, and German. ⊠ *Cerro de la Madera, Apdo. 12, 40880,* ☎ ℻ *755/4–21–12. 6 units. No credit cards.*

$$ ⊞ **Catalina-Sotavento.** Really two hotels in one, this multilevel oldie-but-goodie sits on a cliff overlooking the bay. Below, accessible by extensive stairs, are Playa la Ropa and the hotel's beach bar and lounge chairs. Rooms are large and well maintained, with ceiling fans and ample terraces sporting hammocks and a chaise longue. ⊠ *Playa la Ropa, Apdo. 2, 40880,* ☎ *755/4–20–32,* ℻ *755/4–29–75. 126 rooms. 2 restaurants, 2 bars, pool. AE, DC, MC, V.*

$$ ⊞ **Solimar Inn.** Near the town center, this quiet hotel features large, air-conditioned rooms with cable TV, kitchenettes, and ceiling fans. Guests tend to stay for weeks or longer. ⊠ *Plazas los Faroles, 40880,* ☎ ℻ *755/4–36–92. 12 rooms. Bar, pool. AE, MC, V.*

$$ ⊞ **Villas Miramar.** This pleasant colonial-style hotel is in two sections (divided by a small street). The front section overlooks and has access to Madera Beach, whereas the other part looks to the mountains. The rooms are nicely decorated and have balconies, tile showers, air-conditioning, and ceiling fans. ⊠ *Playa la Madera, Apdo. 211, 40880,* ☎ *755/4–21–06,* ℻ *755/4–21–49. 17 rooms, 1 suite. Restaurant, bar, pool. AE, MC, V.*

$ ⊞ **Ávila.** In the center of town facing the beachside Paseo del Pescador, the Ávila has large, clean rooms (all air-conditioned), TVs, and ceiling fans. Local fishermen stay here during the March fishing tournaments. ⊠ *Calle Juan N. Álvarez 8, 40880,* ☎ *755/4–20–10,* ℻ *755/4–85–92. 27 rooms. AE, MC, V.*

Nightlife

A good way to start an evening is a happy hour at one of Ixtapa's hotels. Sunset is an important daily event, and plans should be made accordingly. Tops for sunset viewing (with live music) is the lobby bar at the **Westin Brisas.** To follow sunset viewing with dancing to tropical music until about 2 AM, take the elevator up to the **Faro Bar** nightclub atop the 85-ft-high faux-lighthouse tower in Marina Ixtapa (☎ 755/3–20–90). **Christine** (☎ 755/3–03–33), at the Krystal in Ixtapa, is the town's liveliest (and most expensive) high-tech disco. Or head over to **Señor Frog's** (⊠ opposite the Presidente Inter-Continental, ☎ 755/3–06–92) for tequila shots and dancing to popular Mexican and international music.

Carlos 'n' Charlie's (⊠ Blvd. Ixtapa, next to the Best Western Posada Real, ☎ 755/3–00–85) has a party atmosphere, with late-night dancing on a raised platform by the beach. There's a desert-inspired disco, complete with blue sky and cactus, at **La Valentina** restaurant–video–bar–disco complex (⊠ Blvd. Ixtapa next to Doubletree hotel, ☎ 755/3–11–90). Some discos have dress codes, so shorts, sandals, and tennis shoes should be left in the closet.

A number of hotels feature **Mexican Fiesta** nights with buffets, handicraft bazaars, and folkloric music and dance performances. In high season you'll find Mexican Fiesta night Monday at the Krystal and Tuesday at the Dorado Pacífico.

Outdoor Activities and Sports

Fishing

Bookings and information about sportfishing can be obtained through **Ixtapa Sportfishing Charters** (⊠ 33 Olde Mill Run, Stroudsburg, PA 18360, ☎ 717/424–8323, FAX 717/424–1016) or **Zihuatanejo** (⊠ Paseo del Pescador 20, ☎ 755/4–37–58). You can also arrange trips at the **Cooperativo de Pescadores** (⊠ Paseo del Pescador 81, ☎ 755/4–20–56), at the Zihuatanejo municipal pier.

Golf

There are two 18-hole championship courses in Ixtapa. Each has its own clubhouse with a restaurant and tennis courts. The **Palma Real Golf Club** (☎ 755/3–10–62), designed by Robert Trent Jones Jr., is on a wildlife preserve that runs from a coconut plantation to the beach. A round costs $45, cart and/or caddie extra. Part of the Marina Ixtapa complex, the challenging **Club de Golf Marina Ixtapa** (☎ 755/3–14–10) was designed by Robert Von Hagge. Greens fees are $85 (including caddie or cart).

Horseback Riding

You can rent horses with guides at **Rancho Playa Linda** (☎ 755/4–30–85) just up the coast from Ixtapa.

Scuba Diving

Some 30 dive sites in the area range from deep canyons to shallow reefs. The waters here are teeming with sea life, and visibility is excellent. At the north end of Playa Cuachalalate on Ixtapa Island, **Centro de Buceo Oliverio** (☎ 755/4–39–92) provides rental equipment, instruction, and guided dives. The **Zihuatanejo Scuba Center** (⊠ Calle Cuauhtémoc 3; ⊠ Puerto Mío marina, Playa del Almacén; ☎ FAX 755/4–21–47), owned and operated by master diver and marine biologist Juan Barnard and his partner Ed Clark, runs one- and two-tank dives as well as an intensive five-day certification course. This authorized NAUI (National

Association of Underwater Instructors) Pro Facility has an enthusiastic and knowledgeable staff.

Tennis

All major Ixtapa hotels have lighted tennis courts, as do the **Palma Real Golf Club** (☎ 755/3–10–62, 755/3–11–63) and the **Club de Golf Marina Ixtapa** (☎ 755/3–14–10). Fees are $10–$12, and equipment rentals are available. In Zihuatanejo, **Villa del Sol** (☎ 755/4–22–39) has courts available to nonguests.

Water Sports

You'll find a variety of water sports along Playa del Palmar in Ixtapa. Parasailing costs about $20 for an eight-minute ride; waterskiing runs about $20 per half hour; banana-boat rides are about $2.50 per person for a 20-minute trip. On Playa la Ropa, next to La Perla restaurant, Hobie Cats rent for about $20 an hour depending on the size of the boat, and classes cost $25 per half hour. Windsurfers—when you can find them—rent for $20 per hour; classes, which include six hours over four days, cost $40.

Shopping

Ixtapa

As you enter Ixtapa from the airport or from Zihuatanejo, you'll see a large handicrafts market, **Mercado de Artesanía Turístico,** on the right side of Boulevard Ixtapa. The result of a state law that banned vendors from the beach, this market is open weekdays 10–10 and hosts some 150 stands, selling handicrafts, T-shirts, folk apparel, and souvenirs.

Across the street from the hotel zone, the shopping area is loosely divided into *centros comerciales,* or malls. These clusters of pleasant colonial-style buildings feature patios containing boutiques, restaurants, cafés, and grocery minimarkets. The first one you'll come to is **Los Patios,** where La Fuente (☎ 755/3–08–12) sells locally designed clothes, art, crafts, and home furnishings. Behind Los Patios, in a terra-cotta-color building, is **Plaza Ixpamar,** host to El Amanecer (☎ 755/3–19–02) and its nice array of folk art. After Plaza Ixpamar comes **Las Fuentes,** where you'll find Nautica (☎ 755/3–12–72); Bye-Bye (☎ 755/3–09–79 ext. 13) beach and casual wear; the ubiquitous sportswear emporium Aca Joe (☎ 755/3–03–02); and the handy Supermercado Scruples (☎ 755/3–21–36). The last mall in the hotel-zone strip is **La Puerta,** which includes Ferrioni Collection (☎ 755/3–23–43), with colorful Scottish terrier–logo casual wear, and Mic-Mac (☎ 755/3–17–33), with crafts and Mexican regional art and clothing.

Zihuatanejo

Downtown Zihuatanejo has a colorful **municipal market** with a labyrinth of small stands on the east side of the town center, on Calle Benito Juárez at Antonio Nava. On the west edge of town, along Calle Cinco de Mayo, is the **Mercado de Artesanía Turístico,** similar to the craft and souvenir market in Ixtapa, but larger, with 255 stands. Good purchases include local hand-painted Guerrero wooden masks and ceramics, huaraches, and silver jewelry. There's a daily **shell market** on the main beach near the municipal pier.

Near the mercado, across from the Aeroméxico office and facing the waterfront, **Casa Marina** (✉ Paseo del Pescador 9, ☎ 755/4–23–73) is a two-story building containing several boutiques, all belonging to the same family. **El Embarcadero** has an extensive selection of folk art from all over Mexico; **Manos** sells handicrafts; **La Zapoteca** features hammocks and hand-loomed rugs. You might want to poke around here first to check prices, and then head for the market, where you'll often pay less for the same wares if you have a good eye and are willing to bargain.

There are a number of interesting shops in the tiny three-block nucleus of central Zihuatanejo. **Galería Maya** (⊠ Calle Nicolás Bravo 31, ☎ 755/4–46–06) is very browseable for its folk art and leather goods. **Lupita's** (⊠ Juan N. Álvarez 5, ☎ 755/4–22–38) and **Botique D' Xochitl** (⊠ Calle Ejido at Cuauhtémoc, ☎ 755/4–21–31) both have good selections of colorful handmade tropical-chic women's apparel from Oaxaca and Chiapas. **Alberto's** (⊠ Calle Cuauhtémoc 12 and 15, ☎ 755/4–21–61) is the best place to find authentic silver jewelry. **Coco Cabaña** (⊠ Agustín Ramírez 1, ☎ 755/4–25–18) is a fascinating folk-art shop at Coconuts restaurant. Over at Playa la Ropa, **Gala Art** (⊠ Villa del Sol, ☎ 755/4–22–39) exhibits and sells paintings and sculptures by prominent local artists.

Arte Mexicano Nopal (⊠ Calle Juan N. Álvarez 13-B, across from Ávila, ☎ 755/4–75–30) stocks quality handmade furniture.

Ixtapa/Zihuatanejo A to Z

Arriving and Departing

BY BUS

Various bus companies run from the **Central de Autobuses** (⊠ Paseo Zihuatanejo at Paseo de la Boquita). **Estrella de Oro** (☎ 755/4–21–75) has deluxe service (with air-conditioning, videos, bathrooms, and soft drinks) between Acapulco and Zihuatanejo. The trip takes less than four hours and costs about $15. The trip from Mexico City takes about five hours, bypassing Acapulco.

BY CAR

The trip from Acapulco is a 3½-hour drive on a good two-lane road that passes through small towns and coconut groves and has some spectacular ocean views for the last third of the way. The drive from Manzanillo is 8–10 hours with a meal stop, and should only be done during daylight, due to reports of car jackings around Playa Azul. Military and police patrols have been increased on Highway 200 in the past year or so, and the number of incidents has dramatically decreased.

BY PLANE

Mexicana (☎ 755/4–22–08, 01–800/50–220) has direct daily flights from Los Angeles, and **Aeroméxico** (☎ 755/3–05–55) flies from multiple U.S. and Mexican cities. **Alaska Airlines** (☎ 800/426–0333) flies from Los Angeles, Portland, San Diego, and Seattle. **America West** (☎ 01–800/363–2597) flies in twice a week from Phoenix, and **Continental** (☎ 01–800/900–5000) flies nonstop from Houston.

From the airport, the taxi fare to the Ixtapa hotel zone is about $10; the trip takes about 20 minutes.

BY SHIP

Several cruise lines, including **Cunard, Holland America Lines, Krystal Cruises, Princess Cruises, Royal Caribbean Cruises,** and **Royal Cruise Lines,** sail to Ixtapa/Zihuatanejo from Los Angeles in winter.

Getting Around

Unless you plan to travel great distances or visit remote beaches, taxis and buses are by far the best way to get around. Taxis are plentiful, clean, and reliable, and fares are reasonable and fixed. The fare from the Ixtapa hotel zone to Zihuatanejo is about $3. Taxis are usually lined up in front of hotels. Two radio taxi companies are **APAAZ** (☎ 755/4–36–80) and **UTAAZ** (☎ 755/4–39–00). Minibuses run every 10–15 minutes between the Ixtapa hotels and between the Ixtapa hotel zone and downtown Zihuatanejo; fare is about 30¢.

Contacts and Resources

CAR RENTAL

Hertz (☎ 755/4–22–55, 755/4–25–90) and **Dollar** (☎ 755/4–23–14) have desks at the airport and in Ixtapa and/or Zihuatanejo. A good local agency is **Quick Rent-A-Car** (✉ across from Doubletree hotel, which is at Blvd. Ixtapa Lote 5–A, ☎ 755/3–18–30). Jeeps are available.

E-MAIL

CDNET Internet Provider (✉ Calle Ejército Mexicano s/n, Zihuatanejo, ☎ 755/4–73–84) offers Internet access.

EMERGENCIES

Police (☎ 755/4–38–37). **Public Safety** (*Seguridad Publica;* ☎ 755/4–71–71). **Hospital de Especialidades Zihuatanejo** (✉ Av. la Perota at Los Hujes, ☎ 755/4–76–28). **Red Cross** (☎ 755/4–20–09).

GUIDED TOURS

Most major hotels have lobby tour desks or travel agencies that have a selection of sight-seeing tours of Ixtapa, Zihuatanejo, and surrounding areas. Another option is a 6½-hour cruise on the 100-passenger trimaran *Tri-Star,* which sets sail from Zihuatanejo Bay. For $60, you get ground transportation, an open bar (domestic drinks), and a fresh-fish lunch at Ixtapa Island. You can also book a three-hour sunset cruise of Zihuatanejo Bay for $30, including open bar and hors d'oeuvres, or a four-hour cruise to Playa Manzanillo, just outside the mouth of the bay, for great snorkeling, swimming, and spinnaker flying (like parasailing). The latter ($52) includes lunch on board and an open bar. Details on all these cruises are available from **Yates del Sol** (☎ 755/4–26–94, 755/4–82–70).

You can hire a fisherman's boat from Zihuatanejo's municipal pier to go to **Los Moros de Potosí,** large white rocks in the ocean where rare web-footed brown boobies congregate with cormorants, egrets, frigates, pelicans, and long-tailed white terns. To see pink flamingos and other birds, take a taxi to **Barra de Potosí** (15 minutes past the airport), where a beautiful *laguna* (lake) is an unofficial bird sanctuary. You can arrange a cruise with the small fishing launches in front of the palapa restaurants there, but the fishermen probably don't speak English.

TRAVEL AGENCY

American Express (✉ Krystal Ixtapa arcade, Blvd. Ixtapa, Ixtapa, ☎ 755/3–08–53, FAX 755/3–12–06) is open Monday–Saturday 9–6.

VISITOR INFORMATION

The **Municipal Tourism Office** (✉ Zihuatanejo City Hall, Plaza Principal, ☎ 755/4–83–01) is open weekdays 9–8. The **Guerrero State Tourism Office** (✉ La Puerta shopping center, across from Presidente Inter-Continental, Ixtapa, ☎ 755/3–19–67) is open weekdays 8–8, Saturday 8–3.

9   ACAPULCO

If Acapulco no longer tops the glitterati top-10 list, it remains both a sentimental favorite and a party-hearty resort town, with miles of beaches and some of the glitziest discos this side of the Pacific. A delightful three-hour drive from Acapulco is Taxco, a colonial treasure, where the Baroque towers of Santa Prisca church overlook cobblestone streets lined with silversmiths.

Updated by
Patricia Alisau

ACAPULCO IS A VIBRANT PORT CITY with one of the most beautiful bays in the world. This, no doubt, is what attracted the Hollywood celebrities of the 1950s who built homes and hotels as hideaways and places for entertaining their friends. The celebrity status continued. This is where John and Jackie Kennedy spent their honeymoon. Likewise, Bill and Hillary Clinton. And it's where Liz Taylor and Michael Todd ventured after tying the knot. In fact, Acapulco still ranks as one of the top honeymoon spots worldwide. Entertainers such as Placido Domingo come to give yearly benefit concerts and singers such as Julio Iglesias and a host of others maintain residences here, carrying on the Hollywood tradition that started long ago.

Acapulco has managed to age gracefully over the years even as it's grown into a town of several million inhabitants. Care is especially lavished on its upkeep. The city fathers initiated a multimillion-dollar beautification program some time ago, which is renewed annually to keep the bay, beaches, and streets landscaped and clean.

Of course, anyone who ventures to this stretch of the Pacific, 433 km (268 mi) south of Mexico City, does so to relax. Translate that as swimming, shopping, and enjoying the nightlife. Everything takes place against a staggeringly beautiful backdrop. The natural harbor of Acapulco Bay is the city's centerpiece. By day the water looks temptingly deep blue; at night it flashes and sparkles with the city lights.

The weather is Acapulco's major draw—warm waters, almost constant sunshine, and year-round temperatures in the 80s. It comes as no surprise, then, that most people plan their day around laying their towel on some part of Acapulco's many kilometers of beach. Both tame and wild water sports are available—everything from waterskiing to snorkeling, diving, and parasailing. Less strenuous possibilities are motorboat rides and fishing trips. Championship golf courses, tennis courts, and the food and crafts markets also lure some visitors away from the beach.

Most people rise from their hammocks, deck chairs, or towels only when impelled by hunger, and eating is one of Acapulco's great pleasures. In addition to the showy places, there are plenty of good no-frills, downhome Mexican restaurants. Eating at one of these joints takes you to the real Mexico.

At night Acapulco rouses itself from the day's torpor and prepares for the long hours ahead. Though Acapulco's heyday is past, its nightlife is legendary, and the constant opening of new and ever more spectacular dance clubs is proof positive that this remains the disco capital of the world. Perpetually crowded, the discos are grouped in twos and threes, and most people go to several places in one night.

The name of the late Teddy Stauffer, a Swiss entrepreneur, is practically synonymous with that of modern Acapulco. He hired the first cliff divers at La Quebrada in Old Acapulco and founded the Boom Boom Room, the town's first dance hall, and Tequila A Go-Go, its first disco. The Hotel Mirador at La Quebrada and the area stretching from Caleta to Hornos beaches, near today's Old Acapulco, were the center of activity in the 1950s, when Acapulco was a town of 20,000 with an economy based largely on fishing.

Since the late 1940s, Acapulco has expanded eastward so that today it is one of Mexico's largest cities, with a population of approximately 2 million. Former President Miguel Alemán Valdés bought up miles of the coast just before the road and airport were built—as his namesake Avenida Costera Miguel Alemán testifies. Under development is a

3,000-acre expanse known as Acapulco Diamante, which encompasses the areas known as Punta Diamante and Playa Diamante and some of the city's most sparkling hotels and residential developments.

Pleasures and Pastimes

Beaches

The lure of sun and sand in Acapulco is legendary. Every sport is available, and you can eat in a beach restaurant, dance, and sleep in a *hamaca* (hammock)—all without leaving the water's edge. There are also plenty of quiet and even isolated beaches within reach.

Dining

Dining in Acapulco is more than just eating out—it is the most popular leisure activity in town. Every night the restaurants fill up, and every night the adventurous diner can sample a different cuisine. The variety of styles matches the range of cuisines: from greasy spoons that serve regional favorites to gourmet restaurants with gorgeous views of Acapulco Bay. Most restaurants fall somewhere in the middle, and on the Costera Miguel Alemán are dozens of beachside restaurants with *palapa* (palm frond) roofs, as well as wildly decorated rib and hamburger joints popular with visitors under 30—not necessarily in age, but definitely in spirit.

Another plus for Acapulco dining is that the food is garden fresh. Each morning the Mercado Municipal is abuzz with restaurant managers and locals buying up the fish, poultry, and vegetables that will appear on plates that evening. Although some top-quality beef is produced in the states of Sonora and Chihuahua, many of the more expensive restaurants claim that they import their beef from the United States. In either case, the beef is excellent in most places. Most establishments that cater to tourists purify their drinking water and use it to cook vegetables.

Lodging

Accommodations in Acapulco run the gamut from sprawling, big-name complexes with nonstop amenities to small, family-run inns where hot water is a luxury. Wherever you stay, however, prices will be reasonable compared with those in the United States, and service is generally good, as Acapulqueños have been catering to tourists for over half a century.

Nightlife

Acapulco has always been famous for its nightlife, and justifiably so. For many visitors the discos and restaurants are just as important as the sun and the sand. The minute the sun slips over the horizon, the Costera comes alive with people milling around window-shopping, deciding where to dine, and generally biding their time till the disco hour. The legendary Acapulco discos are open 365 days a year from about 10:30 PM until they empty out. Obviously you aren't going to find great culture here; theater efforts are few and far between, and except for an occasional benefit concert by Placido Domingo, there is no classical music. However, international pop-music fests along with several film events such as black- and French-cinema festivals are gaining popularity.

Shopping

The abundance of air-conditioned shopping malls and boutiques makes picking up gifts and souvenirs one of the highlights of a visit to Acapulco. The malls are filled with clothing shops, and many others are strung along the Costera. There is also an increasing number of high-fashion boutiques that carry custom-designed clothes. Malls in Acapulco range from the shopping arcades at several of the more lavish hotels to the huge completely enclosed and air-conditioned Plaza Bahía.

There are several good shops specializing in Mexican crafts, and the Mercado Municipal, whose aisles are piled high with fruits, vegetables, poultry, fish, and meats, also is a good source of local handicrafts. Flea markets abound, carrying what seems to be an inexhaustible supply of inexpensive collectibles and souvenirs.

The State of Guerrero is especially known for hand-painted ceramics, items made from *palo de rosa* wood, primitive bark paintings depicting scenes of village life and local flora and fauna, and embroidered textiles. Silver is a real bargain in Mexico. Taxco, three hours away by car (four by bus), is one of the silver capitals of the world.

Sports and the Outdoors

Acapulco has lots for sports lovers to enjoy. Most hotels have pools, and many have private tennis clubs as well as courts. Many of the hotels have gyms, too. Acapulco's waters are teeming with sailfish, marlin, shark, and mahimahi, and although the waters aren't as clear as in the Caribbean (there's little scuba diving), waterskiing is popular as are windsurfing, kayaking, and bronco riding (an activity done in one-person motorboats). Golfers can tee off at the nine-hole municipal course, in town, or at one of the five 18-hole championship courses (three are open to the public) in the Acapulco Diamante area.

EXPLORING

It's possible to get a feel for Acapulco during a short stay if you take in some downtown sights along with your beach activities. Those who have a longer time to spend can really soak up the ambience of the place and can enjoy excursions to some isolated beaches as well as to Taxco.

Numbers in the text correspond to numbers in the margin and on the Acapulco and Taxco Exploring maps.

Great Itineraries

IF YOU HAVE 3 DAYS

Spend the first day enjoying your favorite beach activity, be it parasailing, waterskiing, or simply sunning. That evening, to get the lay of the land, take a sunset cruise that includes a ringside view of Acapulco's daredevil *clavadistas* (divers) at **La Quebrada** ⑧. The following day, experience Acapulco at its most authentic, paying an early visit to the **Mercado Municipal** ④, the **waterfront** ⑥, and the **zócalo** (town square) ⑦. Head for the beach for some rays after all that activity and later take in some late afternoon shopping in the boutiques and handicrafts markets along the Costera Miguel Alemán. Come nightfall, "shake off the dust" (as they say in Mexico) at one of the city's glitzy discos. The next day you'll want to try to land a sailfish, take in the Mexican Fiesta at the **Acapulco International Center** (drinks and show only), and bid farewell to Acapulco with a late candlelit dinner at one of the city's romantic dining spots.

IF YOU HAVE 5 DAYS

Add on to the three-day itinerary a visit to **El Fuerte de San Diego** ⑤, built in the 18th century to protect Acapulco from pirates, and today home of the Anthropology Museum. For a taste of the 1950s Acapulco of John Wayne and Johnny Weissmuller, hire a taxi to take you into the hills above Caleta and Caletilla; make it a point to drop into Los Flamingos Hotel, which Weissmuller once owned with others from the Hollywood gang. Head out to Pie de la Cuesta for a late lunch and boat ride or waterskiing on Coyuca Lagoon, and then cross the road and park your body under a palm-frond umbrella for a spectacular sun-

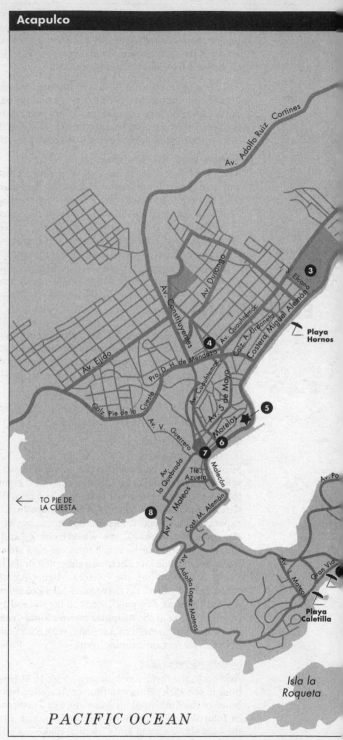

Acapulco

Av. Adolfo Ruiz Cortines

Av. Adolfo Ruiz

Av. Durango

Av. Elcano

3

Av. Constituyentes

Av. Cuauhtémoc

Caliz A. Urdaneta

Costera Miguel Alemán

Playa Hornos

4

Av. Elido

Pro D. H. de Mendoza

Calz. Pie de la Cuesta

Av. Cuauhtémoc

Av. 5 de Mayo

5

Av. V. Guerrero

Morelos

6

7

Tte.
Azueta

Malecón

Av. la Quebrada

Av. L. Mateos

Cost. M. Alemán

← TO PIE DE
LA CUESTA

8

Av. Po

Av. Adolfo Lopez Mateos

Av. Matroi

Gran Vía

**Playa
Caletilla**

*Isla la
Roqueta*

PACIFIC OCEAN

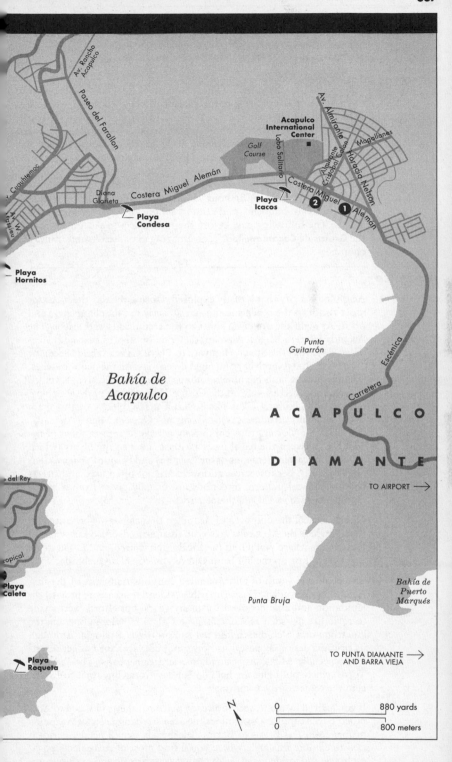

Av. Rancho Acapulco

Paseo del Farallon

Av. Almirante

Acapulco International Center

Golf Course

Lobo Solitario

Magallanes

Av. Almirante Cristóbal Colón

Horacio Nelson

F. Cuauhtémoc

Av. W. Rousseau

Diana Glorieta

Costera Miguel Alemán

Costera Miguel Alemán

Playa Icacos

Playa Condesa

❷

❶

Costera Miguel Alemán

Playa Hornitos

Bahía de Acapulco

Punta Guitarrón

Escénica

A C A P U L C O

Carretera

D I A M A N T E

TO AIRPORT ⟶

del Rey

Bahía de Puerto Marqués

Punta Bruja

ropical

Playa Caleta

Playa Roqueta

TO PUNTA DIAMANTE ⟶
AND BARRA VIEJA

N

0   880 yards

0   800 meters

set on the beach. Save one morning for the thrilling **Shotover Jet** boat ride on the Papagayo River (☞ Participant Sports *in* Outdoor Activities and Sports, *below*). Especially if you're traveling with children, devote a few hours to **Mágico Mundo Marino** ⑨.

IF YOU HAVE 7 DAYS

Follow the five-day itinerary above and then, for a complete change of pace, rent a car or arrange for a tour to **Taxco,** a colonial treasure of twisting cobblestone streets and some 1,000 silver shops, about a three-hour drive from Acapulco; plan to spend the night. For a change from shopping for silver, visit the **Iglesia de San Sebastián y Santa Prisca** ⑩, Taxco's most important landmark, on Plaza Borda, and the **Casa Humboldt** ⑫, which now houses a museum of viceregal art. Try to get a front-row seat at one of the bars or restaurants on the square and spend an hour watching the constant activity: weddings, funerals, baptisms, and vendors selling baskets and animal figurines. The following day, before the return trip to Acapulco, tour the **Grutas de Cacahuamilpa** ⑭, an amazing expanse of subterranean chambers.

Acapulco

Acapulco is a city that is easily explored. During the day the focus for most visitors is the beach and the myriad activities that happen on and off it. At night the attention shifts to the restaurants and discos. The Avenida Costera Miguel Alemán, the wide boulevard that hugs Acapulco Bay from the Scenic Highway to Playa Caleta (about 8 km, or 5 mi), is central to both day and night diversions. All the major beaches, shopping malls, and big hotels—minus the more exclusive Acapulco Diamante properties—are off the Costera. Hence most of the shopping, dining, and clubbing takes place within a few blocks of this main drag, and many an address is listed only as "Costera Miguel Alemán." Although the Costera runs completely across Acapulco, most of the action is between the naval base, La Base, next to the Hyatt (which anchors the eastern terminus of the Costera) and Parque Papagayo (Papagayo Park). Because street addresses are not often used and streets have no logical pattern, directions are usually given from a major landmark, such as CiCi (a theme park).

Old Acapulco, the only area of Acapulco that can easily be visited on foot, is where the Mexicans go to run their errands. Also known as El Centro, it's where you'll find the zócalo, the church, and El Fuerte de San Diego. Just up the hill from Old Acapulco is La Quebrada.

The peninsula south of Old Acapulco contains remnants of the first version of Acapulco. This primarily residential area was prey to dilapidation and abandonment for many years, but efforts were made to revitalize it—such as reopening the Caleta Hotel and opening the aquarium on Caleta Beach and the zoo on Isla la Roqueta. Although its prime is definitely past, it is now a popular area for budget travelers, especially Mexicans, Canadians, and Europeans. The **Plaza de Toros,** where bullfights are held on Sunday from Christmas to Easter, is in the center of the peninsula.

If you arrived by plane, you've already had a royal introduction to Acapulco Bay. **Acapulco Diamante** is the area stretching east of Acapulco proper from Las Brisas to Barra Vieja beach. You'll need a car or a taxi to explore this area, where you'll find most of Acapulco's poshest hotels and residential developments, as well as several exclusive private clubs, pounding surf, and beautiful beaches.

A Good Tour

If you want to get the lay of the land, you might take a drive or taxi ride along the Costera Miguel Alemán, starting on its eastern edge at **La Base,** the Mexican naval base south of Playa Icacos. When you come to Playa Icacos, you'll see the **Casa de la Cultura** ① cultural complex on the beach side (just past the Hyatt Regency hotel); a little farther down is **CiCi** ②, a children's amusement park. About 1 km (½ mi) past CiCi, on the right side of the Costera, lies the **Acapulco International Center** (often called the Convention Center); you might return here in the evening to attend a Mexican fiesta. Continue along through the commercial heart of the Costera until you reach **Parque Papagayo** ③, one of the top municipal parks in the country. When you arrive at the intersection of the Costera with Diego Hurtado de Mendoza, detour a few blocks inland to find Old Acapulco and the sprawling **Mercado Municipal** ④. You'll want to take the bus marked MERCADO or have your taxi drop you off; it's best to navigate this area by foot. A few blocks west and closer to the water, **El Fuerte de San Diego** ⑤ sits on the hill overlooking the harbor next to the army barracks. You'll next see the **waterfront** ⑥ (locally known as the *malecón*) with its series of docks and, adjoining it, the **zócalo** ⑦, the center of Old Acapulco. A 15-minute walk up the hill from the zócalo brings you to **La Quebrada** ⑧, where the famous cliff divers perform their daredevil stunt daily.

Sights to See

❶ **Casa de la Cultura.** This cultural complex includes a small archaeological museum, an exhibit of Mexican and international crafts, and the Ixcateopan art gallery. ⊠ *Costera Miguel Alemán 4834,* ☎ *74/84–40–04.* ▧ *Free.* ☉ *Weekdays 9–2 and 5–8, Sat. 9–2.*

🖐 ❷ **CiCi** (Centro Internacional para Convivencia Infantil). A water-oriented theme park for children, CiCi has dolphin and seal shows, a freshwater pool with wave-making apparatus, a water slide, miniaquarium, and other attractions. ⊠ *Costera Miguel Alemán, across from Hard Rock Cafe,* ☎ *74/84–82–10.* ▧ *$4; $77 to swim with dolphins, including transportation to and from your hotel.* ☉ *Daily 10–6.*

❺ **El Fuerte de San Diego.** Acapulco was originally an important port for the Spanish—who used it to trade with Asian countries, notably the Philippines—and they erected this fortress in the 18th century to protect the city from pirates. Their original fort, destroyed in an earthquake, was built in 1616. The pentagon-shape fort now houses the **Museo Historico de Acapulco.** The exhibits on display in 12 salons portray the city from prehistoric times through Mexico's independence from Spain in 1821. Especially noteworthy are the displays touching on the Christian missionaries sent from Mexico to the Far East and the cultural interchange that resulted. ⊠ *Calle Hornitos and Morelos,* ☎ *74/82–38–28.* ▧ *$1.25, free Sun.* ☉ *Tues.–Sun. 10–5.*

🖐 ❾ **Mágico Mundo Marino.** In addition to an aquarium, the Magic Marine World has a sea lion show, swimming pools, a toboggan, scuba diving, and (for rent) Jet Skis, inner tubes, and kayaks—not to mention clean rest rooms. From **Playa Caleta,** you can take the glass-bottom boat to **Isla la Roqueta** (about 10 minutes each way) for a visit to the small zoo. ⊠ *Playa Caleta,* ☎ *74/83–12–15.* ▧ *Aquarium $3; round-trip ferry service to Isla la Roqueta, including zoo, $3.* ☉ *Mágico Mundo daily 9–6, zoo daily 9–5.*

❹ **Mercado Municipal.** The sprawling municipal market is Acapulco as the locals experience it. They come to purchase their everyday needs, from fresh vegetables and candles to plastic buckets and love potions. The stalls within the mercado are densely packed together, but things stay relatively cool despite the lack of air-conditioning. There are baskets, pottery, hammocks, even a stand offering charms, amulets, and talismans. Come as early as possible to avoid the crowds. ⊠ *Diego Hurtado de Mendoza and Av. Constituyentes, a few blocks west of Costera.* ⊘ *Daily 7–7.*

③ Parque Papagayo. Named for the hotel that formerly occupied the grounds, the park sits on 52 acres of prime real estate on the Costera, just after the underpass that begins at Playa Hornos. Youngsters enjoy the life-size model of a Spanish galleon, made to look like the ones that sailed into Acapulco when it was Mexico's capital of trade with the Orient. There is an aviary, a roller-skating rink, a racetrack with mitesize race cars, a replica of the space shuttle *Columbia,* bumper boats in a lagoon, and other rides. ⊠ *Costera Miguel Alemán,* ☎ *74/85–96–23.* 🚆 *No entrance fee, rides 70¢–$1.80, 10-ride package $4.* ⊘ *Daily 10–8, rides section 4–11 nightly.*

⑧ La Quebrada. High on a hill above downtown Acapulco, La Quebrada (literally "gorge"; in this case cliffs) is home to the Mirador Hotel, *the* place for tourists in the 1940s; it still retains mementos from its glory days. But these days most visitors eventually make the trip here because this is where the famous cliff divers jump from a height of 130 ft daily at 1 PM and evenings at 7:30, 8:30, 9:30, and 10:30. The dives are thrilling, so be sure to arrive early. Before they take the plunge, the brave divers say a prayer at a small shrine near the jumping-off point. Sometimes they dive in pairs; often they carry torches. The hotel's La Perla supper club is the traditional and most comfortable viewing spot, but you will be obligated to buy a drinks-show-tips ($13) or buffet-show-tips package ($23). The tequila, rum, and brandy drinks are watered down and only domestic so be forewarned. By all means, don't let this dissuade you from seeing the show. The divers can also be seen from a general observation deck next to the hotel (about $2). When you exit, some of the divers may also be waiting to greet you—and to ask for tips. (For information about viewing the divers on sunset cruises, *see* Contacts and Resources *in* Acapulco A to Z, *below.*)

⑥ Waterfront. A stroll by the docks will remind you that Acapulco is still a lively commercial port and fishing center. The cruise ships anchor here, and at night Mexicans bring their children to play on the small tree-lined promenade. Farther west, by the zócalo, are the docks for the sightseeing yachts and smaller fishing boats. It's a good spot to join the Mexicans in people-watching. ⊠ *Costera Miguel Alemán, between Calle Escudero on the west and El Fuerte de San Diego on the east.*

⑦ Zócalo. You'll find the hub of downtown and Old Acapulco at this shaded plaza, overgrown with dense trees. All day it's filled with vendors, shoeshine men, and people lining up to use the pay phones. After siesta, they drift here to meet and greet. On Sunday evening there's often music in the bandstand. The zócalo fronts **Nuestra Señora de la Soledad,** the town's modern but unusual church, with its stark-white exterior and bulb-shape blue and yellow spires. ⊠ *Bounded by Calle Felipe Valle on the north, Costera Miguel Alemán on the south, Calle J. Azueta on the west, and Calle J. Carranza on the east.*

NEED A BREAK?	Just off the zócalo, **Sanborns** attracts locals and tourists alike; many linger for hours over a newspaper and a cup of coffee. **Cafetería Astoria** is a little outdoor café on the zócalo where businesspeople stop in for breakfast before work or meet midmorning for a cappuccino and a sweet roll.

Beaches

Some beaches, such as Revolcadero and Pie de la Cuesta, have very strong undertows and surf, so swimming isn't advised. Despite the bay's enticing appearance and officials' efforts to clean it up, it's still polluted—but not as much as before. In addition, although vending on the beach has been officially outlawed, you'll still find yourself approached by souvenir hawkers. A new corps of tourist beach police dressed in blue shorts and white shirts, however, have been somewhat successful in shooing away the vendors. Of course, you can always follow the lead of the Mexican cognoscenti and enjoy the waters at your hotel pool when you're in the mood for a swim.

Beaches in Mexico are public, even those that seem to belong to a big hotel.

Barra Vieja
About 27 km (17 mi) east of Acapulco, between Laguna de Tres Palos and the Pacific, this long stretch of uncrowded beach is somewhat more inviting than Pie de la Cuesta (☞ *below*) because the drive out is much more pleasant. Most people make the trip out here for the solitude and to feast on *pescado à la talla* (fish marinated in spices and grilled over hot coals).

Caleta and Caletilla
On the peninsula in Old Acapulco, these two beaches once rivaled La Quebrada as the main tourist area in Acapulco's heyday. Now they attract families. Motorboats to Isla la Roqueta (☞ Mágico Mundo Marino *in* Exploring, *above*) leave from here.

Condesa
Facing the middle of Acapulco Bay, this stretch of sand has more than its share of tourists, especially singles, and the beachside restaurants are convenient for bites between parasailing flights.

Hornos and Hornitos
Running from the Plaza las Glorias Paraíso to Las Hamacas hotel, these beaches are packed shoulder to shoulder on the weekends with locals and Mexican tourists who know a good thing: graceful palms shade the sand, and there are scads of casual eateries within walking distance.

Icacos
Stretching from the naval base to El Presidente hotel, this beach is less populated than others on the Costera, and the morning waves are especially calm.

Pie de la Cuesta
You'll need a car or cab to reach this relatively unpopulated spot, about a 25-minute drive west of Acapulco, through one of the least picturesque parts of town. A string of rustic restaurants borders the wide beach, and straw palapas provide shade. What attracts people to Pie de la Cuesta, besides the long expanse of beach and spectacular sunsets, is beautiful Coyuca Lagoon, a favorite spot for waterskiing, freshwater fishing, and boat rides. The boats will ferry you to La Laguna restaurant, where, some people claim, the pescado à la talla is even better than at Barra Vieja.

Puerto Marqués
Tucked below the airport highway, this strand is popular with Mexican tourists, so it tends to get crowded on weekends.

Revolcadero
A wide, sprawling beach next to the Vidafel Mayan Palace, Pierre Marqués, and Princess hotels, its water is shallow and its waves are fairly rough. People come here to surf and ride horses.

DINING

The top restaurants in Acapulco can be fun for a splurge and provide very good value. Even at the best places in town, dinner rarely exceeds $35 per person, and the atmosphere and views are fantastic. Ties and jackets are out of place, but so are shorts or jeans. Unless stated otherwise, all restaurants are open daily for lunch and then again for dinner from 6:30 or 7. Several restaurants have two seatings: 6:30 for the gringos and 9 for the Mexican crowd, who head directly to the discos after dinner to dance off the calories.

Note: Loud music blares from many restaurants along the Costera, and proprietors will aggressively try to hustle you inside with offers of drink specials. If you're looking for a hassle-free evening, it's best either to avoid this area or decide in advance precisely where you want to dine.

CATEGORY	COST*
$$$$	over $35
$$$	$25–$35
$$	$15–$25
$	under $15

per person for a three-course meal, excluding drinks, service, and 15% sales tax

American

$$–$$$ ✕ **Hard Rock Cafe.** This link in the international Hard Rock chain is one of the most popular spots in Acapulco, and with good reason. The famous hamburgers and brownies plus southern-style food—fried chicken, ribs—are well prepared, and the portions are more than ample. The taped rock music begins at noon, and a live group starts playing at 11 PM (except Tuesday). ⊠ *Costera Miguel Alemán 37,* ☎ *74/84–66–80. Reservations not accepted. AE, MC, V.*

$$ ✕ **Carlos 'n' Charlie's.** An Acapulco landmark, this is still one of the most popular restaurants in town. Part of the Anderson group (with restaurants in the United States and Spain as well as Mexico), Carlos 'n' Charlie's cultivates an atmosphere of controlled craziness. Prankster waiters, a jokester menu, and eclectic decor add to the chaos. The crowd is mostly young and relaxed, seemingly oblivious to the rush-hour traffic noise that filters up to the covered balcony where people dine. The menu straddles the border, with ribs, stuffed shrimp, and oysters among the best offerings. ⊠ *Costera Miguel Alemán 112,* ☎ *74/84–12–85 or 74/84–00–39. Reservations not accepted. AE, DC, MC, V.*

Belgian

$$ ✕ **La Petite Belgique.** Mexican-born Yolanda Brassart, who spent
★ years in Europe studying the culinary arts, reigns in the kitchen of this small bistro. Guy, her Belgian husband, makes certain that the customers are happy. Diners are greeted by the enticing aromas of goose-liver pâté, home-baked breads, and apple strudel. The menu changes every four months but usually includes boned duck stuffed with almonds and mushrooms and served with a white wine and mushroom sauce. ⊠ *Plaza Marbella,* ☎ *74/84–77–25. AE, MC, V.*

French

$$$ ✕ **Le Jardín des Artistes.** This chic garden hideaway, once a scruffy parking lot, is thoroughly French: the tables bear fresh flowers and Tiffany lamps, and discreet waiters deliver deliciously rich dishes with classic cream and butter sauces. Swiss chef Richard has a local following for his escargots in garlic butter, red-snapper fillet with savory mustard sauce, and smoked trout soufflé. After dinner, stroll through the snazzy art gallery adjoining the garden. ⊠ *Vicente Yañez Pinzón 11,* ☎ *74/ 84–83–44. Reservations essential. AE, DC, MC, V.* ⊙ *Closed Sun.-Wed. in Sept. and Oct. No lunch.*

Health Food

$ ✕ **100% Natural.** Along the Costera Miguel Alemán are several of these 24-hour restaurants that specialize in light, healthful food—yogurt shakes, fruit salads, and sandwiches made with whole-wheat bread. You can order soy burgers or dishes with chicken, about the only meat you'll find on the menu. The service is quick, and the food is a refreshing alternative to heavy meals. You can recognize these eateries by the green signs with white lettering. The original—and best—is across from the Acapulco Plaza hotel. ⊠ *Costera Miguel Alemán 200, near Acapulco Plaza,* ☎ *74/85–39–82;* ⊠ *Next to Oceanic 2000, at Costera Miguel Alemán 3111,* ☎ *74/84–84–40. MC, V.*

International

$$$ ✕ **Coyuca 22.** This is Acapulco's most beautiful restaurant, and more
★ celebrities have eaten here than you can shake a stick at. On hilltop terraces that overlook the bay from Old Acapulco, the understated decor includes Doric pillars and statuary; diners gaze down on an enormous illuminated obelisk and a small pool. It's like eating in a partially restored Greek ruin without the dust. Diners can choose from two fixed menus or order à la carte. Seafood and prime ribs are house specialties. ⊠ *Av. Coyuca 22 (10-min taxi ride from the zócalo),* ☎ *74/82–34–68 or 74/83–50–30. Reservations essential. AE, DC, MC, V. Closed Apr. 30–Nov. 1.*

$$$ ✕ **Madeiras.** A local favorite, Madeiras is very difficult to get into, es-
★ pecially on weekends and during the Christmas and Easter holidays. The bar-reception area is decorated with dramatic coffee tables whose glass tops rest on carved wooden animals; the dishes and flatware were created by silversmiths in nearby Taxco; and all tables afford views back across the bay toward Acapulco. Dinner is served from a four-course, prix-fixe menu and costs about $30 without wine. Specialties include a delicious red snapper baked in sea salt (a Spanish specialty), tasty chilled soups, and a choice of steaks and other seafood. Seatings are every 30 minutes from 7 PM to 10:30 PM. ⊠ *Carretera Escénica 33-B, just past La Vista shopping center,* ☎ *74/84–77–76. Reservations essential. AE, DC, MC, V. No lunch.*

$$–$$$ ✕ **Bella Vista.** This alfresco restaurant in the exclusive Las Brisas area has fantastic sunset views of Acapulco. Its large menu includes items that range from Asian appetizers to Italian and seafood entrées. Try the delicious (and spicy) Thai shrimp, sautéed in sesame oil, ginger, Thai chili, and hoisin sauce; or the red snapper étouffée, cooked in chardonnay, tomato, herbs, basil, and oyster sauce. Part of the restaurant has been enclosed and air-conditioned for those who like it cool. ⊠ *Carretera Escénica 5255,* ☎ *74/84–45–57, ext. 500. Reservations essential. AE, DC, MC, V.*

$$–$$$ ✕ **Costa Constanza.** Mediterranean cuisine can't get much better than
★ it is at this pretty, fresh-looking restaurant, which shares a beach with local fishermen who save the best of the day's catch for the kitchen. Italian-trained Loreli Fernandez assembles creative combinations of Italian, French, and Spanish fish and meat dishes. Tables are set up on a cozy pier at water's edge and in a glass-wrapped, air-conditioned dining room filled with attractive hand-decorated dishware from Michoacán. Consider the creamed oyster soup for starters, then move on

Acapulco Dining and Lodging

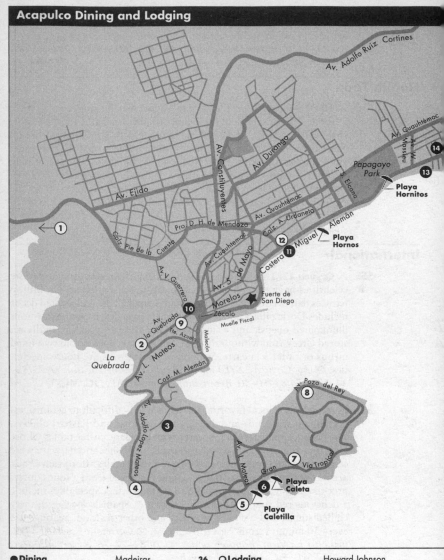

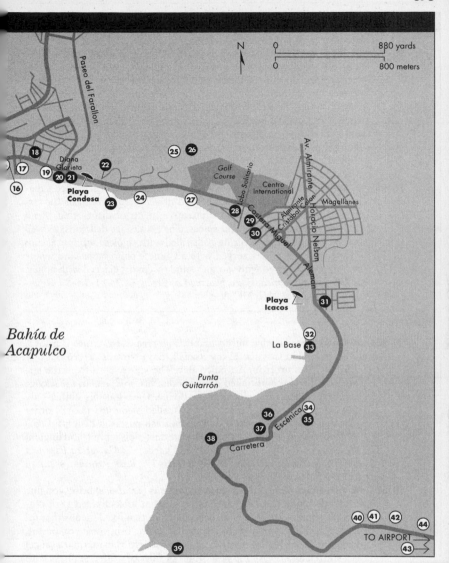

N

| 0 | | 880 yards |
| 0 | | 800 meters |

Paseo del Farallon

18

Diana
Glorieta

17

19

16

20 21

22

**Playa
Condesa**

23

24

25 26

27

*Golf
Course*

Lobo Solitario

*Centro
International*

28

Costera Miguel

Av. Almirante Horacio Nelson

29

30

*Almirante
Cristobal Colón*

Magallanes

Alemán

**Playa
Icacos**

31

*Bahía de
Acapulco*

32

La Base

33

*Punta
Guitarrón*

36

Escénica

34

37

35

38

Carretera

40 41 42 44

TO AIRPORT

43

39

to a grilled salmon steak flavored with yogurt-dill sauce and served with lime rice and sautéed vegetables. ⊠ *Costera Miguel Alemán 239, across from Las Hamacas hotel,* ☎ 74/82–28–61. *AE, MC, V.*

$$–$$$ ✕ **El Olvido.** The view, the foliage, the Mediterranean decor, and the nouvelle cuisine make this one of Acapulco's most popular dining spots, especially for the locals who have made it their social center. A terraced, open-air dining area provides a panoramic vista of the bay for all tables. French chef Daniel Janny blends recipes from many lands with Mexican ingredients, which results in creations such as salmon roll with mango vinaigrette and quail in a honey, pineapple, and *pasilla* chili sauce. For dessert, try the unusual but tasty *guanábana* (soursop sherbet) with black *zapote* (a fruit native to Mexico) sauce. ⊠ *Plaza Marbella,* ☎ 74/81–02–14. *AE, DC, MC, V.*

$$–$$$ ✕ **Spicey.** In addition to another spectacular view of Acapulco's dia-
★   mond-studded bay from the air-conditioned dining room or the ter-race, this restaurant has an innovative menu of dishes that blend international techniques and spices. The results are delicious, as well as a delight to the eye: spring rolls filled with smoked salmon, cream cheese, and vegetables, served with a Chinese plum sauce, and whole red snapper flavored with star anise and rosemary, glacéed with honey. ⊠ *Carretera Escénica, Fracc. Marina Las Brisas,* ☎ 74/81–13–80. *Reservations essential. AE, MC, V.*

Italian

$$–$$$ ✕ **Casa Nova.** Another ultraromantic spot created by Arturo Cordova,
★   the man behind Coyuca 22 (☞ *above*), Casa Nova is carved out of a cliff that rises up from Acapulco Bay. The views, both from the ter-race and the air-conditioned dining room, are spectacular, the service impeccable, and the Italian cuisine divine. Diners at this dinner-only spot can choose the fixed-price menu (called *menu turístico*) or order à la carte. Favorites include antipasto, fresh pastas, a delightful *cos-toletta di vitello* (veal chops with mushrooms), lobster tail, and linguini *alle vongole* (with clams, tomato, and garlic). ⊠ *Carretera Escénica 5256, just past Madeiras,* ☎ 74/84–68–19. *Reservations essential. AE, DC, MC, V.*

$$–$$$ ✕ **Villa Fiore.** Here, the owners of Madeiras (☞ *above*) bring you fine Italian dining in the candlelit garden of what looks like an 18th-cen-tury Venetian villa. Diners can choose from two fixed menus that in-clude appetizer, soup, main course (chicken, fish, meat, or pasta), dessert, and coffee. Opt for the calamari *fritti* (fried in marinara sauce) as a starter, and one of the veal dishes or fillet of stuffed sea bass with artichoke sauce for an entrée. Service is excellent. ⊠ *Av. del Prado 6,* ☎ 74/84–20–40. *AE, DC, MC, V. Closed Wed.*

Japanese

$$$ ✕ **Suntory.** At this traditional Japanese restaurant, you can dine either in a blessedly air-conditioned interior room or in the delightful Asian-style garden. It's one of the few Japanese restaurants in Acapulco and one of the only deluxe restaurants open for lunch. Specialties are the sushi and the teppanyaki, prepared at your table by skilled chefs. ⊠ *Costera Miguel Alemán 36, across from La Palapa hotel,* ☎ 74/84–80–88. *AE, DC, MC, V.*

Mexican

$$ ✕ **Zapata, Villa y Cia.** The music and the excellent food at this Mexi-can version of the Hard Rock Cafe are strictly local, and the memora-bilia recalls the Mexican Revolution—with guns, hats, and photographs

of Pancho Villa. The highlight of an evening here is a visit from a sombrero-wearing baby burro, so be sure to bring your camera. (If per chance the burro is missing, it's likely that the staff is searching for a younger version.) The restaurant isn't open for lunch. ⊠ *Hyatt Regency Acapulco, Costera Miguel Alemán 1,* ☎ *74/69–12–34. AE, DC, MC, V.*

$ ✕ **El Cabrito.** This is a local favorite for true Mexican cuisine and ambience. The name—"The Goat"—is also its specialty. In addition, you can choose among *mole* (spicy chocolate-chili sauce); shrimp in tequila; jerky with egg, fish, and seafood; and other Mexican dishes. ⊠ *Costera Miguel Alemán between CiCi and Centro Internacional,* ☎ *74/84–77–11. Reservations not accepted. AE, MC, V.*

$ ✕ **La Casa de Tere.** Hidden in a commercial district downtown (signs point the way), La Casa de Tere is in a league of its own—expect beer-hall tables and chairs, colorful Mexican decorations, and photos of Acapulco of yore. But that's part of the mix at this spotlessly clean, open-air Bohemian-like establishment. And so is its small but varied menu, which includes an outstanding *sopa de tortilla* (tortilla soup), chicken mole, and flan. ⊠ *Alonso Martín 1721, 2 blocks from Costera Miguel Alemán,* ☎ *74/85–77–35. No credit cards. Closed Mon.*

$ ✕ **Zorrito's.** When Julio Iglesias is in town, this is where he heads in the wee hours of the morning, after the discos close. The menu of this simple, open-air streetside eatery, which is open almost all the time, includes a host of steak and beef dishes, Acapulco's famous green-and-white *pozole* (pork and hominy soup), and the special, *filete tampiqueña* (a strip of tender grilled beef), which comes with tacos, enchiladas, guacamole, and beans—all served on plastic tables with red cloth table covers. ⊠ *Costera Miguel Alemán and Anton de Alaminos, next to Banamex,* ☎ *74/85–37–35. Reservations not accepted. AE, MC, V. Closed 7 AM–9 AM and Tues. 7 AM–2 PM.*

Seafood

$$–$$$ ✕ **La Vela.** Set on a wharf that juts out into Pichilingue Bay, this open-
★ air dining spot is protected by a dramatic roof that simulates a huge white sail. It's very atmospheric after dark, when a stillness hangs over the bay and the lights of Puerto Marqués flicker in the distance. A variety of fish and shellfish dishes are on the menu, but the specialty of the house is the red snapper *à la talla* (basted with chili and other spices and broiled over hot coals). ⊠ *Camino Real Acapulco Diamante, Carretera Escénica, Km 14,* ☎ *74/66–10–10. AE, DC, MC, V.*

$$ ✕ **Beto's.** By day you can eat right on the beach and enjoy live music; by night this palapa-roof restaurant is transformed into a dim and romantic dining area lighted by candles and paper lanterns. Whole red snapper, lobster, and ceviche are recommended. There's another branch next door and a third at Barra Vieja Beach—where the specialty is pescado à la talla. ⊠ *Beto's, Costera Miguel Alemán at Playa Condesa,* ☎ *74/84–04–73;* ⊠ *Beto's Safari, Costera Miguel Alemán, next to Beto's,* ☎ *74/84–47–62;* ⊠ *Beto's Barra Vieja, Barra Vieja Beach,* ☎ *no phone. AE, MC, V.*

$$ ✕ **La Cabaña.** This humble seaside restaurant run by the Alvarez family attracted the likes of Mexican songwriter Agustín Lara and his lady love María Feliz in the 1950s—and other notables craving good seafood ever since. You can see their photo over the bar and sample the same dishes that made the place famous then, such as baby-shark tamales. For heartier appetites, there's steaming seafood casserole or shrimp prepared with sea salt, curry, or garlic. The restaurant is smack in the middle of Playa Caleta and has free lockers if you've dropped in for breakfast, lunch, or dinner. ⊠ *Playa Caleta Lado Ote. s/n, Fracc. Las Playas (a 5-min taxi ride east of town square),* ☎ *74/82–50–07. AE, DC, MC, V.*

\$\$ ✕ **Pipo's.** Situated on a rather quiet part of the Costera, this family-
★   run seafood restaurant doesn't have an especially interesting view, but
diners come here for the fresh fish, good service, and reasonable prices.
Huachinango veracruzano (red snapper baked with tomatoes, peppers,
onion, and olives) and fillet of fish in *mojo de ajo* (garlic butter) are
about as sophisticated as the food preparation gets. ✉ *Costera Miguel
Alemán and Nao Victoria, across from Acapulco International Center,* ☎ *74/84–01–65;* ✉ *Almirante Bretón 3, downtown,* ☎ *74/82–22–
37. Reservations not accepted. AE, MC, V.*

LODGING

Although Acapulco has been an important port since colonial times,
it lacks the converted monasteries and old mansions found in Mexico
City. But the Costera is chockablock with new luxury high-rises and
local franchises of such major U.S. hotel chains as Hyatt and Howard
Johnson. As these hotels tend to be characterless, your choice will depend on location and what facilities are available. All major hotels can
make water-sports arrangements.

In Acapulco, geography is price, so where you stay determines what you
pay. The most exclusive area is the Acapulco Diamante, home to some
of the most luxurious hotels in Mexico—so lush and well equipped that
most guests don't budge from the minute they arrive. The minuses: Playa
Revolcadero is too rough for swimming (although great for surfing), and
this area is a 15- to 25-minute (expensive) taxi ride from the heart of Acapulco. The atmosphere of Acapulco Diamante is refined and revolves around
a game of golf or tennis, dining at some of Acapulco's better restaurants,
and dancing at the glamorous Enigma, Palladium, and Fantasy discos.

There is much more activity on Avenida Costera Miguel Alemán, where
the majority of large hotels, discos, American-style restaurants, and airline offices may be found, along with Acapulco's most popular beaches.
All the Costera hotels have freshwater pools and sun decks, and most
have restaurants and/or bars overlooking the beach, if not on the sand
itself. Hotels across the street are almost always less expensive than those
directly on the beach; because there are no private beaches in Acapulco,
all you have to do is cross the road to enjoy the sand.

Moving west along the Costera leads you to downtown Acapulco. The
beaches and restaurants here are popular with Mexican vacationers;
the hotels attract Canadian and European bargain-hunters.

You can assume that accommodations that cost more than \$50 (dou-
ble) will be air-conditioned (although you can find air-conditioned hotels for less) and will include a telephone, TV, and a view of the bay.
There is usually a range of in-house restaurants and bars, as well as a
pool. Exceptions exist, such as Las Brisas, which, in the name of peace
and quiet, has banned TVs from all rooms. So if such extras are important to you, be sure to ask ahead. If you can't afford air-conditioning,
don't panic. Even the cheapest hotels have cooling ceiling fans.

Note: Most hotels are booked solid Christmas and Easter week, so if
you plan to visit then, it's wise to make reservations months in advance.

CATEGORY	COST*
\$\$\$\$	over \$200
\$\$\$	\$100–\$200
\$\$	\$50–\$100
\$	under \$50

**All prices are for a standard double room, excluding 15% sales (called IVA)
tax and 2% room tax.*

Acapulco Diamante

$$$$ ☷ **Acapulco Princess.** The Princess is one of those megahotels that is
★ always holding at least three conventions. But more rooms equal more
facilities (several of the restaurants and bars close during the off season, May–October), including tennis, golf, and shopping in a cool arcade. The pool near the reception desk is sensational—fantastic tropical
ponds with little waterfalls and a slatted bridge leading into a swim-
ming-sunning area. Rooms are light and airy, with cane furniture and
rugs and curtains in colorful tropical prints. The Modified American
Plan (breakfast and dinner) is obligatory mid-December to mid-April.
⊠ *Playa Revolcadero (A.P. 1351), 39300,* ☎ *74/69–10–00, 800/223–
1818 in the U.S. and Canada,* FAX *74/69–10–16. 927 rooms, 92 suites.
7 restaurants, 7 bars, 5 pools, barbershop, beauty salon, 18-hole golf
course, 7 tennis courts, basketball, exercise room, shops, baby-sitting,
laundry service, concierge, meeting rooms, travel services, car rental.
AE, DC, MC, V.* ✺

$$$$ ☷ **Camino Real Acapulco Diamante.** This stunning hotel is set at the
★ foot of a lush tropical hillside on exclusive Pichilingue Beach, far from
the madding crowd. All rooms are done in luscious pastels, with tile
floors, balcony or terrace, luxurious baths, ceiling fans, and air-conditioning. Each has a view of peaceful Puerto Marqués bay. Eleven extra-
spacious club rooms have their own concierge and extra amenities. Some
rates include a buffet breakfast. A health club was added in 1998. ⊠
Carretera Escénica, Km 14, Calle Baja Catita, 39867, ☎ *74/66–10–
10, 800/722–6466 in the U.S. and Canada,* FAX *74/66–11–11. 145
rooms, 11 suites. 2 restaurants, 2 bars, room service, 3 pools, tennis
court, health club, baby-sitting, meeting rooms. AE, DC, MC, V.* ✺

$$$$ ☷ **Pierre Marqués.** This hotel is especially blessed because guests have
★ access to all the Princess's facilities without the crowds. In addition,
the Pierre Marqués has an 18-hole golf course, three pools, and five
tennis courts. Rooms are furnished identically to those at the Princess
(no TVs here, however), but villas and duplex bungalows with private
patios are also available. The hotel is now an all-inclusive property since
Fairmont and Canadian Pacific are running it. ⊠ *Apdo. 1351, Playa
Revolcadero, 39907,* ☎ *74/66–10–00, 800/223–1818 in the U.S. and
Canada,* FAX *74/66–10–46. 274 rooms, 70 suites. 2 restaurants, bar, 3
pools, 18-hole golf course, 5 tennis courts, shops, baby-sitting, laundry service, concierge, meeting rooms, car rental. AE, DC, MC, V.* ✺

$$$$ ☷ **Quinta Real.** In summer 1998, one of Mexico's most prestigious hotel
chains inaugurated this exclusive low-slung resort in the posh Punta Diamante section, about a 10-minute drive from downtown Acapulco. The
74 suites built on a hillside overlooking the sea have Mexican-made hardwood furniture and earth-tone drapes, rugs, and bedcovers. All have
balconies, climate control, satellite TVs, marble floors, and closet door
handles shaped like iguanas—the hotel's signature motif. Guests take
advantage of the large freshwater pools and the endless stretch of lovely
beach. ⊠ *Paseo de la Quinta Lote 6, Desarrollo Turmstico Real Diamante, 39907,* ☎ *74/69–15–00, 800/457–4000 in the U.S. and Canada,*
FAX *74/69–15–15. 74 suites. Restaurant, bar, 4 pools, exercise room, baby-
sitting, laundry service, concierge, car rental. AE, DC, MC, V.* ✺

$$$$ ☷ **Vidafel Mayan Palace.** This all-suites resort will knock your socks
off. Guests are welcomed in a 100,000-square-ft lobby that's sheltered
under 75-ft palapa roofs. The rooms, on the other hand, are surprisingly subdued. Airy and spacious, they are beautifully appointed with
marble floors, light-wood furniture, and luxurious baths. Canoes and
paddleboats are available to paddle around the man-made, fish-filled
canal, and you can swim in the 850-yard pool. ⊠ *Playa Revolcadero,
39000,* ☎ *74/66–23–93, 800/843–2335,* FAX *74/66–00–38. 366 suites.*

4 restaurants, 3 bars, pool, 18-hole golf course, 12 tennis courts,
beach, shops, billiards, video games. AE, DC, MC, V. 🕸

$$$$ ⊡ **Westin Las Brisas.** Set high on a hillside, Las Brisas remains distinct
★   in Acapulco for the secluded haven it provides its guests. This self-contained luxury complex has accommodations that range from one-bedroom units to deluxe private casitas, complete with small private pools.
All have beautiful bay views. Attention to detail is Las Brisas's claim
to fame: fresh hibiscus blossoms are set afloat in the pools each day.
Transportation is by white-and-pink Jeep. You can rent one for about
$70 a day; or, if you don't mind a wait, the staff will do the driving.
And transport is necessary—it is a good 15-minute walk to the beach
restaurant, and all the facilities are far from the rooms. The rate includes Continental breakfast stylishly delivered to your room each morning. ⊠ *Carretera Escénica 5255, 39868,* ☎ *74/69–69–00, 800/228–
3000,* ℻ *74/84–22–69. 300 rooms. 3 restaurants, 2 bars, in-room data
ports, 3 pools, beauty salon, hot tub, sauna, 5 tennis courts, laundry
service and dry cleaning, concierge, meeting rooms, travel services, car
rental. AE, DC, MC, V.* 🕸

The Costera

$$$$ ⊡ **Villa Vera.** A five-minute drive north of the Costera leads to what
was once one of Acapulco's most exclusive hotels. And although it has
many rivals, the name sells. Some of the villas, which were once private homes, have their own pools, and some standard rooms have been
converted into suites. Units have coffeemakers, video-cassette players,
and other amenities, but are otherwise unremarkable. The main pool,
with its swim-up bar, is the hotel's hub. A health club offering beauty
treatments and massage opened at the end of 1999. Two championship tennis courts host the Veterans tennis tournament. There's no
beach but there are more than a dozen pools on the premises. Children under 16 are not allowed. ⊠ *Apdo. 560, Lomas del Mar 35, 39690,*
☎ *74/84–03–33, 888/554–2361,* ℻ *74/84–74–79. 24 rooms, 25 suites,
6 villas. Restaurant, piano bar, 15 pools, beauty salon, massage, sauna,
2 tennis courts, exercise room. AE, MC, V.*

$$$ ⊡ **Continental Plaza.** Built by former president Miguel Alemán dur-
ing Acapulco's heyday, this landmark hotel—in the center of everything—
is still quite popular, especially with groups. The 390 large and airy
rooms (including 12 suites) have terraces overlooking the bay. There
are several good eating spots, including a Tony Roma's, an excellent
beach, shopping center, and meeting and banquet facilities. Most spec-
tacular is the large and lavish pool that winds around an "island" and
through lush, palm-shaded gardens. A two-night minimum stay is re-
quired. ⊠ *Costera Miguel Alemán, 39580,* ☎ *74/69–05–05, 800/926–
6836,* ℻ *74/84–21–20. 378 rooms, 12 suites. 3 restaurants, 3 bars,
pool, 2 tennis courts, exercise room. AE, DC, MC, V.*

$$$ ⊡ **Elcano.** One of Acapulco's traditional favorites, the hotel has been
★   completely remodeled while still (thankfully) maintaining its '50s fla-
vor. The A+ rooms are snappily done in nautical white and navy blue,
with white tiled floors and beautiful modern bathrooms. There's a delightful beachside restaurant with an outstanding breakfast buffet, a
more elegant indoor one, and a gorgeous pool that seems to float
above the bay, with whirlpools built into its corners. ⊠ *Costera Miguel
Alemán 75, 39690,* ☎ *74/84–19–50,* ℻ *74/84–22–30. 163 rooms, 17
suites. 2 restaurants, bar, pool. AE, DC, MC, V.*

$$$ ⊡ **Fiesta Americana Condesa Acapulco.** The Condesa is right in the
thick of the main shopping and restaurant district, and it is ever pop-
ular with tour operators. And no wonder—it's on one of the best
beaches in town. Newly renovated guest rooms have shed their for-

mer gaudy colors. ⊠ *Costera Miguel Alemán 97, 39690,* ☏ *74/84-28-28, 800/343-7821 in the U.S. and Canada,* 🖷 *74/84-18-28. 492 rooms, 8 suites. 2 restaurants, bar, 2 pools, children's programs (ages 4-12), meeting rooms, travel services. AE, DC, MC, V.* ✎

$$$ 🏨 **Hyatt Regency Acapulco.** A megahotel that you never have to leave, this property is popular with business travelers and conventioneers. The decor is striking, with strong Caribbean colors; in fact, the hotel's glamorous setting has appeared in many a Mexican soap opera. Tennis courts, four eateries (including a kosher restaurant), three bars, and a lavish shopping area are among the reasons for staying put. The Hyatt is also the only hotel in Latin America with an on-site synagogue, supervised by the orthodox rabbinate of Mexico City. The Hyatt is a little out of the way, a plus for those who seek quiet. To avoid the noise of the maneuvers at the neighboring naval base, ask for a room on the west side of the hotel. ⊠ *Costera Miguel Alemán 1, 39869,* ☏ *74/69-12-34, 800/233-1234 in the U.S.,* 🖷 *74/84-30-87. 607 rooms, 17 suites. 3 restaurants, 3 bars, snack bar, 2 pools, massage, 5 tennis courts, exercise room, shops, baby-sitting, laundry service, meeting rooms, travel services, car rental, parking (fee). AE, DC, MC, V.* ✎

$$ 🏨 **Costa Club.** This resort hotel (the former Acapulco Plaza) still has more facilities than many Mexican towns: four bars and as many restaurants, tennis, a sauna, three pools, and a location next to the Plaza Bahía, Acapulco's largest shopping mall. The La Jaula bar, at the mezzanine level, is most extraordinary—a wooden hut, suspended by a cable from the roof, reached by a gangplank and overlooking a garden full of exotic birds. Guest rooms have tile floors and pastel and blond-wood decor, and guests continue to be content with the facilities and service. There's an all-inclusive option for $79 a person. ⊠ *Costera Miguel Alemán 123, 39670,* ☏ *74/85-90-50, 800/712-4156,* 🖷 *74/85-54-93. 506 rooms. 4 restaurants, 4 bars, 3 pools, sauna, 3 tennis courts, health club, meeting rooms. AE, DC, MC, V.* ✎

$$ 🏨 **Las Hamacas.** Las Hamacas is a friendly, old-fashioned Acapulco hotel built in the 1950s with rooms surrounding a large inner courtyard. Across the street from the beach, it has a lovely garden of coconut palms from its former days as a plantation, as well as two pools and a large parking lot. Tile floors, new bathrooms, and air-conditioners are in all of the spacious, light-filled cream and white guest rooms. Junior suites can sleep two adults and two children, which makes the hotel appealing to Mexican families. Twenty second-story rooms have bay views, but also lie above the busy Costera; rooms facing the leafy courtyard are the quietest. The hotel is about a three-minute ride from downtown. ⊠ *Costera Miguel Alemán, 39670,* ☏ *74/83-70-06, 800/448-8355,* 🖷 *74/83-05-75. 100 rooms, 20 suites. Restaurant, bar, 2 pools, beauty salon, meeting rooms, travel services, free parking. MC, V.* ✎

$$ 🏨 **Howard Johnson Maralisa.** Formerly the sister hotel of the Villa Vera
★ (☞ *above*), this property, on the beach side of the Costera, is now part of the Howard Johnson chain. The rooms are light, decorated in whites and pastels. This is a small, friendly place; all rooms have TVs, some have balconies, and the price is right. ⊠ *Apdo. 721, Calle Alemania, 39670,* ☏ *74/85-66-77, 800/446-4656 in the U.S. and Canada,* 🖷 *74/85-92-28. 85 rooms, 5 suites. Restaurant, bar, 2 pools, beach, laundry service and dry cleaning. AE, DC, MC, V.* ✎

$$ 🏨 **Park Hotel & Tennis Center.** A helpful staff and prime location make this hotel an appealing, intimate, and cordial place. In the recent past, rooms were uninspired; now colonial-style wood furniture has been refinished, walls painted, and quiet, individually controlled air-conditioning units installed. Rooms are well-situated around a garden with a good-size pool. Other assets include refrigerators, TVs (Spanish channels only), and plenty of hot water; some rooms have kitchenettes

(for a small fee) and some have balconies, but all are spotlessly clean and well priced. The Park has excellent tennis facilities, and it's only a block to the beach. Since the hotel is right on the Costera, ask for a room overlooking the tennis courts in the back, if you'd prefer quiet. ⊠ *Apdo. 269, Costera Miguel Alemán 127, 39670,* ☎ *74/85–59–92,* FAX *74/85–54–89. 88 rooms. Bar, pool, 3 tennis courts. MC, V.*

Old Acapulco

$$$ 🏨 **Plaza las Glorias El Mirador.** The old El Mirador has been taken over by the Plaza las Glorias chain, which is part of the Sidek conglomerate responsible for marina and golf developments all over Mexico. Very Mexican in style—white with red tiles and hand-carved Mexican furniture—Plaza las Glorias is set high on a hill with a knockout view of Acapulco Bay and La Quebrada, where the cliff divers perform. Many of the suites have hot tubs and stunning ocean vistas. ⊠ *Quebrada 74, 39300,* ☎ *74/83–11–55, 800/342–2644,* FAX *74/82–45–64. 72 rooms, 58 suites. 2 restaurants, bar, 3 pools, beauty salon, sauna, meeting rooms, travel services, free parking. AE, DC, MC, V.*

$$ 🏨 **Los Flamingos.** Almost a historical monument, this hot-pink hotel was the favored hangout of John Wayne, Johnny ("Tarzan") Weissmuller, Errol Flynn, and the rest of the "Hollywood gang" back in the '50s, and their photographs adorn the walls of the lobby. The hotel is strung along a cliff that has some of the finest views in Acapulco— from Pie de la Cuesta all across Acapulco Bay. Los Flamingos attracts plenty of Europeans who come to bask in the ambience of Old Hollywood and toss down the *coco locos,* which barman Esteban Castañeda will tell you were invented here in the 1960s. In 1997 the rooms were spruced up with bright pink walls and flowered print spreads. Baths are spartan (shower only), but adequate. The circular two-bedroom master suite, set apart on a small rise, was once Johnny Weissmuller's digs. The hotel offers free transportation to the beach and downtown. ⊠ *Av. López Mateos,* ☎ *74/82–06–90,* FAX *74/83–98–06. 234 rooms, 2 suites. Restaurant, bar, pool. MC, V.* 🕮

$$ 🏨 **Majestic.** Once upon a time, this dowager hotel served as a Club
★ Med. The stunning decor of the spacious rooms—tile floors, cool colors, and good lighting—is completely unexpected in a hotel in this price category. Entrance is through the seventh-floor lobby, and the rest of the hotel is terraced down a rocky cliff. Many of the rooms in the main building have private terraces and each has a double bed and two studio couches; the villa rooms are smaller. There is no beach at the hotel, but free transportation is provided to the hotel's beach club, next to the Club de Yates (Yacht Club). An all-inclusive plan is also available. ⊠ *Av. Pozo del Rey 73, 39390,* ☎ *74/83–27–13,* FAX *74/84–20–32. 72 rooms, 58 suites. 2 restaurants, 2 bars, 2 pools, tennis court, dance club, parking (fee). AE, DC, MC, V.* 🕮

$$ 🏨 **Suites Alba.** On a quiet hillside in Old Acapulco, the Alba is a resort-style hotel with bargain prices. All suites sleep four and have a kitchenette, private bath, and terrace. There is no extra charge for up to two children under 12 sharing a room with relatives, which makes it especially popular with families. A cable car takes guests to the hotel's beach club on the bay, next door to the Club de Yates, with a 330-ft-long toboggan. During the high season (mid-December–mid-April) there's free transportation from the hotel to Playa Caleta and downtown. ⊠ *Grand Via Tropical 35, 39390,* ☎ *74/83–00–73,* FAX *74/83–83–78. 244 suites. 3 restaurants, bar, 3 pools, tennis court, beach, shops, free parking. AE, DC, MC, V.* 🕮

$ 🏨 **Boca Chica.** This Old Acapulco mainstay may have peeling paint on the facade and an antique switchboard, but its old-time Mexican ambience is the best at a price that's hard to beat. It's a few short steps from a natural swimming cove, and the open-air lobby has lovely views of Caletilla Bay. Rooms are small—with old-fashioned slats on the door, little balconies, tile bathrooms, and nondescript furnishings—but they're very clean and air-conditioned. The property, which also has a pretty palapa restaurant with sushi bar, landscaped jungle garden, and pool, attracts German tourists. An abundant Mexican breakfast is included in the price. ⊠ *Playa Caletilla, across the bay from Isla la Roqueta and Mágico Mundo Marina, 39390,* ☎ *74/83–63–88, 800/ 346–3942. 42 rooms, 3 suites. Restaurant, bar, pool, shops, free parking. AE, MC, V.* ☜

$ ⊞ **Hotel Misión.** Two minutes from the zócalo, this charming, colonial-style hotel surrounds a greenery-rich courtyard with an outdoor dining area that functions only on Thursday. (Ask for the green-and-white pozole.) The rooms are small and by no means fancy, with wrought-iron beds, tile floors, painted brick walls, and ceiling fans (no air-conditioning). Every room has a shower, and there's plenty of hot water. The best rooms are on the second and third floors; the top-floor room is large but hot in the daytime. ⊠ *Calle Felipe Valle 12, 39300,* ☎ *74/ 82–36–43,* ℻ *74/82–20–76. 20 rooms. No credit cards.*

Pie de la Cuesta

$$$ ⊞ **Parador del Sol.** If you want to get away from it all, this is the per-
★ fect place. Traversing both the lagoon and the Pacific Ocean sides of the Pie de la Cuesta road, this all-inclusive property gives the impression that it was designed as a luxury resort. The 150 rooms are distributed among pink villas scattered over gardens. Spacious, with tile floors and baths, each room is air-conditioned and equipped with color TV, phone, and a fan-cooled terrace complete with hammocks. The rate includes all meals and refreshments, domestic drinks, tennis, and nonmotorized water sports. ⊠ *Carretera Pie de la Cuesta–Barra de Coyuca, Km 5, Apdo. 1070, 39300,* ☎ *74/44–40–50,* ℻ *74/44– 40–51. 150 rooms. Restaurant, 2 bars, 2 pools, miniature golf, 4 tennis courts, exercise room, dance club. AE, DC, MC, V.*

NIGHTLIFE AND THE ARTS

The companies listed in the Contacts and Resources section of Acapulco A to Z (☞ *below*) can organize evening jaunts to most of the dance and music places listed below. And don't forget the nightly entertainment at most hotels. The big resorts have live music to accompany the early evening happy hour, and some feature big-name bands from the United States for less than you would pay at home. Many hotels sponsor theme parties—Italian Night, Beach Party Night, and similar festivities.

Cultural Shows

Acapulco International Center (⊠ Costera Miguel Alemán, ☎ 74/84– 32–18), also known as the Convention Center, has a Mexican fiesta Wednesday and Friday, where you can take in mariachi bands, singers, and the *voladores* (flyers) from Papantla. The show with open bar and buffet costs about $35; entrance to the show alone is $20. The performance starts at 8. On Friday at **El Mexicano** restaurant (⊠ Carretera Escénica 5255) in Las Brisas hotel, the Mexican Fiesta starts off with a *tianguis* (marketplace) of handicrafts and ends with a spectacular display of fireworks.

Dance

Salon Q (✉ Costera Miguel Alemán 23, ☎ 74/84–32–52), referred to as the "Cathedral of Salsa," is a combination dance hall and disco where the bands play salsas, merengues, and other Latin rhythms for young and old. There's a live show weekends—mostly impersonations of Mexican entertainers—as well as dance contests.

Discos

Reservations are advisable for a big group; late afternoon or after 9 PM are the best times to call. New Year's Eve requires planning.

Except for Palladium, Fantasy, and Enigma, the discos are clustered on the Costera.

Alebrije is enormous, with seating for 1,200 people in love seats and booths. The most popular night is Friday, when everyone is bathed in foam, with a kind of wet-T-shirt effect. From 10:30 (opening time) to 11:30, the music is slow and romantic; then the disco music and the light show begin, and they go on till dawn. ✉ *Costera Miguel Alemán 3308, across from Hyatt Regency,* ☎ *74/84–59–02.*

Andromeda is proof that Acapulco remains the disco capital of the world. Quite spectacular, even for a city known for its splendiferous discos, this one will impress even the most jaded discoers. Entrance to the Queen of the Sea's "castle" is over a torchlit moat; once inside, the impression is of being in a submarine, with a window to the sea. There are supposedly two dance floors, but the 18–25 crowd dances everywhere to the latest techno and techno-pop sounds. ✉ *Costera Miguel Alemán 15, at Fragata Yucatán,* ☎ *74/84–88–15.*

Baby O is a private club that is known to open its doors to a few select nonmembers. Eschewing the glitz and mirrors of Acapulco's older discos, Baby O resembles a cave in a tropical jungle. The crowd is 25 to 35, mostly well-dressed, wealthy Mexicans. ✉ *Costera Miguel Alemán 22,* ☎ *74/84–74–74.*

Discobeach is Acapulco's only alfresco disco and its most informal one. The under-30 crowd sometimes even turns up in shorts. The waiters are young and friendly—some people find them overly so. (In fact, this is one of Acapulco's legendary pickup spots.) One night they're all in togas carrying bunches of grapes; the next they're in pajamas. Every Wednesday, ladies' night, all the women receive flowers. ✉ *Playa Condesa,* ☎ *74/84–82–30.*

★ **Enigma** (formerly called Extravaganzza) claims to have the ultimate in light and sound and is Acapulco's answer to the Luxor hotel in Las Vegas with its lavish, New Egyptian–theme. It accommodates 700 at a central bar and in comfortable booths, and a glass wall provides an unbelievable view of Acapulco Bay, which includes fireworks on weekends. No food is served, but there are several restaurants nearby. The music (which is for all ages) starts at 10:30. ✉ *On Carretera Escénica to Las Brisas,* ☎ *74/84–71–64.*

★ **Fantasy** attracts a 25–50 crowd—mainly couples—and is one of the few discos where people really dress up, with the men in well-cut pants and shirts and the women in racy outfits and cocktail dresses. Singles gravitate toward the two bars in the back. Fantasy is quite snug, to put it nicely, and people tend to come here earlier than they do to other places. At 2 AM there is a fireworks display. A glassed-in elevator provides an interesting overview of the scene and leads upstairs to a little shop that stocks T-shirts and lingerie. ⊠ *On Carretera Escénica to Las Brisas,* ☎ 74/84–67–27.

Hard Rock Cafe (☞ Dining, *above*), filled with rock memorabilia, is part bar, part restaurant, part dance hall, and part boutique. **Planet Hollywood** (⊠ Costera Miguel Alemán 2917, next to CiCi, ☎ 74/84–42–84) resembles the Hard Rock Cafe, but with Hollywood memorabilia and California-style cuisine.

Palladium is another spectacular production of Tony Rullán, creator of Enigma (☞ *above*). A waterfall that cascades down the hill from the dance-floor level makes this place hard to miss. As at Enigma, the dance floor is nearly surrounded by 50-ft-high windows, giving dancers a wraparound view of Acapulco. ⊠ *On Carretera Escénica to Las Brisas,* ☎ 74/81–03–30.

OUTDOOR ACTIVITIES AND SPORTS

Participant Sports

Fishing

Fishing trips can be arranged through your hotel, downtown at the Pesca Deportiva near the *muelle* (dock) across from the zócalo, or through travel agents. At the docks near the zócalo you can hire a boat for $30 a day (two lines). It is safer to stick with one of the reliable companies whose boats and equipment are in good condition. Boats accommodating 4–10 people cost $200–$500 a day, $45–$60 by chair. Excursions usually leave about 7 AM and return at 1 PM or 2 PM. You are required to get a fishing license ($8–$10, depending on the season) from the Secretaría de Pesca; you'll find their representative at the dock. Don't show up during siesta, between 2 and 4 in the afternoon.

For deep-sea fishing, **Divers de México** (☞ Contacts and Resources *in* Acapulco A to Z, *below*) has well-maintained boats for 4–10 passengers for $200–$800 (six lines). It also has private yacht charters. Small boats for freshwater fishing can be rented at **Cadena's** and **Tres Marías** at Coyuca Lagoon.

Fitness and Swimming

Most of the time, Acapulco weather is like August in the warmest parts of the United States. This means that you should cut back on your workouts and maintain proper hydration by drinking plenty of water.

Acapulco Princess (☞ Acapulco Diamante *in* Lodging, *above*) has the best hotel fitness facilities, including a gym with stationary bikes, Universal machines, and free weights. Because the Princess is about 15 km (9 mi) from the city center and the pollution of Acapulco, you can even swim in the ocean here if you beware of the strong undertow.

Villa Vera Spa and Fitness Center (⊠ Lomas del Mar 35, ☎ 74/84–03–33) has a new spa and fitness center equipped with exercise machines (including step machines), free weights, and benches. Masseuses and cosmetologists give facials, herbal wraps, algae marina treatments, and shiatsu, reflexology, and Swedish massages. Both the beauty center and the gym are open to nonguests.

Westin Las Brisas (☞ Acapulco Diamante *in* Lodging, *above*) is where you should stay if you like to swim but don't like company or competition. Individual casitas come with private or semiprivate pools; the beach club has two saltwater pools. Most of the major hotels in town along the Costera Miguel Alemán also have pools.

Golf

Two 18-hole championship golf courses are shared by the **Acapulco Princess and Pierre Marqués** hotels. Reservations should be made in advance (☎ 74/69–10–00). Greens fees are $65 for guests and $85 for nonguests. A round at the 18-hole **Vidafel Mayan Palace** (☎ 74/66–18–79) course is $42 for guests, $55 for nonguests. There is a public golf course at the **Club de Golf** (☎ 74/84–07–81) on the Costera across from the Acapulco Malibú hotel. Greens fees are $35 for nine holes, $52 for 18. If you're staying at Las Brisas, you can play on the links at Tres Vidas. Otherwise Tres Vidas and Diamante Country Club are reserved for members and their guests.

Jogging

If you don't like beach jogging, the only real venue for running in the downtown area is along the sidewalk next to the Costera Miguel Alemán at the seafront, but you'll have to go very early, before traffic fumes set in. Away from the city center, the best area for running is out at the Acapulco Princess hotel, on the airport road. A 2-km (1-mi) loop is laid out along a lightly traveled road, and in the early morning you can also run along the asphalt trails on the golf course.

Rollerblading

For a change of pace from sand and sea activities, come to **Roller Gran Prix** (✉ Brisamar, east of Costera Miguel Alemán, just before Los Rancheros restaurant, ☎ 74/84–93–13) for rollerblading to disco music and racing Formula One–style go-carts. The $2.50 fee includes blades, and instruction is available. Go-carts cost $2.50 for five minutes.

Scuba Diving

Arnold Brothers (✉ Costera Miguel Alemán 205, near El Fuerte de San Diego, ☎ 74/82–18–77) runs scuba-diving excursions and snorkeling trips. Scuba trips cost $30; snorkeling costs $15.

Tennis

Court fees range from about $8 to $25 an hour during the day and double in the evening. At the hotel courts, nonguests pay about $5 more per hour. Lessons with English-speaking instructors start at about $10 an hour; ball boys get a $2 tip.

There are several places in town to play tennis. **Acapulco Plaza** (☎ 74/85–90–50) has three hard-surface courts, two lighted. In addition to five outdoor courts, the **Acapulco Princess** (☎ 74/69–10–00) has two air-conditioned indoor courts. The **Hyatt Regency** (☎ 74/84–12–25) has three lighted courts at the Municipal Golf Club. There are three lighted courts at the **Park Hotel & Tennis Center** (☎ 74/85–59–92). The **Pierre Marqués** (☎ 74/66–10–00) has five courts. You'll find five courts at **Tiffany's Racquet Club** (✉ Av. Villa Vera 120, ☎ 74/84–79–49). At **Vidafel Mayan Palace** (☎ 74/69–18–79), there are 12 lighted courts. **Villa Vera Hotel** (☎ 74/84–03–33) has two outdoor lighted clay courts and two hard-surface courts.

Water Sports

Waterskiing, broncos (one-person motorboats), and parasailing can all be arranged on the beach. Parasailing is an Acapulco highlight; a five-minute trip costs $15. Waterskiing is about $30 an hour; broncos cost $30–$85 for a half hour, depending on the size. Windsurfing can be arranged at Caleta and most beaches along the Costera but is especially good at Puerto Marqués. The main surfing beach is Revolcadero.

Acapulco's latest attraction, the **Shotover Jet,** is an import from the rivers around Queenstown, New Zealand. For $45, you're driven via air-conditioned coach from the outfit's Acapulco offices to a site near the town of Tierra Colorado (35 minutes each way). There you climb aboard the 12-passenger craft for an exciting 30-minute boat ride on the Papagayo River, complete with several thrilling 360-degree turns—one of the Shotover Jet's trademarks—and vistas of local flora and fauna (cacti, bats, and iguanas). A new addition: shooting the rapids ($30 for an hour of rafting with a guide). For both rides, you pay $61. After the ride, you can return directly to Acapulco or take a later shuttle bus and linger at the riverside property, which has a restaurant, souvenir shop, and an iguana nursery. ⊠ *Continental Plaza, Costera Miguel Alemán, Locale 3,* ☎ *74/84–11–54.*

Spectator Sports

Bullfights

The season runs from about Christmas to Easter, and *corridas* (bullfights) are held on Sunday at 5:30. Tickets are available through your hotel or at the **Plaza de Toros** ticket window (⊠ Av. Circunvalación, across from Playa Caleta, ☎ 74/82–11–81) Monday–Saturday 10–2 and Sunday 10:30–5. Tickets in the shade (*sombra*)—the only way to go—cost about $16. Preceding the fight are performances of Spanish dances and music by the Chili Frito band.

Jai Alai

The **Jai Alai Acapulco Race & Sports Book** (⊠ Costera Miguel Alemán 498, ☎ 74/84–31–95) has two restaurants and a bar, and capacity for 1,500 spectators. The fast-paced games take place Thursday through Sunday at 9 PM, mid-December through January 6, Easter week, and throughout July and August. Entrance is $4.

SHOPPING

The main shopping strip is on the Costera Miguel Alemán from the Acapulco Plaza to the El Presidente Hotel. Here you can find Guess, Peer, Aca Joe, Amarras, Polo Ralph Lauren, and other fashionable sportswear boutiques. Downtown (Old) Acapulco doesn't have many name shops, but this is where you'll find the inexpensive tailors patronized by the Mexicans, lots of little souvenir shops, and a vast flea market with crafts. Also downtown is Sanborns. Most shops are open from 10 to 7 Monday through Saturday and are closed on Sunday.

Department Stores and Supermarkets

Except for the waitresses' uniforms, the food, and a good handicrafts selection, **Sanborns** is very un-Mexican. Still, it is an institution throughout Mexico. It sells English-language newspapers, magazines, and books, as well as a line of high-priced souvenirs. Sanborns's restaurants are popular for their enchiladas *suizas* (prepared with lots of cream and cheese), *molletes* (toasted rolls spread with refried beans and cheese), and their seven-fruit drink. The Calinda branch (⊠ Costera Miguel Alemán 1226, ☎ 74/84–44–13), the Oceanic 2000 branch (⊠ Costera Miguel Alemán 3111, ☎ 74/84–20–25), and the downtown branch (⊠ Costera Miguel Alemán 209, ☎ 74/82–61–67) are open 7 AM to midnight during the high season and 7:30 AM–11 PM the rest of the year.

Branches of **Aurrerá, Gigante, Price Club, Sam's, Wal-Mart** (in case you don't get enough of them back home), and **Comercial Mexicana** are all on the Costera and sell everything from liquor and fresh and frozen food to light bulbs, clothing, garden furniture, and sports equipment.

Malls

Malls in Acapulco range from the delightful air-conditioned shopping arcade at the Princess hotel to rather gloomy collections of shops that sell cheap jewelry and embroidered dresses. Malls are listed below from east to west.

The multilevel **Marbella Mall,** at the Diana Glorieta, is home to Martí, a well-stocked sporting-goods store; a health center (drugstore, clinic, and lab); the Canadian Embassy; and Bing's Ice Cream, as well as several restaurants. **Aca Mall,** which is next door to Marbella Mall, is all white and marble; here you'll find Tommy Hilfiger, Peer, and Aca Joe.

Plaza Bahía, next to the Costa Club hotel, is a place for serious shopping. It is a huge, completely enclosed, air-conditioned mall where you could easily spend an entire day. Stores include Dockers, Mossimo, Nautica, and Ferrioni, for chic casual wear for men and women; Ragazza, which carries an exquisite line of fine lingerie; Aspasia, which sells locally designed, glitzy evening dresses and chunky diamanté jewelry; a large Martí for sporting goods; restaurants and snack bars; and a bowling alley, go-carts, and video-game arcade.

Markets

In addition to fresh produce, meat, fowl, fish, and flowers, the **Mercado Municipal** (☞ Acapulco *in* Exploring, *above*) also is stocked with serapes, piñatas, leather goods, baskets, hammocks, and framed paintings done on velvet of the Virgin of Guadalupe, as well as traditional Mexican cooking utensils. There are even stands offering charms, amulets and talismans, bones, herbs, fish eyes, sharks' teeth, lotions, candles, incense, and soaps said to help one find or keep a mate, increase virility or fertility, or ward off the evil eye.

El Mercado de Artesanías El Parazal, a conglomeration of every souvenir in town, is a 15-minute walk from Sanborns downtown. You'll find fake ceremonial masks, the ever-present onyx chessboards, $15 hand-embroidered dresses, imitation silver, hammocks, ceramics, and even skin cream made from turtles (don't buy it, because turtles are endangered and you won't get it through U.S. Customs). ⊠ *From Sanborns downtown, head away from the Costera to Vásquez de León and turn right 1 block.* ☉ *Daily 9–9.*

In an effort to get the itinerant vendors off the beaches and streets, the local government set up a series of **flea markets** along the Costera, mostly uninviting dark tunnels of stalls that carry what seems to be an inexhaustible supply of inexpensive collectibles and souvenirs, including serapes, ceramics, straw hats, shell sculptures, carved walking canes, and wooden toys. The selections of archaeological-artifact replicas, bamboo wind chimes, painted wooden birds ($5 to $30 each), shell earrings, and embroidered clothes begin to look identical. Prices at the flea markets are often quite low, but it's a good idea to compare prices of items you're interested in with prices in the shops, and bargaining is essential. It's best to buy articles described as being made from semiprecious stones or silver in reputable establishments. If you don't, you may find that the beautiful jade or lapis lazuli that was such a bargain was really cleverly painted paste, or that the silver was simply a facsimile called *alpaca.* One large market with a convenient location is La Diana Mercado de Artesanías, a block from the Continental Plaza hotel, close to the Diana monument.

Specialty Shops

Art
Edith Matison's Art Gallery (⊠ Av. Costera Miguel Alemán 2010, across from Club de Golf, ☎ 74/84–30–84) shows the works of renowned international and Mexican artists, including Calder, Dalí, Siqueiros, and Tamayo, and a large line of Mexican crafts. **Galería Rudic** (⊠ Vicente Yañez Pinzón 9, across from Continental Plaza and adjoining the Jardín des Artistes restaurant, ☎ 74/84–10–04) is one of the best galleries in town, with a good collection of top contemporary Mexican artists, including Armando Amaya, Leonardo Nierman, Gastón Cabrera, Trinidad Osorio, and Casiano García.

Pal Kepenyes (⊠ Guitarrón 140, ☎ 74/84–37–38) gets good press for his sculpture and jewelry, on display in his workshop. The whimsical, painted papier-mâché and giant ceramic sculpture of **Sergio Bustamente** (⊠ Costera Miguel Alemán 120–9, across from Fiesta American Condesa hotel, ☎ 74/84–49–92) can be seen at his gallery.

Boutiques
St. Germaine (⊠ Costera Miguel Alemán, outside the entrance to Fiesta Americana Condesa hotel, ☎ 74/87–37–12; ⊠ Costa Club, Costera Miguel Alemán 123, ☎ 74/85–25–15) carries a sensational line of swimsuits for equally sensational bodies. **Nautica** (⊠ Plaza Bahía, ☎ 74/85–75–11; smaller shop at ⊠ Las Brisas hotel, Carretera Escénica 5255, ☎ 74/84–16–50) is stocked with stylish casual clothing for men. **Armando's** (⊠ Costera Miguel Alemán at the Hyatt Regency, ☎ 74/69–12–34; ⊠ Costera Miguel Alemán 1252–7, in La Torre de Acapulco, ☎ 74/84–51–11) carries its own line of women's dresses, jackets, and vests with a Mexican flavor, as well as some interesting Luisa Conti accessories. **Pit** (⊠ Princess arcade, Playa Revolcadero, ☎ 74/69–10–00) has a smashing line of beach cover-ups and hand-painted straw hats, as well as bathing suits and light dresses.

Custom-Designed Clothes
Esteban's (⊠ Costera Miguel Alemán 2010, across from Club de Golf, ☎ 74/84–30–84) is the most glamorous shop in Acapulco, boasting a clientele of international celebrities and many of the important local families. Esteban's made-to-order clothes are formal and fashionable; his opulent evening dresses range from $200 to $3,000, although daytime dresses average $100. There's a men's clothing section on the second floor. If you scour the sale racks, you can find some items marked down as much as 80%. For a pick-me-up, try the store's café, which serves coffee and pastries.

Handicrafts
AFA (⊠ Horacio Nelson and James Cook, near Hyatt Regency, ☎ 74/84–80–39) is a huge shop offering a vast selection of jewelry, handicrafts, clothing, and leather goods from all over Mexico. **Alebrijes & Caracoles** (⊠ Plaza Bahía, ☎ 74/85–04–90) comprises two shops designed to look like flea-market stalls. Top-quality merchandise is on display, including papier-mâché fruits and vegetables, Christmas ornaments, wind chimes, and brightly painted wooden animals from Oaxaca. **Marielena**(⊠ Hyatt Regency, Costera Miguel Alemán 1, ☎ 74/69–12–34, ext. 8986) has handcrafted candles, dressy women's cocktail jackets, and sculptures of the human form by Mexican Imelda Bravo.

Silver and Jewelry
Antoinette (⊠ Princess arcade, Playa Revolcadero, ☎ 74/69–10–00) has gold jewelry of impeccable design, set with precious and semiprecious stones, that you wouldn't be surprised to find on Fifth Avenue. Also on display is Emilia Castillo's line of brightly colored porcelain ware,

inlaid with silver fish, stars, and birds. It's worth going to window-shop, even if you know you won't buy anything.

Suzett's (✉ Hyatt Regency, Costera Miguel Alemán 1, ☎ 74/69–12–34), a tony shop that's been around for years, has a very laudable selection of gold jewelry.

Tane (✉ Hyatt Regency, Costera Miguel Alemán 1, ☎ 74/84–63–48; ✉ Las Brisas hotel, Carretera Escénica 5255, ☎ 74/81–08–16) carries small selections of the exquisite flatware, jewelry, and objets d'art created by one of Mexico's most prestigious (and expensive) silversmiths.

SIDE TRIP TO TAXCO, THE SILVER CITY

275 km (170 mi) north of Acapulco.

This is Mexico's most medieval-looking city—marvelously preserved colonial buildings nuzzle cobblestone streets that wind up and down the foothills of the Sierra Madre in the state of Guerrero. You could say that its white stucco buildings, red-tile roofs, and quaint inns and cafés make it a centuries-old Mexican town at its best—which is why the government declared the city a national monument in 1928. The city Taxco (pronounced *tahss*-ko) is a living work of art. For centuries its silver mines drew foreign mining companies here. Now its charm, mild temperatures, abundant sunshine, flowers, and silversmiths make Taxco a popular getaway.

Hernán Cortés discovered Taxco's mines in 1522. The silver rush lasted until the next century, when excitement tapered off. Then, in the 1700s, a Frenchman who Mexicanized his name to José de la Borda discovered a rich lode that revitalized the town's silver industry and made him exceedingly wealthy. After Borda, however, Taxco's importance faded, until the 1930s and the arrival of William G. Spratling, a writer-architect from New Orleans. Enchanted by Taxco and convinced of its potential as a silver center, Spratling set up an apprentice shop, where his artistic talent and his fascination with pre-Columbian design combined to produce silver jewelry and other artifacts that soon earned Taxco its worldwide reputation as the Silver City. Spratling's inspiration lives on in his students and their descendants, many of whom are the city's current silversmiths.

⑩ The **Iglesia de San Sebastián y Santa Prisca** has dominated Plaza Borda—one of the busiest and most colorful town squares in all Mexico—since the 18th century. Usually just called Santa Prisca, it was built by French silver magnate José de la Borda in thanks to the Almighty for his having literally stumbled upon a rich silver vein. The style of the church—sort of Spanish Baroque meets rococo—is known as churrigueresque, and its pale pink exterior is a stunning surprise. This is one of Mexico's most beautiful colonial churches and Taxco's most important landmark. ✉ *Southwest side of Plaza Borda.*

NEED A BREAK?
Around Plaza Borda are several *neverías* (ice cream stands) where you can treat yourself to ice cream in exotic flavors such as tequila, corn, avocado, or coconut. **Bar Paco**, directly across the street from Santa Prisca, is a Taxco institution; its terrace is the perfect vantage point for watching the comings and goings on the zócalo while sipping a margarita or a beer.

⑪ The former home of William G. Spratling houses the **Spratling Museum.** This small gallery explains the working of colonial mines and displays Spratling's collection of pre-Columbian artifacts. ✉ *Porfirio Delgado 1,* ☎ *7/622–1660.* 🎟 *$2.* ☉ *Tues.–Sat. 10–5, Sun. 9–3.*

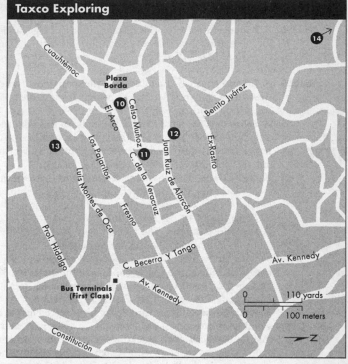

Taxco Exploring

⑫ **Casa Humboldt** was named for the German adventurer Alexander von Humboldt, who stayed here in 1803. The Moorish-style 18th-century house has a finely detailed facade. It now houses a wonderful little museum of colonial art. ⊠ *Calle Juan Ruíz de Alarcón 6,* ☎ *7/622–5501.* ☑ *$1.50.* ۞ *Tues.–Sat. 10–5, Sun. 10–3.*

⑬ If you want to experience a typical Mexican market, with everything from peanuts to electrical appliances, the **Mercado Municipal** is worth a visit. Saturday and Sunday mornings, when locals from surrounding towns come with their produce and crafts, the market spills out onto the surrounding streets. You'll find it directly down the hill from the Church of San Sebastián and Santa Prisca.

⑭ The largest caverns in Mexico, the **Grutas de Cacahuamilpa** (Caves of Cacahuamilpa) are about 15 minutes northeast of Taxco. These 15 large chambers encompass 12 km (7½ mi) of geological formations. All the caves are illuminated, and a tour takes around two hours. ☑ *$3 (includes tour).*

Dining and Lodging

Gastronomes can find everything from tagliatelle to iguana in Taxco restaurants, and meals are much less expensive than in Acapulco. Dress is casual, but less so than at Acapulco resorts. There are several categories of hotel to choose from within Taxco's two types: the small inns nestled on the hills skirting the zócalo and the larger, more modern hotels on the outskirts of town.

$$–$$$ ✕ **El Mural.** This is one of the nicest restaurants in town, with seating
   ★   indoors or on a poolside terrace, where there's a view not only of a Juan O'Gorman mural but of the stunning Santa Prisca church. The chef prepares classic international favorites—filet mignon and surf and turf—and some delicious Mexican specialties, including cilantro

soup, and huitlacoche crepes. ⊠ *Posada de la Misión, Cerro de la Misión 32,* ☎ *7/622–2198. AE, MC, V.*

$$–$$$ ✕ **Pagaduría del Rey.** This restaurant has a long-standing reputation
★ for international fare served in comfortable surroundings. ⊠ *Calle H. Colegio Militar 8 (Col. Cerro de la Bermeja, south of town),* ☎ *7/622– 3467. MC, V.*

$$–$$$ ✕ **Toni's.** Prime rib and lobster are the specialties. There's also a great view and a romantic setting. ⊠ *Monte Taxco Hotel,* ☎ *7/622–1300. AE, MC, V. Closed Sun.*

$$ ✕ **Señor Costilla.** That's right, the name of this whimsical restaurant translates as "Mr. Ribs." The Taxco outpost of the zany Anderson chain serves barbecued ribs and chops in a restaurant with great balcony seating. ⊠ *Plaza Borda 1,* ☎ *7/622–3215. MC, V.*

$–$$ ✕ **Cielito Lindo.** This charming restaurant has a Mexican-international menu. Give the Mexican specialties a try—for example, *pollo en pipian verde* (chicken simmered in a mild, pumpkin seed–based sauce). ⊠ *Plaza Borda 14,* ☎ *7/622–0603. MC, V.*

$ ✕ **Hostería el Adobe.** The lack of view (there are only two window
★ tables) is more than made up for by the original decor—for example, hanging lamps made of a cluster of masks—and the excellent food. Favorites include garlic-and-egg soup and the *queso adobe,* fried cheese on a bed of potato skins, covered with a green tomatillo sauce. ⊠ *Plazuela de San Juan 13,* ☎ *7/622–1416. MC, V.*

$ ✕ **Pizza Pazza.** All nine varieties of pizza served here are tasty, but for
★ a real treat order the *pozole norteño,* a spicy pork and hominy soup that comes with pork cracklings, chopped onion, lemon, and avocado. This cozy place, with scotch-plaid tablecloths and flowering plants, overlooks Plaza Borda. ⊠ *Calle del Arco 1,* ☎ *7/622–5500. Reservations not accepted. MC, V.*

$ ✕ **Santa Fe.** Mexican family-type cooking at its best is served in this simple place. Puebla-style mole, Cornish hen in garlic butter, and enchiladas in green or red chili sauce are among the tasty offerings. There's a daily *comida corrida* (fixed price) meal for $4. ⊠ *Hidalgo 2,* ☎ *7/622–1170. AE, MC, V.*

$$ 🏨 **De la Borda.** Long a Taxco favorite, De la Borda is a bit worn, but the rooms are large and comfortable and the staff couldn't be more hospitable. Ask for a room overlooking town. There's a restaurant, and many bus tours stay here overnight. ⊠ *Apdo. 6, Cerro del Pedregal 2, 40200,* ☎ *7/622–0025,* FAX *7/622–0617. 98 rooms, 4 suites. Restaurant, bar, pool, free parking. AE, MC, V.*

$$ 🏨 **Monte Taxco.** A colonial style predominates at this hotel, which has a knockout view, a funicular, three restaurants, a disco, and nightly entertainment. It *is* a few miles from town, so plan to take taxis to get back and forth. ⊠ *Apdo. 84, Lomas de Taxco, 40210,* ☎ *7/622–1300,* FAX *7/622–1428. 153 rooms, 6 suites, 32 villas. 3 restaurants, 9-hole golf course, 3 tennis courts, horseback riding, dance club. AE, DC, MC, V.*

$$ 🏨 **Posada de la Misión.** Laid out like a colonial-style village, this hotel
★ is within walking distance of town. Rooms range from standard doubles to two-bedroom suites with kitchenettes, fireplaces, and terraces. The pool area is adorned with murals by the noted Mexican artist Juan O'Gorman. Rates include breakfast. ⊠ *Apdo. 88, Cerro de la Misión 32, 40230,* ☎ *7/622–0063,* FAX *7/622–2198. 120 rooms, 30 suites. Restaurant, bar, pool, golf privileges, tennis court, dance club. AE, DC, MC, V.*

$ 🏨 **Agua Escondida.** Popular with some regular visitors to Taxco, this small hotel has simple rooms decorated with Mexican-style furnishings. ⊠ *Guillermo Spratling 4, 40200,* ☎ *7/622–1166,* FAX *7/622– 1306. 50 rooms. Restaurant, bar, café, pool, free parking. MC, V.*

$ ⊞ **Los Arcos.** If you're looking for an affordable place to stay in central Taxco, Los Arcos has basic rooms that surround a pleasant patio. ⊠ *Calle Juan Ruíz de Alarcón 4, 40200,* ☎ *7/622–1836,* ⅺⅺ *7/622–7982. 21 rooms. No credit cards.*

$ ⊞ **Posada de los Castillo.** This in-town inn is straightforward, clean, and good for the price. The Emilia Castillo silver shop is off the lobby. ⊠ *Juan Ruíz de Alarcón 7, 40200,* ☎ *7/622–1396. 14 rooms. MC, V.*

$ ⊞ **Posada de San Javier.** Set somewhat haphazardly around a garden
★ with a pool and a wishing well is this sprawling, very private establishment. In addition to the rooms, there are seven one-bedroom apartments with living rooms and kitchenettes (generally monopolized by wholesale silver buyers). ⊠ *Estacas 32 or Exrastro 6, 40200,* ☎ *7/622–3177,* ⅺⅺ *7/622–2351. 18 rooms, 7 apartments. Pool. No credit cards.*

$ ⊞ **Rancho Taxco-Victoria.** This hotel is under the same management as De la Borda (☞ *above*). Like De la Borda, it is past its prime but exudes a certain charm. The rooms are always freshly painted, and the Mexican decor is simple but attractive. There's also the requisite splendid view. ⊠ *Apdo. 83, Carlos J. Nibbi 5, 40200,* ☎ *7/622–0210,* ⅺⅺ *7/622–0010. 60 rooms, 4 suites. Restaurant, bar, pool. AE, MC, V.*

Nightlife and the Arts

FESTIVALS

Taxco's biggest single cultural event is the Jornadas Alarconianos—which honors one of Mexico's greatest dramatists with theater, dance, and concerts (dates change every year). But it is also known for its abundance of fiestas, which are an integral part of the town's character. These fiestas provide an opportunity to honor almost every saint in heaven with music, dancing, marvelous fireworks (Taxco is Mexico's fireworks capital), and lots of fun. The people of Taxco demonstrate their pyrotechnic skills with set pieces—wondrous blazing "castles" made of bamboo. (Note: Expect high occupancy at local hotels and inns during fiestas.)

January 18–20, the feast of Santa Prisca and San Sebastián, the town's patron saints, is celebrated with music and fireworks.

Holy Week, from Palm Sunday to Easter Sunday, brings processions and events that blend Christian and Indian traditions; the dramas involve hundreds of participants, images of Christ, and, for one particular procession, brown-hooded penitents who flagellate themselves with boughs of thorns following a colonial custom. Most events are centered on Plaza Borda and the Santa Prisca Church. You must reserve a hotel months in advance for Easter week.

September 29, Saint Michael's Day (Dia de San Miguel), is celebrated with regional dances and pilgrimages to the Chapel of Saint Michael the Archangel, on Calle José María Morelos.

In **early November,** on the Monday following the November 1–2 Day of the Dead celebrations, the entire town takes off to a nearby hill for the Fiesta de los Jumil. The *jumil* is a crawling insect, said to taste strongly of iodine, that is considered a great delicacy. Purists eat them alive, but others prefer them stewed, fried, or combined with chili in a hot sauce.

In **late November or early December,** the National Silver Fair (Feria Nacional de la Plata) draws hundreds of artisans from around the world for a variety of displays, concerts, exhibitions, and contests.

NIGHTLIFE

You should satisfy your appetite for fun after dark in Acapulco. Taxco has a few discos, a couple of bars, and some entertainment, but the range is limited.

Still, you might enjoy spending an evening perched on a chair on a balcony or in one of the cafés surrounding the Plaza Borda. Two traditional favorites are the **Bar Paco** (⊠ Plaza Borda 12, ☎ 7/622–0064) and **Bertha's** (⊠ Plaza Borda 9, ☎ 7/622–0172), Taxco's oldest bar, where a tequila, lime, and club soda concoction called a Bertha is the house specialty. It is supposedly the forerunner of today's margarita cocktail. In addition, some of the town's best restaurants have music on weekends.

Or immerse yourself in the thick of things, especially on Sunday evening, by settling in on a wrought-iron bench on the zócalo to watch the action and fellow people-watchers.

There are a few discos, including **La Barra** (⊠ Av. de los Plateros 12, ☎ no phone). Much of Taxco's nighttime activity is at the Monte Taxco hotel's **Windows** discotheque (⊠ Lomas de Taxco) on weekends. Or, on Saturday night, the hotel has a buffet and a terrific fireworks display. **La Pachanga** discotheque (⊠ Cerro de la Misión 32) at Posada de la Misión is open nightly and is popular with townsfolk and tourists.

Outdoor Activities and Sports

You can play golf or tennis, swim, and ride horses at a few hotels around Taxco. Call to see if the facilities are open to nonguests, because the policy seems to change from time to time. Bullfights are occasionally held in the small town of Acmixtla, 6 km (4 mi) from Taxco. Ask at your hotel about the schedule.

Shopping

CRAFTS

Lacquered gourds and boxes from the town of Olinalá and masks, bowls, straw baskets, bark paintings, and many other handcrafted items native to the state of Guerrero are available from strolling vendors and are displayed on the cobblestones at "sidewalk boutiques."

Arnoldo (⊠ Palma 2, ☎ 7/622–1272) has an interesting collection of ceremonial masks; originals come with a certificate of authenticity as well as a written description of origin and use. For $100 per person, Arnoldo will take you on a tour of the villages where the dances using the masks are performed on February 2, December 12, and May 15.

D'Elsa (⊠ Plazuela de San Juan 13, ☎ 7/622–1683), owned by Elsa Ruíz de Figueroa, carries a selection of native-inspired clothing for women, and a wide and well-chosen selection of arts and handicrafts.

Sunday is market day, which means that artisans from surrounding villages descend on the town, as do visitors from Mexico City. It can get crowded, but if you find a seat on a bench in **Plaza Borda,** you're set to watch the show and peruse the merchandise that will inevitably be brought to you.

SILVER

Most of the people who visit Taxco come with silver in mind. Many of the more than 1,000 silver shops carry almost identical merchandise, although a few are noted for their creativity. Three types are available: sterling, which is always stamped .925 (925 parts in 1,000) and is the most expensive (and desirable); plated silver; and the inexpensive alpaca, which is also known as German or nickel silver. Sterling pieces are usually priced by weight according to world silver prices. Fine workmanship will add to the cost. Work is also done with semiprecious stones.

Bangles start at $4, and bracelets range from $10 to $250. William Spratling, Andrés Mejía, and Emilia Castillo, daughter of renowned silversmith Antonio Castillo, are some of the more famous design names. Designs range from traditional bulky necklaces (often inlaid with turquoise) to streamlined bangles and chunky earrings. Just about every hotel has an in-house silver shop or one next door, so you don't have to go far to shop.

Alvaro Cuevas (⊠ Plaza Borda 1, ☎ 7/622–1878) has fine workmanship to match its fine designs.

The stunning pieces at **Galería de Arte en Plata Andrés** (⊠ Av. John F. Kennedy 28, ☎ 7/622–3778) are created by the talented Andrés Mejía.

Emilia Castillo (⊠ Juan Ruíz de Alarcón 7, ☎ 7/622–3471) is the most famous and decidedly one of the most exciting silver shops; it's especially renowned for innovative designs and for combining silver with porcelain (Neiman Marcus sells the wares in its U.S. stores).

Talleres de los Ballesteros (⊠ Florida 14, ☎ 7/622–1076) and their branch, Joyería San Agustín (⊠ Cuauhtémoc 4, ☎ 7/622–3416), carry a large collection of well-crafted silver jewelry and serving pieces. They have three additional branches in Mexico City and one in San Antonio, Texas.

Spratling Ranch (⊠ south of town on the Mexico–Acapulco highway, Km 177, ☎ 7/622–6108) is where the heirs of William Spratling turn out designs using his original molds.

Taxco A to Z

ARRIVING AND DEPARTING

By Bus. First-class **Estrella de Oro** buses leave Acapulco for Taxco five times a day from 7 AM to 6:40 PM from the Terminal Central de Autobuses de Primera Clase (⊠ Av. Cuauhtémoc 158, ☎ 74/85–87–05). The cost for the approximately 4½-hour ride is about $12 one-way for first-class service. The Taxco terminal (☎ 7/622–0648) is at Avenida John F. Kennedy 126. **Sistema Estrella Blanca** buses depart Acapulco several times a day from the Terminal de Autobuses (⊠ Ejido 47, ☎ 74/69–20–28). Purchase your tickets at least one day in advance at the terminal. The one-way ticket is about $11 for first-class service. Buses depart from Taxco (☎ 7/622–0131) at Avenida John F. Kennedy 104.

By Car. It takes about three hours to drive to Taxco from Acapulco, using the expensive (about $28) toll road. It is common practice to take an overnight tour. Check with your hotel for references and prices.

GETTING AROUND

Because of the byways, alleys, and tiny streets, maneuvering anything bigger than your two feet through Taxco will be difficult. Fortunately, almost everything of interest is within walking distance of the zócalo. Wear sensible shoes for negotiating the hilly streets. Minibuses travel along preset routes and charge only a few cents, and Volkswagen "bugs" provide inexpensive (average $1) taxi transportation. Taxco's altitude is 5,800 ft, so if you have come from sea level, take it easy on your first day.

TELEPHONES

Taxco's area code, used when dialing a Taxco number from outside the city, has been changed from 762 to just 7. The 62 has been incorporated into the local phone number, which now has seven digits.

VISITOR INFORMATION

The **tourism office** (⊠ Av. de los Plateros 1, ☎ 7/622–6616) is open weekdays 9–2 and 5–8.

ACAPULCO A TO Z

Arriving and Departing

By Bus

Bus service from Mexico City to Acapulco is excellent. First-class buses, which leave every hour on the hour from the Tasqueña station, are comfortable and in good condition. The trip takes 5½ hours, and a one-way ticket costs about $22. There is also deluxe service, called *Servicio Diamante,* with airplanelike reclining seats, refreshments, rest rooms, air-conditioning, movies, and hostess service. The deluxe buses leave four times a day, also from the Tasqueña station, and cost about $29. *Plus* service (regular reclining seats, air-conditioning, and a rest room) costs $25.

By Car

The trip to Acapulco from Mexico City on the old road takes about six hours. A privately built and run four-lane toll road connecting Mexico City with Acapulco is expensive (about $38 one way) but well maintained, and it cuts driving time between the two cities to 4½ hours. Many people go via Taxco, which can be reached from either road.

By Plane

The **Juan N. Alvarez International Airport** (☎ 74/66–94–34) is located about 20 minutes east of the city. From the United States, **American** (☎ 74/81–01–61) has nonstop flights from Dallas, with connecting service from Chicago and New York. **Continental** (☎ 01–800/90–050) has nonstop service from Houston. **Delta's** (☎ 74/66–90–32) direct flights are from Los Angeles and Atlanta. **Mexicana's** (☎ 74/84–12–15) flights from Chicago and Los Angeles stop in Mexico City before continuing on to Acapulco. **Aeroméxico's** (☎ 74/85–16–00) flight from New York to Acapulco stops in Mexico City. The carrier also has one-stop or connecting service from Atlanta, Chicago, Houston, Los Angeles, New York, Miami, and Orlando.

From New York via Dallas, flying time is 4½ hours; from Chicago, 4¼ hours; from Los Angeles, 3½ hours.

BETWEEN THE AIRPORT AND CITY CENTER

Private taxis aren't permitted to carry passengers from the airport to town, so most people rely on **Transportes Aeropuerto** (☎ 74/62–10–95), a special airport taxi service. The system looks confusing, but there are dozens of helpful English-speaking staff members to help you figure out which taxi to take.

Look for the name of your hotel and its zone number on the overhead sign on the walkway in front of the terminal. Then go to the desk designated with that zone number and buy a ticket for an airport taxi. The ride from the airport to the hotel zone on the strip costs about $5.50 per person for the *colectivo* (shared minivan) and starts at $22 for a nonshared cab, depending on your destination. The drivers are usually helpful and will often take you to hotels that aren't on their list. Tips are optional. The journey into town takes 20–30 minutes.

By Ship

Many cruises include Acapulco as part of their itinerary. Most originate from Los Angeles. Cruise operators include **Celebrity Cruises** (☎ 800/437–3111), **Crystal P&O** (☎ 310/785–9300), **Cunard Line** (☎ 800/528–6273), **Krystal Cruises** (☎ 800/446–6640), **Princess Cruises** (☎ 800/421–0522), and **Royal Caribbean** (☎ 800/327–6700). Bookings are generally handled through a travel agent.

Getting Around

Getting around in Acapulco is quite simple. You can walk to many places, and the bus costs less than 50¢. Taxis cost less than they do in the United States, so most tourists quickly become avid taxi takers.

By Bus

The buses tourists use the most are those that go from Puerto Marqués to Caleta and stop at the fairly conspicuous metal bus stops along the way. New yellow air-conditioned tourist buses, marked ACAPULCO, now run about every 30 minutes along this route. If you want to go from the zócalo to the Costera, catch the bus that says LA BASE (the naval base near the Hyatt Regency). This bus detours through Old Acapulco and returns to the Costera just east of the Ritz Hotel. If you want to follow the Costera for the entire route, take the bus marked HORNOS. Buses to Pie de la Cuesta or Puerto Marqués say so on the front. The Puerto Marqués bus runs about every 10 minutes and is always crowded.

By Car

If you plan to visit some of the more remote beaches or decide to visit Taxco on your own, renting a car is convenient but fairly expensive. Prices start at about $40 a day for a Volkswagen sedan without air-conditioning. Don't expect a full tank; your car will have just about enough gas to get you to the nearest Pemex station.

By Horse and Carriage

Buggy rides up and down the Costera are available evenings. There are two routes: from Parque Papagayo to the zócalo and from Playa Condesa to the naval base. Each costs about $10 (be sure to agree on the price beforehand).

By Taxi

How much you pay depends on what type of taxi you get. The most expensive are hotel taxis. A price list that all drivers adhere to is posted in hotel lobbies. Fares in town are usually about $2.50 to $6; to go from downtown to the Princess Hotel is about $11; to go from the hotel zone to Playa Caleta is about $6. Hotel taxis are by far the roomiest and are kept in the best condition.

Cabs that cruise the streets usually charge by zone. There is a minimum charge of $2; the fare should still be less than it would be at a hotel. Some taxis that cruise have hotel or restaurant names stenciled on the side but aren't affiliated with an establishment. Before you go anywhere by cab, find out what the price should be and agree with the driver on a fare.

A normal—i.e., Mexican-priced—fare is about $2 to go from the zócalo to the International Center. Rates are about 50% higher at night, and although tipping isn't expected, Mexicans usually leave small change.

You can also hire a taxi by the hour or the day. Prices vary from about $10 an hour for a hotel taxi to $8 an hour for a street taxi. Never let a taxi driver decide where you should eat or shop, since many get kickbacks from some of the smaller stores and restaurants.

Contacts and Resources

Car Rental

Car-rental agencies include **Hertz** (☎ 74/85–89–47), **Avis** (☎ 74/62–00–85), **Dollar** (☎ 74/66–94–93), **Quick** (☎ 74/86–34–20), and **Budget** (☎ 74/86–89–55). All have offices at the airport.

Consulates

U.S. Consulate (✉ Continental Plaza Hotel, Costera Miguel Alemán 121–14, ☎ 74/84–03–00); **Canadian Consulate** (✉ Marbella Mall, Suite 23, ☎ 74/84–13–05).

Doctors and Dentists

Your hotel can locate an English-speaking doctor, but they don't come cheap—house calls are about $100. The U.S. consular representative has a list of doctors and dentists, but it's against the consulate's policy to recommend anyone in particular.

E-Mail

More and more Internet facilities are cropping up in Acapulco to keep you connected while traveling. **Smart PCs** (✉ Costera Miguel Alemán 112–4, ☎ 74/84–28–77) is in a shopping arcade next to Carlos 'n' Charlie's restaurant. **iNternet Cyber Café** (✉ Horacio Nelson 40–7A, ☎ 74/84–82–54) is near the Marbella Hotel on the Costera Miguel Alemán.

Emergencies

Police (☎ 74/85–06–50). **Red Cross** (☎ 74/85–41–00). Two reliable hospitals are **Hospital Privado Magallanes** (✉ Wilfrido Massiue 2, ☎ 74/85–65–44) and **Hospital del Pacífico** (✉ Fraile y Nao 4, ☎ 74/87–71–80).

English-Language Bookstores

English-language books and periodicals can be found at **Sanborns** (☞ Department Stores and Supermarkets *in* Shopping, *above*), a reputable American-style department-store chain, and at the newsstands in some of the larger hotels. Many small newsstands carry the Mexico City *News* and the Mexico City *Times*.

Guided Tours

ORIENTATION TOURS

There are organized tours everywhere in Acapulco, from the red-light district to the lagoon. Tours to Mexican fiestas in the evening or the markets in the daytime are easy to arrange. Tour operators have offices around town and desks in many of the large hotels.

If your hotel can't arrange a tour, contact **Mexico Travel Advisors** at La Torre de Acapulco (✉ Costera Miguel Alemán 1252, ☎ 74/84–74–00) or **Viajes Acuario** (✉ Costera Miguel Alemán 186–3, ☎ 74/85–61–00).

SUNSET CRUISES

The famous cliff divers at La Quebrada (☞ Acapulco *in* Exploring, *above*) give one performance in the afternoon and four performances every night. For about $30 a person, **Divers de México** (☎ 74/82–13–98) organizes (December–April only) sunset champagne cruises that provide a fantastic view of the spectacle from the water. For reservations, call or stop by the office downtown near the *Fiesta* and *Bonanza* yachts. The *Fiesta* (☎ 74/82–49–47) runs cruises at 7 PM on Tuesday, Thursday, and Saturday for about $60. The *Bonanza*'s (☎ 74/82–49–47) sunset cruise, with open bar (domestic drinks) and live and disco music, costs about $12. All boats leave from downtown near the zócalo at 4:30. Many hotels and shops sell tickets, as do the ticket sellers on the waterfront.

Telephones

Acapulco now incorporates the 4 from the 74 area code for all calls within the city. The change doesn't affect dialing Acapulco numbers from elsewhere in the country.

Travel Agencies

American Express (✉ La Gran Plaza shopping center, Costera Miguel Alemán 1628, Suites 7–9, ☎ 74/69–11–66); **Viajes Wagon-Lits** (✉ Westin Las Brisas, Carretera Escénica 5255, ☎ 74/84–16–50 ext. 392).

Visitor Information

Procuraduría del Turista (✉ Acapulco International Center, Costera Miguel Alemán, ☎ 74/84–44–16), the State Attorney General's Tourist Office, is open 9 AM–11 PM daily. It's also the place to report a crime or voice a complaint.

10 OAXACA

The geographic, ethnic, and culinary
diversity of Oaxaca has made the state a
favorite of Mexico aficionados. The majority
of residents are descendants of native
Zapotec and Mixtec peoples, who centuries
ago built the Monte Albán and Mitla
complexes near Oaxaca City. Their
contemporary crafts and festivals are
extremely colorful. Although less exotic than
Oaxaca City, the state's coastal
developments of Puerto Escondido and
Bahías de Huatulco are beloved by surfers
and beach bums.

Updated by
Gina Hyams

OAXACA (pronounced woh-*hah*-kah) is both a pre-Columbian and a colonial treasure. The state has a vast geographic and ethnic diversity. Together with neighboring Chiapas, Oaxaca has the largest Indian population in the country, which explains its richness and variety in handicrafts, folklore, culture, and gastronomy. Two out of three Oaxaqueños descend from Zapotec or Mixtec Indians, whose villages dot the valleys, mountainsides, and coastal lowlands. They come from one of 16 distinct linguistic groups and speak 52 dialects—each very different from the other. If they speak Spanish—which many now do—it is a second language to them.

Indigenous tribes flourished in the area thousands of years ago, and the archaeological ruins of Monte Albán, Mitla, and Yagul are among the vivid remnants of their cultures. Located within a 40-km (25-mi) radius of the city of Oaxaca, the ruins bear witness to highly religious, artistic, and advanced civilizations.

The Zapotec and Mixtec civilizations were conquered by the irrepressible Aztecs, who in the 15th century gave Oaxaca its name: *Huaxyaca*. In the Nahuatl language it probably means "by the acacia grove," referring to the location of the Aztec military base. Then came the Spanish conquest in 1528. The Spanish monarch Charles V gave Hernán Cortés the title of *Marqués del Valle de Oaxaca* as a reward for his conquest of Mexico. Cortés preferred to live elsewhere, so an estate was never built on the lands conferred with the title, but Cortés's descendants kept the property until Mexico's bloody 1910 Revolution.

Oaxaca's legacy to Mexican politics has been two presidents: Benito Juárez, the first full-blooded Indian to become chief of state, and Porfirio Díaz, a military dictator who declared himself president-for-life. Juárez, a Zapotec, was a sheepherder from San Pablo Guelatao, a settlement about 64 km (40 mi) north of Oaxaca. As a child he spoke only his native Zapotec tongue. Often referred to as Mexico's Abraham Lincoln, Juárez was trained for the clergy but later studied law and entered politics. He was elected governor of the state (1847), chief justice of the Supreme Court of Mexico (1857), and then president (1858–72), defeating a French effort in 1867 to install Hapsburg Archduke Ferdinand Maximilian of Austria as emperor. Porfirio Díaz, one of Juárez's generals, seized the presidency in his 1877 coup and held office until he was kicked out in 1911.

Oaxaca sits on the vast, fertile, 1½-km (1 mi) high plateau of the Oaxaca Valley, encircled by the majestic Sierra Madre del Sur mountain range. Mexico's fifth largest state, it lies in the southwest, bordered by the states of Chiapas to the east, Veracruz and Puebla to the north, and Guerrero—whose touristic claims to fame are Acapulco and Ixtapa—to the west. The south of Oaxaca state spans 509 km (316 mi) of lush tropical Pacific coast with magnificent beaches. Until recently, these beaches had been relatively unknown and unexploited, except for the long-established small fishing town and seaside hideaway of Puerto Escondido and the even smaller town of Puerto Ángel. But now Bahías de Huatulco (Huatulco Bays), 125 km (77 mi) west of Puerto Escondido, is on the map—thanks to the government working to turn it into a world-class resort.

Note: Assaults and highway banditry have increased throughout Mexico, as the continuing economic crisis exacerbates long-standing poverty. First-class buses are sometimes the target of highway robbery, especially the route between Juchitan, on the Oaxaca coast, and San Cristóbal de las Casas in Chiapas. Night buses are most vulnerable. Although this is indeed cause for concern, occurrences are infrequent.

Pleasures and Pastimes

Dining

One highlight of Oaxaca is its traditional cookery, one of the finest and most elaborate in all Mexico. Oaxaca is known as "the land of seven moles" because of its seven distinct kinds of multispiced mole sauces. One of them, mole *negro,* rivals that of neighboring Puebla in thickness and flavor because of the outstanding local chocolate from which it is made. Tamales, either sweet or stuffed with chicken, are another treat. The home- and factory-made mezcal, the alcoholic drink derived of the blue agave cactus, differs in flavor with each maker and can be as high as 80 proof. The cream variety, thick and sweet, is flavored with orange, lime, or other fruits or nuts.

Oaxacan cuisine—the cheeses, mole sauces, and meats that make dining in the capital memorable—is sadly in short supply along the coast, where seafood is your best bet. Huatulco's restaurants are getting better, and some of the places in Puerto Escondido are very good. With a few exceptions, cooking in Puerto Ángel is mediocre. Dress is casual and reservations are unnecessary at all restaurants unless otherwise noted. Prices are quite inexpensive throughout the state, with the exception of the Huatulco resort.

CATEGORY	COST*
$$$$	over $15
$$$	$10–$15
$$	$5–$10
$	under $5

per person for a three-course meal, excluding drinks and tip

Lodging

Oaxaca City has no luxury resorts, but it does have some magnificently restored properties, including a 16th-century convent and dozens of smaller, moderately priced accommodations, most downtown. These smaller hotels are very popular around December and January and require six months to a year advance booking. Day of the Dead celebrations (October 31–November 2) and Holy Week are also times of high occupancy, so plan accordingly.

Hotel rates vary considerably in the coastal area. In Puerto Escondido and Puerto Ángel, most of the accommodations fall into the $$ or $ price range. Those in Huatulco, where you'll find luxury compounds, are considerably pricier, with the exclusive Quinta Real topping the scale. The high season along the coast runs from mid-December through Holy Week; rates increase 20% or more during this time. Budget accommodations are scarce in Huatulco, although more moderately priced rooms are becoming available, especially in La Crucecita.

CATEGORY	COST*
$$$$	over $120
$$$	$70–$120
$$	$30–$70
$	under $30

All prices are for a standard double room, including 17% tax.

Shopping

Oaxaca City is a magnet for both *mestizos* (people of mixed European and Indian descent) and indigenous people who live in the valley and nearby mountains. They come to town to buy and sell, especially on Saturday. The market might not be as colorful as it was in D. H. Lawrence's *Mornings in Mexico,* but it is an authentic, exotic spectacle. El Central de Abastos is the largest Indian market in Mexico, and only Michoacán and Chiapas have Oaxaca's variety and quality of crafts. Expect hectic activity and bright colors. At markets, listen for the singsong, tonal Zapotec and Mixtec languages, in which changes in the pitch of the voice change the meanings of words. In town, galleries exhibit the pottery, textiles, and fanciful wooden animals called *alebrijes* that have drawn international attention to Oaxaca's artisans.

Surfing

Oaxaca's Puerto Escondido is a household name for serious surfers who migrate to this sunny port for all-out surfing championships each year. These challenging waves have been attracting surfers from all parts of the globe since word first got out in the 1960s.

Exploring Oaxaca

Travelers tend to gravitate toward two parts of Oaxaca: Oaxaca City, the state capital, spread over a valley in the Sierra Madre mountains; and the Pacific Coast area due south of the capital.

Numbers in the text correspond to numbers in the margin and on the Oaxaca City and Oaxaca Coast maps.

Great Itineraries

If you only have three days to spend in the state, choose between Oaxaca City and the coast. Go to Puerto Escondido for unspoiled beaches and wildlife, or if you'd rather spoil yourself, consider the $1 million resorts of Huatulco. Oaxaca City is food for the soul for history and folk-art aficionados, with its magnificent colonial buildings, world-famous crafts, and the ancient temples just outside the city. For a culture-beach combination, plan at least seven days—Oaxaca City and the coast merit three days apiece.

IF YOU HAVE 3 DAYS IN OAXACA CITY

Explore downtown to see the stunning colonial monuments that have been declared World Heritage structures by the United Nations. The first day, take in the **Catedral Metropolitana de Oaxaca** ④, the **Museo de Arte Contemporáneo de Oaxaca** ⑤, the **Iglesia y Ex-Convento de Santo Domingo** ⑦, and the adjoining **Museo de las Culturas** ⑧. On Day 2, beat the crowds by catching a tour or bus right after breakfast for **Monte Albán,** the ruins of an ancient, mountaintop Zapotec capital. After returning to the city and a late lunch, enjoy coffee at the 16th-century **Ex-Convento de Santa Catalina** ⑥, now the Hotel Camino Real, and take in the patio garden with the stone tub where the nuns washed clothes. Visit the **Museo de Arte Prehispánico Rufino Tamayo** ⑩ on Day 3, then shop for regional arts and crafts at the **Central de Abastos** and the **Mercado de Artesanías.** Watch the sun set over Oaxaca from the terrace bar of the **Hotel Victoria,** just above the city proper.

IF YOU HAVE 5 DAYS IN OAXACA CITY

Follow the three-day itinerary, and on Day 4 add a visit to the Mixtec ruins at **Mitla,** stopping on the way or back to see the 2,000-year-old *ahuehuete* cypress in Tule (or, on a Sunday, to experience a country market day in **Tlacolula**); then spend the rest of the afternoon back in Oaxaca City people-watching and dining at the **zócalo** ①, or town square. Day 5, head to the villages near Oaxaca City, where beautiful handicrafts are made before your eyes. Back again in Oaxaca City, visit the **Basílica de Nuestra Señora de la Soledad** ⑪ and the boutiques full of high-quality crafts on **Calle Macedonio Alcalá.**

IF YOU HAVE 3 DAYS IN THE COASTAL BEACH RESORTS

Using **Bahías de Huatulco** ⑭–⑯ as your base, take a boat tour of the bays on the first day, followed by a spell at the beach for a blazing sunset finale. Day 2, tour the small beaches and hidden bays between Huatulco and **Puerto Escondido** ⑫. On Day 3, laze on the beach and, in late afternoon, taxi to **La Crucecita** ⑰ for some strolling, followed by dining at one of the small restaurants on the main square.

IF YOU HAVE 5 DAYS IN THE COASTAL BEACH RESORTS
Follow the three-day itinerary, then sign up for bird-watching on the **Manialtepec Lagoon** on Day 4. Day 5, head inland for a special lunch on the **Coffee Plantation tour.** If you choose laid-back **Puerto Escondido** ⑫ as your base, you might spend Day 4 touring the **Lagoon of Chacahua,** and Day 5 riding horses on the beach in the morning, then relaxing with a soothing Temescal steam bath (a pre-Hispanic–style sauna) and massage in the afternoon.

IF YOU HAVE 7 DAYS OR MORE
You can immerse yourself in the cultural treasures of **Oaxaca City** ①–⑪ and **Monte Albán,** then kick back with some sea and sun. You could spend Days 1–4 at the sights outlined in the first four days of the city itinerary. On Day 5, fly to **Bahías de Huatulco** ⑭–⑯ and, on arrival, sign up for a boat tour of the bays. Take Days 6 and 7 on the beach, or bird-watching and exploring **La Crucecita** ⑰. If you're staying longer, don't miss the **Museum of the Sea Turtle** tour.

When to Tour Oaxaca

Oaxaca celebrates Mexican holidays and its own state's fiestas with an intensity of color, tradition, and talent that attracts hordes. *El Día de Muertos* (Day of the Dead) begins with graveyard celebrations in the city and nearby villages on October 31 and ends in the cemeteries on November 2, when families partake of the favorite food of those they are honoring. The most frequently visited village is Xoxo, but many others, including Atzompa and Xochimilco, also have colorful festivities. On December 23, *Noche de Rábanos* (Night of the Radishes), the zócalo is packed with growers and artists displaying their hybrid radishes carved and arranged in tableaux that depict everything from Nativity scenes to space travel. Prizes are awarded for the biggest and the best, and competition is fierce. Other arrangements are made with *flores inmortales* ("eternal flowers"; small dried flowers) or *totomoxtl* (corn husks, pronounced to-to-*mosh*-tl). Bring plenty of film.

Oaxaca's other major celebration is the *Guelaguetza* (Zapotec for "offering" or "gift"), usually held on the last two Mondays in July. Dancers from all the mountain and coastal communities converge on the city bearing tropical fruits, coffee, and other regional products. They perform elaborate dances in authentic costumes from early morning until early afternoon at the Guelaguetza Auditorium, an open-air amphitheater in the hills just northwest of the city center.

Keep in mind that if you plan to come for these celebrations, you'll need to book far in advance.

OAXACA CITY

Oaxaca City is traditionally Indian, and although cosmopolitan touches are everywhere, women and children still peddle everything from gardenias to chili-seasoned grasshoppers, men and boys offer shoe shines around the city's many parks, and destitute families play accordions along the city streets in the hopes of acquiring spare change.

The city is officially called Oaxaca de Juárez, and it is decidedly the state's major attraction, with a population of about 800,000 and more than a million visitors a year.

Exploring Oaxaca City

The colonial heart of Oaxaca is laid out in a simple grid, with all major attractions within walking distance of one another. Most of the streets in the city's core change names once they pass the zócalo.

A Good Walk

Begin your exploration of Oaxaca at the shady **zócalo** ①, the heart of the city and its pedestrian-only main square. On the south side of the square visit the **Palacio de Gobierno** ②—step inside and check out the mural stretching from the first to the second floor. Upon leaving the government palace, go to the northwest corner of the zócalo and you will reach **El Alameda** ③, a second square that abuts the zócalo. On the east side of the Alameda, you can't miss the **Catedral Metropolitana de Oaxaca** ④. After visiting the cathedral, turn right on Avenida Independencia and left at the next corner. This puts you on the pedestrian mall on Calle Macedonio Alcalá, where you'll see restored colonial mansions in a palate of pastels, and some of Oaxaca's best galleries, shops, museums, and restaurants. It is also lively and well lighted at night, and there are frequent outdoor arts-and-crafts exhibits. After a short 1½ blocks you'll see the **Museo de Arte Contemporáneo de Oaxaca** ⑤ on your right. Continue north on Calle Macedonio Alcalá, turn right on Calle Murguía, and left on the first street, Calle 5 de Mayo. Taking up the entire block on the east side of the street is the **Ex-Convento de Santa Catalina** ⑥, now the Hotel Camino Real. Catercorner from the Camino Real is Parque Labastida, where indigenous artists sell their wares, and musicians sometimes entertain. Continue north until Calle 5 de Mayo ends at Calle Gurrión and the fabulous **Iglesia y Ex-Convento de Santo Domingo** ⑦. You can enter the church from its southern entrance, and leave via the front door onto Calle Macedonio Alcalá. Adjacent to the church is the **Museo de las Culturas** ⑧, which contains priceless artifacts taken from Tomb 7 of Monte Albán, as well as an interesting ethnographic exhibit.

Continue north on Calle Macedonio Alcalá a half block and walk up the steps of La Plazuela del Carmen Alto, where Triqui women in red, beribboned *huipiles* (tunics) sell embroidered blouses, dresses, and other handicrafts. Take a right on Calle García Vigil, and just half a block up, on the left side of the street, you'll find the **Museo Casa de Benito Juárez** ⑨, a museum honoring Oaxaca's most revered statesman. Upon leaving, return south on García Vigil 4½ blocks and turn right on Avenida Morelos. One and a half blocks up on the right, in a beautifully restored colonial mansion, is the **Museo de Arte Prehispánico Rufino Tamayo** ⑩. After seeing the museum, continue west on Morelos 2½ blocks. Descend the steps and cross the large plaza to the massive **Basílica de Nuestra Señora de la Soledad** ⑪. On the left side of the church is a small museum housing items related to Oaxaca's patron saint. Go east on Avenida Independencia past the telegraph office and you'll be back at El Alameda, where you can stop and watch the daily parade of Oaxaqueños.

Sights to See

③ **El Alameda.** This shady square is home to the Catedral Metropolitana de Oaxaca and the post office. Vendors here sell Che Guevara T-shirts, huge balloons, cassette tapes, snacks, and, during festivals, myriad souvenirs and crafts.

⑪ **Basílica de Nuestra Señora de la Soledad.** The Baroque basilica houses the statue of the Virgin of Solitude, Oaxaca's patron saint. According to legend, this statue was found in the pack of a mule that had mysteriously joined a mule train bound for Guatemala; when the mule per-

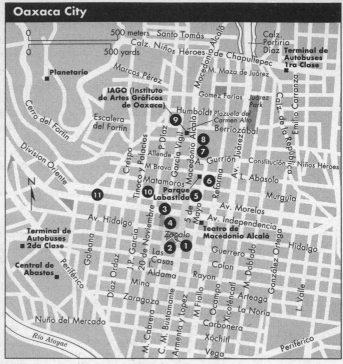

Oaxaca City

ished at the site of the present church and the statue was discovered in its pack, the event was construed as a miracle, and the church was built in 1682 to commemorate it. The Virgin, who is believed to have supernatural healing powers, remains the object of fervent piety for the devout populace. She now stands in a gilded shrine. A small museum at the side of the church displays devotional items left by the faithful over the years. ⊠ *Av. Independencia 107, at Calle Galeana,* ☏ *no phone.* ⊙ *Daily 7–7.*

④ Catedral Metropolitana de Oaxaca. Begun in 1544, the cathedral was destroyed by earthquakes and not finished until 1733. The king of Spain gave the city the wooden-cogged clock that you can see in the facade. ⊠ *Av. Independencia 700,* ☏ *no phone.* ⊙ *Daily 8 AM–9 PM.*

⑥ Ex-Convento de Santa Catalina. This building is now the Hotel Camino Real and, like everything in downtown Oaxaca, is a National Heritage Site. Even if you're not staying here, it's worthwhile to explore the hotel's three courtyards; a large stone basin where the nuns did the convent's laundry 400 years ago still stands in the center of one of the patios. ⊠ *Calle 5 de Mayo 300.*

★ **⑦ Iglesia y Ex-Convento de Santo Domingo.** The most brilliantly decorated church of the city, this 16th-century wonder has an ornately carved facade that stands between two high bell towers. The interior is a profusion of white and gold—real gold leaf—typical of the energy with which Mexico seized on the Baroque style and made of it something unique. The cultural complex of the Ex-Convento is all the more splendid because of the two-year (1997–99) renovation. There are now botanical gardens, a library of antiquarian books, and a café, in addition to the beautifully augmented ☞ **Museo de las Culturas.** ⊠ *Calles Macedonio Alcalá and Gurrión,* ☏ *no phone.* ⊙ *Daily 7 AM–8 PM.*

NEED A
BREAK?
El IAGO (Instituto de Artes Gráficos de Oaxaca), across the street and north of the Ex-Convent of Santo Domingo, has a pretty outdoor café in its back patio. You can relax under the massive bougainvillea over coffee or ice cream, or enjoy a snack or lunch. ✉ *Calle Macedonio Alcalá 507,* ☏ *9/51–66980. No credit cards. Closed Tues.*

❾ Museo Casa de Benito Juárez. Benito Juárez lived in this house as a servant during his youth. The museum re-creates a typical 19th-century house; none of the furnishings or memorabilia belonged to Juárez or his employer/benefactor. ✉ *Calle García Vigil 609,* ☏ *9/51–61860.* 🎟 *About $1.70, free Sun.* ☼ *Tues.–Sat. 10–6, Sun. 10–5.*

★ **❺ Museo de Arte Contemporáneo de Oaxaca.** This museum, also known as the MACO, is housed in an attractive colonial residence. It exhibits works in a variety of media; the permanent collection has that of some of Oaxaca's native sons, including Rufino Tamayo, Rodolfo Morales, and Francisco Toledo. Be sure to check out what remains of the frescoes in the second-floor front gallery. There's a cafeteria on one of the front patios. *Note:* At press time, the museum was closed due to damage sustained in the September 1999 earthquake. Work was in progress. ✉ *Calle Macedonio Alcalá 202,* ☏ *9/51–42228.* 🎟 *About $1.* ☼ *Wed.–Mon. 10:30–8.*

★ **❿ Museo de Arte Prehispánico Rufino Tamayo.** You'll find a small but excellent collection of pre-Hispanic pottery and sculpture at this carefully restored colonial mansion. Originally it was the private collection of the late painter-muralist Rufino Tamayo, who presented it to his hometown in 1979. ✉ *Av. Morelos 503,* ☏ *9/51–64750.* 🎟 *About $1.40.* ☼ *Mon. and Wed.–Sat. 10–4 and 6–7, Sun. 10–3.*

★ **❽ Museo de las Culturas** (formerly called Museo Regional de Oaxaca). Laid out in a series of galleries around the cloister of the ☞ **Ex-Convento de Santo Domingo,** this museum, along with the entire ex-convent, has been totally refurbished. The ground floor now contains temporary galleries, a gift shop, and administrative offices. On the second floor you'll find 14 excellent thematic rooms, including those dedicated to Oaxacan music, medicine, indigenous languages, pottery, and more. Another gallery is dedicated to the treasure taken from the tombs at Monte Albán (☞ Side Trips from Oaxaca City, *below*). The stunning gold jewelry from Tomb 7 was one of the greatest archaeological finds of all time. Tours of the new botanical gardens are available in English Tuesday–Saturday at 1 PM for no additional cost. ✉ *Plaza Santa Domingo,* ☏ *9/51–62991.* 🎟 *$2.50, free Sun.* ☼ *Tues.–Sun. 10–8.*

★ **❷ Palacio de Gobierno.** The splendid 19th-century neoclassical state capitol sits on the south side of the zócalo. The fascinating murals inside depict the history and cultures of Oaxaca (but it's often closed whenever there's a peaceful protest in the zócalo, which is quite often). ✉ *Portal del Palacio,* ☏ *9/51–63850.* ☼ *Daily 9–3 and 6–8.*

★ **❶ Zócalo.** During the day, everyone comes to Oaxaca's shady main plaza, with its green wrought-iron benches and matching bandstand. At night, mariachi and marimba bands play under colonial archways or in the bandstand. ✉ *Bounded by Portal de Clavería on the north, Portal del Palacio on the south, Portal de Flores on the west, and Portal de Mercaderes on the east.*

Dining and Lodging

The open-air cafés surrounding the zócalo are good for drinks, snacks, and people-watching, with the scene changing from serene early mornings to crowded parades with brass bands, floats, and *monos* (giant papier-mâché dolls) on holiday evenings. Most serve the economical *comida corrida* (midday set menu) after 1:30 PM. But you won't be very much out of pocket wherever you choose to dine: the peso devaluation has put most higher-quality restaurants into the $$ price range.

Hotels here fill up quickly during Easter, July, November, and December, so book as far ahead as possible if you'll be visiting then.

$$$ ✕ **El Asador Vasco.** Basque (*vasco*) cuisine is served in this prizewinning restaurant, along with an outstanding Oaxacan version of mole sauce—sweet and mildly spicy, and marvelous on chicken or turkey— and a sumptuous gratiné of oysters in chipotle chili sauce. From 8 to 9 PM, serenading by *tuna* (traditionally dressed student minstrels) evokes medieval Spain. Later, marimba music floats up from the restaurant below. ⊠ *Portal de Flores 11 (west side of zócalo, upstairs),* ☎ *9/51–44755. AE, DC, MC, V.*

$$$ ✕ **El Colibrí.** If you want a restaurant that is quiet and air-conditioned, with romantic background music, free refills of super hot coffee, and fresh rolls and butter on the table, try this one—favored by upscale Mexican families and beeper-toting businesspeople. The menu is extensive: in addition to Oaxacan specialties, there are 10 different salads and five spaghetti dishes, plenty of appetizers, and burgers with fries. ⊠ *Calzada Niños Héroes de Chapultepec 903,* ☎ *9/51–58087. AE, MC, V.*

$$ ✕ **Catedral.** This elegant yet accessible local favorite takes up an entire original colonial house. Favorite dishes include mushroom soup flavored with *epazote* (a pungent local herb), and chicken in squash-blossom sauce, served with rice and a squash blossom stuffed with cheese. You can feast at the lavish Sunday lunch buffet, served 2–7, ending with some of Catedral's great strong coffee. There's dancing in the patio bar Friday and Saturday nights after 9:30. ⊠ *Calle García Vigil 105, at Av. Morelos (1 block north of Catedral Metropolitana de Oaxaca),* ☎ *9/51–63285 or 9/51–63988. AE, DC, MC, V.*

$$ ✕ **El Naranjo.** Melodic music in the background and the work of local artists on the walls lend atmosphere to this large, covered interior patio. Each of Oaxaca's seven moles is featured once a week, and there are many delicious variations of *chiles rellenos* (stuffed peppers)—from mild to hot. Unusual dishes such as a cream soup of smoky chipotle chili and nuts, and a spinach salad with a lovely, light dressing over fresh spinach leaves, jicama, bacon, and red hibiscus flowers, make this restaurant a breath of fresh air for Oaxacan cuisine. ⊠ *Calle Trujano 203,* ☎ *9/51–41878. AE, MC, V.*

$$ ✕ **Nuu-Luu.** The Mixtec name, meaning "picturesque place," couldn't be more appropriate. In a pretty neighborhood in the northern part of town, this open-air restaurant has been a favorite since 1969. Come for Oaxacan specialties, which start off with a free *botana* (appetizer) and a small *donají,* a drink with juice and mescal. Popular dishes include *sopa de guías,* a soup of young squash blossoms, squash, corn, and cornmeal, and *pescado a la yerba santa,* fish topped with a sauce of green tomatoes, herbs, onion, and garlic and steamed in fresh banana leaves. The dining room overlooks a garden. Private transportation is provided for groups of four or more. ⊠ *Iturbide 100, San Felipe del Agua,* ☎ *9/51–53187. AE, MC, V.*

$$ ✕ **La Olla.** The name of this friendly restaurant means "the pot." It doubles as a gallery, and local artists' works hang on the peach-color walls. The menu is varied—its strengths are the large, delicious, and healthy salads and regional dishes that the owner creates herself. A second-floor dining room doubles the restaurant space, and although the rustic rooftop terrace, complete with hammocks, is meant mainly for the adjoining hotel's guests, you can also take a drink up there for a

good view of the city. Service tends to be slow. ⊠ *Calle Reforma 402,* ☎ *9/51–66668. MC, V. Closed Sun.*

$$ ✕ **Terranova.** For delicious mole tamales and a good *caldo tlalpeño* (chicken-based soup with rice, avocado, chili, and tomato), make your way to the east side of the zócalo. One or more musicians are usually on hand 8:30–10:30 PM for some contemporary electric latino sounds. ⊠ *Portal B. Juárez 116,* ☎ *9/51–40533. AE, MC, V.*

$ ✕ **Coffee Beans.** This coffeehouse is a great place for a cup of java, and there's a small selection of cakes and quiches. Different types and roasts of Mexican coffee beans are also on sale. ⊠ *Calle 5 de Mayo 205,* ☎ *no phone. No credit cards.*

$ ✕ **El Gecko.** The mustard-color courtyard of this tranquil coffeehouse is drenched in purple flowering vines. A variety of coffee drinks—including a fabulous iced cappuccino—are offered, as well as light food. You can use the Internet services at Axis, in the same plaza, as you sip your java. ⊠ *Calle 5 de Mayo 412, in Plaza Gonzalo Lucero,* ☎ *9/51–48024. No credit cards. Closed Sun.*

$ ✕ **El Mesón.** Mesón's inviting, inexpensive buffet is right off the zócalo. Stop by for a snack or full meal from the paper menu, where you check off your choices. Tortillas are made on site, and there are 13 types of tacos, as well as *pozole* (hominy soup), *cochinita píbil* (spicy Yucatecan-style pork), and other Mexican dishes. For a sugar fix, have a cup of rich Oaxacan chocolate and a slice of nut or cheese pie. ⊠ *Av. Hidalgo 805, at Calle Valdivieso,* ☎ *9/51–62729. AE, MC, V.*

$$$$ ✕🏠 **Hotel Camino Real Oaxaca.** A monastic air lingers in the breezy ★ patios and enclosed gardens of this beautifully restored former convent (1576), and Gregorian chants float softly through the hotel in the morning hours. The rooms themselves are far from austere, but there is nonetheless a touch of the divine in the atmosphere here. The massive buffets are the main draws at El Refectorio restaurant: the Saturday night spread, accompanied by mariachi music; the elaborate Sunday *comida* (late lunch); and the breakfast buffet. ⊠ *Calle 5 de Mayo 300, 68000,* ☎ *9/51–60611,* 𝔽𝔸𝕏 *9/51–60732. 84 rooms, 7 suites. Restaurant, 2 bars, in-room safes, minibars, room service, pool, baby-sitting, laundry service, travel services. AE, DC, MC, V.*

$$$ ✕🏠 **Casa Oaxaca.** A trio of eccentric Europeans poured their hearts ★ and souls into creating this most unusual bed-and-breakfast. They spent two years restoring a 200-year-old downtown house, combining colonial scale and traditional materials (adobe, cantera stone, etc.) with a distinctly contemporary minimalist sensibility. There is a beautiful indigo-blue-tile pool and a Zapotec shaman-sanctioned sweat lodge. Rooms have fresh flowers, 100% cotton sheets, and marble bathrooms, and serve as a rotating showcase for Oaxaca's modern artists. Nonguests can call a day ahead to make arrangements to sample the B&B's equally imaginative nouvelle Mexican cuisine. ⊠ *Calle García Vigil 407, 68000,* ☎ *9/51–44173,* 𝔽𝔸𝕏 *9/51–64412. 5 rooms, 1 suite. Restaurant, bar, room service, pool, massage, sauna, laundry service. AE, MC, V.*

$$$ ✕🏠 **Hostal de la Noria.** The comfortable rooms in this restored peach– and lilac–painted colonial mansion two blocks off the zócalo are decorated with unique folkloric touches—some with carved wooden headboards, others with wrought-iron or hammered-tin ones. All have marble bathrooms, telephones, and cable TV. Among the house favorites at the hotel's elegant Restaurante Asunción are a delicious chicken mole, and foil-wrapped fish fillets steamed in a mescal sauce. Even more subtle is *pollo a la poblana,* chicken breast stuffed with mild chilies, manchego cheese, and squash blossoms topped with a tomato-chili sauce and melted cheese. ⊠ *Av. Hidalgo 918, 68000,* ☎ *9/51–47844,* 𝔽𝔸𝕏 *9/51–63992. 46 rooms, 4 suites. Restaurant, bar, room service, baby-sitting, laundry service, free parking. AE, MC, V.*

$$$ 🏨 **Hotel Victoria.** Surrounded by terraced grounds and well-kept gar-
★   dens, this sprawling salmon-color complex is perched on a hill over-
        looking the city. Draw back your curtains at dawn and catch your breath
        at the view of Oaxaca awakening under the Sierra Madre. Rooms, bun-
        galows, and suites are available; be sure to request one with a view.
        You can take a shuttle bus on the half hour to the city center, 10 min-
        utes away. El Tule, the veranda dining room that overlooks the hotel
        gardens and the valley below, serves international fare in addition to
        Oaxacan specialties. ✉ *Calle Lomas del Fortín 1, 68070,* ☎ *9/51–52633,*
        FAX *9/51–52411. 59 rooms, 57 suites, 34 bungalows. Restaurant, bar,
        in-room safes, minibars, room service, pool, tennis court, baby-sitting,
        laundry service, travel services, free parking. AE, MC, V.*

$$$ 🏨 **Misión de los Angeles.** Although this resort-style hotel is a long way
        from the zócalo, its peaceful gardens and relaxed ambience make it a
        good choice. It is much closer to El Llano, a city park frequented more
        by locals than by tourists. The hotel's commodious dining room is pop-
        ular with tour groups. ✉ *Calzada Porfirio Díaz 102, 68050,* ☎ *9/51–
        51500,* FAX *9/51–51680. 152 rooms, 21 suites. 2 restaurants, 2 bars,
        room service, pool, tennis court, jogging, recreation room, free park-
        ing. AE, MC, V.*

$$ 🏨 **Las Golondrinas.** This intimate hotel is tastefully ablaze with color,
★   from the profusion of flowering plants to the walls—painted pink, blue,
        mustard, and rust. Guests read or lounge around the blissfully tran-
        quil patios. Plain but cheerful rooms have red-tile floors and comfortable
        beds; none have TV or phone, but there is a TV in the common sitting
        room. Breakfast (not included in room rates) is served 8–10 AM. ✉ *Calle
        Tinoco y Palacios 411, 68000,* ☎ *9/51–43298, 9/51–42126. 24 rooms.
        Laundry service. No credit cards.*

$$ 🏨 **Hotel Cazomalli.** Even the baked-earth floor tiles shine in this lov-
        able hostelry, 15 minutes from downtown Oaxaca in the sleepy, cob-
        blestone barrio of Jalatlaco. The hotel lives up to its name, which in
        Nahuatl means "house of tranquility." Clean, bright, quiet rooms
        have blond pine furnishings and hand-woven bedspreads and cur-
        tains. Rooms have no TVs—there's one in a small second-floor salon—
        but they do have phones. Owner Marina Flores and her family make
        the ambience friendly, and serve breakfast 8–10 AM in either the restau-
        rant or central courtyard, where geraniums bloom en masse. Head up
        to the roof to jump into the small whirlpool or to wash your own clothes.
        ✉ *Calle El Salto 104, at Calle Aldama, Jalatlaco, 68080,* ☎ FAX *9/51–
        38605. 13 rooms, 2 suites. Restaurant, hot tub. AE, MC, V.*

$$ 🏨 **Hotel Rivera del Angel.** This large, plain-looking hotel, formerly called
        the Mesón de Angel, is a favorite with Mexican families, groups, and
        traveling salesmen. Southwest of the zócalo near the markets, it has a
        huge garden pool. The attractive rooms have wide terraces, orthope-
        dic mattresses, desk fans, and phones. Tourist buses to Monte Albán
        leave from here every hour on the half hour until 3:30 PM. ✉ *Calle F.
        J. Mina 518, 68000,* ☎ *9/51–66666,* FAX *9/51–45405. 62 rooms.
        Restaurant, room service, pool, free parking. No credit cards.*

$$ 🏨 **Hotel Señorial.** It's a little worn around the edges, but still a good
        choice if you want a relatively inexpensive hotel right on the zócalo;
        the seven rooms that overlook the square have tiny balconies. Uncar-
        peted rooms have TVs and phones, and the beds are fairly comfort-
        able, although far from firm. The clean bathrooms are tiled in cheerful
        light blue. ✉ *Portal de Flores 6, 68000,* ☎ *9/51–63933,* FAX *9/51–63668.
        126 rooms, 8 suites. Restaurant, café, room service, pool, free park-
        ing. No credit cards.*

$$ 🏨 **Suites Colibrí.** The suites in this business-oriented hotel are a good
        value at about $66. Large rooms have firm beds, cable TV, and phones.
        The three newest units have tile floors and painterly frescoes on the

walls. All rooms have bathtubs. ⊠ *Privada de las Flores 109, off Calzada Niños Héroes de Chapultepec, 68050,* ☎ ꜰAX *9/51–36211. 21 suites. Restaurant, bar, room service, free parking. AE, MC, V.*

Nightlife and the Arts

Oaxaca has plenty of entertainment in evening hours. On almost any night you'll find live marimba, Andean music, or nouveau flamenco in the open-air cafés surrounding the zócalo. There's a slew of discotheques playing salsa or rock, and Sunday at 12:30 PM the **Oaxaca State Band** sets up under the Indian laurel trees in the main square. The **Teatro Macedonio Alcalá** has orchestral and theatrical performances sporadically—even the occasional opera. See the monthly *Guía Cultural* (free at museums and the theater) for information on these and other events.

El Sol y La Luna is *the* place to listen to live music, often jazz or jazzy Mexican and American ballads. You can sit over drinks or order dinner on the outside patio or inside at the latest residence-turned-restaurant, directly across from the Oaxaca Institute of Culture. A cover is charged ($2–$4 depending on the band) when the music begins at 9–9:30 PM. Off-season, there is usually music Thursday–Saturday only. ⊠ *Calle Reforma 502, at Calle Constitución,* ☎ *9/51–48069.*

Every Friday night—and Monday and Wednesday in busier seasons—the **Hotel Camino Real** (⊠ Calle 5 de Mayo 300, ☎ 9/51–60611) hosts the Guelaguetza, a smaller version of the pre-Hispanic Oaxacan dance fête displaying regional dances from throughout the state. The $25 price includes buffet dinner (beginning at 7 PM) and show (8:30 PM) in the former convent's 16th-century chapel. Drinks aren't included in the price. Reservations are recommended. If you want to see a less-expensive Guelaguetza show, check with the tourist office for recommendations.

Shopping

Prospective folk-art buyers in Oaxaca City and surrounding villages should heed one major caveat, or risk being saddled with more than they expected. It isn't too difficult to ship your purchases home from many of the city's shops and shipping services, provided you have a receipt showing that you paid the 15% sales tax on all items purchased. Many artisans have begun giving out official government tax receipts, but if you buy from one who doesn't, you may have a hard time finding someone to ship your goods for you. Ask for receipts and for referrals to shipping agents if you plan to buy more than you can carry home. Also, check out the displays at the shops in town and learn about quality and design before you start spending lots of pesos.

Markets

The Saturday market is held at the functionally named **Central de Abastos** (Supply Center) on the southern edge of the town center. By noon on Saturday the enormous covered market is swarming with thousands of sellers and shoppers—both from Oaxaca and the surrounding villages—and the experience can be quite overwhelming. Don't burden yourself with a lot of camera equipment or purses and bags; you'll have a hard enough time keeping track of companions in the crowd. If you see something you really like, purchase it on the spot because you might never find your way back. The market is active during the rest of the week, too. If you go then, you can check out the mounds of multicolored chilies and herbs, the piles of tropical fruit, and the aisles of baskets, rugs, and fragile green or black pottery. But it's on Saturday that you see the best handicrafts: huipiles that vary with the village of origin; *rebozos* (shawls) of cotton and silk; distinctive pottery from many villages; colorful woven baskets; and wooden and tin toys. Bargaining isn't unexpected, although some sellers quote the actual price these days.

Several other markets in Oaxaca are active daily. **Mercado Benito Juárez** is south of the zócalo between Calles 20 de Noviembre and Miguel Cabrera at Colón. Handicrafts can be found here, as well as cheese, mole, chocolate, fruits, and much more. Locals, budget travelers, and other adventurers eat regional food at the tiny stalls of the **Mercado 20 de Noviembre** (⊠ between Calles 20 de Noviembre and Miguel Cabrera at Calle Aldama). **Mercado de Artesanías** (⊠ Calle J. P. García near Calle Ignacio Zaragoza) sells mostly textiles. Triqui Indian women and children weave wall hangings with simple back-strap looms while they tend their stands.

Each neighborhood has its own market day in a nearby square or structure, although these don't generally sell handicrafts. If you're interested in seeing neighborhood markets, check out **Mercado de Conzatti** (⊠ Calle Reforma at Calle Humboldt) Friday until 4 PM. Sunday is market day for the **Mercado de Merced** (⊠ Calzada de la República at Calle Morelos).

Shops and Galleries

Besides having a mother lode of markets, Oaxaca has some spectacular shops and galleries; some are closed Sunday and others close at midday, so plan your shopping days accordingly.

FINE ARTS

La Mano Mágica (⊠ Calle Macedonio Alcalá 203, ☎ 9/51–64275) is an upscale crafts and fine-arts gallery with a large inventory and high price tags. **Galería Quetzalli** (⊠ Calle Constitución 104, ☎ 9/51–42606) features both established and up-and-coming Oaxacan artists. Prices are high, but the work is excellent. **Galería Arte Mexicano** (⊠ Plaza Santo Domingo, Calle Macedonio Alcalá 407–16, ☎ 9/51–63255) displays local artists' work, and in adjoining rooms, folk art, antiques, and silver jewelry.

HANDICRAFTS

ARIPO (⊠ Calle García Vigil 809, ☎ 9/51–44030) is a government-run artist cooperative with competitive prices and much exclusively Oaxacan work. It's one of the few craft stores open Sunday. The **Fonart** store (⊠ Crespo 114, ☎ 9/51–65764) has a representative selection of quality arts and crafts from elsewhere in Mexico. You can support the women-artists' co-op (open daily) by shopping at the huge warren of shops that makes up **Mujeres Artesanas de las Regiones de Oaxaca** (⊠ Calle 5 de Mayo 204, ☎ 9/51–60670). Selection and quality are good, and prices are reasonable. **Artesanías Chimalli** (⊠ Calle García Vigil 513-A, ☎ 9/51–42101) has an excellent selection of alebrijes—brightly painted copal-wood animals with comical expressions and fantasy shapes. There's also a large assortment of quality crafts from throughout Mexico. Chimalli will cheerfully ship what you buy here, or what you've bought elsewhere. **Artesanías de El Patrón** (⊠ Calle 5 de Mayo 210, at Calle Murguía, ☎ 9/51–62108) specializes in tableware from Michoacán, woven goods, nativities, and elegant stylized statues that reinvent black pottery from San Bartolo Coyotepec. The two-story **Corazón del Pueblo** (⊠ Calle Macedonio Alcalá 307–9, ☎ 9/51–30547) sells beaded Huichol Indian masks, mystical tapestries from Nayarit state, *papel picado* (colorful cutout paper flags), and a good selection of English-language books on Mexican art and history.

Oro de Monte Albán (✉ Calle Macedonio Alcalá 403, ☎ 9/51–43813) is one of several branches of this store, which sells gold and silver reproductions of pre-Columbian jewelry found in the tombs of royalty at Monte Albán (there's also a shop at the archaeological site). Plenty of other fine shops sell jewelry in both traditional and modern styles, many of them along Calle Macedonio Alcalá and adjacent streets, as well as the streets west of Mercado 20 de Noviembre (☞ Markets, *above*).

Side Trips from Oaxaca City

A trip to the colonial city of Oaxaca isn't complete without heading out to see the area's ancient past and the local village life that connects it with the present. The dramatic settings of the Zapotec and Mixtec ruins of Monte Albán, Mitla, and Yagul date back some 2,600 years. And the nearby towns that produce the wares sold in the Oaxaca City market give a taste of traditional regional lifestyles. All of these places are easily reached by public transportation, taxi, or on a tour. Recently, Sedetur, the state tourism board, developed the Tourist Yu'u project, which provides opportunities to experience life outside the city. The project makes available basic, comfortable, clean accommodations in artisan villages and near natural phenomena such as the cold-water springs and fossilized waterfalls at Hierve el Agua. Contact the tourism department (☞ Contacts and Resources *in* Oaxaca City A to Z, *below*) for details and reservations.

Monte Albán

 9 km (5½ mi) southwest of Oaxaca.

The onetime holy city of more than 30,000 Zapotecs, Monte Albán is arguably the most interesting and well-preserved ruin in the state. Experts estimate that a mere 10% of the site is uncovered—excavations are constantly taking place to unearth more knowledge about the fascinating culture of the Zapotec people who lived here.

Monte Albán overlooks the Oaxaca Valley from a flattened mountaintop 1,300 ft high. Either Zapotecs or their predecessors leveled the site around 600 BC. The Zapotecs did construct the existing buildings along a north–south axis, with the exception of one structure thought to have been an observatory, which is more closely aligned with the stars than with the earth's poles. And the varying heights of the site follow the contours of distant mountain ranges. The oldest of the four temples is the **Gallery of the Danzantes** (dancers), so named for the elaborately carved stone figures that once covered the building—the originals are now in the site museum. Experts are unsure whether the figures, mostly male nudes, represent captives, medical cases, or warriors; the theory that they were dancers has been discarded.

Another major point of interest is the **ball court,** where one or more ball games were played. Hips, shoulders, knees, and elbows were probably used to hit a wooden or rubber ball. Some insist the captain of the winning team was sacrificed as an honor, others condemn the losers—the exact outcome of these games is unknown. There is some speculation that the games were a means of solving disputes among factions or villages within the domain.

No one knows for sure whether the Zapotecs abandoned the site gradually or suddenly, but by AD 1000 they had vacated it. Until then, they had expanded the city and taken on Maya influences in buildings and stelae, as had other cultures in the region. The Mixtecs, who took over the site years after the Zapotecs' departure, used Monte Albán as a lofty necropolis, a massive cemetery of lavish tombs. More than 200 tombs and 300 burial sites have been explored to date; in 1932 **Tomb 7**

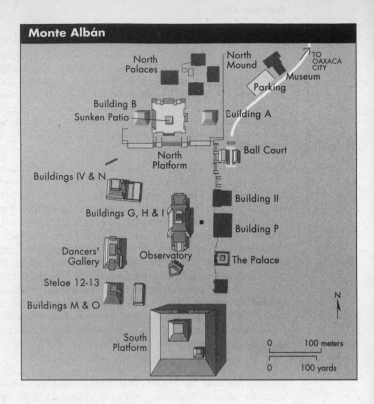

Monte Albán

North Palaces

North Mound

TO OAXACA CITY

Parking

Museum

Building B

Sunken Patio

Building A

Building IV & N

North Platform

Ball Court

Buildings G, H & I

Building II

Building P

Dancers' Gallery

Observatory

The Palace

Stelae 12-13

Buildings M & O

South Platform

0   100 meters

0   100 yards

N

yielded a treasure unequaled in North America. Inside were more than 500 priceless Mixtec objects, including gold breastplates; jade, pearl, ivory, and gold jewelry; and fans, masks, and belt buckles of precious stones and metals. Many of these treasures are now on view at the Museo de las Culturas (☞ Exploring Oaxaca City, *above*). What you'll find here is a small **site museum** with information in Spanish only and an excellent bookstore–gift shop (☎ 9/51–61215). The restaurant isn't half bad and has a great view of the valley of Oaxaca.

Special buses go to Monte Albán from the Hotel Rivera del Angel (☞ Dining and Lodging, *above*) every hour on the half hour from 8:30 to 3:30; the last bus back is at 6 PM. The round-trip fare is about $2; to stay longer than two hours you must pay a 75¢ surcharge. A taxi from the zócalo costs about $5. ✆ *$2.50, free Sun. and holidays.* ☉ *Daily 8–6.*

Mitla

40 km (25 mi) southeast of Oaxaca.

Mitla, like Monte Albán, is a complex of structures started by the Zapotecs and later taken over by the Mixtecs. In fact, the site of these palaces grew even as Monte Albán declined. Mitla's architecture is striking—and unique in the area—for the elegance of its geometric patterns and the brilliance of its stone. Unlike other ancient buildings in North America, there are no human figures or mythological events represented—only abstract designs. The name, from the Aztec word *mictlan*, means "place of the dead." ✆ *$2, free Sun. and holidays.* ☉ *Archaeological zone daily 8–5.*

Yagul

 36 km (22 mi) southeast of Oaxaca.

Although the palace ruins at Yagul aren't nearly as elaborate as those at Monte Albán or Mitla, they stand handsomely atop a hill and are certainly worth a visit, especially if you're interested in Oaxaca's ancient cultures. This city was predominantly a fortress set slightly above a group of palaces and temples; it includes a ball court and more than 30 uncovered underground tombs. ⊠ *$1.50, free Sun. and holidays.* ⊙ *Archaeological zone daily 8–5.*

Indian Villages

Many of the dozen or more villages around Oaxaca City are known for the skills of their artisans, who use both ancient and modern techniques to create their folk-art pieces; they often live among generations of families who have their own special designs for pottery, woven rugs, and wood carvings.

A west-to-south counterclockwise route from the city takes in **Atzompa,** where Dolores Porras, the descendants of Teodora Blanco, and many others in town create fanciful clay pots and sculptures. Other potters make the region's traditional green-glazed plates, bowls, and cups. The Tuesday market day has shrunk recently, however, and some of the town's best wares are found in downtown Oaxaca shops. In **Arrazola,** artists carve alebrijes. On Thursday, **Zaachila** has the most authentic livestock and food market in the area. The southern route goes to **San Bartolo Coyotepec,** the center for glossy, unglazed black pottery sold in people's homes and from a multistall cooperative next to the town square. In **Santo Tomás Jalietza,** women sell belts and table runners from pastel cotton made on small, back-strap looms. **San Martín Tilcajete,** south of Santo Tomás Jalietza on the road to Ocotlán, also is a town full of painted wooden animals. Friday's colorful market in **Ocotlán** is known for its handicrafts, especially handcrafted machetes and knives, famous throughout Mexico.

An eastward route includes **Teotitlán del Valle,** where giant rug looms sit in the front rooms of many houses. One of the town's most respected rug makers is Isaac Vásquez. The small **Museo Comunitario** (closed Monday) on the main square focuses on the anthropology, crafts, and culture of the area. In **Santa Ana del Valle,** Lucio Aquino is the most famous rug maker, although there are many skilled artisans in town. In nearby **Tlacolula,** the Sunday market spreads for blocks around the Baroque 16th-century chapel. On Sunday it seems that all of Oaxaca takes this route, starting at the Tule Tree (☞ *below*), moving to the ruins of Mitla, and then on to the crafts centers and market.

North of the city center, off the road to Mexico City, is **Etla;** its Wednesday market is known for cheeses, mole, bread, and chocolates.

The markets on other routes are held on special days throughout the week, and you can easily fill a week with tours and never see the same sight twice. If you have to budget your time, use tour guides for these trips so you don't miss out on the fascinating details.

The Tule Tree

14 km (8½ mi) east of Oaxaca.

In the town of Santa María del Tule stands a huge ahuehuete cypress estimated to be more than 2,000 years old. One of the largest in the world, it is some 140 ft high, with roots buried more than 60 ft in the earth. It takes 35 adults with their arms outstretched to embrace it. The tree is the traditional center of the town of Santa María and is larger than the church behind it.

OAXACA CITY A TO Z

Arriving and Departing

By Bus

Deluxe buses make the six-hour nonstop run from Mexico City to Oaxaca for about $23. Oaxaca City's first-class terminal is called the **ADO** (✉ Calzada Niños Héroes de Chapultepec 1036, at Calle Emilio Carranza), from which the ADO (☎ 9/51–51703) and Cristóbal Colón (☎ 9/51–51214) bus lines provide service. The second-class bus station, **Central de Autobuses** (✉ Prolongación de Trujano at the Periférico, Oaxaca City, ☎ 9/51–65824) serves intermediate towns within the state. Other lines have desks at one or both terminals.

By Car

From Mexico City, you can take Mexico 190 (Pan American Highway) south and east through Puebla and Izúcar de Matamoros to Oaxaca City—a distance of 546 km (338 mi) along a rather curvy road. This route takes six–seven hours. The toll road, which connects Mexico City to Oaxaca City via Tehuacan, is better. It cuts the driving time by about an hour.

By Plane

Mexicana (☎ 9/51–68414 or 9/51–67352) flies from various U.S. cities (including Chicago, Los Angeles, San Francisco, Miami, and New York) to Oaxaca City with a stop in Mexico City. You will have to change planes in Mexico City on other flights from the United States for **Aeroméxico** (☎ 9/51–61066) or **Mexicana** to get to Oaxaca City's **Benito Juárez Airport,** about 8 km (5 mi) south of town. There is also service for triangle flight itineraries, including the Oaxacan coastal resorts of Bahías de Huatulco or Puerto Escondido.

Domestic service to Oaxaca includes **Aviacsa** (☎ 9/51–45304) from Tuxtla Gutiérrez; **Aero Vega** (☎ 9/51–62777) for charters to and from Puerto Escondido; **Aeromorelos** (☎ 9/51–15100) from Puerto Escondido and Huatulco; and **Aerocaribe** (☎ 9/51–60266, 9/51–60229) to and from Acapulco and Huatulco.

BETWEEN THE AIRPORT AND DOWNTOWN

Transportes Aeropuerto (✉ Alameda de León, ☎ 9/51–44350) will trundle you into the soonest available van and drop you off at your hotel for $1.50. There are usually no taxis in sight. From town, buy a ticket ahead of time for inexpensive airport transportation or hail a regular cab for about $6.

Getting Around

By Car

You won't need a car in Oaxaca City, which is fairly compact. Even outlying sights are easily accessible by taxi or on a tour. That said, a car is a great way for adventurous souls to see the countryside.

By Taxi

Taxis are plentiful, clearly marked, and reasonably priced. You can usually find them at any hour of the day cruising on downtown streets. There are also taxi stands on Avenida Independencia at Calle García Vigil, on one side of Alameda Park, and on Calles Abasolo and Cinco de Mayo, near the Hotel Camino Real. Cabs aren't metered. Determine the fare ahead of time (in town, usually $2–$2.50); for outlying destinations, ask the driver to show you the tariff card.

Contacts and Resources

Car Rental

Cars are available for rent at the airport, in town, and through travel
agencies at various hotels. **Hertz** (⊠ Hotel Marqués del Valle, Portal
de Clavería s/n, Local 7, ☎ FAX 9/51–62434; ⊠ Benito Juárez Airport,
☎ 9/51–15478) has two convenient locations.

Consulate

U.S. Consulate (⊠ Calle Macedonio Alcalá 201, Int. 204, ☎ FAX 9/51–
43054) is open weekdays 10–3. **Canadian Consulate** (⊠ Calle Pino Suarez
700, Local 11-B, ☎ 9/51–33777) is open weekdays 11–2.

E-Mail

There are several Internet cafés downtown. **Axis** (⊠ Calle 5 de Mayo
412, ☎ 9/51–48024), open weekdays 10–8 and Saturday 10–6, charges
$2 an hour.

Emergencies

Dial 060 locally for all emergencies, including police and hospital. **Police** (☎ 9/51–62224). **Hospital–Red Cross** (☎ 9/51–57438).

Guided Tours

Unless you're on a strict budget, take advantage of the many tour companies that offer guided trips to the archaeological sites, colonial
churches and monasteries, outlying towns (some of which have weekly
market days), and folk-art centers. Prices start at $10. Licensed guides
are available as well through travel agencies for approximately $5 per
hour for a minimum of three persons. **Viajes Turísticos Mitla** (⊠ Calle
F. J. Mina 518, in the Hotel Rivera del Angel, ☎ 9/51–66175, FAX 9/
51–43152) and **Agencia Marqués del Valle** (⊠ Portal de Clavería s/n,
☎ 9/51–46970 or 9/51–46962, FAX 9/51–69961) are among the most
established agencies.

Visitor Information

The **Oficina de Turismo** (⊠ Av. Independencia 607, at Calle García Vigil,
☎ 9/51–64828 or 9/51–60123) is open daily 9–8.

THE OAXACA COAST

Oaxaca's 520-km (322-mi) coastline is mainland Mexico's last Pacific
frontier. Huatulco, a project of Fonatur (the government's tourism developers), was launched in the early 1980s. Bahías de Huatulco, as the
entire area is called, covers 51,900 acres of mountain lowlands and
coastal stretches, 40,000 acres of which is supposed to remain a nature reserve. The focal point of the master-planned development is a
string of nine sheltered bays that stretches across 35 km (22 mi) of some
of the Pacific's prettiest coastline.

Huatulco's beauty is arguably best seen from a boat (☞ Contacts and
Resources *in* Oaxaca Coast A to Z, *below*), even though some of the
bays are accessible by road. Bahía Tangolunda is the site of the area's
most exclusive hotels, whereas Bahía Santa Cruz has midrange hotels,
a marina, and a small plaza. Bahía Chahué has been developed in the
past few years, with some moderately priced hotels; a parking lot
makes the beach here quite accessible. The town of La Crucecita, originally built to house the construction crews and workers building Huatulco, has come along nicely: it has a pretty plaza and a recently frescoed
church, as well as some budget hotels and plenty of restaurants.

Puerto Escondido has long been prime territory for international
surfers. The town has the coast's first airport (not international) and
has grown up to tourism in a much more natural, and, to some minds,

pleasant, way than Huatulco. Although the four-block pedestrian walkway—crowded with open-air seafood restaurants, shops, and café bars—is lively, the "real" town above the strip, with its busy market and stores, provides a look at local life and a dazzling view of the coast. The tiny port town of Puerto Ángel, midway between the Puerto Escondido airport and the Bahías de Huatulco airport, has a limited selection of hotels and bungalows tucked into the hills.

Puerto Escondido

⑫ *310 km (192 mi) south of Oaxaca City.*

A coffee-shipping port in the 1920s, Puerto Escondido is the first tourist town on the Oaxaca coast, southeast of Acapulco on Highway 200. The town market, **Mercado Benito Juárez,** is a long walk (but a short cab or bus ride) from most hotels, and it's worth checking out (Saturday and Wednesday). If you want a bit of pampering, cleanse body and soul according to ancient traditions at the **Temazcalli** (⊠ Av. Infraganti, esq. Calle Temazcalli, ☎ 9/58–21023), which claims to combine "the energy of wood, fire, rock, and medicinal herbs." Massages are also offered, and afterward you can watch the sunset from the cliffs above the ocean. Back in town, at the north end of the main beach, you can hire a driver from among the *panga* (small boat) fleet for bay tours or fishing trips. **La Playa Principal** (main beach) and the **Laguna Agua Dulce** are at the south end of the tourist strip, followed by **Marinero Beach**, then a sharp outcropping of rocks, and, finally, the most famous beach of all, **Zicatela** (☞ Beaches, *below*).

The main intersection in Puerto Escondido is at Highway 200 (also called the *carretera costera,* or coast highway) and Avenida Alfonso Pérez Gasga, which meanders south into the tourist zone. On the north side of the highway this street is called Avenida Oaxaca. Traveling down a steep hill, Avenida Gasga passes many of the tourist hotels; at the bottom, traffic is prohibited and the street becomes a four-block-long pedestrian mall lined with shops, restaurants, and lodgings that spread to the sands of the main beach.

The airport is on the northern edge of town, as are the hotels favored by charter groups. **Playa Bacocho,** just south of the airport, is an upscale housing-and-hotel development; some inviting bars, discos, and restaurants have opened in this area, although most of the action still centers around the tourist zone to the south.

Beaches

One of the top 10 surfing beaches in the world, **Zicatela** is a long stretch of cream-color sand battered by the Mexican Pipeline, as this stretch of mighty surf is called. In November international surfing championships are held here, and the town fills with sun-bleached aficionados of both sexes intent on serious surfing and hard partying. Do *not* swim in these waters unless you can withstand deadly undertows and rip currents. Instead, watch the surfers at sunset from the *palapa* (thatch-roof) restaurant at the Arco Iris Hotel.

The safest swimming and snorkeling beaches in Puerto Escondido are **Puerto Angelito** and **Carrizalillo;** both can be reached on foot, but more easily by cab or by boat from the town beach. Transportation is available from the many fishermen who park their pangas on the sand near town and use them as water taxis. The ride should cost about $5.

Dining and Lodging

Understandably, coastal cuisine focuses on fresh seafood dishes, although some savvy townspeople are introducing Italian and vegetarian food

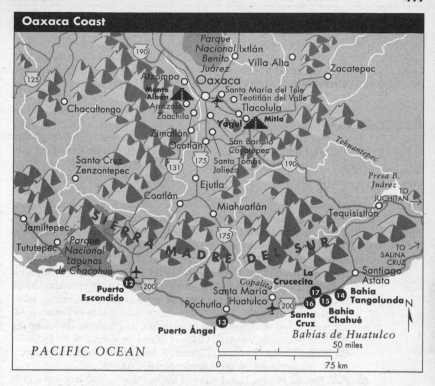

Oaxaca Coast

PACIFIC OCEAN

Bahías de Huatulco

0   50 miles

0   75 km

for variety. For such a small town, Puerto Escondido has more than its share of good restaurants.

$$ ✕ **Mario's Pizzaland.** The proprietor is a courtly, generous Italian who produces in short order pizzas with many exotic toppings, including seafood. Also on the abbreviated menu are vegetarian and meat lasagna, enormous salads, and *bistec alla pizzaiola* (steak smothered in melted cheese and pizza sauce). ⊠ *Av. Gasga east of the tourist zone,* ☎ *9/ 58–20570. No credit cards.*

$$ ✕ **La Perla.** Because it's in the "real" town uphill from the tourist zone, this excellent seafood restaurant has some of the best prices in town. *Pulpo* (octopus) is wonderfully tender. An excellent ceviche comes in a spicy cocktail sauce. It's a bit of a walk but a short, cheap cab ride. ⊠ *Calle 3a Poniente s/n, Sector Juárez,* ☎ *9/58–20461. No credit cards.*

$$ ✕ **Perla Flameante.** Fresh dorado, shark, tuna, and pompano come with teriyaki, Cajun, or garlic seasonings at this second-story bamboo restaurant overlooking the beach. The deep-fried onion rings and zucchini are terrific. Perla is open for breakfast every day except Sunday. ⊠ *Av. Gasga near end of tourist zone,* ☎ *9/58–20167. MC, V.*

$$ ✕ **La Posada del Tiburón.** What's not to like about this place: the waiters are friendly, the food is scrumptious, and you can wiggle your toes in the sand at the tables closest to the beach. Opera music floats over woven tablecloths as waves straggle up the sand along the main beach. Seafood is the specialty here: try a Lyon-style fish fillet in creamy lemon sauce, or the house fillet, topped with fine herbs and slivered almonds. There are also tasty chicken and meat dishes served with baked potato, rice, and steamed vegetables. ⊠ *Av. Gasga s/n, at Playa Principal,* ☎ *9/58–20786. AE, MC, V.*

$ ✕ **Art 'n' Harry's.** Only open during high season, this surfer hangout overlooking the Pipeline is the place to relax with a drink and watch videos or zone out on heavy-metal CDs. The menu offers various stir-fry and spaghetti dishes, salads, and seafood. ⊠ *South end of Zicatela beach,* ☎ *no phone. No credit cards.*

$ ✕ **Carmen's Bakery.** A long-standing favorite for great coffee, whole-
★ grain breads, and sinful pastries, this bakery (a.k.a. La Patisserie) recently moved from its original side-street location to the main drag on Zicatela beach. The breakfast of fruit salad with yogurt and granola is sublime. The same owner runs Cafecito, a happening surfers' hangout down the beach and equally worthy of exploration. ⊠ *Calle del Morro s/n, Zicatela beach,* ☎ *no phone. No credit cards. No dinner.*

$ ✕ **La Gota de Vida.** This small vegetarian café and health-food store on Zicatela beach has all sorts of delicious salads, vegetable soups, tofu and tempeh dishes, and *licuados* (milk shakes made with yogurt and papaya, mango, or banana) as well as fresh vegetable and fruit juices at very reasonable prices. It's often packed with surfers and health-conscious travelers. ⊠ *Calle del Morro s/n,* ☎ *no phone. No credit cards.*

$$$ ✕▦ **Hotel Santa Fe.** Framed by exuberant tropical plants at the north end of Zicatela beach, this pretty hotel has colonial furnishings and curtains and spreads of woven Mexican cloth. Some rooms have balconies overlooking the pools and patios or the beach. The hotel also manages the eight one-bedroom Bungalows Santa Cruz next door, which have well-stocked kitchenettes, cozy furnishings, and wide verandas. By all means treat yourself to at least one meal at the hotel restaurant—whether or not you're a guest. The menu is divided between seafood, vegetarian, and traditional Mexican dishes, and tables overlooking the surf have wonderful views. ⊠ *Calle del Morro s/n, 71980,* ☎ *9/58–20170,* ℻ *9/58–20260. 59 rooms, 2 suites, 8 bungalows. Restaurant, bar, 2 pools, wading pool, shops, laundry service. AE, MC, V.*

$$ ✕▦ **Flor de María.** Hand-painted birds, flowers, and tropical scenes
★ adorn this bright, attractive hotel half a block up from Playa Marinero. Crisp sheets cover firm beds, and rooms are bright and immaculate—with powerful ceiling fans, but no TV or phone. On the roof, you can swing in a row of hammocks, or cool off in the small pool or at the rooftop bar. Like all Zicatela beach hotels, Flor de María is a short but very dark walk from the tourist esplanade. In the outstanding restaurant, Italian-born owner Maria combines New World ingredients with old-world recipes to create delicious pastas, chicken, and steaks in addition to Mexican specialties. ⊠ *Entrance to Playa Marinero s/n, 71980,* ☎ ℻ *9/58–20536. 24 rooms. Restaurant, bar, fans, pool, laundry service. AE, MC, V.*

$$$ ▦ **Hotel Aldea del Bazar.** This sparkling white hotel sits on a bluff overlooking Playa Bacocho, just south of the airport. The restaurant and some of the rooms have a view of the beach below, which can be reached by a ramp—a long walk back up the hill. All the tastefully decorated rooms have small living rooms and color TVs. One of the hotel's best features is the pre-Hispanic–style eucalyptus sauna; the massages are mediocre. ⊠ *Av. Benito Juárez 7, Fracc. Bacocho, 71980,* ☎ ℻ *9/58–20508. 47 rooms. Restaurant, bar, pool, massage, spa. AE, MC, V.*

$$–$$$ ▦ **Paraíso Escondido.** Hidden halfway up the steps of Calle Union, this colonial-style hotel has the charm of a wealthy, eccentric, and somewhat dotty relative's house. No two rooms are alike, and all are furnished with a folkloric mixture of wood dressers, tin mirrors, and brightly colored curtains and spreads. At press time, it was building five new third-floor suites with kitchenettes and private, ocean-view terraces. ⊠ *Calle Union 10, 71980,* ☎ *9/58–20444. 20 rooms, 5 suites. Restaurant, bar, pool. No credit cards.*

$$ ▦ **Studios Tabachín del Puerto.** Special touches such as clocks, vases, and shelves with books give these wonderfully furnished studio apartments a homey feel. Especially wonderful is the fourth-floor "penthouse," with its awesome view of the coast. Each of the six studios, behind the

Hotel Santa Fe near Zicatela beach, has a kitchenette stocked with necessities. Owner don Pablo also manages a small country inn, Posada Nopala, about two hours north of town, which is open October 31 to April 30. It sits in the pine forests of the Oaxaca mountains, amid coffee plantations and crystal-clear rivers. If you have a self-sufficient streak, this comfortable yet rustic lodge is perfect for experiencing life in rural Mexico. Or you can take a day-trip to Nopala; $25 per person includes lunch. ⊠ *Calle de Morro by Zicatela, Apdo. 210, 71980,* ☎ FAX *9/58–21179. 6 apartments. Restaurant. MC, V.*

$–$$ 🏨 **Cabañas de Playa Acali.** A variety of sizes and styles of accommodations is available at this cluster of *cabañas* (cabins) and bungalows on Zicatela beach. Guests mingle around the large central pool. The least expensive rooms are in small, rustic cabañas without air-conditioning; the most expensive, though still a bargain, are eight bungalows with terraces, kitchens, air-conditioning, and dining areas. This is a good choice for groups of four or six surfers sharing expenses and preparing their own meals. ⊠ *Calle del Morro s/n, 71980,* ☎ *9/58–20754. 8 cabañas, 8 bungalows. Kitchenettes, pool. No credit cards.*

$ 🏨 **Hotel Arco Iris.** This sprawling, three-story hotel on Zicatela beach
★ resembles a gracefully aging, old-fashioned guest house. The rooms are simple yet clean, with firm beds and worn but comfortable furnishings. Some rooms have kitchenettes; most have wide verandas (bring a hammock) that overlook the surfing beach just beyond. There is a large pool, a video salon, and a second-story restaurant with a wonderful ocean breeze. ⊠ *Calle del Morro s/n, Col. Marinero, Apdo. 105, 71980,* ☎ FAX *9/58–20432 or 9/58–21494. 26 rooms. Restaurant, bar, pool. MC, V.*

Outdoor Activities and Sports

RIVER TRIPS

Behind El Cafecito restaurant on Calle del Morro at Zicatela beach, **Big Jim's River Trips** (☎ 9/58–21026) organizes 2½-hour trips down the Colotepec River. A half-hour truck ride takes clients to the drop-off point, and a kayak-paddling guide will accompany you downriver as you float idyllically in a truck inner tube. A minimum of two clients is required, and life jackets are provided. Excursions usually depart at 9:30 AM and 2:30 PM and cost about $25.

WATER SPORTS

You can rent boogie boards and surfboards at **Las Olas** (⊠ Calle del Morro s/n, ☎ no phone) for about $6.50 a day. You must pay a deposit of about $80, which will be refunded at the end of the day unless the equipment is damaged.

Puerto Ángel

⑬ *81 km (50 mi) southeast of Puerto Escondido.*

The leading seaport of the state 100 years ago, Puerto Ángel today is a dusty village on a beautiful bay. The region suffered greatly from Hurricane Pauline in the autumn of 1997, but recovered quickly, replacing palapa roofs and rebuilding many destroyed wooden structures in concrete.

The central town beach has been taken over by the navy, and the most popular swimming-and-sunning territory is at **Playa Panteón,** just past the oceanfront cemetery (*panteón* means "cemetery"). Other good (and less populated) swimming and snorkeling beaches are nearby. Six kilometers (4 mi) west of town is **Zipolite,** a bay known for its nude sunbathing. It's a favorite with surfers, aging hippies, and travelers content with a hammock on the beach and little else in the way of creature comforts. The undertow is extremely dangerous here—*zipolite* means killer, and more than a few foolishly brave swimmers die in these waters every year.

The **Centro Mexicano de la Tortuga** (Museum of the Sea Turtle) in Mazunte makes an interesting side trip from Puerto Ángel. The popularity of turtle hunting put the sea creatures, who come to this coastal area to lay eggs each year, in danger of extinction. Mazunte even had its own slaughterhouse for their meat. A 1990 government ban on turtle hunting has for the most part stopped the carnage, and Mazunte is now devoted to protecting the species. A dozen aquariums are filled with turtle specimens that once again flourish in the nearby ocean. From Puerto Ángel, take Highway 200 toward San Pedro Pochutla; about 15 km (9 mi) past town, follow the turnoff marked SAN AGUSTÍN. A few kilometers later at the sign for PLAYA MAZUNTE, ask for directions to the *museo,* which is on the beach. ⊠ *Playa Mazunte,* ☎ *9/58–43055,* 𝔽𝔸𝕏 *9/58–43063.* 🖾 *$2.* ☉ *Tues.–Sat. 10–4:30, Sun. 10–2:30.*

Dining and Lodging

$–$$ ✕🖾 **Posada Cañon Devata.** California comes to Puerto Ángel in this ecological hideaway carved into a wooded canyon. Simple bungalows on the hill offer private quarters; other rooms and buildings are scattered on the hillsides. At the top, the bar El Cielo (Heaven) is a good place to take in the sunset. Windows have screens, and the only drawback to this tranquil space is that there's no hot water. Boat trips and occasional hatha yoga retreats are available. The cool palapa restaurant—open to nonguests (you must reserve ahead for the 7 PM dinner, about $8)—is a find for vegetarians. Meals are healthy and creative, and portions are very generous. ⊠ *Past the cemetery, off Blvd. Virgilio Uribe (Apdo. 10), 70902,* ☎ 𝔽𝔸𝕏 *9/58–43048. 16 rooms, 6 bungalows. Restaurant, bar, massage. No credit cards. Closed May–June.* 🏵

$ ✕🖾 **La Buena Vista.** Some of the clean, simple accommodations here have balconies, some have hammocks just outside, but none have hot water. The third-floor restaurant has one of the most dependable kitchens in town, and rooms at the top level of the hotel have a great view as well as the best breezes. There are a lot of steps to negotiate here, and no elevator. ⊠ *Calle la Buena Compañia (Apdo. 48), 70902,* ☎ 𝔽𝔸𝕏 *9/58–43104. 21 rooms. Restaurant. No credit cards.*

$ 🖾 **La Cabaña de Puerto Ángel.** This plain but adequate hotel is the closest to Playa Panteón, ideal if you want to roll right out of bed in the morning and walk on the beach. Rooms have louvered windows with screens and ceiling fans; some have small, shadeless balconies, but none have closets. It's worth the extra $4 a night to rent the one triple room, which has a fantastic ocean view. ⊠ *Calle Pedro Sainz de Barranda s/n, across from Playa Panteón, 70902,* ☎ *9/58–43105. 23 rooms. No credit cards.*

Bahías de Huatulco

277 km (172 mi) south of Oaxaca City, 111 km (69 mi) east of Puerto Escondido, 48 km (30 mi) east of Puerto Ángel.

Bahías de Huatulco, whose burgeoning development suffered major setbacks because of the 1994 peso devaluation, is still marching forward toward its completion date sometime in the next few years. Three of its nine bays have been developed to date, a fourth (which was originally designated as an ecological zone) is in the planning stages. Huatulco's pristine bays encompass a total of 36 tropical beaches. Because of the fits and starts of its construction, Huatulco has an unfinished look, and this lack of polish makes the area less popular than such places as Cancún and Ixtapa. If you have a car at your disposal, you can drive to several bays that so far haven't been developed and play Robinson Crusoe to your heart's content.

Another popular option is to tour the bays by boat. Standard four- to eight-hour trips—depending on how many bays you visit—might include a lunch of freshly caught fish (which costs extra). Fishing, diving, and snorkeling tours visit the beaches or reefs most suitable for those activities.

⑭ The Huatulco of the future is most evident at **Bahía Tangolunda,** where the poshest hotels are in full swing, and parasailers glide over fleets of sightseeing boats. The site was chosen by developers because of its five beautiful beaches. There is a challenging 18-hole golf course here, the Campo de Golf Tangolunda (☎ FAX 9/58–10059). A small shopping-restaurant center is across from the entrance to the Sheraton, but most of the shopping and dining take place in the towns of Santa Cruz and La Crucecita, each about 10 minutes from the hotels by taxi, or, for the economy-minded, by buses or cooperative taxis.

⑮ **Bahía Chahué,** the most recently developed bay, is a pleasant place to spend a relaxing beach day. The beach parking lot makes it accessible, and there are now several moderately priced hotels and restaurants along the beach.

⑯ **Santa Cruz** is on the bay of the same name. Arrange a glass-bottom-boat or sightseeing tour, or a fishing trip from the marina here. Or spend the day at Tipsy's beach club (⊠ Paseo Mitla beach, ☎ FAX 9/58–70576), where you can rent water toys, take waterskiing lessons, or play volleyball. A central zócalo with a wrought-iron gazebo has been built nearby; tourists and locals mingle in the little plaza, where you can sip a cool drink or cappuccino in the café.

⑰ **La Crucecita,** just off Highway 200, is the only place in Huatulco that resembles a real Mexican town, with its central plaza and a recently constructed church covered inside with frescoes. Modern buildings with arches and balconies are going up along the streets by the park, and this is becoming *the* place for hanging out at sidewalk cafés and shopping in boutiques. The bus station, tourism office, Bing's ice-cream shop, and long-distance telephone office are here, along with a smattering of smaller, less expensive, and more intimate hotels.

Dining and Lodging

$$$ ✕ **Don Porfirio.** You can dine inside or out on the covered patio in this Tangolunda restaurant. There is a good variety of seafood and international dishes; try the combination shish kebab sautéed in tequila, served on a bed of rice with steamed veggies and potato. There is no air-conditioning, and the outdoor patio is loud with street noise, but the food and service are good. ⊠ *Zona Hotelera Tangolunda, across from Hotel Maeva, Bahía Tangolunda,* ☎ *9/58–10001. AE, MC, V.*

$$ ✕ **Restaurant de Doña Celia.** Although the official name of this long-★ time favorite beachfront restaurant is Avalos, everyone knows it by the owner's name: Doña Celia. Even Presidente Ernesto Zedillo has stopped by for a seafood feast. Make your selection from the large menu, and prepare for large portions as well. Tables face the sand and sea at Santa Cruz Bay, just beyond the marina. ⊠ *Bahía Santa Cruz,* ☎ *9/58–70128. No credit cards.*

$$ ✕ **Restaurante María Sabina.** Strangely named for a Oaxaca medicine woman immortalized for her use of "magic" (hallucinogenic) mushrooms, this is a great place from which to watch locals and tourists mingle in La Crucecita's pretty plaza. Grill orders are prepared on the outdoor *parrilla* (grill) and served with grilled onion, baked potato, and sour cream. A favorite plate is *reboso María Sabina,* steak with melted cheese, guacamole, and fresh salsa. ⊠ *Calle Flamboyan, west side of plaza, La Crucecita,* ☎ *9/58–70219. MC, V.*

$$$$ ✕⊡ **Sheraton.** Now offering all-inclusive as well as standard room
★ rates, the Sheraton is the most user-friendly of the upscale hotels on Bahía
Tangolunda. The rooms have bathtubs—a real luxury in these parts.
Water sports and equipment—including kayaks, windsurfers, sailboats,
and catamarans (all-inclusive guests have free use of these)—are considered top notch here, and dive masters are on hand with dive equipment (☞ Water Sports *in* Outdoor Activities and Sports, *below*). The
Casa Real restaurant, which is closed off season, still has the most glamorous dining in Huatulco. The menu emphasizes northern Italian dishes,
and there are elaborate floral arrangements and flickering candles set
out at night. ⊠ *Blvd. Benito Juárez, Bahía Tangolunda 70989,* ☎ *9/
58–10055,* 𝔽𝔸𝕏 *9/58–10113. 347 rooms, 8 suites. 3 restaurants, 3 bars,
2 pools, wading pool, massage, sauna, 4 tennis courts, exercise room,
beach, dive shop, boating, shops, travel services. AE, DC, MC, V.*

$$$$ ⊡ **Camino Real Zaashila.** Previously of the Omni chain, this contemporary stucco Mexican-cum-Mediterranean palace overlooks a secluded lagoon with its own private beach. The resort has 27 landscaped
acres of gardens, fountains, and waterfalls. Ten luxurious suites and
41 rooms have small private pools. The rates are high and, unlike those
at most of the other high-end properties, they aren't all-inclusive. ⊠
Blvd. Benito Juárez 5, Bahía Tangolunda 70989, ☎ *9/58–10460,* 𝔽𝔸𝕏
*9/58–10461. 120 rooms, 10 suites. 3 restaurants, 2 bars, in-room
safes, minibars, 2 pools, wading pool, tennis court, exercise room, beach,
baby-sitting, travel services. AE, DC, MC, V.*

$$$$ ⊡ **Quinta Real.** Opened in 1997, this hilltop resort takes Huatulco lux-
★ ury to new and exclusive heights. A combination of Moorish domes
and thatch palapas, the property's 27 tranquil suites are airy and
plush, each with creamy white leather furnishings, exquisite Guatemalan
tapestries, a Jacuzzi, terrace, and spectacular ocean views. Nine suites
have private pools, and a few are equipped with telescopes for dolphin-
and star-gazing. ⊠ *Blvd. Benito Juárez 2, Bahía Tangolunda 70989,*
☎ *9/58–10428,* 𝔽𝔸𝕏 *9/58–10429. 27 suites. 2 restaurants, bar, in-room
safes, minibars, 2 pools, wading pool, tennis court, beach, baby-sitting, laundry service. AE, DC, MC, V.*

$$$–$$$$ ⊡ **Club Med.** The nearly 500 rooms cut a pastel swath on a hillside
overlooking Bahía Tangolunda. There are three beaches and an end-
less list of amenities. Weeklong fitness programs are particularly pop-
ular. Although some guests are content to never leave the grounds, coastal
excursions and tours to Oaxaca City are offered. Packages with air-
fare included are usually available. This is one of the area's least ex-
pensive all-inclusives. ⊠ *Bahía Tangolunda 70900 (Reservations: 40
W. 57th St., New York, NY 10019),* ☎ *9/58–10033, 800/258–2633,*
𝔽𝔸𝕏 *9/58–10101. 483 rooms. 4 restaurants, 3 bars, in-room safes, 4 pools,
11 tennis courts, exercise room, beach, dance club, children's programs
(ages 4–17), playground. AE, MC, V.*

$$$–$$$$ ⊡ **Royal Maeva.** This all-inclusive resort caters to charter groups and
Mexican families as well as lone travelers. The emphasis is on fun—
and if you're not a fan of loud music, stay in a room away from the
pool. The rooms are spacious, colorful, and adorned with heavy pas-
tel fabrics and light wooden furniture. Considering that the price per
person includes all food, drinks, and access to most water and gym sports,
this is a good deal if you want to do more than just work on your tan.
⊠ *Blvd. Benito Juárez 227, Bahía Tangolunda 70989,* ☎ *9/58–10000,*
𝔽𝔸𝕏 *9/58–10220. 178 rooms, 12 suites. 4 restaurants, 7 bars, in-room
safes, 4 pools, 3 tennis courts, exercise room, beach, dance club, baby-
sitting, children's programs (ages 4–15), car rental. AE, DC, MC, V.*

$$–$$$ ⊡ **Posada Flamboyant.** This is the classiest option if you want to stay
in the town of La Crucecita, about a five-minute cab ride from Bahía
Tangolunda. The ivy-covered, four-story edifice has a vaguely Euro-

pean feel. All rooms have firm beds, cable TVs, and phones, and both the pool and surrounding area are large and inviting. Four comfortable two-bedroom, two-bath suites with well-furnished living rooms and kitchens are available for $100–$200 each per night (depending on the season) for up to six people. ⊠ *Calle Gardenia esq. Tamarindo, La Crucecita 70989,* ☎ *9/58–70113 or 9/58–70105,* ℻ *9/58–70121. 66 rooms, 4 suites. Restaurant, bar, coffee shop, pool, wading pool, baby-sitting, playground, travel services. AE, MC, V.*

$$ ⊞ **Marina Resort Huatulco.** This all-suites resort overlooking the marina on Santa Cruz Bay has plenty of amenities. Each comfortable suite's ample living area contains a small dining table, cable TV, and kitchenette. Upper-floor rooms have the best bay views; all rooms have bathtubs. There's also a disco and a beach club with water sports and a playground. ⊠ *Calle Tehunatepec 112, Bahía Santa Cruz,* ☎ *9/58–70963,* ℻ *9/58–70830. 47 suites. Restaurant, 2 bars, kitchenettes, 2 pools, wading pool, dance club, playground. AE, MC, V.*

$ ⊞ **Hotel Begonias.** Catercorner from the plaza in La Crucecita, this sweet, simple hotel has colonial-style furnishings, ceiling fans, comfortable beds, and color TVs. The hotel's popular restaurant, Oasis, serves an extensive menu of Oaxacan and Japanese dishes. ⊠ *Calle Bugambilias 503, La Crucecita 70989,* ☎ *9/58–70390,* ℻ *9/58– 71390. 9 rooms, 3 suites. Restaurant, bar. AE, MC, V.*

$ ⊞ **Hotel Las Palmas.** Plain but acceptable furnishings and rock-bottom prices (for Huatulco) are what you'll find at this small second-story hotel just a block from the plaza in La Crucecita. The cramped rooms have TVs, hot water, and both fans and air-conditioning. ⊠ *Calle Guamuchil 206, La Crucecita 70989,* ☎ *9/58–70060,* ℻ *9/58–70057. 8 rooms. Restaurant, bar. AE, MC, V.*

Outdoor Activities and Sports

BICYCLING

You can rent mountain bikes from **Motor Tours Huatulco** (☞ Contacts and Resources *in* Oaxaca Coast A to Z, *below*) or **Rent-a-Bike** (⊠ Calle Flamboyant esq. Bugambilias, La Crucecita, ☎ 9/58–70669) for guided or unguided tours.

FISHING

Sportfishing for sailfish, tuna, dorado, and other fish can be arranged through **Sociedad Cooperative Tangolunda,** the boat owners' cooperative at the marina on Santa Cruz Bay (☎ 9/58–70081), or **Cantera Tours** (⊠ Blvd. Benito Juárez, Bahía Tangolunda, ☎ ℻ 9/58–10030), at the Sheraton Hotel in Tangolunda.

WATER SPORTS

The PADI-certified dive masters at **Action Sports Marina** at the Sheraton are among the most reliable in Huatulco. Certification courses are offered, as are dive trips ($50 for one tank, $70 for two) and 1½-hour snorkeling trips ($20). ⊠ *Sheraton Hotel, Paseo Benito Juárez s/n, Bahía Tangolunda,* ☎ *9/58–10055, ext. 842,* ℻ *9/58–10113.*

Shopping

Although Huatulco isn't exactly a shopper's paradise, there are several places worth mentioning. In La Crucecita, **Paradise** boutique (⊠ Calle Gardenia esq. Guarumbo, ☎ 9/58–70268), open daily, has an excellent selection of casual yet stylish beach and resort wear, much of which comes from Bali and India. The batik and hand-painted T-shirts make great gifts, as do the Mexican crafts, including silver jewelry, coconut masks from Guerrero, and black pottery.

The **Museo de Artesanías Oaxaqueñas** (⊠ Calle Flamboyan 216, La Crucecita, ☎ 9/58–71513) is really a store, not a museum, but the artisans who create the fanciful wooden alebrijes, the woven tablecloths, typical pottery, painted tinware, and rugs from throughout the state are on hand to demonstrate how they make their traditional crafts. It's open daily; avoid going at lunchtime, when the artisans take a break. La Crucecita's **Mercado Municipal** (municipal market; ⊠ Calle Guanacaste con Bugambilias, ☎ no phone) is a fun place to shop; in addition to leather sandals, postcards, and other tourist items, you'll see mountains of fresh fruits and vegetables.

OAXACA COAST A TO Z

Arriving and Departing

By Bus

Cristóbal Colón (⊠ Booking office: Calle 20 de Noviembre 204A, ☎ 9/51–46655) has three first-class buses per day leaving from Oaxaca's first-class bus terminal, frequently referred to as the ADO (⊠ Calzada Niños Héroes 1036, ☎ 9/51–51703), to Huatulco (7½ hours; $14). The same bus continues on to Puerto Escondido (nine hours; $16). There are several first-class buses each day to Pochutla (eight hours; $15), where you can connect to Puerto Ángel, but none is direct. Buses return to Oaxaca City from the **Huatulco bus station** (⊠ Calle Gardenias esq. Ocotillo, La Crucecita, ☎ 9/58–70261) and the **Puerto Escondido bus station** (⊠ Calle Primera Nte. 201, ☎ 9/58–21073).

Estrella del Valle's first-class buses run at night; daytime *ordinario* buses make many stops and aren't recommended. Buses leave from Oaxaca's second-class station (⊠ corner of Trujano and the Periférico, ☎ 9/51–45700 or 9/51–65429) for Huatulco and Puerto Escondido ($8). The **Huatulco station** is in La Crucecita (⊠ Calle Jazmin s/n, behind Corona beer warehouse, ☎ 9/58–70193). There is also a **Puerto Escondido station** (⊠ Av. Hidalgo at Calle 3a Ote., ☎ 9/58–20050 or 9/58–20953).

Direct service between Oaxaca City and Puerto Escondido is available on **Autotransportes Turísticos.** Buses leave from Oaxaca City (⊠ Calle Armenta y López 721, ☎ 9/51–40806) and Puerto Escondido (⊠ Av. Hidalgo between 16 de Septiembre and 4a Nte., ☎ 9/58–20953 or 9/58–20050) twice a day.

By Car

The drive from Oaxaca City to the isthmus on Highway 190 is challenging, with plenty of curves and hairpin turns. Highway 175 is another twisting mountain road. The recently inaugurated Highway 131, to Puerto Escondido via Sola de Vega, is an obstacle course of potholes. Do *not* attempt these roads at night. Plan on taking about eight hours, and leave early enough to arrive before dark. At the coast, Highway 200 links Huatulco, Puerto Ángel, and Puerto Escondido. If you want to tool around the various beaches, a car is useful.

By Plane

Aero Vega (☎ 9/58–20151) has daily service to Puerto Escondido from Oaxaca's International Airport. Mexicana subsidiary **AeroCaribe** (☎ 9/58–22024 in Puerto Escondido; 9/58–71220 in Huatulco) connects Puerto Escondido and Oaxaca City five times a week, with daily connections to Huatulco. **Mexicana** (☎ 9/58–70243 or 9/58–70223 in Huatulco) flies to Huatulco from Mexico City, Guadalajara, Cancún, Monterrey, and several other Mexican and U.S. gateways, all with connections in Mexico City.

Aeropuerto Puerto Escondido (✉ Carretera Costera Km 3, ☎ 9/58–20492 or 9/58–20491) is a 10-minute taxi ride from town on Highway 200. **Aeropuerto Bahías de Huatulco** (☎ 9/58–19008) is about 16 km (10 mi) from Tangolunda on Highway 200.

Getting Around

By Bus

Frequent, inexpensive second-class buses connect Puerto Escondido, Puerto Ángel, and Huatulco, but you must stop at Pochutla, just off the highway near Puerto Ángel (☞ Arriving and Departing, *above*). These buses roar down the highway every 15 minutes or so, and each costs about $1.25. If you are going to Huatulco, be sure to specify that your final destination is the bus terminal in La Crucecita, which is closest to the bays.

By Car

Highway 200 from Puerto Escondido to Huatulco should be relatively hassle-free, if potholed. Having a car allows you to turn off the main road onto unmarked dirt roads leading to secluded beaches.

Contacts and Resources

Car Rental

Cars can be rented at the Huatulco airport, in Puerto Escondido, and in the Huatulco Bays area. International firms include **Budget** (✉ Hotel Posada Real, Av. Benito Juárez 11, Puerto Escondido, ☎ 9/58–20312), **National** (✉ Hotel Club Plaza Huatulco, Paseo de Tangolunda 23, ☎ 9/58–10293) in Tangolunda, and **Dollar** (✉ Huatulco: Sheraton Hotel, Blvd. Benito Juárez, ☎ 9/58–10055, ext. 787; Huatulco airport: ☎ 9/58–19004). Rental cars are expensive, starting at $45 a day for a Volkswagen Beetle, for example, and there is an additional drop-off fee if you don't return the car where you picked it up. Nonaffiliated local firms often quote lower rates, but their vehicles may be in questionable condition.

E-Mail

In Huatulco, **Internet Cafe** (✉ Calle 3 de Mayo 203, La Crucecita, ☎ 9/58–70841) is open daily 9–9 and charges $4 an hour.

Emergencies

BAHÍAS DE HUATULCO
Police (☎ 9/58–70020). **Red Cross** (☎ 9/58–71188).

PUERTO ESCONDIDO
Police (☎ 9/58–20111). **Red Cross** (☎ 9/58–20353).

Guided Tours

In Puerto Escondido the most exciting tours are run by ornithologist Michael Malone, who offers dawn and sunset excursions (December–April) into the Manialtepec Lagoon, a prime bird-watching area. Arrange tours (about $35 per person) through your hotel or through **Turismo Rodimar** (✉ Av. Gasga 905–B, ☎ 9/58–20734, FAX 9/58–20737), the most reliable and comprehensive agency in town.

Bahías Plus, with offices in La Crucecita (✉ Calle Carrizal at Calle Guanacastel, ☎ 9/58–70216 or 9/58–70932), is one of the most comprehensive travel agencies in Huatulco; it has tours to Puerto Ángel and Puerto Escondido (van tours start at a bit less than $20 a person in a group of six), as well as plane tours to Oaxaca ($337 a person). Most major hotels also have travel agencies.

Daylong tours into the Sierra Madre are available with the bilingual guides of **Motor Tours Huatulco** (✉ Av. Juárez s/n, Local 9, across from the Sheraton, ☎ 9/58–10323). One of the tours includes a visit to a working coffee plantation, with an elaborate lunch. The cost is approximately $110 to be divided between one to three people. This agency also arranges horse, all-terrain vehicle (ATV), and mountain-bike treks.

Cantera Tours (✉ Sheraton Hotel, Blvd. Benito Juárez, Bahía Tangolunda, ☎ FAX 9/58–10030) has all-day bay cruises for $22–$30 a person, excluding food. It also offers four-hour horse or ATV tours, beginning inland and ending at the beach, for about $38 per person. You can arrange bay trips through the **Sociedad Cooperative Tangolunda,** a boat owners' cooperative at the marina on Santa Cruz Bay (☎ 9/58–70081).

Visitor Information

Puerto Escondido tourism office (✉ Blvd. Benito Juárez, about a block from Aldea del Bazar Hotel at Playa Bacocho development, ☎ FAX 9/ 58–20175) is open weekdays 9–3 and 4–6, Saturday 10–1. The small information desk (☎ no phone) at the north end of the pedestrian walkway is often more helpful than the main tourism office. It's usually open weekdays 10–2 and 4–6, Saturday 10–1.

Oficina Estatal de Turismo (✉ Huatulco state tourism office: Blvd. Benito Juárez s/n, Bahía Tangolunda, in front of Restaurante Misió Fa-Sol, ☎ 9/58–10177, FAX 9/58–10176) is open weekdays 8–5, Saturday 9–1.

11 CHIAPAS AND TABASCO

The state of Chiapas is considered by many to be the most fascinating in Mexico. It is a study in contrasts, with the luxuriant tropical lowlands around Palenque—one of the country's most brilliant Maya ruins—giving way to gorgeous valleys and finally the highlands, home to many of Mexico's most traditional indigenous peoples.

Updated by
Paige Bierma

K NOWN TO MANY foreigners only for the ruins of Palenque and the colonial town of San Cristóbal de las Casas, Chiapas and Tabasco have typically drawn trekkers and travelers rather than tourists. World attention was drawn to Chiapas in early 1994 when indigenous guerrillas staged a brief but decisive rebellion. If you're looking for an outstanding travel experience, a well-planned trip to this area can be very satisfying, particularly if you come during a local festival. Unlike the country's popular beach resorts, Chiapas and Tabasco aren't an easy flight a few hours from major U.S. cities. Substantial ground transportation, either by bus or car, is usually required, although Tuxtla Gutiérrez and Villahermosa have international airports, and Palenque and San Cristóbal de las Casas have national airports with limited routes. Tourist information can be more difficult to obtain in Tabasco than in Chiapas.

A bloody past of exploitation by and fierce confrontation with outsiders remains vividly present, as already impoverished indigenous communities in Chiapas are forced to compete for their lands with developers and new settlers. Because of its isolation, Chiapas has been at the margin of the nation's development. It is one of the poorest states in Mexico, with appallingly high rates of alcoholism, violence, illiteracy, and death due to unhygienic conditions. Land distribution, too, is skewed: 1% of landowners holds 15% of the territory—about 50% of the arable land—keeping the colonial system nearly intact, and repression is rampant. It was the indifference of the Mexican government to their plight that helped bring the anger of the indigenous people to a boil in early 1994, leading the group that calls itself the Zapatista National Liberation Army (EZLN is the Spanish acronym) to an armed uprising. Even though peace talks with the government have been stalled for years, the national and international interest sparked by the indigenous movement bodes well for the possibility of change in the region. The pipe-smoking Zapatista spokesman, Subcomandante Marcos, has become a cult figure in Mexico, his ski-masked image appearing on everything from magazine covers to children's toys, and he puts his poetic communiqués on the Internet for worldwide consumption.

Nominally enriched half a century ago with the discovery of oil in the Gulf of Mexico on its northern border, Tabasco also has a bloody past. During the 1920s and '30s, Tomás Garrido Canabal, a vehemently anticlerical governor, outlawed priests and had all the churches either torn down or converted to other uses. Riots, deportations, and property confiscations were common. When British writer Graham Greene visited Tabasco in 1938, he called it "the Godless state"; his novel *The Power and the Glory* grew out of his experience. All of that said, you won't find much evidence of Tabasco's turbulent past today. A wholly different spirit prevails here than in Chiapas.

Although the Mexican economic crisis has delayed some plans for building more tourism infrastructure, Chiapas is getting a boost from a government promotion program. It's an important segment of the Mundo Maya travel circuit created by the Mexican government in the early 1990s to showcase its Maya ruins and colonial cities in the name of regional development and ecotourism. Development in the past has been a two-edged sword. The Lacandon jungle is already disappearing, its Maya inhabitants being driven to live in a smaller portion of their ancestral lands. Massive erosion and deforestation are taking their toll as new settlers burn the forest and exhaust the soil by raising cattle.

For the present, however, when you set out along tortuous mountain roads—full of dramatic hairpin turns along the edges of mist-filled ravines—you will still find remote clusters of huts and cornfields planted on near-vertical hillsides. You will pass Indian women wrapped in deep-blue shawls and coarsely woven wool skirts, and Indian children selling fruit and flowers by the roadside. Chiapas has nine distinct linguistic groups, primarily the highland-dwelling Tzotzils and the Tzeltals, who live in both highland and lowland areas. In more-isolated regions, many villagers speak only their native language, or a rudimentary Spanish necessary for interaction with the outside world.

Business travelers make up the majority of those who visit Villahermosa, Tabasco's capital. But the city has a superb museum of pre-Columbian archaeology at the CICOM complex and a collection of massive Olmec heads and altars at Parque Museo La Venta. Both provide a good introduction to the Indian heritage of Tabasco and Chiapas. Palenque, with its incredible Maya ruins, is culturally and geographically linked with the lowlands in Tabasco. If you want to get into the great outdoors, there are lakes, lagoons, caves, and wild rivers surging through the jungle.

Note: Although travel in the area is reasonably safe, at press time the U.S. State Department was advising travelers to "exercise extreme caution" in Chiapas because of ongoing sporadic confrontations between government and rebel supporters. Although these skirmishes haven't been near the main tourist destinations—and may be resolved by the time you visit—contact the State Department or any of the Mexican Government Tourist Offices in the United States before you go for the current status. Carry your visa and passport even on day trips throughout the region, as there may be military checkpoints along both main and secondary roads.

Pleasures and Pastimes

Archaeological Sites
Ruins of Maya cities in mysterious, overgrown jungles are a big draw in this area. Unparalleled Palenque has the most appeal, and the lesser known sites of Toniná, Bonampak, and Yaxchilán (pronounced yash-chee-*lan*) are attracting more attention than ever.

Dining
Chiapas has regional specialties but borrows heavily from Yucatán and Oaxaca. Culinary adventurers should try *atole* (a cornmeal drink), the many local variations of tamales, locally smoked ham called *cochito horneado*, candied fruit, and any dishes that contain the tasty Mexican herbs *chipilín* and *yerba santa* (or *mumu*, as locals call it). San Cristóbal's restaurants have an ample choice of Mexican and international cuisines, and most of them have added vegetarian dishes to their menus. Although they can be rated the best in the state, they're not outstanding compared to those in other regions of Mexico.

Prices, however, are quite reasonable: a filling dinner (helped out by tortillas in one of their myriad forms) with beer rarely costs more than $10 a person. There is no dress code to speak of in this part of Mexico, and reservations aren't necessary. San Cristóbal closes down early, so unlike in other parts of Mexico, it is a fairly common practice to eat dinner before 8 PM. As is the case throughout Mexico, lunch is the main meal of the day, served between 1 and 4 PM.

Tabasco saves some of its export beef for the Villahermosa restaurants, which also serve lots of fresh fish from the Gulf and freshwater lakes and rivers. Local specialties—or oddities, if you wish—include *peje-*

lagarto, an ancient fish with the head of an alligator and a strong, sweet flavor. Also try *puchero,* beef stew with vegetables and plantains; river shrimp; *tostones* (fried plantain chips); baked bananas with cream; banana liqueur; and the region's fresh, white cheese.

Generally speaking, the food served in the town of Palenque is modest in both quality and price. Many restaurants are open-air, which is where you want to be in this hot, humid part of Mexico. You'll spend more in the higher priced hotels; most moderate and inexpensive restaurants don't bother to charge sales tax.

CATEGORY	COST*
$$$$	over $15
$$$	$10–$15
$$	$5–$10
$	under $5

per person for a three-course meal, excluding drinks, service, and 15% sales tax

Lodging

Almost all the hotels in San Cristóbal are within walking distance of the major attractions. Most of those listed are colonial—historically and architecturally—in keeping with the rest of the town. All rooms, unless otherwise stated, have showers; air-conditioning isn't necessary at this high altitude and, in fact, fireplaces are welcome.

Tuxtla Gutiérrez lodgings tend to be more functional than frilly; this town is the no-nonsense business and transportation hub of Chiapas. An exception to the rule is the Camino Real, which resembles a small palace perched on a hilltop.

Palenque is no longer the jungle outpost it used to be, fit only for souls who considered rustic amenities colorful. This is a growing tropical town with modern, comfortable hotels. The best and newest are strung along the Palenque–Pakalná highway that goes to the Palenque ruins just outside town. Geared for groups as well as individuals, these hotels have lush gardens, inviting pools, and air-conditioning or ceiling fans. Quite a few new *posadas* (guest houses) have sprung up downtown in the past few years, and there are a couple of agreeable hotels and restaurants in the quiet neighborhood of La Cañada, between the downtown area and the highway.

Villahermosa hotels are relatively expensive, especially when compared with those in San Cristóbal. Fancy four- and five-star hotels geared to business travelers tend to be away from the city center, near Tabasco 2000 and Parque La Venta. But there are comfortable and economical hotels downtown, near the Grijalva River, or in the nearby, pedestrian-friendly Zona Luz (Light Zone), or Zona Remodelada (Remodeled Zone).

Many hotels (especially budget and moderate lodgings) quote prices that already include the 15%–17% tax, which varies from county to county; others do not. Make sure to inquire about this.

CATEGORY	COST*
$$$$	over $90
$$$	$60–$90
$$	$27–$60
$	under $27

All prices are for a standard double room, excluding tax (15%–17%).

Shopping

The artisans of Chiapas, especially in and around San Cristóbal, produce some of the most striking indigenous folk art of Mexico. Best are the embroidered blouses, *huipiles* (tunics), bedspreads, and tablecloths and leather goods, such as belts and purses. Lacandon bows and arrows and the beribboned ceremonial hats worn by local officials also make good souvenirs.

Chiapas is one of the few places in the world that has amber mines, so finely crafted jewelry made from this prehistoric resin is easy to find in San Cristóbal—as are plastic imitations sold by street vendors (stores usually sell amber and street vendors commonly have the fakes, although there is some crossover). San Cristóbal is also known for the quality wrought-iron crosses that bless its rooftops. Although many of the ironworking shops have closed, you can still find the crosses in crafts stores.

Tuxtla Gutiérrez and Palenque, although not known for handicrafts, have a few shops selling quality crafts from throughout the state.

Exploring Chiapas and Tabasco

Where Tabasco is lush, green, and pastoral, the abode of the ancient Olmecs who gave Mexico its mother culture, Chiapas is for the most part mountainous, its Maya ruins and villages isolated from modern Mexico by sinuous roads and footpaths. The colonial city of San Cristóbal once dominated both regions when the Spanish conquistadores held sway over the country. Modern Villahermosa now is the economic force in the two regions because of the petroleum industry.

The highlights of a trip to Chiapas and Tabasco are still the ruins of Palenque and the colonial town of San Cristóbal de las Casas. These and all other major sights are accessible by road from either Tuxtla Gutiérrez or Villahermosa, the only cities with international airports. The once isolated ruins of Yaxchilán and Bonampak are now more accessible—by paved roads or via bush planes that fly from the two internationally connected cities as well as from Palenque, Ocosingo, and Comitán. Palenque and San Cristóbal de las Casas have small new airports that land small-bodied jets on a limited basis. If you're a first-time visitor, and especially if you don't speak Spanish, it's faster, more efficient, and more comfortable to take tours to the area's major attractions.

Numbers in the text correspond to numbers in the margin and on the Chiapas and Tabasco and San Cristóbal de las Casas maps.

Great Itineraries

The farther you wander into the region, the more you'll be fascinated with its natural diversity and its remnants of Maya and Spanish colonial cultures. A three-day trip gives only a superficial glance at what the region has to offer, but it will afford you the opportunity to visit Palenque and San Cristóbal de las Casas, two of Mexico's outstanding attractions. Stays of five to eight or more days will allow you to cover greater distances and get to the lesser-known wonders of Chiapas and Tabasco.

IF YOU HAVE 3 DAYS

Spend the first day and night at the Maya ruins at **Palenque** ㉒, and consider going the proverbial extra mile on a side trip to the lovely jungle waterfalls at **Misol-Há** ㉑ and **Agua Azul** ⑳. Tours from Palenque are the best way to pack it all into one day. The next day, drive south to colonial **San Cristóbal de las Casas** ①–⑧, the oldest city in Chiapas. Spend at least two hours on a walking tour of town, starting at the centuries-old **zócalo** ① (town square). Overnight at San Cristóbal

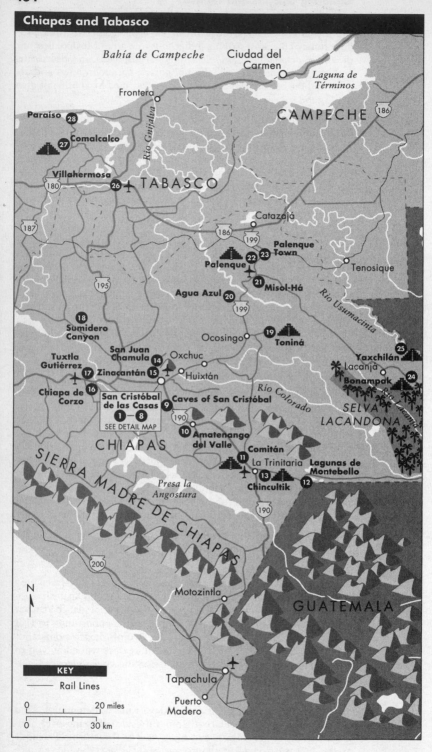

Chiapas and Tabasco

Bahía de Campeche

Ciudad del Carmen

Laguna de Términos

Frontera

CAMPECHE

186

Paraíso **28**

Comalcalco 27

Villahermosa

180

26 ✈ TABASCO

187

Catazajá

199

186

Palenque Town

Palenque **22 23**

195

21 Misol-Há

Agua Azul **20**

199

Tenosique

Río Usumacinta

18

Sumidero Canyon

Ocosingo

19 Toniná

San Juan Chamula

14 Oxchuc

Yaxchilán **25**

Tuxtla Gutiérrez

17 Zinacantán **15**

Huixtán

Lacanjá

Bonampak **24**

Chiapa de Corzo **16**

San Cristóbal de las Casas

1 — **8**

SEE DETAIL MAP

9 Caves of San Cristóbal

Río Colorado

SELVA LACANDONA

10

190

Amatenango del Valle

Comitán

CHIAPAS

11 La Trinitaria

Lagunas de Montebello

13 **12**

Chincultik

Presa la Angostura

190

SIERRA

MADRE

DE

CHIAPAS

GUATEMALA

200

Motozintla

N

KEY

—— Rail Lines

0   20 miles

0   30 km

✈ Tapachula

Puerto Madero

and, on Day 3, visit the Maya villages of **San Juan Chamula** ⑭, known for its Catholic church with pre-Hispanic rituals, and **Zinacantán** ⑮, famous for its handwoven tunics and pink shawls. Return to San Cristóbal to visit the market, shop for Indian crafts, and spend the night.

IF YOU HAVE 5 DAYS

Spend the first day and night in **Villahermosa** ㉖, exploring the giant Olmec heads, the river walkway, and the anthropology museum. Day 2, drive to **Palenque** ㉒, visit the ruins, and stay overnight in Palenque. Day 3, drive to **San Cristóbal de Las Casas** ①–⑧, stopping off at two or more of these sights along the way: the waterfalls at **Misol-Há** ㉑ or **Agua Azul** ⑳, or the Maya site of **Toniná** ⑲, near Ocosingo. Spend the night in San Cristóbal. Day 4, see **San Juan Chamula** ⑭ and **Zinacantán** ⑮ in the morning and then return to San Cristóbal to shop for native crafts and spend another night. On Day 5, drive south on Highway 190 to see the **Lagunas de Montebello** ⑫. After seeing the lakes, visit on the return trip as many of the following as your schedule permits: the small Maya sites of **Chincultik** ⑬ and **Tenam Puente;** the charming town of **Comitán** ⑪; the pottery-producing town of **Amatenango del Valle** ⑩; and the stalactite- and stalagmite-graced **Caves of San Cristóbal** ⑨. For a less rushed visit, plan to spend the night in Comitán and return early the next morning for San Cristóbal or Tuxtla.

IF YOU HAVE 8 DAYS

Spend the first day and night in **Villahermosa** ㉖, as in the five-day itinerary. Next day, drive north of the city to visit the unusual Maya temples at **Comalcalco** ㉗. Return to Villahermosa for a dinner cruise on the *Capitán Buelo* along the Grijalva River and overnight here again. Spend the next four days as on Days 2–5 of the five-day itinerary—seeing **Palenque** ㉒, **Misol-Há** ㉑, **Agua Azul** ⑳, and **Toniná** ⑲ on the way to **San Cristóbal de Las Casas** ①–⑧, from which you can take day trips north and southeast. On Day 7, head west, touring colonial **Chiapa de Corzo** ⑯ and the impressive **Sumidero Canyon** ⑱ by boat en route to **Tuxtla Gutiérrez** ⑰. Spend that night and the next in Tuxtla. On Day 8, visit Tuxtla's zoo, shop at the **Casa de las Artesanías,** and stroll in the **Parque de la Marimba** in the late afternoon.

If you want to go all out seeing Maya sites, add a day trip to **Bonampak** ㉔ and **Yaxchilán** ㉕—which you can take in during a one-day road trip on the new highway from Palenque (chartered planes to the ruins are also sometimes available from Tuxtla Gutiérrez). You can arrange to spend the night at the ecotourism site Escudo Jaguar, on the Usumacinta River near the boat launch for Yaxchilán, or in Palenque. From San Cristóbal, you can still squeeze in a long day trip to **Comitán** ⑪, the **Lagunas de Montebello** ⑫, and **Chincultik** ⑬.

When to Tour

Scheduling your visit to coincide with local festivals is worthwhile. Just make hotel reservations well in advance. Important holidays are January 15–23 for Chiapa de Corzo's San Sebastian festival (also held January 20–22 in Zinacantán); Carnival and Easter Week in San Juan Chamula, where villagers walk over hot coals; every Friday during Lent in Zinacantán; June 22–24 for Chamula's San Juan festival; the July 24–25 festival of the patron saint of San Cristóbal, when brightly decorated trucks, buses, and taxis parade up a hilltop to the San Cristóbal Church; the August 6–11 celebration of San Lorenzo in Zinacantán; the November 1–2 Día de los Muertos (Day of the Dead) celebrations in Zinacantán, with spirited graveside festivals; and the feast of the Virgin of Guadalupe (celebrated for a week in Tuxtla Gutiérrez) on December 12. Several indigenous highland villages hold celebrations on December 31 to install new civil officials. Remember that it's beastly hot in the lowlands most of the year, but especially just prior to the rainy season, February–April.

SAN CRISTÓBAL DE LAS CASAS

San Cristóbal, the most touristic city of the Chiapas highlands, is a pretty town of about 150,000 in a valley of pine forests interspersed with maize fields and orchards. At an altitude of 6,888 ft above sea level, indigenous women with babies tied tightly in colorful shawls share the plaza with backpackers. More Europeans than Americans visit San Cristóbal—perhaps they are less put off by headlines about government troops and the EZLN, or more intrigued by the political ramifications. In truth, the rival sides are more likely to snipe at each other during their rare trips to the negotiating table, or via newspaper editorials or the Internet, than in hostile confrontations.

San Cristóbal is beautiful and inexpensive, the perfect hub for exploring some of the region's lakes, villages, and archaeological sites. Small enough to take in on foot in the course of a day, the town is also captivating enough to invite a stay of three days, a week, or even longer. In addition to viewing colonial monuments, consider planning an early morning visit to see local Indians gather at the *mercado* (market) and browse for crafts, or explore one of the indigenous villages in the vicinity. Sunday is the best day for visiting village markets. Just soaking up the ambience in one of San Cristóbal's little cafés or unpretentious restaurants is a pleasure.

San Cristóbal is among the finest colonial towns in Mexico, and its cool climate is a refreshing change from the sweltering heat of the lower altitudes. On chilly evenings, smoke from chimney fires curls lazily over the red-tile roofs of small, brightly painted stucco houses and elegant colonial mansions. The haunting atmosphere here is intensified by the remarkable quality of the early morning and late-afternoon light.

In 1524 the Spaniards under Diego de Mazariegos decisively defeated the Chiapan Indians at a battle outside town. Mazariegos founded the city, which was called Villareal de Chiapa de los Españoles, in 1528. For most of the viceroyalty, or colonial era, Chiapas, with its capital at San Cristóbal, was a province of Guatemala. Lacking the gold and silver of the north, it was of greater strategic than economic importance to the Spaniards. Under Spanish rule the region's agricultural resources became entrenched in the *encomienda* system, in which wealthy Spanish landowners forced natives to work as slaves. "In this life all men suffer," lamented a Spanish friar in 1691, "but the Indians suffer most of all."

The situation improved only slightly through the efforts of Bartolomé de las Casas, the bishop of San Cristóbal, who in the mid-1500s protested the torture and massacre of the Indians. The Indians protested in another way, murdering priests and other *ladinos* (whites) in infamous uprisings.

Mexico, Guatemala, and the rest of New Spain declared independence in 1821. For just two years, Chiapas remained part of Guatemala, electing by plebescite to join Mexico on September 14, 1824—the date is still celebrated in San Cristóbal and all over Chiapas as the *día de la mexicanidad* (Day of Mexicanization) of Chiapas. In 1892, because of San Cristóbal's allegiance to the Royalists during the War of Independence, the capital was moved to Tuxtla Gutiérrez. With that went all hope that the town would keep pace with the rest of Mexico. It wasn't until the 1950s that the roads into town were paved and the first automobiles arrived. Modern times came late to San Cristóbal, for which many locals and visitors are thankful.

Because of the altitude, it gets cold here at night, and can be chilly during the day as well; pack a warm sweater and plan to layer your clothing. When the sun does appear, it can get quite hot, but most restaurants keep doors open even during cold weather, and hotels are for the most part unheated. The cobblestone and flagstone streets are also best suited to wearing tennis shoes, hiking boots, or other flat-heel sports shoes.

Exploring San Cristóbal de las Casas

San Cristóbal is laid out in a grid pattern centered on the zócalo, with street names changing on either side of the square. For example, Calle Francisco Madero to the east of the square becomes Diego de Mazariegos to the west.

The town was originally divided into several *barrios* (neighborhoods), which now blend together into a city center that is easily negotiated. In colonial times, Indian allies of the triumphant Spaniards were moved onto lands on the outskirts of the nascent city. Each barrio was dedicated to a different occupation. There were Mexican weavers, Tlaxcala fireworks manufacturers, and pig butchers from Cuxtitali. Although these divisions no longer exist, other customs have been kept alive. For example, each Saturday certain houses downtown will put out red lamps to indicate that fresh homemade tamales are for sale.

A Good Walk

Head for the heart of downtown, the Plaza 31 de Marzo, or **zócalo** ① and take in the colonial buildings around the square, many of them homes of the Spanish conquistadores. Note the 16th-century **Casa de Diego de Mazariegos** ② on its southeast corner (now the Hotel Santa Clara). Continue in a northwesterly direction around the square to the neoclassical **Palacio Municipal** ③—which gets painted a different color according to the whim of each new governor—with its numerous arcades. **La Catedral** ④ (cathedral), on the north side of the zócalo, has a fascinating facade painted ochre with details in rust, black, and white. Continue north five blocks along Avenida General Utrilla to the 16th-century **Templo de Santo Domingo** ⑤ with its ornamental baroque facade; walk around the complex to its museum and famous textiles cooperative amid the Indian families selling goods in the large exterior courtyard. Head for Avenida General Utrilla again and walk north three blocks to the **mercado** ⑥ to visit the stalls filled with fruits, vegetables, candles, and other necessities. You can catch a cab, or walk the nine long blocks east on Comitán, to the **Museo Na Bolom** ⑦, a great local repository of Indian artifacts. As the museum is shown by tour only, you'll probably want to time your arrival for the 4:30 tour. To end the day, catch another taxi (or walk five blocks south on Av. Vicente Guerrero and seven blocks west on Calle Real de Guadalupe) back downtown to see the gorgeous regional costumes on display at the **Museo Sergio Castro** ⑧.

Sights to See

② **Casa de Diego de Mazariegos.** One of the most accessible pieces of colonial architecture in San Cristóbal is now the Hotel Santa Clara (☞ Lodging, *below*). The stone mermaid and lions outside it are typical of the period's plateresque style—as ornate and busy as the work of a silversmith. ☒ *Av. Insurgentes 1.*

438

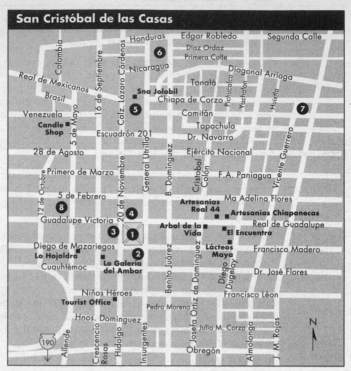

San Cristóbal de las Casas

NEED A
BREAK?
Cozy and relaxing, **La Galería Café** (✉ Calle Hidalgo 3, ½ block south of the zócalo, ☎ 967/8–15–47) is the favorite haunt of local intellectuals and poets who drink their way through cappuccinos, espressos, or beers until midnight. Appetizers, pizza, and hard liquor are also served, and an excellent art gallery and craft store are located inside.

④ La Catedral. Dedicated to San Cristóbal Mártir (St. Christopher the Martyr), it was built in 1528, then demolished, and rebuilt in 1693, with additions during the 18th and 19th centuries. The Baroque facade, recently repainted in ochre with Indian red, black, and white accents, is unforgettable. Inside, don't miss the painting *Nuestra Señora de Dolores* (Our Lady of Sorrows) to the left of the altar, the gold-plated *retablo de los reyes* (altarpiece), the Chapel of Guadalupe, and the gold-washed pulpit. ✉ *Calle Guadalupe Victoria between 20 de Noviembre and Av. Gral. Utrilla; entrance on south side.* ☉ *Daily 7:30–2 and 4–8:30, daily mass at 8 PM.*

⑥ Mercado. This municipal market occupies an eight-block area. Best visited early in the morning—especially on the busiest day, Saturday—the market is the social and commercial center for the Indians from surrounding villages. Stalls overflow with local produce, turkeys, medicinal herbs, flowers, firewood, and wool, as well as huaraches (sandals), grinding stones, candles, and candied fruit. Be discreet about taking photographs. ✉ *Between Av. Gral. Utrilla, Nicaragua, Honduras, and Belisario Domínguez.*

★ **⑦ Museo Na Bolom.** If you are interested in the culture and history of the Maya, particularly that of the Lacandon, set aside an afternoon to tour this institute, a handsome 22-room neoclassical building built as a Christian seminary in 1891. Na Bolom (House of the Jaguar) was purchased by Franz and Gertrude "Trudi" Blom in 1950; Trudi was a social activist born in the Swiss Alps and Franz was a Danish archaeologist. They set it up as an institute dedicated to ethnological and ecological advocacy; this work is still carried on today. The facilities can be used by groups as a base for special events or workshops, combining any permutation of accommodations, meals, and organized tours as they wish. Na Bolom's staff is well connected within San Cristóbal and can arrange tours to artisans' co-ops, villages, and nature reserves that are a bit off the beaten path.

Na Bolom showcases the Bloms' small collection of religious treasures, which had been hoarded in attics during the anticlerical 1920s and 1930s. A museum houses Franz Blom's findings from the Classic Maya site of Moxviquil (pronounced mosh-vee-*keel*), found on the outskirts of San Cristóbal, and his personal effects, such as his Remington typewriter, eyeglasses, and bottle of *mezcal* (agave-based) liquor (he died of cirrhosis of the liver in 1963). Trudi's bedroom contains a case full of silver jewelry, along with her shawls, canes, collection of indigenous handicrafts, and wondrous wardrobe of 95 embroidered dresses. Also on the premises is a room full of objects from the daily life of the Lacandon, a tribe descended from the ancient Maya in the Yucatán; the Bloms documented their traditions and helped to ensure their survival. A library holds more than 10,000 volumes on Chiapas and the Maya. Na Bolom is also a guest house, and revenue from guests, tours, and the gift shop goes to support the work of the institute (☞ Lodging, *below*). The gift shop sells Lacandon crafts such as flutes and bows and arrows, as well as black-and-white photos. Arrange for a meal at Na Bolom, even if you don't stay here (☞ Dining, *below*).

Na Bolom is dedicated to reforestation of the surrounding area, planting thousands of trees each year. Its own extensive nursery/garden is filled with firs, fruit trees, vegetables, and other flowering plants. Trudi, who was born in 1901, received the United Nations' 500 Global Roll of Honor award in 1991 for her lifelong work on the preservation of the environment. She died in 1993, but the private, nonprofit institute is being run by a carefully selected board of directors. ⊠ *Av. Vicente Guerrero 31, between Comitán and Chiapa de Corzo,* ☎ 967/ 8–14–18. 🎫 *Museum and tour $2.* ☉ *Library weekdays 10 AM–12:30 PM, store daily 9:30–1:30 and 3–7, tours in English and Spanish daily at 11:30 and 4:30.*

❽ Museo Sergio Castro. Those interested in regional ethnic apparel might consider a visit to this private gallery. Sergio Castro, an agronomist from northern Mexico who has dedicated himself to building schools in the highlands of Chiapas, has spent nearly 40 years working with the Indians; many of the ceremonial costumes are collector's items. There are around 800 pieces in the collection, including textiles, weavings, and carved wooden saints, musical instruments, and toys. ⊠ *Calle Guadalupe Victoria 61,* ☎ 967/8–42–89. 🎫 *Donations welcome.* ☉ *Daily 5–8.*

❸ Palacio Municipal (Municipal Palace). Perhaps the most famous mansion in San Cristóbal is this building, with its wide colonial arches and tile patio. It was the seat of the state government until 1892, when Tuxtla Gutiérrez became the capital. It now houses municipal government offices. ⊠ *Av. Hidalgo between Calles Diego de Mazariegos and Guadalupe Victoria.* 🎫 *Free.* ☉ *Daily 9–2 and 5–8.*

❺ Templo de Santo Domingo. This three-block-long complex houses a church, former convent, regional history museum, and the **Templo de la Caridad** (Temple of the Sisters of Charity). A two-headed eagle— emblem of the Hapsburg dynasty that once ruled Spain and its American dominions—broods over the pediment of the church, which was built between 1547 and 1569. The pink stone facade (which needs a good cleaning) is carved in an intensely ornamental style known as Baroque Solomonic: saints' figures, angels, and grooved columns overlaid with vegetation motifs abound. The interior is dominated by lavish altarpieces, an exquisitely fashioned pulpit, a sculpture of the Holy Trinity, and wall panels of gilded, carved cedar—one of the precious woods of Chiapas that centuries later lured the woodsmen of Tabasco to the obscure highlands surrounding San Cristóbal. At the southeast corner of the church park lies the tiny and much more humble Templo de la Caridad, built in 1715 to honor the Immaculate Conception. Its highlight is the finely carved altarpiece, and the fact that you'll often find traditional Indians from San Juan Chamula lighting candles and making offerings here (if you can't make the side trip to the town just north of San Cristóbal). *Note:* Do *not* attempt to take photos of the Chamulan Indians.

The Ex-Convento de Santo Domingo, adjacent to the Santo Domingo church, now houses **Sna Jolobil,** an Indian cooperative selling an excellent selection of rather expensive local weavings, embroidered clothing, and colorful postcards. The shop is open Tuesday through Saturday 9–2 and 4–7. The small **Regional History Museum** (☎ 967/8–16–09), also part of the complex, displays archaeological pieces and textiles and is open daily 10–5. Admission is $2, free Sunday. ⊠ *20 de Noviembre s/n near Real de Mexicanos.*

❶ **Zócalo.** This main square around which the colonial city was built has in its center a gazebo used by musicians most evenings and weekend afternoons. You can have a coffee on the top or middle floor of the gazebo; be prepared for small children and women hawking their wares. Surrounding the square are a number of 16th-century buildings, many former mansions of the conquistadores, with wood-beam ceilings and plant-filled central patios. Don't be afraid to go into buildings whose doors are open. ⊠ *Between Avs. Gral. Utrilla and 16 de Septiembre and Calles Diego de Mazariegos and Guadalupe Victoria.*

Outside San Cristóbal. Surrounding San Cristóbal are many small and seldom-visited Indian villages celebrated for the exquisite colors and embroidery work of their inhabitants' costumes. Huixtán (hweesh-*tan*) and Oxchuc (osh-*chuc*) are about 28 km and 43 km (17 mi and 26 mi), respectively, on the road to Ocosingo. Neither is known for its market, although they are visited during their town festivals; Huixtán venerates San Miguel (Saint Michael) on September 29, and Oxchuc celebrates patron San Tomás (Saint Thomas) on July 3. The Thursday market in Tenejapa, 27 km (17 mi) northeast of San Cristóbal, is worth seeing.

Dining

$$$ ✕ **Paris-Mexico.** A cozy, laid-back atmosphere makes this a local fa-
★   vorite for breakfast, lunch, and dinner. Attentive waiters who speak French and Spanish (but no English) serve a range of traditional Mexican and French entrées, soups, and desserts topped off with your choice of a fine French wine or a margarita. ⊠ *Calle Madero 20, corner of Francisco León,* ☎ *967/8–06–95. AE, MC, V.*

$$$ ✕ **Restaurant L'Eden.** Local expats rave about the steaks at this small,
★   charming chalet-style restaurant within the Hotel El Paraíso (☞ Lodging, *below*). It has eight cozy dining tables, piped-in classical music, and pleasant service. The margaritas are the biggest in San Cristóbal. Swiss delights include classic raclette—melted cheese and potato— and beef fondue for two. Homemade lime or raspberry pie makes a perfect finish to a meal. Open for dinner only. ⊠ *Av. 5 de Febrero 19,* ☎ *967/8–00–85. AE, MC, V.*

$$ ✕ **La Casa del Pan.** Organically grown fruits, vegetables, and coffee
★ get top billing at this laid-back vegetarian restaurant—a bit too mel-
low at times, as service tends to be unreasonably slow. Still, the tasty
tamales *chiapanecos* with a spicy cheese filling, hot bean soup, and the
best salads in town draw return visits. The four-course special of the
day, which includes variations on traditional Mexican cooking, really
shines. The bakery sells homemade breads, bagels, coffee, cookies, and
fruit preserves. Musical groups with repertoires from jazz to pop per-
form 8–10 most weekend nights. ✉ *Dr. Navarro 10 at Av. Belisario
Domínguez,* ☎ *967/8–58–95. No credit cards. Closed Mon.*

$$ ✕ **El Fogón de Jovel.** For a truly authentic Chiapan meal and experience, there is no better restaurant than this one, where the waiters dress
in the traditional clothing of the highland Chamulan Indians (black
ponchos and straw hats with colored ribbons). Try the *parrillada chi-
apaneca,* a smorgasbord for two–four people of grilled beef, pork,
chicken, sausage, ribs, onion, pineapple, and various regional sauces;
or opt for the more standard chicken with mole sauce. If you're feeling brave, sample either of two regional drinks: the hefty *posh,* made
from fermented corn and sugarcane and traditionally used for religious
ceremonies, or the sweet but also potent *mistela,* made from local fruits
such as nance, blackberries, or quince. ✉ *Av. 16 de Septiembre 11, in
front of Catedral,* ☎ *967/8–25–57. AE, MC, V.*

$$ ✕ **La Parrilla.** A fireplace warms this horsey restaurant, where saddles
form bar stools and ranch antiques crowd wall shelves. Latino tunes
play discreetly in the background as waiters bring a variety of free ap-
petizers: quesadillas, guacamole, fresh salsa, cheese, and crisp tostadas.
Choose the pizza or a baked potato with three toppings of your choice.
Both the excellent sangria and the *frijoles charro*—bean soup with bits
of bacon and ham—are local favorites. ✉ *Av. Belisario Domínguez 32,*
☎ *967/8–22–20. No credit cards. Closed Mon.*

$$ ✕ **Restaurante el Teatro.** Sunshine streams in the second-story windows
during the day, warming yellow walls decorated with European and
local artwork. At night, candlelight presides. The French owner, Jacky,
keeps the atmosphere unhurried and makes most everything himself,
including the fresh pasta and chocolate mousse. The menu features primarily French and Italian dishes—including chateaubriand and crêpes.
The wood-fired pizzas and shish kebab are also delicious; a few Mexican dishes are served. ✉ *Av. 1 de Marzo 8, at Av. 16 de Septiembre,*
☎ *967/8–31–49. MC, V. Closed Mon.*

$ ✕ **Na Bolom.** Doña Bety, the late Trudi Blom's adoptive daughter, heads
the kitchen at this famous ethnological/ecological museum. Home-cooked
meals emphasizing vegetarian and chicken dishes are the norm here
with foods such as roast chicken, coleslaw, avocado strips, and Mexican *chayote* (a mild green squash). The communal dining table is shared
by international volunteers, Lacandon Indians, resident scholars, travelers, and artists in residence. Breakfast is served 7–11 and a five-course
dinner at 7 (no lunch). If you're not staying at the institute (☞ Lodging, *below*), call at least two hours ahead for a reservation. ✉ *Av. Vicente Guerrero 33,* ☎ *967/8–14–18. No credit cards.*

$ ✕ **La Selva Café.** This coffee shop has more than a dozen organic javas
and assorted coffee-flavored concoctions. The odd menu features no
egg dishes, but mostly sandwiches and cold plates, with exceptions such
as codfish pie, chopped-meat pie, and Chiapas tamales. There's a separate no-smoking section, and a few tables are in the lush garden out
back. ✉ *Crescencio Rosas 9, at Calle Cuauhtémoc,* ☎ *967/8–72–44.
No credit cards.*

Lodging

$$$$ 🔲 **El Jacarandal.** The four guest rooms in this beautiful private estate
★ with a great view of town are by far the most expensive in San Cristóbal,
at $160 per person, double occupancy—but the perfect choice if you
want a special stay. American owners Nancy and Percy Wood, who restored the 19th-century mansion and gardens to magnificence, offer guests
the run of the house, which includes the libraries, sitting rooms, an open
bar, terraces, garden nooks, horseback riding, and excursions to nearby
ruins. All rooms have bathtubs and Mexican and European folk-art furnishings. The kitchen is headed by Doña Fidelia, of Mexico City, who
is equally talented in Continental, American, Mexican, and European
cuisines. Transportation to and from the Tuxtla Gutiérrez airport is available at extra cost. There is a three-day minimum stay. ✉ *Comitán 7,
29220,* ☎ FAX *967/8–10–65. 4 rooms. Restaurant, bar, horseback riding, library, laundry service, free parking. No credit cards.*

$$ 🔲 **Casavieja.** Three blocks east of the zócalo, this spectacular hotel main-
tains the architectural style of the original colonial house, built in
1740. Each plain, comfortable, clean-smelling room is charmingly
decorated in Mexican furnishings and has large windows looking out
onto one of the three interior courtyards. All rooms have phones and
TVs with English channels; suites also have hot tubs. The Espinosas,
who run and own the hotel, are warm and knowledgeable hosts. ✉
Ma. Adelina Flores 27, 29230, ☎ *967/8–03–85,* ☎ FAX *967/8–68–68.
38 rooms, 2 suites. Restaurant, bar, free parking. AE, MC, V.*

$$ 🔲 **Hotel Casa Mexicana.** This beautifully designed hotel in a restored
colonial mansion is colorful, clean, and friendly. Good beds, beam ceil-
ings, and attractive artwork all help make this an outstanding hostelry.
All rooms have phones and satellite TV, and the suites have hot tubs.
The restaurant, which surrounds a lovely, plant-filled courtyard with
bubbling fountain in the middle, serves international dishes, such as
chicken in pistachio sauce and eggplant Parmesan. ✉ *28 de Agosto 1,
29200,* ☎ *967/8–06–98, 967/8–06–83, 967/8–13–48,* FAX *967/8–26–
27. 48 rooms, 2 junior suites, 1 master suite. Restaurant, bar, room
service, massage, sauna, baby-sitting, free parking. AE, MC, V.*

$$ 🔲 **Hotel El Paraíso.** The 13 guest rooms in this charming colonial
home have beam ceilings; some rooms have lofts and carpeting, eight
have phones. Comfortable leather-backed chairs in the guest lounge
overlook a sunny, plant-filled, indoor/outdoor patio area with tables
for breakfasting. The bar-restaurant offers the personal attention of
owners Daniel Suter and his Mexican wife, Teresa, who met as stu-
dents in Switzerland. For more solitude, request a room away from the
street and lounge. ✉ *Av. 5 de Febrero 19, 29200,* ☎ *967/8–00–85,* FAX
967/8–51–68. 13 rooms. Restaurant, bar. AE, MC, V.

$$ 🔲 **Hotel Santa Clara.** Once the home of city founder Diego de Mazariegos, this rambling 16th-century mansion is now a hotel overlooking
the action in the main plaza. It has a tangible air of past grandeur: beam
ceilings, antique furnishings, time-worn hardwood floors, and a slightly
damp smell throughout. Six of the nine extra-roomy units with balconies overlook the zócalo. There is a tiny round pool in the courtyard. For entertainment, Bar Cocodrilos has live Latin rock and pop
most nights. ✉ *Av. Insurgentes 1, 29200,* ☎ *967/8–08–71, 967/8–11–
40,* FAX *967/8–10–41. 39 rooms. Restaurant, bar, coffee shop, pool, travel
services, free parking. AE, MC, V.*

$$ 🔲 **Mansión del Valle.** A few blocks from the zócalo, this 19th-century
property has been converted into a modest yet comfortable hotel with
tasteful Spanish colonial design details. There is a rather plain sitting
room for card-playing or socializing in the large inner atrium. Rooms
on the first floor are dark; the seven second-story rooms with patios

overlooking La Merced church across the street are nicer. ⊠ *Calle Diego de Mazariegos 39, corner of Calle Guadalupe Victoria, 29240,* ☎ *967/8–25–82 or 967/8–25–83,* FAX *967/8–25–81. 40 rooms, 7 suites. Restaurant, bar, coffee shop, meeting room, free parking. AE, MC, V.*

$$ ⊞ **Na Bolom.** Each of the rustic but cozy rooms available at this cen-
★   ter for the study and preservation of the Lacandon Indians and the rain forest is decorated with the accoutrements of a specific indigenous com-munity—including crafts, photographs, and books. About half the rooms have bathtubs; all have fireplaces. Guests staying at Na Bolom receive a free tour of the house (including a documentary presentation) and access to the library. Book well in advance; ask for a garden view. You can share the dining room with staff and volunteers for a sepa-rate charge (☞ Dining, *above*). Groups are welcome, and staff will make travel and tour arrangements for a small fee. ⊠ *Av. Vicente Guerrero 33, 29200,* ☎ *967/8–14–18,* FAX *967/8–55–86. 13 rooms. Restaurant, library, free parking. MC, V.*

$$ ⊞ **Rincón del Arco.** The charming touches at this recently remodeled hotel include a freestanding fireplace in each room. Room 11 is secluded and has a pretty view of the garden. Rooms on the top floor share a wide balcony from which you can sit and enjoy the cityscape: a view of the Church of Guadalupe and ancient houses with red-tile roofs. Ask to see several rooms until you find the one you like best. The cheerful dining room has a fireplace and wrought-iron wagon-wheel chande-liers. ⊠ *Calle Ejército Nacional 66, 29200,* ☎ *967/8–13–13,* FAX *967/ 8–15–68. 50 rooms, 1 suite. Restaurant, bar, free parking. V.*

$–$$ ⊞ **La Catedral.** Reconstructed from a colonial inn and movie house, this four-story hotel has beam ceilings, terrazzo floors, replicas of colonial-era wood furniture, and a San Cristóbal first—solar energy for heating bathwater and the swimming pool. Guest rooms surround a three-story atrium topped with a stained-glass image of San Cristóbal's cathedral; outdoor dining is awkwardly placed in this central patio. Most rooms have central heating (a rarity in town), remote-control satel-lite TV, piped-in music, and tile bathrooms with tubs, phones, and hair dryers; suites have hot tubs. Rooms in the back above the pool have no central heating or tubs but cost almost half the standard rate. ⊠ *Calle Guadalupe Victoria 21, 29200,* ☎ FAX *967/8–13–63, 967/8–53– 56. 62 rooms, 22 suites. Restaurant, bar, pool, beauty salon, health club, business services, travel services, free parking. AE, MC, V.*

$ ⊞ **Hotel Arecife de Coral.** Just four blocks from the zócalo, this colo-nial-style hotel boasts a gorgeous interior courtyard with a resident pea-cock and paradisiacal fruit trees. Rooms have cable TV. ⊠ *Av. Crescencio Rosas 29, corner of Alvaro Obregón,* ☎ *967/8–21–25,* FAX *967/8 28– 98. 50 rooms. Restaurant, bar. MC, V.*

$ ⊞ **Posada Diego de Mazariegos.** This quaint hotel has fine colonial
★   details, beautiful gardens, and skylights throughout. Rooms have high ceilings and lovely tile bathrooms; some rooms have fireplaces the staff will light for you. ⊠ *5 de Febrero 1, corner of Av. Gral. Utrilla,* ☎ *967/8–08–33,* FAX *967/8–08–27. 71 rooms, 3 suites. Restaurant, bar, cafeteria, travel services, car rental, free parking. No credit cards.*

Nightlife and the Arts

The number of cultural offerings in San Cristóbal is on the rise. Ask at the tourist office, La Pared book shop, and El Puente coffee house and cultural center (☞ *below*) about upcoming lectures or concerts.

Museo Na Bolom (☞ Sights to See *in* Exploring San Cristóbal de las Casas, *above*) occasionally sponsors talks and audiovisual presenta-tions. The elegant **Teatro Hermanos Domínguez** (⊠ Diagonal Her-manos Paniagua s/n, just outside the city limits, ☎ 967/8–36–37) features programs such as folkloric dances from Latin America. **El Puente** (⊠ Real de Guadalupe 55, ☎ 967/8–37–23), a casual, hip restaurant-cum-social-center that serves breakfast all day, shows videos most nights, offers Internet access, and hosts occasional art exhibits. It's a good place to hear what's happening around town.

Although nightlife hasn't traditionally been one of San Cristóbal's main draws, there are now several good clubs with live music. **Latinos** (⊠ Francisco y Madero 23, corner of Benito Juárez, ☎ 967/8–20–83) serves up live Latin jazz, salsa, or tropical music after 9:30 Monday through Saturday. Flamenco guitar players perform Thursday through Saturday 9–11 at **Restaurant Bar Margarita** (⊠ Real de Guadalupe 34, ☎ 967/8–09–57), followed by a small salsa band and dancing until 1. **El A-Dove** (⊠ Miguel Hidalgo 2, ☎ 967/8–66–66) is the newest, hippest dance club in town, with a firehouse design and deejay world music until 4 on weekends and 2 Tuesday through Thursday. **Bar Cocodrilos** (⊠ Av. Insurgentes 1, ☎ 967/8–08–71, 967/8–11–40), part of the Hotel Santa Clara, on the zócalo, has a more mellow tavern feel but also hosts live rock and salsa bands most nights from 9:30 to midnight.

Outdoor Activities and Sports

A horseback ride into the neighboring indigenous villages is good exercise for mind and body. Most hotels can arrange for rentals of horses. Guides working through the tourist office and travel agencies can also hire horses and will accompany tourists. Five or six hours are needed to visit area villages or the nature reserve at Huitepec. Novices should be aware, however, that several hours on a horse can be quite—well—a pain. Many outfitters do *not* take experience into account when assigning mounts.

Los Pinguinos (⊠ 5 de Mayo 10–B, ☎ 967/8–02–02) runs mountain-biking tours to neighboring towns ($13–$20) and rents bikes ($1.50 per hour; $6.50 all day).

Shopping

There are no department stores in San Cristóbal. The market, although picturesque, sells more produce than handicrafts. The shops on Avenida Gral. Utrilla, south of the market, have a large selection of goods from Guatemala—not always those of the highest quality. Guatemalan textiles sometimes sell for less in Chiapas than they do in Guatemala, and the Mexican government is considering barring their import because of unfair competition with local producers. For the time being, make sure to bargain for these textiles to get a good price. Most Guatemalan cloth is dark-blue cotton with multicolor cotton needlepoint or trim.

Shops are generally open 9–2 and 4–8. Indian women and children often accost visitors on the streets with their wares—mostly fake amber, woven bracelets, and small dolls—but their selections aren't as varied as those in the shops, and prices won't necessarily be better. You can be assured, though, that the proceeds go directly to the craftspeople.

Among its excellent selection of wares, **Sna Jolobil** (Weaver's House in Tzotzil; ⊠ Ex-Convento de Santo Domingo, Calzada Lázaro Cárdenas 42, ☎ 967/8–71–78), the regional crafts cooperative, sells hand-dyed woolen sweaters and tunics, embroidered pillow covers, and pre-Hispanic-design wall hangings. It's closed Sunday and lunchtime.

Among the smart shops clustered along Real de Guadalupe are two subsidiaries of **El Arbol de la Vida** (⊠ Real de Guadalupe 27 and 28-A, ☎ 967/8–40–85, 967/8–50–50) one block apart. They specialize in attractive designer amber jewelry mixed with silver and gold. **La Galería del Ambar** (⊠ Crescencio Rosas 4A, ☎ 967/8–79–25) has a large selection of amber jewelry.

Artesanías Chiapanecas (⊠ Calle Real de Guadalupe 46C, ☎ no phone) has an excellent selection of embroidered blouses, huipiles, tablecloths, and bags. The government-run **Casa de las Artesanías** (⊠ Calle Niños Héroes and Av. Hidalgo, ☎ FAX 967/8–18–80) has wooden toys, ceramics, embroidered blouses, bags, and handwoven textiles from throughout the state, and a tiny ethnographic museum in back. It's closed Monday. At the Rincón del Arco Hotel, **Textiles Soriano** (⊠ Calle Ejército Nacional 66, ☎ 967/8–13–13) specializes in handwoven bedspreads and other cloth, which can be made to order in a few days. It's open 7:30–3 Monday–Saturday.

Two unique indigenous co-ops are found in old colonial San Cristóbal homes and offer original top-quality crafts as well as free informal tours to observe artisans at work. **Taller Leñateros** (⊠ Flavio A. Paniagua 54, ☎ 967/8–51–74)—run by expat Ambar Past—sells handmade books, boxes, postcards, and writing paper fashioned on the premises out of recycled flower petals, plants, and bark. **Kun Kun SC** (⊠ Talleres Reel de Mexicanos 21, ☎ 967/8–14–17) has an amazing collection of pottery, ceramic tiles, and natural-dyed rugs with Tzeltal and Tzotzil Indian designs.

SOUTH AND EAST OF SAN CRISTÓBAL

Southeast of San Cristóbal lies one of the least explored and most exotic regions of Chiapas: the Selva Lacandona, said to be the second-largest rain forest in the western hemisphere. Incursions of developers, land-hungry settlers, and refugees from neighboring Guatemala are transforming Mexico's last frontier, which for centuries has been the homeland of the Lacandon, a small tribe descended from the Maya of Yucatán. Some of their people still maintain their ancient customs, living in huts and wearing long, plain tunics. However, their custom of not marrying outside the tribe is causing serious problems, and their numbers, never large to begin with, have been reduced to about 350. The fabulous Caves of San Cristóbal (also known as Las Grutas de Rancho Nuevo) are in this region.

The Caves of San Cristóbal

⑨ *13 km (8 mi) southeast of San Cristóbal off Rte. 190.*

Spectacular limestone stalactites and stalagmites are illuminated along a 2,475-ft cement walkway inside these labyrinthine caves, which were discovered in 1960. But the caves were fully explored only a few years ago, prompting the creation of the **San Cristóbal Recreational Park.** The Spanish-speaking gatekeeper (or his kids) is usually available to guide visitors for a small fee. The caves may be closed in inclement weather; if in doubt, check with the San Cristóbal tourist office first. Horses can be rented ($3 per hour) for a ride around the surrounding pine forest, and there is a small restaurant and picnic area on the site. To get here, catch a Teopisca-bound microbus at Boulevard Juan Sabines Gutiérrez, across from the San Diego church. Make sure to tell the driver to let you off at the "grutas." Get off at the signed entrance, and walk about 1 km (½ mi) along the dirt road. Alternatively, catch a taxi from town for about $4. For about twice that price, you can ask him to wait while you explore the caves. ☎ *No phone.* 🎫 *50¢.* 🕐 *Daily 9–5.*

Amatenango del Valle

⑩ *37 km (23 mi) south of San Cristóbal.*

Amatenango del Valle is a Tzeltal village known for the handsome, primitive pottery made principally by the town's women, whose distinctive red and yellow huipiles are also much remarked upon. On the road to Comitán, the village currently has no signage; watch closely for the ocher, black, and natural-clay flowerpots and animal figurines—primarily gray doves—sitting by the side of the road. You can stop at any of these roadside houses, or turn into the town; almost every household has wares to sell. If you go during the dry season, you might get to see some of the pots being fired over open flames (not stoves), as they are done outside and only when rain isn't a threat. Spanish is definitely a second language here, and women negotiate without a lot of chitchat, or use younger children as interpreters.

Comitán

⑪ *55 km (34 mi) southeast of Amatenango del Valle.*

Comitán, whose Maya name, Balún-Canán, means "nine stars" or "guardians," is a pleasant commercial center and agricultural town of about 120,000. It's also the base from which many visitors tour the Lagunas de Montebello (☞ *below*) and the small archaeological sites nearby. Built by the Spaniards, the city flourished early on as a major center linking the lowland temperate plains to the edge of the Maya empire on the Pacific. Even today it serves as the principal trading point for the Tzeltal Indians and such Guatemalan goods as sugarcane liquor and orchids. One of the "Hundred Colonial Cities" now being renovated by a federal government grant, its pretty plaza and surrounding streets and buildings are being refurbished in colonial style.

Two notable churches are **Santo Domingo de Guzmán,** with architecture showing a Moorish influence, and **San Caralampio,** whose Spanish Baroque style shows the influence of Guatemalan artisans.

The **Casa-Museo Dr. Belisario Domínguez,** the lovely former home of a martyr of the revolution, opened as a museum in 1985. It houses a fascinating collection of medical instruments, pharmaceuticals, and late-19th-century furnishings, as well as photographs, documents, and letters from the Mexican revolution, during which the doctor was assassinated for his outspoken criticism of President Victoriano Huerta. ⊠ *Av. Central Sur Dr. Belisario Domínguez 35,* ☎ *963/2–13–00.* ⌨ *$1.* ☉ *Tues.–Sun. 9–5.*

The centrally located **Museo de Arte Hermila Castellanos** shows work by modern Mexican artists, including master painters Rufino Tamayo and Francisco Toledo, both from Oaxaca. In fact, many of the painters represented are Oaxaqueños, and the subject matter deals largely with mestizo and indigenous people, most often in stylized, contemporary depictions. ⊠ *Av. Central Sur Dr. Belisario Domínguez 51,* ☎ *962/2–20–82.* ⌨ *$2.* ☉ *Mon.–Sat. 10–5:45, Sun. 10–1.*

Some 15 km (9 mi) from Comitán, the small Maya site of **Tenam Puente** was discovered by archaeologists Franz Blom and Oliver Le-Farge. Restoration of this primarily ceremonial center, built around the same time as Chincultik (☞ *below*), was begun in 1993, and a royal tomb was discovered in 1996. There are three ball courts, apparently one each for the lower-, middle-, and upper-classes. Admission is free.

Lagunas de Montebello

⑫ *64 km (40 mi) southeast of Comitán.*

The 56 lakes and surrounding pine forest of the Lagunas de Montebello (Lakes of the Beautiful Mountain) constitute a 2,437-acre international park that is shared with Guatemala. A different color permeates each lake, whose waters glow with vivid emerald, turquoise, amethyst, azure, and steel-gray tints, caused by various oxides. The setting is serene and majestic, with clusters of oak, pine, and sweet gum. Practically the only denizens of the more accessible part of the forest are the clamorous goldfinches and mockingbirds. To the east roam puma, jaguar, deer, bear, and the rare quetzal bird.

At the park entrance, the paved road forks. The left fork leads to the Lagunas Coloradas (Colored Lakes). At Laguna Bosque Azul, the last lake along that road, there is a humble sit-down café in addition to the food and beverage stalls that crop up near every lake with a parking lot. Small boys will approach and offer a 45-minute horse-riding expedition to a cave and two cenotes within the forest. You can also tour the lake in a rowboat for $4 (up to four people). Back at the park entrance, the right fork leads past various groupings of lakes to Tziscao Lake (the last) and, just outside the park boundaries, a village of the same name. The only lakes the tourist board recommends for swimming are Tziscao and Montebello. Check with the Comitán tourist offices if you'd like to stay in the park; Tziscao Lodge is the only accommodation and it was being remodeled, with several small cabins expected to be ready by January 2001. Accommodations are available in the lodge's community hostel for $5 per person.

You can pick up a helpful map of the lakes at the tourist office in Comitán. La Angostura (☎ 963/2–60–00) and Transportes Cuxtepeque (☎ 963/2–17–28) buses leave about every half hour from the Comitán bus station (✉ 2da Av. Pte. Sur 17-B, between 2a and 3a Calles Sur Pte.) to both Laguna Bosque Azul and Tziscao. If you take the bus, you'll have to walk or catch the same bus between various lakes; check the map and time your forays to catch the bus on the half-hour. To get to Tziscao from Laguna Bosque Azul you must go to the fork in the road and catch the Bosque Azul bus to the next fork in the road and then board a Tziscao bus.

Chincultik

⑬ *56 km (35 mi) southeast of Comitán.*

The small, Late Classic Maya site of Chincultik makes a lovely stop on the way to or from the Lagunas de Montebello. It's a steep hike of about 10 or 15 minutes to the top of a restored pyramid (as well as a 5-km [3-mi] walk from the highway if you don't come by car). From the top you are rewarded with a fabulous 360-degree view of the Montebello Lakes and the surrounding countryside. You can swim in Cenote Agua Azul, the large sinkhole on the site (ask the guard to point you in the right direction, as signage is poor). The ruins, which are only partially restored, also include a ball court and stelae. ⌧ *About $2, free Sun. ☉ Tues.–Sun. 9–5.*

To get to Chincultik from Comitán, continue south 15 km (9 mi) on Route 190, and turn left at the sign LAGUNAS DE MONTEBELLO outside of La Trinitaria. After 39 km (24 mi), there's a road on the left leading to the ruins, which are 5 km (3 mi) off the highway.

Dining and Lodging

$$ X▣ **Museo Parador Santa María.** Built around the remains of a hacienda from the 1830s, this lodging has an excellent restaurant and five well-appointed rooms. Each room is decorated with a different period of antiques, including plateresque, Chiapas, and French; some have lovely sunken tile bathtubs, a few have fireplaces. This is an excellent place to stop for a special meal after visiting the lakes. All dishes are à la carte, and a meal with wine can easily come to $20 per person. But the regional food here is remarked upon by people throughout the state. ⊠ *Km 22 on the road to the Lagunas de Montebello,* ☎ FAX *963/2– 51–16. 5 rooms. No credit cards.*

NORTH AND WEST OF SAN CRISTÓBAL

San Juan Chamula and Zinacantán are traditional villages in the scenic western outskirts of San Cristóbal. The small colonial town of Chiapa de Corzo will be the first major town you come to when you drive west from San Cristóbal along Route 190. Tuxtla Gutiérrez, the modern state capital, is about 15 km (9 mi) beyond Chiapa de Corzo. Sumidero Canyon is north of Tuxtla; the farthest lookout point is 22 km (14 mi) from the capital.

San Juan Chamula

⑭ *12 km (7½ mi) northwest of San Cristóbal de las Casas.*

The spiritual and administrative center of the Chamula Indians is justly celebrated, as much for its rich past as for its turbulent present. The Chamula are a Tzotzil-speaking Maya group of nearly 52,000 individuals (of a total 300,000 Tzotzils) who live in hamlets throughout the highlands; several thousand of them live in San Juan Chamula.

The Chamula are fiercely religious, a trait that has played an important role in their history. The Chamula uprising of 1869 started when some tribesmen were imprisoned for crucifying a boy in the belief that they should have their own Christ. Some 13,000 Chamula then rose up to demand their leaders' release and massacred scores of ladino villagers in the process. More recently, the infiltration of Protestant evangelists into the community led to the expulsion of the Indian converts by Chamula authorities. In the past 20 years, more than 30,000 have been forced to abandon their ancestral lands and now live on the outskirts of San Cristóbal de las Casas, dressing in conventional clothing and often found selling handicrafts in San Cristóbal's street markets. The Human Rights Commission is trying to mediate their return to the Chamula community.

Physically and spiritually, life in San Juan Chamula revolves around the church, a white stucco building whose doorway is decorated with a flower motif. To get permission to enter the church, pay a token fee (about 50¢) at the tourist office on the main square. A pamphlet gives guidelines about how to conduct yourself in the church and the village.

Extreme discretion must be exercised inside the church. Taking photographs and videos is absolutely prohibited and strictly enforced. There are no pews, and the floor is strewn with fragrant pine needles. The Chamula sit praying silently or chanting while facing colorfully attired statues of saints. For the most part, worshipers appear oblivious to intruders, continuing with their rituals: they burn candles of various colors, drink soft drinks, and may have a live chicken or eggs with them for healing the sick. They "pass" the illness to the chicken or egg, which then gets disposed of outside the church. The church is named

ONE LAST TRAVEL TIP:

Pack an easy way to reach the world.

123 456 7891 2345
J.D. SMITH

Wherever you travel, the MCI WorldCom Card℠ is the easiest way to stay in touch.
You can use it to call to and from more than 125 countries worldwide. And you
can earn bonus miles every time you use your card. So go ahead, travel the world.
MCI WorldCom℠ makes it even more rewarding. For additional access codes,
visit **www.wcom.com/worldphone.**

EASY TO CALL WORLDWIDE

1. Just dial the WorldPhone® access number of
   the country you're calling from.

2. Dial or give the operator your MCI WorldCom
   Card number.

3. Dial or give the number you're calling.

Argentina	0800-222-6249
Belize (A)	557 or 815
Brazil	000-8012
Chile	800-207-300
Colombia ◆	980-9-16-0001
Costa Rica (A) ◆	0800-012-2222
Ecuador ⁙	999-170
Egypt ◆	7955770
El Salvador (A)	800-1567
Guatemala ◆	99-99-189
Honduras (A) ⁙	8000-122
Israel	1-800-920-2727
Mexico	01-800-021-8000
Nicaragua	166
Panama (A)	00800-001-0108
Turkey ◆	00-8001-1177
Venezuela ◆ ⁙	800-11140

(A) Calls back to U.S. only.   ◆ Public phones may require deposit of coin or phone card for dial tone.   ⁙ Limited availability.

EARN FREQUENT FLIER MILES

Bureau de change

Cambio

外国為替

In this city, you can find money on almost any street.

NO-FEE FOREIGN EXCHANGE

The Chase Manhattan Bank has over 80 convenient
locations near New York City destinations such as:

Times Square
Rockefeller Center
Empire State Building
2 World Trade Center
United Nations Plaza

Exchange any of 75 foreign currencies

CHASE

THE RIGHT RELATIONSHIP IS EVERYTHING.®

after Saint John the Baptist, the main god of the universe, according to Chamulan belief; Jesus Christ is revered as his younger brother.

Outside the church there is no taboo against photography, but it is illegal to photograph Chamulan authorities, who wear black ponchos and carry a wand. Flocks of children will pester you to buy small trinkets and will allow you to photograph them in exchange for a small fee (about 50¢ a shot). The best time to visit San Juan Chamula is on Sunday, when the market is in full swing and more-formal religious rites are performed.

To get here from San Cristóbal, head west on Calle Guadalupe Victoria, which forks to the right onto Ramón Larrainzar. Continue 4 km (2½ mi) until you reach the entrance to the village. Most of these roads are paved. Because of the threat of robbery, walking between San Cristóbal, San Juan Chamula, and Zinacantán isn't recommended.

Zinacantán

⑮ *4 km (2½ mi) west of San Juan Chamula.*

The village of Zinacantán (Place of the Bats) is even smaller than San Juan Chamula and is reached via a paved road west just outside San Juan Chamula (from San Cristóbal, take the Tuxtla road about 8 km [5 mi] and look for the signed turnoff on your right). Here photography is totally forbidden, except for the row of village weavers on view along the main street. It is the scenery en route to Zinacantán—terraced hillsides with cornfields and orchards—that draws visitors. There isn't much to see in the village except on Sunday, when people gather from the surrounding parishes, or during religious festivals. The men wear bright pink tunics embroidered with flowers; the women cover themselves with bright pink *rebozos* (shawls). If you take a tour you'll visit the homes of back-strap loom weavers. Watch for the plethora of crosses around the springs and mountains on the way to Zinacantán: they mark a Chamula cemetery of Christian origin.

The **Museo Ik'al Ojov,** on the *calle principal* (main street) behind the church, is located inside a typical home and shows off Zinacantán costumes through the ages. ☎ *No phone.* ✉ *Donation encouraged.* ◷ *Tues.–Sun. 9–5.*

Chiapa de Corzo

⑯ *70 km (43 mi) northwest of San Cristóbal; 15 km (9 mi) east of Tuxtla Gutiérrez.*

Chiapa de Corzo was founded in 1528 by Diego de Mazariegos, who one month later fled the mosquitoes and transported all the settlers to San Cristóbal (then called Chiapa de los Españoles, to distinguish it from Chiapa de los Indios, as Chiapa de Corzo was originally known). The mosquitoes are still here.

Life in this small town on the banks of the Grijalva revolves, inevitably, around the **zócalo,** which is lorded over by *la pila,* a bizarre 16th-century Mozarabic fountain modeled after Queen Isabella's crown. The interior is decorated with stories of the Indians. Several handicraft shops line the square, selling huaraches, ceramics, lacquerware, elaborately carved wooden Parachico masks (used in ceremonial dances), and regional costumes.

Chiapa's **lacquerware museum,** facing the plaza, has a modest collection of delicately carved and painted *jícaras* (gourds). "The sky is no more than an immense blue jícara, the beloved firmament in the form of a

cosmic jícara," explains the *Popul Vuh*, a 16th-century chronicle of
the Quiché Maya. The lacquerware here is both local and imported,
from Michoacán, Guerrero, Chiapas, Guatemala, and Asia. A workshop behind the museum is open during the week and generally keeps
the same hours as the museum. ⊠ *Plaza Angel Albino Corzo 35,* ☎
no phone. ⊠ *Free.* ⊘ *Tues.–Sat. 9–2 and 4–6, Sun. 9–1.*

Dining

$ ✕ **Jardines de Chiapa.** Sample an excellent and inexpensive variety of
regional cuisines in this lovely patio setting. Try the *tasajo* (sun-dried beef
served with pumpkin-seed sauce) and the *chipilín con bolita* soup, made
with balls of ground corn paste cooked in a creamy herbal sauce and
topped with cheese. A marimba band sometimes enlivens the afternoon
meal. ⊠ *Av. Francisco I. Madero 395,* ☎ *961/6–01–98. AE, MC, V.*

Tuxtla Gutiérrez

⑰ *289 km (179 mi) southwest of Villahermosa, 15 km (9 mi) northwest
of Chiapa de Corzo, 85 km (53 mi) northwest of San Cristóbal.*

Tuxtla Gutiérrez is the thriving capital city of the state of Chiapas. In
1939 Graham Greene characterized it as "not a place for foreigners—
the new ugly capital of Chiapas, without attractions. . . . It is like an
unnecessary postscript to Chiapas, which should be all wild mountain
and old churches and swallowed ruins and the Indians plodding by."
That bleak description is slowly changing, as new luxury buildings such
as the Camino Real Hotel add sparkle to the city. Nonetheless, Tuxtla
Gutiérrez is a city through which most visitors to Chiapas will pass
unnoticing, even if it is of vital economic and political importance. It
is the state's transportation hub, and it has what is probably the most
innovative zoo in Mexico. It's also convenient for its proximity to Chiapa de Corzo and the Sumidero Canyon, where there is little in the
way of accommodations.

Tuxtla's first name derives from the Nahuatl word *tochtlan*, meaning
"abundance of rabbits." Its second name, Gutiérrez, honors Joaquín
Miguel Gutiérrez, who fought for the state's independence and incor-
poration into Mexico.

The highway into town is endless. Tuxtla (population 390,000), the
state capital since 1892, doesn't have many conveniences for tourists,
but you can get your bearings best by staying on the main drag, which
will run you smack into the zócalo, known locally as the parque central and fronted by huge government buildings.

Only the most obstinate animal-hater would fail to be captivated by
☪ **Miguel Alvarez del Toro Zoo** (a.k.a. ZooMAT)—where all the species
are native Chiapans, and the more docile creatures roam free. The 100-
plus species on display include jaguars, marsupials, iguanas, quetzal
birds, boa constrictors and other snakes, tapirs, eagles, and monkeys.
Nature videos are often shown Saturday at 11 AM, and you can visit
the tiny museum and the well-stocked gift shop. Admission is free, although the zoo was considering a $6 fee at press time. ⊠ *Calzada Cerro
Hueco s/n, southeast of town off Libramiento Sur,* ☎ *961/2–37–54,
961/2–99–43.* ⊠ *Free.* ⊘ *Tues.–Sun. 9–4.*

Amateur archaeologists and botanists should head for **Parque Madero,**
which includes the **Botanical Garden,** the free **Botanical Museum,** and
the **Regional Museum of Chiapas.** The Regional Museum actually
houses an excellent history museum, an ethnological museum, and a
salon for revolving cultural exhibits. The botanical museum is unim-
pressive, but the garden is pleasant and has labels showing the native

plant species. ⊠ *Northeast of downtown, between Av. Nte. 5a and Calle Ote. 11a,* ☎ *961/3–44–79.* ⛩ *Regional Museum $2, free Sun. and holidays.* ☉ *Garden Tues.–Sun. 9–6, museums Tues.–Sun. 9–5.*

A fine small museum of indigenous Indian cultures in Chiapas opened in 1993 at the government-run **Casa de Artesanías,** which also has a good selection of regional handicrafts for sale. Among the local specialties: amber fashioned into necklaces, earrings, and pendants; hand-embroidered and brocaded table mats, blouses, and huipiles; leather bags; gold filigree jewelry; and lacquerware. ⊠ *Blvd. Dr. Belisario Domínguez 2035,* ☎ *961/2–22–75.* ⛩ *Free.* ☉ *Mon.–Sat. 10–8.*

As its name suggests, **Parque de las Marimbas** (⊠ Av. Central and 8 Pte.) hosts marimba bands, which play old-fashioned dancing music. You can grab a partner and join in—every evening 7–9.

Dining and Lodging

$$$$ ✕ **Montebello.** Prime rib and Mexican specialties headline the menu at this intimate restaurant at the Camino Real (☞ *below*)—where every roll, cake, dessert, and tortilla is made on the premises. Montebello is most romantic at night, when the city lights shimmer into view. The elegance of the earth-tone decor is set off by an unusual white mural of the Sumidero cliffs sculpted into a wall. Live, unobtrusive violin and piano music accompanies diners after 2 PM. ⊠ *Blvd. Dr. Belisario Domínguez 1195,* ☎ *961/7–77–77. AE, DC, MC, V. Closed Sun.*

$$ ✕ **El Asador Castellano** (The Castillian Grill). Tuxtla's best-kept secret
★ is this elegant restaurant. Mouthwatering Spanish dishes such as *calamares a la romana* (Roman calamari) and *poches estofadas con chistorra* (navy beans with sausage) as well as imported choice U.S. beef cuts can be paired with one of more than 50 imported wines difficult to find in Mexico City, let alone Chiapas. Service is very attentive and the presentation flawless. The restaurant is across from the Camino Real and behind Banco Santander. Reservations are recommended on weekends. ⊠ *Blvd. Dr. Belisario Domínguez 2320,* ☎ *961/3–90–00. AE, DC, MC, V. No dinner Sun.*

$$ ✕ **Las Pichanchas.** An outstanding variety of regional dishes, including tamales and cochito horneado, is available here, as well as live marimba music in the afternoon and evening, and folkloric dances 9 PM–10 PM. The restaurant is a favorite among middle-class Mexican families. ⊠ *Av. Central Ote. 837,* ☎ *961/2–53–51. AE, DC, MC, V.*

$$$$ ⛨ **Camino Real.** This hilltop oasis of luxury sets a standard for accom-
★ modations in Chiapas. Rooms surround a huge open-air pool and bar area with exotic vegetation. A concierge floor, business center with computer rentals, and meeting facilities draw many business travelers, who entertain clients in the Azulejos restaurant, enclosed in a sky-blue glass dome (the delicious daily breakfast and lunch buffets are well worth the price), or at the upscale Montebello (☞ *above*). All rooms have a view of the mountains, satellite TVs, room safes, minibars, phones, and full bathroom amenities. At a little more than $100 per night, this member of the Camino Real chain offers more services and amenities than others charging twice as much. ⊠ *Blvd. Dr. Belisario Domínguez 1195, 29060,* ☎ *961/7–77–77, 01–800/901–2300, 800/722–6466,* ⅨⅩ *961/7–77–99. 194 rooms, 26 suites. 2 restaurants, bar, minibar, pool, beauty salon, sauna, 2 tennis courts, health club, concierge floor, business services, meeting rooms, travel services, car rental. AE, DC, MC, V.* ⊛

$$$ ⛨ **Hotel Flamboyant.** For a restful atmosphere and Moorish touches, try one of the rooms in this luxury hotel; all are air-conditioned and have TVs with some channels in English. Twenty-four rooms face the large garden, and a dozen more are off a smaller, tranquil inner garden. Capacious is the byword here: the pool is huge and the public areas vast.

The restaurant is light and airy, and the food is good, but the service is poor; the bar is dark and tacky. A disadvantage is the location—a 10-minute drive west of the town center—but there's a pretty shopping mall next door. ⊠ *Blvd. Dr. Belisario Domínguez, Km 1081, 29000,* ☎ *961/5–08–88, 961/5–09–99,* 🅵🅰🆇 *961/5–00–87. 116 rooms, 2 suites. Restaurant, coffee shop, bar, pool, tennis court, travel services. AE, MC, V.*

$$ 🏨 **Hotel Arecas.** This new four-star hotel is a haven of quiet gardens and tasteful colonial decor in the heart of urban Tuxtla Gutiérrez. Fruit trees, flowering plants, a secluded swimming pool, and bungalow-style junior suites make this hotel a top pick. Both restaurants, the elegant Los Candiles for international cuisine and the more informal La Calabaza for regional dishes, offer relaxing environments and good service. All rooms have air-conditioning and cable TV. ⊠ *Blvd. Dr. Belisario Domínguez 1080, 29020,* ☎ *961/5–11–22, 961/5–11–28,* 🅵🅰🆇 *961/5–11–21. 44 rooms, 16 suites. 2 restaurants, bar, pool, dance club, meeting rooms, free parking. AE, DC, MC, V.*

$$ 🏨 **Hotel María Eugenia.** Although a touch sterile, this air-conditioned downtown hotel has clean rooms with floral spreads as well as a floral scent. There is cable TV and a nice pool surrounded by white wrought-iron furniture. ⊠ *Av. Central Ote. 507, 29000,* ☎ *961/3–37–67, 961/3–37–70,* 🅵🅰🆇 *961/3–28–60. 83 rooms. Restaurant, bar, pool, meeting room, travel services, free parking. AE, MC, V.*

Sumidero Canyon

⑱ *23 km (14 mi) northeast of Tuxtla Gutiérrez.*

Sumidero Canyon came into being about 36 million years ago, with the help of the Grijalva River, which flows north along the canyon's floor. The fissure meanders for some 23 km (14 mi); its near-vertical walls, partly obscured by vegetation, rise 3,500 ft at the highest point. You can admire it from above, as there are five lookout points along the highway; one of them, La Atalaya, has a restaurant.

Viajes Miramar (⊠ Camino Real, Local 2, Tuxtla Gutiérrez, ☎ 961/7–77–77 ext. 7230) offers a five-hour minivan trip for about $7 a person. You can also take a taxi or bus from Tuxtla to Chiapa de Corzo and then a boat trip to the Chicoasen hydroelectric dam; boats leave the Chiapa de Corzo dock between 8 AM and 4 PM daily. The trip there and back takes approximately two hours and costs about $6 a person (there's a four-person minimum). From the boat you can admire the canyon's steep, striated walls, some odd rock formations, and the animals—including ducks, pelicans, herons, raccoons, iguanas, and butterflies—that live inconspicuously at its base. As you visit the canyon, consider the fate of the Chiapa Indians, who jumped into it rather than face slavery at the hands of the Spaniards.

THE ROAD TO PALENQUE AND BEYOND

The road from San Cristóbal to Palenque veers slightly east on Highway 190 upon leaving town, then links up to Highway 199, which heads north to Palenque. You'll pass Ocosingo and the turnoff to Toniná along the first half of the journey, then Agua Azul and Misol-Há before reaching the ruins. It's sierra country most of the way until the mild valleys around Ocosingo; the climate will get progressively hotter and more humid as you approach Palenque. The vegetation will also change, from mountain pine to thick, green tropical foliage. To get to Villahermosa from Palenque, head north for 56 km (35 mi) on Highway 199, and then turn left onto Highway 186 at Catazajá for a leisurely drive on a fairly straight road.

Toniná

 98 km (61 mi) northeast of San Cristóbal; 118 km (73 mi) south and east of Palenque.

Between San Cristóbal and Palenque, on a paved road running along the Jataté River in the mild Ocosingo Valley, is the archaeological site of Toniná. The name means "house of stone" in Tzeltal. Excavations indicate that the vanquished rulers of Palenque and Yaxchilán were brought here as prisoners for execution. Several ball courts and the main pyramid platform (taller than those of Tikal and Teotihuacán) have been uncovered; a small, on-site museum is under construction. Thought to be the last major ceremonial center to flourish in this area, Toniná, with its monumental architecture and noteworthy sculptures, is rapidly adding to our knowledge of Maya civilization. To get to the site, follow the road from Ocosingo, off Route 199. ⛏ $2. ☉ Daily 9:30–4.

Lodging

$ ★ ⊞ **Rancho Esmeralda.** This macadamia-nut farm has eight comfortable wooden cabins just a 15-minute walk from the ruins. The accommodations are rustic, with limited electricity and no phones; there are amazingly clean latrines and a common bathhouse from which you can savor the view as you soak in the extra-long claw-foot tub. The help is friendly, and you could spend an afternoon just talking with the young barman in the thatch-roofed, communal dining area. Delicious, filling meals (especially the buffet breakfast and dinner) are served at extra cost; the coffee is organic—grown, roasted, and ground on the premises. The congenial hosts can help arrange an air excursion to the Bonampak and Yaxchilán ruins (about $100) and white-water rafting trips on the Shumulja River (about $85 a day). Resident cowboy Valentín can take you on a three- to four-hour horseback excursion ($20) through the beautiful Ocosingo Valley, where more than 50 species of exotic birds live year-round. Tent camping is also permitted. ⊠ Turnoff about 8 km (5 mi) along road from Ocosingo to Toniná ruins, Apdo. 68, ☎ no phone, FAX 967/3–07–11. 8 cabins. Restaurant, horseback riding, camping, free parking. No credit cards.

Agua Azul

 68 km (42 mi) northwest of Toniná, 64 km (40 mi) southwest of Palenque.

The series of waterfalls and crystalline blue pools at Agua Azul is breathtaking to behold, especially well into the dry season, from about March through May. The site has lost its sense of isolation since the road was paved in the 1980s, when food shacks and camping facilities sprang up, marring somewhat the natural beauty. Still, it's a breathtaking spot, and you can swim in a series of interconnected pools. The cataracts are surrounded by giant palm fronds and tropical flowers; monkeys and toucans frolic in the vicinity. Six-hour trips (booked via most any travel agency in Palenque and including a visit to Misol-Há) cost about $10 per person and include the entrance fees (50¢ per person or $2 per car). For about $7 a person (including the entrance fee), you can ride with Sociedad Cooperative Chambalum (⊠ Calle Allende at Av. Juárez s/n, Palenque, ☎ no phone) to both sites. Their service is every 30 minutes, 6–6.

Misol-Há

 46 km (29 mi) northeast of Agua Azul, 18 km (11 mi) southwest of Palenque.

If the single cascade at Misol-Há is smaller than those at Agua Azul (☞ *above*), the area surrounding it is also less peopled with vendors and littered with trash. You can swim in the pool formed by the 100-ft cascade, or explore behind the falls, where a cave leads to another, subterranean pool. Surrounded by oversize tropical vegetation, the site has rustic rest rooms, restaurants, and campgrounds. *See* Agua Azul, *above,* for how to get there.

Palenque

 191 km (118 mi) northeast of San Cristóbal de las Casas, 150 km (93 mi) southeast of Villahermosa.

Of all the Maya ruins, none is more sublime than Palenque—only Tikal in Guatemala is its equal. Teotihuacán might be more monumental and Chichén Itzá more expansive, but Palenque possesses a mesmerizing quality, in part because of the intimacy that the surrounding jungle creates. In early morning or late afternoon, sunlight illuminates the structures in a hazy, iridescent glow. Birds call shrilly and eerily, and the local descendants of the Maya wander about collecting banana leaves, oranges, and avocados. You may even see a spider monkey or two, or hear their wild cries.

Antonio de Solis, a Spanish priest, accidently dug into a buried wall here in 1740 while he was trying to plant crops. In 1805 a royal Spanish expedition ventured here to follow up on the discovery. In 1832 an eccentric German count, Jean-Frederic Maximilien de Waldeck, set up house with his mistress for a year in a building known today as the Templo del Conde (Temple of the Count). Explorers John Lloyd Stephens and Frederick Catherwood lived briefly in the palace during their 1840 expedition. Serious excavations began in 1923, under the direction of Franz Blom, cofounder of the Na Bolom foundation in San Cristóbal. Work continued intermittently until 1952, when Alberto Ruz Lhuillier, a Mexican archaeologist, uncovered the tomb of the 7th-century ruler Pacal beneath the Temple of the Inscriptions. Since the early 1970s, groundbreaking work has been done on the Maya by archaeologists, linguists, and astronomers.

Palenque's elegance makes clear why archaeologist Sylvanus Morley honored the Maya as the "Greeks of the New World"—not only for their remarkable buildings, but also for the supple naturalism of the culture's art. The masters at work here shaped stone, stucco, and ceramics into ornate, lyrical designs. Artisans also took liberties here: relief sculpture of great expressiveness replaces the freestanding stelae of other Maya cities.

The most important buildings of the site date from the Mid- to Late Classic period (AD 6th–9th centuries), although Palenque was inhabited as early as 1500 BC. At its zenith, the city dominated the greater part of Tabasco and Chiapas. The site was abandoned around AD 800, making it one of the earliest Maya sites to be deserted in what was a west-to-east pattern of abandonment. The reasons for the inhabitants' departure are still in debate.

Palenque's graceful tower—one of the site's signature structures—sets it apart from other Maya settlements. The Temple of the Inscriptions, a 75-ft pyramid, is another. It was dedicated to Pacal—the "Mesoamer-

THE ROUTE OF THE MAYA: A MESOAMERICAN GIZA

THE MAYA WERE OUTSTANDING ARCHITECTS, without compare in the Americas. They erected immense palaces and towering pyramids in less-than-hospitable climates without the aid of metal tools, the wheel, or beasts of burden. Their ancient cities still resound with the magnificence of their cultures, even though the civilizations have faded.

Río Usumacinta. Builders of pyramids of this style typically gave them additional height by placing them on hillsides or crests—as you'll see at the otherworldly Palenque—and the principal structures were covered with exquisite bas-reliefs carved in stone. The small one-story pyramid-top temples characteristically had vestibules and rooms adorned with vault ceilings. The wide, spacious chambers inside the pyramids had smaller, attached rooms filled with bas-relief carvings of important events that occurred during the reign of the ruler who built the pyramid. Río Usumacinta friezes slope inward, rather than standing perpendicular under the large roof combs. Finest examples: Palenque, Yaxchilán.

Río Bec. Influenced by Guatemala's Petén style, the pitch of these pyramids is rather steep, and the foundations elaborately decorated. The stairways on the outside of some pyramids were built for aesthetic rather than practical purposes, and were "false" (unclimbable). The principal structures were long, one-story affairs containing two or sometimes three tall towers. Each was capped by a large roof comb emboldened with a dramatic stucco facade. Río Bec is found only in what is now the state of Campeche. Finest examples: Calakmul, Xpuhil, Río Bec.

Chenes. Found mainly in Campeche, this style likewise had long, single-story structures. In this case they were divided into three distinct sections, each with its own doorway charmingly surrounded by a face of the rain god, Chaac, whose mouth is the entrance. Facades were smothered in serpentlike embellishments. Finest examples: Hochob, Chicanná.

Puuc. Uxmal is the most striking illustration of the beautifully proportioned Puuc style. Commonly found in the state of Yucatán, it of all styles looks like the "pure" Maya style. The buildings were designed in a low-slung, quadrangle shape and had many, many rooms. Exterior walls were probably kept plain in order to show off the friezes above, which were lavishly embellished with stone-mosaic deities surrounded by geometric and serpentine motifs. The corners of buildings were characteristically lined with the curl-nosed Chaac. Pyramids here didn't have roof combs. Finest examples: Uxmal, Labná, Kabah, Sayil.

Northeast Plains. The fusion of two Maya groups—the early Chichén Maya and later Itzá Maya—produced this Late Classic (AD 600–900) style famously exemplified by Chichén Itzá. Here new forms such as columns and grand colonnades were introduced. Palaces with row upon row of columns carved in the form of serpents looked over private patios, platforms were dedicated to the planet Venus, and pyramids were offered to Kukulcán (the plumed serpent god borrowed from the Toltecs, who called him Quetzalcóatl). Chichén Itzá is also famous for its temple-top, reclining, carved stone chacmool (a reclining figure with an offering tray carved in its middle)—another Itzá addition. Finest examples: Chichén Itzá, Mayapán.

Quintana Roo Coast. Although somewhat influenced by the Itzá Maya, a style entirely different eventually evolved here. The large, squat-looking, one-story buildings have interior columns, wood-beam-supported ceilings, and numerous figures of the descending or Upside Down god that began appearing in the Post-Classic era (900–1530). Friezes were distinctively decorated with small niches. Finest examples: Tulum, El Rey, San Gervasio.

–Patricia Alisau

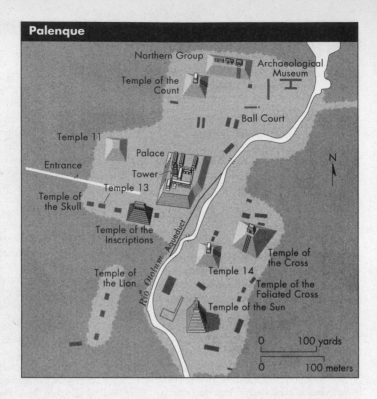

Palenque

Northern Group

Archaeological Museum

Temple of the Count

Ball Court

Temple 11

Palace

Entrance

Tower

Temple 13

Temple of the Skull

Temple of the Inscriptions

Rio Otolum Aqueduct

Temple of the Cross

Temple of the Lion

Temple 14

Temple of the Foliated Cross

Temple of the Sun

N

0 — 100 yards

0 — 100 meters

ican Charlemagne"—who took Palenque to its most glorious heights during his 28- to 38-year reign. He died around AD 692, having become the ruler at age 12 and living into his forties.

The ruling priest-kings communicated life at Palenque in elaborate glyphs and reliefs on the temples. The deciphering of a good portion of Palenque's hieroglyphics in 1988 has revolutionized scholars' understanding of both the Maya and the bloody history of Palenque. Only 800 of the thousands of glyphs have been deciphered, but they have already revealed the complex history of the Palenque dynasties. Exciting finds by archaeologists from the University of Texas in 1998 introduced a new character, Uc-Pakal-Kinich, into the lineage of Palenque rulers. Other clues unearthed at Temple 19 point to a probable liaison between rulers of Palenque and of Copán, in what is now Honduras.

In its heyday, Palenque encompassed an astonishing 128-plus square km (49 square mi). Artificial terraces were built to support the temples, which surrounded plazas, a ball court, altars, and burial grounds. The temples themselves had a complex array of corridors, narrow subterranean stairways, and galleries. And they served as fortresses in time of war. Only about 30% of the site has been excavated. Since late 1994, a huge portion of the ruins around the Temple of the Inscriptions has been reconstructed and is open. Explanations in Spanish, English, and Tzotzil have been placed at all major buildings.

As you enter the site, the first temple on your right is the reconstructed **Temple of the Skull,** which the Maya had painted red and blue in their time. A skull-shape stucco relief, presumed to be that of a rabbit, was found at the small entrance to the temple. It is up the stairway.

The **Temple of the Inscriptions** is just past Temple 13; its nine tiers correspond to the nine-level Maya underworld. Atop this temple and the smaller ones around it are vestiges of roof combs—delicate vertical extensions that are among the features of southern Maya cities. This is the best view of Palenque, and it provides an excellent orientation to the other buildings. Reaching the tomb inside involves a relatively easy, if slow, climb. Once at the summit, turn and take a long look back toward the once-mighty palace on the right. From the top of the Temple of Inscriptions, climb down the steep, damp flight of stairs 80 ft into the **tomb of Pacal,** one of the first crypts found inside a Mexican pyramid. (This is not for claustrophobes.) Pacal's remains along with his diadem and majestic jade, shell, and obsidian mask are in Mexico City's Museum of Anthropology. The intricately carved sarcophagus lid, weighing some 5 tons and measuring 10 by 7 ft, however, remains. A psychoduct—a stone tube in the shape of a snake through which Pacal's soul was thought to have passed to the netherworld—leads up to the temple. It can be difficult to make out the carvings on the slab, but they depict the ruler, prostrate beneath a sacred ceiba tree, who is still revered by the Maya today. The lords of the nine underworlds are carved into stucco reliefs on the walls around him.

In 1994, the small and unassuming **Temple 13,** attached to the Temple of the Inscriptions, revealed a royal tomb hidden in its depths. The tomb, which probably belonged to Pacal's mother or grandmother, is under investigation and currently isn't open to the public.

The patios, galleries, and other buildings that make up the **palace** are set on a 30-ft-high plinth. Stucco work adorns the pillars of the galleries and the inner courtyards. Inside are numerous friezes and masks, most of them depicting Pacal and his dynasty. Steam baths in the southwestern patio suggest that priests once dwelled in the adjoining cellars. The palace's iconic tower was built on three levels, representing the three levels of the universe as well as the movement of the stars.

To the right of the palace, you'll cross the tiny Otulum River, which in ancient times was roofed over to form a 9-ft-high vaulted aqueduct. Cross the river and climb up 80 easy steps to arrive at the reconstructed **Plaza of the Cross,** which contains the Temple of the Foliated Cross, Temple of the Sun, Temple 14, and the Temple of the Cross, the largest of the group. Inside Temple 14, there's an underworld scene in stucco relief, done 260 days after Pacal died. The most exquisite roof combs are found on these buildings, which are open to the public.

To reach the cluster called the **Northern Group,** walk north along the river, passing the palace and then the unexcavated ball court on your left. There are five buildings here in various states of disrepair; the largest and best preserved is the **Temple of the Count.**

A short hike northwest of the Northern Group lies **Grupo C,** an area containing remains of the homes of Maya nobles and a few small temples shrouded in jungle. In order to maintain the natural setting in which the ruins were found, minimal restoration is being done. Human burials, funeral offerings of Jaina figurines, ceramics, and kitchen utensils have been found here as well as in the **Grupo B** area, which lies on the 20-minute "Ecological Path" hike through the jungle and down to the museum. On the way, you'll pass a small waterfall called El Baño de la Reina (The Queen's Bath). The path is poorly marked; be sure to veer left through the Grupo B ruins when you reach them and look for the footbridge that crosses over to the museum.

The on-site **museum** has a remarkable collection of finely preserved heads of Maya deities in elaborate zoomorphic headdresses, discovered in front of the Temple of the Foliated Cross. The group includes 13 figures of the sun god Kinich Ahau. Also noteworthy are the handsome stucco faces of Maya men. Art historians compare their naturalistic execution with that of ancient Greek sculpture. Displays are labeled in English, Spanish, and Tzotzil. There's also a snack bar and a handicrafts store with good weavings, hand-embroidered fabrics, leather, ceramics, amber jewelry, hand-painted wooden crosses, and children's toys.

The museum can also be reached from the main road leading to the ruins; the entrance is about 1 km (½ mi) before the parking-lot entrance to the ruins along the highway. Since explanatory signs inside the ruins are scant and in Spanish, you may want to hire a multilingual guide at the ticket booth. They charge about $35 for a group of up to seven people. ⊠ *Ruins and museum $2.50.* ⊙ *Ruins daily 8–4:45, museum Tues.–Sun. 9–3:45, Pacal's tomb daily 10:30–4.*

Palenque Town

㉓ *8 km (5 mi) north of the ruins.*

Whereas cool highlander San Cristóbal has a polite but reserved exterior, Palenque Town wraps you in a warm tropical embrace. Its days as a sleepy cattle town are far behind, as the city swells with newcomers and longtime residents rush to turn family homes into rent-paying posadas. In only the past few years, thanks to tourism, upgraded services like e-mail servers have arrived; likewise ATMs and 24-hour long-distance phone service. Women and children from San Juan Chamula hawk crafts and souvenirs in front of restaurants and pharmacies along the principal downtown streets.

The principal landmark in Palenque Town is the chalk white "cabeza Maya," a giant sculpture of the head of a Maya chieftain that graces the town's one traffic circle. West of downtown is the quiet neighborhood of La Cañada.

Dining and Lodging

$$$ ✕ **Maya Cañada.** This restaurant in the quiet La Cañada neighbor-
★   hood is the comely baby sister to the aging but still popular Maya downtown. Sixties rock enlivens the atmosphere in the round, thatch-roof restaurant. Try the $3.50 set lunch menu, consisting of soup, a main dish, and dessert, or choose something from the extensive appetizer menu, including tacos and tostadas. Mexican wines are served, and there is a full bar. A trio plays music Thursday through Sunday 9–midnight. ⊠ *Calle Merle Green s/n, La Cañada,* ☎ *934/5–00–42,* FAX *934/5–02–16.* ⊠ *Downtown branch: corner of Av. Hidalgo and Independencia,* ☎ *934/5–00–42. MC, V.*

$$$ ✕ **La Selva.** Although a stop on the tour-group route, this spacious *palapa*
★   (thatch-roof) restaurant is still popular with locals. The setting, surrounded by luxuriant jungle gardens, is superb and so is the food, including the free chips and salsa. There is a scrumptious Sunday brunch buffet after 1 PM for about $9. ⊠ *Carretera Ruinas Km 5,* ☎ *934/5–03–63. MC, V.*

$$ ✕ **El Arbolito.** On the main road to the ruins, this fun and funky restaurant is full of souvenirs of old ranch life. There's a wall full of hats, each inscribed with a different Mexican proverb. Other walls have mounted animal heads and pelts. It's no surprise that the house specialty is meat. Favorites include the spicy *consomé de borrego especial,* a broth with barbecued sheep, onions, and fresh cilantro. Beef tips in smoky chipotle sauce or other, mild chili sauces are served with beans, rice, garnish, and piping hot tortillas. ⊠ *Carretera Palenque–Pakalná Km 1.5, across from Days Inn,* ☎ *934/5–09–00. MC, V.*

$$ ✕ **Casa Grande.** This pleasant, art-filled café has an upstairs terrace overlooking Palenque's zócalo. Typical Mexican fare such as tacos and fried bananas complements the more exotic seafood dishes, which are expertly seasoned with Chiapan spices. Open breakfast, lunch, and dinner, this is the perfect place to perk up with an espresso or wind down with a glass of wine. ⊠ *Av. Hidalgo 6, corner of Jiménez,* ☎ *934/5–01–25. No credit cards.*

$$$$ ⊞ **Misión Palenque.** Four blocks from the zócalo in the downtown area, this hotel is fronted by a huge green lawn and pretty grounds but has plain, motel-like rooms. All are air-conditioned and have cable TV and phones; the tiny patios lack furniture. The terraced restaurant glows nightly with candlelight. Off Route 199, it has a free shuttle bus to the ruins. Tour groups, which constitute a large percentage of the clientele, rotate in and out daily. Note that you'll be quoted a higher price if you call the 800 number. ⊠ *Rancho San Martín de Porres, 29960,* ☎ *934/5–02–41, 800/448–8355,* FAX *934/5–03–00. 208 rooms, 2 suites. Restaurant, bar, pool, steam room, 2 tennis courts, shops, travel services, free parking. AE, DC, MC, V.*

$$$ ⊞ **Chan Kah.** Four kilometers (2½ mi) from the ruins in a paradisia-
★ cal jungle setting that is also a forest reserve, Chan Kah shouldn't be confused with the sister hotel in downtown Palenque. There is a stone-lined, lagoon-style pool, aromatic jasmine bushes, and a stream flowing around the back. The outdoor restaurant is average, and meals are accompanied by recorded Mexican music. But the very comfortable bungalows have wide terraces, mahogany furnishings, and ceiling fans and/or air-conditioning. Bungalows 6–10 have views of the pool and stream. The emphasis here is on tranquility: there are no TVs or phones in the rooms. ⊠ *Carretera Ruinas Km 3.5, 29960,* ☎ *934/5–11–00, 934/5–07–62, 934/5–08–26, 934/5–09–74,* FAX *934/5–08–20. 73 bungalows. Restaurant, bar, pool, free parking. AE, MC, V.*

$$$ ⊞ **Ciudad Real Palenque.** This yellow and white colonial-style hotel sits amid glorious jungle gardens of the type only possible in Palenque. A small waterfall and creek run through the grounds. All rooms have cable TV and air-conditioning as well as a balcony facing the gardens. ⊠ *Carretera Pakal-Na Km 1.5, 29960,* ☎ *934/5–12–85, 934/5–13–15,* FAX *934/5–13–43. 69 rooms, 3 suites. Restaurant, bar, pool, travel services, free parking. AE, MC, V.*

$$$ ⊞ **Days Inn Tulijá.** You can't beat the price or location of this cheerful little hotel, which is about a 10-minute walk from downtown. It has the basics for a comfortable stay: color cable TV, air-conditioning, and firm beds, although rooms are smallish. The 25-m-long pool is a great boon for swimmers. The tequila bar boasts more than 35 brands of the distilled agave liquor. ⊠ *Apdo. 57, Carretera Ruinas Km 27.5, 29960,* ☎ *934/5–01–04, 934/5–01–65, 800/329–7466,* FAX *934/5–01–63. 48 rooms. Restaurant, bar, pool, billiards, laundry service, meeting rooms, travel services, free parking. AE, MC, V.*

$$$ ⊞ **Quality Resorts Palenque Nututún.** This property, a member of the Choice Hotels International chain, has plain, ample rooms with tile floors. There is a $7 difference between rooms with a small, furnitureless terrace and TV and those without. The real draw is the large natural pool formed from a bend in the Nututún River, which runs through the grounds. Camping is permitted near the river for about $5.50 a person. ⊠ *Carretera Palenque–Ocosingo Km 3.5, Apdo. 74, 29960,* ☎ *934/5–01–00, 934/5–01–61, 800/221–2222,* FAX *934/5–06–20. 45 suites, 12 rooms. Restaurant, bar, pool, camping, playground, free parking. AE, MC, V.*

Bonampak

  ⚒️   **24**   *183 km (113 mi) southeast of Palenque.*

Bonampak, which means "painted walls" in Mayan, is renowned for its courtly murals of ancient Maya life. The settlement was built on the banks of the Lacanjá River during the 7th and 8th centuries and remained undiscovered until 1946. Explorer Jacques Soustelle called it "a pictorial encyclopedia of a Mayan city." In remarkable ochre and faience colors, the scenes portrayed in the three rooms of the **Templo de las Pinturas** graphically recall subjects such as life at court and the prelude and aftermath of battle. It's open daily 8–5; admission is $2.50. For an extra $5 a Lacandon guide will join you near the park entrance. Segments of the murals are deteriorating because the high humidity in the area eats away at the colors, and thick white deposits of calcium from dripping water have covered some of the paintings completely. In 1984 Mexican experts devised a technique for cleaning and restoring the murals, and with the help of the National Geographic Society—and computerized, digital amplification techniques—remarkable details and color have come to light. It stands to reason that the reproductions at the archaeological museums in Mexico City and Villahermosa are more legible than the on-site specimens.

Until recently, only the most devoted fans of the Maya attempted the trip to the ruins of Bonampak and Yaxchilán (☞ *below*). Now, however, you can drive or take a three-hour bus ride from Palenque on the newly paved Highway 198 directly to Bonampak. Buses or tour vans will take you all the way to the ruins, or drop you at Lacanjá and let you hike the last 3 km (2 mi) into Bonampak, as was done before the road was built. Getting to Yaxchilán still requires a one-hour jungle boat ride on the Usumacinta River; you must first drive or take a bus to the small town of Frontera Corozal, just off Highway 198, where boats depart for the ruins and Guatemala. This is best arranged through travel agencies or state tourist offices in Mexico City, Palenque, or San Cristóbal de Las Casas, which can also arrange for you to stay at the wonderful Tzeltal Indian cooperative Escudo Jaguar (☞ Lodging *in* Yaxchilán, *below*). Small-plane charter service to Bonampak and Yaxchilán is less available now that the road is finished, but you may still find pilots who leave from Tuxtla Gutiérrez with **Montes Azules** (☎ 961/3–22–56 or 961/3–22–93) or from Comitán with **Servicio Aéreo San Cristóbal** (☎ 963/2–03–09). Be sure to wear sturdy shoes, and bring insect repellent, good sunglasses, and a hat to protect yourself from mosquitoes, ticks, sand flies, undergrowth, and the jungle sun.

Yaxchilán

★ ⚒️   **25**   *50 km (31 mi) northeast of Bonampak, 190 km (118 mi) southeast of Palenque.*

Excavations at Yaxchilán (yash-chee-*lan*), on the banks of the Usumacinta River, have uncovered stunning temples and delicate carvings in an isolated jungle setting. Spider monkeys and toucans are, at this point, more prolific than tourists, and howler monkeys growl like lions from the towering *chico zapote* (fruit tree) and hundred-year-old ceiba trees. Yaxchilán, which means "place of green stones," reached its cultural peak during the Late Classic period, from about AD 680 to 770. It is dominated by two acropolises containing a palace, temples with finely carved lintels, and great staircases. Until recently, the Lacandon, who live in the vicinity, made pilgrimages to this site in the heart of the jungle, leaving behind "god pots" (incense-filled ceramic bowls) in honor of ancient deities. They were particularly awed by the headless sculpture of Yaxachtun (ya-sha-*tun*) at the entrance to the temple (called Structure 33) and believed that the world would end when its head was replaced on its torso.

Yaxchilán was situated on the trade route between Palenque and Tikal, and the existence of a 600-ft bridge crossing the Usumacinta River to connect Yaxchilán to Guatemalan territory has been discovered. The engineering know-how of the people of Yaxchilán is still being deciphered by modern-day engineers. The site was once threatened with destruction by a huge dam to be built by Mexico and Guatemala. Thankfully, plans seem to have been put off indefinitely due to lack of funds. Most people arrive by a combination of land and riverboat (a long day trip from Palenque) or air tour. ☒ *Free.* ☯ *Daily 9–5.*

Lodging

$$ ⊞ **Escudo Jaguar.** This ecotourism project 144 km (89 mi) south of
★ Palenque is run by the local Tzeltal people and is designed to bring people closer to the Maya ruins of Bonampak and Yaxchilán. If you don't mind going a bit rustic, it's the ideal place to stay while you take in the jungle and both archaeological sites. There are 13 comfortable wooden cabins. Each has a wide cement veranda with two large, colorful hammocks for lounging. Inside, the thatch-roof cabins have screened windows, mosquito nets, and fans. The restaurant serves sandwiches and shakes in addition to full lunches and dinners. It's best to book trips to Bonampak and Yaxchilán ahead of time, mentioning that you want to stay overnight at Escudo Jaguar. You must contact the offices in Mexico City for reservations. ✉ *Frontera Corozal, Ocosingo; reservations:* ☎ *5/201–66–40,* Ⅲ *5/201–66–41. 13 cabins. Restaurant, free parking. No credit cards.*

VILLAHERMOSA AND TABASCO

Graham Greene's succinct summation of Tabasco as a "tropical state of river and swamp and banana grove" captures its essence. Although the state played an important role in the early history of Mexico, its past is rarely on view. Instead, it is Tabasco's modern-day status as a supplier of oil that defines it. Set on a humid coastal plain and crisscrossed by 1,930 km (1,197 mi) of rivers, low hills, and unexplored jungles, the land is still rich in banana and cacao plantations. Shantytowns and refineries are for the most part invisible to the visitor, who on bus trips passes small ranches with pastures of tall, green grass feeding horses and beef cattle. The capital city of Villahermosa epitomizes the mercurial development of Tabasco (the airplane was here before the automobile). Thanks to oil and urban renewal, the cramped and ugly neighborhoods in the mosquito-ridden town of the 1970s have been replaced by spacious boulevards, lush green parks, and cultural centers. Sandwiched between the Grijalva River and the historic downtown, the Zona Luz has been redone as a brick-paved pedestrian zone housing galleries and museums in addition to restaurants, ice cream shops, and a Howard Johnson hotel.

This is not to say that the rest of Tabasco has nothing to offer. There are beaches, lagoons, caves, and nature reserves, but the tourism infrastructure is minimal. The fired-brick Maya ruins of Comalcalco attest to the influence of Palenque. Probably the most interesting region is the one to the south and east of Villahermosa, where rivers and canyons are home to jaguars, deer, and alligators. This was where the English pirate Sir Francis Drake hid from the Spanish navy.

Tabasco—specifically the mouth of the Grijalva River—lay along the route of the Spanish explorations of Mexico in 1518–19. At that time, the state's rivers and waterways, along which the Maya lived, served as a trade route between the peoples of the north and those of the south. When the Spaniards came to Tabasco, they had to bridge 50 rivers and contend with swarms of mosquitoes, beetles, and ants—as well as the almost unbearable heat. At the same time, the region was so lush that one early chronicler termed it a Garden of Eden.

The Spanish conquest was made easier by the extreme antipathy and tribal warfare between the Tabascans and their Aztec overlords. Among the 20 slave women turned over to the Spaniards upon their arrival in the Aztec capital was a Chiapan named Malintzín (or Malinche), who was singled out by the Spaniards for her ability to speak both the Maya and the Nahuatl languages. Called Doña Marina by the Spaniards, she learned Spanish and became not only Cortés's mistress and the mother of his illegitimate son but also an interpreter of Indian customs. Marina's cooperation helped the conquistador vanquish both Moctezuma and Cuauhtémoc, the last Aztec rulers. Even today, "La Malinche" is synonymous with "traitor" throughout Mexico.

Until the early 20th century, Tabasco slumbered. It didn't become a state until 1924. After the American Civil War, traders from the southern United States began operating in the region and on its rivers, hauling the precious mahogany trees upstream from Chiapas and shipping them north from the small port of Frontera. This was Tabasco's most prosperous era until the discovery of oil some 50 years ago and the oil boom of the 1980s.

Villahermosa

26 *821 km (509 mi) southeast of Mexico City, 632 km (392 mi) southwest of Mérida.*

There are a good many ways to spend your time in Tabasco's capital. The Zona Luz (a.k.a. Zona Remodelada) is a grid of pedestrian-only streets with restored colonial buildings, sidewalk cafés, galleries, and museums. Most people make a beeline for the **Carlos Pellicer Museo Regional de Antropología** (Regional Museum of Anthropology). Named after the man who donated many of the artifacts and whom the locals call the "poet laureate of Latin America" (1897–1978), the museum is on the right bank of the Grijalva and is part of the huge CICOM cultural complex dedicated to research on the Olmec and Maya (which is what the Spanish acronym CICOM stands for). It provides one of the last tranquil vistas of Villahermosa as it might have looked 50 years ago. Although all the explanations are in Spanish, that shouldn't detract from the visual pleasure of the displays.

Much of the collection is devoted to Tabasco and the Olmec, or "inhabitants of the land of rubber," who flourished in Tabasco as early as 1200 to 1300 BC and disappeared about AD 800. The Olmecs have long been honored as inventors of the numerical and calendrical systems that spread throughout the region. The pyramid is also attributed to them. Some of the most interesting artifacts of the Olmec, apart from the remarkable stone sculptures and giant stone heads on view at Parque Museo La Venta (☞ *below*), are the remnants of their jaguar cult displayed here. The jaguar symbolized the earth fertilized by rain (i.e., procreation), and many Olmec sculptures portray half-human, half-jaguar figures, and jaguar babies. Other sculptures portray human heads emerging from the mouth of a jaguar, bat gods, bird-headed humans, and female fertility figurines.

Many of Mexico's ancient cultures are represented on the upper two floors, from the red-clay dogs of Colima and the nose rings of the Huichol Indians of Nayarit to the huge burial urns of the Chontal Maya, who built Comalcalco. The CICOM complex also houses a theater, restaurant, public library, and handicrafts shop. ✉ *Carlos Pellicer 511, an extension of the malecón (boardwalk)*, ☎ *93/12–63–44.* ✆ *About $1.* ☉ *Tues.–Sun. 9–6.*

The giant stone heads and other figures carved by the Olmec were salvaged from the oil fields of La Venta, on the western edge of Tabasco near the state of Veracruz. They are on display in the 8-hectare **Parque Museo La Venta,** in a tropical garden on the beautiful Lago de las Ilusiones (Lake of Illusions)—also founded by Carlos Pellicer, in 1958. The 6-ft-tall, bold-featured carved stone heads, wearing what look like helmets and weighing up to 20 tons, have sparked endless scholarly debate. It has been theorized that they depict ancient Phoenician slaves or space invaders. The latest and least outlandish (or offensive) theory is that the faces on the sculptures—very similar to today's Tabasco Maya—are actual portraits of successful Olmec athletes, war heroes, and other public figures. La Venta contains 33 sculptures, including jaguars, priests, monsters, stelae, and stone altars. Within the park is a zoo with creatures such as Tabascan river crocodiles, deer, jaguars, coatimundi, monkeys, and wild parrots. There is also a gift shop and several outdoor stands selling embroidered blouses, T-shirts, and souvenirs. ✉ *Blvd. Ruíz Cortines near Paseo Tabasco*, ☎ *93/14–16–52.* ✆ *$1.50.* ☉ *Daily 8–5 (ticket booth closes at 4), zoo closed Mon.*

The small **Museo de la Historia Natural** (Natural History Museum) is just outside the entrance to the park. Of most interest are the displays of Tabasco's native plants and animals, many of which are now under government protection. Other rooms are dedicated to geology, evolution, and the solar system. ✉ *Blvd. Ruíz Cortines near Paseo Tabasco*, ☎ *no phone.* ✆ *$1.* ☉ *Tues.–Sun. 9–5.*

One of Villahermosa's newest attractions is **Yumká,** a nature reserve spread over 250 acres of jungle, savannah, and wetlands. Half-hour guided walking tours take you over a hanging bridge and past free-roaming endangered or threatened species such as spider monkeys, red macaws, toucans, crocodiles, turtles, and native *tepezcuintles* (a giant rodent). Next comes a longer aerial tram ride past Asian and African species such as elephant and zebra. Optional $1 boat tours glide past birds wading or taking flight. ✉ *16 km (10 mi) from downtown past the airport at Poblado Dos Montes,* ☎ *93/56–01–19, 93/56–01–15.* ✆ *$2.* ☉ *Daily 9–5 (ticket window closes at 4).*

Dining and Lodging

$$$$ ✗ **El Mesón del Duende.** This restaurant, which translates as the House of the Elf, adds a regional accent to standard meat and fish dishes. Try the house favorites, *filete en salsa de espinaca y queso* (beef fillet in a spinach and cheese sauce) and *la posta de robalo* (grilled snook). The modest decor is in keeping with the family-style atmosphere. ✉ *Gregorio Méndez 1703,* ☎ *93/15–13–24. AE, MC, V.*

$$$ ✗ **Los Tulipanes.** Tucked between the Esperanza Iris Theater and the Car-
★ los Pellicer Regional Museum of Anthropology in the CICOM complex, spacious Los Tulipanes specializes in seafood and has a soothing river view. Try the regional appetizers, including stuffed tortillas and *empanadas* (turnovers stuffed with crab or shrimp), or the Tabasco specialty pejelagarto, a succulent fish. The same owners run the Capitán Buelo ($$$), a small cruiser that runs 1½-hour dining trips on the Grijalva River twice daily ($5 minimum consumption). Board on the malecón at the foot of Lerdo de Tejada, or call Los Tulipanes for reservations. Daily (except Monday) at 3:30 and 9:30 PM; Sunday 1:30 and 3:30. ✉ *Carlos Pellicer 511,* ☎ *93/12–92–09, 93/12–92–17. AE, MC, V.*

$$ ✕ **Don Lacho.** This popular spot for scrumptious oysters (cooked just about any way you like them) and other seafood features live traditional musicians on weekend nights in the large, air-conditioned section of the restaurant. ✉ *Av. Ruíz Cortines 1506,* ☎ *93/15–34–94. AE, DC, MC, V.*

$$ ✕ **La Fontana Italiana Trattoria.** If you're tiring of Mexican cuisine, enjoy tasty Italian fare (including pizza) at this air-conditioned restaurant a block from the Parque Museo La Venta. It's a favorite among locals. ✉ *Av. Ruíz Cortines 1410, Col. Lopez Mateos,* ☎ FAX *93/14–32–83. AE, MC, V.*

$$$$ ▦ **Camino Real.** This inviting nine-story resort property at the fringe of the Tabasco 2000 shopping complex has air-conditioned rooms with carpet, bathtubs, cable TV, and minibars. The rambling lobby, with rattan furniture in attractive niches, leads to the Tabasco 2000 mall, which has the largest number of upscale stores in Villahermosa. Shaded by bamboo curtains, the restaurant's floor-to-ceiling windows overlook a lovely garden. There's live entertainment in the lobby lounge nightly. Continental breakfast and an appetizer hour are offered for those staying in more-capacious rooms on the executive floor. ✉ *Paseo Tabasco 1407, 86030,* ☎ *93/16–44–00, 800/722–6466,* FAX *93/16–44–00. 180 rooms, 16 suites. Restaurant, bar, coffee shop, room service, pool, beauty salon, exercise room, travel services, car rental, free parking. AE, DC, MC, V.*

$$$$ ▦ **Hyatt Regency Villahermosa.** This American-style luxury hotel built in 1983 offers the amenities of the worldwide Hyatt chain: air-conditioned rooms with cable TV, voice mail, and minibars, and two executive floors with concierge service. Rooms have marble floors and polished wood furnishings. The La Ceiba Café has pleasing tropical decor and a superb daily breakfast buffet ($8) to which local families flock on Sunday. In the lobby, El Plataforma video bar is decked out like the inside of an offshore oil platform with photos of oilmen at work; there is live music nightly at 8 in the El Flamboyant bar. ✉ *Av. Juárez 106, Zona Hotelera, 86050,* ☎ *93/13–44–44, 93/15–12–34, 800/228–9000,* FAX *93/15–58–08, 93/15–12–35. 198 rooms, 9 suites. 2 restaurants, 2 bars, pool, 2 tennis courts, travel services, car rental. AE, DC, MC, V.*

$$$ ▦ **Calinda Viva Villahermosa.** The common areas of this five-story member of the Choice Hotels International chain are more inviting than the ordinary rooms. The enormous square pool is surrounded by lounge chairs and umbrella-shaded tables, and peacocks strut about the grounds or roost on ground-level balconies. All rooms have air-conditioning, FM stereos, color satellite TV, and small balconies. The restaurant serves many regional dishes, with a daily breakfast and lunch buffet. ✉ *Av. Ruíz Cortines at Paseo Tabasco s/n, Col. Linda Vista, 86050,* ☎ *93/15–00–00, 800/221–2222,* FAX *93/15–30–73. 239 rooms, 1 suite. Restaurant, 2 bars, pool, massage, sauna, steam room, exercise room. AE, DC, MC, V.*

$$$ ▦ **Cencali.** This two-story hotel, across from La Venta museum and park, sits on a lagoon and is surrounded by lush greenery; it has the best view in town. Most of the small, cheerfully decorated rooms have lots of light; 30 of the best also have balconies overlooking the lagoon, which is fringed with coconut-palm, mango, and cacao trees. All rooms have bathtubs, air-conditioning, and cable TV. Don't miss the fabulous lobby mural of pre-Columbian indigenous life (inspired by the Maya document *Popol Vuh*) by Tabascan master Daniel Ponce Montúy (1925–). The airy La Isla coffee shop, overlooking the pool and the lagoon, has a daily breakfast buffet ($7.50). ✉ *Av. Juárez and Paseo Tabasco, 86040,* ☎ FAX *93/15–19–19. 120 rooms, 7 suites. Restaurant, bar, coffee shop, pool. AE, DC, MC, V.*

$$$ ⊞ **Maya Tabasco Best Western.** A few blocks from the first-class (ADO) bus station, the Màya Tabasco has rooms with air-conditioning, cable TV, and phones; a rather plain lobby; and an energetic staff. This hotel is outclassed by others of similar price range, but it will do if your first choices are booked. You can check out open-mike night in the new Belle Epoque Trova Bar Café, smack in the middle of the swimming pool. ⊠ *Av. Ruíz Cortines 907, 86000,* ☎ *93/12–11–11, 01–800/237–7700, 800/528-1234,* ℻ *93/12–10–97. 149 rooms, 3 suites. 2 restaurants, bar, café, pool, dance club, travel services, car rental. AE, DC, MC, V.*

$$ ⊞ **Howard Johnson.** This five-story hotel is conveniently located in the pedestrian-only Zona Luz area, not far from the historic downtown and the malecón. It has lots of conveniences for its price range, including cable TV, complimentary newspaper, room service, and an Internet café on the premises. Weekend rates offer a substantial discount (as do most business-oriented hotels here). The coffee shop's attentive waiters serve mugs of hot coffee with real cream and refills. ⊠ *Av. Aldama 404, 86000,* ☎ ℻ *93/14–46–45,* ☎ *800/446–4656 93 rooms, 6 suites. Coffee shop, bar, room service, free parking. AE, DC, MC, V.*

$$ ⊞ **Plaza Independencia.** There's a lot to recommend this attractive hotel besides an excellent location between the Grijalva River and the Plaza de Armas. Common areas are overwashed in Mexican pink, sky blue, and sunny yellow paint, and there's a midsize pool in the back patio. Some of the rooms have wacky decorations, with mint-green and orange furnishings that clash with cotton bedspreads in other bright colors. Others rooms are more subdued. All have room safes, closets, cable TV, and air-conditioning. Ask for a room with a balcony overlooking the river. ⊠ *Av. Independencia 123, 86000,* ☎ *93/12–12–99,* ℻ *93/14–47–24. 89 rooms, 1 suite. Restaurant, bar, pool, free parking. AE, DC, MC, V.*

Comalcalco

🔺 ㉗   *60 km (37 mi) northwest of Villahermosa off Rte. 187.*

Comalcalco, which means "place of the clay griddles" (bricks) in Nahuatl, is the most important Maya site in Tabasco. The abundant cacao trees in the region provided food and livelihood for a booming population during the Late Classic period (AD 600–900); it was founded approximately in the 1st century BC. The site marks the westernmost reach of the Maya, and descendants of its builders, the Chontal, still live in the vicinity. This site is unique among Maya cities for its use of fired brick (made of sand, seashells, and clay), as the Tabasco swamplands lacked the stone for building that was found elsewhere in the empire. The bricks were inscribed and painted with figures of reptiles and birds, geometric figures, and drawings of hands and feet before being covered with stucco. The major pyramid, **Temple IV,** on the Great Eastern Acropolis, is decorated with large stucco masks of the sun god Kinich Ahau and carvings, and the **museum** houses many of the artifacts that were uncovered there. 🎟 *About $2.* ⊘ *Daily 9–4:30.*

Paraíso

㉘   *19 km (12 mi) north of Comalcalco.*

If not seeing the Gulf of Mexico will leave you feeling deprived, you can continue on from Comalcalco to the coast and Paraíso, where you'll get a glimpse of small-town life and a pretty coast. Take a boat ride through mangrove-lined channels or climb nearby **Teodomiro Hill** for a spectacular view of Las Flores lagoon and coconut plantations. Small seafood restaurants and several small hotels dot the shore here; others are a few kilometers inland, in town.

CHIAPAS AND TABASCO A TO Z

Arriving and Departing

By Bus

PALENQUE

First- and luxury-class service is available to Ocosingo (two hours), Villahermosa (2½ hours), San Cristóbal (four hours), Campeche (six hours), Tuxtla Gutiérrez (seven hours), Mérida (eight hours), Cancún (11 hours), and Mexico City (12 hours) on the first-class ADO and Cristóbal Colón. Buses leave from the **ADO bus terminal** (⊠ Av. Juárez near Av. de la Vega, ☎ 934/5–13–44). If you can't get a first-class bus, many of the same destinations can be reached on the second-class buses **Omnibus de Chiapas** (☎ 934/5–13–22) and **Express Plus** (☎ 934/5–10–12), both a few doors away from the ADO bus terminal.

SAN CRISTÓBAL

Cristóbal Colón (⊠ Av. Insurgentes s/n and Blvd. Juan Sabines Gutiérrez, ☎ 967/8–02–91) has first- and second-class buses to major destinations in Chiapas and beyond. The green vans of **Corazón de María** (☎ no phone) leave next door to the Cristóbal Colón terminal for Tuxtla Gutiérrez as soon as they fill up (about every 20 minutes) 5 AM–10 PM and cost about $2.50. Second-class service on **Transportes Tuxtla Express Plus** (☎ 967/8–48–69) to Tuxtla, Palenque, and Mexico City departs from the terminal at Avenida Ignacio Allende, ½ block from Boulevard Juan Sabines Gutiérrez, about four blocks to the west.

TUXTLA GUTIÉRREZ

Cristóbal Colón (⊠ Av. 2a Nte. Pte. 268, ☎ 961/2–16–39, 961/2–26–24) offers deluxe and first- and second-class service between Tuxtla and Oaxaca, Palenque, Villahermosa, Tapachula, Mérida, Mexico City, San Cristóbal, Cancún, Puerto Escondido, and Playa del Carmen. First- and second-class transportation within the state is available on **Sociedad de Transportes Dr. Rodulfo Figueroa** (⊠ 4a Pte. Sur 1060, ☎ 961/3–65–92).

VILLAHERMOSA

Deluxe and first-class service to Campeche, Chetumal, Mérida, Mexico City, Palenque, San Cristóbal, Tapachula, Tuxtla Gutiérrez, Veracruz, and elsewhere is available from the **ADO bus terminal** (⊠ Calle F. J. Mina 297, corner of Lino Merino), which is served by UNO and G. L. (☎ 93/12–76–27, 93/12–76–92) and Cristóbal Colón (☎ 93/12–29–37, 93/12–89–00). There is frequent second-class service to the same cities from the **Central Camionera de 2a Clase** (⊠ Av. Ruíz Cortines s/n, ☎ 93/12–29–77, 93/12–10–91).

By Car

From Tuxtla Gutiérrez, Highway 190 goes east through Chiapa de Corzo to San Cristóbal before continuing southeast to Comitán and the Guatemala border. Highway 199 to Highway 186 (the turnoff is at Catazajá) is the preferred route from San Cristóbal to Villahermosa; it'll take you via Toniná, Agua Azul, and Palenque. The drive from San Cristóbal to Palenque takes about five hours along a winding paved road, and it's another two hours from Palenque to Villahermosa along a fairly straight road.

On the map, Highway 195 may look like the most direct way to travel between San Cristóbal and Villahermosa, but it entails hours of hairpin curves—it's only for the stalwart and absolutely not to be traveled at night because of seasonal fog as well as a lack of reflectors, illumination, and other cars to help in case of emergency.

To get to Villahermosa from Coatzacoalcos and Veracruz, take Highway 180. In all cases, exercise caution during the rainy season (June through October), when roads are slick. Although expensive, car rentals are available at the Tuxtla and Villahermosa airports as well as in San Cristóbal (☞ Car Rental *in* Contacts and Resources, *below*).

By Plane

BONAMPAK AND YAXCHILÁN

For charter flights to the ruins of Bonampak and Yaxchilán, contact the following air charters: in Tuxtla Gutiérrez, **Montes Azules** (☎ 961/3–22–56, 961/3–29–93); in Comitán, **Servicio Aéreo San Cristóbal** (☎ 963/2–03–09, FAX 963/2–29–93).

PALENQUE

Aerocaribe (☞ Tuxtla Gutiérrez, *below*) flies between Palenque and Flores, Guatemala (near the Tikal ruins), and Tuxtla Gutiérrez (with connections to Oaxaca and Mexico City).

SAN CRISTÓBAL

The **San Cristóbal Airport** (✉ Corazón de María Km 17) opened in October 1999. It serves Mexico City daily on Aeromar (☎ 961/4–30–03). The closest major airport is in Tuxtla Gutiérrez (☞ *below*), 85 km (53 mi) to the west. You can get from Tuxtla to San Cristóbal by first-class bus, which leaves several times each day (two hours; about $2.50), or by taxi (1½ hours; $13 for one–four persons). Many travel agencies in both cities provide private taxi service. You can also catch a *colectivo* (shared minivan) to San Cristóbal at either of the two airports in Tuxtla Gutiérrez: from the Llano San Juan Airport, it costs about $6 a person; from the Terán Airport, $4.

TUXTLA GUTIÉRREZ

Two airports serve Tuxtla: **Llano San Juan Airport** (☎ 961/2–29–20), which is in the town of Ocozocoautla, 22 km (14 mi) west of the city, and **Terán Airport** (☎ 961/5–10–11), 8 km (5 mi) southwest of the city center. Flights are routed to one of these two airports depending on meteorological conditions, as fog is frequently a problem. **Aerocaribe** (☎ 961/2–16–92, 961/2–00–20) flies nonstop to Mexico City, Oaxaca, and Villahermosa; from Villahermosa, the flight continues on to Palenque. **Aviacsa** (☎ 961/2–80–81, 961/1–20–00) also has direct flights from Mexico City, Oaxaca, and Tapachula; from Cancún, Guadalajara, and other cities you have to connect through Mexico City. You can catch a colectivo taxi from San Cristóbal to Tuxtla at the corner of Boulevard Juan Sabines Gutiérrez and Avenida Ignacio Allende, across from the second-class bus station. The taxi ($5 per person) will leave when it has four passengers.

VILLAHERMOSA

The **Capitan Carlos A. Rovirosa Pérez Airport** (☎ 93/56–01–57, 93/56–01–56), 15 km (9 mi) to the south, in Rancheria Dos Montes, serves Villahermosa. **Aeroméxico** (☎ 93/12–15–28, 93/12–95–54) has two to three daily nonstop flights from Mexico City and twice a week from Houston, Texas. **Mexicana** (☎ 93/16–31–32, 93/16–31–33, 93/16–31–34, 93/16–31–35) has two–three daily nonstop flights to Mexico City. Both airlines have connecting flights to other Mexican cities. **Aviacsa** (☎ 93/16–57–33) flies nonstop to Mexico City and Mérida. **Aerocaribe,** Mexicana's regional line (☎ 93/16–50–46), serves southwest Mexico, Mexico City, Palenque, Flores, and Tikal.

Getting Around

Palenque

A car or a tour arranged through a local travel agency is the easiest way to reach Palenque's surrounding attractions, although the ruins themselves can easily be reached via private taxi or inexpensive colectivo service from downtown (corner of Av. Hidalgo and Calle Allende) or from the ADO bus station. The local *sitio* (**taxi stand**) is at the town park (☎ 934/5–03–79, 934/8–23–53). The downtown itself is small enough to traverse on foot.

San Cristóbal

As with many other colonial towns, the most enjoyable and thorough way to explore San Cristóbal is on foot. If you do come to town with a car, leave it in the hotel garage until you're ready to take an excursion outside San Cristóbal. Taxis can be found at the **taxi stand** (☎ 967/8–03–96, 967/8–23–53), or sitio, across from the cathedral; there is colectivo service to outlying villages, departing from and returning to the market.

Villahermosa

Of the three rivers surrounding it, Villahermosa is oriented toward the Grijalva River to the east, which is bordered by a malecón. The city is huge, and driving can be tricky. The main road through town, Ruíz Cortines, is almost a highway; exit ramps are about 1 km (½ mi) apart, and tourist destinations aren't clearly marked. There is both *special* (individual) and collective taxi service. Call 93/15–83–33 or 93/15–84–33 for a radio taxi. Information about city buses can be difficult to find.

Contacts and Resources

Car Rental

SAN CRISTÓBAL

Budget (⊠ Calle Diego de Mazariegos 36, ☎ FAX 967/8–18–71, 967/8–31–00) is the only car rental agency in town.

TUXTLA GUTIÉRREZ

Budget (☎ 961/5–13–82, 961/5–06–83) and **Alamo** (☎ 961/2–52–61, 961/2–89–32) are represented at both Tuxtla airports (☞ By Plane *in* Arriving and Departing, *above*).

VILLAHERMOSA

Internationally known companies with offices at the airport and downtown Villahermosa include **Advantage** (☎ 93/15–58–33, 93/15–58–48), **Budget** (☎ 93/14–37–40, 93/56–01–18), **Dollar** (☎ 93/56–02–11), **Hertz** (☎ 93/16–44–00, 93/16–01–63), and **National** (☎ 93/15–12–34 ext. 3710, or 93/56–03–93).

E-Mail

PALENQUE

Cibernet (⊠ Calle Independencia s/n, at Av. 5 de Mayo, ☎ 934/5–1710), the only place for public Internet access in Palenque, is packed with eager elementary-school students and the occasional traveler. At only $1.50 an hour, the Internet access here is fast enough. Cibernet's open Monday–Saturday 8–2 and 4–9.

SAN CRISTÓBAL

The connections at the **CyberC@fe** (⊠ Real de Guadalupe 7, ☎ 967/8–7488), in a small shopping center near the zócalo, are fast. You can have beer, coffee, or dessert while you surf the Web for $4 per hour. It's open 9 AM–9:30 PM daily.

The best Internet café in Tabasco is at the coffee shop of the **Howard Johnson's** hotel (⊠ Aldama 404, ☎ 93/12–96–59), in the popular Zona Luz district. It's open weekdays 8 AM–10 PM, Saturday 8–8, and Sunday noon–8, and charges $2 an hour.

The **CyberCafe** (⊠ 3a Nte. Pte. 1346, ☎ 961/2–3900) is about 10 blocks from the Cristóbal Colón bus station, but the price is right: $1.50 an hour for Internet access. It's open daily 9–9.

Emergencies

In larger cities such as Tuxtla Gutiérrez and Villahermosa, dial **060** for fire, theft, and medical emergencies. If you don't speak Spanish, it might be better to call hotel personnel or the tourist office (during open hours) and ask for an English-speaking representative.

For tourist-related problems contact the **Agencia del Ministerio Público** at the tourist office (☞ Palenque *in* Visitor Information, *below*). Visit the **Centro de Salud** (⊠ Prolongación Juárez s/n, ☎ 934/5–00–25), weekdays 7 AM–8 PM, for medical consultation. In an emergency, the **Hospital General** (☎ 934/5–07–33), next door, is open 24 hours a day, as is **Farmacia Lastra** (⊠ Av. Juárez s/n at Abasolo, downtown, ☎ 934/5–11–19).

Municipal police (⊠ Blvd. Juan Sabines Gutiérrez, s/n, near Unidad Deportiva, ☎ 967/8–05–54); **Federal Highway Police** (⊠ Blvd. Juan Sabines Gutiérrez, s/n, ☎ 967/8–64–66); **Cruz Roja** (Red Cross, ⊠ Prolongación Ignacio Allende 55, ☎ 967/8–07–72, 967/8–65–65); **Hospital General** (⊠ Av. Insurgentes 24, ☎ 967/8–07–70). **Farmacio Regina** (⊠ Crescencio Rosas at Calle Diego de Mazariegos, ☎ 967/8–02–41) is a 24-hour pharmacy.

Farmacia del Ahorro (⊠ Av. Central Pte. 874, ☎ 961/3–88–18) is a 24-hour pharmacy with delivery.

Red Cross Hospital (⊠ Av. Sandino, s/n, Col. Primero de Mayo, ☎ 93/15–55–55, 93/13–35–93); travelers are advised to call the **state tourist office** (☎ 93/16–36–33) for all emergencies. **Farmacia Unión** (⊠ Av. 27 de Febrero 1205, ☎ 93/15–47–17) is a 24-hour pharmacy.

English-Language Bookstores

In San Cristóbal, **Chilam Balam** (⊠ Casa Utrilla at Av. Gral. Utrilla 33 and Dr. Navarro, ☎ 967/8–04–86) has the latest editions of travel, archaeology, and art books along with posters and maps of Mexico. There's a second store at Avenida Insurgentes 18. **La Mercantil** (⊠ Calle Diego de Mazariegos 21) has the best selection of English- and Spanish-language periodicals.

Guided Tours

From the town of Palenque, most tour operators offer half-day guided tours of Palenque ruins for about $6, which includes guide, entrance to the ruins, hotel pickup, and lunch. Also offered are six-hour tours to the waterfalls at Misol-Há and Agua Azul, at about $10 per person—a good deal as it includes entrance to both sites and transportation. Longer trips to San Cristóbal, Toniná, and the Sumidero Canyon are also available. Reliable, recommended tour operators include **Turismo Quetzal** (⊠ Av. Juárez 135, ☎ 934/5–06–01) and **Kukulcán**

(⊠ Av. Juárez s/n at Calle Allende, ☎ 934/5–15–06). Both have one-
and two-day trips to Bonampak and Yaxchilán by land. A one-day trip
costs $30–$40 via land and boat, including transportation, Spanish-
speaking guide, and lunch. Two-day trips overnight in tents at the Lacandon village of Lacanjá and cost about $60, including five meals,
transportation, and guide services. Both companies can arrange river
trips to the Maya ruins at Tikal, in Guatemala, as well as day trips to
Misol-Há and Agua Azul waterfalls near Palenque.

Ceiba Adventures (⊠ Box 2274, Flagstaff, AZ 86003, ☎ 520/527–
0171, FAX 520/527–8127) has guided adventure tours throughout the
Ruta Maya, including excursions to Palenque, Bonampak, Yaxchilán,
and Tikal. Available are cave explorations and river rafting along several Chiapan waterways sunk deep in the jungle.

SAN CRISTÓBAL

Orientation Tours. Full-day city bus tours also cover the village of San
Juan Chamula and the San Cristóbal Caves. Five-hour horseback tours
to the caves or San Juan Chamula can also be arranged.

Guides. Pepe Santiago and his partner lead tours ($8) daily to San Juan
Chamula and Zinacantán, leaving from Na Bolom (☞ Exploring San
Cristóbal de las Casas *in* San Cristóbal de las Casas, *above*) at 10 AM
and returning about 3:30. Mercedes Hernández leaves from the zócalo
at approximately 9 AM; look for her colorful umbrella. She charges about
$5 per person. These guides speak English and are recommended by
the tourist department.

Regional Tours. A.T.C. (⊠ Av. 16 de Septiembre 16, ☎ 967/8–25–50,
967/8–25–57, FAX 967/8–31–45), **Viajes Pakal** (⊠ Calle Cuauhtémoc
6A, ☎ FAX 967/8–28–19), and **Viajes Pedrero** (⊠ Hotel Santa Clara,
Av. Insurgentes 1, ☎ 967/8–69–83, 967/8–11–40, FAX 967/8–10–41)
offer local tours as well as tours of Bonampak, Yaxchilán, Palenque,
Agua Azul, Lagunas de Montebello, Amatenango, Chincultik, Comitán,
Sumidero Canyon, and Tuxtla Gutiérrez; some arrange transportation
to Guatemala, the Yucatán, and Belize. **Pronatura** (⊠ Av. Juárez 11-
B, ☎ 967/8–50–00) offers day trips to the tropical cloud forests of
Reserva Huitepec; profits go to Chiapas conservation and reforestation programs. Most tour operators transport passengers in minibuses
and can arrange hotel pickup. **DANA** (⊠ Dr. Navarro 10, ☎ FAX 967/
8–43–07) offers low-impact four-day guided hiking tours to Laguna
Miramar, the largest natural lake in southwestern Mexico, in the Lacandon rain forest. Here you'll experience camping, swimming, snorkeling, fishing, horseback riding, and visits to small area ruins and
indigenous communities. A three-night stay (the minimum) costs about
$180 if you go by land.

TUXTLA GUTIÉRREZ

Viajes Lido (⊠ Av. Central Pte. 861-A, ☎ 961/5–56–56, FAX 961/2–11–
30) and **Viajes Miramar** (⊠ Camino Real, Local 2, ☎ 961/7–77–77
ext. 7230; FAX 961/5–59–25), run by the Castillo sisters, offer city tours
of Tuxtla Gutiérrez, plus five-hour excursions to Chiapa de Corzo and
Sumidero Canyon for $10.

VILLAHERMOSA

Agencia de Viajes Tabasco (⊠ Hyatt Regency, Av. Juárez 106, Zona
Hotelera, ☎ 93/15–12–34, 93/15–57–90; ⊠ Galería Tabasco 2000,
Local 173, ☎ 93/16–40–88, FAX 93/16–40–90, 93/16–43–37) has city
tours as well as trips to Comalcalco, Palenque, and San Cristóbal.

Visitor Information

The state of Chiapas has a toll-free **tourist information** number, which can be dialed from anywhere in Mexico (☎ 01–800/280–3500), but which isn't always answered.

COMITÁN

Tourist office (✉ ground floor of Municipal Palace, facing zócalo, ☎ 963/2–40–47), open weekdays 9–8, weekends 9–2.

PALENQUE

Tourist information (✉ Av. Juárez and Abasolo, at Plaza de Artesanías, ☎ 934/5–01–41, 934/5–00–13), open weekdays 9–3 and 6–9.

SAN CRISTÓBAL

The people at the **municipal tourist office** (✉ Palacio Municipal [City Hall], ground floor, on zócalo, ☎ 967/8–06–65, 967/8–01–35) have some information about San Cristóbal proper, although they are less than attentive. The people at the **state tourist office** (✉ Miguel Hidalgo 2, ½ block from zócalo, ☎ FAX 967/8–65–70) are very knowledgable and helpful and have information about attractions throughout the state. Both are open Monday through Saturday 9–9, Sunday 9–2.

TUXTLA GUTIÉRREZ

The people at the **state tourist office** (✉ Edificio Plaza de las Instituciones, ground floor, Blvd. Dr. Belisario Domínguez 950, ☎ 961/3–44–99, 01–800/280–3500) are extremely knowledgeable and helpful. The office is open weekdays 9–9, Saturday 9–7, Sunday 9–3.

VILLAHERMOSA

Tourist office (✉ Paseo Tabasco 1504, ☎ 93/16–36–33, 93/16–28–89) is open weekdays 9–3 and 6–9, Saturday 9–1. The auxiliary office at Parque Museo La Venta is open daily 9–4; the information booth at the airport is supposed to be open daily 8–8.

12 VERACRUZ AND THE NORTHEAST

The superb but little-explored pyramids of El Tajín and the raffish charm of Veracruz, the first European city established on the North American mainland, are among Mexico's indisputable highlights. Many Texans get their first taste of Mexico in the northeastern border towns of Nuevo Laredo, Reynosa, and Matamoros. Texan or otherwise, if you venture farther down to Monterrey, you'll find far more-sophisticated dining, shopping, and cultural attractions in the country's third largest city.

T
HERE ARE PLENTY of reasons to make your way down into the
state of Veracruz, not least of which are its culture and history.
You can explore El Tajín—its Temple of the Niches is one of the
most enchanting pre-Columbian buildings in Mexico. Or wander the
venerable port of Veracruz, where the Spanish first landed in 1519; witness the fascinating aerial ritual of the *voladores* (fliers) of Papantla;
and enjoy an archaeological museum second only to the one in Mexico City. You can also stroll the plazas of quaint mountain villages, laze
on sandy beaches, and dine on some of the best seafood in Mexico,
prepared in the famous Veracruz style.

Updated by
Todd Schindler

If the northeasternmost Mexican states of Nuevo León and Tamaulipas are not, for the most part, the Mexico touted in glossy magazines—
which is one reason they are unique—they are by no means bereft of
appeal. A hybrid of Mexican and U.S. culture, the three border cities
of Nuevo Laredo, Reynosa, and Matamoros are good places to pick
up handicrafts and sample authentic Mexican dishes at relatively low
prices. Improved roads have also led more people to take advantage
of the opportunity to visit Monterrey, Mexico's third-largest city. With
its cultural attractions, five-star hotels and restaurants, and, of course,
shops, it is a highlight of the region. In Monterrey, you can arrange
horseback rides, mountain-biking excursions, and treks into the pine
forests of the nearby Sierra Madre.

Pleasures and Pastimes

Dining

The state of **Veracruz** is famous for its signature dish, *huachinango a
là veracruzana* (red snapper in the Veracruz style, covered in tomatoes,
onions, olives, and herbs). Leaving Veracruz without sampling this would
be both a shame and a bit of a feat, as every chef has his own version,
which he will insist you try.

In Veracruz, as befits a hot, breezy port town, the emphasis is on simple, fresh food, mostly *pescado* (fish) and *mariscos* (shellfish). Whether
at night or during the day, a stop at one of the town's cafés is de rigueur—
the 19th-century Café del Portal is known internationally for its atmosphere and its fantastic coffee. **Jalapa** probably has the best restaurants
in the state; the cookery is just as creative as the town's arts and music
scene. It's not uncommon to hear the pat-pat of tortillas being hand-
formed as you eat, and beans, rice, and cheese, and occasionally chilies
(this is, after all, the hometown of the jalapeño) are cleverly integrated
into main dishes of meat and river fish such as trout. You can eat cheaply
and heartily in **Papantla**, but with little variation. Just as **Tuxpán**'s best
attractions are its pretty river and nearby beaches, some of the best places
to eat here are the small, family-run seafood *palapas* (thatch-roof huts)
lining the beach as well as the river, as it makes its way to the gulf at
Playa Tuxpán. If you ask for the *platillo del día* (daily dish), most likely
you'll be treated to a cold shrimp, calamari, or crab cocktail, or a plate
of fried fish or shrimp with Mexican rice and tortillas.

Although **the northeast** isn't especially renowned for its cuisine, you'll
find a nice variety of dishes from around the country. Among the regional specialties are *cabrito* (roast kid), *carne asada* (grilled fillet of
beef), and *café de olla* (a delicious blend of coffee, cinnamon, and brown
sugar brewed in a clay pot).

Very little in the state of Veracruz or the northeast is truly formal. Even
in the cities of Veracruz and Monterrey reservations are almost never
necessary, and a jacket and tie would look out of place almost any-

where (unless we note otherwise). In a town such as Papantla, to say that dress is casual would be an understatement: shorts and a T-shirt won't get a second glance even in the town's fanciest dining room.

CATEGORY	COST*
$$$$	over $20
$$$	$15–$20
$$	$8–$15
$	under $8

*per person for a three-course meal, excluding drinks, service, and tax

Fishing

Northeastern Mexico is a popular place for American anglers. **Lake Vicente Guerrero,** near Ciudad Victoria, has some of the best bass fishing in Mexico. You're likely to hook something at **La Pesca**—its name means "the fish"—on the Tamaulipas coast between Matamoros and Tampico east of Ciudad Victoria and Soto La Marina.

Lodging

The state of **Veracruz** is just starting to get world-class hotels such as the super-deluxe Fiesta Americana in Veracruz. The port city also has a number of inexpensive hotels with plenty of atmosphere, and the moderately priced and more expensive places offer good value for your money—especially in comparison with their counterparts in areas of Mexico that see more foreign tourists.

Although there are plenty of clean, comfortable, and inexpensive options in downtown **Jalapa,** more-upscale choices are limited. The two nicest hotels, the Fiesta Inn and Posada de Coatepec, are a bit out of town, which can be inconvenient if you don't have a car, because local bus service is infrequent and Jalapa's many cultural offerings are concentrated in the *zona centro* (central zone). Many people choose to see **El Tajín** as a day trip from the more developed city of Tuxpán, only passing through Papantla. If you decide to spend a night or two here, your options are limited: **Papantla** has few hotels, and none are exceptional, although the Premier is well equipped. Fortunately, they are concentrated in a five-block radius and almost never fill up, so you can simply walk around town once you arrive and decide which suits you best. **Tuxpán** also has a five-star hotel, a fancy place—for Tuxpán— called Hotel May Palace. Otherwise, there are plenty of safe and comfortable budget rooms in town. Tuxpán sees few foreigners, and aside from during Semana Santa (Holy Week) and July and August, when middle-class Mexicans head en masse for the beach, its hotels are usually empty.

Catering mostly to business travelers and short-term tourists, the hotels in the **border towns** are what you'd expect—not luxurious but reasonably priced and mostly well kept. **Monterrey** affords more choices in all price ranges, and new hotels keep popping up to keep pace with the increase in corporate travelers. The posh Quinta Real typifies the new breed of lodgings.

CATEGORY	COST*
$$$$	over $110
$$	$70–$110
$$	$40–$70
$	under $40

*All prices are for a standard double room, excluding tax.

Exploring Veracruz and the Northeast

The lively port city of Veracruz was of vital importance in the history of the Spanish conquest of Mexico. The lush coastal state of Veracruz also has its share of colonial history, as well as native ruins and newly established adventure-tourism routes.

Northeastern Mexico consists of a string of border towns across from the United States, the city of Monterrey, and some surrounding natural wonders. Although the border towns are worth a visit to sample Mexican cuisine and buy handicrafts at cheaper prices than in the United States, their charm is limited. You might want to linger longer in Monterrey, a major city with some worthwhile restaurants and sights.

Numbers in the text correspond to numbers in the margin and on the Veracruz and East Central Mexico, Veracruz, Northeastern Mexico, and Monterrey maps.

Great Itineraries

The state of Veracruz and Northeast Mexico are separate regions, which is how most travelers approach them when planning a trip. Veracruz is closer to Mexico City and more appealing. Northeast Mexico is closer to Texas and is more often frequented by Texans hopping across the border than by people using Mexico City as a gateway. Our approach to the northeast is therefore from Texas. The drive up the coast from Veracruz is possible, but considering that it's 502 km (311 mi) between Veracruz and Tampico and 1,005 km (623 mi) from Veracruz to Monterrey, the distances look a bit daunting from behind the wheel.

IF YOU HAVE 3 DAYS

If you are flying, head straight for the port of **Veracruz** ①–⑤, the most Caribbean of the Gulf of Mexico cities. You'll have no problem spending two days here: in addition to the excellent aquarium and the museums you'll find some of the country's best cafés, music, and seafood restaurants. On Day 3, take a day trip to the state capital, **Jalapa** ⑧, and its magnificent Museum of Anthropology; stop on the way at **La Antigua** to see the ruins of Hernán Cortés's house, and at the archaeological site of **Cempoala** ⑦, a major Totonac city.

If you are driving down from Texas and have limited time, you could simply explore the area around **Monterrey** ⑮–㉒, the cultural and industrial giant of the northeast, to get a feeling for Mexico. Spend the first day walking around the Gran Plaza area, where the modern-art and history museums are outstanding, and then drive to the **Cuauhtémoc Brewery** ⑳ on the outskirts of town. Devote the next two days to enjoying some of the region's natural attractions, including the **Barranca de la Huasteca** ㉓, an impressive gorge; the ancient **Grutas de García** ㉔; and the **Parque Nacional Cumbres de Monterrey** ㉕, with its spectacular waterfall. For some colonial color, visit downtown **Saltillo** ㉖, where Mexican tiles are made. If you get hooked on its charm, spend one night here instead of driving back to Monterrey.

IF YOU HAVE 5 DAYS

Start in **Veracruz** ①–⑤. On the second day make your way out of the city to the cool hill towns of **Los Tuxtlas** ⑥, where you can consult a *curandero* (healer) for whatever ails you. Then on Day 3 make your way to the city of **Jalapa** ⑧ for its renowned Museum of Anthropology. Plan to spend the two remaining days at **El Tajín** ⑨, overnighting in the nearby town of **Papantla de Olarte** ⑩. Make your way back down the coast to Veracruz, and consider stopping on the way at **La Antigua** and **Cempoala** ⑦.

For five days in the northeast, add an excursion to **Tampico** ㉘, on the Gulf of Mexico, to the three-day jaunt. On Day 4, check out sculptures of Tlazoltéotl, the pre-Hispanic Huastecan Goddess of Love, at the **Museo de la Cultura Huasteca,** or relax with picnicking Mexican families at Playa Miramar. Spend the last day bass fishing (or boating) at **Lake Vicente Guererro** ㉗.

IF YOU HAVE 7 DAYS
In east central Mexico, follow the five-day itinerary above, but extend the trip to include more time around **Jalapa** ⑧ and visit the magnificent falls at **Xico,** overnighting nearby in the picturesque colonial town of Coatepec. The next day, go river rafting on the Río Pescados southeast of Jalapa. If you drive, consider adding a visit to **Los Tuxtlas** ⑥; if you don't have a car, spend a leisurely extra day enjoying the beaches and seafood restaurants of **Boca del Río,** a small fishing village that is quickly turning into a suburb of Veracruz, or visiting more of the sights you missed in the port's downtown.

When to Tour

In Veracruz, the weather is balmy between November and April. The notorious *nortes*—gusty, chilly winds that blow in off the Gulf of Mexico—usually appear between October and February, and especially in December. Pack a sweater and light coat or jacket if you plan to travel during these months. In summer, both the temperature and humidity soar, but the frequent rains afford a respite from the heat.

A great time to visit Veracruz is the week before Ash Wednesday for Carnaval, Mexico's version of Mardi Gras. It's wild and merry but has a small-town ambience that makes it saner and safer than the better-known celebrations in Río or New Orleans. The biggest problem at such times is finding a room (reserve one well in advance), but the local tourist office can usually come up with acceptable accommodations. The same is true during Christmas as well as Easter week, when all of Mexico goes on vacation and heads for the beach.

The hottest months in the northeast are April through June. The cooling rains arrive in July and last through August. There are never any crowds at the border towns or in Monterrey except during major U.S. holidays, when Americans head south for a day or weekend.

THE STATE OF VERACRUZ

A long, skinny crescent of land bordering the Gulf of Mexico, the state of Veracruz is often ignored by travelers, many of whom do no more than glimpse it through the window of a bus barreling toward the Yucatán Peninsula. Although Veracruz's ruins and beaches don't quite compare with those on the Yucatán, the state is popular with vacationing Mexicans, drawn to the cool hill towns of the Sierra de Los Tuxtlas and the liveliness of Veracruz City.

Descending from the volcanic Sierra, the Veracruz coast consists of flat lowlands that have their share of terrible heat and swamps and are pockmarked by noisome oil refineries. As you head inland a ways—Veracruz is only 140 km (87 mi) across at its widest point—the land rises to meet the Sierra Madre Oriental range, with its 6,100-m (20,130-ft) Pico de Orizaba (also called Citlaltépetl), Mexico's highest peak. In the foothills of this range, you'll find the university town and state capital Jalapa, where students share the colonial streets with local farmers marketing their crops. Jalapa is a favored place for foreigners to study Spanish, and the nearby town of Jalcomulco is a base for river-rafting explorations on the Río Pescados. The state does have some good beaches along the coast, particularly around the northern city of Tuxpán, but the real reasons to come are the atmosphere, the history, and the people. All these are at their best in the city of Veracruz, a working port with so many marimba bands in the *zócalo* (main square) on weekend evenings that they have to compete to be heard.

Olmec civilization thrived in Veracruz long before the rise of the Maya. The state's best-preserved ruins, at El Tajín near Papantla, are thought to have been the work of yet another civilization, which had its heyday later, between AD 550 and 1100. By the time Hernán Cortés landed in Veracruz in 1519, the Aztecs held sway, but within a very short time the Indian population was decimated by war and European diseases.

The state of Veracruz played a pivotal role in Cortés's march to Tenochtitlán. A government-sponsored circuit called the Ruta de Cortés (Route of Cortez) traces the Spanish conquistador's footsteps, beginning with his Veracruz landing through to his arrival in Mexico City, where he defeated the Aztec rulers. It's a mélange of soft adventure excursions, such as river rafting, combined with visits to colonial cities, old haciendas, and archaeological zones that were instrumental in the Spanish conquest.

In modern times, the discovery of oil in Veracruz caused a population explosion that saw the number of *veracruzanos* go from about 1 million at the beginning of the century to more than 7 million today. For most foreign visitors, the occasional sulfurous stench of a coastal refinery is an unpleasant intrusion on their tropical reverie, but for many of the state's residents, oil is their bread and butter.

Veracruz

502 km (311 mi) south of Tampico, 345 km (214 mi) west of Mexico City.

Veracruz was the first European city established on the North American mainland. In 1519 Cortés landed about 25 km (16 mi) to the northwest in La Antigua, a tiny slip of a place, but Veracruz became the major gateway for Spanish settlement of Mexico. Its name, which appears throughout Latin America, means "true cross."

To meet their labor needs, the Spanish brought a large number of Africans to Veracruz as slaves. Later, Cuban immigrants flooded the port. This mix in modern days has created an open-minded city, where visitors of all cultural extractions are generously welcomed.

Perhaps the most profound influence of Veracruz's mixed population can be seen in its music and dance. Veracruz is the hometown of "La Bamba," a song that dates back to the 17th century. In addition to its most famous song, the city has a special brand of music, played by lively trios outfitted in white and slapping away at tiny guitars and portable harps. In the evening, mariachis entertain outside sidewalk cafés around the main plaza; night or day, a stop at one of these is de rigueur.

The *danzón*, a languorous two-person dance with lots of subtle hip movement, was brought to the city by penniless refugees fleeing Cuba in 1879 following its Ten Years' War. Most ended up living outside the city walls (only Veracruz aristocrats were allowed to live inside), but the sons of the Mexican elite sneaked into the poor neighborhoods at night and eventually introduced the danzón to high society. Sensuous compared with the stiff and formal dance that had been the norm until this time, the danzón was at first considered scandalous, but it soon won the hearts of even its detractors and became the most popular dance in the city. It later spread throughout the country.

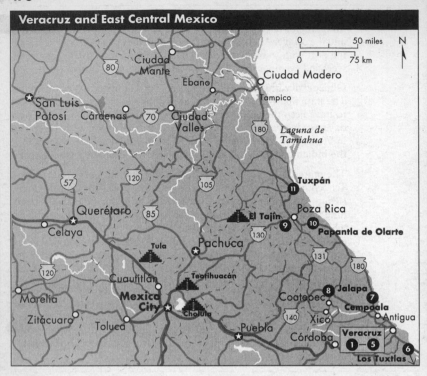

Veracruz and East Central Mexico

Veracruz was Mexico's premier seaside resort and the port of entry for most foreign visitors until a few decades ago; travelers arrived by ship, then boarded a train to Mexico City, often looking back wistfully. Today relatively few foreigners find their way to Veracruz's beaches, but domestic vacationers are lured to the fun-loving town by prices far lower than those found in Acapulco, Puerto Vallarta, or Cancún.

❶ If this is your first visit to the port of Veracruz, a good place to get oriented is the **Museo de la Ciudad.** The region's history is narrated through artifacts and displays, and scale models of the city help you get the lay of the land. Also exhibited are copies of pre-Columbian statues and contemporary indigenous art. A $1 donation pays for a guided tour by a bilingual student. ⊠ *Zaragoza at Morales,* ☎ *29/31–84–10.* 🎫 *Free.* ⊙ *Tues.–Sun. 10–8.*

During the Viceregal era, Veracruz was the only east-coast port permitted to operate in New Spain. As a result, it was frequently attacked **❷** by pirates. The great **Fort of San Juan de Ulúa,** built shortly after the conquest and the last territory in Mexico to be held by the Spanish Royalists, is a monument to that swashbuckling era. A miniature city in itself, the island fort is a maze of moats, ramparts, and drawbridges smack in the middle of the busy port area (it's now connected to the mainland by a causeway). Fortification of the island began in 1535 under the direction of Antonio de Mendoza, the first viceroy of New Spain. Ground coral, sand, and oyster shells were used for the original walls. A few centuries later, the fort was used as a prison, housing such figures as Benito Juárez, who was held here by conservative dictator Santa Anna before being exiled to Louisiana in 1853. After Independence, it was used in unsuccessful attempts to fight off first the invading French, the Americans, then the French again, and, in 1914, the Amer-

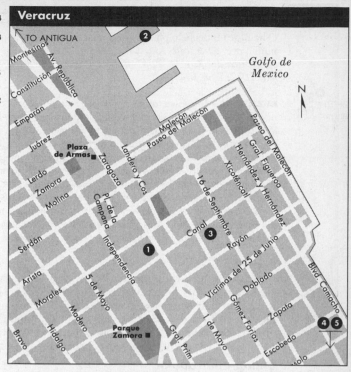

Veracruz

icans yet again. ✉ *Reached via causeway from downtown Veracruz,* ☎ *29/38–51–51.* ✉ *$2, free Sun.* ☉ *Tues.–Sun. 10–4:30.*

❸ The **Baluarte de Santiago,** a fortress and museum, is all that's left of the old city walls; like the Fort of San Juan de Ulúa, the colonial bulwark was built as a defense against pirates (but some 100 years later, in 1635). The structure is impressively solid from the outside and romantically lighted at night. Inside is a small museum that has an exquisite permanent exhibit of gold pre-Columbian jewelry—definitely Spanish plunder—which was discovered by a fisherman 25 years ago and has been on display since 1991. ✉ *Canal at 16 de Septiembre,* ☎ *no phone.* ✉ *$1.75, free Sun.* ☉ *Tues.–Sun. 10–4:30.*

★ ♨ ❹ Since 1992, Veracruz has been the home of the state-of-the-art **Acuario de Veracruz,** one of the three most important aquariums in the world. In addition to its public displays, the complex also houses a marine research center. The main exhibits include a tank with 2,000 species of marine life native to the Gulf of Mexico, including nurse sharks, manta rays, barracudas, sea turtles, and the prehistoric *pejelagartos,* which look like a combination of crocodile and fish. Check out the 18-ft-long outline on the far wall, above the caption THIS IS THE ACTUAL SIZE OF A GREAT WHITE SHARK CAUGHT OFF THE COAST OF TUXPÁN, VERACRUZ. ✉ *Plaza Acuario, Blvd. Manuel Avila Camacho s/n,* ☎ *29/32–79–84, 29/ 32–80–06.* ✉ *$2.* ☉ *Weekdays 10–7, weekends 10–7:30.*

❺ Don't miss the **Casa Museo Agustín Lara,** the museum-home of one of Mexico's most beloved songwriters and singers. Lara's occupations included playing the piano in a house of ill repute and being a bullfighter; he is also famous for marrying seven women, including Mexican screen goddess María Félix. He died in 1970 at age 73 after spending the last years of his life writing and recording music in this house. Among his most famous songs are "María Bonita," which he dedicated to Félix, and "Granada." Newspaper clippings, caricatures, and a replica of the radio station where Lara went on the air nightly with "La Hora Azul" (The Blue Hour) help plunge you into a life that was constantly in the public eye. ✉ *Adolfo Ruíz Cortines s/n, at Av. Manuel Avila Camacho, Boca del Río,* ☎ *29/37–02–09, 29/31–40–78.* 🎫 *$2.* ☉ *Tues.–Sat. 10–7, Sun. 10–5.*

<table>
<tr><td>OFF THE
BEATEN PATH</td><td>LA ANTIGUA – This town, given its name by the Spaniards after they abandoned it, was the site of the first European landing in the New World and the conquistadors' capital for 75 years. Cortés's home, which once had 22 rooms surrounding a huge courtyard, lies abandoned on the northern edge of the village. It's worth seeing if only for its crumbling masonry, taken over by clinging vines and massive tree roots. La Antigua also hosts the first church of New Spain, a little white stucco structure in remarkably good condition. Here, where Cortés and his soldiers prayed and the first converted Indian was baptized, masses are still said today. La Antigua is 25 km (16 mi) northwest of Veracruz, off Highway 180 (toward Poza Rica). The turnoff is just past the toll booth.</td></tr>
</table>

Beaches

Veracruz City's beaches are much less inviting than you might expect: most are somewhat dirty, and the water is polluted. Good beaches begin south of town in **Mocambo,** about 7 km (4½ mi) from downtown, and get better even farther down: about 4 km (2½ mi) south of Playa Mocambo, **Boca del Río** is a small fishing village at the mouth of the Río Jamapa that is quickly getting sucked into Veracruz's orbit.

Dining and Lodging

In addition to the restaurants in Veracruz, you'll want to try one in **Boca del Río.** Many of the village's restaurants—they seem to turn up between every other house—are modest but serve some of the finest seafood in Mexico. Boca del Río holds a spot in *The Guinness Book of Records* for the largest fish fillet stuffed with shellfish—it was 408 ft long and weighed almost two tons, and was prepared at Pardiño's restaurant.

$$$ ✕ **La Casita Blanca.** In the same building as the Agustín Lara museum, this elegant restaurant is decorated with colorful murals and photographs of the popular singer. The menu is equally divided between seafood and thick cuts of steak, and includes a wonderful rendition of a local favorite—*pampano huachinango* (red snapper topped with tomatoes, onions, and herbs). You might find Lara's longtime accompanist, R. Escalante, tickling the ivories of the restaurant piano. ✉ *Adolfo Ruíz Cortines s/n, at Av. Manuel Avila Camacho, Boca del Río,* ☎ *29/ 37–13–38, 29/37–13–63. AE, MC, V.*

$$$ ✕ **Mariscos Villa Rica Mocambo.** This casual, open-air palapa restau-
★   rant on the seafront is worth the small effort to find it. Hidden on a small street that runs parallel to Playa Mocambo, the Villa Rica is a favorite with locals in the know but sees almost no tourists. The menu consists almost entirely of seafood; specialties include mussels, shark, grouper, and octopus prepared as you wish. There are a few meat and poultry dishes, including prime rib and chicken Cordon Bleu. The beverage of choice among loyal patrons is cold Sol (beer) with lime. There's live music Thursday through Sunday, 3 PM–7 PM. ✉ *Calzada Mocambo 527 (near Hotel Mocambo), Boca del Río,* ☎ *29/22–21–13, 29/22–37–43. AE, DC, MC, V.*

$$$ ✕ **Villa Marina Shrimp and Steak House.** You'll find this laid-back restaurant sitting on stilts above the water just off the *malecón* (boardwalk). Waiters bring platters of the day's catch to the table for you to choose from—fresh lobster, shrimp, clams, and sea bass. Then you get to pon-

der the 18 *al gusto* ways your selection can be cooked—breaded, grilled, sautéed in garlic, with cheese sauce, and so on. The menu also lists prime rib, rib eye, and T-bone steaks, as well as a number of pasta dishes. ⊠ *Av. Manuel Avila Camacho s/n,* ☎ *29/35–10–34. MC, V.*

$$ ✕ **Che Tango.** Head to this 10-table Argentine steak house for a departure from Veracruz's typical seafood fare. Huge portions of rib eye, tenderloin, top sirloin, strip steak, and pork are charcoal grilled to order and served sizzling with sautéed onions, jalapeños, fresh tortillas, and a variety of tangy salsas. For starters, try any of the flaky empanadas or the house special, *queso fundido* (a flaming disk of melted provolone cheese smothered in mushrooms or anchovies and accented with Mexican spices). For a digestif, treat yourself to a shot of tequila served with a small glass of *sangrita* (tomato juice, lemon, lime, and a touch of Worcestershire sauce). The white-jacketed waiters are accommodating and happy to make suggestions. ⊠ *Calle 16 de Septiembre 1938, at Calle Enríquez,* ☎ *29/32–17–45, 29/32–17–56. AE, MC, V.*

$$ ✕ **El Gaucho Restaurante.** Since 1983, meat lovers have been packing this cavernous family-friendly ranch-style restaurant morning, noon, and night. The epic menu lists nearly 100 dishes—from spicy chorizo and Veracruz-style tongue to chicken fajitas. The house specialty drink, *jarra de clericot* (red wine with chewy bits of watermelon, pineapple, and cantaloupe), is delicious. ⊠ *Bernal Díaz del Castillo 187, at Colón,* ☎ *29/35–04–11. AE, MC, V.*

$$ ✕ **Pardiño's.** This modest eatery is a star among Boca del Río's many
★ seafood restaurants and a local favorite. Its fame has even spread abroad—it's not unusual for the chef to be invited to gastronomic festivals in France. Plain tables in a nondescript storefront belie the elegant preparation of such dishes as crabs *salpicón* (finely chopped with cilantro, onion, and lime), grilled sea bass, and of course, huachinango à la veracruzana. Also delicious are the simple, fresh appetizers, such as shrimp cocktail with generous chunks of avocado. Owner Rafael Pardiño, who comes from many generations of restaurateurs, has added some of his own creations to the menu—coconut stuffed with succulent seafood plus mouthwatering breaded crab claws. ⊠ *Zamora 40, Boca del Río,* ☎ *29/86–01–35. AE, DC, MC, V.*

$ ✕ **Gran Café de la Parroquia.** Don't be confused if someone tells you this is the wrong Gran Café de la Parroquia: the coffeehouse that long held that name is now called Gran Café del Portal (☞ *below*). Meanwhile, this eatery is run by a black-sheep faction of the Fernandez family, kicked out of del Portal in 1995 after the settlement of a 20-year lawsuit. The menu and music are practically the same at both places and both tend to draw lots of local families. La Parroquia now has two locations, on either end of the same block on the malecón. ⊠ *Paseo del Malecón, at the corners of Gómez Farías and 16 de Septiembre,* ☎ *29/32–25–84. No credit cards.*

$ ✕ **Gran Café del Portal.** Opened by a Spanish immigrant in 1835 in a
★ former monastery, this most famous of Veracruz's sidewalk cafés eventually grew to cover an entire city block. For a long time it was called the Gran Café de la Parroquia, but after a family feud that ousted the cousins who had been running the place, it resumed its original name, Gran Café del Portal, in 1995. An indispensable stop for a *café lechero* (coffee with hot milk)—every Mexican president since Benito Juárez has been here—it's lively from dawn to dusk with the animated babble of customers, the tapping of spoons against glasses to summon waiters, and live marimba music played by the best musicians in town. The menu has a wide selection of egg dishes, as well as soups, sandwiches, a traditional version of huachinango à la veracruzana, and hearty steak and chicken entrées, but the coffee—the formula's a well-guarded

family secret—is the real draw. ✉ *Independencia 1187, across from cathedral,* ☎ *29/31–27–59, 29/32–93–39. No credit cards.*

$$$$ 🖬 **Fiesta Americana.** This splashy hotel on Playa Costa de Oro, inaugurated by the Mexican president in 1996, has the best business facilities in the state of Veracruz. It has seven floors and miles of marble corridors, all of which seem to lead to the giant serpentine pool and lush gardens facing the ocean. Rooms have terraces, voice mail, closet safes, and luxurious bathrooms with tubs, phones, audio systems, and hair dryers. Fiesta Club floors have a business center, concierge service, and a bilingual staff. Guests have access to a nine-hole golf course 20 minutes away. No-smoking rooms and wheelchair-accessible units are available. ✉ *Blvd. Manuel Avila Camacho at Bacalao, Fracc. Costa de Oro 94299,* ☎ *29/89–89–89, 800/343–7821,* 𝐅𝐀𝐗 *29/89–89–07. 211 rooms, 22 suites. 2 restaurants, 3 bars, in-room safes, no-smoking rooms, room service, indoor-outdoor pool, 3 hot tubs, massage, tennis court, dive shop, shops, baby-sitting, children's programs (ages 4+), meeting rooms, travel services, car rental, free parking. AE, DC, MC, V.*

$$$ 🖬 **Hotel Lois.** For those with a sense of humor, this swanky Boca del Río hotel is an over-the-top Postmodern mishmash of Art Deco, '50s kitsch, and riotous neon colors. The coffee shop alone has sparkling ceilings, lavender Naugahyde chairs, etched-glass windows, several random Roman columns, and lots of gleaming chrome. Guest rooms are more conventionally appointed with rattan furniture and cable color TVs and have a subdued pastel palette. ✉ *Adolfo Ruíz Cortines 10, Boca del Río 94249,* ☎ *29/37–82–90, 01–800/712–9136,* 𝐅𝐀𝐗 *29/37–80–89. 112 rooms, 4 suites. Restaurant, 2 bars, coffee shop, in-room safes, minibars, room service, pool, beauty salon, sauna, exercise room, squash, billiards, baby-sitting, children's programs (ages 3–9), meeting rooms, car rental, free parking. AE, MC, V.*

$$$ 🖬 **Torremar.** This deluxe high-rise resort on Playa Mocambo is somewhat excessively decorated in pastels, but you'll find all the amenities here. Suites have small balconies with fantastic views of the Gulf of Mexico. An executive floor, with special concierge service and complimentary breakfast, is also available. Children will like the cascading poolside fountain and the organized activities in the children's play area. ✉ *Adolfo Ruíz Cortines 4300 (Playa Mocambo), Boca del Río 94260,* ☎ *29/89–21–00, 01–800/715–5293,* 𝐅𝐀𝐗 *29/89–21–21. 231 rooms, 18 suites. 2 restaurants, bar, room service, 2 pools, exercise room, baby-sitting, children's programs (ages 3–11), laundry service, concierge floor, car rental, free parking. AE, DC, MC, V.*

$$ 🖬 **Hotel Emporio.** The lobby of this large, elegant hostelry on the
★ malecón is a dramatic sweep of marble and potted palms. Some of the immaculate, light-filled rooms have sea views; all have marble bathrooms with bathtubs (those in the suites are hot tubs), satellite color TVs, and air-conditioning. Dine in the popular restaurant, which is decorated in neoclassical French style, or in the shade of an umbrella at any of the hotel's three pools (one is equipped with a waterfall, slides, and a miniature ship structure nearby for children to play on). ✉ *Paseo del Malecón 210, 91700,* ☎ *29/32–22–22, 29/32–34–10,* 𝐅𝐀𝐗 *29/31–22–61. 182 rooms, 22 suites. Restaurant, bar, coffee shop, room service, 3 pools, sauna, exercise room, shops, children's programs (ages 5–8), meeting rooms, car rental, free parking. AE, MC, V.*

$$ 🖬 **Hotel Hawaii.** This little jewel of a hotel with a prime location on
★ the malecón is one of the best deals in town, offering comfort, class, and personalized service at a reasonable price. All rooms are impeccably maintained and come with air-conditioning, phone, color cable TV, and marble bathrooms. The staff is eager to please, and there's always a bowl of flowers at the check-in desk. You can have all the free

coffee you want at the snug ground-floor coffee shop, and maps are available for the asking. The management also sees to it that each guest gets a bag of fine Veracruz coffee to take home. ⊠ *Paseo del Malecón 458, 91700,* ☎ *29/38–00–88, 29/31–04–27,* ℻ *29/32–55–24. 30 rooms. Coffee shop, room service, indoor pool, laundry service, free parking. AE, MC, V.*

$$ ⊞ **Hotel Mocambo.** When the Mocambo was built in 1934, it was Mexico's only Gulf Coast resort. But what used to be the loveliest and most romantic hotel in the area has lost some of its luster. The spacious, red tile-floor guest rooms have faded floral bedspreads and only modestly effective air-conditioning. And although the hotel's sprawling, terraced gardens exude a magic romanticism worthy of *Arabian Nights,* they also make for a labyrinthine five-level trek to the beaches and pools at palm-lined Playa Mocambo. Dark-wood fixtures and Art Deco touches—such as stained-glass windows in the lobby and flowerlike pillars around the indoor pool—are charming remnants from the Mocambo's more glamorous days. ⊠ *Adolfo Ruíz Cortines 4000 (Playa Mocambo), Boca del Río 94290,* ☎ *29/22–02–05, 01–800/290–0100,* ℻ *29/22–02–12. 116 rooms, 4 suites. Restaurant, 2 bars, coffee shop, room service, 1 indoor and 2 outdoor pools, massage, tennis court, exercise room, baby-sitting, playground, laundry service, car rental, free parking. AE, DC, MC, V.*

$$ ⊞ **Villa del Mar.** This unassuming hotel, just across from one of the nicer sections of the downtown beach, is an ideal place to bring children. The standard, motel-style rooms are spacious and comfortable and surround a large, pretty garden with a tennis court, pool, and small playground. All accommodations have color TVs, phones, and air-conditioning. The staff is very helpful, and some English is spoken at the reception desk. A number of bungalows (accommodating up to five people) are also available: they aren't air-conditioned and are a bit gloomy, but some have kitchenettes. Breakfast is included in the room rate. ⊠ *Blvd. Avila Camacho at Bartolomé de las Casas, 91910,* ☎ *29/31–33–66,* ℻ *29/32–71–35. 91 rooms, 14 bungalows. Restaurant, bar, pool, hot tub, tennis court, playground, laundry service, free parking. MC, V.*

$ ⊞ **Hotel Concha Dorada.** The basically characterless Concha Dorada has the cheapest accommodations on the zócalo. Rooms are cramped but clean, and some have color TVs (local stations only), phones, and air-conditioning. The downstairs restaurant–sidewalk café serves simple fare and is especially popular (read noisy) at lunchtime and on weekend nights. ⊠ *Miguel Lerdo 77, near Zaragoza, 91700,* ☎ *29/31–29–96,* ℻ *29/31–32–46. 46 rooms, 2 suites. Restaurant, bar, room service, laundry service. AE, MC, V.*

$ ⊞ **Hotel Ruiz Milan.** This multistory waterfront hotel is a good value for the price. Guest rooms, although on the small side, are clean, comfortable, and modern. All have color TVs (local stations only), phones, balconies, ample closet space, and sizable bathrooms; about half have air-conditioning. The invitingly cool marble-floor lobby is usually crowded with Mexican businesspeople, and the hotel itself has the amenities of a more expensive establishment, including an indoor pool, a pleasant restaurant, and free covered parking. ⊠ *Paseo del Malecón 432, 91700,* ☎ *29/32–27–72,* ℻ *29/32–37–77 ext. 106. 69 rooms, 19 suites. Restaurant, room service, pool, meeting rooms, free parking. AE, DC, MC, V.*

Nightlife and the Arts

Every Tuesday, Friday, and Saturday night after 8 at the **Plaza de Armas** (zócalo), a local troupe dressed in white performs danzón on stage, then hits the street to involve the townsfolk in this traditional

Veracruz dance, accompanied by live marimba music. On Sunday night, there's danzón at **Parque Zamora** 6–9. The **Instituto Veracruzo de Cultura** (Veracruz Cultural Institute; ⊠ Calles Canal and Zaragoza, ☎ 29/31–69–67) offers danzón classes for a minimal fee.

For authentic Cuban music, head for the unpretentious **El Rincón de la Trova** (⊠ Callejón de Lagunilla 59, ☎ no phone), where people of all ages gather Thursday through Saturday to dance to famous tropical bands until the wee hours; the floors are cement and the ambience is fun and strictly local. El Rincón de la Trova's six-day Cuban music festival in November draws performers and fans from all over Mexico and the Caribbean.

Discos and video bars are plentiful along the waterfront. **Ocean** (⊠ Adolfo Ruíz Cortines 8, at Avila Camacho, ☎ 29/35–23–90) is a flashy, modern discotheque. **Carioca** (⊠ Adolfo Ruíz Cortines 10, at Avila Camacho, ☎ 29/37–82–90) is a dance club in the Hotel Lois. **Blue Ocean** (⊠ Avila Camacho 9, ☎ 29/22–03–66) is a tropical-theme video bar replete with rock sculptures, waterfalls, and a light show. All are packed Friday and Saturday nights with a young, largely local crowd.

Outdoor Activities and Sports

Deep-sea fishing is popular in Veracruz, and you'll find places to windsurf in the coastal areas a few miles south of Boca del Río. An annual **regatta** from the port of Galveston in Texas to the port of Veracruz takes place at the end of May. Check with the Mexican Government Tourist Office (☎ 713/780–3740) in Houston for details.

Shopping

Stands lining the **malecón** sell a variety of ocean-related items: seashells and beauty creams and powders derived from them, black-coral jewelry, ships-in-a-bottle, key rings with miniature sea-life inside, and more. You'll also find Coatepec coffee, T-shirts, bloody crucifixes, and tacky stuffed frogs, iguanas, and armadillos. The **Plaza de las Artesanías** market on the malecón purveys slightly higher-quality goods, including leather and jewelry, with higher prices to match.

For an authentic slice of Mexican daily life, head for the wildly vibrant and chaotic **Mercado Hidalgo** (⊠ bounded by Calles Cortés, Soto, Madero, and Hidalgo), where you'll find artful displays of strawberries and chilies beside heaps of mysterious medicinal herbs and platters of cow eyeballs and chicken feet.

One of the more-unusual shops in town is in the aquarium: **Fiora** (⊠ Plaza Acuario, Blvd. Manuel Avila Camacho s/n, ☎ 29/32–99–50) sells beautiful jewelry designed from miniature flowers grown in Veracruz.

Veracruzanos have eagerly adopted the fashion of neighboring Yucatán, and its famous embroidered *guayabera* shirts are as popular here as mariscos. For the best quality guayabera shirts in the area, visit **Guayaberas Fina Cab** (⊠ Av. Zaragoza 233, between Calles Arista and Serdán, ☎ 29/31–84–27). This family-run shop has a great selection of hand-stitched shirts and dresses, with embroidery ranging from basic interlocking cables to highly elaborate floral designs. At **El Mayab** (⊠ Calle Zamora 78, at Av. Zaragoza, ☎ no phone), you'll find machine-produced guayaberas for slightly lower prices than the hand-embroidered variety goes for elsewhere.

With its sizable Cuban population, Veracruz does a brisk business in cigars. Around Plaza de Armas, there are plenty of streetside stands that specialize in both Mexican and Caribbean tobacco. For the largest variety of cigars, try the small kiosk on Avenida Independencia, in front of Gran Café del Portal; it sells Cuban Cohibas for less than a buck. Although Cuban smokes are the big draw for cigar-puffing tourists, keep in mind that Veracruz upholds its own proud tradition in the tobacco trade. **Cubahi** (⌂ Av. Sarmiento 59, ☎ 29/33–97–10) offers the finest local-tobacco products, and owner José Antonio Sarmiento is happy to make a house call to your hotel.

Los Tuxtlas

❻ *140 km (87 mi) south of Veracruz.*

A small volcanic mountain range, the Sierra de Los Tuxtlas, meets the sea at Los Tuxtlas. The area has lakes, waterfalls, rivers, mineral springs, and access to beaches, making it a popular stopover for travelers heading east from Mexico City to the Yucatán. The region's three principal towns—**Santiago Tuxtla, San Andrés Tuxtla,** and **Catemaco**—are carved into the mountainsides some 600 ft above sea level, lending them a coolness even in summer that's the envy of the perspiring masses on the coastal plain. The Tuxtlas gain an air of mystery from the cool, gray fog that slips over the mountains and lakes and the whisperings among the townspeople about the *brujos* (witches), also called curanderos, who read tarot cards, prescribe herbal remedies, and cast spells here. Today, the economic life of Los Tuxtlas depends on cigar manufacturing (the town of San Andrés Tuxtla is famous for its handrolled variety, which comes in several sizes) and tourism. Tours can be arranged just by showing up at several factories, including **Te-Amo** (⌂ Blvd. 5 de Febrero 10), just outside San Andrés Tuxtla on the highway to Catemaco and Santa Clara, on the bypass road. All have stores open to the public.

Although much of the architecture here is of the 1960s school of looming cement, all three towns are laid out in the colonial style around a main plaza and a church, and all have a certain amount of charm. Santiago Tuxtla has managed to retain more of its colonial character than the other two Tuxtla towns. The region was also a center of Olmec culture, and Olmec artifacts and small ruins abound. A huge stone Olmec head dominates the zócalo at Santiago Tuxtla, and 21 km (13 mi) east are the ruins of **Tres Zapotes,** now decidedly unspectacular but once an important Olmec ceremonial center believed to have been occupied as early as AD 100. The town also has an informative museum, where you can learn about the region's indigenous heritage and contemporary local cultures.

The largest of the three towns, and the only one with an ATM, is San Andrés, but Catemaco is by far the most picturesque and relaxing place to stay. Many of Catemaco's lodgings are on the lake shore, whereas others are grouped around the small square. Catemaco is popular among Mexicans as a summer and Christmas resort and is also the place to go for a *consulta* (consultation) with a brujo or curandero, should you have any problems or questions that require some spiritual clarity or supernatural intervention. Tours of Lake Catemaco, which was formed from the crater of a volcano and which harbors a colorful colony of fish-eating baboons, can be arranged through most local hotels. Beyond Catemaco, a paved road continues over the hills and down to a lovely stretch of undeveloped coastline. Twenty kilometers (12½ mi) from Catemaco is the village of **Sontecomapan,** where you can take a *lancha* (launch) across the lagoon to a desolate beach. A bumpy dirt road follows the coast 19 km (12 mi) north of Sontecomapan to the sleepy fishing village of **Montepío,** which has a wide beach and a couple of inexpensive, basic hotels.

Cempoala

 ❼ *42 km (26 mi) northwest of Veracruz.*

Cempoala (often spelled Zempoala) was the capital of the Totonac nation, whose influence spread throughout Veracruz in pre-Hispanic times. The name means "place of 20 waters," after the sophisticated irrigation system the Totonacs used. The site gained its role in history as the place where, in 1519, Cortés formed his first alliance with a native chief. At the time, the population of Cempoala was estimated at around 20,000. The alliance with the Totonacs enlarged Cortés's paltry army of 200 men and encouraged the Spaniard to push on to Mexico City and fight the Aztecs. In his turn, the leader of the Totonacs—dubbed Fat Chief by his own people because of his enormous girth—was an avowed enemy of the powerful Aztecs, who forced his people to perform human sacrifices to the Aztec war god and put military garrisons on Totonac land.

Cempoala was rediscovered by Francisco del Paso y Troncoso in 1891. Ten of the 60–90 structures at Cempoala have been excavated and can be visited. All are built of river stones, shells, sand, and "glue" made from the whites of turtle and bird eggs. As the story goes, when Cortés first sighted Cempoala at night, the buildings glowed white under a full moon. Cortés thought he had discovered a city of silver.

Upon entering the ruins, you come upon **Circulo de los Gladiadores,** a small circle of waist-high walls to the right of center. This was the site of contests between captured prisoners of war and Totonac warriors: each prisoner was required to fight two armed warriors. One such prisoner, the son of a king from Tlaxcala, won the unfair match and became a national hero. His statue stands in a place of honor in Tlaxcala. Another small structure to the left of the circle marks the spot where an eternal flame was kept lighted during the sacred 52-year cycle of the Totonacs.

The **Templo Mayor,** the main pyramid, is the largest structure on the site. Follow the dirt path that lies straight ahead when you enter. Cortés, after gaining the allegiance of Fat Chief, placed a Christian cross atop this temple—the first gesture of this sort in New Spain—and had mass said by a Spanish priest in his company.

At the smaller **Templo de la Luna** (Temple of the Moon), to the far left of Templo Mayor, outstanding warriors were honored with the title "Eagle Knight" or "Tiger Knight" and awarded an obsidian nose ring to wear as a mark of their status. Just to the left of the Moon Temple is the **Templo del Sol** (Temple of the Sun), where the hearts and blood of sacrificial victims were placed.

Back toward the dirt road and across from it is the **Templo de la Diosa de la Muerte** (Temple of the Goddess of Death), where a statue of the pre-Hispanic deity was found along with 1,700 small idols.

A small on-site **museum** opened in 1997. The voladores of Papantla usually give a performance on weekends. Well-trained guides are available, but tours are mainly in Spanish. ☎ *No phone.* ✉ *$2, free Sun.* ☉ *Tues.–Sun. 10–5.*

Jalapa

❽ *90 km (56 mi) northwest of Veracruz.*

Jalapa, which was a Totonac ceremonial center when Cortés arrived, is perched on the side of a mountain, between the coastal lowlands of Veracruz and the high central plateau. More than 4,000 ft above sea level, the city has a bizarre climate—sun, rain, and fog are all likely to show themselves in the course of a day. However, for perspiration-soaked escapees from the coast, it's an enviable change. The capital and cultural hub of the state of Veracruz, Jalapa is a university town with a diverse population; you are as likely to see long-haired young people sitting around in cafés as you are wizened campesinos walking to work. The town is also home to a symphony orchestra, a ballet company, and a state theater that attracts big-name performers. Jalapa is filled with pretty parks and lakes, and the government buildings downtown—since the grit has been removed from their surfaces—are showing off their stateliness once more.

Much of the city seems to have been built haphazardly, and that is the source of its charm. The hills here pose intriguing engineering problems, and major avenues tend to make 180-degree turns, following level surfaces rather than adhering to a strict grid system. In some places, the twisting cobblestone streets are bordered by 6-ft-high sidewalks to compensate for sudden sharp inclines. Locals refer to the city as a *plato roto* (broken dish) because of this scattered, logic-defying layout. (Note: You'll often see the name of the city spelled Xalapa. Jalapa is the Hispanicized version of the original Nahuatl word.)

The town's prime cultural attraction is the **Museo de Antropología de Jalapa.** With 3,000 of 29,000 pieces on display, it is second only to Mexico City's archaeological museum and is a treasure trove of artifacts from the three main pre-Hispanic cultures of Veracruz: Huastec, Totonac, and most important, Olmec. Its three sections are filled with magnificent stone Olmec heads; carved stelae and offering bowls; terra-cotta jaguars and cross-eyed gods; cremation urns in the forms of bats and monkeys; lovely Totonac murals; and, most touching of all, life-size sculptures of women who died in childbirth (the ancients elevated them to the status of goddesses). At a burial site, you can see ancient bones, ritually deformed skulls, and ceremonial figurines. Tours by English-speaking students are available daily 11–4, but it is best to call in advance and make an appointment, as the tour schedule is unpredictable. ⊠ *Av. Jalapa s/n,* ☎ *28/15–09–20, 28/15–07–08.* 🎟 *$1.50, $10 for tour in English.* ☉ *Daily 9–5.*

Dining and Lodging

$$ ✕ **La Casa de Mamá.** This very popular restaurant is on a busy thor-
★ oughfare just east of the town center. The dark, antique furnishings and lazy ceiling fan almost succeed in giving this place the feel of a northern Mexican hacienda, but the incessant street noise reminds you that you're in a busy capital city. Never mind; you'll be focusing on the generous portions of charcoal-broiled steaks and the succulent shrimp and fish dishes, served with *frijoles charros* (black beans cooked in a spicy sauce) or Mexican rice. The place is known for its desserts, which include flan with caramel and bananas flambéed in brandy. ⊠ *Avila Camacho 113,* ☎ *28/17–31–44,* 𝕱𝕬𝕏 *28/17–31–44. AE, MC, V.*

$$ ✕ **La Casona del Beaterio.** In contrast to the cafeteria-style eateries along Avenida Zaragoza, La Casona dishes up fine local fare in a comfortable, appealing setting. The restaurant's two spacious rooms, surrounding a courtyard garden, are set with sturdy wooden furniture, stained-glass windows, historical photos, and hanging plants. Breakfast specials are a steal, and a typical morning finds locals and business travelers wallowing away a few hours over a cup of strong coffee and *huevos rancheros* (fried eggs with chili sauce, raw onion, grated cheese, and tortillas). The generous steak and seafood dinners, including the house specialty—*cazuela de mariscos* (stew of shrimp, octopus, and clams cooked with chipotle chilies)—draw crowds. This is

java country, so the menu has a dozen different coffee and espresso concoctions. ✉ *Av. Zaragoza 20,* ☎ *28/18–21–19. AE, MC, V.*

$$ ✕ **La Estancia de los Tecajetes.** For fine regional dishes with a dash of
★ creativity, try this rustic, lodgelike restaurant overlooking the lushly tropical Parque los Tecajetes (tucked into a small strip mall, the restaurant can be a bit difficult to find). Inside, it's cozy and relaxing, always buzzing with diners feasting on *cecina* (paper-thin beef fillet) with enchiladas, beans, and avocado; *crepa consentida* (crepes filled with chicken and smothered in poblano chilies and cheese); or *pollo manzana* (a boneless chicken breast cooked in butter, cream, and white wine). Corn tortillas are made on the premises, and the walls are filled with charming sepia-tone photos of Jalapa's past. ✉ *Plaza Tecajetes, Avila Camacho 90–12,* ☎ *28/18–07–32. MC, V.*

$ ✕ **La Fonda.** The entrance to this charming, traditional, breakfast-and-lunch restaurant is hidden on a small pedestrian walkway off busy Calle Enríquez, a block from Parque Juárez. Brightly colored streamers, baskets, flowers, and a mural of Mount Orizaba adorn the walls and ceiling, and the warm corn tortillas served with every meal are made before your eyes. The food is hearty northern Veracruzan fare: beef or chicken and beans, *nopales* (cactus strips), and/or chili are essential elements of almost every dish. ✉ *Antonio M. de Rivera 1 (also known as Callejón del Diamante), at Calle Enríquez,* ☎ *28/18–72–82. No credit cards. Closed Sun. No dinner.*

$ ✕ **La Sopa.** Modest as it may look, this 20-table restaurant draws hearty eaters from all walks of life—local politicians, students, and blue-collar workers—who make a beeline for the bargain *comida corrida* (fixed-price lunch). One of the best-kept secrets in town, La Sopa's four-course attraction might include carrot-and-potato soup, chicken with rice and fresh corn tortillas, and vanilla pudding served with coffee or tea. The menu features light Mexican *antojitos* (appetizers) in the evening, including *chiles rellenos* (green chili peppers stuffed with meat or cheese and fried in egg batter), and tamales. Live music fills the air Thursday (Huastec folk music), Friday (danzón), and Saturday (a harpist), about 7–11. ✉ *Antonio M. de Rivera 3-A (also known as Callejón del Diamante),* ☎ *28/17–80–69. No credit cards. Closed Sun.*

$$$ ⊞ **Fiesta Inn Xalapa.** This attractive chain hotel has the fresh look of a beach property in tropical climes (perhaps to offset the rather gloomy weather typical of Jalapa), and it has the most-upscale amenities. It's a bit out of the way—in a primarily residential neighborhood 10 minutes by car from the center of town—but a good bet if you are looking for a comfortable, quiet, secure, and well-equipped base. The modern guest rooms in the two-story, colonial-style structure have satellite color TVs, phones, air-conditioning, bathtubs, and plenty of morning sunlight. Airport transfers from the port of Veracruz are available for a fee. ✉ *Carretera Xalapa–Veracruz Km 2.5, Fracc. Las Animas 91000,* ☎ *28/12–79–20, 01–800/5–04–50,* ℻ *28/12–79–46. 119 rooms, 4 suites. Restaurant, bar, coffee shop, in-room data ports, room service, pool, exercise room, dance club, free parking. AE, DC, MC, V.*

$$$ ⊞ **Posada Coatepec.** When actor Harrison Ford was filming *Clear and*
★ *Present Danger* in the area, he stayed at this member of the prestigious Small Grand Hotels of Mexico group, a 15-minute drive from Jalapa. Specializing in fine food (but slow service) and catering to French and German travel groups, the Posada (built in 1890) is the former villa of a coffee baron. It has homey guest rooms, each with original decorative tile floors, satellite color TV, and a heater for Coatepec's chilly, rainy winters; ask for one away from the murmur of street noise. The lobby and inner courtyard are splendidly decorated with a fine collection of antiques; a bar framed by lead-crystal windows is cozy and clubby. The hotel can arrange tours to nearby coffee plantations. ✉ *Hidalgo*

9, Coatepec 91500, ☎ *28/16–05–44,* FAX *28/16–00–40, 28/16–05–20. 7 rooms, 16 suites. Restaurant, bar, room service, pool, laundry service. AE, MC, V.*

$$ ⊞ **Hotel Xalapa Finca Real.** The Hotel Xalapa, which sits on a hill above Parque Los Tecajetes, is the most well-equipped downtown hotel, with many of the amenities of a more expensive establishment: phones, color TVs, air-conditioning (in most units), and bathtubs; free covered parking; and a disco. Another 1960s institutional behemoth, the building isn't particularly attractive, and the gaudy pink-and-orange paint job can be tough on the eyes, but the rooms are large, sunny, and quiet. The hotel staff is well meaning, if not particularly competent, and the hot-water supply can be dicey. ⊠ *Victoria at Bustamante, Zona Centro 91000,* ☎ *28/18–22–22, 28/17–70–64,* FAX *28/18–94–24. 170 rooms, 28 suites, 2 villas. 2 restaurants, bar, room service, pool, dance club, baby-sitting, playground, laundry service, car rental, free parking. AE, DC, MC, V.*

$ ⊞ **Hotel Salmones.** Although the lobby's shabby carpeting and ragged reception desk testify to the Salmones' eroding stateliness, some vestiges of its onetime glory remain: its high ceilings, dark-wood fixtures, and large beautiful windows have been untouched by time. The clean rooms (which start at $8) lack air-conditioning but have TVs (local stations only) and phones; some have small balconies. Ask for one of the renovated rooms, which have peach-color walls, smoky-blue carpets, and marble sinks. Rooms in the *antigua* (old) section have threadbare cranberry-red carpets and yellowing walls. ⊠ *Zaragoza 24, 91000,* ☎ *28/17–54–31,* FAX *28/18–27–14. 75 rooms. Restaurant, bar, room service. AE, MC, V.*

$ ⊞ **Mesón del Alférez.** A royal lieutenant of the Spanish Viceroy lived
★ in this colonial house some 200 years ago. Now it's a reasonably priced gem of a hotel, restored with traditional materials such as earthenware tiles, rustic wood, and lime pigment washes on the walls in such luminous hues as lilac, sky blue, and magenta. Rooms surround three small bougainvillea-drenched courtyards and have lovely hand-carved wood headboards, Talavera lamps, and hand-loomed bedspreads, as well as phones and color TVs (local channels only). ⊠ *Sebastián Camacho 2, at Zaragoza, 91000,* ☎ *28/18–63–51, 28/18–01–13, 01–800/ 715–5172, 877/867–9943 in the U.S. and Canada,* FAX *28/12–47–03. 15 rooms, 6 suites. Restaurant, room service, laundry service, free parking. AE, MC, V.*

Nightlife and the Arts

The **Agora** (⊠ Parque Juárez, ☎ 28/18–57–30) cultural center has art exhibits and the occasional folk-music performance and shows classic and avant-garde films in its cinema club. Stop by during the day to see what's planned. The **Teatro del Estado** (⊠ Ignacio de la Llave s/n, ☎ 28/17–31–10) is the big, modern state theater of Veracruz. The Orquesta Sinfónica de Jalapa performs here, often giving free concerts during the off-season (early June–mid-August). Check *Diario Xalapa* (the Jalapa city newspaper in Spanish, available at newsstands) for dates and times of performances, or stop by the Agora. You might find someone who speaks English if you are lucky.

Other nightlife in this student town tends to be youth oriented. **La 7a Estacion** (⊠ 20 de Noviembre near Central Camionera, ☎ 28/17–31– 55) is packed with salsa dancers Wednesday night; Thursday through Saturday you'll find rock and alternative music. **Tempo Libero** (⊠ Av. Camacho 101, ☎ no phone) is a video dance bar that attracts mostly university students with thumping house-music rhythms Tuesday through Sunday. The **Bar Lovento** (⊠ 20 de Noviembre Ote. 641, ☎ 28/17–83–34) heats up with a salsa beat for dancing Wednesday through Saturday nights. A good mix of locals, tourists, and expats jams **Bar Boulevard 93** (✉ Av. Camacho 93, ☎ 28/46–27–93), a tony, neon-lit all-night club across from Parque Los Tecajetes.

Outdoor Activities and Sports

RIVER RAFTING

River rafting along the Río Pescados is gaining in popularity. Most of the operators who run these trips are trained in Canada and are highly professional (☞ Contacts and Resources *in* Veracruz A to Z, *below*). Base camps with tents, rafting equipment, and dining facilities are near the river at Jalcomulco, 42 km (26 mi) southeast of Jalapa.

Shopping

Mexico's finest export coffee is grown in this region, specifically in the highlands around the picturesque colonial towns of Coatepec and Xico, less than 10 km (6 mi) from Jalapa. Shops selling the prized *café de altura* (coffee of the highlands) abound in the main squares of both places. In Jalapa, **Café Colón** (✉ Calle Primo Verdad 15, between Avs. Zaragoza and Enríquez, ☎ 28/17–60–97) sells 20 varieties of coffee for about $2 a pound.

The **Mercado Jareguí** (✉ Av. Revolución and Calle Altamirano), open daily, is a wild indoor bazaar where you can find everything from jewelry, blankets, and fresh vegetables to some rather dubious-looking natural "healing" potions and supposedly aphrodisiacal body pastes.

Side Trip to Xico

19 km (12 mi) south of Jalapa on road to Coatepec.

If you close your eyes and try to imagine the ideal Mexican small town, it couldn't be any more perfect than Xico. Aside from the occasional passing automobile, this village seems untouched by time; donkeys hauling burlap sacks of fresh beans clip-clop along the quaint cobblestone streets, followed by coffee-picking locals, machetes tied to their waists with red sashes. Lying in Mexico's premier coffee-growing region at the base of the mist-filled Perote foothills, Xico is famous for its native cuisine (*mole xiqueno,* a tasty mix of poblano chili and chocolate sauce) and its raucous summer festival (beginning July 22) celebrating the town's patron saint, Mary Magdalene, which includes a running of the bulls.

But Xico is perhaps even better-known for its natural wonders, notably the **Cascada de Texolo,** a majestic waterfall set in a deep gorge of tropical greenery. The setting for much of the 1984 film *Romancing the Stone,* this lush, scenic area is great for exploring; numerous paths lead off from the main falls through forests of banana trees to smaller cascades and crystal-blue pools, perfect for a refreshing swim. There's also a steep staircase that will take you from the observation deck to the base of the falls, a favorite spot for picnicking locals.

The falls are about 3 km (2 mi) from the center of town. To reach them, start from the red-and-white church where Calles Zaragosa and Matamoros meet and follow the cobblestone street downhill, bearing right when you reach the small roadside shrine to the Virgin Mary. Continue through the coffee plantations, following the signs for "La Cascada" until you reach the main observation deck, which includes a small restaurant and a plaque commemorating the establishment of a nearby hydroelectric dam by President Porfirio Díaz in 1898. Entry is free.

El Tajín

★ ⚑ ❾ *13 km (8 mi) west of Papantla.*

The extensive ruins of El Tajín—the Totonac word means "thunder"—
express the highest degree of artistry of any ancient city in the coastal
area. The city remained hidden until 1785, when a Spanish engineer
came upon it. Early theories attributed the complex—believed to be a
religious center—to a settlement of Maya-related Huastecs, one of the
most important cultures of the Veracruz area. Because of its immense
size and unique architecture, however, scholars now believe it may have
been built by a distinct El Tajín cultural group related to the Maya.
Although much of the site has been restored, many structures are still
hidden under thick jungle growth.

El Tajín is thought to have reached its peak between AD 600 and 1200.
During this time, hundreds of structures of native sandstone were built
here, including temples, double-storied palaces, ball courts, large retaining walls, and hundreds of houses. But El Tajín was already an important religious and administrative center during the first three
centuries AD. Its influence is in part attributed to the fact that it had
large reserves of cacao beans, used as money in pre-Hispanic times.

Evidence suggests that the southern half of the uncovered ruins—the
area around the lower plaza—was reserved for ceremonial purposes.
Its centerpiece is the 60-ft-high **Pyramid of the Niches,** surely one of
the finest pre-Columbian buildings in Mexico. The finely wrought
seven-level structure has 365 coffers—one for each day of the solar year—
built-in around its seven friezes. The reliefs on the pyramid depict the
ruler, 13-Rabbit—all the rulers' names were associated with sacred animals—and allude also to El Tajín's main god, the benign Quetzalcóatl.
One panel on the pyramid tells the tale of heroic human sacrifice and
of the soul's imminent descent to the underworld, where it is rewarded
with the gift of sacred *pulque,* a milky alcoholic beverage made from
cactus, from the gods.

Just south of the pyramid is a series of 10 I-shape **ball courts**—more
than at any other site in Mesoamerica—where the sacred pre-Columbian
ball game was played. The walls are covered with relief sculpture. Note
that the crosslike glyphs on the facades are related to the planet Venus.
This game, played throughout Mesoamerica, is similar in some ways
to soccer—players used a hard rubber ball that could not be touched
with the hands, and suited up in knee pads and body protectors—but
far more deadly. Intricate carvings at this and other complexes indicate that the games ended with human sacrifice. It's still a subject of
debate whether the winner or loser of the match was the sacrificial victim. It is surmised that the players may have even been high-standing
members of the priest or warrior classes.

El Tajín Chico, to the north, is thought to have been the secular part
of the city, administrative and residential. It was likely the location of
the elite's living quarters. Floors and roofing were made with a pre-
Columbian cement of volcanic rock and limestone. The most important structure here is the Complejo de los Columnos (Complex of the
Columns). The columns once held up the cement ceilings, but early settlers in Papantla removed the ceiling stones to construct houses.

A small museum at the entrance displays some pottery and sculpture
and tells what little is known of the site. But because guided tours of
El Tajín aren't available, the rest is left to your imagination. The area
outside the entrance is lined with covered stalls that sell inexpensive
meals and tacky souvenirs, and there's a large, cafeteria-style restau-

rant at the site. If you're prepared to work your way through the thick jungle, you can see some more-recent finds along the dirt paths that lead over the nearby ridges. ⌸ *$2.50, free Sun.* ☉ *Daily 9–5.*

Papantla de Olarte

⑩ *250 km (155 mi) northwest of Veracruz.*

Papantla de Olarte sits amid tropical hills, the center of a vanilla-producing region. A distinctive mix of Spanish colonial and indigenous influence can be seen here: Totonac men in flowing white pants lead their donkeys through the crowded streets, and palm trees shade the traditional, tile zócalo. The town is best known for its voladores, who twirl off an 82-ft pole next to Papantla's ornate cathedral. This ritual was originally performed as a tribute to the god of sun and rain. The four fliers begin the dance on a platform at the top of the ceremonial pole, each facing one of the cardinal directions. They start their descent from the side of the platform facing east—where the sun rises and the world awakes—twisting left for 13 full rotations each. Between them, the four fliers circle the pole 52 times, representing the sacred 52-year cycle of the Totonacs (the Maya calendar had the same 52-year cycle). A fifth man, the prayer giver, sits atop the pole, playing a small flute while keeping rhythm on a drum as the fliers descend. Originally the ceremony was held on the vernal equinox, but now the voladores fly for the crowds every Saturday and Sunday at 12:45 PM and give special shows on Corpus Christi.

Dining and Lodging

$ ✕ **Restaurante Sorrento.** With more than 200 items on the menu, this
★ is the most popular restaurant in Papantla, crowded with locals who come to enjoy the cheap regional seafood and to catch a few minutes of the *telenovela* (soap opera) on the corner set. Tilework lines the lavender dining room. ⊠ *Enríquez 105-B,* ☏ *784/2-00-67. No credit cards.*

$ ✕ **Restaurant Tajín.** The Hotel Tajín's sunny restaurant is comparatively elegant and hardly more expensive than the storefront eateries near the second-class bus station. House specialties include a fillet of fish stuffed with shellfish, *jaibas rellenas* (stuffed crab), chili-marinated rabbit, and Yucatecan *pollo píbil* (chicken in a mild orange-achiote sauce). Don't be alarmed by the misleading bilingual menu—the *tasajo cerdo* is not, in fact, "steak porpoise" but marinated pork. ⊠ *Hotel Tajín, Nuñez y Domínguez 104,* ☏ *784/2-06-44. MC, V.*

$$ 🛏 **Hotel Premier.** Right on Papantla's pretty, lively zócalo, the Premier is the town's swankiest hotel and a real bargain. The lobby is lined with mirrors and furnished with small purple chairs that were once dedicated to the no-longer-functional bar. The rooms are spotless and good-sized and have tiny balconies overlooking the square. Amenities include tile bathrooms, air-conditioning, phones, and satellite color TVs. ⊠ *Enríquez 103, 93400,* ☏ *784/2-16-45,* 📠 *784/2-10-62. 16 rooms, 4 suites. Room service, free parking. MC, V.*

$ 🛏 **Hotel Tajín.** The Tajín is less expensive and has more amenities than the slightly more central Hotel Premier, but the trick is getting the right room; some rooms have black-and-white TVs rather than color, ceiling fans instead of air-conditioning, lumpy beds, and phones that don't always work. But all in all, the rooms are spotless, and this is still a decent deal. The hillside perch makes for nice views. Hotel services are in an annex adjoining the main building; there's usually an English-speaking staff member at the reception desk. ⊠ *Nuñez y Domínguez 104, 93400,* ☏ *784/2-01-21,* 📠 *784/2-10-62. 59 rooms. Restaurant, bar, room service, beauty salon, free parking. MC, V.*

Shopping

Half a block downhill from the zócalo, along Avenida 20 de Noviembre, is a teeming **street market** selling native Totonac costumes, carvings, woven baskets, handbags, cassettes, and food. The quality is not great, but if you poke around, you can find some good deals. The real draw is vanilla, the chief product of this region, which is sold in every conceivable form—beans and extract are common, but for a real souvenir, pick up a box of vanilla-flavored cigars.

Tuxpán

⓫ *193 km (120 mi) south of Tampico, 309 km (192 mi) northwest of Veracruz, 89 km (55 mi) north of Papantla.*

Tuxpán is a peaceful riverside town with graceful winding streets—and the Río Tuxpán is even clean enough to swim in. **Juárez,** the main street, running parallel to the river, is lined with diners, hotels, and shops. The **Parque Reforma** is the center of social activity in town, with more than a hundred tables set around a hub of cafés and fruit stands. It has a memorial to Fausto Vega Santander, a member of the 201st Squadron of the Mexican Air Force and the first Mexican to be killed in combat during World War II. Lanchas shuttle passengers across the river to the **Casa de Fidel Castro,** where Castro lived for a time while planning the overthrow of Fulgencio Batista. A replica of the *Granma,* the ship that carried Fidel's men from Tuxpán to Cuba, molders outside. Inside, the casa is bare save some black-and-white photos of Fidel.

Beaches

Tuxpán's main appeal is the untouristed miles of beaches that begin just 7 km (4½ mi) east of town. The first, and most accessible beach from Tuxpán, is **Playa Tuxpán.** The surf here isn't huge, but there's enough action to warrant breaking out your surf or boogie board. Of the palapas on Playa Tuxpán, the most established is Restaurant Miramar, which has an extensive menu and also provides umbrellaed beach chairs for customers.

Dining and Lodging

$$ ✕ **Antonio's.** Next to the Hotel Reforma on Avenida Juárez and serving as its restaurant, Antonio's is a quiet, comparatively elegant eatery with a varied menu. The cazuela de mariscos is excellent, as are the prawns, served grilled or in garlic sauce. A number of beef dishes and sandwiches are also available, as well as cocktails from the full bar. ⊠ *Av. Juárez 25, at Garizurieta,* ☎ *783/4–16–02. AE, MC, V.*

$$ ✕ **Berra de Mariscos.** This unpretentious, open-air eatery on Tuxpán's main drag is an ideal place to spend a relaxing lunch hour people-watching. Don't be fooled by the white plastic tables and the bare-bones decor—the quality of the seafood dishes here easily rivals the most expensive restaurants in town. Hunker down with a cold beer and a plate of *pulpos* (octopus and squid cooked with onions, butter, and garlic) or the house specialty, *camarones a la diabla* (a spicy concoction of grilled prawns and chilies) and take in the afternoon action along busy Avenida Juárez. The wait staff is friendly and prompt, and all meals are preceded by a generous serving of freshly made tortilla chips. ⊠ *Av. Juárez 44, at Calle Mina,* ☎ *783/4–46–01. No credit cards.*

$ ✕ **Taqueria 2 Amigos.** If you've got the nerve and the elbow power, wade into the greasy-spoon madness of 2 Amigos, Tuxpán's reigning king of under-a-buck dining. A virtual closet next to Hotel May Palace, this noisy neighborhood favorite specializes in savory tacos and thick *tortas* (sandwiches filled with pork, beef, or chicken with tomatoes and onions), all cooked on a sizzling grill just inside the doorway. With the constant clamor and crowds (and only four small tables), it can be nearly impossible to get a seat at mealtime, so grab your snack and skip across the street to one of the many outdoor tables at Parque Reforma. ⊠ *Av. Juárez s/n at Plaza Reforma,* ☎ *no phone. No credit cards.*

$$ 🏨 **Hotel May Palace.** The most luxurious lodgings in Tuxpán can be secured at this five-star hotel in the center of town. The modern five-story property is geared to a business clientele. The rooms are swathed in pastels and set off by rattan furniture designed for the hotel. All units have phones, satellite TVs, and air-conditioning. Guest services include a small video bar, a restaurant specializing in seafood and regional dishes, a rooftop pool, and meeting salons. ⊠ *Av. Juárez 44, facing Parque Reforma, 92800,* ☎ FAX *783/4–88–82, 783/4–44–61. 68 rooms, 2 suites. Restaurant, bar, room service, pool, exercise room, laundry service, meeting rooms, free parking. AE, DC.*

$$ 🏨 **Hotel Plaza Palmas.** In a sleepy suburban neighborhood five min-
★ utes from the city center, this sprawling bi-level hostelry is a welcome respite from Tuxpán's riverfront bustle. And although the mounted stag heads overseeing the spare lobby give the Palmas a rather incongruous tropical-motel-cum-hunting-lodge quality, the wackiness ends there. Quaint cobblestone paths lead to the accommodations, which are housed in two U-shape buildings surrounding a large palm-lined pool area with tables and a small seafood bar. Rooms are spacious and clean with blue-tile floors, brick and stucco walls, two double beds, air-conditioning, phone, and cable TV. ⊠ *Libramiento Carretera s/n, 92800,* ☎ *783/4–35–29, 783/4–35–74,* FAX *783/4–35–35, 783/4–27–42. 98 rooms, 3 suites. Restaurant, bar, room service, pool, 2 tennis courts, playground, laundry service, meeting rooms, free parking. AE, MC, V.*

$ 🏨 **Hotel Florida.** Don't be deceived by the harsh fluorescent light in
★ the lobby or the cramped elevator: this is the best hotel deal in down-town Tuxpán. The rooms, all with phones, cable TV, and air-conditioning, are decorated in soft pastels; most have ample light and space as well as immaculate bathrooms. A note of caution: a few of the basic rooms, particularly those facing the inner courtyard, have fallen into disrepair, with stained carpeting and tattered bedspreads. You'd do best to stay in one of the slightly more expensive, better-maintained outer rooms, which have terraces and views of the cathedral and waterfront. ⊠ *Av. Juárez 23, across from cathedral, 92800,* ☎ *783/4–02–22, 783/ 4–06–02,* FAX *783/4–06–50. 75 rooms. Restaurant, bar, room service, meeting rooms, free parking. DC, MC, V.*

$ 🏨 **Hotel Reforma.** The Reforma is a lovely building a block from the waterfront in the heart of downtown. It lacks a lobby but has a central courtyard with a number of skylights, a fountain, and a few wrought-iron tables where guests often congregate in the afternoon. Rooms are carpeted and have phones, cable color TVs, air-conditioning, and good-size bathrooms. Street noise can be a problem on the first floor. ⊠ *Av. Juárez 25, 92800,* ☎ *783/4–06–18, 783/4–02–10,* FAX *783/4–06–25. 88 rooms, 10 suites. Restaurant, bar, room service, laundry service, meeting room, free parking. AE, MC, V.*

$ 🏨 **Hotel Tajín.** This hotel's real selling point is its location on the banks of the river, across from the city center. Despite its swanky modern exterior, well-manicured grounds, a 1999 face-lift, and a long list of amenities, the Tajín doesn't quite deliver the first-class luxury it promises. Rooms, although bright and comfortable—with nice views and phones and color TVs—tend toward the bland. The battered furniture in some rooms looks like it was picked up at a frat-house yard sale, and the fresh coat of paint on the hotel's exterior can't quite hide the slow tropical decay. But the Tajín isn't entirely charmless: its spacious, tile lobby, lovely restaurant, boutiques, disco, basketball and tennis courts, and three pools (one with a 15-ft water slide), as well as the availability of water sports, are sure to please resort-minded guests. If you don't have a car, you must take a longish taxi ride from the city center or catch a beach-bound bus to the Paso de Esquifes La Peñita, where a skiff will shuttle you across the river. The hotel is a three-minute walk from the landing. ✉ *Carretera a Cobos, Km 2.5, 92800,* ☎ *783/4–22–60, 783/4–25–72,* FAX *783/ 4–25–19. 110 rooms, 10 suites, 40 villas. 2 restaurants, bar, room service, 3 pools, 2 tennis courts, basketball, volleyball, dock, dance club, shops, children's programs (ages 3–12), playground, laundry service, meeting room, free parking. AE, DC, MC, V.*

Outdoor Activities and Sports

WATER SPORTS

For scuba diving, head to **Tamiahua,** a small village just north of Tuxpán, where you can hire a fishing boat for the 45-minute journey to the prime diving around **Isla Lobos** (Wolf Island), a protected eco-reserve that shares its space with a military outpost and a lighthouse. In the shallow water offshore you'll find a few shipwrecks and colorful reefs that are home to a large variety of sea life, including puffer fish, parrot fish, damselfish, and barracuda. **Aquasport** (☎ 783/7–02–59), just west of Playa Tuxpán, arranges scuba-diving trips to Isla Lobos and also has deep-sea fishing excursions. Other outfits run trips to the island, which include permits, scuba gear, lunch, and transportation.

VERACRUZ A TO Z

Arriving and Departing

By Car

The city of Veracruz can be reached within about eight hours by traveling south from Tampico via Mexico 180, or within six hours from Mexico City via Mexico 150. The highways throughout the state, paved and kept up with oil money, are generally very good.

By Plane

Both **Mexicana** (☎ 29/32–22–42, 29/32–86–99) and **Aeroméxico** (☎ 29/35–08–33, 29/35–02–83) provide nonstop service from Mexico City to the port of Veracruz. **Heriberto Jara International Airport** (☎ 29/34–00–08) is about 8 km (5 mi) south of downtown Veracruz.

BETWEEN THE AIRPORT AND DOWNTOWN

A cab to the city center costs $8.50. No city bus serves the airport. An air-conditioned minivan ($10) runs between the airport and the downtown office of **Transavion** (✉ Hidalgo 826, between Canal and Morales, ☎ 29/37–87–19, 29/37–89–78).

Getting Around

By Bus

Veracruz's main **bus terminal** (✉ Díaz Mirón 1698, ☎ 29/37–57–44) is about 4 km (2½ mi) south of the zócalo. The main bus company is **ADO** (☎ 29/37–29–22, 29/35–07–83), with daily service to Jalapa every 20 minutes 6 AM–midnight and round-the-clock departures for Mexico City. ADO also offers first- and second-class service to Reynosa, on the Texas border. If you are headed north and east, the deluxe bus line **UNO** (☎ 29/35–07–83, 29/37–29–22) goes to Jalapa, Puebla, and Mexico City. Second-class **Cuenca** buses (☎ 29/35–54–05) go south to Oaxaca. **Cristóbal Colón** (☎ 29/37–57–44) offers frequent first- and second-class service to Los Tuxtlas.

Contacts and Resources

Car Rental

Jalapa. Renta de Autos Sánchez (✉ Ignacio de la Llave 14, ☎ 28/17–70–46) is the only rental agency in town.

Veracruz. Avis (✉ Heriberto Jara International Airport, ☎ 29/32–16–76), **Dollar** (✉ Víctimas del 5 y 6 de Julio 883, ☎ 29/35–52–31, 29/35–33–77), **Hertz** (✉ Hotel Costa Verde, Avila Camacho 3797, Boca del Río, ☎ 29/37–41–00), and **National** (✉ Díaz Mirón 1036, ☎ 29/31–17–56, 29/31–33–12) are represented.

Currency Exchange

Jalapa. About seven blocks from Parque Juárez, **Casa de Cambio Jalapa** (✉ Zamora 36, ☎ 28/17–20–60) has good rates; it's open 9–3 and 5–7:30 weekdays. You can also change money in the morning at several banks on Parque Juárez. Most have 24-hour ATMs.

Papantla. There are plenty of banks surrounding the zócalo, most of which change money weekday mornings. **Banamex** (✉ Enríquez 102) changes both cash and traveler's checks weekdays 9–noon and has a 24-hour ATM that accepts Cirrus, Plus, Visa, and MasterCard.

Tuxpán. Banamex (✉ Av. Juárez at Calle Corregidora) changes cash and traveler's checks 9–5 weekdays; it has a 24-hour ATM. **Bancomer** (✉ Av. Juárez at Escuela Médico Militar, ☎ 783/4–00–09) has a 24-hour ATM and changes cash and traveler's checks weekdays 8:30–2:30.

Veracruz. The best rates in town are at **Bancomer** (✉ Av. Juárez at Independencia, ☎ 29/31–00–95, 29/89–80–00), but money-changing hours are limited to 9–noon weekdays, so you'll have to arrive early to make it through the lines. The **Casa de Cambio Puebla** (✉ Av. Juárez 112, ☎ 29/31–24–50) is open weekdays 9–6. Or use an ATM.

Emergencies

Jalapa. Police (☎ 28/18–74–90, 28/18–71–99); for an ambulance, call the **Cruz Roja** (Red Cross; ☎ 28/17–34–31, 28/17–81–58).

Papantla. Police (☎ 784/2–00–75); **Cruz Roja** (☎ 784/2–01–26).

Tuxpán. Police (☎ 783/4–02–52); **Cruz Roja** (☎ 783/4–01–58).

Veracruz. Dial **06** for medical, fire, and theft emergencies. **Oficinas Para la Seguridad de la Turista** (☎ 01–800/903–9200) has a country-wide 24-hour toll-free hot line to provide legal and medical help for tourists. **Police** (✉ Playa Linda 222, ☎ 29/38–06–64, 29/38–06–93); **Hospital General de Veracruz** (✉ 20 de Noviembre s/n, ☎ 29/31–04–52, 29/31–04–85); **Cruz Roja** (☎ 29/37–55–00).

Guided Tours

Jalapa. Expediciones Mexico Verde (✉ Homero 526, Int. 801, Col. Polanco, Mexico, D.F. 11560, ☎ 5/255–44–00, 01/800–362–8800, ☎ FAX 5/255–4465) has river rafting along the Río Pescados near Jalapa. One-day or overnight excursions are available. All equipment, including life jackets, helmets, and oars, is provided. The outfit also runs 7- or 10-day trips on the Cortés Route, which includes Veracruz City, La Antigua, Cempoala, Jalapa, and Coatepec (in the state of Veracruz) and continues on to conquistador-related sites in the states of Tlaxcala, Puebla, and Mexico. English is spoken.

The Jalapa tourist office also recommends the following two bilingual river-rafting outfits: **Veraventuras** (✉ Santos Degollado 81, Int. 8, ☎ 28/18–97–79, 01–800/2–65–72) and **Iguana Expediciones** (✉ Cotaxtla Sur 16, Col. Petrolera, Boca del Río, ☎ FAX 29/21–15–50).

Veracruz. Boat tours of the bay depart from the malecón daily 7–7. Boats leave whenever they're full, and the $2.50 half-hour ride includes a (Spanish-language) talk on Veracruz history. Longer trips to nearby **Isla Verde** (Green Island) and **Isla de Enmedio** (Middle Island) leave daily from the shack marked PASEO EN LANCHITA near Plaza Acuario. Boats wait until they're full to set off, so it's best to be in a group. The cost should be about $3–$5 per person, but feel free to bargain.

Martin Sandoval Tours (✉ Balboa 327, between Washington and Martí, ☎ 29/30–40–23, 🖷 FAX 29/35–31–72) has city tours as well as trips to El Tajín and Papantla, Los Tuxtlas, and Jalapa. Diving and fishing trips are available, too. There are also travel desks at the Torremar, Emporio, and Fiesta Americana hotels.

Letters and E-Mail

Jalapa. Mail and fax services are available at the main **post office** (✉ Av. Zamora 70, at Calle Diego Leno). For e-mail, **Caseta Telefonica** (✉ Av. Enríquez 16, ☎ 28/17–36–86, 28/12–24–62) has three computers, charges $1.50 an hour, and is open weekdays 7 AM–10 PM, and weekends 8 AM–9 PM. **Compupapel** (✉ Calle Primo Verdad 23, at Av. Zaragoza, ☎ 28/17–23–22), has eight computers; it's open daily 9–8:30 and charges $1 an hour.

Papantla. Several blocks from the zócalo, **PC's Palafox** (✉ Aquiles Serdán 500, at Calle Galeana, ☎ 784/2–13–57) has 10 machines and offers Internet access for $1.50 an hour 8 AM–9 PM weekdays, 8–7 Saturday, and 8–5 Sunday.

Tuxpán. The **post office** (✉ Calle Morelos 12) is half a block from Avenida Juárez. There are a number of Internet cafés in the downtown area and all charge about $1.50 an hour. **Instituto Cristóbal Colón** (✉ Av. Juárez 44, ☎ no phone) has a dozen machines and is open daily 10–8:30. (Enter through the pedestrian walkway and go past the stores to the back of the building.) **Sesico** (✉ Av. Juárez 52, off Parque Reforma, ☎ 783/4–45–05) is open Monday–Saturday 9–8:30 and Sunday 10–3; it has 10 computers.

Veracruz. The main **post office** (✉ Plaza República 213) is a five-block walk from the zócalo. For Internet access, **Web Café** (✉ Calle Rayon 579-A, between Avs. Independencia and Zaragoza, ☎ no phone) has the fastest machines, for $1.80 an hour, with slightly cheaper rates for students. It's open 10–10 daily. **Netcha Boys** (✉ Calle Miguel Lerdo 369, ☎ no phone), open weekdays 9–9 and weekends noon–8, will run you $1.50 an hour for Internet access.

Pharmacies

Jalapa. Calle Enríquez is lined with pharmacies. For 24-hour service, the **Farmacia Plus** (✉ Revolución 173, at Sagayo, ☎ 28/17–27–77, 28/17–27–97) is your best option.

Papantla. Farmacia de Descuento (✉ Gutiérrez Zamora 103, ☎ 784/2–19–41), open daily 7:30 AM–10 PM, is the largest pharmacy in town.

Tuxpán. In the downtown area, try **Farmacia El Fenix** (✉ Calle Morelos 1, at Av. Juárez, ☎ 783/4–30–23), open daily 8 AM–10 PM.

Veracruz. Farmacia del Ahorro (✉ Paseo del Malecón 342, at Calle Fariaz, ☎ 29/37–35–25) is a big, convenient drugstore downtown; it closes at 10 PM daily. For late-night service, try **Farmacia El Mercado** (✉ Independencia 1197, ☎ 29/31–08–83), open until 2 AM.

Visitor Information

The **Jalapa tourist office** (✉ Blvd. Cristóbal Colón 5, Jardines de las Animas, ☎ 28/12–85–00 ext. 130, 🖷 FAX 28/12–59–36) is in the large office building on the way out of town toward Veracruz (known as Torre Animas) and is open weekdays 9–9. There's a **Jalapa tourist information booth** (✉ Calle Enríquez 14) in front of the Palacio Municipal; it's open daily 9–9.

The **Tuxpán tourist office** (✉ Av. Juárez 26, ☎ 783/4–01–77) is open daily 8–3 and 4–6.

The **Veracruz Dirección Municipal de Turismo** (✉ Palacio Municipal on zócalo, ☎ 29/32–19–99, 𝖥𝖠𝖷 29/32–75–93) is open Monday–Saturday 9–9, Sunday 10–1.

THE NORTHEAST

Few travelers go out of their way to visit northeastern Mexico, an arid area that's becoming increasingly industrial as more and more multinational companies establish *maquiladoras* (foreign-owned factories in duty-free zones) along the border and create more and more air pollution. But day- and weekend-trippers from Texas enjoy the foreign color and cuisine of border towns such as Nuevo Laredo, Matamoros, and Reynosa. And only about three hours from the border is Monterrey, a fast-paced city that's home to Mexico's major brewery, some good museums, and one of Latin America's finest universities.

Nature lovers can enjoy the Parque Nacional Cumbres de Monterrey, northwest of the city, with its impressive Cola de Caballo waterfall. Also near Monterrey is the dramatic cut of the Barranca de la Huasteca, as well as the Grutas de García, caves with an underground lake and a stalactite and stalagmite forest. Anglers and hunters are lured farther into the area by the magnificent fish and game at Lake Vicente Guerrero, not far from Ciudad Victoria. And Tampico is known both for its seaside appeal and its interesting architectural sights.

Nuevo Laredo

⑫ *1½ km (1 mi) south of Laredo, Texas.*

Of all the eastern border towns, Nuevo Laredo receives the largest onslaught of American souvenir-seekers. Shopping is the primary pursuit here, and you'll find a warren of stalls and shops as well as a large crafts market concentrated on Avenida Guerrero in a seven-block stretch that extends from the International Bridge to the main plaza. In addition to the standard border-town curios, Nuevo Laredo shops stock a good selection of high-quality handicrafts from all over Mexico, at somewhat inflated prices. Wander a few blocks off the main drag in any direction for better prices and smaller crowds.

Nuevo Laredo was founded after the Treaty of Guadalupe Hidalgo in 1848, which ended the Mexican-American War. The treaty established the Río Bravo (or Rio Grande) as the border between the two countries and forced Mexico to give up a substantial amount of territory. Many of Laredo's Mexican residents, who suddenly found themselves living in the United States, crossed the river and founded Nuevo Laredo on what had been the outskirts of town. Today, Nuevo Laredo's economy depends greatly on gringos who head south for a few days of drunken revelry, returning home with a bottle of tequila, suitcases full of souvenirs, and a mean hangover.

Dining and Lodging

$$$ ✕ **Restaurant Victoria 3020.** Set back from the street and surrounded
★ by a garden, the Victoria offers the swankiest dining in town. In the pastel-hue main room, amid abstract paintings and sculptures by Mex-

Northeastern Mexico

ico's top artists, diners feast on such rich creations as broiled New York
steak topped with demiglace burgundy and marrow butter, frog legs
sautéed in garlic and white-wine sauce, and rainbow trout in a sweet
almond sauce. The white-jacketed waiters won't let you get away
without trying the *tunas borrachas victoria* (prickly pear and kiwi
served with tequila and vanilla ice cream) for dessert. The candlelit courtyard in back is perfect for a quiet, romantic dinner. ⊠ *Victoria 3020,
at Matamoros,* ☎ *87/12–69–00, 87/13–30–20. AE, MC, V.*

$$ ✕ **El Dorado.** Dating from the Prohibition era, this spot is a favorite
with the Texas crowd—a hangout better known for its atmosphere than
for its cuisine. Try the combination plate of grilled meat, which includes
two selections of either goat, quail, or frogs' legs. ⊠ *Ocampo at Calle
Belden,* ☎ *87/12–00–15. AE, MC, V.*

$$ ✕ **México Típico.** This establishment, gaily decorated in bright Mexican colors, offers indoor and outdoor dining, with mariachis coming
in from the street to entertain. The patio, partially covered, features a
waterfall. Specialties are carne asada and cabrito. True to its name, México Típico serves the typical Mexican plate of beef or chicken enchiladas with rice and refried beans. ⊠ *Av. Guerrero 934,* ☎ *87/12–15–
25. MC, V.*

$$$ ⊞ **Hotel Hacienda Real.** Although the sign threatening electrocution
for guests who touch the stuffed stag displayed in the hotel lobby
might seem like a sick taxidermist's joke (it's ostensibly to keep tots
from climbing on it), the accommodations here are pleasant. The
bright, immaculate rooms, overlooking a central garden and palm-lined
pool area, all have hand-carved wooden furniture, embroidered bed-
spreads, large tile bathrooms, air-conditioning, and cable TV. And it's
really the small touches—such as the wrought-iron balconies and Eu-
ropean-style streetlamps along the walkways—that make the Hacienda
Real well worth the 15-minute trip from the city center. ⊠ *Av. Reforma*

5530, 88280, ☎ *87/17–00–00, 01–800/718–7470,* FAX *87/17–04–20. 72 rooms, 2 suites. Restaurant, bar, room service, pool, beauty salon, tennis court, basketball, meeting rooms, free parking. AE, MC, V.*

$ 🗹 **Hotel Reforma.** An older hotel just a half block south of Plaza Hidalgo, Reforma has a restaurant, marble lobby, and secure parking. Rooms in the older section, although somewhat small and rather nondescript, are comfortable; the junior suites in the newer section are slightly bigger and have fresh carpets and curtains, although the hallways smell musty. All units come with shower, air-conditioning, cable color TVs, and phones. ⊠ *Av. Guerrero 822, 88000,* ☎ *87/12–62–50,* FAX *87/12–67–14. 45 rooms. Restaurant, bar, room service, free parking. MC, V.*

Nightlife and the Arts

Victoria's, three blocks from International Bridge 1, is a noisy favorite; the **El Dorado** is somewhat more sedate; and **Quintana Rock** and the new **Plaza San Miguel** are the local discos. All of the above dance clubs are on Avenida Guerrero in the heart of the shopping district.

Shopping

On the stretch where International Bridge 1 leads into Avenida Guerrero, you'll find most of Nuevo Laredo's shops—classy and junky alike. **Granada** (⊠ Av. Guerrero 504, ☎ 87/12–86–44) has better-quality items than many of the other vendors, including lead crystal and serapes. Artisan shops selling lots of leather goods and ceramics are in the **Nuevo Mercado de la Reforma,** a market three blocks south of International Bridge 1, at Avenida Guerrero and Calle Belden. The **Maria Cristina** mall, at Avenida Guerrero 631, houses about three dozen curio outlets. Most stores remain open until 8 PM.

Reynosa

⑬ *16 km (10 mi) south of McAllen, Texas.*

Because of its manageable size and mellow attitude, Reynosa is one of the most pleasant points of entry into Mexico. It is also a convenient starting point if you're bound for Mexico City, Monterrey, or Veracruz. That said, Reynosa is still an industrial border town of limited charm, driven economically by the petrochemicals industry, agriculture, and the ever-present tourist trade. As you enter town, you'll see the **Zona Rosa** (Pink Zone) tourist district, with a few curio shops and a couple of bars and restaurants. The heart of the city, around **Plaza Principal,** is about five blocks from the International Bridge. An urban renewal project that was started in 1996 enlarged sidewalks and put in park benches, cobblestone streets, and new street signs. After leaving downtown, the rest of Reynosa is a jumble of tacky border-town urban sprawl.

Plaza Principal is in many ways a typical Mexican town center, but its original colonial church has been joined like a Siamese twin to an ultramodern newer addition with arches and stained-glass windows, bordered on one side by a movie theater and on the other by a Nike outlet store. **Hidalgo Street,** a colorful pedestrian mall of shops and street vendors, leads off from the plaza. Many Texans save money by having their teeth fixed south of the Rio Grande—which explains the many dental offices you'll see in this area.

Dining and Lodging

$$ ✕ **La Fogata.** Baby goat, stuffed goat intestines, lamb ribs, and a variety of beef cuts are all prepared on a smoky open grill at the back of this popular cabrito joint. The herculean portions of slow-roasted meat are served in the classic northern style, with side dishes of guacamole, lime, jalapeños, and tortillas. The menu also includes chicken fajitas, quail, and Cornish hen. Give yourself a couple of hours to work

your way to the bottom of your plate. ⊠ *Matamoros 750, at Chapa,* ☎ *89/22–47–72, 89/22–82–16. AE, MC, V.*

$$ ✕ **Sam's.** Wild game such as quail and dove served in season (November–January) and seafood are the reasons to come here. Desserts are limited to flan and cheesecake. In winter, Sam's is frequented by Americans from the Rio Grande Valley and snowbirds from Minnesota. ⊠ *Allende 1100,* ☎ *89/22–00–34, 89/22–34–34. AE, MC, V.*

$$ 🏨 **Astromundo.** Downtown and handy to the market and the few good local restaurants, this popular hotel gets a lot of traffic from weekending Texans. ⊠ *Juárez 675, 88500,* ☎ *89/22–56–25,* FAX *89/22–98–88. 90 rooms, 6 suites. Restaurant, bar, room service, free parking. AE, MC, V.*

$$ 🏨 **Hacienda.** Along the highway to Monterrey about 16 km (10 mi) from the U.S. border, this sparkling hotel is luxurious by Reynosa standards. Its tile lobby is decorated with colonial-style furniture and handicrafts, which carry over into the light-filled, cheerful rooms; all have color cable TVs, air-conditioning, and direct-dial phones. ⊠ *Blvd. Hidalgo 2013, 88650,* ☎ *89/24–60–10,* FAX *89/23–59–62. 20 rooms, 13 suites. Restaurant, bar, room service, meeting room, travel services, car rental, free parking. AE, MC, V.*

$ 🏨 **San Carlos.** This five-story hotel on the square has air-conditioned rooms with colonial-style furniture and satellite TVs. Business travelers and tourists appreciate its central location, close to the square and shopping center, and the friendly staff. ⊠ *Hidalgo 970, 88500,* ☎ *89/22–12–80, 89/22–40–00,* FAX *89/22–26–20. 66 rooms, 10 suites. Restaurant, room service, laundry service, free parking. MC, V.*

Nightlife and the Arts

The **Imperial** (⊠ Av. Virreyes 1087, entrance at the back of gift shop, ☎ no phone) offers slow-dance music on weeknights and disco on weekends; don't get too close to the live chained monkey on the patio—he bites! The Zona Rosa has several discos and **Treviño's** (⊠ Av. Virreyes 1075, ☎ 89/22–14–44), a cocktail lounge and piano bar.

Shopping

Treviño's (⊠ Av. Virreyes 1075, ☎ 89/22–14–44) has a good selection of Mexican arts and crafts, sculpture, papier-mâché, perfumes, liquors, and clothing. There's a cocktail lounge in the rear (☞ Nightlife and the Arts, *above*).

Matamoros

14 *1 km (about ½ mi) south of Brownsville, Texas.*

Matamoros, across from Brownsville, Texas, is the most historic of the border towns, dating from the 18th century. It actually is named H. Matamoros, or Heroic Matamoros, for one of the many rebellious priests who were executed by the Spanish during the War of Independence (1810–21). The first major battle of the Mexican-American War was fought here when guns in Matamoros began shelling Fort Brown on the north side of the Rio Grande. Shortly afterward, troops of Zachary Taylor occupied Matamoros and began their march south.

Today Matamoros is the commercial center of a rich agricultural area and a manufacturing center for multinational corporations. Some 20 years ago, **Avenida Alvaro Obregón,** which leads from the main bridge, was spruced up to "dignify" the Mexican side of the border, and of the three border towns, it makes the prettiest entryway. This is where you'll find the town's best shops, restaurants, and accommodations. Also of interest is the **Casa Mata Museum** in the remains of Fort Mata, built in 1845 to defend the city against American invasion. The fortress wasn't completed in time, and Zachary Taylor's troops were able to capture Matamoros easily. Casa Mata now displays photos and artifacts, mostly from the Mexican Revolution. ⊠ *Guatemala and Santos Degollado,* ☎ *88/13–59–29.* 🎟 *Free.* ☉ *Mon.–Sat. 9:30–5, Sun. 9:30–3.*

Beach

Playa Bagdad is about 30 km (18 mi) from downtown Matamoros. It's worth a visit only if you hanker for the Gulf of Mexico. It's the site of the Confederacy's only open harbor during the U.S. Civil War. Freighters skirting the Union naval blockade unloaded their war supplies and loaded up with Confederate cotton destined for Europe. Today, there's an air of decrepit charm about the place: about 100 palapas are lined up neatly along the gritty shore waiting for visitors, accompanied by a couple of seafood restaurants that seem to be barely surviving. On weekends, hordes of Mexican middle-class families pour into the place. The entrance fee is about $1.50 a vehicle.

Dining and Lodging

$$ ★ X **Garcia's.** Rebuilt and redecorated over its own parking garage, this is a romantic place for dancing and dining on lobster or steak and your choice of a dozen fine tequilas. An elevator from the garage takes you up to a gift shop with wares from all over Mexico as well as to the restaurant and a bar. ⊠ *Av. Alvaro Obregón 82,* ☎ *88/12–39–29; 88/13–18–33. AE, MC, V.*

$ X **Los Norteños.** A goat slow-roasting over hot coals in the window is the not-so-subtle advertisement for the best cabrito in town. A dozen plain tables with plastic tablecloths are the setting for an equally spare menu—goat, guacamole, and quesadillas. All meals are served with a tasty black-bean soup and a heaping pile of tortillas. ⊠ *Calle Matamoros between 8 and 9,* ☎ *88/13–00–37. No credit cards.*

$$$ ★ 🏨 **Gran Hotel Residencial.** The best hotel in the city, this pleasant low-rise built along Spanish colonial lines is near the center of Matamoros. All rooms have terraces, two queen- or one king-size bed, and color cable TVs. There's also a large pool and a children's play area in the lush garden. ⊠ *Av. Alvaro Obregón 249, at Amapola, 87330,* ☎ *88/13–98–11, 01–800/718–8230,* 🖷 *88/13–27–77. 109 rooms, 5 suites. Restaurant, bar, room service, pool, meeting rooms, travel services, car rental, free parking. AE, MC, V.*

$$ ★ 🏨 **Hotel Plaza Matamoros.** A good alternative to the expensive luxury hotels on one hand and the grubby downtown digs on the other, this member of the Best Western chain has comfortable, clean rooms near the center of town. All have heavy wooden furniture, thick burgundy carpeting, air-conditioning, phones, and cable TVs, and look out over a central indoor restaurant. ⊠ *Calle 9 No. 1421, at Bravo, 87330,* ☎ *88/16–16–96, 88/16–16–02,* 🖷 *88/16–16–87. 40 rooms. Restaurant, bar, room service, pool, shop, laundry service, meeting room, free parking. AE, MC, V.*

Nightlife and the Arts

The **Teatro Reforma** (⊠ Calle 6 and Abasolo, ☎ 88/16–62–07, 88/12–51–20), Matamoros's cultural hub, presents music and dance performances from around the country. Call for dates and times.

Garcia's and the **Gran Hotel Residencial** (☞ Dining and Lodging, *above*) are good places for a relaxed drink. If you're looking for some dance action, head out to Avenida Alvaro Obregón toward the International Bridge, where you'll find several discos, including **Crazy Lazy, Zero Zone,** and **Mr. Lee's Dragon Club.**

Shopping

The most appealing shops are on Avenida Alvaro Obregón, which leads from the border bridge to the center of town. The salmon-color building that houses **Garcia's** restaurant (☞ Dining and Lodging, *above*) also contains a huge gift shop, where you can buy everything from big sombreros to quality tequila, silver, Oaxaca wedding dresses, and leather jackets. Across from Garcia's, **Aztlan** (⊠ Av. Alvaro Obregón 75, ☎ 88/16–29–47) has high-quality jewelry, pewter, clothes, some modern artwork, and wooden and stone carvings. **Barbara** (⊠ Av. Alvaro Obregón 37, ☎ 88/16–54–56) sells attractive craft items, home furnishings, good costume jewelry, and imported cosmetics. It's also the only store that prepares free margaritas for shoppers. But beware: "You Break, You Buy!" The covered, block-long **Mercado Juárez** downtown, between Calle 9 and Matamoros, is the place to haggle for bargains; you get what you pay for.

Monterrey

235 km (146 mi) southwest of Nuevo Laredo, 225 km (140 mi) west of Reynosa, 325 km (201 mi) west of Matamoros.

Monterrey is a favorite with weekenders and "winter Texans" from the Rio Grande Valley who find the city so near—a three-hour drive from the border or a short flight from Dallas, Houston, or San Antonio—and yet so foreign. The top hotels are clustered downtown in the Zona Rosa or Barrio Antiguo (Old Quarter). Several streets, including Avenida Morelos—the main drag—are now pedestrian malls.

In 1996 Monterrey celebrated the 400th anniversary of its founding. It is Mexico's third-largest city and the capital of the state of Nuevo León. This industrial center is a brewer of beer and forger of steel, with nothing in the way of a laid-back lifestyle. It is where some of the country's most powerful captains of industry hold sway—a fact that earned the city its nickname, the Sultan of the North. Monterrey also has the country's most sophisticated convention center—a high-tech facility called Cintermex—and built a gigantic sports arena to host international events.

The impressive **Gran Plaza**—at 100 acres, one of the country's largest squares—was completed in 1985 as part of an urban renewal project that also includes the first stages of a San Antonio–style riverwalk with cafés and shops. The plaza is within walking distance of the downtown hotels. Better known as Macroplaza, it extends from the modernistic Palacio Municipal (City Hall) several blocks past the newly painted cathedral, the old City Hall, and the Legislative Palace to the Palacio de Gobierno (State House).

⑮ Towering above the plaza, opposite the neoclassical **Palacio de Gobierno,** is a giant orange concrete slab topped by the Beacon of Commerce, a laser beam that flashes from 8 to 11 nightly. It was designed by Luis Barragán to commemorate the 100th anniversary of the founding of the city's Chamber of Commerce. Handsome Saddle Mountain and the craggy Sierra Madre provide a majestic backdrop to this austere modern monument. The grandly lighted Palacio de Gobierno stays open all night, piping out soft classical music over a loudspeaker, and makes for a wonderful evening visit. ⊠ *Between 5 de Mayo, 15 de Mayo, and Avs. Zaragoza and Zuazua.*

★ ⑯ The opulent **Museo de Arte Contemporaneo** (Museum of Contemporary Art) is the principal sight on the Gran Plaza. Designed in the style of a Moorish palace by renowned Mexican architect Ricardo Legorretta, it has 11 galleries that display the cutting-edge art of Mexico and

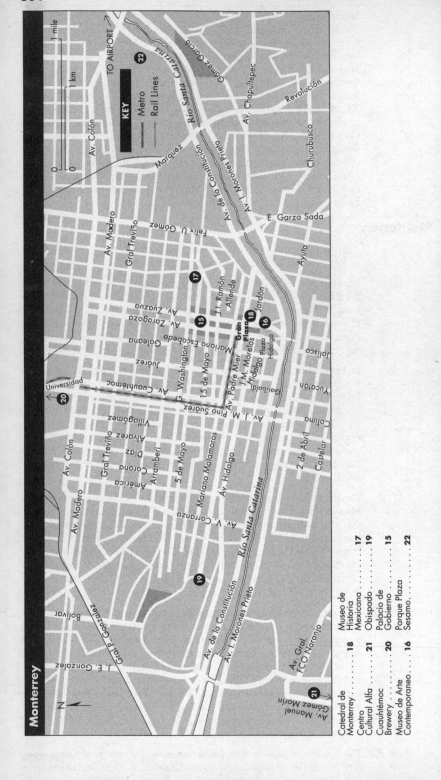

Monterrey

KEY
Metro
Rail Lines

TO AIRPORT

Catedral de
Monterrey **18**
Centro
Cultural Alfa **21**
Cuauhtémoc
Brewery **20**
Museo de Arte
Contemporaneo **16**

Museo de
Historia
Mexicana **17**
Obispado **19**
Palacio de
Gobierno **15**
Parque Plaza
Sesamo. **22**

Latin America and, at times, of other parts of the world. There's an outstanding collection of art books for sale at the gift shop. You can listen to live music alongside a reflecting pool on the beautiful marble patio Wednesday evening (6–8) and watch the candlelit tables fill up with culture vultures sipping coffee and nibbling on pie. ⊠ *Gran Plaza at Av. Zuazua and Jardón,* ☎ 8/342–4820. ⊒ *About $3, free Wed.* ⊙ *Tues. and Thurs.–Sun. 10–6, Wed. 10–8.*

⑰ The **Museo de Historia Mexicana** (Mexican History Museum) has a mini riverwalk with cafés and a boat ride on its grounds. It displays the country's most complete history of its 1910–20 Revolution. Battles, marches, and political protagonists come to life in the newsreels of the period, part of a sophisticated multimedia show held inside a railroad car that served as a troop carrier for the insurgents. Life-size plaster-of-paris casts of the Villistas (soldiers under the command of Pancho Villa) sit shotgun on the roof of a car that we are led to believe has just been "liberated" from the Mexican army. Other exhibits include the first bottle-capping machine used by Coca-Cola, a history of Mexican cinema, and pre-Columbian Huastec artifacts. Free guided tours are available in English (call ahead to confirm that an English-speaking guide is available). ⊠ *Dr. Coss 445 Sur,* ☎ 8/345–9898. ⊒ *$1, free Tues.* ⊙ *Tues.–Thurs. 11–7, Fri.–Sun. 11–8.*

Monterrey's Spanish history began in 1596, and for its first couple of
⑱ centuries it was little more than an outpost. Construction of the **Catedral de Monterrey** began in 1600 but took some 250 years to finish. As a result, a Baroque facade is set off by neoclassical columns and two huge ornate plateresque medallions on the main door. Murals by local artists frame the main altar. ⊠ *Gran Plaza at Av. Zuazua and Jardón.*

⑲ The **Obispado** (Bishop's House) is the only landmark to be completed in the colonial era (1788). Built on a hilltop as a home for retired prelates, it was used as a fort during the Mexican-American War (1847), the French Intervention (1862), and again during the Mexican Revolution (1915). Today it houses the **Museo Regional de Nuevo León El Obispado,** with exhibits that focus on the history of the entire area. The museum's major appeal, however, is its splendid view of Monterrey. ⊠ *Far west end of Av. Padre Mier, at Rafael José Berger,* ☎ 8/346–0404. ⊒ *$1.25.* ⊙ *Tues.–Sun. 10–5.*

The explosion of the popularity of Mexican beer in recent years owes
⑳ much to the **Cuauhtémoc Brewery,** which opened a century ago. Named after a famous Aztec chief, the brewery is the heart of an industrial empire that produces Carta Blanca and Tecate beer. The brewery complex includes the Mexican Baseball Hall of Fame, a sports museum, the Museo de Monterrey Electronic Arts Gallery, and a beer garden with free beer—obviously the big draw. ⊠ *Av. Alfonso Reyes 2202 Nte.,* ☎ 8/328–5746, 8/375–2200 to book a brewery tour. ⊒ *Free.* ⊙ *Tues.–Sun. 11–8. Brewery tours by request, weekdays 9–1 and 3–6.*

The Cuauhtémoc Brewery spawned a glass factory for bottles, a steel mill for caps, a carton factory, and, eventually, several industrial con-
㉑ glomerates. One of the last, Alfa, gave Monterrey the **Centro Cultural Alfa** (Alfa Cultural Center), probably the best museum of science and technology in the country. The museum has many hands-on exhibits and an IMAX theater. Free buses to the museum run from the downtown *alameda* (main square) hourly 3–8 daily. ⊠ *Roberto Garza Sada 1000,* ☎ 8/303–0002. ⊒ *$3.50.* ⊙ *Tues.–Fri. 3–9, Sat. 2–9, Sun. noon–9.*

The newest recreational/educational play area for children is the clev-
㉒ erly designed **Parque Plaza Sesamo** (Sesame Plaza Park), a sprawling

theme park built on the grounds of Parque Fundidora that also houses the city's Cintermex convention complex. There are three main areas. One has a world of water sports with 17 water toboggans, pint-size pools, interactive games, and minirivers. A second area has a computer center where children can plug into the Internet and play nonviolent video games. The last section is taken up by restaurants and theaters where the park's own personalities put on musical shows. Families can easily spend an entire day here. ⊠ *Calle Agricola 3700–1 Ote., Col. Agricola in Parque Fundidora,* ☎ *8/354–5400.* ☜ *$10.* ☉ *June–Aug., daily 11–9:30; Sept.–May, daily 3–8.*

Dining and Lodging

$$$$ ✕ **Luisiana.** Perhaps the most elegant dining room downtown, this is
  ★   a taste of how New Orleans is imagined in Mexico. There are no Cajun specialties on the menu, but the deepwater crawfish are divine. Wonderfully prepared steak and seafood dishes make this one of the best restaurants in the country. The waiters wear tuxedos, and there's always soft piano music playing at dinnertime. ⊠ *Av. Hidalgo Ote. 530,* ☎ *8/340–3753, 8/343–1561. AE, MC, V.*

$$$ ✕ **Residence.** A clubby meeting place for Monterrey's high-powered
  ★   industrialists and executives, Residence has a menu featuring both Mexican specialties and Continental dishes such as prime rib cooked slowly in its juice. ⊠ *Degollado 605 Sur, at Matamoros,* ☎ *8/342– 7230, 8/345–5040, or 8/345–5478. AE, DC, MC, V.*

$$ ✕ **El Rey de Cabrito.** The restaurant's name ("King of Cabrito") is no lie: this is *the* place to try what is probably the best roast kid you'll ever eat. (The owner keeps his own goat herds.) The hunting lodge–theme restaurant covers half a city block and has become so well known that it's constantly filling out-of-town orders. You can fill up on steaks and fried blood, as well as the famous cabrito. ⊠ *Constitución 817, at Dr. Coss,* ☎ *8/345–3232, 8/345–3292. MC, V.*

$ ✕ **Sanborns.** Part of a national chain that is a Mexican institution, this is the place for hamburgers and malts as well as tacos and enchiladas. ⊠ *Escobedo Sur 920, off Plaza Hidalgo,* ☎ *8/343–1834. AE, MC, V.*

$$$$ ☷ **Fiesta Americana Centro Monterrey.** In the center of the Zona Rosa, this spiffy-looking pink sandstone building has a striking atrium lobby that is abuzz with business travelers. The light-filled units (all of them two-room suites) are tastefully decorated and have burgundy carpets. Rooms facing the plaza have fabulous mountain views. ⊠ *Av. Corregidora Ote. 519, Zona Rosa, 64000,* ☎ *8/319–0900, 01–800/504– 5000,* ℻ *8/319–0980. 207 suites. Restaurant, bar, minibars, no-smoking rooms, room service, indoor pool, exercise room, baby-sitting, laundry service, concierge, parking (fee). AE, DC, MC, V.*

$$$$ ☷ **Quinta Real.** This elegant all-suites business hotel holds sway among
  ★   Monterrey's financial elite and exudes the aura of a prosperous hacienda of bygone days. The high-dome lobby is set with French furnishings in soothing colors, huge bowls of flowers, and carvings of classic Mexican handicrafts, many of them one-of-a-kind works. A collection of finely executed indigenous weavings and embroideries lines the long lobby corridors. The suites have either two double beds or one king, robes, color TVs, and luxury bathroom soaps and lotions. The hotel's restaurant serves excellent French and Mexican cuisine and has built up quite a local following. ⊠ *Av. Diego Rivera 500, Fracc. Valle Ote., San Pedro Garza García 66260,* ☎ *8/368–1000, 800/445–4565,* ℻ *8/368–1070. 125 suites. Restaurant, bar, minibars, no-smoking rooms, room service, sauna, exercise room, baby-sitting, laundry service, concierge, travel services, car rental, free parking. AE, DC, MC, V.*

$$$$ ☷ **Radisson Plaza Gran Hotel Ancira.** Built in 1912, this hotel is rem-
  ★   iniscent of the grand hotels of Europe: an elegant spiral staircase dom-

inates an expansive Art Deco lobby accented by a black-and-white tile floor and crystal chandeliers. Legend has it that Pancho Villa, taken with the place, settled in and stabled his horse in the lobby. Rooms are conservatively decorated with tasteful pastel walls and matching furnishings. All have minibars, cable TVs, and large marble baths. The Plaza Club business-floor suites have impeccable concierge service. ⊠ *Hidalgo at Escobedo, 64000,* ☎ *8/345–7575, 800/333–3333,* FAX *8/ 150–7000. 236 rooms, 26 suites. Restaurant, 2 bars, coffee shop, minibars, no-smoking rooms, pool, beauty salon, outdoor hot tub, sauna, exercise room, baby-sitting, laundry service, concierge floor, travel services, car rental, free parking. AE, MC, V.*

$$$$ ⊞ **Sheraton Ambassador.** One of the best hotels in this part of Mex-
★ ico, this downtown landmark has spacious rooms and an executive floor where units have data ports, work areas, and complimentary Continental breakfast in the executive lounge. There's also a concierge with secretarial and fax service. A health club, an upscale Mediterranean restaurant, and a piano bar with a stained-glass ceiling are among the other amenities. ⊠ *Hidalgo 310 Ote., 64000,* ☎ *8/380–7000, 800/ 325–3535,* FAX *8/380–7039. 223 rooms, 16 suites. 2 restaurants, bar, minibars, no-smoking rooms, room service, pool, massage, tennis court, health club, racquetball, laundry service, concierge floor, meeting rooms, travel services, free parking. AE, DC, MC, V.*

$$$ ⊞ **Hotel Chipinque.** If you have a car, this hilltop resort overlooking the city on 700 acres of forest land is a tranquil choice. The view from the restaurant is extraordinary, especially at night. All rooms have either a king or two queen-size beds, satellite TVs, and phones; some have fireplaces. ⊠ *Meseta de Chipinque 1000, San Pedro Garza García, 66297,* ☎ *8/378–1100, 8/378–6600, 888/237–3316 in the U.S.,* FAX *8/378–1338. 58 rooms, 13 suites. Restaurant, bar, air-conditioning, room service, pool, outdoor hot tub, tennis court, racquetball, billiards, meeting rooms, free parking. AE, MC, V.*

$$ ⊞ **Royalty.** You get your money's worth at this downtown hotel, where prices are lower than usual for this expensive city. The interior, including the lobby and terrace restaurant, is dominated by a cheerful pink-and-white color scheme. Extras include a tiny outdoor pool, a bar with live music nightly, cable TVs, happy hour every evening, and a complimentary American-style breakfast Friday through Sunday. ⊠ *Hidalgo 402 Ote., at Emilio Carranza, 64000,* ☎ *8/340–2800,* FAX *8/340– 5812. 57 rooms, 5 suites. Restaurant, bar, room service, pool, health club (for men only), laundry service, free parking. AE, DC, MC, V.*

$ ⊞ **Colonial.** This no-frills hotel—the oldest in Monterrey—has an ideal central-downtown location and budget-price rooms. The small lobby has one of the last remaining manually operated elevators in the city— it's more than 100 years old. Rooms have cable TVs, carpeting, and air-conditioning units. At night, rooms facing the street get an earful from the noisy men's club next door. ⊠ *Hidalgo 475 Ote., 64000,* ☎ *8/343–6791,* ☎ FAX *8/342–1169. 100 rooms. Air-conditioning, laundry service, dry cleaning, free parking. AE, DC, MC, V.*

Nightlife and the Arts

Fashionable folk, residents, and visitors flock to downtown hotels for after-dark action. The pianist at the **Sheraton Ambassador** (⊠ Hidalgo 310 Ote., ☎ 8/340–7000) is rather reserved, as is the lobby-bar jazz combo at the **Fiesta Americana Centro Monterrey** (⊠ Av. Corregidora Ote. 519, ☎ 8/319–0900). **Monasterio** (⊠ Escobedo and Morelos, ☎ no phone), presents an eclectic mix of live music—from rock to romantic Mexican ballads—Tuesday through Saturday nights. **Vat-Kru,** (⊠ Blvd. Constitución 3050 Pte., ☎ 8/333–5241), bizarre name and all, is one of the hottest discos in town.

Shopping

Top-quality shops center on Plaza Hidalgo, near the major hotels. Leather and cowboy boots are the local specialties. Owner Porfirio Sosa handpicks all the items he sells at the upscale **Carápan** (⊠ Hidalgo 305 Ote., ☎ 8/345–4422) and loves to tell you about them. His array of Mexican antiques, hand-loomed rugs, shawls, clay figures from Michoacán, metal sculptures, and handblown glassware rivals that of stores anywhere in the country. **Sanborns** (⊠ Escobedo 920, off Plaza Hidalgo, ☎ 8/343–1834) offers a standard selection of silver, onyx, and other Mexican craft items. **Plaza Fiesta San Agustín** (⊠ Av. Real de San Agustín at Lázaro Cárdenas, San Pedro Garza García) is an enormous mall where Monterrey socialites shop for evening gowns, precious gems, and imported perfumes. The **Mercado Indio** (⊠ Bolivar Nte. 1150) is a typical Mexican market with dozens of stalls, although the selections are a little monotonous.

Sports

GOLF

Some of the larger hotels can arrange temporary memberships in one of Monterrey's three golf courses.

ICE SKATING

🖑 **Pista de Hielo San Pedro** (⊠ Plaza San Pedro Local 10, ☎ 8/356–7293) is a popular ice-skating rink. It's open weekdays 10–3 and 4:30–8, weekends 10–8.

ROCK CLIMBING

Antonio Rodriguez Tours (☎ 8/134–8164) offers climbing and hiking tours to Barranca de la Huasteca and Las Grutas de García (☞ *below*).

Barranca de la Huasteca (Huastec Canyon)

🖑 **㉓**   *23 km (14 mi) southwest of Monterrey.*

The Barranca de la Huasteca, with its 1,000-ft-deep gorge, is spectacular for the striated grooves etched into its walls that make it resemble a giant piece of Lalique glassware. A children's play area has a miniature train ride and two pools. ⊠ *From Monterrey, 20 km (12 mi) west on Hwy. 40 to Santa Catarina, then 3 km (2 mi) south on marked road to canyon,* ☎ *no phone.* 🎟 *$1 per car and 10¢ per person.* ☉ *Daily 9–6.*

Grutas de García (Garcia Caves)

㉔   *49 km (30 mi) northwest of Monterrey.*

The Grutas García are an estimated 50–60 million years old and at one time were submerged by an ocean. Petrified sea animals are visible in some of its walls. From the entrance, you can hike the steep 1 km (½ mi) to the caves or hop on a swaying funicular. Guides lead the way through a strenuous mile of underground grottoes and caverns. ⊠ *From Monterrey, Hwy. 40 west for 40 km (25 mi) to Saltillo, then 9 km (5½ mi) on marked road to caves,* ☎ *no phone.* 🎟 *$3, $5 with funicular.* ☉ *Daily 9–5.*

Parque Nacional Cumbres de Monterrey

㉕   *90 km (56 mi) northwest of Monterrey.*

One of the highlights of a trip to the Parque Nacional Cumbres de Monterrey, tucked into the Sierra Madre, is a view of **La Cascada Cola de Caballo** (Horsetail Falls), a dramatic 75-ft-high waterfall that tumbles down from the pine-forested heights. The waterfall is about 1 km (½ mi) from the park's entrance, up a cobblestone road. You can rent a docile horse or burro for about $3 an hour from the local kids who hang out by the ticket booth, or hop on a horse-drawn carriage for $2. ⊠ *From Monterrey, Hwy. 85 northwest 90 km (56 mi) to falls,* ☎ *no phone.* 🎟 *$1.50.* ⊙ *Daily 9–7.*

Saltillo

㉖ *40 km (25 mi) southwest of Monterrey.*

Spanish captain Alberto de Canto founded Saltillo in 1577. Occupying a strategic position along the Camino Real, the main artery from Mexico City north into what is now Texas, the city was a crucial colonial outpost in its heyday. It was the capital of the Mexico-controlled Texas territory in 1824–36.

Saltillo is perhaps best known these days for the unglazed terra-cotta tiles it produces. Knockoffs of these plain but attractive tiles line patios and floors throughout Mexico and the southwest United States. This prosperous city has a great deal of industrial sprawl, but city fathers have preserved the historic **main plaza,** which is surrounded by buildings dating from the colonial period. Much smaller than Monterrey, Saltillo nonetheless has its own convention center and some outstanding hotels and restaurants.

Lake Vicente Guerrero

㉗ *316 km (196 mi) southwest of Matamoros, 304 km (188 mi) southeast of Monterrey.*

The man-made Lake Vicente Guerrero is a favorite with American bass fishermen year-round and, in winter, an excellent place to hunt duck and white-wing dove. Several camps in the area, such as El Tejón and El Sargento lodges, cater to Americans. ⊠ *From Monterrey, 288 km (181 mi) south on Hwy. 85 to Ciudad Victoria, then 16 km (10 mi) northeast on Hwy. 101 to lake.*

Tampico

㉘ *504 km (312 mi) south of Matamoros, 583 km (361 mi) southeast of Monterrey.*

Tampico is a picturesque port adjoining Ciudad Madero, now an oil-refining center. In 1828 the Spaniards attempted to reconquer then-independent Mexico by landing troops at Tampico, but they were soundly defeated. After later invasions by the Americans and the French, the port languished until oil was discovered in the region a century ago. The British and Americans developed the industry until it was nationalized in 1938. Petroleum helped Tampico to prosper, but it isn't the kind of thing to enhance tourism. And the Río Pánuco is so polluted that it no longer attracts tarpon fishermen, although the big ocean freighters are an impressive sight.

Still, because of its relative proximity to the border, Tampico gets a smattering of U.S. visitors. (Usually a low-profile place, Tampico made big news in 1995 when it was discovered to be the hometown of the elusive Subcomandante Marcos, spokesman of the Zapatista rebels in Chiapas.) And it is a fascinating place to wander around for a spell—the old part of town has something of the feel of a run-down New Orleans French Quarter. **Plaza de la Libertad,** near the harbor, is surrounded by old colonial buildings. A block away is the regal **Plaza de Armas,** its majestic City Hall guarded by towering palms. The **cathedral** here, started in 1823, was completed with funds donated by Edward L. Doheny, an oil magnate implicated in the U.S.'s Teapot Dome scandal of the 1920s.

In Ciudad Madero (between Tampico and the coast), the small but impressive **Museo de la Cultura Huasteca** (Museum of Huastec Culture) houses an exquisite collection of pre-Hispanic ceramics, shellwork and costumes, and some pots dating as far back as 1100 BC. ⊠ *Instituto Tecnológico, 1 de Mayo at Sor Juana Inés de la Cruz, Ciudad Madero,* ☎ *12/10–22–17.* ⊡ *Donations.* ⊘ *Mon.–Sat. 10–5.*

Beaches

Playa Miramar, about 5 km (3 mi) from town, is a favorite with locals. For a fee, lounge chairs, towels, and showers are available from the hotels and restaurants along the beach. Public transportation is available from Tampico for about 35¢.

Dining and Lodging

$$ ✕ **Restaurant La Troya.** Exceedingly rich meat and seafood dishes are the focus of this restaurant, in one of Tampico's oldest buildings. House specialties include *paella a la troya* (a saffron-flavored stew of chicken, pork, seafood, and vegetables) and *caldo gallego* (Spanish broth with pork, sausage, beans, potatoes, and chard). The best tables are out on the balcony, overlooking the Plaza de la Libertad. Downstairs, in the lobby of the Hotel Posada del Rey, is where Brigadier General Don Isidor Barrados surrendered to Mexican troops September 11, 1829, ending Spain's final attempt to reconquer Mexico. ⊠ *Calle Madero 218 Ote., at Av. Juárez,* ☎ *12/14–11–55. AE, MC, V.*

$ ✕ **Café y Nevería Elite.** This is a popular gathering spot for breakfast, coffee, and ice-cream treats. Don't be put off by the noise and the rather worn Formica tables; it's all part of the local color. ⊠ *Av. Díaz Mirón 211 Ote.,* ☎ *12/12–03–64. MC, V.*

$$$ ⊡ **Camino Real.** Attractively decorated, this low-rise property 20 minutes from the city center is a resort hotel—the best you'll find in Tampico (in spite of the name, it's not part of the Camino Real chain). Its rooms and bungalows surround a huge garden overflowing with tropical trees and flowers. Rooms contain Chippendale-style furniture, minibars, cable color TVs, and direct-dial phones. Fishing excursions can be booked through the hotel's travel agency. ⊠ *Hidalgo 2000, 89140,* ☎ *12/13–88–11, 01–800/570–0000,* 𝖥𝖠𝖷 *12/13–92–26. 100 rooms, 3 suites. Restaurant, bar, room service, minibars, pool, tennis court, laundry service, travel services, car rental. AE, DC, MC, V.*

$ ⊡ **Plaza.** This centrally located budget hotel is clean and comfortable, if a little drab. Rooms are small but air-conditioned, and all have phones and cable color TVs. ⊠ *Madero 204, 89000,* ☎ *12/14–17–84. 60 rooms. No credit cards.*

Nightlife and the Arts

Eclipse (⊠ Universidad 2004, ☎ no phone) has dancing Thursday; the rest of the week, it's a video bar. **Byblos** (⊠ Byblos 1, ☎ 12/13–08–27) is a popular disco. The bar at the **Camino Real** hotel (⊠ Hidalgo 2000, ☎ 12/13–88–11) has evening piano music, except Sunday.

Outdoor Activities and Sports

FISHING

Although the river is polluted, tarpon and snapper fishing is still popular at **Chairel Lagoon,** with boats and equipment available for rent (just don't plan to eat what you hook). You can arrange for a boat, guide, and equipment through the **Camino Real** hotel (⊠ Hidalgo 2000, ☎ 12/13–88–11, 01–800/570–0000).

GOLF

Lagunas de Miralta Country Club (☎ 12/24–00–03) sells day passes at Centro Commercial Tres Arcos on Hidalgo for its golf course at Km 26.1 on the Carretera Tampico–Altamira. Ask at your hotel about passes or special discounts at other local clubs.

THE NORTHEAST A TO Z

Arriving and Departing

By Car

With unleaded gasoline now more widely available, a growing number of motorists from up north are exploring Mexican highways. A car trip is not without its red tape, however (☞ Smart Travel Tips A to Z *in* Chapter 14). **Sanborn's Mexican Insurance** (✉ 2009 S. 10th St., McAllen, TX 78503, ☎ 800/222–0158 in the U.S. and Canada, FAX 956/686–0732) can help you complete the paperwork in advance— free if you buy insurance there, otherwise for a fee.

Distances are deceiving in this part of Mexico because of mountainous driving in the Sierra Madre Oriente. It generally takes three hours to drive from the border to Monterrey. From Monterrey to Ciudad Victoria, it's another four hours.

BORDER TOWNS

Downtown Nuevo Laredo is reached by two bridges: International Bridge 1 in town, and the Columbia–Laredo Bridge (42 km, or 26 mi, northwest of Laredo). Both have facilities for clearing you for travel to the interior of Mexico. (When parking your vehicle in Nuevo Laredo, use only parking lots with attendants on duty—there have been a number of reports of theft of luggage and car stereos.)

The New Bridge is the best route from Brownsville to Matamoros. U.S. 281 leads down to Hidalgo, Texas, and the bridge into Reynosa. For brief excursions across the border, consider leaving your car in Texas and walking over. This eliminates the long wait—often a half hour or more—to bring a car back into the United States.

From Matamoros, Mexico 180 runs down the Gulf coast to Tampico, Veracruz, and beyond. A turnoff on Mexico 101 leads to the hunting and fishing camps at Lake Vicente Guerrero. Mexico 97 leads from Reynosa to Mexico 101/180, which meet up for a bit. From Reynosa, you can drive the free routes Mexico 40 to Mexico 35 to Linares; here Mexico 58 will lead you across to San Roberto (and Mexico 57) via a spectacular road with a most unusual mural by Frederico Cantú chiseled out of the side of a mountain.

MONTERREY

From Laredo, the old Pan-American Highway, Mexico 85 Libre (free), and the four-lane Mexico 85 Cuota (toll) both lead to Monterrey, some 242 km (150 mi) south. The latter road, which ends in Monterrey, is a much better one, although the toll is expensive (about $15). It's around the same price to take the toll road Mexico 40 to Monterrey from Reynosa. Although the Laredo route is more scenic, traversing some nice mountains, Laredo itself is more congested to get through than Reynosa. The Reynosa road, although flat and dull, is more convenient to downtown Monterrey.

TAMPICO

The port is roughly a seven-hour drive from Matamoros on Mexico 180, or eight hours from Monterrey via Mexico 85, which connects with Mexico 80.

By Plane

BORDER TOWNS

From Mexico City, **Aeroméxico** has service to Matamoros (☎ 88/12–24–60) and Reynosa (☎ 89/22–11–15). **Mexicana** flies to Nuevo Laredo (☎ 87/12–20–52).

MONTERREY

Mexicana (☎ 8/356–3050) has flights from Chicago, Denver, Los Angeles, New York, San Antonio, and San Francisco to Monterrey, via Mexico City. **Aeroméxico** (☎ 8/343–5560) has direct service to Houston and Los Angeles and flights to New York via Mexico City. **Continental** (☎ 8/348–4282) flies from Chicago, Las Vegas, Los Angeles, Miami, and New York, via Houston. **American** (☎ 8/340–3031) has six flights a day to Monterrey from Dallas. **Aerolitoral** (☎ 8/386–2070) has service from McAllen and San Antonio, Texas. **Taesa** (☎ 8/369–0847) flies from Mexico City.

Monterrey's **Aeropuerto Internacional Mariano Escobedo** (☎ 8/345–4432), equipped with luggage storage ($4 a day) and a money-exchange booth, is 6 km (4 mi) northeast of downtown. The only way to get here is by taxi, which will cost about $14.

TAMPICO

Aerolitoral (☎ 12/28–41–97) has nonstop flights to Tampico from Mexico City. Both **Aeroméxico** (☎ 12/13–96–00) and **Mexicana** (☎ 12/13–96–00) have flights between Tampico and Mexico City.

By Train

There is no first-class train service from the border to Monterrey or Tampico. Information about schedules and prices for second-class service is available from **Mexico by Train** (☎ FAX 210/725–3659) in Laredo, Texas.

Getting Around

By Bus

Northeastern Mexico is well connected by buses, which are becoming downright luxurious while fares remain low. Information on Mexican bus service is available from **Transportes del Norte** (☎ 8/372–4965) in Laredo (Valley Transit, ☎ 956/723–4324), McAllen (Valley Transit, ☎ 956/686–5479), and Brownsville (Valley Transit, ☎ 956/546–7171). In conjunction with Greyhound, Transportes del Norte goes from San Antonio, Dallas, and Houston to Monterrey.

By Subway

The Monterrey metro, which runs along elevated tracks across the city, is modern and efficient. There are only two lines. Magnetic cards are used to enter the station. Buy them from station vending machines in units of one, three, or five rides. Each ride costs less than 50¢. The metro runs 6 AM–midnight daily.

By Taxi

Taxis are pretty scarce and expensive in border towns but plentiful and moderately priced in Monterrey. In Monterrey, **Metrotaxi** (☎ 8/342–2069) provides reliable on-call service.

Contacts and Resources

Consulates

Matamoros. U.S. Consulate (⊠ Calle 1 No. 232, ☎ 88/12–44–02).

Monterrey. Canadian Consulate (⊠ Edificio Kalos, Calle Mariano Escobedo and Av. Constitución, Suite 108, ☎ 8/344–3200, 8/344–

2753). **U.S. Consulate** (✉ Av. Constitución 411 Pte., ☎ 8/343–7124, 8/345–2120).

Currency Exchange

Some banks won't cash traveler's checks, but most have ATMs.

Matamoros. There are plenty of banks downtown, mostly around Plaza Hidalgo, that change money and traveler's checks. Money-changing hours at banks generally end at 3 PM weekdays, so if you arrive late, try **Turismo Axis** (✉ Morelos 94–107, at Calle 5), which stays open until 5 PM.

Monterrey. Banks in the Zona Rosa generally change money and traveler's checks weekdays 9–3. For later service, **Eurodivisas** (✉ Morelos 359 Ote., ☎ 8/340–1683) stays open until 8 PM Sunday through Friday, 9 PM Saturday.

Reynosa. There are many casas de cambio along Avenida Alemán as you enter town via the International Bridge. Most banks change money but won't cash traveler's checks. One exception: **Citibank** (✉ Av. Alemán 100, ☎ 89/22–56–19, 89/22–56–60) will change traveler's checks weekdays 9–2. You can find the best exchange rates closer to the city center, around Plaza Principál and along Calle Hidalgo.

Tampico. Citibank (✉ Aduana 309 Sur, ☎ 12/12–92–40) changes money and traveler's checks weekdays 9–3. **Banamex** (✉ Madero 403 Ote., ☎ 12/14–02–30) changes money and traveler's checks until 5 PM. **Casa de Cambio** (✉ Juárez 215 Sur, ☎ 12/12–90–00) is open weekdays 9–6, Saturday 9–1:30.

Emergencies

Matamoros. Police (✉ Pedro Cárdenas and Soledad, ☎ 88/17–22–05). **Cruz Roja Hospital** (✉ García and L. Caballero, ☎ 88/12–00–44).

Monterrey. Police (✉ Gonzalitos and Lincoln, ☎ 8/151–6000). **Cruz Roja** (✉ Av. Alfonso Reyes 2503, ☎ 8/375–1212).

Nuevo Laredo. Police (✉ Maclovio Herréra and Ocampo, ☎ 87/12–21–46). **Cruz Roja** (✉ Independencia 1619 and San Antonio, ☎ 87/12–09–49, 87/12–09–89).

Reynosa. Police (✉ Morelos between Veracruz and Nayarit, ☎ 89/22–00–08, 89/22–07–90). **Cruz Roja** (✉ ☎ 89/22–13–14, 89/22–62–50).

Hospital Santander (✉ Fco. Madero and Ortiz Rubyo, ☎ 89/22–96–22, 89/22–93–97).

Tampico. Police (✉ Sor Juana Inés de la Cruz and Tamaulipas, ☎ 12/12–10–32). **Cruz Roja Hospital** (✉ Tamaulipas and Colegio Militar, Zona Centro, ☎ 12/12–13–33).

Guided Tours

Sanborn's Viva Tours (✉ 2015 S. 10th St., McAllen, TX 78503, ☎ 956/682–9872, 800/395–8482 in the U.S. and Canada) runs shopping and sightseeing tours to the border towns and coach excursions into the interior, including to El Tajín (☞ State of Veracruz, *above*). **Osetur Tours** (✉ Calles San Francisco and Loma Larga, Monterrey, ☎ 8/347–1599, 8/347–1614) has sightseeing trips in the area, as does **Tours Gray Line** (✉ Av. Eugenio Garza Sada 2256, Monterrey, ☎ 8/369–6472, 8/369–6473).

Letters and E-Mail

Monterrey. The central **post office** (✉ Washington, between Zaragoza and Zuazua) is at the far northern end of Macro Plaza. **Ships 2000** (✉ Escobedo 819 Sur, ☎ 8/343–2568), above the video arcade, offers the only Internet service in the Zona Rosa and the rates are steep at $3.50 an hour. It's open daily 10–10.

Reynosa. The **post office** is on the corner of Díaz and Colón. **Cyber-space Internet Café** (⊠ Hidalgo and Allende, ☎ no phone) and **Computadores** (⊠ Allende and Av. Juárez, ☎ 89/22–55–73) offer Internet services and are generally open weekdays 9–9, weekends until 4. Both charge about $1.50 an hour.

Tampico. There's a **post office** (⊠ Madero 309 Ote.) just off the Plaza de la Libertad. **Coffee Net** (⊠ Carranza 106 Pte., ☎ 12/14–13–90) has 10 computers with Internet access for $1.50 an hour; it's open Monday through Saturday 9–9.

Pharmacies

Matamoros. Pharmacy Benavides (⊠ Av. Obregón 65, ☎ 88/12–53–78), near the International Bridge, and **Farmacia El Fenix** (⊠ Abosolo 806, ☎ 88/12–29–09) downtown are open daily 8 AM–10 PM.

Monterrey. Farmacia Benavides (⊠ Morelos 499, at Escobedo, ☎ 8/345–0257) is open daily 8 AM–10 PM.

Nuevo Laredo. For 24-hour service, use **Farmacia Calderón** (⊠ Guerrero 704, ☎ 87/12–51–77).

Reynosa. Farmacia Sucursal Aduana (⊠ Av. Alemán 115-B, ☎ 87/12–51–77) is open 24 hours.

Tampico. Off Plaza de la Libertad, **Farmacia Droguería del Pueblo** (⊠ Juárez 308 Sur, ☎ 12/12–15–42) is open daily 8 AM–9:30 PM. For service until 11 PM, try **Farmacia El Fenix** (⊠ Díaz Mirón at Olmos, ☎ 12/12–43–51), near Plaza de Armas.

Visitor Information

In the U.S. The best information about this part of Mexico is found in Texas border towns, especially at places that sell the (mandatory) Mexican automobile insurance. These include **Sanborn's Viva Tours** (⊠ 2015 S. 10th St., McAllen, TX 78503, ☎ 956/682–9872, 800/395–8482 in the U.S. and Canada), **Sanborn's Mexican Insurance** (⊠ 2009 S. 10th St., McAllen, TX 78503, ☎ 800/222–0158, FAX 956/686–0732), **Bravo Insurance** (⊠ 2212 Santa Ursula St., Laredo, TX, ☎ 956/723–3657, FAX 956/723–0000), and **Johnny Ginn's Travel** (⊠ 1845 Expressway 77, Brownsville, TX, ☎ 956/542–5457, FAX 956/504–2919). The **Brownsville Chamber of Commerce** (⊠ 1600 E. Elizabeth St., 1 block from International Bridge, ☎ 956/542–4341) is open daily 9–5.

In Mexico. Matamoros Tours-Transport (⊠ Tamaulipas and Av. Alvaro Obregón, a few blocks from International Bridge, ☎ 88/12–21–18) is open daily 8–6. **Nuevo Laredo** (⊠ Calles Herrera and Juárez, ☎ 87/12–73–97) is open daily 8–8. **Reynosa** (⊠ Puente Internacional/International Bridge, ☎ 89/22–11–89 or 89/22–24–49) is open weekdays 7:30 AM–8 PM. Also near the International Bridge, you'll find cab drivers and roving tourist-department representatives who are glad to dispense free information to travelers. **Monterrey Infotour** (⊠ Hidalgo 441 Ote., ☎ 8/345–0870, 8/345–0902, 01–800/83–222, 800/235–2438) is open Tuesday through Sunday 10–5. **Tampico** (⊠ 20 de Noviembre 218 Ote., ☎ 12/12–26–68, 12/12–00–07) is open weekdays 9–7.

13 THE YUCATÁN PENINSULA

The Yucatán Peninsula is Mexico's perennial favorite for more reasons than you can count—the high-profile sparkle of Cancún, the laid-back beachcombing of Isla Mujeres, the spectacular seas around Cozumel, the fascinating Spanish-Maya mix of Mérida, and the evocative Maya ruins of Tulum, Chichén Itzá, and Uxmal. And if the heart of nature moves your blood, there are two huge coastal eco-zones: Sian Ka'an Biosphere Reserve and Parque Natural Río Lagartos, migration stopovers for thousands of flamingos and other birds.

F OR MOST PEOPLE, Mexico's great appeal is its beaches and its ancient ruins. Cancún and the Yucatán have the best of both. Cancún is Mexico's most popular tourist mecca, and it rises against a backdrop of Maya culture—both ancient ruins and modern villages. Although much of the Yucatán Peninsula is vast, scrubby desert with a smattering of jungles and hills, its eastern coastline on the clear, turquoise waters of the Caribbean has superb natural features. In addition to a semitropical climate, the Caribbean coast has unbroken stretches of beach and the world's second-longest barrier reef, starting off the coast of Cancún and extending in its entirety down into South America. Isla Mujeres (Isle of Women) and Cozumel are also part of the Yucatán. And on the west side of the peninsula, Mérida, one of Mesoamerica's first Spanish cities, has colonial atmosphere rare in this part of Mexico.

In its entirety, the 113,000-square-km (43,600-square-mi) peninsula encompasses the Mexican states of Yucatán, Campeche, and Quintana Roo, as well as Belize and part of Guatemala. Within its bounds are tremendous bird-watching, water sports, archaeology, handicrafts, and savory Yucatecan cuisine. Above all, there are the Yucatecos themselves—short and dark like their Maya ancestors, with prominent cheekbones and aquiline noses. Veteran travelers to Mexico often remark on the openness and friendliness of these people.

As many activities as there are on the Yucatán, there is an equal range of accommodations, from the never-leave-the-site resorts of Cancún to more modest properties near the ruins and humble but adequate beach shacks. That means that you'll see a broad range of travelers: package-tour groups, backpackers, people tripping around in rental cars. International airports at Cancún and Cozumel provide nonstop service from several North American cities. The Mérida airport handles primarily domestic flights. Cruise ships call at Cozumel and Playa del Carmen, and other harbor facilities are being developed at Progreso on the north coast off the Gulf of Mexico.

Pleasures and Pastimes

Beaches

Cancún and the rest of the Yucatán have a wonderful variety of beaches: Those who thrive on the resort atmosphere will probably enjoy Playa Chacmool and Playa Tortugas on the bay side of Cancún, which is calmer, if less beautiful, than the windward side. On the north end of Isla Mujeres, Playa Norte (or Playa Cocoteros) offers handsome sunset vistas. Beaches on the relatively sheltered leeward side of Cozumel are wide and sandy. The Caribbean Coast abounds with hidden and not-so-hidden beaches—at Puerto Morelos, Playa del Secreto, Paamul, Chemuyil, Xcacel, Punta Bete, and along the Xcalak peninsula. There are also long stretches of white sand, usually filled with sunbathers, at Playa del Carmen, Akumal, and Tulum. Around Campeche and Progreso, the gulf waters are deep green, shallow, and tranquil.

Bird-Watching

The Yucatán Peninsula is one of the finest areas for birding in Mexico. Habitats range from wildlife and bird sanctuaries to unmarked lagoons, estuaries, and mangrove swamps. Frigates, tanagers, warblers, and macaws inhabit Isla Contoy (off Isla Mujeres) and the Laguna Colombia on Cozumel. There is an even greater variety of species in the Sian Ka'an Biosphere Reserve on the Boca Paila Peninsula south of Tulum. Along the north and west coasts of Yucatán—at Río Lagartos,

Laguna Rosada, and Celestún—flamingos, herons, ibis, cormorants, pelicans, and peregrine falcons thrive.

Dining

The mystique of Yucatecan cooking has a lot to do with generous doses of local spices and herbs, although generally the spices aren't too fiery hot. Among the specialties are *cochinita pibíl* and *pollo pibíl* (succulent pork or chicken baked in banana leaves with a spicy, pumpkin-seed-and-chili sauce), *poc chuc* (Yucatecan pork marinated in sour-orange sauce with pickled onions), *tikinchic* (fried fish prepared with sour orange), *panuchos* (fried tortillas filled with black beans and topped with turkey, chicken, or pork, pickled onions, and avocado), *papadzules* (tortillas stuffed with hard-boiled eggs and drenched in a sauce of pumpkin seed and fried tomato), and *codzitos* (rolled tortillas in pumpkin-seed sauce). *Achiote* (annatto), cilantro, and the fiery chili habañero are heavily favored condiments.

The following price categories apply everywhere outside of Cancún and Cozumel, which are more expensive than the rest of the Yucatán, and Isla Mujeres. We have included separate price charts in the relevant sections of this chapter.

CATEGORY	COST*
$$$$	over $20
$$$	$15–$20
$$	$8–$15
$	under $8

per person for a three-course meal, excluding drinks and service

Fishing

The rich waters of the Caribbean and the Gulf of Mexico support hundreds of species of tropical fish, making the Yucatán coastline and the outlying islands a paradise for deep-sea fishing, fly-fishing, and bonefishing. Particularly between April and July, the waters off Cancún, Cozumel, and Isla Mujeres teem with sailfish, marlin, red snapper, tuna, barracuda, and wahoo. Bill fishing is so rich around Cozumel, Isla Mujeres, Puerto Morelos, and Puerto Aventuras that each holds its own annual tournament.

Farther south, along the Boca Paila Peninsula, banana fish, bonefish, mojarra, shad, permit, and sea bass provide great sport for flat fishing and fly-fishing, while oysters, shrimp, and conch lie on the bottom of the Gulf of Mexico near Campeche and Isla del Carmen. At Progreso, on the north coast, sportfishing for grouper, dogfish, and pompano is quite popular.

Lodging

Accommodations in the Yucatán range from the ultraglitzy megaresorts of Cancún to the charming colonial mansions in Mérida and the rustic but character-filled lodgings near the ruins. The following price categories apply everywhere outside of Cancún and Cozumel, which are more expensive than the rest of the destinations in the Yucatán, and Isla Mujeres. We have included separate price charts in the relevant sections of this chapter.

CATEGORY	COST*
$$$$	over $90
$$$	$60–$90
$$	$25–$60
$	under $25

All prices are for a standard double room in the high season, excluding service charges and 17% tax.

Ruins

Amateur archaeologists will find heaven in the Yucatán. Pick your period and your preference, whether for well-excavated sites or overgrown, out-of-the-way ruins barely touched by scholars' shovels. The major Maya sites are Cobá and Tulum on the Caribbean Coast and Chichén Itzá and Uxmal in the state of Yucatán, but smaller ruins scattered throughout the peninsula are often equally fascinating.

Scuba Diving and Snorkeling

The clear turquoise waters of Cozumel, Akumal, Puerto Morelos, Isla Mujeres, and other parts of Mexico's Caribbean Coast are filled with exquisitely colored fish swimming in the brilliant coral formations. Currents allow for drift diving, and there are both reefs and offshore wrecks to dive to, many of which are safe enough for neophytes. The peninsula's cenotes (natural sinkholes) also provide unusual dive experiences.

Water Sports

Along the Yucatán's coasts, you can do it all—jet skiing, catamaran sailing, sailboarding, waterskiing, sailing, sea kayaking, parasailing.

Exploring the Yucatán Peninsula

Numbers in the text correspond to numbers in the margin and on the Cancún, Isla Mujeres, Cozumel, North Caribbean Coast, State of Yucatán, Mérida, and Campeche City maps.

Great Itineraries

If you go to the major beach resorts of Cancún and Cozumel, you are likely to settle in for the entire stay, perhaps taking side trips to the ruins of Tulum or Chichén Itzá or the city of Mérida. As for beach experiences, Cancún has a higher profile and is more expensive. Isla Mujeres tends to be more relaxed. The following itineraries are designed to keep you on the move from a base either in one of the Caribbean Coast towns or in Mérida. The first is ideal for water sports, the others for steeping yourself in Maya civilization.

IF YOU HAVE 3 DAYS

If you want to base yourself on the Caribbean Coast, get a room in **Playa del Carmen** ㉒, and start out by visiting the ruins of the Maya city of **Tulum** ㉛. Afterward, climb down to the small beach alongside it for a dip in the ocean. Day 2, head to **Xel-Há** ㉙, where you can snorkel, swim, sunbathe, and see some more modest ruins back on land. Day 3, head for **Akumal** ㉖ for diving, deep-sea fishing, snorkeling, or swimming. Later in the day visit the tiny lagoon of **Yalkú** ㉗, which was around during the time of the Maya traders.

An alternative is to spend two days in **Mérida** ㉞–㊵, savoring the city's unique character as you make your way among its historic churches and mansions, and enjoy its parks and restaurants. You can easily devote a day to exploring the heart of downtown, including the **zócalo** (main square) ㉞ and its surrounding buildings. Take a second, more leisurely day to visit the Museum of Anthropology and History in the **Palacio Cantón** ㊼ and, perhaps, the **Museo de Arte Popular** ㊽ or the **El Centenario Zoo** ㊿. On Day 3, drive or take a tour to one of Yucatán's most famous Maya ruins—**Chichén Itzá** ㊾ or **Uxmal** ㊼. Each is within about two hours of Mérida.

IF YOU HAVE 7 DAYS

Again basing yourself in **Playa del Carmen** ㉒, visit **Tulum** ㉛ on the first day, and then spend Day 2 touring **Xcaret** ㉓, a Disney-like ecological theme park. Day 3, start the morning at the Maya ruins of **Cobá** ㉜ and spend the afternoon at **Xel-Há** ㉙, cooling off in the water. Day 4, head for **Akumal** ㉖ and its water sports. Day 5, sign up for a tour of the

Sian Ka'an Biosphere Reserve ㉝. On Days 6 and 7, head west for the colonial city of **Mérida** ㉞–㊿. Spend one day in the city and the next out at **Chichén Itzá** (52) or **Uxmal** (57).

On a weeklong trip in and around Mérida, take in the city's sights first and then take two separate overnight excursions. First, head for Uxmal and overnight at one of the nearby archaeological hotels. The next day explore the Ruta Puuc, the series of lost cities south of Uxmal that includes **Kabah, Sayil,** and **Labná,** as well as the fascinating **Loltún Caves.** On the second excursion, to Chichén Itzá, allow as much as a full day en route to explore some of the present-day Maya villages along the way, especially **Izamal** (51). After seeing the Chichén Itzá ruins, beat the afternoon heat in the **Cave of Balancanchén** (54) or on a swim in one of the cool subterranean cenotes nearby. An alternate side trip—go north of **Valladolid** (55) to see the flamingo nesting grounds at **Parque Natural Río Lagartos** (56).

IF YOU HAVE 10 DAYS

With even more time, consider continuing from **Mérida** ㉞–㊿ to **Campeche City** (59)–(78). After spending a day seeing the city's sights—almost all those of interest are within the compact historic district—head inland the next morning to **Edzná,** a magnificently restored ceremonial center an hour's drive from the city. Return to your Campeche City hotel and set out the next day to the **Hopelchén** region, beyond Edzná, where you can explore the little-known Maya temples at **Hochob** and **Dzibilnocac,** as well as **Las Grutas de Xtacumbilxunaan** near **Bolonchén de Rejón,** one of the large cave systems on the peninsula.

When to Tour the Yucatán Peninsula

Thousands of people swarm to Chichén Itzá for the vernal equinox on the first day of spring to see the astronomical phenomenon that makes a shadow resembling a snake—which represented the plumed serpent god Kukulcán—appear on the side of the main pyramid. The phenomenon also occurs on the first day of fall, but the rainy autumnal weather tends to discourage visitors. Both the capital and outlying villages of Campeche state celebrate the Day of the Dead (November 1–2) with special fervor because it corresponds to a similar observance in ancient Maya tradition.

High season in the states of Yucatán and Campeche generally corresponds to high season in the rest of Mexico: Christmastime, Easter week, and July and August. Rainfall is heaviest and—humidity most uncomfortable—from May to October or November. On the Caribbean Coast, including Cancún, Cozumel, and Isla Mujeres, the peak tourist times are mid-December through late March. In less visited towns, levels of service differ drastically between the high and low seasons (when staff and activities may be cut back), so be prepared for the trade-off. The rainy season isn't a bad time to visit if you don't mind the afternoon showers and the sometimes reduced tourist attentions. On the coast, hurricane season is September–October.

CANCÚN

Updated by Shelagh McNally

If you want dazzle for your dollar, Cancún is the place, with beachside high-rise hotels, glitzy discos, air-conditioned malls, and miles and miles of sand. For a glimpse of a more "real" Mexico, head downtown to the markets and restaurants for a taste of authentic Yucatecan specialties.

Flying into Cancún, you see nothing but green treetops for miles. It's clear from the air that this resort was literally carved out of the jungle. When development began here in 1974, the beaches were deserted except for birds and iguanas. Now luxury hotels, shopping malls, and restaurants line Cancún's oceanfront. More vacationers come here than to any other part of Mexico, and many come again and again for the white-sand beaches, crystalline turquoise waters, sizzling nightlife, numerous restaurants, and the proximity of Maya ruins.

Cancún has two very different sides. On the mainland is the actual Ciudad Cancún (Cancún City), the commercial center that is also informally known as El Centro. The other half, the Zona Hotelera (Hotel Zone), is the tourist mecca. The Zone is actually a 22½-km (14-mi) barrier island off the Yucatán Peninsula. It has evolved into a resort that pleases average American tastes: most people speak English, and there are fast-food outlets, cable TV, and brand-name stores. Shopping, eating, and lounging in the year-round tropical warmth are the main activities. (The sun shines an average of 240 days a year, reputedly more than at almost any other Caribbean spot. Temperatures linger at about 80°F.) At night you can enjoy the variety of activities, including knocking back tequila slammers at a bar, listening to great music at clubs, watching folkloric dance performances, and sampling Yucatecan food.

But there is more to Cancún than plopping yourself down under a *palapa* (thatched roof). Downtown offers a more authentic glimpse into the sights and sounds of Mexico. For diving and snorkeling, the reefs off Cancún and nearby Cozumel, Puerto Morelos, and Isla Mujeres are among the best in the world. Cancún also makes a relaxing base for venturing to the stupendous ruins of Chichén Itzá, Tulum, and Cobá.

The most important buildings in Cancún, however, are the modern hotels. The resort has followed the typical course of any tourist resort area, first attracting the jet set and gradually welcoming less affluent tourists. Today there are large numbers of package tourists and college students, particularly during spring break when hordes of tanned young bodies fill the beaches and restaurants.

As for Cancún's history, not much was written about it before its birth as a resort. The Maya people did settle the area during the Pre-Classic era, around AD 200, and remained until the 14th or 15th century. But little is known about them. Other explorers seem to have overlooked the barrier island. It doesn't appear on early navigators' maps. It was never heavily populated, perhaps because its terrain of mangroves and marshes discouraged settlement. Some minor Maya ruins were discovered in the mid-19th century, but archaeologists didn't get around to studying them until the 1950s. In 1967, the Mexican government, under the leadership of Luis Echeverría, commissioned a study to pinpoint the ideal place for an international Caribbean resort. The computer choose Cancún, and the transformation began. At the time the area's only residents were the three caretakers of a coconut plantation. In 1972 work began on the first hotel, and the island and city grew from there. Today there are more than 25,000 hotel rooms in the Zona Hotelera alone.

Success has come with a price. Cancún's natural environment has suffered. Its lagoons and mangrove swamps have been polluted, and a number of species, such as conch and lobster, are dwindling. Parts of the coral reef are dead. Although the beaches still appear pristine for the most part, an increased effort will have to be made in order to preserve the physical beauty that is the resort's prime appeal.

Exploring

Cancún is divided into two parts: the hotel zone, Zona Hotelera, a numeral 7–shaped island; and Cancún City or downtown Cancún, known as El Centro, 4 km (2½ mi) west of the hotel zone on the mainland.

Boulevard Kukulcán is the main drag in the hotel zone, and since the island is less than 1 km (½ mi) wide, you can see both the Caribbean and the lagoons from either side of it. The hotel zone consists entirely of hotels, restaurants, shopping complexes, marinas, and time-share condominiums, with few residential areas. It's not the sort of place you can get to know by walking, although there is now a bicycle/walking path that starts at the Convention Center, ending downtown.

A Good Tour

Cancún's scenery consists mostly of its beautiful beaches and crystal-clear waters, but there are also a few intriguing historical sites tucked away among the modern hotels. In addition to the attractions listed below, two modest vestiges of the ancient Maya civilization are worth a visit for dedicated archaeology buffs. Neither is identified by name. On the 12th hole of Pok-Ta-Pok golf course (⊠ Blvd. Kukulcán Km 6.5)—the name means ball game in Maya—stands a ruin consisting of two platforms and the remains of other buildings. And the ruin of a tiny Maya shrine is cleverly incorporated into the architecture of the Hotel Camino Real, on the beach at Punta Cancún.

You don't need a car in Cancún, but if you've rented one to make extended trips, start in the southern Hotel Zone at **Ruinas del Rey** ① and **San Miguelito** ②, drive north to **Yamil Lu'um** ③, and then stop in at the **Cancún Convention Center** ④ before heading west to **El Centro** ⑤.

Sights to See

④ **Cancún Convention Center.** This strikingly modern venue for cultural events is the jumping-off point for a 1-km-long (½-mi-long) string of shopping malls that extends west to the Presidente Inter-Continental Cancún. In the Convention Center complex itself, **Inter Plaza** contains 15 restaurants, 21 boutiques, a bank, and several airline offices. ⊠ *Blvd. Kukulcán Km 9,* ☎ *98/83–01–99.*

The **National Institute of Anthropology and History,** a small museum on the ground floor of the Convention Center, traces Maya culture with a fascinating collection of 1,000- to 1,500-year-old artifacts collected throughout Quintana Roo. ⊠ *Blvd. Kukulcán Km 9,* ☎ *98/83–03–05.* 🎟 *About $3, free Sun.* ⊙ *Tues.–Sun. 9–7. Guided tours in English, French, German, and Spanish.*

⑤ **El Centro** (Downtown Cancún). Markets offer a glimpse into a more provincial Mexico. The main street, **Avenida Tulum,** is easily recognizable for the huge seashell sculpture in the roundabout, which adds drama to the city when lit up at night. Many restaurants and shops are located along this street. **Ki Huic** is the largest crafts market in Cancún. If you're looking for shopping bargains, however, you'll generally find better prices on the parallel **Avenida Yaxchilán,** particularly in **Mercado Veinteocho** (Market 28). Just off Avenida Yaxchilán and Sunyaxchén, this is the hub of downtown, filled with shops and restaurants frequented by locals.

⛰ ① **Ruinas del Rey** (Ruins of the King). Large signs on the Zone's lagoon side, roughly opposite the Playa de Oro and El Pueblito hotels, point out these small ruins, which have been incorporated into the Caesar Park Beach & Golf Resort complex. Skeletons interred both at the apex and at the base indicate the site may have been a royal burial ground. ⊠ *Blvd. Kukulcán Km 17,* ☎ *no phone.* 🎟 *About $3, free Sun.* ⊙ *Daily 8–5.*

⛰ ② **San Miguelito.** On the east side of Boulevard Kukulcán is a very small stone building, about the size of a shack, with a number of columns about 4 ft high. Local archaeologists have plans to do more work on this site. ⊠ *Blvd. Kukulcán Km 16.5,* ☎ *no phone.*

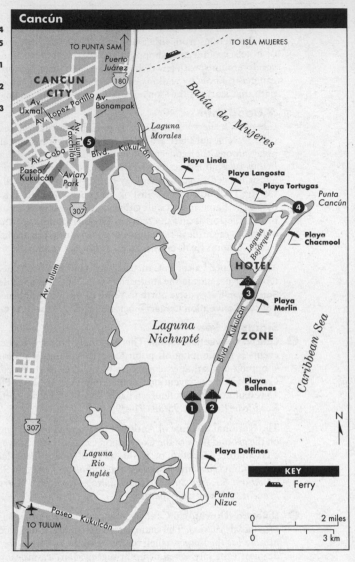

Cancún

TO PUNTA SAM

TO ISLA MUJERES

Puerto
Juárez

180

CANCÚN
CITY

Av. Uxmal

Av. López Portillo

Av. Bonampak

Av. Tulum Yaxchilán

Laguna
Morales

5

Blvd. Kukulcán

Av. Cobá

Paseo
Kukulcán

Aviary
Park

307

Playa Linda

Playa Langosta

Playa Tortugas

Punta
Cancún

4

Playa
Chacmool

Bahía de Mujeres

Laguna
Bojórquez

HOTEL

3

Playa
Merlin

Av. Tulum

Laguna
Nichupté

ZONE

Blvd. Kukulcán

Caribbean Sea

Playa
Ballenas

1 2

307

Laguna
Rio
Inglés

Playa Delfines

N

Punta
Nizuc

KEY

Ferry

Paseo Kukulcán

TO TULUM

0   2 miles

0   3 km

🔺 **3** **Yamil Lu'um.** A small sign at the Sheraton will direct you to the dirt
path leading to this site, which stands on the highest point of Cancún.
The name Yamil Lu'um means "hilly land." Although it comprises two
structures—one probably a temple, the other probably a lighthouse—
this is the smallest of Cancún's ruins. ⊠ *Blvd. Kukulcán Km 12,* ☎
no phone.

Dining

With more than 1,200 restaurants in Cancún, finding the right restaurant might be the hardest work you do while on vacation. Both the
Hotel Zone and downtown have plenty of great places to eat. There
are some pitfalls: restaurants that line noisy Avenida Tulum often have
tables spilling onto sidewalks, with gas fumes and hordes of people de-
tracting from the romantic outdoor-café ambience. In the Hotel Zone,
restaurants often cater to what they assume is a tourist preference for
bland, not-too-foreign-tasting food.

One key to eating well in Cancún is to find the local haunts, most of which are in the downtown area. Parque de las Palapas, just off Avenida Tulum, is where locals go for Yucatecan-style food prepared by experts. Farther into the city center, you can find the freshest seafood and other traditional Mexican fare at Mercado 28. There are dozens of small restaurants there that serve great food at reasonable prices.

Sumptuous breakfast or brunch buffets are the latest Cancún dining trend. They are especially pleasant at palapa restaurants on the beach. With prices ranging from $7 to $15, the brunches are a good value. Eat on the late side and you won't need to eat again until dinner.

Generally speaking, dress is casual here, but many restaurants will not allow bare feet, short shorts, or no shirts. At more upscale restaurants, wear pants or a skirt or dress instead of shorts for dinner. Unless otherwise stated, restaurants serve lunch and dinner daily.

CATEGORY	COST*
$$$$	over $40
$$$	$25–$40
$$	$15–$25
$	under $15

per person, excluding drinks and service

Hotel Zone
Hotel Zone restaurants are located on the Cancún Hotel Zone Dining and Lodging map.

$$$$ ★ ✕ **Club Grill.** Simply the best. The intimate dining rooms of Cancún's Ritz-Carlton (☞ Hotel Zone *in* Lodging, *below*) are the hands-down favorite for exceptional food and romantic dining. The elegant rooms have tall windows overlooking a courtyard fountain. Classic dishes have been given a distinctly Mexican flavor. The sautéed foie gras with caramelized mango is a good starter, followed by the bean and lentil soup with habañero chili. Don't forget the wickedly delicious desserts. The live jazz accompanying your meal is the best you will hear in Cancún. ⊠ *Blvd. Kukulcán (Retorno del Rey 36),* ☎ 98/85–08–08. AE, MC, V. *No lunch.*

$$$$ ✕ **La Dolce Vita.** The grande dame of Cancún restaurants, this place is loved by many. The kitchen uses the finest ingredients in creative ways to produce superbly presented variations on classic Italian dishes. It has a romantic, casual elegance enhanced by the incredible view of Laguna Nichupté, especially on a full-moon night. Favorites from the excellent Northern Italian menu include *boquinete dolce vita* (snapper in puff pastry) and veal ravioli in rosemary sauce. ⊠ *Blvd. Kukulcán Km 14.5, across from the Marriott Hotel,* ☎ 98/85–01–50, 98/85–01–61. AE, MC, V.

$$$$ ★ ✕ **The Plantation House.** Cancún's latest gourmet sensation, this restaurant re-creates the plantation era of the Caribbean. A clever design has the lounge/bar overlooking the dining room. Classical piano music adds to the refined atmosphere. Among the inspired seafood dishes is lobster au gratin with coconut and pineapple. For more exotic fare, try the marinated pheasant. There is also a superb wine list. Expect a memorable meal. ⊠ *Blvd. Kukulcán Km 10.5,* ☎ 98/85–14–55, 83–21–20. *Reservations essential.* AE, MC, V. *No lunch.*

$$$ ★ ✕ **La Destileria.** Be prepared to have your perceptions about tequila changed forever. This combination restaurant and tequila museum has more than 100 kinds of tequila available by the glass—or opt for the impressive margaritas. The traditional Northern Mexican food is served by seriously charming waiters. The *sopa de elote* (spiced corn soup) is a delicious appetizer; the *pescado con flor de calabaza* (fish

with pumpkin flowers) is a tasty main course. The title of the dessert menu, "Favorite Sins," says it all. ⊠ *Blvd. Kukulcán Km 12.65 (across from Kukulcán Plaza)*, ☎ *98/83–10–87. AE, MC, V.*

$$$ ✕ **Lorenzillos.** Named after a 17th-century pirate, this is one of the handsomest waterfront restaurants in the Hotel Zone. Built right on the water with an outdoor terrace overlooking the lagoon, it's the perfect spot to watch the sun set. It has its own lobster farm, so the delicacy is offered year-round. The soft-shell crab and whole fish Veracruz style are also great. ⊠ *Blvd. Kukulcán Km 10.5,* ☎ *98/83–12–54. MC, V.*

$$$ ✕ **Maria Bonita.** Here is the authentic Mexico in food, music, and atmo-
★ sphere. This delightful restaurant overlooking the water is divided into sections named after three states of Mexico: Jalisco, Michoacán, and Oaxaca. The menu includes food from these areas, as well as other Mexican specialties. Worth trying are the various mole dishes or the four-chili beef fillet. This is a fine place to learn about Mexican cuisine. The menu even explains the different chilies the kitchen uses. The service matches the wonderful food. ⊠ *Hotel Camino Real, Punta Cancún,* ☎ *98/83–17–30. MC, V. No lunch.*

$$ ✕ **The Captain's Cove.** There are two Cancún branches of this restaurant. Both have waterfront locations and serve vast, inexpensive breakfast buffets. The decor is decidedly nautical. The restaurant near the Casa Maya Hotel overlooks the Caribbean. The other is beside the Nichupté Lagoon. Both have lunch and dinner menus filled with seafood dishes and charbroiled steak. Parents appreciate the lower-priced children's menu, an unusual feature in Cancún. ⊠ *Blvd. Kukulcán Km 16.5, lagoon side across from Royal Mayan Hotel,* ☎ *98/85–00–16; beach side next to Casa Maya Hotel,* ☎ *98/85–00–16. AE, MC, V.*

$$ ✕ **Cenacola.** This is a favorite neighborhood restaurant, perfect for lunch
★ or dinner. The interior is quiet, decorated with Italian art and stained glass. Outside is a bustling, plant-filled patio overlooking Boulevard Kukulcán. The food is consistently marvelous. Highlights include the salad of mixed greens, ricotta ravioli, lasagna with béchamel, and sliced filet mignon in balsamic vinegar. The staff is lovely and will spoil you completely. ⊠ *Kukulcán Plaza,* ☎ *98/85–36–03. AE, MC, V.*

$ ✕ **100% Natural.** Looking for something healthy? Head to one of the four locations of this cheery open-air restaurant. All have identical menus with special appeal to vegetarians: soups, fruit and veggie salads, fresh fruit drinks, and other nonmeat items. Also look for egg dishes, sandwiches, and grilled chicken and fish. The branch at Plaza Terramar is open around the clock. ⊠ *Blvd. Kukulcán at Kukulcán Plaza,* ☎ *98/ 85–29–04;* ⊠ *Plaza Terramar,* ☎ *98/83–11–80;* ⊠ *Forum Plaza, Blvd. Kukulcán Km 9.5,* ☎ *no phone;* ⊠ *Downtown: Av. Sunyaxchen 62,* ☎ *98/84–36–17. Reservations not accepted. AE, MC, V.*

Downtown

Downtown restaurants are located on the Downtown Cancún Dining and Lodging map.

$$$ ✕ **La Habichuela** (The Green Bean). Once an elegant home, this Can-
★ cún landmark is now an enchanting garden restaurant decorated with Maya sculpture. The garden, lit up at night, is bewitching. Don't miss the famous *crema de habichuela* (a rich, cream-based seafood soup) or the *cocobichuela* (lobster and shrimp in a light curry sauce served inside a coconut). Finish off your meal with Xtabentun (Maya coffee). ⊠ *Margaritas 25, Sm 22,* ☎ *98/84–31–58. AE, DC, MC, V.*

$$ ✕ **Bisquets Obregon.** With its cheery colors, two levels of tables, and
★ sit-down luncheon counter, this cafeteria-style spot is *the* place to have breakfast downtown. Begin your day with hearty Mexican classics such as *huevos rancheros* (eggs sunnyside-up on tortillas, covered with tomato sauce) or *huaraches* (thick tortillas with a variety of toppings).

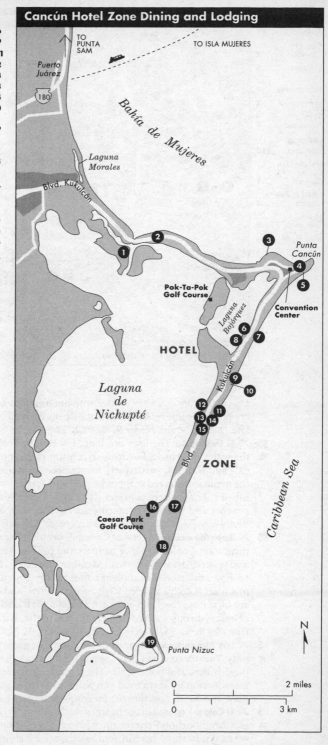

Cancún Hotel Zone Dining and Lodging

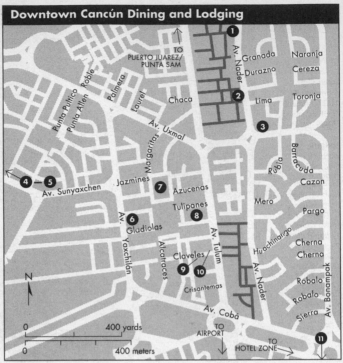

Downtown Cancún Dining and Lodging

Dining

Los Almendros ..11

Bisquets Obregon 2

El Cejas 5

La Habichuela ...7

El Pescador ..8

Rosa Mexicano 9

Lodging

Antillano ...10

Holiday Inn Centro Cancún 1

Hotel el Rey Caribe 3

Hotel Tankah 4

Mex Hotel ...6

Do try the *cafe con leche* (coffee with hot milk). Just watching the waiters pour it is impressive. The place opens early (7 AM) and stays open late (1 AM). ⊠ *Av. Nader 9,* ☎ 98/87–68–76, 98/87–68–77. *MC, V.*

$$ ✕ **El Pescador.** The lines are long, but the the seafood here is worth
★ the wait. This rustic, Mexican-style restaurant is popular with both locals and tourists, particularly for its open-air patio. Heavy hitters on the menu include red snapper broiled with garlic, and charcoal-broiled lobster. For dessert consider sharing ice-cream cake covered with peaches and strawberry marmalade. ⊠ *Av. Tulipanes 28, Sm 22,* ☎ 98/84–26–73. *Reservations not accepted. AE, MC, V.*

$$ ✕ **Rosa Mexicano.** At one of Cancún's prettiest Mexican colonial–style restaurants, colorful paper banners and piñatas hang from the ceiling, and waiters dress as *charros* (Mexican cowboys). For extra romance, reserve a table on the candlelit patio. Savory appetizers include *nopalitos* (cactus strips sautéed with corn, cilantro, and cheese). Specialties are *filete* Rosa (beef and onions in a tequila-orange sauce) and *camarones al ajillo* (shrimp sautéed in olive oil and garlic, with chili peppers). ⊠ *Claveles 4,* ☎ 98/84–63–13. *AE, DC, MC, V. No lunch.*

$ ✕ **Los Almendros.** Illustrations take some of guesswork out of the to-
★ tally Yucatecan menu here. Specialities include lime soup, poc chuc, papadzules, and pollo pibíl. The service is excellent. This is the best introduction to Maya food you will find in these parts. ⊠ *Av. Bonampark and Sayil, opposite the bullring,* ☎ 98/87–13–32. *AE.*

$ ✕ **El Cejas.** Located in the heart of the bustling, lively Mercado 28, this
★ is a neighborhood restaurant with an international reputation. The seafood is fresh, wonderful, and half the price it is elsewhere. Their cocktail Vuelva la Vida (Return to Life) really does have restorative powers. ⊠ *Mercado 28, Av. Sunyaxchen,* ☎ *no phone. No credit cards.*

Lodging

Cancún has a bewildering variety of hotels to choose from. For the most part the downtown hotels don't offer anything near the luxury or amenities of the Hotel Zone properties. They will, however, give you the opportunity to stay in a popular resort without paying resort prices, and many places have free shuttle service to the beach. At downtown hotels you'll also be closer to Ki Huic, Cancún's crafts market, and restaurants that are more authentic—and less costly—than what you'll find in the Zone.

Expect minibars, satellite TV, laundry and room service, private safes (check to see if there is an extra charge for safe use), and bathroom hair dryers in hotels in the $$$$ category; in addition almost every major hotel has suites, rooms for people with disabilities, no-smoking rooms, an in-house travel agency and/or a car-rental concession, guest parking, water-sports facilities, beauty salon and spa, fully equipped gymnasium, and a daily schedule of games and activities for guests. Unless otherwise noted, all hotels have air-conditioning and private baths. Hotel Zone hotels have a beach unless otherwise indicated. All Cancún hotels are within the 77500 postal code.

CATEGORY	COST*
$$$$	over $200
$$$	$120–$200
$$	$50–$120
$	under $50

*All prices are for a standard double room, excluding 12% tax.

Hotel Zone

Hotels in this section appear on the Cancún Hotel Zone Dining and Lodging map.

$$$$ ★   **Baccará.** Beautiful rooms are furnished individually with authentic Mexican pieces and art. Living and dining rooms overlook the ocean, and all guest rooms have fully equipped kitchens. The lobby is intimate and informally elegant. The lovely bar leads out to the artfully designed pool area. The staff only adds to the warmth Baccará exudes. ⊠ *Blvd. Kukulcán Km 11.5,* ☎ *98/83–20–77, 888/784–2801,* ℻ *98/83–21–73. 34 rooms. 3 restaurants, 3 bars, pool, car rental. AE, DC, MC, V.* ✍

$$$$ **Caesar Park Beach & Golf Resort.** Liberal use of Mérida marble, Mexican tile murals, and colorful oil paintings give this appealing Westin property a distinctly Mexican flavor. The guest rooms continue the theme with terra-cotta tile floors, rattan furniture, and local artwork. Some have a private balcony with a view of the ocean. A few let you see the championship 18-hole golf course across Boulevard Kukulcán. Seven interconnecting pools wind through palm-dotted lawns. The Royal Beach Club section comprises 80 luxurious oceanfront villas with extra-spacious rooms. ⊠ *Blvd. Kukulcán Km 17 (Apdo. 1810),* ☎ *98/81–80–00, 800/228–3000,* ℻ *98/81–80–80. 426 rooms, 4 suites. 3 restaurants, 3 bars, lobby lounge, 7 pools, beauty salon, 2 hot tubs, 2 saunas, 18-hole golf course, 2 tennis courts, aerobics, exercise room, shops, children's programs. AE, DC, MC, V.* ✍

$$$$ **Meliá Cancún.** This boldly modern version of a Maya temple is flanked by a sheer black marble wall and a sleek waterfall. The ultrachic atrium has lush tropical flora dappled with sunlight, which floods in from corner windows and the pyramid skylight overhead. The luxurious guest rooms have private balconies or terraces. The upscale spa has an array of pampering and rejuvenating body treatments. ⊠ *Blvd. Kukulcán Km 16,* ☎ *98/81–11–00, 800/336–3542,* ℻ *98/85–12–63. 536 rooms, 10*

suites. 5 restaurants, 3 bars, 2 pools, spa, 18-hole golf course, 3 tennis courts, health club, paddle tennis, shops. AE, DC, MC, V. ☜

$$$$ 🏨 **Le Meridien.** The newest luxury hotel in Cancún is refined yet re-
★ laxed. The architecture is an updated Art Deco style, with subtle Maya influences. High on a hill, the property offers rooms with spectacular views. The gigantic spa (the best in town) offers the newest European techniques and equipment and a state-of-the-art gymnasium that over-looks an outdoor Jacuzzi and waterfall. Fine dining can be found at Côté Sud. ⊠ *Retorno Del Rey Lote 37,* ☎ *98/81–22–00, 800/225–5843,* FAX *98/81–22–01. 187 rooms, 24 suites, 2 presidential suites. 3 restaurants, 2 bars, 3 pools, hot tub, spa, 2 tennis courts, health club, children's programs (ages 5–12), shops. AE, MC, V.* ☜

$$$$ 🏨 **Ritz-Carlton Cancún.** Ultraposh, ornate, and sumptuous, the Ritz
★ radiates an Old World elegance with a lobby richly appointed with thick carpets, plush furniture, and fine European and American antiques and oil paintings. Rooms have large balconies overlooking the Caribbean. Travertine marble bathrooms are fitted with telephones and separate tubs and showers. The hotel's elegant restaurants, especially the Club Grill (☞ Hotel Zone *in* Dining, *above*) and Fantino (which serves North-ern Italian dinners), are standouts. ⊠ *Blvd. Kukulcán, Retorno del Rey 36,* ☎ *98/85–08–08, 800/241–3333,* FAX *98/85–10–15. 365 rooms, 40 suites. 3 restaurants, 2 bars, 3 pools, hot tub, spa, 3 tennis courts, health club, pro shop, shops. AE, DC, MC, V.* ☜

$$$$ 🏨 **Westin Regina Resort Cancún.** A location on the southern end of the Hotel Zone on Punta Nizuc gives this luxury resort more seclusion than many other Hotel Zone properties. The low-rise, postmodern-style hotel was designed by one of Latin America's leading architects, Ricardo Legorreta. From the lobby you can look down on a stylish restaurant with stunning ocean views. The rooms are even more elegant. This is one of the few hotels with direct access to both a 1,600-ft beach and Laguna Nichupté. ⊠ *Blvd. Kukulcán Km 20 (Apdo. 1808),* ☎ *98/85–00–86, 98/85–05–37, 800/228–3000,* FAX *98/85–00–74. 293 rooms, 24 suites. 4 restaurants, 3 bars, 5 pools, 6 hot tubs, 2 tennis courts, exer-cise room, children's programs (ages 4–12). AE, MC, V.* ☜

$$$ 🏨 **Hyatt Regency Cancún.** A cylindrical 14-story tower with the Hyatt trademark—a striking central atrium filled with tropical greenery and topped by a sky-lighted dome—affords a 360° view of the sea and the lagoon. This hotel, much larger and livelier than its sister property far-ther south in the Zone, has an enormous two-level pool with a wa-terfall. Cilantro, the hotel's pretty waterfront dining room, serves a good breakfast buffet. ⊠ *Blvd. Kukulcán (Apdo. 1201),* ☎ *98/83–09–66, 98/83–12–34, 800/233–1234,* FAX *98/83–14–38. 300 rooms. 2 restau-rants, 3 bars, pool, health club, recreation room. AE, MC, V.* ☜

$$$ 🏨 **Piramides Cancún.** These twin pyramids were formerly an often-over-
★ looked part of the Sheraton hotel. New management and renovations in 1999 have created a hotel that sometimes surpasses its parent. Stan-dard suites have two double beds and full baths. Each of the Ambas-sador suites has a kitchen, a living room/dining room, three double beds, and a full bath. Some have a private Jacuzzi and terrace either facing the lagoon or the ocean. The beachside presidential suite has a remarkable view of the Maya ruin Yamil Lu'um. The property also has two pools joined by a waterfall, a lovely beach, and a well-stocked, reasonably priced grocery store. ⊠ *Blvd. Kukulcán Km 12.5,* ☎ *98/85–13–33,* FAX *98/85–01–13. 232 rooms, 54 suites. Restaurant, bar, 2 pools, ex-ercise room, shops, children's program (ages 4–12), travel services. AE, MC, V.* ☜

$$$ 🏨 **El Pueblito Beach Hotel.** El Pueblito, which means "little town," is
★ a sweet name and a perfect description for this all-inclusive property, built on hill above the sea with clusters of guest rooms in tri-level units

that evoke Old Mexico. Pathways lined with tropical foliage lead to terrace pools with waterfalls and stone archways. There's also a long, separate water slide for children. Rooms, which are large for the price, have marble floors and simple rattan furnishings. A few have kitchenettes. Ask for an oceanfront room. ⊠ *Blvd. Kukulcán Km 17.5,* ☎ *98/85–88–00,* FAX *98/85–07–31. 239 rooms. 3 restaurants, bar, 5 pools, tennis court, shops, travel services. AE, MC, V.*

$$ 🏨 **Club Las Velas.** Delightfully private, Las Velas is a replica of a Mex-
★ ican village, complete with central plaza, fountains, and lush gardens. Winding stone pathways connect the Mexican colonial–style attached villas and four five-story towers with the Laguna Nichupté beachfront, palapa restaurant, and pools. Tower rooms from the second floor up all have balconies. The duplex villas are especially suited to families. ⊠ *Blvd. Kukulcán and Galeon,* ☎ *98/83–22–22, 800/707–8815,* FAX *98/83–21–18. 226 rooms, 59 villas. 2 restaurants, 2 bars, snack bar, 2 pools, 2 tennis courts, aerobics, exercise room, shops, children's programs (ages 3–12). AE, MC, V.*

Downtown

Downtown hotels appear on the Downtown Cancún Dining and Lodging map.

$$ 🏨 **Antillano.** Right on the main strip, this pleasant hotel is beautifully
★ maintained and stands out from the others in its league. Each room is fitted with wood furnishings, one or two double beds, a sink area separate from the bath, red-tile floors, and a small television. There is a cozy little lobby bar and decent-size pool. The quietest rooms are those facing the interior—avoid the noisier rooms that face Avenida Tulum. ⊠ *Av. Tulum at Claveles,* ☎ *98/84–15–32,* FAX *98/84–18–78. 48 rooms. Pool, shops, baby-sitting services. AE, DC, MC, V.*

$$ 🏨 **Holiday Inn Centro Cancún.** This is the place to stay if you want to
★ be downtown, close to restaurants and shops, but still have all the luxury hotel amenities. It's less expensive than similar properties in the Hotel Zone, and it provides free transportation to the Crown Princess Club beach. The attractive pink four-story building houses rooms that are motel modern, with appealing Mexican touches. All rooms overlook the terrific pool. ⊠ *Av. Nader 1, Sm 2,* ☎ *98/87–44–55, 800/465–4329,* FAX *98/84–79–54. 246 rooms. 2 restaurants, 2 bars, pool, beauty salon, tennis court, exercise room, nightclub, coin laundry, travel services, car rental. AE, DC, MC, V.* ✧

$$ 🏨 **Hotel El Rey del Caribe.** A marvel in downtown Cancún, El Rey del
★ Caribe has been designed to have zero impact on the environment, in part by using solar energy for electricity, a water-recycling plan, and special composting toilets. And its luxurious garden, which blocks the heat and noise of downtown, makes it an oasis. Rooms are on the small side, but are pleasant and have convenient kitchenettes. The hotel is within walking distance of all downtown shops and restaurants. ⊠ *Corner of Uxmal and Nader,* ☎ *98/84–20–28,* FAX *98/84–98–57. 26 rooms. Pool, hot tub. AE, MC, V.*

$$ 🏨 **Mex Hotel.** This three-story Spanish colonial–style hotel has a small shopping plaza that fronts the busy street. Rooms are in back, decorated with pleasant Mexican touches: tile floors, terra-cotta pottery, and textiles in tasteful earth tones. Within walking distance of restaurants, shops, and open-air concerts in the Parque de las Palapas, it's extremely popular with students, Europeans, and Canadians. ⊠ *Av. Yaxchilán 31,* ☎ *98/84–30–78, 800/221–6509,* FAX *98/34–78–81. 81 rooms. Restaurant, bar, pool. AE, DC, MC, V.*

$ 🏨 **Hotel Tankah.** Minutes away from Mercado 28, this basic hotel boasts
★ some lovely Mexican architecture in the lobby. Rooms are simply furnished. All offer local TV, decent beds, and bathrooms. Some have a

small sitting room. The property is quite secure. ⊠ *Av. Tankah 69,* ☎ *98/84–44–46,* ℻ *98/84–48–44. 40 rooms. MC, V.*

Nightlife and the Arts

The Arts

The **Casa de Cultura** (⊠ Prol. Av. Yaxchilán, Sm 21, ☎ 98/84–83–64) hosts local cultural events, such as art exhibits, dance performances, plays, and concerts throughout the year.

FESTIVALS

Cancún's **Jazz Festival** is an annual weeklong event in late May that draws a huge international crowd from the United States, South America, and Europe. The Cancún Hotel Association (⊠ Av. Ign. García de la Torre, Sm 1, Lote 6, Cancún, Quintana Roo, 77500, ☎ 98/84–70–83) can provide information about this popular gathering.

Each November the state of Quintana Roo hosts the **Caribbean Culture Festival.** Cancún and other regional cities present a series of events that range from Caribbean music to readings by Mexican poets and exhibits by Latin American painters and sculptors. The real draw, however, is the variety of salsa music, performed by groups from throughout the Caribbean. Consult your hotel's concierge for event schedules.

PERFORMANCES

The **Ballet Folklórico de Cancún** performs nightly at the Convention Center (⊠ Blvd. Kukulcán Km 9, ☎ 98/83–01–99). This popular ballet folklórico dinner show has upbeat music and dances from across Mexico. Cocktails are at 6:30; dinner, a typical Mexican buffet, is at 7; and the dance production goes on at 8. Tickets start at around $35.

Nightlife

Nightlife happens all over Cancún in a variety of places. Numerous restaurants do double duty as party centers; discos offer music (sometimes taped, sometimes live) and light shows; and most nightclubs have live music and dancing.

DINNER CRUISES

AquaWorld's **Cancún Queen** (⊠ AquaWorld Marina, Blvd. Kukulcán Km 15.2, ☎ 98/85–22–88) is the only paddle wheeler in Mexico. It offers cruises of the lagoon, complete with a three-course dinner, starting at $65. The 62-ft galleon **Columbus** (⊠ Royal Yacht Club, Blvd. Kukulcán Km 16.6, ☎ 98/83–14–88) offers Lobster Dinner Cruises at sunset (5 PM) and star cruises at 8 PM. **Pirates Night** (⊠ Playa Langosta Dock, Blvd. Kukulcán Km 5.5, ☎ 98/83–14–88) offers trips to Treasure Island and a buffet dinner. Children under 12 are half–price. The modern sailboat is decked out like a pirate ship, the crew like pirates. Reservations are recommended for all dinner cruises.

DISCOS

Cancún wouldn't be Cancún without its glittering discos, which generally start jumping about 10:30. **Christine** (⊠ Krystal Cancún Hotel, ☎ 98/83–17–93) is the grande dame of the disco scene and puts on an incredible light show. The wild, wild **Coco Bongo** (⊠ Blvd. Kukulcán Km 9.5, across the street from Dady'O, ☎ 98/83–05–92) has no chairs, and everyone dances on the spot or on top of their tables. **Dady'O** (⊠ Blvd. Kukulcán Km 9.5, ☎ 98/83–33–33) has been around for a while but is still a very *in* place. **Dady Rock** (⊠ Blvd. Kukulcán Km 9.5, ☎ 98/83–33–33) draws a high-energy crowd with live music, a giant screen, contests, and food specials. The high-tech **Liquid Club** (⊠ Blvd. Kukulcán Km 9.5, Party Center, ☎ 98/83–31–47) is a disco with high-tech lighting and sound. **Fat Tuesday** (⊠ Blvd. Kukulcán Km 6.5, ☎ 98/82–26–76) has a large daiquiri bar and live and taped disco music. Two new dance clubs have opened at La Isla Shopping Village (⊠ Blvd. Kukulcán Km 1.5): **Alebrije/The Myth** (☎ 98/83–45–25) has a huge bar and continual laser shows; **Ma'Ax'O** (☎ 98/83–55–99) offers the latest music and a wild dance floor. **Up and Down** (⊠ Hotel Oasis, Blvd. Kukulcán Km 15.5, ☎ 98/85–08–67) holds foam parties popular with spring-breakers. **La Boom** (⊠ Blvd. Kukulcán Km 3.5, ☎ 98/83–11–52) is always the last place to close; it has a video bar with a light show and regular weekly events.

MUSIC

Azucar (⊠ Hotel Camino Real, ☎ 98/83–01–00) showcases the very best of Latin American bands; proper dress is required. **Batacha** (⊠ Hotel Miramar Misión, ☎ 98/83–17–55) is a terrific spot for Latin American and Mexican music. **Cat's Reggae Bar** (⊠ Blvd. Kukulcán Km 9, ☎ 98/83–19–00) imports the hottest reggae bands from the United States and from Caribbean islands. The classy downtown **Roots Bar** (⊠ Av. Tulipanes 26, near Parque de las Palapas, ☎ 98/84–24–37) is the place for jazz, flamenco, blues, and modern Brazilian music. **El Camarote** (⊠ Avs. Uxmal and Nader, ☎ 98/84–32-18) offers a bohemian style and alternative music.

RESTAURANT PARTY CENTERS

While the food at the following restaurants is usually quite good, the real draw at each spot is the nightly parties that usually have live music until dawn. At **Carlos 'n' Charlie's** (⊠ Blvd. Kukulcán Km 5.5, ☎ 98/83–08–46) zany waiters perform on stage with live rock bands. Just as fun is **Senor Frogs** (⊠ Blvd. Kukulcán Km 12.5, ☎ 98/83–10–92). **Pat O'Briens** (⊠ Blvd. Kukulcán Km 11.5, ☎ 98/83–04–18) brings the New Orleans party scene to the Zone with live rock bands and its famous cocktails. **Mango Tango** (⊠ Blvd. Kukulcán Km 12.5, ☎ 98/83–03–03) has a Las Vegas–style dinner theater show with Caribbean music and dance.

Outdoor Activities and Sports

Bullfights

The Cancún **bullring,** a block south of the Pemex station, hosts year-round bullfights. A matador, charros, a mariachi band, and flamenco dancers entertain during the hour preceding the bullfight (from 2:30 PM). ⊠ *Blvd. Kukulcán at Av. Bonampak,* ☎ *98/84–83–72, 98/84–82-48.* ≊ *About $40.* ☉ *Fights Wed. at 3:30.*

Golf

The main course is at **Pok-Ta-Pok** (⊠ Blvd. Kukulcán between Km 6 and Km 7, ☎ 98/83–12–30), a club with fine views of both sea and lagoon, whose 18 holes were designed by Robert Trent Jones, Sr. Greens fees are $70 ($55 after 2 PM); carts are $25. There is an 18-hole championship golf course at the **Cáesar Park Beach & Golf Resort** (⊠ Blvd. Kukulcán Km 17, ☎ 98/81–80–16); greens fees are $95 ($75 for hotel guests), and carts are included. The 18-hole executive course (par 53) at the **Hotel Meliá Cancún** (⊠ Blvd. Kukulcán Km 12, ☎ 98/85–11–60) shares the property's beautiful ocean views. The greens fee is about $20.

Water Sports

Aqua Fun (⊠ Blvd. Kukulcán Km 16.5, ☎ 98/85–32–60) and **Aqua World** (⊠ Blvd. Kukulcán Km 15.2, ☎ 98/85–22–88, ℻ 98/85–22–99) maintain full-service marinas with large fleets of water toys. **Parque Nizuc** (⊠ Blvd. Kukulcán Km 25, ☎ 98/85–30–33) is the area's newest marine park. It includes Wet n' Wild, a water theme park offering seven different water slides; Baxal-Há, a snorkel area that's home to gentle sharks and manta rays; and Atlántida, an aquarium where visitors can interact with dolphins. Cancún also has numerous places to go parasailing (about $35 for eight minutes); waterskiing ($70 per hour); or jet skiing ($70 per hour, or $60 for Wave Runners, double-seated Jet Skis). Paddleboats, kayaks, catamarans, and banana boats are also readily available.

FISHING

Some 500 species of tropical fish, including sailfish, bluefin, marlin, barracuda, and red snapper, live in the waters adjacent to Cancún. Deep-sea fishing boats and gear may be chartered from outfitters for about $350 for four hours, $450 for six hours, and $550 for eight hours. Charters generally include a captain, a first mate, gear, bait, and beverages.

Marina del Rey (✉ Blvd. Kulkulcán Km 15.5, ☎ 98/83–05–54); **Mundo Marina** (✉ Blvd. Kulkulcán Km 5.5, ☎ 98/83–04–42); **Aqua Tours** (✉ Blvd. Kulkulcán Km 6, ☎ 98/83–02–27); and **Barracuda Marina** (✉ Blvd. Kulkulcán Km 14, ☎ 98/85–34–44) each charter boats for deep-sea fishing. Trips last from four to eight hours. Prices include soft drinks, bait, and fishing gear.

SAILBOARDING AND KAYAKING

The **International Windsurfer Sailing School** (☎ 98/84–20–23) rents windsurfing equipment at the Club International Beach for $40 per day and has two-hour lessons for $25. Many of the hotels now have their own kayaks, which are available to guests free of charge.

SNORKELING AND SCUBA DIVING

Snorkeling is best at Parque Nizuc (☞ *above*), Punta Cancún, and Playa Tortugas, although you should be especially careful of the strong currents at the last. You can generally rent gear for $10 per day from many of the scuba-diving places, and most hotels and resorts have their own gear for rent. If you've brought your own snorkeling gear and want to save money, just take a city bus down to Club Med and walk along the resort's beach for less than 1 km (½ mi) until you get to Punta Nizuc.

Barracuda Marina (✉ Blvd. Kulkulcán Km 14, ☎ 98/85–24–44) has a two-hour Wave Runner jungle tour through the mangroves, which ends with snorkeling at the Punta Nizuc coral reef. The $38.50 fee includes snorkeling equipment, life jackets, and refreshments.

Scuba diving has gained in popularity in Cancún. A word of caution about one-hour courses offered as a freebie by the resorts: this does not prepare you to dive in the ocean, no matter what the high-pressure concession operators tell you. A one-hour lesson in a controlled environment such as a pool differs vastly from the open ocean. If you have caught the scuba bug, invest in a few more lessons and prepare yourself properly so you can enjoy the experience. Remember that scuba-diving accidents can be fatal.

The secret of a good scuba company is personal attention. Ask to meet the dive master and check out the company's equipment and certifications thoroughly. **Scuba Cancún** (✉ Blvd. Kulkulcán Km 5, ☎ 98/83–10–11) specializes in diving trips and offers NAUI, CMAS, and PADI instruction. It's operated by Luis Hurtado, who has more than 35 years of experience. **Blue Peace Diving** (✉ Blvd. Kulkulcán Km 16.2, ☎ 98/85–14–47) has two-tank dives for $85 with NAUI, SSI, and PADI instruction. **Ocean Sports** (✉ Av. Cobá 51, ☎ 98/84–60–34) also runs some scuba courses.

Shopping

Resort wear and handicrafts are the most popular purchases in Cancún, but prices are high and the selection standard. If you're traveling elsewhere in Mexico, postpone your shopping spree until you get to another town. Bargaining is expected in the markets; stores usually have fixed prices. If you can do without plastic, you may get the 12% sales tax lopped off at shops that don't want to pay high commissions to credit-card companies.

In Cancún, shopping hours are generally weekdays 10–1 and 4–7, although more and more stores are staying open throughout the day rather than closing for siesta 1–4. Many shops keep Saturday morning hours, and some are now open Sunday until 1. Shops in the malls tend to be open weekdays from 9 AM or 10 AM to 8 PM or 10 PM.

Downtown

There's a wide variety of shops downtown along Avenida Tulum (between Avs. Cobá and Uxmal). **Fama** (⊠ Av. Tulum 105, ☎ 98/84–65–86) is a department store that sells clothing, English reading matter, sports gear, toiletries, liquor, and *latería* (crafts made of tin). **Ultrafemme** (⊠ Av. Tulum and Calle Claveles, ☎ 98/85–08–04) is another popular downtown store that carries duty-free perfume, cosmetics, and jewelry. The oldest and largest of Cancún's crafts markets is **Ki Huic** (⊠ Av. Tulum 17, between Bancomer and Bital, ☎ 98/84–33–47), which is open daily 9 AM–10 PM and houses about 100 vendors. Another good spot to check out souvenirs is **Mercado Veinteocho** (Market 28). Just off Avenida Yaxchilán and Sunyaxchen, this popular market is filled with shops selling many of the same souvenir items found in the Hotel Zone, but at half the price.

Plaza las Americas (⊠ Av. Tulum, Sm 4 and 9, ☎ 98/87–58–93) is the newest shopping center in downtown Cancún. Its 50-plus stores, three restaurants, eight movie theaters, video arcade, fast-food outlets, and three large department stores will make you think you're back home.

Hotel Zone

Fully air-conditioned malls—*centros comerciales*—are as streamlined and well kept as any in the United States or Canada.

There is only one open-air market in the Hotel Zone. **Coral Negro,** next to the Convention Center, is a collection of about 50 stalls selling craft items. It's open daily until late evening. Everything here is overpriced, but bargaining does work.

Kukulcán Plaza (⊠ Blvd. Kukulcán Km 13) is a mall that never seems to end, with around 130 shops (including Benetton and Harley Davidson boutiques), 12 restaurants, a bar, a liquor store, a bank, a three-screen cinema, bowling lanes, and a video arcade.

Flamingo Plaza (⊠ Blvd. Kukulcán Km 11.5, across from the Hotel Flamingo) is a small, high-tech plaza beautifully decorated with marble. It has designer, duty-free, and sportswear shops, an exchange booth, and two boutiques selling Guatemalan imports.

Forum-by-the-Sea (⊠ Blvd. Kukulcán Km 9.5) is a sparkling entertainment/shopping plaza in the Zone. This three-level plaza offers Cancún's biggest selection of cinemas, brand-name stores, and restaurants in a circuslike atmosphere.

The largest and most contemporary of the malls, **Plaza Caracol** (⊠ Blvd. Kukulcán Km 8.5) is north of the Convention Center. It houses about 200 shops and boutiques, including two pharmacies, art galleries, a currency exchange, and folk-art and jewelry shops, as well as cafés and restaurants. Boutiques include Benetton, Bally, Gucci, and Ralph Lauren, with prices lower than at their U.S. counterparts.

Plaza Mayafair has a large open-air center filled with restaurants, bars, and shops. An adjacent indoor shopping mall is decorated to resemble a rain forest. The mall has more than 30 shops and a free nightly show of Maya dance and music.

The glittering, ultratrendy (and ultraexpensive) **La Isla Shopping Village** (⊠ Blvd. Kukulcán Km 1.5) is on the Nichupte Lagoon under a giant canopy. A series of canals and small bridges are designed to give the place a Venetian look. In addition to a wide range of shops, the mall has a marina, an aquarium, a disco, restaurants, and movie theaters.

Specialty Shops

GALLERIES

The **Renato Dorfman Gallery** (⊠ Avs. Sunyaxchen and Yaxchilán 63, Sm 25, ☎ 98/87–46–15; ⊠ La Isla Shopping Village, Blvd. Kukulcán 12.5, ☎ 98/83–03–59, 98/83–55–73) carries Dorfman's original pieces as well as his hand-carved replicas of Maya art and stelae. The **Huichol Collection** (⊠ Plaza Kukulcán and Plaza Caracol, ☎ 98/83–50–59) sells beadwork and embroidery made by the Huichol Indians of the West Coast. You can visit the store and watch one of the visiting tribe members doing this amazing work.

Cancún A to Z

Arriving and Departing

BY BUS

The downtown **bus terminal** (⊠ Avs. Tulum and Uxmal, ☎ 98/84–13–78, 98/84–39–48) has first-class buses making the trip from Mexico City and first- and second-class buses coming from Puerto Morelos, Playa del Carmen, Tulum, Chetumal, Cobá, Valladolid, Chichén Itzá, and Mérida. Public buses (Route 8) run to Puerto Juárez and Punta Sam for the ferries to Isla Mujeres, and taxis will take you from the bus station to Puerto Juárez for about $2.

BY CAR

Route 180 runs from Matamoros at the Texas border through Campeche, Mérida, Valladolid, and into Cancún. The trip from Texas can take up to three days. **Route 307** runs south from Cancún through Puerto Morelos, Tulum, and Chetumal, then into Belize. There are few gas stations on these roads, so keep your tank full. Route 307 has two Pemex stations between Cancún and Playa del Carmen.

BY PLANE

Cancún International Airport is 16 km (9 mi) southwest of the heart of Cancún City, 10 km (6 mi) from the southernmost point of the Hotel Zone. **Aeroméxico** (☎ 98/84–10–97, 98/84–35–71) flies nonstop from Houston, Miami, and New York. **American** (☎ 98/86–00–86) has nonstop service from Dallas and Miami. **Continental** (☎ 98/86–00–40) offers daily direct service from Houston. **Mexicana** (☎ 98/87–44–44, 98/83–48–81) nonstop flights depart from Los Angeles, Miami, and New York. In Cancún, Mexicana subsidiaries **Aerocaribe** (☎ 98/84–20–00, 98/86–00–83) and **Aerocozumel** (☎ 98/84–20–00, 98/86–01–62) fly to Cozumel, the ruins at Chichén Itzá, Mérida, and other Mexican cities.

Between the Airport and Hotels. No buses are allowed into the airport. The options are taxis or *colectivos* (vans). A counter at the airport exit sells colectivo and taxi tickets. Prices range from $15 to $40, depending on the destination. Getting back to the airport for your trip home is cheaper. Taxi rates to the airport range from $10 to $22. Hotels post the most current rates. Be sure to agree on a price before getting into the taxi.

Getting Around

Motorized transport of some sort is necessary, as sights are somewhat spread out. Public buses are good, taxis relatively inexpensive.

ADDRESSES

"Sm" in Cancún addresses stands for Super Manzana. All neighborhoods are labeled with such a number (Sm 23, Sm 25, etc.), with the various main streets running around them. Each Sm has its own park or square and the area streets are fashioned around the park.

BY BOAT

North of Cancún City, boats leave Puerto Juárez and Punta Sam for Isla Mujeres every half hour or so (☞ Arriving and Departing *in* Isla Mujeres A to Z, *below*).

BY BUS

Public buses run between the Hotel Zone and downtown 6 AM–midnight. The cost is about 3 pesos. There are designated bus stops, but you can also flag down drivers along Boulevard Kukulcán. The service is frequent and quite reliable. Buses from the Zone do not go into downtown Cancún but will drop you off at Avenida Tulum, where you can catch a connecting bus. Taking the bus can save you a considerable amount of money on taxis, particularly if you are staying in the Hotel Zone.

BY CAR AND MOPED

Mopeds are extremely dangerous. Essentially, you're risking your life using one either in the Zone or downtown. Renting a car in Cancún is an unnecessary expense that entails tips for valet parking, gasoline, and rather high rental rates. Driving is harrowing with the many one-way streets, *glorietas* (traffic circles), poor traffic lights, ill-placed *topes* (speed bumps), lots of pedestrians, and large potholes. Be sure to observe all speed limits in the Zone and downtown, because the traffic police are vigilant. If you do plan to explore beyond Cancún, using it as a base, roads are excellent within a 100-km (62-mi) radius.

BY TAXI

Taxi rides within the Hotel Zone cost $5–$7; between the Hotel Zone and downtown, $8 and up; and to the ferries at Punta Sam or Puerto Juárez, $15–$20 or more. Prices depend on distance, your negotiating skills, and whether you pick up the taxi in front of a hotel or decide to save a few dollars by going onto the avenue to hail one yourself (look for green city cabs). Most hotels list rates at the door. Confirm the price with your driver *before* you set out. If you lose something in a taxi or have questions or a complaint, call the **Sindicato de Taxistas** (☎ 98/88–69–85).

Contacts and Resources

BANKS

Banks in Cancún are generally open weekdays 9–5, with money-exchange desks open 9–1:30. Go early to avoid long lines. Downtown locations are along Avenida Tulum. Some larger banks have locations scattered along the Hotel Zone. The larger banks are: **Banamex** (✉ Av. Tulum 19, next to City Hall, ☎ 98/84–54–11; ✉ Plaza Terramar, Blvd. Kukulcán Km 37, ☎ 98/83–31–00); **Bital** (✉ Av. Tulum 15, ☎ 98/84–33–481; ✉ Plaza Caracol, ☎ 98/83–46–52); and **Bancomer** (✉ Av. Tulum 20, ☎ 98/84–44–00; ✉ Plaza Caracol and next to the Convention Center, ☎ 98/83–11–28).

CAR AND MOPED RENTAL

Rental cars are available at the airport and in town. Most are standard-shift subcompacts and jeeps. For air-conditioned cars with automatic transmission, reserve well in advance. Rental agencies include: **Avis** (five locations; ✉ airport, ☎ 98/86–02–22); **Econo-Rent** (✉ Av.

Bonampak, ☏ 98/87–64–87); **Global** (✉ Tropical Plaza, Av. Tulum 192, ☏ 98/87–25–74); **Hertz** (nine locations; ✉ airport, ☏ 98/86–01–50); **Localiza Rent a Car** (five locations; ✉ Dos Playas, ☏ 98/83–19–17); **National** (seven locations; ✉ airport, ☏ 98/86–01–52); **Thrifty's** (five locations; ✉ airport, ☏ 98/86–03–33); and **Zipp Rental Cars** (✉ Baccará Hotel, Blvd. Kukulcán Km 11.5, ☏ 98/83–20–77).

Mopeds and scooters are available on the island. They are fun, but the accident rate is high, especially downtown, and no insurance is available for driver or vehicle. Rates start around $25 per day.

CONSULATES

The **U.S. Consulate** (✉ Plaza Caracol, 3rd floor, HZ, ☏ 98/83–02–72) is open weekdays 9–1.

The **Canadian Consulate** (✉ Plaza Caracol 11, 3rd floor, Local 330, ☏ 98/84–37–16, ⨳ 98/83–32–32) is open daily 11–1. For after-hours emergencies, call the Canadian Embassy in Mexico City (☏ 5/724–7900).

EMERGENCIES

To report an emergency, dial **06.** Other emergency numbers: **Municipal Police** (☏ 98/84–19–13), **Traffic Police** (☏ 98/84–07–10), **Highway Police** (☏ 98/84–24–45), **Immigration Office** (☏ 98/84–17–49), **Red Cross** (✉ Av. Xcaret and Labná, Sm 21, ☏ 98/84–16–16), **Fire Department** (☏ 98/84–12–02). **Hospital Americano** (✉ Viento 15, ☏ 98/84–61–33) is a well-equipped hospital but is notorious for grossly overcharging tourists. **Total Assist** (✉ Claveles, Sm 22, ☏ 98/84–10–92, 98/84–81–16) has English-speaking staff members and reasonable fees. Both provide emergency medical care.

GUIDED TOURS

Air Tours. Grupo Taca (✉ Cancún Airport, ☏ 98/87–41–10, 98/84–39–38) flies between Cancún and Guatemala City, continuing on to Flores and the ruins at Tikal, for $290 round-trip. This one-day tour covers all ground transfers, departure taxes, entrance to ruins, tour guide, and lunch. The most efficient way to get tickets is through a local travel agent.

Day Cruises. Day cruises to Isla Mujeres are popular. They generally include snorkeling, shopping downtown, open-bar buffet lunches, and listening to music or lounging at Playa Norte. While there are plenty of tour operators offering such trips, it's just as simple and far cheaper to plan your own. All you have to do is catch the ferries to Isla Mujeres that leave every half hour or so from Puerto Juárez and Punta Sam, both north of Cancún City. If you do want someone else to do the planning and don't mind spending the money, **Captain Hook** (✉ Blvd. Kukulcán Km 4.5, ☏ 98/83–37–36) runs an Isla Mujeres day tour that departs at 10 AM from the pier in front of Fat Tuesday's and returns at 5 PM. It costs about $55.

Dolphin Discovery (✉ Playa Langosta, ☏ 98/83–07–77, 98/83–07–79) sails daily from Playa Langosta and Playa Tortugas to the company's dock on Isla Mujeres. The program includes an instruction video, a 30-minute swim session with the dolphins, and time to explore the island.

Jungle Ecotours. While many claim to have jungle tours, few actually deliver. An exception is **Reserva Ecológica El Eden** (✉ A.P. 308, Postal 770, 77500, Cancún, Quintana Roo, ☏ ⨳ 98/80–50–32). The 500,000-acre reserve, 48 km (30 mi) northwest of Cancún, abounds with flora and fauna. Tours include bird-watching, animal tracking, stargazing, crocodile ecology, and exploring cenotes and archaeological sites. Prices include transportation to and from Cancún, one to two nights' accommodation at La Savanna Research Station, meals, cocktails, guided nature walks, and all tours. Two-day/one-night excursions start at $235, three-day/two-nights at $315.

Submarine Cruises. *Nautibus* (☎ 98/83–35–52, 98/83–21–19), or the "floating submarine," has a 1½-hour Caribbean-reef cruise. *Nautibus* departure times change often, so check in advance. The $30 price includes music and drinks. The **Atlantis** (⊠ Aqua Tours, Blvd. Kukulcán Km 6.25, ☎ 98/83–04–00) offers submarine trips that actually go underwater (others float on the surface and have window seats below). Tours depart every hour 10–3 and include an hour-long cruise to Playa Indios on Isla Mujeres, a 45-minute tour to the reefs, food and drink at the Atlantis Bar & Grill, showers, towels, and locker service, all for about $69.

LATE-NIGHT PHARMACIES

Among the downtown pharmacies that offer delivery service are **Canto** (⊠ Avs. Kabah and Cobá, ☎ 98/87–70–93) and **Pharmacia Cancún** (⊠ Av. Tulum 17, ☎ 98/84–12–83); **Paris** (⊠ Av. Yaxchilán, ☎ 98/84–30–05) delivers around the clock. In the Hotel Zone try **Extra** (⊠ Plaza Caracol, ☎ 98/83–28–27), which delivers to hotels 9 AM–10 PM.

TRAVEL AGENCIES AND TOUR OPERATORS

American Express (⊠ Av. Tulum 208, ☎ 98/84–20–01), **Intermar Caribe** (⊠ Av. Tulum, ☎ 98/84–42–66), **Mayaland Tours** (⊠ 225 Party Center, Blvd. Kukulcán Km 9, ☎ 98/83–06–79), and **Aviomar** (⊠ Av. Yaxchilán 82, ☎ 98/84–88–31) all offer day trips. Shop around for the best price or call the **Travel Agency Association** (⊠ Plaza Mexico, Av. Tulum 200, Suite 301, ☎ 98/87–16–70, FAX 98/84–37–38) for further information.

VISITOR INFORMATION

Cancún Tips (⊠ Av. Tulum 29, Suites 1–5, ☎ 98/84–14–58) is open daily 9–9. Twice a year the company publishes a free pocket-size guide to hotels, restaurants, shopping, and recreation with excellent maps and discount coupons.

The Mexican Ministry of Tourism has a toll-free 24-hour English-language **help line** for tourists (☎ 01–800/9–03–92). There are also the **State Tourism Office—Quintana Roo** (Sectur; ⊠ Government Palace, Av. Tulum, ☎ 98/84–04–37) and the **State Tourism Information Center** (⊠ Av. Tulum 23, ☎ 98/84–80–73).

ISLA MUJERES

Updated by
Shelagh
McNally

Isla Mujeres (*ees*-lah moo-*hair*-ayce) has a magic all its own that defies change. This tiny, fish-shape island 8 km (5 mi) off Cancún is a tranquil alternative to its bustling western neighbor. Only about 8 km (5 mi) long by 1 km (½ mi) wide, Isla has flat sandy beaches on its northern end and steep rocky bluffs to the south.

No one remembers who gave the isle its name, which means "isle of women." Many believe it was the ancient Maya who used the island as a religious center for worshiping Ixchel (ee-*shell*), the Maya goddess of rainbows, fertility, and childbirth. Another popular legend has the Spanish conquistador, Hernández de Córdoba, naming the island when he landed in 1517, blown off course from Cuba. When he and his crew came on shore they saw only women (the men were out fishing) and found hundreds of female-shape clay idols dedicated to Ixchel and her daughters. Still others claim the name is a legacy from pirate days when, like many other Caribbean islands in the 17th century, Isla was a haven for buccaneers and smugglers. These pirates would stash their women on Isla before heading out to rob ships at sea.

After its popularity waned with pirates and smugglers, Isla settled into life as a quiet fishing village. In the late '70s, day-trippers came over from Cancún, bringing Isla's hotel, restaurant, and shop owners more business than ever. Isla has withstood the onslaught, managing to keep its character as a peaceful island retreat with a rich history and culture centered on the sea.

Exploring

To get your bearings, think of Isla Mujeres as an elongated fish, the head being the southern tip, the northern prong the tail. The island's only town, known simply as El Pueblo, extends the full width of Isla's northern "tail" and is sandwiched between sand and sea to the south, west, and east, with no high-rises to block the view.

A Good Tour

The best way to explore the whole island is to take a taxi or rent either a moped or golf cart. You can walk to Isla's historic **cemetery** ⑥ by going north from the ferry piers on Avenida Lopez Mateos. Then head south along Avenida Rueda Medina past the piers to reach the Mexican naval base. It's off-limits to tourists, and the Mexican navy doesn't like anyone photographing the crew, base, or ships. But you can see the flag ceremonies from the road at sunrise and sunset. Continue south out of town and after 2½ km (1½ mi) you'll come to **Laguna Makax** ⑦ on the right.

At the south end of the lagoon, a dirt road to the left leads to the remains of the **Hacienda Mundaca** ⑧. About a block southeast of the hacienda, turn right off the main road at the sign that says SAC BAJO to a smaller, unmarked side road, which loops back north. Approximately ½ km (¼ mi) farther on the left is the entrance to the **Tortugranja** ⑨.

Return to Avenida Rueda Medina and head south past Playa Lancheros to **El Garrafón National Park** ⑩. Slightly more than ½ km (¼ mi) along the same road, on the windward side of the tip of Isla Mujeres, is the site of a small **Maya ruin** ⑪, which stood for centuries but was destroyed by Hurricane Gilbert in 1988. Follow the paved eastern perimeter road north back into town. Known as the Corredor Panoramico (Panoramic Highway), this is a scenic drive with a few pull-off areas along the way, perfect for a secluded picnic. Swimming is not recommended along this coast because of the strong currents and rocky shore.

Sights to See

⑥ **Cemetery.** You'll find Isla's unnamed cemetery, with its 100-year-old gravestones, on Avenida Lopez Mateos, the road that parallels Playa Norte. Filled with carved angels and flowers, the most beautiful of the decorated tombs are those in memory of children. Hidden among them is the tomb of the notorious Fermín Mundaca (☞ Hacienda Mundaca, *below*). This 19th-century slave trader—who's often billed more glamorously as a pirate—carved his own skull-and-crossbones tombstone with the ominous epitaph: AS YOU ARE, I ONCE WAS; AS I AM, SO SHALL YOU BE. Mundaca's grave is empty, however; his remains lie in Mérida, where he died. The monument is not easy to find—ask a local to point out the unidentified marker.

⑩ **El Garrafón National Park.** Bought by the owners of Xcaret (☞ North Caribbean Coast, *below*), this national marine park has undergone a major revamping. The grounds have been cleaned of garbage, landscaped, and expanded. A three-floor facility with restaurants, bathrooms, gift shops, and walkways has been built. The park has long been a snorkeling mecca for day-trippers from Cancún, and as a result much of the coral reef here has died. In an attempt to restore it, the new own-

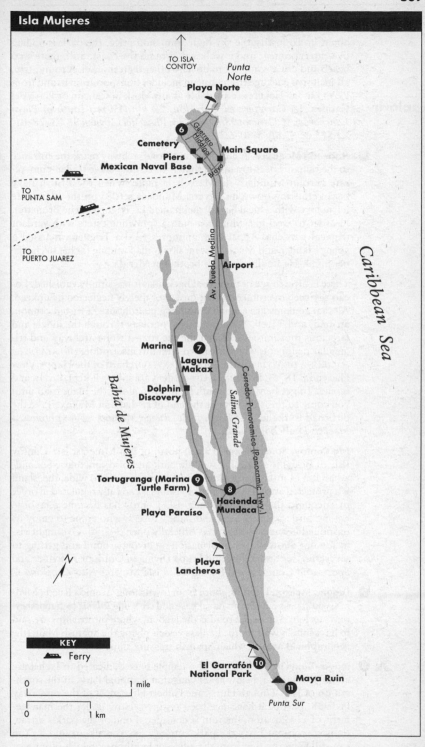

Isla Mujeres

TO ISLA CONTOY

Punta Norte

Playa Norte

6

Guerrero Hidalgo

Cemetery

Piers

Main Square

Mexican Naval Base

Playa

TO PUNTA SAM

TO PUERTO JUAREZ

Caribbean Sea

Av. Rueda Medina

Airport

Bahía de Mujeres

Marina

7

Laguna Makax

Corredor Panorámico (Panoramic Hwy.)

Salina Grande

Dolphin Discovery

Tortugranga (Marina Turtle Farm)

9

8

Hacienda Mundaca

Playa Paraíso

Playa Lancheros

KEY

Ferry

0   1 mile

0   1 km

El Garrafón National Park

10

Maya Ruin

11

Punta Sur

ers have blocked off most of the reef and restricted access to 700 visitors per day. There are still some sea creatures to be seen, but that's about it. To justify the sky-high admission price, the park is adding live entertainment and a walkway around the coast. Still, there's no beach and not a whole lot to do here other than snorkel. A round-trip, all-inclusive package from Cancún includes transportation to and from Playa Linda. Tickets are available at any kiosk in Cancún or Playa del Carmen. ⊠ *Carretera El Garrafón, 2½ km (1½ mi) south of Playa Lancheros.* ☎ *Cancún 98/83–32–33; Playa del Carmen 987/3–28–01.* ☜ *$15.* ⊙ *Daily 8:30–6:30.*

❽ Hacienda Mundaca. A dirt drive and stone archway mark the entrance to the remains of the mansion that 19th-century slave trader–cum–pirate Fermín Mundaca de Marechaja built. When the British navy began cracking down on slavers, Mundaca settled on the island. He fell in love with a local beauty nicknamed La Trigueña (The Brunette). In order to woo her, Mundaca built a sprawling estate with verdant tropical gardens. Apparently unimpressed, La Trigueña married a young islander, and Mundaca went slowly mad waiting for her to change her mind. He finally died in a brothel in Mérida.

There is little to see of the actual hacienda. It has simply vanished. Locals say the government tore it down, or merely neglected its upkeep. All that remains are a small crumbling guardhouse, a rusted cannon, an arch, and a well. You must push your way through the jungle and ferocious mosquitoes to reach the the ruined stone archway and triangular pediment, which is carved with this inscription: HUERTA DE LA HACIENDA DE VISTA ALEGRE MDCCCLXXVI (Orchard of the Happy View Hacienda, 1876). In contrast, the gardens are still well-kept, lovely, and serene. To get here, drive south from town along the main road until you come to the "S" curve at the end of ☞ **Laguna Makax**. Take the dirt road to the left. ⊠ *East off Av. Rueda Medina,* ☎ *no phone.* ☜ *Free.* ⊙ *Daily dawn–dusk.*

Isla Contoy. Some 30 km (19 mi) north of Isla Mujeres, Isla Contoy (Isle of Birds) is a national wildlife park and bird sanctuary. Six-and-a-half km (4 mi) long and less than 1 km (about ½ mi) wide, the island is a protected area. The number of visitors is carefully regulated in order to safeguard the flora and fauna. Isla Contoy has become a favorite among birders, snorkelers, and nature lovers, who come to enjoy its unspoiled beauty. The island is officially open 9–5:30. Overnight visits are not allowed. For information on diving around and getting to the island, *see* Snorkeling and Scuba Diving *in* Outdoor Activities and Sports *and* Contacts and Resources *in* Isla Mujeres A to Z, *below.*

❼ Laguna Makax. Heading south from town along Avenida Rueda Medina, you'll pass a Mexican naval base and see some *salinas* (salt marshes) on your left. Across the road is the lagoon, where pirate ships are said to have lain in wait for the hapless vessels plying the Spanish Main (the geographical area in which Spanish treasure ships trafficked).

⛰ ⓫ Maya ruin. The sad vestiges of a temple once dedicated to Ixchel are about 1 km (½ mi) below ☞ **El Garrafón National Park**, at the southern tip of Isla. Though Hurricane Gilbert blew most of the ruin away in 1988, part of it has since been restored. Now under the management of El Garrafón, the ruin is considered one of the park's attractions so you must pay the park entrance fee to walk around it. You can still view the ruin from the adjacent **lighthouse**, which is not part of the park. For a small tip the keeper will allow you to climb to the top, where there is an incredible view of the open ocean on one side and Mujeres Bay on the other. The ruin is located at the point where the road turns northeast into the **Corredor Panorámico,** which has some of the most breathtaking coastline scenery on the island.

9 **Tortugranja** (Marina Turtle Farm). Run by an outfit called Eco Caribe, this facility is dedicated to the study and preservation of sea turtles. During hatching season, May–September, upward of 6,000 turtles are hatched along the coast of Quintana Roo. Some are brought to the farm to be raised until they are large enough to survive at sea. Visitors can view hatchlings and young turtles of various species in outdoor tanks. There is also a small but well-designed museum explaining the various stages of turtle life and different parts of the coral reef. *Follow the main road to the fork, about a block southeast of Hacienda Mundaca. Take the right-hand fork, the smaller road that loops back north. About ½ km (¼ mi) to the left is the entrance to the turtle farm.* ☎ 987/ 7-05-95. 🎫 *$2.* �} *Daily 9–5.*

Beaches

The superb **Playa Norte** (or Playa Cocoteros), at the extreme northwest of the island, is simple to find: go north on any of the north–south streets in town. There the turquoise sea is as calm as a lake, and you can wade out for 40 yards in waist-deep water. Playa Norte is famous for its congenial atmosphere. There are quite a few palapa bars where you can sit and enjoy a drink or snack. Las Palapas de Chimbo and Buho's are popular with locals and tourists, who gather to chat, eat fresh seafood, drink cold beer, and watch the sunset. Also along the beach are stands where you can rent snorkeling gear, Jet Skis, floats, and sailboards.

Between Laguna Makax and El Garrafón, you'll find **Playa Paraíso** and **Playa Lancheros,** good spots for lunch or for shopping at the small stands selling local handicrafts, souvenirs, and T-shirts. At Playa Lancheros are some pet sea turtles and harmless *tiburones gatos* (nurse sharks) housed in sea pens. A tourist attraction lets you have your picture taken with one of the sharks. **Playa Indios,** southeast of Laguna Makax, has a lovely beach, but it's also the staging point for *Atlantis* submarine tours (☞ Contacts and Resources *in* Cancún A to Z, *above*), which means lots of people milling about while announcements boom over a public-address system.

Dining

As in the rest of Mexico, locals eat their main meal during siesta hours, 1–4, and then have a light dinner in the evening. Unless otherwise stated, restaurants are open daily for lunch and dinner.

CATEGORY	COST*
$$$	over $15
$$	$10–$15
$	under $10

per person, excluding drinks and service

$$$ ✕ **Chez Magaly.** This pleasant pool-side restaurant is on the grounds of the shocking-pink Nautibeach Condo-Hotel. Inside, the decor is more subdued: wood floors, hanging plants, white and blue tables, and a palapa roof. After a day at the beach, it's the perfect spot to enjoy a romantic dinner and watch the sunset. Caribbean–French fare is the served; specialties include tender steaks, succulent lobster, and tasty shrimp. ✉ *Av. Rueda Medina, Playa Norte,* ☎ *987/7-02-59, 987/7-04-36. MC, V. Closed Mon. and 2 wks in June.*

$$$ ✕ **Maria's Kan Kin.** A charming beachside eatery, it's located near El Garrafón (☞ Exploring, *above*). Fresh lobster (trapped by locals) is prepared with a French twist. Other noteworthy dishes include lobster bisque, fresh fish, and snails. Three flagstone terraces overlook a small garden. Come for a romantic late-afternoon lunch that extends into watching the sunset. ⊠ *Carretera Garrafón,* ☎ *Isla Mujeres 987/ 7–00–15, Cancún 98/83–14–20. AE, MC, V.*

$$$ ✕ **Zazil-Ha.** This fine restaurant, on the grounds of the Na Balam hotel
★ (☞ Lodging, *below*), serves delicious vegetarian dishes and regional specialties. The indoor eating area is a cozy palapa dining room decorated with light-wood furniture, tile floors, and Mexican pottery. Outside there is a lovely shaded terrace with wooden tables. Look for daily seafood specials such as *chaya* (Maya spinach) with pasta. The breakfast menu includes homemade bread, tropical fruits, a variety of egg dishes, and good coffee. ⊠ *Hotel Na Balam, Calle Zazil-Ha 118,* ☎ *987/7–02–79. AE, MC, V.*

$$ ✕ **Bucanero.** This large outdoor café has a great menu of seafood and Yucatecan specialities for breakfast, lunch, and dinner. Try *huevos motuleños* (fried eggs on a corn tortilla heaped with beans, ham, cheese, peas, and marinated red onions covered in tomato sauce) or a classic American breakfast, which costs around $3.50. Lunch and dinner specialties include avocado stuffed with shrimp and *mar y cielo* ("sea and sky"—a fish fillet and a chicken breast with french fries and onions). ⊠ *Av. Hidalgo 11,* ☎ *987/7–02–10. Reservations not accepted. MC, V.*

$$ ✕ **Café Cito.** This is one of the prettiest cafés on the island, decorated
★ in shades of pink and blue, with stained-glass windows and mobiles. Glass tops on tables cover arrangements of sand and shells. Drink great cappuccino or espresso with a breakfast of fresh waffles, fruit-filled crepes, or egg dishes. For dinner, the chef whips up different daily specials. You can join the island's Harley Davidson Club here, or have your tarot cards read by Sabrina. ⊠ *Avs. Juárez and Matamoros,* ☎ *987/7–04–38. Reservations not accepted. No credit cards.*

$ ✕ **Lonchería La Lomita.** The word here is home-style. Although the bright
★ aqua decor isn't much to look at, the servings of chicken, steak, and seafood cooked to order (grilled, fried, or sautéed) are hearty and filling. Octopus sautéed in butter and garlic is particularly tasty. Breakfast is amazingly low-priced. ⊠ *Av. Juárez 25-B, past Av. Allende,* ☎ *no phone. Reservations not accepted. No credit cards.*

$ ✕ **Red Eye Café.** The logo says it all: a bloodshot eye obviously in need of a cup of joe. This is the place to get your morning caffeine fix. Gus and Inga know their coffee and serve it with hearty American-style breakfasts with a German flair. Fresh sausages, made by a German sausage maker in Cancún, accompany the egg dishes. ⊠ *Av. Hidalgo between Avs. Maramoros and Mateos,* ☎ *no phone. No credit cards. Closed Tues.*

$ ✕ **Velazquez.** This family-owned palapa-style restaurant on the beach
★ serves the freshest seafood on the island. Do try the regional speciality, tikinchic. You haven't eaten Yucatecan until you've had tikinchic. Feasting on a fantastic fish meal while you sit outside and watch the boats go by is a true Isla experience. ⊠ *Av. Rueda Medina, two blocks west of the ferry docks,* ☎ *no phone. No credit cards.*

Lodging

There is no shortage of hotels on Isla. Generally the older, more modest places are in town, and the newer, more expensive resorts front the beach around Punta Norte or on the peninsula near the lagoon. Most hotels have ceiling fans, some have air-conditioning, but few have TVs or phones. Luxurious, self-contained time-share condominiums are another option, which you can learn more about from local travel agencies. All hotels share the 77400 postal code.

CATEGORY	COST*
$$$$	over $100
$$$	$60–$100
$$	$25–$60
$	under $25

All prices are for a standard double room, excluding 12% tax.

$$$$ ⊞ **La Casa de los Sueños.** Tucked away at Isla's south end, this daz-
★ zling residence turned (no-smoking) bed-and-breakfast is honeymoon-
perfect. You enter through a large interior courtyard that leads to a
sunken, open-air living room, which in turn extends into a open-air
terrace that ends with a two-tier swimming pool on a cliff overlooking the ocean. All nine rooms have ocean-view balconies or terraces.
The master suite has a Jacuzzi with a sunset view. Included in the price
is a full American breakfast; scuba lessons in the pool; and the use of
bicycles, kayaks, and snorkeling equipment. ⊠ *Carretera El Garrafón,*
☎ *987/7–06–51; 800/551–2558; 212/679–3099 in New York;* FAX *987/
7–07–08. 9 rooms. Air-conditioning, fans, pool, beach, dock, snorkeling, boating, bicycles. AE, MC, V.*

$$$$ ⊞ **Na Balam.** This intimate hotel set on Playa Norte will satisfy all your
★ tropical-paradise fantasies. Each room in the main hotel building has
a palapa roof, eating area, large bathroom, and either a patio or balcony facing the ocean. Decorated with Mexican folk art or photographs, the rooms are simple, yet elegant. Across the street are eight
more spacious rooms, each with a balcony, sitting area, double bed,
and palapa roof. There's also a pool, garden, and meditation room,
where you can receive a massage or, during the off season, attend
courses in massage, Maya medicine, and other holistic disciplines.
Breakfast at the Zazil-Ha restaurant (☞ Dining, *above*) is a delightful way to kick off the day. ⊠ *Calle Zazil-Ha 118,* ☎ *987/7–02–79,
800/552–4550,* FAX *987/7–04–46. 31 rooms. Restaurant, bar, air-conditioning, pool, beach. AE, MC, V.* ✍

$$$ ⊞ **Cabañas María del Mar.** This establishment offers an eclectic mix
★ of rooms in three different locations. Farthest from the beach (and there-
fore cheapest) are the simply furnished bungalows, with patios that face
a lovely garden and pool. Rooms in The Tower are decorated with Mex-
ican folk art and offer ocean-view balconies, air-conditioning, refrig-
erators, and large beds. Across the street is The Castle, where rooms
decorated with hand-carved wood furnishings have air-conditioning,
refrigerators, bathrooms with Mexican tiles and hand-painted sinks,
and large terraces overlooking Playa Norte. Rates include a Continental
breakfast. The property also has a terrific beach bar, Buho's (☞
Nightlife *in* Nightlife and the Arts, *below*). ⊠ *Av. Carlos Lazos 1,* ☎
987/7–01–79, 800/223–5695, FAX *987/7–02–13. 42 rooms, 14 cabañas.
Restaurant, bar, air-conditioning (some), refrigerators, pool, motorbikes,
travel services. MC, V.*

$$ ⊞ **Hotel Frances Arlene.** This small peach-color hotel is a real deal: bud-
★ get prices with five-star standards. The Magaña family runs it behind
the family home and takes great care to maintain both the property
and its relaxed ambience. Rooms are centered on a pleasant courtyard
and are fitted with double beds, bamboo furniture, and refrigerators.
Some have kitchenettes. From its central location, the beach and downtown are a short stroll away. ⊠ *Av. Guerrero 7,* ☎ *987/7–04–30,* FAX
*987/7–04–29. 11 rooms. Refrigerators, air-conditioning, fans, kitch-
enettes (some). AE, MC, V.*

$ ⊞ **Hotel Osorio.** This heart-of-town hotel is one of the cheapest on the
island. Rooms are basic (double bed, small bathroom) and open onto

a courtyard. ⊠ *Corner of Avs. Juárez and Madero,* ☏ *no phone. 40 rooms. Fans. No credit cards.*

Nightlife and the Arts

The Arts

The island celebrates many religious holidays and festivals in the main square, usually with live entertainment on the outdoor stage. Carnival is in February and is spectacular fun. Other popular events are the springtime regattas. The **Isla Mujeres International Music Festival** takes place the second week in October, and the island is filled with music and dancers from around the world. Founding Day, August 17, marks the day the island was officially founded by the Mexican government.

Nightlife

Nightlife on Isla is laid-back. Most restaurant bars have a happy hour each evening 5–7, with two drinks for the price of one. Check out **YaYa's** (⊠ Av. Rueda Medina 42, near the lighthouse and Playa Norte, ☏ no phone), which serves up Texas steaks, chili dogs, and shrimp along with live jazz, rock, and reggae jam sessions until 2 or 3 AM. **Buho's** (⊠ Av. Carlos Lazo 1, Playa Norte, ☏ 987/7–14–79), the bar/restaurant at Cabañas María del Mar (☞ Lodging, *above*), is a good choice for a relaxing drink at sunset or later at night. **Daniels Bar & Grill** (⊠ Av. Hidalgo, two doors down from the park, ☏ no phone) is a fun bar with friendly staff, funky decor, great Mexican food, live music, and more than 100 kinds of tequila. **Chiles Loco** (⊠ Plaza Isla Mujeres, Local A-4, ☏ no phone) has live music until midnight.

Outdoor Activities and Sports

For water sports, beaches on the north and west sides are the calmest.

Fishing

Bahía Dive Shop (⊠ Av. Rueda Medina 166, across from the pier, ☏ FAX 987/7–03–40) has hourly rates ($20) for offshore fishing (barracuda, snapper, and smaller fish) and day rates ($200–$250) for deep-sea fishing and casting (tarpon, snook, and bonefish). The **Sociedad Cooperativa Turistica** (☏ 987/7–02–74) offers four hours of fishing close to shore for $100. Eight hours farther out are $240. If you're interested in participating in the **Red Cross Billfish Tournament,** held in the spring, contact Michael Creamer (⊠ A.P. 54 Isla Mujeres, Quintana Roo, Mexico 77400, ☏ FAX 987/7–04–43).

Snorkeling and Scuba Diving

There's good snorkeling near **Playa Norte** on the north end. In the waters near *el farolito* (the lighthouse) is a partially buried but still visible statue of the Virgin Mary. There's excellent diving and snorkeling at **Xlaches** (pronounced *ees*-lah-chayss) reef, due north on the way to Isla Contoy. One of Contoy's most alluring dives is the **Cave of the Sleeping Sharks,** east of the northern tip. At the extreme southern end of the island on the leeward side lies **Los Manchones.** A 1-ton, 9¾-ft bronze cross was sunk here, making for a dramatic, fascinating dive. **Los Cuevones,** to the southwest near La Bandera, reaches a depth of 45 ft. On the windward side of the islet north of Mujeres is an unnamed site complete with two sunken galleons. Dive shops are able to direct you to this spot and others.

Bahía Dive Shop (⊠ Av. Rueda Medina 166, across from the pier, ☏ FAX 987/7–03–40) rents snorkeling and scuba equipment and runs three-hour boat and dive trips to the reefs and the Cave of the Sleeping Sharks. Snorkel gear goes for $5 a day; tanks, $45–$60, depending on the length of the dive. **Mexico Divers** (⊠ Avs. Rueda Medina and Madero, a block from the ferry, ☎ 987/7–01–31), also called Buzos de México, runs three-hour snorkeling tours for $15. Two-tank scuba trips start at $55 for a reef dive and $75 for the shark-cave dive. Rental gear is available. **Coral Scuba Dive Center** (✉ Av. Matamoros 13-A, ☎ 987/7–03–71) offers manta-ray dives during the months of May, June, and July for $80; shipwreck dives for $50–$125; photo dives starting at $59; and snorkel trips for $14.

Swimming with Dolphins

Dolphin Discovery (☎ 98/83–07–77 in Cancún) offers humans the chance to play with the delightful sea mammals in a small, supervised group in a pool. There are four swims daily, at 9, 11, 1, 3. Each session lasts an hour—a 30-minute instruction video, then 30 minutes in the water. The cost is $134 and includes the boat ride from Cancún and an all-you-can-eat Mexican buffet.

Shopping

Shopping on Isla Mujeres used to be limited to T-shirts, suntan lotion, beer, and groceries. Those shops are still around, but now there are more places selling Mexican crafts—silver, folk art, handcrafted jewelry, textiles, and clothes. Most shops accept credit cards. Shopping hours are generally 10–1 and 4–7 daily, although quite a few stores now stay open through siesta. Many shops close Sunday.

Casa del Arte Mexica (✉ Av. Hidalgo 6, ☎ 987/7–04–59) has a good selection of fine limestone carvings along with silver jewelry, batiks, rubbings, wood carvings, leather, and hammocks. Some carved wooden masks and animals from Oaxaca, beautiful boxes and clothes from Guatemala, and a large display of handcrafted jewelry are available at **La Loma** (✉ Av. Guerrero, ☎ no phone). **Van Cleef & Arpels** (✉ Avs. Juáres and Morelos, ☎ 987/7–03–31, ℻ 987/7–04–76) offers an incredible selection of jewelry. **Cosmic Cosas** (✉ Matamoros 82, ☎ 987/ 7–08–06) is the only English-language bookstore on the island; it also has e-mail and computer services.

Isla Mujeres A to Z

Arriving and Departing

BY BOAT

Speedboats and passenger ferries run between the main dock on Isla and Puerto Juárez on the mainland. There are also faster and more expensive shuttles to Isla's main dock from Playa Linda, Plaza Caracol, and Playa Tortuga on Cancún. Municipal ferries carry vehicles and passengers between Isla's dock and Cancún's Punta Sam.

Passenger Ferries and Speedboats. Passenger ferries *Sultana del Mar* and *Blanca Beatriz* are the slowest and least expensive options. A one-way ticket is $1.50 and the trip takes about 45 minutes. Delays and crowding aren't unknown, but often there is live music on board, which starts an instant party. The faster speedboats *Caribbean Lady* and *Miss Valentina* (☎ 987/7–02–54, 987/7–02–53) are air-conditioned cruisers with bar service. A one-way ticket costs $2.50 and the crossing takes about 20 minutes. Passenger ferries and speedboats leave every half hour from Cancún and Isla Mujeres 5 AM–8 PM. There's one final ferry from Isla to Puerto Juárez at 9 PM and from Isla to Puerto Juárez at 11:30 PM. Always check the times posted at the dock, as the schedule is subject to change depending on the season and weather conditions. You can reach the **ferry office** at ☎ 987/7–00–65.

Shuttles. Faster but more expensive than the ferries, the shuttles cost about $15 round-trip and take approximately 30 minutes depending on weather conditions. The **Colon Tours** shuttle (☎ 98/84–53–33) departs from Playa Linda at 9:30 AM and leaves Isla at 4 PM. **Asterix Water Taxi** (☎ 98/86–48–47) departs Plaza Caracol at 9, 11, 1, and 3, with return trips from Isla at 10, noon, 2, and 5. The **Isla shuttle** (☎ 98/83–34–48) leaves Playa Tortuga at 9, 11, 1, and 3:45 and returns from Isla at 10, 12:30, 2:30, and 5. Call ahead, as schedules change according to demand.

Municipal Ferries. Cars are unnecessary on Isla, but there are ferries that bring vehicles over. The ride takes about 45 minutes and the fare is just under $2 per person and about $11 per vehicle. From Punta Sam, the ferry leaves at 8, 11, 2:45, 5:30, 6:45, and 8:15. Departing Isla, times are 6:30, 9:30, 12:45, 3, 4:15, 5:30, and 7:15. Again, check the schedule. Landlubbers note: This ferry offers the smoothest ride when the sea is rough.

Getting Around

BY BICYCLE
Bicycles are available but keep in mind the hot sun and tricky road conditions (especially those unexpected speed bumps). Don't ride at night. Many of the roads have no streetlights. **Rent Me Sport Bike** (⊠ Avs. Juárez and Morelos, a block from the main pier, ☎ no phone) rents five-speed cycles starting at less than $3 per hour. A full day costs about $7. You can leave your driver's license in lieu of a deposit. The place is open daily 8–6.

BY BUS
Municipal buses (☎ 987/7–05–29, 987/7–41–73) run at 20- to 30-minute intervals daily 6 AM–10 PM, generally following the ferry schedule. The route goes from the Posada del Mar hotel on Avenida Rueda Medina out to Colonia Salinas on the windward side. As you might expect, service is slow because the buses make frequent stops.

BY CAR
There is little reason to bring a car to Isla Mujeres, because there are plenty of other forms of transportation that cost far less than renting and transporting a private vehicle. Moreover, though the main road is paved, speed bumps abound, and some areas are poorly lighted.

BY GOLF CART
This is a fun way to get around Isla. Many places rent golf carts (including most of the moped rental shops listed below). The best prices on the island can be found at **Ciro's Motorent** (Av. Guerrero Nte. 11 at Av. Matamoros, ☎ 987/7–05–78), with rates as low as $50 for 24 hours. It has more than 30 carts and accepts credit cards. Be prepared to move to the side of the road to let faster vehicles pass you.

BY MOPED
Compared with riding a moped in Cancún, riding one on Isla is an enjoyable affair. It's also the locals' favored mode of transportation, so there are lots of moped rental shops. **Motorent Kankin** (⊠ Av. Abasolo 15, ☎ no phone) provides a two-seat, three-speed Honda for about $5 per hour or $20 per day; a $20 deposit, credit card, or passport is required. **P'pe's Rentadora** (⊠ Av. Hidalgo 19, ☎ 987/7–00–19) has fully automatic Honda Aeros starting at $5 per hour (two-hour minimum). **Ciro's Motorent** (Av. Guerrero Nte. 11, at Av. Matamoros, ☎ 987/7–05–78) has Honda Tact 50 mopeds and offers some great deals. In addition to moped rentals, **Richa's Mopeds** (⊠ Av. Abasolo 13, ☎ 987/5–35–66) has a convenient location—the cheapest laundromat in town is next door.

BY TAXI
If your time is limited you can hire a **taxi** (⊠ Av. Rueda Medina, ☎ 987/7–00–66) for a private island tour at about $15 an hour. Fares run

$1–$2 from the ferry or downtown to the hotels on the north end, at Playa Norte. Taxis line up right by the ferry dock around the clock.

Contacts and Resources

BANKS

Bital (✉ Av. Rueda Medina 3, ☎ 987/7–01–04, 987/7–00–05), the only bank on the island, is open 8–7 and exchanges money 10–noon. Be sure to save some money for the ferry ride back to the mainland, as the ATM machine is often empty by day's end. You can also exchange money at the small **change booth** on Avenida Hidalgo at Francisco Madero weekdays 8:30–7 and Saturday 9–2.

BOAT TOURS

Cooperativa Lanchera (✉ Waterfront near dock, ☎ no phone) has four-hour trips to the submerged Virgin statue, the lighthouse, the turtles at Playa Lancheros, the coral reefs at Los Manchones, and El Garrafón, for about $25 including lunch. **Cooperativa Isla Mujeres** (✉ Av. Rueda Medina near ferry, ☎ 987/7–02–74) rents boats for a maximum of four hours and six people ($120). An island tour with lunch (minimum six people) costs $15 per person.

***Atlantis* Submarine Adventure** (✉ Marina Aqua Tours, Blvd. Kukulcán Km 6.25, Cancún, ☎ 98/83–30–21) leaves from Cancún, but you can catch up with the tour by going to the *Atlantis* site on Playa Indios. The ride lasts approximately 45 minutes and allows you to see the bottom of the ocean without getting all wet. Tickets ($69) include food and drink for the day. Book one day in advance.

Sociedad Cooperativa "Isla Mujeres" (✉ Pier, ☎ 987/7–05–00) and **La Isleña** (✉ ½ block from the pier, Avs. Morelos and Juárez, ☎ 987/7–05–78) offer boat trips to the Isla Contoy national wildlife park and bird sanctuary. Boats depart daily at 8:30 AM. They return at 4 PM. The trip takes about 45 minutes, depending on the weather and the boat. The cost is $30–$40.

EMERGENCIES

Police (☎ 987/7–00–82); **Port Captain** (☎ 987/7–00–95). Isla has an excellent **Red Cross Clinic** (✉ Colonia La Gloria, south side of the island, ☎ 987/7–02–80). The **Centro de Salud** (✉ Av. Guerrero 5, on the plaza, ☎ 987/7–02–17) provides 24-hour emergency service and accepts regular visits 8–8.

LATE-NIGHT PHARMACIES

Farmacia Isla Mujeres (✉ Av. Juárez 8, ☎ 987/7–01–78) is open 9 AM–10 PM Monday through Saturday, 9–3 Sunday. **Farmacia La Gloria** (✉ Carretera al Garrafón, MZ 67, Lt5, ☎ 987/7–08–85) is open daily 8 AM–11 PM, with 24-hour service available.

TOUR OPERATORS

Mundaca Travel (✉ Av. Hidalgo, ☎ 987/7–00–25, 987/7–00–26, FAX 987/7–00–76), a state-of-the-art travel agency, sells plane and bus tickets, sends Federal Express packages, and arranges airport transfers, tours, and house rentals.

VISITOR INFORMATION

The **Isla Mujeres tourist office** (✉ Plaza Isla Mujeres, north end of main shopping street, ☎ 987/7–03–16) is open weekdays 9–2 and 7–9.

COZUMEL

Updated by
Shelagh
McNally

The 490-square-km (189-square-mi) island 19 km (12 mi) east of the Yucatán peninsula, Cozumel is mostly flat with an interior covered by parched scrub, dense jungle, and marshy lagoons. White sandy beaches with calm waters line the island's leeward (western) side, which is fringed by a spectacular reef system, while the windward (eastern) side, facing the Caribbean Sea, features powerful surf and rocky strands. Most of Cozumel is undeveloped, with a good deal of the land and the shores set aside as national parks. A few Maya ruins provide what limited sightseeing there is aside from the island's glorious natural attractions. San Miguel is the only town.

The island's name comes from the Maya word *Ah-Cuzamil-Peten,* which means "land of the swallows." For the Maya, Cozumel was the sacred site of the fertility goddess Ixchel, as well as a key center of trade and navigation. For the Spanish, it was useful as a naval base in the late 16th century. For pirates, its safe harbors and the catacombs and tunnels the Maya dug were ideal for their treasure-gathering and -storing needs. After cycles of settlement and abandonment that included an economic boom based on the island's abundant supply of zapote trees, which produce chicle, a chewing-gum industry staple, Jacques Cousteau discovered Cozumel's incredible reefs and diving opportunities in 1961, and the trajectory of its current life was set.

Despite the inevitable effects of cruise ships that dock here, the island's earthy charm remains largely intact, and the relaxing atmosphere remains typically Mexican—friendly and unpretentious. A mainstay of Cozumel's mood is the isleños, descendents of the Maya who have inhabited the island for centuries.

Exploring

Cozumel is some 53 km (33 mi) long and 15 km (9 mi) wide, but only a small percentage of its roads—primarily those in the southern half—is paved. Navigating the dirt roads requires a bit of care and a four-wheel-drive vehicle.

A Good Tour

It's worth renting some kind of vehicle to explore Cozumel, which has more sights than either Cancún or Isla Mujeres. Be forewarned that most car-rental companies have a policy that voids your insurance when you leave paved roads. Most of the dirt roads are not maintained, so proceed with great caution, especially after a rain.

Head south from Cozumel's principal town, **San Miguel** ⑫, and in about 15 minutes you'll come to **Parque Chankanaab** ⑬. Continue past Parque Chankanaab to reach the beaches: Playa Corona, Playa San Francisco, Playa San Clemente, and Playa Sol. If you stay on this road you will eventually reach the turnoff for the ruins of **El Cedral** ⑭. The road to this ruin is not navigable unless you have four-wheel drive. About 3 km (2 mi) inland, you'll reach the village and what is left of the ruin.

Once back on the main coast road, continue south until you reach the turnoff for Playa del Palancar, where the famous reef lies offshore. Here the roads turn west. If you continue to the point where the road swings north, you come to the entrance of the island's newest park **Parque Punta Sur** ⑮. The park encompasses Laguna Colombia and Laguna Chunchacaab as well as the ancient Maya lighthouse El Caracol and the modern lighthouse **Punta Celerain Faro** ⑯. You will have to leave your car at the gate and use either the bicycles, small carts, or public bus provided by the park.

At Punta Sur the coast road swings north, passing one beach after another: Playa Paradiso, Punta Chiqueros, Playa Bonita, Playa San Martin, Playa Chen Río, and Punta Morena. Just north of Playa Paradiso are the minuscule ruins of El Mirador and El Trono. At Playa Oriente,

Cozumel

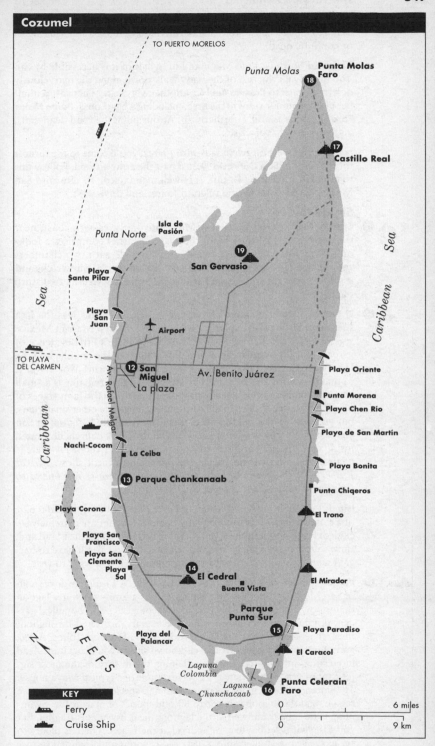

TO PUERTO MORELOS

Punta Molas

Punta Molas Faro

18

17 **Castillo Real**

Punta Norte

Isla de Pasión

Sea

19 **San Gervasio**

Playa Santa Pilar

Playa San Juan

Airport

Caribbean Sea

TO PLAYA DEL CARMEN

12 **San Miguel**
La plaza

Av. Benito Juárez

Playa Oriente

Caribbean

Punta Morena

Playa Chen Río

Playa de San Martín

Nachi-Cocom

La Ceiba

13 **Parque Chankanaab**

Playa Bonita

Punta Chiqeros

Playa Corona

El Trono

Playa San Francisco

Playa San Clemente
Playa Sol

14 **El Cedral**

Buena Vista

El Mirador

Parque Punta Sur

Playa del Palancar

15 **Playa Paradiso**

El Caracol

Laguna Colombia

Laguna Chunchacaab

16 **Punta Celerain Faro**

R E E F S

N

KEY

▲ Ferry

⛴ Cruise Ship

0   6 miles

0   9 km

the coast road intersects with Avenida Benito Juárez, which crosses the island to the east coast. You can take this road west back into San Miguel or continue north.

The road north is quite rough and only half of it is accessible by car. You must walk the rest of the way. Walk north along the marvelously deserted beach to **Castillo Real** ⑰, another Maya site. There are a number of other minor ruins in the area, including a lighthouse, **Punta Molas Faro** ⑱, at the island's northern tip. At this point the road dead-ends, and you have to turn back.

If you travel west on Avenida Benito Juárez, you'll come to the turnoff for the ruins of **San Gervasio** ⑲, just past the army airfield. Follow this road north for 7 km (4½ mi). It is well maintained. To return to San Miguel, go back to Avenida Benito Juárez and drive west.

Sights to See

⚠ ⑰ **Castillo Real** (Royal Castle). A Maya site on the eastern coast, near the northern tip of the island, the *castillo* (castle) comprises a lookout tower, the base of a pyramid, and a temple with two chambers capped by a false arch. The waters here harbor several shipwrecks and it's a fine spot for snorkeling because there are few visitors to disturb the fish.

⚠ ⑭ **El Cedral.** Once the hub of Maya life on Cozumel, this was the first site found by Spanish explorers in 1518, and the first Mass in Mexico was reportedly celebrated here. These days, there's little evidence of its past glory. Conquistadors tore down much of the temple, and the U.S. Army Corps of Engineers destroyed the rest during World War II to make way for the island's first airport. All that remains is a small structure with an arch; be sure to look inside to see the faint traces of paint and stucco. Hidden in the surrounding jungle are other small ruins, but you will need a guide to find them (they usually hang out at San Gervasio). Nearby is a green and white cinder-block church, decorated inside with crosses shrouded in embroidered lace. Every May there is a fair here, with dancing, music, bullfights, and a cattle show. *Turn at Km 17.5 off the main island road, then drive 3 km (2 mi) inland to the site,* ☎ *no phone.* 🎟 *Free.* ☉ *Dawn–dusk.*

Isla de Pasión. In Abrigo Bay, east of Punta Norte, this tiny island is part of a state reserve. Accessible only by boat, its beaches are extremely secluded. Fishing is permitted, but there are no facilities on the island and, since so few people come here, no scheduled tours. You'll have to bargain with a local boat owner for transportation if you want to visit.

⚠ ☉ ⑬ **Parque Chankanaab** (Chankanaab Nature Park). A 15-minute drive south of San Miguel, Chankanaab ("small sea") is a lovely saltwater lagoon that is now a national park with an archaeological park, botanical garden, dolphin aquarium, and wildlife sanctuary. Scattered throughout the archaeological park are 60 reproductions of Olmec, Toltec, Aztec, and Maya stone carvings from well-known sites in Mexico. Guides lead interesting, informative tours, explaining the history of the most significant pieces. Also on site is a good example of a typical Maya house. The botanical garden houses more than 450 species of plants from the region, and the lagoon is home to 60-odd species of marine life. Swimming is no longer allowed at the lagoon (the ecosystem is fragile), but you can swim, scuba dive, or snorkel at the beach. There is plenty to see in the sea: a sunken ship, crusty old cannons and anchors, statues of Jesus Christ, a Maya Chacmool (the revered rain god), along with hordes of brilliant fish. At the dolphin aquarium, visitors can swim with the fascinating marine mammals. Also on the premises are four dive shops, two restaurants, three gift shops, a snack stand, and a dressing room with lockers and showers. Come early, as the park fills up fast. ⊠ *Carretera Sur Km 9,* ☎ *no phone.* 🎟 *$7, free after 5 PM.* ☉ *Daily 7–6.*

⑮ **Parque Punta Sur.** Mexico's newest national park is at the southernmost tip of Cozumel. The 247-acre preserve, home to numerous birds and animals such as crocodiles, flamingos, foxes, egrets, and herons, has been kept natural and pristine. No cars are allowed. Visitors must use park transportation (bicycles, small carts, or public buses). From observation towers you can spot crocodiles and birds in **Laguna Columbia** or **Laguna Chunchacaab.** Or visit the ancient Maya lighthouse **El Caracol.** At the southernmost point of the park (and the is-
⑯ land) is the **Punta Celerain Faro,** a lighthouse with a navigational museum. The beaches here are deserted and wide, and there's great snorkeling offshore. Snorkeling equipment is available for rent, as are kayaks. There's a snack bar, a restaurant, an information center, a souvenir shop, and rest rooms. A round-trip taxi ride from town is $30. ⊠ *Southernmost point on the coastal road,* ☎ *no phone.* 🎟 *$10, free after 3 PM.* ☉ *Daily 7–4.*

⑱ **Punta Molas Faro** (Molas Point Lighthouse). At the northernmost point of Cozumel, the lighthouse is an excellent spot for sunbathing, birding, and camping. The jagged shoreline and the open sea offer magnificent views, making it well worth the time-consuming and somewhat difficult trip. Be prepared to walk some of the way. Your car-rental company will actively discourage you from driving here. Access is easier by boat, or you may prefer to take the guided tour (☞ Contacts and Resources *in* Cozumel A to Z, *below*).

⛏️ ⑲ **San Gervasio.** Standing in lovely forest, these remarkable ruins are the largest existing Maya and Toltec site on Cozumel. San Gervasio was once the island's capital and ceremonial center, dedicated to the fertility goddess Ixchel. The Classic– and Post-Classic–style buildings were continuously occupied AD 300–1500. Typical architectural features include limestone plazas and arches atop stepped platforms, as well as stelae and bas-reliefs. Be sure to see the "hands" temple, which has red hand imprints all over its altar. Plaques clearly identify each of the ruins in Maya, Spanish, and English. You'll find a snack bar and some gift shops at the entrance. If you want a rugged hike, take the 15-km (9-mi) dirt road that travels north to the coast and ☞ **Castillo Real.** ⊠ *Av. Juárez east to San Gervasio access road; follow road north for 7 km (4½ mi).* 🎟 *Access to road $1, ruins $3.50.* ☉ *Daily 8–5. Closed Oct.*

⑫ **San Miguel.** Cozumel's only town has kept some of the flavor of a Mexican village, although its streets are dotted with shops and restaurants trying to draw crowds of tourists. Stroll along the malecón and take in the ocean breeze. The main square is where townspeople and visitors hang out, particularly on Sunday night when mariachi bands join the assortment of food and souvenir vendors.

🐚 **Museo de la Isla de Cozumel** (Museum of the Island of Cozumel). The museum is housed on two floors of what was once the island's first luxury hotel. The first floor is dedicated to natural history, with exhibits about the origins of the island. Upstairs, the history of Cozumel is illustrated with Maya artifacts, cannons and swords of the conquistadors, and maritime instruments. Guided tours are available. ⊠ *Av. Rafael Melgar between Calles 4 and 6 Norte,* ☎ *987/2–14–75.* 🎟 *$3.* ☉ *Daily 10–6.*

Beaches

Cozumel's beaches vary from long, treeless, sandy stretches to isolated coves and rocky shores. Most development is on the leeward (west) side, where the coast is relatively sheltered by the proximity of the mainland 19 km (12 mi) to the west. The best sand beaches lie along the southern half of Cozumel's leeward side, some 5 km (3 mi) long—from **Playa Corona** south to **Punta Celerain.** In between them, **Playa San Francisco** and **Playa Sol** tend to get cruise ship crowds. **Playa del Palancar** is often less crowded than those two.

Getting to the east coast requires transportation, but the succession of mostly deserted rocky coves and narrow, powdery beaches—sadly garbage-strewn in spots—poised dramatically against the turquoise water is worth the trip. **Playa Oriente** has pounding surf; there is also a café for light meals and drinks. **Punta Chiqeros** is a moon-shaped cove sheltered by an offshore reef. The cove is part of Playa Bonita, which also has a café. Swimming on parts of the east coast can be treacherous if you go too far out or if a southwest wind is blowing—in some parts a deadly undertow can sweep you out to sea in a matter of minutes—but the beaches are still great for solitary sunbathing.

Dining

Dining options on Cozumel reflect the nature of the place as a whole: breezy and relaxed with the occasional harmless pretensions. There are more than 80 restaurants in the downtown core, so you can choose among American fast-food outlets, simple outdoor eateries that serve great regional dishes, and dining spots offering gourmet seafood and romantic settings. Most restaurants accept credit cards; café-type places generally take only cash. A tip: don't be influenced by cab drivers' suggestions—usually they are paid to recommend restaurants.

CATEGORY	COST*
$$$	over $25
$$	$15–$25
$	under $15

per person for a three-course meal, excluding drinks and service

$$$ ✕ **Arrecife.** A well-trained staff and impeccably prepared dishes put this casually elegant hotel restaurant in a class by itself. Tall windows providing excellent views of the sea complement the stylish decor. Live music adds to the romantic mood. The rack of lamb, fish, and homemade pasta dishes are exceptional. ⊠ *Presidente Inter-Continental Cozumel, Carretera Chankanaab Km 6.5,* ☎ *987/2–03–22. AE, DC, MC, V. Closed Sept. and Oct. No lunch.*

$$$ ✕ **La Cabaña del Pescador Lobster House.** Walk the gangplank to this palapa restaurant with seashells and nets hanging from the walls. It's kitschy and cutesy, but worth it if you're looking for the freshest lobster on the island. The crustaceans are sold by weight, but the rest of your meal—including the delicious *Ixtabentun* (an eggnoglike drink)—is included in the price of your lobster. ⊠ *Carretera San Juan Km 4 across from Playa Azul Hotel,* ☎ *987/2–07–95. AE, MC, V. No lunch.*

$$$ ✕ **La Cocay.** The name is Maya for firefly and, like its namesake, this
★ place is a bit magical. Located atop a small hill, the restaurant offers some of the most innovative and flavorful cuisine on the island. The chef and manager create a new menu every month or so. Sample creations include spiced-nut-and-tamarind-crusted chicken breast, pumpkin-stuffed *medialunas* (half-moon pasta) with sage and Parmesan butter sauce, and rack of lamb with a red-onion reduction sauce. The decor is simple yet sophisticated, and an open-air kitchen lets you watch the chefs do their magic. Desserts are phenomenal. Accompanying the exquisite fare is a well thought out wine list. ⊠ *Av. 17 Sur 1000,* ☎ *987/2–55–33. No credit cards. Closed Sun. and Oct. No lunch.*

$$ ✗ **El Capi Navegante.** When the captain's motto is "The fish we serve today slept in the sea last night," you know the fish will be fresh. This blue and white restaurant is one of oldest on the island and was one of the first to introduce inventive ways to serve fish. Specialties such as whole red snapper and stuffed squid are skillfully prepared and sometimes flambéed at your table. The conch ceviche is highly recommended. ⊠ *Av. 10 Sur 312, at Calle 3,* ☎ *987/2–17–30. MC, V.*

$$ ✗ **La Choza.** With its white stucco walls, open kitchen, and thatch roof, this family-run restaurant resembles a large Maya home. Doña Elisa Espinosa is assisted by her four daughters, and together they create local favorites such as *pozole* (corn soup) or *pollo en relleno negro* (chicken in a blackened sauce). To finish, try their signature frozen avocado pie. Open all day, this is a popular place with both locals and tourists, so the staff is often rushed and there's frequently a long wait for a table. ⊠ *Rosada Salas 198, at Av. 10 Sur,* ☎ *987/2–09–58. Reservations not accepted. AE, MC, V.*

$$ ✗ **Prima.** Located on a breezy second-floor terrace, this is the best Ital-
★ ian restaurant on the island. Everything is fresh: the meat is flown in daily from the States and the vegetables come from local gardens. Start off with the house speciality, conch fritters, and move on to angel-hair pasta with lobster, jumbo shrimp stuffed with crabmeat au gratin, or the seafood combo dish. The salads, coffee, and desserts are also exemplary. The first-floor store sells Mexico's finest wines and pricey Cuban cigars. ⊠ *Rosado Salas 109-A,* ☎ *987/2–42–42, 987/2–24–77. AE, MC, V. No lunch.*

$$ ✗ **La Veranda.** This charming wooden Caribbean house oozes ro-
★ mance. Inside there is comfortable rattan furniture, soft lighting, and good music. Outside, a terrace looks into a lush tropical garden. The Mexican chef, Miguel Garcia Lopez, has introduced a fusion menu based on Mexican–Caribbean cuisine. Try the poblano chilies stuffed with sun-dried tomato, seafood, and goat cheese. The flambé desserts are sensational. ⊠ *Calle 4 Nte. 140,* ☎ *987/2–41–32. AE, MC, V. No lunch.*

$ ✗ **Chen Río Restaurant.** On the east side of the island at Chen Río beach,
★ this place serves the best fish on Cozumel. It's run by a Maya family whose sons go out in the morning to catch the fish they serve for lunch. Relax under the coconut trees, watch the surf, or go for a swim while you wait for your meal to arrive. The combo plate—with shrimp, lobster, fish, rice, and vegetables—is a phenomenal bargain. ⊠ *East coast road Km 28,* ☎ *no phone. No credit cards.*

$ ✗ **El Foco.** Here's a fun spot to grab a *cerveza* (beer) and a bite to eat. This traditional Mexican joint is essentially a *taquería* (taco stand), where you'll find soft tacos stuffed with pork, chorizo, cheese, or chilies. The graffiti on the walls provide the entertainment. ⊠ *Av. 5 Sur 13-B, between Calles Rosado Salas and 3 Sur,* ☎ *no phone. No credit cards.*

$ ✗ **El Moro.** This restaurant has been serving Cozumeleños for more than 40 years. It's also quite popular with divers. The ghastly decor becomes unimportant once you taste the delicious and hearty food and meet the sweet staff. Try the substantial *pollo Ticuleño,* a layered medley of tomato sauce, mashed potatoes, crispy baked tortillas, and batter-fried chicken topped with shredded cheese. Take a taxi here. El Moro is too far a walk and too difficult to find. ⊠ *Calle 75 Nte. between Calles 2 and 4,* ☎ *987/2–30–29. MC, V. Closed Thurs.*

$ ✗ **El Turix.** About 10 minutes by cab from downtown, this simple, wel-
★ coming place is worth the trip for a chance to experience true Yucatecan cuisine. Don't miss the pollo pibíl or the poc chuc. There are also daily specials, and paella on request. ⊠ *Av. 20 Sur between Calles 17 and 19,* ☎ *987/2–52–34. No credit cards. No lunch.*

Lodging

All of Cozumel's hotels are on the leeward (west) side of the island. Hotels north and south of San Miguel tend to be larger, all-inclusive resorts, while less expensive places are in town. Because of the proximity of the reefs, divers and snorkelers tend to congregate at the southern properties, while sailors and anglers prefer the hotels to the north, where the beaches are better. Most budget hotels are in town. All hotels have air-conditioning unless otherwise noted, and all share the 77600 postal code.

CATEGORY	COST*
$$$$	over $160
$$$	$90–$160
$$	$40–$90
$	under $40

All prices are for a standard double room in the high season, excluding service charges and 10% tax.

North Hotel Zone

$$$$ ⊞ **Coral Princess Hotel & Resort.** Tasteful and elegant, this is one of
★   the newer hotels in the North Hotel Zone. The lobby features a fountain and sculptures of wrought iron and glass; the rooms are decorated with Mexican furnishings and artwork. Each of the Princess Villas has two bedrooms, two bathrooms, a kitchen, a dining room, and private terrace. The Coral Villas have one bedroom with a combined kitchen/dining area and terrace. Studios units have two double beds and a small balcony. There isn't much of a beach but there is a wonderful pool and huge deck with palapas and stairs leading down to the ocean. The lovely bar is perfect for a romantic drink before moving on to El Galeón restaurant. ⊠ *Zona Hotelera Norte Km 2.5,* ☎ *987/2–32–00, 800/253–2702,* FAX *987/2–15–22. 100 rooms, 37 villas, 2 penthouses. Restaurant, bar, pool, dive shop, dock, snorkeling, fishing, volleyball, car rental. AE, MC, V.* ✎

$$$ ⊞ **Playa Azul Hotel.** At this quiet, comfortable hotel, airy rooms have either great ocean views or face beautiful tropical gardens. All have sliding doors leading to sun-filled terraces. Some of the rooms have couches that convert to beds. Along the beach, small palapas are set up with comfortable chairs. Snorkeling, scuba diving, and fishing trips depart daily from Playa Azul's own dock. The Palma Azul restaurant serves delicious meals centered on fresh fish. ⊠ *Zona Hotelera Norte, Carretera San Juan Km 4, Apdo. 31,* ☎ *987/2–01–99,* FAX *987/2–01–10. 31 rooms. Restaurant, 2 bars, pool, massage, dive shop, dock, snorkeling, fishing, billiards, car rental. AE, MC, V.* ✎

South Hotel Zone

$$$$ ⊞ **Allegro Resort.** This southernmost all-inclusive hotel, located on Playa San Francisco, resembles a luxury camp for adults. There are lots of organized activities, with much of the action centered around the nearby Palancar Reef. Standard rooms, arranged in groups of eight in two-story palapa villas, are small. The duplex suites are much larger and can easily accommodate three or four people. Guests here have access to the facilities at other Allegro hotels in Cancún and Playa del Carmen. Pack bug spray—at dusk the mosquitoes arrive in droves. ⊠ *San Francisco Palancar Km 16.5,* ☎ *987/2–35–54, 800/858–2258,* FAX *987/2–45–08. 292 rooms, 8 suites. 3 restaurants, 4 bars, 2 pools, beauty salon, 4 tennis courts, aerobics, basketball, shuffleboard, volleyball, snorkeling, bicycles, motorbikes, shops, children's programs (ages 4–12), car rental. AE, MC, V.* ✎

$$$$ 🏨 **Presidente Inter-Continental Cozumel.** Luxury, comfort, and privacy
★ are hallmarks of the Presidente. Most units have a full ocean view. The
deluxe rooms have their own private terraces in front of the beach or
gardens. The beach and the pool are both among the nicest on the island, and there's incredible snorkeling just a few feet off the beach. A
professional dive and water-sports center is also on the premises. The
staff is noted for its warmth and efficiency, and the restaurant, Arrecife
(☞ Dining, *above*), is highly recommended. ⊠ *Carretera Chankanaab
Km 6.5,* ☎ *987/2–03–22, 800/327–0200,* FAX *987/2–13–60. 253 rooms.
2 restaurants, 3 bars, coffee shop, pool, hot tub, 2 tennis courts, dive
shop, motorbikes, shops, children's program (ages 4–12), car rental.
AE, DC, MC, V.* ☜

$$$ 🏨 **Fiesta Americana Cozumel Reef.** Reasonable prices and a good lo-
cation have made this bright orange hotel one of the most popular on
the island. It's ideally situated for snorkeling and scuba diving—although
the building itself is across the road from the water, a pedestrian walk-
way provides easy access to the dive shop, dock, beach, pool, and restau-
rant. Standard rooms are large, with light-wood furnishings; all have
ocean-front balconies. There is also a 56-room semicircular cluster of
villas with patios and ocean views. ⊠ *Carretera Chankanaab Km 7.5,*
☎ *987/2–26–22, 800/343–7821,* FAX *987/2–26–66. 172 rooms, 56
villa rooms. 3 restaurants, 3 bars, 2 pools, 2 tennis courts, dive shop,
dock, motorbikes, travel services, car rental. AE, MC, V.* ☜

$$ 🏨 **Casa del Mar.** Each of the cheerful rooms at this three-story diver's
hotel has a small balcony with a view of either the pool or the ocean
across the road. The bi-level cabañas, which sleep three or four, are a
very good buy. The hotel has been set up to accommodate divers
(rooms for equipment, lots of showers and towels). Close by is the Del
Mar Dive Shop, along with several boutiques, sports shops, bars, and
restaurants. Eight miles south is the property's new beach club, Nachi
Cocom. ⊠ *Carretera Chankanaab Km 4,* ☎ *987/2–19–44, 800/877–
4383,* FAX *987/2–18–55. 98 rooms, 8 cabañas. 2 restaurants, 2 bars,
pool, hot tub, dive shop, travel services, car rental. AE, MC, V.* ☜

Downtown Hotels

$$ 🏨 **Sun Village San Miguel.** This hotel has an outdoor café and a bar
that are popular with locals. The rooms are clean and functional, with
balconies overlooking the main square. There's also a lovely pool and
a game room with pool tables. Shops are nearby and there's often some-
thing happening right outside the front door. ⊠ *Main square, Av.
Juárez,* ☎ FAX *987/2–02–33,* ☎ *800/221–5835. 97 rooms. Pool, mas-
sage, bicycles, shops, baby-sitting, laundry service. MC, V.*

$$ 🏨 **Tamarindo Bed & Breakfast.** The owners of this five-room charmer
have created a place that combines the flavor of Mexico with the ele-
gance of France. Rooms are gracefully decorated with individual
touches. The staff will arrange diving expeditions, and there is a rinse
tank and gear-storage facility on the premises. ⊠ *Calle 4 Nte. 421, between Avs. 20 and 25,* ☎ FAX *987/2–36–14. 5 rooms. Massage, bicycles, baby-sitting, laundry service. MC, V.*

$$ 🏨 **Villas Las Anclas.** Conveniently located parallel to the malecón, these
villas are furnished apartments for rent by the day, week, or month.
Each of the duplexes has a downstairs sitting room, a dining area, and
a fully equipped kitchenette. A spiral staircase leads up to a small bed-
room overlooking a quiet courtyard garden. ⊠ *Apdo. 25, Av. 5 Sur
325, between Calles 3 and 5,* ☎ *987/2–14–03,* FAX *987/2–54–76. 7 units.
Kitchenettes, refrigerators. No credit cards.*

$ 🏨 **Charrito's.** This charming B&B with a Western flavor is run by a
★ hospitable Mexican-American husband-and-wife team. Its quiet loca-
tion in a typical neighborhood seven blocks from the beach gives you

a chance to experience a slice of Mexico. Each of the five rooms is extremely comfortable, with individual decor and a private bath. Upstairs is a charming terrace for sunbathing or taking in sunsets. Sandy and Marcos will help you arrange dive trips and other outings. The full Mexican breakfast is delicious. ⊠ *Calle 21 Sur, between Felipe Angeles and Av. 40 Sur,* ☎ FAX *987/2–47–60. 5 rooms. Ceiling fans. No credit cards.*

Nightlife and the Arts

For a bit of local culture check out the folkloric dance performances held Thursdays at the **Fiesta Americana** (☎ 987/2–26–22). The whole island explodes with music, costumes, dancing, parades and parties for **Carnival,** which takes place just before the start of Lent in February.

Bars
For a quiet drink and good people-watching, try **Video Bar Aladino** (☎ 987/2–02–33) at the Sun Village San Miguel, at the north end of the plaza. Serious barhoppers like the wild, raucous (and at times obnoxious) **Carlos 'n' Charlie's** (⊠ Av. Rafael Melgar 11, between Calles 2 and 4 Nte., ☎ 987/2–01–91). Sports fiends can play video games or catch all the news on ESPN at **Sports Page Video Bar and Restaurant** (⊠ Av. 5 Nte. and Calle 2, ☎ 987/2–11–99); the hamburgers aren't bad either.

Discos
Neptuno (⊠ Av. Rafael Melgar at Calle 11 Sur, ☎ 987/2–15–37), preferred by the teenage set and locals, can be loud and fun, although it's pretty quiet on weekdays. **Viva Mexico** (⊠ Av. Rafael E. Melgar, ☎ 987/2–07–99) has a DJ who plays dance music until the wee hours.

Live Music
Sunday evening, 8–10, locals head for the **zócalo** (plaza) to hear mariachis and island musicians play tropical tunes. **Hog's Breath** (⊠ Av. Rafael Melgar, ☎ no phone) has live music every night. The food is ★ risky at **Joe's Lobster House** (⊠ Av. 10 Sur 229, between Calles Rosada Salas and 3 Sur, ☎ 987/2–32–75), but the reggae and salsa are great (nightly 10:30 until dawn). For sophisticated jazz, smart cocktails, and great cigars, check out the **Havana Club** (⊠ Av. Rafael Melgar between Calles 6 and 8, second floor, ☎ 987/2–65–99).

Outdoor Activities and Sports

Most people come to Cozumel for the water sports—scuba diving, snorkeling, and fishing are particularly big, but jet skiing, sailboarding, waterskiing, and sailing are also popular. You'll find services and rentals throughout the island, especially through major hotels and water-sports centers such as **Scuba Du** (⊠ Calle 3 Sur 33, between Avs. Rafael Melgar and 5 Sur, ☎ 987/2–19–94) and **Del Mar Aquatics** (⊠ Carretera Chankanaab Km 4, ☎ 987/2–16–65, 800/877–4383, FAX 987/ 2–18–33). For small group or individual lessons, try **Eagle Ray Dive School** (⊠ Avs. Chichén and Pamuul, ☎ 987/2–57–35).

Fishing
Regulations forbid commercial fishing, sportfishing, spear fishing, and the collection of any marine life between the shore and El Cantil Reef and between the cruise-ship dock and Punta Celerain. It's illegal to kill certain species, including billfish. The annual **International Billfish Tournament** (⊠ Apdo. 442, Cozumel 77600, ☎ 800/253–2701, FAX 987/ 2–09–99), held the last week in April or the first week in May, draws anglers from around the world.

You can charter high-speed fishing boats for $300 for a half day or $350 for a full day, for a maximum of six people, from the **Club**

Naútico de Cozumel (✉ Puerto de Abrigo, Av. Rafael Melgar, Apdo. 341, ☎ 987/2–01–18, 800/253–2701, FAX 987/2–11–35), the island's headquarters for game fishing. Daily charters are easily arranged from the dock or at your hotel, but you might also try **Aquarius Fishing and Tours** (✉ Calle 3 Sur, ☎ 987/2–10–92) or **Dive Cozumel** (✉ Rosado Salas 72, at Av. 5 Sur, ☎ 987/2–41–10, FAX 987/2–18–42).

Scuba Diving

With more than 30 charted reefs whose average depths range from 50 to 80 ft and a water temperature that hits about 75°F–80°F during peak diving season (June–August, when the hotel rates are at their lowest), Cozumel is far and away Mexico's no. 1 diving destination. Diverse diving options include deep dives, drift dives, shore dives, wall dives, and night dives, as well as theme dives focusing on ecology, archaeology, sunken ships, and photography.

DIVE SHOPS AND TOUR OPERATORS

You can choose from a variety of two-tank boat trips and specialty dives ranging from $45 to $60; two-hour resort courses cost about $50–$60, and 1½-hour night dives $30–$35. Basic certification courses, such as PADI's Discover Scuba or Naui's introductory course, are available for about $350, while advanced certification courses cost as much as $700. Equipment rental is relatively inexpensive, from $6 for tanks or a lamp to $8–$10 for a regulator and BC vest. Underwater-camera rentals can cost as much as $35, video-camera rentals run about $75, and professionally shot and edited videos of your own dive are about $160.

Before choosing a dive shop, check credentials, look over the boats and equipment, and consult experienced divers who are familiar with the operators here. Look for places that focus on smaller groups and offer individual attention. Make sure your instructor has PADI certification (or FMAS, the Mexican equivalent) and is affiliated with the **SSS recompression chamber** (✉ Calle 5 Sur 21B, between Avs. Rafael Melgar and 5a Sur, next to Discover Cozumel, ☎ 987/2–23–87, 987/2–18–48) or the recompression chamber at the **Hospital Civil** (✉ Av. 11 Sur, between Calles 10 and 15, ☎ 987/2–01–40, 987/2–05–25). Also consider getting DAN (Divers Alert Network) insurance, which covers dive accidents.

The following are some of the dive shops in town. In addition, many hotels have their own operations and offer dive and hotel packages starting at about $350 for three nights, double occupancy, and two days of diving.

Aqua Safari (✉ Av. Rafael Melgar 429, between Calles 5 and 7 Sur, ☎ 987/2–01–01); **Black Shark** (✉ Av. 5 Sur between Calles Rosado Salas and 3 Sur, ☎ 987/2–56–57); **Blue Angel** (✉ Av. Rafael Melgar next to Hotel Villablanca, ☎ 987/2–16–31); **Blue Bubble** (✉ Av. 5 Sur at Calle 3, ☎ 987/2–18–65); **Chino's Scuba** (✉ Rosado Salas 16-A, ☎ 987/2–44–87); **Dive Cozumel** (✉ Rosado Salas 72, at Av. 5 Sur, ☎ 987/2–41–10, FAX 987/2–18–42); **Dive Paradise** (✉ Av. Rafael Melgar 602, ☎ FAX 987/2–10–07); **Eagle Ray Dive School** (✉ Avs. Chichén and Pamuul, ☎ 987/2–57–35); **Michelle's Dive Shop** (✉ Av. 5 Sur 201, at Rosado Salas, ☎ 987/2–09–47); **Nitrox Solutions** (✉ Calle 3 Sur between the waterfront and Av. 5 ☎ FAX 987/2–56–66); **Ramone Zapata Divers** (✉ Chankanaab Park, ☎ 987/2–05–02); **Scuba Du** (✉ Presidente Inter-Continental Cozumel Hotel, ☎ 987/2–03–22, 987/2–13–79, FAX 987/2–41–30); **Studio Blue** (✉ Rosado Salas 121, between Avs. 5 and 10 Sur, ☎ FAX 987/2–43–30); **Tico's Dive Center** (✉ Av. 5 Nte. 121, between Calles 2 and 4, FAX 987/2–02–76).

Snorkeling

Snorkeling equipment is available at the Presidente Inter-Continental, La Ceiba, Chankanaab Bay, Playa San Francisco, and Club Cozumel Caribe hotels, and directly off the beach near the Fiesta Americana Cozumel Reef and Playa Corona for less than $10 a day.

Snorkeling tours run $25–$50, depending on the length, and take in the shallow reefs off Palancar, Colombia, and Yucab. **Eagle Ray Dive School** (⊠ Avs. Chichén and Pamuul, ☎ 987/2–57–35) specializes in combined diving and snorkeling trips for families where only one member dives. **Fiesta Cozumel** (⊠ Calle 11 Sur 598, between Avs. 25 and 30, ☎ 987/2–07–25, FAX 987/2–13–89) runs snorkeling tours from the 45-ft catamarans *El Zorro* and *Fury.* Rates begin at about $50 per day and include equipment, a guide, soft drinks and beer, and a box lunch.

Shopping

Cozumel's main shopping area is downtown on the waterfront along Avenida Rafael Melgar, and on some of the side streets around the plaza (there are more than 150 shops in this area alone). There is also a **crafts market** (⊠ Calle 1 Sur, behind the plaza), which sells a respectable assortment of Mexican wares. In addition, small clusters of shops can be found at **Plaza del Sol** (on the east side of the main plaza), **Villa Mar** (on the north side of the main plaza), and **Plaza Confetti** (on the south side of the main plaza). As a general rule, the newer, trendier shops line the waterfront, while the area around Avenida 5a houses the better crafts shops. South of the city, past Casa del Mar, is **Plaza Maya,** a collection of shops selling low-end souvenirs at high-end prices. The craft market at **Puerto Maya,** where the cruise ships dock, has some crafts at good prices. For fresh produce, try the **town market** (⊠ Rosada Salas, between Avs. 20 and 25 Sur) or the grocery store **Chedraui** (⊠ Carretera Chankanaab Km 1.5).

Department Stores

Relatively small and more like U.S. variety stores than department stores, the following nevertheless carry a relatively wide array of goods, from the useful to the frivolous. **Fama** (⊠ Av. 5 Nte. 50, ☎ 987/2–50–20) carries clothes, CDs, books, and shoes. **Pama** (⊠ Av. Rafael Melgar Sur 9, ☎ 987/2–00–90), near the pier, carries imported luxury items. **Prococo** (⊠ Av. Rafael Melgar Norte 99, ☎ 987/2–18–75, 987/2–19–64) offers a good selection of liquor, jewelry, and gift items. **Viva México** (⊠ Av. Rafael Melgar at Rosada Salas, ☎ 987/2–07–91) sells souvenirs and handicrafts from all over Mexico.

Specialty Stores

CLOTHING

Several trendy sportswear stores line Avenida Rafael Melgar between Calles 2 and 6. **Miro** (⊠ Av. Rafael Melgar, one block from the town pier, ☎ 987/2–02–60) has a wide variety of Mexican resort wear with the latest designs and styles. **Poco Loco** (⊠ Av. Rafael Melgar 18 and Av. Benito Juárez 2-A, ☎ 987/2–54–99) sells casual wear and beach bags. **Bikinis do Brasil** (⊠ Calle 1 Sur, between Avs. 10 and 15, ☎ 987/2–02–60) features a collection of Brazilian swimwear and sundresses.

JEWELRY

Jewelry on Cozumel is pricey, but it tends to be of higher quality than what you'll find in many other Yucatán towns. **Diamond Creations** (⊠ Av. Rafael Melgar Sur 131, ☎ 987/2–53–30) lets you custom-design a piece of jewelry from its collection of loose gems. You'll find silver, gold, and coral jewelry—bracelets and earrings especially—at **Joyería Palancar** (⊠ Av. Rafael Melgar Nte. 15, ☎ 987/2–14–68). Quality gemstones and striking designs are the strong point at **Rachat & Romero** (⊠ Av. Rafael Melgar 101, ☎ 987/2–05–71). Innovative designs and top-quality stones can be found at **Van Cleef & Arpels** (⊠ Av. Rafael Melgar Nte. across from the ferry, ☎ 987/2–65–40).

MEXICAN CRAFTS

Bugambilias (⊠ Av. 10 Sur between Calles Rosado Salas and 1 Sur, ☎ 987/2–62–82) sells handmade Mexican linens. **Los Cinco Soles** (⊠ Av. Rafael Melgar Nte. 27, ☎ 987/2–01–32, 987/2–20–40) is the best bet for one-stop shopping. **El Sombrero** (⊠ Av. Rafael Melgar 29, ☎ 987/2–03–74) stocks a fine selection of leather clothing and accessories. **Talavera** (⊠ Av. 5 Sur 349, ☎ 987/2–01–71) carries beautiful ceramics from all over Mexico. **Xtabay** (⊠ Av. 5 Sur 203, ☎ no phone) has beautiful work by artists from all over Mexico.

Cozumel A to Z

Arriving and Departing

BY CRUISE SHIP

At least a dozen cruise lines call at Cozumel and/or Playa del Carmen, including, from Fort Lauderdale, **Celebrity Cruises** (☎ 800/437–3111), **Cunard Line** (☎ 800/221–4770), and **Princess Cruises** (☎ 800/568–3262); from Miami, **Carnival Cruise Lines** (☎ 800/327–9501), **Costa Cruise Lines** (☎ 800/327–2537), **Norwegian Cruise Line** (☎ 800/327–7030), **Premier Cruises** (☎ 800/222–1003), and **Royal Caribbean** (☎ 800/327–6700); from New Orleans, **Commodore Cruise Line** (☎ 800/327–5617); and from Tampa, **Holland America Line** (☎ 800/426–0327).

BY FERRY

Passenger-only ferries depart from the dock at **Playa del Carmen** (☎ 987/2–15–08) for the 45-minute trip to the main pier in Cozumel. They leave approximately every hour on the hour 5 AM–11 PM. Call to verify the regularly changing schedule. **Maritima Chankanaab** (☎ 987/2–08–27) runs a car ferry to Cozumel from Calica, just south of Playa del Carmen; the trip takes only two hours. The ferry departs from Calica at 10 AM and 7 PM; return trips leave Cozumel at 8 AM and 5:30 PM. The car ferry from **Puerto Morelos** (☎ 987/2–17–22), on the mainland north of Playa del Carmen, is not recommended; the trip takes three to four hours.

BY HYDROFOIL

A water-jet catamaran and two large speedboats make the trip between Cozumel (downtown pier at the zócalo) and Playa del Carmen. This service, operated by **Aviomar** (⊠ Av. 5 Nte., between Calles 2 and 4, ☎ 987/2–05–88, 987/2–04–77), costs the same as the ferry and takes almost as much time, but the vessel is considerably more comfortable and offers onboard videos and refreshments. The boats make at least 10 crossings a day, leaving Playa del Carmen approximately every one to two hours 5:15 AM–8:45 PM and returning from Cozumel 4 AM–8 PM. Tickets are sold at the piers in both ports one hour before departure. Call to confirm the schedule as it tends to be erratic.

BY PLANE

The **Cozumel Airport** (☎ 987/2–09–28) is 3 km (2 mi) north of town. **Continental** (☎ 987/2–04–87) provides nonstop service from Houston; **Mexicana** (☎ 987/2–01–57) flies nonstop from Miami and San Francisco; **Aerocaribe** (☎ 987/2–05–03) and **Aerocozumel** (☎ 987/2–09–28), both Mexicana subsidiaries, fly to Cancún and other destinations in Mexico, including Chichén Itzá, Chetumal, Mérida, and Playa del Carmen. The airport departure tax is $16.

Between the Airport and Hotels. Because of an agreement between the taxi drivers' and bus drivers' unions, there is taxi service *to* the airport but *not from* the airport. The *colectivo,* a van that seats a maximum of eight, takes arriving passengers to their hotels; the fare is $5. If you want to avoid waiting for the van to fill or for other passengers to be dropped off, you can hire an *especial*—an individual van. A trip via an especial to one of the hotel zones costs a little under $20. A trip to the city runs about $8. Another alternative is walking out of the terminal to where the road begins and flagging a taxi exiting the airport after a drop-off. Taxis to the airport cost about $8 from the hotel zones and approximately $5 from downtown.

Getting Around

BY BICYCLE, MOPED, AND MOTORCYCLE

Mopeds and motorcycles are very popular here, but also extremely dangerous because of heavy traffic, potholes, and hidden stop signs. Accidents happen all too frequently. Mexican law requires all passengers to wear helmets. It's a $25 fine if you don't. Drive slowly, check for oncoming traffic, and don't ride the moped when it's raining or if you've been drinking. For the best rates and newest machines, try **RC Scooter Rentals** (⊠ Av. 30 Nte. 700, between Calles 7 and 11 Sur, ☎ 987/2–50–09). They will deliver to your hotel. Other good places include: **Auto Rent** (⊠ Carretera Costera Sur, ☎ 987/2–08–44 ext. 712), **Rentadora Cozumel** (⊠ Rosada Salas 3-B, ☎ 987/2–15–03; ⊠ Av. 10 Sur at Calle 1, ☎ 987/2–11–20), and **Rentadora Marlin** (⊠ Av. Adolfo López Mateos, ☎ 987/2–15–86). Mopeds go for about $25 per day; insurance is included.

BY BUS

Because of a union agreement with taxi drivers, no public buses operate in the north and south hotel zones. Local bus service runs mainly within the town of San Miguel, although there is a route from town to the airport. Service is irregular but inexpensive.

BY CAR

A rental car is a great way to get around the island. To get to the more secluded beaches and ruins you will need a jeep or some other vehicle with four-wheel drive (check to make sure that it hasn't been disconnected). Your insurance will not cover trips off the main roads. Many of the smaller companies carry only standard-transmission cars, so request an automatic in advance. There are two gas stations on Cozumel: one at the corner of Avenida Benito Juárez and Avenida 30 on the way to San Gervaiso, the other on Pedro Joaquin Coldwell and Avenida Benito Juárez. Both are open daily 7 AM–midnight.

BY TAXI

Taxi service is available 24 hours a day, with a 25% surcharge midnight–6 AM, at the main office (⊠ Calle 2 Nte., ☎ 987/2–00–41, 987/2–02–36) or at the malecón, at the main pier in town. Cabs also wait at all the major hotels. The fixed rates are: about $1 for a taxi ride within town, $3 to go between town and either hotel zone, about $8 from most hotels to the airport, and about $10–$15 from the northern hotels or town to Chankanaab Park or San Francisco Beach. However, cruise-ship passengers taking taxis to or from the international terminal are often charged about twice as much as tourists staying on the island. The cost from the cruise-ship terminal to San Miguel should be $4.

Contacts and Resources

CAR RENTAL

The following firms handle two- and four-wheel-drive vehicles (all the major hotels have rental offices). Rates start at $50 a day: **Hertz** (⊠ airport, ☎ 987/2–38–88); **J & E Rent a Car** (⊠ Plaza Las Glorias, ☎ 987/

2–49–59; ✉ Fiesta Americana Coral Reef, ☎ 987/2–27–77; ✉ Hotel Meson San Miguel, ☎ 987/22–44–63); **National Interrent** (✉ Av. Benito Juárez, Lote 10, near Av. 10, ☎ 987/2–32–63, 987/2–41–01); and **Rentadora Aguilla** (✉ Av. Rafael Melgar 685, ☎ 987/2–07–29).

Police (✉ Anexo del Palacio Municipal, ☎ 987/2–04–09). **Red Cross** (✉ Rosada Salas at Av. 20 Sur, ☎ 987/2–10–58). **Air Ambulance** (☎ 987/2–40–70). **Recompression Chamber** (✉ Calle 5 Sur 21-B, between Avs. Rafael Melgar and 5 Sur, ☎ 987/2–14–30). The **Centro de Salud** clinic (✉ Av. 20 Sur at Calle 11, ☎ 987/2–01–40) provides 24-hour emergency care, and the **Medical Specialties Center** (✉ Av. 20 Nte. 425, ☎ 987/2–14–19, 987/2–29–19) offers 24-hour air-ambulance service and a 24-hour pharmacy.

See Travel Agencies and Tour Operators, *below,* for addresses and telephone numbers of the companies mentioned here.

Air Tours. Caribe Tours goes to Chichén Itzá by plane; the $145 price includes the flight, transfers to the ruins, buffet lunch, and a guide. The company also flies to the Sian Ka'an Biosphere Reserve. In addition to lunch, this $160 trip includes a boat ride through the biosphere's mangroves.

Horseback Tours. Rancho Buenavista (☎ 987/2–15–37) runs four-hour guided horseback tours that visit three Maya ruins tucked away in Cozumel's tropical forest. The tour departs from Restaurant Acuario (✉ Av. Rafael Melgar at Calle 11) weekdays at noon and Saturday at 11. The price ($60) includes transportation to the ranch and soft drinks or beer during the tour. **Rancho San Manuel** (✉ Playa Paraíso, Av. Rafael Melgar [Coastal Road] Km 3.5, ☎ no phone) has seven horses and great jungle tours for $20 per hour.

Specialty Tours. If you want to get to Punta Molas Faro at the northern end of the island without all the hassles, consider **Wild Tours** (☎ 987/2–58–76, 987/2–67–47), which offers a 2½-hour excursion in hardy all-terrain vehicles (ATVs). To see the brilliant underwater life around Cozumel without getting wet, contact **Fiesta Cozumel,** which offers three-hour trips aboard the *Principe,* a glass-bottom boat, or *Nautilus IV,* a semi-submarine that goes partially underwater. Each tour is $26, including soft drinks and beer. ***Atlantis* Submarines** (✉ Carretera Chankanaab Km 4, across from Hotel Casa del Mar, ☎ 987/2–56–71) offers a 1½-hour submarine ride through the Chankanaab Reef. Tickets are $74 for adults, $38 for children.

Off-island tours to Tulum and Xel-Há run by Fiesta Cozumel, Turismo Aviomar, and Caribe Tours cost $63–$75 and include the 30-minute ferry trip to Playa del Carmen, the 45-minute bus ride to Tulum, 1½–2 hours at the ruins, entrance fees, guides, lunch, and a stop for snorkeling at Xel-Há Lagoon.

Fiesta Cozumel also has day trips to the eco-archaeological theme park Xcaret, about halfway between Playa del Carmen and Tulum. The $50 price includes round-trip ferry to Playa del Carmen, entrance to the park, and a bilingual guide.

The island's largest drugstore, **Farmacia Dori** (✉ Rosada Salas between Avs. 15 and 20 Sur, ☎ 987/2–05–59), is open daily 7 AM–midnight. **Farmacia Joaquín** (✉ north side of the plaza, ☎ 987/2–25–20) is open Monday–Saturday 8 AM–10 PM and Sunday 9–1 and 5–9. **Farmacias Canto** (☎ 987/2–53–77) is open 24 hours and delivers to hotels.

Caribe Tours (✉ Av. Rafael Melgar at Calle 5 Sur, ☎ 987/2–31–00), **Fiesta Cozumel Holidays/American Express** (in all major hotel lobbies; ✉ Calle 11 Sur 598, between Avs. 25 and 30, ☎ 987/2–07–25), **IMC** (Calle 2 Nte. 101–8, ☎ 987/2–15–35, ᖴᑎᕽ 987/2–08–95), **Turismo Aviomar** (in several hotel lobbies, including El Presidente; ✉ Av. 5 Nte. 8, between Calles 2 and 4, ☎ 987/2–05–88).

The **state tourism office** (✉ upstairs in the Plaza del Sol mall, at the east end of the main square, ☎ ᖴᑎᕽ 987/2–09–72) is open weekdays 9–2:30. A good source of information on lodgings (and many other things) is the **Cozumel Island Hotel Association** (✉ Calle 2 Nte. at Av. 15, ☎ 987/2–31–32, ᖴᑎᕽ 987/2–28–09), open weekdays 8–2 and 4–7.

THE NORTH CARIBBEAN COAST

Updated by
Shelagh
McNally

South of Cancún, the coast of the Yucatán Peninsula runs the gamut of tropical possibilities. Whereas Puerto Morelos retains the relaxed atmosphere of a Mexican fishing village, the once laid-back town of Playa del Carmen now has resorts as glitzy as those in Cancún and Cozumel. The beaches, from Punta Bete to Tulum, are beloved by scuba divers, snorkelers, birders, and beachcombers, and there are accommodations to suit every budget, from campsites and bungalows to condos and luxury hotels. Rustic but comfortable fishing and scuba diving lodges on the even more secluded Boca Paila in the Sian Ka'an Biosphere Reserve and on the Xcalak Peninsula have a well-deserved reputation for excellent bonefishing and superb diving on virgin reefs. At the same time this coast is one of the most threatened by development, and concerned environmentalists are supporting the rise of ecotourism programs such as the ones at Xcacel that get visitors involved in helping to save the threatened sea-turtle population.

Against this backdrop is the Maya culture. The modern Maya live in the cities and villages along the coast; the legacy of the ancient inhabits the ruins. The dramatic remains of Tulum stand on a bluff overlooking the Caribbean. A short distance inland, at Cobá, there are towering jungle-shrouded pyramids, a testament to the site's importance as a leading center of commerce in the ancient Maya world.

The coast is divided into two areas: Puerto Morelos to Tulum, which has the most ancient sites and places to lodge; and south of Tulum to Chetumal, where civilization thins out quite a bit. We detail the coast as far as the Sian Ka'an Biosphere Reserve just south of Tulum. If you want to venture farther, you'll be rewarded with remote beaches, coves, inlets, lagoons, and tropical landscapes.

Puerto Morelos

㉟ *36 km (22 mi) south of Cancún on Highway 307.*

For years, Puerto Morelos was known as the small coastal town where the car ferry left for Cozumel. This lack of regard has actually been its saving grace; it has escaped the hysteria of development engulfing other communities, retaining the authentic and relaxed atmosphere of a Mexican fishing village. More and more people are discovering that Morelos makes a great base for exploring the region, because it is exactly halfway between Cancún and Playa del Carmen.

In ancient times this was a point of departure for Maya women making pilgrimages by canoe to Cozumel, the sacred isle of the fertility goddess, Ixchel. Remnants of Maya ruins do exist along the coast here,

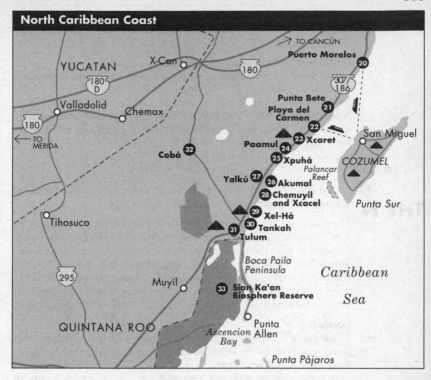

North Caribbean Coast

but nothing has been restored. The town itself is small with a central plaza; a number of shops and restaurants line the streets surrounding the square. The town's trademark is a leaning lighthouse.

Puerto Morelos' greatest attraction is the superb coral reef only 1,800 ft offshore, which provides excellent snorkeling and scuba diving. Dive sites include an intact Spanish galleon with coral-crusted cannons and the caves of the sleeping sharks (of documentary-movie fame), 8 km (5 mi) east of the town. The proximity of the reef creates an exceptionally calm and safe beach. It has been declared a national park, which should help to protect its fragile ecosystem.

Dining and Lodging

$ ✕ ★ **La Otra Cordobeza.** Owned by a friendly family from Veracruz, this simple restaurant serves good, inexpensive Mexican breakfasts. Lunch and dinner are also good and basic: sandwiches, tortillas, and a daily special. ✉ *Directly across the street from the police station,* ☎ *no phone. No credit cards.*

$$ ▣ ★ **Casa Caribe.** This small, pretty hotel sits just a few blocks from the center and five minutes from the beach. The breezy rooms offer Mexican furnishings, refrigerators, roomy baths, and terra-cotta tiles. Terraces have hammocks and views of the ocean or the mangroves. A large kitchen is available for guests' use. The grounds include a fragrant tropical garden. ✉ *Av. Rojo Gomez and Ejercito Mexicano,* ☎ *9/87–10–049, 517/784–9146 in the U.S. 6 rooms. Bar. No credit cards.*

$$ ▣ **Hotel Ojo de Agua.** A friendly, family-run hotel, it offers a peaceful atmosphere and a beachfront location. Half the guest rooms have kitchenettes, and all rooms have ceiling fans and views of the sea or the courtyard gardens. An open-air restaurant serves up great burgers, fish, and cocktails near the small pool. There's great snorkeling directly out front, including Ojo de Agua, an underwater cenote sink-

hole shaped like an eye. ⊠ *Av. Rojo Gomez, 3 blocks north of town,*
☎ FAX *9/87–10–027. 24 rooms. Kitchenettes (some), pool, beach, dive
shop, snorkeling. MC, V.*

Outdoor Activities and Sports

For snorkeling and fishing trips, contact **Almost Heaven Adventures**
(☎ 9/87–10–230) or **El Faro Trips** (☎ 9/87–10–275), both on the
town's main square. For scuba lessons and excursions, contact **Sub-
Aqua Explorers** (☎ 9/87–10–018) or divemaster **David Sanchez** (☎ 9/
87–10–006). Deep-sea fishing expeditions can be arranged with **Secret
Reef** (☎ 9/87–10–244).

Punta Bete

㉑ *22 km (14 mi) south of Puerto Morelos on Highway 307, then about
2 km (1 mi) off the main road.*

The roads into Punta Bete may be paved with good intentions, but they
aren't paved with anything resembling asphalt. Once you finish the bumpy
2⅓-km (1½-mi) ride through the jungle, you *will* arrive at a 6½-km-
(4-mi-) long isolated beach dotted with bargain bungalow-style hotels
and thatch-roof restaurants. If you want to spare yourself some grit in
your personal belongings, there are more comfortable accommodations up the road at the Posada del Capitán Lafitte (☞ Lodging, *below*).

Lodging

$$$$ ▥ **Kai Luum II.** A much-loved vacation spot is back in operation after
★   being wiped out by the 1996 Hurricane Roxanne. Right on the beach,
Kai Luum offers "tentalapas"—large canvas tents under palapa roofs
with ocean-view porches and hammocks. Inside are double beds with
clean sheets, fluffy pillows, and bedside tables. Bathrooms and showers are shared. The outdoor restaurant, serving Yucatecan specialities,
is lit by oil lamps (there is no electricity here). ⊠ *Hwy. 307 Km 62,
beyond Posada del Capitán Lafitte,* ☎ *no phone.* ⊠ *Reservations:
Turquoise Reef Group, Box 2664, Evergreen, CO 80439,* ☎ *800/538-
6802, 303/674–9615,* FAX *303/674–8735. 29 tents. Restaurant, bar,
beach, snorkeling. AE, MC, V.* 🐾

$$$$ ▥ **Posada del Capitán Lafitte.** Set on an invitingly long stretch of
beach just 10 km (6 mi) north of Playa del Carmen, this retreat is famous for its warm atmosphere. There are clusters of three-unit cabañas
as well as some duplexes suitable for families; opt for one of the newer
cabañas on the north end of the beach. Groups activities such as
snorkeling trips and horseback riding are encouraged here. The on-site
dive shop offers PADI certification courses for guests and nonguests
alike. Rates include breakfast and dinner. ⊠ *Hwy. 307 Km 62 (look
for the brightly colored sculpture),* ☎ *9/87–30–214,* FAX *9/87–30–212.*
⊠ *Reservations: Turquoise Reef Group, Box 2664, Evergreen, CO
80439,* ☎ *800/538–6802, 303/674–9615,* FAX *303/674–8735. 62 rooms.
Restaurant, bar, pool, beach, dive shop, airport shuttle, car rental. AE,
MC, V.* 🐾

Playa del Carmen

㉒ *10 km (6 mi) south of Punta Bete, 68 km (42 mi) south of Cancún.*

Once upon a time, Playa del Carmen was an innocent fishing village
with a ravishing, deserted beach. Now it's the fastest growing city on
the coast, with a population of more than 30,000. The beach is still
delightful—alabaster-white sand, turquoise-blue waters—it's just not
deserted. The most consistent sound you will hear throughout Playa
del Carmen is that of the jackhammer. For the past few years a construction boom has been going on that regularly transforms the city

every few months. Hotels, restaurants, and shops are multiplying faster than you can say *Kukulcán*.

The busiest parts of town are down by the **ferry pier,** along the commercial strip **Avenida Juárez,** and along the pedestrian walkway **Avenida 5.** Take a stroll north from the pier along the beach and you'll find a more peaceful part of town—simple restaurants roofed with palm fronds, where people sit around drinking beer for hours; overgrown tropical foliage; and a few campgrounds. On the south side of the pier the massive Playacar Resort begins. In the middle of the development, there is an excellent open-air aviary—the best on the coast. Though peace and quiet may not be the operative words in most of Playa, the place is a fun introduction to the Caribbean coast. It is no longer a budget destination. Prices are steadily increasing.

Dining and Lodging

There are hundreds of hotels in Playa, and more keep opening each day. The more luxurious rooms are to be found at Playacar; more modest rooms are available in town. Most will ask for a deposit (usually the price of one night) before taking your reservation.

$$$ ✕ **La Carmela.** Craving some *filete en un negra tormenta de verano*
★ (steak in a black summer storm) or *la envidia de vecindario pollo* (envy of the neighborhood chicken)? These whimsical names reflect the playful and sophisticated atmosphere of this restaurant. At night the lights of the patio create true romance. A well-rounded wine list and more than 50 types of tequila complement the authentic Mexican fare. ⊠ *Av. 10 at Plaza Antiqua, Playacar,* ☎ 9/87–31-662. *AE, MC, V.*

$$$ ✕ **Da Gabi.** If you can tolerate the slightly pretentious air, you'll be re-
★ warded with high-quality Italian fare. Enjoy the Maya chef's homemade fettuccine, spinach ravioli, or oven-baked pizza. Or try daily specials such as salmon antipasto. ⊠ *Da Gabi Hotel, Av. 1 and Calle 12,* ☎ 9/87–30–048. *No credit cards. No lunch.*

$$$ ✕ **Johnny Cairo's.** With a sumptuous menu, attentive service, and in-
★ credible ambience, this is the one local dining spot you shouldn't miss. To begin, try the veal liver pâté with Spanish sherry, and then move on to the succulent roasted duck with chili, honey, and aged tequila. Finish off your meal with an extra-rich dessert. The tasting menu gives you a chance to try everything. ⊠ *Quinta Maya Hotel, Calle 5 between Calles 12 and 14,* ☎ 9/87–30-111. *AE, MC, V. No lunch.*

$$ ✕ **Media Luna.** This casual place with a great vegetarian menu is decorated with textiles from Guatemala. For breakfast try the spinach and mushroom crepes; for lunch, Greek salads or black-bean quesadillas; for dinner, fresh grilled fish. Everything that comes from the kitchen is scrumptious. ⊠ *Av. 5 at Calle 8,* ☎ *no phone. No credit cards.*

$$ ✕ **New Máscaras.** Named for the masks that hang on its walls, this eatery produces exceptionally good thin-crust pizza and bread, and the homemade pasta is very tasty. Popular with locals, it is a central gathering spot with a view of the goings-on at the main plaza. ⊠ *Av. Juárez across from plaza,* ☎ 9/87–31–053. *AE, DC, MC, V.*

$$ ✕ **Yaxche.** At this celebration of Maya culture, the chef creates deli-
★ cious dishes such as papadzules and pollo pibíl. It's a refreshing change from the pizza, pasta, and burgers in town. ⊠ *Calle 8 at Avs. 5 and 10,* ☎ 9/87–32–502. *No credit cards.*

THE PLAYACAR RESORT

$$$$ ⊞ **Continental Plaza Playacar.** A blush-color palace, this hotel is the centerpiece of the Playacar development, with all the amenities of its competitors at the larger resort towns. The rooms have ocean-view balconies or patios, air-conditioning, and marble baths. The beach is one of the nicest in Playa del Carmen, far less crowded than those to the north. The main restaurant and the palapa pool restaurant both offer good Mexican and international dishes. There is also a full-scale watersports facility and an 18-hole championship golf course; ask about golf packages. ⊠ *Fracc. Playacar (north end of Playacar development),* ☎ *9/87–30–100, 800/882–6684,* 𝔽𝔸𝕏 *9/87–30–105. 188 rooms, 16 suites. 2 restaurants, bar, pool, 18-hole golf course, tennis court, dive shop, beach, shops, travel services, car rental. AE, MC, V.*

$$$$ ▣ **Iberostar Tucan and Quetzal.** This is a unique, luxurious, all-inclu-
★   sive resort. The Quetzal side is decorated with Mexican colonial art and furniture, while the Tucan has reproductions of famous stelae and carvings from Maya ruins. The hotel has worked hard at preserving the natural surroundings, and among the resident animals are flamingos, ducks, hens, turtles, fish, toucans—even a family of monkeys. Spacious air-conditioned rooms have ocean- or jungle-view private balconies. The restaurants serve up decent Mexican and international fare. Also on the premises are a fully equipped water-sports center, a gym, and a health club. Playa del Carmen is a 20-minute walk or a $4 cab ride north. ⊠ *Fracc. Playacar,* ☎ *9/87–30–200, 888/923–2722,* 𝔽𝔸𝕏 *9/87– 30–424. 700 rooms. 3 restaurants, 2 bars, 4 pools, spa, 2 tennis courts, basketball, health club, dive shop, shops, nightclub, children's program (ages 4–12). AE, MC, V.* ☙

HOTELS IN TOWN

$$$$ ▣ **Baal Nah Kah.** True to its name, which means "home hidden among
★   the gum trees" in Maya, this small hotel is quite homey. Guests have the use of a large kitchen, common sitting room, and barbecue pit. The five bedrooms and one studio are on different levels, affording complete privacy. Two rooms have spacious balconies with a panoramic view of the ocean; all offer tile baths, fans, double or king-size beds, and Mexican decor. A small café next door serves breakfast, snacks, and light meals. The beach is one block away. ⊠ *Calle 12 between Avs. 5 and 1,* ☎ *9/87–30–110,* 𝔽𝔸𝕏 *9/87–30–050. 5 rooms, 1 apartment. No credit cards.* ☙

$$$$ ▣ **Porto Real Resort & Suites.** The largest building on the north end of the beach, this all-inclusive hotel sticks out like a sore thumb. But inside it is quite lovely. Each unit has an ocean-view balcony and an oversize, luxurious bathroom and air-conditioning. There are plenty of facilities to keep you occupied here. ⊠ *End of Av. Constituyentes,* ☎ *9/87–34–000, 800/216–5500,* 𝔽𝔸𝕏 *98/81–73–25. 192 junior suites, 2 master suites. 3 restaurants, 2 bars, pool, tennis court, exercise room, beach, travel services. AE, MC, V.* ☙

$$$ ▣ **Mosquito Blue.** This beautiful hotel has become a landmark in Playa
★   for its artistic design and architecture. With their lovely mahogany furniture and Indonesian decor, the air-conditioned rooms are at once casual and elegant. The lobby has a curving staircase and an open-air bar; outside there is a cloistered courtyard with a garden and pool. A dive shop is on site and the beach is a short walk away. The Water Grill restaurant is also making a name for itself with its superb seafood meals. ⊠ *Av. 5 between Calles 12 and 14,* ☎ 𝔽𝔸𝕏 *9/87–31–335. 16 rooms, 8 suites. Bar, pool, massage, dive shop. AE, MC, V.* ☙

$$$ ▣ **El Tucan Condotel Villas and Beach Club.** This complex looks very
★   exclusive and expensive but in fact is quite affordable. Rooms and suites are well separated from one another and offer private terraces, tiny kitchenettes, and attractive accents such as burnished tile floors and painted wood furniture and air-conditioning. The large jungle garden has a pool and a natural cenotec. Included in the rate is buffet breakfast at the Tucan Maya restaurant across the street. ⊠ *Av. 5 between Calles 14*

and 16, ☏ *9/87–30–417,* FAX *9/87–30–668. 56 rooms, 55 suites. Restaurant, bar, grocery, pool, beach, bicycles. MC, V.*

$$ ▣ **Alejari.** This two-story complex set amid flower-filled gardens is one of the most pleasant accommodations on Playa's north beach. It's not as tranquil as it once was, thanks to the late-night revelers at bars close by. Some rooms have kitchenettes. All have fans or air-conditioning. A hearty breakfast is included in the rates, and the Mexican family that owns the hotel is extremely friendly. ✉ *Calle 6 Nte. at Av. 5,* ☏ *9/87–30–372,* FAX *9/87–30–005. 29 rooms. Restaurant, air-conditioning (some), fans, kitchenettes (some). AE, MC, V.*

$$ ▣ **Delfín.** Right in the heart of Playa, although not on the beach, the Delfín is a good choice for its bright, airy rooms cooled by sea breezes. Rooms also have fans or air-conditioning, safety-deposit boxes, refrigerators, and wonderful ocean views. Everything you need or want in Playa is within close walking distance. The management is exceptionally helpful. There is a 5% fee on credit-card payments. ✉ *Av. 5 at Calle 6,* ☏ FAX *9/87–30–176. 14 rooms. Air-conditioning (some), fans, in-room safes, refrigerators. MC, V.* 🍽

$$ ▣ **Hotel Casa Tucan.** The owners have worked hard at creating a cozy
★ community just up from the main drag. The peaceful gardens here are home to a small menagerie of rabbits, ducks, birds, and turtles, and there are a variety of clean and cheerful rooms geared to different budgets. The property also includes a restaurant, a game room, a meditation palapa, a TV bar, a language school, and a specially designed dive pool that is used by the on-site dive center. ✉ *Calle 2 between Avs. 10 and 15,* ☏ *9/87–30–054. 24 rooms. Restaurant, bar, pool, dive shop, shops, billiards. MC, V.*

$ ▣ **Elefante.** Three blocks from the beach, this three-story, family-run hotel is well kept—and the best deal around for the price. The only sore spot is the unkempt field you pass on the way to the rooms. All the bare-bones units overlook a small plant-filled walkway and each has tile floors, a bathroom, two double beds, and fans; some have kitchenettes. Many restaurants and bars are nearby. ✉ *Av. 12 and Calle 10,* ☏ *9/87–91–987. 38 rooms. Fans, kitchenettes (some). No credit cards.*

Outdoor Activities and Sports

The oldest dive shop in town, **Tank–Ha Dive Shop** (☏ FAX *9/87–31–355*) has PADI-certified teachers and runs diving and snorkeling trips to the reefs and caverns. **The Abyss** (☏ *9/87–32–164*) offers training courses in addition to dive trips. **Yucatek Divers** (☏ *9/87–30–054*) specializes in cenote dives, diving packages, and technical training.

Shopping

Avenida 5 between Calles 4 and 10 is definitely the best place to shop in Playa, if not along the whole coast. Unique shops and boutiques sell folk art and textiles from around Mexico, and clothing shops carry original designs created from hand-painted Indonesian batiks. Except where indicated, the shops listed below are open from about 10 in the morning to 9 or 10 at night.

Amber Museum Shop (✉ Av. 5 between Calles 4 and 6, ☏ FAX *9/87–30–446*) has elegantly crafted amber jewelry by a local designer who imports the amber from Chiapas. **La Calaca** (✉ Av. 5 between Calles 6 and 8; Av. 5 and Calle 4, ☏ *987/3–01–77* for both locations) has an eclectic collection of wooden masks and other carvings; of note are the playful devils and angels. **Telart** (✉ Av. Juarez 10, ☏ *9/87–30–066*) carries textiles from all over Mexico. **Manas Huellas** (✉ Calle 5 Nte. between Avs. 10 and 12, ☏ no phone) is a small store that sells art, textiles, and handicrafts from Oaxaca and Chiapas.

Xcaret

  ㉓ *10 km (6 mi) south of Playa del Carmen and 72 km (45 mi) south of Cancún.*

South of Playa del Carmen is where Disney meets the Maya. Xcaret, once a sacred Maya city and port, is a 250-acre ecological theme park on a gorgeous stretch of coastline. You can't escape it since it's the most heavily advertised park on the coast, with its own buses, magazines, and stores. Billed as "nature's sacred paradise," it's expensive, contrived, and crowded. If you're a Walt Disney World fan, you will love Xcaret.

Highlights of the park include an aviary, a butterfly pavilion, botanical gardens, riding stables, a tropical aquarium with a sea-turtle nursery, an artificially created beach for snorkeling and swimming, a dive center with myriad sporting activities, a replica of a Maya village, a small zoo, some Maya ruins, and an underground river ride where you snorkel through a series of caves. There is even a Dolphinarium, where you can attend a dolphin workshop and even swim with the dolphins for a hefty fee (book early because only 36 people a day are allowed).

Evenings, there are folkloric extravaganzas that begin with a reenactment of the Maya ball game and end with a performance by the famed Voladores de Papantla (Fliers of Papantla) from Veracruz. Plan to spend the day and plenty of money. The $39 (per person) entrance fee just covers getting into the grounds and the exhibits. Other costs: snorkel mask $8, fins $3, life vest $3, towel $3.50, locker $1, strollers $8, snorkel tour $23, swim with dolphins $80, horseback riding $30 per hour, hot dog and soft drink $7, water $2.50. You can buy tickets from any travel agency or major hotel along the coast. ☎ 987/1–40–00. ⌨ *Theme park, Mon.–Sat. $39 including show; Sun. $30, no show.* ⊙ *Apr.–Oct., daily 8:30 AM–10 PM; Nov.–Mar., daily 8:30 AM–9 PM.*

Paamul

㉔ *10 km (6 mi) south of Xcaret.*

Beachcombers and snorkelers are fond of Paamul, a crescent-shape lagoon with clear, placid waters sheltered by a coral reef at the lagoon's mouth. Shells, sand dollars, and even glass beads—some from the sunken pirate ship at Akumal—wash onto the sandy parts of the beach. Trailer camps, cabañas, and tent camps are scattered along the shore; a restaurant sells beer and fresh fish; and in June and July you can see sea-turtle hatchlings on the beach, one of Paamul's chief attractions.

Lodging

$$$$ **Cabañas Paamul.** If you're looking for seclusion and comfort, you'll be thrilled with this small hostelry on a perfect white-sand beach. Seven bungalows face the sea; all have two double beds, ceiling fans, and hot-water showers. The property includes 140 full-service hookups (gas, water, and drainage) for motor homes and tents, and a full-service dive shop. This place sees many repeat visitors. ⊠ *Hwy. 307 Km 85,* ☎ *9/87–62–691. 7 rooms. Restaurant, bar, beach, dive shop. No credit cards.*

Xpuhá

㉕ *15 km (9 mi) south of Paamul.*

This used to be a tranquil little beach, until developers snatched it up and immediately made it an all-inclusive "eco-park," where you can snorkel, swim in the cenote, and dive for $40 per person—all of which you used to be able to do for free. The area is being developed, so there are fences along the beach, but be persistent with the security guards at the gates. Look for the sign on the middle dirt road off Highway 307 to find **Kiin-Xuna** (☎ 987/69–945) a four-room hotel offering inexpensive rooms and meals. The beach, luckily, remains pristine.

Akumal

㉖ *37 km (23 mi) south of Playa del Carmen, 102 km (63 mi) south of Cancún.*

The Maya name means "Place of the Turtle," and for hundreds of years, this beach has been a nesting ground for turtles. The place first attracted international attention in 1926, when explorers discovered the *Mantanceros,* a Spanish galleon that sank in 1741. In 1958, Pablo Bush Romero, a wealthy businessman who loved diving these pristine waters, created the first resort, which became the headquarters for the club he formed—the Mexican Underwater Explorers Club (Cedam). Akumal soon became a gathering spot for wealthy underwater adventurers who flew in on private planes and searched the waters for sunken treasures. Hotel rooms are at a premium during the high season, December 15 to April 30—reserve well in advance.

Akumal consists of three distinct areas. **Half Moon Bay** to the north is lined with private homes, hotels, and condominiums. It has some of the prettiest beaches and best snorkeling in the area. **Akumal Proper** consists of a large resort with a market, grocery stores, laundry facilities, and pharmacy. Farther up the highway is a small Maya community. There's also a nature center next to the dive shop with a staff of ecologists. More condos and homes and an all-inclusive resort are at **Akumal Aventuras** to the south. The biggest attraction, of course, is diving.

㉗ For great snorkeling, check out the blessedly undeveloped lagoon of **Yalkú,** a couple of miles north of Akumal along an unmarked dirt road. A series of small lagoons that gradually reach the ocean, Yalkú is home to schools of parrot fish in clear water with visibility to 160 ft. It has recently been given "eco-park" status, which means that you now find a toilet, a small parking lot, and an entrance fee of about $6. Enjoy it while it lasts, for it too is scheduled for development.

Dining and Lodging

$$$ ✕ **Lol Ha.** The restaurant serves delectable food in a romantic, tropical-beach setting. Menu highlights include homemade sweet rolls, delicious Yucatecan specialties, fantastically prepared fresh fish, and grilled steaks. The staff is delightful, and at night there is a Yucatecan folk-dancing show. ⊠ *Club Akumal Caribe (follow signs off Hwy. 307),* ☎ 987/59–01–12. *AE, MC, V.*

$$ ✕ **La Lunita.** Located in Half Moon Bay, this converted one-bedroom condo has a breakfast and dinner menu that changes daily. The cuisine is eclectic and delicious. Look for fresh fish served with a lime and cilantro sauce. The atmosphere is friendly. You'll be sure to pick up some tips on local events. ⊠ *Hacienda de la Tortuga, through the entrance way at Club Akumal Caribe, then left (north) at the dirt road to Half Moon Bay,* ☎ 987/2–24–21 *for the condo office. No credit cards.*

$$$$ 🏨 **Club Oasis Akumal.** This all-inclusive luxury hotel used to be the private preserve of millionaire Pablo Bush Romero, a friend of the late Jacques Cousteau. Today, the beach—protected by an offshore reef—and the pier are used as the starting point for canoeing, snorkeling, diving, fishing, and windsurfing expeditions. Apartments have air-conditioning, full kitchens, and dining areas. All rooms have balconies with a view of either the ocean or the garden. ⊠ *South of Akumal off*

Hwy. 307, ☎ *987/59–000,* ℻ *987/59–009. 120 rooms, 4 apartments. Restaurant, 2 bars, 2 pools, tennis court, beach, dive shop, bicycles, travel services, car rental. AE, MC, V.* ✎

$$$ 🏨 **Club Akumal Caribe & Villas Maya.** Accommodations at this con-
★ genial resort on the edge of a cove overlooking a small harbor range
from rustic-but-comfortable garden-view bungalows (Villas Maya) to
beachfront rooms in a modern three-story hotel building (Club Aku-
mal Caribe). Also available are the more secluded one-, two-, and three-
bedroom condominiums called the Villas Flamingo, on Half Moon Bay
with their own beach and pools (definite bargains). By the hotel are
two dive shops. Snorkeling, windsurfing, kayaking, and deep-sea fish-
ing are also available. An optional meal plan includes breakfast and
dinner. ✉ *Hwy. 307 Km 104,* ☎ *987/59–012. Reservations:* ✉ *Aku-
trame, Box 13326, El Paso, TX 79913,* ☎ *800/351–1622, 800/343–
1440 in Canada. 21 rooms, 40 bungalows, 4 villas, 5 condos. 3 restau-
rants, bar, grocery, ice cream parlor, pizzeria, snack bar, air-conditioning,
pool, beach, 2 dive shops, shops, children's program (ages 5–14). AE,
MC, V.* ✎

Outdoor Activities and Sports

Akumal Dive Center (✉ about 10 min north of Club Akumal Caribe,
☎ 987/59–068) rents equipment, runs dive trips, and has certification
programs. For dive packages, including accommodations, contact **Aku-
trame Inc.** (✉ Box 13326, El Paso, TX 79913, ☎ 800/351–1622 or
915/584–3552 in the U.S., 800/343–1440 in Canada). **Mike Madden's
CEDAM Dive Center** is in the Club Omni Puerto Aventuras Hotel (☎
987/3–51–29).

Chemuyil and Xcacel

㉘ *7 km (4½ mi) south of Akumal.*

You may find **Cheyumil** open, or you may find it closed. It's been tar-
geted for development and a chain-link fence now cuts off the road to
this lovely bay with its fine powdery beach, calm turquoise waters, and
shady coconut palms. To get through to the beach you may have be a
bit persistent with the security guard at the gate, but it's worth it.

Cheyumil's sister beach, **Xcacel,** is the scene of an international envi-
ronmental dispute that has become the symbol of what has gone wrong
along the coast. For decades this beach has been the most important
breeding ground for Atlantic green and loggerhead turtles—both en-
dangered species. It was a federal reserve until the infamous ex-gov-
ernor Mario Villanueva sold it in 1998 to a Spanish conglomerate for
a measly $2.2 million dollars—the price of a Cancún condo. Plans for
a 450-room hotel, an 18-hole golf course, and an "eco-disco" were put
on hold after local environmentalists alerted the world to what was
happening. The battle for the beach continues, but do come to say hello
to the brave volunteers and enjoy the nearby cenote and gorgeous beach
while you can—it may be soon gone, along with the turtles.

Xel-Há

㉙ *2 km (1 mi) south of Laguna de Xcacel.*

Brought to you by the people who now manage Xcaret (☞ *above*), Xel-
Há (pronounced shel-*hah*) is a natural aquarium made from coves, in-
lets, and lagoons cut out of the limestone shoreline. The name means
"where the water is born," and the river here forms a natural spring
that flows out to meet the saltwater, creating a perfect habitat for trop-
ical marine life. Scattered throughout the park are small Maya ruins,
including **Na Balaam,** known for a yellow jaguar painted on one of

its walls. Low wooden bridges over the lagoons allow for leisurely walks around the park, and there are spots to rest or swim. While there seem to be fewer fish each year, and the mixture of fresh- and saltwater can cloud visibility, there is still enough here to impress novice snorkelers.

Certain areas are off-limits to swimmers, but because the lagoons are quite large, you can swim far out or explore one of the underwater caves or the cenotes deep in the jungle, finally floating back to the coastline with the current. Also on the grounds are a huge but overpriced souvenir shop, food stands, and a small museum housing pre-Columbian artifacts. Bring your own towel and snorkeling gear if you can, as they're not included in the entrance fee and are not cheap to rent. Don't apply sunscreen, as it's not allowed. It kills the fish. If you come with a huge appetite, the all-inclusive package ($36) is a bargain. It's best to arrive early in the morning before the tour buses arrive. ☎ 987/5–40–70, 987/5–40–71. 🎫 $15. ⊙ Daily 8–8.

🔺 If you're sick of tour buses, head across the road to the compact, little-visited **Xel-Há Archaeological Site.** Its squat structures are thought to have been inhabited from the Late Preclassic until the Late Post-Classic periods. The most interesting sights are on the north end of the ruins, where remains of a Maya *sacbé* (road) and mural paintings in the **Jaguar House** sit near a tranquil, deep cenote. ☎ No phone. 🎫 $1.50, free Sun. and holidays. ⊙ Daily 8–5.

Tankah

③⓪ 9½ km (6 mi) south of Xel-Há.

Tankah is no longer the secluded beach it once was, but it is still surprisingly tranquil and has great swimming, snorkeling, diving, and fishing.

Dining and Lodging

$$$ ✕🏨 **Tankah Inn.** A friendly East Texas family runs this exquisite guest
★ house located on a sunny strip of beach. The inn is popular with divers, who come in small groups to take advantage of the nearby reefs, top-notch equipment, and full-service, personal attention. The five spacious rooms have their own balconies or terraces, some with incredible ocean views. Upstairs is a large airy restaurant with a terrace. ✉ Tankah Bay 16, ☎ 987/42–188; 409/636–7721; 📠 987/12–092. 5 rooms. Restaurant, beach, dive shop. No credit cards.

Tulum

🔺 ③① 2 km (1 mi) south of Tankah, 130 km (81 mi) south of Cancún.

The spectacle of Tulum's limestone temples against the blue-green Caribbean waters is nothing less than riveting. This is the largest coastal city that the Maya built, and the only Maya city known to have been inhabited when the conquistadors arrived. Unfortunately, you'll share the site with roughly half the tourist population of Quintana Roo on any given day, even if you arrive early. And no longer can you climb or enter Tulum's most impressive buildings (only three, described below, really merit close inspection), which means that you can see the ruins in two hours. You might, however, want to allow extra time for a swim or a stroll on the beach, where no doubt the ancient Maya beached their canoes.

The first significant structure you'll see is the two-story **Temple of the Frescoes,** to the left of the entrance. The temple's vaulted roof and corbeled (triangular) arch are examples of classic Maya architecture. Faint traces of blue-green frescoes outlined in black on the inner and outer walls refer to ancient Maya beliefs. One scene portrays the rain god seated on a four-legged animal—probably a reference to the Spaniards on their horses.

The largest and most famous building, the **Castillo,** looms at the edge of a 40-ft limestone cliff just past the Temple of the Frescoes. Atop the castle, at the end of a broad stairway, sits a temple with stucco ornamentation on the outside and traces of fine frescoes inside the two chambers. (The stairway has been roped off, so the top temple is inaccessible.) The regal structure overlooks the rest of Tulum and an expanse of dense jungle to the west. Researchers think the Castillo may have functioned as a watchtower to monitor enemy approaches by sea. To the left of the Castillo is the **Temple of the Descending God**—so called for the carving of a winged god plummeting to earth over the doorway.

At the old turnoff on Highway 307 to the ruins, called the crucero (it no longer provides access), there are two small hotels, two restaurants, and a gas station. A few feet south is the new entrance to the ruins, clearly marked with overhead signs. Still farther south is the turnoff for the road leading to the coast and eventually the Sian Ka'an preserve. The majority of hotels, cabañas, campgrounds, beaches, and restaurants are along this route. Back on the highway about 4 km (2½ mi) south of the ruins is the present-day village of Tulum. Markets, restaurants, shops, services, and auto-repair shops continue to spring up along the road. In the process, the pueblo has become rather unsightly, with a wide four-lane highway running down the middle. However, the town does have some remarkably fine restaurants.

Dining and Lodging

$$$$ ✕⌸ **Cabañas Ana y José.** Several two-story buildings face the beach at this small, well-loved hotel south of the ruins. All rooms have fans, tile floors, and colorful Mexican furniture and art. Those on the second floor are cooler, thanks to sea breezes. The restaurant serves unique Mexican cuisine. Tours to the Sian Ka'an Biosphere leave from here. The one sour note is the noisy generator next door. But the lovely beach makes up for it. ⊠ *Road to Boca Baila, 6 km (4 mi) south of the ruins,* ☎ *98/80–60–22,* 𝔽𝔸𝕏 *98/80–60–21. 16 rooms. Restaurant, fans, pool, beach. MC, V.* 🐢

$$$ ⌸ **Las Ranitas** (The Froggies). Run by a French couple (thus the hu-
★ morous name), this ingenious ecological hotel uses wind-generated electricity, solar energy, and recycled water. But what you really notice is how chic the rooms are. The grounds, which include a pool and tennis court, are equally luxurious, and there's a restaurant on the premises as well. Attention to detail upgrades the property from being comfortable to absolute bliss. ⊠ *Road to Sian Ka'an, last hotel before Boca Paila,* ☎ *98/42–60–82,* 𝔽𝔸𝕏 *987/30–934. 16 rooms. Restaurant, pool, tennis, beach. MC, V.* 🐢

Cobá

▲ ㉜ *49 km (30 mi) northwest of Tulum, 167 km (104 mi) southwest of Cancún.*

Cobá—the Maya word means "water stirred by the wind"—flourished AD 800–1100, with a population of as many as 55,000 inhabitants. Now, the jungle having reclaimed many of its buildings, Cobá stands in a solitude pierced by the occasional shriek of a spider monkey or the call of a bird. Archaeologists estimate that some 6,500 structures are present in the area, but only 5% have been uncovered, and it will take decades before the work is completed. Discovered by Teobert Maler in 1891, Cobá subsequently was explored in 1926 by the Carnegie Institute but not excavated until 1972. At present there is no restoration work under way.

Sited on five lakes between coastal watchtowers and inland cities, Cobá exercised economic control over the region through a network of at least 16 *sacbeob* (white stone roads), one of which measures 100 km (62 mi), the longest in the Maya world. The city once covered 70 square km (43 square mi), which makes it a noteworthy sister nation to Tikal in northern Guatemala, to which it had close cultural and commercial ties. It's noted for its massive, soaring temple-pyramids, one of which stands 138-ft tall, the largest and highest in northern Yucatán.

Because it is easy to get lost here, stay on the main road and don't be tempted by the narrow paths leading into the jungle—unless you have a qualified guide with you.

The first major grouping, off a path to your right as you enter the ruins, is the **Cobá Group**, whose pyramids are built around a sunken patio. At the near end of the group, facing a large plaza, you'll see the 79-ft-high *Iglesia* (church), where some Indians still place offerings and light candles in hopes of improving their harvests. Farther along the main path to your left is the **Chumuc Mul Group**, little of which has been excavated. The principal pyramid here is covered with the stucco remains of vibrantly painted motifs (*chumuc mul* means "stucco pyramid"). A kilometer (½ mile) past the Chumuc Mul Group is the **Nohoch Mul Group** (Large Hill Group), the highlight of which is the pyramid of the same name. It is the tallest at Cobá, its uppermost chamber evocatively perched at treetop height. The pyramid, which has 120 steps, shares a plaza with **Temple 10**. The Descending God (also seen at Tulum) is depicted on a facade of the temple atop Nohoch Mul, from which the view is excellent. The unrestored **Crossroad Pyramid** opposite Nohoch Mul was the meeting point for three sacbeob.

Beyond the Nohoch Mul Group is the **Castillo**. Its nine chambers are reached by a stairway. To the south are the remains of a ball court, including the stone ring through which the ball was hurled. From the main route, follow the sign to **Las Pinturas Group**, named for the still discernible polychromatic friezes on the inner and outer walls of its large, patioed pyramid. Take the minor path for 1 km (½ mi) to the **Macanxoc Group**, not far from the lake of the same name. The main pyramid at Macanxoc is accessible by a stairway. Many of the stelae here are intricately carved with Maya dates (their time-keeping methods were incomparable) and other symbols of the history of Cobá.

Cobá is a 35-minute drive northwest of Tulum, down a well-marked, paved road that leads straight through the jungle. You can comfortably see Cobá in a half day. Spending the night is highly advised as you'll be able to visit the ruins in solitude when they open at 8 AM. Even on a day trip, consider taking time out for lunch to escape from the intense heat and mosquito-thick humidity of the ruins. Buses depart Cobá for Playa del Carmen and Valladolid twice daily. Check with your hotel and the clerk at the ruins for times, which may not be exact. ⌧ *$1.75, free Sun. and holidays.* ⊙ *Daily 8–5.*

Lodging

$$ ⊞ **Villa Arqueológica Cobá.** A 10-minute walk from the ruins, this Club Med property overlooks one of the region's vast lakes. The hotel has a clean, airy feel, although the rooms themselves are quite small. There is a decent library, along with a large-screen TV and a pool table. The restaurant food, alas, is mediocre but expensive, and it is not included in the room rates. ⊠ *Lagoon road, west of the ruins.* ⊠ *Reservations:* ☎ *5/254–7077,* ☏ *5/255–3164. 40 rooms, 3 suites. Restaurant, bar, pool, tennis court, shops, library. AE, MC, V.* 🐌

$ ⛏ **El Bocadito.** Though not as lavish as the Villa Arqueológica Cobá (☞ *above*), El Bocadito is much more congenial. It's a satisfactory budget alternative, only a five-minute walk from the ruins. Each of the basic rooms has two double beds, a ceiling fan, a toilet, and a cold-water shower. Rooms here fill up quickly—if you're thinking of spending the night, stop here before visiting the ruins. ⊠ *On the road to the ruins,* ☎ *987/4–20–87. 10 rooms. AE, V.*

Sian Ka'an and the Boca Paila Peninsula

15 km (9½ mi) south of Tulum to Boca Paila turnoff, located within Sian Ka'an; 137 km (85 mi) south of Cancún.

Sian Ka'an ("where the sky is born") was first settled by the Maya in the 5th century AD. In 1986 the Mexican Government established the 1.3-million-acre **Sian Ka'an Biosphere Reserve** as an internationally protected area. The next year, it was named a World Heritage Site by the United Nations Educational, Scientific, and Cultural Organization (UNESCO). In 1996 the reserve was extended by 200,000 acres.

This is one of the last undeveloped stretches of coastline in North America. The reserve constitutes 10% of the land in Quintana Roo and covers 100 km (62 mi) of coast. Freshwater and coastal lagoons, mangrove swamps, watery cays, savannahs, tropical forests, a barrier reef, hundreds of species of local and migratory birds, fish, other animals and plants, and fewer than 1,000 local residents (primarily Maya) share this area. Many species of the once-flourishing wildlife have fallen into the endangered category, but the waters here still teem with fish (and crocodiles). Fishing the flats for wily bonefish is especially popular, and the peninsula's few lodges also run deep-sea fishing trips. The beaches are wide and white, and although many of the palms have succumbed to the yellowing palm disease imported from Florida, the vegetation is growing back. There are approximately 27 ruins (none excavated) linked by a unique canal system—one of the few of its kind in the Maya world in Mexico.

In order to see the sites you must take a guided tour offered by a private, nonprofit organization such as Amigos de Sian Ka'an (⊠ Crepúsculo 18, Sm 44, Manzana 13, Cancún, Quintana Roo 77506, ☎ 98/48–16–18, 98/48–21–36, 98/80–60–24, FAX 98/87–30–80). The four-hour boat tour includes bird-watching, a visit to the Maya ruins of Xlapak (where you can jump into one of the channels and float downstream), and a tour of the mangroves. Tour groups depart from Cabañas Ana y José (☞ Dining and Lodging *in* Tulum, *above*) every Wednesday and Saturday morning; the fee includes a bilingual guide and binoculars.

To explore on your own, follow the road past Boca Paila to the secluded 35-km (22-mi) coastal strip of land that is part of the reserve. You'll be limited to swimming, snorkeling, and camping on the beaches, as there are no trails into the surrounding jungle. The narrow, extremely rough dirt road down the peninsula is filled with monstrous potholes and after a rainfall is completely impassable. Don't attempt it unless you have four-wheel drive. Most fishing lodges along the way close for the rainy season in August and September, and accommodations are hard to come by. The road ends at **Punta Allen,** a fishing village whose main catch is spiny lobster, which was becoming scarce until ecologists taught the local fishing cooperative how to build and lay special traps to conserve the species. There are several small expensive guest houses. If you haven't booked ahead, start out early in the morning so you can get back to civilization before dark.

Lodging

$$$$ 🏨 **Boca Paila Fishing Lodge.** In the midst of the Sian Ka'an Biosphere Reserve, this charming lodge has nine spacious cottages with two double beds, couches, large bathrooms, and separate screened-in sitting areas. Catering principally to anglers, the lodge provides boats and guides for fly-fishing and bonefishing; guests can bring their own tackle or rent some at the lodge. Meals, included in the room rate, are excellent. The beach is exceptionally lovely and tranquil. Beware: Credit cards can only be used by arrangement with Frontiers, the reservations agent. ⊠ *Boca Paila Peninsula,* ☎ *no phone.* ⊠ *Reservations: Frontiers, Box 959, Wexford, PA 15090,* ☎ *800/245–1950, 724/935–1577,* 🖷 *724/935–5388. 9 cottages. Restaurant, bar. No credit cards.*

$$$$ 🏨 **Casa Blanca Lodge.** Punta Pájaros, to which this remote fishing resort
★ provides unique access, is reputed to be one of the best places in the world for light-tackle saltwater fishing. The American-managed, all-inclusive lodge—just 100 ft from the ocean—is set on a rocky outcrop covered with palm trees. The lodge's 10 guest rooms are large and modern; there's also an open-air bar and a living and dining area. Rates are highest March through June, lowest January through March. During the high season, Saturday–Saturday stays and a 50% prepayment are required. Rates include a charter flight from Cancún to the lodge, all meals, a boat, and a guide. ⊠ *Reservations: Frontiers, Box 959, Wexford, PA 15090,* ☎ *800/245–1950, 724/935–1577,* 🖷 *724/935–5388;* ⊠ *Outdoor Travel,* ☎ *713/526–3739, 800/533–7299. 10 rooms. Restaurant, bar, fishing. MC, V.*

The North Caribbean Coast A to Z

Arriving and Departing

BY BUS

The **ADO** line (⊠ Av. Juárez at Av. 5, ☎ 9/87–30–109) has first-class and deluxe service between Playa del Carmen and Cancún, Valladolid, Chichén Itzá, Chetumal, Tulum, Xel-Há, Mexico City, and Mérida daily. **Mayab** (⊠ Av. Juárez, ☎ no phone) runs second-class buses to the above destinations, and deluxe express buses to Chetumal. **Autotransportes Oriente** (⊠ Av. Juárez, ☎ no phone) has express service to Mérida eight times daily, and one bus daily to Cobá. **TRP** (⊠ Av. Juárez at Av. 5, ☎ no phone) offers first-class service about every 15 minutes to Cancún.

BY FERRY

Passenger-only ferries and two large speedboats depart from the dock at Playa del Carmen (☎ 9/87–21–508) for the 45-minute trip to the main pier in Cozumel. They leave approximately every hour on the hour 5 AM–11 PM with no ferry at noon, 2, 8 or 10. Return service to Playa runs every hour on the hour 4 AM–10 PM with no ferry at 5, 11, 1, 7, or 9 PM. Call (☎ 9/87–20–588, 9/87–20–477) to verify the regularly changing schedule.

Getting Around

BY CAR

The entire coast from Punta Sam near Cancún to the main border crossing to Belize at Chetumal is traversable on Highway 307. This straight road is entirely paved and has been widened into four lanes south to Xcaret. Drive with caution—many locals, remembering the rutted roads of yesterday, like to speed on the new highway. Gas stations are becoming more abundant, but it's still a good idea to fill the tank whenever you can. There are gas stations in Cancún, Puerto Morelos, Playa del Carmen, Tulum, Felipe Carrillo Puerto, and Chetumal.

BY PLANE

The airstrip in Playa del Carmen is near the Continental Plaza Hotel, and there is occasional shuttle service to Cozumel.

BY TAXI

You can hire taxis in Cancún to go as far as Playa del Carmen, Tulum, or Akumal, but the price is steep unless you have many passengers. Fares run about $55 or more to Playa alone; between Playa and Tulum or Akumal, expect to pay at least $25. It's much cheaper from Playa to Cancún, with taxi fare running about $30; negotiate before you hop into the cab. Taxis wait eagerly for passengers by the bus station in Playa, and there's a taxi stand at the entrance to Akumal.

Contacts and Resources

CAR RENTAL

In Playa del Carmen, car-rental agencies proliferate around the ferry pier and Avenida Juárez. Rental agencies include **Hertz** (⊠ White Sands Travel, ☎ 9/87–31–130, 9/87–30–703; ⊠ Hotel Continental Plaza Playacar, ☎ 9/87–30–033) and **National** (⊠ Hotel Molcas, ☎ 9/87–30–360, 9/87–30–883). If you want air-conditioning, reserve your car in advance.

EMERGENCIES

Playa del Carmen. Police (⊠ Av. Juárez between Avs. 15 and 20, ☎ 9/87–30–291). **Red Cross** (⊠ Av. Juárez at Av. 25, ☎ 9/87–31–233). For medical emergencies, contact **Centro de Salud** (⊠ Av. Juárez at Av. 15, ☎ 987/2–12–30 ext. 147).

GUIDED TOURS

Although some guided tours are available in this area, the roads are quite good for the most part, so renting a car is an efficient and enjoyable alternative: most of the sights you'll see along this stretch are natural, and you can hire a guide at the ruins sites.

Air Tours. In Playa del Carmen, **Aero Saab** (⊠ Playa del Carmen airport, ☎ 9/87–30–804) will take you on a panoramic flight to see your hotel from the sky or on a guided tour to Isla Holbox to visit the bird sanctuary (lunch is included).

Ecotours. Visit the ruins of Cobá and the Maya village of Pac-Chen located deep in the jungle with **Alltournative Expeditions** (⊠ Av. 10 1, Plaza Antigua, Playa del Carmen, ☎ 9/87–32–036). It offers a variety of other ecotours as well.

Maya Ruins. In Playa del Carmen, **Tierra Maya Tours** (⊠ Av. 5 at Calle 6, ☎ 9/87–31–385, FAX 9/87–31–386) runs trips to the ruins of Chichén Itzá, Uxmal, Palenque, and Tikal. It can also help you with transfers, tickets, and booking hotel rooms. Many first-class hotels in Playa del Carmen and Puerto Aventuras can arrange day tours to Tulum, Chichén Itzá, and Cobá.

TRAVEL AGENCIES

There are more major travel agencies and tour operators up and down the coast than before, and first-class hotels in Playa del Carmen, Puerto Aventuras, and Akumal usually have their own in-house travel services.

VISITOR INFORMATION

The Playa del Carmen **tourist information booth** (⊠ Av. Juárez by the police station, ☎ 9/87–32–804) is open Monday to Saturday 8 AM–9 PM. The office is filled with helpful brochures and information. Tourist police are also located just outside the bus station and can answer many of your questions.

THE STATE OF YUCATÁN

Updated by
Patricia Alisau

Almost five centuries after the conquest, Yucatán state remains one of the last great strongholds of Mexico's indigenous population. To this day, in fact, many Maya do not even speak Spanish, primarily because of the peninsula's geographic and, hence, cultural isolation from the rest of the country.

Physically, too, Yucatán differs from the rest of the country. Its geography and wildlife have more in common with Florida and Cuba—with which it was probably once connected—than with the central Mexican plateau and mountains. A mostly flat limestone slab possessing almost no bodies of water, it is rife with underground cenotes, caves with stalactites, small hills, and intense jungle.

The celebrated Maya ruins at Chichén Itzá and Uxmal are the stars of Yucatán, but small towns such as Valladolid have their own unpretentious charm. Mérida, the capital, has excellent restaurants and markets and a unique mix of Maya, Spanish, and French architectural styles.

Mérida

There is a marvelous eccentricity about Mérida. Fully urban, with maddeningly slow-moving traffic, it has a self-sufficient, self-contented air that would suggest a small town, more than a state capital of some 1.5 million inhabitants. Gaily pretentious turn-of-the-century buildings have an Iberian–Moorish flair for the ornate, but most of the architecture is low-lying, and although the city sprawls, it is not imposing. Grandiose colonial facades adorned with iron grillwork, carved wooden doors, and archways conceal marble tiles and lush gardens that hark back to the city's heyday as the wealthiest capital in Mexico.

Mérida is a city of subtle contrasts, from its opulent facades to its residents, very European yet very Maya. The Indian presence is unmistakable: people are short with square faces and almond-shaped eyes. Women pad about in *huipiles* (hand-embroidered, sacklike white dresses), and craftsmen and vendors from outlying villages come to town in their huaraches.

Mérida is the cultural and intellectual center of the peninsula, with museums, schools, and attractions that provide great insight into the history and character of Yucatán. Consider making it one of the first stops in your travels, and make sure you come on a Sunday, when traffic is light, the city seems to revert to a more gracious era, and admission to archaeological sites is free.

㉞ The **zócalo,** which Méridanos also call by its traditional names—the Plaza Principal and Plaza de la Independencia—was laid out in 1542 on the ruins of T'hó, the Maya city demolished to make way for Mérida. Recently revamped, it is still the focal point around which the most important public buildings cluster. The plaza is bordered east and west by Calles 60 and 62, north and south by Calles 61 and 63.

㉟ Francisco Montejo—father and son—conquered the peninsula and founded Mérida in 1542. They built the stately **Casa de Montejo** (⊠ Calle 63 on the south side of the zócalo) 10 years later. The palace remained with the family until the late 1970s, when it was restored and converted into a bank. Built in the French style during Mérida's heyday as the world's henequen capital, it now represents the city's finest—and oldest—example of elaborately decorated, colonial plateresque architecture. Step into the building weekdays between 9 and 5 for a glimpse of the lushly foliated inner patio.

㊱ The west side of the main square is occupied by the 18th-century **Palacio Municipal**—the city hall—which is painted yellow and trimmed with white arcades, balustrades, and the national coat of arms. ⊠ *Calle 62 between Calles 61 and 63.* ☉ *Weekdays 8–7, Sat. 8–2.*

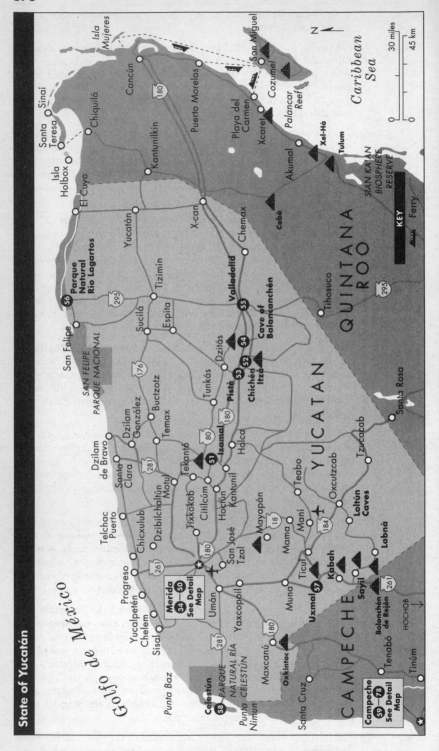

State of Yucatán

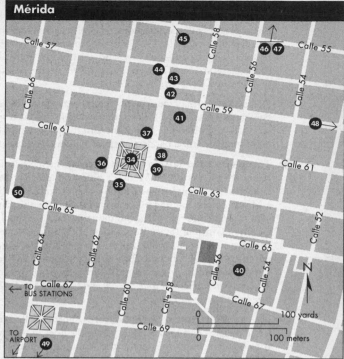

③⑦ On the northeast corner of the zócalo, the **Palacio del Gobierno** (State Government Palace) was built in 1885 on the site of the Casa Real (Royal House). The upper floor of the palace contains Fernando Castro Pacheco's vivid murals of the bloody history of the conquest of Yucatán, painted in 1978. ⊠ *Calle 61 between Calles 60 and 62.* ⊙ *Daily 8 AM–11 PM.*

③⑧ The second-oldest **catedral** on the North American mainland (and oldest in Mexico) stands catercorner from the Palacio del Gobierno. Begun in 1561, it took several hundred Maya laborers, working with stones from the pyramids of the ravaged Maya city, 36 years to complete. Its somber Renaissance-style facade is stark and unadorned. Inside, the black Cristo de las Ampollas (Christ of the Blisters), on a side altar to the left of the main one, is a replica of the original, which was destroyed during the Revolution. According to legend, the Christ figure burned all night. It appeared the next morning covered only with blisters—hence its name.

③⑨ **Museo de Arte Contemporáneo** (Museum of Contemporary Art). Originally designed as an art school but used until recently as a convent, this enormous two-story building is full of light, just perfect for an art museum. It showcases the works of Yucatecan artists and has excellent international art exhibits in the second-floor galleries. These make up for the halfhearted reproductions of some of the world's masterpieces in the World History of Art room below. There's also a bookstore (closed Sunday). ⊠ *Pasaje de la Revolución 1907, between Calles 58 and 60 on the main plaza,* ☎ *99/28-32-58, 99/28-32-36.* ⊠ *$2, free Sun.* ⊙ *Wed.–Mon. 10–5:30.*

Two picturesque 19th-century edifices house the main post office and
④⓪ telegraph buildings. Behind them sprawls the pungent, labyrinthine **Mercado Municipal,** filled with local color, where almost every patch of

ground is occupied by Indian women selling chilies, herbs, fruit, and essential plasticware. On the second floor of the main building is the **Bazar de Artesanías Municipales,** the principal handicrafts market, where you can buy jewelry (gold or gold-dipped filigree earrings), pottery, embroidered clothes, hammocks, and straw bags. Only about one-fifth of the stalls are open Sundays. ⊠ *Calle 65 between Calles 56 and 58.* ☉ *Weekdays 8–7, Sat. 8–5, Sun. 8–1.*

41 Half a block north of the main plaza is the cozy **Parque Hidalgo,** or Cepeda Peraza, as it is officially known. Renovated mansions-turned-hotels and sidewalk cafés stand at two corners of the park, which comes alive at night with marimba bands and street vendors. ⊠ *Calles 60 and 59.*

42 The **Iglesia de la Tercera Orden de Jesús,** facing Parque Hidalgo on the north side, is one of Mérida's oldest buildings and the first Jesuit church in the Yucatán. The church was built in 1618 of limestone from a Maya temple that had previously stood on the site. The former convent rooms in the rear of the building now host the small **Pinoteca Juan Gamboa Guzmán** (State Repository of Paintings). One of the rooms displays striking bronze sculptures of the Yucatán's indigenous people by its most celebrated 20th-century sculptor, Enrique Gottdiener. On the second floor are about 20 forgettable oil paintings. ⊠ *Calle 59 between Calles 60 and 58,* ☎ *99/24–79–12.* 🎫 *$1, free Sun.* ☉ *Tues.–Sat. 8–8, Sun. 8–2.*

43 The Italianate **Teatro Peón Contreras,** north of Parque Hidalgo on Calle 60, was designed in 1908 along the lines of the grand European turn-of-the-century theaters and opera houses. Today, in addition to performing arts, the theater also houses temporary art exhibits and the main Centro de Información Turística (☎ 99/24–92–90), to the right of the lobby. A café spills out to a patio from inside the theater.

44 The arabesque **Universidad Autonoma de Yucatán** plays a major role in the city's cultural and intellectual life. The folkloric ballet performs on the patio of the main building Fridays at 9 PM. Photographic and other art or cultural exhibits are often on view in its various salons, and the library has interesting frescoes of regional heroes. The 1711 building has crownlike Moorish-style upper reaches and uncloistered archways. ⊠ *Calle 60 between Calles 57 and 59,* ☎ *99/24–80–00.*

45 The rather plain **Parque de Santa Lucia** draws crowds to the Thursday-night serenades of local musicians and folk dancers starting at 9. The small 1575 church opposite the park was built as a place of worship for the African and Caribbean slaves who lived here. The churchyard functioned as the cemetery until 1821. ⊠ *Calle 60 at Calle 55.*

46 North of downtown, the 10-block-long street known as the **Paseo Montejo** exemplifies the Parisian airs the city took on in the late 19th century, when wealthy plantation owners built opulent, impressive mansions. The broad boulevard, lined with tamarinds and laurels, is sometimes wistfully referred to as Mérida's Champs-Élysées. Although the once-stunning mansions fell into disrepair a few years ago, their stateliness is being restored by a citywide beautification program. This part of town is where posh new hotels are opening.

The most compelling of the Paseo Montejo mansions, the pale peach **47 Palacio Cantón** houses the **Museum of Anthropology and History,** dedicated to Maya culture and history. Although it's not that impressive compared with its counterparts in other Mexican cities, it serves as an opener to visiting nearby archaeological sites. Bilingual legends accompany the displays, but lengthier explanations are in Spanish only. Private guides are available for hire, and there's a bookstore on site. ⊠ *Calle 43 at Paseo Montejo,* ☎ *99/23–05–57.* 🎟 *$1.60, free Sun.* ◔ *Tues.–Sat. 8–8, Sun. 8–2; bookstore closed Sun.*

㊽ Several blocks east of the main plaza is the **Museo de Artes Popular** (Museum of Folk Art), housed in a fine old mansion. The ground floor is devoted to Yucatecan arts and crafts, and the second floor focuses on the popular arts of the rest of Mexico. ⊠ *441 Calle 59, at Calle 50,* ☎ *no phone.* 🎟 *Free.* ◔ *Tues.–Sat. 9–8, Sun. 8–2.*

At the south end of the city, about nine blocks below the square, **㊾** stands the 1748 **Ermita de Santa Isabel,** part of a Jesuit monastery also known as the Hermitage of the Good Trip. A resting place in colonial days for travelers heading to Campeche, the restored chapel is an enchanting spot to visit at sunset. Next door is a huge garden with a waterfall. The church hours are irregular, but the garden is almost always open during the day. ⊠ *Calles 66 and 77.*

㊿ ㊿ **El Centenario Zoological Park,** Mérida's great children's attraction, is a large, somewhat tacky amusement complex consisting of playgrounds, rides (including ponies and a small train), a roller-skating rink, snack bars, and cages with more than 300 marvelous native monkeys, birds, reptiles, and other animals. There are also pleasant wooded paths, picnic areas, and a small lake where you can rent rowboats. On Sunday morning, special events, such as puppet shows, are hosted for kids. ⊠ *Av. Itzaes between Calles 59 and 65 (entrances on Calles 59 and 65),* ☎ *no phone.* 🎟 *Free.* ◔ *Daily 9–6.*

Dining and Lodging

$$$ ✕ **Alberto's Continental Patio.** Widely praised for its food and setting, **★** this restaurant is in a lovely 1727 building. There are two dining rooms and an inner patio surrounded by rubber trees. Lebanese choices include shish kebab, fried *kibi* (ground beef, wheat germ, and spices), and tabbouleh. Mexican dishes are on the menu as well. ⊠ *Calle 64 No. 482, at Calle 57,* ☎ *99/28–53–67. AE, MC, V.*

$$$ ✕ **Habichuela.** Intended for the discriminating diner who expects ex- **★** cellence in both food and service, this elegant place is a good alternative to the tourist restaurants around the main square. For starters, try the seafood crepes or salmon pâté. Main dishes include butterflied shrimp with ginger, tamarind, or fruit sauce. The chocolate-mousse cake is the star of the dessert menu. ⊠ *Calle 1 No. 416, Col. Mexico Oriente, about 20 minutes by car or cab from the main square,* ☎ *99/26–36– 26. AE, MC, V. No breakfast or dinner Sun.*

$$ ✕ **Los Almendros.** This Mérida classic takes credit for the invention of the regional specialty poc chuc, although some dispute the claim. The menu provides a good introduction to the variety of Yucatecan cuisine; it includes cochinita pibíl and papadzules. Ask for the English-language menu. There is live music daily 2–5 and 7:30–11, and a regional show Friday at 8. ⊠ *Calle 50 No. 493,* ☎ *99/23–81–35, 99/ 28–54–59. AE, MC, V.*

$$ ✕ **Amaro.** This historic home takes on a romantic glow at night, with candlelit tables on the open patio. Once strictly vegetarian, Amaro has expanded its menu to include poultry and red meats. Recommended dishes include eggplant curry and soup made with *chaya,* a local vegetable. ⊠ *Calle 59 No. 507,* ☎ *99/28–24–51. No credit cards. Closed Sun. Apr.–Nov.*

$$ ✕ **La Casona.** This pretty mansion-turned-restaurant near Parque Santa Ana has an inner patio, arcade, and ceiling fans. A bar features live romantic music on weekends. The accent is Yucatecan, with poc chuc, pollo pibíl, and *huachinango* (red snapper baked in banana leaves) among the recommended dishes. There are some Italian offerings as well. ⊠ *Calle 60 No. 434,* ☎ *99/23–99–96. MC, V. Closed Sun.*

$$ × **Pórtico del Peregrino.** The softly lit outdoor patio is lovely, but the
★ indoor sections of this old colonial home are equally appealing. The
house special is a robust *zarzuela de mariscos* (seafood casserole cooked
in white wine); the eclectic menu also includes a delicious tortilla soup,
pollo pibíl, shish kebab, and chicken liver brochettes. For dessert try
coconut ice cream with Kahlúa. ⊠ *Calle 57 No. 501,* ☎ *99/28–61–
63. AE, MC, V.*

$ × **Café La Havana** Overwhelmingly popular with locals, this new café
★ recalls old Havana with its old-fashioned ceiling fans and elegant
wicker furniture. Sixteen javas are offered, including Irish, espresso,
and Arab. The menu has light fare such as lime soup, as well as some
entrées, including enchiladas, fajitas, and breaded shrimp. A few blocks
north of the main square, it's open around the clock. ⊠ *Corner of Calles
59 and 62,* ☎ *99/28–65–02. No credit cards.*

$$$$ ×🍽 **Hacienda Katanchel.** This romantic, rambling 17th-century
★ henequin hacienda on 740 acres has been restored to its original splen-
dor. The guest suites are outfitted with overhead fans, hammocks,
huge tile bathrooms, and plunge pools. The former processing plant
has been turned into a gorgeous restaurant serving contemporary Yu-
catecan cuisine. The menu offers such selections as cream of avocado
soup with shrimp and goat cheese; chicken in *pipian* (pumpkin seed)
and pistachio sauce; and candied papaya with white cheese. The price
of a room includes a full breakfast. But be warned: some but not all
the rooms have air-conditioning. ⊠ *25 km (15 mi) east of Mérida on
Rte. 180 (toward Cancún),* ☎ *99/20–09–97, 800/223–6510,* 🅵🅰🆇 *888/
882–9470. 39 suites. Restaurant, bar, air-conditioning (some), pools,
travel services, airport shuttle, car rental, free parking. AE, MC, V.* 🍽

$$$$ 🍽 **Casa del Balam.** This very pleasant hotel on well-heeled Calle 60
★ was built more than 60 years ago as the home of the Barbachano fam-
ily, pioneers of Yucatán tourism. Today the hotel—owned and man-
aged by Carmen Barbachano—offers capacious, well-maintained rooms
with wrought-iron accessories and refrigerator-minibars. Cocktails
and light meals are served in the lobby courtyard; there's also a restau-
rant. ⊠ *Calle 60 No. 488 (Apdo. 988),* ☎ *99/24–88–44, 99/24–21–
50, 800/624–8451,* 🅵🅰🆇 *99/24–50–11. 51 rooms, 3 suites. Restaurant,
2 bars, minibars, no-smoking rooms, pool, travel services, car rental,
free parking. AE, DC, MC, V.* 🍽

$$$$ 🍽 **Fiesta Americana Mérida.** The lovely pink facade of this posh hotel
★ and shopping/business center mirrors the architecture of Paseo Mon-
tejo mansions on an epic scale. The colonial echoes carry into the grand
and spacious upper lobby, and the theme of bygone elegance is con-
tinued in the guest rooms, which also offer all the modern conve-
niences, including minibars, data ports, and three phones. ⊠ *Av. Colón
451, at Paseo Montejo,* ☎ *99/20–21–94, 800/343–7821,* 🅵🅰🆇 *99/20–
21–98. 323 rooms, 27 suites. 2 restaurants, 2 bars, in-room data ports,
minibars, no-smoking rooms, health club, shops, concierge floor, travel
services, car rental, free parking. AE, MC, V.* 🍽

$$$$ 🍽 **Hyatt Regency Mérida.** The first of the deluxe hotels to open on Paseo
Montejo, the 18-story Hyatt brought a new level of service to Mérida.
The rooms are regally decorated and offer satellite TV and minibars.
Amenities not commonly found in Mérida include a top-notch busi-
ness center and the city's only tapas bar, not to mention bathtubs and
hair dryers. ⊠ *Av. Colón 344, at Calle 60,* ☎ *99/42–02–02, 99/42–
12–34, 800/233–1234,* 🅵🅰🆇 *99/25–70–02. 296 rooms, 4 suites. 2 restau-
rants, 2 bars, no-smoking rooms, pool, tennis court, travel services,
car rental, free parking. AE, DC, MC, V.* 🍽

$$$ 🍽 **Mérida Misión Park Inn Plaza.** The Misión has two major assets: an
excellent location in the heart of downtown and a genuine colonial am-
bience. Forty-five units in the old colonial section are set around a pretty

courtyard; rooms in the modern 11-story annex don't have as much character, but the ones on the upper floors have good city views. All rooms are equipped with cable TV, hair dryers, minibars, and safes. There's also a pool and a bar with romantic music nightly. ⊠ *Calle 60 No. 491,* ☎ *99/23–95–00, 888/224–8837 in the U.S.,* 𝔽𝔸𝕏 *99/23–76–65. 137 rooms, 8 suites. Restaurant, bar, snack bar, no-smoking rooms, pool, travel services, car rental, free parking. AE, DC, MC, V.* ✎

$$ ⌸ **Casa Mexilio.** This choice B&B has wonderfully eclectic decor—Middle Eastern wall hangings, French tapestries, colorful tile floors and sinks, and folk-art furniture. Casa Mexilio lacks the amenities of the larger hotels—only five rooms have air-conditioning—but if you enjoy the more casual feeling of staying in a private home, you'll be happy here. ⊠ *Calle 68 No. 495,* ☎ 𝔽𝔸𝕏 *99/28–25–05.* ⊠ *Reservations in the U.S.:* ☎ *800/538–6802, 303/674–9615,* 𝔽𝔸𝕏 *303/674–8735. 8 rooms. Breakfast room, pool. MC, V.* ✎

$$ ⌸ **Gran Hotel.** Cozily situated on Parque Hidalgo, this legendary 1901 hotel is the oldest in the city, and it still lives up to its name. The guest rooms have high ceilings and antique furniture. Thirteen units have balconies—request one of these if you don't mind noise from the park (most of the others have no windows at all). The rooms on the second floor in the back are the quietest. Fidel Castro chose one of these when he stayed here; Porfirio Díaz stayed in one of the sumptuous corner rooms, which have small living and dining areas. All rooms have air-conditioning and fans. ⊠ *Calle 60 No. 496,* ☎ *99/23–69–63, 99/24–76–32,* 𝔽𝔸𝕏 *99/24–76–22. 25 rooms, 7 suites. Restaurant, bar, pizzeria, travel services, free parking. MC, V.* ✎

$ ⌸ **Casa San Juan.** This B&B is housed in a beautifully restored colonial mansion built by a Portuguese family in the 1860s. Designated a historical monument, the house has many original components, such as high ceilings decorated with Belgium railroad ties, tile floors, a stone fountain, and 10-ft-high mahogany doors. Three patios and a sitting room surround an interior garden. All guest rooms are extra large with double beds and ceiling and floor fans; two have air-conditioning. Be warned: Credit cards can only be used when booking from the U.S. ⊠ *Calle 62 No. 545-A,* ☎ *99/23–68–23,* 𝔽𝔸𝕏 *99/86–29–37. 6 rooms. Breakfast room, parking $2 a day. MC, V.* ✎

Nightlife and the Arts

Mérida enjoys an unusually active and diverse cultural life, including free government-sponsored music and dance performances most nights, as well as sidewalk art shows in local parks. On Saturday check out the Noche Mexicana, a free, outdoor spectacle of music, dance, and regional handicrafts where you'll see more locals than tourists. It happens 8 PM–11 PM at the foot of Paseo Montejo at Calle 47. On Sunday, when six blocks around the zócalo are closed off to traffic, there's live music at Plaza Santa Lucia and Parque Hidalgo (usually at 11 AM); mariachis, marimbas, folkloric dance, and other treats at the main plaza (1 PM). For more information on these and other performances, consult the tourist office, the local newspapers, or the billboards and posters at the **Teatro Peón Contreras** (⊠ Calle 60 at Calle 57), **Universidad Autónoma de Yucatán,** or **Café Pop** (⊠ Calle 57 between Calles 60 and 62).

DANCING

A number of restaurants have live music and dancing, including **El Tucho** (⊠ Calle 60 No. 482, ☎ 99/24–23–23) and **Xtabay** (⊠ above El Tucho, Calle 60 No. 482, ☎ 99/28–09–61). **Pancho's** (⊠ Calle 59 x 60 y 62, ☎ 99/23–09–42) attracts locals and foreigners for a mix of live salsa and Western music. **Vatizia** (⊠ Hotel Fiesta Americana, Av. Colón 451, at Paseo Montejo, ☎ 99/42–11–11) has different theme nights.

FOLKLORIC SHOWS

Fancy Paseo Montejo hotels such as the **Fiesta Americana, Hyatt Regency,** and **Holiday Inn** stage dinner shows with folkloric dances; check with concierges for schedules. The **Folkloric Ballet of the University of Yucatán** presents "The Roots of Today's Yucatán," a combination of music, dance, and theater, every other Wednesday at 8 PM at the Teatro Peón Contreras (⊠ Calle 60 at Calle 57, ☎ 99/23–73–54); tickets are $8. On alternate Fridays "University Serenade" is held at 9 PM at the university (Calle 60 at Calle 57); the show includes music, folkloric dance, and poetry; tickets are $1. **Tianos** (⊠ Calle 60 No. 461, ☎ 99/23–71–18) hosts a colorful show of regional dancing nightly at 8 (with dinner or drinks only).

Outdoor Activities and Sports

BULLFIGHTS

Bullfights are held sporadically between October and May and during other holiday periods at the **Plaza de Toros** (⊠ Paseo de la Reforma near Calle 25, Col. Garcia Gineres, ☎ 99/25–79–96). Contact the travel desk at your hotel or one of the tourist information centers.

GOLF

The 18-hole championship golf course at **Club de Golf La Ceiba** (⊠ Carretera Mérida-Progreso Km 14.5, ☎ 99/22–00–53, 99/22–00–54) is open to the public. It is about 16 km (10 mi) north of Mérida.

Shopping

CRAFT MARKETS AND STORES

On the second floor of the **Mercado Municipal** (⊠ between Calles 65 and 67 and Calles 54 and 56), you'll find crafts, food, flowers, and live birds, among other items. The government-run **Casa de Artesanías** (⊠ Calle 63 No. 503, ☎ 99/23–53–92) has folk art from throughout Mexico. The **Bazar García Rejón** (⊠ Calle 65 at Calle 62) has leather items, palm hats, and handmade guitars, among other things. The streets north of the main square, especially **Calle 60,** are lined with crafts and jewelry stores. Sunday brings an array of wares into Mérida. The **Handicraft Bazaar** (⊠ in front of the Municipal Palace across from the main square) is filled with huipiles, hats, and costume jewelry. The **Popular Art Bazaar** (⊠ Parque Santa Lucía, corner of Calles 60 and 55) offers the same, and sometimes work by local artists.

SPECIALTY STORES

Clothing. Look for expensive designer cotton clothing inspired by regional dress at **Mexicanísimo** (⊠ Calle 60 No. 496, on Parque Hidalgo, ☎ 99/23–81–32). For a good selection of *guayaberas,* the shirts worn by Mexican men, try **Camisería Canul** (⊠ Calle 62 No. 484, ☎ 99/23–01–58). Pick up a *jipi* at **El Becaleño** (⊠ Calle 65 No. 483, ☎ 99/85–05–81)—the famous hats are made at Becal in Campeche by the González family.

Galleries. Contemporary paintings and photographs are showcased in the **Teatro Peón Contreras** (⊠ Calle 60 between Calles 57 and 59, ☎ 99/23–73–54), the **Galería Casa Colón** (⊠ Av. Colón 507, ☎ 99/25–79–52, 99/25–82–53), the **Galería Ateneo Peninsular** (⊠ Calle 60 between Calle 61 and Pasaje Revolución, ☎ 99/25–79–52, 90/25–82–53), and the **Palacio del Gobierno** (⊠ Calle 61 between Calles 60 and 62, ☎ 99/23–19–44).

Jewelry. La Perla Maya (⊠ Calle 60 Nos. 485–487, ☎ 99/28–58–86) sells old-fashioned silver Yucatecan filigree earrings and pins. **La Canasta** (⊠ Calle 60 No. 500, ☎ 99/28–19–78) has a good selection of filigree jewelry, both sterling silver and gold-dipped. **Tane** (⊠ Hyatt Regency Hotel, Calle 60 No. 344, ☎ 99/42–02–02) is an outlet for exquisite (and expensive) silver earrings, necklaces, and bracelets, some using ancient Maya designs.

The Scenic Route to Chichén Itzá

Although you can get to Chichén Itzá (120 km [74 mi] east of Mérida) along the shorter Route 180, it's far more scenic to follow Route 80 until it ends at Tekantó, and then head south to Citilcúm, east to Dzitas, and south again to Pisté. These roads have no signs, but are the only paved roads going in these directions. Ask directions frequently.

Izamal

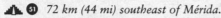 *72 km (44 mi) southeast of Mérida.*

Izamal is nicknamed Ciudad Amarillo (Yellow City) because its buildings are painted earth-tone yellow, according to city ordinance in colonial times. In the center of town stands the enormous 16th-century **Convento de San Antonio de Padua,** perched on—and built from—the remains of a pyramid devoted to Itamná, god of the heavens, day, night, and the dew. The monastery's church, which Pope John Paul II visited in 1993, has a gigantic columned portico (claimed to be second only to that of the Vatican in size) and, in the entranceway next to the gift shop, newly discovered frescoes of saints and of Christ. The Virgin of the Immaculate Conception, to whom the church is dedicated, is the patron saint of the Yucatán. Miracles are ascribed to her, and a yearly pilgrimage takes place in her honor. Another pyramid, called **Kinich Kakmó** (macaw of fire), is all that remains of a royal Maya city that flourished here hundreds of years ago.

On Sunday a special air-conditioned car attached to the regular train makes a round-trip excursion between Mérida and Izamal. The cost ($18) includes train fare, lunch, a folkloric show, and a city tour in a horse-drawn carriage. Tickets can be purchased through any travel agent (☞ Contacts and Resources *in* State of Yucatán A to Z, *below*). The train leaves the **Mérida train station** (⊠ Calle 55 at Calle 48, ☎ 99/27–77–01, 99/26–20–91) Sunday at 8 AM and returns at 5 PM.

Chichén Itzá

 *116 km (72 mi) from Mérida.*

One of the four best-known Maya ruins, Chichén Itzá (chee-*chen* eet-*zah*) was probably the most important city in Yucatán from the 10th to the 12th century. An architectural mélange, Chichén was altered by each successive wave of inhabitants. Evidence suggests the site was first settled in AD 432, abandoned for an unknown period, then rediscovered in 964 by the Maya-speaking Itzá people, who are believed to have come from the Petén rain forest around Tikal, in what is now northern Guatemala. The building style is very similar to what's found in the southern Maya empire—an area extending from the Petén south to Honduras. *Chichén Itzá* means "the mouth of the well of the Itzás." By 1224, after some 260 years, the Itzás had deserted the site.

The majesty and enormity of this site are unforgettable. Chichén Itzá encompasses approximately 6 square km (4 square mi), though only 20 to 30 buildings of the several hundred at the site have been fully explored. It's divided into two parts, called Old and New, although architectural motifs from the Classic period are found in both sections. A more convenient distinction is topographical, since there are two major complexes of buildings separated by a dirt path.

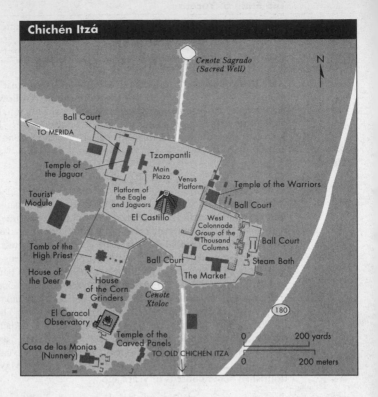

Chichén Itzá

The iconic 98-ft-tall pyramid called **El Castillo** (the castle), which dominates the site, represents a marriage of styles: the martial, imperial architecture of the Itzá and the more cerebral design genius and astronomical expertise of the earlier Maya. Atop the castle is a temple dedicated to Kukulcán—the Maya name for Quetzalcóatl, that legendary priest-king from Tula in the Valley of Mexico who was incarnated as the plumed serpent. The structure was constructed so that twice a year, at the spring and fall equinoxes, the play of light and shadow would create an image of the god Kukulcán snaking his way down the sides of the pyramid. A more ancient temple inside the Castillo is open to the public for only a few hours in the morning and again in the afternoon. Claustrophobes should think twice before entering: the stairs are narrow, dark, and winding. An evening sound-and-light show highlights the architectural details in the Castillo and other buildings with a clarity the eye doesn't see in daylight, but its narrative has inaccuracies.

The temple rests on a massive trapezoidal square, on the west side of which is Chichén Itzá's largest ball court, one of seven on the site. The game played here was something like soccer (no hands were used), but it had a strictly religious significance. Bas-relief carvings at the court depict a player being decapitated. Other bas-reliefs once believed to depict the Toltecs playing against the Maya are actually the Itzá playing against a Maya enemy.

Between the ball court and El Castillo stands a **Tzompantli** (stone platform) carved with rows of human skulls. In ancient times it was actually covered with stakes on which the heads of enemies were impaled. In the **Sacred Well**—a cenote 65 yards in diameter that sits 1 km (½ mi) north of El Castillo at the end of a 900-ft-long sacbe—skeletons of about 50 people were found. Thousands of artifacts made of gold, jade, and other precious materials, most of them not of local provenance, have been recovered from the brackish depths. The well's excavation by Mexican diver/businessman Pablo Bush Romero launched the field of underwater archaeology.

Returning to the causeway, you will see on your left the **Group of the Thousand Columns** with the famous **Temple of the Warriors,** a masterful example of the Itzá influence here. Scientists have shown that this temple was used as an official meeting place for members of the council of Lords of Chichén. Murals of village life and scenes of war can be viewed here, and you can see an artistic representation of the defeat of the Maya on the interior murals of the adjacent **Temple of the Jaguar.**

To get to the less visited cluster of structures at New Chichén Itzá—often confused with "Old" Chichén Itzá—take the main road south from the Temple of the Jaguar past El Castillo and turn right onto a small path opposite the ball court on your left. Archaeologists are currently restoring several buildings, including the **Tomb of the High Priest,** where several tombs with skeletons and jade offerings were found, and the northern part of the site, which was used by the military. The most impressive structure in this area is the astronomical observatory, **El Caracol.** The name, meaning "snail," refers to the spiral staircase at the building's core. Although definitely used for observing the heavens, it also served a religious function. After leaving El Caracol, continue south several hundred yards to the beautiful **Casa de las Monjas** (Nunnery) and its annex, which have long carved panels.

At Old Chichén Itzá, "pure Maya" style—with playful latticework, Chaac masks, and gargoyle-like serpents on the cornices—dominates. Highlights include the **Date Group** (so named because of the complete series of hieroglyphic date inscriptions), the **House of the Phalli,** and the **Temple of the Three Lintels.** Maya guides will lead you down the path by an old narrow-gauge railroad track to even more ruins, barely unearthed, if you ask. A fairly good restaurant and great ice-cream stand are in the entrance building, and there are refreshment stands by the cenote and on the pathway near El Caracol. ▩ *Site and museum $7.50, free Sun. and holidays; sound-and-light show $3.50 in Spanish, $5 in English; parking $1; use of video camera $7.* ☉ *Daily 8–5; sound-and-light show: Spanish version Apr.–Oct. 8 PM, Nov.–Mar. 7 PM; English version Apr.–Oct. 9 PM, Nov.–Mar. 8 PM.*

Lodging

$$$$ ▦ **Mayaland.** The hotel closest to the ruins, this charming 1920s lodg-
★ ing belongs to the Barbachano family, whose name is practically synonymous with tourism in Yucatán. In addition to a main hotel building, a wing and several bungalows are set in a large garden on the 100-acre site. You can see part of Chichén-Itzá from the gardens and the hotel has its own private walkway into the ruins. All units have cable TV and minibars; five suites have hot tubs. Tour buses fill the road in front of the hotel, so choose a room at the back. The 24 bungalows at the rear of the hotel are the prettiest (and most expensive) accommodations. Light meals served poolside and at tables overlooking the garden are a better choice than the expensive fixed-price meals served in the dining room. ✉ *Carretera Mérida–Pto. Juárez Km 120,* ☎ *985/1–01–29,* FAX *985/1–01–29. Reservations: Mayaland Tours,* ✉ *Apdo. 407, Mérida,* ☎ *99/24–20–99, 800/235–4079,* FAX *99/24–62–90. 91 rooms, 10 suites. 4 restaurants, 2 bars, air-conditioning, minibars, 3 pools, tennis courts, shuffleboard, volleyball, meeting rooms, free parking. AE, DC, MC, V.*

$$$ ▦ **Hacienda Chichén.** A converted 16th-century hacienda, this hotel
★ once served as the home of U.S. Consul General Edward S. Thomp-

son. All rooms, which are simply furnished in colonial Yucatecan style, have air-conditioning, private bathrooms, and verandas but no phones or TVs. There's a color satellite TV in the library. An enormous old pool sits in the midst of the landscaped garden. Fairly good meals are served on the patio overlooking the grounds, and there's an air-conditioned restaurant; stick with the Yucatecan specialties. ⊠ *Carretera Mérida–Pto. Juárez Km 120,* ☎ *985/1–00–45, 99/24–21–50, 99/24–50–11, 800/624–8451,* ℻ *99/24–50–11. 22 rooms, 3 suites. Restaurant, bar, air-conditioning, pool, chapel, free parking. AE, DC, MC, V.* ✎

Pisté

🟢 *1 km (½ mi) west of Chichén Itzá on Route 180.*

The town of Pisté serves mainly as a base camp for travelers to Chichén Itzá. Hotels, campgrounds, restaurants, and handicrafts shops tend to be cheaper here than south of the ruins. At the west end of town is a Pemex gas station. On the outskirts of Pisté, a short walk from the ruins, **Pueblo Maya,** a pseudo-Maya village, has a shopping and dining center for tour groups. The restaurant serves a bountiful buffet at lunch ($10). Right in town, across from the Dolores Alba hotel is **Parque Ik Kil** (Place of the Winds). The park is built around a lovely cenote where you can swim 8–6 for $2.50, and the restaurant serves national and international fare. Recent additions to the park include a swimming pool, bungalows inspired by Maya dwellings, and a row of shops where artisans demonstrate their crafts. ⊠ *Carretera Libre Pisté–Cancún Km 112,* ☎ *no phone.*

Lodging

$$ ✕🖼 **Pirámide Inn Resort.** The rooms (27 air-conditioned) in this two-story, American-owned '50s-style motel are clean and comfortable, with tile floors and large square desks, but no phones or TVs. The garden contains a small Maya pyramid and an enormous rectangular swimming pool, and the restaurant is one of the best in Pisté. Some good vegetarian dishes are available, in addition to regional cuisine. ⊠ *Calle 15A No. 30, Carretera Mérida–Pto. Juárez Km 117, 97751,* ☎ *985/1–01–15,* ℻ *985/1–01–14. 35 rooms. Restaurant, pool. MC, V.*

$$ 🖼 **Dolores Alba.** The best low-budget choice near the ruins is this family-run hotel, a longtime favorite in the area south of Pisté. The rooms are simple, clean, and comfortable; half have air-conditioning. Hammocks hang by one of the two pools, and breakfast and dinner are served family-style in the main building. Free transportation to the ruins is provided, and there is a covered, guarded parking lot. ⊠ *Carretera Mérida–Cancún Km 122, 3 km (2 mi) south of Chichén Itzá. Reservations:* ⊠ *Calle 63 No. 464, Mérida,* ☎ *99/28–56–50,* ℻ *99/28–31–63. 28 rooms. Restaurant, 2 pools, free parking. AE.* ✎

Cave of Balancanchén

⛰ 🟢 *5 km (3 mi) northeast of Chichén Itzá.*

The Cave of Balancanchén, a shrine whose Maya name translates as "throne of the jaguar," remained virtually undisturbed from the time of the conquest until its discovery in 1959. Inside is a large collection of artifacts—mostly vases, jars, and incense burners. Although there are seven chambers, only three are open. You'll walk past stalactites and stalagmites until you come to an underground lake filled with blind fish; an altar to the rain god rises above it. In order to explore the shrine you must take one of the guided tours, which depart almost hourly. Also at the site is a sound-and-light show that fancifully recounts

Maya history. A small museum at the entrance is very informative. You can catch a bus or taxi to the caves from Chichén Itzá. ☒ *Caves (including tour) $4, free Sun.; show $4; parking $1.* ⊙ *Daily 9–5; tours leave daily at 11, 1, 3 (English); 9, noon, 2, 4 (Spanish); 10 (French).*

Valladolid

⑤⑤ *44 km (27 mi) east of Chichén Itzá.*

The second-largest city in the state of Yucatán, Valladolid is a picturesque provincial town (pop. 70,000). It's enjoying growing popularity among travelers traveling to or from Chichén Itzá or Río Lagartos who want a change from the more touristy places. Montejo founded Valladolid in 1543 on the site of the Maya town of Sisal. The city suffered during the Caste War—when the Maya in revolt killed nearly all Spanish residents—and again during the Mexican Revolution.

Today, however, placidity reigns in this agricultural market town. The center is mostly colonial, although it has many 19th-century structures. The main sights are the colonial churches, principally the large **cathedral** on the central square and the 16th-century **San Bernardino Church and Convent** three blocks southwest. Both were pillaged during the Caste War. A briny, muddy cenote in the center of town draws only the most resolute swimmers; instead, visit the adjacent **ethnographic museum.** Outside town you can swim with the catfish in lovely, mysterious **Cenote Dzitnup,** located in a cave lit by a small natural skylight ($2).

Valladolid is renowned for its cuisine, particularly its sausages; try one of the restaurants within a block of the square. You can find good buys on sandals, baskets, and the local liqueur, Xtabentún, flavored with honey and anise.

Lodging

$$ 🏨 **El Mesón del Marqués.** This building, on the north side of the main square, is a well-preserved, very old hacienda built around a lovely courtyard. All rooms have air-conditioning, phones, and cable TV, and are attractively furnished with rustic and colonial touches. The 25 junior suites have large bathrooms with bathtubs. The restaurant serves Yucatecan specialties such as pollo pibíl and local sausage dishes. ☒ *Calle 39 No. 203, 97780,* ☎ *985/6–20–73, 985/6–30–42,* FAX *985/6–22–80. 58 rooms, 25 junior suites. Restaurant, bar, pool, shops. AE.*

$ 🏨 **María de la Luz.** Another choice on the main plaza, this hotel is built around a shallow, kidney-shape swimming pool surrounded by banana trees. The plain rooms have tile bathrooms, air-conditioning, firm beds, and color cable TV. The street-side restaurant serves tasty Mexican dishes. ☒ *Calle 42 No. 193-C, 97780,* ☎ FAX *985/6–20–71, 985/6–11–81. 51 rooms. Restaurant, bar, pool, free parking. MC, V.*

Parque Natural Río Lagartos

⑤⑥ *101 km (63 mi) north of Valladolid, 150 km (93 mi) northeast of Mérida.*

If you're a flamingo fan, don't miss Parque Natural Río Lagartos, especially between June and March, when you'll see the largest number of flamingos. Spanning a long estuary, the 116,000-acre park was developed with ecotourism in mind—even though the alligators for which it and the village were named were hunted to near extinction years ago. In addition to flamingos, look for egrets, herons, ibis, cormorants, pelicans, and even peregrine falcons. Fishing is good, too, and endangered hawksbill and green turtles lay their eggs on the beach.

The offices of the Reserva are in Tizimín (Flamingo Reserve; ☒ Calle 47 No. 415-A, ☎ 986/3–28–54), open weekdays 9–2 and 6–9, for information. With three days' notice, it can arrange for a bilingual guide. The helpful people who work at the information module ½ km (¼ mi) from the entrance into Río Lagartos also call up a guide with a boat for you. The Isla de Contoy restaurant in town (✉ Calle 19 No. 12, 2 blocks from the estuary in Río Lagartos, ☎ 986/3–26–68) also runs boat tours. Three-hour boat tours cost $15 an hour for a boat that accommodates 8–10 people.

Uxmal, the Ruta Puuc, and the Coast

Passing through the large Maya town of Umán on Mérida's southern outskirts, you enter one of the least populated areas of the Yucatán. The highway to Uxmal and Kabah is a fairly traffic-free route through uncultivated woodlands. The forest seems to become more dense beyond Uxmal, which was connected to a number of smaller ceremonial centers in ancient times by *caminos blancos* (white roads). Several of these satellite sites, including **Kabah,** with its 250 Chaac masks; **Sayil,** with its majestic, three-story palace; and **Labná,** with its iconic, vaulted *Puerta* (gateway), are open to the public along a side road known as the Ruta Puuc, which winds its way eastward and eventually joins busy Highway 184, a major highway. Along this route you'll also find the **Loltún Caves,** the largest known cave system in the Yucatán, containing wall paintings and stone artifacts from Maya and pre-Maya times. You can make a loop to all of these sites, ending the loop in the little town of **Plaza,** which produces much of the pottery you'll see around the peninsula. **Ticul** is a convenient alternative to spending the night at the hotels just outside the Uxmal ruins, and the reasonable **Plaza** hotel (☎ 997/2–04–84), a block from the town square, is a suitable place to stay.

Uxmal

★ ⛰ ⑤ *78 km (48 mi) south of Mérida on Hwy. 261.*

If Chichén Itzá is the most monumental Maya ruin in Yucatán, Uxmal is arguably the most graceful. Where the former has a dramatic grandeur, the latter seems more understated and elegant—pure Maya, as people often say. The architecture reflects the Late Classic renaissance of the 7th to 9th centuries and is contemporary with that of Palenque and Tikal, among other great Maya metropolises of the southern highlands.

The site is considered the finest and largest example of Puuc architecture (*puuc* means "low hill" in Maya), which embraces such details as ornate stone mosaics and friezes on the upper walls, intricate cornices with curled noses, rows of columns, and soaring vaulted arches. Lines are clean and uncluttered, with the horizontal—especially the parallelogram—preferred to the vertical.

Although most of Uxmal remains unrestored, three buildings merit attention. The most prominent, the **Pyramid of the Magician,** is, at 125 ft, the tallest structure at the site. Unlike most other Maya pyramids, which are stepped and angular, it has a strangely elliptical design. Built five times, each time over the previous structure, the pyramid has a stairway on its western side that leads through the mouth of a giant Chaac mask to two temples at the summit.

West of the pyramid lies the **Nunnery,** or Quadrangle of the Nuns, considered by some to be the architectural jewel of Uxmal. You can enter the four buildings. Each comprises a series of low, gracefully repetitive chambers that look onto a central patio. Elaborate decoration blankets the upper facades. The name of the building came from the Spaniards because it reminded them of a convent building in old Spain. However, recent findings say it was the palace and living quarters of the high lord of Uxmal, named Chaan Chak, which means "abundance of rain."

Continue walking south and you'll pass the ball court before reaching the **Palace of the Governor,** which archaeologist Victor von Hagen considered the most magnificent building ever erected in the Americas. Interestingly, the palace faces east whereas the rest of Uxmal faces west. Archaeologists believe this is because the palace was used to sight the planet Venus. Covering five acres and rising over an immense acropolis, the palace lies at the heart of what must have been Uxmal's administrative center. Intricate friezes decorating the facade consist of some 20,000 individually cut stones.

First excavated in 1929 by the Danish explorer Franz Blom, the site served in 1841 as home to John Lloyd Stephens. Today a sound-and-light show recounts Maya legends and focuses on the people's dependence on rain—thus the cult of Chaac. The show is performed nightly in English and is one of the best of such productions. ⌧ *Site and museum $7.50, free Sun. and holidays; sound-and-light show in Spanish $3.50, in English $5; parking $1; use of video camera $8.* ◷ *Daily 8–5; sound-and-light show: in Spanish Apr.–Oct. 8 PM, Nov.–Mar. 7 PM; in English Apr.–Oct. 9 PM, Nov.–Mar. 8 PM.*

Dining and Lodging

$ ✕ **Las Palapas.** A great alternative to the hotel dining rooms at Uxmal, this family-run restaurant specializes in delicious Yucatecan dishes served with homemade tortillas. When tour groups request it in advance, the owners prepare a traditional feast, roasting the chicken or pork pibíl-style in a pit in the ground. If you see a tour bus in the parking lot, stop in—you may chance upon a memorable fiesta. ⌧ *Hwy. 261, 5 km (3 mi) north of the ruins,* ☎ *no phone. No credit cards.*

$$$$ ⊞ **Hacienda Uxmal.** The oldest hotel at the Maya site, built in 1955 and still owned and operated by the Barbachano family, this pleasant colonial-style building has lovely floor tiles, ceramics, and iron grillwork. The rooms—all with ceiling fans, cable TV, and air-conditioning—are fronted with wide verandas where you can enjoy the fresh air. The large courtyard features a garden and pools. The ruins are across the road and about 100 yards south. ⌧ *Within walking distance of the ruins,* ☎ 𝖥𝖠𝖷 *99/49–47–54. Reservations: Mayaland Tours* ⌧ *Calle 60 between Calles 59 and 61, Mérida,* ☎ *99/24–20–99, 800/235–4079,* 𝖥𝖠𝖷 *99/24–62–90. 78 rooms, 2 suites. 2 restaurants, bar, room service, 2 pools, Ping-Pong, billiards, free parking. AE, MC, V.* ⊜

$$$ ⊞ **Villas Arqueológicas Uxmal.** This two-story Club Med property, just down the street from the ruins, is run by a French-American couple. Rooms are small and functional, with garden views, cozy niches for the beds, and powerful but quiet air-conditioners. The French and Continental food served in the restaurant can be a delightful change from regional fare. Day-trippers have free of use the pool—towels are even provided. The price is very reasonable considering its proximity to the ruins. ⌧ *Carretera Uxmal Km 76 (Apdo 449, Mérida 97000),* ☎ *99/28–06–44, 800/ 258–2633,* 𝖥𝖠𝖷 *99/28–06–44. 40 rooms, 3 suites. Restaurant, bar, pool, tennis court, billiards, library, free parking. AE, MC, V.* ⊜

Celestún

🟢 *90 km (56 mi) west of Mérida on Routes 180 and 281.*

This tranquil fishing village, with its air of unpretentiousness, sits at the end of a spit of land separating the Celestún estuary from the gulf on the western hump of the Yucatán. It is the only point of entry to the **Parque Natural Ría Celestún,** a 100,000-acre wildlife reserve with extensive mangrove forests and salt flats and one of the largest colonies of flamingos in North America. June through March, clouds of pink wings soar over the pale blue backdrop of the estuary, up to 18,000 at a time. It also has more than 200 other species of birds and a large sea-turtle population. Rocks, islets, and white-sand beaches enhance the park's lovely setting. There is good fishing in both the river and the gulf, and if you're lucky you can see deer and armadillo roaming the surrounding land. Bring a bathing suit for a dip in one of the cenotes.

Celestún Expeditions (⊠ Calle 10 No. 97, ☎ 991/6–20–49) is a small company run by two natives of Celestún, David and Feliciano. In addition to the standard flamingo tours, they offer guided bike tours, jungle walks, crocodile tours, bird-watching excursions, and trips to the Maya ruins and haciendas. Tours range from $15–$70 per person.

Dining and Lodging

$–$$ ✕ **La Palapa.** A facade made entirely of conch shells leads you to the best seafood place in town, famous for its *camarones a la palapa* (fried shrimp smothered in a garlic and cream sauce). ⊠ *Calle 12 No. 105,* ☎ *991/6–20–63. MC, V.*

$$$$ ⊡ **Hotel Eco Paraíso Xixim.** In a nature reserve outside town on an old coconut plantation, this hotel features thatch-roof bungalows, with porches and hammocks, right on the 5-km- (3-mi-) long beach. Bring strong insect repellent, as mosquitoes can be vicious, especially in the rainy season. Room rates include ample breakfasts and dinners at the clubhouse. Tours and kayaks are available. ⊠ *Camino Viejo a Sisal Km 10, 97367,* ☎ *991/6–21–00, 888/264–5792,* ☒ *991/6–21–11. 15 cabañas. Restaurant, bar, fans, in-room safes, pool, beach, billiards, library. AE, MC, V.* ☜

$ ⊡ **Hotel Sol y Mar.** A half block from the town beach, this is definitely the best hotel of this category around. Rooms are spare but clean, with two double beds, small table and chairs, tile bathrooms, and either air-conditioning (in three rooms for $5 more) or overhead fans. ⊠ *Calle 12 No. 104, 97367,* ☎ *991/6–21–66. 8 rooms. No credit cards.*

The State of Yucatán A to Z

Arriving and Departing

BY BUS

Mérida's first-class buses, including **ADO** (☎ 99/24–78–68) and **UNO** (☎ 99/24–83–91) serve Akumal, Cancún, Chichén Itzá, Playa del Carmen, Tulum, Uxmal, Valladolid, and other major Mexican cities from the **CAME Station** (⊠ Calle 70 No. 555, ☎ 99/24–83–91, 99/24–92–63). ADO also has a branch at the **Fiesta Americana Hotel** (⊠ Paseo Montejo, ☎ 99/20–01–26, 99/25–09–10). Several other first-class lines have stations near CAME, including **Super Expreso** (⊠ Calle 70 No. 555, ☎ 99/24–83–91) and **ADO** (⊠ Terminal Unica, Calle 69 between Calles 68 and 70, ☎ 99/23–22–87, 99/24–08–30). These have frequent buses to Cancún, Valladolid, and other places east of Mérida.

You can also access major destinations within the Yucatán Peninsula via older, frequent-stopping second-class buses from the **second-class bus station** (⊠ Calle 69 No. 544, ☎ 99/22–23–87, 99/23–22–87). These buses also go to small and intermediate towns.

BY CAR

Most of the roads in this region are paved and have two lanes, and the government is accelerating the pace at which its fixing up the rest. Route 180, the main road along the Gulf coast from the Texas border to Cancún, runs into Mérida. Mexico City is 1,550 km (960 mi) to the west; Cancún, 320 km (198 mi) due east. The *autopista,* a four-lane toll highway between Cancún and Mérida, runs somewhat parallel to Route 180 and cuts driving time between Cancún and Mérida—formerly around 4½ hours—by about 1 hour.

BY PLANE

The following airlines serve Mérida: **Aeroméxico** (☎ 99/20–12–60, 99/ 20–12–65) flies direct from Miami with a stop (but no plane change) in Cancún; **Mexicana** (☎ 99/46–13–32) has a connecting flight from Newark via Cancún, and a number of connecting flights from the United States via Mexico City; **Delta** (☎ 800/241–4141) has flights from Atlanta to Mérida via Mexico City with a change of planes; **Aerocaribe** (☎ 99/28–67–90), a subsidiary of Mexicana, has flights from Cancún, Chetumal, Cozumel, Oaxaca, Tuxtla Gutiérrez, and Villahermosa, and there is additional service to Veracruz, Monterrey, and Havana.

Between the Airport and City Center. Mérida's **Manuel Crescencio Rejón International Airport** is 7 km (4½ mi) west of the city's central square, about a 20-minute ride. A private taxi costs about $8; there is only collective service for groups (usually a Volkswagen minibus), about $3. For both, pay the taxi-ticket vendor at the airport, not the driver. The inexpensive but irregular Bus No. 79 goes from the airport to downtown.

Getting Around

BY BUS

Mérida's municipal buses run daily 5 AM–midnight, but service is somewhat confusing until you master the system. In the downtown area, buses go east on Calle 59 and west on Calle 61, north on Calle 60 and south on Calle 62. You can catch a bus heading north to Progreso on Calle 56. Unfortunately, there is no direct bus service from the hotels around the plaza to the long-distance bus station.

BY CAR

Driving in Mérida can be frustrating because of the one-way streets (many of which end up being one lane because of the parked cars) and because traffic is dense. But having your own wheels is the best way to take excursions from the city. Prices can be lower if you arrange your rental in advance through one of the large international agencies.

BY CARRIAGE

You can hail horse-drawn *calesas* (pony traps) with sad-looking horses along Calle 60. A one-way ride to Saturday's Noche Mexicana, at Paseo Montejo and Calle 47, will cost about $5; a round-trip from downtown, along Paseo Montejo and back downtown, is $9–$10. Bargaining is acceptable.

BY TAXI

Taxis are available at 13 taxi stands around the city, including **Sitio Parque de la Madre** (☎ 99/28–53–22) and **Sitio Mejorada** (☎ 99/28– 55–89), or in front of the large hotels. The minimum fare is $2. Taxis operate around the clock.

Contacts and Resources

CAR RENTAL

There are almost 20 car-rental agencies in town, including **Budget** (⊠ Hyatt Regency, Calle 60 No. 344, ☎ 99/42–12–26, 99/25–54–53; ⊠ Holiday Inn, Av. Colón 498, at Calle 60, ☎ 99/25–54–53; ⊠ airport, ☎ 99/46–13–80); **National** (⊠ Fiesta Americana, ☎ 99/25–75–24; ⊠ airport, ☎ 99/46–13–94); **Hertz** (⊠ Fiesta Americana, ☎ 99/25–75– 95; ⊠ Calle 60 between Calles 55 and 57, ☎ 99/24–28–34, 99/84–

00–28; ⊠ airport, ☎ 99/46–13–55, 99/46–25–54); and **Thrifty** (⊠ Calle 60 No. 446-C, ☎ 99/23–34–40; ⊠ airport, ☎ 99/46–25–15).

CONSULATES

United States (⊠ Paseo Montejo 453, ☎ 99/25–50–11, 99/25–54–09). **United Kingdom** (⊠ Calle 58 No. 450, ☎ 99/28–61–52).

EMERGENCIES

Mérida. Police (☎ 99/28–25–52); **Red Cross** (⊠ Calle 68 No. 583, ☎ 99/24–98–13, 99/83–02–43); **Fire** (☎ 99/24–92–42); **general emergency** (☎ 06).

Clínica Yucatán (⊠ Calle 66 No. 528, ☎ 99/24–93–91) and **Red Cross Hospital** (⊠ Calle 68 No. 533, ☎ 99/28–53–91).

GUIDED TOURS

There are more than 50 tour operators in Mérida, and they generally go to the same places. What differs is how you go—in a private car, a van, or a bus—and whether or not the vehicle is air-conditioned and insured. A day trip to Chichén Itzá, with guide, entrance fee, and lunch, runs some $47. For about the same price you can see the ruins of Uxmal and Kabah in the Puuc region, and for a few more dollars you can add the neighboring sites of Sayil, Labná, and the Loltún Caves. Afternoon departures to Uxmal allow you to take in the sound-and-light show at the ruins and return by 11 PM, for $47 (including dinner). There is also the option of a tour of Chichén Itzá followed by a drop-off in Cancún for about $67. Most operators take credit cards.

Special-Interest Tours. Several of the tour operators in Mérida run overnight excursions to archaeological sites farther afield, notably Cobá, Tulum, Edzná, and Palenque. Adventure tours of the Mundo Maya, including sites in Mexico, Guatemala, and Belize, are available from **Ceiba Adventures** (⊠ Box 2274, Flagstaff, AZ 86003, ☎ 520/527–0171, FAX 520/527–8127). **Ecoturismo Yucatán** (⊠ Calle 3 No. 235, Col. Pensiones, ☎ 99/20–27–72, FAX 99/25–90–47) specializes in bird-watching, natural history, anthropology, kayaking, diving in cenotes, and the Mundo Maya. **Emerald Planet** (⊠ 4076 Crystal Court, Boulder, CO 80304, ☎ 800/883–3260, 303/541–9688, FAX 303/541–9683) runs bird-watching and orchid tours and other trips into wildlife reserves—often combined with stops at archaeological ruins.

TRAVEL AGENCIES AND TOUR OPERATORS

Mérida's local agencies and operators include **American Express** (⊠ Calle 56 No. 494, ☎ 99/42–82–00, 99/24–43–26, FAX 99/42–82–70); **Carmen Travel Service** (⊠ Hotel María del Carmen, Calle 63 No. 550, ☎ 99/24–12–12, FAX 99/24–12–88); **Felgueres Tours** (⊠ Holiday Inn, Av. Colón 498, ☎ 99/20–44–77, 99/20–34–44, FAX 99/25–63–89); **Betanzos Internacional** (⊠ Calle 60 No. 463, Depto. 1, ☎ 99/23–99–66, 99/23–85–94, FAX 99/23–99–66); **Mayaland Tours** (⊠ Calle 57 between Calles 59 and 61, ☎ 99/28–30–75, 800/235–4079, FAX 99/28–30–77; ⊠ Fiesta Americana, Calle Colón at Calle 60, ☎ FAX 99/24–62–90); **Turismo Aviomar** (⊠ Calle 58A 500-C, Glorieta San Fernando, ☎ 99/20–04–44, 99/20–04–43, FAX 99/25–50–64); and **Yucatán Trails** (⊠ Calle 62 No. 482, ☎ 99/28–59–13, 99/28–25–82, FAX 99/24–19–28).

24-HOUR PHARMACIES

Farmacia Yza (☎ 99/2–66–66) has many branches; call for delivery or to find the nearest branch.

VISITOR INFORMATION

Mérida. State Tourist Information Center (⊠ Teatro Peón Contreras, Calle 60 between Calles 57 and 59, ☎ 99/24–92–90), open daily 8–

8. **Information kiosks:** at the airport (☎ no phone), open daily 8–8; at the second-class bus station (✉ Calle 69 between Calles 68 and 70, ☎ no phone). **City Tourist Information Center** (✉ Calle 59 No. 514, ☎ 99/28–65–47), open weekdays 8–2 and 5–7.

THE STATE OF CAMPECHE

Updated by
Shelagh
McNally

Campeche, the least-visited and most underrated corner of the Yucatán, is the perfect place for adventure. Here you'll find friendly people with a genuine welcome for visitors, colonial cities and towns that retain an air of innocence, and, outside the cities, protected biospheres, farmland, and jungle. The forts of Campeche City have 300-year-old cannons pointing across the Gulf of Mexico, relics from pirate days that give the city an aura of romance and history. Beyond its walls, the ancient pyramids and ornate temples of ancient Maya kingdoms—some of the most important discoveries in the Maya empire to date—lie waiting in tropical forests.

The terrain of the state of Campeche varies from the northeastern flatlands to the rolling mountains of the south. More than 60% of the territory is covered by jungle, which is filled with precious mahogany and cedar. The Gulf Stream keeps temperatures at about 26°C (78°F) year-round, and the humid, tropical climate is eased by evening breezes. Campeche's economy is based on agriculture, fishing, logging, salt, tourism, and, since the 1970s, hydrocarbons—it is the largest producer of oil in Mexico. Ninety oil platforms dot the Campeche coast, but most of the oil industry is concentrated at the western end of the state, near Ciudad del Carmen.

Campeche City

The city of Campeche has a lovely, time-weathered air: no self-conscious, ultramodern tourist glitz here, just a friendly city by the sea, population 270,000, that is proud of its heritage and welcomes all to share in it. That good-humored, open-minded attitude is enshrined in the Spanish adjective *campechano,* meaning easygoing and cheerful.

Because it has been walled since 1686, most of the historic downtown is neatly contained in an area measuring five by nine blocks. The old city, or Viejo Campeche, looks fresh with newly painted and remodeled historic buildings from the 16th–19th centuries and signs guiding tourists to attractions along the streets. Seven *baluartes* (bastions) in various stages of disrepair or reconstruction are strategically placed around the perimeter of the old city. These were once connected by a 3-km (2-mi) wall in a hexagonal fortification that was built to safeguard the city against the pirates who kept ransacking it—and it was not until 1771, when Fuerte San Miguel was built on a hilltop on the outskirts of town, that pirates finally ceased their attacks. Only short stretches of the wall exist, and two stone archways—one facing the sea, the other the land—are all that remain of the four gates that provided the only means of access to Campeche.

66 Avenida Ruíz Cortines is Campeche's waterfront boulevard, with a broad pedestrian walkway called the **malecón.** The sidewalk runs the length of the waterfront, from the Ramada Inn south to the outskirts of town, and is popular with joggers and strollers enjoying the cool sea breezes and view at sunset.

67 A modernistic building resembling a flying saucer houses the **Congreso del Estado** (State Congress building), where the state legislature holds session. One block inland from the malecón, on Avenida 16 de

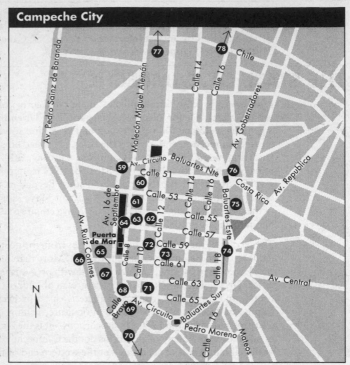

Campeche City

⑥⑤ Septiembre, the Congreso del Estado shares a broad plaza with the much taller **Palacio del Gobierno** (State Government Palace), which locals have dubbed "El Tocadiscos" (the jukebox) because of its elaborate facade.

⑥⑧ The **Baluarte San Carlos,** the bastion where Avenida 16 de Septiembre curves around and becomes Circuito Baluartes, houses the **Sala de las Fortificaciones** (Chamber of the Fortifications), containing scale models of the original defense system, and the **Museo Gráfico de la Ciudad** (Graphics Museum), with photographs of the city as it developed. Don't miss the dungeon inside the bastion, where captured pirates were jailed, and the rooftop view, especially at sunset.

⑦① The **Ex-Templo de San José,** built by the Jesuits in 1756, occupies the full city block between Calles 10 and 12 and Calles 63 and 65. Its portal is completely covered with blue and yellow Talavera tiles and crowned by seven narrow stone finials that resemble the roof combs on many Maya temples. Campeche's first lighthouse, built in 1864, sits atop the right-hand tower. Cultural events are held here Tuesday evenings starting at 7. ☉ *The Ex-Templo is officially closed; ask a guard at the Instituto Campechano, next door, to show you the interior.*

⑥⑨ The **Iglesia de San Román** became central to the lives of the Indians when an ebony image of Christ, the "Black Christ," arrived in about 1565. The legend goes that a ship that refused to carry the statue was wrecked, whereas the ship that did take it on board reached Campeche in record time. To this day, the Feast of San Román—when the icon is carried through the streets as part of a procession, on August 31— is the biggest such celebration in Campeche. ⊠ *Calle 10 at Calle Bravo,* ☉ *Daily 7–1 and 3–7.*

⑦② On **Calle 59,** between Calles 8 and 18, stand some of Campeche's finest homes, some of which have been partially or totally converted for other uses. The richest inhabitants built as close to the sea as possible, in case escape became necessary. Since 1987, a citywide beautification project has restored more than 1,600 facades of buildings on this and many adjoining streets.

73 Just east of Calle 12, the architecture and ambience of the tiny **Iglesia de San Francisquito** do justice to historic Calle 59's old-fashioned beauty. ✉ *Calle 59 at Calle 12.* ☉ *Daily 8:30–noon and 5–7.*

74 Old Campeche ends at the **Puerta de Tierra** (land gate), the only one of the four original (and two remaining) city gates with its basic structure intact. There is a two-hour light show in Spanish and English Tuesday–Saturday at 8:30 PM. ✉ *Calle 18 at Calle 59.* 🎟 *$1.50.* ☉ *8–6.*

To take in the heart of a true Mexican inner city, stroll through the **75** **Mercado Municipal** (municipal market), where locals congregate en masse to shop for seafood, produce, and housewares daily from dawn to dusk. ✉ *Av. Circuito Baluartes Este between Calles 51 and 55.*

76 North of the mercado is **Baluarte San Pedro,** built in 1686. The bastion's thick walls, flanked by watchtowers, now house a handicrafts and souvenir shop and a satellite office for the Secretary of Tourism, where you can book an English tour guide. Many of the tours to ruins leave from this point. ✉ *Avs. Gobernadores and Circuito Baluartes,* ☎ *no phone.* 🎟 *Free.* ☉ *Tues.–Sat. 9–8.*

63 The unpretentious **Parque Principal** (main square), or **Plaza de la Independencia** (Independence Plaza), dating from 1540 or 1541, occupies the heart of the old city. Its southern side (Calle 57) is lined with several modest cafés and hotels. Band concerts are held here Sunday at dusk. ✉ *Bounded by Calles 10, 8, 55, and 57.*

★ **64** On the south side of Parque Principal, the **Baluarte de la Soledad** (Bastion of Our Lady of Solitude) was built between 1690 and 1692 to protect one of the four city gates, the **Puerte de Mar** (sea door). It houses the **Museo de los Estela,** which has 20 Maya stelae and a few other pieces, but no plaques. The largest of the bastions, this one has relatively complete parapets and embrasures that offer a view of the cathedral, the municipal buildings, and a sliver of sea. ✉ *Calle 8 at Calle 57,* ☎ *no phone.* 🎟 *40¢.* ☉ *Tues.–Sat. 8–8, Sun. 8–1.*

62 Across from the main plaza, **Casa Seis** (House No. 6) was one of the first colonial homes built in Campeche and is now the Cultural Center. It has been beautifully restored, and still has its original frescoes, some dating from 1500. The courtyard has Moorish architecture offset by lovely 18th-century stained-glass windows. An art gallery, bookstore, and restaurant are also on the premises. ✉ *Calle 57 No. 6,* ☎ *no phone.* 🎟 *Free.* ☉ *Daily 9–9.*

An exception to the generally somber architecture of colonial Campeche, **61** the **catedral** combines neoclassical and Renaissance elements. The present cathedral—which took two centuries (1650–1850) to build—occupies the site of Montejo's original church, which went up in 1540. Inside is the magnificent ebony Holy Sepulcher, decorated with stamped silver and an army of angels. ✉ *Calle 55 between Calles 8 and 10.* ☉ *Daily 6–noon and 5:30–8.*

Built in the early 20th century by one of the wealthiest plantation owners in Yucatán, the opulent, eclectic **Mansión Carvajal** did time as the **60** Hotel Señorial before arriving at its present role as an office for the Family Institute, run by the governor's wife. ✉ *Calle 10 No. 584,* ☎ *981/6–76–44.* 🎟 *Free.* ☉ *Weekdays 8–2.*

⑤⑨ The **Baluarte Santiago,** the last of the bastions to be built (1704), is now the site of the **X' much Haltún Botanical Gardens,** with more than 200 plant species from the region; plants and trees are labeled in Latin and sometimes Maya. The original bastion was demolished at the turn of the century, then rebuilt in the 1950s. ✉ *Calle 8 and Av. Circuito Baluartes,* ☎ *no phone.* 🎟 *Donation.* ☉ *Tues.–Sat. 9–8.*

⑦⑦ Away from the city center, in a residential neighborhood, stands the beautifully restored **Iglesia de San Francisco,** the oldest church site (1546) in Campeche, constructed on the base of a Maya temple. Some contend it marks the spot where the first Mass on the North American continent was said, in 1517 (the same claim has been made for Veracruz and Cozumel). One of Cortés's grandsons was baptized here, and the baptismal font still stands. ✉ *Avs. Miguel Alemán and Mariano Escobedo.* ☉ *Daily 8–noon and 5–7.*

⑦⑧ The lofty **Fuerte San José el Alto** (*el alto* means "the tall"), at the northern boundary of the old city, is home to the **Museo de Armas y Barcos** (Museum of Arms and Boats). The displays focus on 18th-century weapons used in the many wars against the pirates. Also look for scale ships-in-a-bottle, manuscripts, and religious art. The view is terrific from the top of the ramparts, which were used for spotting invading ships. ✉ *Av. Francisco Morazán s/n, north of town,* ☎ *no phone.* 🎟 *50¢.* ☉ *Tues.–Sat. 8–8, Sun. 8–1.*

★ ⑦⓪ At the opposite end of town from Fuerte San José is **Fuerte de San Miguel.** The scenic Avenida Ruíz Cortines near the south end of the city winds its way to a hilltop, where this fort commands one of the grandest views overlooking the city and the Gulf of Mexico. Built in 1771, the fort was positioned to bombard enemy ships with cannonballs. But as soon as it was completed, pirates stopped attacking the city. Its impressive cannons were fired only once, in 1842, when Gen. Santa Anna used the fort to put down a revolt by Yucatecan separatists seeking independence from Mexico. The fort now houses the excellent **Museo Cultura Maya.** The collection of Campeche Maya artifacts—with explanations in English—is not to be missed. The six exquisite jade funeral masks found in tombs at Calakmul alone are worth a visit. ✉ *South of downtown on Av. Escénica s/n,* ☎ *no phone.* 🎟 *$1.* ☉ *Tues.–Sat. 8–8, Sun. 8–1.*

Dining and Lodging

$$ ✕ **La Pigua.** A favorite with local professionals, La Pigua is arguably
★ the best seafood restaurant in town, with the most pleasant ambience. A truly ambitious lunch would start with a seafood cocktail or plate of cold crab claws, followed by *camarones al coco* (fried shrimp with a layer of crispy coconut), and, for dessert, liqueur-drenched local peaches. ✉ *Av. Miguel Alemán 197-A,* ☎ *981/1–33–65. MC, V. No dinner.*

$ ✕ **Marganzo.** This rustically furnished restaurant, conveniently lo-
★ cated a half block south of the plaza, has colorful decor and waitstaff dressed in traditional clothing to go along with the traditional Campeche cuisine. You can't go wrong with such specials as *pampano en escabeche* (grilled fish with chilies and orange juice). ✉ *Calle 8 No. 267,* ☎ *981/ 1–38–98. AE, MC, V.*

$ ✕ **Miramar.** This restaurant attracts locals and foreign visitors with its fabulous *huevos motuleños* (fried eggs smothered in refried beans and garnished with peas, ham, cheese, and tomato sauce), fresh fish, and excellent soups. The heavy furnished wooden tables and chairs give it a colonial feel. Stop in for an afternoon beer—you'll be rewarded with a free appetizer. ✉ *Calle 8 No. 293A,* ☎ *981/6–28–83. No credit cards.*

$ ✕ **La Palapa del Balneario Popular.** One of the few seaside restaurants in Campeche, this place has live music and great ambience. Sit and watch the fishing boats out on the gulf or enjoy a drink while the sun sets. Naturally, the fish and seafood cocktails are the freshest in town. ✉ *Av. Insurgentes,* ☎ *981/6–59–18. AE, MC, V.*

$$$ ▥ **Ramada Inn.** This is the fanciest hotel in town—even if by inter-
★ national standards it is quite average—and it has the most amenities. Rooms are fairly large, with air-conditioning, color cable TV, and bal-conies overlook the pool or the bay across the street. The lobby cof-fee shop is extremely popular with locals. ✉ *Av. Ruíz Cortines 51, on the waterfront,* ☎ *981/6–22–33, 800/228–9898,* FAX *981/1–16–18. 138 rooms, 11 suites. Restaurant, coffee shop, pool, dance club, travel services, free parking. AE, MC, V.* ✑

$$ ▥ **Debliz.** Located east of the center, this large hotel caters to tour groups. The rooms are huge, with two double beds, balconies that look out onto the pool, cable TV, and air-conditioning. There's also a very good restaurant and a nice bar. You will need to take a cab to the historical center—it's just a little too far to walk. ✉ *Av. Las Palmas 55,* ☎ *981/ 5–22–22,* FAX *981/5–22–77. 143 rooms. Restaurant, bar, snack bar, air-conditioning, pool, parking (fee). AE, MC, V.*

$$ ▥ **Del Paseo.** In the quiet San Román neighborhood, a block from the ocean, this pretty hotel is cheerful and comfortable. Rooms have tiny balconies, cable TV, and air-conditioning. A lovely, glass-roof atrium with park benches and many plants shelters the small hotel complex, which includes the lobby, a restaurant, a beauty parlor, and a car-rental agency. ✉ *Calle 8 No. 215,* ☎ *981/1–00–84, 981/1–01–00,* FAX *981/ 1–00–97. 48 rooms, 2 suites. Restaurant, bar, air-conditioning, room service, beauty shop, car rental, free parking. AE, MC, V.*

$ ▥ **Colonial.** The former home of a high-ranking army lieutenant, this
★ building dates back to 1812, but was converted into a hotel in the 1940s. All rooms are delightfully different, as befits a colonial mansion, with ceiling fans or air-conditioning (in four of the rooms). Rooms 16, 18, 28, and 27 have wonderful views of the cathedral and city at night. Public areas include two leafy patios, a small sunroof, and a sitting room. ✉ *Calle 14 No. 122,* ☎ *981/6–22–22, 981/6–26–30. 30 rooms. Air-conditioning (some), fans. No credit cards.*

$ ▥ **Lopez.** This cheerful little three-story hotel, with balconies in an un-dulating design, is a pleasant place if you're on a budget. Smallish stan-dard rooms (lit by fluorescent lights) have tiny closets, armoires, luggage stands, and easy chairs. Bathrooms are small but clean. Ancient ceiling fans, however, have only two speeds: OFF and GALE-FORCE WINDS. Other units have equally loud but less blustery air-conditioning. ✉ *Calle 12 No. 189,* ☎ *981/6–33–44, 981/6–24–88,* FAX *981/6–30–21. 39 rooms. Air-conditioning (some), ceiling fans. No credit cards.*

$ ▥ **El Regis.** This seven-room hotel two blocks from the plaza is a good bargain. Though a bit run-down, the Regis is a lovely old two-story colonial home with high ceilings, balconies, and an airy inner atrium. All rooms are spick-and-span, with two double beds. On the down-side: unfriendly staff, tiny bathrooms, poor lighting, and lackluster air-conditioning. The front doors are locked at 11, but the night watchman will let you in. ✉ *Calle 12 No. 148,* ☎ *981/6–31–75. 7 rooms. Air-conditioning, fans. No credit cards.*

Nightlife and the Arts

If you're in the mood to dance, try Campeche's discos: **Lafitte's** (✉ Ra-mada Inn, ☎ 981/6–22–33) is where politicians go to party; **El Dragon** (✉ Sajuge complex at Av. Resurgimiento No. 87, near the university, ☎ 981/1–18–10, 981/6–42–89) is student-oriented. Both places are open Thursday through Saturday nights. The new high-tech **Millenium** (✉

Av. Resurgimento 112, ☎ 981/8–45–55) offers laser shows and loud dance music Friday and Saturday. To listen to some live music, check out **Eclipso Bar** (✉ Av. López Matoes 426, ☎ no phone). It's open Wednesday through Saturday nights.

For a fun, free evening, mix with the locals at the **Sabadito Alegre** (Happy Saturday) cultural fair. From 7 to 10:30 on Saturday evening, the streets around the main square are closed to traffic and filled with folk and popular dance performances, singers, comics, handicrafts, and food and drink stands.

Outdoor Activities and Sports

Hunting, fishing, and birding are popular throughout the state of Campeche. Contact **Don José Sansores** at his office in the Hotel Castelmar (✉ Calle 61 No. 2, ☎ FAX 981/1–06–24) or at the Snook Inn in Champotón (✉ Calle 30 No. 1, ☎ FAX 982/8–00–18) to arrange sportfishing or wildlife photo excursions in the Champotón area. **Francisco Javier Hernandez Romero** (✉ La Pigua, Av. Miguel Alemán 179–A, ☎ 811/33–65) can arrange boat or fishing trips to the Peten Ecological Reserve.

Shopping

Because Campeche is a seaport, ships-in-a-bottle, tacky statues made of seashells, and mother-of-pearl and black coral jewelry are everywhere. (Note: Buying black coral is environmentally incorrect; there are restrictions regarding bringing it into the United States.) You can also find a limited selection of basketry, straw hats, embroidered cloth, and clay trinkets.

Visit the **Municipal Market** (✉ Av. Circuito Baluartes between Calles 51 and 55) for food and some craft items. **Casa de Artesanía Tukulna** (✉ Calle 10 No. 333, ☎ 981/6–90–88) is set in a lovely old mansion; well-made embroidered dresses, blouses, pillow coverings, hammocks, Panama hats, posters, jewelry, baskets, and stucco reproductions of Maya motifs are sold here. The expensive **Veleros** (✉ Ah-Kin-Pech shopping center, ☎ 981/1–24–46) is owned by craftsman David Pérez and stocks his miniature ships, seashells, furniture with nautical motifs, and jewelry fashioned from sanded and polished bull's horns (a legal alternative to tortoiseshell).

From Campeche City to Mérida on Highway 261

This is by far the longer—and more interesting—way to reach the Yucatán capital. The highway takes you past low-growing jungle beyond which cornfields and citrus orchards grow. Dairy and beef cows graze on the wide, open pasturelands, and you'll skirt—and sometimes pass through—villages of traditional round adobe huts with thatch roofs and tiny, weathered wooden doors. If you're driving you can take short detours to see underground caves, Maya ruins, and colonial churches and to get a feel for how people live outside the relative modernity of Mérida and Campeche City.

Edzná

 55 km (34 mi) southeast of Campeche City.

Archaeologists consider Edzná one of the peninsula's most important ruins because of the crucial transitional role it played among several architectural styles. It was occupied from 300 BC to AD 1450, reaching its pinnacle between AD 600 and 900. It was rediscovered in 1927. Although restoration work is going ahead now, there was little funding for it after its initial excavation in 1943. There are information plaques in Spanish, English, and Maya in front of all of the structures, and a tourist facility on site has a snack shop, rest rooms, and a small book and souvenir store.

The 6-square-km (4-square-mi) expanse of savanna lies in a broad valley that is prone to flooding. Surrounding the site are vast networks of irrigation canals, the remnants of a highly sophisticated hydraulic system that channeled rainwater and water from the Champotón River into human-made *chultunes,* or wells. Commanding center stage in the **Gran Acrópolis** (Great Acropolis complex) is the **Pirámide de los Cinco Pisos** (Five-Story Pyramid), which rises 102 ft. The temple was so constructed that, in spring (May 1–3) and summer (August 7–9), the setting sun would illuminate the mask of the sun god located inside one of the pyramid's rooms. Carved into the Gran Acrópolis's **Temple of the Stone Masks** (Building 414) are various images of the sun deity. On the east side are portrayals of the dawn sun; those of the afternoon sun are logically found on the west side of the temple. Perhaps the most compelling image, however, is the anthropomorphic head with its huge and sinister protruding eye sockets. Local lore holds that Edzná, which means "house of the gestures" (or "grimaces"), may have been named for these images. More recent theories say the name comes from "Home of the Echo," as there is an acoustic effect between the main buildings; or that it means "Home of the Itzás," a Maya group native to southwest Campeche.

If you're not driving, consider taking one of the inexpensive day trips offered by most travel agencies in Campeche; this is far easier than trying to get to Edzná by municipal bus. Servicios Turísticos Picazh (✉ Calle 16 No. 348, ☎ 981/6–44–26) offers transportation only or guided service to Edzná at reasonable prices. ✉ *Rte. 261 east from Campeche City for 44 km (27 mi) to Cayal, then Rte. 188 southeast for 18 km (11 mi),* ☎ *no phone.* 🎟 *$2, free Sun. and holidays.* ⊙ *Daily 8–5.*

Hopelchén

41 km (25 mi) east of the Edzná turnoff on Hwy. 261.

Hopelchén—the name means "place of the five wells"—is a traditional Maya town noted for the lovely **Franciscan church** built in honor of St. Francis of Padua in 1667. Corn, beans, squash, tobacco, fruit, and henequen are cultivated in this rich agricultural center. There's also a community of blond-haired, blue-eyed Mennonites living here who make a living tilling the soil and selling homemade cheese.

Bolonchén de Rejón

34 km (21 mi) north of Hopelchén.

Just short of the state line between Campeche and Yucatán and a few miles before Bolonchén de Rejón are the **Grutas de Xtacumbilxunaan**—(shta-*cum*-bil-shu-nan), the "caverns of the hidden women" in Spanish and Maya—where legend says a Maya girl disappeared after going for water. In ancient times cenotes deep in the extensive cave system provided an emergency water source during droughts. Only a few chambers are open to the public because the rock surfaces are dangerously slippery and the depth of the caverns is 240 ft. In the upper part of the caves you can admire the delicate limestone formations, which have been given whimsical names such as "witch's ball." The two-hour tour should be booked through the tourist office in Campeche or in Hopelchén; there are sometimes guides at the site, but don't count on it. 🎟 *$1.50.* ⊙ *Daily 8–5.*

Hochob

 14 km (9 mi) south of Dzibalchén, 55 km (34 mi) south of Hopelchén.

The small Maya ruin of Hochob is an excellent example of the Chenes architectural style, which flowered in the Classic period from about AD 200 to 900. Found throughout central and southern Campeche, temples in the Chenes style are easily recognized by their elaborate stucco facades forming giant masks of jaguars, birds, or other creatures, with doorways representing the beasts' open jaws. Since work began at Hochob in the early 1980s, three temples and palaces have been excavated at the site. *Southwest of Hopelchén on Dzibalchén–Chencho road,* ☎ *no phone.* ☜ *Free.* ☺ *Daily 8–5.*

Dzilibnocac

 18 km (11 mi) northeast of Dzibalchén, 30 km (19 mi) northeast of Hochob.

To get to the rarely visited archaeological site of Dzibilnocac, you must first reach the village of **Dzibalchén** by traveling south on Route 261. From there you proceed north on a small side road to **Vincente Guerrero,** also known as Iturbide, a farming community 19 km (11½ mi) north—literally at the end of the road. Each corner of the town square has a small stone guardhouse built in 1850 during the War of the Castes, and the road around them eventually turns into a dirt path passing houses and ending at the ruins. Dzibilnocac was a fair-size ceremonial center AD 250–900. Although at least seven temple pyramids have been located here, the only one that has been partially excavated is the **Palacio Principal,** a palace with three separate pyramids, combining elements of the Puuc and Chenes architectural styles. Only one pyramid has been cleared, revealing a one-room, square temple at the top with beautifully executed carvings of Chaac on the outside walls. The middle pyramid, partially cleared on top, has two small underground chambers accessed through a Maya arch. ☎ *No phone.* ☜ *Free.* ☺ *Daily 8–5.*

The State of Campeche A to Z

Arriving and Departing

BY BUS

ADO (✉ Av. Gobernadores 289, at Calle 45, along Rte. 261 to Mérida, ☎ 981/1–43–34, 981/6–34–45), a first-class line, runs buses to Campeche City from Mérida almost every hour, and to Ciudad del Carmen, Mexico City, Tampico, Veracruz, and Villahermosa regularly, but less frequently. Adjacent to the ADO station, from the second-class bus station, there is service on **Autobuses del Sur** (☎ 981/6–34–45, 981/ 6–28–02 ext. 2405) to intermediate points throughout the Yucatán Peninsula, as well as less desirable service to Chetumal, Ciudad del Carmen, Escárcega, Mérida, Palenque, Tuxtla Gutiérrez, and Villahermosa. Half a block from the ADO station, **Nuevos Horizontes** (✉ Av. Gobernadores 575, ☎ 981/1–02–61) has first-class service to Mérida, Ciudad del Carmen, Mexico City, Veracruz, Cancún, Jalapa, Puebla, and Villahermosa at least once a day.

Note: Avoid an extended stopover in Escárcega, along Route 261. Until the government beefed up security it was an unsafe spot for tourists, with bus passengers the targets of robberies and assaults. Things have calmed down but Escárcega is still not a place to linger.

BY CAR

Campeche is about 1½ hours from Mérida along the 160-km (99-mi) *via corta* (short way), Route 180. The alternative route, the 250-km (155-mi) *via larga* (long way), Route 261, takes at least six hours but passes the major Maya ruins of Uxmal, Kabah, and Sayil. A four-lane toll road runs from Campeche City to Champotón. The toll is $3 (one way) and it shaves 20 km (12 mi) off the 68-km (42-mi) trip.

BY PLANE

Aeroméxico (☎ 981/6–56–78) has one flight daily from Mexico City to Campeche City.

Getting Around

BY BUS

The municipal bus system covers all of Campeche City, but you can easily visit the major sights on foot. Public buses run along Avenida Ruíz Cortines and cost about 30¢.

BY TAXI

Taxis can be commissioned in Campeche City from the **main taxi stand** (⊠ Calle 8 between Calles 55 and 53, ☎ 981/5–30–36) or at stands by the bus stations and market. Because of the scarcity of taxis, it's quite common to share them with other people headed in the same direction. Don't be surprised to see one already occupied slow down to where you are standing, or flash its lights if the cab driver thinks he can pick up another fare. A shared cab ride will cost under $1. If you have one to yourself, it's $1.50–$3.

Contacts and Resources

CAR RENTAL

There are two reliable rental agencies: **AutoRent** (⊠ Hotel del Paseo, Calle 8 No. 215, ☎ 981/1–01–00), which charges $45 a day including insurance and allows 200 km (120 mi) per day, and the slightly more expensive **Maya Rent a Car** (⊠ Ramada Hotel, Ruíz Cortines at Calle 59, ☎ 981/6–22–33, FAX 981/1–16–18), which rents small Chevys for $59 a day, including insurance and unlimited mileage.

EMERGENCIES

Throughout the state, call **06** locally in case of emergency.

Campeche City. Police (⊠ Av. Resurgimiento 77, Col. Lazareto, ☎ 981/6–23–09); **Red Cross** (⊠ Av. Las Palmas at Ah-Kim-Pech, ☎ 981/5–24–11). For emergency roadside assistance call the **Green Angels** (☎ 981/6–09–34, 981/1–25–44). **Hospital General** (⊠ Av. Central at Av. Circuito Baluartes, ☎ 981/6–09–20, 981/6–42–33) and **Social Security Clinic** (⊠ Av. Lopez Mateos and Talamantes, ☎ 981/6–18–55, 981/6–52–02) are both open 24 hours for emergencies.

GUIDED TOURS

Trolley tours of Campeche City leave from the Plaza Principal daily at 9:30, 6, and 8. The one-hour, bilingual tour costs 70¢. On weekends there is an additional tour at 7 PM. You can buy tickets on board the trolley or ahead of time in the municipal tourist office next to the cathedral, also on the plaza. One route takes you through the city and another goes to the forts; check to see which route is being offered before boarding.

TRAVEL AGENCIES AND TOUR OPERATORS

Campeche City. American Express/VIPs (⊠ Prolongación Calle 59, Edificio Belmar, Depto. 5, ☎ 981/1–10–10, 981/1–10–00, FAX 981/6–83–33); **Destinos Maya** (⊠ Av. Miguel Alemán 162 Altos, Locale 106, ☎ 981/1–09–34, 713/440–0291, FAX 981/1–09–34); **Viajes Campeche** (⊠ Calle 10 No. 329, ☎ 981/6–52–33, FAX 981/6–28–44). The **Secretería de Turismo** (⊠ Av. Ruíz Cortines s/n, Plaza Moch/Couah, ☎ 981/6–55–93, 981/6–73–64, FAX 981/6–67–67) can arrange tours with English guides throughout the state.

Campeche City. The **tourist office** (✉ Av. Ruíz Cortines s/n, Plaza Moch-Couoh, ☎ 981/6–55–93, ☎ FAX 981/6–67–67) is open daily 9–3 and 5–8. On weekends a guard hands out maps and literature but has little knowledge. The **municipal tourist office** (✉ Calle 55 just west of the cathedral, ☎ 981/1–39–89, 981/1–39–90) is open daily 8–2:30 and 4–8. The staff speaks very little English, but you'll find maps, and you can book a city trolley tour.

14 BACKGROUND AND ESSENTIALS

Portrait of Mexico

Chronology

Maps of Mexico

Smart Travel Tips A to Z

LIFE BEHIND THE HEADLINES

Mexico these days is about where East Berlin found itself circa 1989. In this case there was no brick wall to tear down, but rather a slow crumbling of 70-year rule by one party, the Institutional Revolutionary Party (PRI). The party, not coincidentally, shares the colors of the Mexican flag. Instead of barbed wire to keep its citizens in, Mexico has a porous 2,000-mi border with the United States that serves as a pressure valve during hard times. But demand for change has grown from within. There is greater competition from the ballot box to the board room every day. From the scathing editorials in the growing free press to the customer-service hot lines at once indifferent monopolies, Mexico has been going through a political and economic transition all the more dramatic in part because it does not always make the nightly news.

Mexico, for all its ancient history, is a young country. About a third of the population is between 15 and 29 years old. Many of these young people were raised on economic and political turmoil. Mexicans today are tired of seeing themselves as downtrodden. Many prefer to look for inspiration to actress Salma Hayek—a Veracruz native—or to the successful young Harvard Business School entrepreneur, Miguel Angel Davila, who started the Cinemex movie chain. Signs of modern Mexico are everywhere: cash machines even in some small towns, *People en Español*, and forgery-proof voter I.D. cards. But as ever, modernity does not come all at once. In much of Mexico, a brand new VW Beetle may share the road with a burro. Mexico's struggle with progress is like a Latin dance: two steps forward, one step back.

As the country opened economically over the past two decades, a slow push for political opening followed.

Those growing up now are often dubbed the NAFTA generation, after the free-trade agreement: they are more outward looking, more free-enterprise savvy, and more cynical about the old one-party system. That old system failed them when the bottom fell out of the economy just after the 1994 presidential election, and the memory of what Mexicans simply call *la crisis* is very much alive. People are still shy of bank accounts, credit cards, and home loans, which have been practically nonexistent since the peso crashed. Wages remain below what they were before the crisis, full-time jobs are always in short supply, and the government keeps tightening the belt. Much of Mexico, however, is booming. Exports—driven by the free-trade agreement with the United States—are thriving. Investors have returned, betting on the perennial comeback. The economy is still vulnerable to global recession, but it is much more stable than it was before la crisis.

Hopes had been running high that presidential elections July 2, 2000, would firmly establish Mexico as a democracy. Still, despite the burgeoning of two major opposition parties—the liberal Democratic Revolutionary Party (PRD) and the conservative National Action Party (PAN)—over recent years, public-opinion polls were giving PRI presidential candidate Francisco Labastida Ochoa a strong lead over the opposition candidates as the election drew closer. However, it was the PAN candidate, the swashbuckling *norteño* (northern) governor Vicente Fox, who won. A former CEO of Coca-Cola in Mexico, Fox campaigned so intensely during the three years leading up to the election that he earned the nickname Ausente Fox (Absent Fox) in his home state of Guanajuato. The PRD had pinned its hopes on Cuauhtémoc Cárdenas. This former

PRI politician also had lost a presidential race to Carlos Salinas in a 1988 election suspected of fraud but captured the mayorship of Mexico City in 1997. Although Cárdenas is popular among peasants and on the left, his failure to conquer the city's daunting crime and smog problems during his term as mayor probably dragged down his showing at the polls.

But though change has been painstakingly slow in Mexico's presidential politics, democracy has achieved a respectable pace in other areas of government. Recent state elections voted out 10 PRI governors (six states went to the PAN; four to the PRD) and gave opposition parties real power in Congress for the first time in modern history. Congressmen used to be called *levantadedos* (finger lifters) because all they did was vote the president's bidding. Today, there is competition—even the occasional fistfight—on the House floor.

One thing's for sure: the monarchical Mexican presidency has come to an end. No one used to look the Mexican president in the eye. Such was his power. Then some political commentators used the informal *tu* (you) when addressing President Ernesto Zedillo. He was pilloried regularly in political cartoons. Satirists even dubbed him "presidente lite." In fact, Zedillo was an accidental candidate, stepping in for Luis Donaldo Colosio, who was assassinated in 1994—a tragedy from which Mexico has never fully recovered. But during his *sexenio* (six-year term), Zedillo had proven himself more of an accidental reformer. By not playing the role of iron-clad president, he opened the door to the opposition. He expanded political funding for all parties, returned some power and money to the country's 31 states, and relinquished his traditional right to name his successor. This PRI tradition of handpicking the next president, called the *dedazo* (literally "the finger-pointing"), existed from the time the PRI took power in 1929 until 1999, when the party held its first-ever primaries to choose its presidential candidate.

Many have predicted the demise of the PRI. But like Cuba's Fidel Castro, it keeps hanging on. Considering that the PRI machine makes Chicago's ward politics look like amateur hour, it's no wonder. Mexico is hardly free of the old dirty dealings, such as vote buying and bullying from party bosses, but these days electoral fraud is much less common, especially in cities. Ballot boxes are transparent, and there is a national voter registry.

The PRI's grip on power—for a long time—had more to do with the opposition's immaturity, the party's ability to learn from its mistakes, and the longing many older Mexicans felt for the security the party once provided. The PRI has never been an ideological party, and it often managed to change to suit the national mood. It's already making a comeback in state elections, in part, by moving away from its technocrats—the term refers to the young reformers epitomized by former president Salinas. The "Harvard-trained economist," as he was invariably described, brought Mexico free trade, privatization, and all the promises of neoliberalism.

Salinas also brought discredit on his party and his country. Not only did his dream of First World membership die with the peso crisis, but his administration is now considered one of the most corrupt in Mexican history. Salinas lives in self-imposed exile in Dublin, Ireland, but he is still called Mexico's favorite villain. Street vendors sell masks of his face with his inimitable big ears. Bankers who cashed in under Salinas's privatizations have gone on the lam. And Salinas's older brother, Raúl, has been sentenced to 50 years for allegedly masterminding the murder of a former PRI leader. (The decision is under appeal). Meanwhile, Swiss investigators seized $114 million from Raúl's Swiss bank accounts in 1998 claiming that the money was proceeds from protecting drug traffickers. Now Mexico is investigating drug ties in the Salinas administration.

There has been a kind of don't-ask-don't-tell attitude about drug-trafficking in Mexico for years. Since Mexico became the main transportation route for Colombian cocaine growers in the 1980s, drug cartels have insinuated themselves into Mexican life, and Mexican cartels are now every bit as powerful as their Colombian counterparts. Drug use is up, and drug culture, touching everything from clothing to music, is spreading. People wink and nudge each other about the gaudy hotels and new shopping complexes, especially along the U.S. border, that they assume were built with drug money. But they shrug it off. And although both the Mexican and U.S. governments are working together to fight traffickers, it may be too little too late. Drug violence hasn't hurt the average citizen enough (except in border cities such as Juárez and Tijuana) for Mexicans to get really angry about it. But increased crime—driven by corruption, and not poverty—has. Most Mexicans' biggest concern, they'll tell you, is public safety. Although crime is still no worse than in many big U.S. cities, poor policing and weak courts make it seem that way.

As in much of Latin America, hardliners are making a comeback. Some Mexicans are beginning to clamor for the death penalty, something almost unheard of in Catholic countries. The army has been called in to help fight street crime, drugs, and guerillas. And the human-rights situation, especially in states considered guerilla-friendly, is bleak. In December 1997, paramilitary forces massacred 45 peasants thought sympathetic to the Zapatista rebels in Acteal in the southern state of Chiapas. Peace talks with the Zapatistas, who sprang up in 1995, are stalled even though the cease-fire holds. The Zapatistas, or EZLN, are only the most publicity-savvy of a few small guerilla groups. They—with their charismatic spokesman Subcomandante Marcos—are still a leftist cause célèbre. At first, Mexicans had a brief romance with the pipe-smoking Marcos because he seemed to speak for the downtrodden. Now, they say they are mostly weary of the violence.

Can Mexico become a truly modern democracy? It's an ongoing debate on the editorial pages. Some claimed it simply couldn't happen as long as the PRI had a stranglehold on the presidency. Although the opposition supports most of the country's liberal economic changes, just what role the state will play in the future is fuzzy. Many Mexicans still believe that the government should provide, whereas the NAFTA generation wants to be free of the state's shackles. For most Mexicans, democracy largely remains a buzzword. But every day Mexicans have more choices and opportunities, and greater freedom.

– Martha Brandt and Paige Bierma

MEXICO AT A GLANCE

Pre-Columbian Mexico

ca. 50,000 BC Asian nomads cross land bridge over the Bering Strait to North America, gradually migrate south.

ca. 5000–2000 BC Archaic period, which marked the beginnings of agriculture and village life.

ca. 2000–200 BC Formative or pre-Classic period: development of pottery, incipient political structures.

ca. 1500–900 BC The powerful and sophisticated Olmec civilization develops along the Gulf of Mexico in the present-day states of Veracruz and Tabasco. Olmec culture, the "mother culture" of Mexico, flourishes along Gulf coast.

ca. 200 BC–AD 900 Classic period: height of pre-Columbian culture. Three centers at Teotihuacán (near Mexico City), Monte Albán (Oaxaca), and Maya civilization in the Yucatán. Priest-run city-states produce impressive art and architecture.

650–900 Decline of Classic cultures: fall of Teotihuacán ca. 650 leads to competition among other city-states, exacerbated by migrations of northern tribes.

ca. 900–1521 Post-Classic period: rule passes to military; war and war gods gain prominence.

ca. 900–1150 Toltecs, a northern tribe, establish a flourishing culture at their capital of Tula under the legendary monarch Topiltzin-Quetzalcóatl.

ca. 1200 Rise of Mixtec culture at Zapotec sites of Monte Albán and Mitla; notable for production of picture codices, which include historical narratives.

ca. 1000–1450 Maya culture, declining in south, emerges in the Yucatán; under Toltec rule, Chichén Itzá dominates the peninsula.

1111 Aztecs migrate to mainland from island home off the Nayarit coast. They are not welcomed by the peoples of central Mexico.

1150–1350 Following the fall of Tula, first the Chichimecs, then the Tepanecs assert hegemony over central Mexico. The Tepanec tyrant Tezozómoc (1320–1426), like his contemporaries in Renaissance Italy, establishes his power with murder and treachery.

1376 Tezozómoc grants autonomy to the Aztec city of Tenochtitlán, built in the middle of Lake Texcoco.

1420–1500 Aztecs extend their rule to much of central and southern Mexico. A warrior society, they build a great city at Tenochtitlán.

1502 Moctezuma II (1466–1520) assumes throne at the height of Aztec culture and political power.

1517 Spanish expedition under Francisco Hernandez de Córdoba (1475–1526) lands on Yucatán coast.

1519 Hernán Cortés (1485–1547) lands in Cozumel, founds Veracruz, and determines to conquer. Steel weapons, horses, and smallpox, combined with a belief that Cortés was the resurrected Topiltzin-Quetzalcóatl, minimize Aztec resistance. Cortés enters Tenochtitlán and captures Moctezuma.

The Colonial Period

1520–21 Moctezuma is killed; Tenochtitlán falls to Cortés. The last Aztec emperor, Cuauhtémoc, is executed.

1528 Juan de Zumarraga (1468–1548) arrives as bishop of Mexico City, gains title "Protector of the Indians"; native conversion to Catholicism begun.

1535 First Spanish viceroy arrives in Mexico.

1537 Pope Paul III issues a bull declaring that native Mexicans are indeed human and not beasts. First printing press arrives in Mexico City.

1546–48 Silver deposits discovered at Zacatecas.

1547 Spanish conquest of Aztec Empire—now known as "New Spain"—completed, at enormous cost to native peoples.

1553 Royal and Pontifical University of Mexico, first university in the New World, opens.

1571 The Spanish Inquisition established in New Spain; it is not abolished until 1820.

1609 Northern capital of New Spain established at Santa Fe (New Mexico).

1651 Birth of Sor (Sister) Juana Inés de la Cruz, greatest poet of colonial Mexico (d. 1695).

1718 Franciscan missionaries settle in Texas, which becomes part of New Spain.

1765 Charles III of Spain (1716–88) sends José de Galvez to tour New Spain and propose reforms.

1769 Franciscan Junípero Serra establishes missions in California, extending Spanish hegemony.

1788 Death of Charles III; his reforms improved administration, but also raised social and political expectations among the colonial population, which were not fulfilled.

1808 Napoléon invades Spain, leaving a power vacuum in New Spain.

The War of Independence

1810 September 16: Father Miguel Hidalgo y Costilla (1753–1811) preaches his *Grito de Dolores,* sparking rebellion.

1811 Hidalgo is captured and executed; leadership of the movement passes to Father José Maria Morelos y Pavón (1765–1815).

1813 Morelos calls a congress at Chilpancingo, which drafts a Declaration of Independence.

1815 Morelos is captured and executed.

The Early National Period

1821 Vicente Guerrero, a rebel leader, and Agustín de Iturbide (1783–1824), a Spanish colonel converted to the rebel cause, rejuvenate the Independence movement. Spain recognizes Mexican independence with the Treaty of Córdoba.

1822 Iturbide is named Emperor of Mexico, which stretches from California through Central America.

1823 After 10 months in office, Emperor Agustín is turned out.

1824 A new constitution creates a federal republic, the Estados Unidos Mexicanos; modeled on the U.S. Constitution, the Mexican version retains the privileges of the Catholic Church and gives the president extraordinary "emergency" powers.

1829 President Vicente Guerrero abolishes slavery. A Spanish attempt at reconquest is halted by General Antonio López de Santa Anna (1794–1876), already a hero for his role in the overthrow of Emperor Agustín.

1833 Santa Anna is elected president by a huge majority; he holds the office for 11 of its 36 changes of hands by 1855.

1836 Although voted in as a liberal, Santa Anna abolishes the 1824 constitution. Already dismayed at the abolition of slavery, Texas—whose population is largely American—declares its independence. Santa Anna successfully besieges the Texans at the Alamo. But a month later he is captured by Sam Houston following the Battle of San Jacinto. Texas gains its independence as the Lone Star Republic.

1846 The U.S. decision to annex Texas leads to war.

1848 The treaty of Guadalupe Hidalgo reduces Mexico's territory by half, ceding present-day Texas, New Mexico, Arizona, California, Nevada, Utah, and part of Colorado to the United States.

1853 Santa Anna agrees to the Gadsden Purchase, ceding a further 48,000 square km (30,000 square mi) to the United States.

The Reform and French Intervention

1855 The Revolution of Ayutla topples Santa Anna and leads to the period of The Reform.

1857 The liberal Constitution of 1857 disestablishes the Catholic Church, among other measures.

1858–61 The civil War of the Reform ends in liberal victory. Benito Juárez (1806–72) is elected president. France, Spain, and Britain agree jointly to occupy the customs house at Veracruz to force payment of Mexico's huge foreign debt.

1862 Spain and Britain withdraw their forces; the French, seeking empire, march inland. On May 5, General Porfirio Díaz repulses the French at Puebla.

1863 Strengthened with reinforcements, the French occupy Mexico City. Napoléon III of France appoints Archduke Ferdinand Maximilian of Austria (1832–67) as Emperor of Mexico.

1864 Maximilian and his empress Charlotte, known as Carlotta, land at Veracruz.

1867 With U.S. assistance, Juárez overthrows Mexico's second empire. Maximilian is executed; Carlotta, pleading his case in France, goes mad.

1872 Juárez dies in office. The Mexico City–Veracruz railway is completed, symbol of the new progressivist mood.

The Porfiriato

1876 Porfirio Díaz (1830–1915) comes to power in the Revolution of Tuxtepec; he holds office nearly continuously until 1911. With his advisors, the *cientificos,* he forces modernization and balances the budget for the first time in Mexican history. But the social cost is high.

1886 Birth of Diego Rivera (d. 1957).

1890 José Schneider, who is of German ancestry, founds the Cerveceria Cuauhtémoc, brewer of Carta Blanca.

1900 Jesús, Enrique, and Ricardo Flores Magón publish the anti-Díaz newspaper *La Regeneración.* Suppressed, the brothers move their campaign to the United States, first to San Antonio, then to St. Louis.

1906 The Flores Magón group publish their Liberal Plan, a proposal for reform. Industrial unrest spreads.

The Second Revolution

1907 Birth of Frida Kahlo (d. 1954).

1910 On the centennial of the Revolution, Díaz wins yet another rigged election. Revolt breaks out.

1911 Rebels under Pascual Orozco and Francisco (Pancho) Villa (1878–1923) capture Ciudad Juárez; Díaz resigns. Francisco Madero is elected president; calling for land reform, Emiliano Zapata (1879–1919) rejects the new regime. Violence continues.

1913 Military coup: Madero is deposed and murdered. In one day Mexico has three presidents, the last being General Victoriano Huerta (1854–1916). Civil war rages.

1914 American intervention leads to dictator Huerta's overthrow. Villa and Zapata briefly join forces at the Convention of Aguascalientes, but the Revolution goes on. Birth of poet-critic Octavio Paz.

1916 Villa's border raids lead to an American punitive expedition under Pershing. Villa eludes capture.

1917 Under a new constitution, Venuziano Carranza, head of the Constitutionalist Army, is elected president. Zapata continues his rebellion, which is brutally suppressed.

1918 CROM, the national labor union, is founded.

1919 On order of Carranza, Zapata is assassinated.

1920 Carranza is assassinated; Alvaro Obregón (1880–1928), who helped overthrow dictator Huerta in 1914, is elected president, beginning a period of reform and reconstruction. Schools are built and land is redistributed. In the next two decades, revolutionary culture finds expression in the art of Diego Rivera and José Clemente Orozco (1883–1949), the novels of Martin Luis Guzmán and Gregorio Lopez y Fuentes, and the music of Carlos Chavez (1899–1978).

1923 Pancho Villa is assassinated. The United States finally recognizes the Obregón regime.

1926–28 Catholics react to government anticlericalism in the Cristero Rebellion.

1934–40 The presidency of Lázaro Cárdenas (1895–1970) leads to the fullest implementation of revolutionary reforms.

1938 Cárdenas nationalizes the oil companies, removing them from foreign control.

1940 On August 20, exiled former Soviet leader Leon Trotsky murdered in his Mexico City home.

Post-Revolutionary Mexico

1951 Mexico's segment of the Pan-American Highway is completed, confirming the industrial growth and prosperity of post-war Mexico. Culture is increasingly Americanized; writers such as Octavio Paz and Carlos Fuentes express disillusionment with the post-revolution world.

1968 The Summer Olympics in Mexico City showcase Mexican prosperity, but massive demonstrations indicate underlying social unrest.

1981–82 Recession and a drop in oil prices severely damage Mexico's economy. The peso is devalued.

1985 Thousands die in the Mexico City earthquake.

1988 American-educated economist Carlos Salinas de Gortari is elected president; for the first time since 1940, support for the PRI, the national political party, seems to be slipping.

1993 North American Free Trade Agreement (NAFTA) is signed with United States and Canada.

1994 Uprising by the indigenous peoples of Chiapas, led by the Zapatistas and their charismatic ski-masked leader, Subcomandante Marcos; election reforms promised as a result.

Popular PRI presidential candidate Luis Donaldo Colosio assassinated while campaigning in Tijuana. Ernesto Zedillo, generally thought to be more of a technocrat and "old boy"-style PRI politician, replaces him and wins the election.

Zedillo, blaming the economic policies of his predecessor, devalues the peso in December.

1995 Recession sets in as a result of the peso devaluation. The former administration is rocked by scandals surrounding the assassinations of Colosio and another high-ranking government official; ex-President Carlos Salinas de Gortari moves to the United States.

1996 Mexico's economy, bolstered by a $28 billion bailout program led by the United States, turns upward, but the recovery is fragile. The opposition National Action Party (PAN), which is committed to conservative economic policies, gains strength. New details of scandals of the former administration continue to emerge.

1997 Mexico's top antidrug official is arrested on bribery charges. Nonetheless, the United States recertifies Mexico as a partner in the war on drugs. The Zedillo administration faces midterm party elections.

1998 Death of Octavio Paz.

1999 Raúl Salinas, brother of the former president Carlos Salinas de Gortari (in exile in Ireland), sentenced for the alleged murder of a PRI leader.

2000 Spurning long-ruling PRI, Mexicans elect opposition candidate Vicente Fox president.

614

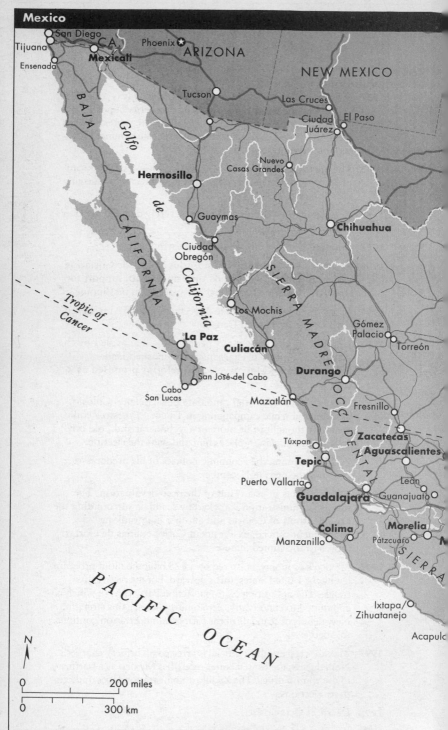

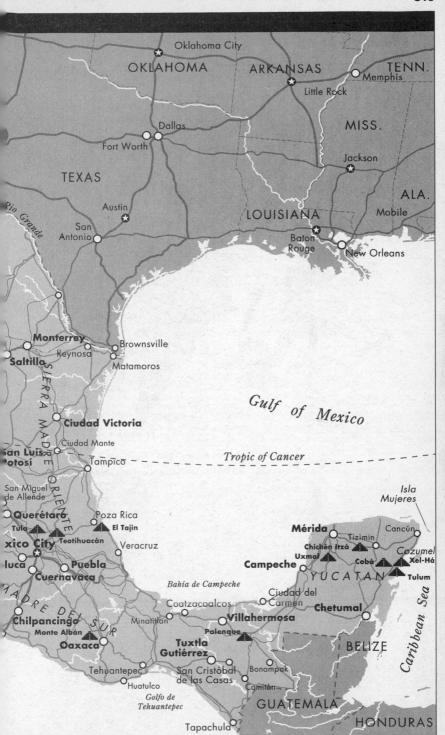

Mexican States and Capitals

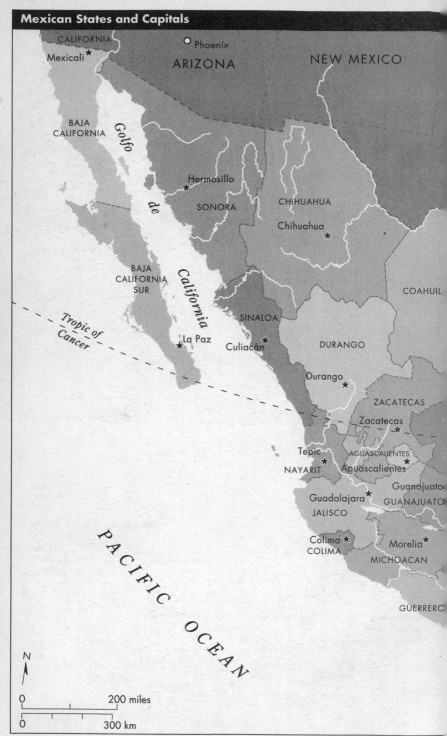

CALIFORNIA

Mexicali ★

○ Phoenix

ARIZONA

NEW MEXICO

BAJA
CALIFORNIA

Golfo

de

California

Hermosillo ★

SONORA

CHIHUAHUA

Chihuahua ★

COAHUIL

BAJA
CALIFORNIA
SUR

SINALOA

DURANGO

Tropic of
Cancer

La Paz ★

Culiacán ★

Durango ★

ZACATECAS

Zacatecas ★

Tepic ★

NAYARIT

AGUASCALIENTES

Aguascalientes ★

Guanajuato ★

GUANAJUATO

Guadalajara ★

JALISCO

Colima ★

COLIMA

Morelia ★

MICHOACAN

GUERRERO

PACIFIC OCEAN

N

0   200 miles

0   300 km

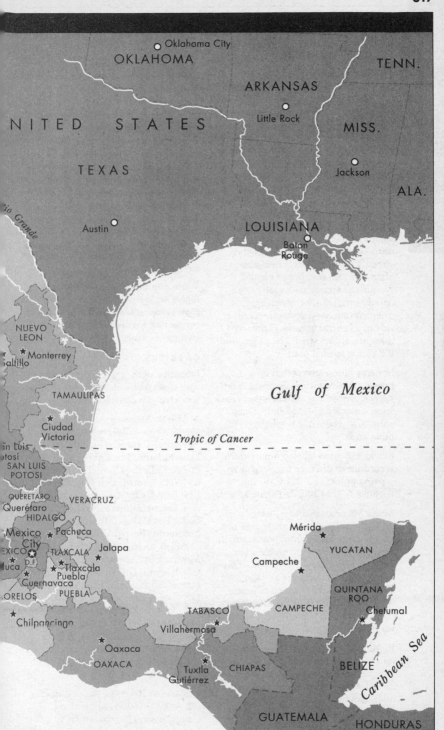

ESSENTIAL INFORMATION

ADDRESSES

The Mexican method of naming streets can be exasperatingly arbitrary, so **be patient when searching for street addresses.** Streets in the centers of many colonial cities (those built by the Spanish) are laid out in a grid surrounding the *zócalo* (main square) and often change names on different sides of the square. Other streets simply acquire a new name after a certain number of blocks. Numbered streets are usually designated *norte/sur* (north/south) or *oriente/poniente* (east/west) on either side of a central avenue. (Three of these are abbreviated: Nte., Ote., and Pte. Sur is spelled out.)

In many cities, streets that have proper names, such as Avenida Benito Juárez, change names when they cross some other street—and only a map will show where one begins and the other ends.

Blocks are often labeled numerically, according to distance from a chosen starting point, as in "la Calle de Pachuca," "2a Calle de Pachuca," etc.

Many Mexican addresses have "s/n" for *sin número* (no number) after the street name. This is common in small towns where there aren't many buildings on a block. Similarly, many hotels give their address as "Km 30 Carr. a Querétaro," which indicates that the property is at the 30th kilometer on the *carretera* (main highway) to Querétaro.

In Mexico City (and other cities), most addresses include their *colonia* (neighborhood), which is abbreviated as Col. Other abbreviations used in addresses include: Av. (*avenida,* or avenue); Calz. (*calzada,* or road); Fracc. (*fraccionamiento,* or housing estate); and Int. (interior).

As in Europe, addresses in Mexico are written with the street name first, followed by the street number. A five-digit *código postal* (postal code) precedes, rather than follows, the name of the city. Apdo. (*apartado*) means box; Apdo. Postal, or A.P., means post-office box number. Here is a sample address: *Hacienda Paraíso, Calle Allende 211, 68000 Oaxaca, Oax.*

AIR TRAVEL

BOOKING

When you book **look for nonstop flights** and **remember that "direct" flights stop at least once.** Try to avoid connecting flights, which require a change of plane.

CARRIERS

Domestic plane travel costs about four times as much as the bus, but it will save you considerable travel time.

➤ MAJOR AIRLINES: **American** (☎ 800/433–7300) to Mexico City, Acapulco, Cancún, Guadalajara, León/El Bajío, Los Cabos, Monterrey, Puerto Vallarta. **Continental** (☎ 800/ 231–0856) to Mexico City, Cancún, Chihuahua City, Cozumel, Guadalajara, Ixtapa/Zihuatanejo, León/El Bajío, Los Cabos, Mazatlán, Mérida, Monterrey, Puerto Vallarta, Veracruz, Tampico. **Delta** (☎ 800/241–4141) to Mexico City, Acapulco, Cancún, Guadalajara, Guaymas, Hermosillo, Ixtapa/Zihuatanejo, León/El Bajío, Los Cabos, Los Mochis, La Paz, Mérida, Puerto Vallarta. **Northwest** (☎ 800/447–4747) to Mexico City, Cancún, Cozumel, Puerto Vallarta. **United** (☎ 800/241–6522) to Mexico City. **US Airways** (☎ 800/428–4322) to Cancún.

➤ SMALLER AIRLINES: **AeroCalifornia** (☎ 800/237–6225) to Mexico City, Guadalajara, Hermosillo, La Paz, Loreto, Los Cabos, Manzanillo, Mazatlán, Monterrey, Puebla, Tepic, Tijuana. **Aeroméxico** (☎ 800/237– 6639) to Mexico City, Acapulco,

Cancún, Cozumel, Guadalajara, Guaymas/San Carlos, Ixtapa/Zihuatanejo, León/El Bajío, Los Cabos, Mérida, Monterrey. **America West** (☎ 800/235–9292) to Mexico City, Acapulco, Guaymas, Ixtapa/Zihuatanejo, Los Cabos, Manzanillo, Mazatlán, Puerto Vallarta. **Mexicana** (☎ 800/531–7921) to Mexico City, Acapulco, Cancún, Guadalajara, Ixtapa/Zihuatanejo, León/El Bajío, Los Cabos, Mazatlán, Mérida, Morelia, Puerto Vallarta, Zacatecas.

➤ FROM THE U.K.: **British Airways** (☎ 0845/773–3377) has a nonstop flight from London to Mexico City. Other airlines flying to Mexico, with brief stops en route, include **Air France** (☎ 0181/742–6600), via Paris; **American** (☎ 020/8572–5555; ☎ 0345/789789 outside London), from London via Chicago, Dallas, or Miami; **Continental** (☎ 01293/776464), from London via Houston, and from Birmingham and Manchester via Newark; **Delta** (☎ 0800/414767), via Atlanta; **Iberia** (☎ 0171/830–0011), via Madrid; **KLM** (☎ 0181/750–9820), via Amsterdam; **Lufthansa** (☎ 0181/750–3535), via Frankfurt; and **United** (☎ 0181/990–9900), via Chicago or Washington, D.C.

➤ DOMESTIC AIRLINES: **AeroCalifornia** (☎ 800/237–6225) serves Guadalajara, Loreto, Puebla, Tepic, Tijuana, and several other gateways. **Aerocaribe** (reserve through Mexicana) serves the Yucatán and the Southeast. **Aerolitoral** (reserve through Aeroméxico or Mexicana) serves northeastern Mexico. **Aeromar** (reserve through Mexicana or Aeroméxico) serves central Mexico. **Aviacsa** (☎ 961/2–80–81 in Chiapas; 5/448–8900 in Mexico City) serves Cancún, Chetumal, and Mérida. **Taesa** (☎ 800/328–2372) serves Mexico City, Acapulco, Cancún, Morelia, Oaxaca City, Puerto Vallarta, Tijuana, Zacatecas.

CHECK-IN & BOARDING

Assuming that not everyone with a ticket will show up, airlines routinely overbook planes. When everyone does, airlines ask for volunteers to give up their seats. In return, these volunteers usually get a certificate for a free flight and are rebooked on the next flight out. If there are not enough volunteers, the airline must choose who will be denied boarding. The first to get bumped are passengers who checked in late and those flying on discounted tickets, so **get to the gate and check in as early as possible,** especially during peak periods.

Always **bring a government-issued photo I.D. to the airport.** You may be asked to show it before you are allowed to check in.

CUTTING COSTS

The least-expensive airfares to Mexico must usually be purchased in advance and are nonrefundable. It's smart to **call a number of airlines, and when you are quoted a good price, book it on the spot**—the same fare may not be available the next day. Always **check different routings** and look into using different airports. Travel agents, especially low-fare specialists (☞ Discounts & Deals, *below*), are helpful.

Consolidators are another good source. They buy tickets for scheduled international flights at reduced rates from the airlines, then sell them at prices that beat the best fare available directly from the airlines, usually without restrictions. Sometimes you can even get your money back if you need to return the ticket. Carefully read the fine print detailing penalties for changes and cancellations, and **confirm your consolidator reservation with the airline.**

When you **fly as a courier,** you trade your checked-luggage space for a ticket deeply subsidized by a courier service. There are restrictions on when you can book and how long you can stay.

➤ CONSOLIDATORS: **Cheap Tickets** (☎ 800/377–1000). **Discount Airline Ticket Service** (☎ 800/576–1600). **Unitravel** (☎ 800/325–2222). **Up & Away Travel** (☎ 212/889–2345). **World Travel Network** (☎ 800/409–6753).

➤ COURIERS: **Air Courier Association** (☎ 800/693–8333, www.aircourier. com). **Air Facility** (☎ 718/712–1769, www.airfacility.com). **Now Voyager** (☎ 212/431–1616).

ENJOYING THE FLIGHT

For more legroom, **request an emergency-aisle seat.** Don't sit in the row in front of the emergency aisle or in front of a bulkhead, where seats may not recline. If you have dietary concerns, **ask for special meals when booking.** These can be vegetarian, low-cholesterol, or kosher, for example. On long flights, try to maintain a normal routine, to help fight jet lag. At night, **get some sleep.** By day, **eat light meals, drink water** (not alcohol), and **move around the cabin** to stretch your legs.

FLYING TIMES

Mexico City is 4½ hours from New York, 4 hours from Chicago, and 3½ hours from Los Angeles. Cancún is 3½ hours from New York and from Chicago, 4½ hours from Los Angeles. Acapulco is 6 hours from New York, 4 hours from Chicago, and 3½ hours from Los Angeles.

From London, Mexico City is a 12½-hour flight, Cancún 11¾ hours.

HOW TO COMPLAIN

If your baggage goes astray or your flight goes awry, complain right away. Most carriers require that you **file a claim immediately.**

➤ AIRLINE COMPLAINTS: U.S. Department of Transportation Aviation Consumer Protection Division (✉ C-75, Room 4107, Washington, DC 20590, ☎ 202/366–2220, airconsumer@ost. dot.gov, www.dot.gov/airconsumer). Federal Aviation Administration Consumer Hotline (☎ 800/322–7873).

AIRPORTS

The main gateway to Mexico is **Aeropuerto Internacional Benito Juárez** in Mexico City.

➤ AIRPORT INFORMATION: **Mexico City** (Aeropuerto Internacional Benito Juárez, ☎ 5/571–3600). **Acapulco** (General Juan Alvarez airport, ☎ 74/66–9434). **Cancún** (Cancún airport, ☎ 98/860–049). **Cozumel** (Cozumel airport, ☎ 987/2–04–85). **Guadalajara** (Ramón F. Quintanilla García airport, ☎ 3/688–51–20). **Ixtapa** (Manuel Zúrita Gallegos airport, ☎ 755/42–070). **Los Cabos** (Licenciado Alberto de la Mora airport, ☎ 114/2–03–41). **Manzanillo** (Playa de Oro airport, ☎ 333/32–525). **Mazatlán** (Juan Buelna airport, ☎ 69/82–23–99). **Mérida** (Hector José Navarrete Muñoz airport, ☎ 99/43–13–40). **Puerto Vallarta** (Gustavo Díaz Ordaz airport, ☎ 322/1–12–98).

BIKE TRAVEL

Bike travel in Mexico is a rough-and-ready proposition. Some roads have never seen a bicycle, and drivers are not accustomed to cyclists. In addition, most Mexican roads lack shoulders and are often pitted. Despite these drawbacks, cycling in Mexico can be fun if you plan ahead, and bikes are especially useful for travel to places where there are only dirt roads or tracks, or where public transportation is scant. In the Yucatán, for example, bikes are a primary form of transportation for locals, and bike-repair shops are common even in smaller towns. When planning your trip, consult an up-to-date AAA, Pemex, or Guía Roji map. You can find Pemex and Guía Roji maps in Mexico at most Sanborns restaurant/shops and major supermarket chains—such as Superama, Aurrera, and Commercial Mexicana—for less then $10. Be sure to carry plenty of water and everything you might need to repair your bike. Pack extra patch kits, as shards of glass often litter the roads. If you can take your bike apart and fold it up, buses will allow you to store it in the cargo space; likewise on trains in the Copper Canyon.

Bicycling Mexico (Hunter Publishing Inc.), by Ericka Weisbroth and Eric Ellman, is the bible of bicyclists, complete with maps, color photos, historical information, and a kilometer-by-kilometer breakdown of every route possible. For a list of companies that run organized bike tours of Mexico, *see* Tours & Packages, *below*.

BIKES IN FLIGHT

Most airlines accommodate bikes as luggage, provided they are dismantled and boxed. For bike boxes, which are often free at bike shops, from airlines you'll pay about $5. International travelers can sometimes substitute a bike for a piece of checked luggage at no charge; otherwise, the cost is about $100. Domestic and Canadian airlines charge $25–$50.

BUS TRAVEL

Getting to Mexico by bus is no longer for just the adventurous or budget-conscious. In the past, bus travelers were required to change to Mexican vehicles at the border, and vice versa. Now, however, in an effort to bring more American visitors and their tourist dollars to off-the-beaten-track markets and attractions, the Mexican government has removed this obstacle, and a growing number of trans-border bus tours are available.

Gateway cities in Texas, such as El Paso, Del Rio, Laredo, McAllen, Brownsville, and San Antonio, along with Tijuana, are served by several small private bus lines as well as by **Greyhound** (☎ 800/231–2222). If you'll be leaving Mexico by bus, you can buy tickets for the U.S. leg of your trip from the Greyhound representative in Mexico City (✉ Paseo de la Reforma 35, ☎ 5/592–3766).

The Mexican bus network is extensive, far more so than that of the railroads. Buses go where trains do not, service is more frequent, tickets can be purchased on the spot (except during holidays and on long weekends, when advance purchase is crucial), and first-class buses are punctual, faster, and much more comfortable than trains. On all overnight bus rides, **bring something to eat** in case you don't like the restaurant where the bus stops, and **carry toilet tissue,** as rest rooms might not have any.

In large cities, bus stations are a good distance from the center of town. Though there's a trend toward consolidation, some towns have different stations for each bus line. Bus service in Mexico City is well organized, operating out of four terminals.

CLASSES

For travel within Mexico, buses run the gamut from comfortable air-conditioned coaches with bathrooms, video movies, reclining airline-like upholstered seats with individual seat belts, refreshments, and hostess service (premier or deluxe) to dilapidated "vintage" buses (second and third class) on which pigs and chickens travel and frequent stops are made. A lower-class bus ride can be interesting if you are not in a hurry and want to see the sights and experience the local culture—and the fares generally are up to 30% cheaper than those in the premium categories. Still, you should be prepared for cracked windows and litter in the aisles. But for comfort's sake alone, if you are planning a long-distance haul, **buy tickets for first class or better when traveling by bus within Mexico.**

Smoking is prohibited on all first-class and deluxe buses.

There are several first-class bus lines. **ADO** (☎ 5/785–9659, 01–800/702–8000) serves Cancún, Oaxaca, Tampico, Veracruz, Villahermosa, and Yucatán from Mexico City; **ADO GL** (☎ 5/785–9659) offers deluxe service to the same destinations. **Cristóbal Colón** (☎ 5/756–9926) goes to Chiapas, Oaxaca, Puebla, and the Guatemala border from Mexico City. **Estrella Blanca** (☎ 5/729–0707) goes from Mexico City to Manzanillo, Mazatlán, Monterrey, and Nuevo Laredo. **ETN** (☎ 5/273–0251) goes to Mexico City, Manzanillo, Morelia, Puerto Vallarta, and Toluca. **Estrella Blanca** (☎ 5/729–0707) has first-class and deluxe service to all states but Yucatán, Quintana Roo, and Chiapas. You can take **Estrella de Oro** (☎ 5/549–8520) from Mexico City to Acapulco, Cuernavaca, Ixtapa, and Taxco.

PAYING

For the most part, you should plan to pay in pesos, although some of the deluxe bus services have started accepting credit cards such as Visa and Mastercard.

RESERVATIONS

Tickets for first class or better—unlike tickets for the other classes—can and should be reserved in advance.

BUSINESS HOURS

BANKS & OFFICES

Banks are generally open weekdays 9–3. In larger cities, most are open until 5 or 7. Many of the larger banks keep a few branches open Saturday from 9 or 10 to 2:30 and Sunday 10–1:30; however, the extended hours are often for deposits or check cashing only. Banks will give you cash advances in pesos (for a fee) if you have a major credit card. Government offices are usually open to the public 8–3; along with banks and most private offices, they are closed on national holidays.

GAS STATIONS

Gas stations in general are open 7 AM–10 PM. Those near major thoroughfares in big cities stay open 24 hours, including most holidays.

MUSEUMS & SIGHTS

Along with theaters and most archaeological sights, museums are closed on Monday, with few exceptions. Museums across the country have free admission on Sunday. Hours are normally 9–5 or 6.

SHOPS

Stores are generally open weekdays and Saturday from 9 or 10 AM to 7 or 8 PM; in resort areas, shops may also be open on Sunday. In some resort areas and small towns, shops may close for a two-hour lunch break—about 2–4. Airport shops are open for business seven days a week.

CAMERAS & PHOTOGRAPHY

You should **always ask permission before taking photos of indigenous people** as they are especially sensitive about cameras. They may ask you for a *propina,* or tip, in which case a few pesos is customary. Some churches in Chiapas and elsewhere forbid cameras. Two subjects to capture on film: mariachi musicians and a village religious celebration.

➤ PHOTO HELP: **Kodak Information Center** (☎ 800/242–2424). *Kodak Guide to Shooting Great Travel Pictures,* available in bookstores or from Fodor's Travel Publications (☎ 800/533–6478; $16.50 plus $5.50 shipping).

EQUIPMENT PRECAUTIONS

Always **keep your film and tape out of the sun.** Carry an extra supply of batteries, and **be prepared to turn on your camera or camcorder** to prove to airport security personnel that the device is real. Always **ask for hand inspection of film,** which becomes clouded after repeated exposure to airport X-ray machines, and **keep videotapes away from metal detectors.**

FILM & DEVELOPING

Film—especially Kodak and Fuji brands—is fairly easy to find in many parts of Mexico. If purchased in a major city, a roll of 36-exposure print film costs about the same as in the United States; the price is slightly higher in more-remote places, where finding film might not be as easy. Advantix wasn't available in Mexico at press time, but is likely to become so in the near future. It's a good idea to **pack more film than you think you'll need** on your trip. Overnight film developing is fairly common in Mexico, although the quality isn't consistently good.

VIDEOS

Videotapes are good quality and can easily be found in urban areas. A 120-minute tape costs about $3.

CAR RENTAL

When you think about renting a car, bear in mind that you may be sharing the road with bad local drivers—sometimes acquiring a driver's license in Mexico is more a question of paying someone off than of having tested skill. In addition, the highway system is very uneven from state to state: in some regions, modern, well-paved superhighways prevail; in others—particularly the mountains—potholes, untethered livestock, and dangerous, unrailed curves are the rule. Check on local road conditions before you rent. *See* Car Travel, *below,* for further information on driving in Mexico.

Mexico manufactures Chrysler, General Motors, Ford, and Volkswagen vehicles. With the exception of Volkswagen, you can get the same kind of midsize and luxury cars in Mexico that you can rent in the United States and Canada. Economy usually refers to a Volkswagen Beetle, which may or may not come with air-conditioning.

Rates begin at $65 a day and $445 a week in Mexico City and $35 a day and $235 a week in Acapulco for an economy car with air-conditioning, a manual transmission, and unlimited mileage. This doesn't include tax on car rentals, which is 15%, or insurance, which runs about $100 a week. *See* Insurance *in* Car Travel, *below.* Avoid local car-rental agencies; **stick with the major companies** because they tend to be more reliable.

You can also hire a car (limousine) with a driver; they're normally available through hotels and charge around $20 an hour within town, with a three-hour minimum requirement. Rates for out-of-town trips are higher. **Negotiate a price beforehand** if you will need the service for more than one day. If your hotel can't arrange limousine service, ask the concierge to refer you to a reliable *sitio* (cab stand); the rate will be lower.

➤ MAJOR AGENCIES: **Alamo** (☎ 800/ 522–9696; 0181/759–6200 in the U.K.). **Avis** (☎ 800/331–1084; 800/ 879–2847 in Canada; 02/9353–9000 in Australia; 09/525–1982 in New Zealand). **Budget** (☎ 800/527–0700; 0144/227–6266 in the U.K.). **Dollar** (☎ 800/800–6000; 0181/897–0811 in the U.K., where it is known as Eurodollar; 02/9223–1444 in Australia). **Hertz** (☎ 800/654–3001; 800/ 263–0600 in Canada; 0181/897– 2072 in the U.K.; 02/9669–2444 in Australia; 03/358–6777 in New Zealand). **National InterRent** (☎ 800/227–3876; 0345/222525 in the U.K., where it is known as Europcar InterRent).

CUTTING COSTS

To get the best deal, **book through a travel agent who will shop around.**

INSURANCE

When driving a rented car you are generally responsible for any damage to or loss of the vehicle as well as for any property damage or personal injury that you may cause. Before you rent, see what coverage your personal auto-insurance policy and credit cards already provide. In Mexico you must have Mexican auto insurance (☞ Car Travel, *below,* for more information).

REQUIREMENTS & RESTRICTIONS

In Mexico your own driver's license is acceptable. An International Driver's Permit is a good idea; it's available from the U.S. and Canadian automobile associations, and, in the United Kingdom, from the Automobile Association or Royal Automobile Club. These international permits are universally recognized, and having one in your wallet may save you a problem with the local authorities.

SURCHARGES

Before you pick up a car in one city and leave it in another, **ask about drop-off charges or one-way service fees,** which can be substantial. Note, too, that some rental agencies charge extra if you return the car before the time specified in your contract. To avoid a hefty refueling fee, **fill the tank just before you turn in the car,** but be aware that gas stations near the rental outlet may overcharge.

CAR TRAVEL

There are two absolutely essential points to remember about driving in Mexico. First and foremost is to **carry Mexican auto insurance.** (☞ Insurance, *below.*)

Point No. 2: **if you enter Mexico with a car, you must leave with it.** In recent years, the high rate of U.S. vehicles being sold illegally in Mexico has caused the Mexican government to enact stringent regulations for bringing a car into the country—at great inconvenience to motoring American tourists. In order to drive into the country, **you must cross the border with the following documents:** title or registration for your vehicle; a birth certificate or passport; a credit card (AE, DC, MC, or V); a valid driver's license with a photo. The title holder, driver, and credit-card owner must be one and the same—that is, if your spouse's name is on the title of the car and yours isn't, you cannot be the one to bring the car into the country. For financed, leased, rental, or company cars, **you must bring a notarized letter of permission** from the bank, lien holder, rental agency, or company.

When you submit your paperwork at the border and pay a $12 charge on your credit card, you will receive a tourist visa, a car permit, and a sticker to put on your vehicle, all valid for up to six months. **Be sure to turn in the permit and the sticker** at the border prior to their expiration date; otherwise you could incur high fines.

One alternative to going through this hassle when you cross is to **have your paperwork done in advance** at a branch of Sanborn's Mexican Insurance; look in the Yellow Pages for an office in almost every town on the U.S.–Mexico border. You'll still have to go through some of the procedures at the border, but all your paperwork will be in order, and Sanborn's express window will ensure that you get through relatively quickly. There is a $10 charge for this service. The fact that you drove in with a car is stamped on your tourist card, which you must give to immigration authorities at departure. If an emergency arises and you must fly home, there are complicated customs procedures to face.

For day trips and local sightseeing, **consider engaging a car and driver** (who often acts as a guide) for a day; this can be a hassle-free, more economical way to travel than renting a car and driving yourself. Hotel desks will know which taxi companies to call, and you can negotiate a price with the driver.

EMERGENCY SERVICES

To help motorists on major highways, the Mexican Tourism Ministry operates a fleet of more than 350 pickup trucks, known as the Angeles Verdes, or Green Angels. The bilingual drivers provide mechanical help, first aid, radio-telephone communication, basic supplies and small parts, towing, tourist information, and protection. Services are free, and spare parts, fuel, and lubricants are provided at cost. Tips are always appreciated (figure $5–$10 for big jobs, $2–$3 for minor repairs). The Green Angels patrol fixed sections of the major highways twice daily 8–8 (later on holiday weekends). If you break down, **pull off the road as far as possible,** lift the hood of your car, hail a passing vehicle, and ask the driver to **notify the patrol.** Most bus and truck drivers will be quite helpful. If you witness an accident, do not stop to help—inform the nearest official.

➤ CONTACTS: **Green Angels, Mexico City** (☎ 5/250–8221).

GASOLINE

Pemex franchises all gas stations in Mexico. Stations are located at most road junctions and in cities and towns and gas is measured in liters instead of gallons. Gas stations usually do not accept U.S. or Canadian credit cards or dollars. Fuel prices vary from region to region. They tend to be on the lower end in Mexico City and surroundings and near the U.S. border, increasing the farther you get from these areas. Overall, prices run slightly to moderately higher than in the United States. Premium unleaded gas (called Magna Premio) and regular unleaded gas (Magna Sin) is available nationwide, but it's still a good idea to **fill up whenever you can.** Fuel quality is generally lower than that in the United States and Europe. Vehicles with fuel-injected engines are likely to have problems after driving extended distances.

Gas-station attendants pump the gas for you and may also wash your windshield and check your oil and tire air pressure. A five- or 10-peso tip is customary depending on the number of services rendered. **Keep a close eye on the gas meter** to make sure the attendant is starting it at "0" and that you pay the price that is shown afterward. Even though standards of cleanliness have improved considerably in most gas stations in cities and on the major highways, especially *franquicia* (franchised) stations, some still leave a lot to be desired.

INSURANCE

You must **carry Mexican auto insurance,** which you can purchase near border crossings on either the U.S. or Mexican side. If you injure anyone in an accident, you could well be jailed—whether it was your fault or not—unless you have insurance. Guilty until proven innocent is part of the country's Code Napoléon. Purchase enough Mexican automobile insurance at the border to cover your estimated trip. It's sold by the day, and if your trip is shorter than your original estimate, some companies might issue a prorated refund for the unused time upon application after you exit the country.

▶ CONTACTS: **Instant Mexico Auto Insurance** (✉ 223 Via de San Ysidro, San Ysidro, CA 92173, ☎ 619/428–3583). **Oscar Padilla** (✉ 4330 La Jolla Village Dr., San Diego, CA 92122, ☎ 800/258–8600). **Sanborn's Mexican Insurance** (✉ 2009 S. 10th St., McAllen, TX 78503, ☎ 210/686–0711).

ROAD CONDITIONS

There are several well-kept toll roads in Mexico—most of them four lanes wide. However, these *carreteras* (major highways) don't go too far out of the capital into the countryside. (*Cuota* means toll road; *libre* means no toll, and such roads are two lanes and usually not as smooth.) Some excellent new roads have opened in the past seven or so years, making car travel safer and faster. These include highways connecting Acapulco and Mexico City; Cancún and Mérida; Nogales and Mazatlán; León and Aguascalientes; Guadalajara and Tepic; Mexico City, Morelia, and Guadalajara; Mexico City, Puebla, Teotihuacán, and Oaxaca; and Nuevo Laredo and Monterrey. However, tolls as high as $40 one way can make using these thoroughfares prohibitively expensive. Approaches to most of the large cities are also in good condition.

In rural areas, roads are quite poor: **use caution, especially during the rainy season,** when rock slides and potholes are a problem, and watch out for animals. Driving in Mexico's central highlands may also necessitate adjustments to your carburetor. Generally, driving times are longer than for comparable distances in the United States. *Topes* (speed humps) are also common; it's best to slow down when approaching a village.

Common sense goes a long way: if you have a long distance to cover, **start early and fill up on gas**; don't let your tank get below half-full. Allow extra time for unforeseen occurrences as well as for the trucks that seem to be everywhere. By day, **be alert to animals,** especially cattle and dogs.

Traffic can be horrendous in cities, particularly in Mexico City. As you would in metropolitan areas anywhere, **avoid rush hour** (7–9 AM and 6–8 PM) and when schools let out (2–3 PM). Signage is not always adequate in Mexico, so if you aren't sure where you're going, **travel with a companion and a good map.** Always lock your car, and never leave valuable items in the body of the car (the trunk will suffice for daytime outings, but don't pack it in front of prying eyes).

The Mexican Tourism Ministry distributes free road maps from its tourism offices outside the country. Guía Roji and Pemex (the government petroleum monopoly) publish current city, regional, and national road maps, which are available in bookstores and big supermarket chains for under $10; gas stations generally do not carry maps.

RULES OF THE ROAD

When you sign up for Mexican car insurance, you should receive a booklet on Mexican rules of the road. Read this booklet in order to avoid breaking laws that differ from those of your native country.

Illegally parked cars are either towed or have wheel blocks placed on the tires, which can require a trip to the traffic-police headquarters for payment of a fine. When in doubt, **park in a lot instead of on the street**; your car will probably be safer there anyway.

If an oncoming vehicle flicks its lights at you in daytime, slow down: it could mean trouble ahead. When approaching a narrow bridge, the first vehicle to flash its lights has right of way. One-way streets are common. One-way traffic is indicated by an arrow; two-way, by a double-pointed arrow. A circle with a diagonal line superimposed on the letter *E* (for *estacionamiento*) means "no parking." Other road signs follow the now widespread system of international symbols, a copy of which will usually be provided when you rent a car in Mexico.

In Mexico City, **watch out for "Hoy no Circula" notices.** Because of pollution, all cars in the city are prohibited from driving one day a week (two days a week during high-alert periods). Posted signs show certain letters or numbers paired with each day of the week, indicating that vehicles with those letters or numbers in their license plates are not allowed to drive on the corresponding day. Foreigners are not exempt.

Mileage and speed limits are given in kilometers: 100 kph and 80 kph (62 and 50 mph, respectively) are the most common maximums. A few of the newer toll roads allow 110 kph (68 mph). In cities and small towns, **observe the posted speed limits,** which can be as low as 20 kph (12 mph).

SAFETY ON THE ROAD

First of all, **never drive at night** in Mexico, especially in remote and rural areas. *Banditos* are one concern, but so are potholes, free-roaming animals, cars with no working lights, road-hogging trucks, and difficulty in getting assistance. It's best to use toll roads whenever possible; although costly, they are much safer. Plan driving times, and if night is falling, find a nearby hotel.

If you are driving from Manzanillo to Ixtapa/Zihuatanejo—about 8–10 hours with a meal stop—make the trip only during daylight hours, due to reports of car jackings around the area of Playa Azul. Military and police patrols have been increased on Highway 200 and the number of incidents has dramatically decreased; still, exercise caution.

Some of the biggest hassles on the road might be from police who pull you over for supposedly breaking the law, or for being a good prospect for a scam. Remember to **be polite**— displays of anger will only make matters worse—and be aware that a police officer might be pulling you over for something you didn't do. Corruption is a fact of life in Mexico, and the $5 it costs to get your license back is definitely supplementary income for the officer who pulled you over with no intention of taking you down to police headquarters.

If you are stopped for speeding, the officer is supposed to take your license and hold it until you pay the fine at the local police station. But the officer will always prefer a *mordida* (small bribe) to wasting his time at the police station. If you decide to dispute a charge that seems preposterous, do so with a smile, and tell the officer that you would like to talk to the police captain when you get to the station. The officer usually will let you go rather than go to the station.

When walking, **look both ways for oncoming traffic** when crossing streets, even with the light. Although pedestrians have the right of way by law, drivers disregard it. And more often than not, if a driver hits a pedestrian, he'll drive away as fast as he can without stopping, to avoid jail. Many Mexican drivers do not carry auto insurance, so you will have to shoulder your own medical expenses.

CHILDREN IN MEXICO

Mexico has one of the strictest policies about children entering the country. All children, including infants, must have proof of citizenship for travel to Mexico. All children up to age 18 traveling with a single parent must also have a notarized letter from the other parent stating that the child has his or her permission to leave their home country. If the other parent is deceased or the child has only one legal parent, a notarized statement saying so must be obtained as proof. In addition, parents must now fill out a tourist card for each child over the age of 10 traveling with them.

If you are renting a car, don't forget to **arrange for a car seat** when you reserve.

FLYING

If your children are two or older, **ask about children's airfares.** As a general rule, infants under two not occupying a seat fly at greatly reduced fares or even free. When booking, **confirm carry-on allowances** if you're traveling with infants. In general, for babies charged 10% of the adult fare you are allowed one carry-on bag and a collapsible stroller; if the flight is full, the stroller may have to be checked or you may be limited to less.

Experts agree that it's a good idea to use safety seats aloft for children that weigh under 40 pounds. Airlines set their own policies: U.S. carriers usually require that the child be ticketed, even if he or she is young enough to ride free, since the seats must be strapped into regular seats. Do **check your airline's policy about using safety seats during takeoff and landing.** And since safety seats are not allowed everywhere in the plane, get your seat assignments early.

When reserving, **request children's meals or a freestanding bassinet** if you need them. But note that bulkhead seats, where you must sit to use the bassinet, may lack an overhead bin or storage space on the floor.

FOOD & SUPPLIES

Fresh milk isn't readily available, though necessities such as disposable diapers can be found in almost every small town.

LODGING

Most hotels in Mexico allow children under a certain age to stay in their parents' room at no extra charge, but others charge for them as extra adults; be sure to **find out the cutoff age for children's discounts** before booking accommodations.

Many hotel chains in Mexico offer services that make it easier to travel with children. They include connecting family rooms, play areas such as kiddie pools and playgrounds, and kids' clubs with special activities and outings. Check with your hotel before booking to see if the services are included in the price or if there is an extra charge.

SIGHTS & ATTRACTIONS

The larger tourist areas have plenty of activities for children. Places in this book that are especially appealing to children are indicated by a rubber-duckie icon in the margin.

COMPUTERS ON THE ROAD

Internet cafés have sprung up all over Mexico, making e-mail by far the easiest way to get in touch with people back home—or anywhere for that matter.

If you have a Toshiba or Macintosh laptop, bear in mind that having it serviced might be hopeless. Parts for these machines are hard to come by in Mexico.

Carry a spare battery because replacement batteries are expensive and difficult to find. Always check with your hotel about surge protection, especially if the property isn't part of a major chain and/or is in an out-of-the-way place. Extreme electrical fluctuations and surges can damage or destroy your computer. Check with IBM for its pen-size modem tester that plugs into a telephone and jack to test if the line is safe.

CONSUMER PROTECTION

Whenever shopping or buying travel services in Mexico, **pay with a major credit card** so you can cancel payment or get reimbursed if there's a problem. If you're doing business with a particular company for the first time, **contact your local Better Business Bureau and the attorney general's offices** in your own state and the company's home state, as well. Have any complaints been filed? Finally, if you're buying a package or tour, always **consider travel insurance** that includes default coverage (☞ Insurance, *below*).

➤ BBBs: **Council of Better Business Bureaus** (✉ 4200 Wilson Blvd., Suite 800, Arlington, VA 22203, ☎ 703/276–0100, FAX 703/525–8277, www.bbb.org).

CUSTOMS & DUTIES

When shopping, **keep receipts** for all purchases. Upon reentering the country, **be ready to show customs officials what you've bought.** If you feel a duty is incorrect or object to the way your clearance was handled, note the inspector's badge number and ask to see a supervisor. If the problem isn't resolved, write to the appropriate authorities, beginning with the port director at your point of entry.

IN AUSTRALIA

Australian residents who are 18 or older may bring home A$400 of souvenirs and gifts (including jewelry), 250 cigarettes or 250 grams of tobacco, and 1,125 milliliters of alcohol (including wine, beer, and spirits). Residents under 18 may bring back A$200 in goods. Prohibited items include meat products. Seeds, plants, and fruits need to be declared upon arrival.

➤ INFORMATION: **Australian Customs Service** (Regional Director, ✉ Box 8,

Sydney, NSW 2001, ☎ 02/9213–2000, FAX 02/9213–4000).

IN CANADA

Canadian residents who have been out of Canada for at least seven days may bring home C$500 worth of goods duty-free. If you've been away fewer than seven days but more than 48 hours, the duty-free allowance drops to C$200; if your trip lasts 24 to 48 hours, the allowance is C$50. You may not pool allowances with family members. Goods claimed under the C$500 exemption may follow you by mail; those claimed under the lesser exemptions must accompany you. Alcohol and tobacco products may be included in the seven-day and 48-hour exemptions but not in the 24-hour exemption. If you meet the age requirements of the province or territory through which you reenter Canada, you may bring in, duty-free, 1.14 liters (40 imperial ounces) of wine or liquor *or* 24 12-ounce cans or bottles of beer or ale. If you are 16 or older you may bring in, duty-free, 200 cigarettes and 50 cigars. Check ahead of time with Revenue Canada or the Department of Agriculture for policies regarding meat products, seeds, plants, and fruits.

You may send an unlimited number of gifts worth up to C$60 each duty-free to Canada. Label the package UNSOLICITED GIFT—VALUE UNDER $60. Alcohol and tobacco are excluded.

➤ INFORMATION: **Revenue Canada** (✉ 2265 St. Laurent Blvd. S, Ottawa, Ontario K1G 4K3, ☎ 613/993–0534; 800/461–9999 in Canada; FAX 613/957–8911, www.ccra-adrc.gc.ca).

IN MEXICO

Upon entering Mexico, you will be given a baggage declaration form and asked to itemize what you're bringing into the country. You are allowed to bring in 2 liters of spirits or wine for personal use; 400 cigarettes, 50 cigars, or 250 grams of tobacco; a reasonable amount of perfume for personal use; one movie camera and one regular camera and 12 rolls of film for each; and gift items not to exceed a total of $300. If driving across the U.S. border, gift items must not exceed $50. You aren't allowed to bring firearms,

meat, vegetables, plants, fruit, or flowers into the country.

IN NEW ZEALAND

Homeward-bound residents 17 or older may bring back NZ$700 worth of souvenirs and gifts. Your duty-free allowance also includes 4.5 liters of wine or beer; one 1,125-milliliter bottle of spirits; and either 200 cigarettes, 250 grams of tobacco, 50 cigars, or a combination of the three up to 250 grams. Prohibited items include meat products, seeds, plants, and fruits.

➤ INFORMATION: **New Zealand Customs** (Custom House, ✉ 50 Anzac Ave., Box 29, Auckland, New Zealand, ☎ 09/359–6655, FAX 09/359–6732).

IN THE U.K.

From countries outside the EU, including Mexico, you may bring home, duty-free, 200 cigarettes or 50 cigars; 1 liter of spirits or 2 liters of fortified or sparkling wine or liqueurs; 2 liters of still table wine; 60 milliliters of perfume; 250 milliliters of toilet water; plus £136 of other goods, including gifts and souvenirs. Prohibited items include meat products, seeds, plants, and fruits.

➤ INFORMATION: **HM Customs and Excise** (✉ Dorset House, Stamford St., Bromley, Kent BR1 1XX, ☎ 0171/202–4227).

IN THE U.S.

U.S. residents who have been out of the country for at least 48 hours (and who have not used the $400 allowance or any part of it in the past 30 days) may bring home $400 worth of foreign goods duty-free.

U.S. residents 21 and older may bring back 1 liter of alcohol duty-free. In addition, regardless of your age, you are allowed 200 cigarettes and 100 non-Cuban cigars. Antiques, which the U.S. Customs Service defines as objects more than 100 years old, enter duty-free, as do original artworks done entirely by hand, including paintings, drawings, and sculptures.

You may also send packages home duty-free: up to $200 worth of goods for personal use, with a limit of one parcel per addressee per day (except alcohol or tobacco products or perfume worth more than $5); label the package PERSONAL USE and attach a list of its contents and their retail value. Do not label the package UNSOLICITED GIFT or your duty-free exemption will drop to $100. Mailed items do not affect your duty-free allowance on your return.

➤ INFORMATION: **U.S. Customs Service** (✉ 1300 Pennsylvania Ave. NW, Washington, DC 20229, www.customs.gov; inquiries ☎ 202/354–1000; complaints c/o ✉ Office of Regulations and Rulings; registration of equipment c/o ✉ Resource Management, ☎ 202/927–0540).

DINING

Mexican restaurants run the gamut from humble hole-in-the-wall shacks, street stands, *taquerías,* and American-style fast-food joints to internationally acclaimed gourmet restaurants. Prices, naturally, follow suit. To save money, **look for the fixed-menu lunch** known as *comida corrida* or *menú del día,* which is served 1–4 almost everywhere in Mexico.

The restaurants we list are the cream of the crop in each price category. For more information on local foods throughout Mexico, *see* the Cocina Mexicana box in Mexico City (Chapter 1) and the Dining sections that appear under Pleasures and Pastimes at the beginning of each chapter.

MEALTIMES

In Mexico, lunch is the big meal; dinner is rarely served before 8 PM. Unless otherwise noted, the restaurants listed in this guide are open daily for lunch and dinner.

PAYING

Credit cards—especially American Express, MasterCard, and Visa—are widely accepted at pricier restaurants. Bargains are usually cash only.

RESERVATIONS & DRESS

Reservations are always a good idea: we mention them only when they're essential or not accepted. Book as far ahead as you can, and reconfirm as soon as you arrive. We mention dress only when men are required to wear a jacket or a jacket and tie.

DISABILITIES & ACCESSIBILITY

Mexico is poorly equipped for travelers with disabilities. There are no special discounts or passes for such travelers in Mexico, nor is public transportation, including the Mexico City Metro, wheelchair accessible. An exception is the city of Veracruz, where street corners have ramps in the downtown area. Roads and sidewalks are most often crowded and without ramps—in colonial cities cobblestone sidewalks and streets are unnavigable—and people on the street will not usually assist you unless expressly asked. You cannot rent vehicles outfitted for travelers with disabilities in Mexico, so your best bet for exploring comfortably is to **bring a car or van.**

Most hotels and restaurants have at least a few steps, and while rooms considered "wheelchair accessible" by hotel owners are usually on the ground floor, the doorways and bathroom may not be maneuverable. It's a good idea to call ahead to find out what a hotel or restaurant can offer. Despite these barriers, Mexicans with disabilities manage to negotiate places that most travelers outside Mexico would not consider accessible.

LODGING

The best choices of accessible lodging are found in major resort towns such as Acapulco, Cancún, and Mazatlán, and big cities such as Mexico City and Guadalajara.

RESERVATIONS

When discussing accessibility with an operator or reservations agent, **ask hard questions.** Are there any stairs, inside or out? Are there grab bars next to the toilet *and* in the shower/tub? How wide is the doorway to the room? To the bathroom? For the most extensive facilities meeting the latest legal specifications, **opt for newer accommodations.**

➤ COMPLAINTS: **Disability Rights Section** (✉ U.S. Department of Justice, Civil Rights Division, Box 66738, Washington, DC 20035-6738, ☎ 202/514–0301, 800/514–0301;

TTY 202/514–0301, 800/514–0301; FAX 202/307–1198) for general complaints. **Aviation Consumer Protection Division** (☞ Air Travel, *above*) for airline-related problems. **Civil Rights Office** (✉ U.S. Department of Transportation, Departmental Office of Civil Rights, S-30, 400 7th St. SW, Room 10215, Washington, DC 20590, ☎ 202/366–4648, FAX 202/366–9371) for problems with surface transportation.

TRAVEL AGENCIES

In the United States, the Americans with Disabilities Act requires that travel firms serve the needs of all travelers. Some agencies specialize in working with people with disabilities.

➤ TRAVELERS WITH MOBILITY PROBLEMS: **Access Adventures** (✉ 206 Chestnut Ridge Rd., Rochester, NY 14624, ☎ 716/889–9096, dltravel@prodigy.net), run by a former physical-rehabilitation counselor. **CareVacations** (✉ 5-5110 50th Ave., Leduc, Alberta, Canada T9E 6V4, ☎ 780/986–6404, 877/478–7827, FAX 780/986–8332, www.carevacations.com), for group tours and cruise vacations. **Flying Wheels Travel** (✉ 143 W. Bridge St., Box 382, Owatonna, MN 55060, ☎ 507/451–5005, 800/535–6790, FAX 507/451–1685, thq@ll.net, www.flyingwheels.com). **Hinsdale Travel Service** (✉ 201 E. Ogden Ave., Suite 100, Hinsdale, IL 60521, ☎ 630/325–1335, FAX 630/325–1342, hinstrvl@interaccess.com).

➤ TRAVELERS WITH DEVELOPMENTAL DISABILITIES: **New Directions** (✉ 5276 Hollister Ave., Suite 207, Santa Barbara, CA 93111, ☎ 805/967–2841, 888/967–2841, FAX 805/964–7344, newdirec@silcom.com, www.silcom.com/ánewdirec/). **Sprout** (✉ 893 Amsterdam Ave., New York, NY 10025, ☎ 212/222–9575, 888/222–9575, FAX 212/222–9768, sprout@interport.net, www.gosprout.org).

DISCOUNTS & DEALS

Be a smart shopper and **compare all your options** before making decisions. A plane ticket bought with a promotional coupon from travel clubs, coupon books, and direct-mail offers may not be cheaper than the least expensive fare from a discount ticket agency. And always keep in mind that what you get is just as important as what you save.

DISCOUNT RESERVATIONS

To save money, **look into discount reservations services** with toll-free numbers, which use their buying power to get a better price on hotels, airline tickets, even car rentals. When booking a room, always **call the hotel's local toll-free number** (if one is available) rather than the central reservations number—you'll often get a better price. Always ask about special packages or corporate rates.

When shopping for the best deal on hotels and car rentals, **look for guaranteed exchange rates**, which protect you against a falling dollar. With your rate locked in, you won't pay more, even if the price goes up in the local currency.

➤ AIRLINE TICKETS: ☎ 800/FLY–4–LESS. ☎ 800/FLY–ASAP.

➤ HOTEL ROOMS: **Players Express Vacations** (☎ 800/458–6161, www.playersexpress.com). **Steigenberger Reservation Service** (☎ 800/223–5652, www.srs-worldhotels.com).

PACKAGE DEALS

Don't confuse packages and guided tours. When you buy a package, you travel on your own, just as though you had planned the trip yourself. Fly/drive packages, which combine airfare and car rental, are often a good deal.

ELECTRICITY

For U.S. and Canadian travelers, electrical converters are not necessary because Mexico operates on the 60-cycle, 120-volt system; however, many Mexican outlets have not been updated to accommodate three-prong and polarized plugs (those with one larger prong), so to be safe **bring an adapter.**

If your appliances are dual-voltage you'll need only an adapter. Don't use 110-volt outlets, marked FOR SHAVERS ONLY, for high-wattage appliances such as blow-dryers. Most laptops operate equally well on 110 and 220 volts and so require only an adapter.

EMBASSIES

All embassies are in Mexico City. If you need assistance in an emergency, you can go to your country's embassy. Proof of identity and citizenship are generally required to enter.

➤ AUSTRALIA: **Australian Embassy** ✉ Rubén Darío 55, Col. Polanco, ☎ 5/531–5225.

➤ CANADA: **Canadian Embassy** ✉ Schiller 529, Col. Polanco, ☎ 5/724–7900.

➤ NEW ZEALAND: **New Zealand Embassy** ✉ José Luis LaGrange 103, 10th fl., Col. Polanco, ☎ 5/281–5486.

➤ UNITED KINGDOM: **British Embassy** ✉ Río Lerma 71, ☎ 5/207–2449.

➤ UNITED STATES: **U.S. Embassy** (✉ Paseo de la Reforma 305, Col. Cuauhtémoc, ☎ 5/209–9100).

EMERGENCIES

You're not protected by the laws of your native land once you're on Mexican soil. If you get into a scrape with the law, you can call the Citizens' Emergency Center in the United States. You can also call the 24-hour English-language hot line of the Procuraduría de Protecciónal Turista (Attorney General for the Protection of Tourists) in Mexico City; it can provide immediate assistance as well as general, nonemergency guidance. **In an emergency, dial 07 from any phone.**

➤ CONTACTS: **Citizens' Emergency Center**(☎ 202/647–5225 weekdays 8:15 AM–10 PM EST, Sat. 9AM–3 PM; ☎ 202/634–3600 after hours and-Sun.). **Procuraduría de Protección al Turista** (Attorney General for the Protection of Tourists; ☎ 01–800/903–9200, 800/482–9832 from the U.S.).

ENGLISH-LANGUAGE MEDIA

English-language magazines and books can be found at some of the larger grocery stores in Mexico, but they are expensive—usually at least double what you'd pay back home. Several stores in Mexico City sell English-language publications (☞ Mexico City A to Z *in* Chapter 1) and you can probably find at least one place in other major cities to buy them. However, in most smaller towns, you won't have much luck.

NEWSPAPERS & MAGAZINES

Mexico has two major English-language newspapers: *The Mexico City Times* and *The News,* available at hotels and newsstands in the tourist areas.

ETIQUETTE & BEHAVIOR

In the United States, for example, being direct, efficient, and succinct is highly valued. But in Mexico, where communication tends to be more subtle, this style is often perceived as rude and aggressive. Mexicans are extremely polite, so losing your temper over delays or complaining loudly will get you branded as rude and make people less inclined to help you. **Remember that things move at a slow pace** here and that there's no stigma attached to being late; **accept this** gracefully. Learning basic phrases in Spanish such as "please" and "thank you" will make a big difference in how people respond to you.

BUSINESS ETIQUETTE

Personal relationships always come first here, so developing rapport and trust is essential. A handshake and personal greeting is appropriate along with a friendly inquiry about family, especially if you have met the family. In established business relationships, do not be surprised if you are greeted with a kiss on the check or a hug. Always be respectful toward colleagues in public and keep confrontations private. Meetings may or may not start on time, but you should be patient. When invited to dinner at the home of a client or associate, bring a gift and be sure to send a thank-you note afterward.

GAY & LESBIAN TRAVEL

Mexican same-sex couples keep a low profile, and it's a good idea for foreign same-sex couples to do the same. Two people of the same gender can often have a hard time getting a *cama matrimonial* (double bed), especially in smaller hotels. This could be attributed to the influence of the Catholic Church—Mexico is a devoutly Catholic country. The same rule that applies all over the world holds in Mexico as well: alternative lifestyles (whether they be homosexuality or any other bending of conventional roles) are more easily accepted in cosmopolitan areas, such as Mexico City, Acapulco, Ajijic, Cancún, Cuernavaca, Guadalajara, Puerto Vallarta, San Miguel de Allende, and Veracruz City.

➤ GAY- & LESBIAN-FRIENDLY TRAVEL AGENCIES: **Different Roads Travel** (✉ 8383 Wilshire Blvd., Suite 902, Beverly Hills, CA 90211, ☎ 323/651–5557, 800/429–8747, FAX 323/651–3678, leigh@west.tzell.com). **Kennedy Travel** (✉ 314 Jericho Turnpike, Floral Park, NY 11001, ☎ 516/352–4888, 800/237–7433, FAX 516/354–8849, main@kennedytravel.com, www.kennedytravel.com). **Now Voyager** (✉ 4406 18th St., San Francisco, CA 94114, ☎ 415/626–1169, 800/255–6951, FAX 415/626–8626, www.nowvoyager.com). **Skylink Travel and Tour** (✉ 1006 Mendocino Ave., Santa Rosa, CA 95401, ☎ 707/546–9888, 800/225–5759, FAX 707/546–9891, skylinktvl@aol.com, www.skylinktravel.com), serving lesbian travelers.

HEALTH

AIR POLLUTION

Air pollution in Mexico City can pose a health risk. The sheer number of cars and industries in the capital, thermal inversions, and the inability to process sewage have all contributed to the high levels of lead, carbon monoxide, and other pollutants in Mexico City's atmosphere. Though the long-term effects are not known, children, the elderly, and those with respiratory problems are advised to avoid jogging, participating in outdoor sports, and being outdoors more than necessary on days of high smog alerts. If you have heart problems, keep in mind that Mexico City is, at 7,556 ft, the highest metropolis on the North American continent. This compounded with the smog may pose a serious health risk, so check with your doctor before planning a trip.

The Australian, British, Canadian, New Zealand, and U.S. embassies in Mexico City can provide lists of English-speaking doctors.

DIVERS' ALERT

Do not fly within 24 hours of scuba diving.

FOOD & DRINK

In Mexico the major health risk, known as *turista,* or traveler's diarrhea, is caused by eating contaminated fruit or vegetables or drinking contaminated water. So **watch what you eat.** Stay away from ice, uncooked food, and unpasteurized milk and milk products, and **drink only bottled water** or water that has been boiled for at least 20 minutes (*quiero el agua hervida por viente minutos*), even when you're brushing your teeth. Mild cases may respond to Imodium (known generically as loperamide or Lomotil) or Pepto-Bismol (not as strong), both of which can be purchased over the counter. Drink plenty of purified water or tea; chamomile tea (*te de manzanilla*) is a good folk remedy and it's readily available in restaurants throughout Mexico. In severe cases, rehydrate yourself with Gatorade or a salt–sugar solution (½ teaspoon salt and 4 tablespoons sugar per quart of water).

When ordering cold drinks at untouristed establishments, **skip the ice:** *sin hielo.* (You can usually identify ice made commercially from purified water by its uniform shape and the hole in the center.) Hotels with water-purification systems will post signs to that effect in the rooms. *Tacos al pastor*—thin pork slices grilled on a spit and garnished with the usual cilantro, onions, and chili peppers— are delicious but dangerous. It's also a good idea to pass up *ceviche,* raw fish cured in lemon juice—a favorite appetizer, especially at seaside resorts. The Mexican Department of Health warns that marinating in lemon juice does not constitute the "cooking" that would make the shellfish safe to eat. Also, be wary of hamburgers sold from street stands, because you can never be certain what meat they are made with (horse meat is common).

MEDICAL PLANS

No one plans to get sick while traveling, but it happens, so **consider sign-**

ing up with a medical-assistance company. Members get doctor referrals, emergency evacuation or repatriation, hot lines for medical consultation, cash for emergencies, and other assistance.

➤ MEDICAL-ASSISTANCE COMPANIES: **International SOS Assistance** (✉ 8 Neshaminy Interplex, Suite 207, Trevose, PA 19053, ☎ 215/245–4707, 800/523–6586, ℻ 215/244–9617; ✉ 12 Chemin Riantbosson, 1217 Meyrin 1, Geneva, Switzerland, ☎ 4122/785–6464, ℻ 4122/785–6424; ✉ 331 N. Bridge Rd., 17-00, Odeon Towers, Singapore 188720, ☎ 65/338–7800, ℻ 65/338–7611; www.internationalsos.com).

PESTS & OTHER HAZARDS

Caution is advised when venturing out in the Mexican sun. Sunbathers lulled by a slightly overcast sky or the sea breezes can be burned badly in just 20 minutes. To avoid overexposure, **use strong sunscreens and avoid the peak sun hours** of noon to 2 PM. Sunscreen, including many American brands, can be found in pharmacies, supermarkets, and resort gift shops.

SHOTS & MEDICATIONS

According to the U.S. National Centers for Disease Control and Prevention (CDC), there is a limited risk of malaria and dengue fever in certain rural areas of Mexico. In most urban or easily accessible areas you need not worry. However, if you plan to visit remote regions or stay for more than six weeks, **check with the CDC's International Travelers Hotline.** In areas where malaria and dengue, both of which are carried by mosquitoes, are prevalent, use mosquito nets, wear clothing that covers the body, apply repellent containing DEET, and use spray for flying insects in living and sleeping areas. Repellents (*repelentes contra moscas*) and sprays (*repelentes de sprie contra moscas*) can be purchased at pharmacies. In some places you see mosquito coils (*espirales contra moscas*) used; they can be purchased in hardware stores (*ferretería*) as well as in pharmacies. Also **consider taking antimalarial pills** if you are doing serious adventure activities in subtropical areas. There is no vaccine to combat dengue, which

if you are reasonably healthy is usually not serious (only dengue hemorrhagic fever is potentially fatal).

➤ HEALTH WARNINGS: **National Centers for Disease Control and Prevention** (CDC; National Center for Infectious Diseases, Division of Quarantine, Traveler's Health Section, ✉ 1600 Clifton Rd. NE, M/S E-03, Atlanta, GA 30333, ☎ 888/232–3228, ℻ 888/232–3299, www.cdc.gov).

HOLIDAYS & FESTIVALS

Mexico is the land of festivals; if you reserve lodging well in advance, they're a golden opportunity to have a thoroughly Mexican experience. January is full of long, regional festivals. Notable are the **Fiesta de la Inmaculada Concepción** (Feast of the Immaculate Conception), which transforms the city of Morelia into a sea of lights and flowers for much of the month, and a series of folkloric dances in Chiapa de Corzo, Chiapas, that culminates in the **Feast of San Sebastián,** the third week in January.

Banks and government offices close during Holy Week (the week leading to Easter Sunday) and on Cinco de Mayo, Día de la Raza, and Day of the Dead. Government offices usually have reduced hours and staff from Christmas through New Year's Day.

WINTER

➤ JAN. 1: **New Year's Day** is a major celebration throughout the country. Agricultural and livestock fairs are held in the provinces.

➤ JAN. 6: **Feast of Epiphany** is the day the Three Kings bring gifts to Mexican children.

➤ JAN. 17: **Feast of San Antonio Abad** honors animals all over Mexico. Pets and livestock are decked out with flowers and ribbons and taken to church for a blessing.

➤ FEB. 2: **Día de la Candelaria,** or Candlemas Day, means fiestas, parades, bullfights, and lantern-decorated streets. Festivities include a running of the bulls through the streets of Tlacotalpan, Veracruz.

➤ FEB.–MAR.: **Carnaval** is celebrated throughout Mexico—most notably in

Mazatlán and Veracruz, with parades of floats and bands.

SPRING

➤ MAR. 21: **Benito Juárez's Birthday,** a national holiday, is most popular in Guelatao, Oaxaca, where Juárez, the beloved 19th-century president of Mexico and champion of the people, was born. This is also the day that Cuernavaca's **Fiesta de la Primavera** marks the beginning of spring.

➤ MAR.–APR.: **Semana Santa** (Holy Week), the week leading to Easter Sunday, is observed with parades and passion plays.

➤ APR.–MAY: **San Marcos National Fair,** held in Aguascalientes, is one of the country's best fairs. It features Indian *matachnes* (dances performed by grotesque figures), mariachi bands, and bullfights. Also during this time, the 10-day **Festival de las Artes** (Arts Festival) brings music, theater, and dance troupes from all over Latin America to San Luis Potosí.

➤ MAY 1: **Labor Day** is a day for workers to parade through the streets.

➤ MAY 5: **Cinco de Mayo** marks, with great fanfare countrywide, the anniversary of the French defeat by Mexican troops in Puebla in 1862.

➤ MAY 15: **Feast of San Isidro Labrador** is noted nationwide by the blessing of new seeds and animals. In Cuernavaca, a parade of oxen wreathed in flowers is followed by street parties and feasting.

SUMMER

➤ JUNE 1: **Navy Day** is commemorated in all Mexican seaports and is especially colorful in Acapulco, Mazatlán, and Veracruz. The **Feast of Corpus Christi** is celebrated in different ways. In Mexico City, children are dressed in native costumes and taken to the cathedral on the zócalo for a blessing. In Papantla, Veracruz, the Dance of the Flying Birdmen—a pre-Hispanic ritual to the sun—is held throughout the day.

➤ JUNE 24: **Saint John the Baptist Day,** a popular national holiday, sees many Mexicans observing a tradition of tossing a "blessing" of water on most anyone within reach.

➤ EARLY JULY: The **Feria Nacional** (National Fair) in Durango runs from the Day of Our Lady of Refuge (July 4) to the anniversary of the founding of Durango in 1563 (July 22). The old-time agricultural fair has become known across the country for its carnival rides, livestock shows, and music. The **Guelaguetza Dance Festival,** a pre-Columbian Oaxacan affair, usually falls on the first and third Monday of July.

➤ JULY 16: **Our Lady of Mt. Carmel Day** is celebrated with fairs, bullfights, fireworks, even a major fishing tournament.

➤ LATE JULY: The **Feast of Santiago** features *charreadas*, Mexican-style rodeos.

➤ AUG.: The **Feast of St. Augustine** brings a month of music, dance, and fireworks to Puebla. On August 26 (feast day) it is customary to prepare the famous *chiles en nogada*.

➤ AUG. 15: **Feast of the Assumption of the Blessed Virgin Mary** is celebrated nationwide with religious processions. In Huamantla, Tlaxcala, the festivities include a running of the bulls and a carpet of flowers laid out in front of the church.

➤ AUG. 25: **San Luis Potosí Patron Saint Fiesta** is the day the town honors its patron, San Luis Rey, with traditional dance, music, and foods.

AUTUMN

➤ SEPT. 15–16: **Independence Day** is marked throughout Mexico with fireworks and parties that outblast those on New Year's Eve. The biggest celebrations are in Mexico City.

➤ SEPT. 29: **San Miguel Day** honors St. Michael, the patron saint of all towns with San Miguel in their names—especially San Miguel de Allende—with bullfights, folk dances, concerts, and fireworks.

➤ OCT.: **October Festival** means a month of cultural and sporting events in Guadalajara.

➤ OCT. 4: **Feast of St. Francis of Assisi** is a day for processions dedicated to St. Francis in parts of the country.

➤ OCT. 12: **Día de la Raza** (Day of the Race) is comparable to Columbus Day in the United States.

➤ OCT.–NOV.: **International Cervantes Festival** in Guanajuato is a top cultural event that attracts dancers, singers, and actors from various countries.

➤ OCT. 31–NOV. 2: On **All Souls' and All Saints' Day,** or Day of the Dead, families welcome back the spirits of departed relatives to elaborate altars and refurbished gravesites. Especially intriguing are the celebrations in Pátzcuaro and Oaxaca.

➤ NOV. 20: **Anniversary of the Mexican Revolution** is a national holiday.

➤ NOV.–DEC.: **National Silver Fair,** an annual Taxco event, is an occasion for even more silver selling than usual, the crowning of a Silver Queen, and jewelry and silver exhibitions.

➤ DEC. 12: On **Feast Day of the Virgin of Guadalupe,** Mexico's patron saint is feted with processions and native folk dances, particularly at her shrine in Mexico City. In Puerto Vallarta, 12 days of processions and festivities lead up to the night of Dec. 12.

➤ DEC. 16–25: **The Posadas and Christmas** include candlelight processions that lead to holiday parties and the breaking open of piñatas. Mexico City is brightly decorated, but don't expect any snow.

➤ DEC. 23: **Night of the Radishes,** a pre-Christmas tradition in Oaxaca, is one of the most colorful in Mexico: participants carve giant radishes into amusing shapes and display them in the city's main plaza.

INSURANCE

The most useful travel-insurance plan is a comprehensive policy that includes coverage for trip cancellation and interruption, default, trip delay, and medical expenses (with a waiver for preexisting conditions).

Without insurance you will lose all or most of your money if you cancel your trip, regardless of the reason. Default insurance covers you if your tour operator, airline, or cruise line goes out of business. Trip-delay covers expenses that arise because of bad weather or mechanical delays. Study the fine print when comparing policies.

If you're traveling internationally, a key component of travel insurance is coverage for medical bills incurred if you get sick on the road. Such expenses generally are not covered by Medicare or private policies. British and Australian citizens need extra medical coverage when traveling overseas. U.K. residents can buy a travel-insurance policy valid for most vacations taken during the year in which it's purchased (but check preexisting-condition coverage). Always **buy travel policies directly from the insurance company**; if you buy them from a cruise line, airline, or tour operator that goes out of business you probably will not be covered for the agency or operator's default, a major risk. Before making any purchase, **review your existing health and home-owner's policies** to find what they cover away from home.

➤ TRAVEL INSURERS: In the U.S.: **Access America** (✉ 6600 W. Broad St., Richmond, VA 23230, ☎ 804/285–3300, 800/284–8300, FAX 804/673–1583, www.previewtravel.com), **Travel Guard International** (✉ 1145 Clark St., Stevens Point, WI 54481, ☎ 715/345–050, 800/826–1300, FAX 800/955–8785, www.noelgroup.com). In Canada: **Voyager Insurance** (✉ 44 Peel Center Dr., Brampton, Ontario L6T 4M8, ☎ 905/791–8700, 800/668–4342).

➤ INSURANCE INFORMATION: In the U.K.: **Association of British Insurers** (✉ 51–55 Gresham St., London EC2V 7HQ, ☎ 0171/600–3333, FAX 0171/696–8999, info@abi.org.uk, www.abi.org.uk). In Australia: **Insurance Council of Australia** (☎ 03/9614–1077, FAX 03/9614–7924)

LANGUAGE

Spanish is the official language of Mexico, although Indian languages are spoken by approximately 20% of the population and those people speak no Spanish at all. Basic English is widely understood by most people employed in tourism, less so in the less developed areas. At the very least, shopkeepers will know the numbers for bargaining purposes.

As in most other foreign countries, knowing the mother tongue has a way of opening doors, so **learn some Spanish words and phrases.** Mexicans welcome even the most halting attempts to use the language.

Castilian Spanish—which is different from Latin American Spanish not only in pronunciation and grammar but also in vocabulary—is most widely taught outside Mexico. Words or phrases that are harmless or everyday in one country can offend in another. Unless you are lucky enough to be briefed on these nuances by a native coach, the only way to learn is by trial and error.

LANGUAGE-STUDY PROGRAMS

Language institutes are pretty widespread in Mexico, and attending one is an ideal way not only to learn Mexican Spanish but also to acquaint yourself with the customs and the people of the country. For total immersion, most language schools offer boarding with a Mexican family, but your choice of lodgings and of length of stay is generally flexible.

➤ LANGUAGE INSTITUTES: Recommended places to learn Spanish and live with a Mexican family include: **Centro de Idiomas de la Universidad Autónoma Benito Juárez** (Burgoa at Bustamante, Oaxaca 68000, ☎ FAX 951/1–03–55), which offers classes in Mixtec and Zapotec as well as in Spanish; **Centro Internacional de Estudios para Estranjeros** (✉ Tomás V. Gómez 125, Guadalajara, Jalisco 44600, ☎ 3/616–4399; ✉ Libertad 42, Local 1, Puerto Vallarta, Jalisco 48360, ☎ 322/3–20–82, FAX 322/3–29–82); **Cetlalic** (✉ Apdo. 1-201 Cuernavaca, Morelos, CP 62000, ☎ 73/13–35–79), with an emphasis on social justice as well as language acquisition; **Iberoamerican University Programs for Foreign Students** (✉ Prolongacion Paseo de la Reforma 880, Lomas de Santa Fe, Mexico, D.F. 01210, ☎ FAX 5/267–4111 ext. 4931); **Instituto Allende** (✉ A.P. 85-A, San Miguel de Allende, Guanajuato 37700, ☎ 465/2–01–90, FAX 465/2–45–38); **Instituto Falcon** (✉ Callejón de la Mora 158, Guanajuato 36000, ☎ 4/731–0745, www.infonet.com.

mx/falcon); **Instituto Jovel, A.C.** (✉ A.P. 62, Ma. Adelina Flores 21, San Cristóbal de las Casas, Chiapas 29200, ☎ FAX 967/8–40–69); **National Autonomous University of Mexico School for Foreign Students** (✉ A.P. 70, Taxco, Guerrero 40200, ☎ FAX 7/622–01–24); and the **SLI– Spanish Language Institute** (✉ A.P. 2–3, Cuernavaca, Morelos 62191, ☎ FAX 73/17–52–94); in the U.S. contact **Language Link Inc.** ✉ Box 3006, Peoria, IL 61612, ☎ 800/552–2051, FAX 309/692–2926).

AmeriSpan Unlimited (✉ Box 40513, Philadelphia, PA 19106, ☎ 800/879–6640, FAX 215/985–4524) can arrange for language study and homestays.

LANGUAGES FOR TRAVELERS

A phrase book and language-tape set can help get you started.

➤ PHRASE BOOKS & LANGUAGE-TAPE SETS: *Fodor's Spanish for Travelers* (☎ 800/733–3000 in the U.S.; 800/668–4247 in Canada; $7 for phrasebook, $16.95 for audio set).

LODGING

The price and quality of accommodations in Mexico vary about as much as the country's restaurants: from superluxurious, international-class hotels and all-inclusive resorts to modest budget properties, seedy places with shared bathrooms, *casas de huéspedes* (guest houses), youth hostels, and *cabañas* (beach huts). You may find appealing bargains while you're on the road, but if your comfort threshold is high, **look for an English-speaking staff, guaranteed dollar rates, and toll-free reservation numbers.**

The lodgings we list are the cream of the crop in each price category. We always list the facilities that are available—but we don't specify whether they cost extra; when pricing accommodations, **always ask what's included and what costs extra.** Lodgings are denoted in the text with a house icon, ⌂ ; establishments with restaurants that warrant a special trip have ✕⌂ .

Hotel rates are subject to the 15% value-added tax (it's 10% in the states of Quintana Roo, Baja California, and Baja California Sur). In addition, many states are charging a 2% hotel tax, and the revenue is being used for tourism promotion. Service charges and meals generally are not included in the hotel rates. The Mexican government categorizes hotels, based on qualitative evaluations, into *gran turismo* (superdeluxe, or six-star, properties, of which there are only about 50 nationwide); five-star down to one-star; and economy class. Keep in mind that many hotels that might otherwise be rated higher have opted for a lower category to avoid higher interest rates on loans and financing.

High- versus low-season rates can vary significantly (☞ When to Go, *below*). Hotels in this guide have air-conditioning and private bathrooms with showers, unless stated otherwise; bathtubs are not common in inexpensive hotels and properties in smaller towns.

It's essential to **reserve in advance** if you are traveling during high season or holiday periods. Overbooking is a common practice in some parts of Mexico, such as Cancún and Acapulco. Travelers to remote areas will encounter little difficulty in obtaining rooms on a walk-in basis unless it's during a holiday season.

If you are particularly sensitive to noise, you should **call ahead to learn if your hotel of choice is located on a busy street.** Many of the most engaging accommodations in Mexico are on downtown intersections that experience heavy automobile and pedestrian traffic. And large hotels are known to have lobby bars with live music in the middle of an open-air atrium leading directly to rooms. When you book, **request a room far from the bar.**

APARTMENT & VILLA RENTALS

If you want a home base that's roomy enough for a family and comes with cooking facilities, **consider a furnished rental.** These can save you money, especially if you're traveling with a group. Home-exchange directories sometimes list rentals as well as exchanges.

➤ INTERNATIONAL AGENTS: **At Home Abroad** (✉ 405 E. 56th St., Suite 6H, New York, NY 10022, ☎ 212/421–9165, FAX 212/752–1591, athomabrod@aol.com, www.member.aol.com/athomabrod/index.html). **Hideaways International** (✉ 767 Islington St., Portsmouth, NH 03801, ☎ 603/430–4433, 800/843–4433, FAX 603/430–4444, info@hideaways.com www.hideaways.com; membership $99). **Vacation Home Rentals Worldwide** (✉ 235 Kensington Ave., Norwood, NJ 07648, ☎ 201/767–9393, 800/633–3284, FAX 201/767–5510, vhrww@juno.com, www.vhrww. com). **Villas and Apartments Abroad** (✉ 1270 Avenue of the Americas, 15th floor, New York, NY 10020, ☎ 212/897–5045, 800/433–3020, FAX 212/897–5039, vaa@altour.com, www.vaanyc.com). **Villas International** (✉ 950 Northgate Dr., Suite 206, San Rafael, CA 94903, ☎ 415/499–9490, 800/221–2260, FAX 415/499–9491, villas@best.com, www.villasintl.com).

B&BS

The B&B craze hasn't missed Mexico, and the same delights that you find elsewhere in the world apply here, too—personable service, interesting local furnishings and decorative talent, and tasty morning meals. San Miguel de Allende and other Heartland cities have their share of charming places, as do Mexico City and parts of the Yucatán.

➤ RESERVATION SERVICES: If you arrive in Mexico City without a reservation, the **Mexico City Hotel and Motel Association** (☎ 5/571–3268, 5/571–3262) operates a booth at the airport that will assist you.

CAMPING

A host of camping opportunities exist in Mexico, but don't expect the typical U.S.-style campground. Mexico's are usually trailer parks with running water, cooking areas, and room to pitch tents; sites can cost $1–$10. To enjoy more-rustic surroundings, you can set up camp off the road or on the beach in relative safety, and save loads of money. Usually, you can camp at an *ejido* (farming community) or on someone's land for free as long as you ask permission first; ask locals about the safest and best spots. **Be alert and don't camp alone;** the beaches at night aren't as safe as they once were. And don't camp at archaeological sites.

Camping supplies are scarce in Mexico. Before you begin packing loads of camping gear, however, consider how much camping you will actually do versus how much trouble it will be to haul around your tent, sleeping bag, stove, and accoutrements. Finding a place to store your gear can be difficult—lockers tend to be small.

In many towns along the Pacific and Caribbean coasts, beachside *palapas* (thatch-roof huts) are an excellent alternative to tent camping. All you'll need for a night in a palapa is a hammock (they don't cost much in Mexico), some mosquito netting, and a padlock for stashing your belongings in a locker.

HOME EXCHANGES

If you would like to exchange your home for someone else's, **join a home-exchange organization,** which will send you its updated listings of available exchanges for a year and will include your own listing in at least one of them. It's up to you to make specific arrangements.

➤ EXCHANGE CLUBS: HomeLink International (✉ Box 650, Key West, FL 33041, ☎ 305/294–7766, 800/638–3841, ℻ 305/294–1448, usa@homelink.org, www.homelink.org; $98 per year).

HOSTELS

No matter what your age, you can **save on lodging costs by staying at hostels.** In Mexico, however, high-school and college students are more often the norm at hostels than older travelers. In some 5,000 locations in more than 70 countries around the world, Hostelling International (HI), the umbrella group for a number of national youth-hostel associations, offers single-sex, dorm-style beds and, at many hostels, rooms for couples and family accommodations. Membership in any HI national hostel association, open to travelers of all ages, allows you to stay in HI-affili-

ated hostels at member rates; one-year membership is about $25 for adults (C$26.75 in Canada, £9.30 in the U.K., A$30 in Australia, and NZ$30 in New Zealand); hostels run about $10–$25 per night. Members have priority if the hostel is full; they're also eligible for discounts around the world, even on rail and bus travel in some countries.

➤ ORGANIZATIONS: Australian Youth Hostel Association (✉ 10 Mallett St., Camperdown, NSW 2050, ☎ 02/9565–1699, ℻ 02/9565–1325, www.yha.com.au). Hostelling International—American Youth Hostels (✉ 733 15th St. NW, Suite 840, Washington, DC 20005, ☎ 202/783–6161, ℻ 202/783–6171, www.hiayh.org). Hostelling International—Canada (✉ 400–205 Catherine St., Ottawa, Ontario K2P 1C3, ☎ 613/237–7884, ℻ 613/237–7868, www.hostellingintl.ca). Youth Hostel Association of England and Wales (✉ Trevelyan House, 8 St. Stephen's Hill, St. Albans, Hertfordshire AL1 2DY, ☎ 01727/855215, 01727/845047, ℻ 01727/844126, www.yha.uk). Youth Hostels Association of New Zealand (✉ Box 436, Christchurch, ☎ 03/379–9970, ℻ 03/365–4476, www.yha.org.nz).

HOTELS

After choosing a hotel, it's best to **reserve ahead,** especially for the high season (December through the second week after Easter). Rooms in hotels listed have private baths unless otherwise noted.

➤ TOLL-FREE NUMBERS: Best Western (☎ 800/528–1234, www.bestwestern.com). Choice (☎ 800/221–2222, www.hotelchoice.com). Doubletree and Red Lion Hotels (☎ 800/222–8733, www.doubletreehotels.com). Four Seasons (☎ 800/332–3442, www.fourseasons.com). Hilton (☎ 800/445–8667, www.hiltons.com). Holiday Inn (☎ 800/465–4329, www.holiday-inn.com). Howard Johnson (☎ 800/654–4656, www.hojo.com). Hyatt Hotels & Resorts (☎ 800/233–1234, www.hyatt.com). Inter-Continental (☎ 800/327–0200, www.interconti.com). Marriott (☎ 800/228–9290, www.marriott.com). Le Meridien (☎ 800/543–4300, www.forte-hotels.com). **Nikko Hotels International** (☎ 800/645–5687, www. nikko.com). **Omni** (☎ 800/843–6664, www.omnihotels.com). **Radisson** (☎ 800/333–3333, www.radisson.com). **Ritz-Carlton** (☎ 800/241–3333, www.ritzcarlton.com). **Sheraton** (☎ 800/325–3535, www.sheraton.com). **Westin Hotels & Resorts** (☎ 800/228–3000, www.starwood.com).

MAIL & SHIPPING

The Mexican postal system is notoriously slow and unreliable; **never send packages** or expect to receive them, as they may be stolen. (For emergencies, use a courier service or the express-mail service, with insurance). If you are an American Express cardholder, your best bet is to send a package to the AmEx office nearest the recipient.

Post offices (*oficinas de correos*) are found in even the smallest villages. International postal service is all airmail, but even so your letter will take anywhere from 10 days to six weeks to arrive. Service within Mexico can be equally slow.

OVERNIGHT SERVICES

Federal Express, DHL, and United Parcel Service are available in major cities and many resort areas, but Federal Express is the most widespread. They offer office or hotel pickup with 24-hour advance notice and are very reliable. From Mexico City to anywhere in the U.S., the minimum charge is around $15 for a package weighing less than 8 ounces. Starting prices are higher for Australia, Canada, New Zealand, and the U.K., and deliveries take longer.

➤ MAJOR SERVICES: In Mexico City: **Federal Express** (☎ 5/228–9904); **DHL** (☎ 5/227–0299); and **United Parcel Service** (☎ 5/228–7900).

POSTAL ABBREVIATIONS

Mexican states have postal abbreviations of two or more letters. If you plan to send mail to Mexico, here is a short list of Mexican state postal codes: **Baja California**: B.C.; **Baja California Sur**: B.C.S.; **Campeche**: Camp.; **Chiapas**: Chis.; **Chihuahua**: Chih.; **Distrito Federal (Mexico City)**: D.F.; **Guanajuato**: Gto.; **Guerrero**:

Gro.; **Jalisco**: Jal.; **Estado de Mexico**: Edo. de Mex.; **Michoacán**: Mich.; **Morelos**: Mor.; **Nuevo Leon**: N.I.; **Oaxaca**: Oax.; **Querétaro**: Qro.; **Quintana Roo**: Q. Roo; **Sinaloa**: Sin.; **Sonora**:Son.; **Tabasco**: Tab.; **Veracruz**: Ver.; **Yucatán**: Yuc.; **Zacatecas**: Zac.

POSTAL RATES

It costs 3.50 pesos to send a postcard or letter weighing under 20 grams to the United States or Canada, and 4.40 pesos to Great Britain.

RECEIVING MAIL

To receive mail in Mexico, you can have it sent to your hotel or use *poste restante* at the post office. In the latter case, the address must include the words "a/c Lista de Correos" (general delivery), followed by the city, state, postal code, and country. To use this service, you must first register with the post office at which you wish to receive your mail. The post office posts and updates daily a list of names for whom mail has been received. Holders of American Express cards or traveler's checks can have mail sent to them in care of the local American Express office. For a list of offices worldwide, write for the *Traveler's Companion* from **American Express** (✉ Box 678, Canal Street Station, New York, NY 10013).

MONEY MATTERS

Prices in this book are quoted most often in U.S. dollars. We would prefer to list costs in pesos, but because the value of the currency fluctuates considerably, what costs 90 pesos today might cost 120 pesos in six months.

Mexico has a reputation for being inexpensive, particularly compared with other North American vacation spots, such as the Caribbean; the devaluation of the peso, started in late 1994, has made this especially true, though prices of the large chain hotels, calculated in dollars, have not gone down, and some restaurant owners and merchants have raised their prices to compensate for the devaluation. In general, costs will vary with the when, where, and how of your travel in Mexico. "When" is discussed in When to Go, *below*. As to "how," if you are looking for a place as much as possible like home, travel only by air or package tour, stay at international hotel-chain properties, eat at restaurants catering to tourists, and shop at fixed-price tourist-oriented malls, you might not find Mexico such a bargain. If you want a closer look at the country and are not wedded to standardized creature comforts, you can spend as little as $25 a day on room, board, and local transportation. Speaking Spanish is also helpful in bargaining situations and when asking for dining recommendations. As a rule, region by region, costs decrease as the amount of English that people speak decreases.

Cancún, Puerto Vallarta, Mexico City, Monterrey, Acapulco, Ixtapa, Los Cabos, Manzanillo, and, to a lesser extent, Mazatlán and Huatulco are the most expensive places to visit in Mexico. All the beach towns, however, offer budget accommodations, and the smaller, less accessible ones are often more moderately priced, examples being the Gulf coast and northern Yucatán, parts of Quintana Roo, some of the less developed spots north and south of Puerto Vallarta in the states of Jalisco and Nayarit, Puerto Escondido, and the smaller Oaxacan coastal towns as well as those of Chiapas and Tabasco.

Average costs in major cities vary, although less than in the past because of an increase in business travelers. A stay in one of Mexico City's top hotels can cost more than $200 (as much or more than at the coastal resorts), but you can get away with a tab of $45 for two at what was once an expensive restaurant.

Probably the best value for your travel dollar is in smaller, inland towns, such as San Cristóbal de las Casas, Mérida, Morelia, Guanajuato, and Oaxaca, where tourism is less developed. Although Oaxaca lodging can run more than $150 a night, simple colonial-style hotels with adequate accommodations for under $40 can be found, and tasty, filling meals are rarely more than $15.

Prices throughout this guide are given for adults. Substantially reduced fees are almost always available for children, students, and senior citizens. For information on taxes, *see* Taxes, *below*.

ATMS

ATMs (*caja automática*) are becoming commonplace in more and more Mexican towns and cities. Cirrus and Plus are the most commonly found networks in Mexico. Before you leave home, **ask what the transaction fee will be** for withdrawing money in Mexico. (It's usually $3 a pop.) Many Mexican ATMs cannot accept PINs (personal identification numbers) that have more than four digits; if yours is longer, **ask your bank about changing your PIN (*numero de clave*) before you leave home,** and keep in mind that processing such a change often takes a few weeks.

If your transaction still cannot be completed—an annoyingly common occurrence—chances are that the computer lines are busy or that the machine has run out of money or is being serviced.

For cash advances, plan to use Visa or MasterCard, as many Mexican ATMs don't accept American Express. The ATMs at Banamex, one of the oldest nationwide banks, tend to be the most reliable. Bancomer is another bank with many ATM locations, but they usually provide only cash advances. The newer Serfín banks have reliable ATMs that accept credit cards as well as Plus and Cirrus cards.

See Safety, *below*, on avoiding ATM robberies.

CREDIT CARDS

Traveler's checks and all major U.S. credit cards are accepted in most tourist areas of Mexico. Smaller, less expensive restaurants and shops, however, tend to take only cash. In general, credit cards aren't accepted in small towns and villages, except for tourist-oriented hotels. Diner's Club is usually accepted only in major hotel chains; the most widely accepted cards are Mastercard and Visa. When shopping, you can usually get better prices if you **pay with cash.**

At the same time, when traveling internationally you will **receive wholesale exchange rates** when you make purchases with credit cards. These exchange rates are usually better than rates that banks give you for changing money. In Mexico the decision to pay cash or use a credit card might depend on whether the establishment in which you are making a purchase finds bargaining for prices acceptable. To avoid fraud, it's wise to **make sure that "pesos" is clearly marked on all credit-card receipts.**

Throughout this guide, the following abbreviations are used: **AE,** American Express; **DC,** Diner's Club; **MC,** MasterCard; and **V,** Visa.

➤ REPORTING LOST CARDS: Before you leave for Mexico, be sure to **find out your credit-card companies' toll-free card-replacement numbers** that work at home as well as in Mexico; they could be impossible to find once you get to Mexico, and the calls you place to cancel your cards can be long ones. **Carry these numbers separately from your wallet** so you'll have them if you need to call to report lost or stolen cards.

CURRENCY

At press time, the peso was still "floating" after the devaluation enacted by the Zedillo administration in late 1994. While exchange rates have been as favorable as 9.92 pesos to US$1, 6.40 pesos to C$1, 15.40 pesos to £1, 6.10 pesos to A$1, and 4.85 pesos to NZ$1, the market and prices continue to adjust. **Check with your bank or the financial pages of your local newspaper for current exchange rates.** For quick estimates of how much something costs in U.S. dollar terms, divide prices given in pesos by 10. For example, 50 pesos would be about $5.

Mexican currency comes in denominations of 10-, 20-, 50-, 100-, 200-, 500-, and 1,000-peso bills. Coins come in denominations of 20, 10, and 5 pesos and 50, 20, 10, and 5 centavos. Many of the coins and bills are very similar, so check carefully.

U.S. dollar bills (but not coins) are widely accepted in many parts of the Yucatán, particularly in Cancún and Cozumel, where you'll often find prices in shops quoted in dollars. However, you'll get your change in pesos. Many tourist shops and market vendors as well as virtually all hotel service personnel also accept dollars.

CURRENCY EXCHANGE

ATM transaction fees may be higher abroad than at home, but ATM currency-exchange rates are the best of all because they are based on wholesale rates offered only by major banks. And if you take out a fair amount of cash per withdrawal, the transaction fee becomes less of a strike against the exchange rate (in percentage terms). However, most ATMs allow only up to $150 a transaction. Banks and *casas de cambio* (money-exchange houses) have the second-best exchange rates. The difference from one place to another is usually only a few centavos.

Most banks change money on weekdays only until 1 (though they stay open until 5), while casas de cambio generally stay open until 6 and often operate on weekends. Bank rates are regulated by the federal government and are therefore invariable, while casas de cambio have slightly more-variable rates. Some hotels also exchange money, but for providing you with this convenience they help themselves to a bigger commission than banks.

You can do well at most airport exchange booths, except in Cancún, but not necessarily at rail and bus stations, in hotels, in restaurants, or in stores. If the airport rate isn't favorable, you can exchange just enough money to pay for transportation to your hotel and then find an exchange house near there.

When changing money, count your bills before leaving the bank or casa de cambio, and don't accept any partially torn or taped-together notes; they won't be accepted anywhere. Also, many shop and restaurant owners are unable to make change for large bills. Enough of these encounters may compel you to request *billetes chicos* (small bills) when you exchange money.

➤ EXCHANGE SERVICES: **International Currency Express** (☎ 888/278–6628 for orders, www.foreignmoney.com). **Thomas Cook Currency Services** (☎ 800/287–7362, www.us.thomascook. com).

TRAVELER'S CHECKS

Do you need traveler's checks? It depends on where you're headed. If you're going to rural areas and small towns, go with cash; traveler's checks are best used in cities. Lost or stolen checks can usually be replaced within 24 hours. To ensure a speedy refund, buy your own traveler's checks—don't let someone else pay for them: irregularities like this can cause delays. The person who bought the checks should make the call to request a refund.

OUTDOORS & SPORTS

Mexico offers golf, waterskiing, diving, and hiking. Mexico City, Guadalajara, Monterrey, and smaller cities as well as beach resorts all have golf facilities. Courses abound in Los Cabos, an area that's been gearing up to become Mexico's premier golf resort.

Waterskiing is very popular at beach resorts, while the scuba diving in Cozumel, the Caribbean coast, and Cancún is excellent. Renting equipment isn't a problem in the larger resort areas.

Mexico's volcanoes and mountains provide many hiking opportunities. The Copper Canyon is a favorite destination for this.

PASSPORTS & VISAS

When traveling internationally, **carry your passport even if you don't need one** (it's always the best form of I.D.) and **make two photocopies of the data page** (one for someone at home and another for you, carried separately from your passport). If you lose your passport, promptly call the nearest embassy or consulate and the local police.

ENTERING MEXICO

For stays of up to 180 days, **Americans must prove citizenship through either a valid passport, certified copy of a birth certificate, or voter-registration card (the last two must be accompanied by a government-issue photo ID).** Minors traveling with one parent need notarized permission from the absent parent. For stays of more than 180 days, all U.S. citizens, even infants, need a valid passport to enter

Mexico. Minors also need parental permission.

Canadians need only proof of citizenship to enter Mexico for stays of up to six months.

U.K. citizens need only a valid passport to enter Mexico for stays of up to three months.

Mexico has instituted a $15 visitor fee that applies to all visitors except those entering by sea at Mexican ports who stay less than 72 hours and those entering by land who do not stray past the 26–30-km (16–18-mi) checkpoint into the country's interior. For visitors arriving by air, the fee, which covers visits of more than 72 hours and up to 30 days, is usually tacked on to the airline-ticket price. You must pay the fee each time you extend your 30-day tourist visa.

PASSPORT OFFICES

The best time to apply for a passport or to renew is in fall and winter. Before any trip, check your passport's expiration date, and, if necessary, renew it as soon as possible.

➤ AUSTRALIAN CITIZENS: **Australian Passport Office** (☎ 131–232, www.dfat.gov.au/passports).

➤ CANADIAN CITIZENS: **Passport Office** (☎ 819/994–3500, 800/567–6868, www.dfait-maeci.gc.ca/passport).

➤ NEW ZEALAND CITIZENS: **New Zealand Passport Office** (☎ 04/494–0700, www.passports.govt.nz).

➤ U.K. CITIZENS: **London Passport Office** (☎ 0990/210–410), for fees and documentation requirements and to request an emergency passport.

➤ U.S. CITIZENS: **National Passport Information Center** (☎ 900/225–5674; calls are 35¢ per minute for automated service, $1.05 per minute for operator service).

REST ROOMS

Expect to find clean flushing toilets, toilet tissue, soap, and running water in the major tourist destinations. Other places should have simple but clean toilets. The more-primitive rest rooms, usually in public areas with little tourist traffic, will have no paper, no water at times, and no toilet seats. Some public places, like bus stations, charge one or two pesos to use the facility, but toilet paper is included in the fee. Still, it's always a good idea to carry some tissue.

SAFETY

The U.S. State Department has warned of "critical levels" of crime against tourists in Mexico, noting an increase in the level of violence of the crimes committed and what appeared to be a significant incidence of sexual assaults against women. Reports indicated that uniformed police officers were on occasion perpetrating the nonviolent crimes, sometimes stopping cars and seeking money (☞ Safety on the Road *in* Car Travel, *above*).

The largest increase in crime has taken place in Mexico City, where the age-old problem of pickpocketing has been overshadowed by robberies at gunpoint. Another development has been abductions and robberies in taxicabs hailed from the street (as opposed to hired from a hotel or taxi stand).

Many foreigners are aware of Mexico's reputation for corruption. The patronage system is a well-entrenched part of Mexican politics and industry, and workers in the public sector—notably policemen and customs officials—are notoriously underpaid. Everyone has heard some horror story about highway assaults, pickpocketing, bribes, or foreigners languishing in Mexican jails. It is important to note that these reports of crimes apply in large part to Mexico City and more-remote areas of Oaxaca and Chiapas. So far, crime is not such a problem in the Heartland (cities like San Miguel de Allende), Puerto Vallarta, Cancún, and much of the rest of the country. Pickpocketing is usually the biggest concern.

Use common sense everywhere, but **exercise particular caution in Mexico City.** In addition, it is best to **avoid remote, less-traveled areas of Oaxaca and Chiapas** as crime in these areas can be more life-threatening. Do not

pick up hitchhikers or hitchhike yourself. Also, try to use luxury buses (rather than second- or third-class vehicles), which use the safer toll roads—and it's best to travel only during the day. For the time being, **women should not venture alone onto uncrowded beaches,** and everyone should **avoid urges to get away from it all on your own (even as a couple) to go hiking in remote national parks.**

In Mexico City, **do not wear any valuables, including watches,** and try not to act too much like a tourist. Wear a money belt, put valuables in hotel safes, avoid driving on untraveled streets and roads at night, and carry your own baggage whenever possible, unless in a luxury hotel. Also, you won't need your passport in the city, so leave it in the hotel safe—replacing it would be more trouble than you need.

Take only registered hotel taxis or have a hotel concierge call a *sitio* (stationed cab)—do not hail taxis on the street under any circumstances. If you must use an ATM, do so during the day and in big, enclosed commercial areas. Avoid the glass-enclosed street variety of banks where you may be more vulnerable to thieves who force you to withdraw money for them; abduction is also possible. This cannot be stressed strongly enough.

Bear in mind that reporting a crime to the police is often a frustrating experience unless you speak excellent Spanish and have a great deal of patience. If you are the victim of an assault, contact your local consular agent or the consular section of your country's embassy in Mexico City, especially if you need medical attention (☞ Mexico City A to Z *in* Chapter 1).

WOMEN IN MEXICO

Women traveling alone are likely to be subjected to *piropos* (catcalls). To avoid this, try not to wear tight or provocative clothes or enter street bars or cantinas alone; in some very conservative rural areas, even sleeveless shirts or Bermuda shorts may seem inappropriate to the locals. Your best strategy is always to try and ignore the offender, do not speak to him, and go on about your business. If the situation seems to be getting out of hand, do not hesitate to ask someone for help. Piropos are one thing, but outright harassment of women is not considered acceptable behavior. If you express outrage, you should find no shortage of willing defenders.

SENIOR-CITIZEN TRAVEL

To qualify for age-related discounts, **mention your senior-citizen status up front** when booking hotel reservations (not when checking out) and before you're seated in restaurants (not when paying the bill). When renting a car, ask about promotional car-rental discounts, which can be cheaper than senior-citizen rates.

Mexican senior citizens must present a special government-issued credential to obtain discounts at any facility; foreign-issued credentials (such as from AARP) are not recognized in the country, and it's not enough to mention that you are a senior citizen.

➤ EDUCATIONAL PROGRAMS: **Elderhostel** (✉ 75 Federal St., 3rd floor, Boston, MA 02110, ☎ 877/426–8056, ℻ 877/426–2166, www.elderhostel.org). **Interhostel** (✉ University of New Hampshire, 6 Garrison Ave., Durham, NH 03824, ☎ 603/862–1147, 800/733–9753, ℻ 603/862–1113, www.learn.unh.edu).

SHOPPING

At least three varieties of outlets sell Mexican crafts: indoor and outdoor municipal markets, shops run by Fonart (a government agency to promote Mexican crafts), and tourist boutiques in towns, shopping malls, and hotels. If you buy in the municipal shops or markets, you can avoid the value-added tax (VAT), but you should pay in pesos because paying in dollars won't give you a good exchange rate most of the time. Be sure to **take your time and inspect merchandise closely**: you'll find bargains, but quality can be inconsistent. Fonart shops are a good reference for quality and prices (the latter are fixed), and they accept credit cards. Boutiques also accept credit cards if not dollars; although their prices may be higher, they are convenient and sometimes carry one-of-a-kind items.

(You may be asked to pay up to 10% more on credit-card purchases; savvy shoppers with cash have greater bargaining clout.) The 15% VAT (10% in the states of Quintana Roo, Baja California, and Baja California Sur) is charged on most purchases but is often included in the price or disregarded by eager or desperate vendors.

It is not always true that the closer you are to the source of an article, the better the selection and price are likely to be. Mexico City, Guadalajara, Páztcuaro, San Miguel de Allende, Puerto Vallarta, Oaxaca, San Cristóbal de las Casas, and Mérida have some of the best selections of crafts—and bargains as well. Prices are usually higher and selections more touristy at beach resorts.

Bargaining is widely accepted in markets, but you should understand that not all vendors will start out with outrageous prices. If you feel the price quoted is too high, start off by offering no more than half the asking price and then slowly go up, usually to about 70% of the original price. Always **shop around.** In major shopping areas such as San Miguel, shops will wrap and send purchases back to the United States via a package-delivery company. Items made from tortoiseshell and black coral are not allowed into the United States.

STUDENTS IN MEXICO

➤ I.D.S & SERVICES: **Council Travel** (CIEE; ✉ 205 E. 42nd St., 14th floor, New York, NY 10017, ☎ 212/822–2700 or 888/268–6245, ℻ 212/822–2699, info@councilexchanges.org, www.councilexchanges.org) for mail orders only, in the U.S. **Travel Cuts** (✉ 187 College St., Toronto, Ontario M5T 1P7, ☎ 416/979–2406 or 800/667–2887, www.travelcuts.com) in Canada.

TAXES

Mexico charges an airport departure tax of US$18 or the peso equivalent for international and domestic flights. This tax is usually included in the price of your ticket, but check to be certain. Traveler's checks and credit cards are not accepted at the airport as payment for this.

Many states are charging a 2% tax on accommodations, the funds from which are being used for tourism promotion.

VALUE-ADDED TAX

Mexico has a value-added tax of 15% (10% in the states of Quintana Roo, Baja California, and Baja California Sur), called I.V.A. (*impuesto de valor agregado*), which is occasionally (and illegally) waived for cash purchases. Other taxes and charges apply for phone calls made from your hotel room.

TAXIS

Government-certified taxis have a license with a photo of the driver and a taxi number prominently displayed, a meter, and either an orange or green stripe at the bottom of the license plate. In many cities, taxis charge by zones. In this case, be sure to agree on a fare before setting off. For reasons of security, especially in Mexico City, it is always best to call a *sitio* (stationed) cab rather than to flag one on the street. Tipping is not necessary unless the driver helps you with your bags, in which case a few pesos are appropriate.

AT THE AIRPORT

From the airport, **take the authorized taxi service.** Purchase the taxi vouchers sold at stands inside or just outside the terminal, which ensure that your fare is established beforehand. However, before you purchase your ticket, it's wise to locate the taxi originating and destination zones on a map and make sure your ticket is properly zoned; if you only need a ticket to Zone 3, don't pay for a ticket to Zone 4 or 5. Don't leave your luggage unattended while making transportation arrangements.

IN CITIES & BEACH RESORTS

In Mexican cities, **take a taxi rather than public transportation,** which, though inexpensive, is frequently slow and sometimes patrolled by pickpockets. (The exceptions are the air-conditioned buses in Acapulco, Cancún, and Mérida.) Always **establish the fare beforehand,** and **count your change.** In most of the beach resorts, there are inexpensive fixed-route fares, but if you don't ask, or your Spanish isn't great, you may get taken. In cities, especially the capital, be certain that the meter runs before getting in, and remember that there is usually an extra charge after 10 PM. For out-of-town and hourly services, negotiate a rate in advance; many drivers will start by asking how much you want to pay to get a sense of how street-smart you are. In all cases, if you are unsure of what a fare should be, ask your hotel's front-desk personnel or bell captain.

Hire taxis only from hotels and taxi stands (*sitios*), or use those that you have summoned by phone. Street taxis might be the cheapest, but an alarming increase in abductions and violent crime involves street cabs—for safety's sake, under no circumstances should you take one. And never leave luggage unattended in a taxi.

In addition to private taxis, many cities have bargain-price collective taxi services using Volkswagen minibuses (called *combis*) and sedans. The service is called *colectivo* or *pesero*. Peseros run along fixed routes, and you hail them on the street and tell the driver where you are going. The fare—which you pay before you get out—is based on distance traveled. We recommend that you take only the *colectivos* (special airport taxis) that transport passengers from—and sometimes to— airports. In places like Cozumel you'll find that colectivos only—not taxis— are permitted to take passengers from airport terminals into town.

(For information on taxis in Mexico City, *see* Chapter 1.)

TELEPHONES

Thanks to its 1991 privatization, Teléfonos de México (Mexico's phone service)—which for so long was exasperatingly inefficient—is gradually being overhauled. As of January 1997, Teléfonos de México's monopoly ended, enabling competition from several long-distance services, including MCI and AT&T. Many phones, especially in the better city hotels, have Touch-Tone (digital) circuitry. If you think you'll need to access an automated phone system or voice mail in the United States or elsewhere and you don't know what phone service will be available, it's a good idea to take along a Touch-Tone simulator (you can buy one for about $17 at most electronics stores). With the increased installation of new phone and fax lines in major Mexican cities, many phone numbers are in the process of being changed; a recording may offer the new number, so it's useful to learn the Spanish words for numbers 1 through 9.

AREA & COUNTRY CODES

The country code for Mexico is 52. When calling a Mexico number from abroad, dial the country code and then all of the numbers listed for the entry.

DIRECTORY & OPERATOR ASSISTANCE

Directory assistance is 040 nationwide. For international assistance, dial 00 first for an international operator and most likely you'll get one that speaks English; tell her in what city, state, and country you require directory assistance and she will connect you with directory assistance there.

INTERNATIONAL CALLS

To make a call to the United States or Canada, **dial 001 before the area code and number**; to call Europe, Latin America, or Japan, **dial 00** before the country and city codes. When calling home, the country code for the U.S. and Canada is 1, the U.K. 44, Australia 61, New Zealand 64, and South Africa 27.

LOCAL AND LONG-DISTANCE CALLS

The number of digits you need to dial for local calls varies. Numbers preceding the / in our listings are the area or city codes, to be dialed when calling long distance within Mexico. However, in some cities, such as Mexico City, even when calling locally you now must dial the area code as well as the regular number.

For local or long-distance calls, one option is to find a **caseta de larga distancia,** a telephone service usually operated out of a store such as a *papelería* (stationery store), phar-

macy, restaurant, or other small business; look for the phone symbol on the door. Casetas may cost more to use than pay phones, but you have a better chance of immediate success. To make a direct long-distance call, tell the person on duty the number you'd like to call, and he or she will give you a rate and dial for you. Rates seem to vary widely, so shop around. Sometimes you can make collect calls from casetas, and sometimes you cannot, depending on the individual operator and possibly your degree of visible desperation. Casetas will generally charge 50¢–$1.50 to place a collect call (some charge by the minute); it's usually better to call *por cobrar* (collect) from a pay phone.

LONG-DISTANCE SERVICES

AT&T, MCI, and Sprint access codes make calling long distance relatively convenient, but you may find the local access number blocked in many hotel rooms. First ask the hotel operator to connect you. If the hotel operator balks, ask for an international operator, or dial the international operator yourself. One way to improve your odds of getting connected to your long-distance carrier is to travel with more than one company's calling card (a hotel may block Sprint, for example, but not MCI). If all else fails, call from a pay phone.

➤ ACCESS CODES: **AT&T Direct** (☎ 01–800/462–4240). **MCI World-Phone** (☎ 01–800/674–7000). **Sprint International Access** (☎ 01–800/877–8000).

PHONE CARDS

In most parts of the country now, pay phones accept prepaid cards, called Ladatel cards, sold in 30-, 50- or 100-peso denominations (approximately $3, $5, and $10, respectively) at newsstands or pharmacies. Many pay phones in Mexico only accept these cards; coin-only pay phones are usually broken. Still other phones have two unmarked slots, one for a Ladatel (a Spanish acronym for "long-distance direct dialing") card and the other for a credit card. These are primarily for Mexican bank cards, but some accept Visa or MasterCard, though *not* U.S. telephone credit cards.

To use a Ladatel card, simply insert it in the appropriate slot, dial 001 (for calls to the States) or 01 (for calls in Mexico), and the area code and number you're trying to reach. Credit is deleted from the card as you use it, and your balance is displayed on a small screen on the phone.

PUBLIC PHONES

There are two basic kinds of phones in the country. Occasionally you'll see traditional black, square phones with push buttons or dials; although they have a coin slot on top, you may make local calls on them for free. Other, new phones have an unmarked slot for Ladatel cards (☞ *above*).

TOLL-FREE NUMBERS

Toll-free numbers in Mexico start with an 800 prefix. To reach them, you need to dial 01 before the number. In this guide, Mexico-only toll-free numbers appear as follows: 01–800/12–345 (numbers can also have six or seven digits). Most of the 800 numbers in the book work in the U.S. only and are listed simply: 800/123–4567. Toll-free numbers that work in Canada are labeled accordingly, as are those that work in more than one country.

TIME

Mexico has three time zones; most of the country falls in Central Standard Time, which includes Mexico City and is in line with Chicago. Baja California is on Pacific Standard Time—the same as California. Baja Californa Sur and parts of the northwest coast, including Sonora, are on Mountain Standard Time.

TIPPING

When tipping in Mexico, remember that the minimum wage is the equivalent of $3 a day and that the vast majority of workers in the tourist industry live barely above the poverty line. However, there are Mexicans who think in dollars and know, for example, that in the United States porters are tipped about $2 a bag; many of them expect the peso equivalent from foreigners but are sometimes happy to accept 5 pesos (about 5¢) a bag from Mexicans. They will complain either verbally or with a facial expression if they feel they deserve more—you and your conscience must decide. Following are some guidelines. Naturally, larger tips are always welcome.

Porters and bellboys at airports and at moderate and inexpensive hotels: $1 per bag.

Porters at expensive hotels: $2 per person.

Maids: $1 per night (all hotels).

Waiters: 10%–15% of the bill, depending on service (make sure a 10%–15% service charge hasn't already been added to the bill, although this practice is more common in resorts).

Taxi drivers: Tipping is necessary only if the driver helps with your bags—5 pesos to 10 pesos should be sufficient, depending on the extent of the help.

Tour guides and drivers: at least $1 per half day, minimum.

Gas-station attendants: 3 pesos to 5 pesos; if they check the oil, tires, etc., tip more.

Parking attendants and theater ushers: 5 pesos to 10 pesos. Some restaurants and theaters charge for valet-parking service; it's still customary to tip the attendant at least 10 pesos.

TOURS & PACKAGES

Because everything is prearranged on a prepackaged tour or independent vacation, you'll spend less time planning—and often get it all at a good price.

BOOKING WITH AN AGENT

Travel agents are excellent resources. But it's a good idea to collect brochures from several agencies as some agents' suggestions may be influenced by relationships with tour and package firms that reward them for volume sales. If you have a special interest, **find an agent with expertise in that area**; ASTA (☞ Travel Agencies, *below*) has a database of specialists worldwide.

Make sure your travel agent knows the accommodations and other services of the place they're recommending. Ask about the hotel's location, room size, beds, and whether it has a pool, room service, or programs for children, if you care about these. Has your agent been there in person or sent others whom you can contact?

Do some homework on your own, too: local tourism boards can provide information about lesser-known and small-niche operators, some of which may sell only direct.

BUYER BEWARE

Each year consumers are stranded or lose their money when tour operators—even large ones with excellent reputations—go out of business. So **check out the operator.** Ask several travel agents about its reputation, and try to **book with a company that has a consumer-protection program.** (Look for information in the company's brochure.) In the United States, members of the National Tour Association and the United States Tour Operators Association are required to set aside funds to cover your payments and travel arrangements in the event that the company defaults. It's also a good idea to choose a company that participates in the American Society of Travel Agents' Tour Operator Program (TOP); ASTA will act as mediator in any disputes between you and your tour operator.

Remember that the more your package or tour includes the better you can predict the ultimate cost of your vacation. Make sure you know exactly what is covered, and **beware of hidden costs.** Are taxes, tips, and transfers included? Entertainment and excursions? These can add up.

➤ Tour-Operator Recommenda- tions: **American Society of Travel Agents** (☞ Travel Agencies, *below*). **National Tour Association** (NTA; ✉ 546 E. Main St., Lexington, KY 40508, ☎ 606/226–4444, 800/682–8886, www.ntaonline.com). **United States Tour Operators Association** (USTOA; ✉ 342 Madison Ave., Suite 1522, New York, NY 10173, ☎ 212/599–6599, 800/468–7862, FAX 212/599–6744, ustoa@aol.com, www. ustoa.com).

THEME TRIPS

➤ Art & Archaeology: **Archaeolog- ical Conservancy** (✉ 5301 Central Ave. NE, #1218, Albuquerque, NM 87108-1517, ☎ 505/266–1540). **Crow Canyon Archaeological Center** (✉ 2339 Road K, Cortez, CO 81321, ☎ 970/565–8975, 800/422–8975, FAX 970/565–4859). **Far Horizons Archaeological & Cultural Trips** (✉ Box 91900, Albuquerque, NM 87199-1900, ☎ 505/343–9400, 800/552–4575, FAX 505/343–8076).

➤ Birding: **Field Guides** (✉ 9433 Bee Cave Rd., Bldg. 1, Suite 150, Austin, TX 78733, ☎ 512/327–4953, 800/728–4953, FAX 512/327–9231). **Victor Emanuel Nature Tours** (✉ 2525 Wallingwood Rd., Bldg. 10, Austin, TX 78746, ☎ 512/328–5221, 800/328–8368, FAX 512/328–2919). **Wings** (✉ 1643 N. Alvernon Way, Suite 105, Tucson, AZ 85712, ☎ 520/320–9868, FAX 520/320–9373).

➤ Bicycling: **Backroads** (✉ 801 Cedar St., Berkeley, CA 94710-1800, ☎ 510/527–1555, 800/462–2848, FAX 510/527–1444). **Edelweiss Bike Travel** (✉ 129 Hillside Ave., Willis- ton Park, NY 11596, ☎ 516/746–6761, 800/877–2784, FAX 516/746–6690). **Imagine Tours** (✉ Box 123, Davis, CA 95617, ☎ 530/758–8782, 888/592–8687, FAX 530/758–8778).

➤ Butterfly Sanctuaries: **Natural Habitat Adventures** (✉ 2945 Center Green Ct., Boulder, CO 80301, ☎ 303/449–3711, 800/543–8917, FAX 303/449–3712). **Remarkable Journeys** (✉ Box 31855, Houston, TX 77231-1855, ☎ 713/721–2517, 800/856–1993, FAX 713/728–8334).

➤ Horseback Riding: **Equitour FITS Equestrian** (✉ Box 807, Dubois, WY 82513, ☎ 307/455–3363, 800/545–0019, FAX 307/455–2354).

➤ Walking: **Backroads** (☞ Bicycling, *above*). **Butterfield & Robinson** (✉ 70 Bond St., Toronto, Ontario, Canada M5B 1X3, ☎ 416/864–1354, 800/678–1147 in the U.S. and Canada, FAX 416/864–0541).

➤ Whale-Watching: **American Cetacean Society** (✉ 801 Stanley Ave., Long Beach, CA 90804, ☎ 562/438–8960, FAX 310/548–6950). **Planet Expeditions** (✉ 2549 Center Green Ct. S., Suite H, Boulder, CO 80301, ☎ 800/233–2433, FAX 303/349–3712).

TRAIN TRAVEL

By late 1997 private companies operating the Mexican railroads decided that passenger service was not profitable enough, mainly because of the North American Free Trade Agreement, which is making use of the freight service at a bigger profit to the Mexicans. Private rooms and berths were taken out, and only general first-class service, *clase única primera*, remained, entitling passengers to a reserved reclining seat. As first-class bus service proliferates throughout the country, however, first-class rail cars and schedules are practically nonexistent.

As a result, rail travel in Mexico is not recommended, excepting the spectacular train ride through the Copper Canyon (the train was privatized in 1998 and remodeled cars went into service in 1999) (☞ Chapter 5), which you can do either on the new Mexican train or on privately run trains that originate in the United States. Another new service is the limited Tequila Express, which runs between Guadalajara and Tequila.

➤ TRAIN INFORMATION: At press time there was no central office in Mexico with train information. From the United States, you can get some information on trains and rail-hotel packages by contacting **Mexico by Train** (☎ FAX 956/725–3659, ☎ 800/321–1699).

TRAVEL AGENCIES

A good travel agent puts your needs first. Look for an agency that has been in business at least five years, emphasizes customer service, and has someone on staff who specializes in your destination. In addition, **make sure the agency belongs to a professional trade organization.** The American Society of Travel Agents, with 27,000 agents in some 170 countries, is the largest and most influential in the field. Operating under the motto "Integrity in Travel," it maintains and enforces a strict code of ethics and will step in to help mediate any agent-client disputes if necessary. ASTA also maintains a Web site that includes a directory of agents. (If a travel agency is also acting as your tour operator, *see* Buyer Beware *in* Tours & Packages, *above*.)

➤ LOCAL AGENT REFERRALS: **American Society of Travel Agents** (ASTA; ☎ 800/965–2782 24-hr hot line, FAX 703/684–8319, www.astanet. com). **Association of British Travel Agents** (✉ 68–71 Newman St., London W1P 4AH, ☎ 0171/637–2444, FAX 0171/637–0713, abta.co.uk, www. abtanet.com). **Association of Canadian Travel Agents** (✉ 1729 Bank St., Suite 201, Ottawa, Ontario K1V 7Z5, ☎ 613/521–0474, FAX 613/521–0805, acta.ntl@sympatico.ca). **Australian Federation of Travel Agents** (✉ Level 3, 309 Pitt St., Sydney 2000, ☎ 02/9264–3299, FAX 02/9264–1085, www.afta.com.au). **Travel Agents' Association of New Zealand** (✉ Box 1888, Wellington 10033, ☎ 04/499–0104, FAX 04/499–0827, taanz@tiasnet. co.nz).

VISITOR INFORMATION

➤ MEXICAN GOVERNMENT TOURIST OFFICES (MGO): **United States:** (☎ 800/446–3942 nationwide; ✉ 31 East 63rd St., 3rd fl., New York, NY 10021, ☎ 212/821–0314, FAX 212/821–0367; ✉ 300 North Michigan Ave., 4th fl., Chicago, IL 60601, ☎ 312/606–9273, FAX 312/606–9015; ✉ 2401 West 6th St., 5th fl., Los Angeles, CA 90057, ☎ 213/351–2069, FAX 213/351–2074; ✉ 10440 West Office Dr., Houston, TX 77042, ☎ 713/780–3740, FAX 713/780–8367; ✉ 1200 NW 78th Ave., Suite 203, Miami, FL 33126, ☎ 305/381–6996, FAX 305/381–8982).

Canada: (✉ 1 Place Ville Marie, Suite 1510, Montréal, Québec H3B 2B5, ☎ 514/871–1052, FAX 514/871–3825; ✉ 2 Bloor St. W, Suite 1502, Toronto, Ontario M4W 33E2, ☎ 416/925–0704, FAX 416/925–6061; ✉ 999 W. Hastings St., Suite 1610, Vancouver, British Columbia V6C 2WC, ☎ 604/669–2845, FAX 604/669–3498).

United Kingdom: (✉ 60 Trafalgar Sq., London WC2N 5DS, ☎ 0171/734–1058, FAX 0171/930–9202).

Mexico: (✉ Presidente Masaryk 172, Mexico, D.F. 11550, ☎ 5/250–0123).

➤ U.S. GOVERNMENT ADVISORIES: **U.S. Department of State** (✉ Overseas

Citizens Services Office, Room 4811 N.S., 2201 C St. NW, Washington, DC 20520, ☎ 202/647–5225 for interactive hot line, 301/946–4400 for computer bulletin board, FAX 202/647–3000 for interactive hot line); enclose a self-addressed, stamped, business-size envelope.

WEB SITES

Do check out the World Wide Web when you're planning. You'll find everything from current weather forecasts to virtual tours of famous cities. Fodor's Web site, www.fodors.com, is a great place to start your online travels. When you see a 🐚 in this book, go to www.fodors.com/urls for an up-to-date link to that destination's site.

WHEN TO GO

Mexico is sufficiently large and geographically diverse enough that you can find a place to visit any time of year. October through May are generally the driest months; during the peak of the rainy season (June–September), it may rain for a few hours daily. But the sun often shines for the rest of the day, and the reduced off-season rates may well compensate for the reduced tanning time.

From December through the second week after Easter, the Mexican resorts—where the vast majority of tourists go—are the most crowded and therefore the most expensive. This also holds true for July and August, school-vacation months, when Mexican families crowd hotels. To avoid the masses, the highest prices, and the worst rains, **consider visiting Mexico during October, November, April, or May,** just not during the traditional holiday periods. Hotel rates at the beach resorts can fall as much as 30% in the shoulder season, 50% in the off-season.

Mexicans travel during traditional holiday periods—Christmas through Jan. 6, Three Kings Day, *Semana Santa* (Holy Week, the week before Easter), the week after Easter—and summertime school vacations as well as over extended national holiday weekends, called *puentes* (bridges). Festivals play a big role in Mexican national life. If you plan to travel during a major national event, reserve both lodgings and transportation well in advance.

CLIMATE

The variations in Mexico's climate are not surprising considering the size of the country. The coasts and low-lying sections of the interior are often very hot if not actually tropical, with temperatures ranging from 17°C to 31°C (63°F to 88°F) in winter and well above 32°C (90°F) in summer. A more temperate area ranging from 16°C to 21°C (60°F to 70°F) is found at altitudes of 1,220–1,830 meters (4,000–6,000 feet). In general, the high central plateau on which Mexico City, Guadalajara, and many of the country's colonial cities are located is springlike year-round.

➤ FORECASTS: **Weather Channel Connection** (☎ 900/932–8437), 95¢ per minute from a Touch-Tone phone.

ACAPULCO (PACIFIC COAST)

Jan.	88F	31C	May	90F	32C	Sept.	90F	32C
	72	22		75	24		75	24
Feb.	88F	31C	June	90F	32C	Oct.	90F	32C
	72	22		77	25		75	24
Mar.	88F	31C	July	90F	32C	Nov.	90F	32C
	72	22		77	25		73	23
Apr.	90F	32C	Aug.	91F	33C	Dec.	88F	31C
	73	23		77	25		71	22

COZUMEL (CARIBBEAN COAST)

Jan.	84F	29C	May	91F	33C	Sept.	89F	32C
	66	19		73	23		75	24
Feb.	84F	29C	June	89F	32C	Oct.	87F	31C
	66	19		75	24		73	23

Mar.	88F	31C	July	91F	33C	Nov.	86F	30C
	69	21		73	23		71	22
Apr.	89F	32C	Aug.	91F	33C	Dec.	84F	29C
	71	22		73	23		68	20

ENSENADA (BAJA CALIFORNIA)

Jan.	66F	19C	May	70F	21C	Sept.	79F	26C
	45	7		52	11		59	15
Feb.	68F	20C	June	73F	23C	Oct.	75F	24C
	45	7		54	12		54	12
Mar.	68F	20C	July	77F	25C	Nov.	72F	22C
	46	8		61	16		48	9
Apr.	69F	21C	Aug.	79F	26C	Dec.	68F	20C
	48	9		61	16		45	7

LA PAZ (BAJA CALIFORNIA SUR)

Jan.	73F	23C	May	91F	33C	Sept.	95F	35C
	54	12		59	15		73	23
Feb.	77F	25C	June	95F	35C	Oct.	91F	33C
	54	12		64	18		66	19
Mar.	80F	27C	July	97F	36C	Nov.	84F	29C
	54	12		71	22		61	16
Apr.	86F	30C	Aug.	97F	36C	Dec.	77F	25C
	55	13		73	23		54	12

MEXICO CITY (CENTRAL MEXICO)

Jan.	70F	21C	May	79F	26C	Sept.	72F	22C
	44	6		54	12		52	11
Feb.	73F	23C	June	77F	25C	Oct.	72F	22C
	45	7		54	12		50	10
Mar.	79F	26C	July	73F	23C	Nov.	72F	22C
	48	9		52	11		46	8
Apr.	81F	27C	Aug.	73F	23C	Dec.	70F	21C
	50	10		54	12		45	7

MONTERREY (NORTHEAST MEXICO)

Jan.	68F	20C	May	88F	31C	Sept.	88F	31C
	48	9		68	20		70	21
Feb.	73F	23C	June	91F	33C	Oct.	81F	27C
	52	11		72	22		63	17
Mar.	79F	26C	July	91F	34C	Nov.	73F	23C
	57	14		72	22		55	13
Apr.	86F	30C	Aug.	93F	34C	Dec.	70F	21C
	64	18		72	22		50	10

SAN MIGUEL DE ALLENDE (HEARTLAND)

Jan.	75F	24C	May	88F	31C	Sept.	79F	26C
	45	9		59	15		59	15
Feb.	79F	26C	June	88F	30C	Oct.	79F	26C
	48	9		59	15		54	12
Mar.	86F	30C	July	82F	28C	Nov.	75F	24C
	54	12		59	15		50	10
Apr.	88F	31C	Aug.	82F	28C	Dec.	75F	24C
	57	14		59	15		46	8

INDEX

NOTES

NOTES

NOTES

NOTES

NOTES

NOTES

NOTES

NOTES

NOTES

FODOR'S MEXICO 2001

EDITOR: Christine Swiac

Editorial Contributors: Patricia Alisau, Paige Bierma, Mary Callahan, Shane Christensen, Gina Hyams, Shelagh McNally, Charles Runnette, Todd Schindler, Daniel Taras

Editorial Production: Frank Walgren

Maps: David Lindroth, *cartographer;* Rebecca Baer, Robert Blake, *map editors*

Design: Fabrizio La Rocca, *creative director;* Guido Caroti, *art director;* Jolie Novak, *photo editor;* Melanie Marin, *photo researcher*

Cover Design: Pentagram

Production/Manufacturing: Robert B. Shields

COPYRIGHT

SPECIAL SALES

IMPORTANT TIP

Although all prices, opening times, and other details in this book are based on information supplied to us at press time, changes occur all the time in the travel world, and Fodor's cannot accept responsibility for facts that become outdated or for inadvertent errors or omissions. So **always confirm information when it matters,** especially if you're making a detour to visit a specific place.

PHOTOGRAPHY

Joan Iaconetti, *cover* (Cancún).

Baja California Tours, 8 top, 9 bottom, 19C.

Corbis Images, 1, 2 top left, 2 top right, 2 bottom left, 2 bottom center, 2 bottom right, 3 top left, 3 top right, 3 bottom left, 3 bottom right, 6C, 13C, 30E.

Pablo Garber, 6A, 7F, 19 bottom left, 19D.

Peter Guttman, 8A.

Hotel Chan-Kah, 30J.

The Image Bank: Carolyn Brown, 15E. Luis Catañeda, 21C, 24G, 29 top. Angelo Cavalli, 22A, 23D, 24H, 25I. Steve Dunwell, 16A, 16C. Tom Owen Edmunds, 7E, 11A, 21B. Grant V. Faint, 23C, 25 bottom. Andre Gallant, 15C. Cyril Isy-Schwart, 20A, 20C. Gill C. Kenny, 10A. Don Klumpp, 12A. Mahaux Photography, 17B, 22B. Michael Melford, 8B. Andrea Pistolesi, 24F. Anne Rippy, 13B, 28C, 30H. Guido Alberto Rossi, 4-5, 7D, 9C, 14B, 20B. Harald Sund, 6B. Roberto Valladares, 16B, 32. Luis Veiga, 23E, 29 bottom.

La Casa de Espiritus Alegres, 30F.

Las Ventanas al Paraíso, 30B.

Marcella Martinez Associates, Inc., 26A, 30C.

Museo de Arte Contemporaneo de Monterrey (MARCO), 30I.

Christie Parker, 14 top.

Ashlesha Patel, 30D.

PhotoDisc, 15D, 17A, 18A, 18B, 21A.

Querétaro Tourism, 27B.

Quinta Real, 30G.

SNA Jolobil, S.C., 27 bottom, 30A.

Westin Brisas Resort, 17C.

Nik Wheeler, 9D, 10B, 10C, 11B, 11C, 13D, 14A.

ABOUT OUR WRITERS

Every trip is a significant trip. Acutely aware of that fact, we've pulled out all stops in preparing *Fodor's Mexico 2001*. To help you zero in on what to see in Mexico, we've gathered some great color photos of the key sights in every state. To show you how to pull it all together, we've created great itineraries. And to direct you to the places that are truly worth your time and money, we've rallied the team of know-it-alls we're pleased to call our writers. If you knew them, you'd poll them for tips yourself.

So drawn to the surrealism of Mexico that she turned a one-week vacation into a 20-year sojourn, **Patricia Alisau** has traveled just about every inch of the country on assignment for Mexican and U.S. journals. She has written for Mexico's *Vogue* magazine and, as a foreign correspondent, for the *New York Times,* the *Chicago Tribune,* and the Associated Press. This year, she updated our Acapulco chapter, Smart Travel Tips, and sections of the Mexico City and Yucatán Peninsula chapters.

Paige Bierma, who updated the Mexico City and Side Trips and Chiapas and Tabasco chapters for us, covers political and social issues for major U.S. newspapers and magazines. After working as a reporter for several years in her native Iowa and in California, she headed south of the border to bring Mexican news to the breakfast tables of the north-of-the-border public. It took her six years to leave.

A native of southern California, **Shane Christensen,** who updated our Guadalajara and Pacific Coast Resorts chapters, grew up surrounded by Mexican–American culture and learned Spanish at an early age. He has written extensively for us in South America but says he has yet to discover a country more hospitable than Mexico.

In 1997 **Gina Hyams** and her husband and toddler daughter traded in their San Francisco yuppie lifestyle for the good life in Mexico. She is at work on a family travel memoir about their experience, currently titled *Escape Artists,* excerpts of which appeared on-line in *Salon* magazine. They live in San Miguel de Allende. Gina updated the Heartland and Oaxaca chapters for us this year.

Intrepid, discerning Yucatán Peninsula updater **Shelagh McNally** braved the slings and arrows of contentious hotel owners to separate the wheat from the chaff on the Caribbean coast for us. Her reporter's persistence and objectivity—along with her knowledge of Yucatán ecosystems—refresh our perspective on this popular corner of Mexico.

The son of an airline executive, **Charles Runnette** has traveled to many a place, including Mexico's Copper Canyon for this guide. He has been a writer/editor for *New York* magazine, Microsoft's Sidewalk, and New York Times Electronic Media. He also developed the Travel channel for StarMedia.com.

Despite being approached to pose for a youth-oriented clothing magazine in Monterrey, **Todd Schindler** decided to keep working as a freelance writer and documentary filmmaker in New York City. Todd has written about music, architecture, and boxing, as well as travel. For this guide, he traveled to Veracruz and the Northeast region of Mexico.

When not out on the road, **Daniel J. Taras,** a geographer, chef, and writer, works on perfecting his tortilla-soup recipe. A 1994 graduate of the University of Wisconsin, he's spent the past six years crossing the globe, with extended layovers in Oregon, Hawaii, Mexico, and New York. He updated our Baja California chapter.

We'd also like to acknowledge Aeroméxico for its considerable assistance with travel arrangements.

Don't Forget to Write

We love feedback—positive and negative—and follow up on all suggestions. So contact the Mexico editor at editors@ fodors.com or c/o Fodor's, 280 Park Avenue, New York, New York 10017. Have a wonderful trip!

Karen Cure

Karen Cure
Editorial Director